McDougal Littell

THE LANGUAGE OF
LITERATURE

EMILY DICKINSON

HOMER

AMY TAN

STEPHEN KING

BARBARA KINGSOLVER

MAYA ANGELOU

NELSON MANDELA

STEPHEN VINCENT BENET

AGATHA CHRISTIE

O. HENRY

W. H. AUDEN

JACK LONDON

FRANK McCOURT

RICHARD WRIGHT

LANGSTON HUGHES

SANDRA CISNEROS

JUDITH ORTIZ COFER

RITA DOVE

BERYL MARKHAM

ROBERT FROST

JULIA ALVAREZ

GUY DE MAUPASSANT

TIM O'BRIEN

TRUMAN CAPOTE

EDGAR ALLAN POE

GABRIEL GARCÍA MÁRQUEZ

SAKI

WILLIAM SHAKESPEARE

MARTIN LUTHER KING, JR.

DORIS LESSING

McDougal Littell

THE LANGUAGE OF
LITERATURE

Arthur N. Applebee

Andrea B. Bermúdez

Sheridan Blau

Rebekah Caplan

Peter Elbow

Susan Hynds

Judith A. Langer

James Marshall

McDougal Littell

A HOUGHTON MIFFLIN COMPANY

Evanston, Illinois • Boston • Dallas

Acknowledgments

Unit One

Estate of Williams Forrest: "Plainswoman" by Williams Forrest, from *The Saturday Evening Post*, 24 September 1960. Reprinted by permission of Mrs. Elaine Forrest.

Harcourt Brace & Company: "The Necklace" by Guy de Maupassant, from *Adventures in Reading*, Laureate Edition, Grade 9. Copyright © 1963 by Harcourt Brace & Company and renewed 1991 by Deborah Jean Lodge, Alice Lodge, Jeanne M. Shutes, Jessica Sand, Lydia Winderman, Florence F. Potell, and Mary Rivers Bowman. Reprinted by permission of the publisher.

Brandt & Brandt Literary Agents: "The Most Dangerous Game" by Richard Connell. Copyright © 1924 by Richard Connell. Copyright renewed © 1952 by Louise Fox Connell. Reprinted by permission of Brandt & Brandt Literary Agents, Inc.

Business Week: "Games People Probably Shouldn't Play," from *Business Week*, 24 September 1984, page 144. Reprinted from the September 24, 1984, issue of *Business Week* by special permission. Copyright © 1984 by The McGraw-Hill Companies, Inc.

Tim O'Brien: "Where Have You Gone, Charming Billy?" by Tim O'Brien, from *Redbook*, May 1975. Copyright © 1975 by Tim O'Brien. Reprinted by permission of the author.

Eugenia Collier: "Marigolds" by Eugenia Collier, originally published in *Negro Digest*, November 1969. Copyright © 1994 by Eugenia Collier. Reprinted by permission of the author.

Putnam Berkley: "Two Kinds," from *The Joy Luck Club* by Amy Tan. Copyright © 1989 by Amy Tan. Reprinted by permission of Putnam Berkley, a division of Penguin Putnam Inc.

Estate of William Stafford: "The Osage Orange Tree" by William Stafford, originally published in *Oregon Centennial Anthology, 1859–1959*. Copyright © 1959 by William Stafford. Reprinted by permission of the Estate of William Stafford.

Continued on page 1240

ISBN 13: 978-0-395-93172-1
ISBN 10: 0-395-93172-X

15 16 17 18 19 20 0868 12 11 10 09

Senior Consultants

The senior consultants guided the conceptual development for *The Language of Literature* series. They participated actively in shaping prototype materials for major components, and they reviewed completed prototypes and/or completed units to ensure consistency with current research and the philosophy of the series.

Arthur N. Applebee Professor of Education, State University of New York at Albany; Director, National Research Center on English Learning and Achievement; Senior Fellow, Center for Writing and Literacy

Andrea B. Bermúdez Professor of Studies in Language and Culture; Director, Research Center for Language and Culture; Chair, Foundations and Professional Studies, University of Houston-Clear Lake

Sheridan Blau Senior Lecturer in English and Education and former Director of Composition, University of California at Santa Barbara; Director, South Coast Writing Project; Director, Literature Institute for Teachers; Past President, National Council of Teachers of English

Rebekah Caplan Coordinator, English Language Arts K-12, Oakland Unified School District, Oakland, California; Teacher-Consultant, Bay Area Writing Project, University of California at Berkeley; served on the California State English Assessment Development Team for Language Arts

Peter Elbow Professor of English, University of Massachusetts at Amherst; Fellow, Bard Center for Writing and Thinking

Susan Hynds Professor and Director of English Education, Syracuse University, Syracuse, New York

Judith A. Langer Professor of Education, State University of New York at Albany; Director, National Research Center on English Learning and Achievement; Director, Albany Institute for Research on Education

James Marshall Professor of English and English Education, University of Iowa, Iowa City

Contributing Consultants

Tommy Boley Associate Professor of English, University of Texas at El Paso

Lucila A. Garza ESL Consultant, Austin, Texas

Jeffrey N. Golub Assistant Professor of English Education, University of South Florida, Tampa

William L. McBride, Ph.D. Reading and Curriculum Specialist; former middle and high school English instructor

Sharon Sicinski-Skeans, Ph.D. Assistant Professor of Reading, University of Houston-Clear Lake

Multicultural Advisory Board

The multicultural advisors reviewed literature selections for appropriate content and made suggestions for teaching lessons in a multicultural classroom.

Julie A. Anderson, English Department Chairperson, Dayton High School, Dayton, Oregon

Vikki Pepper Ascuena, Meridian High School, Meridian, Idaho

Dr. Joyce M. Bell, Chairperson, English Department, Townview Magnet Center, Dallas, Texas

Linda F. Bellmore, Livermore High School, Livermore, California

Dr. Eugenia W. Collier, Author; lecturer; Chairperson, Department of English and Language Arts; Teacher of Creative Writing and American Literature, Morgan State University, Maryland

Dr. Bill Compagnone, English Department Chairperson, Lawrence High School, Lawrence, Massachusetts

Kathleen S. Fowler, President, Palm Beach County Council of Teachers of English, Boca Raton Middle School, Boca Raton, Florida

Jan Graham, Cobb Middle School, Tallahassee, Florida

Barbara J. Kuhns, Camino Real Middle School, Las Cruces, New Mexico

Patricia J. Richards, Prior Lake, Minnesota

Janna Rigby, Clovis High School, Clovis, California

Continued on page 1251

Teacher Review Panels

The following educators provided ongoing review during the development of the tables of contents, lesson design, and key components of the program.

Texas

Dana Davis, English Department Chairperson, Irving High School, Irving Independent School District

Susan Fratcher, Cypress Creek High School, Cypress Fairbanks School District

Continued on page 1251

Manuscript Reviewers

The following educators reviewed prototype lessons and tables of contents during the development of *The Language of Literature* program.

David Adcox, Trinity High School, Euless, Texas

Carol Alves, English Department Chairperson, Apopka High School, Apopka, Florida

Jacqueline Anderson, James A. Foshay Learning Center, Los Angeles, California

Continued on page 1253

Student Board

The student board members read and evaluated selections to assess their appeal for 9th-grade students.

Nancy Beirne, St.Francis DeSales, Ohio

Isabel Benros, Kennedy High School, New York

Gia Brophy, Nottingham High School, New Jersey

Anne S. Burke, Nichols School, New York

Cristin Cammon, Arvada West High School, Colorado

Ruth El-Jamal, Centennial High School, Illinois

Jason Esler, Lyons Township High School, Illinois

Yahaira Ferreira, Miami Sunset Junior High School, Florida

Zenon Iracheta, Lopez High School, Texas

Angie Lang, Lee's Summit High School, Missouri

Amanda Leonard, East Bay High School, Florida

Aric C. Lewis, E. F. Lindop School, Illinois

Michael Allen Little, J. Lupton Simpson Middle School, Virginia

Peter Lum, Centennial High School, Illinois

Douglas McCallum, Central High School, Michigan

William Caleb McDaniel, Clark High School, Texas

Sarah Middleton, Henry Clay High School, Kentucky

Catherine Murriel, Kingsberry High School, Tennessee

Scott Navarro, Downington Senior High School, Pennsylvania

LaShannon Petit, Hialeah High School, Florida

Vu Quang, Center Street Middle School, Ohio

Erica Rey, Plainview High School, Texas

Erica Scully, Illinois

Jefrey Sherman, Clark High School Academy of Math and Science, Nevada

Matt Siler, Aloha High School, Oregon

Joshua Taylor III, H-B Woodlawn Program, Virginia

James Whatley, Longview High School, Texas

Navy Yort, Jordan High School, Texas

Cristina Zuccarello, Rhodes Junior High School, Arizona

THE Language OF LITERATURE

OVERVIEW

Literature Connections

Each of the books in the *Literature Connections* series combines a novel or play with related readings—poems, stories, plays, personal essays, articles—that add new perspectives on the theme or subject matter of the long work.

The Miracle Worker
WILLIAM GIBSON

WITH THESE RELATED READINGS

Helen Keller	*from* **Three Days to See**
Harold Krents	**Darkness at Noon**
Joanna Greenberg	**And Sarah Laughed**
Judith Ortiz Cofer	**The Game**
Arthur Cavanaugh	**Miss Awful**
Nina Cassian	**A Man**
Annie Dillard	*from* **Seeing**

Listed below are some of the most popular choices to accompany the Grade 9 anthology:

The Autobiography of Miss Jane Pittman
ERNEST J. GAINES

To Kill a Mockingbird: The Screenplay
HORTON FOOTE

The Friends
ROSA GUY

Animal Farm
GEORGE ORWELL

The Chosen
CHAIM POTOK

Picture Bride
YOCHIKO UCHIDA

The Chocolate War
ROBERT CORMIER

1984
GEORGE ORWELL

Fahrenheit 451
RAY BRADBURY

West with the Night
BERYL MARKHAM

Kaffir Boy
MARK MATHABANE

The New Novel (1877), Winslow Homer, Watercolor, 9½″ × 20½″. Museum of Fine Arts, Springfield, Massachusetts. Horace P. Wright Collection.

UNIT ONE
PAGE 20

The *Power* of *Storytelling*

Voices
of
Experience

Family (1992), Varnette P. Honeywood. Collage, Copyright © 1992 Varnette P. Honeywood.

UNIT FOUR
PAGE 586

All in the Family

The Mighty Hand (1885), Auguste Rodin. Bronze, 18″ × 11½″ × 7½″, collection of the First National Bank of Chicago.

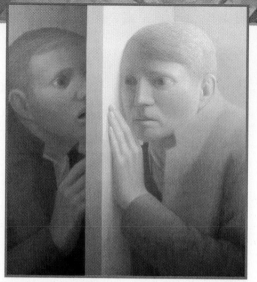

Voice I (1963), George Tooker. Egg tempera gesso panel, 19½″ × 17½″. Private collection, courtesy DC Moore Gallery, New York.

UNIT FIVE
PAGE 736

A World of Mysteries

Winged Victory, Victor Higgins. Oil on canvas, 40″ × 43¼″. Collection of the Museum of Fine Arts, Museum of New Mexico, Gift of Joan Higgins Reed. Photo by Blair Clark.

UNIT SIX
PAGE 884

The *Classic Tradition*

Student *Resource Bank*

Selections by Genre

Speeches

Poetry

Electronic Library

The *Electronic Library* is a CD-ROM that contains additional fiction, nonfiction, poetry, and drama for each unit in *The Language of Literature*. Here is a sampling from the titles included in Grade 9.

Special Features in This Book

Writing Workshops

Communication Workshops

Building Vocabulary

Assessment Pages

The Power of Storytelling

Why did Homer's Odyssey *show up thousands of years later as a made-for-television movie? Why has the story of* Romeo and Juliet *been told and retold throughout generations? Why is this week's mountain-climbing expedition next week's bestselling novel?*

People everywhere love a good story, whether it is as ancient as the tale of Odysseus or as current as today's news. Perhaps this is because a powerful story, no matter when it was written, explores conflicts, relationships, and emotions that all of us have experienced in our own lives. This is why some stories seem to live forever. And this is why we keep reading them.

Armand Assante in
Homer's Odyssey, a
television movie

"All good books are alike in that they are truer than if they had really happened and after you are finished reading one you will feel that all that happened to you and afterwards it all belongs to you. . . ."

**—Ernest Hemingway
Pulitzer Prize–winning author**

Mountain climber on ridge of Mt. Everest

Leonardo DiCaprio and Claire Danes in *Romeo and Juliet*, a 20th-Century-Fox film (1996)

"In books I have traveled, not only to other worlds, but into my own. I learned who I was and who I wanted to be, what I might aspire to, and what I might dare to dream about my world and myself."

—*Anna Quindlen*
contemporary author

Leonard Whiting and Olivia Hussey in *Romeo and Juliet*, directed by Franco Zeffirelli (1968)

- **What makes some stories capture the imagination of generations of readers?**
- **What kinds of stories most appeal to you?**
- **How can you find excitement and relevance in the literature you read?**

The answers lie on the next few pages.

Get Involved with the Literature

The activities you may enjoy—sports, art, music, drama—involve techniques that you have learned to understand and appreciate. You probably didn't stand back and watch for too long before wanting to participate yourself. After all, almost any activity is more exciting when you are actively involved in it. Reading literature works in the same way. You can't simply sit back and let the literature speak to you. You need to interact with the words on a page.

Your Reader's Notebook

Almost any kind of notebook can be used to help you interact with literature. Use your Reader's Notebook to keep track of what's going on inside your mind as you read. Here are three ways to interact.

> ### ❶ Record Your Thoughts
>
> In your 📖 **READER'S NOTEBOOK**, jot down ideas, responses, connections, and questions before, while, and after you read a selection. (See "Strategies for Reading," page 7.) Summarize important passages, and include sketches and charts, too, if they will help. If you wish, compare your ideas with those of a classmate.

"The Plainswoman"
by William Forrest

(page 18) What allows Nora to face the dreaded task before her?

<u>Important Idea</u>
The woman rises to the challenges that meet her on the harsh western frontier. People can adapt to new circumstances and do what they need to do to survive.

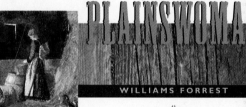

READING MODEL

Alongside "Plainswoman" are transcripts of the spoken comments made two ninth-grade students, Bryan Dobkin and Alexis Owen, while they were the story. Their comments provide a glimpse into the minds of readers acti engaged in the process of reading. You'll notice that in the course of their Bryan and Alexis quite naturally used the Strategies for Reading that were introduced on pages 6–7.

To benefit most from this model of active reading, read the story first, jo down your own responses in your 📖 **READER'S NOTEBOOK**. (Cover up side comments with a sheet of paper if you're tempted to peek.) Then read and Alexis's comments and compare their processes of reading with your o

PLAINSWOMA

WILLIAMS FORREST

The cold of the fall was sweeping over the plains, and No husband, Rolf, and his men had ridden off on the round She was left on the ranch with Pleny, a handy man, who to do the chores and lessen her fears.

Her pregnancy told her that she should hurry back East befo the solemn grip of winter fell on the land. She was afraid to ha the child touch her within, acknowledge its presence, when the long deep world below the mountains closed in and no exit wa available—for the body and for the spirit.

Her baby had not yet wakened, but soon it would. But gus wind and a forbidding iron shadow on the hills told her that t greatest brutality of this ranch world was about to start. And one morning Pleny came in for his breakfast, holding the long of his left hand in the fingers of his right. For some time he ha concealed his left hand from her, holding it down or in his po

Bryan: I don't really understand this description.
]UESTIONING

!ADING MODEL

Complete the specific ▯▯ **READER'S NOTEBOOK**
activity on the first page of each literature lesson.
This activity will help you apply an important skill
as you read the selection.

❸ **Collect Ideas for Writing**

Be aware of intriguing themes, passages,
and thoughts of your own as you read or
complete follow-up activities. In a special
section of your ▯▯ **READER'S NOTEBOOK**,
jot down anything that may later be a
springboard to your own writing.

d from the way he had held himself, she had thought it was a
rt of his chivalry, his wish to have table manners, use his right
nd and sit up straight with a lady. But now he held it before him
e a trophy, and one he did not wish to present.
Nora had been thinking of New England when Pleny came in—of
e piano and the gentle darkness of her mother's eyes, of frost on
e small windowpanes, and the hearth fires, of holidays and the
rish of sleighs, of men with businesslike faces and women who
ank tea and read poetry, of deep substantial beds and the way the
ls and the sea prescribed an area, making it intimate, and the way
e towns folded into the hills. She was thinking of home and
mfort, and then Pleny walked in; the dust trailed around his
kles, and the smell of cattle seemed to cling to his boots. A
ousand miles of cattle and plains and work and hurt were clung
e webs in his face.
Nora had made eggs, ham, bread and coffee for the breakfast,
t Pleny made them objects of disgust as he extended his hand, as
ly but as definitely as a New England lad asking for a dance, and
d, "I got the mortification, ma'am. I have to let you see it."

he looked at his index finger and saw the mortification of the
flesh, the gangrene. He held the finger pointed forward, his
other fingers closed. He pressed the finger with his other hand,
and the darkened skin made a crackling sound like that of
cient paper or dangerous ice over a pond. And above the finger
me yellow streaks were like arrows pointing to the hairs and veins
ove his wrist.
Nora smelled the food, gulped, stood up and turned away.
"I got to come to you, ma'am," said Pleny. "I finally got to come
you."
He spoke firmly but shyly, but she did not hear his tone; she
ard only his demand. And her emotion rejected it and any part of
Her emotion said that he should not have come to her and that
e had nothing to do with it, and would not and could not. She
alked toward the fireplace, staring into the low flames. She heard
e wind coax the sides of the house. She said, pretending nothing
se had been mentioned, "Pleny, there's your breakfast." She
mized it, as if the words could barricade her against him.
ggs . . . ham . . . bread . . . hot coffee—hot coffee."
But after she had spoken she heard nothing but his steady,
iting breathing behind her. And she understood that she would
ve to turn and face it. She knew he was not going away and
uld not happily sit down to eat and would not release her.

*Alexis: I don't know that word,
chivalry, but I can just picture him
standing there, holding his finger.*
QUESTIONING/VISUALIZING

*Bryan: The story jumps here into
something else. I know the parts
have something to do with each
other, but it's confusing.*
EVALUATING

*Bryan: I'm not quite sure what the
words mortification and gangrene
mean. But this part is very
descriptive.*
QUESTIONING/EVALUATING

*Alexis: I'm not sure what they're
talking about. It would be nice to
know where they were.*
EVALUATING/QUESTIONING

PLAINSWOMAN   **9**

"The Plainswoman"
by William Forrest

Writing Ideas
• I could imagine what this woman would have written in a
letter to her family back home.
• It might be interesting to write about the woman from the
husband's point of view.

Your Working Portfolio

Artists and writers keep portfolios in which
they store works in progress or the works
they are most proud of. Your portfolio can
be a folder, a box, or a notebook—the form
doesn't matter. Just make sure to keep adding
to it—with drafts of your writing experiments,
summaries of your projects, and your own goals
and accomplishments as a reader and writer.
Later in this book, on the Reflect and Assess
pages, you will choose your best or favorite
work to place in a *Presentation Portfolio.*

Become an Active Reader

The strategies you need to become an active reader are already within your grasp. In fact, you use them every day to make sense of the images and events in your world. Whether watching a movie, observing your surroundings, or viewing the news, you already know how to employ such strategies.

Take a look at this striking photograph. Read the comments alongside it, made by one student. As you will see, this student used three different strategies— Clarify, Question, Connect—to understand and interpret the situation shown in the photograph. These and the other reading strategies on the next page can help you interact with literature as well.

Clarify *I think this is the Vietnam War Memorial. I bet the man was in the war and lost someone close to him.*

Question *Is the man the boy's father, or could he be an uncle or family friend? Why is the boy kissing the memorial? Who is being remembered?*

> **Connect** *This image reminds me of when I was young. My uncle used to carry me on his shoulders, which was always an adventure.*

Strategies for Reading

Following are specific reading strategies that are introduced and applied throughout this book. Use them when you read and interact with the various literature selections. Occasionally **monitor** how well the strategies are working for you and, if desired, modify them to suit your needs.

PREDICT Try to figure out what will happen next and how the selection might end. Then read on to see how accurate your guesses were.

VISUALIZE Visualize characters, events, and setting to help you understand what's happening. When you read nonfiction, pay attention to the images that form in your mind as you read.

CONNECT Connect personally with what you're reading. Think of similarities between the descriptions in the selection and what you have personally experienced, heard about, and read about.

QUESTION Question what happens while you read. Searching for reasons behind events and characters' feelings can help you feel closer to what you are reading.

CLARIFY Stop occasionally to review what you understand, and expect to have your under-standing change and develop as you read on. Reread and use resources to help you clarify your understanding. Also watch for answers to questions you had earlier.

EVALUATE Form opinions about what you read, both while you're reading and after you've finished. Develop your own ideas about characters and events.

On the next page, you will see how two readers applied these strategies to the story "Plainswoman."

Go Beyond the Text If you really become an active reader, your involvement doesn't stop with the last line of the text. Decide what else you'd like to know. Discuss your ideas with others, do some research, or jump on the Internet.

 More Online
www.mcdougallittell.com

Alongside "Plainswoman" are transcripts of the spoken comments made by two ninth-grade students, Bryan Dobkin and Alexis Owen, while they were reading the story. Their comments provide a glimpse into the minds of readers actively engaged in the process of reading. You'll notice that in the course of their reading, Bryan and Alexis quite naturally used the Strategies for Reading that were introduced on page 7.

To benefit most from this model of active reading, read the story first, jotting down your own responses in your 📖 **READER'S NOTEBOOK.** (Cover up the side comments with a sheet of paper if you're tempted to peek.) Then read Bryan's and Alexis's comments and compare their processes of reading with your own.

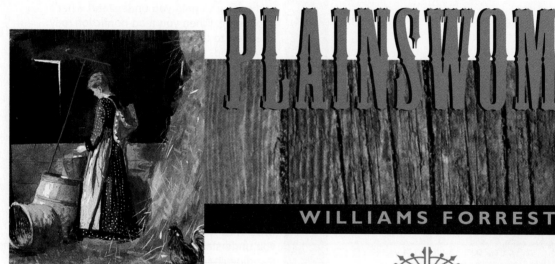

PLAINSWOMAN

WILLIAMS FORREST

The cold of the fall was sweeping over the plains, and Nora's husband, Rolf, and his men had ridden off on the roundup. She was left on the ranch with Pleny, a handy man, who was to do the chores and lessen her fears.

Her pregnancy told her that she should hurry back East before the solemn grip of winter fell on the land. She was afraid to have the child touch her within, acknowledge its presence, when the long deep world below the mountains closed in and no exit was available—for the body and for the spirit.

Her baby had not yet wakened, but soon it would. But gusts of wind and a forbidding iron shadow on the hills told her that the greatest brutality of this ranch world was about to start. And then one morning Pleny came in for his breakfast, holding the long finger of his left hand in the fingers of his right. For some time he had concealed his left hand from her, holding it down or in his pocket;

Bryan: *This woman must be worried about having her baby in the winter when it's hard to get around.*
CLARIFYING

Alexis: *Something must be wrong with his finger.*
CLARIFYING

and from the way he had held himself, she had thought it was a part of his chivalry, his wish to have table manners, use his right hand and sit up straight with a lady. But now he held it before him like a trophy, and one he did not wish to present.

Nora had been thinking of New England when Pleny came in—of the piano and the gentle darkness of her mother's eyes, of frost on the small windowpanes, and the hearth fires, of holidays and the swish of sleighs, of men with businesslike faces and women who drank tea and read poetry, of deep substantial beds and the way the hills and the sea prescribed an area, making it intimate, and the way the towns folded into the hills. She was thinking of home and comfort, and then Pleny walked in; the dust trailed around his ankles, and the smell of cattle seemed to cling to his boots. A thousand miles of cattle and plains and work and hurt were clung like webs in his face.

Nora had made eggs, ham, bread and coffee for the breakfast, but Pleny made them objects of disgust as he extended his hand, as shyly but as definitely as a New England lad asking for a dance, and said, "I got the mortification, ma'am. I have to let you see it."

She looked at his index finger and saw the mortification of the flesh, the gangrene. He held the finger pointed forward, his other fingers closed. He pressed the finger with his other hand, and the darkened skin made a crackling sound like that of ancient paper or dangerous ice over a pond. And above the finger some yellow streaks were like arrows pointing to the hairs and veins above his wrist.

Nora smelled the food, gulped, stood up and turned away.

"I got to come to you, ma'am," said Pleny. "I finally got to come to you."

He spoke firmly but shyly, but she did not hear his tone; she heard only his demand. And her emotion rejected it and any part of it. Her emotion said that he should not have come to her and that she had nothing to do with it, and would not and could not. She walked toward the fireplace, staring into the low flames. She heard the wind coax the sides of the house. She said, pretending nothing else had been mentioned, "Pleny, there's your breakfast." She itemized it, as if the words could barricade her against him. "Eggs . . . ham . . . bread . . . hot coffee—hot coffee."

But after she had spoken she heard nothing but his steady, waiting breathing behind her. And she understood that she would have to turn and face it. She knew he was not going away and would not happily sit down to eat and would not release her.

Alexis: I can just picture him standing there, holding his finger.
VISUALIZING

Bryan: The story jumps here into something else. I know the parts have something to do with each other, but it's confusing.
EVALUATING

Bryan: I think gangrene is a really bad infection, or something like that. Anyway, this part is very descriptive.
CLARIFYING/EVALUATING

Alexis: What does he mean when he says, "I got to come to you"?
QUESTIONING

Bryan: I guess "death . . . in his finger" is another way to say gangrene.
CLARIFYING

The fire spoke and had no answer, even though it was soft. She turned and saw the weather on Pleny's face, the diamonds of raised flesh, the scars. And she knew that death was in his finger and was moving up his arm and would take all of him finally, as fully as a bullet or freezing or drowning.

"What do you expect of me, Pleny?" she said.

He moved with a crinkling hard sound of stained dungarees, hardened boots and his dried reluctant nature. "Ma'am," he said, "I don't want you to think I'm a coward. I just wouldn't want you to get that notion. I'll take my bumps, burns and cuts, just like I did with this finger on the lamp in the bunkhouse and then on the gate before it could heal. I'll take it without complaining, but I sure don't like to doctor myself." His lake-blue eyes were narrowed with thought, and the erosion in his face was drawn together, as if wind and sun were drawing his face closer together the way they did the land in the drought. "I just can't bear to cut on myself," he said, lowering his head with a dry shame. He lifted his head suddenly and said, "I suppose I'd do it out on the plain, in the mountains, alone. But I can't do it here."

His Adam's apple wobbled as he sought in his throat for words. His lips were cracked and did not easily use explanations. "It just seems sinful, ma'am," he said, "for a man to hack on himself." Suddenly his eyes were filled with burning knowledge. He spoke reasonably, without pleading, but an authority was in his voice. "Ma'am, you never saw a man do that, did you, when somebody else was around to doctor him?"

She had watched and listened to his explanation without a stirring in her; she had done so as if she were mesmerized, like a chicken before a snake. Gradually his meaning penetrated her and told her what he meant.

"Ma'am," he said, "would you do me the kindness to take off this here finger?"

She ran senselessly, as if she were attempting to run long, far, back to New England. The best she could do was run through the rooms of the haphazardly laid-out house and get to her room and close the door and lean against it. She was panting, and her eyes were closed, and her heart was beating so hard that it hurt her chest. Slowly she began to feel the hurts on her shoulders, where she had struck herself against the walls and doors. Rolf had started this house with one room and had made rooms and halls leading off from it as time went on. She had careered through the halls to her room, as if fighting obstacles.

Bryan: I can't believe he just asked her to chop off his finger!
EVALUATING

Alexis: Why did she run to her room?
QUESTIONING

She went to her bed, but did not allow herself to fall down on it. That would be too much weakness. She sat on the edge of the bed, with her hands in her lap. Her wish to escape from this place was more intense than ever within her. And her reasons for it ran through her brain like a cattle stampede, raising acrid dust and death and injury—and fear, most of all.

Her fear had begun in the first frontier hotel in which she had spent a night. Rolf had been bringing her West from New England to his ranch in the springtime. The first part of the ride on the railroad had been a pure delight. Rolf's hand was big, brown, with stiff red hairs on the back, a fierce, comforting hand; and her own had lain within it as softly as a trusting bird. The railroad car had had deep seats and decor that would have done credit to a fine home. As those parts of the world she had never seen went past, mountain, stream and hamlet, she had felt serene; and the sense of adventure touched her heart like the wings of a butterfly. She was ready to laugh at each little thing and she had a persistent wish to kiss Rolf on the cheek, although she resisted such an unseemly act in front of other people.

"I know I'll be happy," she said. And his big quiet hand around hers gave her the feeling of a fine, strong, loving, secure world.

But the world changed. After a time they were on a rough train that ran among hills and plains, and after a while there was nothing to see but an endless space with spring lying flat on it in small colorful flowers and with small bleak towns in erratic spaces, and the men on the train laughed roughly and smelled of whisky. Some men rode on the roof of the car and kicked their heels, fired guns and sang to a wild accordion.

Rolf's hand seemed smaller. His tight, strong burned face that she had so much admired seemed remote; he was becoming a stranger, and she was becoming alone with herself. She, her love for him, her wish for adventure were so small, it seemed, in comparison to the spaces and the crudity.

One night the train stopped at a wayside station, and the passengers poured out as if Indians were attacking. They assailed the dining room of the canvas-and-board hotel as if frenzied with starvation. In the dining room Rolf abruptly became a kind of man she had never known. He grabbed and speared at plates like any of the others and smiled gently at her after he had secured a plateload of food for her that made her stomach turn. After affectionately touching her hand, he fought heartily with the others to get an immense plateload for himself. Then he winked at her and started to eat, in the same ferocious way as the others. His manners in

Bryan: I can imagine the scene on the railroad car, but what does it have to do with what is going on?
VISUALIZING/QUESTIONING

Bryan: The lady in the story thinks that she and Rolf are drifting apart.
CLARIFYING

Alexis: She seems scared. Why is she scared?
CLARIFYING/QUESTIONING

Bryan: I'm not sure if Nora's still in that flashback or if this part is happening now. I'd better go back and reread a few paragraphs.
MONITORING

New England had seemed earthy, interesting and powerful—a tender animal. But here, here he was one more animal.

That night they shared a bedroom with five other people, one a woman who carried a pistol. Rolf had bought sleeping boards and blankets, so that they would not have to share beds with anyone. The gun-carrying woman coughed and then said, "Good night, all you no-good rascals."

Rolf laughed.

The spring air flipped the canvas walls. The building groaned with flimsiness and people. Nora had never before heard the sounds of a lot of sleeping people. She put her face against Rolf's chest and pulled his arm over her other ear.

Alexis: *Why is she crying?*
QUESTIONING

Late at night she woke crying. Or was she crying? There was crying within her, and there were tears on her face. But when she opened her eyes, the night was around her, without roof or walls, but there was the water of rain on her cheeks. Rolf bent over her. "We're outside," he said. "You were suffering. Exhausted, suffering, and you spoke out loud in your sleep."

"Why did you bring me out here?" The blankets were wet, but she felt cozy. He was strong against her. The night was wet but sweet after the flapping, moaning hotel.

Some water fell from his face to hers. Was Rolf crying? No, not Rolf, no. But when he spoke, his voice was sad. "I told you how it would be, didn't I?"

"I didn't know," she said. "I didn't know how awful it could be."

He spoke powerfully, but troubledly. "I can't always take you outside, away from things. I can't do that. There'll be times when I can't do for you, when only you can do it yourself."

"Don't be disturbed," she said, holding him closer. "Don't be disturbed." The smell of the wet air was sweet, and it was spring, and they were alone and small again in an enclosed world, made of them both, and she was unafraid again. "I'll be all right," she promised. "Rolf, I will be all right."

Alexis: *This sounds like a strange place.*
EVALUATING

She slept with that promise, but it did not last through the next day. The train stopped after noontime in the midst of the plain. Cattle ran from the train. A lone horseman rode toward them out of curiosity. The sky was burning. Some flowers beside the tracks lifted a faint gossamer odor. Men were drinking and making tea on the stove of the car. Then they all were told that a woman two cars ahead was going to have a child, now. Nora was asked to go forward to attend her.

The impressions of the next few hours had smitten her ever since. The car in which the woman lay on a board suspended between seats across the aisle was empty except for herself and the third

Shadows of the Past (1989), Al Stine. Courtesy of the artist.

woman on the train. The cars before and after this one had also been emptied. The woman helping her said that the men were not even supposed to hear the cries of the woman in labor. It would not be proper. But were the men proper anyway? From the sounds in the distance, Nora could tell they were shouting, singing and shooting, and maybe fighting and certainly drinking.

She had seen labor before, when the doctor was unavailable, blocked away by snow, so she was good enough here, and there were no complications. But there was no bedroom with comforters, a fire and gentle women about. The woman helping her was the one who wore a pistol, and she cussed.

When the child, a boy, was born, the gun-toting woman shouted the word out the window, and the air was rent with shouts and shooting. The woman on the board lifted her wet head, holding her blanketed baby. "A boy to be a man," she said. "A boy to be a man." She laughed, tears streaming from her eyes.

The woman with the gun said softly, "God rest Himself. A child of the plains been born right here and now."

The train started up. Nora sat limply beside the mother and child. Men walked into the car, looked down and smiled.

Bryan: *What was the title of this story? "Plainswoman."*
QUESTIONING/CLARIFYING

Alexis: *It is explained well when Nora helps the woman on the train deliver her baby.*
EVALUATING

"Now, that's a sight of a boy."

"Thank you kindly," said the woman.

"Now, ma'am, that boy going to be a cattleman?" said another.

"Nothing else."

"Hope we wasn't hoorawing too much, ma'am," said a tall man.

"Jus' like my son was born Fourth of July. Thank you kindly."

"Just made this tea, but it ain't strong's should be," said a man carrying a big cup.

"Thank you kindly."

Another man came up timidly—strange for him; he was huge. It turned out he was the husband. He did not even touch his wife. He looked grimly at his son. The woman looked up at him. "All these folks been right interested," he said.

The woman smiled. The train jerked and pulled. Her face paled. The man put his hand on her forehead. "Now, just don't fret," he said. "Just don't fret."

"Thank you kindly," she said.

In her own seat, next to Rolf, Nora was pale. She flinched when the train racketed over the road. Rolf gripped her hand.

"Rolf?"

"Yes, honey?"

"She's all right. The woman with the baby—she's all right."

"I know."

"Then be quiet, don't be disturbed. I can tell from your hand. You're disturbed."

He looked out the window at the plains, at the spring. "The trip took longer than I thought," he said. "It's time for spring roundup. I ought to be at the ranch."

She was shocked. This great, terrible, beautiful thing had happened, and he was thinking of the roundup. Her hand did not feel small and preserved in his; it felt crushed, even though his fingers were not tightly closed.

"Rolf?" Her shock was low and hurt and it told in her voice. "Rolf. That woman had a baby on the train. It could have been awful. And all you can think of now is the roundup."

He looked around at the others in the car. Then he lowered decorum a little and put his arm around her.

He whispered, "Honey, I tried to tell you—I tried. Didn't you listen? On the plains we do what has to be done. Why, honey, that woman's all right, and now we've got to get to roundup."

"But can't we—can't we be human beings?" she said.

He held her. "We are, honey," he said. "We are. We're the kind of human beings that can live here."

Bryan: They're putting a lot of emphasis on the new baby. I think there's going to be a connection to the title, but I'm not sure yet.
CLARIFYING/PREDICTING

Alexis: It's pretty sad that Rolf doesn't care that the woman had a baby.
EVALUATING

Bryan: I can tell that Nora's upset that Rolf is paying no attention to the new baby. He's just talking about the cattle and the roundup.
CLARIFYING

She remembered all that and she remembered also that within two days after they had got to the ranch, Rolf had gone out with the men on spring roundup. That time, too, Pleny had been left with her to take care of the home ranch. She had been sad, and he had spoken to her about it in a roundabout fashion at supper one night. Pleny ate with her in the big kitchen when the others were gone, instead of in the bunkhouse. And he was shy about it, but carried a dignity on his shyness.

"Don't suppose you know that the cattle're more important than anything out here?" he said.

"It seems I have to know it," said Nora.

Pleny was eating peas with a knife. She heard about it, but had never been sure it was possible.

"Couldn't live here without the cattle," he said.

"It seems to me that living here would be a lot better if people thought more about people."

"Do. That's why cattle's more important."

"I fail to understand you."

Pleny worked on steak meat. "Ma'am, cattle's money, and money's bread. Not jus' steak, but bread, living. Why, ma'am, if a man out here wants a wife, he has to have cattle first. Can't make out well enough to have a wife and kids without you have cattle."

"I don't think it's right," she had said then in the springtime. "I don't think it's right that it should be that way."

And Pleny had replied, "Don't suppose you're wrong, ma'am. I really don't." He wiped his mouth on his sleeve. "Only trouble is, that's the way it is here, if you want to stay."

She hadn't wanted to stay. As soon as she was sure she was pregnant, she wanted to go home. The spring had passed, and the summer hung heavy over the plains. The earth, the sky, the cattle, the people had dry mouths, and dogs panted with tongues gone gray. The wind touched the edges of the windmills, and water came from the deep parts of the earth, but you could not bathe in it. The water was golden and rationed, and coffee sometimes became a luxury—not because you didn't have the coffee, but because the cool watery heart of the earth did not wish to serve you.

The fall roundup time came; and just before the outfit moved out, a cowboy, barely seventeen years old, had broken his leg. Rolf had pulled the leg straight, strapped a board to it and put the boy on a horse with a bag of provisions. "Tie an extra horse to him," Rolf had commanded Pleny, "in case something happens."

Pleny had done so. Rolf had asked the boy, "Got your money?"

"Got it right here."

Alexis: Maybe this place is a farm because there are cows.
CONNECTING

Bryan: Nora's still upset about what happened on the train.
CLARIFYING

Alexis: Why did she want to go home when she found out she was pregnant? Maybe because people here care more about cattle than other people.
QUESTIONING/CLARIFYING

"Now, you get to that doctor."

"Sure enough try."

"Now, when you're fixed up," said Rolf, "you come back."

"Sure enough will."

Nora knew that it would take eight to ten days for the boy to get to the nearest doctor. She ran toward the boy and the horses. She held the reins and turned on Rolf. "How can you let him go alone? How? How?"

Rolf's face had been genial as he talked to the boy, but now it hardened. But the boy, through a dead-white pain in his face, laughed. "Ma'am," he said, "now who's going to do my work and that other man's?"

"Rolf?" she said.

Rolf turned to her, took her hands. "Nora, there isn't anybody that can go with him. He knows that."

The boy laughed. "Mr. Rolf," he said, "when I get my own spread, I'm going to go out East there to get a tender woman. I swear." He spurred with his good leg and, still laughing, flashed off into dust with his two horses.

"Rolf? He might die."

Rolf bowed his head, then fiercely lifted it. "Give him more credit."

"But you can't—" she began.

"We can!" he said. Then he softened. "Nora, I don't know what to say. Here—here there's famine, drought, blizzard, locusts. Here—here we have to know what we must do if we want to stay."

"I don't like it," she said.

A wind lifted and moved around them, stirring grass and dust. In the wind was the herald of the fall—and therefore the primary messenger of the bitter winter. In the wind was the dusty harbinger of work, of the fall roundup.

"Soon I'll have to go," he said, "for the roundup."

"I know."

"The plains are mean," he said. "I know. I came here and found it. But I—I don't hate it. I feel—I feel a—a bigness. I see—I see rough prettiness." He bowed his head. "That isn't all I mean." He looked at her. "Soon I have to go. You'll be all right. Pleny will take care of you."

She hadn't told him that she was sure she had a child within her. She felt that she must keep her secret from this wild place, because even if it were only spoken, the elements might ride like a stampede against her, hurting her and her child, even as they did in the dark when she was alone and the wind yelled against the walls beside her bed and told her how savage was the place of the world in which she lived.

Ringside (1994), William Matthews. Courtesy of the
William Matthews Gallery, Denver, Colorado.

There was a knock on her door. She looked up. Her hands, folded in her lap, gripped each other. She did not answer.

"Ma'am?"

She said nothing.

"It's Pleny. I just can't sit down and eat, ma'am, worrying about this mortification of the flesh I got. I just can't sit down to anything like that. I just have to do something."

She made her hands relax in her lap.

"I have it wrapped up in my kerchief, ma'am," said Pleny, "but that ain't going to do it no good."

She closed her eyes, but opened them at once, staring at the door.

Pleny said, "I ain't going to leave you and the ranch, ma'am. Couldn't do that. I have my chores to do."

A small unbidden tear touched the edge of her eye and slipped down.

There was a silence, and then he said quietly, "The doc's so far away, don't 'spect I could get there before that mortification took more of my flesh. Sure would hate that. Sure would hate that."

A second tear burned silver on the edge of her eye and dropped and burned golden down her cheek and became acid on her line of chin, and her wrist came up and brushed it away.

She heard the wind and many messages and she imagined Pleny waiting. She felt a sense of response, of obligation, of angry maternal love, as if all the wistful hope and female passion of her nature had been fused, struck into life, made able because she was woman, and was here, and birth, survival, help, lay potent, sweet, powerful in her heart and in her hands.

She stood up. "Pleny?"

"Yes, ma'am?"

"What must I do?"

He was silent, and she opened the door. Angrily, then firmly, she said, "Let's go outside, Pleny."

"Yes, ma'am."

She held the kindling ax. Pleny had his finger on the block. He closed his eyes. The wind pulled her skirts. She looked up for a moment at the whirling light. Then, in necessity and tenderness, she swiftly did what must be done.

They were coming, the men were coming home from the roundup. The screen of dust was on the plain. She had been working on the meal and now it was the bread she was kneading. Working on the bread, she felt a kick against her abdomen.

She stopped, startled a moment, her hands deep, gripping in the dough—the kick again, strong.

Suddenly, in a way that would have shocked her mother, in a way that would have shocked herself not so long ago, she threw back her head and laughed, a fierce song of love and expectancy. She made bread and was kicked; she expected her man and she laughed, fiercely and tenderly. She was kicked, and a child of the plains had awakened within her.

Fresh Eggs (1874), Winslow Homer. Collection of Mr. and Mrs. Paul Mellon, Copyright © 2000, Board of Trustees, National Gallery of Art, Washington D.C.

Bryan: *Does this mean a child is about to be born or the feeling of the baby kicking? The story ended suddenly. I don't know how Rolf is going to react to the baby.*
QUESTIONING

Alexis: *This story was confusing at first, but then I understood it more.*
EVALUATING

The Power of

No tears in

the writer,

no tears in

the reader.

No surprise for

the writer,

no surprise for

the reader.

ROBERT FROST

The New Novel (1877), Winslow Homer. Watercolor, 9½″ × 20½″.
Museum of Fine Arts, Springfield, Massachusetts. Horace P. Wright Collection.

Storytelling

PART 1 Crisis and Conflict

It's the first day of school, and you're late for class, but you can't find your schedule. You think you're ready to stay out a little later with your friends, but your mom disagrees. Crisis and conflict are a part of life—the challenge is not to avoid them, but to deal with them. Part of what makes literature enjoyable and worthwhile is seeing how another person responds to a crisis and whether he or she can resolve conflict. As you read the selections in this part of Unit One, think about how the fictional characters and real people portrayed in them meet the challenges life throws at them. Ask yourself how you would behave in similar situations.

LEARNING the Language of *Literature*

*F*iction refers to works of prose that have imaginary elements. Although fiction can be inspired by actual events and real people, it usually springs from writers' imaginations. Fiction is meant to entertain, but it can also provide the reader with a deeper understanding of life. The two major types of fiction are novels and short stories. A novel is a long, often complex work. A short story is much shorter than a novel and can usually be read at one sitting. Both novels and short stories contain four basic elements: **plot, character, setting, and theme.** Use the following passages from "Plainswoman" by Williams Forrest to learn more about the elements of fiction.

Plot

The sequence of events in a story is called the story's **plot.** The plot is like a blueprint of what happens, when it happens, and to whom it happens. Plots are almost always built around conflicts—problems or struggles between opposing forces. Although plots differ, a plot usually includes the four stages of development described in the diagram below: **exposition** (introductory material that gives the background of the story), **rising action, climax,** and **falling action** (sometimes called **resolution**).

YOUR TURN Read the passage at the right, which is taken from the exposition of "Plainswoman." What potential conflict is introduced? Is there only one?

PLOT

Her pregnancy told her that she should hurry back East before the solemn grip of winter fell on the land. She was afraid to have the child touch her within, acknowledge its presence, when the long deep world below the mountains closed in and no exit was available—for the body and for the spirit.

Her baby had not yet wakened, but soon it would. But gusts of wind and a forbidding iron shadow on the hills told her that the greatest brutality of this ranch world was about to start. And then one morning Pleny came in for his breakfast, holding the long finger of his left hand in the fingers of his right.

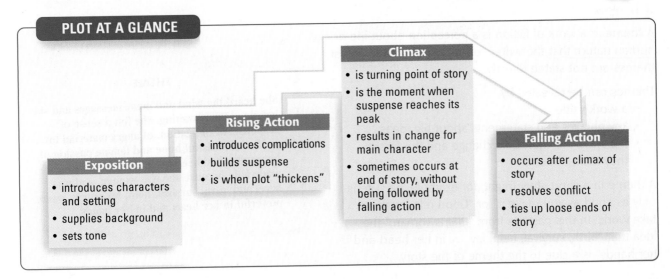

PLOT AT A GLANCE

Exposition
- introduces characters and setting
- supplies background
- sets tone

Rising Action
- introduces complications
- builds suspense
- is when plot "thickens"

Climax
- is turning point of story
- is the moment when suspense reaches its peak
- results in change for main character
- sometimes occurs at end of story, without being followed by falling action

Falling Action
- occurs after climax of story
- resolves conflict
- ties up loose ends of story

Character

The **characters** in a story are the people, animals, or imaginary creatures who take part in the action. In most stories, the events center on one or more **main characters.** The other characters, called **minor characters,** interact with the main characters and help move the story along. Characters can be dynamic or static. **Dynamic** characters change as a result of events, whereas **static** characters remain unchanged. Writers show characters' growth and change by presenting carefully chosen details.

YOUR TURN What details in this passage give you clues to understanding the very different characters of Nora and Pleny?

CHARACTER

Nora had been thinking of New England when Pleny came in— . . . of men with businesslike faces and women who drank tea and read poetry. . . . She was thinking of home and comfort, and then Pleny walked in; the dust trailed around his ankles, and the smell of cattle seemed to cling to his boots. A thousand miles of cattle and plains and work and hurt were clung like webs in his face.

Setting

The **setting** of a story is the particular time and place in which the events occur. A story may be set in a real or an imaginary place. The events may occur in the past, the present, or the future. Vivid descriptions help readers picture the setting in their minds. Setting can play an important role in what happens to the characters and how they respond to problems.

YOUR TURN In this passage, what words and phrases help evoke the setting?

SETTING

After a time they were on a rough train that ran among hills and plains, and after a while there was nothing to see but an endless space with spring lying flat on it in small colorful flowers and with small bleak towns in erratic spaces, and the men on the train laughed roughly and smelled of whiskey. Some men rode on the roof of the car and kicked their heels, fired guns and sang to a wild accordion.

Theme

A **theme** in a work of fiction is a perception about life or human nature that the writer conveys to the reader. Most themes are not stated directly.

Themes can be revealed by
- a work's title
- key phrases and statements about big ideas
- the ways the characters change and the lessons they learn about life

A theme in a short story might, for example, be "Life is only as good as you make it" or "Good relationships take work." In this passage from "Plainswoman," the idea that "birth, survival, help, lay . . . in her heart and in her hands" is a clue to the theme of the story.

THEME

She heard the wind and many messages and she imagined Pleny waiting. She felt a sense of response, of obligation, of angry maternal love, as if all the wistful hope and female passion of her nature had been fused, struck into life, made able because she was woman, and was here, and birth, survival, help, lay potent, sweet, powerful in her heart and in her hands.

The power of fiction to entertain and instruct is an effect of compelling plots, engaging characters, detailed descriptions of settings, and universal themes. Although every story is unique, the reading strategies explained here can help you get the most from every work of fiction you read.

Need More Help?

Remember that active readers use the essential reading strategies explained on page 7: **visualize, predict, clarify, question, connect, evaluate, monitor.**

Reading Fiction

Strategies for Using Your 📖 READER'S NOTEBOOK

As you read, take notes to
- **connect** what you read about people, places, and situations with your personal experiences
- record any phrases, passages, or ideas you find particularly exciting
- record any questions you have about plot, character, setting, or theme

1 Strategies for Understanding Plot
- Keep track of the events as they develop. A chart like this one might help you to **visualize** the sequence of events.

Event 1	Event 2	Event 3	Event 4	Event 5
Nora thinks about leaving.	Pleny reveals he has gangrene.			

- Identify the main conflict and the causes of it. Note the minor problems or difficulties that the characters encounter along the way.
- Note how the characters react to problems they encounter. **Predict** what they might do next.
- Ask yourself whether the ending is what you expected.

2 Strategies for Exploring Character
- Use the details the writer provides to **visualize** the characters. Note any special aspects of their appearance that might be clues to their personalities.
- Look for clues to the characters' motives.
- Note the ways in which characters change during the story. Watch for signs of internal conflict—that is, conflict within a character's mind.
- Try using a chart like the one at the right to help you get to know the characters you encounter.

"Plainswoman"	
Character	Nora
Words & actions	
Thoughts	"I'll never adjust to this place."
Appearance	
What others think	

3 Strategies for Visualizing Setting
- Look for specific adjectives that help you imagine how the opening scene might look. Watch for details that help you **visualize** the setting.
- Pay attention to ways in which setting influences the characters, the plot, or the mood of the story.

4 Strategies for Determining Theme
- **Question** whether the title offers any clues to the theme.
- Think about what any accompanying illustrations reveal about the story.
- Note any sentences or ideas that you find especially intriguing. They might be clues to the theme.

"She was one of those pretty and charming girls."

The Necklace

Short Story by GUY DE MAUPASSANT (gē′ də mō-pă-säN′)

Connect to Your Life

Where Do You Stand? Status is defined as the standing a person has in a group to which he or she belongs. With your classmates, consider the role status plays in a group to which you belong, such as your school. Discuss these questions with your classmates: What are some things that give a person status? How can you tell that a person has status? What are some benefits of status? What are some possible harmful effects of concern about status?

Build Background

Status for Sale "The Necklace" takes place in Paris in the second half of the 19th century. At that time, the life of a typical French woman was dictated by the income and social class of her father or her husband. A wealthy woman of the upper class could look forward to a life of luxury. A middle-class woman was expected to find happiness in taking care of her family and modest home. A woman of the lower class could expect a life of poverty and hard work. The only way a woman could improve her status was by marrying someone in a higher class. A major obstacle to such a marriage, however, was the tradition of the dowry—money or property that the bride's family was expected to give her new husband.

WORDS TO KNOW **Vocabulary Preview**		
adulation	gamut	ruinous
aghast	pauper	vexation
askew	privation	
exorbitant	prospects	

LaserLinks: Background for Reading
Historical Connection

Focus Your Reading

LITERARY ANALYSIS **PLOT** The **plot** of a story is made up of a sequence of events or actions that moves the story forward by introducing **conflicts,** adding **complications,** and providing **resolution.** For example, in the story you are about to read, a woman who is unhappy with her social life is surprised by an invitation to a party. While this event seems to resolve one conflict in her life, it also introduces another. As you read this story, identify the basic conflicts and note the important events that complicate or resolve them.

ACTIVE READING **CAUSE AND EFFECT** Events in a **plot** are sometimes linked causally; that is, one event causes another, which causes another, and so on until the end of the story. A series of events linked in this way is called a chain of **cause and effect.**

READER'S NOTEBOOK Using a diagram like the one shown, see if you can connect the major events of the story in an unbroken chain of cause and effect. Use as many links as you think are necessary.

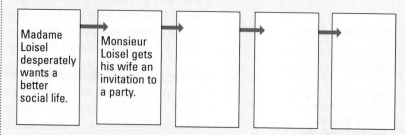

Madame Loisel desperately wants a better social life. → Monsieur Loisel gets his wife an invitation to a party. →

The Necklace

Guy de Maupassant

She was one of those pretty and charming girls, born, as if by an accident of fate, into a family of clerks.

With no dowry, no prospects, no way of any kind of being met, understood, loved, and married by a man both prosperous and famous, she was finally married to a minor clerk[1] in the Ministry of Education.

She dressed plainly because she could not afford fine clothes, but was as unhappy as a woman who has come down in the world; for women have no family rank or social class. With them, beauty, grace, and charm take the place of birth and breeding. Their natural poise, their instinctive good taste, and their mental cleverness are the sole guiding principles which make daughters of the common people the equals of ladies in high society.

She grieved incessantly, feeling that she had been born for all the little niceties and luxuries of living. She grieved over the shabbiness of her apartment, the dinginess of the walls, the worn-out appearance of the chairs, the ugliness of the draperies. All these things, which another woman of her class would not even have noticed, gnawed at her and made her furious. The sight of the little Breton[2] girl who did her humble housework roused in her disconsolate[3] regrets and wild daydreams. She would dream of silent chambers, draped with Oriental tapestries and lighted by tall bronze floor lamps, and of two handsome butlers in knee breeches, who, drowsy from the heavy warmth cast by the central stove, dozed in large overstuffed armchairs.

She would dream of great reception halls hung with old silks, of fine furniture filled with priceless curios,[4] and of small, stylish, scented sitting rooms just right for the four o'clock chat with intimate friends, with distinguished and sought-after men whose attention every woman envies and longs to attract.

When dining at the round table, covered for the third day with the same cloth, opposite her husband, who would raise the cover of the soup tureen, declaring delightedly, "Ah! A good stew! There's nothing I like better . . . ," she would dream of fashionable dinner parties, of gleaming silverware, of tapestries making the walls alive with characters out of history and strange birds in a fairyland forest; she would dream of delicious dishes served on wonderful china, of gallant compliments whispered and listened to with a sphinxlike[5] smile as one eats the rosy flesh of a trout or nibbles at the wings of a grouse.

She had no evening clothes, no jewels, nothing. But those were the things she wanted; she felt that was the kind of life for her. She so much longed to please, be envied, be fascinating and sought after.

She had a well-to-do friend, a classmate of convent-school days whom she would no longer go to see, simply because she would feel so distressed on returning home. And she would weep for days on end from vexation, regret, despair, and anguish.

Then one evening, her husband came home proudly holding out a large envelope.

"Look," he said, "I've got something for you."

She excitedly tore open the envelope and pulled out a printed card bearing these words:

ACTIVE READING

CLARIFY Why is the woman so unhappy?

---

1. **clerk:** office worker who handles routine tasks such as letter writing and record keeping.
2. **Breton** (brĕt'n): of or relating to the province of Brittany in northwestern France.
3. **disconsolate:** very unhappy; beyond cheering up.
4. **curios:** rare or unusual ornamental objects.
5. **sphinxlike:** mysterious; from the Greek myth of the sphinx, a winged creature that killed those who could not answer its riddle.

WORDS TO KNOW
prospects (prŏs'pĕkts') *n.* chances or possibilities, especially for success or profit
vexation (vĕk-sā'shən) *n.* anger or annoyance

"The Minister of Education and Mme. Georges Ramponneau[6] beg M. and Mme. Loisel[7] to do them the honor of attending an evening reception at the Ministerial Mansion on Friday, January 18."

Instead of being delighted, as her husband had hoped, she scornfully tossed the invitation on the table, murmuring, "What good is that to me?"

"But, my dear, I thought you'd be thrilled to death. You never get a chance to go out, and this is a real affair, a wonderful one! I had an awful time getting a card. Everybody wants one; it's much sought after, and not many clerks have a chance at one. You'll see all the most important people there."

She gave him an irritated glance and burst out impatiently, "What do you think I have to go in?"

He hadn't given that a thought. He stammered, "Why, the dress you wear when we go to the theater. That looks quite nice, I think."

He stopped talking, dazed and distracted to see his wife burst out weeping. Two large tears slowly rolled from the corners of her eyes to the corners of her mouth; he gasped, "Why, what's the matter? What's the trouble?"

By sheer willpower she overcame her outburst and answered in a calm voice while wiping the tears from her wet cheeks:

ACTIVE READING

CAUSE AND EFFECT Why does the invitation have the opposite effect on Madame Loisel from the one her husband expected?

"I'm not sure exactly, but I think with four hundred francs I could manage it."

"Oh, nothing. Only I don't have an evening dress and therefore I can't go to that affair. Give the card to some friend at the office whose wife can dress better than I can."

He was stunned. He resumed.

"Let's see, Mathilde.[8] How much would a suitable outfit cost—one you could wear for other affairs too—something very simple?"

She thought it over for several seconds, going over her allowance and thinking also of the amount she could ask for without bringing an immediate refusal and an exclamation of dismay from the thrifty clerk.

Finally, she answered hesitatingly, "I'm not sure exactly, but I think with four hundred francs[9] I could manage it."

He turned a bit pale, for he had set aside just that amount to buy a rifle so that, the following summer, he could join some friends who were getting up a group to shoot larks on the plain near Nanterre.

However, he said, "All right. I'll give you four hundred francs. But try to get a nice dress."

---

6. **Mme. Georges Ramponneau** (zhôrzh′ räN-pô-nō′): *Mme.* is an abbreviation for *Madame* (mə-däm′), a title of courtesy for a married French woman.

7. **M. and Mme. Loisel** (lwä-zĕl′): *M.* is an abbreviation for *Monsieur* (mə-syœ′), a title of courtesy for a Frenchman.

8. **Mathilde** (mä′tēld).

9. **francs** (frăngks): the franc is the basic monetary unit of France.

As the day of the party approached, Mme. Loisel seemed sad, moody, and ill at ease. Her outfit was ready, however. Her husband said to her one evening, "What's the matter? You've been all out of sorts for three days."

And she answered, "It's embarrassing not to have a jewel or a gem—nothing to wear on my dress. I'll look like a pauper: I'd almost rather not go to that party."

He answered, "Why not wear some flowers? They're very fashionable this season. For ten francs you can get two or three gorgeous roses."

She wasn't at all convinced. "No. . . . There's nothing more humiliating than to look poor among a lot of rich women."

But her husband exclaimed, "My, but you're silly! Go see your friend Mme. Forestier[10] and ask her to lend you some jewelry. You and she know each other well enough for you to do that."

She gave a cry of joy, "Why, that's so! I hadn't thought of it."

The next day she paid her friend a visit and told her of her predicament.

Mme. Forestier went toward a large closet with mirrored doors, took out a large jewel box, brought it over, opened it, and said to Mme. Loisel, "Pick something out, my dear."

At first her eyes noted some bracelets, then a pearl necklace, then a Venetian cross, gold and gems, of marvelous workmanship. She tried on these adornments in front of the mirror, but hesitated, unable to decide which to part with and put back. She kept on asking, "Haven't you something else?"

"Oh, yes, keep on looking. I don't know just what you'd like."

All at once she found, in a black satin box, a superb diamond necklace; and her pulse beat faster with longing. Her hands trembled as she took it up. Clasping it around her throat, outside her high-necked dress, she stood in ecstasy looking at her reflection.

Then she asked, hesitatingly, pleading, "Could I borrow that, just that and nothing else?"

"Why, of course."

She threw her arms around her friend, kissed her warmly, and fled with her treasure.

The day of the party arrived. Mme. Loisel was a sensation. She was the prettiest one there, fashionable, gracious, smiling, and wild with joy. All the men turned to look at her, asked who she was, begged to be introduced. All the Cabinet officials wanted to waltz with her. The minister took notice of her.

ACTIVE READING

QUESTION Why do you think Mme. Loisel finally chooses only the diamond necklace?

She danced madly, wildly, drunk with pleasure, giving no thought to anything in the triumph of her beauty, the pride of her success, in a kind of happy cloud composed of all the adulation, of all the admiring glances, of all the awakened longings, of a sense of complete victory that is so sweet to a woman's heart.

She left around four o'clock in the morning. Her husband, since midnight, had been dozing in a small empty sitting room with three other gentlemen whose wives were having too good a time.

He threw over her shoulders the wraps he had brought for going home, modest garments of everyday life whose shabbiness clashed with the stylishness of her evening clothes. She felt this and longed to escape, unseen by the other women who were draped in expensive furs.

Loisel held her back.

"Hold on! You'll catch cold outside. I'll call a cab."

_____

10. **Forestier** (fô-rĕs-tyā').

WORDS
TO
KNOW

pauper (pô′pər) _n._ a poor person, especially one who depends on public charity
adulation (ăj′ə-lā′shən) _n._ excessive praise or flattery

Too Early (1873), Jacques-Joseph Tissot. Guildhall Gallery, London/Art Resource, New York.

But she wouldn't listen to him and went rapidly down the stairs. When they were on the street, they didn't find a carriage; and they set out to hunt for one, hailing drivers whom they saw going by at a distance.

They walked toward the Seine,[11] disconsolate and shivering. Finally on the docks they found one of those carriages that one sees in Paris only after nightfall, as if they were ashamed to show their drabness during daylight hours.

It dropped them at their door in the Rue des Martyrs,[12] and they climbed wearily up to their apartment. For her, it was all over. For him, there was the thought that he would have to be at the Ministry at ten o'clock.

Before the mirror, she let the wraps fall from her shoulders to see herself once again in all her glory. Suddenly she gave a cry. The necklace was gone.

Her husband, already half-undressed, said, "What's the trouble?"

---

11. **Seine** (sĕn): the principal river of Paris.

12. **Rue des Martyrs** (rü′ dā mär-tēr′): a street in Paris.

She turned toward him despairingly, "I . . . I . . . I don't have Mme. Forestier's necklace."

"What! You can't mean it! It's impossible!"

They hunted everywhere, through the folds of the dress, through the folds of the coat, in the pockets. They found nothing.

He asked, "Are you sure you had it when leaving the dance?"

"Yes, I felt it when I was in the hall of the Ministry."

"But if you had lost it on the street, we'd have heard it drop. It must be in the cab."

"Yes. Quite likely. Did you get its number?"

"No. Didn't you notice it either?"

"No."

They looked at each other aghast. Finally Loisel got dressed again.

"I'll retrace our steps on foot," he said, "to see if I can find it."

And he went out. She remained in her evening clothes, without the strength to go to bed, slumped in a chair in the unheated room, her mind a blank.

Her husband came in about seven o'clock. He had had no luck.

He went to the police station, to the newspapers to post a reward, to the cab companies, everywhere the slightest hope drove him.

That evening Loisel returned, pale, his face lined; still he had learned nothing.

"We'll have to write your friend," he said, "to tell her you have broken the catch and are having it repaired. That will give us a little time to turn around."

She wrote to his dictation.

At the end of a week, they had given up all hope.

And Loisel, looking five years older, declared, "We must take steps to replace that piece of jewelry."

The next day they took the case to the jeweler whose name they found inside. He consulted his records. "I didn't sell that necklace, madame," he said. "I only supplied the case."

Then they went from one jeweler to another hunting for a similar necklace, going over their recollections, both sick with despair and anxiety.

They found, in a shop in Palais Royal, a string of diamonds which seemed exactly like the one they were seeking. It was priced at forty thousand francs. They could get it for thirty-six.

They asked the jeweler to hold it for them for three days. And they reached an agreement that he would take it back for thirty-four thousand if the lost one was found before the end of February.

Loisel had eighteen thousand francs he had inherited from his father. He would borrow the rest.

He went about raising the money, asking a thousand francs from one, four hundred from another, a hundred here, sixty there. He signed notes, made ruinous deals, did business with loan sharks, ran the whole gamut of money-

At the end of a week, they had given up all hope.

WORDS   **aghast** (ə-găst′) *adj.* filled with shock or horror
TO   **ruinous** (ro͞o′ə-nəs) *adj.* bringing ruin or downfall; disastrous
KNOW   **gamut** (găm′ət) *n.* the entire range or series of something

lenders. He compromised[13] the rest of his life, risked his signature without knowing if he'd be able to honor it, and then, terrified by the outlook for the future, by the blackness of despair about to close around him, by the prospect of all the <u>privations</u> of the body and tortures of the spirit, he went to claim the new necklace with the thirty-six thousand francs which he placed on the counter of the shopkeeper.

When Mme. Loisel took the necklace back, Mme. Forestier said to her frostily, "You should have brought it back sooner; I might have needed it."

She didn't open the case, an action her friend was afraid of. If she had noticed the substitution, what would she have thought? What would she have said? Would she have thought her a thief?

Mme. Loisel experienced the horrible life the needy live. She played her part, however, with sudden heroism. That frightful debt had to be paid. She would pay it. She dismissed her maid; they rented a garret[14] under the eaves.

She learned to do the heavy housework, to perform the hateful duties of cooking. She washed dishes, wearing down her shell-pink nails scouring the grease from pots and pans; she scrubbed dirty linen, shirts, and cleaning rags, which she hung on a line to dry; she took the garbage down to the street each morning and brought up water, stopping on each landing to get her breath. And, clad like a peasant woman, basket on arm, guarding sou[15] by sou her scanty allowance, she bargained with the fruit dealers, the grocer, the butcher, and was insulted by them.

Each month notes had to be paid, and others renewed to give more time.

Her husband labored evenings to balance a tradesman's accounts, and at night, often, he copied documents at five sous a page.

And this went on for ten years.

Finally, all was paid back, everything including the <u>exorbitant</u> rates of the loan sharks and accumulated compound interest.

Mme. Loisel appeared an old woman, now. She became heavy, rough, harsh, like one of the poor. Her hair untended, her skirts <u>askew</u>, her hands red, her voice shrill, she even slopped water on her floors and scrubbed them herself. But, sometimes, while her husband was at work, she would sit near the window and think of that long-ago evening when, at the dance, she had been so beautiful and admired.

What would have happened if she had not lost that necklace? Who knows? Who can say? How strange and unpredictable life is! How little there is between happiness and misery!

Then one Sunday when she had gone for a walk on the Champs Élysées[16] to relax a bit from the week's labors, she suddenly noticed a woman strolling with a child. It was Mme. Forestier, still young-looking; still beautiful, still charming.

Mme. Loisel felt a rush of emotion. Should she speak to her? Of course. And now that everything was paid off, she would tell her the whole story. Why not?

She went toward her. "Hello, Jeanne."

The other, not recognizing her, showed astonishment at being spoken to so familiarly by this

ACTIVE READING

PREDICT How do you think the story will end?

---

13. **compromised:** exposed to danger.
14. **garret:** room just below the sloping roof of a building; attic.
15. **sou** (so͞o): a French coin of small value.
16. **Champs Élysées** (shäɴ zā-lē-zā'): a famous wide street in Paris.

WORDS	**privation** (prī-vā'shən) *n.* lack of basic necessities or comforts of life
TO	**exorbitant** (ĭg-zôr'bĭ-tənt) *adj.* much too high; excessive
KNOW	**askew** (ə-sky͞o') *adj.* crooked; to one side

33

common person. She stammered. "But . . . madame . . . I don't recognize . . . You must be mistaken."

"No, I'm Mathilde Loisel."

Her friend gave a cry, "Oh, my poor Mathilde, how you've changed!"

"Yes, I've had a hard time since last seeing you. And plenty of misfortunes—and all on account of you!"

"Of me . . . How do you mean?"

"Do you remember that diamond necklace you loaned me to wear to the dance at the Ministry?"

"Yes, but what about it?"

"Well, I lost it."

"You lost it! But you returned it."

"I brought you another just like it. And we've been paying for it for ten years now. You can imagine that wasn't easy for us who had nothing. Well, it's over now, and I am glad of it."

Mme. Forestier stopped short, "You mean to say you bought a diamond necklace to replace mine?"

"Yes. You never noticed, then? They were quite alike."

And she smiled with proud and simple joy. Mme. Forestier, quite overcome, clasped her by the hands. "Oh, my poor Mathilde. But mine was only paste.[17] Why, at most it was worth only five hundred francs!" ❖

---

17. **paste:** a hard, glassy material used in making imitations of precious stones.

Girl Sweeping (1912), William McGregor Paxton. Oil on canvas, 40¼″ × 30⅜″, courtesy of the Museum of American Art of the Pennsylvania Academy of the Fine Arts, Philadelphia, Joseph E. Temple Fund (1912.4).

Connect to the Literature

1. What Do You Think? What was your reaction to the surprise ending? Share your thoughts with a classmate.

> **Comprehension Check**
> - Why is Madame Loisel unhappy with her life at the beginning of the story?
> - Why does Madame Loisel borrow a necklace from Madame Forestier?
> - Why do the Loisels live like paupers for ten years?

Think Critically

2. What might be Madame Loisel's thoughts and feelings right after she learns that the diamond necklace was only paste?

3. How does Madame Loisel change as a result of her experiences?

 THINK ABOUT
- what she values in life
- her positive and negative **character traits**
- her behavior toward others

4. Madame Loisel pays dearly for jumping to a wrong conclusion. Do you think it ultimately ruins her life or saves her life? Explain your answer.

5. **ACTIVE READING** **CAUSE AND EFFECT** Look over the diagram you made in your **READER'S NOTEBOOK** of the sequence of major events in "The Necklace." In your opinion, what would have been the best point in the story for Madame Loisel to break the chain of **cause and effect?** Support your answer with evidence from the story.

Extend Interpretations

6. Critic's Corner The literary critic Edward D. Sullivan declares that "The Necklace" is not just a story pointing to a moral, such as "Honesty is the best policy," but a story showing that in people's lives "blind chance rules." Do you agree or disagree with Sullivan's argument? Cite evidence to support your opinion.

7. What If? Suppose that Madame Loisel had not lost the necklace. On the basis of her feelings and actions up to that point in the story, what do you think her future would have been like?

8. Connect to Life Do people still chase after wealth and social status today? Do you think the pursuit of status is worthwhile? Explain your opinion.

Literary Analysis

PLOT The events that make up the **plot** of a story can be divided into **rising action** and **falling action.** The rising action consists of the **conflict** and **complications** that the main character faces leading up to the **climax,** or turning point, of the story. The falling action, sometimes called the **resolution,** occurs at the end of the story and shows how the conflicts faced by the main character are resolved.

Cooperative Learning Activity With a small group, outline the events in "The Necklace" that form the **rising action,** the **climax,** and the **falling action.**

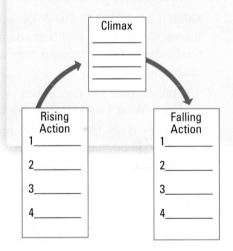

Choices & CHALLENGES

Writing Options

1. Necklace Sequel What do you think Madame Loisel's life will be like now that she has paid off her debt and found out the real value of the necklace? Draft a sequel to the story that explains how she has come to terms with what's happened.

2. Speech Plan Apply the saying "Success is getting what you want, but happiness is wanting what you get" to the characters in "The Necklace." Explain your ideas in notes for a speech.

Activities & Explorations

Video Storyboard View the video version of "The Necklace."

How does it compare with the way you imagined the story when you read it? Choose any scene that you visualized or interpreted differently and create a storyboard for a video that would embody your vision of the story. ~ **VIEWING AND REPRESENTING**

 **Literature in Performance**

Inquiry & Research

The Chemistry of Elegance Find out what materials are used to make artificial jewels and how jewelers can tell real jewels from fakes. You might look in books about costume jewelry or talk to a jeweler. Share your findings with your class.

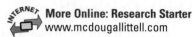 **More Online: Research Starter** www.mcdougallittell.com

Vocabulary in Action

EXERCISE A: CONTEXT CLUES On your paper, write the vocabulary word that best completes each of the following photo captions from a fashion magazine article.

1. What's out? The rags of last year's _____ look. What's in? Elegance like this!

2. In this classy, elegant outfit, any _____ you feel will be quickly forgotten.

3. This beautiful suit is the perfect thing to wear in seeking new job _____.

4. Although those with traditional taste may be _____ at this wedding gown in black and crimson, the gown is making its mark on the fashion scene.

5. This one-of-a-kind design by Tanto Denaro will save its wearer the _____ of running into three other women in the same dress.

6. Wearing this hat straight would be too dull for designer Baka Kyappu, so all of her carefree and oh-so-current headwear is worn _____.

7. With this fabulous creation, Modéliste Vaniteux proves that he deserved the _____ his talent received last season.

8. This sporty number, combining glittering rhinestones and sturdy denim, shows just one of the looks available in the full _____ of Jaquette Atroce's new designs.

9. Although some may feel that the $87,000 price of this outfit is _____, it was the most photographed design at the fashion show.

10. This lovely frock demonstrates how completely The House of Pelea has recovered from the nearly _____ dispute between its two top designers.

EXERCISE B Tell a "round robin" story in which one person begins the story and must keep talking until he or she has used one of the vocabulary words. Then, another person continues the story, using another word. Continue the story until all ten vocabulary words are used.

Building Vocabulary
For an in-depth study of context clues, see page 103.

| WORDS TO KNOW | adulation | askew | gamut | privation | ruinous |
| | aghast | exorbitant | pauper | prospects | vexation |

Grammar in Context: Abstract and Concrete Nouns

In the opening paragraphs of "The Necklace," Maupassant describes women like Madame Loisel:

> Their natural **poise,** their instinctive good **taste,** and their mental **cleverness** . . . make [them] the equals of ladies in high society.

The words in blue type are **abstract nouns,** which refer to ideas or qualities. In the example, Maupassant uses abstract nouns to establish the refined qualities of Madame Loisel. Later he uses concrete nouns, shown below in red type, to give evidence of her "instinctive good taste."

> All at once [Mme. Loisel] found, in a black satin **box,** a superb diamond **necklace.**

As you may recall, **concrete nouns** refer to objects that can be seen, heard, smelled, touched, or tasted.

WRITING EXERCISE Read each sentence. Then complete the sentence starter in parentheses, using abstract nouns if the original sentence contains concrete nouns, or concrete nouns if the original selection contains abstract nouns.

Example: _Abstract noun_ Although poor, Mme. Loisel has great <u>ambitions</u> for herself. (Mme. Loisel wants . . .)

Rewritten Mme. Loisel wants to be invited to the best <u>parties</u>, meet distinguished <u>men</u>, and give elaborate <u>dinners</u>.

1. Mme. Loisel fantasizes about Oriental <u>tapestries</u>, bronze floor <u>lamps</u>, and handsome <u>butlers</u>. (Mme. Loisel is a . . .)

2. Monsieur Loisel works hard to obtain an important <u>invitation</u> for his wife and buys her an expensive <u>dress</u>. (Monsieur Loisel shows great . . .)

3. At the party, Mme. Loisel is a <u>sensation</u>. (Everyone admires her beautiful clothes . . .)

Grammar Handbook Nouns, p. 1180

Guy de Maupassant
1850–1893

Other Works
"A Piece of String"
"The Umbrella"

A Tortured Life Guy de Maupassant was born in northwestern France to an upper-middle-class family. When the family fortune ran out, he was forced into tiring work as a government clerk, which he pursued from 1872 to 1882, until he achieved success as a writer. Although his writing eventually brought him modest wealth, Maupassant led a tortured life. From 1877 until his death, he suffered from an incurable disease, experiencing occasional hallucinations. As the infection spread to his brain, Maupassant became insane and died in a Paris asylum at age 42.

Writing from Experience Maupassant may be the best-known French writer outside France. His hundreds of stories excel in portraying everyday life, and his subjects reflect his background. He wrote about peasants in the countryside near his home, government clerks, upper-class society—and madness. One critic has noted that Maupassant's strength is not his subject matter but his style, which is clear and to the point: he had the "remarkable ability to suggest character with one deft stroke of the pen—a single phrase, a couple of well-chosen verbs." A biographer of Maupassant claims that the "brevity and brisk pace" of his writing gave the short story genre "both a worthy literary form and a new popularity."

Author Activity

As a young man, Maupassant found a second father and mentor in a family friend—the writer Gustave Flaubert. Find out what kinds of stories Flaubert wrote. Then, with classmates, discuss whether you think Flaubert was a father to Maupassant artistically as well as personally.

The Most Dangerous Game

Short Story by RICHARD CONNELL

"The world is made up of two classes— the hunters and the huntees."

Connect to Your Life

Survival! A sudden storm traps hikers in the mountains. A hurricane leaves thousands homeless. The daily news is filled with stories of life-threatening events like these. With a partner, think about one or two similar situations you have experienced or heard about. Using a chart like the one shown, mark what you think are the three most important qualities that would help a person survive each ordeal. Discuss your choices with a partner.

What Does It Take to Survive?

Character traits	trapped in the mountains	hurricane
intelligence		
determination		
experience		
luck		
physical condition		
speed		

Build Background

Big Game Hunting "The Most Dangerous Game" presents two characters who have experienced the dangers and thrills of hunting "big game"—elephants, Cape buffaloes, lions, leopards, and rhinoceroses. Big game hunting was a popular sport of the wealthy class early in the 20th century, the **setting** of this story. Such people had the desire, the money, and the time to travel the world, seeking challenging animals to hunt. The danger and excitement of the chase were a major part of the appeal.

WORDS TO KNOW
Vocabulary Preview

affable	droll	solicitously
amenity	elude	stamina
condone	imperative	tangible
deplorable	quarry	uncanny
disarming	scruple	zealous

LaserLinks: Background for Reading
Cultural Connection

Focus Your Reading

LITERARY ANALYSIS **CONFLICT** Every story **plot** centers on a key **conflict,** or struggle. This struggle may exist between people, or between people and nature or society. Sometimes, though, the struggle may go on inside a character, as it does in this passage from the story you are about to read:

> *I was lying in my tent with a splitting headache one night when a terrible thought pushed its way into my mind. Hunting was beginning to bore me! And hunting, remember, had been my life.*

As you read this story, look for other examples of conflicts and try to **predict** how they will affect the plot of the story.

ACTIVE READING **PREDICTING** A **prediction** is an attempt to answer the question "What will happen next?" To make predictions, notice the following as you read:

- interesting details about **character, plot,** and **setting**
- unusual statements by the main **characters**
- **foreshadowing**—hints about future plot twists

READER'S NOTEBOOK As you read this story, jot down at least three predictions, as well as a few reasons for each guess. Remember, though, that a good suspense story is like a game of cat-and-mouse. The writer will often try to mislead you.

THE MOST DANGEROUS GAME

RICHARD CONNELL

"OFF THERE TO THE RIGHT—SOMEWHERE—
is a large island," said Whitney. "It's rather a mystery—"

"What island is it?" Rainsford asked. "The old charts
call it 'Ship-Trap Island,'" Whitney replied. "A suggestive
name, isn't it? Sailors have a curious dread of the place. I
don't know why. Some superstition—"

"Can't see it," remarked Rainsford, trying to peer through the dank tropical night that was palpable as it pressed its thick warm blackness in upon the yacht.

"You've good eyes," said Whitney, with a laugh, "and I've seen you pick off a moose moving in the brown fall bush at four hundred yards, but even you can't see four miles or so through a moonless Caribbean night."

"Nor four yards," admitted Rainsford. "Ugh! It's like moist black velvet."

"It will be light enough in Rio," promised Whitney. "We should make it in a few days. I hope the jaguar guns have come from Purdey's. We should have some good hunting up the Amazon. Great sport, hunting."

"The best sport in the world," agreed Rainsford.

"For the hunter," amended Whitney. "Not for the jaguar."

"Don't talk rot, Whitney," said Rainsford. "You're a big-game hunter, not a philosopher. Who cares how a jaguar feels?"

"Perhaps the jaguar does," observed Whitney.

"Bah! They've no understanding."

"Even so, I rather think they understand one thing—fear. The fear of pain and the fear of death."

"Nonsense," laughed Rainsford. "This hot weather is making you soft, Whitney. Be a realist. The world is made up of two classes—the hunters and the huntees. Luckily, you and I are hunters. Do you think we've passed that island yet?"

"I can't tell in the dark. I hope so."

"Why?" asked Rainsford.

"The place has a reputation—a bad one."

"Cannibals?" suggested Rainsford.

"Hardly. Even cannibals wouldn't live in such a Godforsaken place. But it's gotten into sailor

lore, somehow. Didn't you notice that the crew's nerves seemed a bit jumpy today?"

"They were a bit strange, now you mention it. Even Captain Nielsen—"

"Yes, even that tough-minded old Swede, who'd go up to the devil himself and ask him for a light. Those fishy blue eyes held a look I never saw there before. All I could get out of him was: 'This place has an evil name among seafaring men, sir.' Then he said to me, very gravely: 'Don't you feel anything?'—as if the air about us was actually poisonous. Now, you mustn't laugh when I tell you this—I did feel something like a sudden chill.

"There was no breeze. The sea was as flat as a plate-glass window. We were drawing near

Untitled [Nyack] (1973), Julio Larraz. Private collection, courtesy of Nohra Haime Gallery, New York.

the island then. What I felt was a—a mental chill; a sort of sudden dread."

"Pure imagination," said Rainsford. "One superstitious sailor can taint the whole ship's company with his fear."

"Maybe. But sometimes I think sailors have an extra sense that tells them when they are in danger. Sometimes I think evil is a <u>tangible</u> thing—with wavelengths, just as sound and light have. An evil place can, so to speak, broadcast vibrations of evil. Anyhow, I'm glad we're getting out of this zone. Well, I think I'll turn in now, Rainsford."

"I'm not sleepy," said Rainsford. "I'm going to smoke another pipe up on the afterdeck."

"Good night, then, Rainsford. See you at breakfast."

"Right. Good night, Whitney."

There was no sound in the night as Rainsford sat there but the muffled throb of the engine that drove the yacht swiftly through the darkness, and the swish and ripple of the wash of the propeller.

Rainsford, reclining in a steamer chair, indolently puffed on his favorite brier.[1] The sensuous drowsiness of the night was on him. "It's so dark," he thought, "that I could sleep without closing my eyes; the night would be my eyelids—"

---

1. **brier** (brī′ər): a tobacco pipe.

WORDS TO KNOW   **tangible** (tăn′jə-bəl) *adj.* capable of being touched or felt; having actual form and substance

An abrupt sound startled him. Off to the right he heard it, and his ears, expert in such matters, could not be mistaken. Again he heard the sound, and again. Somewhere, off in the blackness, someone had fired a gun three times.

Rainsford sprang up and moved quickly to the rail, mystified. He strained his eyes in the direction from which the reports had come, but it was like trying to see through a blanket. He leaped upon the rail and balanced himself there, to get greater elevation; his pipe, striking a rope, was knocked from his mouth. He lunged for it; a short, hoarse cry came from his lips as he realized he had reached too far and had lost his balance. The cry was pinched off short as the blood-warm waters of the Caribbean Sea closed over his head.

He struggled up to the surface and tried to cry out, but the wash from the speeding yacht slapped him in the face, and the salt water in his open mouth made him gag and strangle. Desperately he struck out with strong strokes after the receding lights of the yacht, but he stopped before he had swum fifty feet. A certain cool-headedness had come to him; it was not the first time he had been in a tight place. There was a chance that his cries could be heard by someone aboard the yacht, but that chance was slender and grew more slender as the yacht raced on. He wrestled himself out of his clothes and shouted with all his power. The lights of the yacht became faint and ever-vanishing fireflies; then they were blotted out entirely by the night.

Rainsford remembered the shots. They had come from the right, and doggedly he swam in that direction, swimming with slow, deliberate strokes, conserving his strength. For a seemingly endless time he fought the sea. He began to count his strokes; he could do possibly a hundred more and then—

Rainsford heard a sound. It came out of the darkness, a high, screaming sound, the sound of an animal in an extremity of anguish and terror.

He did not recognize the animal that made the sound; he did not try to; with fresh vitality he swam toward the sound. He heard it again; then it was cut short by another noise, crisp, staccato.

"Pistol shot," muttered Rainsford, swimming on.

Ten minutes of determined effort brought another sound to his ears—the most welcome he had ever heard—the muttering and growling of the sea breaking on a rocky shore. He was almost on the rocks before he saw them; on a night less calm he would have been shattered against them. With his remaining strength he dragged himself from the swirling waters. Jagged crags appeared to jut up into the opaqueness; he forced himself upward, hand over hand. Gasping, his hands raw, he reached a flat place at the top. Dense jungle came down to the very edge of the cliffs. What perils that tangle of trees and underbrush might hold for him did not concern Rainsford just then. All he knew was that he was safe from his enemy, the sea, and that utter weariness was on him. He flung himself down at the jungle edge and tumbled headlong into the deepest sleep of his life.

When he opened his eyes, he knew from the position of the sun that it was late in the afternoon. Sleep had given him new vigor; a sharp hunger was picking at him. He looked about him, almost cheerfully.

"Where there are pistol shots, there are men. Where there are men, there is food," he thought. But what kind of men, he wondered, in so forbidding a place? An unbroken front of snarled and ragged jungle fringed the shore.

He saw no sign of a trail through the closely

knit web of weeds and trees; it was easier to go along the shore, and Rainsford floundered along by the water. Not far from where he had landed, he stopped.

Some wounded thing, by the evidence a large animal, had thrashed about in the underbrush; the jungle weeds were crushed down, and the moss was lacerated; one patch of weeds was stained crimson. A small, glittering object not far away caught Rainsford's eye, and he picked it up. It was an empty cartridge.

"A twenty-two," he remarked. "That's odd. It must have been a fairly large animal, too. The hunter had his nerve with him to tackle it with a light gun. It's clear that the brute put up a fight. I suppose the first three shots I heard was when the hunter flushed[2] his quarry and wounded it. The last shot was when he trailed it here and finished it."

He examined the ground closely and found what he had hoped to find—the print of hunting boots. They pointed along the cliff in the direction he had been going. Eagerly he hurried along, now slipping on a rotten log or a loose stone, but making headway; night was beginning to settle down on the island.

Bleak darkness was blacking out the sea and jungle when Rainsford sighted the lights. He came upon them as he turned a crook in the coastline, and his first thought was that he had come upon a village, for there were many lights. But as he forged along, he saw to his great astonishment that all the lights were in one enormous building—a lofty structure with pointed towers plunging upward into the gloom. His eyes made out the shadowy outlines of a palatial château;[3] it was set on a high bluff, and on three sides of it cliffs dived down to where the sea licked greedy lips in the shadows.

"Mirage," thought Rainsford. But it was no mirage, he found, when he opened the tall spiked iron gate. The stone steps were real enough; the massive door with a leering gargoyle[4] for a knocker was real enough; yet about it all hung an air of unreality.

He lifted the knocker, and it creaked up stiffly as if it had never before been used. He let it fall, and it startled him with its booming loudness. He thought he heard steps within; the door remained closed. Again Rainsford lifted the heavy knocker and let it fall. The door opened then, opened as suddenly as if it were on a spring, and Rainsford stood blinking in the river of glaring gold light that poured out. The first thing Rainsford's eyes discerned was the largest man Rainsford had ever seen—a gigantic creature, solidly made and black-bearded to the waist. In his hand the man held a long-barreled revolver, and he was pointing it straight at Rainsford's heart.

Out of the snarl of beard two small eyes regarded Rainsford.

"Don't be alarmed," said Rainsford, with a smile which he hoped was disarming. "I'm no robber. I fell off a yacht. My name is Sanger Rainsford of New York City."

The menacing look in the eyes did not change. The revolver pointed as rigidly as if the giant were a statue. He gave no sign that he understood Rainsford's words, or that he had even heard them. He was dressed in uniform, a black uniform trimmed with gray astrakhan.[5]

"I'm Sanger Rainsford of New York," Rainsford began again. "I fell off a yacht. I am hungry."

---

2. **flushed:** forced out of a hiding place.

3. **palatial château** (pə-lā'shəl shă-tō'): palacelike mansion.

4. **gargoyle** (gär'goil): an ornamental figure in the shape of a bizarre, monstrous creature.

5. **astrakhan** (ăs'trə-kăn'): a fur made from skins of young lambs.

WORDS TO KNOW **quarry** (kwôr'ē) *n.* the object of a hunt; prey
disarming (dĭs-är'mĭng) *adj.* removing or overcoming suspicion; inspiring confidence

Waiting for Henry Morgan (1984), Julio Larraz. Oil on canvas, 49½″ × 47″, private collection, courtesy of Nohra Haime Gallery, New York.

The man's only answer was to raise with his thumb the hammer of his revolver. Then Rainsford saw the man's free hand go to his forehead in a military salute, and he saw him click his heels together and stand at attention. Another man was coming down the broad marble steps, an erect, slender man in evening clothes. He advanced to Rainsford and held out his hand.

In a cultivated[6] voice marked by a slight accent that gave it added precision and deliberateness, he said: "It is a very great pleasure and honor to welcome Mr. Sanger Rainsford, the celebrated hunter, to my home."

Automatically Rainsford shook the man's hand.

"I've read your book about hunting snow leopards in Tibet, you see," explained the man. "I am General Zaroff."

Rainsford's first impression was that the man was singularly handsome; his second was that there was an original, almost bizarre quality about the general's face. He was a tall man past middle age, for his hair was a vivid white; but his thick eyebrows and pointed military moustache were as black as the night from which Rainsford had come. His eyes, too, were black and very bright. He had high cheekbones, a sharp-cut nose, a spare, dark face, the face of a man used to giving orders, the face of an aristocrat. Turning to the giant in uniform, the general made a sign. The giant put away his pistol, saluted, withdrew.

"Ivan is an incredibly strong fellow," remarked the general, "but he has the misfortune to be deaf and dumb. A simple fellow, but, I'm afraid, like all his race, a bit of a savage."

---

6. **cultivated:** educated and cultured.

"Is he Russian?"

"He is a Cossack,"[7] said the general, and his smile showed red lips and pointed teeth. "So am I.

"Come," he said, "we shouldn't be chatting here. We can talk later. Now you want clothes, food, rest. You shall have them. This is a most restful spot."

Ivan had reappeared, and the general spoke to him with lips that moved but gave forth no sound.

"Follow Ivan, if you please, Mr. Rainsford," said the general. "I was about to have my dinner when you came. I'll wait for you. You'll find that my clothes will fit you, I think."

It was to a huge, beam-ceilinged bedroom with a canopied bed big enough for six men that Rainsford followed the silent giant. Ivan laid out an evening suit, and Rainsford, as he put it on, noticed that it came from a London tailor who ordinarily cut and sewed for none below the rank of duke.

The dining room to which Ivan conducted him was in many ways remarkable. There was a medieval magnificence about it; it suggested a baronial hall of feudal times with its oaken panels, its high ceiling, its vast refectory table where two score men could sit down to eat. About the hall were the mounted heads of many animals—lions, tigers, elephants, moose, bears; larger or more perfect specimens Rainsford had never seen. At the great table the general was sitting, alone.

"You'll have a cocktail, Mr. Rainsford," he suggested. The cocktail was surpassingly good; and, Rainsford noted, the table appointments were of the finest—the linen, the crystal, the silver, the china.

They were eating *borsch*, the rich red soup with whipped cream so dear to Russian palates. Half apologetically General Zaroff said: "We do our best to preserve the amenities of civilization here. Please forgive

> "HERE IN MY PRESERVE ON THIS ISLAND," HE SAID, IN THE SAME SLOW TONE, "I HUNT MORE DANGEROUS GAME."

any lapses. We are well off the beaten track, you know. Do you think the champagne has suffered from its long ocean trip?"

"Not in the least," declared Rainsford. He was finding the general a most thoughtful and affable host, a true cosmopolite.[8] But there was one small trait of the general's that made Rainsford uncomfortable. Whenever he looked up from his plate, he found the general studying him, appraising him narrowly.

"Perhaps," said General Zaroff, "you were surprised that I recognized your name. You see, I read all books on hunting published in English, French, and Russian. I have but one passion in my life, Mr. Rainsford, and it is the hunt."

---

7. **Cossack** (kŏs´ăk): a member of a southern Russian people formerly famous as cavalrymen.

8. **cosmopolite** (kŏz-mŏp´ə-līt´): a sophisticated person who can handle any situation well.

WORDS TO KNOW

amenity (ə-měn´ĭ-tē) *n.* something that adds to one's comfort or convenience
affable (ăf´ə-bəl) *adj.* friendly, pleasant, and easy to talk to

45

Casanova (1987),
Julio Larraz.
Oil on canvas,
60″ × 69½″,
private collection,
courtesy of Nohra
Haime Gallery,
New York.

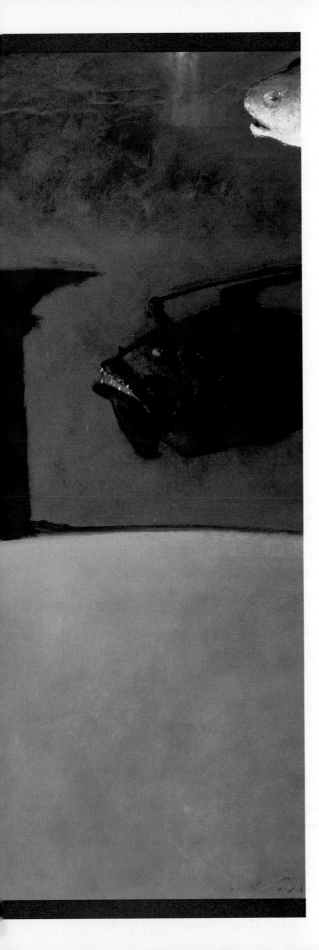

"You have some wonderful heads here," said Rainsford as he ate a particularly well cooked filet mignon. "That Cape buffalo is the largest I ever saw."

"Oh, that fellow. Yes, he was a monster."

"Did he charge you?"

"Hurled me against a tree," said the general. "Fractured my skull. But I got the brute."

"I've always thought," said Rainsford, "that the Cape buffalo is the most dangerous of all big game."

For a moment the general did not reply; he was smiling his curious red-lipped smile. Then he said slowly: "No. You are wrong, sir. The Cape buffalo is not the most dangerous big game." He sipped his wine. "Here in my preserve on this island," he said, in the same slow tone, "I hunt more dangerous game."

Rainsford expressed his surprise. "Is there big game on this island?"

The general nodded. "The biggest."

"Really?"

"Oh, it isn't here naturally, of course. I have to stock the island."

"What have you imported, General?" Rainsford asked. "Tigers?"

The general smiled. "No," he said. "Hunting tigers ceased to interest me some years ago. I exhausted their possibilities, you see. No thrill left in tigers, no real danger. I live for danger, Mr. Rainsford."

The general took from his pocket a gold cigarette case and offered his guest a long black cigarette with a silver tip; it was perfumed and gave off a smell like incense.

"We will have some capital hunting, you and I," said the general. "I shall be most glad to have your society."

"But what game—" began Rainsford.

"I'll tell you," said the general. "You will be amused, I know. I think I may say, in all modesty, that I have done a rare thing. I have invented a new sensation. May I pour you another glass of port, Mr. Rainsford?"

"Thank you, General."

The general filled both glasses and said: "God makes some men poets. Some he makes kings, some beggars. Me he made a hunter. My hand was made for the trigger, my father said. He was a very rich man with a quarter of a million acres in the Crimea,[9] and he was an ardent sportsman. When I was only five years old, he gave me a little gun, specially made in Moscow for me, to shoot sparrows with. When I shot some of his prize turkeys with it, he did not punish me; he complimented me on my marksmanship. I killed my first bear in the Caucasus[9] when I was ten. My whole life has been one prolonged hunt. I went into the army—it was expected of noblemen's sons—and for a time commanded a division of Cossack cavalry, but my real interest was always the hunt. I have hunted every kind of game in every land. It would be impossible for me to tell you how many animals I have killed."

The general puffed at his cigarette.

"After the debacle[10] in Russia I left the country, for it was imprudent[11] for an officer of the Tsar to stay there. Many noble Russians lost everything. I, luckily, had invested heavily in American securities, so I shall never have to open a tearoom in Monte Carlo or drive a taxi in Paris. Naturally, I continued to hunt—grizzlies in your Rockies, crocodiles in the Ganges,[12] rhinoceroses in East Africa. It was in Africa that the Cape buffalo hit me and laid me up for six months. As soon as I recovered, I started for the Amazon to hunt jaguars, for I had heard they were unusually cunning. They weren't." The Cossack sighed. "They were no match at all for a hunter with his wits about him, and a high-powered rifle. I was bitterly disappointed. I was lying in my tent with a splitting headache one night when a terrible thought pushed its way into my mind. Hunting was beginning to bore me! And hunting, remember, had been my life. I have heard that in America businessmen often go to pieces when they give up the business that has been their life."

"Yes, that's so," said Rainsford.

The general smiled. "I had no wish to go to pieces," he said. "I must do something. Now, mine is an analytical mind, Mr. Rainsford. Doubtless that is why I enjoy the problems of the chase."

"No doubt, General Zaroff."

"So," continued the general, "I asked myself why the hunt no longer fascinated me. You are much younger than I am, Mr. Rainsford, and have not hunted as much, but you perhaps can guess the answer."

"What was it?"

"Simply this: hunting had ceased to be what you call 'a sporting proposition.' It had become too easy. I always got my quarry. Always. There is no greater bore than perfection."

The general lit a fresh cigarette.

"No animal had a chance with me any more. That is no boast; it is a mathematical certainty. The animal had nothing but his legs and his instinct. Instinct is no match for reason. When I thought of this, it was a tragic moment for me, I can tell you."

Rainsford leaned across the table, absorbed in what his host was saying.

"It came to me as an inspiration what I must do," the general went on.

"And that was?"

The general smiled the quiet smile of one who has faced an obstacle and surmounted it with success. "I had to invent a new animal to hunt," he said.

"A new animal? You're joking."

"Not at all," said the general. "I never joke about hunting. I needed a new animal. I found one. So I bought this island, built this house,

---

9. **Crimea** (krī-mē′ə) . . . **Caucasus** (kô′kə-səs): regions in the southern part of the former Russian Empire, near the Black Sea.

10. **debacle** (dǐ-bä′kəl): a disastrous defeat; rout (a reference to the 1917 Russian Revolution that overthrew the czar).

11. **imprudent**: showing poor judgment; unwise.

12. **Ganges** (găn′jēz′): a river in northern India.

and here I do my hunting. The island is perfect for my purposes—there are jungles with a maze of trails in them, hills, swamps—"

"But the animal, General Zaroff?"

"Oh," said the general, "it supplies me with the most exciting hunting in the world. No other hunting compares with it for an instant. Every day I hunt, and I never grow bored now, for I have a quarry with which I can match my wits."

Rainsford's bewilderment showed in his face.

"I wanted the ideal animal to hunt," explained the general. "So I said: 'What are the attributes of an ideal quarry?' And the answer was, of course: 'It must have courage, cunning,

"EVERY DAY I HUNT, AND I NEVER GROW BORED

NOW, FOR I HAVE A QUARRY WITH WHICH I CAN MATCH MY WITS."

and, above all, it must be able to reason.'"

"But no animal can reason," objected Rainsford.

"My dear fellow," said the general, "there is one that can."

"But you can't mean—" gasped Rainsford.

"And why not?"

"I can't believe you are serious, General Zaroff. This is a grisly[13] joke."

"Why should I not be serious? I am speaking of hunting."

"Hunting? Good God, General Zaroff, what you speak of is murder."

The general laughed with entire good nature. He regarded Rainsford quizzically. "I refuse to believe that so modern and civilized a young man as you seem to be harbors romantic ideas about the value of human life. Surely your experiences in the war—"

"Did not make me <u>condone</u> cold-blooded murder," finished Rainsford, stiffly.

Laughter shook the general. "How extraordinarily <u>droll</u> you are!" he said. "One does not expect nowadays to find a young man of the educated class, even in America, with such a naïve, and, if I may say so, mid-Victorian point of view. It's like finding a snuffbox in a limousine. Ah, well, doubtless you had Puritan ancestors. So many Americans appear to have had. I'll wager you'll forget your notions when you go hunting with me. You've a genuine new thrill in store for you, Mr. Rainsford."

"Thank you, I'm a hunter, not a murderer."

"Dear me," said the general, quite unruffled, "again that unpleasant word. But I think I can show you that your scruples are quite ill-founded."

"Yes?"

"Life is for the strong, to be lived by the strong, and, if needs be, taken by the strong. The weak of the world were put here to give the strong pleasure. I am strong. Why should I not use my gift? If I wish to hunt, why should I not? I hunt the scum of the earth—sailors from tramp ships—lascars,[14] blacks, Chinese, whites, mongrels—a thoroughbred horse or hound is worth more than a score of them."

"But they are men," said Rainsford, hotly.

---

13. **grisly** (grĭz′lē): horrible; ghastly.

14. **lascars** (lăs′kərz): sailors from India.

WORDS TO KNOW	**condone** (kən-dōn′) *v.* to overlook, forgive, or disregard
	droll (drōl) *adj.* amusingly odd or comical
	scruple (skrōō′pəl) *n.* an uneasy feeling arising from one's conscience or principles

"Precisely," said the general. "That is why I use them. It gives me pleasure. They can reason, after a fashion. So they are dangerous."

"But where do you get them?"

The general's left eyelid fluttered down in a wink. "This island is called Ship Trap," he answered. "Sometimes an angry god of the high seas sends them to me. Sometimes, when Providence is not so kind, I help Providence a bit. Come to the window with me."

Rainsford went to the window and looked out toward the sea.

"Watch! Out there!" exclaimed the general, pointing into the night. Rainsford's eyes saw only blackness, and then, as the general pressed a button, far out to sea Rainsford saw the flash of lights.

The general chuckled. "They indicate a channel," he said, "where there's none: giant rocks with razor edges crouch like a sea monster with wide-open jaws. They can crush a ship as easily as I crush this nut." He dropped a walnut on the hardwood floor and brought his heel grinding down on it. "Oh, yes," he said, casually, as if in answer to a question, "I have electricity. We try to be civilized here."

"Civilized? And you shoot down men?"

A trace of anger was in the general's black eyes, but it was there for but a second, and he said, in his most pleasant manner: "Dear me, what a righteous young man you are! I assure you I do not do the thing you suggest. That would be barbarous. I treat these visitors with every consideration. They get plenty of good food and exercise. They get into splendid physical condition. You shall see for yourself tomorrow."

"What do you mean?"

"We'll visit my training school," smiled the general. "It's in the cellar. I have about a dozen pupils down there now. They're from the Spanish bark *Sanlúcar* that had the bad luck to go on the rocks out there. A very inferior lot, I regret to say. Poor specimens and more accustomed to the deck than to the jungle."

He raised his hand, and Ivan, who served as waiter, brought thick Turkish coffee. Rainsford, with an effort, held his tongue in check.

"It's a game, you see," pursued the general, blandly. "I suggest to one of them that we go hunting. I give him a supply of food and an excellent hunting knife. I give him three hours' start. I am to follow, armed only with a pistol of the smallest caliber and range. If my quarry eludes me for three whole days, he wins the game. If I find him"—the general smiled—"he loses."

"Suppose he refuses to be hunted?"

"Oh," said the general, "I give him his option, of course. He need not play that game if he doesn't wish to. If he does not wish to hunt, I turn him over to Ivan. Ivan once had the honor of serving as official knouter[15] to the Great White Tsar, and he has his own ideas of sport. Invariably, Mr. Rainsford, invariably they choose the hunt."

"And if they win?"

The smile on the general's face widened. "To date I have not lost," he said.

Then he added, hastily: "I don't wish you to think me a braggart, Mr. Rainsford. Many of them afford only the most elementary sort of problem. Occasionally I strike a tartar.[16] One almost did win. I eventually had to use the dogs."

"The dogs?"

"This way, please. I'll show you."

The general steered Rainsford to a window. The lights from the windows sent a flickering

---

15. **knouter** (nout′ər): a person who whipped criminals in Russia.

16. **strike a tartar:** encounter a fierce opponent.

WORDS TO KNOW   **elude** (ĭ-lōōd′) v. to escape, especially by means of daring, cleverness, or skill

illumination that made grotesque patterns on the courtyard below, and Rainsford could see moving about there a dozen or so huge black shapes; as they turned toward him, their eyes glittered greenly.

"A rather good lot, I think," observed the general. "They are let out at seven every night. If anyone should try to get into my house—or out of it—something extremely regrettable would occur to him." He hummed a snatch of song from the Folies Bergère.[17]

"And now," said the general, "I want to show you my new collection of heads. Will you come with me to the library?"

"I hope," said Rainsford, "that you will excuse me tonight, General Zaroff. I'm really not feeling at all well."

"Ah, indeed?" the general inquired, solicitously. "Well, I suppose that's only natural, after your long swim. You need a good, restful night's sleep. Tomorrow you'll feel like a new man, I'll wager. Then we'll hunt, eh? I've one rather promising prospect—"

Rainsford was hurrying from the room.

"Sorry you can't go with me tonight," called the general. "I expect rather fair sport—a big, strong black. He looks resourceful— Well, good night, Mr. Rainsford; I hope you have a good night's rest."

 **THE BED WAS GOOD, AND THE** pajamas of the softest silk, and he was tired in every fiber of his being, but nevertheless Rainsford could not quiet his brain with the opiate of sleep. He lay, eyes wide open. Once he thought he heard stealthy steps in the corridor outside his room. He sought to throw open the door; it would not open. He went to the

window and looked out. His room was high up in one of the towers. The lights of the château were out now, and it was dark and silent, but there was a fragment of sallow moon, and by its wan light he could see, dimly, the courtyard; there, weaving in and out in the pattern of shadow, were black, noiseless forms; the hounds heard him at the window and looked up, expectantly, with their green eyes. Rainsford went back to the bed and lay down. By many methods he tried to put himself to sleep. He had achieved a doze when, just as morning began to come, he heard, far off in the jungle, the faint report of a pistol.

General Zaroff did not appear until luncheon. He was dressed faultlessly in the tweeds of a country squire. He was solicitous about the state of Rainsford's health.

"As for me," sighed the general, "I do not feel so well. I am worried, Mr. Rainsford. Last night I detected traces of my old complaint."

To Rainsford's questioning glance the general said: "Ennui. Boredom."

Then, taking a second helping of crêpes suzettes, the general explained: "The hunting was not good last night. The fellow lost his head. He made a straight trail that offered no problems at all. That's the trouble with these sailors; they have dull brains to begin with, and they do not know how to get about in the woods. They do excessively stupid and obvious things. It's most annoying. Will you have another glass of Chablis, Mr. Rainsford?"

"General," said Rainsford, firmly, "I wish to leave this island at once."

The general raised his thickets of eyebrows; he seemed hurt. "But, my dear fellow," the general protested, "you've only just come.

---

17. **Folies Bergère** (fô-lē′ běr-zhĕr′): a music hall in Paris, famous for its variety shows.

WORDS TO KNOW **solicitously** (sə-lĭs′ĭ-təs-lē) *adv.* with an expression of care or concern

You've had no hunting—"

"I wish to go today," said Rainsford. He saw the dead black eyes of the general on him, studying him. General Zaroff's face suddenly brightened.

He filled Rainsford's glass with venerable Chablis from a dusty bottle.

"Tonight," said the general, "we will hunt—you and I."

Rainsford shook his head. "No, General," he said. "I will not hunt."

The general shrugged his shoulders and delicately ate a hothouse grape. "As you wish, my friend," he said. "The choice rests entirely with you. But may I not venture to suggest that you will find my idea of sport more diverting than Ivan's?"

He nodded toward the corner to where the giant stood, scowling, his thick arms crossed on his hogshead of chest.

"You don't mean—" cried Rainsford.

"My dear fellow," said the general, "have I not told you I always mean what I say about hunting? This is really an inspiration. I drink to a foeman worthy of my steel—at last."

The general raised his glass, but Rainsford sat staring at him.

"You'll find this game worth playing," the general said, enthusiastically. "Your brain against mine. Your woodcraft against mine. Your strength and stamina against mine. Outdoor chess! And the stake is not without value, eh?"

"And if I win—" began Rainsford, huskily.

"I'll cheerfully acknowledge myself defeated if I do not find you by midnight of the third day," said General Zaroff. "My sloop will place you on the mainland near a town."

The general read what Rainsford was thinking.

"Oh, you can trust me," said the Cossack. "I will give you my word as a gentleman and a sportsman. Of course, you, in turn, must agree to say nothing of your visit here."

"I'll agree to nothing of the kind," said Rainsford.

"Oh," said the general, "in that case— But why discuss that now? Three days hence we can discuss it over a bottle of Veuve Cliquot, unless—"

The general sipped his wine.

Then a businesslike air animated him. "Ivan," he said to Rainsford, "will supply you with hunting clothes, food, a knife. I suggest you wear moccasins; they leave a poorer trail. I suggest, too, that you avoid the big swamp in the southeast corner of the island. We call it Death Swamp. There's quicksand there. One foolish fellow tried it. The deplorable part of it was that Lazarus followed him. You can imagine my feelings, Mr. Rainsford. I loved Lazarus; he was the finest hound in my pack. Well, I must beg you to excuse me now. I always take a siesta after lunch. You'll hardly have time for a nap, I fear. You'll want to start, no doubt. I shall not follow till dusk. Hunting at night is so much more exciting than by day, don't you think? Au revoir,[18] Mr. Rainsford, au revoir."

General Zaroff, with a deep, courtly bow, strolled from the room.

From another door came Ivan. Under one arm he carried khaki hunting clothes, a haversack of food, a leather sheath containing a long-bladed hunting knife; his right hand rested on a cocked revolver thrust in the crimson sash about his waist. . . .

Rainsford had fought his way through the bush for two hours. "I must keep my nerve. I must keep my nerve," he said, through tight teeth.

He had not been entirely clear-headed when

---

18. **au revoir** (ō′ rə-vwär′): goodbye; farewell until we meet again

WORDS TO KNOW

stamina (stăm′ə-nə) *n.* physical or moral strength; endurance
deplorable (dĭ-plôr′ə-bəl) *adj.* deeply regrettable; unfortunate

the château gates snapped shut behind him. His whole idea at first was to put distance between himself and General Zaroff, and, to this end, he had plunged along, spurred on by the sharp rowels of something very like panic. Now he had got a grip on himself, had stopped, and was taking stock of himself and the situation.

He saw that straight flight was futile; inevitably it would bring him face to face with the sea. He was in a picture with a frame of water, and his operations, clearly, must take place within that frame.

"I'll give him a trail to follow," muttered Rainsford, and he struck off from the rude path he had been following into the trackless wilderness. He executed a series of intricate loops; he doubled on his trail again and again, recalling all the lore of the fox hunt, and all the dodges of the fox. Night found him leg-weary, with hands and face lashed by the branches, on a thickly wooded ridge. He knew it would be insane to blunder on through the dark, even if he had the strength. His need for rest was <u>imperative</u>, and he thought, "I have played the fox; now I must play the cat of the fable." A big tree with a thick trunk and outspread branches was nearby, and, taking care to leave not the slightest mark, he climbed up into the crotch and, stretching out on one of the broad limbs, after a fashion, rested. Rest brought him new confidence and almost a feeling of security. Even so <u>zealous</u> a hunter as General Zaroff could not trace him there, he told himself; only the devil himself could follow that complicated trail through the jungle after dark. But perhaps the general was a devil—

 **An apprehensive night** crawled slowly by like a wounded snake, and sleep did not visit Rainsford, although the silence of a dead world was on the jungle. Toward morning, when a dingy gray was varnishing the sky, the cry of some startled bird focused Rainsford's attention in that direction. Something was coming through the bush, coming slowly, carefully, coming by the same winding way Rainsford had come. He flattened himself down on the limb, and through a screen of leaves almost as thick as tapestry, he watched. The thing that was approaching was a man.

It was General Zaroff. He made his way along with his eyes fixed in utmost concentration on the ground before him. He paused, almost beneath the tree, dropped to his knees, and studied the ground. Rainsford's impulse was to hurl himself down like a panther, but he saw that the general's right hand held something metallic—a small automatic pistol.

The hunter shook his head several times, as if he were puzzled. Then he straightened up and took from his case one of his black cigarettes; its pungent, incenselike smoke floated up to Rainsford's nostrils.

Rainsford held his breath. The general's eyes had left the ground and were traveling inch by inch up the tree. Rainsford froze there, every muscle tensed for a spring. But the sharp eyes of the hunter stopped before they reached the limb where Rainsford lay; a smile spread over his brown face. Very deliberately he blew a smoke ring into the air; then he turned his back on the tree and walked carelessly away, back along the trail he had come. The swish of the underbrush against his hunting boots grew fainter and fainter.

The pent-up air burst hotly from Rainsford's lungs. His first thought made him feel sick and numb. The general could follow a trail through the woods at night; he could follow an extremely difficult trail; he must have <u>uncanny</u> powers; only by the merest chance had the Cossack failed to see his quarry.

Rainsford's second thought was even more terrible. It sent a shudder of cold horror through his whole being. Why had the general smiled? Why had he turned back?

Rainsford did not want to believe what his reason told him was true, but the truth was as evident as the sun that had by now pushed through the morning mists. The general was playing with him! The general was saving him

for another day's sport! The Cossack was the cat; he was the mouse. Then it was that Rainsford knew the full meaning of terror.

"I will not lose my nerve. I will not."

He slid down from the tree and struck off again into the woods. His face was set, and he forced the machinery of his mind to function. Three hundred yards from his hiding place he stopped where a huge dead tree leaned precariously on a smaller, living one. Throwing off his sack of food, Rainsford took his knife from its sheath and began to work with all his energy.

The job was finished at last, and he threw himself down behind a fallen log a hundred feet away. He did not have to wait long. The cat was coming again to play with the mouse.

Following the trail with the sureness of a bloodhound came General Zaroff. Nothing escaped those searching black eyes, no crushed blade of grass, no bent twig, no mark, no matter how faint, in the moss. So intent was the Cossack on his stalking that he was upon the thing Rainsford had made before he saw it. His foot touched the protruding bough[19] that was the trigger. Even as he touched it, the general sensed his danger and leaped back with the agility of an ape. But he was not quite quick enough; the dead tree, delicately adjusted to rest on the cut living one, crashed down and struck the general a glancing blow on the shoulder as it fell; but for his alertness, he must have been smashed beneath it. He staggered, but he did not fall; nor did he drop his revolver. He stood there, rubbing his injured shoulder, and Rainsford, with fear again gripping his heart, heard the general's mocking laugh ring through the jungle.

"Rainsford," called the general, "if you are within sound of my voice, as I suppose you are, let me congratulate you. Not many men know how to make a Malay man-catcher.

> THE COSSACK WAS THE CAT; HE WAS THE MOUSE. THEN IT WAS THAT RAINSFORD KNEW THE FULL MEANING OF TERROR.

---

19. **protruding bough** (bou): a tree branch that extends or juts out.

The Voice of the Casuarina (1985), Julio Larraz. Oil on canvas, 60½″ × 60½″, private collection, courtesy of Nohra Haime Gallery, New York.

Luckily for me I, too, have hunted in Malacca.[20] You are proving interesting, Mr. Rainsford. I am going now to have my wound dressed; it's only a slight one. But I shall be back. I shall be back."

When the general, nursing his bruised shoulder, had gone, Rainsford took up his flight again. It was flight now, a desperate,

hopeless flight, that carried him on for some hours. Dusk came, then darkness, and still he pressed on. The ground grew softer under his moccasins; the vegetation grew ranker, denser;

---

20. **Malay** (mə-lā′) . . . **Malacca** (mə-lăk′ə): The Malays are a people of southeast Asia. Malacca is a region they inhabit, just south of Thailand.

insects bit him savagely. Then, as he stepped forward, his foot sank into the ooze. He tried to wrench it back, but the muck sucked viciously at his foot as if it were a giant leech. With a violent effort he tore his foot loose. He knew where he was now. Death Swamp and its quicksand.

His hands were tight closed as if his nerve were something tangible that someone in the darkness was trying to tear from his grip. The softness of the earth had given him an idea. He stepped back from the quicksand a dozen feet or so, and like some huge prehistoric beaver, he began to dig.

Rainsford had dug himself in in France when a second's delay meant death. That had been a placid pastime compared to his digging now. The pit grew deeper; when it was above his shoulders, he climbed out and from some hard saplings cut stakes and sharpened them to a fine point. These stakes he planted in the bottom of the pit with the points sticking up. With flying fingers he wove a rough carpet of weeds and branches, and with it he covered the mouth of the pit. Then, wet with sweat and aching with tiredness, he crouched behind the stump of a lightning-charred tree.

He knew his pursuer was coming; he heard the padding sound of feet on the soft earth, and the night breeze brought him the perfume of the general's cigarette. It seemed to Rainsford that the general was coming with unusual swiftness; he was not feeling his way along, foot by foot. Rainsford, crouching there, could not see the general, nor could he see the pit. He lived a year in a minute. Then he felt an impulse to cry aloud with joy, for he heard the sharp crackle of the breaking branches as the cover of the pit gave way; he heard the sharp scream of pain as the pointed stakes found their mark. He leaped up from

his place of concealment. Then he cowered back. Three feet from the pit a man was standing, with an electric torch in his hand.

"You've done well, Rainsford," the voice of the general called. "Your Burmese tiger pit has claimed one of my best dogs. Again you score. I think, Mr. Rainsford, I'll see what you can do against my whole pack. I'm going home for a rest now. Thank you for a most amusing evening."

AT DAYBREAK RAINSFORD, lying near the swamp, was awakened by a sound that made him know that he had new things to learn about fear. It was a distant sound, faint and wavering, but he knew it. It was the baying of a pack of hounds.

Rainsford knew he could do one of two things. He could stay where he was and wait. That was suicide. He could flee. That was postponing the inevitable. For a moment he stood there, thinking. An idea that held a wild chance came to him, and, tightening his belt, he headed away from the swamp.

The baying of the hounds grew nearer, then still nearer, nearer, ever nearer. On a ridge Rainsford climbed a tree. Down a watercourse, not a quarter of a mile away, he could see the bush moving. Straining his eyes, he saw the lean figure of General Zaroff; just ahead of him, Rainsford made out another figure whose wide shoulders surged through the tall jungle weeds; it was the giant Ivan, and he seemed pulled forward by some unseen force; Rainsford knew that Ivan must be holding the pack in leash.

They would be on him any minute now. His mind worked frantically. He thought of a native trick he had learned in Uganda. He slid down the tree. He caught hold of a springy young sapling, and to it he fastened his hunting knife, with the blade pointing down the trail; with a bit of wild grapevine he tied back the sapling. Then he ran for his life. The hounds raised their voices as they hit the fresh scent. Rainsford knew now how an animal at bay feels.

He had to stop to get his breath. The baying of the hounds stopped abruptly, and Rainsford's heart stopped, too. They must have reached the knife.

He shinned excitedly up a tree and looked back. His pursuers had stopped. But the hope that was in Rainsford's brain when he climbed died, for he saw in the shallow valley that General Zaroff was still on his feet. But Ivan was not. The knife, driven by the recoil of the springing tree, had not wholly failed.

Rainsford had hardly tumbled to the ground when the pack took up the cry again.

"Nerve, nerve, nerve!" he panted, as he dashed along. A blue gap showed between the trees dead ahead. Ever nearer drew the hounds. Rainsford forced himself on toward that gap. He reached it. It was the shore of the sea. Across a cove he could see the gloomy gray stone of the château. Twenty feet below him the sea rumbled and hissed. Rainsford hesitated. He heard the hounds. Then he leaped far out into the sea. . . .

When the general and his pack reached the place by the sea, the Cossack stopped. For some minutes he stood regarding the blue-green expanse of water. He shrugged his shoulders. Then he sat down, took a drink of brandy from a silver flask, lit a perfumed cigarette, and hummed a bit from *Madama Butterfly*.[21]

General Zaroff had an exceedingly good dinner in his great paneled dining hall that evening. With it he had a bottle of Pol Roger and half a bottle of Chambertin. Two slight annoyances kept him from perfect enjoyment. One was the thought that it would be difficult to replace Ivan; the other was that his quarry had escaped him; of course the American hadn't played the game—so thought the general as he tasted his after-dinner liqueur. In his library he read, to soothe himself, from the works of Marcus Aurelius.[22] At ten he went up to his bedroom. He was deliciously tired, he said to himself, as he locked himself in. There was a little moonlight, so before turning on his light he went to the window and looked down at the courtyard. He could see the great hounds, and he called "Better luck another time" to them. Then he switched on the light.

A man, who had been hiding in the curtains of the bed, was standing there.

"Rainsford!" screamed the general. "How in God's name did you get here?"

"Swam," said Rainsford. "I found it quicker than walking through the jungle."

The general sucked in his breath and smiled. "I congratulate you," he said. "You have won the game."

Rainsford did not smile. "I am still a beast at bay," he said, in a low, hoarse voice. "Get ready, General Zaroff."

The general made one of his deepest bows. "I see," he said. "Splendid! One of us is to furnish a repast[23] for the hounds. The other will sleep in this very excellent bed. On guard, Rainsford. . . ."

He had never slept in a better bed, Rainsford decided. ❖

---

21. *Madama Butterfly:* a famous opera.
22. **Marcus Aurelius** (mär′kəs ô-rē′lē-əs): an ancient Roman emperor and philosopher.
23. **repast** (rĭ-păst′): meal.

Connect to the Literature

1. What Do You Think? Explain what you think happens to Rainsford and Zaroff at the end of the story.

> **Comprehension Check**
> - Before arriving at the island, what is Rainsford's position on hunting?
> - Why has Zaroff begun hunting human "game"?
> - What tricks does Rainsford use to avoid capture?

Think Critically

2. **ACTIVE READING** **PREDICTING** How accurate were the **predictions** you made in your **READER'S NOTEBOOK** as you read the story? Discuss with a classmate the **details** in the story that either helped or misled you.

3. What is your reaction to Zaroff's statement: "We try to be civilized here"? Explain your answer.

4. Look over the chart of qualities that you created for the Connect to Your Life activity on page 38. In your opinion, which of these **character traits** most help Rainsford win the game? Support your choices with details from the story.

5. Why do you think Rainsford chooses to confront Zaroff in the end, rather than simply ambush him?

6. Do you think that Rainsford's views on hunting have been permanently changed by his experience of being hunted? Why or why not?

> **THINK ABOUT**
> - Rainsford's conversation with Whitney at the beginning of the story
> - his last encounters with Ivan and Zaroff
> - the last line of the story

Extend Interpretations

7. What If? Imagine that Rainsford's friend, Whitney, has formed a search party that lands on the island. Find a point in the **plot** of the story where Whitney's arrival might take place and describe the possible consequences of this event.

8. Connect to Life Early in the story, Rainsford declares that "the world is made up of two classes—the hunters and the huntees." Do you agree? Explain your opinion.

Literary Analysis

CONFLICT Most stories are built around a central **conflict**, or struggle. This story, for example, centers on the deadly competition between Zaroff and Rainsford. A conflict may be either external or internal. An **external conflict** involves a character pitted against an outside force, such as nature, a physical obstacle, or another character. An **internal conflict** is one that occurs within a character's own mind.

Cooperative Learning Activity Make a chart like the one shown below. Working with a partner, go back through the story and list as many instances of each kind of conflict as you can. When you are done with your chart, discuss the following questions with a larger group:
- Which conflicts added the most excitement to the story?
- Which conflicts revealed something important about one of the characters? Explain.
- Why do you think Connell chose to include each of the other examples you found?

> Internal Conflict
> Zaroff |
> Rainsford |
>
> External Conflict
> person vs. person |
> person vs. nature |
> person vs. obstacle |

Writing Options

1. Recollection Diary Rainsford's experience on the island probably haunted his thoughts for years. Think of an experience you have had that has affected you deeply. Record the experience in a diary entry. Place the entry in your **Working Portfolio.**

2. Comparison of the Hunters In what ways are Zaroff and Rainsford similar and different? You could use a Venn diagram to record your thoughts. Then write a paragraph in which you highlight similarities and differences between the characters.

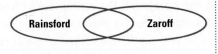

Rainsford   Zaroff

Writing Handbook
See page 1155: Compare–Contrast.

Activities & Explorations

1. Trial Arguments Are Rainsford's actions justified at the end of the story? Write either the defense's or the prosecution's opening arguments in his trial. Present your argument to your class. **~ SPEAKING AND LISTENING**

2. Illustrated Map What other dangers has Zaroff hidden on his nightmarish hunting ground? Create an illustrated map of the island. Include details from the story, such as the château and Death Swamp. Then add your own features with notes explaining the dangers of each one. **~ ART**

3. Book on Tape Adapt a scene from the story as an audio book excerpt. Decide whether you want to keep all the narration or turn the scene into a drama by adding dialogue. **~ SPEAKING AND LISTENING**

Inquiry & Research

War Games Today, a nonlethal version of Zaroff's "game" takes place in arcades and on mock battlefields in many countries around the world. In these games, participants "shoot" each other with lasers and paintballs. Players call these war games "harmless fun." Do you agree? What is your opinion of war games?

Real World Link
Read the magazine article on page 61 before writing your opinion.

Vocabulary in Action

EXERCISE A: CONTEXT CLUES On your paper, fill in each blank with the word that best completes the sentence.

1. Rainsford will _____ the hunter by using a trick he learned in Uganda.
2. Society does not _____ the actions of a cold-blooded murderer.
3. His _____ and strength made the general believe that he had found a worthwhile opponent.
4. A _____ sense of humor amuses some people.
5. Zaroff's _____ behavior at the beginning of the story contrasts with his businesslike approach to the hunt.

EXERCISE B: ASSESSMENT PRACTICE Identify the relationship between each pair of words by writing *Synonyms* or *Antonyms*.

1. **solicitously**–indifferently
2. **affable**–disagreeable
3. **tangible**–physical
4. **quarry**–trapper
5. **imperative**–required
6. **disarming**–offensive
7. **zealous**–passionate
8. **stamina**–vigor
9. **amenity**–crudeness
10. **deplorable**–distressing

WORDS TO KNOW					
affable	deplorable	elude	scruple	tangible
amenity	disarming	imperative	solicitously	uncanny
condone	droll	quarry	stamina	zealous

Building Vocabulary
For an in-depth lesson on word relationships such as synonyms and antonyms, see page 849.

Grammar in Context: Choosing Precise Verbs

In the following excerpt from "The Most Dangerous Game," carefully chosen verbs help convey Rainsford's complete exhaustion after his escape from the sea.

> He **flung** himself down at the jungle edge and **tumbled** headlong into the deepest sleep of his life.

Think about how the tone of the sentence would change had the author written, "He <u>lay</u> down at the jungle edge and <u>went</u> into the deepest sleep of his life." Experienced writers often avoid using such common verbs as *be, have, make, go, say,* and *lie.* Although there is nothing wrong with these verbs, more precise verbs often work better.

Apply to Your Writing Using precise verbs in your writing can help you

- clarify meaning and characters' actions
- create vivid images
- strengthen the mood or tone of a story

WRITING EXERCISE In the sentences below, replace each underlined verb with a verb that creates a more vivid picture. **Usage Tip:** Make sure the verbs you select agree in number with their subjects.

Example: Original General Zaroff <u>sits</u> back in his chair and <u>says</u> what he is thinking.
Rewritten General Zaroff <u>settles</u> back in his chair and <u>reveals</u> what he is thinking. (Both new verbs are singular to agree with the singular subject.)

1. Rainsford <u>walks</u> over the uneven ground.
2. His heart <u>beats</u> wildly as he runs.
3. Rainsford <u>climbs</u> up the tree.
4. General Zaroff <u>follows</u> him.

Connect to the Literature Look at the paragraph on page 42 that begins, "Rainsford sprang up . . ." In three places in the paragraph the author could have used the word *jumped,* but he chose more precise verbs instead. Can you name the verbs he used? How do they improve the story?

Grammar Handbook Subject-Verb Agreement, pp. 1204–1206

Richard Connell
1893–1949

Other Works
Ironies

Early Years Even as a young boy, Richard Connell loved to write. When he was only 10 years old, he covered baseball games for his father's daily newspaper in Poughkeepsie, New York. By 16, Connell was city editor for the *Poughkeepsie News-Press.* As a Harvard student, he edited two school publications, the *Daily Crimson* and the humor magazine *The Lampoon.*

His Varied Career While a soldier during World War I, Connell edited his army division's newspaper. In 1919, he became a freelance fiction writer.

Though he focused mostly on short stories, publishing over 300 in American and British magazines, he also wrote novels and screenplays. His career flowered in the 1920s and 1930s, bringing him fame and wealth. Yet for all that he produced, his writings today are for the most part unknown to the public. "The Most Dangerous Game" is the only one of his stories that is still widely read.

Author Activity

From Story to Film Later in his career, Connell became a screenwriter. Find out what movies he wrote the screenplay for. Then, with classmates, discuss other books, movies, or TV shows that may have been inspired by Connell's story.

 LaserLinks: Background for Reading
Contemporary Connection

GAMES PEOPLE PROBABLY SHOULDN'T PLAY

②

③ **A**ccording to the company that started the trend, some 18,000 people in hundreds of different weekend groups in the U.S. and Canada pay $30, $50, or more per person to take part in an outdoor "game" that you might want to consider carefully—very carefully—before anyone in your family joins in. Called by such names as "Skirmish," "The War Game," and "Survival" (it was originated by National Survival Games of New London, N.H.), the game has two teams of players competing in a woodland setting to capture each other's flag. But to reach the flag, players "kill" their rivals—by shooting them with realistic pistols that fire gelatin pellets filled with red dye.

④ The game is supposedly safe—players wear goggles—but reports of eye damage have rival companies arguing over whose guns are less likely to cause injury. It's also said to be wholesome fun, according to some 400 to 500 franchised dealers who rent guns to use on playing fields

⑤ across the country (and in West Germany, Britain, and Japan, says Toronto-based Adventure Game of America). But Georgia Lanoil, a psychologist on the board of the *Journal of Preventive Psychiatry*, disputes claims that playing provides a harmless release for pent-up aggressions. A conclusion drawn from studies on anger, she says, is that hostile behavior often is a rehearsal for future action. "It's one step beyond viewing violent films, and isn't like football, where you try to get past your opponent to the goal. Here, the goal is annihilation." Adds Dr. Robert London, director of short-term psychotherapy at New York University Medical Center-Bellevue: "Why anyone would get high on people-hunting and simulated murder is something they should discuss with their therapist."

BUSINESSWEEK **①**

Reading for Information

Do you believe everything you read? You shouldn't! When you read an article, you need to decide whether the information is accurate and reliable.

EVALUATING SOURCES

A writer's viewpoint, or **bias,** can influence his or her choice of what to report and how to report it.

YOUR TURN Use the questions and activities below to evaluate this article.

① Consider the source of the article. Would you expect it to be fair and balanced? Why or why not?

② Read the article's title. What does it tell you about the writer's viewpoint?

③ A **fact** is a statement that can be proved to be true or untrue. What facts are given here?

④ An **opinion** is something a person believes. What clues in the second paragraph reveal the writer's opinion?

⑤ Identify the various opinions given about the games. What are the credentials of each source?

Identifying Bias What is the writer's bias? Support your opinion with evidence.

Inquiry & Research

Activity Link: "The Most Dangerous Game," p. 59. Has the opinion of war games you formed while reading "The Most Dangerous Game" changed now that you have read this article? Write a paragraph explaining your opinion.

Where Have You Gone, Charming Billy?

Short Story by TIM O'BRIEN

"Then they found him. Green and covered with algae."

Connect to Your Life

Nerves of Steel? Some people seem to have nerves of steel. They always appear calm, no matter what they are feeling inside. Most people, however, show their feelings when they are very afraid or extremely anxious. What are some ways of showing fear or anxiety that you have observed in yourself or other people? Which of them seem "normal," and which are surprising? Discuss your responses with your classmates.

Build Background

Vietnam War "Where Have You Gone, Charming Billy?" takes place in the Southeast Asian country of Vietnam during a war in which nearly 58,000 Americans died. The Vietnam War grew out of a conflict over communism. South Vietnamese rebels, with the aid of Communist-ruled North Vietnam, began trying to take over South Vietnam in 1957. To help prevent the spread of communism, the United States entered the war as an ally of the South Vietnamese government in 1964. Between 1965 and 1973, over 2 million Americans were sent to Vietnam. Although the soldiers were given special training, few were prepared for the kind of fear and anxiety they would face in the jungles and rice fields of that unfamiliar land.

WORDS TO KNOW
Vocabulary Preview

casually	elegantly	silhouetted
conical	execute	transparent
consolation	inertia	
diffuse	primitive	

Focus Your Reading

LITERARY ANALYSIS **CHARACTER** Most stories center on the experiences and actions of one or more **main characters.** Other characters, who interact with the main characters and help move the story along, are called **minor characters.** As you read this story, notice who the main character is and identify the details that indicate that he is the focus of the story. Also notice who the minor characters are and what they contribute to the story.

ACTIVE READING **MAKING INFERENCES** When you make a logical guess about something in a story, based on information in the story and your own common sense, you are making an **inference.** As you read this story, record clues that help you understand who Paul Berlin is and what he is going through. Pay special attention to

- what he does with his body
- what he notices in his surroundings
- what he thinks about

READER'S NOTEBOK Use a chart like the one shown to record your observations.

Private First Class Paul Berlin

Statement in Story	Common Sense	Inference
"He pretended he was not a soldier."	People pretend that things they wish were true <u>are</u> true.	Paul does not like being a soldier.

Tim O'Brien

Where Have You Gone, Charming Billy?

The platoon of twenty-six soldiers moved slowly in the dark, single file, not talking.

One by one, like sheep in a dream, they passed through the hedgerow,[1] crossed quietly over a meadow and came down to the rice paddy.[2] There they stopped. Their leader knelt down, motioning with his hand, and one by one the other soldiers squatted in the shadows,

---

1. **hedgerow:** a thick hedge separating fields or farms.
2. **rice paddy:** a flooded field in which rice is grown.

vanishing in the <u>primitive</u> stealth of warfare. For a long time they did not move.

Except for the sounds of their breathing, . . . the twenty-six men were very quiet: some of them excited by the adventure, some of them afraid, some of them exhausted from the long night march, some of them looking forward to reaching the sea where they would be safe. At the rear of the column, Private First Class Paul Berlin lay quietly with his forehead resting on the black plastic stock of his rifle, his eyes closed. He was pretending he was not in the war, pretending he had not watched Billy Boy Watkins die of a heart attack that afternoon. He was pretending he was a boy again, camping with his father in the midnight summer along the Des Moines River. In the dark, with his eyes pinched shut, he pretended. He pretended that when he opened his eyes, his father would be there by the campfire and they would talk softly about whatever came to mind and then roll into their sleeping bags, and that later they'd wake up and it would be morning and there would not be a war, and that Billy Boy Watkins had not died of a heart attack that afternoon. He pretended he was not a soldier.

In the morning, when they reached the sea, it would be better. The hot afternoon would be over, he would bathe in the sea and he would forget how frightened he had been on his first day at the war. The second day would not be so bad. He would learn.

There was a sound beside him, a movement and then a breathed: "Hey!"

He opened his eyes, shivering as if emerging from a deep nightmare.

"Hey!" a shadow whispered. "We're *moving*. . . . Get up."

"Okay."

"You sleepin', or something?"

"No." He could not make out the soldier's face. With clumsy, concrete hands he clawed for his rifle, found it, found his helmet.

The soldier-shadow grunted. "You got a lot to learn, buddy. I'd shoot you if I thought you was sleepin'. Let's go."

Private First Class Paul Berlin blinked.

Ahead of him, <u>silhouetted</u> against the sky, he saw the string of soldiers wading into the flat paddy, the black outline of their shoulders and packs and weapons. He was comfortable. He did not want to move. But he was afraid, for it was his first night at the war, so he hurried to catch up, stumbling once, scraping his knee, groping as though blind; his boots sank into the thick paddy water and he smelled it all around him. He would tell his mother how it smelled: mud and algae and cattle manure and chlorophyll,[3] decay, breeding mosquitoes and leeches as big as mice, the fecund[4] warmth of the paddy waters rising up to his cut knee. But he would not tell how frightened he had been.

Though he was afraid, he now knew that fear came in many degrees and types and peculiar categories...

Once they reached the sea, things would be better. They would have their rear guarded by three thousand miles of ocean, and they would swim and dive into the breakers and hunt crayfish and smell the salt, and they would be safe.

He followed the shadow of the man in front of him. It was a clear night. Already the Southern Cross[5] was out. And other stars he could not yet name—soon, he thought, he would learn their names. And puffy night clouds. There was not yet

---

3. **chlorophyll** (klôr′ə-fĭl): a green pigment found in plants.
4. **fecund** (fē′kənd): producing much growth; fertile.
5. **Southern Cross:** a cross-shaped group of stars visible in the Southern Hemisphere.

Infantry (1997), James E. Faulkner. Oil on canvas. Collection of
Nature's Nest Gallery, Golden, Colorado. Courtesy of the artist.

a moon. Wading through the paddy, his boots made sleepy, sloshing sounds, like a lullaby, and he tried not to think. Though he was afraid, he now knew that fear came in many degrees and types and peculiar categories, and he knew that his fear now was not so bad as it had been in the hot afternoon, when poor Billy Boy Watkins got killed by a heart attack. His fear now was <u>diffuse</u> and unformed: ghosts in the tree line, nighttime fears of a child, a boogieman in the closet that his father would open to show empty, saying "See? Nothing there, champ. Now you can sleep." In the afternoon it had been worse: the fear had been bundled and tight and he'd been on his hands and knees, crawling like an insect, an ant escaping a giant's footsteps and thinking nothing, brain flopping like wet cement in a mixer, not thinking at all, watching while Billy Boy Watkins died.

Now as he stepped out of the paddy onto a narrow dirt path, now the fear was mostly the fear of being so terribly afraid again.

He tried not to think.

There were tricks he'd learned to keep from thinking. Counting: He counted his steps, concentrating on the numbers, pretending that the steps were dollar bills and that each step through the night made him richer and richer, so that soon he would become a wealthy man, and he kept counting and considered the ways he might spend the money after the war and what he would do. He would look his father in the eye and shrug and say, "It was pretty bad at first, but I learned a lot and I got used to it." Then he would tell his father the story of Billy Boy Watkins. But he would never let on how frightened he had been. "Not so bad," he would say instead, making his father feel proud.

Songs, another trick to stop from thinking: *Where have you gone, Billy Boy, Billy Boy, Oh, where have you gone, charming Billy? I have gone to seek a wife, she's the joy of my life, but she's a young thing and cannot leave her mother,* and other songs that he sang in his thoughts as he walked toward the sea. And when he reached the sea he would dig a deep hole in the sand and he would sleep like the high clouds, and he would not be afraid any more.

The moon came out. Pale and shrunken to the size of a dime.

The helmet was heavy on his head. In the morning he would adjust the leather binding. He would clean his rifle, too. Even though he had been frightened to shoot it during the hot afternoon, he would carefully clean the breech and the muzzle and the ammunition so that next time he would be ready and not so afraid. In the morning, when they reached the sea, he would begin to make friends with some of the other soldiers. He would learn their names and laugh at their jokes. Then when the war was over he would have war buddies, and he would write to them once in a while and exchange memories.

Walking, sleeping in his walking, he felt better. He watched the moon come higher.

Once they skirted a sleeping village. The smells again—straw, cattle, mildew. The men were quiet. On the far side of the village, buried in the dark smells, a dog barked. The column stopped until the barking died away; then they marched fast away from the village, through a graveyard filled with <u>conical</u>-shaped burial mounds and tiny altars made of clay and stone. The graveyard had a perfumy smell. A nice place to spend the night, he thought. The mounds would make fine battlements, and the smell was nice and the place was quiet. But they went on, passing through a hedgerow and across another paddy and east toward the sea.

He walked carefully. He remembered what he'd been taught: Stay off the center of the path, for

66

that was where the land mines and booby traps were planted, where stupid and lazy soldiers like to walk. Stay alert, he'd been taught. Better alert than inert.[6] Ag-ile, mo-bile, hos-tile.[7] He wished he'd paid better attention to the training. He could not remember what they'd said about how to stop being afraid; they hadn't given any lessons in courage—not that he could remember—and they hadn't mentioned how Billy Boy Watkins would die of a heart attack, his face turning pale and the veins popping out.

> **"I don't wanna scare you. You'll get used to it soon enough..."**

Private First Class Paul Berlin walked carefully.

Stretching ahead of him like dark beads on an invisible chain, the string of shadow-soldiers whose names he did not yet know moved with the silence and slow grace of smoke. Now and again moonlight was reflected off a machine gun or a wrist watch. But mostly the soldiers were quiet and hidden and far-away-seeming in a peaceful night, strangers on a long street, and he felt quite separate from them, as if trailing behind like the caboose on a night train, pulled along by inertia, sleepwalking, an afterthought to the war.

So he walked carefully, counting his steps. When he had counted to three thousand, four hundred and eighty-five, the column stopped.

One by one the soldiers knelt or squatted down.

The grass along the path was wet. Private First Class Paul Berlin lay back and turned his head so that he could lick at the dew with his eyes closed, another trick to forget the war. He might have slept. "I *wasn't* afraid," he was screaming or dreaming, facing his father's stern eyes. "I wasn't afraid," he was

saying. When he opened his eyes, a soldier was sitting beside him, quietly chewing a stick of Doublemint gum.

"You sleepin' again?" the soldier whispered.

"No," said Private First Class Paul Berlin. . . .

The soldier grunted, chewing his gum. Then he twisted the cap off his canteen, took a swallow and handed it through the dark.

"Take some," he whispered.

"Thanks."

"You're the new guy?"

"Yes." He did not want to admit it, being new to the war.

The soldier grunted and handed him a stick of gum. "Chew it quiet—okay? Don't blow no bubbles or nothing."

"Thanks. I won't." He could not make out the man's face in the shadows.

They sat still and Private First Class Paul Berlin chewed the gum until all the sugars were gone; then the soldier said, "Bad day today, buddy."

Private First Class Paul Berlin nodded wisely, but he did not speak.

"Don't think it's always so bad," the soldier whispered. "I don't wanna scare you. You'll get used to it soon enough. . . . They been fighting wars a long time, and you get used to it."

"Yeah."

"You will."

They were quiet awhile. And the night was quiet, no crickets or birds, and it was hard to imagine it was truly a war. He searched for the soldier's face but could not find it. It did not matter much. Even if he saw the fellow's face, he would not know the name; and even if he knew the name, it would not matter much.

---

6. **inert:** lifeless; dead.

7. **ag-ile, mo-bile, hos-tile:** a chant reminding soldiers to be light on their feet (agile), ready to move (mobile), and aggressive (hostile).

WORDS TO KNOW   **inertia** (ĭ-nûr′shə) *n.* the tendency of an object to keep moving once it has started moving

"Haven't got the time?" the soldier whispered.

"No."

"Rats. . . . Don't matter, really. Goes faster if you don't know the time, anyhow."

"Sure."

"What's your name, buddy?"

"Paul."

"Nice to meet ya," he said, and in the dark beside the path they shook hands. "Mine's Toby. Everybody calls me Buffalo, though." The soldier's hand was strangely warm and soft. But it was a very big hand. "Sometimes they just call me Buff," he said.

And again they were quiet. They lay in the grass and waited. The moon was very high now and very bright, and they were waiting for cloud cover.

The soldier suddenly snorted.

"What is it?"

"Nothin'," he said, but then he snorted again. "A bloody *heart attack!*" the soldier said. "Can't get over it—old Billy Boy croaking from a lousy heart attack. . . . A heart attack—can you believe it?"

The idea of it made Private First Class Paul Berlin smile. He couldn't help it.

"Ever hear of such a thing?"

"Not till now," said Private First Class Paul Berlin, still smiling.

"Me neither," said the soldier in the dark. ". . . Dying of a heart attack. Didn't know him, did you."

"No."

"Tough as nails."

"Yeah."

"And what happens? A heart attack. Can you imagine it?"

"Yes," said Private First Class Paul Berlin. He wanted to laugh. "I can imagine it." And he imagined it clearly. He giggled—he couldn't help it. He imagined Billy's father opening the telegram:

SORRY TO INFORM YOU THAT YOUR SON BILLY BOY WAS YESTERDAY SCARED TO DEATH IN ACTION IN THE REPUBLIC OF VIETNAM, VALIANTLY SUCCUMBING TO[8] A HEART ATTACK SUFFERED WHILE UNDER ENORMOUS STRESS, AND IT IS WITH GREATEST SYMPATHY THAT . . . He giggled again. He rolled onto his belly and pressed his face into his arms. His body was shaking with giggles.

The big soldier hissed at him to shut up, but he could not stop giggling and remembering the hot afternoon, and poor Billy Boy, and how they'd been drinking Coca-Cola from bright-red aluminum cans, and how they'd started on the

---

8. **valiantly succumbing** (văl′yənt-lē sə-kŭm′ĭng) **to:** bravely dying from.

Mine on Patrol (1966), John Steel. Acrylic on canvas, 7″×10″.
United States Navy Combat Art Collection.

day's march, and how a little while later poor Billy Boy stepped on the mine, and how it made a tiny little sound—*poof*—and how Billy Boy stood there with his mouth wide-open, looking down at where his foot had been blown off, and how finally Billy Boy sat down very <u>casually</u>, not saying a word, with his foot lying behind him, most of it still in the boot.

He giggled louder—he could not stop. He bit his arm, trying to stifle it, but remembering: "War's over, Billy," the men had said in <u>consolation</u>, but Billy Boy got scared and started crying and said he was about to die. "Nonsense," the medic said, Doc Peret, but Billy Boy kept bawling, tightening up, his face going pale and <u>transparent</u> and his veins popping out. Scared stiff. Even when Doc Peret stuck him with morphine,[9] Billy Boy kept crying.

"Shut up!" the big soldier hissed, but Private First Class Paul Berlin could not stop. Giggling and remembering, he covered his mouth. His eyes stung, remembering how it was when Billy Boy died of fright.

"Shut up!"

But he could not stop giggling, the same way Billy Boy could not stop bawling that afternoon.

Afterward Doc Peret had explained: "You see, Billy Boy really died of a heart attack. He was scared he was gonna die—so scared, he had himself a heart attack—and that's what really killed him. I seen it before."

So they wrapped Billy in a plastic poncho, his eyes still wide-open and scared stiff, and they carried him over the meadow to a rice paddy, and then when the Medevac[10] helicopter arrived they carried him through the paddy and put him aboard, and the mortar rounds[11] were falling everywhere, and the helicopter pulled up and Billy Boy came tumbling out, falling slowly and then faster, and the paddy water sprayed up as if Billy Boy had just <u>executed</u> a long and dangerous dive, as if trying to escape Graves Registration, where he would be tagged and sent home under a flag, dead of a heart attack.

"Shut up, . . . !" the soldier hissed, but Paul Berlin could not stop giggling, remembering: scared to death.

---

9. **morphine** (môr′fēn′): a powerful drug used as a painkiller and tranquilizer.
10. **Medevac** (mĕd′ĭ-văk′): used for the transportation of injured people by air to places where they can receive medical care. (The word is a contraction of "medical evacuation.")
11. **mortar rounds:** shells fired from small, portable cannons.

Later they waded in after him, probing for Billy Boy with their rifle butts, <u>elegantly</u> and delicately probing for Billy Boy in the stinking paddy, singing—some of them—*Where have you gone, Billy Boy, Billy Boy, Oh, where have you gone, charming Billy?* Then they found him. Green and covered with algae, his eyes still wide-open and scared stiff, dead of a heart attack suffered while—

"Shut up, . . . !" the soldier said loudly, shaking him.

But Private First Class Paul Berlin could not stop. The giggles were caught in his throat, drowning him in his own laughter: scared to death like Billy Boy.

Giggling, lying on his back, he saw the moon move, or the clouds moving across the moon. Wounded in action, dead of fright. A fine war story. He would tell it to his father, how Billy Boy had been scared to death, never letting on . . . He could not stop.

The soldier smothered him. He tried to fight back, but he was weak from the giggles.

The moon was under the clouds and the column was moving. The soldier helped him up. "You okay now, buddy?"

"Sure."

"What was so bloody funny?"

"Nothing."

"You can get killed, laughing that way."

"I know. I know that."

"You got to stay calm, buddy." The soldier handed him his rifle. "Half the battle, just staying calm. You'll get better at it," he said. "Come on, now."

He turned away and Private First Class Paul Berlin hurried after him. He was still shivering.

He would do better once he reached the sea, he thought, still smiling a little. A funny war story that he would tell to his father, how Billy Boy Watkins was scared to death. A good joke. But even when he smelled salt and heard the sea, he could not stop being afraid. ❖

I like a look of Agony
Emily Dickinson

I like a look of Agony,
Because I know it's true—
Men do not sham Convulsion,
Nor simulate, a Throe—

5   The Eyes glaze once—and that is
      Death—
Impossible to feign
The Beads upon the Forehead
By homely Anguish strung.

3 sham Convulsion: pretend to have a seizure.
4 Throe: sudden surge of pain.

6 feign (fān): fake.

WORDS TO KNOW

elegantly (ĕl′ĭ-gənt-lē) *adv.* with grace and style

Connect to the Literature

1. What Do You Think?
What was your reaction to the narrator's statement, at the end of the story, that Paul "could not stop being afraid"?

Comprehension Check
- What are the soldiers in this story doing?
- How did Billy Boy Watkins die?
- Why does Toby want to shut Paul up?

Think Critically

2. **ACTIVE READING** **MAKING INFERENCES** With a classmate, look over the chart of **inferences** about Paul Berlin in your **READER'S NOTEBOOK**. On the basis of your inferences, what kind of person do you think he is, and how well do you think he is going to adjust to being in a war?

3. Why does Paul worry about being as "terribly afraid" as he was when he watched Billy Boy die?

4. Why do you think Paul decides not to tell his parents that he was afraid on his first day of combat?

5. In your opinion, what amuses Toby and Paul about Billy Boy's death from a heart attack?

6. Would you say that Paul's giggling is normal or unusual? Explain your answer.

THINK ABOUT
- the effect a death like Billy Boy's might have on a new soldier
- the song the other soldiers sang while looking for Billy in the rice paddy
- Paul's way of dealing with his fear and anxiety
- the real feelings Paul is experiencing

Extend Interpretations

7. What If? How might Paul's first day in combat be different if Billy Boy were killed by the mine instead of by fright?

8. Comparing Texts On the basis of this story, do you think Tim O'Brien would agree with the **speaker** of Emily Dickinson's poem (page 70) about the look of agony on a person's face?

9. Connect to Life Do you think that the experience of being in combat builds character? Explain your answer.

Literary Analysis

CHARACTER Characters are the people (or animals or imaginary creatures) who take part in the action of a story. A short story usually contains one or two **main characters** whose experiences, reactions, and changes are the focus of the story. **Minor characters** interest us mainly because of the effects they have on main characters or the ways in which their actions move a story forward. In this story, Paul is the main character, and Billy Boy and Toby are minor characters.

Cooperative Learning Activity With a partner, make a **spider map** like the one below to show how the minor characters affect the main character in this story. Then discuss with a larger group: Which characters contribute to Paul's **conflict,** and which help Paul resolve his conflict? How do they do so?

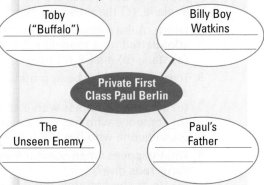

REVIEW **CONFLICT** A **conflict,** or struggle, may be either external or internal. In an **external conflict,** a character struggles against an outside force, such as nature, a physical object, or another character. An **internal conflict** is a struggle within the character's own mind. Is Paul's conflict primarily external or internal?

Choices & CHALLENGES

Writing Options

1. Letter from the War Imagine that Paul Berlin's younger brother is thinking of enlisting. As Paul, write a letter to him in which you offer your perspective and advice.

2. Training Manual Write a training-manual entry that might help prepare soldiers for experiences like those described in the story.

Activities & Explorations

1. Live Report from the Field With a partner, stage a dialogue between Paul Berlin and a war correspondent. Begin by imagining the questions that the correspondent would ask and the ways in which Paul might answer them. Enact your dialogue for the class. **~ SPEAKING AND LISTENING**

2. A Soldier's Story Interview someone who served in the Vietnam War. Gather as much factual information about the person's tour of duty as you can. Also ask the person to give you personal impressions of the war and to describe its effect on his or her life. Present your findings to the class. **~ HISTORY**

Inquiry & Research

Guerrilla Warfare Most American soldiers who were sent to Vietnam had no combat experience, and even those with experience were not fully prepared for the guerrilla warfare they faced in the jungles of Vietnam. Use history books and interviews with people who served in the war to prepare a report on the tactics involved in guerrilla warfare.

 More Online: Research Starter www.mcdougallittell.com

Vocabulary in Action

EXERCISE: MEANING CLUES Write the letter of the best answer to each question.

1. Which of the following is **conical**?
   (a) the lid of a barrel, (b) the nose of an airplane, (c) the tires on a bicycle

2. Which of the following might you see **silhouetted** on a moonlit night?
   (a) stars, (b) a lake, (c) trees

3. To whom would it be appropriate to offer **consolation**?
   (a) someone who has won a competition, (b) someone who has requested your advice, (c) someone who has lost a loved one

4. What happens when someone **executes** a dangerous dive?
   (a) He or she performs the dive successfully. (b) He or she prevents others from performing the dive. (c) He or she teaches others to perform the dive.

5. Which weapon would be considered the most **primitive**?
   (a) a metal arrow, (b) a tank, (c) a rock

6. Which of the following is most likely to move **elegantly**?
   (a) a wounded soldier, (b) a ballet dancer, (c) a child playing tag

7. Which of the following illustrates **inertia**?
   (a) a baseball rolling across an outfield, (b) a person screaming in fear, (c) a tree's leaves changing color in autumn

8. What would be an example of **diffuse** light?
   (a) the beam of a flashlight, (b) the light of a lamp that illuminates every corner of a room, (c) the glow of a warning light on a car's dashboard

9. What might a girl who is dressed **casually** be wearing?
   (a) a prom dress, (b) blue jeans and a T-shirt, (c) a work uniform

10. Which item would you describe as **transparent**?
    (a) a stained-glass window, (b) a piece of paper, (c) a pottery jar

WORDS TO KNOW	casually	consolation	elegantly	inertia	silhouetted
	conical	diffuse	execute	primitive	transparent

Building Vocabulary
For an in-depth lesson on how to expand your vocabulary, see page 572

Grammar in Context: Adverbs

Notice how the adverbs, in red type, affect the meaning of the sentence about Private Berlin.

when   where
Now as he stepped **out** of the paddy onto a

when   how much
narrow dirt path, **now** the fear was **mostly** the

to what extent how much   when
fear of being **so terribly** afraid **again**.

You may recall that an **adverb** is a word that modifies a verb, an adjective, or another adverb. As the labels in the example show, adverbs supply additional information about when, where, how much, or to what extent something happens or is done. They help readers more clearly visualize or understand a scene or character.

WRITING EXERCISE For each sentence, supply an adverb that gives the reader more detail about how, when, or to what extent each action was performed. *Usage Tip:* To avoid confusing your reader, place each adverb close to the word that it modifies.

> **Example:** *Original* He grabs his rifle and <u>searches</u> for his helmet.
> *Rewritten* He grabs his rifle and <u>frantically</u> <u>searches</u> for his helmet.

1. The soldiers <u>wade</u> into the paddy.
2. He <u>follows</u> the soldier in front of him.
3. His fear <u>strangles</u> him.
4. He <u>trudges</u>, counting his steps.

Connect to the Literature Look at the adverbs used to describe the soldiers' search for Billy's body in the first paragraph on page 70. What kinds of additional information do these adverbs supply?

<u>Grammar Handbook</u> Modifiers, pp. 1186–1188

Tim O'Brien
1946–

Other Works
Going After Cacciato
The Nuclear Age
The Things They Carried
In the Lake of the Woods

Young Writer While growing up in Minnesota, Tim O'Brien displayed an early flair for writing. He wrote his first story, "Timmy of the Little League," at the age of nine. He wrote his first novel when he was a student at Macalester College in St. Paul—although today he is thankful it was never published!

Vietnam War Shortly after graduating from college, O'Brien was drafted into the U.S. Army. Opposed to the Vietnam War, he thought seriously about fleeing to Canada or going to prison to avoid military service. He changed his mind, though, and was shipped to Vietnam in 1969. Although his war experiences were extremely unpleasant, they prompted him to write and provided much

material to write about. In 1973, O'Brien published his first book, a personal memoir called *If I Die in a Combat Zone, Box Me Up and Ship Me Home.* The Vietnam War has been the main subject of his writing for over 20 years.

Other Pursuits In 1970, O'Brien moved to the Boston area, where he studied for a doctoral degree in government at Harvard University. He also worked briefly as a news reporter for the *Washington Post* and as a teaching assistant. O'Brien still lives in Massachusetts but now spends most of his time writing.

Author Activity

Writing and Experience O'Brien served in the Vietnam War for over a year. In your opinion, which details in "Where Have You Gone, Charming Billy?" could have been written only by someone who had actually experienced the war? Which details seem to be products of the author's artistic imagination? Share your opinions with classmates.

Marigolds

Short Story by EUGENIA COLLIER

"I feel again the chaotic emotions of adolescence."

Connect to Your Life

Why Did I Do That? Think of a time when you did something in a fit of anger or frustration that you regretted later. Did you perhaps destroy something or hurt someone, simply because you were mad, depressed, or having a hard time? Discuss this experience with another classmate.

Build Background

Hard Times "Marigolds" takes place during the Great Depression, which began in 1929 with the stock market crash and the resulting failure of many banks. In the aftermath, factories closed, businesses went bankrupt, fortunes were destroyed, and unemployment soared. At the time, there were no programs such as unemployment insurance to help people who had lost all sources of income. In many towns, the poor lived in shacks in areas called shantytowns. Although many Americans suffered, African Americans were particularly hard hit. The percentage of unemployed African Americans was higher because they were often the last to be hired and the first to be fired.

WORDS TO KNOW
Vocabulary Preview

bravado	impoverished
compassion	perverse
degradation	poignantly
futile	squalor
impotent	stoicism

Focus Your Reading

LITERARY ANALYSIS **SETTING**   A story's **setting**—the time and place of its action—often plays an important role in the **plot** and makes a strong contribution to the story's overall impact and meaning. "Marigolds" is set in an African-American shantytown during the Great Depression. As you read the story, notice how this setting influences the **narrator's** childhood experiences and the conflicts that she faces.

ACTIVE READING **DRAWING CONCLUSIONS**   Understanding literature requires you to **draw conclusions** about events, causes of events, characters, and so on. In drawing conclusions, you combine information from the text with your own prior knowledge. For example, reading that all the narrator seems to remember of her hometown is dust, and knowing that people usually remember pleasant experiences, you might conclude that she didn't have many pleasant experiences there.

READER'S NOTEBOOK   As you read this story, note places where you find yourself drawing a conclusion that helps you make sense of the story. Use a chart like the one shown to record your conclusions.

Drawing Conclusions About "Marigolds"

Text Information	Prior Knowledge	Conclusion
All the narrator remembers of her hometown is the dust.	People remember pleasant experiences.	The narrator didn't have many pleasant experiences in her hometown.

MARIGOLDS

Eugenia Collier

WHEN I THINK OF THE HOME TOWN OF MY YOUTH, ALL THAT I SEEM TO REMEMBER IS DUST—THE BROWN, CRUMBLY DUST OF LATE SUMMER—ARID, STERILE DUST THAT GETS INTO THE EYES AND MAKES THEM WATER, GETS INTO THE THROAT AND BETWEEN THE TOES OF BARE BROWN FEET. I DON'T KNOW WHY I SHOULD REMEMBER ONLY THE DUST. SURELY THERE MUST HAVE BEEN LUSH GREEN LAWNS AND PAVED STREETS UNDER LEAFY SHADE TREES SOMEWHERE IN TOWN; BUT MEMORY IS AN ABSTRACT PAINTING—IT DOES NOT PRESENT THINGS AS THEY ARE, BUT RATHER AS THEY *FEEL*. AND SO, when I think of that time and that place, I remember only the dry September of the dirt roads and grassless yards of the shanty-town where I lived. And one other thing I remember, another incongruency of memory—a brilliant splash of sunny yellow against the dust—Miss Lottie's marigolds.

ACTIVE READING

CONNECT What sight, smell, sound, or feeling from your childhood stands out in your memory?

Whenever the memory of those marigolds flashes across my mind, a strange nostalgia comes with it and remains long after the picture has faded. I feel again the chaotic emotions of adolescence, illusive as smoke, yet as real as the potted geranium before me now. Joy and rage and wild animal gladness and shame become tangled together in the multicolored skein of 14-going-on-15 as I recall that devastating moment when I was suddenly more woman than child, years ago in Miss Lottie's yard. I think of those marigolds at the strangest times; I remember them vividly now as I desperately pass away the time waiting for you, who will not come.

I suppose that futile waiting was the sorrowful background music of our impoverished little community when I was young. The Depression that gripped the nation was no new thing to us, for the black workers of rural Maryland had always been depressed. I don't know what it was that we were waiting for; certainly not for the prosperity that was "just around the corner," for those were white folks' words, which we never believed. Nor did we wait for hard work and thrift to pay off in shining success as the American Dream[1] promised, for we knew better than that, too. Perhaps we waited for a miracle, amorphous in concept but necessary if one were to have the grit to rise before dawn each day and labor in the white man's vineyard until after dark, or to wander about in the September dust, offering one's sweat in return for some meager share of bread. But God was chary[2] with miracles in those days, and so we waited —and waited.

We children, of course, were only vaguely aware of the extent of our poverty. Having no radios, few newspapers, and no magazines, we were somewhat unaware of the world outside our community. Nowadays we would be called "culturally deprived" and people would write books and hold conferences about us. In those days everybody we knew was just as hungry and ill-clad as we were. Poverty was the cage in which we all were trapped, and our hatred of it was still the vague, undirected restlessness of the zoo-bred flamingo who knows that nature created him to fly free.

As I think of those days I feel most poignantly the tag-end of summer, the bright dry times when we began to have a sense of shortening days and the imminence of the cold.

By the time I was 14 my brother Joey and I were the only children left at our house, the older ones having left home for early marriage or the lure of the city, and the two babies having been sent to relatives who might care for them better than we. Joey was three years younger than I, and a boy, and therefore vastly inferior. Each morning our mother and father trudged wearily down the dirt road and around

---

1. **American Dream:** the belief that through hard work one will achieve a comfortable and prosperous life.

2. **chary** (châr'ē): sparing or stingy.

WORDS TO KNOW	**futile** (fyōōt'l) *adj.* having no useful result; without effect
	impoverished (ĭm-pŏv'ər-ĭsht) *adj.* poor
	poignantly (poin'yənt-lē) *adv.* in a profoundly moving manner

Two Figures, Still Pond (1990), W. Joe Innis. Acrylic on canvas, 22″ × 28″, collection of Dr. Nobuyoshi Hagino, San Antonio, Texas.

the bend, she to her domestic job, he to his daily unsuccessful quest for work. After our few chores around the tumbledown shanty, Joey and I were free to run wild in the sun with other children similarly situated.

For the most part, those days are ill-defined in my memory, running together and combining like a fresh water-color painting left out in the rain. I remember squatting in the road drawing a picture in the dust, a picture that Joey gleefully erased with one sweep of his dirty foot. I remember fishing for minnows in a muddy creek and watching sadly as they eluded my cupped hands, while Joey laughed uproariously. And I remember, that year, a strange restlessness of body and of spirit, a feeling that something old and familiar was ending, and something unknown and therefore terrifying was beginning.

One day returns to me with special clarity for some reason, perhaps because it was the beginning of the experience that in some inexplicable way marked the end of innocence.

ACTIVE READING

QUESTION What questions or thoughts do you have about the story so far?

I was loafing under the great oak tree in our yard, deep in some reverie which I have now forgotten except that it involved some secret, secret thoughts of one of the Harris boys across the yard. Joey and a bunch of kids were bored now with the old tire suspended from an oak limb which had kept them entertained for a while.

"Hey, Lizabeth," Joey yelled. He never talked when he could yell. "Hey, Lizabeth, let's us go somewhere."

I came reluctantly from my private world. "Where you want to go? What you want to do?"

The truth was that we were becoming tired of the formlessness of our summer days. The idleness whose prospect had seemed so beautiful during the busy days of spring now had degenerated to an almost desperate effort to fill up the empty midday hours.

"Let's go see can we find some locusts on the hill," someone suggested.

Joey was scornful. "Ain't no more locusts there. Y'all got 'em all while they was still green."

The argument that followed was brief and not really worth the effort. Hunting locust trees wasn't fun any more by now.

"Tell you what," said Joey finally, his eyes sparkling. "Let's go over to Miss Lottie's."

The idea caught on at once, for annoying Miss Lottie was always fun. I was still child enough to scamper along with the group over rickety fences and through bushes that tore our already raggedy clothes, back to where Miss Lottie lived. I think now that we must have made a tragicomic spectacle, five or six kids of different ages, each of us clad in only one garment—the girls in faded dresses that were too long or too short, the boys in patchy pants, their sweaty brown chests gleaming in the hot sun. A little cloud of dust followed our thin legs and bare feet as we tramped over the barren land.

When Miss Lottie's house came into view we stopped, ostensibly to plan our strategy, but actually to reinforce our courage. Miss Lottie's house was the most ramshackle of all our ramshackle homes. The sun and rain had long since faded its rickety frame siding from white to a sullen gray. The boards themselves seemed to remain upright not from being nailed together but rather from leaning together like a house that a child might have constructed from cards. A brisk wind might have blown it down, and

the fact that it was still standing implied a kind of enchantment that was stronger than the elements. There it stood, and as far as I know is standing yet—a gray rotting thing with no porch, no shutters, no steps, set on a cramped lot with no grass, not even any weeds—a monument to decay.

In front of the house in a squeaky rocking chair sat Miss Lottie's son, John Burke, completing the impression of decay. John Burke was what was known as "queer-headed." Black and ageless, he sat, rocking day in and day out in a mindless stupor, lulled by the monotonous squeak-squawk of the chair. A battered hat atop his shaggy head shaded him from the sun. Usually John Burke was totally unaware of everything outside his quiet dream world. But if you disturbed him, if you intruded upon his fantasies, he would become enraged, strike out at you, and curse at you in some strange enchanted language which only he could understand. We children made a game of thinking of ways to disturb John Burke and then to elude his violent retribution.

But our real fun and our real fear lay in Miss Lottie herself. Miss Lottie seemed to be at least a hundred years old. Her big frame still held traces of the tall, powerful woman she must have been in youth, although it was now bent and drawn. Her smooth skin was a dark reddish-brown, and her face had Indian-like features and the stern stoicism that one asso- ciates with Indian faces. Miss Lottie didn't like intruders either, especially children. She never left her yard, and nobody ever visited her. We never knew how she managed those necessities that depend on human interaction—how she ate, for example, or even whether she ate. When we were tiny children, we thought Miss Lottie was a witch and we made up tales, that we half believed ourselves, about her exploits. We were far too sophisticated now, of course, to believe the witch-nonsense. But old fears have a way of clinging like cobwebs, and so when we sighted the tumble-down shack, we had to stop to reinforce our nerves.

ACTIVE READING

PREDICT What do you think the children are going to do to Miss Lottie?

"Look, there she is," I whispered, forgetting that Miss Lottie could not possibly have heard me from that distance. "She's fooling with them crazy flowers."

"Yeh, look at 'er."

Miss Lottie's marigolds were per- haps the strangest part of the picture. Certainly they did not fit in with the crumbling decay of the rest of her yard. Beyond the dusty brown yard, in front of the sorry gray house, rose suddenly and shockingly a dazzling strip of bright blossoms, clumped together in enormous mounds, warm and passionate and sun-golden. The old black witch-woman worked on them all summer, every summer, down on her creaky knees, weeding and cultivating and arranging, while the house crumbled and John Burke rocked. For some perverse reason, we children hated those marigolds. They interfered with the perfect ugliness of the place; they were too beautiful; they said too much that we could not understand; they did not make sense. There was something in the vigor with which the old woman destroyed the weeds that intimidated us. It should have been a comical sight—the old woman with the man's hat on her cropped white head, leaning over the bright mounds, her big backside in the air—but it wasn't com- ical, it was something we could not name. We had to annoy her by whizzing a pebble into her flowers or by yelling a dirty word, then dancing away from her rage, reveling in our youth and mocking her age. Actually, I think it was the flowers we wanted to destroy, but nobody had the nerve to try it, not even Joey, who was usually fool enough to try anything.

"Y'all git some stones," commanded Joey now, and was met with instant giggling obedience as everyone except me began to gather pebbles from the dusty ground. "Come on, Lizabeth."

I just stood there peering through the bushes, torn between wanting to join the fun and feel- ing that it was all a bit silly.

"You scared, Lizabeth?"

I cursed and spat on the ground—my favorite gesture of phony bravado. "Y'all children get the stones; I'll show you how to use 'em."

I said before that we children were not consciously aware of how thick were the bars of our cage. I wonder now, though, whether

WORDS
TO
KNOW

stoicism (stō'ĭ-sĭz'-əm) *n.* indifference to pleasure or pain; not showing emotion
perverse (pər-vûrs') *adj.* stubbornly contrary; wrong; harmful
bravado (brə-vä'dō) *n.* a false show of courage or defiance

Maudell Sleet's Magic Garden (1978), Romare Bearden. From the Profile/Part 1: The Twenties series (Mecklenburg County). Collage on board 10⅛″ × 7″. Copyright © Romare Bearden Foundation/Licensed by VAGA, New York.

we were not more aware of it than I thought. Perhaps we had some dim notion of what we were, and how little chance we had of being anything else. Otherwise, why would we have been so preoccupied with destruction? Anyway, the pebbles were collected quickly, and everybody looked at me to begin the fun.

"Come on, y'all."

We crept to the edge of the bushes that bordered the narrow road in front of Miss Lottie's place. She was working placidly, kneeling over the flowers, her dark hand plunged into the golden mound. Suddenly "zing"—an expertly-aimed stone cut the head off one of the blossoms.

"Who out there?" Miss Lottie's backside came down and her head came up as her sharp eyes searched the bushes. "You better git!"

We had crouched down out of sight in the bushes, where we stifled the giggles that insisted on coming. Miss Lottie gazed warily across the road for a moment, then cautiously returned to her weeding. "Zing"—Joey sent a

pebble into the blooms, and another marigold was beheaded.

Miss Lottie was enraged now. She began struggling to her feet, leaning on a rickety cane and shouting, "Y'all git! Go on home!" Then the rest of the kids let loose with their pebbles, storming the flowers and laughing wildly and senselessly at Miss Lottie's impotent rage. She shook her stick at us and started shakily toward the road crying, "Git 'long! John Burke! John Burke, come help!"

Then I lost my head entirely, mad with the power of inciting such rage, and ran out of the bushes in the storm of pebbles, straight toward Miss Lottie chanting madly, "Old witch, fell in a ditch, picked up a penny and thought she was rich!" The children screamed with delight, dropped their pebbles and joined the crazy dance, swarming around Miss Lottie like bees and chanting, "Old lady witch!" while she screamed curses at us. The madness lasted only a moment, for John Burke, startled at last, lurched out of his chair, and we dashed for the bushes just as Miss Lottie's cane went whizzing at my head.

I did not join the merriment when the kids gathered again under the oak in our bare yard. Suddenly I was ashamed, and I did not like being ashamed. The child in me sulked and said it was all in fun, but the woman in me flinched at the thought of the malicious attack that I had led. The mood lasted all afternoon. When we ate the beans and rice that was supper that night, I did not notice my father's silence, for he was always silent these days, nor did I notice my mother's absence, for she always worked until well into evening. Joey and I had a particularly bitter argument after supper; his exuberance got on my nerves.

Finally I stretched out upon the palette in the room we shared and fell into a fitful doze.

When I awoke, somewhere in the middle of the night, my mother had returned, and I vaguely listened to the conversation that was audible through the thin walls that separated our rooms. At first I heard no words, only voices. My mother's voice was like a cool, dark room in summer—peaceful, soothing, quiet. I loved to listen to it; it made things seem all right somehow. But my father's voice cut through hers, shattering the peace.

"Twenty-two years, Maybelle, twenty-two years," he was saying, "and I got nothing for you, nothing, nothing."

"It's all right, honey, you'll get something. Everybody's out of work now, you know that."

"It ain't right. Ain't no man ought to eat his woman's food year in and year out, and see his children running wild. Ain't nothing right about that."

"Honey, you took good care of us when you had it. Ain't nobody got nothing nowadays."

"I ain't talking about nobody else, I'm talking about *me*. God knows I try." My mother said something I could not hear, and my father cried out louder, "What must a man do, tell me that?"

"Look, we ain't starving. I git paid every week, and Mrs. Ellis is real nice about giving me things. She gonna let me have Mr. Ellis' old coat for you this winter—"

"Damn Mr. Ellis' coat! And damn his money! You think I want white folks' leavings? Damn, Maybelle"—and suddenly he sobbed, loudly and painfully, and cried helplessly and

hopelessly in the dark night. I had never heard a man cry before. I did not know men ever cried. I covered my ears with my hands but could not cut off the sound of my father's harsh, painful, despairing sobs. My father was a strong man who would whisk a child upon his shoulders and go singing through the house. My father whittled toys for us and laughed so loud that the great oak seemed to laugh with him, and taught us how to fish and hunt rabbits. How could it be that my father was crying? But the sobs went on, unstifled, finally quieting until I could hear my mother's voice, deep and rich, humming softly as she used to hum to a frightened child.

The world had lost its boundary lines. My mother, who was small and soft, was now the strength of the family; my father, who was the rock on which the family had been built, was sobbing like the tiniest child. Everything was suddenly out of tune, like a broken accordion. Where did I

fit into this crazy picture? I do not now remember my thoughts, only a feeling of great bewilderment and fear.

Long after the sobbing and the humming had stopped, I lay on the palette, still as stone with my hands over my ears, wishing that I too could cry and be comforted. The night was silent now except for the sound of the crickets and of Joey's soft breathing. But the room was too crowded with fear to allow me to sleep, and finally, feeling the terrible aloneness of 4 A.M., I decided to awaken Joey.

"Ouch! What's the matter with you? What you want?" he demanded disagreeably when I had pinched and slapped him awake.

"Come on, wake up."

"What for? Go 'way."

I was lost for a reasonable reply. I could not say, "I'm scared, and I don't want to be alone," so I merely said, "I'm going out. If you want to come, come on."

The promise of adventure awoke him. "Going out now? Where to, Lizabeth? What you going to do?"

I was pulling my dress over my head. Until now I had not thought of going out. "Just come on," I replied tersely.

I was out the window and halfway down the road before Joey caught up with me.

"Wait, Lizabeth, where you going?"

I was running as if the Furies[3] were after me, as perhaps they were— running silently and furiously until I came to where I had half-known I was headed: to Miss Lottie's yard.

The half-dawn light was more eerie than complete darkness, and in it the old house was like the ruin that my world had become—foul and crumbling, a grotesque caricature. It looked haunted, but I was not afraid because I was haunted too.

"Lizabeth, you lost your mind?" panted Joey.

I had indeed lost my mind, for all the smoldering emotions of that summer swelled in me and burst—the great need for my mother who was never there, the hopelessness of our poverty and degradation, the bewilderment of being neither child nor woman and yet both at once, the fear unleashed by my father's tears. And these feelings combined in one great impulse toward destruction.

"Lizabeth!"

I leaped furiously into the mounds of marigolds and pulled madly, trampling and pulling

ACTIVE READING

PREDICT What do you suppose Lizabeth has on her mind now?

---

3. **Furies:** In Greek and Roman mythology, the Furies were three goddesses of vengeance, or revenge.

WORDS TO KNOW   **degradation** (dĕg′rə-dā′shən) *n.* a decline to a lower condition, with loss of dignity

and destroying the perfect yellow blooms. The fresh smell of early morning and of dew-soaked marigolds spurred me on as I went tearing and mangling and sobbing while Joey tugged my dress or my waist crying, "Lizabeth stop, please stop!"

And then I was sitting in the ruined little garden among the uprooted and ruined flowers, crying and crying, and it was too late to undo what I had done. Joey was sitting beside me, silent and frightened, not knowing what to say. Then, "Lizabeth, look."

I opened my swollen eyes and saw in front of me a pair of large calloused feet; my gaze lifted to the swollen legs, the age-distorted body clad in a tight cotton night dress, and then the shadowed Indian face surrounded by stubby white hair. And there was no rage in the face now, now that the garden was destroyed and there was nothing any longer to be protected.

"M-miss Lottie!" I scrambled to my feet and just stood there and stared at her, and that was the moment when childhood faded and womanhood began. That violent, crazy act was the last act of childhood. For as I gazed at the immobile face with the sad, weary eyes, I gazed upon a kind of reality that is hidden to childhood. The witch was no longer a witch but only a broken old woman who had dared to create beauty in the midst of ugliness and sterility. She had been born in squalor and lived in it all her life. Now at the end of that life she had nothing except a falling-down hut, a wrecked body, and John Burke, the mindless son of her passion. Whatever verve[4] there was left in her, whatever was of love and beauty and joy that had not been squeezed out by life, had been there in the marigolds she had so tenderly cared for.

Of course I could not express the things that I knew about Miss Lottie as I stood there awkward and ashamed.

The years have put words to the things I knew in that moment, and as I look back upon it, I know that that moment marked the end of innocence. People think of the loss of innocence as meaning the loss of virginity, but this is far from true. Innocence involves an unseeing acceptance of things at face value, an ignorance of the area below the surface. In that humiliating moment I looked beyond myself and into the depths of another person. This was the beginning of compassion, and one cannot have both compassion and innocence.

The years have taken me worlds away from that time and that place, from the dust and squalor of our lives and from the bright thing that I destroyed in a blind childish striking out at God-knows-what. Miss Lottie died long ago and many years have passed since I last saw her hut, completely barren at last, for despite my wild contrition she never planted marigolds again. Yet, there are times when the image of those passionate yellow mounds returns with a painful poignancy. For one does not have to be ignorant and poor to find that one's life is barren as the dusty yards of one's town. And I too have planted marigolds. ❖

ACTIVE READING

DRAW CONCLUSIONS
Why is Lizabeth suddenly able to see Miss Lottie as she really is and feel compassion for her?

---

4. **verve** (vûrv): vitality, enthusiasm.

WORDS
TO
KNOW

squalor (skwŏl′ər) *n.* a filthy and wretched condition
compassion (kəm-păsh′ən) *n.* deep awareness of the suffering of another coupled with the wish to relieve it

Connect to the Literature

1. What Do You Think? How did you react to Lizabeth's destruction of the marigolds?

> **Comprehension Check**
> - Who is telling the story?
> - What time in her life is the narrator telling about?
> - Why does Lizabeth become upset in the middle of the night?
> - Why does Miss Lottie's garden become completely barren?

Think Critically

2. Why does Lizabeth destroy Miss Lottie's marigolds?

 THINK ABOUT
- the contrast between the marigolds and the shantytown in which Lizabeth lives
- the anger and frustration in Lizabeth's family
- Lizabeth's feelings about herself

3. How does the **climax** of the story—Lizabeth's destruction of the marigolds—begin a rite of passage from childhood to the beginning of womanhood?

 THINK ABOUT
- Lizabeth's new understanding of Miss Lottie and her marigolds
- what the **narrator** says about compassion and innocence

4. Why does Miss Lottie never plant marigolds again, despite Lizabeth's "wild contrition"—her sincere remorse?

5. What do you think the narrator means at the end of the story when she says that she too has planted marigolds?

6. **ACTIVE READING** **DRAWING CONCLUSIONS** What are some conclusions you noted in your **READER'S NOTEBOOK** ? Compare your notes with those of your classmates. Did you come to the same conclusions? After finishing the story, do you want to revise any of your conclusions?

Extend Interpretations

7. Comparing Texts Compare Lizabeth's rite of passage in this story with Paul's in "Where Have You Gone, Charming Billy?" Which **main character** do you think is more deeply changed by the experience? Give reasons for your opinion.

8. Connect to Life Lizabeth's "wild contrition" does not seem to make Miss Lottie feel better or want to go back to raising marigolds. What do you think is the best way to make it up to someone we have deliberately hurt? What should we do if that person does not forgive us?

Literary Analysis

SETTING The time and place of action of a story is called the **setting.** In some stories, such as "Where Have You Gone, Charming Billy?" the setting is simple and straightforward—Vietnam during the Vietnam War. In other stories, such as "Marigolds," the setting can be more complex. The story takes place in a small town during the Great Depression. But it also takes place in the private world of Lizabeth's adult memory. As she admits, memory "does not present things as they are, but rather as they *feel.*"

Paired Activity With a partner, review the story and locate at least two passages where the description of the setting seems to express the narrator's feelings. Then, choose descriptive phrases from the passages to create a poem. Use the example below as a model.

Beyond the dusty brown yard, in front of the sorry gray house, rose suddenly and shockingly a dazzling strip of bright blossoms, clumped together in enormous mounds, warm and passionate and sun-golden. (p. 79)

dusty brown yard
sorry gray house
dazzling blossoms
warm and passionate
sun-golden

Give your poem a title and share it with the class.

Writing Options

1. Interpretive Essay The narrator says, "This was the beginning of compassion, and one cannot have both compassion and innocence." Using details from the story to support your opinion, write a draft of an essay explaining what you think she means.

Writing Handbook
See page 1157: Analysis.

2. Mood Diary Think back to the incident you recalled in the Connect to Your Life activity in which you acted out of anger or frustration. Write a diary entry that describes the incident, focusing on the change in your feelings when you began to regret what you had done. Place the entry in your **Working Portfolio.**

Activities & Explorations

1. Dramatic Dialogue With a partner, act out a conversation that might have occurred between Miss Lottie and Lizabeth after the destruction of the marigolds. ~ **SPEAKING AND LISTENING**

2. Abstract Painting The narrator says that memory is "an abstract painting—it does not present things as they are, but rather as they *feel.*" Create an abstract painting or collage to convey the mixture of emotions that Lizabeth feels in this story. Show your work to the class. ~ **VIEWING AND REPRESENTING/ART**

Inquiry & Research

The Great Depression Research books on the Great Depression of the 1930s. Look for information about shantytowns, such as where they were usually located and what the conditions were. Report your findings to the class, using photographs from the books as visual aids.

Art Connection

Look again at the collage by Romare Bearden on page 80. The subject, Maudell Sleet, lived in the artist's hometown. She had a green thumb and shared the produce from her garden with Bearden and his mother. This collage is one of several he created in her memory. How do you think Lizabeth as a child would portray Miss Lottie in art? How would the adult Lizabeth portray her? How would each portrayal compare with Bearden's?

Maudell Sleet's Magic Garden (1978), Romare Bearden. From the Profile/Part 1: The Twenties series (Mecklenburg County). Collage on board 10⅛" × 7". Copyright © Romare Bearden Foundation/Licensed by VAGA, New York.

Vocabulary in Action

EXERCISE: CONTEXT CLUES Write the vocabulary words that best complete the sentences.

During the Great Depression, many Americans lost their jobs. Without an income, many became _____. People looked for work, but often their efforts were _____. Many experienced a _____ of their living standards, and some were forced to exist in terrible conditions of _____. Showing a sensitivity to people's suffering, literature and photography of the period _____ captured the distress these hardships caused. People reacted to their predicament in various ways. Some felt helpless and _____. Some, in a show of _____, took _____ pleasure in spending money on foolish luxuries. Still others reacted calmly and with _____. Meanwhile, many charities showed _____ for the poor.

Building Vocabulary
Several Words to Know in this lesson contain prefixes and suffixes. For an in-depth study of word parts, see page 473.

WORDS TO KNOW				
bravado	degradation	impotent	perverse	squalor
compassion	futile	impoverished	poignantly	stoicism

Grammar in Context: Compound Adjectives

In the following passage, Eugenia Collier uses adjectives that show the contrast between a garden of marigolds and a poor community in rural Maryland.

> Beyond the dusty brown yard, in front of the sorry gray house, rose suddenly and shockingly a dazzling strip of bright blossoms, clumped together in enormous mounds, warm and passionate and sun-golden.

Remember that an **adjective** modifies a noun or pronoun. When two or more adjectives modify the same noun or pronoun, they are called compound adjectives. In the passage above, adjectives are shown in colored type. Compound adjectives are shown in blue type.

Punctuation Tip: When compound adjectives are not separated by the word *and,* they usually should be separated by commas. Do not use commas in compound adjectives before or after an adjective that refers to age, color, number, shape or size—for example, the *dusty brown* yard.

WRITING EXERCISE Insert compound adjectives to modify the underlined nouns. Choose adjectives that are compatible with the descriptions of the town in Collier's story.

Example: *Original* Lizabeth races through the town, dodging stones in the streets.
Rewritten Lizabeth races through the dusty, tattered town, dodging stones in the streets.

1. One autumn day a wind blasts through the town.
2. The dogs scramble for shelter, knowing a storm would blow dust before the rain came.
3. The towering oaks let go of their leaves.
4. The tire swing sways like a pendulum.
5. The sheds and shanties look frail under the sky.

Connect to the Literature Look for a sentence on page 83 that contains two examples of compound adjectives. How does this sentence help create the mood of the story?

Grammar Handbook Modifiers, pp. 1186–1188

Eugenia Collier
1928–

Other Works
Breeder and Other Stories
Spread My Wings

A Family Tradition of Education Eugenia Collier was born in Baltimore, Maryland, where she now lives. Her father was a physician and her mother a teacher. She graduated with high honors from Howard University in Washington, D.C., in 1948 and earned her master of arts from Columbia University in 1950. Collier has taught English at Howard, Baltimore Community College, and Morgan State University in Baltimore.

Seeing Life from Both Sides For a time, Collier was a case worker with the Baltimore Department of Public Welfare. She started teaching college in 1955 and later began writing. One of her first efforts, "Marigolds," won the Gwendolyn Brooks Award for Fiction in 1969. Her stories, poems, and critical essays have appeared in many anthologies and magazines. Collier says that the source of her creativity is "the richness, the diversity, the beauty of my black heritage."

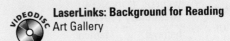

LaserLinks: Background for Reading
Art Gallery

Two Kinds

Short Story by AMY TAN

"You could become instantly famous."

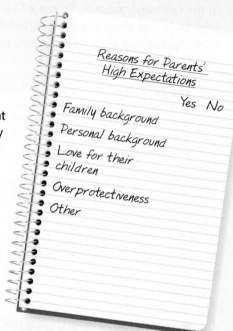

Reasons for Parents'
High Expectations

Yes No

Family background
Personal background
Love for their children
Overprotectiveness
Other

Connect to Your Life

You Can Do It! You can probably think of at least one time when someone in authority had high expectations of you—so high you were not sure you could meet them. Perhaps a bandleader gave you a difficult solo or a coach put you in a game at a critical moment. With a partner, think about why many parents in particular often have high expectations of their children. To help you sort out your thoughts on this issue, create a chart similar to the one shown here.

Build Background

Unlimited Possibilities During the 1930s and 1940s, China was invaded by Japan and racked by political upheavals that led to a bitter civil war. Some Chinese citizens escaped these dangers by emigrating to the United States. To many Chinese immigrants, life in the United States was so different from life in war-torn China that anything seemed possible, especially for their children. Parents had high expectations for their children and wanted them to pursue the American dream of material success, but without sacrificing the traditional Chinese values of obedience and respect for one's elders. "Two Kinds" is narrated by a young woman who, like Amy Tan herself, is the daughter of Chinese immigrants.

WORDS TO KNOW
Vocabulary Preview

betrayal	lament
devastate	prodigy
discordant	ream
fiasco	reproach
indignity	reverie

Focus Your Reading

LITERARY ANALYSIS **THEME** **Theme** is the main idea, or message, in a work of fiction. It is a perception about life or human nature that the writer shares with the reader. Often, a theme reveals itself through a **character** who is confronted with a particular **conflict** during the course of a story. As you read, take note of the key conflicts and decide whether they suggest a theme.

ACTIVE READING **MAKING JUDGMENTS** In this story, the mother and daughter each have a number of complaints about the other. In order to **make a judgment** about which of these complaints is justified, decide what criteria or standards you would apply to the situation. For example, you might think the mother's complaint that her daughter doesn't try is not justified, because the mother is not being realistic.

READER'S NOTEBOOK List what you think are the most important criteria. Then, as you read the story, jot down two or three complaints made by each character and note whether they are justified according to your criteria.

TWO KINDS

AMY TAN

My mother believed you could be anything you wanted to be in America. You could open a restaurant. You could work for the government and get good retirement. You could buy a house with almost no money down. You could become rich. You could become instantly famous.

Detail of *Laundryman's Daughter* (1988), Tomie Arai.

"Of course you can be <u>prodigy</u>, too," my mother told me when I was nine. "You can be best anything. What does Auntie Lindo know? Her daughter, she is only best tricky."

America was where all my mother's hopes lay. She had come here in 1949 after losing everything in China: her mother and father, her family home, her first husband, and two daughters, twin baby girls. But she never looked back with regret. There were so many ways for things to get better.

We didn't immediately pick the right kind of prodigy. At first my mother thought I could be a Chinese Shirley Temple.[1] We'd watch Shirley's old movies on TV as though they were training films. My mother would poke my arm and say, *"Ni kan"*—You watch. And I would see Shirley tapping her feet, or singing a sailor song, or pursing her lips into a very round O while saying, "Oh my goodness."

"Ni kan," said my mother as Shirley's eyes flooded with tears. "You already know how. Don't need talent for crying!"

Soon after my mother got this idea about Shirley Temple, she took me to a beauty training school in the Mission district[2] and put me in the hands of a student who could barely hold the scissors without shaking. Instead of getting big fat curls, I emerged with an uneven mass of crinkly black fuzz. My mother dragged me off to the bathroom and tried to wet down my hair.

"You look like Negro Chinese," she lamented, as if I had done this on purpose.

The instructor of the beauty training school had to lop off these soggy clumps to make my hair even again. "Peter Pan is very popular these days," the instructor assured my mother. I now had hair the length of a boy's, with straight-across bangs that hung at a slant two inches above my eyebrows. I liked the haircut, and it made me actually look forward to my future fame.

In fact, in the beginning, I was just as excited as my mother, maybe even more so. I pictured this prodigy part of me as many different images, trying each one on for size. I was a dainty ballerina girl standing by the curtains, waiting to hear the right music that would send me floating on my tiptoes. I was like the Christ child lifted out of the straw manger, crying with holy <u>indignity</u>. I was Cinderella stepping from her pumpkin carriage with sparkly cartoon music filling the air.

In all of my imaginings, I was filled with a sense that I would soon become *perfect.* My mother and father would adore me. I would be beyond <u>reproach</u>. I would never feel the need to sulk for anything.

But sometimes the prodigy in me became impatient. "If you don't hurry up and get me out of here, I'm disappearing for good," it warned. "And then you'll always be nothing."

Every night after dinner, my mother and I would sit at the Formica[3] kitchen table. She would present new tests, taking her examples from stories of amazing children she had read in *Ripley's Believe It or Not,* or *Good Housekeeping, Reader's Digest,* and a dozen other magazines she kept in a pile in our bathroom. My mother got these magazines from people whose houses she cleaned. And since she cleaned many houses each week, we had a great assortment. She would look through them all,

---

1. **Shirley Temple:** a popular child movie star of the 1930s.
2. **Mission district:** a residential neighborhood in San Francisco.
3. **Formica** (fôr-mī′kə): a heat-resistant plastic used on tops of kitchen counters, tables, and the like.

WORDS TO KNOW
prodigy (prŏd′ə-jē) *n.* a young person who is exceptionally talented or intelligent
indignity (ĭn-dĭg′nĭ-tē) *n.* a loss of dignity or honor; a source of such loss
reproach (rĭ-prōch′) *n.* blame; criticism

searching for stories about remarkable children.

The first night she brought out a story about a three-year-old boy who knew the capitals of all the states and even most of the European countries. A teacher was quoted as saying the little boy could also pronounce the names of the foreign cities correctly.

"What's the capital of Finland?" my mother asked me, looking at the magazine story.

All I knew was the capital of California, because Sacramento was the name of the street we lived on in Chinatown. "Nairobi!"[4] I guessed, saying the most foreign word I could think of. She checked to see if that was possibly one way to pronounce "Helsinki" before showing me the answer.

The tests got harder—multiplying numbers in my head, finding the queen of hearts in a deck of cards, trying to stand on my head without using my hands, predicting the daily temperatures in Los Angeles, New York, and London.

One night I had to look at a page from the Bible for three minutes and then report everything I could remember. "Now Jehoshaphat[5] had riches and honor in abundance and . . . that's all I remember, Ma," I said.

And after seeing my mother's disappointed face once again, something inside of me began to die. I hated the tests, the raised hopes and failed expectations. Before going to bed that night, I looked in the mirror above the bathroom sink and when I saw only my face staring back—and that it would always be this ordinary face—I began to cry. Such a sad, ugly girl! I made high-pitched noises like a crazed animal, trying to scratch out the face in the mirror.

And then I saw what seemed to be the prodigy side of me—because I had never seen that face before. I looked at my reflection, blinking so I could see more clearly. The girl staring back at me was angry, powerful. This girl and I were the same. I had new thoughts, willful thoughts, or rather thoughts filled with lots of won'ts. I won't let her change me, I promised myself. I won't be what I'm not.

So now on nights when my mother presented her tests, I performed listlessly, my head propped on one arm. I pretended to be bored. And I was. I got so bored I started counting the bellows of the foghorns out on the bay while my mother drilled me in other areas. The sound was comforting and reminded me of the cow jumping over the moon. And the next day, I played a game with myself, seeing if my mother would give up on me before eight bellows. After a while I usually counted only one, maybe two bellows at most. At last she was beginning to give up hope.

Two or three months had gone by without any mention of my being a prodigy again. And then one day my mother was watching *The Ed Sullivan Show*[6] on TV. The TV was old and the sound kept shorting out. Every time my mother got halfway up from the sofa to adjust the set, the sound would go back on and Ed would be talking. As soon as she sat down, Ed would go silent again. She got up, the TV broke into loud

> I won't let her change me, I promised myself. I won't be what I'm not.

---

4. **Nairobi** (nī-rō′bē): the capital of the African nation of Kenya.

5. **Jehoshaphat** (jə-hŏsh′ə-făt′): a king of Judah in the ninth century B.C.

6. *The Ed Sullivan Show*: a popular weekly variety show on television from 1948 to 1971.

Laundryman's Daughter (1988), Tomie Arai. Silkscreen print, 22″ × 30″ unframed, printed in an edition of 35 by Avocet Editions.

piano music. She sat down. Silence. Up and down, back and forth, quiet and loud. It was like a stiff, embraceless dance between her and the TV set. Finally she stood by the set with her hand on the sound dial.

She seemed entranced by the music, a little frenzied piano piece with this mesmerizing quality, sort of quick passages and then teasing lilting ones before it returned to the quick playful parts.

"*Ni kan*," my mother said, calling me over with hurried hand gestures, "Look here."

I could see why my mother was fascinated by the music. It was being pounded out by a little Chinese girl, about nine years old, with a Peter Pan haircut. The girl had the sauciness of a Shirley Temple. She was proudly modest like a proper Chinese child. And she also did this fancy sweep of a curtsy, so that the fluffy skirt of her white dress cascaded slowly to the floor like the petals of a large carnation.

In spite of these warning signs, I wasn't worried. Our family had no piano and we couldn't afford to buy one, let alone <u>reams</u> of sheet music and piano lessons. So I could be generous in my comments when my mother bad-mouthed the little girl on TV.

"Play note right, but doesn't sound good! No singing sound," complained my mother.

"What are you picking on her for?" I said carelessly. "She's pretty good. Maybe she's not the best, but she's trying hard." I knew almost immediately I would be sorry I said that.

"Just like you," she said. "Not the best. Because you not trying." She gave a little huff as she let go of the sound dial and sat down on the sofa.

The little Chinese girl sat down also to play an encore of "Anitra's Dance" by Grieg.[7] I remember the song, because later on I had to learn how to play it.

Three days after watching *The Ed Sullivan Show*, my mother told me what my schedule would be for piano lessons and piano practice. She had talked to Mr. Chong, who lived on the first floor of our apartment building. Mr. Chong was a retired piano teacher and my mother had traded housecleaning services for weekly lessons and a piano for me to practice on every day, two hours a day, from four until six.

When my mother told me this, I felt as though I had been sent to hell. I whined and then kicked my foot a little when I couldn't stand it anymore.

"Why don't you like me the way I am? I'm *not* a genius! I can't play the piano. And even if I could, I wouldn't go on TV if you paid me a million dollars!" I cried.

My mother slapped me. "Who ask you be genius?" she shouted. "Only ask you be your best. For you sake. You think I want you be genius? Hnnh! What for! Who ask you!"

"So ungrateful," I heard her mutter in Chinese. "If she had as much talent as she has temper, she would be famous now."

Mr. Chong, whom I secretly nicknamed Old Chong, was very strange, always tapping his fingers to the silent music of an invisible orchestra. He looked ancient in my eyes. He had lost most of the hair on top of his head and he wore thick glasses and had eyes that always looked tired and sleepy. But he must have been younger than I thought, since he lived with his mother and was not yet married.

I met Old Lady Chong once and that was enough. She had this peculiar smell like a baby that had done something in its pants. And her fingers felt like a dead person's, like an old peach I once found in the back of the refrigerator; the

---

7. **Grieg** (grēg): the Norwegian composer Edvard Grieg (1843–1907).

skin just slid off the meat when I picked it up.

I soon found out why Old Chong had retired from teaching piano. He was deaf. "Like Beethoven!"[8] he shouted to me. "We're both listening only in our head!" And he would start to conduct his frantic silent sonatas.

Our lessons went like this. He would open the book and point to different things, explaining their purpose: "Key! Treble! Bass! No sharps or flats! So this is C major! Listen now and play after me!"

And then he would play the C scale a few times, a simple chord, and then, as if inspired by an old, unreachable itch, he gradually added more notes and running trills and a pounding bass until the music was really something quite grand.

I would play after him, the simple scale, the simple chord, and then I just played some nonsense that sounded like a cat running up and down on top of garbage cans. Old Chong smiled and applauded and then said, "Very good! But now you must learn to keep time!"

So that's how I discovered that Old Chong's eyes were too slow to keep up with the wrong notes I was playing. He went through the motions in half-time. To help me keep rhythm, he stood behind me, pushing down on my right shoulder for every beat. He balanced pennies on top of my wrists so I would keep them still as I slowly played scales and arpeggios.[9] He had me curve my hand around an apple and keep that shape when playing chords. He marched stiffly to show me how to make each finger dance up and down, staccato[10] like an obedient little soldier.

> **I also learned I could be lazy and get away with mistakes, lots of mistakes.**

He taught me all these things, and that was how I also learned I could be lazy and get away with mistakes, lots of mistakes. If I hit the wrong notes because I hadn't practiced enough, I never corrected myself. I just kept playing in rhythm. And Old Chong kept conducting his own private reverie.

So maybe I never really gave myself a fair chance. I did pick up the basics pretty quickly, and I might have become a good pianist at that young age. But I was so determined not to try, not to be anybody different, that I learned to play only the most ear-splitting preludes,[11] the most discordant hymns.

Over the next year, I practiced like this, dutifully in my own way. And then one day I heard my mother and her friend Lindo Jong both talking in a loud, bragging tone of voice so others could hear. It was after church, and I was leaning against the brick wall wearing a dress with stiff white petticoats. Auntie Lindo's daughter, Waverly, who was about my age, was standing farther down the wall about five feet away. We had grown up together and shared all the closeness of two sisters squabbling over crayons and dolls. In

---

8. **Beethoven** (bā′tō′vən): the German composer Ludwig van Beethoven (1770–1827), who began losing his hearing in 1801 and was deaf by 1819.

9. **arpeggios** (är-pĕj′ē-ōz′): chords in which the notes are played separately in quick sequence rather than at the same time.

10. **staccato** (stə-kä′tō): producing distinct, abrupt breaks between successive tones.

11. **preludes** (prĕl′yōōdz′): short piano compositions, each usually based on a single musical theme.

WORDS TO KNOW

reverie (rĕv′ə-rē) *n.* a daydream
discordant (dĭ-skôr′dnt) *adj.* having a disagreeable or clashing sound; not in harmony

other words, for the most part, we hated each other. I thought she was snotty. Waverly Jong had gained a certain amount of fame as "Chinatown's Littlest Chinese Chess Champion."

"She bring home too many trophy," lamented Auntie Lindo that Sunday. "All day she play chess. All day I have no time do nothing but dust off her winnings." She threw a scolding look at Waverly, who pretended not to see her.

"You lucky you don't have this problem," said Auntie Lindo with a sigh to my mother.

And my mother squared her shoulders and bragged: "Our problem worser than yours. If we ask Jing-mei[12] wash dish, she hear nothing but music. It's like you can't stop this natural talent."

And right then, I was determined to put a stop to her foolish pride.

A few weeks later, Old Chong and my mother conspired to have me play in a talent show which would be held in the church hall. By then, my parents had saved up enough to buy me a secondhand piano, a black Wurlitzer spinet[13] with a scarred bench. It was the showpiece of our living room.

For the talent show, I was to play a piece called "Pleading Child" from Schumann's[14] *Scenes from Childhood*. It was a simple, moody piece that sounded more difficult than it was. I was supposed to memorize the whole thing, playing the repeat parts twice to make the piece sound longer. But I dawdled over it, playing a few bars and then cheating, looking up to see what notes followed. I never really listened to what I was playing. I daydreamed about being somewhere else, about being someone else.

The part I liked to practice best was the fancy curtsy: right foot out, touch the rose on the carpet with a pointed foot, sweep to the side, left leg bends, look up and smile.

My parents invited all the couples from the Joy Luck Club to witness my debut.[15] Auntie Lindo and Uncle Tin were there. Waverly and her two older brothers had also come. The first two rows were filled with children both younger and older than I was. The littlest ones got to go first. They recited simple nursery rhymes, squawked out tunes on miniature violins, twirled Hula-Hoops,[16] pranced in pink ballet tutus,[17] and when they bowed or curtsied, the audience would sigh in unison, "Awww," and then clap enthusiastically.

When my turn came, I was very confident. I remember my childish excitement. It was as if I knew, without a doubt, that the prodigy side of me really did exist. I had no fear whatsoever, no nervousness. I remember thinking to myself, This is it! This is it! I looked out over the audience, at my mother's blank face, my father's yawn, Auntie Lindo's stiff-lipped smile, Waverly's sulky expression. I had on a white dress layered with sheets of lace, and a pink bow in my Peter Pan haircut. As I sat down I envisioned people jumping to their feet and Ed Sullivan rushing up to introduce me to everyone on TV.

And I started to play. It was so beautiful. I was so caught up in how lovely I looked that at first I didn't worry how I would sound. So it was a surprise to me when I hit the first wrong note and I realized something didn't sound

---

12. **Jing-mei** (jǐng′mā′).

13. **spinet** (spǐn′ǐt): a small upright piano.

14. **Schumann's** (sho͞o′mänz′): of Robert Schumann (1810–1856), a German composer famous for his piano works.

15. **debut** (dā-byo͞o′): first public performance.

16. **Hula-Hoops:** plastic hoops that are whirled around the body by means of hip movements similar to those of the hula, a Hawaiian dance.

17. **tutus** (to͞o′to͞oz): short layered skirts worn by ballerinas.

quite right. And then I hit another and another followed that. A chill started at the top of my head and began to trickle down. Yet I couldn't stop playing, as though my hands were bewitched. I kept thinking my fingers would adjust themselves back, like a train switching to the right track. I played this strange jumble through two repeats, the sour notes staying with me all the way to the end.

When I stood up, I discovered my legs were shaking. Maybe I had just been nervous and the audience, like Old Chong, had seen me go through the right motions and had not heard anything wrong at all. I swept my right foot out, went down on my knee, looked up and smiled. The room was quiet, except for Old Chong, who was beaming and shouting, "Bravo! Bravo! Well done!" But then I saw my mother's face, her stricken face. The audience clapped weakly, and as I walked back to my chair, with my whole face quivering as I tried not to cry, I heard a little boy whisper loudly to his mother, "That was awful," and the mother whispered back, "Well, she certainly tried."

And now I realized how many people were in the audience, the whole world it seemed. I was aware of eyes burning into my back. I felt the shame of my mother and father as they sat stiffly throughout the rest of the show.

We could have escaped during intermission. Pride and some strange sense of honor must have anchored my parents to their chairs. And so we watched it all: the eighteen-year-old boy with a fake mustache who did a magic show and juggled flaming hoops while riding a unicycle. The breasted girl with white makeup who sang from *Madama Butterfly*[18] and got honorable mention. And the eleven-year-old boy who won first prize playing a tricky violin song that sounded like a busy bee.

After the show, the Hsus,[19] the Jongs, and the St. Clairs from the Joy Luck Club came up to my mother and father.

"Lots of talented kids," Auntie Lindo said vaguely, smiling broadly.

"That was somethin' else," said my father, and I wondered if he was referring to me in a humorous way, or whether he even remembered what I had done.

Waverly looked at me and shrugged her shoulders. "You aren't a genius like me," she said matter-of-factly. And if I hadn't felt so bad, I would have pulled her braids and punched her stomach.

But my mother's expression was what <u>devastated</u> me: a quiet, blank look that said she had lost everything. I felt the same way, and it seemed as if everybody were now coming up, like gawkers at the scene of an accident, to see what parts were actually missing. When we got on the bus to go home, my father was humming the busy-bee tune and my mother was silent. I kept thinking she wanted to wait until we got home before shouting at me. But when my father unlocked the door to our apartment, my mother walked in and then went to the back, into the bedroom. No accusations. No blame. And in a way, I felt disappointed. I had been waiting for her to start shouting, so I could shout back and cry and blame her for all my misery.

I assumed my talent-show <u>fiasco</u> meant I never had to play the piano again. But two days later, after school, my mother came out of the kitchen and saw me watching TV.

"Four clock," she reminded me as if it were any other day. I was stunned, as though she were asking me to go through the talent-show

---

18. *Madama* (mä-dä′mä) *Butterfly:* a famous opera by the Italian composer Giacomo Puccini.

19. **Hsus** (shüz).

WORDS
TO
KNOW

devastate (dĕv′ə-stāt′) *v.* to destroy or overwhelm
fiasco (fē-ăs′kō) *n.* a complete failure

The Stairway (1970), Will Barnet. Photo courtesy of Terry Dintenfass Gallery, New York.
© 1995 Will Barnet/Licensed by VAGA, New York, NY.

torture again. I wedged myself more tightly in front of the TV.

"Turn off TV," she called from the kitchen five minutes later.

I didn't budge. And then I decided. I didn't have to do what my mother said anymore. I wasn't her slave. This wasn't China. I had listened to her before and look what happened. She was the stupid one.

She came out from the kitchen and stood in the arched entryway of the living room. "Four clock," she said once again, louder.

"I'm not going to play anymore," I said nonchalantly. "Why should I? I'm not a genius."

She walked over and stood in front of the TV. I saw her chest was heaving up and down in an angry way.

"No!" I said, and I now felt stronger, as if my true self had finally emerged. So this was what had been inside me all along.

"No! I won't!" I screamed.

She yanked me by the arm, pulled me off the

floor, snapped off the TV. She was frighteningly strong, half pulling, half carrying me toward the piano as I kicked the throw rugs under my feet. She lifted me up and onto the hard bench. I was sobbing by now, looking at her bitterly. Her chest was heaving even more and her mouth was open, smiling crazily as if she were pleased I was crying.

"You want me to be someone that I'm not!" I sobbed. "I'll never be the kind of daughter you want me to be!"

"Only two kinds of daughters," she shouted in Chinese. "Those who are obedient and those who follow their own mind! Only one kind of daughter can live in this house. Obedient daughter!"

"Then I wish I wasn't your daughter. I wish you weren't my mother," I shouted. As I said these things I got scared. It felt like worms and toads and slimy things crawling out of my chest, but it also felt good, as if this awful side of me had surfaced, at last.

"Too late change this," said my mother shrilly.

And I could sense her anger rising to its breaking point. I wanted to see it spill over. And that's when I remembered the babies she had lost in China, the ones we never talked about. "Then I wish I'd never been born!" I shouted. "I wish I were dead! Like them."

It was as if I had said the magic words. Alakazam!—and her face went blank, her mouth closed, her arms went slack, and she backed out of the room, stunned, as if she were blowing away like a small brown leaf, thin, brittle, lifeless.

> "Only two kinds
> of daughters,"
> she shouted in Chinese.
> "Those who are obedient
> and those who follow
> their own mind!"

It was not the only disappointment my mother felt in me. In the years that followed, I failed her so many times, each time asserting my own will, my right to fall short of expectations. I didn't get straight A's. I didn't become class president. I didn't get into Stanford. I dropped out of college.

For unlike my mother, I did not believe I could be anything I wanted to be. I could only be me.

And for all those years, we never talked about the disaster at the recital or my terrible accusations afterward at the piano bench. All that remained unchecked, like a betrayal that was now unspeakable. So I never found a way to ask her why she had hoped for something so large that failure was inevitable.

And even worse, I never asked her what frightened me the most: Why had she given up hope?

For after our struggle at the piano, she never mentioned my playing again. The lessons stopped. The lid to the piano was closed, shutting out the dust, my misery, and her dreams.

So she surprised me. A few years ago, she offered to give me the piano, for my thirtieth birthday. I had not played in all those years. I saw the offer as a sign of forgiveness, a tremendous burden removed.

"Are you sure?" I asked shyly. "I mean, won't you and Dad miss it?"

"No, this your piano," she said firmly. "Always your piano. You only one can play."

"Well, I probably can't play anymore," I said. "It's been years."

"You pick up fast," said my mother, as if she knew this was certain. "You have natural talent. You could been genius if you want to."

"No I couldn't."

"You just not trying," said my mother. And she was neither angry nor sad. She said it as if to announce a fact that could never be disproved. "Take it," she said.

But I didn't at first. It was enough that she had offered it to me. And after that, every time I saw it in my parents' living room, standing in front of the bay windows, it made me feel proud, as if it were a shiny trophy I had won back.

Last week I sent a tuner over to my parents' apartment and had the piano reconditioned, for purely sentimental reasons. My mother had died a few months before and I had been getting things in order for my father, a little bit at a time. I put the jewelry in special silk pouches. The sweaters she had knitted in yellow, pink, bright orange—all the colors I hated—I put those in mothproof boxes. I found some old Chinese silk dresses, the kind with little slits up the sides. I rubbed the old silk against my skin, then wrapped them in tissue and decided to take them home with me.

After I had the piano tuned, I opened the lid and touched the keys. It sounded even richer than I remembered. Really, it was a very good piano. Inside the bench were the same exercise notes with handwritten scales, the same second-hand music books with their covers held together with yellow tape.

I opened up the Schumann book to the dark little piece I had played at the recital. It was on the left-hand side of the page, "Pleading Child." It looked more difficult than I remembered. I played a few bars, surprised at how easily the notes came back to me.

And for the first time, or so it seemed, I noticed the piece on the right-hand side. It was called "Perfectly Contented." I tried to play this one as well. It had a lighter melody but the same flowing rhythm and turned out to be quite easy. "Pleading Child" was shorter but slower; "Perfectly Contented" was longer, but faster. And after I played them both a few times, I realized they were two halves of the same song. ❖

Thinking through the LITERATURE

Connect to the Literature

1. What Do You Think?
How would you describe your impressions of the two main characters?

Comprehension Check
- What does the narrator's mother want her to become?
- How does the narrator feel after the talent show?
- When the narrator is 30, what does her mother offer to give her?

Think Critically

2. **ACTIVE READING** **MAKING JUDGMENTS** Look over the list you made in your **READER'S NOTEBOOK** of complaints the **narrator** and her mother have about each other. Based on your judgment about which of these complaints is justified, do you think the daughter is just as unreasonable as the mother? Explain your answer.

3. Why do you think the mother had such high expectations for her daughter? Use evidence from the story to support your ideas. You might also review the chart you made for the Connect to Your Life on page 88.

4. Why do you think the narrator's feelings about being a prodigy change during the story?

THINK ABOUT
- her daydreams at the beginning of the story
- her response to her mother's expectations
- her opinions about herself

5. What might the narrator mean by saying that "Pleading Child" and "Perfectly Contented" are "two halves of the same song"?

Extend Interpretations

6. Comparing Texts Compare the ways in which Madame Loisel and the narrator in this story respond to the pressures and expectations of their communities or families.

7. The Writer's Style Although Amy Tan's story deals with the serious problem of a parent's unrealistic expectations, **humor** plays an important role in it. Go through the story again and identify places where events or descriptions add a humorous **tone** to the story. What effect does the humor have on your view of the narrator's **conflict?**

8. Connect to Life In this story, the mother's high expectations have a negative effect on the narrator. When can high expectations have a positive effect? Explain, drawing on your own experience.

Literary Analysis

THEME The **theme** of a work of literature is a main idea—a belief about life or human nature—that a writer hopes the reader will learn from the work. Often, the theme must be **inferred** from the **characters** and situations in a story. Sometimes, the theme is similar to what the characters themselves learn in the story. Consider what the mother and the daughter learn from the mother's high expectations for the daughter. Based on the story, what do you think is the author's opinion about these expectations?

Cooperative Learning Activity With a small group of classmates, discuss what theme you think the author wants to convey to the reader. Then, as a group, compose a sentence or two in which you state the theme of the story as you understand it. Share your statement of theme with other groups and compare any differences of interpretation.

REVIEW **CHARACTER** Most stories center around the experiences and actions of one or more **main characters.** The **minor characters** in a story interact with the main characters and help move the story along. In "Two Kinds," do you see the mother more as a main character or a minor character?

Choices & CHALLENGES

Writing Options

1. Mom's Diary Write a diary entry in which the mother explains her hopes, dreams, and expectations for her daughter, as well as her sense of frustration.

2. Personality Profile Write a personality profile of either the mother or the daughter. Describe your subject's distinctive traits.

Activities & Explorations

1. Stage-Mom Dialogue With a classmate, role-play a conversation between the narrator's mother and Auntie Lindo, in which the narrator's mother describes her daughter's talent-show performance.
~ SPEAKING AND LISTENING

2. "America" Collage Many of the mother's ideas about the United States come from television and popular magazines. Collect pictures from various magazines and create a collage showing the misleading impression of American life that an immigrant might derive from these publications. **~ VIEWING AND REPRESENTING**

Inquiry & Research

Chinese Americans The 1930s and 1940s were not the only period of time when large numbers of people emigrated from China to the United States. Consult history books or encyclopedias to find out about the influx of Chinese immigrants during the mid-1800s. Present your findings in an oral report to the class.

Vocabulary in Action

EXERCISE: ASSESSMENT PRACTICE On your paper, match each word on the left with a synonym on the right.

1.	**prodigy**	**a.**	mourn
2.	**indignity**	**b.**	disaster
3.	**reproach**	**c.**	genius
4.	**discordant**	**d.**	ruin
5.	**lament**	**e.**	disloyalty
6.	**ream**	**f.**	humiliation
7.	**reverie**	**g.**	condemnation
8.	**devastate**	**h.**	daydream
9.	**fiasco**	**i.**	heap
10.	**betrayal**	**j.**	inharmonious

<u>Building Vocabulary</u>

For an in-depth lesson on how to build your vocabulary, see page 572.

Grammar in Context: Verb Phrases

Amy Tan, in her story "Two Kinds," uses repetition of verb phrases to emphasize the conflict between the mother and her daughter.

> My mother believed . . . You could open a restaurant. . . . You could buy a house with almost no money down. You could become rich. . . .
>
> I didn't get straight A's. I didn't become class president. I didn't get into Stanford.

Remember that a **verb phrase** consists of two or more words: a **main verb** (in red type) and **helping,** or **auxiliary, verbs** (in blue type). In the example above, the verb phrases show the mother's beliefs about life in America (*could open, could buy, could become*) contrasted with the daughter's rebellion (*didn't get, didn't become, didn't get*). The rhythm of these verb phrases emphasizes each character's main trait.

Apply to Your Writing Repetition of verb phrases helps

- convey information about a character or scene
- emphasize a particular trait or quality
- compare characters' other characteristics

WRITING EXERCISE Using repetition of verb phrases, write several sentences comparing the mother and daughter. Choose one or more helping verbs from the list below, then combine them with main verbs. You can use any verb tense you like.

Examples: The mother should have listened to her daughter. She should have stopped the piano lessons. She should have asked what her daughter wanted.
Jing-mei did not want to be a prodigy. She did not practice the piano. She did not try her best.

Helping Verbs
is, are, was, were, be, have, has, had, do, does, did, will, could, should, would, might
Main Verbs
practice, teach, recognize, stop, perform, listen, ask, shout, try, play, applaud, dream, cry, discover

Connect to the Literature Skim through the story. Where else does the writer use repetition of verb phrases? What information about her characters does she convey through this technique?
Grammar Handbook Verbs, pp. 1183–1185

Amy Tan
1952–

Other Works
"Mother Tongue"
The Kitchen God's Wife
The Hundred Secret Senses

First Career Amy Tan, the daughter of Chinese immigrants, was born in Oakland, California. She earned a bachelor's degree in linguistics and English and a master's degree in linguistics at San Jose State University, and then went on to become a successful business writer before turning her talents to fiction.

A Stunning Success "Two Kinds" is part of her popular work *The Joy Luck Club*, a book that weaves together separate stories about four Chinese mothers and their American-born daughters. After its release in 1989, the book spent eight months on the *New York Times* bestseller list; in 1993, it was made into a movie. *The Joy Luck Club* was a finalist for the National Book Award and the National Book Critics Circle Award, and it received the 1990 Bay Area Book Reviewers Award for Fiction. It has been translated into more than 15 languages, including Chinese.

Author Activity

Mothers and Daughters Find out more about Waverly and Auntie Lindo by reading the chapter "Rules of the Game" in Amy Tan's *The Joy Luck Club*. In a small group, compare the mother-daughter relationship in that story with the one in "Two Kinds."

Clues to Meaning

Have you ever heard an unfamiliar word and been momentarily confused until the sentences that followed made it clear? Look at the excerpt on the right from Eugenia Collier's story "Marigolds." See if you can figure out the meaning of the word *ramshackle* by thinking about the **context,** or the surrounding words of the passage.

The meaning of the word *ramshackle* is made clear by the descriptive details that follow—"rickety frame" and "the boards . . . leaning together like a house . . . constructed from cards." From these clues, you know that *ramshackle* means "shaky, broken-down." By

Miss Lottie's house was the most ramshackle of all our ramshackle homes. The sun and rain had long since faded its rickety frame siding from white to a sullen gray. The boards themselves seemed to remain upright, not from being nailed together but rather from leaning together like a house that a child might have constructed from cards.

—Eugenia Collier, "Marigolds"

looking for such **context clues,** you will often be able to figure out the meaning of unfamiliar words.

Strategies for Building Vocabulary

In the example above, a type of context clue known as a **description clue** helped you understand an unfamiliar word. Here are some other types of context clues you should learn to recognize.

❶ **Definition and Restatement Clues** In these context clues, a word is accompanied by a **definition clue,** or a restatement of the word's meaning. For example, look at the context surrounding *appraising* in this excerpt.

. . . he found the general studying him, appraising him narrowly.
—Richard Connell, "The Most Dangerous Game"

The phrase "studying him" is a **restatement clue**—it suggests that *appraising* means "studying." Restatement clues are often signaled by a comma or by words such as *or, that is, in other words,* or *also called.*

❷ **Example Clues** An **example clue** is a type of context clue that uses examples to demonstrate a word's meaning. An example clue may be signaled by words and phrases like *including* and *such as.* Notice in the following sentence how the meaning of the word *privations* is illustrated by examples.

Mathilde faced many privations, such as giving up her maid and getting by on a tiny allowance.

❸ **Comparison and Contrast Clues** A comparison clue compares a word to a similar word or idea. Sometimes a comparison clue is found in a **simile,** a comparison between two things using the word *like* or *as.* Look at the following sentence for an example of a comparison clue.

The necklace scintillated like the stars on a fine Paris night.

The simile *like the stars* helps you understand that *scintillated* means "sparkled."

In **contrast clues,** on the other hand, an unfamiliar word is contrasted with another word or idea. Contrast clues often use the signal words *although, but, however, yet, on the other hand,* and *in contrast.*

EXERCISE Use context clues to define each underlined word. Then identify the kind of context clue that led you to each definition.

1. She wore a chic evening gown, a stark contrast to her dull, out-of-fashion work clothes.

2. After the bombing, the roof lay askew, like a hat on a sleeping cowboy.

3. She had no prospects, in other words, no possibilities for improving her life.

4. Horrified and shocked by the destruction, he stood in the plaza, aghast at the sight of his village.

5. He was such a garrulous man; for example, he often cornered Papa and kept talking to him for hours.

The *Osage Orange* Tree

William Stafford

On that first day of high school in the prairie town where the tree was, I stood in the sun by the flagpole and watched, but pretended not to watch, the others. They stood in groups and talked and knew each other, all except one—a girl though—in a faded blue dress, carrying a sack lunch and standing near the corner looking everywhere but at the crowd.

I might talk to her, I thought. But of course it was out of the question.

That first day was easier when the classes started. Some of the teachers were kind; some were frightening. Some of the students didn't care, but I listened and waited; and at the end of the day I was relieved, less conspicuous from then on.

But that day was not really over. As I hurried to carry my new paper route I was thinking about how in a strange town, if you are quiet, no one notices, and some may like you, later. I was thinking about this when I reached the north edge of town where the scattering houses dwindle. Beyond them to the north lay just openness, the plains, a big swoop of nothing. There, at the last house, just as I cut across a lot and threw to the last customer, I saw the girl in the blue dress coming along the street, heading on out of town, carrying books. And she saw me.

"Hello."

"Hello."

And because we stopped we were friends. I didn't know how I could stop, but I didn't hurry on. I stood. There was nothing to do but to act as if I were walking on out too. I had three papers left in the bag, and I frantically began to fold them—box them, as we called it—for throwing. We had begun to walk and talk. The girl was timid; I became more bold. Not much, but a little.

"Have you gone to school here before?" I asked.

"Yes, I went here last year."

A long pause. A meadowlark sitting on a fencepost hunched his wings and flew. I kicked through the dust of the road.

I began to look ahead. Where could we possibly be walking to? I couldn't be walking just because I wanted to be with her.

Fortunately, there was one more house, a gray house by a sagging barn, set two hundred yards from the road.

"I thought I'd see if I could get a customer here," I said, waving toward the house.

"That's where I live."

"Oh."

We were at the dusty car tracks that turned off the road to the house. The girl stopped. There was a tree at that corner, a straight but little tree with slim branches and shiny dark leaves.

"I could take a paper tonight to see if my father wants to buy it."

A great relief, this. What could I have said to her parents? I held out a paper, dropped it, picked it up, brushing off the dust. "No, here's a new one"—a great action, putting the dusty paper in the bag over my shoulder and pulling out a fresh one. When she took the paper we stood there a minute. The wind was coming in over the grass. She looked out with a tranquil expression.

She walked away past the tree, and I hurried quickly back toward town. Could anyone in the houses have been watching? I looked back once. The girl was standing on the small bridge halfway in to her house. I hurried on.

The next day at school I didn't ask her whether her father wanted to take the paper. When the others were there I wouldn't say anything. I stood with the boys. In American history the students could choose their seats, and I saw that she was too quiet and plainly dressed for many to notice her. But I crowded in with the boys, pushing one aside, scrambling for a seat by the window.

That night I came to the edge of town. Two papers were left, and I walked on out. The meadowlark was there. By some reeds in a ditch by the road a dragonfly—snake feeders, we called them—glinted. The sun was going down, and the plains were stretched out and lifted, some way, to the horizon. Could I go on up to the house? I didn't think so, but I walked on. Then, by the tree where her road turned off, she was standing. She was holding her books. More confused than ever, I stopped.

"My father will take the paper," she said.

She told me always to leave the paper at the foot of the tree. She insisted on that, saying their house was too far; and it is true that I was far off my route, a long way, a half-mile out of my territory. But I didn't think of that.

And so we were acquainted. What I remember best in that town is those evening walks to the tree. Every night—or almost every night—the girl was there. Evangeline was her name. We didn't say much. On Friday night of the first week she gave me a dime, the cost of the paper. It was a poor newspaper, by the way, cheap, sensational, unreliable. I never went up to her house. We never talked together at school. But all the time we knew each other; we just happened to meet. Every evening.

There was a low place in the meadow by that corner. The fall rains made a pond there, and in the evenings sometimes ducks would be coming in—a long line with set wings down the wind, and then a turn, and a skimming glide to the water. The wind would be blowing and the grass bent down. The evenings got colder and colder. The wind was cold. As winter came on the time at the tree was dimmer, but not dark. In the winter there was snow. The pond was frozen over; all the plains were white. I had to walk down the ruts of the road and leave the paper in the crotch of the tree, sometimes, when it was cold. The wind made a sound through the black branches. But usually, even on cold evenings, Evangeline was there.

At school we played ball at noon—the boys did. And I got acquainted. I learned that Evangeline's brother was janitor at the school. A big dark boy he was—a man, middle-aged I thought at the time. He didn't ever let on that he knew me. I would see him sweeping the halls, bent down, slow. I would see him and Evangeline take their sack lunches over to the south side of the building. Once I slipped away from the ball game and went over there, but he looked at me so steadily, without moving, that I pretended to be looking for a book, and quickly went back, and got in the game, and struck out.

You don't know about those winters, and especially that winter. Those were the dust years. Wheat was away down in price. Everyone was poor—poor in a way that you can't understand. I made two dollars a week, or something like that, on my paper route. I could tell about working for ten cents an hour—and then not getting paid; about families that ate wheat, boiled, for their main food, and burned wheat for fuel. You don't know how it would be. All through that hard winter I carried a paper to the tree by the pond, in the evening, and gave it to Evangeline.

In the cold weather Evangeline wore a heavier dress, a dark, straight, heavy dress, under a thick black coat. Outdoors she wore a knitted cap that fastened under her chin. She was dressed this way when we met and she took the paper. The reeds were broken now. The meadowlark was gone.

And then came the spring. I have forgotten to tell just how Evangeline looked. She was of medium height, and slim. Her face was pale, her forehead high, her eyes blue. Her tranquil face I remember well. I remember her watching the wind come in over the grass. Her dress was long, her feet small. I can remember her by the tree, with her books, or walking on up the road toward her house and stopping on the bridge halfway up there, but she didn't wave, and I couldn't tell whether she was watching me or not. I always looked back as I went over the rise toward town.

And I can remember her in the room at school. She came into American history one spring day, the first really warm day. She had changed from the dark heavy dress to the dull blue one of the last fall; and she had on a new belt, a gray belt, with blue stitching along the edges. As she passed in front of Jane Wright, a girl who sat on the front row, I heard Jane say to the girl beside her, "Why look at Evangeline— that old dress of hers has a new belt!"

Mansfield (1980), Billy Morrow Jackson. Oil on canvas, 42″ × 42″. Collection of Drs. Thomas and Judith Chused.

"Stop a minute, Evangeline," Jane said, "let me see your new dress."

Evangeline stopped and looked uncertainly at Jane and blushed. "It's just made over," she said, "it's just. . . ."

"It's cute, Dear," Jane said; and as Evangeline went on Jane nudged her friend in the ribs and the friend smothered a giggle.

Well, that was a good year. Commencement time came, and—along with the newspaper job—I had the task of preparing for finals and all. One thing, I wasn't a student who took part in the class play or anything like that. I was just one of the boys—twenty-fourth in line to get my diploma.

And graduation was bringing an end to my paper-carrying. My father covered a big territory in our part of the state, selling farm equipment; and we were going to move at once to a town seventy miles south. Only because of my finishing the school year had we stayed till graduation.

I had taught another boy my route, always leaving him at the end and walking on out, by myself, to the tree. I didn't really have to go around with him that last day, the day of graduation, but I was going anyway.

At the graduation exercises, held that May afternoon, I wore my brown Sunday suit. My mother was in the audience. It was a heavy day. The girls had on new dresses. But I didn't see *her*.

I suppose that I did deserve old man Sutton's "Shhh!" as we lined up to march across the stage, but I for the first time in the year forgot my caution, and asked Jane where Evangeline was. She shrugged, and I could see for myself that she was not there.

We marched across the stage; our diplomas were ours; our parents filed out; to the strains of a march on the school organ we trailed to the hall. I unbuttoned my brown suit coat, stuffed the diploma in my pocket, and sidled out of the group and upstairs.

Evangeline's brother was emptying wastebaskets at the far end of the hall. I sauntered toward him and stopped. I didn't know what I wanted to say. Unexpectedly, he solved my problem. Stopping in his work, holding a partly empty wastebasket over the canvas sack he wore over his shoulder, he stared at me, as if almost to say something.

"I noticed that—your sister wasn't here," I said. The noise below was dwindling. The hall was quiet, an echoey place; my voice sounded terribly loud. He emptied the rest of the wastebasket and shifted easily. He was a man, in big overalls. He stared at me.

"Evangeline couldn't come," he said. He stopped, looked at me again, and said, "She stole."

"Stole?" I said. "Stole what?"

He shrugged and went toward the next wastebasket, but I followed him.

"She stole the money from her bank—the money she was to use for her graduation dress," he said. He walked stolidly on, and I stopped. He deliberately turned away as he picked up the next wastebasket. But he said something else, half to himself. "You knew her. You talked to her . . . I know." He walked away.

I hurried downstairs and outside. The new carrier would have the papers almost delivered by now; so I ran up the street toward the north. I took a paper from him at the end of the street and told him to go back. I didn't pay any more attention to him. No one was at the tree, and I turned, for the first time, up the road to the house. I walked over the bridge and on up the narrow, rutty tracks. The house was gray and lopsided. The ground of the yard was packed; nothing grew there. By the back door, the door to which the road led, there was a grayish-white place on the ground where the dishwater had been thrown. A gaunt shepherd dog trotted out growling.

And the door opened suddenly, as if someone had been watching me come up the track. A woman came out—a woman stern-faced, with a shawl over her head and a dark lumpy dress on— came out on the back porch and shouted, "Go 'way, go 'way! We don't want no papers!" She waved violently with one hand, holding the other on her shawl, at her throat. She coughed so hard that she leaned over and put her hand against one of the uprights of the porch. Her face was red. She glanced toward the barn and leaned toward me. "Go 'way!"

Behind me a meadowlark sang. Over all the plains swooped the sky. The land was drawn up somehow toward the horizon.

I stood there, half-defiant, half-ashamed. The dog continued to growl and to pace around me, stiff-legged, his tail down. The windows of the house were all blank, with blinds drawn. I couldn't say anything.

I stood a long time and then, lowering the newspaper I had held out, I stood longer, waiting, without thinking of what to do. The meadowlark bubbled over again, but I turned and walked away, looking back once or twice. The old woman continued to stand, leaning forward, her head out. She glanced at the barn, but didn't call out any more.

My heels dug into the grayish place where the dishwater had been thrown; the dog skulked along behind.

At the bridge, halfway to the road, I stopped and looked back. The dog was lying down again; the porch was empty; and the door was closed. Turning the other way, I looked toward town. Near me stood our ragged little tree—an Osage orange tree it was. It was feebly coming into leaf, green all over the branches, among the sharp thorns. I hadn't wondered before how it grew there, all alone, in the plains country, neglected. Over our pond some ducks came slicing in.

Standing there on the bridge, still holding the folded—boxed—newspaper, that worthless paper, I could see everything. I looked out along the road to town. From the bridge you could see the road going away, to where it went over the rise.

Glancing around, I flipped that last newspaper under the bridge and then bent far over and looked where it had gone. There they were—a pile of boxed newspapers, thrown in a heap, some new, some worn and weathered, by rain, by snow. ❖

William Stafford
1914–1993

Other Works
Traveling Through the Dark
Allegiances
Down in My Heart
Stories That Could Be True

William Stafford was born in Hutchinson, Kansas, and grew up in small towns scattered across the Kansas plains. A conscientious objector during World War II, Stafford lived in U.S. Forest Service work camps with other conscientious objectors during those years. In 1948, he began teaching English at Lewis and Clark College in Oregon, where he remained for much of his life.

Primarily a poet, Stafford described the work of writing as an exploration. Writers don't necessarily know many of the things they write about until they begin to write, he explained. All of his poems started out as experiments and, despite his many successes, most of them— "thousands"—were never completed.

Stafford was highly respected as a poet, winning numerous awards and honors. His book *Traveling Through the Dark* received the National Book Award in 1963. He was named poetry consultant for the Library of Congress in 1970 and served as poet laureate of the state of Oregon from 1975 to 1993. Stafford also won the Shelley Memorial Award in 1964 and the American Academy and Institute of Arts and Letters Award in Literature in 1981. In 1986, he was named one of America's ten major living poets by his peers in a poll in *Writer's Digest*.

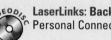 **LaserLinks: Background for Reading**
Personal Connection

Storytelling Across Genres

from **The Perfect Storm** *Nonfiction by* SEBASTIAN JUNGER	**The Wreck of the Hesperus** *Poetry by* HENRY WADSWORTH LONGFELLOW

What's the Connection?

Shipwreck! You are about to read two works of literature about disasters at sea. While one is a true-life adventure and the other a poem, both tell a kind of story that has fascinated readers for generations.

Why do sea-disaster stories captivate us? One reason is the sea itself—an awesome force of nature that challenges human strength and courage. Another is the admiration or sympathy we feel for the people who brave the sea. Can you think of other reasons?

The Enduring Appeal of Sea-Disaster Stories: Leonardo DiCaprio tries to keep his head above water in the film *Titanic*.

Points of Comparison

Evaluating Storytelling Across Genres In this unit so far, you have studied the elements of storytelling in short fiction. But stories can be told in other genres as well. In the pages that follow, you will compare two stories about disasters at sea—one in the form of nonfiction, and the other in poetry—to decide which you think is more effective. You will begin by establishing points of comparison.

Critical Thinking: Establishing Criteria

The first step in comparing and evaluating two works of literature is to establish some criteria, or standards, of success. To evaluate a sea-disaster story, decide what you think are the most important elements of such a story and what would make each element especially powerful and compelling. Use a chart like the one below to develop your ideas.

Storytelling Elements	Criteria for a Powerful Sea-Disaster Story
people in the story	we should care about them
action/conflict	should be exciting and believable
setting	should make you feel as though you are there

READER'S NOTEBOOK As you read the two selections that follow, jot down any additional qualities you think a good sea-disaster story should have.

"When you're on the rescuing side you're very aware of life and death."

from **The Perfect Storm**

Nonfiction by SEBASTIAN JUNGER

Connect to Your Life

Acts of Courage You are about to read a true story of the courageous actions that took place at the scene of a sinking boat. Have you or has someone you know ever faced a situation that called for you to act courageously? Was your challenge a physical one or one that required you to take a stand? What risks were involved? In what ways did your actions surprise you? Discuss your answers with a small group of your classmates.

Build Background

Storm of the Century In October 1991, off the northeastern coast of Canada, several weather patterns came together to produce one of the worst storms in history. Meteorologists labeled this freak occurrence "the perfect storm." The following excerpt from Sebastian Junger's *The Perfect Storm* focuses on the struggle of the *Satori*, a 32-foot sailboat, to stay afloat at the end of the storm, near the New England coast. The boat was caught in hurricane-force winds and 60-foot swells. A wave had knocked down the poles that held its sails, its life raft had disappeared, and water had poured from an open hatch into its cabin. Crew member Sue Bylander sent a distress call.

WORDS TO KNOW
Vocabulary Preview

amalgam	hypothermic
despondent	incredulously
flail	intermittently
hoist	maelstrom
hull	tether

Focus Your Reading

LITERARY ANALYSIS **NARRATIVE NONFICTION** *The Perfect Storm* is a work of **nonfiction,** writing that is about real people, places, and events. It is also a work of **narrative nonfiction.** The selection provides factual information, yet it may remind you of adventure tales you've read. Writers of narrative nonfiction bring facts to life by presenting them in a storylike way. While you're reading the selection, pay attention to how the events unfold. Also notice the conflicts that arise.

ACTIVE READING **IDENTIFYING ELEMENTS OF STORYTELLING** As you read this nonfiction account of a disaster at sea, pay attention to the way the author tells the story. Notice how people in the story are like **characters** in a work of fiction. Look for important moments of **action** or **conflict,** and pay close attention to the **setting.**

READER'S NOTEBOOK Use a chart like the one shown to record your observations.

Storytelling Elements in The Perfect Storm

people in the story:
Captain Leonard worried about losing Satori
action/conflict:
setting:

THE PERFECT Storm

Sebastian Junger

AT 11:15 PM, OCTOBER 29TH, A FREIGHTER OFF LONG ISLAND PICKS UP A WOMAN'S TERRIFIED VOICE ON THE VHF:[1] THIS IS THE SATORI, THE SATORI, 39:49 NORTH AND 69:52 WEST, WE ARE THREE PEOPLE, THIS IS A MAYDAY.[2] IF ANYONE CAN HEAR US, PLEASE PASS OUR POSITION ON TO THE COAST GUARD. REPEAT, THIS IS A MAYDAY, IF ANYONE CAN HEAR US, PASS OUR POSITION ON TO THE COAST GUARD.

---

1. *VHF:* a two-way radio that transmits and receives very-high-frequency radio waves.

2. **mayday:** a distress signal; call for help.

The freighter, the *Gold Bond Conveyor,* relays the message to Coast Guard operations in Boston, which in turn contacts the Coast Guard cutter *Tamaroa* in Provincetown Harbor. The *Tamaroa* has just come off Georges Bank, where she was conducting spot checks on the fishing fleet, and now she's waiting out the weather inside Cape Cod's huge flexed arm. A small Falcon jet scrambles from Air Station Cape Cod and the *Tamaroa,* 1,600 tons and 205 feet, weighs anchor at midnight and heads down the throat of the storm.

The crew of the *Satori* have no way of knowing whether the radio is working, they just have to keep repeating the mayday and hope for the best. And even if the radio *is* working, they still have to be within two or three miles of another vessel for the signal to be heard. That's a lot to ask for on a night like this. Bylander, wedged behind the nav table,[3] broadcasts their name and position <u>intermittently</u> for half an hour without any response at all; they're alone out there, as far as she can tell. She keeps trying— what else is there to do?—and Stimpson goes back on deck to try to keep the *Satori* pointed into the seas. She's not there long when she hears the sound of an airplane fading in and out through the roar of the storm. She looks around frantically in the darkness, and a minute later a Falcon jet, flying low under the cloud cover, shrieks overhead and raises Bylander on the VHF. "Sue was so excited she was giddy," Stimpson says, "but I wasn't. I remember not feeling elated or relieved so much as like, instantly, I'd rejoined the world of the living."

The Falcon pilot circles just below cloud level and discusses what to do next over the VHF with Bylander. The *Tamaroa* won't be there for

another twelve hours, and they've got to keep the boat afloat until then, even if that means burning out the engine. They can't afford to risk any more knockdowns. Bylander, against Leonard's wishes, finally toggles the starter switch, and to her amazement it turns over. With the storm jib up and the prop turning away they can now get a few degrees to the weather.[4] It's not a lot, but it's enough to keep from getting broached by the seas.

Throughout the night the Falcon pilot flies over them, reassuring Bylander that they're going to come out of this alive. Stimpson stays at the helm[5] and Leonard lies on his bunk, contemplating the impending loss of his boat. When the *Tamaroa* arrives he'll have to abandon ship, which is an almost unthinkable act for a captain. The *Satori* is his home, his life, and if he allows himself to be taken off by the Coast Guard he'll probably never see her again. Not intact, anyway. At some point that night, lying on his bunk waiting for dawn, Ray Leonard decides he won't get off the boat. The women can leave if they want to, but he'll see the vessel into port.

Throughout that night the *Tamaroa* slugs her way through the storm. She's a bulldog of a vessel, built to salvage crippled battleships in World War Two, and she can "tow anything afloat," according to her literature. The sea state is so high, though, that the most she can make is three or four

---

3. **nav table:** a table for spreading out the charts used in plotting a boat's course.

4. **With the storm jib up . . . to the weather:** With a small triangular sail raised and the propeller operating, they can turn the *Satori* a bit more toward the direction from which the wind is blowing.

5. **helm:** the steering gear of a boat or ship—usually a tiller or wheel.

WORDS
TO   **intermittently** (ĭn'tər-mĭt'nt-lē) *adv.* at intervals; from time to time
KNOW

knots[6]—roughly walking pace. On the larger swells she plunges into the crest, stalls, and launches out the far side, spray streaming off her bridge and greenwater sheeting out her scuppers.[7] She crosses Cape Cod Bay, threads the canal, leaves the Elizabeth Islands to starboard,[8] and finally turns the corner around Martha's Vineyard. Commander Lawrence Brudnicki, chief officer on board, estimates that they'll arrive on-scene late the next afternoon; the *Satori* crew has to stay afloat until then. They have no life raft or survival suits on board, and the nearest helicopter base is an hour away. If the *Satori* goes down, the crew is dead.

Brudnicki can't speak directly to the *Satori*, but he can relay messages via the Falcon that's circling above them. Both ship and plane are also in contact with the First District Command Center in Boston—D1 Comcen, as it's referred to in Coast Guard reports. D1 Comcen is responsible for coordinating all the Coast Guard vessels and aircraft on the rescue, and developing the safest strategy for taking the people off the boat. Every decision has to be approved by them. Since the *Satori* isn't sinking yet, they decide to have the Falcon fly cover until the *Tamaroa* arrives, and then take the crew off by raft. Air rescue in such conditions can be riskier than actually staying with the boat, so it's used as a last resort. As soon as day breaks, the Falcon will be relieved by an H-3 rescue helicopter, and H-3's will fly cover in shifts until the *Tamaroa* shows up. Helicopters have a limited amount of flying time—generally about four hours—but they can pluck people out of the water if need be. Falcon jets can't do much for people in the water except circle them and watch them drown.

---

6. **three or four knots:** a speed of three or four nautical miles per hour.

7. **scuppers** (skŭp'ərz): openings in the side of a ship at deck level to allow water to run off.

8. **leaves . . . to starboard:** passes to the left of the Elizabeth Islands.

From the incident log, D1 Comcen:

2:30 AM—s/v [sailing vessel] is running out of fuel, recommend we try to keep Falcon o/s [on-scene] until Tamaroa arrives.

5:29 AM—Falcon has lost comms [communication] with vessel, vessel is low on battery power and taking on water. Pumps are keeping up but are run by ele [electric].

7:07 AM—Falcon o/s, vessel has been located. Six hours fuel left. People on board are scared.

The H-3 arrives on scene around 6:30 and spends half an hour just trying to locate the *Satori*. The conditions are so bad that she's vanished from the Falcon's radar, and the H-3 pilot is almost on top of her before spotting her in the foam-streaked seas. The Falcon circles off to the southwest to prepare a life-raft drop while the H-3 takes up a hover directly over the boat. In these conditions the Falcon pilot could never line up on something as small as a sailboat, so the H-3 acts as a stand-in. The Falcon comes back at 140 knots, radar locked onto the helicopter, and at the last moment the H-3 falls away and the jet makes the drop. The

pilot comes screaming over the *Satori's* mast[9] and the copilot pushes two life-raft packages out a hatch in the floorboards. The rafts are linked by a long nylon <u>tether</u>, and as they fall they cartwheel apart, splashing down well to either side of the *Satori*. The tether, released at two hundred feet into a hurricane-force wind, drops right into Bylander's hand.

The H-3 hovers overhead while the *Satori* crew haul in the packages, but both rafts have exploded on impact. There's nothing at either end of the line. The *Tamaroa* is still five hours away and the storm has retrograded[10] to within a couple of hundred miles of the coast; over the next twenty-four hours it will pass directly over the *Satori*. A daylight rescue in these conditions is difficult, and a nighttime rescue is out of the question. If the *Satori* crew is not taken off in the next few hours, there's a good chance they won't be taken off at all. Late that morning the second H-3 arrives and the pilot, Lieutenant Klosson, explains the situation to Ray Leonard. Leonard radios back that he's not leaving the boat.

It's unclear whether Leonard is serious or just trying to save face. Either way, the Coast Guard is having none of it. Two helicopters, two Falcon jets, a medium-range cutter, and a hundred air- and seamen have already been committed to the rescue; the *Satori* crew are coming off now. *"Owner refuses to leave and says he's sailed through hurricanes before,"* the Comcen incident log records at 12:24 that afternoon. *"Tamaroa wants manifestly unsafe voyage so that o/o [owner-operator] can be forced off."*

A "manifestly unsafe voyage" means that the vessel has been deemed an unacceptable risk to her crew or others, and the Coast Guard has the legal authority to order everyone off.

Commander Brudnicki gets on the radio with District One and requests a manifestly unsafe designation for the *Satori*, and at 12:47 it is granted. The *Tamaroa* is just a couple of miles away now, within VHF range of the *Satori*, and Brudnicki raises Leonard on the radio and tells him he has no choice in the matter. Everyone is leaving the boat. At 12:57 in the afternoon, thirteen hours after weighing anchor, the *Tamaroa* plunges into view.

There's a lot of hardware circling the *Satori*. There's the Falcon, the H-3, the *Tamaroa*, and the freighter *Gold Bond Conveyor*, which has been cutting circles around the *Satori* since the first mayday call. Hardware is not the problem, though; it's time. Dark is only three hours away, and the departing H-3 pilot doesn't think the *Satori* will survive another night. She'll run out of fuel, start getting knocked down, and eventually break apart. The crew will be cast into the sea, and the helicopter pilot will refuse to drop his rescue swimmer because he can't be sure of getting him back. It would be up to the *Tamaroa* to maneuver alongside the swimmers and pull them on board, and in these seas it would be almost impossible. It's now or never.

The only way to take them off, Brudnicki decides, is to shuttle them back to the *Tamaroa* in one of the little Avons. The Avons are 21-foot inflatable rafts with rigid <u>hulls</u> and outboard engines; one of them could make a run to the *Satori*, drop off survival suits and then come back again to pick up the three crew. If anyone wound up in the water, at least they'd be insulated and afloat. It's not a particularly complicated maneuver, but no one has done it

---

9. **mast:** a vertical pole that supports the sails of a sailing vessel.

10. **retrograded:** backed up.

in conditions like this before. No one has even seen conditions like this before. At 1:23 PM the *Tamaroa* crew gathers at the port davits,[11] three men climb aboard the Avon, and they lower away.

It goes badly from the start. What passes for a lull between waves is in fact a crest-to-trough change of thirty or forty feet. Chief bosun[12] Thomas Amidon lowers the Avon half way down, gets lifted up by the next wave, can't keep up with the trough and freefalls to the bottom of the cable. The lifting eye[13] gets ripped out of its mount and Amidon almost pitches overboard. He struggles back into position, finishes lowering the boat, and makes way from the *Tamaroa*.

The seas are twice the size of the Avon raft. With excruciating slowness it fights its way to the *Satori*, comes up bow-to-stern,[14] and a crew member flings the three survival suits on deck. Stimpson grabs them and hands them out, but Amidon doesn't back out in time. The sailboat rides up a sea, comes down on the Avon, and punctures one of her air bladders. Things start to happen very fast now: the Avon's bow collapses, a wave swamps her to the gunwales,[15] the engine dies, and she falls away astern.[16] Amidon tries desperately to get the engine going again and finally manages to, but they're up to their waists in water and the raft is crippled. There's no way they can even get themselves back onto the *Tamaroa*, much less save the crew of the *Satori*. Six people, not just three, now need to be rescued.

The H-3 crew watches all this incredulously. They're in a two o'clock hover[17] with their jump door open, just over the tops of the waves. They can see the raft dragging heavily through the seas, and the *Tamaroa* heaving through 90-degree rolls. Pilot Claude Hessel finally gets on the radio and tells Brudnicki and Amidon that he may have another way of doing this. He can't hoist the

Satori crew directly off their deck, he says, because the mast is flailing too wildly and might entangle the hoist. That would drag the H-3 right down on top of the boat. But he could drop his rescue swimmer, who could take the people off the boat one at a time and bring them up on the hoist. It's the best chance they've got, and Brudnicki knows it. He consults with District One and then gives the okay.

The rescue swimmer on Hessel's helicopter is Dave Moore, a three-year veteran who has never been on a major rescue. ("The good cases don't come along too often—usually someone beats you to them," he says. "If a sailboat gets in trouble far out we usually get a rescue, but otherwise it's just a lot of little stuff.") Moore is handsome in a baby-faced sort of way—square-jawed, blue-eyed, and a big open smile. He has a dense, compact body that is more seal-like than athletic. His profession of rescue swimmer came about when a tanker went down off New York in the mid-1980s. A Coast Guard helicopter was hovering overhead, but it was winter and the tanker crew were too hypothermic to get into the lift basket. They all drowned. Congress decided they wanted something done, and the Coast Guard adopted the Navy rescue

---

11. **port davits:** small cranes on the left side of the ship, used for lowering and raising the inflatable rafts.

12. **bosun** (bō'sən): an officer in charge of a ship's boat crews and maintenance crews.

13. **lifting eye:** a metal ring through which the rope used to lower the boat passes.

14. **bow-to-stern:** from behind the *Satori*.

15. **swamps her to the gunwales** (gŭn'əlz): fills the boat with water to the top of its sides.

16. **falls away astern:** is left behind by the *Satori*.

17. **in a two o'clock hover:** hovering so that the boat is 60 degrees to the right of straight ahead.

WORDS
TO
KNOW

incredulously (ĭn-krĕj'ə-ləs-lē) *adv.* in a way that expresses disbelief
hoist (hoist) *v.* to raise or haul up
flail (flāl) *v.* to move vigorously or erratically; thrash about
hypothermic (hī'pə-thûr'mĭk) *adj.* having an abnormally low body temperature

program. Moore is 25 years old, born the year Karen Stimpson graduated from high school.

Moore is already wearing a neoprene[18] wetsuit. He puts on socks and hood, straps on swim fins, pulls a mask and snorkel down over his head, and then struggles into his neoprene gloves. He buckles on a life vest and then signals to flight engineer Vriesman that he's ready. Vriesman, who has one arm extended, gate-like, across the jump door, steps aside and allows Moore to crouch by the edge. That means that they're at "ten and ten"—a ten foot hover at ten knots. Moore, who's no longer plugged into the intercom, signals final corrections to Vriesman with his hands, who relays them to the pilot. This is it; Moore has trained three years for this moment. An hour ago he was in the lunch line back on base. Now he's about to drop into the <u>maelstrom</u>.

Hessel holds a low hover with the boat at his two o'clock. Moore can see the crew clustered together on deck and the *Satori* making slow, plunging headway into the seas. Vriesman is seated next to Moore at the hoist controls, and avionicsman[19] Ayres is behind the copilot with the radio and search gear. Both wear flightsuits and crash helmets and are plugged into the internal communication system in the wall. The time is 2:07 PM. Moore picks a spot between waves, takes a deep breath, and jumps.

It's a ten-foot fall and he hits feet-first, hands at his side. He comes up, clears his snorkel, settles his mask, and then strikes out for the *Satori*. The water is lukewarm—they're in the Gulf Stream—and the seas are so big they give him the impression he's swimming uphill and downhill rather than over individual waves. Occasionally the wind blows a crest off, and he has to dive under the cascade of whitewater before setting out again. The *Satori* appears and disappears behind the swells and the H-3 thunders overhead, rotors blasting a lily-pad of flattened water into

THE BOAT'S UNDER POWER AND THERE'S NO WAY HE'S GOING TO CATCH HER.

the sea. Vriesman watches anxiously through binoculars from the jump door, trying to gauge the difficulty of getting Moore back into the helicopter. Ultimately, as flight engineer, it's his decision to deploy[20] the swimmer, his job to get everyone safely back into the aircraft. If he has any doubts, Moore doesn't jump.

Moore swims hard for several minutes and finally looks up at Vriesman, shaking his head. The boat's under power and there's no way he's going to catch her, not in these seas. Vriesman sends the basket down and Moore climbs back in. Just as he's about to ride up, the wave hits.

It's huge and cresting, fifty or sixty feet. It avalanches over Moore and buries both him and the lift basket. Vriesman counts to ten before Moore finally pops up through the foam, still inside the basket. It's no longer attached to the hoist cable, though; it's been wrenched off the hook and is just floating free. Moore has such tunnel vision[21] that he doesn't realize the basket has come off; he just sits there, waiting to be hoisted. Finally he understands that he's not going anywhere, and swims the basket over to the cable and clips it on. He climbs inside, and Vriesman hauls him up.

---

18. **neoprene** (nē′ə-prēn′): a synthetic rubber.

19. **avionicsman** (ā′vē-ŏn′ĭks-mən): the person in charge of an aircraft's electronic equipment.

20. **deploy:** make use of.

21. **has such tunnel vision:** is so focused on his mission.

This time they're going to do things differently. Hessel banks the helicopter to within fifty feet of the *Satori* and shows a chalk board that says, "Channel 16." Bylander disappears below, and when Hessel has her on the VHF, he tells her they're going to do an in-the-water pick-up. They're to get into their survival suits, tie the tiller down,[22] and then jump off the boat. Once they're in the water they are to stay in a group and wait for Moore to swim over to them. He'll put them into the hoist basket and send them up one at a time.

Bylander climbs back up on deck and gives the instructions to the rest of the crew. Moore, looking through a pair of binoculars, watches them pull on their suits and try to will themselves over the gunwale. First, one of them puts a leg over the rail, then another does, and finally all three of them splash into the water. It takes four or five minutes for them to work up the nerve. Leonard has a bag in one hand, and as he goes over he loses his grip and leaves it on deck. It's full of his personal belongings. He claws his way down the length of the hull and finally punches himself in the head when he realizes he's lost it for good. Moore takes this in, wondering if Leonard is going to be a problem in the water.

Moore sheds his hood and gloves because the water's so warm and pulls his mask back down over his face. This is it; if they can't do it now, they can't do it at all. Hessel puts the *Satori* at his six o'clock[23] by lining them up in a little rearview mirror and comes down into a low hover. It's delicate flying. He finally gives Moore

---

22. **tie the tiller down:** tie down the handle used for steering the boat, so that it can't move.

23. **puts the *Satori* at his six o'clock:** moves the helicopter so that the *Satori* is directly behind it.

the go-ahead, and Moore breathes in deep and pushes off. "They dropped Moore and he just skimmed over the top of the water, flying towards us," says Stimpson. "When he gets there he says, 'Hi, I'm Dave Moore your rescue swimmer, how are you?' And Sue says, 'Fine, how are you?' It was very cordial. Then he asks who's going first, and Sue says, 'I will.' And he grabbed her by the back of the survival suit and skimmed back across the water."

Moore loads Bylander into the rescue basket, and twenty seconds later she's in the helicopter. Jump to recovery takes five minutes (avionicsman Ayres is writing everything down in the hoist log). The next recovery, Stimpson's, takes two minutes, and Leonard's takes three. Leonard is so <u>despondent</u> that he's deadweight in the water, Moore has to wrestle him into the basket and push his legs in after him. Moore's the last one up, stepping back into the aircraft at 2:29. They've been on-scene barely two hours.

Moore starts stripping off his gear, and he's got his wetsuit half-way off when he realizes the helicopter isn't going anywhere. It's hovering off the *Tamaroa's* port quarter.[24] He puts his flight helmet on and hears the *Tamaroa* talking to Hessel, telling him to stand by because their Avon crew still needs to be recovered. . . . Moore pulls his gear back on and takes up his position at the jump door. Hessel has decided

on another in-the-water rescue, and Moore watches the three Coast Guardsmen grab hands and reluctantly abandon ship. Even from a distance they look nervous. Hessel comes in low and puts them at his six o'clock again, barely able to find such a small target in his rearview mirror. Moore gets the nod and jumps for the third time; he's got the drill down now and the entire rescue takes ten minutes. Each Coast Guardsman that makes it into the aircraft gives Stimpson a thumbs-up. Moore comes up last—"via bare hook," as the report reads—and Vriesman pulls him in through the door. The H-3 banks, drops her nose, and starts for home.

"When I got up into the helicopter I remember everyone looking in my and Sue's faces to make sure we were okay," says Stimpson. "I remember the intensity, it really struck me. These guys were *so* pumped up, but they were also human—real humanity. They'd take us by the shoulders and look us in the eyes and say, 'I'm so glad you're alive, we were with you last night, we prayed for you. We were worried about you.' When you're on the rescuing side you're very aware of life and death, and when you're on the rescued side, you just have a sort of numb awareness. At some point I stopped seeing the risk clearly, and it just became an <u>amalgam</u> of experience and observation." ❖

YOU

JUST

HAVE A

SORT OF

NUMB

AWARENESS.

---

24. **the *Tamaroa's* port quarter:** the rear part of the *Tamaroa's* left side.

121

Connect to the Literature

1. **What Do You Think?** Did you enjoy this true-life account as an adventure story? Explain why or why not.

Comprehension Check
- Whom did the Coast Guard first attempt to rescue?
- How did the sailboat manage to stay afloat?
- How did Dave Moore help those in danger?

Think Critically

2. **ACTIVE READING** **IDENTIFYING ELEMENTS OF STORYTELLING**
    READER'S NOTEBOOK Using the chart you made, discuss with classmates what you think are the most important elements of the story.

3. Which person in the story did you find the most interesting? Support your answer with evidence from the selection.

4. Consider how Dave Moore handled conflicts during the rescue. What personal traits do you think he displayed?

   THINK ABOUT {
   - his rescues before this one
   - how he reacted to sudden changes
   - how he treated the *Satori* crew

5. Did you find the author's description of the **setting** clear and complete enough for you to picture the scene of the rescue? Explain your answer.

6. Do you think the struggle for survival presented in this nonfiction account is more or less gripping than a fictional tale would be?

Extend Interpretations

7. **What If?** How might the story have ended if the crew members of the *Satori* had refused to jump into the water?

8. **Connect to Life** How would you define *courage?* To which people in this account would you apply this definition? Explain your answer.

9. **Points of Comparison** Look again at the list of criteria you made for a good sea-disaster story. Based on the chart of storytelling elements you made for this excerpt from *The Perfect Storm,* how well do you think it succeeds as a sea-disaster story? Cite evidence to support your answer.

Literary Analysis

NARRATIVE NONFICTION

Nonfiction is prose writing that deals with real people, places, and events. *The Perfect Storm* is an example of **narrative nonfiction.** It uses elements typically found in fiction, such as **plot, character,** and **setting,** to present factual information and to bring events to life for the reader. For example, the "plot" of this excerpt consists of the steps of the rescue, presented in logical order. **Descriptions** of the stormy setting read like ones you might find in a **short story.** Conversations between people often resemble the **dialogue** of fictional characters. Also, as in fiction, **conflicts** arise that draw readers into the action. For example, consider the following situation:

They have no life raft or survival suits on board, and the nearest helicopter base is an hour away. If the Satori *goes down, the crew is dead.*

Paired Activity With a partner, review the selection and choose a paragraph with details that seem storylike. Then rewrite the paragraph in a way that is strictly informative, without the intensity or dramatic emphasis of a story. How does this change affect your enjoyment of the paragraph?

Choices & CHALLENGES

Writing Options

Disaster Narrative Write about a real-life disaster that you have experienced or heard about. Use elements of storytelling, such as characterization, dialogue, action, conflict, suspense, and details of setting, to help bring your story to life. Place the narrative in your **Working Portfolio.**

Activities & Explorations

Comic Strip Review the steps taken in rescuing the *Satori* crew. Depict the incident in the form of an action comic strip. ~ **ART**

Inquiry & Research

Tracking Hurricanes The *Satori* is wrecked by the great whirling winds of a hurricane. Discover how hurricanes form and how the National Hurricane Center observes their formation and tracks them.

 **More Online: Research Starter** www.mcdougallittell.com

Vocabulary in Action

EXERCISE A: SYNONYMS For each phrase in the first column, write the letter of the rhyming phrase in the second column that has similar meaning.

1. stir **intermittently**
2. damaged **hull**
3. **despondent** young man
4. **hoist** the cow
5. hang calmly from a **tether**

a. raise the grazer
b. cope on a rope
c. blend now and then
d. maimed frame
e. sad lad

EXERCISE B: WORD MEANING Answer these questions on your paper.

1. Could you develop a **hypothermic** condition by sitting in a heated pool?
2. Would a recipe be an **amalgam** of ingredients?
3. Would you stare **incredulously** at someone who looked perfectly normal?
4. Which weather condition could be described as a **maelstrom**—a light snowfall or a thunderstorm?
5. Which person would be more likely to **flail** his or her arms—an orchestra conductor or a soccer player?

Building Vocabulary
For an in-depth lesson on word relationships such as synonyms and antonyms, see page 849.

Sebastian Junger
1962–

Life on the Edge Danger is nothing new to Sebastian Junger, a native of Belmont, Massachusetts. He spent several years as a freelance journalist, contributing articles to action-oriented magazines. As a newspaper writer, he trekked across politically unstable regions. Junger has always been intrigued by dangerous professions. According to the author, "Whether you're on the border between two fighting countries or on the edge of the sea . . . things happen on the edge."

From Tree Cutter to Best-Selling Author Working as a tree cutter to supplement his income in the early 1990s, Junger injured his leg. In the free time that resulted, he began the three-year project of researching and writing *The Perfect Storm*. The rescue of the *Satori* is a small part of the book. *The Perfect Storm* focuses mainly on the last days of the crew of the *Andrea Gail*, a swordfishing vessel from Gloucester, Massachusetts. This real-life account became a phenomenal bestseller.

The Wreck of the Hesperus

Poetry by HENRY WADSWORTH LONGFELLOW

"I fear a hurricane."

Connect to Your Life

No Problem! Everyone knows that you need confidence to succeed. But having too much confidence can be a problem. Think of a time when you or someone you knew had too much confidence in facing a particular challenge. With a partner, describe what happened and what you learned from it. Then, with a larger group, discuss this question: What are the risks of having too much confidence?

Build Background

A Haunting Wreck In 1839, poet Henry Wadsworth Longfellow read a report of a wreck that had occurred off Norman's Reef near Gloucester, Massachusetts. According to the report, 20 bodies had washed ashore with the wreckage of a schooner (illustrated below), named the *Hesperus.* Longfellow's thoughts turned repeatedly to the fate of the people aboard. Then, weeks later, it occurred to him to write a poem about the disaster.

spar
masts

Two-Masted Schooner

Focus Your Reading

LITERARY ANALYSIS **NARRATIVE POETRY** In Longfellow's time, gathering at home to read aloud by the fireside was a popular activity. Many of Longfellow's works are **narrative poems,** poems that tell stories. Like **fiction,** narrative poems contain the elements of **character, setting,** and **plot.** Notice how "The Wreck of the Hesperus" opens in a way that a story might:

> *It was the schooner Hesperus,*
> *That sailed the wintry sea;*

As you read this poem, pay attention to what happens to the ship and its passengers.

ACTIVE READING **IDENTIFYING ELEMENTS OF STORYTELLING** Just as you did with *The Perfect Storm,* pay attention to the way this poem about a disaster at sea tells a story. Notice how **character** is developed in the poem. Note important moments of action or **conflict,** and pay close attention to how the **setting** is described.

📖 **READER'S NOTEBOOK** As with the previous selection, use a chart like the one shown to record your observations.

Storytelling Elements in
"The Wreck of the Hesperus"

people in the story:

action/conflict:

setting:

The Wreck of the Hesperus

HENRY WADSWORTH LONGFELLOW

Moonlit Shipwreck at Sea (1901), Thomas Moran. Christie's Images.

It was the schooner Hesperus,
    That sailed the wintry sea;
And the skipper had taken his little daughter,
    To bear him company.

5 Blue were her eyes as the fairy-flax,
    Her cheeks like the dawn of day,
And her bosom white as the hawthorn buds,
    That ope in the month of May.

  The skipper he stood beside the helm,
10   His pipe was in his mouth.
And he watched how the veering flaw did blow
    The smoke now West, now South.

  Then up and spake an old Sailor,
    Had sailed to the Spanish Main,
15 "I pray thee, put into yonder port,
    For I fear a hurricane.

  "Last night, the moon had a golden ring,
    And to-night no moon we see!"
The skipper, he blew a whiff from his pipe,
20   And a scornful laugh laughed he.

  Colder and louder blew the wind,
    A gale from the Northeast,
The snow fell hissing in the brine,
    And the billows frothed like yeast.

25 Down came the storm, and smote amain
    The vessel in its strength;
She shuddered and paused, like a frighted steed,
    Then leaped her cable's length.

8 ope: open.

11 veering flaw: a gust of wind that changes direction.

15 yonder port: the harbor over there.

23 brine: seawater.

24 billows frothed: great waves foamed.

25 smote (smōt) **amain:** struck with great force.

"Come hither! come hither! my little
    daughter,
30 And do not tremble so;
For I can weather the roughest gale
    That ever wind did blow."

He wrapped her warm in his seaman's
    coat
    Against the stinging blast;
35 He cut a rope from a broken spar,
    And bound her to the mast.

"O father! I hear the church-bells ring,
    Oh say, what may it be?"
"'Tis a fog-bell on a rock-bound coast!"—
40   And he steered for the open sea.

Holding the Lines, James E. Buttersworth. Christie's Images.

"O father! I hear the sound of guns,
    Oh say, what may it be?"
"Some ship in distress, that cannot live
    In such an angry sea!"

45 "O father! I see a gleaming light,
    Oh say, what may it be?"
But the father answered never a word,
    A frozen corpse was he.

Lashed to the helm, all stiff and stark,
50   With his face turned to the skies,
The lantern gleamed through the gleaming snow
    On his fixed and glassy eyes.

Then the maiden clasped her hands and prayed
    That savèd she might be;
55 And she thought of Christ, who stilled the wave,
    On the Lake of Galilee.

And fast through the midnight dark and drear,
    Through the whistling sleet and snow,
Like a sheeted ghost, the vessel swept
60   Tow'rds the reef of Norman's Woe.

29 hither (hĭth'ər): here (that is, toward the speaker).

35 spar: pole.

36 bound her to the mast: tied her to one of the vertical poles supporting the ship's sails (to prevent her being washed overboard).

49 lashed: tied with a rope.

And ever the fitful gusts between
    A sound came from the land;
It was the sound of the trampling surf
    On the rocks and the hard sea-sand.

65 The breakers were right beneath her bows,
    She drifted a dreary wreck,
And a whooping billow swept the crew
    Like icicles from her deck.

She struck where the white and fleecy waves
70   Looked soft as carded wool,
But the cruel rocks, they gored her side
    Like the horns of an angry bull.

Her rattling shrouds, all sheathed in ice,
    With the masts went by the board;
75 Like a vessel of glass, she stove and sank,
    Ho! ho! the breakers roared!

At daybreak, on the bleak sea-beach,
    A fisherman stood aghast,
To see the form of a maiden fair,
80   Lashed close to a drifting mast.

The salt sea was frozen on her breast,
    The salt tears in her eyes;
And he saw her hair, like the brown sea-weed,
    On the billows fall and rise.

85 Such was the wreck of the Hesperus,
    In the midnight and the snow!
Christ save us all from a death like
      this,
    On the reef of Norman's Woe!

65 breakers: waves breaking into foam against a shoreline; **bows:** front section.

67 whooping: roaring.

70 carded wool: wool combed clean.

73 shrouds: ropes supporting the masts; **sheathed:** covered.

74 by the board: overboard.

75 stove: broke up.

78 aghast (ə-găst'): struck with amazement or horror.

Rising of the Moon (1906),
Thomas Moran. Christie's Images.

Connect to the Literature

1. What Do You Think?
How did you react when the skipper's daughter was discovered?

> **Comprehension Check**
> - Why does the skipper bring his daughter along on the voyage?
> - How does the skipper die?
> - Why does the ship sink?

Think Critically

2. **ACTIVE READING** | **IDENTIFYING ELEMENTS OF STORYTELLING**

 READER'S NOTEBOOK Using the chart you made, discuss with classmates what you think are the most important elements of the story told in this poem. Did you find it easier or harder to identify storytelling elements in the poem than in the **nonfiction** account from *The Perfect Storm?* Explain your answer.

3. How would you describe the **character** of the skipper of the *Hesperus?*

> **THINK ABOUT**
> - his response to the old sailor
> - what he says to his daughter
> - what he does to protect her

4. What do you learn about the skipper's daughter from the **dialogue?**

5. How realistic do you find the **setting** of the poem compared to that of the excerpt from *The Perfect Storm?*

Extend Interpretations

6. What If? If Longfellow had written "The Wreck of the Hesperus" as a short story rather than as a poem, do you think it would have been more or less compelling? Explain.

7. Connect to Life Some think that people reveal their true character in the face of danger. Do you agree? Support your opinion.

8. **Points of Comparison** Look again at the list of criteria you made for a good sea-disaster story. Based on the chart of storytelling elements you made for "The Wreck of the Hesperus," how well do you think the poem succeeds as a sea-disaster story?

9. **Points of Comparison** Who do you think would make a better character in a **short story,** the skipper of the *Satori* or the skipper of the *Hesperus?*

Literary Analysis

NARRATIVE POETRY | **Narrative poems** are poems that tell stories. Like fiction, narrative poems contain characters, setting, plot, and sometimes dialogue. The events in a narrative poem may be real or a combination of the real and the imaginative. For example, "The Wreck of the Hesperus" is based on what happened to a real ship of the same name, but the characters are completely imaginary. "The Wreck of the Hesperus" is a **ballad,** a kind of narrative poem that is meant to be sung or recited.

Cooperative Learning Activity In small groups, discuss the subject matter of "The Wreck of the Hesperus" and the overall feeling the poem conveys. Take turns reading lines from the poem that reflect this feeling. If the poem were sung, what kind of music might fit this feeling? Suggest some song titles or hum some tunes that are familiar to your classmates.

Writing Options

Interpretive Essay Why do you think the skipper of the *Hesperus* fails to protect his daughter and his ship from danger? In a brief essay, explain your interpretation.

Activities & Explorations

1. Sound Effects Obtain a recording of ocean sounds. Read "The Wreck of the Hesperus" aloud, accompanied by the sounds of crashing waves and distant bells. ~ **SPEAKING AND LISTENING**

2. Imaginary Map The *Hesperus* wreck took place near what is now Gloucester, Massachusetts. Locate the region on a map. Using details from the poem and your imagination, draw a map that illustrates the final journey of the *Hesperus.* ~ **VIEWING AND REPRESENTING/ART**

Inquiry & Research

The Discovery of the *Titanic* The grand ocean liner *Titanic* sank in the North Atlantic on April 15, 1912, and remained lost for the next 73 years. On September 1, 1985, it was finally discovered, at a depth of 2½ miles, by members of the Woods Hole Oceanographic Institute and the French oceanographic organization IFREMER. Find out what enabled these scientists to locate and explore the wreck after so many others had failed and what their efforts revealed.

 **More Online: Research Starter** www.mcdougallittell.com

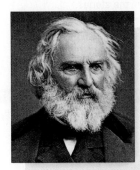

Henry Wadsworth Longfellow
1807–1882

OTHER WORKS
The Song of Hiawatha
Evangeline
"Paul Revere's Ride"

Scholarly Background Born in Portland, Maine, Henry Wadsworth Longfellow entered Bowdoin College at the age of 15. He could speak several languages and showed such promise as a translator that he was the first to qualify at Bowdoin as a professor in the new field of modern languages. At age 32, Longfellow published his first book of poetry, *Voices in the Night,* launching a writing career that would span nearly half a century.

America's Poet Longfellow was the most popular American poet of his time. As a poet, he helped to establish a lively and distinctive identity for American literature. Everyday people took pride in memorizing his poems. As a translator, Longfellow introduced his nation's readers to the works of the Italian poet Dante and to other major European writers.

England's Honoree In 1868–1869, Longfellow toured Europe. While in England, he received honorary degrees from Oxford and Cambridge and was granted an audience with Queen Victoria, who noted the range of the poet's popularity across society's classes. Upon his death, Longfellow became the first American writer to be honored with a bust in the Poets' Corner of London's Westminster Abbey.

Author Activity

Poets' Corner Longfellow was the first American author to be honored in the Poets' Corner of Westminster Abbey. Who are some of the other writers celebrated there? Why do you think Longfellow was the first American to receive the honor?

Comparing Literature: Assessment Practice

In writing assessment, you will often be asked to compare and evaluate two literary works like the excerpt from *The Perfect Storm* and "The Wreck of the Hesperus." You are now going to practice writing an essay with this kind of focus.

PART 1 · Reading the Prompt

Often you will be asked to write in response to a prompt like the one below. First, read the entire prompt carefully. Then read through it again, looking for key words that help you identify the purpose of the essay and decide how to approach it.

Writing Prompt

The excerpt from *The Perfect Storm* is a true-life account of the sinking of the *Satori* and the rescue of its crew. "The Wreck of the Hesperus" is a poem that describes the fate of a schooner overcome by a hurricane. In an essay, compare ① the selections and explain which one you think ② tells a better, more powerful story of a disaster at sea. Cite evidence from the selections to ③ support your opinion.

STRATEGIES IN ACTION

① I have to **compare** two stories about disasters at sea.

② I have to **evaluate** them— to say which one is more powerful.

③ I need to include **examples** or **quotations** from the stories.

PART 2 · Planning an Evaluative Essay

- Choose your criteria. (Refer to the chart of storytelling elements you developed on page 111. You may want to revise it.)

- Rate each work against the criteria. (Refer to the Points of Comparison questions on pages 122 and 128.)

- Decide which selection is more powerful and why.

- Create a graphic like the one shown.

Which Is a Better, More Powerful Sea-Disaster Story?

Criteria	*Perfect Storm*	"Hesperus"	My Choice

PART 3 · Drafting Your Essay

Introduction Begin by clearly stating the main point of your essay—your opinion about which selection is a more powerful sea-disaster story.

Organization Evaluate each selection individually, or take one storytelling element at a time and relate it to each selection. Include relevant examples from the selections to illustrate your points.

Conclusion End your essay with a strong statement of *why* you think one selection is more successful than the other.

Revision If possible, allow some time at the end of your writing session to review your work. Make sure it is clear, well-supported, and free of mistakes.

Writing Handbook
See page 1155: Compare and Contrast.

Writing Workshop

Telling a story...

From Reading to Writing In "Marigolds," the narrator remembers an adolescent act that led to disaster and the beginning of compassion. In "Two Kinds," the writer remembers incidents involving a mother and daughter. These narratives involve events that left a lasting impact on the characters. Writing a **personal narrative** is one way you can explore discoveries and experiences that happened to you or to someone you know. We hear or read about people's experiences every day from personal conversation to newspaper stories.

For Your Portfolio

WRITING PROMPT Write a narrative about something that actually happened to you or to someone you know.

Purpose: To inform and entertain
Audience: Your classmates, friends, or family

Basics in a Box

Personal Narrative at a Glance

Beginning

Introduces the incident, including the people and place involved

Middle

- Describes the event using descriptive details and possibly dialogue
- Makes the significance clear

End

- Tells the outcome or result of the event
- Presents the writer's feelings about the experience

RUBRIC Standards for Writing

A successful narrative should

- focus on a clear, well-defined incident
- make the importance or significance of the event clear
- show clearly the order in which events occurred
- use descriptive details that appeal to the senses to describe characters and setting
- use dialogue to develop characters
- maintain a consistent tone

Analyzing a Student Model

Joe Hasley
Linn-Mar Senior High School

RUBRIC IN ACTION

Patella (Alias the Kneecap)

I've never been an exceptional student, but there is one scientific term you can bet I'll never forget.

It was a cool day in the middle of May. The kind near the end of the school year that just drags on and on. Perhaps the most tedious thing about the last weeks of school was that I was so looking forward to junior high. I hated being treated like a kid all the time and being told where to sit at lunch and that I should keep my desk clean because, "It will lead to good habits in the future." Yes, the last days of school were tedious.

Except, of course, for the time that could easily be classified as The Greatest Day of My Career as a Student.

The time for science had arrived. Mr. Winnekamp asked, "Would anyone like to try the bone chart today?"

There was an "Oh yeah, right" and a "Dream on," but all the snickering in the room turned to a dead hush when I said, "Yeah, Mr. Winnekamp. I'd like to take the challenge."

Now, granted, in order to understand the magnitude of the moment, you may need some background. It had been announced the previous day that anyone who could name all twenty-six bones on the chart at the back of the room would receive twenty extra-credit points and get his or her name on the "I Know My Bones" chart and would receive an official membership certificate to the "I Know My Bones" Club. But, as is always the case when such fame and glory are at stake, there was a catch: You only had one chance to take the membership test. One mistake, one wrong word, and your chance to be the best of the best went down the tubes in one fell swoop.

So now that you know the reason for the class's amazement, I can continue where I left off.

Mr. Winnekamp and I walked to the back of the room with the class still reeling in shock. When we finally arrived, the chart seemed like a giant peering down to seal my doom. The intensity was nerve-racking.

After an eternity, the solemn silence was broken by the sound of Mr. Winnekamp's voice. "What is the name of this bone?" he asked, pointing to the head of the skeleton on the life-sized poster. I looked around. Every eye was on me. For a brief second—and only a second, mind you—I might have felt a bit of nervousness run up and down my spine. But, being a Hasley of noble character, I straightened my back, looked him in the eye, and answered him. "That's the cranium."

The class let out a huge sigh of relief, but then became as mesmerized as they had been only seconds before when they realized that there were still twenty-five bones to go.

❶ Captures readers' interest with an intriguing statement
Other Options:
• Start with dialogue.
• Create a brief anecdote.

❷ Uses dialogue to introduce the incident

❸ Gives important background information

❹ Signals the organizational structure

❺ This writer uses exaggeration to maintain the humorous tone.

So on we went, me naming each bone he pointed to, in a process that seemed to take hours. After the first couple of bones, though, the class seemed to relax and feel confident I would answer them all correctly. Everyone was pulling for me and cheering every time I got one right. I felt like I was shooting free throws in the final game of the NCAA tournament. Finally we got to the last bone. It was the knee bone. The class, which seconds earlier had been buzzing with anticipation, now fell dead silent.

Now, usually I'm pretty cool under pressure. I've gotten up in front of large groups before and it's no big deal. But this, this was entirely different. Every eye was on me. Mouths hung open. No one breathed. Mr. Winnekamp even started to sweat. The temperature outside was a mild fifty degrees, but you could have fried an egg on my head. The air was so thick you could have hung a map in midair just by driving nails through it. (Well, maybe not that thick, but close!)

People were turning blue because they had forgotten to breathe, so I decided it was time to take some final, decisive action. Calmly, coolly, I started to answer—and then my mind went blank! I couldn't remember! Oh no! My chance for fame and glory shot down because I couldn't remember the scientific name for kneecap. I thought so hard I thought my head would explode. Then, at my lowest moment, when I was in the pit of despair, at the end of my rope, about to lose faith, it hit me.

I looked up. The class was hanging on my every breath. My throat was as dry as carpet. I straightened myself from my hunched position, grabbed hold of my overall straps, looked at the chart, and casually said, "Ah . . . I'm pretty sure that's the patella."

The whole room just exploded. Everyone was yelling and standing on their desks and patting me on the back and hugging me. I think I even saw some tears of joy wiped back. Mr. Winnekamp came up, shook my hand, and presented me with the award.

"It's possible that they may rename the school after you, ya know."

"Gee, I don't know," I said, trying not to appear ungrateful. "Having the school named after me might interfere with my chances of having a 'normal' childhood."

Mr. Winnekamp said he understood.

There were three really good things that happened to me as a result of being the first in my class admitted to the "I Know My Bones" Club. First, I could wear my corduroy overalls to school and not have to worry about anyone picking me up by the straps. Second, I had a lot of new friends. And third, I have missed a lot of questions on a lot of tests, but you can bet that I'll never be at a loss for the answer to the question, "What is the scientific name for the kneecap?"

6 Creates suspense

7 Uses descriptive details to build suspense

8 Uses dialogue to increase the humor

9 Tells the significance of the incident

IDEABank

1. Your Working Portfolio 📁

Look for ideas in the **Writing Options** you completed earlier in this unit:

- **Recollection Diary,** p. 59
- **Mood Diary,** p. 86
- **Disaster Narrative,** p. 123

2. Interviews
Ask three or four people of different ages and with diverse experiences to talk about the most significant event of their lives. Choose one for a narrative and ask additional questions.

3. Superlative Chart
Make a chart showing the incidents you've experienced, seen, or heard about in the last year for each of the following categories: saddest, funniest, scariest, and most exciting.

Writing Your Personal Narrative

❶ Prewriting

Your life, though it may seem average to you, is a new and exotic world to other people. Don't be afraid to write about your personal experiences.

Joe Hasley, student writer

Begin by thinking about interesting or unusual events that really happened. First, **recall** personal experiences that have been funny, sad, frightening, or unforgettable. Then, **brainstorm** similar incidents that you were not part of but witnessed. Finally, **list** incidents you have heard about from others. See the **Idea Bank** in the margin for more suggestions. After you select an incident, follow the steps below.

Planning Your Personal Narrative

▶ **1. Analyze the nature of the incident.** What was its significance? Why does it stand out in your mind?

▶ **2. Decide on the tone you want to create.** How did the incident make you feel when you experienced, saw, or heard about it? What is the main feeling you want to create in your audience?

▶ **3. Make a time line.** List all the parts of the event in time order. For each part, stop and list who was involved, where it happened, and some of the significant details. When the list is finished, decide which parts to include in your narrative and which parts you can condense or skip in order to keep the narrative focused and lively.

▶ **4. Decide which parts of the narrative to enliven with dialogue or with details that appeal to the senses.** What details could help you show what happened rather than simply telling about it? What dialogue would move your narrative along and make it more realistic?

❷ Drafting

You could **begin** by describing the setting or an important character. Or you might give background information or flash forward to an event further along in the narrative. Use your **time line** to help you remember the order of events. As you tell what happened, keep in mind what tone you want to create. Use **dialogue** and plenty of **descriptive details** to help move the narrative along. **End** by telling the outcome.

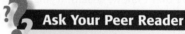

Ask Your Peer Reader

- Did you understand the order of events?
- Was the tone I used appropriate to the incident?
- How might I increase the audience's interest?
- Which parts may need more details?

❸ Revising

TARGET SKILL ▶ WORD CHOICE Paying attention to word choice, or diction, will make your narrative more lively and interesting. Try to choose specific nouns, verbs, and modifiers. For example, if you are describing someone who laughed, a word like *chuckle, snicker, giggle, guffaw,* or *roar* will show the exact nature of that laugh. Use modifiers, like *velvety* or *shrill,* that appeal to the senses. Use a thesaurus to find specific synonyms for vague words. Check a dictionary for the precise meaning of words you find in a thesaurus before using them.

Need revising help?

Review the **Rubric,** p. 131

Consider **peer reader** comments

Check **Revision Guidelines,** p. 1143

> Mr. Winnekamp and I walked to the back of the room
> *reeling in*
> with the class still ~~in a state of~~ shock. When we finally ~~got~~ *arrived*
> *peering*
> ~~there,~~ the chart seemed like a giant ~~looking~~ down to ~~arrange~~ *seal*
> *doom*   *nerve-racking*
> my ~~fate.~~ The intensity was ~~awful.~~ After a while, the serious
>
> silence was ended by the sound of Mr. Winnekamp's voice.

❹ Editing and Proofreading

TARGET SKILL ▶ PRONOUN–ANTECEDENT AGREEMENT In your narrative, make sure each pronoun you use agrees with its antecedent in number, gender, and person. When the antecedent is an indefinite pronoun, decide whether it is singular or plural. The indefinite pronouns *each, neither, someone,* and *anyone* are singular, so you must use singular pronouns to agree with them, as in "Did anyone forget her book?"

Stumped by pronoun and antecedent agreement?

See the **Grammar Handbook,** p. 1205

> It had been announced the previous day that anyone who could
>
> name all twenty-six bones on the chart at the back of the room
> *his or her*
> would receive twenty extra-credit points and get ~~their~~ name on
>
> the "I Know My Bones" chart and receive an official member-
>
> ship certificate to the "I Know My Bones" Club.

Publishing IDEAS

- Illustrate your personal narrative and post it on a bulletin board with others by your classmates.
- Record your personal narrative on audio-tape and play it for the class or your family.

More Online: Publishing Options

❺ Reflecting

FOR YOUR WORKING PORTFOLIO What did you discover about writing a personal narrative? What methods helped you to create a specific tone? Attach your answer to your finished work. Save your true narrative in your **Working Portfolio.**

Read this opening from the first draft of a personal narrative. The underlined sections may include the following kinds of errors:

- **incorrect verb forms**
- **sentence fragments**
- **lack of pronoun-antecedent agreement**
- **double negatives**

For each underlined section, choose the revision that most improves the writing.

> Plumbing work isn't hardly easy. I should know—I learned the hard way.
> (1)
> Last summer our basement sink had a slow drip. After a few weeks, the
> basement floor has become wet and slimy. Our two beagles, Mabel and Billie,
> (2)
> stopped sleeping in the cool basement because they couldn't find a dry spot to lie
> (3)
> on. My mother decided to call the plumber. Who arrived with two assistants.
> (4)
> Unfortunately, they didn't finish the work that day. The sink was still leaking
> when they left. One of the workers had left their tools behind. That's when I
> (5)
> made my first mistake: I decided to use it to fix the leak myself.
> (6)

1. **A.** Plumbing work isn't scarcely easy.
   B. Plumbing work is hardly easy.
   C. Plumbing work isn't barely easy.
   D. Correct as is

2. **A.** had become
   B. had became
   C. has became
   D. Correct as is

3. **A.** Mabel and Billie
   B. she
   C. them
   D. Correct as is

4. **A.** My mother decided to call the plumber who arrived, with two assistants.
   B. My mother decided to call the plumber: who arrived with two assistants.
   C. My mother decided, to call the plumber, who arrived with two assistants.
   D. My mother decided to call the plumber, who arrived with two assistants.

5. **A.** Some of the workers had left his tools behind.
   B. The workers had left his tools behind.
   C. One of the workers had left her tools behind.
   D. Correct as is

6. **A.** that
   B. them
   C. theirs
   D. Correct as is

Need extra help?

See the **Grammar Handbook**

Double Negatives, p. 1188

Pronoun-Antecedent Agreement, p. 1181

Sentence Fragments, pp. 1197, 1204

Verbs, pp. 1183–1186

One way we know we are deeply involved in a work of literature is that we begin to care about what happens. Yet part of what makes some stories entertaining is that the writer withholds information so that we *don't* know what has happened or what is going to happen. The writer may keep us in suspense or give us information that we didn't anticipate, surprising us with the unexpected.

ACTIVITY

With a small group of classmates, write down on a piece of notebook paper a situation—real or imaginary—that your group thinks could be the basis of a story. Include at least one important conflict. For example, your situation might be that of a teenager who wants to be a jockey but is allergic to horses. Then pass your idea to another group. Take the idea that your group receives and agree on a surprise ending to the story. Try to make your solution to the conflict something unexpected, but effective. Jot down your ending at the bottom of the notebook page. With the other groups, take turns reading the story ideas and surprise endings aloud to the whole class and discuss which ones you think are the most intriguing.

LEARNING the Language of *Literature*

Poetry is the most compact form of literature. The French poet Paul Valéry once said that prose is like walking but poetry is like dancing. In **poetry,** ideas and emotions are tightly compressed into a package where everything—the meanings and sounds of words, the line breaks, even the empty spaces—is designed to create an effect or to convey a message or an experience. Despite vast differences in style, all poems contain some or all of these elements: **form, sound,** a **speaker, figurative language,** and **imagery.** Use the following excerpts from "The Wreck of the Hesperus" to help you learn more about these elements of poetry.

Form

The distinctive way a poem is laid out on the page is called the poem's **form.** Poems are usually divided into **lines,** which may or may not be sentences. In some poems the lines are arranged in groups, called **stanzas.** A poem's stanzas may have the same number of lines or varying numbers of lines. Each stanza plays a part in conveying the overall meaning of the poem. In other words, a stanza is like a piece of a puzzle—it is closely connected to the other pieces and contributes to the building up of the overall "picture."

YOUR TURN Read this passage from "The Wreck of the Hesperus." How would you describe the form of the passage? Refer to the number of lines and stanzas in your answer.

> **FORM**
>
> The skipper he stood beside the helm,
> His pipe was in his mouth.
> And he watched how the veering flaw did blow
> The smoke now West, now South.
>
> Then up and spake an old Sailor,
> Had sailed to the Spanish Main,
> "I pray thee, put into yonder port,
> For I fear a hurricane."

Sound

The effect that a poem has on the reader frequently depends on the sounds of its words. The following are some techniques that poets use to achieve different sound effects.

- **Rhyme** is a likeness of sounds at the ends of words, as in *suite, heat,* and *complete.* **Internal rhyme** is the use of rhyming words within a line; **end rhyme** is the use of such words at the ends of lines. A pattern of end rhymes in a poem is called the poem's **rhyme scheme.** To describe a rhyme scheme, you can assign each line a letter of the alphabet, starting with *a* for the first line and assigning lines that rhyme the same letter. Look at the pattern of end rhymes in the stanza at the right.

> **RHYME**
>
> It was the schooner Hesperus,   a
> That sailed the wintry sea;   b
> And the skipper had taken his little daughter,   c
> To bear him company.   b

- **Rhythm** is the pattern of sound created by the arrangement of stressed and unstressed syllables in a line. In some poems the lines have a repeated rhythmic pattern, or **meter.** The first two lines of the stanza at the right have the stressed syllables (ˊ) and the unstressed syllables (˘) marked. Read those lines aloud to hear their rhythmic pattern.

- **Alliteration** is a repetition of consonant sounds at the beginning of words. Think about the effect of the repetition of *b* in the line "The <u>b</u>reakers were right <u>b</u>eneath her <u>b</u>ows." Is the sound harsh, or is it soothing?
- **Assonance** is a repetition of vowel sounds in nonrhyming words, as in "Some sh*i*p in d*i*stress, that cannot l*i*ve."
- **Consonance** is a repetition of consonant sounds within or at the end of words, like the repetition of *r* and *d* in "But the father answe**rd** never a wo**rd**."
- **Onomatopoeia** is the use of words that sound like what they refer to, like *buzz, hiss, crunch,* and *thump.*

YOUR TURN Copy the last two lines of the stanza above, marking the stressed and unstressed syllables.

Speaker

The **speaker** of a poem is the voice that relates the ideas or story of the poem. Remember that the speaker is not necessarily the poet. Of course, poets sometimes write as themselves, speaking directly to the reader.

Figurative Language and Imagery

Imagery is language that appeals to the reader's sense of sight, hearing, smell, taste, or touch. In "The Wreck of the Hesperus," for example, the lines "He wrapped her warm in his seaman's coat / Against the stinging blast" draw us into the feeling of the poem by appealing to our sense of touch.

   Figurative language communicates ideas besides the ordinary, literal meanings of the words. There are three basic types of figurative language. **Personification** is the attribution of human qualities to an object, animal, or idea, as in "the wind's gentle cry." A **simile** is a comparison indicated by the word *like* or *as.* "Strong as a boulder" is an example of a simile. A **metaphor** is a more direct comparison, as in "This room is a war zone."

YOUR TURN Read the stanza at the right. What things are compared in these lines? Are the comparisons similes or metaphors?

The various elements of poetry combine to convey meaning and to create an overall effect on the reader. The form, sound, speaker, figurative language, and imagery in a poem all help the reader to imagine the experience that the writer is sharing. The following reading strategies can help you get the most from every poem you read.

Reading Poetry

Strategies for Using Your 📖 READER'S NOTEBOOK

As you read, take notes to
- **connect** your personal experiences to what the poet presents
- record any intriguing images and other poetic elements you encounter
- write down questions or thoughts you may have

1 Strategies for Understanding Form
- Observe the arrangement of words.
- Notice the length and arrangement of lines. Are the lines short, simple phrases, or do they resemble sentences? What visual effect do the lines have on you?
- Note whether the lines are grouped into stanzas. If they are, what idea, emotion, or information does each stanza convey?

2 Strategies for Analyzing Sound
- Read the poem out loud, listening to how it sounds.
- Notice any internal or end rhymes. Is there a rhyme scheme?
- Analyze the rhythm. How does it add to the effect of the poem?
- Look for other sound devices the writer uses, such as alliteration, assonance, consonance, or onomatopoeia.

Examples of sound devices
alliteration:
assonance:
consonance:
onomatopoeia:

3 Strategies for Evaluating the Speaker
- Look for clues that reveal something about the speaker.
- **Connect** the speaker's feelings, ideas, and values to your own to form an impression of the speaker.

4 Strategies for Understanding Imagery and Figurative Language
- **Visualize** comparisons that are made, either by means of similes or metaphors. How do they contribute to the overall effect of the poem?
- Look for the use of personification. Notice if an animal or object is described as having human features, characteristics, or emotions.
- Use a chart similar to the one shown to keep track of imagery. Determine which of the senses (sight, touch, smell, taste, or hearing) the poet is appealing to, as well as the effects the imagery has on you.

Image	Sense It Appeals To	Its Effect on Me

Need More Help?

Remember that active readers use the essential reading strategies explained on page 7: **visualize, predict, clarify, question, connect, evaluate, monitor.**

O What Is That Sound

Poetry by W. H. AUDEN

"O what are they doing with all that gear?"

Connect to Your Life

In Suspense A telephone rings suddenly in the night. Or a strange package arrives, or maybe an unexpected letter. Or perhaps you hear a weird sound outside that you've never heard before. At what point does your curiosity turn into a feeling of suspense—and then become anxiety? With a partner, brainstorm some situations that could be exciting but that have a strong element of the mysterious or the unknown—something that might make you uneasy.

Build Background

Long Ago and Far Away? Many details in the poem you are about to read—the references to drums, horses, and the red uniforms of soldiers—suggest a faraway time, perhaps around the time of the American Revolution. However, the poem was written in the 1930s—a time that its author, W. H. Auden, called "the age of anxiety." Along with some thrilling events in those days came serious economic depression and a terrible war. Ordinary citizens were never sure when they might be swept away by events beyond their control.

Focus Your Reading

LITERARY ANALYSIS **POETIC FORM: BALLAD** "O What Is That Sound" is a **ballad,** a poem that tells a story and is meant to be sung or recited. Like many traditional ballads, this poem tells its story entirely in dialogue. Without descriptive details, you must infer what is happening. As you read, be aware of the fact that there are two speakers. Which stanza has only one of them speaking?

ACTIVE READING **MAKING INFERENCES ABOUT SPEAKERS** An **inference** is a logical guess or conclusion based on facts. As a reader you normally infer much from what characters say to each other. In this poem, everything you learn about the story and the feelings of the characters is based on the dialogue between the speakers.

READER'S NOTEBOOK Make a chart like the one shown, and as you read this poem, use the reactions of the speakers to imagine what is happening. Look for changes in either speaker's attitude as the action takes place. Fill in the chart, using information that you have inferred about the speakers in the poem. Indicate who the two people might be and how they react to the sound—at first and then later in the poem.

	Identity	First Reaction to Sound	Later Reaction to Sound
First speaker			
Second speaker			

O What Is That Sound

W. H. Auden

O what is that sound which so thrills the ear
    Down in the valley drumming, drumming?
Only the scarlet soldiers,[1] dear,
    The soldiers coming.

5   O what is that light I see flashing so clear
    Over the distance brightly, brightly?
Only the sun on their weapons, dear,
    As they step lightly.

O what are they doing with all that gear,
10   What are they doing this morning, this morning?
Only their usual maneuvers,[2] dear,
    Or perhaps a warning.

---

1. **scarlet soldiers:** British soldiers, who wore bright red coats.
2. **maneuvers:** training exercises carried out by troops.

O why have they left the road down there,
    Why are they suddenly wheeling, wheeling?
15 Perhaps a change in their orders, dear.
    Why are you kneeling?

O haven't they stopped for the doctor's care,
    Haven't they reined their horses, their horses?
Why, they are none of them wounded, dear.
20   None of these forces.

O is it the parson they want, with white hair,
    Is it the parson, is it, is it?
No, they are passing his gateway, dear,
    Without a visit.

25 O it must be the farmer who lives so near.
    It must be the farmer so cunning, so cunning?
They have passed the farmyard already, dear,
    And now they are running.

O where are you going? Stay with me here!
30   Were the vows you swore deceiving, deceiving?
No, I promised to love you, dear,
    But I must be leaving.

O it's broken the lock and splintered the door,
    O it's the gate where they're turning, turning;
35 Their boots are heavy on the floor
    And their eyes are burning.

16 What does this line suggest about the state of mind of the first speaker?

31–32 From these lines, what inference can you make about the second speaker?

33–36 What do you think it means that these lines are spoken by one person? What do you think has happened?

Connect to the Literature

1. What Do You Think? What emotion did you feel most strongly by the end of this poem?

> **Comprehension Check**
> - Whom do the speakers observe in the distance?
> - Which speaker seems calmer?
> - What happens to the second speaker?
> - What do the soldiers do?

Think Critically

2. **ACTIVE READING** **MAKING INFERENCES** Look at the chart that you made in your **READER'S NOTEBOOK** identifying the **speakers'** reactions. Who do you think these two people might be?

3. Describe what you think is happening in the poem.

THINK ABOUT
- what is causing anxiety for one of the speakers
- the actions that are taking place
- the possible reasons for these actions

4. How do the two people react to the soldiers and to each other as the situation changes? Demonstrate this change with a partner by acting out in pantomime the three scenes described in **stanzas** one, four, eight, and nine.

Extend Interpretations

5. Comparing Texts Look back at Longfellow's "The Wreck of the Hesperus." How are the two poems alike and different? Compare them in terms of **stanza, rhythm, author's purpose,** and use of **dialogue.**

6. Connect to Life Under what kinds of circumstances might the action in this poem take place today?

Literary Analysis

BALLAD A narrative poem that can be sung or recited is called a **ballad.** Some ballads contain nothing but dialogue. In "O What Is That Sound," one speaker asks a series of questions, and a second speaker gives answers. Each stanza notches up the tension a little further until the final stanza, which is apparently spoken entirely by the first speaker.

Cooperative Learning Activity With a group of five classmates, have two read the poem aloud, each taking the part of one of the speakers. After the poem has been read, have the rest of the group ask the readers questions about the situation described in the poem and the feelings of the two speakers.

SOUND DEVICES The sounds of words are always important in poetry, especially in ballads, which are meant to be sung or read aloud. Note that in "O What Is That Sound" the **rhyme scheme** *(abab)* is the same in each stanza. Also strong in this ballad is **rhythm,** the pattern created by the arrangement of stressed and unstressed syllables. Rhythm in poetry is like the beat in music. Try tapping your foot to a regular beat while you read the stanzas aloud, listening to the rhythm. In what way does this rhythmic effect seem appropriate for this poem?

Writing Options

1. Letter to a Prisoner Suppose that the first speaker in the poem ends up in prison. Write a letter that the second speaker might send to this person in prison.

2. Imaginary Dialogue Imagine how this story might continue. Write a dialogue showing what happens next, such as a soldier questioning the first speaker.

3. A New Ballad Refer to your list of mysterious situations that might cause you anxiety. Draft a ballad modeled on "O What Is That Sound" that tells about one of these situations.

Activities & Explorations

1. Poetic Illustration Sketch a picture to illustrate this poem. What do you imagine the two speakers look like? What are they doing as they speak? Show and explain your sketch to the class.
~ **ART**

2. Musical Setting Try setting the words of this ballad to music. Or choose or compose a piece of music that captures the suspense and tension in this poem and play it for the class.
~ **MUSIC**

Inquiry & Research

American Ballads Many American ballads are about heroes, famous outlaws, or disasters. Examples are "John Henry," "Casey Jones," "The Titanic," "The Wreck of the C & O," "The Johnstown Flood," "Jesse James" and "The Streets of Laredo." Locate recordings of these or other American ballads and play them for the rest of the class. Explain if they were based on actual events or persons.

Woody Guthrie (left) was a famous writer and singer of ballads.

W. H. Auden
1907–1973

Other Works
Another Time
The Age of Anxiety
The Shield of Achilles
The English Auden
Collected Poems

A Major Figure W. H. Auden, one of the most important poets of the 20th century, was a prolific writer whose works explored political, personal, and religious values. Known and respected for his lyrical, inventive, and thoughtful poetry, Auden won both the Pulitzer Prize and the National Book Award.

From Biology to English Wystan Hugh Auden was born in York, England, the third son of a doctor and a nurse, and received a traditional English boarding school education. He first majored in biology at Christ Church College, Oxford, but changed his field of study to English. By then he had decided to become a "great poet." In his first years after graduating, Auden quickly established his reputation with the publication of a book of poetry, *The Orators*. Soon he became the best known of a group of young British writers of the 1930s.

Becoming an American Just before the outbreak of World War II, Auden immigrated to the United States. He wanted to live "deliberately without roots" by breaking away from English literary and political life and from his family. "America may break one completely," he wrote to a friend, "but the best of which one is capable is more likely to be drawn out of one here than anywhere else." As an American citizen he became a part of New York City's intellectual and artistic community, writing, teaching, and lecturing.

Author Activity

Auden in Song Some of Auden's work is obscure, but he was quite versatile and also wrote ballads and blues, limericks and light verse. Some of his songs can be found in *Another Time* (1940). Find out more about this lighter side of Auden.

Incident in a Rose Garden

Poetry by DONALD JUSTICE

Connect to Your Life

Image of Death If you were suddenly to encounter the figure of death, waiting for you, what do you think he—or she, or it—might look like? Would it be an animal? Would it have wings? Would it be a human figure? What kind of qualities or personality would it have? Would it be carrying anything? Draw the picture you imagine and share your sketch with a classmate. Discuss the qualities of death that your image emphasizes. As you read this poem, compare your sketch with the image presented by the poet.

Build Background

An Old Idea Down through the ages, different cultures of the world have sometimes imagined death as a human figure. In Western cultures, the standard image of death is often that of a skeleton or a scary, hooded figure, dressed in black. The figure often carries a scythe (sīth), an implement with a long, curved blade attached to a long handle, used for cutting down tall grasses for harvest. Thus, death is imagined as a "grim reaper," someone who comes to "harvest" human beings. Throughout the ages, writers and artists have created different variations of this standard image.

Focus Your Reading

LITERARY ANALYSIS FIGURATIVE LANGUAGE Language that communicates meaning beyond the literal meaning of words is called **figurative language.** Examples are **similes** and **metaphors.** Each of these **figures of speech** makes a comparison between two things that are actually unlike but that have something in common. A simile uses the word *like* or *as.* For example, this poem describes the death figure as "thin as a scythe." Describing death as a human figure is an example of another kind of figurative language: **personification.** As you read, look for figurative language in the poem.

ACTIVE READING VISUALIZING The process of forming a mental picture from a written description is called **visualizing.** The writer provides details to help you picture in your mind the following:

- the physical **setting**
- the physical appearance of the **characters**
- the **events** that take place

READER'S NOTEBOOK As you read this poem, jot down any details that help you visualize the setting, characters, and events.

INCIDENT
IN A Rose Garden

DONALD JUSTICE

The gardener came running.
An old man, out of breath.
Fear had given him legs.

    Sir, I encountered Death
5   *Just now among the roses.*
    Thin as a scythe he stood there.

    I knew him by his pictures.
    He had his black coat on,
    Black gloves, a broad black hat.

10   *I think he would have spoken,*
    Seeing his mouth stood open.
    Big it was, with white teeth.

    As soon as he beckoned, I ran.
    I ran until I found you.
15   *Sir, I am quitting my job.*

    I want to see my sons
    Once more before I die.
    I want to see California.

We shook hands; he was off.

20 And there stood Death in the garden.
    Dressed like a Spanish waiter.
    He had the air of someone
    Who because he likes arriving
    At all appointments early
25 Learns to think himself patient.
    I watched him pinch one bloom off
    And hold it to his nose—
    A connoisseur of roses—
    One bloom and then another.
30 They strewed the earth around him.
        Sir, you must be that stranger
        Who threatened my gardener.
        This is my property, sir.
        I welcome only friends here.

35 Death grinned, and his eyes lit up
    With the pale glow of those lanterns
    That workmen carry sometimes
    To light their way through the dusk.
    Now with great care he slid
40 The glove from his right hand
    And held that out in greeting,
    A little cage of bone.
        Sir, I knew your father,
        And we were friends at the end.
45   *As for your gardener,*
        I did not threaten him.
        Old men mistake my gestures.
        I only meant to ask him
        To show me to his master.
50   *I take it you are he?*

                    for Mark Strand

28 connoisseur (kŏn′ə-sûr′): an expert or authority in some field, especially in the fine arts or in matters of taste.

Thinking through the LITERATURE

Connect to the Literature

1. **What Do You Think?** What effect did the ending of "Incident in a Rose Garden" have on you? Discuss your response with a partner.

> **Comprehension Check**
> - How does the gardener recognize Death?
> - Why is the gardener afraid of Death?
> - For whom has Death come?

Think Critically

2. Explain any **ironies,** or unexpected twists, that you see in this poem.

3. Contrast the gardener's and the master's attitudes toward Death. Why do you think they have such different attitudes?

THINK ABOUT
- the **description** of the gardener in the first three lines
- the master's description of Death in lines 21–25
- the master's attitude when speaking to Death, in lines 31–34

4. **ACTIVE READING** **VISUALIZING** Think about the descriptive visual details of Death's appearance that you jotted down in your **READER'S NOTEBOOK.** How do these details help explain why the gardener was so frightened?

Extend Interpretations

5. **Comparing Texts** Like W. H. Auden's "O What Is That Sound," "Incident in a Rose Garden" is a **narrative poem,** a poem that tells a story. Compare and contrast the narrative elements of characters, setting, plot, and theme in the two poems.

6. **Connect to Life** Sketch the image of death as it is portrayed in this poem. How does this image compare with the image you sketched for the Connect to Your Life activity on page 146?

Literary Analysis

FIGURATIVE LANGUAGE

Sometimes language goes beyond the literal meanings of words in order to produce more precise descriptions. One kind of **figurative language** is the **metaphor,** which points out a similarity between two things that are otherwise not alike. A **simile** does the same thing but uses the word *like* or *as.* These **figures of speech** add flavor and dimension to language. For example, Death is described as "thin as a scythe" and "dressed like a Spanish waiter," with eyes like lanterns carried through darkness. His hand is described metaphorically as a "cage of bone." Finally, the death figure itself is an example of **personification**—a figure of speech giving human qualities to something not human, like an animal, an object, or even an idea.

Cooperative Learning Activity
Make a chart like the one shown below. Working with a partner, identify each figure of speech as a simile or a metaphor and describe how you think it adds to the effect of the description. Then with a larger group discuss this question: How does figurative language contribute to the overall feeling or effect of this poem?

Description	Figure of Speech	Effect Created
Death: human figure	Personification	
Death: Spanish waiter		
Death's eyes: lanterns		
Death's hand: cage of bone		

Writing Options

1. Garden Dialogue Extend "Incident in a Rose Garden" by writing a description or dialogue of how the master might respond to Death's question at the end.

Writing Handbook
See pages 1151–1152: Descriptive Writing.

2. Profile of the Visitor Based on the evidence of the poem, what kind of a "person" is Death? Write a brief profile of him, emphasizing his personality and manners and suggesting whether these make him seem more menacing. A word web might help get you started.

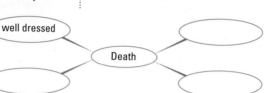

Activities & Explorations

1. Dramatic Scene Form a group of three to perform a skit based on "Incident in a Rose Garden." If time allows, you can create costumes or use props that are suggestive of the three characters. ~ DRAMA

2. Collage Put together a collage of pictures and words inspired by the themes and images in "Incident in a Rose Garden." ~ ART

Inquiry & Research

Death in Art The concept of death has been given human qualities by artists throughout history, and particularly in medieval Christian art. Prepare a representative selection of these images to show the class. You may want to bring in art books or get photocopies of particular works.

 More Online: Research Starter
www.mcdougallittell.com

Donald Justice
1925–

Other Works
The Summer Anniversaries
Night Light
The Sunset Maker
A Donald Justice Reader
New and Selected Poems

Depression Child Donald Justice was born in 1925, in Miami, Florida, and grew up during the Great Depression in circumstances he describes as "near poor." Justice graduated from the University of Miami and received a doctorate from the University of Iowa. He has taught at these schools as well as at Syracuse University, the University of California, Princeton University, and the University of Virginia.

Honors and Awards As one critic has noted, Justice has long been fascinated with "the ease with which [language] creates worlds." His *Selected Poems* (1979) earned him a Pulitzer Prize. He received the Bollingen Prize in Poetry in 1991 and was elected a Chancellor of the Academy of American Poets in 1997.

Author Activity

Dialogue Only Justice often experiments with poetic form. He wrote "Incident in a Rose Garden" in two versions—an original one using dialogue only and the revised version here, with its descriptive passages. Find both of these in *Selected Poems* (1979). Which do you like more?

 LaserLinks: Background for Reading
Art Gallery

The Gift of the Magi

Short Story by O. HENRY

"There was clearly nothing to do but flop down on the shabby little couch and howl."

Connect to Your Life

Sacrifice Think of your most prized possession—the one thing you'd want to rescue if your house were burning down. Think of some of the reasons this possession is important to you. Then try to imagine under what circumstances you might give it up. For what, or for whom, would you sacrifice it? Using a chart like the one shown, identify the possession, list reasons for its importance, and suggest when or how you might ever be prepared to part with it.

My Prized Possession

| Why I want to hang on to it | Why I might give it up |

Build Background

Bearers of Gifts In this story, O. Henry makes an **allusion,** or reference, to the Magi. According to Christian tradition, the Magi were three wise men or kings named Balthasar, Melchior, and Gaspar. They traveled from the east to Bethlehem, guided by a miraculous star, to present gifts of gold, frankincense, and myrrh to the infant Jesus. These gifts were prized possessions, having not only monetary but medicinal and ceremonial value. They are sometimes thought of as the first Christmas presents.

WORDS TO KNOW
Vocabulary Preview

agile	inconsequential
assertion	instigate
cascade	predominating
chronicle	prudence
coveted	vestibule

Focus Your Reading

LITERARY ANALYSIS **IRONY** **Irony** is the difference between what we expect to happen and what actually happens. When you get a high grade on the one paper that you spent the least time working on, it's an unexpected surprise—and it's **ironic.** When the quietest kid you know turns into a debating champ, that's ironic too; it was the last thing you expected. O. Henry is well known for writing stories with ironic surprises like these. As you read "The Gift of the Magi," be ready for the unexpected.

ACTIVE READING **PREDICTING** If a story is well written, it will keep you wondering what happens next. You may ask yourself questions and find yourself **predicting** possible answers. In this story, for example, what can you predict from the title?

READER'S NOTEBOOK As you are reading this story, wondering how it will come out, jot down two or three **predictions.** Then see whether you were right—or whether O. Henry managed to surprise you.

The
GIFT
of the
MAGI

O. Henry

One dollar and eighty-seven cents. That was all. And 60 cents of it was in pennies. Pennies saved one and two at a time by bulldozing the grocer and the vegetable man and the butcher until one's cheeks burned with the silent imputation of parsimony[1] that such close dealing implied. Three times Della counted it. One dollar and eighty-seven cents. And the next day would be Christmas.

There was clearly nothing to do but flop down on the shabby little couch and howl. So Della did it. Which <u>instigates</u> the moral reflection that life is made up of sobs, sniffles, and smiles, with sniffles <u>predominating</u>.

While the mistress of the home is gradually subsiding from the first stage to the second, take a look at the home. A furnished flat at $8 per week. It did not exactly beggar description, but it certainly had that word on the lookout for the mendicancy squad.[2]

In the <u>vestibule</u> below belonged to this flat a letterbox into which no letter would go and an electric button from which no mortal finger could coax a ring. Also appertaining[3] thereunto was a card bearing the name "Mr. James Dillingham Young."

ACTIVE READING

CLARIFY Why is Della crying?

The "Dillingham" had been flung to the breeze during a former period of prosperity when its possessor was being paid $30 per week. Now, when the income was shrunk to $20, the letters of "Dillingham" looked blurred, as though they were thinking seriously of contracting to a modest and unassuming D. But whenever Mr. James Dillingham Young came home and reached his flat above, he was called "Jim" and greatly hugged by Mrs. James Dillingham Young, already introduced to you as Della. Which is all very good.

Della finished her cry and attended to her cheeks with the powder rag. She stood by the window and looked out dully at a gray cat walking a gray fence in a gray backyard. Tomorrow would be Christmas Day, and she had only $1.87 with which to buy Jim a present. She had been saving every penny she could for months, with this result. Twenty dollars a week doesn't go far. Expenses had been greater than she had calculated. They always are. Only $1.87 to buy a present for Jim. Her Jim. Many a happy hour she had spent planning for something nice for him. Something fine and rare and sterling—something just a little bit near to being worthy of the honor of being owned by Jim.

There was a pier glass[4] between the windows of the room. Perhaps you have seen a pier glass in an $8 flat. A very thin and very <u>agile</u> person may, by observing his reflection in a rapid sequence of longitudinal strips, obtain a fairly accurate conception of his looks. Della, being slender, had mastered the art.

Suddenly she whirled from the window and stood before the glass. Her eyes were shining brilliantly, but her face had lost its color within twenty seconds. Rapidly she pulled down her hair and let it fall to its full length.

Now, there were two possessions of the James Dillingham Youngs in which they both

---

1. **imputation** (ĭm'pyŏŏ-tā'shən) **of parsimony** (pär'sə-mō'nē): suggestion of stinginess.
2. **mendicancy** (mĕn'dĭ-kən-sē) **squad:** a police unit assigned to arrest beggars. The author here is making a play on the word *beggar*, used earlier in the sentence to mean "make inadequate."
3. **appertaining** (ăp'ər-tā'nĭng): belonging as a part; attached.
4. **pier glass:** a narrow mirror set in a wall section between windows.

WORDS TO KNOW

instigate (ĭn'stĭ-gāt') *v.* to stir up; provoke
predominating (prĭ-dŏm'ə-nā'tĭng) *adj.* most important or frequent **predominate** *v.*
vestibule (vĕs'tə-byōōl') *n.* a small entryway within a building
agile (ăj'əl) *adj.* able to move quickly and easily

took a mighty pride. One was Jim's gold watch that had been his father's and his grandfather's. The other was Della's hair. Had the Queen of Sheba[5] lived in the flat across the air shaft, Della would have let her hair hang out the window some day to dry and mocked at Her Majesty's jewels and gifts. Had King Solomon[6] been the janitor, with all his treasures piled up in the basement, Jim would have pulled out his watch every time he passed, just to see him pluck at his beard from envy.

So now Della's beautiful hair fell about her, rippling and shining like a cascade of brown waters. It reached below her knee and made itself almost a garment for her. And then she did it up again nervously and quickly. Once she faltered for a minute and stood still while a tear or two splashed on the worn red carpet.

On went her old brown jacket; on went her old brown hat. With a whirl of skirts and with the brilliant sparkle still in her eyes, she fluttered out the door and down the stairs to the street.

ACTIVE READING

PREDICT Where is Della going?

Where she stopped, the sign read "Mme. Sofronie. Hair Goods of All Kinds." One flight up Della ran and collected herself, panting, before Madame, large, too white, chilly, and hardly looking the "Sofronie."

"Will you buy my hair?" asked Della.

"I buy hair," said Madame. "Take yer hat off and let's have a sight at the looks of it."

Down rippled the brown cascade.

"Twenty dollars," said Madame, lifting the mass with a practiced hand.

"Give it to me quick," said Della.

Oh, and the next two hours tripped by on rosy wings. Forget the hashed metaphor. She was ransacking the stores for Jim's present.

She found it at last. It surely had been made for Jim and no one else. There was none other like it in any of the stores, and she had turned all of them inside out. It was a platinum fob chain[7] simple and chaste in design, properly proclaiming its value by substance alone and not by meretricious ornamentation[8]—as all good things should do. It was even worthy of The Watch. As soon as she saw it, she knew that it must be Jim's. It was like him. Quietness and value—the description applied to both. Twenty-one dollars they took from her for it, and she hurried home with the 87 cents. With that chain on his watch Jim might be properly anxious about the time in any company. Grand as the watch was, he sometimes looked at it on the sly on account of the old leather strap that he used in place of a chain.

When Della reached home, her intoxication gave way a little to prudence and reason. She got out her curling irons and lighted the gas and went to work repairing the ravages made by generosity added to love. Which is always a tremendous task, dear friends—a mammoth task.

Within forty minutes her head was covered with tiny, close-lying curls that made her look

AS SOON AS SHE SAW IT, SHE KNEW THAT IT MUST BE JIM'S. IT WAS LIKE HIM.

---

5. **Queen of Sheba:** in the Bible, a rich Arabian queen.

6. **King Solomon:** a biblical king of Israel, known for his wisdom and wealth.

7. **fob chain:** a short chain for a pocket watch.

8. **meretricious** (mĕr´ĭ-trĭsh´əs) **ornamentation:** cheap, gaudy decoration.

WORDS TO KNOW

cascade (kă-skād´) *n.* a waterfall
prudence (prōod´ns) *n.* the use of good judgment and common sense

Golden Fall (1940), Joseph Stella. Oil on canvas, 26″ × 20″, courtesy of Spanierman Gallery, New York.

wonderfully like a truant schoolboy. She looked at her reflection in the mirror long, carefully, and critically.

"If Jim doesn't kill me," she said to herself, "before he takes a second look at me, he'll say I look like a Coney Island chorus girl. But what could I do—oh, what could I do with a dollar and eighty-seven cents!"

At 7 o'clock the coffee was made, and the frying pan was on the back of the stove hot and ready to cook the chops.

Jim was never late. Della doubled the fob chain in her hand and sat on the corner of the table near the door that he always entered. Then she heard his step on the stair away down on the first flight, and she turned white for just a moment. She had a habit of saying little silent prayers about the simplest everyday things, and now she whispered: "Please, God, make him think I am still pretty."

The door opened, and Jim stepped in and closed it. He looked thin and very serious. Poor fellow, he was only twenty-two—and to be burdened with a family! He needed a new overcoat, and he was without gloves.

Jim stopped inside the door, as immovable as a setter at the scent of a quail. His eyes were fixed upon Della, and there was an expression in them that she could not read, and it terrified her. It was not anger, nor surprise, nor disapproval, nor horror, nor any of the sentiments that she had been prepared for. He simply stared at her fixedly with that peculiar expression on his face.

ACTIVE READING

CLARIFY What is Jim's reaction to Della's hair?

Della wriggled off the table and went for him.

"Jim, darling," she cried, "don't look at me that way. I had my hair cut off and sold it because I couldn't have lived through Christmas without giving you a present. It'll grow again—you won't mind, will you? I just had to do it. My hair grows awfully fast. Say 'Merry Christmas!' Jim, and let's be happy. You don't know what a nice— what a beautiful, nice gift I've got for you."

"You've cut off your hair?" asked Jim, laboriously, as if he had not arrived at that patent fact yet even after the hardest mental labor.

"Cut it off and sold it," said Della. "Don't you like me just as well, anyhow? I'm me without my hair, ain't I?"

Jim looked about the room curiously.

"You say your hair is gone?" he said, with an air almost of idiocy.

"You needn't look for it," said Della. "It's sold, I tell you—sold and gone too. It's Christmas Eve, boy. Be good to me, for it went for you. Maybe the hairs of my head were numbered," she went on with a sudden serious sweetness, "but nobody could ever count my love for you. Shall I put the chops on, Jim?"

Out of his trance Jim seemed to quickly wake. He enfolded his Della. For ten seconds let us regard with discreet scrutiny[9] some inconsequential object in the other direction. Eight dollars a week or a million a year—what is the difference? A mathematician or a wit would give you the wrong answer. The magi brought valuable gifts, but that was not among them. This dark assertion will be illuminated later on.

Jim drew a package from his overcoat pocket and threw it upon the table.

"Don't make any mistake, Dell," he said, "about me. I don't think there's anything in the way of a haircut or a shave or a shampoo that could make me like my girl any less. But

---

9. **scrutiny** (skrōōt'n-ē): careful observation.

WORDS TO KNOW

inconsequential (ĭn-kŏn'sĭ-kwĕn'shəl) *adj.* of no importance
assertion (ə-sûr'shən) *n.* a statement

156

if you'll unwrap that package, you may see why you had me going awhile at first."

White fingers and nimble tore at the string and paper. And then an ecstatic scream of joy, and then, alas! a quick feminine change to hysterical tears and wails, necessitating the immediate employment of all the comforting powers of the lord of the flat.

For there lay The Combs—the set of combs, side and back, that Della had worshiped for long in a Broadway window. Beautiful combs, pure tortoise shell, with jeweled rims—just the shade to wear in the beautiful vanished hair. They were expensive combs, she knew, and her heart had simply craved and yearned over them without the least hope of possession. And now, they were hers, but the tresses[10] that should have adorned the coveted adornments[11] were gone.

But she hugged them to her bosom, and at length she was able to look up with dim eyes and a smile and say, "My hair grows so fast, Jim!"

And then Della leaped up like a little singed cat and cried, "Oh, oh!"

Jim had not yet seen his beautiful present. She held it out to him eagerly upon her open palm. The dull, precious metal seemed to flash with a reflection of her bright and ardent spirit.

"Isn't it a dandy, Jim?" I hunted all over town to find it. You'll have to look at the time a hundred times a day now. Give me your watch. I want to see how it looks on it."

Instead of obeying, Jim tumbled down on the couch and put his hands under the back of his head and smiled.

"Dell," said he, "let's put our Christmas presents away and keep 'em a while. They're too nice to use just at present. I sold the watch to get the money to buy your combs. And now suppose you put the chops on."

The magi, as you know, were wise men—wonderfully wise men—who brought gifts to the Babe in the manger. They invented the art of giving Christmas gifts. Being wise, their gifts were no doubt wise ones, possibly bearing the privilege of exchange in case of duplication. And here I have lamely related to you the uneventful chronicle of two foolish children in a flat who most unwisely sacrificed for each other the greatest treasures of their house. But in a last word to the wise of these days let it be said that of all who give gifts these two were of the wisest. Of all who give and receive gifts, such as they are the wisest. Everywhere they are the wisest. They are the magi. ❖

"MY HAIR GROWS SO FAST, JIM!"

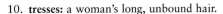

---

10. **tresses:** a woman's long, unbound hair.

11. **adornments:** things intended to beautify; ornaments.

NIKKI GIOVANNI
LUXURY

i suppose living
in a materialistic society
luxury
to some would be having
5 more than what you need

living in an electronic age seeing
the whole world by
    pushing a button
the *nth* degree might
    perhaps be
adequately represented
    by having
10 someone there to push
the buttons for you

i have thought if only
i could become rich and famous
    i would
live luxuriously in new york
    knowing
15 famous people eating
in expensive restaurants calling
long distance anytime i want

but you held me
one evening and now i know
20 the ultimate luxury
of your love

Seated Man (1922), Jacques Lipchitz. Bronze,
20¼″ × 10½″ × 10⅝″. Copyright © Estate of Jacques
Lipchitz/Licensed by VAGA, New York/Marlborough
Gallery, New York.

Connect to the Literature

1. **What Do You Think?** How did you react to the ending of the story?

Comprehension Check
- What are the Youngs' two prized possessions?
- What two gifts do they buy each other?
- How does each get the money to buy the other a gift?

Think Critically

2. Think of three words you might use to describe Jim and Della's relationship.

3. O. Henry calls Della and Jim "foolish," but he also says, "These two were of the wisest." What does he mean?

   THINK ABOUT { • what the last sentence of the story suggests
   • what you think true wisdom consists of

4. Look again at the **title** of this story. What "gift" do you think O. Henry had in mind? How might it suggest a **theme** of the story?

5. **ACTIVE READING** **PREDICTING** Look at the predictions that you made in your **READER'S NOTEBOOK** as you read the story. How do these predictions relate to the irony of the story?

6. What connection do you see between this story and Nikki Giovanni's poem "Luxury"?

Extend Interpretations

7. **Comparing Texts** Compare Jim and Della to Madame Loisel and her husband in Guy de Maupassant's "The Necklace." What similarities and differences do you see between the two couples?

8. **Connect to Life** Do you think the spirit of sacrifice in the holiday season is still alive and well today, or has it disappeared? Have you experienced gift giving in the spirit described in this story?

Literary Analysis

IRONY The contrast between what is expected to happen and what actually exists or happens is called **irony.** There are several kinds of irony, but the most common is **situational irony.** In a story, this occurs when a **character**—or the reader—expects one thing to happen but something entirely different occurs. In this story, for example, you might expect somebody named Mr. James Dillingham Young to be a rich man, but he makes only 20 dollars a week.

Activity To explain the irony of the situation in "The Gift of the Magi," make a chart like the one below. For each character, identify what is expected to happen and what actually happens. There is a double irony here. How are the two ironies related?

Situational Irony	
What Della plans:	What actually happens:
What Jim plans:	What actually happens:

Choices&CHALLENGES

Writing Options

1. Interior Monologue What might Jim be thinking when he notices Della's short hair? Write an inner monologue that expresses his thoughts.

2. TV Talk Show Who do you think makes the greater sacrifice—Della or Jim? Imagine that the couple appears on a TV talk show. Make notes for what you would say if you were a member of the audience. State your reasons. Place your notes in your **Working Portfolio.**

3. Special Gift List A gift that costs nothing can be the most valuable gift of all. Make a list of gifts that cost little or nothing but that you think have special value. Share your list with the class.

Activities & Explorations

1. Plot Collage Review the main events of this story. Then work with classmates to create a collage that represents the key events. Your collage might modernize the story by showing how the events could happen in today's world. Exhibit your collage in class. ~ **VIEWING AND REPRESENTING**

2. Work of Art "The Gift of the Magi" is a story of romantic love and mutual sacrifice. Create a drawing, painting, or sculpture that serves as a symbol of Jim and Della's relationship and that could be used to illustrate the story. ~ **ART**

Inquiry & Research

Wigs Do some research on the history of wigs and hairpieces. Find out about the use of both natural and synthetic hair in wigs, as well as their uses in theatrical productions and daily life. Prepare a report on your findings.

Art Connection

Look again at the painting by Joseph Stella on page 155. Stella's decision to obscure the subject's face contributes to the overall effect of mystery. How would the effect of this painting be different if the figure's face was visible?

Vocabulary in Action

EXERCISE: WORD MEANING On your paper, write the letter of the word that is most different in meaning from the other words in the set. Use a dictionary if you need help.

1. (a) stop, (b) stir, (c) urge, (d) instigate
2. (a) predominating, (b) dominating, (c) ruling, (d) missing
3. (a) culvert, (b) vestibule, (c) foyer, (d) anteroom
4. (a) history, (b) record, (c) chronicle, (d) prediction
5. (a) stream, (b) river, (c) brook, (d) cascade
6. (a) assertion, (b) declaration, (c) denial, (d) statement
7. (a) desired, (b) coveted, (c) craved, (d) unwanted
8. (a) carelessness, (b) caution, (c) prudence, (d) wisdom
9. (a) limber, (b) agile, (c) clumsy, (d) flexible
10. (a) important, (b) unnecessary, (c) inconsequential, (d) insignificant

Building Vocabulary
For an in-depth lesson on word relationships such as synonyms and antonyms, see page 849.

WORDS TO KNOW					
	agile	cascade	coveted	instigate	prudence
	assertion	chronicle	inconsequential	predominating	vestibule

Grammar in Context: Pronouns

In "The Gift of the Magi," Della is overwhelmed after she opens her Christmas present:

> **They were expensive combs, she knew, and her heart had simply craved and yearned over them without the least hope of possession.**

O. Henry uses several pronouns in the sentence above to make his writing flow smoothly. A **pronoun** is a word that takes the place of a noun or another pronoun. Try rewriting the sentence in the example above without using any pronouns.

Apply to Your Writing Pronouns can help you
- avoid repeating proper nouns
- reflect the way people think and talk
- make your writing flow more smoothly

Usage Tip: Make sure your readers will understand what word each pronoun refers to.

WRITING EXERCISE Rewrite the sentences in the next column, substituting pronouns for nouns.

Example: *Original* The door opens. Jim steps inside and then closes the door. Jim stares at Della, while Della waits for Jim to say something. ***Rewritten*** The door opens. Jim steps inside and then closes it. He stares at Della, while she waits for him to say something.

1. Della approaches Jim. Della starts to speak but can see that Jim is upset. Della decides to wait until later to speak with Jim.
2. Jim knows that Della yearns to have the combs, and Jim decides to buy the combs for Della.
3. When Della opens Jim's present, Della screams with joy. Then Della bursts into tears.

Connect to the Literature Look at the paragraph at the top of the second column on page 153 ("Della finished her cry . . . "). How does O. Henry's use of pronouns help make the paragraph effective?

Grammar Handbook Pronouns, pp. 1181–1183

O. Henry
1862–1910

Other Works
*The Four Million
Heart of the West
Voice of the City
Waifs and Strays
The Collected Works of O. Henry*

Surprising Life Using the pen name O. Henry, William Sydney Porter wrote nearly 300 short stories that brought him worldwide fame. During the two decades following his death, his stories were more popular than those of any other American writer. Moreover, the twists and turns of his own life sound like one of his stories. He was born in Greensboro, North Carolina, and raised by his grandmother and aunt after his mother's death. At 16, he left school to work in his uncle's drugstore. Later he moved to Texas and worked on a ranch there. At the age of 25, he married Athol Estes. After the birth of their child, they moved to Austin, Texas, where Porter became a bank clerk.

Several years after leaving this position, he was suspected of having embezzled bank funds. Porter fled to Central America to avoid trial. When he returned to visit his dying wife, he was arrested, convicted, and jailed for three years. Throughout, he maintained his innocence.

Practice in Prison It was in jail that Porter refined his short story style. When he came out of prison he was already selling stories to magazines under his new pen name. Today, the most renowned annual collection of new American short stories still bears that name—the O. Henry Awards.

Author Activity

Expecting the Unexpected O. Henry's short stories are famous for his use of the surprise ending, where the reader experiences a sudden reversal in a character or story line. To further appreciate his use of this technique, read "The Ransom of Red Chief," "The Furnished Room," or "A Retrieved Reformation."

The Sniper

Short Story by LIAM O'FLAHERTY

"There was a flash and a bullet whizzed over his head."

Connect to Your Life

Enemies What causes people to become enemies? Why is world peace so difficult to achieve? Think about different issues that might cause one person or a group of people to become your enemy. Using a chart like the one shown, list some of these issues. Then number them to show how valid or important each one is to you, with number 1 being the most important, or most likely to make someone your enemy. Discuss your opinions with classmates.

What Causes People to Become Enemies?	
Issues	Level of Importance

Build Background

Troubles "The Sniper" takes place in Dublin, Ireland, during a civil war that erupted in 1922–1923. This war, which killed many innocent civilians, resulted from internal opposition to Ireland's move toward independence from England. The Irish Free Staters wanted Ireland to govern itself but still remain a part of the British Empire. The Irish Republican Army (or the Republicans) wanted complete independence from England.

WORDS TO KNOW
Vocabulary Preview

ascetic	lodge
beleaguered	spasmodically
enveloped	reel
fanatic	remorse
identity	ruse

Focus Your Reading

LITERARY ANALYSIS **SUSPENSE** **Suspense** is the excitement or tension that readers feel as they get involved in a story and become eager to know the outcome. Notice how the author builds suspense in this passage from the story you are about to read:

The sniper could hear the dull panting of the motor. His heart beat faster. It was an enemy car. He wanted to fire, but he knew it was useless.

As you read this story, look for ways in which O'Flaherty creates suspense.

ACTIVE READING **NOTING DETAILS** To create suspense in a story, a writer usually includes **details** that are intended to arouse the reader's curiosity about what will happen next. Your enjoyment and understanding of any story can be broadened if you pay attention to these details.

READER'S NOTEBOOK As you read this story, jot down some of the details about the setting, the characters, and the action that help create suspense.

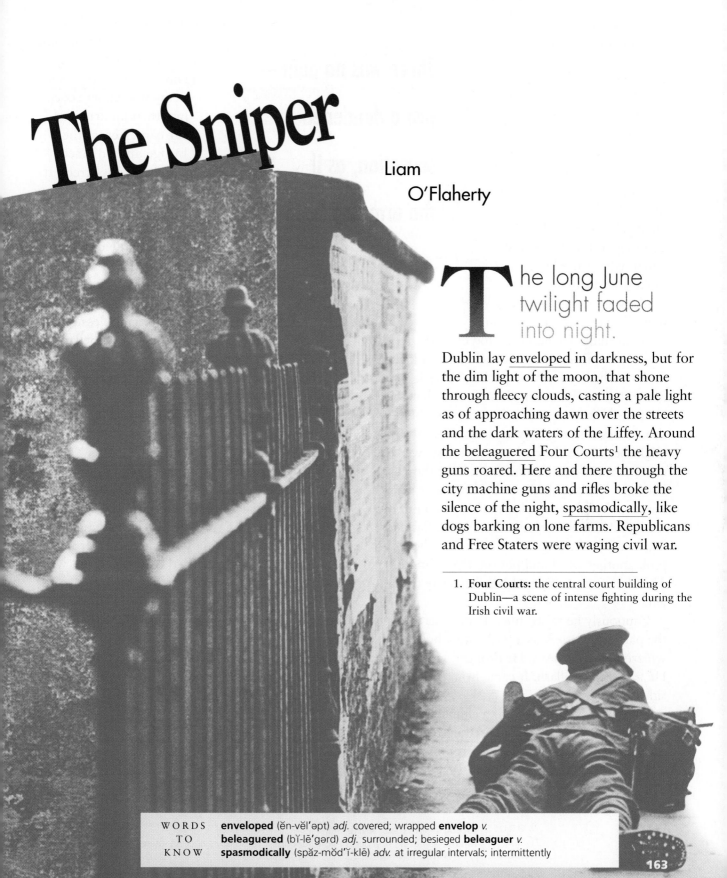

The Sniper

Liam O'Flaherty

The long June twilight faded into night.

Dublin lay enveloped in darkness, but for the dim light of the moon, that shone through fleecy clouds, casting a pale light as of approaching dawn over the streets and the dark waters of the Liffey. Around the beleaguered Four Courts[1] the heavy guns roared. Here and there through the city machine guns and rifles broke the silence of the night, spasmodically, like dogs barking on lone farms. Republicans and Free Staters were waging civil war.

---

1. **Four Courts:** the central court building of Dublin—a scene of intense fighting during the Irish civil war.

WORDS TO KNOW

enveloped (ĕn-vĕl′əpt) *adj.* covered; wrapped **envelop** *v.*
beleaguered (bĭ-lē′gərd) *adj.* surrounded; besieged **beleaguer** *v.*
spasmodically (spăz-mŏd′ĭ-klē) *adv.* at irregular intervals; intermittently

On a roof-top near O'Connel Bridge, a Republican sniper lay watching. Beside him lay his rifle and over his shoulders were slung a pair of field-glasses. His face was the face of a student—thin and ascetic, but his eyes had the cold gleam of the fanatic. They were deep and thoughtful, the eyes of a man who is used to looking at death.

He was eating a sandwich hungrily. He had eaten nothing since morning. He had been too excited to eat. He finished the sandwich, and taking a flask of whiskey from his pocket, he took a short draught. Then he returned the flask to his pocket. He paused for a moment, considering whether he should risk a smoke. It was dangerous. The flash might be seen in the darkness and there were enemies watching. He decided to take the risk. Placing a cigarette between his lips, he struck a match, inhaled the smoke hurriedly and put out the light. Almost immediately, a bullet flattened itself against the parapet[2] of the roof. The sniper took another whiff and put out the cigarette. Then he swore softly and crawled away to the left.

Cautiously he raised himself and peered over the parapet. There was a flash and a bullet whizzed over his head. He dropped immediately. He had seen the flash. It came from the opposite side of the street.

He rolled over the roof to a chimney stack in the rear, and slowly drew himself up behind it, until his eyes were level with the top of the

> **There was no pain—just a deadened sensation, as if the arm had been cut off.**

parapet. There was nothing to be seen—just the dim outline of the opposite housetop against the blue sky. His enemy was under cover. Just then an armored car came across the bridge and advanced slowly up the street. It stopped on the opposite side of the street fifty yards ahead. The sniper could hear the dull panting of the motor. His heart beat faster. It was an enemy car. He wanted to fire, but he knew it was useless. His bullets would never pierce the steel that covered the grey monster.

Then round the corner of a side street came an old woman, her head covered by a tattered shawl. She began to talk to the man in the turret of the car. She was pointing to the roof where the sniper lay. An informer.

The turret opened. A man's head and shoulders appeared, looking towards the sniper. The sniper raised his rifle and fired. The head fell heavily on the turret wall. The woman darted toward the side street. The sniper fired again. The woman whirled round and fell with a shriek into the gutter.

Suddenly from the opposite roof a shot rang out and the sniper dropped his rifle with a curse. The rifle clattered to the roof. The sniper thought the noise would wake the dead. He stopped to pick the rifle up. He couldn't lift it. His forearm was dead. . . . He muttered, "I'm hit."

---

2. **parapet** (păr′ə-pĭt): a low wall along the edge of a roof or balcony.

Dropping flat on to the roof, he crawled back to the parapet. With his left hand he felt the injured right forearm. The blood was oozing through the sleeve of his coat. There was no pain—just a deadened sensation, as if the arm had been cut off.

Quickly he drew his knife from his pocket, opened it on the breastwork of the parapet and ripped open the sleeve. There was a small hole where the bullet had entered. On the other side there was no hole. The bullet had lodged in the bone. It must have fractured it. He bent the arm below the wound. The arm bent back easily. He ground his teeth to overcome the pain.

Then, taking out his field dressing, he ripped open the packet with his knife. He broke the neck of the iodine bottle and let the bitter fluid drip into the wound. A paroxysm[3] of pain swept through him. He placed the cotton wadding over the wound and wrapped the dressing over it. He tied the end with his teeth.

Then he lay still against the parapet, and closing his eyes, he made an effort of will to overcome the pain.

In the street beneath all was still. The armored car had retired speedily over the bridge, with the machine gunner's head hanging lifeless over the turret. The woman's corpse lay still in the gutter.

The sniper lay for a long time nursing his wounded arm and planning escape. Morning must not find him wounded on the roof. The enemy on the opposite roof covered his escape. He must kill that enemy and he could not use his rifle. He had only a revolver to do it. Then he thought of a plan.

Taking off his cap, he placed it over the muzzle of his rifle. Then he pushed the rifle slowly upwards over the parapet, until the cap was visible from the opposite side of the street. Almost immediately there was a report,[4] and a bullet pierced the center of the cap. The sniper slanted the rifle forward. The cap slipped down into the street. Then, catching the rifle in the middle, the sniper dropped his left hand over the roof and let it hang, lifelessly. After a few moments he let the rifle drop to the street. Then he sank to the roof, dragging his hand with him.

Crawling quickly to the left, he peered up at the corner of the roof. His ruse had succeeded. The other sniper seeing the cap and rifle fall, thought that he had killed his

---

3. **paroxysm** (păr′ək-sĭz′əm): sudden attack.

4. **report:** an explosive noise; bang.

man. He was now standing before a row of chimney pots, looking across, with his head clearly silhouetted against the western sky.

The Republican sniper smiled and lifted his revolver above the edge of the parapet. The distance was about fifty yards—a hard shot in the dim light, and his right arm was paining him. . . . He took a steady aim. His hand trembled with eagerness. Pressing his lips together, he took a deep breath through his nostrils and fired. He was almost deafened with the report and his arm shook with the recoil.[5]

Then, when the smoke cleared, he peered across and uttered a cry of joy. His enemy had been hit. He was reeling over the parapet in his death agony. He struggled to keep his feet, but he was slowly falling forward, as if in a dream. The rifle fell from his grasp, hit the parapet, fell over, bounded off the pole of a barber's shop beneath and then clattered on to the pavement.

Then the dying man on the roof crumpled up and fell forward. The body turned over and over in space and hit the ground with a dull thud. Then it lay still.

The sniper looked at his enemy falling and he shuddered. The lust of battle died in him. He became bitten by remorse. The sweat stood out in beads on his forehead. Weakened by his wound and the long summer day of fasting and watching on the roof, he revolted[6] from the sight of the shattered mass of his dead enemy. His teeth chattered. He began to gibber[7] to himself, cursing the war, cursing himself, cursing everybody.

He looked at the smoking revolver in his hand and with an oath he hurled it to the roof at his feet. The revolver went off with the concussion,[8] and the bullet whizzed past the sniper's head. He was frightened back to his senses by the shock. His nerves steadied. The cloud of fear scattered from his mind and he laughed.

Taking the whiskey flask from his pocket, he emptied it at a draught. He felt reckless under the influence of the spirits.[9] He decided to leave the roof and look for his company commander to report. Everywhere around was quiet. There was not much danger in going through the streets. He picked up his revolver and put it in his pocket. Then he crawled down through the sky-light to the house underneath.

When the sniper reached the laneway on the street level, he felt a sudden curiosity as to the identity of the enemy sniper whom he had killed. He decided that he was a good shot whoever he was. He wondered if he knew him. Perhaps he had been in his own company before the split in the army. He decided to risk going over to have a look at him. He peered around the corner into O'Connell Street. In the upper part of the street there was heavy firing, but around here all was quiet.

The sniper darted across the street. A machine gun tore up the ground around him with a hail of bullets, but he escaped. He threw himself face downwards beside the corpse. The machine gun stopped.

Then the sniper turned over the dead body and looked into his brother's face. ❖

---

5. **recoil:** the jerking back of a gun when it is fired.

6. **revolted:** turned away in disgust.

7. **gibber** (jĭb′ər): to speak rapidly and incoherently.

8. **concussion:** impact.

9. **spirits:** liquor.

WORDS   **reel** (rēl) *v.* to fall off balance; lurch
TO   **remorse** (rĭ-môrs′) *n.* bitter regret
KNOW   **identity** (ī-děn′tĭ-tē) *n.* the quality of being a unique person; individuality

166

Connect to the Literature

1. **What Do You Think?** What were your first thoughts at the end of the story?

> **Comprehension Check**
> - Why is the sniper on the roof?
> - How does the sniper's arm become injured?
> - What trick does the sniper play on the other gunman?

Think Critically

2. In your opinion, does the sniper have any other choice than to kill the man on the opposite roof? Give reasons for your answer.

3. How do you think the sniper would justify killing the old woman?

4. How do you think the sniper feels about what he is doing?

THINK ABOUT

- the description of his eyes at the beginning of the story
- his first reaction to shooting the other gunman
- his reactions while watching the other gunman fall

5. **ACTIVE READING** **NOTING DETAILS** In your opinion, which of the **details** that you listed in your 📖 **READER'S NOTEBOOK** contribute most to the suspense in this story?

Extend Interpretations

6. **Critic's Corner** One critic has said that "O'Flaherty's characters are marked by wild mood swings and often by bizarre, contradictory behavior. . . ." Did you find any evidence of mood swings or contradictory behavior in O'Flaherty's characterization of the sniper? Explain your answer.

7. **Connect to Life** In this story, a civil war turns brothers into enemies. Can you imagine any issue that would be important enough to make a family member your enemy? Think about the list of issues you made earlier. Then discuss your thoughts.

Literary Analysis

SUSPENSE AND SURPRISE ENDING The excitement or tension readers feel as they become involved in the story and become curious about what will happen next is called **suspense.** O'Flaherty begins creating suspense early in this story by describing the **setting** as a city "enveloped in darkness" with the silence broken only by the sounds of machine guns. Often, stories that contain suspense also have a **surprise ending,** an unexpected turn of events at the conclusion of the story.

Cooperative Learning Activity The graph below shows five major events of the story in the order in which they happen. Place a dot for each event to show your level of suspense at that point in the story, with 1 being the *least* suspenseful and 5 the *most* suspenseful. Draw a line to connect the dots. Then compare your graph with those of your classmates.

Suspense in "The Sniper"

Level of Suspense	Sniper eats sandwich.	Sniper shoots informer.	Sniper is wounded.	Sniper kills enemy.	Sniper identifies body.
5					
4					
3					
2					
1					

REVIEW **SITUATIONAL IRONY**
Situational irony is the contrast between what is expected and what actually happens. The situational irony in this story centers around the identity of the other gunman. Discuss these questions with classmates: How important is the situational irony in this story? How would your reaction to the story be different if the sniper did not know the other gunman?

Choices & CHALLENGES

Writing Options

1. Sniper Sequel Imagine what might happen next to the sniper. How will he react to his brother's death? How will his family and friends react? Will he continue his wartime activities? Write a short summary for a sequel to this story.

Writing Handbook

See pages 1153–1154: Narrative Writing.

2. Thoughts in Verse Write a short poem in which you express your reaction to one or more of the events described in the story.

Activities & Explorations

1. Eulogy Pretend you are a member of the same family as the two brothers. Prepare a eulogy you would deliver at the dead brother's funeral. Present your eulogy to the class. **~ SPEAKING AND LISTENING**

2. Voice-Mail Message It has been said that in war no side really wins. Decide whether you agree or disagree with this statement. Then, using examples from this story and from another source (such as a movie or a newspaper), express your opinion in a voice-mail message to the Pentagon. **~ SPEAKING AND LISTENING**

Inquiry & Research

1. Irish Republican Army The Irish Republican Army, or IRA, still exists today. Find out more about this organization—or about the Republican political party Sinn Fein. What do they represent? How have they affected Irish history since the civil war described in "The Sniper"? Present your findings in an oral report to your classmates.

 More Online: Research Starter www.mcdougallittell.com

2. Breaking the Cycle In Northern Ireland, Catholics and Protestants have feared and resented each other for generations. Children have grown up there in an atmosphere of distrust. How do you think this cycle of suspicion might be broken?

 Real World Link Read "A Respite from 'The Troubles'" on pages 170–171 before forming your opinion.

Vocabulary in Action

EXERCISE A: ASSESSMENT PRACTICE On your paper, identify each pair of words below as synonyms or antonyms.

1. **fanatic**—enthusiast
2. **spasmodically**—continuously
3. **lodge**—catch
4. **remorse**—gladness
5. **ascetic**—outgoing
6. **beleaguered**—liberated
7. **ruse**—prank
8. **identity**—character
9. **reel**—stagger
10. **enveloped**—released

Building Vocabulary

For an in-depth lesson on synonyms and antonyms, see page 849.

EXERCISE B: MEANING CLUES Choose the Word to Know that is most clearly related to the situation described in each sentence.

1. Enemy soldiers border the city on all sides.
2. The woman would absolutely never miss a Rangers' game.
3. A man hopes the spinach he's eating won't get stuck between his teeth.
4. A prisoner puts on a disguise and slips past the guards.
5. The boy feels sorry about having broken the window.

Grammar in Context: Adverb Placement

One way that experienced writers emphasize certain words and change the meaning of sentences is through careful placement of adverbs. In the following sentences, notice where Liam O'Flaherty places adverbs (shown in blue).

> **Cautiously** he raised himself and peered over the parapet.

> He had **only** a revolver to [kill the enemy].

How would the emphasis change if *cautiously* were moved toward the end of the first sentence? In the second example, how would the meaning change if *only* appeared before *He?*

Apply to Your Writing Varying the placement of adverbs can help you

- change emphasis in a sentence or phrase
- change the meaning of a sentence

WRITING EXERCISE Change the placement of the underlined adverbs. Briefly describe how the change affects the meaning of the sentence.

Example: *Original* The sniper drops his rifle and slumps to the ground <u>suddenly</u>.
Rewritten <u>Suddenly</u> the sniper drops his rifle and slumps to the ground. (emphasis shifts from *slumps* to *drops*)

1. <u>Quickly</u> the sniper draws the knife from his pocket and cuts open his sleeve.
2. He pours the iodine <u>slowly</u> and <u>awkwardly</u> bandages the wound.
3. The sniper <u>only</u> has a chance to escape from the roof.
4. His hand trembles <u>nervously</u> as he takes aim with the revolver.
5. <u>Once</u> he makes it past the machine gun, he learns the identity of the dead sniper.

Grammar Handbook Modifiers, pp. 1186–1188

Liam O'Flaherty
1896–1984

Other Works
The Informer
Civil War
Famine

Irish Roots As a child, Liam O'Flaherty lived on one of the Aran Islands, an isolated and stormy area off the west coast of Ireland. He was later educated in Dublin, where he studied briefly for the Roman Catholic priesthood. After leaving the seminary, he enrolled in a Dublin university. During World War I, O'Flaherty left college to join the Irish Guards, a branch of the British army. During a brutal combat in Belgium, he was badly shell-shocked and forced to return home.

The Wanderer While still a young man, O'Flaherty set out on a series of wanderings throughout the world. To pay for his travel, he worked at various odd jobs, including that of seaman, miner, lumberjack, bellboy, and bank clerk. He tried writing stories about his adventures, but no one wanted to publish them.

Irish Republican In 1920, O'Flaherty finally returned to Ireland, where he became involved with the Irish Republican Army. Like the sniper in the story, he supported the Irish Republicans in their war against the Irish Free Staters. In 1922, after taking part in a rebellion of unemployed workers, he was forced to flee to England to avoid being imprisoned. In 1923, he published his first story, "The Sniper," which is undoubtedly based, in part, on O'Flaherty's own experience during Ireland's civil war.

Author Activity

Liam O'Flaherty wrote novels as well as short stories. His first novel was published in 1923 and his last one in 1950. Find out which of his novels was made into a movie, what year the movie was released, and whether or not it was popular. Also, try to learn what the novel and movie are about. Share your findings with classmates.

Reading for Information

In 1969, fighting broke out between the Protestant majority and the Roman Catholic minority in Northern Ireland. The violence that resulted became known as "the Troubles." One challenge faced by newspapers, magazines, and other news sources is that of making prolonged political conflicts like this one real and relevant to readers far away from the scenes of the strife.

http://www.abcnews.com

❶ A Respite[1] from "The Troubles"
by Gayle Tzemach

❷ For the children of Northern Ireland, violence is embedded in the rituals of daily life. Early curfews are the norm, public places are commonly avoided, and Catholics and Protestants rarely venture outside their own neighborhoods.

Since sectarian violence began in 1969, generations of Belfast youngsters have known only "the Troubles"—and many have grown up to repeat the cycles of terrorism and despair. Project Children aims to change all that, child by child, lifting them out of Northern Ireland and placing them with American host families for six weeks in hopes of showing them what life is like when peace is the norm.

"My host family showed me that there is a lot more to the world, that I can achieve anything," said James Dawson, a 16-year-old participating in Project Children for the sixth summer. "You grow up in Belfast and always thought that Protestants were different, or Catholics were different, and you realize that they're just the same."

Project Children Began Humbly
As all-party peace talks approach, those behind Project Children say they are more hopeful than ever that their vision of a peaceful Northern Ireland can become reality.

"There are great hopes for peace right now," says Denis Mulcahy, an NYPD bomb-squad detective who began the program in 1975 with just $1,800 and six children. "I think that what we do right now is more important than ever because it gives the kids an opportunity to be together, to see that really there isn't any difference."

❸ Since then, the project has brought more than 13,000 children to the United States, including 630 Irish youngsters in 19 states this year. The trips are paid for by private donations.

The mixing of Catholic and Protestant children so accustomed to segregated ghettos and mutual mistrust creates "magic," according to Margaret Dawson, who coordinates the Belfast contingent.

---

1. **respite** (rĕs′pĭt): a short period of rest or relief.

READING NEWS SOURCES

An effective news article usually begins by dealing with the "five W's"—*who, what, where, when,* and *why* (along, sometimes, with *how*). The rest of the article then fleshes out the story with facts, descriptions, and quotations.

YOUR TURN Use the questions and activities below to explore this news article.

❶ Analyzing Headings Feature articles often contain headlines and subheadings that summarize the information they present. What ideas do the headings in this article convey?

❷ Evaluating These two paragraphs provide the reader with basic background information. Determine whether the information in the paragraphs covers the five W's.

❸ How do the facts presented in this paragraph show that the program has been successful?

④ How do the quoted statements by the Belfast coordinator and the two participants help you understand the ways in which the program has improved children's lives?

`http://www.abcnews.com`

Peace Talks Bring Optimism

She too is optimistic that September's round of talks may be the ones to bring change to the children's lives.

"What's going to make it better this year is [the Irish Republican Army's] ceasefire," she says. "[If we get peace, the children] will be able to keep in touch with each other more. There's just a good feeling about it all this year."

④ For their part, Project Children's children say the experience is unforgettable. "It was brilliant," says Belfast native Sandra O'Hara. "I found out that everything is not as wild as Belfast, and not everybody is fighting over here. It was quiet, and it was nice meeting other people."

"There's no fighting, it's calm," says another young Irish visitor, John Ireland. "You can go out without anything happening, you know you can stay out late."

Americans Also Benefit

And the host families involved say they gain as much as they give. "Once they begin to see what America is like, no bombs or anything like that, they begin to act like a normal child," says four-time participant Kevin Macleod. "It is very rewarding as a host parent to see that."

Macleod and the rest of those who play a part in Project Children say it is in these young lives that the peace must truly take hold if it is to last. And they are hopeful that in the end, a durable peace can be created, one child at a time.

"It's not going to happen overnight," says Mulcahy. "But hopefully there is light at the end of the tunnel, and in a few years we won't have to do this anymore."

Looking around at the children as they gathered for their return trip home this year, Dawson stressed the hope she felt now that Protestant and Catholic leaders have joined the talks.

"Hopefully we are on our way," she said. "We're always hopeful. If we didn't have hope, we'd have despair."

Inquiry & Research

Activity Link: *from* **The Sniper, p. 168**
What is being done to try to end the cycle of suspicion and violence in Northern Ireland? If Protestants and Catholics have ended the bloodshed, what are the prospects that this period of peace will be lasting? Write your own feature article to answer one of these questions.

Scenes like this one occurred regularly in Northern Ireland.

The Possibility of Evil

Short Story by SHIRLEY JACKSON

(Connect to Your Life)

First Impressions How do you form an opinion of people you meet for the first time? Think about the first time you met a new friend. What traits or qualities caught your attention? Do you think now that your first impressions were accurate? Make a list of the traits, qualities, and behavior patterns that normally help you form an opinion about someone you meet for the first time. Discuss your list with classmates.

How I Form First Impressions
The traits I notice:
nice smile
The qualities I notice:
friendly
The behavior I notice:
opens doors for people

Build Background

Eerie Tales Shirley Jackson is known as a writer of eerie, "catch-you-by-surprise" stories. Shortly after she wrote her most famous story, "The Lottery," Jackson received hundreds of letters from readers, most of whom were shocked by the plot of this now famous tale. Many of her plots involve events that appear normal but conceal an evil or twisted reality. Often, her characters are isolated from others—people who lack feeling, display contradictory personalities, and are capable of bizarre behavior. You can decide for yourself if "The Possibility of Evil" fits these patterns.

> WORDS TO KNOW
> **Vocabulary Preview**
>
> appropriation   potential
> banished   proverbial
> consequently   rapt
> degraded   reprehensible
> indulgently   unchecked

Focus Your Reading

LITERARY ANALYSIS **CHARACTERIZATION** **Characterization** refers to the way a writer develops a character's personality and traits. A writer creates characterization by using any of four methods: (1) describing a character's physical appearance; (2) describing a character's speech, thoughts, feelings, or actions; (3) describing other characters' speech, thoughts, feelings, or actions; (4) using the narrator to directly comment on a character. All four methods of characterization appear in the story you are about to read, as shown by these examples:

1. Miss Adela Strangeworth came daintily along Main Street. . . .

2. Miss Strangeworth . . . thought that there was nothing in the world like a fragrant summer day.

3. Half a dozen people turned . . . to wave at her or call out good morning.

4. Miss Strangeworth never gave away any of her roses. . . .

As you read the story, look for more examples of these four ways that Shirley Jackson uses to develop her main character, Miss Adela Strangeworth.

ACTIVE READING **MAKING INFERENCES ABOUT CHARACTER** In the course of a story, a writer often provides details that turn out to be subtle clues to a character's personality.

📖READER'S NOTEBOOK Draw a word web like the one shown. As you read the story, jot down any details that help you form an opinion of Miss Strangeworth.

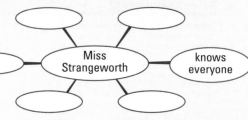

The Possibility of Evil

SHIRLEY JACKSON

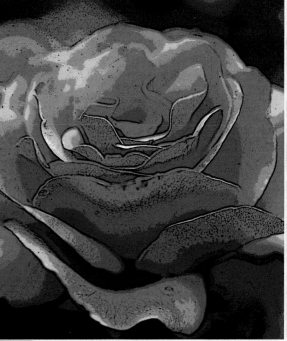

Miss Adela Strangeworth came daintily along Main Street on her way to the grocery. The sun was shining, the air was fresh and clear after the night's heavy rain, and everything in Miss Strangeworth's little town looked washed and bright. Miss Strangeworth took deep breaths and thought that there was nothing in the world like a fragrant summer day.

She knew everyone in town, of course; she was fond of telling strangers—tourists who sometimes passed through the town and stopped to admire Miss Strangeworth's roses—that she had never spent more than a day outside this town in all her long life. She was seventy-one, Miss Strangeworth told the tourists, with a pretty little dimple showing by her lip, and she sometimes found herself thinking that the town belonged to her. "My grandfather built the first house on Pleasant Street," she would say, opening her blue eyes wide with the wonder of it. "This house, right here. My family has lived here for better than a hundred years. My grandmother planted these roses, and my mother tended them, just as I do. I've watched my town grow; I can remember when Mr. Lewis, Senior, opened the grocery store, and the year the river flooded out the shanties[1] on the low road, and the excitement when some young folks wanted to move the park over to the space in front of where the new post office is today. They wanted to put up a statue of Ethan Allen"[2]—Miss Strangeworth would frown a little and sound stern—"but it should have been a statue of my grandfather. There wouldn't have been a town here at all if it hadn't been for my grandfather and the lumber mill."

Miss Strangeworth never gave away any of her roses, although the tourists often asked her. The roses belonged on Pleasant Street, and it bothered Miss Strangeworth to think of people wanting to carry them away, to take them into strange towns and down strange streets. When the new minister came, and the ladies were gathering flowers to decorate the church, Miss Strangeworth sent over a great basket of gladioli; when she picked the roses at all, she set them in bowls and vases around the inside of the house her grandfather had built.

Walking down Main Street on a summer morning, Miss Strangeworth had to stop every minute or so to say good morning to someone or to ask after someone's health. When she came into the grocery, half a dozen people turned away from the shelves and the counters to wave at her or call out good morning.

"And good morning to you, too, Mr. Lewis," Miss Strangeworth said at last. The Lewis family had been in the town almost as long as

Old-Fashioned Roses (about 1915), Bessie Hoover. Courtesy of the Cincinnati Art Club Collection.

---

1. **shanties** (shăn′tēz): roughly built cabins; shacks.
2. **Ethan Allen**: a Revolutionary War hero who led a group of soldiers, called the Green Mountain Boys, from what is now Vermont.

the Strangeworths; but the day young Lewis left high school and went to work in the grocery, Miss Strangeworth had stopped calling him Tommy and started calling him Mr. Lewis, and he had stopped calling her Addie and started calling her Miss Strangeworth. They had been in high school together, and had gone to picnics together, and to high-school dances and basketball games; but now Mr. Lewis was behind the counter in the grocery, and Miss Strangeworth was living alone in the Strangeworth house on Pleasant Street.

"Good morning," Mr. Lewis said, and added politely, "Lovely day."

"It is a very nice day," Miss Strangeworth said, as though she had only just decided that it would do after all. "I would like a chop, please, Mr. Lewis, a small, lean veal chop. Are those strawberries from Arthur Parker's garden? They're early this year."

"He brought them in this morning," Mr. Lewis said.

"I shall have a box," Miss Strangeworth said. Mr. Lewis looked worried, she thought, and for a minute she hesitated, but then she decided that he surely could not be worried over the strawberries. He looked very tired indeed. He was usually so chipper, Miss Strangeworth thought, and almost commented; but it was far too personal a subject to be introduced to Mr. Lewis, the grocer, so she only said, "And a can of cat food and, I think, a tomato."

Silently, Mr. Lewis assembled her order on the counter, and waited. Miss Strangeworth looked at him curiously and then said, "It's Tuesday, Mr. Lewis. You forgot to remind me."

"Did I? Sorry."

"Imagine your forgetting that I always buy my tea on Tuesday," Miss Strangeworth said gently. "A quarter pound of tea, please, Mr. Lewis."

"Is that all, Miss Strangeworth?"

"Yes thank you, Mr. Lewis. Such a lovely day, isn't it?"

"Lovely," Mr. Lewis said.

Miss Strangeworth moved slightly to make room for Mrs. Harper at the counter. "Morning, Adela," Mrs. Harper said, and Miss Strangeworth said, "Good morning, Martha."

"Lovely day," Mrs. Harper said, and Miss Strangeworth said, "Yes, lovely," and Mr. Lewis, under Mrs. Harper's glance, nodded.

"Ran out of sugar for my cake frosting," Mrs. Harper explained. Her hand shook slightly as she opened her pocketbook. Miss Strangeworth wondered, glancing at her quickly, if she had been taking proper care of herself. Martha Harper was not as young as she used to be, Miss Strangeworth thought. She probably could use a good strong tonic.[3]

"Martha," she said, "you don't look well."

"I'm perfectly all right," Mrs. Harper said shortly. She handed her money to Mr. Lewis, took her change and her sugar, and went out without speaking again. Looking after her, Miss Strangeworth shook her head slightly. Martha definitely did *not* look well.

Carrying her little bag of groceries, Miss Strangeworth came out of the store into the bright sunlight and stopped to smile down on the Crane baby. Don and Helen Crane were really the two most infatuated young parents she had ever known, she thought indulgently, looking at the delicately embroidered baby cap and the lace-edged carriage cover.

"That little girl is going to grow up expecting luxury all her life," she said to Helen Crane.

---

3. **tonic:** a medicine for restoring and energizing the body.

Helen laughed. "That's the way we want her to feel," she said. "Like a princess."

"A princess can see a lot of trouble sometimes," Miss Strangeworth said dryly. "How old is Her Highness now?"

"Six months next Tuesday," Helen Crane said, looking down with rapt wonder at her child. "I've been worrying, though, about her. Don't you think she ought to move around more? Try to sit up, for instance?"

"For plain and fancy[4] worrying," Miss Strangeworth said, amused, "give me a new mother every time."

"She just seems—slow," Helen Crane said.

"Nonsense. All babies are different. Some of them develop much more quickly than others."

"That's what my mother says." Helen Crane laughed, looking a little bit ashamed.

"I suppose you've got young Don all upset about the fact that his daughter is already six months old and hasn't yet begun to learn to dance?"

"I haven't mentioned it to him. I suppose she's just so precious that I worry about her all the time."

"Well, apologize to her right now," Miss Strangeworth said. "*She* is probably worrying about why you keep jumping around all the time." Smiling to herself and shaking her old head, she went on down the sunny street, stopping once to ask little Billy Moore why he wasn't out riding in his daddy's shiny new car; and talking for a few minutes outside the library with Miss Chandler, the librarian, about the new novels to be ordered and paid for by the annual library appropriation. Miss Chandler seemed absentminded and very much as though she were thinking about something else. Miss Strangeworth noticed that Miss Chandler had not taken much trouble with her hair that morning, and sighed. Miss Strangeworth hated sloppiness.

Many people seemed disturbed recently, Miss Strangeworth thought. Only yesterday the Stewarts' fifteen-year-old Linda had run crying down her own front walk and all the way to school, not caring who saw her. People around town thought she might have had a fight with the Harris boy, but they showed up together at the soda shop after school as usual, both of them looking grim and bleak. Trouble at home, people concluded, and sighed over the problems of trying to raise kids right these days.

From halfway down the block, Miss Strangeworth could catch the heavy scent of her roses, and she moved a little more quickly. The perfume of roses meant home, and home meant the Strangeworth House on Pleasant Street. Miss Strangeworth stopped at her own front gate, as she always did, and looked with deep pleasure at her house, with the red and pink and white roses massed along the narrow lawn, and the rambler[5] going up along the porch; and the neat, the unbelievably trim lines of the house itself, with its slimness and its washed white look. Every window sparkled, every curtain hung stiff and straight, and even the stones of the front walk were swept and clear. People around town wondered how old Miss Strangeworth managed to keep the house looking the way it did, and there was a legend about a tourist once mistaking it for the local museum and going all through the place without finding out about his mistake. But the town was proud of Miss Strangeworth and her roses and her house. They had all grown together.

Miss Strangeworth went up her front steps, unlocked her front door with her key, and went into the kitchen to put away her groceries. She

---

4. **plain and fancy:** every kind of.

5. **rambler:** a rose plant that grows upward like a vine, by clinging to a support.

WORDS TO KNOW

rapt (răpt) *adj.* deeply delighted; enchanted
appropriation (ə-prō′prē-ā′shən) *n.* money set aside for a specific purpose

debated about having a cup of tea and then decided that it was too close to midday dinnertime; she would not have the appetite for her little chop if she had tea now. Instead she went into the light, lovely sitting room, which still glowed from the hands of her mother and her grandmother, who had covered the chairs with bright chintz[6] and hung the curtains. All the furniture was spare and shining, and the round hooked rugs on the floor had been the work of Miss Strangeworth's grandmother and her mother. Miss Strangeworth had put a bowl of her red roses on the low table before the window, and the room was full of their scent.

Miss Strangeworth went to the narrow desk in the corner and unlocked it with her key. She never knew when she might feel like writing letters, so she kept her notepaper inside and the desk locked. Miss Strangeworth's usual stationery was heavy and cream-colored, with STRANGEWORTH HOUSE engraved across the top; but, when she felt like writing her other letters, Miss Strangeworth used a pad of various-colored paper bought from the local newspaper shop. It was almost a town joke, that colored paper, layered in pink and green and blue and yellow; everyone in town bought it and used it for odd, informal notes and shopping lists. It was usual to remark, upon receiving a note written on a blue page, that so-and-so would be needing a new pad soon—here she was, down to the blue already. Everyone used the matching envelopes for tucking away recipes, or keeping odd little things in, or even to hold cookies in the school lunchboxes. Mr. Lewis sometimes gave them to the children for carrying home penny candy.

Miss Strangeworth **hated** *sloppiness.*

Although Miss Strangeworth's desk held a trimmed quill pen that had belonged to her grandfather, and a gold-frosted fountain pen that had belonged to her father, Miss Strangeworth always used a dull stub of pencil when she wrote her letters; and she printed them in a childish block print. After thinking for a minute, although she had been phrasing the letter in the back of her mind all the way home, she wrote on a pink sheet: DIDN'T YOU EVER SEE AN IDIOT CHILD BEFORE? SOME PEOPLE JUST SHOULDN'T HAVE CHILDREN SHOULD THEY?

She was pleased with the letter. She was fond of doing things exactly right. When she made a mistake, as she sometimes did, or when the letters were not spaced nicely on the page, she had to take the discarded page to the kitchen stove and burn it at once. Miss Strangeworth never delayed when things had to be done.

After thinking for a minute, she decided that she would like to write another letter, perhaps to go to Mrs. Harper, to follow up the ones she had already mailed. She selected a green sheet this time and wrote quickly: HAVE YOU FOUND OUT YET WHAT THEY WERE ALL LAUGHING ABOUT AFTER YOU LEFT THE BRIDGE CLUB ON THURSDAY? OR IS THE WIFE REALLY ALWAYS THE LAST ONE TO KNOW?

Miss Strangeworth never concerned herself with facts; her letters all dealt with the more negotiable[7] stuff of suspicion. Mr. Lewis would never have imagined for a minute that his grandson might be lifting petty cash[8] from the store register if he had not had one of Miss

---

6. **chintz:** a colorful printed cotton fabric.

7. **negotiable** (nĭ-gō′shə-bəl): having a practical use.

8. **petty cash:** a small fund of money kept handy for miscellaneous expenses.

Strangeworth's letters. Miss Chandler, the librarian, and Linda Stewart's parents would have gone unsuspectingly ahead with their lives, never aware of possible evil lurking nearby, if Miss Strangeworth had not sent letters opening their eyes. Miss Strangeworth would have been genuinely shocked if there had been anything between Linda Stewart and the Harris boy; but, as long as evil existed <u>unchecked</u> in the world, it was Miss Strangeworth's duty to keep her town alert to it. It was far more sensible for Miss Chandler to wonder what Mr. Shelley's first wife had really died of than to take a chance on not knowing. There were so many wicked people in the world and only one Strangeworth left in the town. Besides, Miss Strangeworth liked writing her letters.

She addressed an envelope to Don Crane after a moment's thought, wondering curiously if he would show the letter to his wife, and using a pink envelope to match the pink paper. Then she addressed a second envelope, green, to Mrs. Harper. Then an idea came to her and she selected a blue sheet and wrote: YOU NEVER KNOW ABOUT DOCTORS. REMEMBER THEY'RE ONLY HUMAN AND NEED MONEY LIKE THE REST OF US. SUPPOSE THE KNIFE SLIPPED ACCIDENTALLY. WOULD DR. BURNS GET HIS FEE AND A LITTLE EXTRA FROM THAT NEPHEW OF YOURS?

She addressed the blue envelope to old Mrs. Foster, who was having an operation next month. She had thought

of writing one more letter, to the head of the school board, asking how a chemistry teacher like Billy Moore's father could afford a new convertible, but, all at once, she was tired of writing letters. The three she had done would do for one day. She could write more tomorrow; it was not as though they all had to be done at once.

She had been writing her letters—sometimes two or three every day for a week, sometimes no more than one in a month—for the past year. She never got any answers, of course, because she never signed her name. If she had been asked, she would have said that her name, Adela Strangeworth, a name honored in the town for so many years, did not belong on such trash. The town where she lived had to be kept clean and sweet, but people everywhere were lustful and evil and <u>degraded</u>, and needed to be watched; the world was so large, and there was

Mailboxes & Cosmos, Carl Schmalz, W.H.S. Watercolor. Courtesy of the artist.

178

only one Strangeworth left in it. Miss Strangeworth sighed, locked her desk, and put the letters into her big black leather pocketbook, to be mailed when she took her evening walk.

She broiled her little chop nicely, and had a sliced tomato and a good cup of tea ready when she sat down to her midday dinner at the table in her dining room, which could be opened to seat twenty-two, with a second table, if necessary, in the hall. Sitting in the warm sunlight that came through the tall windows of the dining room, seeing her roses massed outside, handling the heavy, old silverware and the fine, translucent[9] china, Miss Strangeworth was pleased; she would not have cared to be doing anything else. People must live graciously, after all, she thought, and sipped her tea. Afterward, when her plate and cup and saucer were washed and dried and put back onto the shelves where they belonged, and her silverware was back in the mahogany silver chest, Miss Strangeworth went up the graceful staircase and into her bedroom, which was the front room overlooking the roses, and had been her mother's and her grandmother's. Their Crown Derby dresser set[10] and furs had been kept there, their fans and silver-backed brushes and their own bowls of roses; Miss Strangeworth kept a bowl of white roses on the bed table.

She drew the shades, took the rose satin spread from the bed, slipped out of her dress and her shoes, and lay down tiredly. She knew that no doorbell or phone would ring; no one in town would dare to disturb Miss Strangeworth during her afternoon nap. She slept, deep in the rich smell of roses.

After her nap she worked in her garden for a little while, sparing herself because of the heat; then she came in to her supper. She ate asparagus from her own garden, with sweet-butter sauce and a soft-boiled egg; and, while she had her supper, she listened to a late-evening news broadcast and then to a program of classical music on her small radio. After her dishes were done and her kitchen set in order, she took up her hat—Miss Strangeworth's hats were <u>proverbial</u> in the town; people believed that she had inherited them from her mother and her grandmother—and, locking the front door of her house behind her, set off on her evening walk, pocketbook under her arm. She nodded to Linda Stewart's father, who was washing his car in the pleasantly cool evening. She thought that he looked troubled.

There was only one place in town where she could mail her letters, and that was the new post office, shiny with red brick and silver letters. Although Miss Strangeworth had never given the matter any particular thought, she had always made a point of mailing her letters very secretly; it would, of course, not have been wise to let anyone see her mail them. <u>Consequently</u>, she timed her walk so she could reach the post office just as darkness was starting to dim the outlines of the trees and the shapes of people's faces, although no one could ever mistake Miss Strangeworth, with her dainty walk and her rustling skirts.

There was always a group of young people around the post office, the very youngest roller-skating upon its driveway, which went all the way around the building and was the only smooth road in town; and the slightly older ones already knowing how to gather in small groups and chatter and laugh and make great, excited plans for going across the street to the soda shop in a minute or two. Miss

---

9. **translucent** (trăns-loo′sənt): allowing light to shine through.
10. **Crown Derby dresser set:** a hairbrush, comb, and hand mirror made of fine china.

Strangeworth had never had any self-consciousness before the children. She did not feel that any of them were staring at her unduly or longing to laugh at her; it would have been most reprehensible for their parents to permit their children to mock Miss Strangeworth of Pleasant Street. Most of the children stood back respectfully as Miss Strangeworth passed, silenced briefly in her presence, and some of the older children greeted her, saying soberly, "Hello, Miss Strangeworth."

Miss Strangeworth smiled at them and quickly went on. It had been a long time since she had known the name of every child in town. The mail slot was in the door of the post office. The children stood away as Miss Strangeworth approached it, seemingly surprised that anyone should want to use the post office after it had been officially closed up for the night and turned over to the children. Miss Strangeworth stood by the door, opening her black pocketbook to take out the letters, and heard a voice which she knew at once to be Linda Stewart's. Poor little Linda was crying again, and Miss Strangeworth listened carefully. This was, after all, her town, and these were her people; if one of them was in trouble she ought to know about it.

"I can't tell you, Dave," Linda was saying—

Senility (1962), Simon Samsonian. Oil on canvas, 50″×35″. Museum of Fine Art, Yerevan, Armenia.

so she *was* talking to the Harris boy, as Miss Strangeworth had supposed—"I just *can't*. It's just *nasty*."

"But why won't your father let me come around any more? What on earth did I do?"

"I can't tell you. I just wouldn't tell you for *any*thing. You've got to have a dirty, dirty mind for things like that."

"But something's happened. You've been

WORDS
TO
KNOW

reprehensible (rĕp′rĭ-hĕn′sə-bəl) *adj.* deserving of blame

crying and crying, and your father is all upset. Why can't *I* know about it, too? Aren't I like one of the family?"

"Not any more, Dave, not any more. You're not to come near our house again; my father said so. He said he'd horsewhip you. That's all I can tell you: You're not to come near our house any more."

"But I didn't *do* anything."

"Just the same, my father said . . ."

Miss Strangeworth sighed and turned away. There was so much evil in people. Even in a charming little town like this one, there was still so much evil in people.

She slipped her letters into the slot, and two of them fell inside. The third caught on the edge and fell outside, onto the ground at Miss Strangeworth's feet. She did not notice it because she was wondering whether a letter to the Harris boy's father might not be of some service in wiping out this <u>potential</u> badness. Wearily Miss Strangeworth turned to go home to her quiet bed in her lovely house, and never heard the Harris boy calling to her to say that she had dropped something.

"Old lady Strangeworth's getting deaf," he said, looking after her and holding in his hand the letter he had picked up.

"Well, who cares?" Linda said. "Who cares any more, anyway?"

"It's for Don Crane," the Harris boy said, "this letter. She dropped a letter addressed to Don Crane. Might as well take it on over. We pass his house anyway." He laughed. "Maybe it's got a check or something in it, and he'd be just as glad to get it tonight instead of tomorrow."

"Catch old lady Strangeworth sending anybody a check," Linda said. "Throw it in the post office. Why do anyone a favor?" She sniffled. "Doesn't seem to me anybody around here cares about us," she said. "Why should we care about them?"

"I'll take it over anyway," the Harris boy said. "Maybe it's good news for them. Maybe they need something happy tonight, too. Like us."

Sadly, holding hands, they wandered off down the dark street, the Harris boy carrying Miss Strangeworth's pink envelope in his hand.

iss Strangeworth awakened the next morning with a feeling of intense happiness and, for a minute wondered why, and then remembered that this morning three people would open her letters. Harsh, perhaps, at first, but wickedness was never easily <u>banished</u>, and a clean heart was a scoured heart. She washed her soft old face and brushed her teeth, still sound in spite of her seventy-one years, and dressed herself carefully in her sweet, soft clothes and buttoned shoes. Then, coming downstairs and reflecting that perhaps a little waffle would be agreeable for breakfast in the sunny dining room, she found the mail on the hall floor and bent to pick it up. A bill, the morning paper, a letter in a green envelope that looked oddly familiar. Miss Strangeworth stood perfectly still for a minute, looking down at the green envelope with the penciled printing, and thought: It looks like one of my letters. Was one of my letters sent back? No, because no one would know where to send it. How did this get here?

Miss Strangeworth was a Strangeworth of Pleasant Street. Her hand did not shake as she opened the envelope and unfolded the sheet of green paper inside. She began to cry silently for the wickedness of the world when she read the words:

LOOK OUT AT WHAT USED TO BE YOUR ROSES.

WORDS TO KNOW

potential (pə-tĕn′shəl) *adj.* possible, but not yet existing
banish (băn′ĭsh) *v.* to force to go away; drive out

181

Connect to the Literature

1. What Do You Think?
What words would you use to describe Miss Strangeworth? Share them with a classmate.

> **Comprehension Check**
> - How does Miss Strangeworth secretly warn people about "the possibility of evil"?
> - How is her secret activity discovered?
> - What happens to make her cry at the end of the story?

Think Critically

2. **ACTIVE READING** | **MAKING INFERENCES ABOUT CHARACTER**
Analyze the details that you included in the word web in your **READER'S NOTEBOOK.** Does the author provide any **foreshadowing,** or clues early in the story, about Miss Strangeworth's real personality? Give examples to support your answer.

3. Why do you think Miss Strangeworth writes her letters?

> THINK ABOUT
> - her lifestyle
> - what she values most
> - her attitude toward other people

4. Do you think Miss Strangeworth realizes that she has done something wrong? Give reasons for your answer.

Extend Interpretations

5. What If? Suppose that some of the townspeople decided to confront Miss Strangeworth directly instead of destroying her roses. What might have happened?

6. Comparing Texts Of the stories you have read so far in this unit, which one has the most surprising ending? Support your opinion.

7. Connect to Life Miss Strangeworth thinks there is "so much evil in people." Do you agree with her? Discuss with your classmates.

Literary Analysis

CHARACTERIZATION

There are four basic methods of **characterization,** or ways of developing characters. A writer may use any or all of the following:

- descriptions of a character's physical appearance
- a character's speech, thoughts, feelings, or actions
- the speech, thoughts, feelings, or actions of other characters
- the narrator's direct comments about a character

Through these methods, a writer can make his or her characters come to life for the reader.

Paired Activity With a partner, use a chart like the one shown to examine the methods of characterization used in this story. Go back through the story and look for details that help characterize Miss Strangeworth. Be sure to use the details you included in your word web. Tell what each piece of information suggests about the main character, and identify the method of characterization being used by the author. A few examples have been given.

Miss Strangeworth		
What the story says	**What it tells me about her**	**Method of characterization**
She walked daintily	Very proper and careful	Physical appearance
Knew everyone in town	Well-known; long-time resident	Direct comment

Choices & CHALLENGES

Writing Options

1. Personal Narrative Write a short narrative about meeting someone for the first time. Then tell whether or not your first impression was accurate. You might use a chart like the one shown to organize your thoughts.

Meeting a New Friend	
First Impressions	Later Impressions

Writing Handbook
See pages 1153–1154: Narrative Writing.

2. Letter to the Editor Pretend that you are one of the townspeople in this story. Write a letter to the editor of your local newspaper and express your opinion about Miss Strangeworth's behavior and about how she could make amends for what she has done.

Place the letter in your **Working Portfolio.**

3. Script of a Chat Imagine how Mrs. Harper might react the next time she meets Miss Strangeworth. Write the script for a conversation between the two women.

Activities & Explorations

1. Two-Faced Drawing How would you describe the two "faces" of Miss Strangeworth? Create a drawing that illustrates two different aspects of her life and personality. ~ **ART**

2. News Interview How do you think Miss Strangeworth would react to the questions of a local news reporter? With a partner, prepare a list of questions that you would like to ask Miss Strangeworth and the answers you think she would give. Then conduct your news interview in front of other classmates.
~ **SPEAKING AND LISTENING**

Inquiry & Research

Unexpected Behavior Many incidents in real life involve the unexpected, sometimes criminal, behavior of a seemingly well-mannered person. Often, family and friends are completely surprised by what the person has done. Look for reports of such incidents in newspapers, magazines, or television broadcasts. Write a paragraph summarizing one such incident. Read your paragraph to classmates and then discuss this question: Is it possible for family and friends to miss early warnings of a person's unexpected behavior?

Vocabulary in Action

EXERCISE: CONTEXT CLUES On your paper, write the Words to Know that best fill the blanks in the passage below.

Everyone respects Miss Strangeworth. Her gracious way of life is ___1___ among the townspeople, who often speak of it with pride. They gaze with ___2___ pleasure at her roses. They appreciate her concern about how the library spends its ___3___.

She does not, however, return the respect that the townspeople feel for her. She keeps her feelings hidden, of course, and speaks ___4___ to everyone. Inwardly, though, she regards her neighbors as ___5___ people, wicked through and through. They have done few wrongs so far, but she sees their ___6___ evil. She believes that if this evil goes ___7___, it will take over the world.

It is ___8___ strange that the most ___9___, or blameworthy, actions in the story are performed by Miss Strangeworth. Her cruel letters are all based on suspicions, which she finds much easier to deal with than facts. One of the persons who receives a letter, however, gets revenge on Miss Strangeworth. This person doesn't ___10___ her, making her leave forever; the person just kills what she loves most in the world—her roses.

Building Vocabulary
For an in-depth study of context clues, see page 103.

WORDS TO KNOW				
appropriation	consequently	indulgently	proverbial	reprehensible
banished	degraded	potential	rapt	unchecked

Grammar in Context: Proper Nouns

The following passage explains why the main character in the short story "The Possibility of Evil" does not sign her name to the nasty letters she writes.

> If she had been asked, she would have said that her name, Adela Strangeworth, a name honored in the town for so many years, did not belong on such trash.

A **proper noun** names a specific person, place, or thing. Writers sometimes use proper nouns to provide clues about a character or place and to add realism or precision to a story. For example, the name *Strangeworth* underscores the main character's odd nature.

Apply to Your Writing In fiction writing, carefully chosen proper nouns can help you

- suggest traits of a character or place
- create a more real-world feel to a story
- convey tone and attitude

Usage Tip: Always capitalize proper nouns.

WRITING EXERCISE For each sentence, make up a proper noun that suggests traits of a character or place, adds realistic details, or conveys a certain tone.

Example: *Original* No one, including her cousin, Mayor _____, cares about the damage to her roses.

Rewritten No one, including her cousin, Mayor Bosswell, cares about the damage to her roses.

1. Adela thinks of her town, named _____, as something that belonged to her.
2. Miss Strangeworth's favorite rose is called _____.
3. Helen and Don Crane feed their baby only the best food, _____.
4. Miss Strangeworth's neighbors, the _____, hope she will leave them money when she dies.
5. The librarian's assistant is reading _____ when Miss Strangeworth walks in.

Connect to the Literature Miss Strangeworth lives on Pleasant Street. Why do you think the author chose the name Pleasant Street? Explain your answer.

Grammar Handbook Capitalization, p. 1203

Shirley Jackson
1916–1965

Other Works
The Sundial
The Haunting of Hill House

Novelist at 16 When Shirley Jackson was just 16 years old, she grew weary of the book she was reading and decided to write her own. She hurriedly composed a murder mystery and then read it to her family. She was disappointed by their lukewarm reaction, however, and decided never to write again. Fortunately, Jackson changed her mind. By the time she was a student at Syracuse University in New York, she had already chosen writing as a career and had set a goal for herself of writing at least 1,000 words a day.

A Little Humor Jackson guarded her privacy and was hesitant to discuss her family in public. Still, some of her stories are undoubtedly auto-biographical. These are not, however, her stories of cruelty, evil, prejudice, and mass hysteria. Jackson also wrote two collections of extremely funny stories called *Life Among the Savages* and *Raising Demons.* They describe hilarious events that apparently occurred in her own family while she and her husband were raising their four children in North Bennington, Vermont.

A Sad Ending While writing one of her last novels, Jackson began to suffer from health problems, including asthma, arthritis, and anxiety. In spite of her illness, however, she wrote *We Have Always Lived in the Castle*, a bestseller that was eventually turned into a Broadway play. A few years later, while working on her last novel, Jackson died quite suddenly from heart failure at the age of 48.

The Censors

Short Story by **LUISA VALENZUELA** (lōō-ē′sä vä′len-zwĕ′lä)

"These things happen the minute you're careless."

Connect to Your Life

Watch What You Say What does the word *censorship* mean to you? With your class, create a word web, like the one shown, to explore the meaning of censorship and to give examples of different types of censorship.

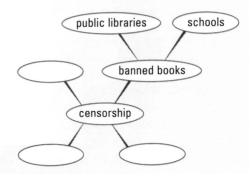

Build Background

A Heavy Hand Although every form of government has employed censorship to some degree, especially in times of war, the strictest censorship is most often found in dictatorships. In the 1960s and 1970s, a number of Latin American countries, including Luisa Valenzuela's native Argentina, were governed by military dictators. These leaders often employed censorship to control their opponents and limit the free expression of ideas. Their controls included the closing of newspapers and magazines, the suppression of public meetings, and censorship of the arts, especially literature. "The Censors" focuses on a common type of censorship—the reading of personal letters in order to control the flow of information and guard against acts of rebellion. The story, inspired by the political situation in Argentina, takes place in a fictional Latin American setting.

> WORDS TO KNOW
> **Vocabulary Preview**
> conniving   subtle
> irreproachable   subversive
> staidness

Focus Your Reading

LITERARY ANALYSIS **IRONY** When something happens that is just the opposite of what you'd expect—or when you say one thing but you obviously mean something else—that is **irony.** Irony can be playful and poke fun at something, or it can be deadly serious or tragic. Irony is what you have when the fire station burns down. As you read this story, see if you notice anything **ironic** about it.

ACTIVE READING **IDENTIFYING AUTHOR'S PURPOSE** A writer can have various purposes for writing. Usually these include one or more of the following:

- to entertain
- to inform or explain
- to express an opinion
- to persuade

READER'S NOTEBOOK As a writer of fiction, Valenzuela surely wanted to tell a good, entertaining story. Still, as you read "The Censors," think about what other purposes she may have had in mind, and jot them down.

Luisa Valenzuela

THE CENSORS

P oor Juan!¹ One day they caught him with his guard down before he could even realize that what he had taken as a stroke of luck was really one of fate's dirty tricks. These things happen the minute you're careless, as one often is. Juancito² let happiness—

a feeling you can't trust—get the better of him when he received from a confidential source Mariana's new address in Paris and knew that she hadn't forgotten him. Without thinking twice, he sat down at his table and wrote her a letter. *The* letter that now keeps his mind off his job during the day and won't let him sleep at night (what had he scrawled, what had he put on that sheet of paper he sent to Mariana?).

Juan knows there won't be a problem with the letter's contents, that it's irreproachable, harmless. But what about the rest? He knows that they examine, sniff, feel, and read between the lines of each and every letter, and check its tiniest comma and most accidental stain. He knows that all letters pass from hand to hand and go through all sorts of tests in the huge

---

1. **Juan** (hwän).
2. **Juancito** (hwän-sē'tô): an affectionate nickname for Juan.

186

censorship offices and that, in the end, very few continue on their way. Usually it takes months, even years, if there aren't any snags; all this time the freedom, maybe even the life, of both sender and receiver is in jeopardy. And that's why Juan's so troubled: thinking that something might happen to Mariana because of his letters. Of all people, Mariana, who must finally feel safe there where she always dreamt she'd live. But he knows that the Censor's Secret Command operates all over the world and cashes in on the discount in air fares; there's nothing to stop them from going as far as that hidden Paris neighborhood, kidnapping Mariana, and returning to their cozy homes, certain of having fulfilled their noble mission.

Well, you've got to beat them to the punch, do what everyone tries to do: sabotage the machinery, throw sand in its gears, get to the bottom of the problem so as to stop it.

This was Juan's sound plan when he, like many others, applied for a censor's job—not because he had a calling[3] or needed a job: no, he applied simply to intercept his own letter, a consoling albeit unoriginal idea. He was hired immediately, for each day

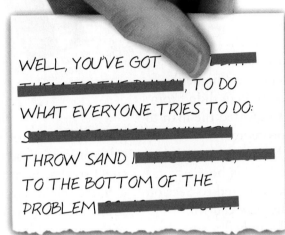

WELL, YOU'VE GOT ~~THEM TO THE PUNCH~~, TO DO WHAT EVERYONE TRIES TO DO: ~~SABOTAGE THE MACHINERY~~ THROW SAND I~~N ITS GEARS, GET~~ TO THE BOTTOM OF THE PROBLEM ~~SO AS TO STOP IT.~~

more and more censors are needed and no one would bother to check on his references.

Ulterior motives[4] couldn't be overlooked by the Censorship Division, but they needn't be too strict with those who applied. They knew how hard it would be for the poor guys to find the letter they wanted and even if they did, what's a letter or two when the new censor would snap up so many others? That's how Juan managed to join the Post Office's Censorship Division, with a certain goal in mind.

The building had a festive air on the outside that contrasted with its inner <u>staidness</u>. Little by little, Juan was absorbed by his job, and he felt at peace since he was doing everything he could to get his letter for Mariana. He didn't even worry when, in his first month, he was sent to Section K where envelopes are very carefully screened for explosives.

It's true that on the third day, a fellow worker had his right hand blown off by a letter, but the division chief claimed it was sheer negligence on the victim's part. Juan and the other

---

3. **had a calling:** had an inner urge to go into a particular occupation or career.
4. **ulterior motives:** reasons for doing something that are concealed in order to deceive.

WORDS TO KNOW   **staidness** (stād'nĭs) *n.* a quiet, often strait-laced dignity

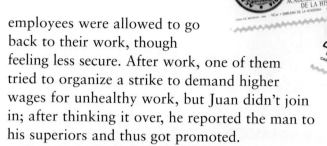

employees were allowed to go back to their work, though feeling less secure. After work, one of them tried to organize a strike to demand higher wages for unhealthy work, but Juan didn't join in; after thinking it over, he reported the man to his superiors and thus got promoted.

You don't form a habit by doing something once, he told himself as he left his boss's office. And when he was transferred to Section F, where letters are carefully checked for poison dust, he felt he had climbed a rung in the ladder.

By working hard, he quickly reached Section E, where the job became more interesting, for he could now read and analyze the letters' contents. Here he could even hope to get hold of his letter, which, judging by the time that had elapsed, had gone through the other sections and was probably floating around in this one.

Soon his work became so absorbing that his noble mission blurred in his mind. Day after day he crossed out whole paragraphs in red ink, pitilessly chucking many letters into the censored basket. These were horrible days when he was shocked by the <u>subtle</u> and <u>conniving</u> ways employed by people to pass on <u>subversive</u> messages; his instincts were so sharp that he found behind a simple "the weather's unsettled" or "prices continue to soar" the wavering hand of someone secretly scheming to overthrow the Government.

His zeal brought him swift promotion. We don't know if this made him happy. Very few letters reached him in Section B—only a handful passed the other hurdles—so he read them over and over again, passed them under a magnifying glass, searched for microprint with an electronic microscope, and tuned his sense of smell so that he was beat by the time he made it home. He'd barely manage to warm up his soup, eat some fruit, and fall into bed, satisfied with having done his duty. Only his darling mother worried, but she couldn't get him back on the right track. She'd say, though it wasn't always true: Lola called, she's at the bar with the girls, they miss you, they're waiting for you. Or else she'd leave a bottle of red wine on the table. But Juan wouldn't overdo it: any distraction could make him lose his edge, and the perfect censor had to be alert, keen, attentive, and sharp to nab cheats. He had a truly patriotic task, both self-denying and uplifting.

His basket for censored letters became the best fed as well as the most cunning basket in the whole Censorship Division. He was about to congratulate himself for having finally discovered his true mission, when his letter to Mariana reached his hands. Naturally, he censored it without regret. And just as naturally, he couldn't stop them from executing him the following morning, another victim of his devotion to his work. ❖

Translated by David Unger

Connect to the Literature

1. What Do You Think?
What was your reaction to the ending of the story?

> **Comprehension Check**
> • Why does Juan become a censor?
> • What does Juan do when he finds his letter?
> • What finally happens to Juan?

Think Critically

2. What is your opinion of Juan? What kind of **character** is he? Support your opinion with examples from the story.

3. Explain how and why Juan seems to change during the course of his work as a censor.

> **THINK ABOUT**
> • his initial **motivations**
> • his attitude toward work and duty
> • his gradual changes in attitude

4. **ACTIVE READING** **IDENTIFYING AUTHOR'S PURPOSE** Look at what you wrote in your **READER'S NOTEBOOK** about this writer's purpose. In addition to telling an entertaining story, what else do you think Valenzuela's purpose might be?

> **THINK ABOUT**
> • issues of censorship
> • issues of patriotism

Extend Interpretations

5. What If? Valenzuela includes no **dialogue** in this story but refers to conversations that take place. Choose such a moment in the story and write what you imagine the dialogue would be. For example, you might write the actual conversation between Juan and his supervisor as he reports the planned strike or the talk between Juan and his worried mother.

6. Connect to Life Why do you think censorship is more severe in dictatorships than in democracies? Do you think that censorship is necessary in certain circumstances?

Literary Analysis

IRONY **Irony** is the contrast between what happens and what is expected to happen. In this story it is ironic that a man who is afraid of censorship should go to work as a censor. This is an example of **situational irony.**

Verbal irony occurs when one expresses a meaning by using words that carry the opposite meaning. In the middle of a blizzard you say, "What a beautiful day!" This is sometimes called **sarcasm.**

Finally, imagine watching a movie in which a man is walking in the woods. You the viewer can see a snake waiting in the path ahead, but the man walks on, still unaware of the danger. This is **dramatic irony**—the contrast between what a character knows and what the reader or audience knows.

Cooperative Learning Activity With a partner, make a chart like the one below, and fill in the blanks. Then look for one or two more examples of irony to add to the chart.

Example of Irony	Type of Irony
Juan is afraid of censorship.	Situational irony
BUT: Juan becomes a censor.	
Kidnapping is _____ .	
BUT: Kidnapping is called "a noble mission."	

Choices & CHALLENGES

Writing Options

1. Dramatic Scene Imagine living in a dictatorship in which the government censors all writing and people can be arrested for what they say. Write a brief dramatic scene depicting life in such a society.

2. Juan's Letter Write the letter that Juan writes to Mariana. Then censor it as you think Juan might have. Explain to the class how you decided to censor it.

3. List of Rules Create a list of regulations for the workers in the Post Office's Censorship Division. Include at least five do's and five don'ts.

Activities & Explorations

1. Report Card With a partner, evaluate Juan as a citizen. Create a list of criteria by which to judge him, and then give him a grade for each of these qualities. Share your results with your classmates.
~ SPEAKING AND LISTENING

2. Teacher Interviews Conduct interviews with administrators or teachers to learn if there are any official policies about censorship that apply to the school library, the school newspaper, or the classroom. **~ SPEAKING AND LISTENING**

Inquiry & Research

American Freedoms "The Censors" is a reaction to modern totalitarianism. Could it ever happen here? Read the Bill of Rights to find the amendments limiting the power of the U.S. government to impose censorship. Research the roles of the Central Intelligence Agency (CIA) and the Federal Bureau of Investigation (FBI) to find out whether censorship of mail or tapping of phone calls is ever legal in the United States. Summarize your findings in a brief report.

 More Online: Research Starter
www.mcdougallittell.com

Vocabulary in Action

EXERCISE: WORD MEANING Use your understanding of the boldfaced words below to complete each of the sentences.

1. An **irreproachable** censor would (a) never work, (b) always do his job well, (c) whine about the demands of the job.

2. A **subtle** message in a letter would (a) be easy to understand, (b) reveal the ignorance of the writer, (c) not be immediately obvious.

3. **Conniving** citizens might be expected to (a) try to fool the authorities, (b) follow all the rules, (c) be reluctant to take action of any kind.

4. A government agency characterized by **staidness** would (a) have a festive air, (b) be noted for its efficiency, (c) be a sober place to work.

5. A **subversive** employee might (a) dutifully attend to details, (b) work to topple the government, (c) look for ways to advance his or her career.

Building Vocabulary
For an in-depth lesson on analyzing the roots of words, see page 191.

Luisa Valenzuela
1938–

Other Works
Something to Smile About
The Heretics
Open Door
Strange Things Happen Here

An Early Start When Luisa Valenzuela was very young, her older sister used to read her horror stories to make her eat. "I would open my mouth in fright and she would stuff it," she reports. Her mother was a well-known writer, and their home in Buenos Aires, Argentina, was often visited by literary figures. At age 17 she published her first short story.

Traveling and Writing Feeling stifled by Argentina's political situation, Valenzuela lived abroad when she could, working in Paris for a broadcasting agency, attending the Writers' Program at the University of Iowa, and becoming a writer-in-residence at Columbia University in New York City. Her best work communicates her ideas about power, politics, and human relationships.

Roots and Base Words

Every day you use words that originate from two ancient languages, and you probably don't give it a thought. Modern English includes many words derived from the ancient Greek and Latin languages. For example, the word *monotone* in the excerpt at the right comes from two Greek words: *mono*, meaning "one," and *tonos*, meaning "tone."

Other words have been formed by combining a Greek or a Latin word part with an English word. Such is the case with the word *monorail*, which is composed of the Greek word *mono* and the Middle English word *raile*.

> And the people—ah, the people
> They that dwell up in the steeple
>   All alone,
> And who, tolling, tolling, tolling,
>   In that muffled monotone . . .
>   —Edgar Allan Poe, "The Bells"

Strategies for Building Vocabulary

Mono is an example of a Greek **root.** A root is a word part that helps to form words. A root cannot stand by itself but must be combined with other word parts, such as prefixes and suffixes. In English, many roots come from Greek and Latin. Knowing the meanings of roots can help you figure out the meaning of unfamiliar English words.

❶ **Understanding Word Families** English words that have the same root may also have related meanings. Such words make up a **word family.** Knowing the meaning of one word in a word family can help you figure out the meanings of other words in the word family. For example, the Latin root *sens,* meaning "to feel," is found in the words *sense, sensory, sensation, sensible, sensitive,* and *resent.* Because these words are in the same word family, their meanings are related. By knowing the meaning of *sense,* you can then figure out the meanings of *sensory* and *resent.*

❷ **Remembering Word Roots** The best way to unlock the meaning of many English words is to recognize word roots. Here is a short list of Greek and Latin word roots you can learn to help you expand your vocabulary. Notice how each word in a word family is related to the meaning of its root.

Greek Root	Meaning	Example
aster, astr	star	asteroid, asterisk, astrology
chron	time	chronology, chronicle
dem	people	democracy, demographics
geo	earth	geography, geology
log	word	logic, dialogue
soph	wise, wisdom	sophomore, sophisticated
tele	far, distant	telephone, telecommunication

Latin Root	Meaning	Example
ject	throw, hurl	eject, reject
junct	join	junction, conjunction
scrib, script	write	description, scripture
solus, sol	alone	solitude, solitary, solo
ten	hold, keep	detention, tenant, tenure
ven, vent	come	convention, event, advent
vol	wish	volunteer, volition

EXERCISE Identify the root for each word pair and give its meaning. Then write a sentence using each word.

1. inject/deject
2. sophistry/sophistical
3. desolate/solitaire
4. scribe/prescription
5. logistics/illogical

THE PRINCESS AND THE TIN BOX
JAMES THURBER

A fable is a brief tale with a moral. It is often meant to instruct the young. You may have read some of Aesop's fables. So when one of America's finest humorists decides to write a fable, here is how it comes out.

Once upon a time, in a far country, there lived a king whose daughter was the prettiest princess in the world. Her eyes were like the cornflower, her hair was sweeter than the hyacinth, and her throat made the swan look dusty.

From the time she was a year old, the princess had been showered with presents. Her nursery looked like Cartier's window.[1] Her toys were all made of gold or platinum or diamonds or emeralds. She was not permitted to have wooden blocks or china dolls or rubber dogs or linen books, because such materials were considered cheap for the daughter of a king.

When she was seven, she was allowed to attend the wedding of her brother and throw real pearls at the bride instead of rice. Only the nightingale, with his lyre of gold, was permitted to sing for the princess. The common blackbird, with his boxwood flute,[2] was kept out of the palace grounds. She walked in silver-and-samite slippers to a sapphire-and-topaz bathroom and slept in an ivory bed inlaid with rubies.

On the day the princess was eighteen, the king sent a royal ambassador to the courts of five neighboring kingdoms to announce that he would give his daughter's hand in marriage to the prince who brought her the gift she liked the most.

The first prince to arrive at the palace rode a swift white stallion and laid at the feet of the princess an enormous apple made of solid gold which he had taken from a dragon who had guarded it for a thousand years. It was placed on a long ebony table set up to hold the gifts of the princess's suitors. The second prince, who came on a gray charger,[3] brought her a nightingale made of a thousand diamonds, and it was placed beside the golden apple. The third prince, riding on a black horse, carried a great jewel box made of platinum and sapphires, and it was placed next to the diamond nightingale. The fourth prince, astride a fiery yellow horse, gave the princess a gigantic heart made of rubies and pierced by an emerald arrow. It was placed next to the platinum-and-sapphire jewel box.

Now the fifth prince was the strongest and handsomest of all the five suitors, but he was the son of a poor king whose realm had been overrun by mice and locusts and wizards and mining engineers so that there was nothing much of value left in it. He came plodding up to the palace of the princess on a plow horse and he brought her a small tin box filled with mica and feldspar and hornblende[4] which he had picked up on the way.

The other princes roared with disdainful laughter when they saw the tawdry[5] gift the fifth prince had brought to the princess. But she examined it with great interest and squealed with

---

1. **Cartier's** (kär-tyāz′) **window:** the show window of a well-known jewelry store.
2. **lyre** (līr) **of gold . . . boxwood flute:** The nightingale's voice is likened to a golden harp; the blackbird's voice is likened to a cheap wooden flute.
3. **charger:** warhorse.
4. **mica** (mī′kə) **and feldspar and hornblende** (hôrn′blĕnd′): three common minerals.
5. **tawdry** (tô′drē): flashy but cheap.

delight, for all her life she had been glutted with precious stones and priceless metals, but she had never seen tin before or mica or feldspar or hornblende. The tin box was placed next to the ruby heart pierced with an emerald arrow.

"Now," the king said to his daughter, "you must select the gift you like best and marry the prince that brought it."

The princess smiled and walked up to the table and picked up the present she liked the

most. It was the platinum-and-sapphire jewel box, the gift of the third prince.

"The way I figure it," she said, "is this. It is a very large and expensive box, and when I am married, I will meet many admirers who will give me precious gems with which to fill it to the top. Therefore, it is the most valuable of all the gifts my suitors have brought me and I like it the best."

The princess married the third prince that very day in the midst of great merriment and high revelry.[6] More than a hundred thousand pearls were thrown at her and she loved it.

Moral: All those who thought the princess was going to select the tin box filled with worthless stones instead of one of the other gifts will kindly stay after class and write one hundred times on the blackboard "I would rather have a hunk of aluminum silicate[7] than a diamond necklace." ❖

---

6. **revelry** (rĕv′əl-rē): noisy celebrating.
7. **aluminum silicate** (sĭl′ĭ-kāt′): the type of chemical compound of which mica, feldspar, and hornblende consist.

James Thurber
1894–1961

Other Works
The Thurber Carnival
My Life and Hard Times

Comedy and Cartoons James Thurber is one of the great humorists of American literature. He made a career out of poking fun at society and created hundreds of stories, essays, and cartoon drawings. Often, his stories center around strong, aggressive women who bully and terrify weak, timid men. This theme is central to one of Thurber's best-known stories, "The Secret Life of Walter Mitty." In his drawings Thurber did not consider himself an artist, but his cartoons had a distinctive style and became as popular as his stories.

The New Yorker After accepting one of his stories, *The New Yorker* magazine gave him a full-time job.

The New Yorker gave Thurber his fame, while he was making important contributions to its style. Although he remained on its staff for only six years, he continued to create stories and cartoons for the magazine for 30 more years. Eventually he contributed 365 short stories, along with articles, essays, poems, and cartoons. He thus played a significant role in creating the sophisticated style that *The New Yorker* still has today.

Near-Blindness Thurber grew up in Ohio and attended Ohio State University. However, an eye injury prevented him from completing all his college courses. This injury occurred during his childhood when Thurber was hit in the eye by an arrow. It led to his near-blindness by the age of 57. When his vision began to fail completely, Thurber started dictating his stories to a secretary. His memory was so sharp that he could easily compose a 2,000-word story in his mind, remember it overnight, and dictate it to his secretary the next day.

Author Study
EDGAR ALLAN POE

> "The story of Edgar Allan Poe is one of the great tragedies of literature."
>
> —David Sinclair

HIS LIFE
HIS TIMES

A Life of Tragedy and Mystery

1809–1849

One of America's literary giants, Edgar Allan Poe has fascinated generations of readers with his haunting poetry and tales of horror. Perhaps because of his own tormented life, Poe had a brilliant talent for depicting the dark side of the mind and heart.

In this Author Study, you will learn more about the life and the literature of this troubled yet intriguing author.

"MANY AND MANY A YEAR AGO" He was born Edgar Poe in Boston on January 19, 1809, the second son of traveling actors. His father deserted the family a year later, and his mother moved to Richmond, Virginia, where she was well-known on stage for her singing and dancing. Her death at the tender age of 24 dealt two-year-old Edgar a crushing blow, from which he never quite recovered.

The orphaned Poe was then taken in by his mother's friend Frances Allan and her husband, John, a successful Richmond merchant. By the time Poe was a teenager, he had received the education and mannerly upbringing of an upperclass gentleman.

1809 Is born Jan. 19 in Boston	1811 Becomes foster son of the Allans	John Allan	1820 Returns to Virginia after five-year stay in Europe
1810		**1815**	**1820**
	1812 United States declares war with Britain.		1821 President James Monroe begins his second term.

"SOME PLACE IN THIS WIDE WORLD" At age 17, Poe entered the University of Virginia. But after his first term, he quarreled with John Allan over money and impulsively ran away. In his bitter parting letter to his foster father, he expressed his hopes of finding "some place in this wide world, where I will be treated—not as you have treated me."

Poe ended up in Boston, where he published his first book of poetry. Although the book didn't sell, Poe had officially begun his chosen career. To keep from starving, however, he enlisted in the U.S. Army at Fort Independence in Boston

Poe's Baltimore, Maryland, home from 1832 to 1835

Harbor and served as a model soldier for 18 months.

Then suddenly Poe received word from John Allan that his beloved foster mother had died. Grief-stricken at her death, both foster father and son attempted a reconciliation. Although Allan refused to give Poe money to pursue a literary career, he did agree to send him to the U.S. Military Academy in West Point, New York, so that Poe could become an officer. The reconciliation was short-lived, however, and Allan eventually disowned Poe.

While he was waiting for his application to West Point to be processed, Poe went to Baltimore to visit his father's family. There he met his aunt, the widow Maria Clemm, and her daughter, Virginia, among

LITERARY Contributions

The most tragic aspect of Edgar Allan Poe's career is that full recognition of his genius did not come in his lifetime. Yet nearly 150 years after his death his work continues to influence writers.

Master of the Short Story Along with Nathaniel Hawthorne, Poe helped to shape and define the short story form with such works as the following:

"Ligeia" (1838)
"The Fall of the House of Usher" (1839)
"The Masque of the Red Death" (1842)
"The Pit and the Pendulum" (1842)
"The Black Cat" (1843)
"The Gold Bug" (1843)
"The Tell-Tale Heart" (1843)
"The Cask of Amontillado" (1846)

Father of the Detective Story In the following works, Poe introduced the first amateur detective, inspiring countless more:

"The Murders in the Rue Morgue" (1841)
"The Purloined Letter" (1845)

Prolific Poet "The Raven" (1845) is not only Poe's most famous poem, it may be the most famous poem ever written. His other poems include the following:

"To Helen" (1831)
"Lenore" (1831)
"Annabel Lee" (1849)
"For Annie" (1849)
"The Bells" (1849)
"El Dorado" (1849)

Poe's room at the University of Virginia

| 1826 Enrolls in the University of Virginia | 1827 Publishes *Tamerlane and Other Poems* | 1829 Frances Allan dies. | 1830 Writes "To Helen"; enters West Point | 1831 Publishes *Poems: Second Edition* |

1825 **1830**

| 1823 Mexico becomes a republic. | 1824 Beethoven completes Symphony No. 9. | 1828 Noah Webster publishes *An American Dictionary of the English Language;* Andrew Jackson is elected president. | 1830 Nat Turner leads slave rebellion in Virginia. |

other relatives. Poe was warmly welcomed by these relatives, especially Maria Clemm, who mothered him like a son.

Poe was desperately unhappy during his stay at West Point. Although he excelled in his studies, his personality was not suited to the life of a soldier. He also missed his new-found family in Baltimore, and he sought escape from his loneliness in alcohol.

"THE MOST NOBLE OF PROFESSIONS"

After about eight months, Poe left West Point determined to be a writer. He returned to Baltimore to join the loving but poverty-stricken Clemm household and to devote himself to literature. His big break came in 1833 when he won the $50 first prize for his story "Ms. Found in a Bottle."

Over the next ten years, Poe worked for several leading literary magazines, contributing stories, poems, and reviews. Despite his success at getting published, however, Poe was never able to make very much money. His great comfort continued to be his adopted family, and in 1836, Poe married his cousin Virginia, shortly before her 14th birthday. The marriage occasioned some gossip at the time, but by all accounts it was a happy one.

Then in 1842, another tragedy rocked Poe's life. Virginia burst a blood vessel while she was singing and almost died. She never fully recovered. Five years later, she died of consumption, an infectious disease also known as pulmonary tuberculosis. By this time, Poe was a wreck emotionally, physically, and mentally. In the last year of his life, he rallied somewhat and frequently traveled among the literary centers of the country—New York, Boston, Philadelphia, Baltimore, and Richmond—to give readings and lectures. And he never regretted his choice of a career. In his last year, he wrote to a friend: "Literature is the most noble of professions. In fact, it is about the only one fit for a man."

In the end, Poe's death at age 40 was as mysterious as it was tragic. He was found semiconscious, wandering around a polling place in Baltimore. After four days in a hospital, during which he never fully regained consciousness, Poe died of what was diagnosed as "congestion of the brain." Theories explaining the actual cause of his death are debated today. He remains a figure shrouded in mystery.

 More Online: Author Link
www.mcdougallittell.com

 LaserLinks: Background for Reading
Author Background

| 1835 Becomes editor of *Southern Literary Messenger* in Richmond | 1836 Marries Virginia Clemm | 1839 Publishes *Tales of the Grotesque and Arabesque* | 1841 Becomes editor of *Graham's Magazine* |

Poe

1835 — **1840**

| 1835 Samuel Colt patents the revolver. | 1837 Nathaniel Hawthorne publishes *Twice-Told Tales*. | 1838 Underground Railroad is organized; Frederick Douglass escapes slavery. |

The Masque of the Red Death, 1964

The Pit and the Pendulum, 1961

The Black Cat, 1934

Murders in the Rue Morgue, 1964

Books to Film

Starting in the silent-film era and continuing through the 1960s, Hollywood adapted several of Poe's horror classics for the big screen. Low on budget and high on eerie, gothic settings, these movies often strayed from Poe's plots and generally produced more guffaws than goosebumps. Sinister characters were portrayed by Hollywood's own masters of horror, including Boris Karloff, Bela Lugosi, and Vincent Price.

Illness and Poverty

Imagine what it was like about 150 years ago, before electricity, central heating, bathrooms, aspirin, antiseptic, and antibiotics. Back then, a fever or a bad cold could kill you. Now imagine what it was like to be poor and without those basics. In the winter of 1846, Edgar and Virginia Poe, along with her mother, Mrs. Clemm, were living in the small town of Fordham, New York. A friend who visited them wrote this poignant description of the ailing Virginia:

> There was nothing on the bed, . . . but a snow white counterpane and sheets. The weather was cold, and the sick lady had the dreadful chills that accompany the hectic fever of consumption. She lay on the straw bed, wrapped in her husband's great coat, with a large tortoiseshell cat on her bosom. The wonderful cat seemed conscious of her great usefulness. The coat and the cat were the sufferer's only means of warmth.

Virginia Clemm Poe

1845
Publishes "The Raven," which makes him famous

1847
Virginia dies.

1848
Moves back to Richmond

1849
Dies Oct. 7 in Baltimore; "Annabel Lee" is published.

1845 — **1850**

1844
First telegraph line opens from Washington, D.C., to Baltimore.

1846
War erupts between United States and Mexico.

1848
First women's rights convention is held in Seneca Falls, New York.

Poe's grave in Baltimore

"The death of a beautiful woman is, unquestionably, the most poetical topic in the world."
—Edgar Allan Poe

Annabel Lee ❧ The Bells

Poetry by EDGAR ALLAN POE

Connect to Your Life

Why Poetry? Think of the last time you read a poem or listened to a song. What effect did the experience have on you? Why do you think writers sometimes choose to express feelings or thoughts in a poem rather than in another form of writing? Jot down your responses.

Build Background

Poetry of Poe Edgar Allan Poe believed the death of a beautiful woman to be the topic most worthy of poetry. The first poem you will read, "Annabel Lee," is his loving tribute to his young wife, Virginia. He probably started composing the poem even before she died, as a way of coping with the agony of her five-year illness. The poem was published on the day of Poe's own death.

Poe also felt that a poem should possess musical qualities, for he viewed music as one of the highest forms of artistic expression. The second poem, "The Bells," was written by Poe as an experiment with the more musical aspects of poetry.

Focus Your Reading

LITERARY ANALYSIS **SOUND DEVICES** Poe used every poetic technique available to transform his words into music, including the following:

Rhyme: similar sounds at the ends of two or more words (ag<u>o</u> and kn<u>ow</u>)

Alliteration: repetition of consonant sounds at the beginnings of words (<u>s</u>ounding <u>s</u>ea)

Assonance: repetition of a vowel sound within nonrhyming words (n<u>i</u>ght, t<u>i</u>de, l<u>ie</u>)

While you are reading the poems, notice how "Annabel Lee" becomes increasingly musical and how closely "The Bells" echoes the actual sounds of bells.

ACTIVE READING **UNDERSTANDING POETRY** Be aware that Poe's vocabulary and complex sentence structure may challenge you. Use these suggestions:

- Try reading the poems aloud to help you hear the musical quality of the words.
- Pay attention to the punctuation, which signals where an idea breaks or stops. Punctuation can also suggest the mood or emotion behind a phrase.
- Refer to the Guide for Reading annotations for definitions of difficult words or phrases.
- Read each poem more than once.

📖 **READER'S NOTEBOOK** Record any questions you may have about the poems as you read.

Annabel Lee

Study of a Head for The Mill, Sir Edward Coley Burne-Jones (1833–1898). Graphite and wash, 7¼″ × 6½″, Bankside Gallery, London.

It was many and many a year ago,
   In a kingdom by the sea,
That a maiden there lived whom you may know
   By the name of Annabel Lee;—
5   And this maiden she lived with no other thought
   Than to love and be loved by me.

She was a child and *I* was a child,
   In this kingdom by the sea,
But we loved with a love that was more than love—
10   I and my Annabel Lee—
With a love that the wingéd seraphs of Heaven
   Coveted her and me.

And this was the reason that, long ago,
   In this kingdom by the sea,
15 A wind blew out of a cloud by night
   Chilling my Annabel Lee;

11 seraphs (sĕr′əfs): any of the highest order of angels.
12 coveted: envied.

So that her high-born kinsmen came
    And bore her away from me,
To shut her up in a sepulcher
20   In this kingdom by the sea.

The angels, not half so happy in Heaven,
    Went envying her and me;
Yes! that was the reason (as all men know,
    In this kingdom by the sea)
25 That the wind came out of the cloud chilling
    And killing my Annabel Lee.

But our love it was stronger by far than the love
    Of those who were older than we—
    Of many far wiser than we—
30 And neither the angels in Heaven above
    Nor the demons down under the sea
Can ever dissever my soul from the soul
    Of the beautiful Annabel Lee:—

For the moon never beams without bringing me dreams
35   Of the beautiful Annabel Lee;
And the stars never rise but I feel the bright eyes
    Of the beautiful Annabel Lee;
And so, all the night-tide, I lie down by the side
Of my darling, my darling, my life and my bride
40   In her sepulcher there by the sea—
    In her tomb by the side of the sea.

19 sepulcher (sĕp'əl-kər): a place for burial; tomb.

32 dissever: disunite; separate.

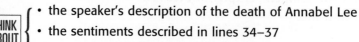

Thinking Through the Literature

1. After reading "Annabel Lee," what images linger in your mind?

2. What effect does this poem have on you? What words, phrases, or images do you think contribute to this effect?

3. How well is the speaker coping with his bride's death?

> THINK ABOUT
> - the speaker's description of the death of Annabel Lee
> - the sentiments described in lines 34–37
> - the speaker's nightly activities, described in lines 38–41

4. How would you define the speaker's love for Annabel Lee? Would you want to feel or be the object of such a love? Explain why or why not.

The Bells

I

Hear the sledges with the bells—
    Silver bells!
What a world of merriment their melody foretells!
    How they tinkle, tinkle, tinkle,
5   In the icy air of night!
    While the stars that oversprinkle
    All the Heavens, seem to twinkle
        With a crystalline delight;
    Keeping time, time, time,
10   In a sort of Runic rhyme,
To the tintinnabulation that so musically wells
    From the bells, bells, bells, bells,
        Bells, bells, bells—
        From the jingling and the tinkling of the bells.

II

15   Hear the mellow wedding bells—
        Golden bells!
What a world of happiness their harmony foretells!
    Through the balmy air of night
    How they ring out their delight!—
20   From the molten-golden notes,
            And all in tune,
        What a liquid ditty floats
To the turtle-dove that listens while she gloats
        On the moon!
25   Oh, from out the sounding cells,
What a gush of euphony voluminously wells!
            How it swells!
            How it dwells
        On the Future!—how it tells
30   Of the rapture that impels
        To the swinging and the ringing
            Of the bells, bells, bells!—
        Of the bells, bells, bells, bells,
            Bells, bells, bells—
35   To the rhyming and the chiming of the bells!

GUIDE FOR READING

1 sledges (slĕj′ĭz): sleighs.

10 Runic (rōō′nĭk): magical.
11 tintinnabulation
(tĭn′tĭ-năb′yə-lā′shən): ringing.

18 balmy (bä′mē): mild.

22 ditty: a simple song.
23 turtle-dove: a bird resembling a pigeon; **gloats:** gazes with delight.

26 euphony (yōō′fə-nē): sweet sound or harmony; **voluminously** (və-lōō′mə-nəs-lē): so as to fill a large space.

32–34 What effect do you think Poe creates with this use of repetition?

THE BELLS   **201**

III

Hear the loud alarum bells—
Brazen bells!
What tale of terror, now, their turbulency tells!
In the startled ear of Night
40   How they scream out their affright!
Too much horrified to speak,
They can only shriek, shriek,
Out of tune,
In a clamorous appealing to the mercy of the fire—
45   In a mad expostulation with the deaf and frantic fire,
Leaping higher, higher, higher,
With a desperate desire
And a resolute endeavor
Now—now to sit, or never,
50   By the side of the pale-faced moon.
Oh, the bells, bells, bells!
What a tale their terror tells
Of despair!
How they clang and clash and roar!
55   What a horror they outpour
In the bosom of the palpitating air!
Yet the ear, it fully knows,
By the twanging
And the clanging,
60   How the danger ebbs and flows:—
Yes, the ear distinctly tells,
In the jangling
And the wrangling,
How the danger sinks and swells,
65   By the sinking or the swelling in the anger of the bells—
Of the bells—
Of the bells, bells, bells, bells,
Bells, bells, bells—
In the clamor and the clangor of the bells.

37 brazen (brā′zən): made of brass; also, loud or harsh.

40 affright: fear.

45 expostulation (ĭk-spŏs′chə-lā′shən): argument.

56 palpitating (păl′pĭ-tā′tĭng): trembling.

65 by the sinking . . . of the bells: Visualize what is happening at this point. How does this scene contrast with those described earlier in the poem?

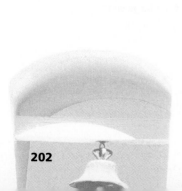

IV

Hear the tolling of the bells—
Iron bells!
What a world of solemn thought their monody compels!
In the silence of the night
How we shiver with affright
75 At the melancholy meaning of the tone!
For every sound that floats
From the rust within their throats
Is a groan.
And the people—ah, the people
80 They that dwell up in the steeple
All alone,
And who, tolling, tolling, tolling,
In that muffled monotone,
Feel a glory in so rolling
85 On the human heart a stone—
They are neither man nor woman—
They are neither brute nor human,
They are Ghouls:—
And their king it is who tolls:—
90 And he rolls, rolls, rolls, rolls
A Paean from the bells!
And his merry bosom swells
With the Paean of the bells!
And he dances and he yells;
95 Keeping time, time, time,
In a sort of Runic rhyme,
To the Paean of the bells—
Of the bells:—
Keeping time, time, time,
100 In a sort of Runic rhyme,
To the throbbing of the bells—
Of the bells, bells, bells—
To the sobbing of the bells:—
Keeping time, time, time,
105 As he knells, knells, knells,
In a happy Runic rhyme,
To the rolling of the bells—
Of the bells, bells, bells:—
To the tolling of the bells—
110 Of the bells, bells, bells, bells,
Bells, bells, bells—
To the moaning and the groaning of the bells.

70 tolling: sounding slowly in repeated single tones.

72 monody (mŏn′ə-dē): poem in which the speaker mourns another's death.

83 monotone: a succession of sounds or words uttered in a single tone of voice.

91 Paean (pē′ən): a song of joyful praise.

105 knells: rings slowly and solemnly.

Connect to the Literature

1. **What Do You Think?**
   What was the first thought you had as you finished "The Bells"?

   Comprehension Check
   - What four types of bells are described in the poem?
   - In what kinds of situations do bells ring?

Think Critically

2. Review the poem, noticing the changes from stanza to stanza. What overall effect on his readers do you think Poe wanted to achieve?

   THINK ABOUT
   - Poe's use of repetition
   - his change of setting from stanza to stanza
   - his choice of words in each stanza

3. Which type of bell could you "hear" most clearly? Explain your response.

4. **ACTIVE READING** **UNDERSTANDING POETRY** Review any notes you took about the poems in your **READER'S NOTEBOOK**. Which line or passage from "The Bells" seemed hardest to understand when you first read it? Briefly explain what techniques you used to make its meaning clearer.

Extend Interpretations

5. **Comparing Texts** Read the two poems again, paying special attention to how they are alike and how they are different. Use a chart like the one shown to record your ideas.

	Annabel Lee	The Bells
Speaker		
Topic		
Effects		

6. **Critic's Corner** To his American contemporary Ralph Waldo Emerson, Poe was merely "the jingle-man," not worthy of respect as a poet. But to the French poets of the late 19th and early 20th centuries, Poe was a great master. After studying these two poems, how do you rate Poe as a poet? How do his poems compare to others you've read?

7. **Connect to Life** Do you agree with Poe's judgment that the death of a beautiful woman is the most poetic topic? If not, what do you think is the most poetic subject?

Literary Analysis

SOUND DEVICES You have seen how Poe uses sounds to create a particular effect and emphasize ideas. Following are three of the devices he uses most often:

- **Rhyme** is the occurrence of a similar or identical sound at the ends of two or more words. Internal rhyme in poetry occurs within a line, such as "chilling / And killing" in "Annabel Lee" and "the swinging and the ringing" in "The Bells." **End rhyme** occurs at the ends of lines in both poems.

- **Alliteration** is the repetition of consonant sounds at the beginnings of words. Most of the alliteration in "The Bells" is done simply through the use of repeated words.

From the bells, bells, bells, bells

- **Assonance** is the repetition of vowel sounds within nonrhyming words.

mellow wedding bells

Activity Go through the poems and find examples of rhyme, alliteration, and assonance. As you find more examples, try to explain what effects you think these sound devices create.

Letter to Maria Clemm

Letter by Edgar Allan Poe

Preparing to Read

Build Background

In the summer of 1835, the 26-year-old Poe was working in Richmond, Virginia, and sending some of his meager paycheck ($10 a week) to help support his aunt Maria Clemm and her 13-year-old daughter, Virginia, in Baltimore. Then Poe received a letter from his aunt saying that a cousin, Neilson Poe, had offered to educate and support Virginia in his home. Poe's reply to his aunt expressed what he thought of this proposed arrangement.

Focus Your Reading

Letters, diaries, newspaper articles, and other firsthand accounts are called **primary sources**. When you read such a document by a historical figure, look for evidence of the author's personality or for details that can provide insights about his or her work. Also look for reflections of the times he or she lived in.

Aug: 29th

My dearest Aunty,

I am blinded with tears while writing this letter—I have no wish to live another hour. Amid sorrow, and the deepest anxiety your letter reached [me]—and you well know how little I am able to bear up under the pressure of grief—My bitterest enemy would pity me could he now read my heart—My last my last my only hold on life is cruelly torn away—I have no desire to live and *will not*. But let my duty be done. I love, *you know* I love Virginia passionately devotedly. I cannot express in words the fervent devotion I feel towards my dear little cousin—my own darling. But what can [I] say. Oh think for me for I am incapable of thinking. All [my] thoughts are occupied with the supposition that both you & she will prefer to go with N. Poe; I do sincerely believe that your *comforts* will for the present be secured—I cannot speak as regards your peace—your happiness. You have both tender hearts —and you will always have the reflection that my agony is more than I can bear—that you have driven me to the grave—for love like mine can never be gotten over. It is useless to disguise the truth that when Virginia goes with N. P. that I shall never behold her again—that is absolutely sure. Pity me, my dear Aunty, pity me. I have no one now to fly to—I am among strangers, and my wretchedness is more than I can bear. It is useless to expect advice from me—what can I say? Can I, in honour & in truth say—Virginia! do not go!—do not go where you can be comfortable & perhaps happy—and on the other hand can I calmly resign my—life itself. If she had truly loved me would she not have rejected the offer with scorn? Oh God have mercy on me! If she goes with N. P. what are you to do, my own Aunty?

I had procured a sweet little house in a retired situation on Church hill—newly done up and with a large garden and [ever]y convenience—at only $5 month. I have been dreaming every day & night since of the rapture I should feel in [havin]g my only friends—all I love on Earth with me there, [and] the pride I would take in making you both comfor[table] & in calling her my wife. But the dream is over. Have mercy on me. What have I to live for? Among strangers with *not one soul to love me.* . . .

Adieu my dear Aunty. I *cannot advise you*. Ask Virginia. Leave it to her. Let me have, under her own hand, a letter, bidding me *good bye*—forever—and I may die—my heart will break—but I will say no more.

E A P.

Kiss her for me—a million times

Thinking Through the Literature

1. How do you think Mrs. Clemm and Virginia reacted to Poe's message?

2. What new insights into Edgar Allan Poe did you get from this letter?

3. **Comparing Texts** Reread the poem "Annabel Lee" on page 199 and the paragraphs on pages 196 and 197 that have to do with Virginia Clemm. After reading this primary source, what guesses might you make about the content of the poem?

The Cask of Amontillado

Short Story by EDGAR ALLAN POE

"I must not only punish, but punish with impunity."

Connect to Your Life

Revenge! In the first paragraph of this story, the narrator, Montresor (môn'trĕ-sôr'), vows revenge. He not only wants to make known the wrongs he feels have been done to him, but he also wants to punish the wrongdoer. Think about a time when you felt wronged or unfairly treated. In the heat of the moment, did you feel like getting even? How did you eventually react? Discuss one or two such incidents with a partner.

Build Background

Carnival This story takes place in a European country, perhaps Italy or France, during carnival. Mainly celebrated in Roman Catholic regions, carnival is a time of festival just before the 40-day period of fasting known as Lent. During carnival, people wear fanciful costumes, attend balls, and participate in feasts. Mardi Gras in New Orleans originated from this European celebration.

> **WORDS TO KNOW**
> **Vocabulary Preview**
>
> accost   impunity   termination
> destined   preclude   virtuoso
> fetter   repose
> implore   subside

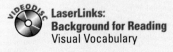 **LaserLinks:**
Background for Reading
Visual Vocabulary

Focus Your Reading

LITERARY ANALYSIS **MOOD** One element that adds an extra chill to Poe's tale is **mood**—the feeling or atmosphere the writer creates for the reader. For example, think about the following description:

> *We passed through a range of low arches, descended, passed on, and descending again, arrived at a deep crypt, in which the foulness of the air caused our flambeaux rather to glow than flame.*

What mood is created by the description of darkness and foul air? As you read, think about other descriptive details that contribute to the mood of the story.

ACTIVE READING **MAKING INFERENCES** You make an **inference** every time you figure something out on the basis of evidence. Usually you infer by combining clues in the text with what you already know from your experiences or other reading. Montresor, who tells this story, is also one of its two main characters. As you read, think about the narrator's actions, his thoughts, and his feelings. Look for insights into his motivation and state of mind. Here is an example of the kind of inference you might make about Montresor, based on clues presented in the story.

READER'S NOTEBOOK
As you read, record any observations that provide clues about the narrator's state of mind in a chart like the one shown.

What the Narrator Says	What I Can Infer
The thousand injuries of Fortunato I had borne as I best could; but when he ventured upon insult, I vowed revenge.	The narrator feels that he has been injured by Fortunato's insults.

THE CASK OF

EDGAR ALLAN POE

AMONTILLADO

The thousand injuries of Fortunato[1] I had borne as I best could; but when he ventured upon insult, I vowed revenge. You, who so well know the nature of my soul, will not suppose, however, that I gave utterance to a threat. *At length* I would be avenged; this was a point definitively settled—but the very definitiveness with which it was resolved, precluded the idea of risk. I must not only punish, but punish with impunity.

ACTIVE READING

CLARIFY What terms does Montresor set up for his revenge here?

A wrong is unredressed when retribution overtakes its redresser. It is equally unredressed when the avenger fails to make himself felt as such to him who has done the wrong.

It must be understood, that neither by word nor deed had I given Fortunato cause to doubt my good-will. I continued, as was my wont, to smile in his face, and he did not perceive that my smile *now* was at the thought of his immolation.[2]

He had a weak point—this Fortunato—although in other regards he was a man to be respected and even feared. He prided himself on his connoisseurship[3] in wine. Few Italians have the true virtuoso spirit. For the most part their enthusiasm is adopted to suit the time and opportunity—to practice imposture[4] upon the British and Austrian *millionaires*. In painting and gemmary[5] Fortunato, like his countrymen, was a quack—but in the matter of old wines he was sincere. In this respect I did not differ from him materially; I was skilful in the Italian vintages myself, and bought largely whenever I could.

It was about dusk, one evening during the supreme madness of the carnival season, that I encountered my friend. He accosted me with excessive warmth, for he had been drinking much. The man wore motley.[6] He had on a tight-fitting parti-striped dress, and his head was surmounted by the conical cap and bells.

---

1. **Fortunato** (fôr′chə-nä′tō).
2. **immolation** (ĭm′ə-lā′shən): death or destruction.
3. **connoisseurship** (kŏn′ə-sûr′shĭp): expertise or authority, especially in the fine arts or in matters of taste.
4. **imposture:** deception.
5. **gemmary** (jĕm′ə-rē): knowledge of precious gems.
6. **motley:** the costume of a court jester or clown.

W O R D S
T O
K N O W

preclude (prĭ-klōōd′) *v.* to make impossible, especially by taking action in advance; prevent
impunity (ĭm-pyōō′nĭ-tē) *n.* freedom from punishment, penalty, or harm
virtuoso (vûr′chōō-ō′sō) *adj.* characteristic of a person with masterly knowledge or skill
accost (ə-kôst′) *v.* to approach and speak to in an aggressive or hostile manner

I was so pleased to see him, that I thought I should never have done wringing his hand.

I said to him: "My dear Fortunato, you are luckily met. How remarkably well you are looking to-day! But I have received a pipe[7] of what passes for Amontillado,[8] and I have my doubts."

"How?" said he. "Amontillado? A pipe? Impossible! And in the middle of the carnival!"

"I have my doubts," I replied; "and I was silly enough to pay the full Amontillado price without consulting you in the matter. You were not to be found, and I was fearful of losing a bargain."

"Amontillado!"

"I have my doubts."

"Amontillado!"

"And I must satisfy them."

"Amontillado!"

"As you are engaged, I am on my way to Luchesi.[9] If anyone has a critical turn, it is he. He will tell me—"

"Luchesi cannot tell Amontillado from Sherry."

"And yet some fools will have it that his taste is a match for your own."

"Come, let us go."

"Whither?"

"To your vaults."

"My friend, no; I will not impose upon your good nature. I perceive you have an engagement. Luchesi—"

"I have no engagement;—come."

"My friend, no. It is not the engagement, but the severe cold with which I perceive you are afflicted. The vaults are insufferably damp. They are encrusted with niter."[10]

"Let us go, nevertheless. The cold is merely nothing. Amontillado! You have been imposed upon. And as for Luchesi, he cannot distinguish Sherry from Amontillado."

Thus speaking, Fortunato possessed himself of my arm. Putting on a mask of black silk, and drawing a *roquelaure*[11] closely about my person, I suffered him to hurry me to my palazzo.[12]

There were no attendants at home; they had absconded to make merry in honor of the time. I had told them that I should not return until the morning, and had given them explicit orders not to stir from the house. These orders were sufficient, I well knew, to insure their immediate disappearance, one and all, as soon as my back was turned.

I took from their sconces two flambeaux,[13] and giving one to Fortunato, bowed him through several suites of rooms to the archway that led into the vaults. I passed down a long and winding staircase, requesting him to be cautious as he followed. We came at length to the foot of the descent and stood together on the damp ground of the catacombs of the Montresors.

The gait of my friend was unsteady, and the bells upon his cap jingled as he strode.

"The pipe?" said he.

"It is farther on," said I; "but observe the white web-work which gleams from these cavern walls."

He turned toward me, and looked into my eyes with two filmy orbs that distilled the rheum of intoxication.[14]

---

7. **pipe:** a wine barrel with a capacity of 126 gallons.

8. **Amontillado** (ə-mŏn´tl-ä´dō): a pale dry sherry.

9. **Luchesi** (lōō-kä´sē).

10. **niter:** a white, gray, or colorless mineral, consisting of potassium nitrate.

11. *roquelaure* (rôk-lōr´) *French:* a man's knee-length cloak, popular during the 18th century.

12. **palazzo** (pə-lät´sō): a palace or mansion.

13. **from . . . flambeaux** (flăm´bōz´): from their wall brackets two lighted torches.

14. **filmy . . . intoxication:** eyes clouded and watery from drunkenness.

"Niter?" he asked, at length.

"Niter," I replied. "How long have you had that cough?"

"Ugh! ugh! ugh!—ugh! ugh! ugh!—ugh! ugh! ugh!—ugh! ugh! ugh!—ugh! ugh! ugh!"

My poor friend found it impossible to reply for many minutes.

"It is nothing," he said, at last.

"Come," I said, with decision, "we will go back; your health is precious. You are rich, respected, admired, beloved; you are happy, as once I was. You are a man to be missed. For me it is no matter. We will go back; you will be ill, and I cannot be responsible. Besides, there is Luchesi—"

"Enough," he said; "the cough is a mere nothing; it will not kill me. I shall not die of a cough."

"True—true," I replied; "and, indeed, I had no intention of alarming you unnecessarily; but you should use all proper caution. A draft of this Medoc[15] will defend us from the damps."

Here I knocked off the neck of a bottle that I drew from a long row of its fellows that lay upon the mold.

"Drink," I said, presenting him the wine.

He raised it to his lips with a leer. He paused and nodded to me familiarly, while his bells jingled.

"I drink," he said, "to the buried that repose around us."

"And I to your long life."

He again took my arm, and we proceeded.

"These vaults," he said, "are extensive."

"The Montresors," I replied, "were a great and numerous family."

"I forget your arms."[16]

"A huge human foot d'or,[17] in a field azure; the foot crushes a serpent rampant whose fangs are imbedded in the heel."

"And the motto?"

"*Nemo me impune lacessit.*"[18]

"Good!" he said.

The wine sparkled in his eyes and the bells jingled. My own fancy grew warm with the  Medoc. We had passed through walls of piled bones, with casks and puncheons[19] intermingling, into the inmost recesses of the catacombs. I paused again, and this time I made bold to seize Fortunato by an arm above the elbow.

"The niter!" I said; "see, it increases. It hangs like moss upon the vaults. We are below the river's bed. The drops of moisture trickle among the bones. Come, we will go back ere it is too late. Your cough—"

"It is nothing," he said; "let us go on. But first, another draft of the Medoc."

I broke and reached him a flagon of De Grâve.[20] He emptied it at a breath. His eyes flashed with a fierce light. He laughed and threw the bottle upward with a gesticulation[21] I did not understand.

I looked at him in surprise. He repeated the movement—a grotesque one.

"You do not comprehend?" he said.

"Not I," I replied.

"Then you are not of the brotherhood."

"How?"

"You are not of the masons."[22]

---

15. **Medoc** (mā-dôk′): a red Bordeaux wine.

16. **arms:** coat of arms—a design that represents one's ancestry and family heritage. (In the following paragraph, Montresor describes his family's coat of arms.)

17. **d'or** (dôr) *French:* gold colored.

18. ***Nemo me impune lacessit*** (nā′mō mā ĭm-pōō′nĕ lä-kĕs′ĭt) *Latin:* Nobody provokes me with impunity.

19. **casks and puncheons:** large containers for storing wine.

20. **De Grâve** (də gräv′): a red Bordeaux wine.

21. **gesticulation** (jə-stĭk′yə-lā′shən): a vigorous motion or gesture.

22. **of the masons:** a Freemason, a member of a social organization with secret rituals and signs.

WORDS TO KNOW   **repose** (rĭ-pōz′) *v.* to lie dead or at rest

"Yes, yes," I said; "yes, yes."

"You? Impossible! A mason?"

"A mason," I replied.

"A sign," he said.

"It is this," I answered, producing a trowel from beneath the folds of my *roquelaure*.

"You jest," he exclaimed, recoiling a few paces. "But let us proceed to the Amontillado."

"Be it so," I said, replacing the tool beneath the cloak, and again offering him my arm. He leaned upon it heavily. We continued our route in search of the Amontillado. We passed through a range of low arches, descended, passed on, and descending again, arrived at a deep crypt,[23] in which the foulness of the air caused our flambeaux rather to glow than flame.

At the most remote end of the crypt there appeared another less spacious. Its walls had been lined with human remains, piled to the vault overhead, in the fashion of the great catacombs of Paris. Three sides of this interior crypt were still ornamented in this manner. From the fourth the bones had been thrown down, and lay promiscuously[24] upon the earth, forming at one point a mound of some size. Within the wall thus exposed by the displacing of the bones, we perceived a still interior recess, in depth about four feet, in width three, in height six or seven. It seemed to have been constructed for no especial use within itself, but formed merely the interval between two of the colossal supports of the roof of the catacombs, and was backed by one of their circumscribing walls of solid granite.

It was in vain that Fortunato, uplifting his dull torch, endeavored to pry into the depth of the recess. Its <u>termination</u> the feeble light did not enable us to see.

ACTIVE READING

PREDICT What do you think Montresor plans to do to Fortunato?

"Proceed," I said; "herein is the Amontillado. As for Luchesi—"

"He is an ignoramus," interrupted my friend, as he stepped unsteadily forward, while I followed immediately at his heels. In an instant he had reached the extremity of the niche, and finding his progress arrested by the rock, stood stupidly bewildered. A moment more and I had <u>fettered</u> him to the granite. In its surface were two iron staples, distant from each other about two feet, horizontally. From one of these depended a short chain, from the other a padlock. Throwing the links about his waist, it was but the work of a few seconds to secure it. He was too much astounded to resist. Withdrawing the key I stepped back from the recess.

"Pass your hand," I said, "over the wall; you cannot help feeling the niter. Indeed it is *very* damp. Once more let me *implore* you to return. No? Then I must positively leave you. But I must first render you all the little attentions in my power."

"The Amontillado!" ejaculated my friend, not yet recovered from his astonishment.

"True," I replied; "the Amontillado."

As I said these words I busied myself among the pile of bones of which I have before spoken. Throwing them aside, I soon uncovered a quantity of building stone and mortar. With these materials and with the aid of my trowel, I began vigorously to wall up the entrance of the niche.

I had scarcely laid the first tier of the masonry[25] when I discovered that the intoxication of Fortunato had in a great measure worn off. The

---

23. **crypt:** an underground chamber serving as a burial place.

24. **promiscuously** (prə-mĭs′kyōō-əs-lē): randomly.

25. **masonry:** stonework.

WORDS TO KNOW	**termination** (tûr′mə-nā′shən) *n.* the end of something; limit or edge
	fetter (fĕt′ər) *v.* to restrain with chains or shackles
	implore (ĭm-plôr′) *v.* to beg; earnestly ask for

earliest indication I had of this was a low moaning cry from the depth of the recess. It was *not* the cry of a drunken man. There was then a long and obstinate silence. I laid the second tier, and the third, and the fourth; and then I heard the furious vibrations of the chain. The noise lasted for several minutes, during which, that I might hearken to it with the more satisfaction, I ceased my labors and sat down upon the bones. When at last the clanking <u>subsided</u>, I resumed the trowel, and finished without interruption the fifth, the sixth, and the seventh tier. The wall was now nearly upon a level with my breast. I again paused, and holding the flambeaux over the mason-work, threw a few feeble rays upon the figure within.

A succession of loud and shrill screams, bursting suddenly from the throat of the chained

form, seemed to thrust me violently back. For a brief moment I hesitated—I trembled. Unsheathing my rapier,[26] I began to grope with it about the recess; but the thought of an instant reassured me. I placed my hand upon the solid fabric of the catacombs, and felt satisfied. I reapproached the wall. I replied to the yells of him who clamored. I re-echoed—I aided—I surpassed them in volume and in strength. I did this, and the clamorer grew still.

It was now midnight, and my task was drawing to a close. I had completed the eighth, the ninth, and the tenth tier. I had finished a portion of the last and the eleventh; there remained but a single stone to be fitted and plastered in. I struggled with its weight; I placed it partially in its <u>destined</u> position. But now there came from out the niche a low laugh that erected the hairs upon my head. It was succeeded by a sad voice, which I had difficulty in recognizing as that of the noble Fortunato. The voice said—

"Ha! ha! ha!—he! he!—a very good joke indeed—an excellent jest. We will have many a rich laugh about it at the palazzo—he! he! he! —over our wine—he! he! he!"

"The Amontillado!" I said.

"He! he! he!—he! he! he!—yes, the Amontillado. But is it not getting late? Will not they be awaiting us at the palazzo, the Lady Fortunato and the rest? Let us be gone."

"Yes," I said, "let us be gone."

"For the love of God, Montresor!"

"Yes," I said, "for the love of God!"

But to these words I hearkened in vain for a reply. I grew impatient. I called aloud,

"Fortunato!"

No answer. I called again,

"Fortunato!"

No answer still. I thrust a torch through the remaining aperture[27] and let it fall within. There came forth in return only a jingling of the bells. My heart grew sick—on account of the dampness of the catacombs. I hastened to make an end of my labor. I forced the last stone into its position; I plastered it up. Against the new masonry I re-erected the old rampart[28] of bones. For the half of a century no mortal has disturbed them. *In pace requiescat!*[29] ❖

---

26. **rapier** (rā′pē-ər): a long, slender sword.

27. **aperture** (ăp′ər-chər): an opening, such as a hole or a gap.

28. **rampart:** fortification; protective barrier.

29. *In pace requiescat* (ĭn pä′kĕ rĕ-kwē-ĕs′kät) *Latin:* May he rest in peace.

WORDS
TO
KNOW

subside (səb-sīd′) *v.* to become less agitated or active; lessen
destined (dĕs′tĭnd) *adj.* determined beforehand; fated **destine** *v.*

THE STORY BEHIND "THE CASK OF AMONTILLADO"

Edward Rowe Snow

While at Fort Independence, Poe [who was a private there in 1827] became fascinated with the inscriptions on a gravestone on a small monument outside the walls of the fort. . . .

Beneath this stone are deposited the remains of Lieut. ROBERT F. MASSIE, of the U. S. Regt. of Light Artillery. . . .

During the summer of 1817, Poe learned, twenty-year-old Lieutenant Robert F. Massie of Virginia had arrived at Fort Independence as a newly appointed officer. Most of the men at the post came to enjoy Massie's friendship, but one officer, Captain Green, took a violent dislike to him. Green was known at the fort as a bully and a dangerous swordsman.

When Christmas vacations were allotted, few of the officers were allowed to leave the fort, and Christmas Eve found them up in the old barracks hall, playing cards. Just before midnight, at the height of the card game, Captain Green sprang to his feet, reached across the table and slapped Lieutenant Massie squarely in the face. "You're a cheat," he roared, "and I demand immediate satisfaction!" . . .

The duel began. Captain Green, an expert swordsman, soon had Massie at a disadvantage and ran him through. Fatally wounded, the young Virginian was carried back to the fort, where he died that afternoon. His many friends mourned the passing of a gallant officer. . . .

Feeling against Captain Green ran high for many weeks, and then suddenly he completely vanished. Years went by without a sign of him, and Green was written off the army records as a deserter.

According to the story which Poe finally gathered together, Captain Green had been so detested by his fellow officers at the fort that they decided to take a terrible revenge on him for Massie's death. . . .

Visiting Captain Green one moonless night, they pretended to be friendly and plied him with wine until he was helplessly intoxicated. Then, carrying the captain down to one of the ancient dungeons, the officers forced his body through a tiny opening which led into the subterranean casemate.[1] . . .

By this time Green had awakened from his drunken stupor and demanded to know what was taking place. Without answering, his captors began to shackle him to the floor, using the heavy iron handcuffs and footcuffs fastened into the stone. Then they all left the dungeon and proceeded to seal the captain up alive inside the windowless casemate, using bricks and mortar. . . .

Captain Green shrieked in terror and begged for mercy, but his cries fell on deaf ears. The last brick was finally inserted, mortar applied, and the room sealed up, the officers believed, forever. Captain Green undoubtedly died a horrible death within a few days. . . .

[In 1905, workmen repairing the fort found the dungeon. To their amazement, they found a skeleton inside, shackled to the floor, with a few fragments of an old army uniform clinging to the bones.]

---

1. **subterranean casemate** (sŭb′tə-rā′nē-ən kās′māt′): a fortified underground or partly underground room with small windows for firing weapons from.

Connect to the Literature

1. **What Do You Think?** Why does Montresor end his story with the Latin phrase meaning "May he rest in peace"?

Comprehension Check
- Why does Montresor want revenge?
- What weakness of Fortunato's does Montresor take advantage of in order to carry out his plan?
- What happens to Fortunato?

Think Critically

2. **ACTIVE READING** **MAKING INFERENCES** Briefly refer to the notes in your **READER'S NOTEBOOK** about the narrator's state of mind. What is your evaluation of Montresor? Is he sane or insane, reliable or unreliable? Are his actions justified, or is he evil and malicious? Support your response with evidence from the text.

3. Do you think Montresor achieves the kind of revenge he says he wants in the first paragraph? Defend your answer.

4. Look back at "The Story Behind 'The Cask of Amontillado'" on page 215. Why might the incident described have captured Poe's imagination? Explain.

Extend Interpretations

5. **Critic's Corner** It has been said that "The Cask of Amontillado" is more powerful because Poe does not include more specific information about Fortunato's insult. Do you agree? Explain why or why not.

6. **Different Perspectives** Some readers feel that Montresor suffers for his crimes, feeling haunted by guilt. Others see him as a criminal for seeming to gloat about his evil act. What do you think will happen to Montresor?

THINK ABOUT
- his deliberate actions
- his reaction to Fortunato's moans and groans
- his state of mind at the end of the story

7. **Comparing Texts** Poe is as well-known for his poetry as for his short stories. Now that you've read examples of each, which form of his writing do you prefer? Discuss your choice with someone who prefers the other form.

8. **Connect to Life** Recall your own experiences with feelings of revenge. Do you think revenge is ever justified on a personal level, or is it better to forgive and forget? Explain.

Literary Analysis

MOOD The overall feeling or atmosphere the writer creates for the reader is called **mood.** Descriptive words, the setting, and figurative language contribute to the mood of a work, as do the sound and rhythm of the language used. Think about the use of repeated sounds in the following example, and notice the effect they create:

I must not only punish, but punish with impunity. A wrong is unredressed when retribution overtakes its redresser.

What mood is created by the repetition? How does the sound of the language affect you? Say this passage aloud, and note what words and sounds are being emphasized.

Activity Find two or three other examples that help create the mood of the story. Identify what kind of mood is being created, and explain how the mood is developed.

POINT OF VIEW The **point of view** is the perspective from which events in a short story or novel are related. A story told in the **first-person point of view** has a narrator who is a character in the story and tells everything in his or her own words. "The Cask of Amontillado" is told from the first-person point of view. You know what Montresor is thinking and feeling, but what can you infer about Fortunato's thoughts and feelings from Montresor's description in this passage?

But now there came from out the niche a low laugh that erected the hairs upon my head. It was succeeded by a sad voice, which I had difficulty in recognizing as that of the noble Fortunato.

THE AUTHOR'S STYLE

Poe's Sinister Stylings

Style is the particular way in which something is written. Word choice, sentence length, imagery, and tone all contribute to a writer's style. Part of Poe's genius comes from the slightly different style he creates for each one of his tales, depending on who's telling the story and what effect or impact Poe wants the story to have.

Key Aspects of Poe's Style

- short sentences or sentences with dashes and other interruptions
- repeated or italicized words that draw attention to the narrator or to a concept
- frequent use of first-person point of view
- rhythm that conveys the intensity of the narrator's thoughts

Analysis of Style

At the right are excerpts from the openings of three famous Poe tales. Study the chart above, and then read each opening carefully. Complete the following activities:

- Find several examples of each stylistic device in the passages. Decide what effect Poe was trying to create in each case.
- Find at least two or three additional stylistic devices that you see at work in any of the three examples.
- Look again at the two poems, the story, and the letter. Choose one, and discuss with other readers the stylistic devices you see being used.

Applications

1. Changing Style Working with a partner, rewrite one of the opening passages, expressing the same ideas but in simpler language. Then read your version and the original aloud, and compare them. What's missing in the changed version? Share your observations with your classmates.

2. Imitation of Style Choose one of the three openings, and write a continuation of the story in the style that Poe has established. Then entertain your classmates with a reading of the piece.

3. Speaking and Listening Alone or with a group, give each opening a dramatic reading to reveal the different characters and moods expressed through Poe's style. Have the class discuss the differences they hear in each of these oral interpretations.

---

from "The Tell-Tale Heart"

True!—nervous—very, very dreadfully nervous I had been and am; but why *will* you say that I am mad? The disease had sharpened my senses—not destroyed—not dulled them. Above all was the sense of hearing acute. I heard all things in the heaven and in the earth. I heard many things in hell. How, then, am I mad? Hearken! and observe how healthily—how calmly I can tell you the whole story.

from "The Black Cat"

For the most wild, yet most homely narrative which I am about to pen, I neither expect nor solicit belief. Mad indeed would I be to expect it, in a case where my very senses reject their own evidence. Yet, mad am I not—and very surely do I not dream. But to-morrow I die, and to-day I would unburthen my soul.

from "The Fall of the House of Usher"

During the whole of a dull, dark, and soundless day in the autumn of the year, when the clouds hung oppressively low in the heavens, I had been passing alone, on horseback, through a singularly dreary tract of country; and at length found myself, as the shades of the melancholy evening drew on, within view of the melancholy House of Usher. I know not how it was—but, with the first glimpse of the building, a sense of insufferable gloom pervaded my spirit.

Writing Options

1. Program Introduction Using language that is appropriate to a formal setting, create a TV host's introduction for "The Cask of Amontillado."

2. Fortunato's Version Retell your favorite part of the story as though Fortunato were the narrator. Be sure to include your impressions of your "friend" and his actions. Put your version of the story in your **Working Portfolio.**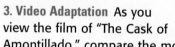

Writing Handbook
See page 1153: Narrative Writing.

Activities & Explorations

1. Sinister Readings Select passages from the story that characterize Montresor as either sincere or insincere. Do an oral interpretation of these passages for classmates. ~ **SPEAKING AND LISTENING**

2. Flow Chart How does someone commit a "perfect" crime? What steps does Montresor take? Make a flow chart that graphically represents each step of Montresor's plan. ~ **VIEWING AND REPRESENTING**

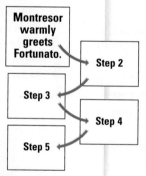

Montresor warmly greets Fortunato.
Step 2
Step 3
Step 4
Step 5

3. Video Adaptation As you view the film of "The Cask of Amontillado," compare the mood created in the film with that evoked in the story. Which did you find more powerful, the story or the film? Discuss your responses with your classmates. ~ **VIEWING AND REPRESENTING**

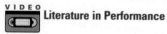
VIDEO Literature in Performance

Inquiry & Research

Science and Medicine Find out how long Fortunato could last in the walled-up niche. What would happen to him after being deprived of fresh air, water, and food? From these gruesome facts, draw some conclusions about how the human body reacts under certain conditions.

Edgar Allan Poe

Author Study Project
CREATING A MULTIMEDIA BIOGRAPHY

Working with a small group, with a partner, or alone, create a multimedia biography of Poe. You may wish to focus on one facet of his life that especially intrigues you: his career, his personal life, or his influence on later writers. Your biography might take the form of a video, a web page, a slide show, a performance, or some combination of products like these. Following is a list of sources and suggestions that can help you complete your research:

Books and Periodicals Look in these resources for images not only of Poe, but also of other writers of his day, including Charles Dickens and Elizabeth Barrett Browning. Possible causes of Poe's death are still debated today, so don't overlook recent newspapers or magazines.

Films and Readings Look for biographies of Poe or performances of his work on videotape or audiotape. Several actors have even taken on the role of Poe himself in one-man performances. Edit excerpts from these performances into a "Best of Poe" presentation.

Computers Try to find as many nonprint materials as possible for your presentation. Use CD-ROMs and the Internet as resources. Try contacting Poe appreciation societies or museums. Look for images of Poe and samples of his handwriting as well as for photographs of his many rented residences.

 **More Online: Research Starter**
www.mcdougallittell.com

Grammar in Context: Compound Verbs

Poe often uses long, carefully crafted sentences to create a sort of "special effect" with words. One way he builds such sentences is through the use of **compound verbs.**

verb
We passed through a range of low arches,
verb   verb
descended, passed on, and descending again,
verb
arrived at a deep crypt.

Notice how this "special-effect" sentence helps the reader to get a sense of the long, twisting path down into the catacombs.

Apply to Your Writing You can use compound verbs to combine several short sentences into longer, more interesting thoughts. Start out by trying two verbs with one subject.

WRITING EXERCISE Use compound verbs to combine the following sets of sentences into one sentence. **Punctuation Tip:** Be sure to follow each verb or verb phrase in a series with a comma.

> **Example: *Original*** The mongrel yelped. It whined. It ran in circles.
> ***Rewritten*** The mongrel yelped, whined, and ran in circles.

1. Carmine picked up the key. She brushed the dirt from it. She turned it over in her hands, examining it.
2. After the masquerade, one quiet figure returned. He glanced around the empty square. He chuckled softly to himself.
3. Montresor bowed politely. He smiled at his friend. Then he reached for the first brick.

Grammar Handbook Punctuation, pp. 1201–1202

Vocabulary in Action

EXERCISE A: CONTEXT CLUES Complete this story summary by choosing the best vocabulary word for each sentence.

Once Montresor had decided to get revenge on Fortunato, then Fortunato's death seemed __1__ to happen. Always careful, Montresor took precautions to __2__ anyone from finding out. Then, one night, Montresor __3__ Fortunato in a friendly way and persuaded him to taste some wine stored in the Montresor family catacombs. Fortunato was quite a __4__ in wine, so he wasn't suspicious. While they were descending into the catacombs, Fortunato began to cough severely. Montresor stopped and __5__ his friend to go back, but Fortunato waved away his concern. Once Fortunato's coughs had __6__, the two men continued on their way. At the __7__ of one corridor was a small recess with a chain and padlock. Swiftly Montresor used the chain and padlock to __8__ Fortunato to the wall, and then he bricked up the recess. Fortunato screamed for help, but no one came. For 50 years, Fortunato has __9__ with Montresor's dead ancestors. Montresor had gotten his revenge with __10__.

EXERCISE B: ASSESSMENT PRACTICE A knowledge of word parts often can help you unlock the meaning of words. The following three prefixes are drawn from your Words to Know.

im- **"not"**   *pre-* **"before"**   *sub-* **"under"**

Use these prefixes to help you choose the best definition for each word below.

1. **precognizant** (a) in disguise (b) a type of cement (c) knowing beforehand
2. **impervious** (a) not vulnerable (b) haughty (c) eager
3. **subterranean** (a) unfamiliar (b) mysterious (c) beneath the earth

Building Vocabulary

Most of the Words to Know in this lesson come from Latin. For an in-depth study of word origins, see page 973.

WORDS TO KNOW					
	accost	fetter	impunity	repose	termination
	destined	implore	preclude	subside	virtuoso

Writing Workshop

Expressing an opinion . . .

From Reading to Writing As you read "The Censors," "The Sniper," and other selections in this unit, you might have felt strongly the unfairness of life that their writers expressed. From time to time, certain issues will move you to speak out as well. One way to make your voice heard is to write an **opinion statement**, in which you express your point of view and back it up with reasons and facts.

For Your Portfolio

WRITING PROMPT Write an opinion statement about an issue that interests you.

> **Purpose:** To give reasons for the opinion you express
>
> **Audience:** Your classmates and friends, members of your community

---

Basics in a Box

Opinion Statement at a Glance

Presents the issue and states your opinion — Introduction

WHY I BELIEVE IT

| Supporting evidence | Supporting evidence | Supporting evidence | — Body |

Summary of opinion — Conclusion

RUBRIC Standards for Writing

A successful opinion statement should

- clearly state the issue and your opinion on it in the introduction
- support your opinion with convincing examples, facts, and statistics
- use language and details appropriate for your audience
- sum up your opinion in the conclusion

Analyzing a Student Model

Joel Goldman
Spring Dale High School

Should School Newspapers Be Censored?

The First and Fourteenth Amendments to the U.S. Constitution guarantee Americans' rights to freedom of speech and freedom of the press—unless those Americans happen to be students. More and more principals are censoring articles in school newspapers, and the courts are upholding their right to do it.

The editors and writers of school newspapers are aware that they cannot print material that is obscene or damaging to anyone's character. As long as they keep those restrictions in mind, I think they should be allowed to include any other material they choose in their publications. School administrators, however, have recently censored articles that are not obscene or libelous, but that merely make the administrators uncomfortable.

In a famous case in Hazelwood, Missouri, the principal removed two articles from the school newspaper—one about the effects of divorce on students and the other about teen pregnancies—that he said were "unsuitable for student readers." Several students sued the school district, saying that the action violated their constitutional rights to freedom of expression. The students took the case all the way to the Supreme Court, which, in 1988, upheld the school principal's right to censor the articles. In my opinion, the Supreme Court was wrong.

I think that one of the most important responsibilities of the educational system is to teach students how to discuss controversial issues in a free society. How can that happen if school administrators won't even allow certain issues to be mentioned? Some administrators say that they are trying to protect students from inappropriate and controversial subject matter. The fact is, though, that censoring stories in the school newspaper does not protect students from inappropriate information. It just makes that information harder to get.

Student editors and writers have a responsibility to discuss issues that their readers are concerned about and need to know. If there is a drug problem in the school, for example, the student newspaper should be able to confront it openly. Not bringing the problem to students' attention will not

RUBRIC
IN ACTION

❶ States the issue and his position on it clearly in the introduction

❷ This writer gives an example to support his statement.
Other Options:
• Quote an expert.
• Provide facts or statistics.

❸ Presents a reason supporting his first point

❹ Uses an example to support his second point

make it go away. It will only make students lose respect for the publication. It will also prevent the editorial staff from learning valuable lessons in freedom and responsibility.

Those who support the rights of school administrators to censor student publications think that student reporters have no more rights than other reporters to have their stories printed. Censorship, they say, is just a lesson in the realities of the publishing world, where the publisher has all the power. Even a reporter for The New York Times, for example, might not get an article on gangs published if the editor of that paper decided against using it for any reason.

My answer to that position is that high school is not the place for student journalists to learn such a lesson. They did not become involved in a demanding extracurricular activity to learn how to be controlled by the administration. The school should give them the opportunity to develop their skills as responsible thinkers, organizers, writers, and citizens, which means exercising their freedoms of speech and of the press. The school's social studies classes teach the value of those freedoms; its extracurricular activities should allow students to put them into practice.

Censorship supporters want students to realize that the people who own their school newspaper—the administrators—are responsible for its content. My position, however, is that the administrators don't own the newspaper; we, the students, and our parents do. The paper is funded with our parents' tax or tuition money. The principal and other administrators have no financial investment in it. Because we actually own the school newspaper, we, therefore, should have the power to control its content.

School newspapers should provide the opportunity for student journalists to gain experience seeking out and reporting on issues that concern students at their school. Student journalists need to use this opportunity to explore and express their constitutional freedoms, not to have those freedoms censored.

> **⑤ Presents the opposing position and answers it with logically developed reasons**

> **⑥ Summarizes his opinion strongly in the conclusion**

Writing Your Opinion Statement

I share no man's opinions; I have my own.
**Ivan Sergeyevich Turgenev,
novelist and playwright**

IDEABank

1. Your Working Portfolio
Look for ideas in one of the **Writing Options** you completed earlier in this unit.
- **TV Talk Show**, p. 160
- **Letter to the Editor**, p. 183

2. Surf the Net
Go online and check into some chat groups. What are the topics of conversation? What is your opinion of them?

3. Get It on Paper
Explore issues that matter to you by freewriting about them. Which do you feel strongest about? Which do you know the most about? Choose one to develop for your opinion statement.

❶ Prewriting

You might generate ideas for your opinion statement by **looking through your journal** to identify issues that interest or bother you. What issues do you mention over and over again? What have you tried to do about those issues? See the **Idea Bank** in the margin for more suggestions. After you select an issue, develop it by following the suggestions below.

Planning Your Opinion Statement

▶ **1. Examine the issue.** Make sure you understand the issue thoroughly. Get all the facts and become familiar with opposing opinions.

▶ **2. Analyze your opinion.** Why do you feel the way you do about the issue? What facts or other evidence supports your opinion?

▶ **3. Gather information.** What additional evidence do you need to support your opinion? Where will you look for this evidence?

▶ **4. Identify your audience.** Who will read your opinion statement? What do they know and feel about the issue? How might you address their opposing views?

▶ **5. Consider the tone of your statement.** Would a humorous or a more serious tone be most effective with your audience? Which approach would you be most comfortable using?

❷ Drafting

The most important aspect of drafting is putting your ideas in writing. You can organize and refine your writing later. Remember, though, that you eventually will need to state your opinion clearly and support it with convincing evidence, such as **examples, facts,** and **statistics.** One way to **organize** your paper is to state each reason and give its supporting details. You also might want to give possible **opposing arguments** and answer them. Be sure as you rework your draft that you present your opinion in the **introduction** and summarize it in the **conclusion.**

Ask Your Peer Reader

- What is my opinion about this issue?
- What were my strongest supporting points?
- What information was weak or unnecessary?
- What more would you like to know about the issue or my opinion?

Need revising help?

Review the **Rubric**, p. 220

Consider **peer reader** comments

Check **Revision Guidelines**, p. 1143

❸ Revising

TARGET SKILL ▶ SUPPORTING STATEMENTS WITH FACTS AND EXAMPLES No matter how strongly you feel about your opinion, your readers will not be convinced unless you give them concrete evidence supporting it. As you revise, look for ways to add facts, statistics, examples, quotations, and other details to your writing.

> *editors and writers*
> Students have a responsibility to discuss issues that their
>
> readers are concerned about and need to know. Not bringing
>
> the problem to students' attention will not make it go away.
>
> *If there is a drug problem in the school, for example,*
>
> *the student newspaper should be able to confront*
>
> *it openly.*

❹ Editing and Proofreading

TARGET SKILL ▶ SUBJECT-VERB AGREEMENT For your opinion statement to be convincing, it must not confuse your readers. Look for verbs that do not agree with their subjects and make them agree in number. Remember that a verb must agree with the main subject of the sentence, not with the noun closest to it.

> Censorship supporters wants students to realize that the people
>
> who own their school newspaper—the administrators—*are* ~~is~~
>
> responsible for its content. My position, however, ~~are~~ *is* that the
>
> administrators don't own the newspaper; we, the students, and
>
> our parents ~~does~~ *do*.

Stumped by subject-verb agreement?

See the **Grammar Handbook**, p. 1205

Publishing IDEAS

• Post your opinion statement on an Internet chat group.

• Submit your opinion statement to your local or school newspaper.

More Online: Publishing Options www.mcdougallittell.com

❺ Reflecting

FOR YOUR WORKING PORTFOLIO What did you enjoy most about writing your opinion statement? How did your opinion change or become strengthened as you wrote? Write responses to these questions and keep them with your opinion statement in your **Working Portfolio.**

Read this opening from the first draft of an opinion statement. The underlined sections may include the following kinds of errors:

- **lack of parallel structure**
- **lack of subject-verb agreement**
- **comma errors**
- **misplaced modifiers**

For each underlined section, choose the revision that most improves the writing.

> Every informed voter in the community <u>support</u> the bill to build an addition
> to our public library. <u>The addition will help solve the library's space problem
> and it will create a more pleasant environment.</u> Currently, the rooms are too
> small to accommodate the number of patrons who <u>use</u> the library. <u>Every day,
> looking for a place to sit, the library is crowded with students and other</u>
> visitors. These people must compete <u>for the available computers and for the
> reference librarians' time.</u> As a high school student, I go to the library <u>to
> conduct research, to use the computers, and for studying.</u>

1. **A.** was supporting
   B. supports
   C. are supporting
   D. Correct as is

2. **A.** The addition will help solve, the library's space problem, and it will create a more pleasant environment.
   B. The addition will help solve, the library's space problem and it will create a more pleasant environment.
   C. The addition will help solve the library's space problem, and it will create a more pleasant environment.
   D. Correct as is

3. **A.** uses
   B. used
   C. is using
   D. Correct as is

4. **A.** Every day the library is crowded with students and other visitors, looking for a place to sit.
   B. Looking for a place to sit, the library is crowded every day with students and other visitors.
   C. The library every day is crowded with students looking for a place to sit and other visitors.
   D. Every day the library crowds students and visitors looking for a place to sit.

5. **A.** for the available computers, and for the reference librarians' time.
   B. for the available computers; and, for the reference librarians' time.
   C. for the available computers, and, for the reference librarians' time.
   D. Correct as is

6. **A.** to research, to use the computers, and for studying
   B. to conduct research, to use the computers, and to study
   C. for researching, using computers, and to study
   D. Correct as is

Need extra help?

See the **Grammar Handbook**

Misplaced Modifiers, p. 1188

Punctuation Chart, pp. 1201–1202

Subject-Verb Agreement, pp. 1198–1199

The Power of Storytelling

In this unit, you have read a variety of stories told in a number of different ways. What impact did these stories have on you? Explore this question by completing one or more of the options in each of the following sections.

The New Novel (1877), Winslow Homer, Watercolor, 9½" × 20½". Museum of Fine Arts, Springfield, Massachusetts. Horace P. Wright Collection.

Reflecting on Theme

OPTION 1

Identifying Conflict and Resolution For some of the fictional characters or real people in this unit, resolving conflict means finding a solution to the problem that confronts them; for others, it means living with the consequences. Make a list of the conflicts portrayed in these selections and the ways in which they are or are not resolved. Then compare the list with the one you made on page 22. Are any of the conflicts common to both lists?

OPTION 2

Examining Endings Think about the stories in this unit that created a strong feeling of suspense for you. When you read the ending of these stories, were you surprised or did things turn out as you had expected? Which stories did you find more satisfying—the ones that met your expectations or those with surprise endings? After discussing these questions with your classmates, look back at the list of story ideas and surprise endings that you made on page 137. Choose the idea that seems to you most promising and turn it into a one-page story summary.

OPTION 3

Evaluating Storytelling Discuss the following questions with your classmates: What makes a good story? Which stories did you like best in this unit and why? Which stories in this unit do you think teach lessons that can be applied to life? Support your opinions with examples from the selections.

Self ASSESSMENT

📖 READER'S NOTEBOOK

Based on your likes and dislikes in this unit, what can you say about your own taste in stories?

Reviewing Literary Concepts

OPTION 1

Analyzing Conflict Most of the fictional characters in Unit One face conflicts that force them to grow or change. Make a chart like the one shown to analyze the conflicts in the selections you have read.

Selection	Type of Conflict	Description of Conflict	Effect on Main Character
"The Most Dangerous Game"	External	The main character is hunted like an animal by another man.	Rainsford learns to see things from the perspective of the hunted.
"The Necklace"	Internal		

OPTION 2

Judging the Impact of Suspense In most stories of life-and-death struggles, readers are carried along by a feeling of tension or anticipation as they wonder what will happen next. Think of the selections you have read in this unit. Which ones do you think would register the highest on a "suspense thermometer"? In a paragraph, explain your choices and describe what exactly contributes to the suspense in the selections.

Self ASSESSMENT

READER'S NOTEBOOK

On a sheet of paper, copy the following literary terms introduced in this unit. Next to each term, jot down a brief definition. If you don't understand a particular concept very well, refer to the **Glossary of Literary Terms** on page 1131.

plot	characterization
conflict	sound devices
complication	rhyme
resolution	alliteration
character	assonance
setting	speaker
theme	figurative
narrative	language
nonfiction	simile
narrative poetry	metaphor
ballad	personification
irony	mood
suspense	point of view
surprise ending	

Building Your Portfolio

- **Writing Options** Several Writing Options in this unit asked you to expand upon the situation in a story. From your responses, choose the one that you feel best captures the spirit of the story that it is based on. Write a note explaining the reasons for your choice. Then attach the note to the response, and place it in your **Presentation Portfolio.**

- **Writing Workshops** In this unit you wrote a Personal Narrative. You also wrote an Opinion Statement. Reread these two pieces and decide which you think does a better job of communicating your personal perspective. Explain your choice on a cover page, attach it to the piece you have selected, and place it in your **Presentation Portfolio.**

- **Additional Activities** Think back to any of the assignments you completed under **Activities & Explorations** and **Inquiry & Research**. Keep a record in your portfolio of any assignments that you especially enjoyed, found helpful, or would like to do further work on.

Self ASSESSMENT

At this point, you may just be beginning your **Presentation Portfolio.** Are the pieces you have chosen ones you think you'll keep, or do you think you will be replacing them as the year goes on?

Setting GOALS

As you worked through the reading and writing activities in this section, you probably identified certain skills that you want to work on. Look back through your assignments, worksheets, and

READER'S NOTEBOOK.

Then make a list of the skills or concepts that you'd like to work on in the next unit.

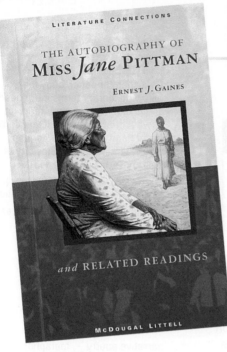

LITERATURE CONNECTIONS

The Autobiography of Miss Jane Pittman

ERNEST J. GAINES

In this fictionalized autobiography, a 110-year-old woman tells the story of her life, from her childhood as a slave during the Civil War to the early years of the civil rights movement of the 1960s. Proud and independent, Jane Pittman endures tragedy and loss but never loses hope. In times of crisis, she provides strength and wise counsel to those in her community.

These thematically related readings are provided along with *The Autobiography of Miss Jane Pittman*:

A Conspiracy of Grace
BY ETHEL MORGAN SMITH

Keeping the Thing Going While Things Are Stirring
BY SOJOURNER TRUTH

"It's Such a Pleasure to Learn"
BY WALLACE TERRY

To Be of Use
BY MARGE PIERCY

Booker T. and W. E. B.
BY DUDLEY RANDALL

from Having Our Say: The Delany Sisters' First 100 Years
BY SARAH AND A. ELIZABETH DELANY WITH AMY HILL HEARTH

The First Time I Sat in a Restaurant
BY JO CARSON

The Great White Myth
BY ANNA QUINDLEN

The Old Demon
BY PEARL S. BUCK

And Even *More* . . .

Profiles in Courage

JOHN F. KENNEDY

John F. Kennedy won the Pulitzer Prize for biography in 1957 for this collection of eight essays on U. S. senators who made hard decisions, often at the expense of their careers. These thought-provoking essays provide insight into the lives and careers of such statesmen as Daniel Webster, Sam Houston, and John Quincy Adams.

Books

41 Stories by O. Henry
O. HENRY
Forty-one stories filled with plot twists, surprise endings, and insights into human behavior

Further Fables for Our Time
JAMES THURBER
A collection of fables by the famous humorist

The Haunting of Hill House
SHIRLEY JACKSON
A suspenseful, subtle horror novel

To Kill a Mockingbird: The Screenplay

HORTON FOOTE

This screenplay adapts Harper Lee's Pulitzer Prize-winning novel of two young children experiencing rites of passage in a small Alabama town during the Great Depression. The children learn about justice from their lawyer father who, in the face of impossible odds, stands up for what he believes is right. They also learn that they can never really understand a person until they "climb inside his skin and walk around in it."

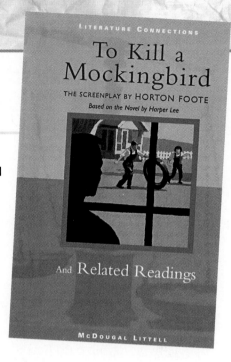

These thematically related readings are provided along with *To Kill a Mockingbird: The Screenplay*:

from **Growing Up in the Great Depression**
BY RICHARD WORMSER

The Right Thing to Do at the Time
BY GEORGE GARRETT

Lawyer Clark Blues
BY SLEEPY JOHN ESTES

Strange Fruit
BY LEWIS ALLAN

The Thanksgiving Visitor
BY TRUMAN CAPOTE

The Hidden Songs of a Secret Soul
BY BOB GREENE

Freedom
BY LANGSTON HUGHES

You Wouldn't Understand
BY JOSÉ EMILIO PACHECO

Kaffir Boy
MARK MATHABANE
The true story of a young black youth's coming of age in apartheid South Africa

The Kitchen God's Wife
AMY TAN
The story of a woman's struggle for survival in the harsh world of China before and during World War II

Other Media
The Autobiography of Miss Jane Pittman
Actress Cicely Tyson stars in this acclaimed dramatization of Gaines's best-selling novel.
(VIDEOCASSETTE)

Edgar Allan Poe Short Stories
Edward Blake reads several of Poe's best-known stories, including "The Cask of Amontillado."
(AUDIOCASSETTES)

Titanic: Adventure Out of Time
This game allows the player to explore the great ship and—possibly—rewrite history.
(CD-ROM)

To Kill a Mockingbird
Horton Foote's screenplay of Harper Lee's novel brought to life.
(VIDEOCASSETTE)

PASSAGES

Things do
not change;
we
change.

Henry David Thoreau

East Twelfth Street (1946), Ben Shahn. Tempera, 22″ × 30″, collection of Mr. and Mrs. Albert Hackett, New York. Copyright © 1995 Estate of Ben Shahn/Licensed by VAGA, New York.

PART 1   Journeys of Discovery

A travel ad used to proclaim, "Getting there is half the fun." The same could be said for the process of becoming an adult. Growing up is not just a means to an end, but a journey of discovery. In this part of Unit Two, fictional characters and real people learn that even painful experiences can lead to sudden insights and unexpected joys. As you read these selections, look for discoveries that might help you through the next difficult situation you encounter.

LEARNING *the* Language of *Literature*

*N*onfiction is writing about real people, places, and events. You encounter nonfiction when you read a movie review, a newspaper editorial, or a history textbook. Unlike fiction, nonfiction contains mostly factual information, although the writer selects the information in accordance with his or her purpose. Nonfiction includes a wide variety of writing, from recipes and speeches to sports articles and encyclopedias. Use the following descriptions and examples to learn more about the characteristics of nonfiction.

Biography

A **biography** is a writer's account of another person's life. Typically the subject of a biography is well-known, either in history or in contemporary life. The biographer must research the subject's life, using both primary and secondary sources, in order to present the facts accurately. The best biographers strive to produce balanced accounts of their subjects, including strengths and weaknesses, successes and failures.

Autobiography

An **autobiography** is a writer's account of his or her own life. Autobiographies generally focus on their writers' personal experiences over a period of time. A **personal narrative** is a short autobiographical work that focuses on a specific experience in the writer's life. **Diaries, journals,** and **letters** are also forms of autobiographical writing.

YOUR TURN In the passage at the right, Frank McCourt describes his hospitalization for typhoid fever as a child. What aspects of the passage help you to understand how he felt?

> **AUTOBIOGRAPHY**
> My ankles and the back of my hand are throbbing from the tubes bringing in the blood and I don't care about boys praying for me. I can hear the swish of Sister Rita's habit and the click of her rosary beads when she leaves the room. I fall asleep and when I wake it's dark and Dad is sitting by the bed with his hand on mine.
>
> —Frank McCourt, *Angela's Ashes*

Essay

An **essay** is a relatively short piece of writing on a single subject. Some essays are **formal**—that is, tightly structured and written in an impersonal style. Others are **informal,** with a looser structure and a more personal style. There are three common types of essays:

- **Expository essays** present or explain information and ideas.
- **Persuasive essays** present arguments and attempt to convince readers to adopt particular points of view.
- **Personal essays** express writers' thoughts and feelings about subjects.

YOUR TURN Is the passage at the right from an expository, a persuasive, or a personal essay? How do you know?

> **ESSAY**
> For Christmas, I begged for go-go boots. The rest of my life would be endurable if I had a pair of those white, calf-high confections with the little black heels. . . . Never mind that those little black heels are like skate blades in inclement weather. I would walk on air.
>
> —Barbara Kingsolver, "Life Without Go-Go Boots"

Informative Article

An **informative article** provides facts about a specific subject. This type of writing takes two basic forms:

- **News stories** give objective, or unbiased, accounts of current events.
- **Feature articles** appear in magazines as well as newspapers. Many of them are human-interest stories, focusing on interesting people or events.

Informative writing also can be found in textbooks, encyclopedias, and reference books.

YOUR TURN Do you think the excerpt at the right is from a news story or from a feature article? Give reasons for your conclusion.

INFORMATIVE ARTICLE

For the children of Northern Ireland, violence is embedded in the rituals of daily life. Early curfews are the norm, public places are commonly avoided, and Catholics and Protestants rarely venture outside their own neighborhoods.

Since sectarian violence began in 1969, generations of Belfast youngsters have known only "the Troubles"—and many have grown up to repeat the cycles of terrorism and despair. Project Children aims to change all that, child by child, lifting them out of Northern Ireland and placing them with American host families for six weeks in hopes of showing them what life is like when peace is the norm.

—Gayle Tzemach, "A Respite from 'The Troubles'"

Interview

An **interview** is a conversation in which one person asks questions of another to obtain information. The interviewer takes notes or tape-records the conversation. Using those notes, the interviewer may then write a **profile** of the person. A profile may include the writer's own interpretations of the interviewee's responses, along with information from other sources. Another approach is for the interviewer to present interesting parts of the interview word for word, as an edited **transcript.** A transcript of an interview lets the personality of the interviewee come through in his or her own words. This is the approach used in "Unfinished Business" (page 260).

True-Life Adventure

Nonfiction can be every bit as exciting and dramatic as fiction. True tales of heroism, survival, and adventure are the subject of many popular books and articles. The excerpt at the right is a good example.

YOUR TURN The events in this excerpt happened in the past, but the writer used the present tense to relate them. What is the effect of this use of the present tense?

TRUE-LIFE ADVENTURE

Dark is only three hours away, and the departing H-3 pilot doesn't think the *Satori* will survive another night. She'll run out of fuel, start getting knocked down, and eventually break apart. The crew will be cast into the sea, and the helicopter pilot will refuse to drop his rescue swimmer because he can't be sure of getting him back. It would be up to the *Tamaroa* to maneuver alongside the swimmers and pull them on board, and in these seas it would be almost impossible. It's now or never.

—Sebastian Junger, *The Perfect Storm*

Reading Nonfiction

Nonfiction writing entertains and informs readers as it tells about real people, places, and events. The reading strategies explained here can help you to enjoy and interpret the many types of nonfiction you will encounter.

1 Strategies for Understanding Autobiography and Biography

- Keep track of the people who are mentioned in the narrative. Use a web diagram like this one or a family tree to record important relationships.
- Be aware of cause-and-effect relationships among events.
- In a biography, **question** whether the writer allowed a personal bias to influence the presentation of information.

mother		father
	subject	sister

2 Strategies for Evaluating an Essay

- Be sure to distinguish between facts and opinions. A statement of fact can be proved or disproved. An opinion expresses a belief about which people can agree or disagree but which cannot be proved or disproved. Use a chart like the one at the right to keep track of facts and opinions.
- **Analyze** whether the writer primarily wants to express ideas and feelings, to inform, to entertain, or to persuade.
- **Evaluate** the writer's ideas and reasoning. Does the writer support opinions with facts? Do you agree with the writer's conclusions?
- **Clarify** your understanding by summarizing the main ideas as you read.

Essay:
Writer:
Facts	Opinions

3 Strategies for Reading an Informative Article or Interview

- Before reading the article or interview, skim it to learn what its subject is. Look at any headings or captions.
- Read the article or interview slowly, looking for key facts and ideas.
- When reading an article, identify details that support the main ideas.
- When reading an interview, note the impressions that you form of the interviewee on the basis of the information presented.
- Reread any passages that do not seem clear.

4 Strategies for Exploring a True-Life Adventure

- **Visualize** the people and events as the narrative unfolds.
- Keep track of the sequence of events. Try to **predict** what will happen next.
- List words and phrases that help to create a sense of danger, suspense, excitement, or mystery.

Need More Help?

Remember that active readers use the essential reading strategies explained on page 7: **visualize, predict, clarify, question, connect, evaluate, monitor.**

Life Without Go-Go Boots

Personal Essay by BARBARA KINGSOLVER

"High fashion has the shelf life of potato salad."

Connect to Your Life

What's in Fashion? Fashion means different things to different people. Every year the world's most famous models, at fancy shows in New York or Paris, introduce the latest clothing styles created by the world's most famous fashion designers. However, these fashions are not necessarily the ones sought by teenagers, or even by the majority of adults. What types of clothing are now in fashion among teenagers in your school or community or your circle of friends? Do you like these fashions? How important is fashion to you? Discuss your thoughts with classmates.

Build Background

Fashions of the 60s In "Life Without Go-Go Boots," Barbara Kingsolver mentions women's fashions that were popular in the 1960s when she was a young girl. Chief among these was the miniskirt—a straight skirt that ended above the knee. In a society accustomed to skirts worn well below the knee, the arrival of the miniskirt was a shocker! A popular accessory to the miniskirt was a calf-high boot with a small heel, known as a "go-go" boot. The term "go-go" described the type of fast-paced music played at the discos, or dance clubs, where miniskirts and go-go boots were the preferred fashion.

WORDS TO KNOW
Vocabulary Preview

compel	inscrutable
conventional	irreparable
indulge	

Focus Your Reading

LITERARY ANALYSIS   PERSONAL ESSAY   A **personal essay** is a short form of nonfiction in which the writer expresses his or her thoughts, feelings, and opinions about a subject. Personal essays are often autobiographical, focusing on incidents or experiences in the writer's own life. Most personal essays are written with more than a single purpose in mind. As you read "Life Without Go-Go Boots," try to determine Kingsolver's purpose for writing this essay.

ACTIVE READING   CHRONOLOGICAL ORDER   Writers of essays always give their work some kind of structure. In other words, the events or experiences they describe are deliberately presented in a specific order. In "Life Without Go-Go Boots," the writer's experiences are presented in chronological order, that is, the order in which they happened.

READER'S NOTEBOOK   Draw a time chart like the one shown. Then, as you read the essay, record the writer's experiences to show the order in which they occur.

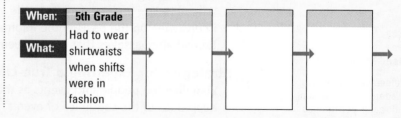

When:	5th Grade			
What:	Had to wear shirtwaists when shifts were in fashion			

Fashion nearly wrecked my life.

I grew up beyond its pale, convinced

that this would stunt me in some

<u>irreparable</u> way. I don't think it

has, but for a long time

it was touch and go.

Photo by Irving Solero. Courtesy of the Museum at the Fashion Institute of Technology, New York.

Life Without Go-Go Boots

BARBARA KINGSOLVER

We lived in the country, in the middle of an alfalfa field; we had no immediate access to Bobbie Brooks sweaters. I went to school in the hand-me-downs of a cousin three years older. She had excellent fashion sense, but during the three-year lag her every sleek outfit turned to a pumpkin. In fifth grade, when girls were wearing straight shifts with buttons down the front, I wore pastel shirtwaists with cap sleeves and a multitude of built-in petticoats. My black lace-up oxfords, which my parents perceived to have orthopedic value, carried their own weight in the spectacle. I suspected people noticed, and I knew it for sure on the day Billy Stamps announced to the lunch line: "Make way for the Bride of Frankenstein."

I suffered quietly, casting an ever-hopeful eye on my eighth-grade cousin whose button-front shifts someday would be mine. But by the time I was an eighth grader, everyone with an iota[1] of social position wore polka-dot shirts and miniskirts. For Christmas, I begged for go-go boots. The rest of my life would be endurable if I had a pair of those white, calf-high confections[2] with the little black heels. My mother, though always <u>inscrutable</u> near Christmas, seemed sympathetic; there was hope. Never mind that those little black heels are like skate blades in inclement weather. I would walk on air.

On Christmas morning I received white rubber boots with treads like a pair of Michelins. My mother loved me, but had missed the point.

In high school I took matters into my own hands. I learned to sew. I contrived to make an apple-green polyester jumpsuit that was supremely fashionable for about two months. Since it took me forty days and forty nights to make the thing, my moment of glory was brief. I learned what my mother had been trying to tell me all along: high fashion has the shelf life of potato salad. And when past its prime, it is similarly deadly.

Once I left home and went to college I was on my own, fashion-wise, having bypassed my cousin in stature and capped the arrangement off by moving to another state. But I found I still had to reckon with life's limited choices. After classes I worked variously as a house cleaner, typesetter, and artists' model. I could spend my wages on trendy apparel (which would be useless to me in any of my jobs, particularly the latter), or on the lesser gratifications of food and textbooks. It was a tough call, but I opted for education. This was Indiana and it was cold; when it wasn't cold, it was rainy. I bought an army surplus overcoat, with zip-out lining, that reached my ankles, and I found in my parents' attic a green pith helmet.[3] I became a known figure on campus. Fortunately, this was the era in which army boots were a fashion option for coeds. And besides, who knew? Maybe under all that all-weather olive drab was a Bobbie Brooks sweater. My social life picked right up.

As an adult, I made two hugely fortuitous choices in the women's-wear department: first, I moved out West, where the buffalo roam and hardly anyone is ever arrested for being unstylish. Second, I became a novelist. Artists (also mathematicians and geniuses) are greatly <u>indulged</u> by society when it comes to matters of grooming. If we happen to look like an unmade bed, it's

---

1. **an iota** (ī-ō′tə): a little bit.
2. **confections:** fancy articles of clothing.
3. **pith helmet:** a light, rigid hat worn in tropical countries as protection from the sun.

presumed we're preoccupied with plot devices or unifying theories or things of that ilk.

Even so, when I was invited to attend an important author event on the East Coast, a friend took me in hand.

"Writers are supposed to be eccentric," I wailed.

My friend, one of the people who loves me best in the world, replied: "Barbara, you're not eccentric, you're an anachronism,[4]" and marched me down to an exclusive clothing shop.

It was a very small store; I nearly hyperventilated. "You could liquidate the stock here and feed an African nation for a year," I whispered. But under pressure I bought a suit, and wore it to the important author function. For three hours of my life I was precisely in vogue.

Since then it has reigned over my closet from its dry-cleaner bag, feeling unhappy and out of place, I am sure, a silk ambassador assigned to a flannel republic. Even if I go to a chichi[5] restaurant, the suit stays home. I'm always afraid I'll spill something on it; I'd be too nervous to enjoy myself. It turns out I would rather converse than make a statement.

Now, there is fashion, and there is style. The latter, I've found, will serve, and costs less. Style is mostly a matter of acting as if you know very well what you look like, thanks, and are just delighted about it. It also requires consistency. A friend of mine wears buckskin moccasins every day of her life. She has daytime and evening moccasins. This works fine in Arizona, but when my friend fell in love with a Tasmanian geologist and prepared to move to a rain forest, I worried. Moccasins instantaneously decompose in wet weather. But I should have known, my friend has sense. She bought clear plastic galoshes to button over her moccasins, and writes me that she's happy.

I favor cowboy boots. I don't do high heels, because you never know when you might actually have to get somewhere, and most other entries in the ladies-shoes category look to me like Ol' Dixie and Ol' Dobbin trying to sneak into the Derby, trailing their plow. Cowboy boots aren't trying. They say, "I'm no pump, and furthermore, so what?" That characterizes my whole uniform, in fact: oversized flannel shirts, jeans or cotton leggings, and cowboy boots when weather permits. In summer I lean toward dresses that make contact

---

4. **anachronism** (ə-năk′rə-nĭz′əm): something out of its proper time period (like an automobile in a movie about the Middle Ages).

5. **chichi** (shē′shē): stylish or chic in a showy way.

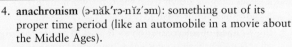

my mother loved me, but had missed the point.

239

I am happy.

with the body (if at all) only on the shiatsu acupressure points;[6] maybe also a Panama hat; and sneakers. I am happy.

I'm also a parent, which of course calls into question every decision one ever believes one has made for the last time. Can I raise my daughter as a raiment renegade?[7] At present she couldn't care less. Maybe obsessions skip a generation.

> **ACTIVE READING**
>
> **CLARIFY** What distinction do you think the author is making between fashion and style?

She was blessed with two older cousins whose sturdy hand-me-downs she has worn from birth, with relish. If she wasn't entirely a fashion plate, she also escaped being typecast. For her first two years she had no appreciable hair, to which parents can clamp those plastic barrettes that are gender dead giveaways. So when I took her to the park in cousin Ashley's dresses, strangers commented on her blue eyes and lovely complexion; when she wore Andrew's playsuits emblazoned with trucks and airplanes (why is it we only decorate our boys with modes of transportation?), people always commented on how strong and alert my child was—and what's his name?

This interests me. I also know it can't last. She's in school now, and I'm very quickly remembering what school is about: two parts ABCs to fifty parts Where Do I Stand in the Great Pecking Order of Humankind? She still rejects stereotypes, with extraordinary good humor. She has a dress-up collection to die for, gleaned from Goodwill and her grandparents' world travels, and likely as not will show up to dinner wearing harem pants, bunny ears, a glitter-bra over her T-shirt, wooden shoes, and a fez.[8] But underneath it all, she's only human. I have a

feeling the day might come when my daughter will beg to be a slave of conventional fashion.

I'm inclined to resist, if it happens. To press on her the larger truths I finally absorbed from my own wise parents: that she can find her own path. That she will be more valued for inward individuality than outward conformity. That a world plagued by poverty can ill afford the planned obsolescence of haute couture.[9]

> **ACTIVE READING**
>
> **EVALUATE** The author has presented events in chronological order. How does this help her bring the essay to a more effective close?

But a small corner of my heart still harbors the Bride of Frankenstein, eleven years of age, haunting me in her brogues[10] and petticoats. Always and forever, the ghosts of past anguish compel us to live through our children. If my daughter ever asks for the nineties equivalent of go-go boots, I'll cave in.

Maybe I'll also buy her some of those clear plastic galoshes to button over them on inclement days. ❖

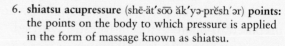

---

6. **shiatsu acupressure** (shē-ät′so͞o ăk′yə-prĕsh′ər) **points:** the points on the body to which pressure is applied in the form of massage known as shiatsu.

7. **raiment** (rā′mənt) **renegade:** clothing rebel.

8. **fez:** a cap shaped like a flat-topped cone, usually with a tassel hanging down from the top—worn mainly by men in the Middle East.

9. **the planned obsolescence** (ŏb′sə-lĕs′əns) **of** *haute couture* (ōt′ ko͞o-to͞or′): fashion designers' continual creation of new styles in an effort to sell more clothes.

10. **brogues** (brōgz): sturdy leather shoes.

WORDS TO KNOW	**conventional** (kən-vĕn′shə-nəl) *adj.* conforming to accepted standards; traditional **compel** (kəm-pĕl′) *v.* to force

Connect to the Literature

1. **What Do You Think?** Do you agree with any of the author's thoughts about fashion? Share your opinions with classmates.

> **Comprehension Check**
> - What did the author want to wear as a child?
> - What does she want to wear as an adult?
> - What concerns does she have about her daughter?

Think Critically

2. How would you describe the author of this essay?

THINK ABOUT
- her attitude toward fashion now
- the distinction she makes between fashion and style
- what she hopes her daughter will learn
- her writing **style**

3. Why do you think the author was so concerned about fashion in the fifth grade?

4. Do you think the author's daughter will benefit from the experiences of her mother? Support your opinion.

5. **ACTIVE READING** **CHRONOLOGICAL ORDER** Study the time chart that you constructed in your **READER'S NOTEBOOK.** In your opinion, is the order in which Kingsolver describes her experiences important? Explain.

Extend Interpretations

6. **Critic's Corner** One critic has said that Kingsolver helps us "find instructions for life in surprising places." To what extent is this true of "Life Without Go-Go Boots"? Explain your answer.

7. **Connect to Life** Kingsolver believes that school is "two parts ABCs to fifty parts Where Do I Stand in the Great Pecking Order of Humankind?" How does this view compare with your experiences in school?

Literary Analysis

PERSONAL ESSAY "Life Without Go-Go Boots" is a **personal essay.** It is a short piece of nonfiction in which the author expresses her thoughts, feelings, and opinions about the topic of women's fashions. As with all personal essays, the work is **autobiographical,** focusing on experiences from the author's own life and on the insights or lessons she has gained from those experiences. Most personal essays are written for more than one purpose. The author may want to share personal thoughts and experiences, to entertain readers, to inform readers about a subject, or to persuade readers to act, think, or feel a certain way. The essay form also allows Kingsolver to indulge her whimsical sense of humor and enjoyment of wordplay.

Cooperative Learning Activity
Review Kingsolver's essay. Then answer the following questions:

- What is the author's attitude toward her subject matter?
- What lessons did the author learn from her experiences?
- What is the author's purpose for writing the essay?

Compare your responses with those of some of your classmates.

"Life Without Go-Go Boots"

Author's Attitude:

Lessons Learned:

Author's Purpose for Writing:

Writing Options

Personal Essay Write your own personal essay. Tell about a time when you desperately wanted something that you could not have. Describe how you reacted and what you thought at the time. Then explain what you think about the experience now. You might use a time chart like the one on page 236 to organize your thoughts. Place your essay in your **Working Portfolio.**

Activities & Explorations

Fashion Survey With a group of classmates, prepare a list of questions for a survey on what kinds of clothes teenagers like and how important fashion is to them. Then use your questions to take a fashion survey of students in your school. Compile the results of your survey, and display your findings in the form of a bar or line graph. **~MATH**

Inquiry & Research

Yesterday's Fashions With a group of classmates, create a display of photographs or drawings that illustrate the styles from an earlier decade of the 20th century. Then give an oral report, describing these fashions and showing any resemblance to clothes worn today.

 More Online: Research Starter www.mcdougallittell.com

Vocabulary in Action

EXERCISE: SYNONYMS For each group of words below, write the letter of the word that is a synonym of the boldfaced Word to Know.

1. **conventional:** (a) political, (b) religious, (c) usual
2. **indulge:** (a) swallow, (b) pamper, (c) shove
3. **inscrutable:** (a) tight, (b) complicated, (c) interior
4. **irreparable:** (a) incurable, (b) immovable, (c) unblemished
5. **compel:** (a) weaken, (b) communicate, (c) coerce

Building Vocabulary
Several Words to Know in this lesson contain prefixes and suffixes. For an in-depth study of affixes, see page 473.

Barbara Kingsolver
1955–

Other Works
The Bean Trees
Animal Dreams
Pigs in Heaven

Biologist to Writer Barbara Kingsolver began writing stories as a child but never dreamed that she could earn a living as a writer. In college, she started writing poetry but turned to science for her future career. In 1977, Kingsolver graduated from DePauw University in Indiana with a major in biology. She later received a master's degree, also in science, from the University of Arizona. When she took a job writing scientific articles, Kingsolver finally realized that writing could be a career. In 1987, she became a full-time writer and published her first novel the following year.

Awards and Admiration Kingsolver has won many awards for her writing, including the American Library Association Award for *The Bean Trees* and the Los Angeles Times Book Award for *Pigs in Heaven*. Her work has appeared in numerous popular magazines, including *McCall's, Redbook,* and *Mademoiselle,* and *The Bean Trees* has been published in over 65 different countries.

Author Activity

Barbara Kingsolver writes novels, short stories, nonfiction, and poetry. In her writing, she often reveals her personal concerns about political and social issues—especially human rights, the environment, and racial injustice. Find out the subject matter of one or more of Kingsolver's novels or essays. Share your findings with classmates.

from Angela's Ashes

Memoir by FRANK McCOURT

"She's a very stern nurse from the County Kerry and she frightens me."

Connect to Your Life

Get Well Soon! Cards, flowers, balloons—can any of these "get-well" gifts really make you feel better? Think about the last time you were very ill or recovering from an injury. What cheered you or helped you pass the time while you were recovering? Discuss your experiences with classmates.

Build Background

Typhoid and Diphtheria Thanks to vaccines and to healthy living conditions, most of us will never be sick from typhoid fever or diphtheria. Frank McCourt, however, growing up in a poor family in a poverty-stricken area of Ireland, was not so lucky. In this excerpt from *Angela's Ashes,* he recalls a childhood experience when he was quite ill. Typhoid, in addition to causing a high fever, leads to severe weakness and sometimes death. Diphtheria, a contagious respiratory infection, may also lead to death. Though not familiar to most of us, these dreadful diseases do still exist, especially in areas where people live in crowded, unclean conditions.

WORDS TO KNOW
Vocabulary Preview

clamoring	potent
exception	privilege
induced	recite
pagan	relapse
perfidy	torrent

Focus Your Reading

LITERARY ANALYSIS MEMOIR   *Angela's Ashes* is a **memoir,** a form of **nonfiction** in which a person recalls significant events in his or her life. Unlike an autobiography, a memoir may describe just one period or aspect of a writer's life, for example, a memorable journey or a special relationship. In *Angela's Ashes*, Frank McCourt describes his childhood in Ireland in the 1940s. He recalls past events but describes them as if they were happening in the present, as shown in this passage from the selection you are about to read:

> *Sister Rita comes in and tells Dad he has to go. I don't want him to go because he looks sad. When he looks sad it's the worst thing in the world and I start crying.*

As you read the selection, notice the author's use of the present tense and how it affects you as a reader.

ACTIVE READING MAKING INFERENCES   Every time you use bits of evidence to figure something out, you are **making inferences.** You are combining facts with what you already know from personal experience. Making inferences is an important skill in reading nonfiction as well as fiction. It allows you to learn more about people, places, or events that you encounter in your reading.

READER'S NOTEBOOK   Create a chart like the one shown. Use it to record the facts you learn from your reading and to record any inferences you make. Also jot down clues that help you make the inferences.

What I Know as Fact	What I Can Infer
Frank's relationship with his father	Sister Rita's attitude toward children
Frank's knowledge of poetry	Seamus's attitude toward children

Frank McCourt

Angela's

Frank McCourt *(right front)* in the playground of
Leamy's School in Limerick, Ireland, about 1938.
Reprinted with the permission of Scribner,
a Division of Simon & Schuster, from Angela's
Ashes: *A Memoir* by Frank McCourt.
Copyright © 1996 by Frank McCourt.

Ashes

Mam comes with Dr. Troy. He feels my forehead, rolls up my eyelids, turns me over to see my back, picks me up and runs to his motor car. Mam runs after him and he tells her I have typhoid fever. Mam cries, . . . am I to lose the whole family? Will it ever end? She gets into the car, holds me in her lap and moans all the way to the Fever Hospital at the City Home.

The bed has cool white sheets. The nurses have clean white uniforms and the nun, Sister Rita, is all in white. Dr. Humphrey and Dr. Campbell have white coats and things hanging from their necks which they stick against my chest and all over. I sleep and sleep but I'm awake when they bring in jars of bright red stuff that hang from tall poles above my bed and they stick tubes into my ankles and the back of my right hand. Sister Rita says, You're getting blood, Francis. Soldier's blood from the Sarsfield Barracks.

Mam is sitting by the bed and the nurse is saying, You know, missus, this is very unusual.

> " . . . am I to lose the whole family?"

No one is ever allowed into the Fever Hospital for fear they'd catch something but they made an exception for you with his crisis coming. If he gets over this he'll surely recover.

I fall asleep. Mam is gone when I wake but there's movement in the room and it's the priest, Father Gorey, from the Confraternity[1] saying Mass at a table in the corner. I drift off again and now they're waking me and pulling down the bedclothes. Father Gorey is touching me with oil and praying in Latin. I know it's Extreme Unction and that means I'm going to die and I don't care. They wake me again to receive Communion. I don't want it, I'm afraid I might get sick. I keep the wafer on my tongue and fall asleep and when I wake up again it's gone.

It's dark and Dr. Campbell is sitting by my bed. He's holding my wrist and looking at his watch. He has red hair and glasses and he always smiles when he talks to me. He sits now and hums and looks out the window. His eyes close and he snores a little. . . .

Sister Rita's white habit is bright in the sun that comes in the window. She's holding my wrist, looking at her watch, smiling. Oh, she says, we're awake, are we? Well, Francis, I think we've come through the worst. Our prayers are answered and all the prayers of those hundreds of little boys at the Confraternity. Can you imagine that? Hundreds of boys saying the rosary[2] for you and offering up their communion.

My ankles and the back of my hand are throbbing from the tubes bringing in the blood and I don't care about boys praying for me. I can hear the swish of Sister Rita's habit and the click of her rosary beads when she leaves the room. I fall asleep and when I wake it's dark and Dad is sitting by the bed with his hand on mine.

Son, are you awake?

I try to talk but I'm dry, nothing will come out and I point to my mouth. He holds a glass of water to my lips and it's sweet and cool. He presses my hand and says I'm a great old soldier and why wouldn't I? Don't I have the soldier's blood in me?

The tubes are not in me anymore and the glass jars are gone.

Sister Rita comes in and tells Dad he has to go. I don't want him to go because he looks sad. When he looks sad it's the worst thing in the world and I start crying. Now what's this? says Sister Rita. Crying with all that soldier blood in you? There's a big surprise for you tomorrow, Francis. You'll never guess. Well, I'll tell you, we're bringing you a nice biscuit[3] with your tea in the morning. Isn't that a treat? And your father will be back in a day or two, won't you, Mr. McCourt?

Dad nods and puts his hand on mine again. He looks at me, steps away, stops, comes back, kisses me on the forehead for the first time in my life and I'm so happy I feel like floating out of the bed.

The other two beds in my room are empty. The nurse says I'm the only typhoid patient and I'm a miracle for getting over the crisis.

The room next to me is empty till one morning a girl's voice says, Yoo hoo, who's there?

I'm not sure if she's talking to me or someone in the room beyond.

Yoo hoo, boy with the typhoid, are you awake?

I am.

Are you better?

I am.

---

1. **Confraternity:** a religious society or association.
2. **rosary** (rō′zə-rē): a series of prayers repeated by Roman Catholics as a form of devotion to the Virgin Mary— usually counted off on a string of beads as they are said.
3. **biscuit:** cookie.

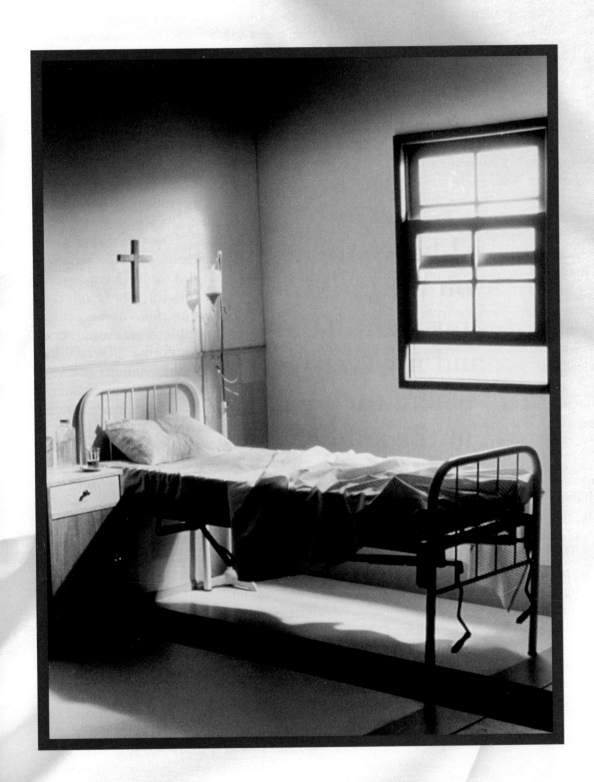

Well, why are you here?

I don't know. I'm still in the bed. They stick needles in me and give me medicine.

What do you look like?

I wonder, What kind of a question is that? I don't know what to tell her.

Yoo hoo, are you there, typhoid boy?

I am.

What's your name?

Frank.

That's a good name. My name is Patricia Madigan. How old are you?

Ten.

Oh. She sounds disappointed.

But I'll be eleven in August, next month.

Well, that's better than ten. I'll be fourteen in September. Do you want to know why I'm in the Fever Hospital?

I do.

I have diphtheria and something else.

What's something else?

They don't know. They think I have a disease from foreign parts because my father used to be in Africa. I nearly died. Are you going to tell me what you look like?

I have black hair.

You and millions.

I have brown eyes with bits of green that's called hazel.

You and thousands.

I have stitches on the back of my right hand and my two feet where they put in the soldier's blood.

Oh, . . . did they?

They did.

> **I have stitches on the back of my right hand and my two feet where they put in the soldier's blood.**

You won't be able to stop marching and saluting.

There's a swish of habit and click of beads and then Sister Rita's voice. Now, now, what's this? There's to be no talking between two rooms especially when it's a boy and a girl. Do you hear me, Patricia?

I do, Sister.

Do you hear me, Francis?

I do, Sister.

You could be giving thanks for your two remarkable recoveries. You could be saying the rosary. You could be reading *The Little Messenger of the Sacred Heart*[4] that's beside your beds. Don't let me come back and find you talking. She comes into my room and wags her finger at me. Especially you, Francis, after thousands of boys prayed for you at the Confraternity. Give thanks, Francis, give thanks. She leaves and there's silence for awhile. Then Patricia whispers, Give thanks, Francis, give thanks, and say your rosary, Francis, and I laugh so hard a nurse runs in to see if I'm all right. She's a very stern nurse from the County Kerry and she frightens me. What's this, Francis? Laughing? What is there to laugh about? Are you and that Madigan girl talking? I'll report you to Sister Rita. There's to be no laughing for you could be doing serious damage to your internal apparatus.[5]

She plods out and Patricia whispers again in a heavy Kerry accent, No laughing, Francis, you could be doin' serious damage to your internal

---

4. *The Little . . . Heart:* a Roman Catholic magazine.

5. **internal apparatus** (ăp′ə-rā′təs): the internal organs of the body.

apparatus. Say your rosary, Francis, and pray for your internal apparatus.

Mam visits me on Thursdays, I'd like to see my father, too, but I'm out of danger, crisis time is over, and I'm allowed only one visitor. Besides, she says, he's back at work at Rank's Flour Mills and please God this job will last a while with the war on and the English desperate for flour. She brings me a chocolate bar and that proves Dad is working. She could never afford it on the dole.[6] He sends me notes. He tells me my brothers are all praying for me, that I should be a good boy, obey the doctors, the nuns, the nurses, and don't forget to say my prayers. He's sure St. Jude pulled me through the crisis because he's the patron saint of desperate cases and I was indeed a desperate case.

Patricia says she has two books by her bed. One is a poetry book and that's the one she loves. The other is a short history of England and do I want it? She gives it to Seamus, the man who mops the floors every day, and he brings it to me. He says, I'm not supposed to be bringing anything from a diphtheria room to a typhoid room with all the germs flying around and hiding between the pages and if you ever catch diphtheria on top of the typhoid they'll know and I'll lose my good job and be out on the street singing patriotic songs with a tin cup in my hand, which I could easily do because there isn't a song ever written about Ireland's sufferings I don't know. . . .

Oh, yes, he knows Roddy McCorley. He'll sing it for me right enough but he's barely into the first verse when the Kerry nurse rushes in. What's this, Seamus? Singing? Of all the people in this hospital you should know the rules against singing. I have a good mind to report you to Sister Rita.

Ah, . . . don't do that, nurse.

Very well, Seamus. I'll let it go this one time. You know the singing could lead to a <u>relapse</u> in these patients.

When she leaves he whispers he'll teach me a few songs because singing is good for passing the time when you're by yourself in a typhoid room. He says Patricia is a lovely girl the way she often gives him sweets from the parcel her mother sends every fortnight.[7] He stops mopping the floor and calls to Patricia in the next room, I was telling Frankie you're a lovely girl, Patricia, and she says, You're a lovely man, Seamus. He smiles because he's an old man of forty and he never had children but the ones he can talk to here in the Fever Hospital. He says, Here's the book, Frankie. Isn't it a great pity you have to be reading all about England after all they did to us, that there isn't a history of Ireland to be had in this hospital.

The book tells me all about King Alfred and William the Conqueror and all the kings and queens down to Edward, who had to wait forever for his mother, Victoria, to die before he could be king. The book has the first bit of Shakespeare I ever read.

I do believe, <u>induced</u> by <u>potent</u> circumstances
That thou art mine enemy.

The history writer says this is what Catherine, who is a wife of Henry the Eighth, says to Cardinal Wolsey, who is trying to have her head cut off. I don't know what it means and I don't care because it's Shakespeare and it's like having jewels in my mouth when I say the words. If I had a whole book of Shakespeare they could keep me in the hospital for a year.

Patricia says she doesn't know what induced means or potent circumstances and she doesn't

---

6. **on the dole:** receiving government unemployment payments.

7. **fortnight:** two weeks.

WORDS   **relapse** (rē'lăps') *n.* a worsening of an illness after a partial recovery
TO   **induced** (ĭn-dōost') *adj.* persuaded; influenced **induce** *v.*
KNOW   **potent** (pōt'nt) *adj.* powerful

care about Shakespeare, she has her poetry book and she reads to me from beyond the wall a poem about an owl and a pussycat that went to sea in a green boat with honey and money[8] and it makes no sense and when I say that Patricia gets huffy and says that's the last poem she'll ever read to me. She says I'm always reciting the lines from Shakespeare and they make no sense either. Seamus stops mopping again and tells us we shouldn't be fighting over poetry because we'll have enough to fight about when we grow up and get married. Patricia says she's sorry and I'm sorry too so she reads me part of another poem which I have to remember so I can say it back to her early in the morning or late at night when there are no nuns or nurses about,

> The wind was a <u>torrent</u> of darkness among the gusty trees,
> The moon was a ghostly galleon tossed upon cloudy seas,
> The road was a ribbon of moonlight over the purple moor,
> And the highwayman came riding
> Riding riding
> The highwayman came riding, up to the old inn-door.
> He'd a French cocked-hat on his forehead, a bunch of lace at his chin,
> A coat of the claret velvet, and breeches of brown doe-skin,
> They fitted with never a wrinkle, his boots were up to the thigh.
> And he rode with a jeweled twinkle,
> His pistol butts a-twinkle,
> His rapier hilt a-twinkle, under the jeweled sky.[9]

Every day I can't wait for the doctors and nurses to leave me alone so I can learn a new verse from Patricia and find out what's happening to the highwayman and the landlord's red-lipped daughter. I love the poem because it's exciting and almost as good as my two lines of Shakespeare. The redcoats are after the highwayman because they know he told her, I'll come to thee by moonlight, . . .

I'd love to do that myself, come by moonlight for Patricia in the next room. . . . She's ready to read the last few verses when in comes the nurse from Kerry shouting at her, shouting at me, I told ye there was to be no talking between rooms. Diphtheria is never allowed to talk to typhoid and visa versa. I warned ye. And she calls out, Seamus, take this one. Take the by.[10] Sister Rita said one more word out of him and upstairs with him. We gave ye a warning to stop the blathering but ye wouldn't. Take the by, Seamus, take him.

Ah, now, nurse, sure isn't he harmless. 'Tis only a bit o' poetry.

Take that by, Seamus, take him at once.

He bends over me and whispers, Ah, . . . I'm sorry, Frankie. Here's your English history book. He slips the book under my shirt and lifts me from the bed. He whispers that I'm a feather. I try to see Patricia when we pass through her room but all I can make out is a blur of dark head on a pillow.

Sister Rita stops us in the hall to tell me I'm a great disappointment to her, that she expected me to be a good boy after what God had done for me, after all the prayers said by hundreds of boys at the Confraternity, after all the care from

---

8. **a poem . . . money:** "The Owl and the Pussycat," a humorous poem by the 19th-century British poet and artist Edward Lear.

9. **The wind . . . jeweled sky:** the opening lines of "The Highwayman," a narrative poem by the 20th-century British writer Alfred Noyes.

10. **by:** boy (spelled thus to indicate the nurse's dialectal pronunciation).

WORDS TO KNOW

recite (rĭ-sīt´) v. to say out loud something memorized
torrent (tôr´ənt) n. a rushing stream

the nuns and nurses of the Fever Hospital, after the way they let my mother and father in to see me, a thing rarely allowed, and this is how I repaid them lying in the bed reciting silly poetry back and forth with Patricia Madigan knowing very well there was a ban on all talk between typhoid and diphtheria. She says I'll have plenty of time to reflect on my sins in the big ward upstairs and I should beg forgiveness for my disobedience reciting a <u>pagan</u> English poem about a thief on a horse and a maiden with red lips who commits a terrible sin when I could have been praying or reading the life of a saint. She made it her business to read that poem so she did and I'd be well advised to tell the priest in confession.

The Kerry nurse follows us upstairs gasping and holding on to the banister. She tells me I better not get the notion she'll be running up to this part of the world every time I have a little pain or a twinge.

There are twenty beds in the ward, all white, all empty. The nurse tells Seamus put me at the far end of the ward against the wall to make sure I don't talk to anyone who might be passing the door, which is very unlikely since there isn't another soul on this whole floor. She tells Seamus this was the fever ward during the Great Famine[11] long ago and only God knows how many died here brought in too late for anything but a wash before they were buried and there are stories of cries and moans in the far reaches of the night. She says 'twould break your heart to think of what the English did to us, that if they didn't put the blight[12] on the potato they didn't do much to take it off. No pity. No feeling at all for the people that died in this very ward, children suffering and dying here while the English feasted on roast beef and guzzled the

> # There are twenty beds in the ward, all white, all empty.

---

11. **Great Famine** (făm'ĭn): a devastating food shortage in Ireland in the late 1840s, caused by a failure of the potato crop. Almost a million Irish people died of starvation during the famine, and about 1.5 million emigrated, mainly to the United States.

12. **blight:** a plant disease—in this case, the one that destroyed the Irish potato crop.

WORDS TO KNOW   **pagan** (pā'gən) *adj.* non-Christian

251

best of wine in their big houses, little children with their mouths all green from trying to eat the grass in the fields beyond, God bless us and save us and guard us from future famines.

Seamus says 'twas a terrible thing indeed and he wouldn't want to be walking these halls in the dark with all the little green mouths gaping at him. The nurse takes my temperature, 'Tis up a bit, have a good sleep for yourself now that you're away from the chatter with Patricia Madigan below who will never know a gray hair.[13]

She shakes her head at Seamus and he gives her a sad shake back.

Nurses and nuns never think you know what they're talking about. If you're ten going on eleven you're supposed to be simple like my uncle Pat Sheehan who was dropped on his head. You can't ask questions. You can't show you understand what the nurse said about Patricia Madigan, that she's going to die, and you can't show you want to cry over this girl who taught you a lovely poem which the nun says is bad.

The nurse tells Seamus she has to go and he's to sweep the lint from under my bed and mop up a bit around the ward. Seamus tells me . . . that you can't catch a disease from . . . he never heard the likes of it, a little fella shifted upstairs for saying a poem and he has a good mind to go to the *Limerick Leader*[14] and tell them print the whole thing except he has this job and he'd lose it if ever Sister Rita found out. Anyway, Frankie, you'll be outa here one of these fine days and you can read all the poetry you want though I don't know about Patricia below, I don't know about Patricia. . . .

He knows about Patricia in two days because she got out of the bed to go to the lavatory when she was supposed to use a bedpan and collapsed and died in the lavatory. Seamus is mopping the floor and there are tears on his cheeks and

he's saying, 'Tis a dirty rotten thing to die in a lavatory when you're lovely in yourself. She told me she was sorry she had you reciting that poem and getting you shifted from the room, Frankie. She said 'twas all her fault.

It wasn't, Seamus.

I know and didn't I tell her that.

Patricia is gone and I'll never know what happened to the highwayman and Bess, the landlord's daughter. I ask Seamus but he doesn't know any poetry at all especially English poetry. He knew an Irish poem once but it was about fairies and had no sign of a highwayman in it. Still he'll ask the men in his local pub where there's always someone reciting something and he'll bring it back to me. Won't I be busy meanwhile reading my short history of England and finding out all about their perfidy. That's what Seamus says, perfidy, and I don't know what it means and he doesn't know what it means but if it's something the English do it must be terrible.

He comes three times a week to mop the floor and the nurse is there every morning to take my temperature and pulse. The doctor listens to my chest with the thing hanging from his neck. They all say, And how's our little soldier today? A girl with a blue dress brings meals three times a day and never talks to me. Seamus says she's not right in the head so don't say a word to her.

The July days are long and I fear the dark. There are only two ceiling lights in the ward and they're switched off when the tea tray is taken away and the nurse gives me pills. The nurse tells me go to sleep but I can't because I see people in

---

13. **never know a gray hair:** won't live to be old.

14. *Limerick Leader:* a newspaper published in the Irish city of Limerick.

WORDS
TO
KNOW

perfidy (pûr′fĭ-dē) *n.* dishonesty; treachery

Royal Hospital, Kilmainham. The Irish Architectural Archive, Dublin.

the nineteen beds in the ward all dying and green around their mouths where they tried to eat grass and moaning for soup Protestant soup[15] any soup and I cover my face with the pillow hoping they won't come and stand around the bed clawing at me and howling for bits of the chocolate bar my mother brought last week.

No, she didn't bring it. She had to send it in because I can't have any more visitors. Sister Rita tells me a visit to the Fever Hospital is a privilege and after my bad behavior with Patricia Madigan and that poem I can't have the privilege anymore. She says I'll be going home in a few weeks and my job is to concentrate on getting better and learn to walk again after being in bed for six weeks and I can get out of bed tomorrow after breakfast. I don't know why she says I have to learn how to walk when I've been walking since I was a baby but when the nurse stands me by the side of the bed I fall to the floor and the nurse laughs, See, you're a baby again.

I practice walking from bed to bed back and forth back and forth. I don't want to be a baby. I don't want to be in this empty ward with no Patricia and no highwayman and no red-lipped landlord's daughter. I don't want the ghosts of children with green mouths pointing bony fingers at me and clamoring for bits of my chocolate bar.

Seamus says a man in his pub knew all the verses of the highwayman poem and it has a very sad end. Would I like him to say it because he never learned how to read and he had to carry the poem in his head? He stands in the middle of the ward leaning on his mop and recites,

Tlot-tlot, in the frosty silence! Tlot-tlot in the echoing night!

Nearer he came and nearer! Her face was like a light!
Her eyes grew wide for a moment, she drew one last deep breath,
Then her finger moved in the moonlight,
Her musket shattered the moonlight,
Shattered her breast in the moonlight and warned him—with her death.

He hears the shot and escapes but when he learns at dawn how Bess died he goes into a rage and returns for revenge only to be shot down by the redcoats.

Blood-red were his spurs in the golden noon; wine-red was his velvet coat,
When they shot him down on the highway,
Down like a dog on the highway,
And he lay in his blood on the highway, with a bunch of lace at his throat.

Seamus wipes his sleeve across his face and sniffles. He says, There was no call at all to shift you up here away from Patricia when you didn't even know what happened to the highwayman and Bess. 'Tis a very sad story and when I said it to my wife she wouldn't stop crying the whole night till we went to bed. She said there was no call for them redcoats to shoot that highwayman, they are responsible for half the troubles of the world and they never had any pity on the Irish, either. Now if you want to know any more poems, Frankie, tell me and I'll get them from the pub and bring 'em back in my head. ❖

---

15. **Protestant soup:** soup provided by the hated English.

WORDS TO KNOW

privilege (prĭv′ə-lĭj) *n.* a special benefit or advantage
clamoring (klăm′ər-ĭng) *adj.* making loud demands; crying out **clamor** *v.*

Connect to the Literature

1. What Do You Think?
What is your reaction to the way Frank is treated in the Fever Hospital?

Comprehension Check
- Why is Frank in the hospital?
- What rules does he disobey?
- How does he meet Patricia?

Think Critically

2. What do you think motivates Sister Rita to forbid Frank to talk to Patricia?

THINK ABOUT
- the kind of behavior she expects from children
- her profession
- what she knows about Patricia

3. How would you describe Seamus?

4. Do you think Frank benefited in any way from his experiences in the Fever Hospital? Explain your answer.

5. **ACTIVE READING** **MAKING INFERENCES** What **inferences** did you make about Frank's relationship with his father? What clues in the story helped you make these inferences? Use the notes you took in your ▮▮ **READER'S NOTEBOOK.**

Extend Interpretations

6. Critic's Corner One critic has said that, while reading *Angela's Ashes,* "you never know whether to weep or roar—and find yourself doing both at once." Did you think any of the incidents described in this selection were, at the same time, both sad and humorous? Give examples to support your answer.

7. Connect to Life What kinds of hospital experience do you think are best for children recovering from serious illness?

Literary Analysis

MEMOIR In a **memoir,** a writer usually describes important events from his or her own life. Most memoirs share the following characteristics: (1) they use the **first-person point of view;** (2) they are true accounts of actual events; (3) although basically personal, they may also deal with historical events or social issues; (4) they often include the writers' feelings and opinions about historical or social issues.

Paired Activity Make a chart like the one shown below. Working with a partner, go back through the selection and list instances where the author refers to historical or social issues. Also, describe any opinions about these issues that are expressed either by the author or by someone else in the selection. When you have finished, discuss what the evidence in your chart tells you about Ireland and the Irish people during the time of this memoir.

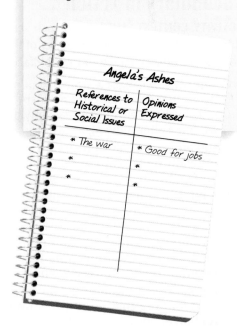

Angela's Ashes

References to Historical or Social Issues	Opinions Expressed
* The war	* Good for jobs
*	*
*	*

Writing Options

1. Personal Memoir Think about a time when you needed comfort or assistance and a friend, family member, or new acquaintance came to your aid. Write a brief personal memoir, describing the events as they actually happened. If possible, include any conversations that took place during the experience. Place your personal memoir in your **Working Portfolio.**

2. Caregivers Comparison In what ways do Sister Rita and Seamus differ? Write a paragraph in which you highlight the differences between these two caregivers.

Writing Handbook
See page 1155: Compare-Contrast.

3. Letter to the Editor Imagine that Seamus wants to tell the *Limerick Leader,* a local newspaper, about recent events in the Fever Hospital. Write the letter to the editor that you think Seamus might dictate if he were not worried about losing his job.

Activities & Explorations

1. Dramatic Reading Find a copy of "The Highwayman" by Alfred Noyes, the poem that Frank hears for the first time in the hospital. Practice reading the poem aloud, and then give a dramatic reading of it in front of a group of classmates. ~ **PERFORMING**

2. Stage Set Think of this excerpt as it might be performed on stage. Sketch the set design for such a production as you imagine it would look. ~ **ART**

Inquiry & Research

1. The Great Famine According to the nurse, Frank's empty ward was the "fever ward during the Great Famine." She is referring to a famine that devastated Ireland during the 1840s. Look for more information about the causes and effects of this disaster. Present your findings in an oral report to the class. Then discuss with class-mates why you think the Great Famine was still so important to the Irish 100 years later.

2. Disease Carriers Frank nearly died of typhoid fever, caused by poor sanitation. Some people can spread this disease without coming down with it themselves. Find out more about the restrictions placed on people who have infectious diseases. Are these restrictions warranted?

 Real World Link In the process of forming your opinion, read the Internet article about Typhoid Mary on page 258.

Vocabulary in Action

ACTIVITY: CONTEXT CLUES Read each sentence below. Then, on your paper, write the letter of the phrase that best clarifies the meaning of the boldfaced word.

1. Someone who calls a story **pagan** probably thinks that it (a) does not have any religious or moral value, (b) is not a real story, (c) was written a short time ago.

2. You are most likely to **recite** a poem if you (a) wrote it yourself, (b) want someone to hear it, (c) find it hard to understand.

3. A **relapse** of the flu usually means (a) it is hard to get well, (b) it is time for a flu shot, (c) it is time to go back to school or work.

4. A **clamoring** patient probably (a) disobeys all the rules, (b) appreciates the care he or she is receiving, (c) wants more attention from a nurse.

5. A **potent** medication would be most likely to be used for (a) a cold, (b) a diaper rash, (c) pneumonia.

6. A **torrent** of water could most likely be produced by (a) a leaky hose, (b) a large rain cloud, (c) a spray bottle.

7. If you can **induce** a friend to join you on a boring errand, you are probably good at (a) persuading others, (b) getting things done, (c) working alone.

8. Experiencing an act of **perfidy** might make you (a) travel in the wrong direction, (b) feel angry and betrayed, (c) decide to read historical fiction.

9. A nurse making an **exception** for you might (a) prepare your daily medication, (b) break a hospital rule, (c) take your temperature.

10. A patient given a **privilege** would most likely have (a) a serious illness, (b) bad behavior, (c) a private room.

Building Vocabulary
For an in-depth lesson on context clues, see page 103.

Grammar in Context: Compound Predicates

In the example below, a compound predicate expresses concisely a series of actions that might otherwise have taken many more words to explain.

> Mam comes with Dr. Troy. He feels my forehead, rolls up my eyelids, turns me over to see my back, picks me up **and** runs to his motor car.

A **predicate** is the part of a sentence that tells what the subject does or is or what happens to the subject. The predicate includes the sentence's verb or verbs. A compound predicate is made up of two or more predicates that share a subject. Using compound predicates can help you make your writing more concise and show how ideas are related.

Usage Tip: Make sure all of the verbs in a compound predicate refer to the same noun.

WRITING EXERCISE Rewrite each group of sentences as a single sentence with a compound predicate.

> **Example: Original** Sister Rita comes into my room. She wags her finger at me. She scolds me. Then she disappears into the hallway.
> **Rewritten** Sister Rita comes into my room, wags her finger at me, scolds me, and then disappears into the hallway.

1. The priest says mass in a corner. Then he touches me with oil. He prays in Latin.
2. Now Dr. Campbell sits by my bed. He holds my wrist. He hums.
3. In a whisper Patricia mocks the stern nun. She makes me laugh loudly.
4. Seamus brings me Patricia's book. He teaches me songs. He chats with me.
5. To pass the time, I practice walking. I read books. I imagine the past.

Grammar Handbook The Sentence and Its Parts, p.1190

Frank McCourt
1930–

Irish Roots Frank McCourt was born in Brooklyn, New York, where his parents had recently immigrated from Ireland. When his father had trouble keeping a job in New York, the family moved back to their homeland. McCourt was four years old at the time and lived with his family in Limerick, Ireland, until he was 19. It is this period of his life that the author describes in his memoir *Angela's Ashes*.

Family Poverty Because of a serious drinking problem, McCourt's father was fired from most of his jobs and usually spent whatever money he made in the pubs. Consequently, the family often had little money for food and was forced to seek help from local charities and the Irish welfare program. McCourt's mother, Angela, struggled constantly to keep the family clothed and fed. His baby sister and twin brothers died from childhood diseases that might have been prevented with better living conditions and proper medical care.

Musical Revue to Bestseller When he was 19, McCourt returned to the United States, where he eventually attended New York University. In one of his first careers, he and his brother Malachy performed a musical act about their Irish background. For many years McCourt was a high school writing teacher in New York City, where he still lives today. Published in 1996, *Angela's Ashes* earned outstanding reviews, quickly became a bestseller, and won prestigious awards.

Author Activity

A Pulitzer Prize In 1997, Frank McCourt was awarded the Pulitzer Prize for *Angela's Ashes*. Find out more about this award—the significance of winning a Pulitzer Prize, how recipients are chosen, and in what different categories the award is given.

FDA *Consumer*, June 1989

Mary Mallon's
Trail of Typhoid

by Catherine Carey

Salmonella in eggs! Botulism from garlic-in-oil! Listeria in cheese! It seems that every day newspapers are shouting headlines about outbreaks of food-borne illnesses. But these recent outbreaks, serious as they are, can't match the 11-year reign of typhoid epidemics caused by one person at the beginning of the 20th century.

Mary Mallon, known to history as "Typhoid Mary," was born sometime around 1870. She was the first typhoid carrier identified in the United States who never displayed a single symptom of the disease herself. But before she was captured and quarantined for life, she directly infected at least 51 people, three of whom died, and indirectly infected countless others.

Typhoid, or typhoid fever, is an acute infectious disease caused by Salmonella typhi bacteria. The bacteria enter the body through contaminated food or water, penetrate the small intestine, and thus invade the bloodstream, where they cause blood poisoning and carry infection into other parts of the body.

Early symptoms of the disease begin suddenly with headache, general aches and restlessness, coughing, nosebleeds, bloody diarrhea or constipation, and fever. A rash on the torso appears a week or two later. If the victim manages to survive, the fever begins to decline after about four weeks and gradually returns to normal. But if complications arise, such as heart failure and ulceration or perforation of the intestinal wall, typhoid is generally fatal.

About 30 percent of people infected with typhoid remain carriers, excreting the organism in their stool or urine for weeks or months. About 5 percent are long-term carriers, like Mary Mallon, who shed the organism for years. These carriers show no apparent ill effects but harbor the bacteria in their gallbladders and bile ducts.

Mallon's case came to light in 1904 when an epidemic of typhoid spread through New York's Oyster Bay and adjacent

Reading for Information

This article describes a disease outbreak that had an impact on many lives nearly a century ago. While the scientific understanding gained about typhoid was important, the article also shows how an incident that appears isolated or unimportant can have a huge impact on the world at large.

CAUSE AND EFFECT

To appreciate the impact of an event or action, look beyond the individual event itself. Try to see how it relates to events that come before or after it. Often these events have a cause-and-effect relationship; that is, one event directly causes the other. Being aware of this can lead to new insights about what you are reading.

- A **cause** is an event or action that directly results in another event. Clue words used to indicate cause include *because, due to,* and *since.*

- An **effect** is the direct outcome of an event or action. Words that indicate effect include *led to, as a result, consequently,* and *therefore.*

YOUR TURN To help you recognize cause and effect in this article, use the questions and activities that follow.

❶ Here, the writer provides specific information about how typhoid fever spreads throughout a population and describes its devastating effects. What does this important passage suggest about Mary Mallon's role in the outbreak?

towns on Long Island. A sanitary engineer with New York City's Department of Health named George Soper was asked to investigate. He found that Mallon had been employed as a cook in each of the stricken households. When he confronted her with his suspicion and offered medical care at no charge, she vehemently refused, going so far as to threaten the investigator with a rolling pin. She then disappeared.

But a persistent Soper, convinced Mallon was a typhoid carrier, tracked her for three years. He found her again in 1907, working as a cook in a Park Avenue home in Manhattan. Mallon was brought—literally kicking and screaming—to the Riverside Hospital for Communicable Diseases on North Brother Island, where, upon examination, she was found to be, in Soper's words, "a living culture tube" of typhoid bacteria. The authorities committed her to the isolation center, and, despite a legal appeal that was ultimately denied by the U.S. Supreme Court, she stayed at the center until 1910, when she was released after promising never to work as a food handler again.

But four years later, when typhoid epidemics broke out at a sanatorium in Newfoundland, New Jersey, and Sloane Maternity Hospital in Manhattan, Soper learned that Mallon had worked as a cook at both places and the search was on again.

She was found at last in 1915 and arrested at a friend's home in suburban Westchester County, New York, while making dessert. She was returned to Riverside, where she remained for the rest of her life. In her later years, she worked as a hospital volunteer and did a creditable job. A paralytic stroke led to her slow death in 1938.

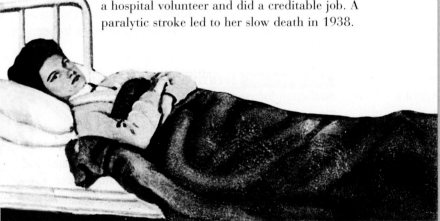

This old newsphoto shows Mary Mallon at the isolation center.

❷ What caused Mary Mallon to disappear?

❸ Review the events in these paragraphs. Use a graphic like this one to trace the pattern of events in Mary Mallon's life. Start with her disappearance and conclude with the number of infections that she is known to have directly caused. What can you infer about the "ripple" effects of Mary's actions—in other words, what impact might those 51 infected people have had on the general population?

Cause and Effect

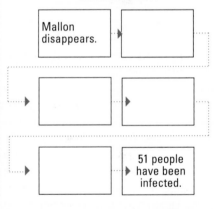

Mallon disappears.	
	51 people have been infected.

Inquiry & Research

Activity Link: *from* **"Angela's Ashes," p. 256** How did this article help you understand Frank McCourt's illness and treatment as described in the excerpt from *Angela's Ashes?* Write a short report explaining whether you believe the restrictions placed on Mary Mallon's activities were reasonable.

"Dying patients literally teach you about life."

Unfinished Business

ELISABETH KÜBLER-ROSS
Interview by LYNN GILBERT *and* GAYLEN MOORE

Connect to Your Life

How Would You Cope? In this selection, a psychiatrist tells about her work with a dying child and the child's family. Think about how you might react if you or a loved one were dying from an incurable illness. Look at the chart shown here, and jot down the phrases that describe what you think your reaction would be. Add any other reactions you think you might have.

Reactions to Dying	
accept it	get angry
avoid thinking about it	learn from it
become depressed	make the most of time left
deny it	try to bargain with God
face it	view it as a horrible thing
fear it	view it as a natural process
fight it	

Build Background

Therapy in Art Adults often think children are too young to understand what dying is. But even though young children may not be able to express in words their understanding of death, there is a way that they can share their inner awareness and their deepest feelings. In this selection, you will read how Elisabeth Kübler-Ross helped three children use drawing as a kind of "symbolic language" to describe their feelings about their dying sister. As you read, notice the drawings accompanying the selection. They were not made by the children Kübler-Ross describes but by the children from another family after their nine-month-old brother Kevin died as the result of a heart defect. The drawings by Sean, Mary Kate, and Kerry Cullen provide an example of the kind of "symbolic language" by which, Kübler-Ross says, even the very young can teach us about life and death.

> WORDS TO KNOW
> **Vocabulary Preview**
>
> bland
> concretely
> contaminated
> convey
> devastated
> procrastinating
> punitive
> spontaneous
> transcend
> uniqueness

Focus Your Reading

LITERARY ANALYSIS INTERVIEW An **interview** is an exchange of questions and answers between two people. What you are about to read comes out of an interview with Elisabeth Kübler-Ross, conducted by Lynn Gilbert and Gaylen Moore. However, the questions asked by the interviewers have been omitted. The result is a casual, conversational style that gives a vivid impression of this famous psychiatrist. As you read "Unfinished Business," pay attention to the impressions you get of Kübler-Ross as well as to her message about dying.

ACTIVE READING IDENTIFYING THE MAIN IDEA Most nonfiction focuses on a **main idea**—a central idea, message, or opinion that the writer wants to communicate to the reader. Sometimes the main idea is only implied or suggested. Other times it is stated directly. Typically, a main idea is broad and general and is supported by more specific ideas and details.

READER'S NOTEBOOK As you read "Unfinished Business," jot down some of the author's ideas as you come to them and mark the one that you think is the most general or main idea.

UNFINISHED BUSINESS

ELISABETH KÜBLER-ROSS

INTERVIEW BY LYNN GILBERT AND GAYLEN MOORE

I love to work with dying children. They're just so beautiful.

Nobody knows what pearls they are. They have all the wisdom in

the world. They know that they are dying. They know how and

when they are dying. They teach you all about life if you can hear,

if you can listen to them. They use an incredible symbolic language to convey to you how much they know. If people would only understand their symbolic language.

One of my girls, I took her home to die, but she couldn't die. She was just lying there week after week after week. And the father couldn't communicate with her. He was a very nonverbal man. The mother was very verbal and a

They know they are going to die, and they share their concepts of life and death and unfinished business in their pictures.

practicing Catholic. Every family member was at a different stage and used his own coping mechanism.[1] That's the time when you have to help always the ones who limp behind because they're going to hurt the most and they're going to have the most unfinished business. We try to help them finish the unfinished business *before* somebody dies, otherwise they have all the grief work afterward.

Grief is the most God-given gift to get in touch with your losses. You shed your tears and then stand up and start again like a child who falls and hurts his knees, cries for fifteen seconds and then jumps up and plays ball again. That's a natural thing. My work is preventive psychiatry, it's to finish as much as possible before death, like we bring flowers to our patients before they die so we don't have to pile them up on the casket afterward. If I love somebody, I tell them "I love you" now, so I can skip the schmaltzy eulogies[2] afterward.

One day I asked the father of this twelve-year

old girl if he would give me permission to talk to the other children, six, ten and eleven years old. He said, "They don't know about it." I said, "Come, your child's arms and legs are like pieces of chalk, and her belly is like she's nine months pregnant, and she's lying there slowly dying in the living room. How can a six-, ten- and eleven-year-old not know?" I said, "All I want is for you to give your permission for me to sit with them without grownups, and I'll ask them to draw me a picture." We used the Susan Bach method. She's a Jungian analyst[3] from London who worked in Zurich in my hospital there with children who had brain tumors. She saw that children who had brain tumors, little children, show in their pictures that they know they are going to die, and they share their concepts of life and death and unfinished business in their pictures.

I use this technique daily. In a few minutes I can evaluate the whole family and know who needs the most help and who's O.K. and who's in pain. You don't need hours and hours of psychiatric evaluation, which is just talking and just touches the surface. This is all preconscious[4] material. It's the same material that you would get if you had ten consecutive dreams, but I can get it at a morgue, at a wake, in a church, in a school, in a motel, in a shack in Alaska in an Eskimo family, with Aborigines in Australia; it costs nothing, it takes five minutes, it transcends language, it's human. All

---

1. **coping mechanism:** way of thinking or behaving that helps one deal with problems, troubles, or sorrows.
2. **schmaltzy eulogies** (shmält'sē yoo'lə-jēz): overly sentimental talk in praise of a dead person.
3. **Jungian** (yŏong'ē-ən) **analyst:** psychiatrist who follows the teachings of Carl Jung (1875–1961), a Swiss psychiatrist.
4. **preconscious:** having to do with memories or feelings that are not part of one's immediate awareness but that can be recalled through conscious effort.

Kerry, age 5, drew this picture of herself with Kevin in the bathtub.

Mary Kate, age 7, shows her sorrow and her love in this collage done on a round lid.

human beings are the same anyway.

So the father finally gave me permission, and I went there at three-thirty when school was out so that the father wouldn't be back, you know, and have second thoughts and give in to his own anxiety. The children were absolutely gorgeous. I locked the dining room with a key so no grownup could interfere, and I said, "Let's have a competition. We're going to draw a picture and we have ten minutes." I limit the time so they don't start thinking, so it's as genuine and authentic and <u>spontaneous</u> as possible. In every picture these children revealed they knew that their sister was dying. I just said, "Use any color and draw a picture."

Anyway, the six-year-old was just gorgeous. His picture was so clear. I talked with him about it in the presence of the others. I said to him, "What your picture is telling is that your sister is dying." He said, "Yes." I said, "Well, if

His sister lifted her arms up with her last strength and fell over his shoulders, and hanging on to him she started to sob and sob.

she's going to die tomorrow, is there anything you haven't done, because this is your last chance to say or do anything you want to do, so that you don't have to worry about it afterwards when it's too late. That's what grownups do, but you don't have to do that." That challenged him. He said, "Yeah, I guess I'm supposed to tell her I love her." I said, "You're already a phoney-baloney at six years old." Children shouldn't be that <u>contaminated</u>.

I said, "I've never seen a six-year-old who goes to a twelve-year-old and says, 'I love you.' There must have been a lot of things that she did that drove you up the wall, that she was unfair, you know, negative stuff." I said, "You can only really love her when you get rid of all the negative stuff, all the fights that you had, and when you get rid of that, then you love her so much that you don't need to say it, because she'll know it anyway and you'll know it."

He was fidgeting around at the table, and I said, "Come on, you're the youngest"—and the younger, the more honest they are—"get it out, what bugs you?" And he said, "Well, I really would like to tell her to get it over with already. I would like her to drop dead already." And I said, "Yes, naturally," as carefully as I could. And I said, "Why does it bug you that it takes so long?" He said, "I can't slam the doors ever, I can't bring my friends home, and I can't watch television anymore, and it's sickening how long it takes." You know, very natural, honest answers for a six-year-old.

I'm sitting there putting fuel on the fire and encouraging him to talk. The ten- and eleven-year-olds just sat there and stared at him. I said, "I wonder if you're honest enough and have the courage to share that with your sister." He said, "One ought not to do that." I said, "Who says? Do you think it's better to swallow this down, and then after she dies you have all these guilt trips and later on need counseling, or is it better to share it with your sister now and then you can love each other or forgive each other, whatever is necessary? And then you'll really feel super-duper. You will still miss her." They will have grief, you understand, but not grief *work*. He said, "Oh, I would love to be able to do that."

So you have to visualize . . . we go out into this living room where she lies there. And the

265

In this picture, Sean, age 9, imagines playing football with Kevin as an older boy. Sean praises Kevin with the words "nice throw."

six-year-old sits next to her, and I'm behind him, then the ten-year-old is behind me and the eleven-year-old behind her, then the mother came in and at the very end, the father behind her. And the arrangement was very symbolically beautiful. They came in the right chronological order in the courage they had to do that. Then the six-year-old starts <u>procrastinating</u> a little, and I gave him a little nudge in the pants with my foot. Then he blurted it out and said to her, "You know, sometimes it takes so long, sometimes I pray to get it over with."

He was just ready to explain, and something very beautiful happened with that symbolic language. His sister lifted her arms up with her last strength and fell over his shoulders, and hanging on to him she started to sob and sob and cry, not painful crying but tremendous relief. It was just like floodgates opening. In her sobbing she kept repeating, "Thank God, thank God, thank God. I prayed for the last three days for God to take me already because it really is getting too much now. And every time I finish my prayer, Mom comes in and stands in the doorway and said she spent the whole night sitting up, praying to God to keep me." And she said, "If you help me, then together we can outdo Mom."

WORDS TO KNOW

procrastinating (prō-krăs′tə-nā′tĭng) *n.* putting off doing something until later; delaying **procrastinate** *v.*

Children take everything very concretely. And he was the proudest man in the world, he was just beaming, and they were holding onto each other, crying and laughing. It was one of the most moving moments of house calls, and I've made lots of them. The other siblings naturally were envious that they weren't the ones who had the courage to do that.

About three days later I went back to see not just how she was doing, but how the six-year-old was doing, if he had any second thoughts about it. He was in super shape, he was high. But the girl couldn't die and so I asked the mother, I said, "If you don't mind, I'm just going to ask her straightforward, not in symbolic language, why she can't die, if that's O.K. with you. And I want you to come in and see how I'm doing that so you're never worried that I'm hurting anybody." She had great faith in me.

So I walked into the living room, and I looked at her and I said, "You just can't die, can you?" She said, "No." I said, "Why?" She said, "Because I can't get to heaven." I said, "Who told you that?" She said she was always taught for twelve years that nobody gets to heaven unless you have loved God more than anybody else in the whole world. Then she lifted her arms up and whispered in my ear as if she would try to prevent God from hearing her. She whispered very quietly, "You understand that I love my mommy and daddy better than anybody in the whole world."

That made me very sad that children have to apologize for that. What you then have to do is to set aside your own anger at the people who teach this kind of punitive approach. I said, "We're not going to get into an argument about who is right and who is wrong, because each one believes what they need to believe. I can only work with you and talk with you the way I always have. You and I always talked about school, and the biggest dream of your life was to be a schoolteacher. The only time I ever saw you devastated was in September when the school buses rolled up and school started after the summer vacation, and your brothers and sisters boarded the school bus, and you looked through this window and you really looked devastated." I said, "I think what happened was that at that moment it began to dawn on you that you will never again go back to your beloved school and you will never become a teacher." I said, "I want to ask only one question. Sometimes your teacher gives very tough assignments to some students." It was in the back of my mind that she was an honor student. I said, "Does she give these assignments to her lousy students? Does she give it to everybody in the class without discrimination, or does she give it to a very few of her hand-picked, chosen students?" Then her face lit up and she said, "Oh, she gives it to very few of us." I said, "Since God is also a teacher, do you think He gave you a tough assignment? Or an assignment he could give to any child?"

What she did then was symbolic language. At first she didn't answer me in words. Ever so slowly she looked down at her belly and her arms which were not thicker than my thumb, and her belly full of cancer. She very slowly looked down her body, and then she looked at me and said, "I don't think God could give a tougher assignment to any child."

She died about two and a half or three days later. My last communication with her was totally nonverbal and to me very beautiful because I knew that it helped her. I thought at that time she was in a coma, and I came then so as not to disturb the family in the last day or two. I stood in the doorway and took another look at her, and she suddenly opened her eyes. She couldn't speak anymore at that

WORDS TO KNOW   **concretely** (kŏn-krēt′lē) *adv.* in a real, solid, material way
punitive (pyōō′nĭ-tĭv) *adj.* punishing or having to do with punishment
devastated (dĕv′ə-stā′tĭd) *adj.* destroyed; stunned and overwhelmed **devastate** *v.*

267

time. And she looked down at her belly and her legs, and she had a big smirk on her face. And I nodded. She knew what I talked about and I knew what she talked about. It was totally nonverbal. It was very beautiful.

I learn always from dying patients. Instead of always looking at the negative, what you see is the <u>uniqueness</u> and strength in every single human being. I have patients who never share, never communicate. They live a very <u>bland</u> life, and anybody who looked at them would say, Is this all there is to it? and then you really get to know those people. There is a beauty in them that very few see. And all you have to do is look.

Dying patients look back at their lives, and they review and evaluate what they would do over again if they had a second chance, and that's very instructive because dying patients throw overboard all the following: they don't have to impress you anymore, they do not have to pretend. They're not interested in material things. They have no secondary gains except to honestly share what life is all about and what lessons they have learned too late. And they pass it on to you, and I pass it on to others so they don't have to wait until they're on their deathbed and say the same thing. Dying patients literally teach you about life. ❖

"Good Night, Willie Lee, I'll See You in the Morning"

Alice Walker

Looking down into my father's
dead face
for the last time
my mother said without
5   tears, without smiles
without regrets
but with *civility*[1]
"Good night, Willie Lee, I'll see you
in the morning."

10   And it was then I knew that the healing
of all our wounds
is forgiveness
that permits a promise
of our return
at the end.

---

1. **civility:** politeness, especially of a merely formal kind.

WORDS
TO
KNOW

uniqueness (yōō-nēk′nĭs) *n.* the quality or condition of being like no other
bland (blănd) *adj.* smooth and untroubled but also ordinary or dull

Thinking through the LITERATURE

Connect to the Literature

1. **What Do You Think?** Jot down words and phrases that describe your reactions to this selection. Then discuss your reactions with other classmates.

> **Comprehension Check**
> - What is the work that Kübler-Ross does?
> - What does she often ask children and families to do, so that she can find out how they feel?
> - Why was the 12-year-old girl having trouble dying?

Think Critically

2. **ACTIVE READING** **IDENTIFYING THE MAIN IDEA** Look at what you jotted down in your **READER'S NOTEBOOK** as you read the interview. What would you say is Kübler-Ross's **main idea**? Suggest one or two of her related ideas.

3. Consider the **title.** What do you think Kübler-Ross means by "unfinished business"?

4. What do you think of the approach that Kübler-Ross uses in trying to help the dying girl and her family?

> **THINK ABOUT**
> - "You're already a phoney-baloney at six years old."
> - "You can only really love her when you get rid of all the negative stuff."
> - "I'm just going to ask her straightforward . . . why she can't die."

5. What impressions of Kübler-Ross do you get from reading this **interview**?

6. What do you think people can learn from those who are dying?

Extend Interpretations

7. **Comparing Texts** Consider the death in "Good Night, Willie Lee, I'll See You in the Morning." Do you think there is any unfinished business here? Explain.

8. **Connect to Life** Look over the notes you made in the Connect to Your Life activity on page 260. Now that you have read the selection, would you change any of your notes? Explain.

Literary Analysis

INTERVIEW An **interview** is a series of questions and answers between two people. The interviewer usually comes away with notes and often with a tape recording. He or she then may present the questions and answers as they occurred or may shape the information into a **biographical essay** or **profile.** Another approach—the one used here by Gilbert and Moore—is to edit a taped interview, focusing on the best parts of the conversation and allowing the person being interviewed to speak directly to the reader. This format allows the person's personality to emerge clearly.

Paired Activity Since this selection is based not on written but on spoken remarks, it tends to have a looser, more conversational style. Working with a partner, go back through the selection and pick out three passages that sound like conversational speech rather than like a written essay. Read these passages aloud to a larger group, and discuss whether this casual style enhances or detracts from Kübler-Ross's **main idea.**

Choices & CHALLENGES

Writing Options

1. Interview Questions Imagine that you have been asked to do a follow-up interview of Kübler-Ross. Write a list of interview questions that you would ask her.

2. Character Sketch Write a brief profile or character sketch of Kübler-Ross, drawing upon the impressions you gained from reading this interview. Place your sketch in your **Working Portfolio.** 📁

Activities & Explorations

1. Artistic Rendering For most people, death is the ultimate uncharted territory. In a sketch or a painting, communicate the impressions of the experience of dying that you gained from reading this selection. ~ **ART**

2. Video Interviews Interview several people you know well about their attitudes toward dying. Videotape the interviews and, with the subjects' permission, share them in class. Discuss the different reactions that people have to the subject. ~ **VIEWING AND REPRESENTING**

Art Connection

Sean, Mary Kate, and Kerry Cullen drew their pictures in an art-therapy program run by Rose Richardson, a licensed clinical social worker. The children express their feelings in a safe environment with others their own age who have experienced similar losses. In Kerry's drawing (p. 263), you'll notice that both Kerry and Kevin are smiling, but dark geometric shapes cover the top part of the picture. How do you interpret this picture? Mary Kate's colorful collage (p. 264) includes stars, hearts, and other shiny decorations. What feelings does this picture communicate to you? In Sean's drawing (p. 266), why do you think Kevin is depicted as an older boy?

Vocabulary in Action

EXERCISE A: MEANING CLUES Write the vocabulary word that goes with each clue below.

1. This word describes rivers that industries dump waste products into.
2. Charities need to be supported in this way, as well as with kind thoughts.
3. You don't have to speak or write to do this; body language can do it.
4. Both fines and jail sentences can be described with this word.
5. If this word describes your life, you might feel you need to spice up your life a bit.
6. If you wanted to advise someone against doing this, you might say, "Make hay while the sun shines."
7. Things made on an assembly line or with a cookie cutter do not have this quality.
8. People who have suffered a terrible tragedy may describe their lives with this word.
9. A great work of art will often do this to any verbal attempt to describe the work.
10. If you suddenly want to have a picnic and you throw some sandwiches in a bag and go, your decision is this kind.

EXERCISE B Working with a partner, see how quickly you can communicate each of the vocabulary words by saying things that call that word to mind—but without using synonyms. For example, for bland, you might say, "Mashed potatoes, the color beige, boring movies, baby food . . . ," continuing until the correct word is guessed. Note that anything that could help your partner guess the word is allowed—a phrase, a description, an example—anything but a synonym. You might be the clue giver for half of the list and the guesser for the other half.

Building Vocabulary
For an in-depth study of context clues, see page 103.

WORDS TO KNOW	bland	contaminated	devastated	punitive	transcend
	concretely	convey	procrastinating	spontaneous	uniqueness

Grammar in Context: Simple Sentences

Elisabeth Kübler-Ross uses simple, uncomplicated sentences in describing her work with dying children.

> I love to work with dying children. They're just so beautiful. . . . They have all the wisdom in the world.

A **simple sentence** contains a subject and a verb and expresses a complete thought. It has only one main clause and no subordinate clauses. Using simple, direct sentences can be a very forceful way to signal the importance of ideas and to communicate feelings and thoughts. The use of simple sentences in combination with other types of sentences can produce interesting, rhythmic prose.

WRITING EXERCISE The following paragraph contains no simple sentences. Decide which ideas in it would be more effective if they stood alone. Then add sentence variety to the paragraph by rewriting it, using simple sentences to express those ideas.

Young children can recognize approaching death, and they can accept the truth and die in peace. Sometimes they can express their feelings more easily than adults can, since children do not rely just on words and they can use symbolic language. The pictures they draw and the colors they use provide insights into their thoughts, and a trained psychologist can use information gathered from pictures to help both the child and family members.

Grammar Handbook The Sentence and Its Parts, p. 1190

Elisabeth Kübler-Ross

1926–

Other Works
On Death and Dying
Death: The Final Stage of Growth
On Children and Death

Early Insights Elisabeth Kübler-Ross is one of the great humanitarians of our time. Raised in an upper-middle-class Swiss family, she decided early in life to become a doctor. Her father opposed this idea, however, so she postponed her medical education and took a position as a domestic servant. At the age of 18, she volunteered to help with war relief. While visiting the concentration camp of Majdanek in Poland, she was struck by pictures of butterflies scratched on the prison walls. She realized that doomed children, nearing their deaths in the gas chamber, must have viewed their spirits as butterflies leaving the cocoons of their bodies. This image of hope amid despair made a deep impression on her.

A Country Doctor Always determined, Kübler-Ross eventually gained her medical degree and worked as a country doctor in Switzerland. After immigrating to New York, she worked in a state mental hospital and achieved remarkable success in helping mentally ill patients who had been labeled hopeless.

Her True Work As a psychiatrist at Billings Hospital of the University of Chicago, Kübler-Ross began a series of seminars in which she interviewed dying patients. These seminars attracted national attention and publicity. Meanwhile, Kübler-Ross continued to help countless people view life and death as "a challenge and not a threat." She left the University of Chicago in 1969 and began giving workshops all over the world. Her work has inspired the establishment of hospice programs, which support terminally ill patients and their families.

Author Activity

On Telling the Truth A frequent question in dealing with the dying is how much to tell them about their condition. How can honesty best be balanced against hope? Find out what Kübler-Ross's answer is to this question. A good place to look is her classic work, *On Death and Dying*.

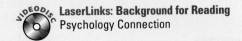

LaserLinks: Background for Reading
Psychology Connection

A Christmas Memory

Short Story by TRUMAN CAPOTE

"There is the question of money. Neither of us has any."

Connect to Your Life

Special Memories Think of a person that made a lasting impression on you. What kinds of scenes or activities—accompanied by special sights, sounds, smells, tastes, and sensations—remind you of this person? Jot down in a chart some details from your memories. Use the five senses as headings for the chart. As you read Truman Capote's story, based on his own childhood memories, notice the details that found their way into his narrative.

Special Memories	
Sight	
Smell	
Hearing	
Taste	
Touch	

Build Background

The Facts Behind the Fiction
Truman Capote grew up in the rural South during the Great Depression of the 1930s, a time of poverty and hardship for many Americans. He was raised by relatives in a small Alabama town. There he developed a close relationship with a much older female cousin, Sook Faulk. More than 20 years later, Capote details a lasting impression of Sook, creating a Christmas season representing memories of the experiences he had over the years with his cousin.

WORDS TO KNOW
Vocabulary Preview

cavort	inaugurate
conspiracy	noncommittal
exhilarate	prosaic
garish	sever
goad	squander

LaserLinks:
Background for Reading
Visual Vocabulary

Focus Your Reading

LITERARY ANALYSIS **AUTOBIOGRAPHICAL FICTION** The line between fiction and nonfiction is easy to cross. In creating a story, a writer may take material from anywhere, including experiences from his or her own life. Or the writer may set out to write an autobiography in the first place—but then shape and alter the material so much that it becomes more like a short story. That seems to be the case with "A Christmas Memory." For example, the following could come from Capote's own life:

The person to whom she is speaking is myself. I am seven; she is sixty-something.

But from the very opening lines of the story, the language is rich in the crafts of fiction: the shaping of character, setting, plot, and theme. These are the very things that turn memory into art. As you read the story, you'll find that it won't matter which details are strictly factual and which are not.

ACTIVE READING **NOTING SENSORY DETAILS** Good descriptive writing is usually rich in **imagery**—words and phrases that appeal to the various senses. Capote gives us a vivid, lasting impression of his holiday memory by creating descriptions that appeal to one or more of the five senses.

READER'S NOTEBOOK Make a chart like the one below. Then as you read, jot down the phrases or details from the selection that you find especially striking. Check off the senses that are appealed to in each case.

Description	Sight	Smell	Hearing	Taste	Touch
Cracking open the pecans	✔		✔	✔	

Imagine a morning in late November. A coming of winter morning more than twenty years ago.

A Christmas Memory

Truman Capote

Consider the kitchen of a spreading old house in a country town. A great black stove is its main feature; but there is also a big round table and a fireplace with two rocking chairs

placed in front of it. Just today the fireplace commenced its seasonal roar.

A woman with shorn white hair is standing at the kitchen window. She is wearing tennis shoes and a shapeless gray sweater over a summery calico dress. She is small and sprightly, like a bantam hen; but, due to a long youthful illness, her shoulders are pitifully hunched. Her face is remarkable—not unlike Lincoln's, craggy like that, and tinted by sun and wind; but it is delicate too, finely boned, and her eyes are sherry-colored and timid. "Oh my," she exclaims, her breath smoking the windowpane, "it's fruitcake weather!"

The person to whom she is speaking is myself. I am seven; she is sixty-something. We are cousins, very distant ones, and we have lived together—well, as long as I can remember. Other people inhabit the house, relatives; and though they have power over us, and frequently make us cry, we are not, on the whole, too much aware of them. We are each other's best friend. She calls me Buddy, in memory of a boy who was formerly her best friend. The other Buddy died in the 1880's, when she was still a child. She is still a child.

"I knew it before I got out of bed," she says, turning away from the window with a purpose-ful excitement in her eyes. "The courthouse bell sounded so cold and clear. And there were no birds singing; they've gone to warmer country, yes indeed. Oh, Buddy, stop stuffing biscuit and fetch our buggy. Help me find my hat. We've thirty cakes to bake."

It's always the same: a morning arrives in November, and my friend, as though officially inaugurating the Christmas time of year that exhilarates her imagination and fuels the blaze of her heart, announces: "It's fruitcake weather! Fetch our buggy. Help me find my hat."

The hat is found, a straw cartwheel corsaged with velvet roses out-of-doors has faded: it once belonged to a more fashionable relative. Together, we guide our buggy, a dilapidated baby carriage, out to the garden and into a grove of pecan trees. The buggy is mine; that is, it was bought for me when I was born. It is made of wicker, rather unraveled, and the wheels wobble like a drunkard's legs. But it is a faithful object; springtimes, we take it to the woods and fill it with flowers, herbs, wild fern for our porch pots; in the summer, we pile it with picnic paraphernalia and sugar-cane fishing poles and roll it down to the edge of a creek; it has its winter uses, too: as a truck for hauling firewood from the yard to the kitchen, as a warm bed for Queenie, our tough little orange and white rat terrier who has survived distemper[1] and two rattlesnake bites. Queenie is trotting beside it now.

Three hours later we are back in the kitchen hulling a heaping buggyload of windfall pecans. Our backs hurt from gathering them: how hard they were to find (the main crop having been shaken off the trees and sold by the orchard's owners, who are not us) among the concealing leaves, the frosted, deceiving grass. Caarackle! A cheery crunch, scraps of miniature thunder sound as the shells collapse and the golden mound of sweet oily ivory meat mounts in the milk-glass bowl. Queenie begs to taste, and now and again my friend sneaks her a mite, though insisting we deprive ourselves. "We mustn't, Buddy. If we start, we won't stop. And there's scarcely enough as there is. For thirty cakes." The kitchen is growing dark. Dusk turns the window into a mirror: our reflections mingle with the rising moon as we work by the fireside

---

1. **distemper:** an infectious viral disease of dogs.

| WORDS TO KNOW | **inaugurate** (ĭn-ô′gyə-rāt′) *v.* to make a formal beginning of |
| | **exhilarate** (ig-zĭl′ə-rāt′) *v.* to make merry or lively |

in the firelight. At last, when the moon is quite high, we toss the final hull into the fire and, with joined sighs, watch it catch flame. The buggy is empty, the bowl is brimful.

We eat our supper (cold biscuits, bacon, blackberry jam) and discuss tomorrow. Tomorrow the kind of work I like best begins: buying. Cherries and citron, ginger and vanilla and canned Hawaiian pineapple, rinds and raisins and walnuts and whiskey and oh, so much flour, butter, so many eggs, spices, flavorings: why, we'll need a pony to pull the buggy home.

But before these purchases can be made, there is the question of money. Neither of us has any. Except for skinflint sums persons in the house occasionally provide (a dime is considered very big money); or what we earn ourselves from various activities: holding rummage sales, selling buckets of hand-picked blackberries, jars of homemade jam and apple jelly and peach preserves, rounding up flowers for funerals and weddings. Once we won seventy-ninth prize, five dollars, in a national football contest. Not that we know a fool thing about football. It's just that we enter any contest we hear about: at the moment our hopes are centered on the fifty-thousand-dollar Grand Prize being offered to name a new brand of coffee (we suggested "A.M."; and, after some hesitation, for my friend thought it perhaps sacrilegious, the slogan "A.M.! Amen!"). To tell the truth, our only *really* profitable enterprise was

the Fun and Freak Museum we conducted in a back-yard woodshed two summers ago. The Fun was a stereopticon[2] with slide views of Washington and New York lent us by a relative who had been to those places (she was furious when she discovered why we'd borrowed it); the Freak was a three-legged biddy chicken hatched by one of our own hens. Everybody hereabouts wanted to see that biddy: we charged grownups a nickel, kids two cents. And took in a good twenty dollars before the museum shut down due to the decease of the main attraction. But one way and another we do each year accumulate Christmas savings, a Fruitcake Fund. These moneys we keep hidden in an ancient bead purse under a loose board under the floor under a chamber pot under my friend's bed. The purse is seldom removed from this safe location except to make a deposit or, as happens every Saturday, a withdrawal; for on Saturdays I am allowed ten cents to go to the picture show. My friend has never been to a picture show, nor does she intend to: "I'd rather hear you tell the story, Buddy. That way I can imagine it more. Besides, a person my age shouldn't <u>squander</u> their eyes. When the Lord comes, let me see him clear." In addition to never having seen a movie, she

---

2. **stereopticon** (stĕr′ē-ŏp′tĭ-kŏn): an early slide projector that could merge two images of the same scene on a screen, resulting in a 3-D effect.

WORDS TO KNOW   **squander** (skwŏn′dər) *v.* to spend or use wastefully

has never: eaten in a restaurant, traveled more than five miles from home, received or sent a telegram, read anything except funny papers and the Bible, worn cosmetics, cursed, wished someone harm, told a lie on purpose, let a hungry dog go hungry. Here are a few things she has done, does do: killed with a hoe the biggest rattle-snake ever seen in this county (sixteen rattles), dip snuff[3] (secretly), tame hummingbirds (just try it) till they balance on her finger, tell ghost stories (we both believe in ghosts) so tingling they chill you in July, talk to herself, take walks in the rain, grow the prettiest japonicas[4] in town, know the recipe for every sort of old-time Indian cure, including a magical wart remover.

ACTIVE READING

QUESTION What questions or thoughts do you have about the characters and situation so far?

Now, with supper finished, we retire to the room in a faraway part of the house where my friend sleeps in a scrap-quilt-covered iron bed painted rose pink, her favorite color. Silently, wallowing in the pleasures of <u>conspiracy</u>, we take the bead purse from its secret place and spill its contents on the scrap quilt. Dollar bills, tightly rolled and green as May buds. Somber fifty-cent pieces, heavy enough to weight a dead man's eyes.[5] Lovely dimes, the liveliest coin, the one that really jingles. Nickels and quarters, worn smooth as creek pebbles. But mostly a hateful heap of bitter-odored pennies. Last summer others in the house contracted to pay us a penny for every twenty-five flies we killed. Oh, the carnage of August: the flies that flew to heaven! Yet it was not work in which we took pride. And, as we sit counting pennies, it is as though we were back tabulating dead flies. Neither of us has a head for figures; we count

To tell the truth, our only really profitable enterprise was the Fun and Freak Museum we conducted in a back-yard woodshed two summers ago.

---

3. **dip snuff:** to rub (dip) a finely ground tobacco (snuff) on one's teeth and gums.
4. **japonica** (jə-pŏn′ĭ-kə): an ornamental bush with red flowers.
5. **heavy enough to weight a dead man's eyes:** from the custom of putting coins on the closed eyes of corpses to keep the eyelids from opening.

WORDS TO KNOW   **conspiracy** (kən-spîr′ə-sē) *n.* a joining or acting together in a secretive way, often with wrongful motives

277

slowly, lose track, start again. According to her calculations, we have $12.73. According to mine, exactly $13. "I do hope you're wrong, Buddy. We can't mess around with thirteen. The cakes will fall. Or put somebody in the cemetery. Why, I wouldn't dream of getting out of bed on the thirteenth." This is true: she always spends thirteenths in bed. So, to be on the safe side, we subtract a penny and toss it out the window.

Of the ingredients that go into our fruitcakes, whiskey is the most expensive, as well as the hardest to obtain: State laws forbid its sale. But everybody knows you can buy a bottle from Mr. Haha Jones. And the next day, having completed our more prosaic shopping, we set out for Mr. Haha's business address, a "sinful" (to quote public opinion) fish-fry and dancing café down by the river. We've been there before, and on the same errand; but in previous years our dealings have been with Haha's wife, an iodine-dark Indian woman with brassy peroxided hair and a dead-tired disposition. Actually, we've never laid eyes on her husband, though we've heard that he's an Indian too. A giant with razor scars across his cheeks. They call him Haha because he's so gloomy, a man who never laughs. As we approach his café (a large log cabin festooned inside and out with chains of garish-gay naked light bulbs and standing by the river's muddy edge under the shade of river trees where moss drifts through the branches like gray mist) our steps slow down. Even Queenie stops prancing and sticks close by. People have been murdered in Haha's café. Cut to pieces. Hit on the head. There's a case coming up in court next month.

Naturally these goings-on happen at night when the colored lights cast crazy patterns and the Victrola[6] wails. In the daytime Haha's is shabby and deserted. I knock at the door, Queenie barks, my friend calls: "Mrs. Haha, ma'am? Anyone to home?"

Footsteps. The door opens. Our hearts overturn. It's Mr. Haha Jones himself! And he *is* a giant; he *does* have scars; he *doesn't* smile. No, he glowers at us through Satan-tilted eyes and demands to know: "What you want with Haha?"

For a moment we are too paralyzed to tell. Presently my friend half-finds her voice, a whispery voice at best: "If you please, Mr. Haha, we'd like a quart of your finest whiskey."

His eyes tilt more. Would you believe it? Haha is smiling! Laughing, too. "Which one of you is a drinkin' man?"

"It's for making fruitcakes, Mr. Haha. Cooking."

This sobers him. He frowns. "That's no way to waste good whiskey." Nevertheless, he retreats into the shadowed café and seconds later appears carrying a bottle of daisy-yellow unlabeled liquor. He demonstrates its sparkle in the sunlight and says: "Two dollars."

We pay him with nickels and dimes and pennies. Suddenly, as he jangles the coins in his hand like a fistful of dice, his face softens. "Tell you what," he proposes, pouring the money back into our bead purse, "just send me one of them fruitcakes instead."

"Well," my friend remarks on our way home, "there's a lovely man. We'll put an extra cup of raisins in *his* cake."

The black stove, stoked with coal and firewood, glows like a lighted pumpkin. Eggbeaters whirl, spoons spin round in bowls of butter and sugar, vanilla sweetens the air,

---

6. **Victrola:** a trademark for a brand of old record player that would play grooved black discs with a needle.

278

ACTIVE READING

CONNECT Remember the smell of something cooking? List several foods you remember smelling as they cooked.

ginger spices it; melting, nose-tingling odors saturate the kitchen, suffuse the house, drift out to the world on puffs of chimney smoke. In four days our work is done. Thirty-one cakes, dampened with whiskey, bask on windowsills and shelves.

Who are they for?

Friends. Not necessarily neighbor friends: indeed, the larger share is intended for persons we've met maybe once, perhaps not at all. People who've struck our fancy. Like President Roosevelt. Like the Reverend and Mrs. J. C. Lucey, Baptist missionaries to Borneo who lectured here last winter. Or the little knife grinder who comes through town twice a year. Or Abner Packer, the driver of the six o'clock bus from Mobile, who exchanges waves with us every day as he passes in a dust-cloud whoosh. Or the young Wistons, a California couple whose car one afternoon broke down outside the house and who spent a pleasant hour chatting with us on the porch (young Mr. Wiston snapped our picture, the only one we've ever had taken). Is it because my friend is shy with everyone *except* strangers that these strangers, and merest acquaintances, seem to us our truest friends? I think yes. Also, the scrapbooks we keep of thank-you's on White House stationery, time-to-time communications from California and Borneo, the knife grinder's penny post cards, make us feel connected to eventful worlds beyond the kitchen with its view of a sky that stops.

Now a nude December fig branch grates against the window. The kitchen is empty, the cakes are gone; yesterday we carted the last of them to the post office, where the cost of stamps turned our purse inside out. We're broke. That rather depresses me, but my friend insists on celebrating—with two inches of whiskey left in Haha's bottle. Queenie has a spoonful in a bowl of coffee (she likes her coffee chicory-flavored and strong). The rest we divide between a pair of jelly glasses. We're both quite awed at the prospect of drinking straight whiskey; the taste of it brings screwed-up expressions and sour shudders. But by and by we begin to sing, the two of us singing different songs simultaneously. I don't know the words to mine, just: *Come on along, come on along, to the dark-town strutters' ball.* But I can dance: that's what I mean to be, a tap dancer in the movies. My dancing shadow rollicks on the walls; our voices rock the chinaware; we giggle: as if unseen hands were tickling us. Queenie rolls on her back, her paws plow the air, something like a grin stretches her black lips. Inside myself, I feel warm and sparky as those crumbling logs, carefree as the wind in the chimney. My friend waltzes round the stove, the hem of her poor calico skirt pinched between her fingers as though it were a party dress: *Show me the way to go home,* she sings, her tennis shoes squeaking on the floor. *Show me the way to go home.*

Enter: two relatives. Very angry. Potent with eyes that scold, tongues that scald. Listen to what they have to say, the words tumbling together into a wrathful tune: "A child of seven! whiskey on his breath! are you out of your mind? feeding a child of seven! must be loony! road to ruination! remember Cousin Kate? Uncle Charlie? Uncle Charlie's brother-in-law? shame! scandal! humiliation! kneel, pray, beg the Lord!"

Queenie sneaks under the stove. My friend gazes at her shoes, her chin quivers, she lifts her skirt and blows her nose and runs to her room.

Long after the town has gone to sleep and the house is silent except for the chimings of clocks and the sputter of fading fires, she is weeping

Having stuffed
our burlap sacks
with enough
greenery and
crimson to
garland a dozen
windows, we
set about
choosing a tree.

❧

into a pillow already as wet as a widow's handkerchief.

"Don't cry," I say, sitting at the bottom of her bed and shivering despite my flannel nightgown that smells of last winter's cough syrup, "don't cry," I beg, teasing her toes, tickling her feet, "you're too old for that."

"It's because," she hiccups, "I *am* too old. Old and funny."

"Not funny. Fun. More fun than anybody. Listen. If you don't stop crying you'll be so tired tomorrow we can't go cut a tree."

She straightens up. Queenie jumps on the bed (where Queenie is not allowed) to lick her cheeks. "I know where we'll find real pretty trees, Buddy. And holly, too. With berries big as your eyes. It's way off in the woods. Farther than we've ever been. Papa used to bring us Christmas trees from there: carry them on his shoulder. That's fifty years ago. Well, now: I can't wait for morning."

Morning. Frozen rime[7] lusters the grass; the sun, round as an orange and orange as hot-weather moons, balances on the horizon, burnishes the silvered winter woods. A wild turkey calls. A renegade hog grunts in the undergrowth. Soon, by the edge of knee-deep, rapid-running water, we have to abandon the buggy. Queenie wades the stream first, paddles across barking complaints at the swiftness of the current, the pneumonia-making coldness of it. We follow, holding our shoes and equipment (a hatchet, a burlap sack) above our heads. A mile more: of chastising thorns, burrs and briers that catch at our clothes; of rusty pine needles brilliant with gaudy fungus and molted

ACTIVE READING

CLARIFY How would you describe Buddy's friend? Explain how she's different from most people her age.

---

7. **rime:** a white frost.

feathers. Here, there, a flash, a flutter, an ecstasy of shrillings remind us that not all the birds have flown south. Always, the path unwinds through lemony sun pools and pitch-black vine tunnels. Another creek to cross: a disturbed armada of speckled trout froths the water round us, and frogs the size of plates practice belly flops; beaver workmen are building a dam. On the farther shore, Queenie shakes herself and trembles. My friend shivers, too: not with cold but enthusiasm. One of her hat's ragged roses sheds a petal as she lifts her head and inhales the pine-heavy air. "We're almost there; can you smell it, Buddy?" she says, as though we were approaching an ocean.

And, indeed, it is a kind of ocean. Scented acres of holiday trees, prickly-leafed holly. Red berries shiny as Chinese bells: black crows swoop upon them screaming. Having stuffed our burlap sacks with enough greenery and crimson to garland a dozen windows, we set about choosing a tree. "It should be," muses my friend, "twice as tall as a boy. So a boy can't steal the star." The one we pick is twice as tall as me. A brave handsome brute that survives thirty hatchet strokes before it keels with a creaking rending cry. Lugging it like a kill, we commence the long trek out. Every few yards we abandon the struggle, sit down and pant. But we have the strength of triumphant huntsmen; that and the tree's virile, icy perfume revive us, goad us on. Many compliments accompany our sunset return along the red clay road to town; but my friend is sly and noncommittal when passers-by praise the treasure perched in our buggy: what a fine tree, and where did it come from?

"Yonderways," she murmurs vaguely. Once a car stops, and the rich mill owner's lazy wife leans out and whines: "Giveya two-bits[8] cash for that ol tree." Ordinarily my friend is afraid of saying no; but on this occasion she promptly shakes her head: "We wouldn't take a dollar." The mill owner's wife persists. "A dollar, my foot! Fifty cents. That's my last offer. Goodness, woman, you can get another one." In answer, my friend gently reflects: "I doubt it. There's never two of anything."

Home: Queenie slumps by the fire and sleeps till tomorrow, snoring loud as a human.

A trunk in the attic contains: a shoebox of ermine[9] tails (off the opera cape of a curious lady who once rented a room in the house), coils of frazzled tinsel gone gold with age, one silver star, a brief rope of dilapidated, undoubtedly dangerous candylike light bulbs. Excellent decorations, as far as they go, which isn't far enough: my friend wants our tree to blaze "like a Baptist window," droop with weighty snows of ornament. But we can't afford the made-in-Japan splendors at the five-and-dime. So we do what we've always done: sit for days at the kitchen table with scissors and crayons and stacks of colored paper. I make sketches and my friend cuts them out: lots of cats, fish too (because they're easy to draw), some apples, some

---

8. **two-bits:** twenty-five cents.
9. **ermine** (ûr'mĭn): the soft, white fur of a weasel of northern regions.

281

Anna Kuerner (1971), Andrew Wyeth. Tempera on panel, private collection. Copyright © 1995 Andrew Wyeth.

watermelons, a few winged angels devised from saved-up sheets of Hershey-bar tin foil. We use safety pins to attach these creations to the tree; as a final touch, we sprinkle the branches with shredded cotton (picked in August for this purpose). My friend, surveying the effect, clasps her hands together. "Now honest, Buddy. Doesn't it look good enough to eat?" Queenie tries to eat an angel.

After weaving and ribboning holly wreaths for all the front windows, our next project is the fashioning of family gifts. Tie-dye scarves for the ladies, for the men a home-brewed lemon and licorice and aspirin syrup to be taken "at the first

EVALUATE

EVALUATE What do you think of Buddy and his friend's Christmas decorations?

Symptoms of a Cold and after Hunting." But when it comes time for making each other's gift, my friend and I separate to work secretly. I would like to buy her a pearl-handled knife, a radio, a whole pound of chocolate-covered cherries (we tasted some once, and she always swears: "I could live on them, Buddy, Lord yes I could—and that's not taking his name in vain"). Instead, I am building her a kite. She would like to give me a bicycle (she's said so on several million occasions: "If only I could, Buddy. It's bad enough in life to do without something *you* want; but confound it, what gets my goat is not being able to give somebody something you want *them* to have. Only one of these days I will, Buddy. Locate you a bike. Don't ask how. Steal it, maybe"). Instead, I'm fairly certain that she is building me a kite—the same as last year and the year before: the year before that we exchanged slingshots. All of which is fine by me. For we are champion kite fliers who study the wind like sailors; my friend, more accomplished than I, can get a kite aloft when there isn't enough breeze to carry clouds.

Christmas Eve afternoon we scrape together a nickel and go to the butcher's to buy Queenie's traditional gift, a good gnawable beef bone. The bone, wrapped in funny paper, is placed high in the tree near the silver star. Queenie knows it's there. She squats at the foot of the tree staring up in a trance of greed: when bedtime arrives she refuses to budge. Her excitement is equaled by my own. I kick the covers and turn my pillow as though it were a scorching summer's night. Somewhere a rooster crows: falsely, for the sun is still on the other side of the world.

"Buddy, are you awake?" It is my friend, calling from her room, which is next to mine; and an instant later she is sitting on my bed holding a candle. "Well, I can't sleep a hoot," she declares. "My mind's jumping like a jack rabbit. Buddy, do you think Mrs. Roosevelt will serve our cake at dinner?" We huddle in the bed, and she squeezes my hand I-love-you. "Seems like your hand used to be so much smaller. I guess I hate to see you grow up. When you're grown up, will we still be friends?" I say always. "But I feel so bad, Buddy. I wanted so bad to give you a bike. I tried to sell my cameo Papa gave me. Buddy"—she hesitates, as though embarrassed—"I made you another kite." Then I confess that I made her one, too; and we laugh. The candle burns too short to hold. Out it goes, exposing the starlight, the stars spinning at the window like a visible caroling that slowly, slowly daybreak silences. Possibly we doze; but the beginnings of dawn splash us like cold water: we're up, wide-eyed and wandering while we wait for others to waken. Quite deliberately my friend drops a kettle on the kitchen floor. I tap dance in front of closed doors. One by one the household emerges, looking as though they'd like to kill us both; but it's Christmas, so they can't. First, a gorgeous breakfast: just everything you can imagine—from flapjacks[10] and fried squirrel to hominy grits and honey-in-the-comb. Which puts everyone in a good humor except my friend and me. Frankly, we're so impatient to get at the presents we can't eat a mouthful.

Well, I'm disappointed. Who wouldn't be? With socks, a Sunday school shirt, some handkerchiefs, a hand-me-down sweater, and a year's subscription to a religious magazine for children. *The Little Shepherd.* It makes me boil. It really does.

My friend has a better haul. A sack of satsumas,[11] that's her best present. She is proudest, however, of a white wool shawl knitted by her married sister. But she *says* her favorite gift is the kite I built her. And it *is* very beautiful; though not as beautiful as the one she made me, which is blue and scattered with gold and green Good Conduct stars;[12] moreover, my name is painted on it, "Buddy."

"Buddy, the wind is blowing."

The wind is blowing, and nothing will do till we've run to a pasture below the house where Queenie has scooted to bury her bone (and where, a winter hence, Queenie will be buried, too). There, plunging through the healthy waist-

ACTIVE READING

CONNECT Have you ever been disappointed with gifts you couldn't wait to open? Jot down your most disappointing gifts.

---

10. **flapjacks:** pancakes.

11. **satsumas** (săt-soō′məz): fruit similar to tangerines.

12. **Good Conduct stars:** small, shiny, glued paper stars often awarded to children for good behavior or perfect attendance.

high grass, we unreel our kites, feel them twitching at the string like sky fish as they swim into the wind. Satisfied, sun-warmed, we sprawl in the grass and peel satsumas and watch our kites cavort. Soon I forget the socks and hand-me-down sweater. I'm as happy as if we'd already won the fifty-thousand-dollar Grand Prize in that coffee-naming contest.

"My, how foolish I am!" my friend cries, suddenly alert, like a woman remembering too late she has biscuits in the oven. "You know what I've always thought?" she asks in a tone of discovery and not smiling at me but a point beyond. "I've always thought a body would have to be sick and dying before they saw the Lord. And I imagined that when he came it would be like looking at the Baptist window: pretty as colored glass with the sun pouring through, such a shine you don't know it's getting dark. And it's been a comfort: to think of that shine taking away all the spooky feeling. But I'll wager it never happens. I'll wager at the very end a body realizes the Lord has already shown himself. That things as they are"—her hand circles in a gesture that gathers clouds and kites and grass and Queenie pawing earth over her bone—"just what they've always seen, was seeing him. As for me, I could leave the world with today in my eyes."

This is our last Christmas together.

Life separates us. Those who Know Best decide that I belong in a military school. And so follows a miserable succession of bugle-blowing prisons, grim reveille-ridden[13] summer camps. I

ACTIVE READING

CONNECT Recall a time when you were happy with something simple and inexpensive.

have a new home too. But it doesn't count. Home is where my friend is, and there I never go.

And there she remains, puttering around the kitchen. Alone with Queenie. Then alone. ("Buddy dear," she writes in her wild hard-to-read script, "yesterday Jim Macy's horse kicked Queenie bad. Be thankful she didn't feel much. I wrapped her in a Fine Linen sheet and rode her in the buggy down to Simpson's pasture where she can be with all her Bones. . . ."). For a few Novembers she continues to bake her fruitcakes single-handed; not as many, but some: and, of course, she always sends me "the best of the batch." Also, in every letter she encloses a dime wadded in toilet paper: "See a picture show and write me the story." But gradually in her letters she tends to confuse me with her other friend, the Buddy who died in the 1880's; more and more, thirteenths are not the only days she stays in bed: a morning arrives in November, a leafless birdless coming of winter morning, when she cannot rouse herself to exclaim: "Oh my, it's fruitcake weather!"

And when that happens, I know it. A message saying so merely confirms a piece of news some secret vein had already received, severing from me an irreplaceable part of myself, letting it loose like a kite on a broken string. That is why, walking across a school campus on this particular December morning, I keep searching the sky. As if I expected to see, rather like hearts, a lost pair of kites hurrying toward heaven. ❖

---

13. **reveille-ridden** (rĕv′ə-lē): dominated by an early-morning signal, as on a bugle, to wake soldiers or campers.

WORDS
TO
KNOW

cavort (kə-vôrt′) v. to leap or romp about
sever (sĕv′ər) v. to cut off

Connect to the Literature

1. **What Do You Think?** What emotions did this holiday story trigger in you? Jot down your response.

> **Comprehension Check**
> - Who is Buddy's best friend?
> - What is different about this particular Christmas in Buddy's memory?
> - What causes the two friends to be separated?
> - What happens to Buddy's friend?

Think Critically

2. Describe the image you have of Buddy's best friend. What **details** helped create this image in your mind?

3. Buddy is seven; his cousin is over 60. Why do you think they become good friends?

THINK ABOUT
- Buddy's statement, "She is still a child."
- their status in the household
- the things that give them pleasure
- the way the cousin treats Buddy

4. **ACTIVE READING** **NOTING SENSORY DETAILS** Look over the descriptive passages and **sense images** that you noted in your 📖 **READER'S NOTEBOOK**. Which description impressed you the most? What kind of sense images did it use? Explain why the passage impressed you.

5. What might the two kites at the end of the story represent or be a **symbol** of?

Extend Interpretations

6. **Comparing Texts** This story, like the selection from *Angela's Ashes*, describes the interaction of a young person with various adults around him. How would you compare and contrast the two situations?

7. **Connect to Life** Have you ever known anyone who was an "outcast"—someone who was different from other people, causing him or her to be alone? What do you think a community's role should be in including an outsider? What should your role be? Explain your answer.

Literary Analysis

> **AUTOBIOGRAPHICAL FICTION**

Autobiography is the story of a person's life written by that person. A work of **fiction** is a narrative that springs from the imagination of the writer, though it may be based on actual events and real people. "A Christmas Memory" combines both of these forms. Capote combined various memories and incidents as if they had happened in a single season.

Cooperative Learning Activity
With a group, discuss the following questions about Capote's use of the elements of fiction:
- Who are the **main characters** and who are the **minor** ones?
- Trace the **rising action** to the point you would call the **climax**, and identify the **falling action.**
- Describe the **setting** in this story. What does it add to the piece?
- What do you think is the **theme**?

Characters:
Main:
Minor:
Plot:
Climax:
Falling Action:
Setting:
Theme:

Choices & CHALLENGES

Writing Options

1. Friendly Letter Write one of the letters Buddy's cousin might have sent him after he left for military school.

2. Respectful Epitaph An epitaph is a brief inscription on a tombstone honoring the person buried there. Write the epitaph that Buddy might have composed for his friend.

3. Personal Narrative Use the writing you did before reading this story as the basis for a short narrative about a holiday that made a lasting impression on you. Place the entry in your **Working Portfolio.**

Activities & Explorations

1. Panel Discussion Rent a videotape of the 1966 TV production of "A Christmas Memory," starring Geraldine Page. Watch it as a class, and hold a panel discussion on how it compares with the story that you have read. ~ **VIEWING AND REPRESENTING**

2. Sensory Collage Create a collage that sums up for you the spirit of this story, especially its setting and characters. You might base it on your chart of the most vivid and memorable sensory details. ~ **ART**

LaserLinks:
Background for Reading
Literary Connection
Art Gallery

Inquiry & Research

Winter Celebrations Celebrations of holidays such as Christmas vary from family to family as well as from culture to culture. Find out how people you know celebrate winter holidays by interviewing from five to seven people—classmates, friends, relatives, and/or neighbors from different religions or cultural backgrounds. Ask especially about particular foods, decorations, and rituals that people have for these holidays.

Christmas fiesta in San Antonio, Texas.

Vocabulary in Action

EXERCISE: WORD MEANING Write the letter of the word that is not related in meaning to the other words in the set.

1. (a) **exhilarate** (b) depress (c) invigorate (d) excite
2. (a) begin (b) start (c) finish (d) **inaugurate**
3. (a) **cavort** (b) bound (c) prance (d) goad
4. (a) **squander** (b) waste (c) conserve (d) misuse

5. (a) virile (b) robust (c) **prosaic** (d) forceful
6. (a) retreat (b) urge (c) spur (d) **goad**
7. (a) cut (b) separate (c) join (d) **sever**
8. (a) **conspiracy** (b) privacy (c) solitude (d) isolation
9. (a) willing (b) eager (c) **noncommittal** (d) agreeable
10. (a) glaring (b) simple (c) flashy (d) **garish**

Building Vocabulary

For an in-depth lesson on how to build your vocabulary, see page 572.

Grammar in Context: Imperative Sentences

At the beginning of "A Christmas Memory," Capote uses imperative sentences to speak directly to readers. He invites them into the kitchen of a home in rural Alabama to watch events unfold.

> **Imagine a morning in late November. . . .**
> **Consider the kitchen of a spreading old house**
> **in a country town.**

An **imperative sentence** gives a command, makes a request, or gives an instruction. How would the beginning of the narrative be different if the first sentence were "It was a morning in late November"?
Punctuation Tip: Some imperative sentences are exclamatory sentences and should be punctuated with exclamation marks.

WRITING EXERCISE Rewrite the following paragraph, changing some sentences to imperative sentences.

Example: *Original* It's not good to eat all the pecans. You have to save some for the cake.
Rewritten Don't eat all the pecans. Save some for the cake.

After reading "A Christmas Memory," you can easily develop a formula for a memorable holiday. First, it is important to plan and prepare the food. You should try to include a favorite of each person. Store-bought presents and decorations aren't important. You can make your own. Perhaps the best part is the warmth of being with family and friends. It's important to enjoy one another!

Grammar Handbook The Sentence and Its Parts, p. 1192

Truman Capote
1924–1984

Other Works
"Thanksgiving Visitor"
A Tree of Night
Other Voices, Other Rooms
The Dogs Bark
Music for Chameleons
One Christmas

What He Wanted to Be Mainly through appearances on TV talk shows during his later life, Truman Capote became nearly as famous for being an eccentric media "personality" as he was for being a major writer. He had become part of flashy New York and Hollywood social circles, having once told an interviewer, "I always knew that I wanted to be a writer and that I wanted to be rich and famous."

Lonely Beginnings Born in New Orleans, Capote spent his early years in the care of various Southern relatives, including his "friend" in "A Christmas Memory." Capote began writing as a lonely child of 10. At 13 he was sent to a military boarding school, and at 17 he went to work as a clerk for *The New Yorker* magazine. He soon quit his job and concentrated on writing, achieving almost immediate success through the distinctive style, rhythms, and sounds of his prose. He subsequently published a succession of short story collections and novels, as well as travel essays, play adaptations, and film scripts.

Success and Popularity Capote's two most famous books are *Breakfast at Tiffany's,* a short novel set in New York City, and *In Cold Blood,* a sensational work that tells the true story of the 1959 mass murder of a wealthy farm family in Kansas. Capote's idea in *In Cold Blood* was to create what he called a nonfiction novel, a new literary form that combined fiction and research journalism. The project took nearly six years and left him physically and emotionally drained. "If I had known what that book was going to cost in every conceivable way . . . I never would have started it," he later confessed.

Difficult Last Years Capote published little after 1966, a period of his life generally considered to be dominated by severe writer's block, the pursuit of celebrity, and various physical ailments that included alcoholism.

Song of the Open Road
Poetry by WALT WHITMAN

The Road Not Taken
Poetry by ROBERT FROST

Connect to Your Life

Outward Bound The Chinese philosopher Lao-tzu wrote that "A journey of a thousand miles begins with a single step." But when the journey is your own life, how do you decide what step to take? Think about some decisions you've made in the past or may face in the future—such as choosing the right job or deciding on a college. Then create a chart that shows your decision-making process and share it with a classmate. An example is shown. Your chart can be different, as long as it is clear to others how you could reach a decision.

Decision: Should I Learn to Ski?	
Reasons for Yes	**Reasons for No**
I might really enjoy it.	It might be difficult or expensive.
I'll definitely learn something new.	I might not like it (but then I could quit, so not a good reason).
There's a club I could join, so I'll meet people.	
Choice: Yes	

Build Background

Journeys Think of all the ways we use the word *road*. For example, there are the phrases "the road to success," "on the road," and "taking the high road." Singer Bob Dylan asked, "How many roads must a man walk down, before you call him a man?" Clearly, the image of a road has become a kind of **metaphor,** as in "the road of life." Often a destination is implied, such as a dream, a career, or an ideal. Sometimes what attracts us is not the goal at the end; it's the journey itself. In the following poems, Whitman speaks of the "open road"—a very American idea—and Frost considers the problem of choosing one road over another.

Focus Your Reading

LITERARY ANALYSIS **RHYME SCHEME/FREE VERSE** Not all poetry rhymes, but when it does, there is usually a **rhyme scheme,** a pattern or sequence of rhyme sounds at the ends of lines.

Poetry that has no regular pattern of rhyme or **rhythm** is called **free verse.** The lines in free verse often flow more naturally than do rhymed, **metrical** lines. They achieve a rhythm more like that of everyday speech. As you read the following poems, notice where you find regular rhyme or rhythm and where you do not. In the case of free verse, what other sound devices do you think the poet uses?

ACTIVE READING **PARAPHRASING** **Paraphrasing** is simply putting things in your own words. It is often useful in helping you better understand a poem. Paraphrasing often uses simpler forms or words, but it is not necessarily shorter, since it is not a summary but a reshaping of information. To be able to paraphrase, you need to

- find the **main idea** of what a writer is saying
- notice **details** that indicate what the writer feels or sees
- if possible, think of simpler or more familiar ways of saying what the writer has written

READER'S NOTEBOOK As you read these poems, be thinking of ways you might paraphrase them. This is difficult with poetry; a paraphrase will often lack the power and subtlety of the original. But look for main ideas that you could state in your own words and jot them down.

OPEN ROAD

WALT WHITMAN

Afoot and light-hearted I take to the open road,
Healthy, free, the world before me,
The long brown path before me leading wherever I choose.
Henceforth I ask not good fortune, I myself am good fortune,
5 Henceforth I whimper no more, postpone no more,
   need nothing,
Done with indoor complaints, libraries, querulous criticisms,
Strong and content I travel the open road.

4 henceforth: from this time forward.

6 indoor complaints: illnesses caused by a lack of fresh air and outdoor exercise;
querulous (kwĕr′ə-ləs): complaining; grumbling.

Thinking Through the Literature

1. **Comprehension Check** What does Whitman's road look like?
2. Based on the poem, what kind of person do you think the **speaker** is?
3. What kind of change do you think the speaker has decided to make in his or her life?

- the apparent state of mind of the speaker
- what the speaker might have been doing previously, based on the poem

THE ROAD NOT TAKEN

ROBERT FROST

Two roads diverged[1] in a yellow wood,
And sorry I could not travel both
And be one traveler, long I stood
And looked down one as far as I could
5 To where it bent in the undergrowth;

Then took the other, as just as fair,
And having perhaps the better claim,
Because it was grassy and wanted wear;
Though as for that the passing there
10 Had worn them really about the same,

And both that morning equally lay
In leaves no step had trodden[2] black.
Oh, I kept the first for another day!
Yet knowing how way leads on to way,
15 I doubted if I should ever come back.

I shall be telling this with a sigh
Somewhere ages and ages hence:
Two roads diverged in a wood, and I—
I took the one less traveled by,
20 And that has made all the difference.

---

1. **diverged** (dĭ-vûrjd′): branched out; went in different directions.
2. **trodden** (trŏd′n): walked or trampled.

Thinking through the LITERATURE

Connect to the Literature

1. **What Do You Think?** Which road appeals to you more, Whitman's or Frost's? Explain.

Comprehension Check
- Where do Frost's roads diverge?
- Which road did the speaker in Frost's poem choose?

Think Critically

2. **ACTIVE READING** **PARAPHRASING** Select one of the two poems and rewrite it, or a portion of it, in your own words. Consult the notes you took in your **READER'S NOTEBOOK** for ideas. Your paraphrase should include the important elements of the poem you choose. Be prepared to share your paraphrase with the class.

3. In Frost's poem, the speaker chooses between two different paths in the wood. What alternatives does Whitman's speaker choose between?

4. How do you think the different roads in these poems might **symbolize** or represent the situations of the two speakers?

> **THINK ABOUT**
> - Whitman's descriptions of the road and the speaker
> - what that speaker has rejected
> - the state of mind of the speaker in Frost's poem

Extend Interpretations

5. **Comparing Texts** Suppose the speakers of the two poems should meet each other on the road. What advice do you think each would have for the other?

6. **Connect to Life** Consider how the **themes** of these two poems could apply to your life today. Is there still an "open road" to be found? Are there life choices for you to make, as in Frost's poem?

Literary Analysis

RHYME SCHEME Frost's poem uses **rhyme,** that is, similar or identical sounds at the ends of words. Like most rhyming poems, this one has a distinctive **rhyme scheme.** A rhyme scheme is charted by using letters of the alphabet to represent the sounds. Lines that rhyme are given the same letter. Whenever a new sound is introduced at the end of a line, it gets a new letter. Read "The Road Not Taken" aloud and listen for the pattern of rhymes at the ends of lines. In contrast, "Song of the Open Road" does not use rhyme. It also lacks a regular rhythmic pattern. For these reasons it is called **free verse.** Although free verse makes no regular use of rhyme, it often uses other sound devices that strike the ear and help hold the poem together. One of these is **repetition.** Read this poem aloud, too, to hear how it differs from the Frost poem.

Activity Chart the rhyme scheme of "The Road Not Taken." Remember that you need a new letter of the alphabet for each new sound. Once you have charted the first stanza, decide whether its pattern repeats itself, with different letters, in the other stanzas. Now look again at "Song of the Open Road." In Whitman's poem, look for examples of repetition of words or phrases. What is their effect? In what way do you think the **form** of each of these poems fits the spirit or thought of that poem?

Stanza 1
1. a
2.
3.
4.
5.

Writing Options

Path Description In these poems the speakers reveal a great deal about themselves by describing roads and why they chose them. Think of a setting that says something about you and what you're like—a country road, a city sidewalk, a warm kitchen, a bookstore, a playing field. Write a paragraph describing the setting and how it reflects your personality.

Writing Handbook
See page 1151: Descriptive Writing.

Activities & Explorations

Board Game Design a board game that represents a real-life journey—a trip you've either taken or dreamed about or a goal you've pursued. Make sure there are places along the way where "roads diverge" and choices must be made. Illustrate the game board with pictures that are appropriate to the journey you have chosen. ~ **ART**

Inquiry & Research

Quotation Anthology Using a book of quotations, such as *Bartlett's Quotations,* create a collection of sayings and phrases that include the idea of a road in some form. You might also get the help of a librarian to create a bibliography of stories and books that use the road as an idea, metaphor, or setting for the action. Be prepared to share your findings with the class.

Walt Whitman
1819–1892

Other Works
"Song of Myself"
"Crossing Brooklyn Ferry"
"When Lilacs Last in the Dooryard Bloom'd"
"I Sing the Body Electric"
"O Captain! My Captain!"

Robert Frost
1874–1963

Other Works
"Nothing Gold Can Stay"
"Out, Out—"
"Birches"
"Fire and Ice"
"Mending Wall"
"Stopping by Woods on a Snowy Evening"

An American Voice Walt Whitman is considered one of America's most loved and original writers. He seemed determined to see and experience everything that America had to offer, and this joyous attitude toward life was evidenced in his first book of poetry, *Leaves of Grass.*

Revolutionary Poet In both form and content, Whitman's poems were radical and unconventional for their time. He used language that was close to living speech, and he often wrote in the first person, even referring to himself by name. Because no publisher was interested in his strange new poetry, written free-form with no rhyme, Whitman himself paid for the printing of *Leaves of Grass.* His new verse forms and stubborn refusal to follow traditional poetic conventions opened the door to a new literary freedom for future poets.

Difficult Beginnings Robert Frost was born to a family whose New England ancestors dated back eight generations. He excelled in school but was forced by illness to leave Harvard College. Frost married and worked at odd jobs such as mill hand and shoe salesman. He then moved with his growing family to a farm in New Hampshire, where he wrote some of his best-known poems. When he was 38, the farm failed and he moved his family to England, where he concentrated on writing poetry.

Affirmation of Life The hardships in Frost's life included years of poverty, a sister and a child who suffered from mental illness, and the deaths of his wife and four of their six children. Still, although some of his poems deal with fear, doubt, and death, his work is seen largely as an affirmation of life. He was issued a special Congressional medal in 1960 and is the only American poet to win four Pulitzer Prizes. In 1961 he was asked to read his work at the inauguration of President John F. Kennedy.

American History

Short Story by JUDITH ORTIZ COFER (ôr-tēs' kō'fər)

"Once school started I looked for him in all my classes."

Connect to Your Life

A Fateful Event What do you know about the death of President John F. Kennedy in 1963? Create a cluster diagram similar to the one shown to help you record your thoughts. Afterwards, meet with a small group of classmates to share your knowledge. Then brainstorm to identify some significant public events that have occurred in your lifetime. Jot down these events for possible use later.

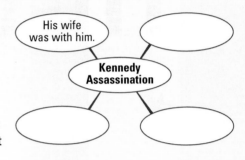

Build Background

End of an Era In 1960, John F. Kennedy became the second youngest man and the first Roman Catholic ever elected U.S. President. He sought to energize Americans in the defense of freedom and the struggle against poverty. His appeal was heightened by his charisma and the charm of his family, and he became a popular president. However, his term was short-lived. On November 22, 1963, he was assassinated while riding in an open motorcade through downtown Dallas. His murder left Americans shocked and numbed, and many people came to view his passing as the end of a unique period of boundless optimism in American society.

WORDS TO KNOW
Vocabulary Preview

abusive	infatuated
dilapidated	maneuvering
distraught	martyrs
elation	resigned
hierarchy	solace

LaserLinks: Background for Reading
Historical Connection
Visual Vocabulary

Focus Your Reading

LITERARY ANALYSIS **PLOT** **Rising action** refers to the events in a story that move the **plot** forward by adding **complications** or expanding the **conflict.** As the action rises, it builds **suspense** to a **climax,** or **turning point** in the story. The part of the story that follows the turning point is called the **falling action.**

The story you are about to read begins as the narrator shares her memories of the **setting.** Then the rising action begins to build. As you read the story, look for the point at which the rising action reaches its greatest intensity. Identify the climax and the falling action of the story.

ACTIVE READING **IDENTIFYING SEQUENCE OF EVENTS**
The events of a plot are not always described in the same **sequence** in which they take place. A story may move back and forth in time. It may include a **flashback,** which stops the forward movement of the plot to describe earlier events. In order to fully understand a story, the reader must be able to follow the **sequence of events** of its plot.

READER'S NOTEBOOK As you read the story, jot down the important events that take place—both the public and the private ones. Then number them in the sequence in which they actually happen.

American History

Judith
Ortiz
Cofer

I once read in a "Ripley's Believe It or Not" column that Paterson, New Jersey, is the place where the Straight and Narrow (streets) intersect. The Puerto Rican tenement known as *El*[1] *Building* was one block up from Straight. It was, in fact, the corner of Straight and Market; not "at" the corner, but *the* corner. At almost any hour of the day, El Building was like a monstrous jukebox, blasting out *salsas*[2] from open windows as the residents, mostly new immigrants just up from the island,[3] tried to drown out whatever they were currently enduring with loud music. But the day President Kennedy was shot there was a profound silence in El Building; even the <u>abusive</u> tongues of viragoes,[4] the cursing of the unemployed, and the screeching of small children had been somehow muted. President Kennedy was a saint to these people. In fact, soon his photograph would be hung alongside the Sacred Heart[5] and over the spiritist altars[6] that many women kept in their apartments. He would become part of the <u>hierarchy</u> of <u>martyrs</u> they prayed to for favors that only one who had died for a cause would understand.

On the day that President Kennedy was shot, my ninth grade class had been out in the fenced playground of Public School Number 13. We had been given "free" exercise time and had been ordered by our P.E. teacher, Mr. DePalma, to "keep moving." That meant that the girls should jump rope and the boys toss basketballs through a hoop at the far end of the yard. He in the meantime would "keep an eye" on us from just inside the building.

It was a cold gray day in Paterson. The kind that warns of early snow. I was miserable, since

I had forgotten my gloves, and my knuckles were turning red and raw from the jump rope. I was also taking a lot of abuse from the black girls for not turning the rope hard and fast enough for them.

"Hey, Skinny Bones, pump it, girl. Ain't you got no energy today?" Gail, the biggest of the black girls had the other end of the rope, yelled, "Didn't you eat your rice and beans and pork chops for breakfast today?"

The other girls picked up the "pork chop" and made it into a refrain: "pork chop, pork chop, did you eat your pork chop?" They entered the double ropes in pairs and exited without tripping or missing a beat. I felt a burning on my cheeks and then my glasses fogged up so that I could not manage to coordinate the jump rope with Gail. The chill was doing to me what it always did; entering my bones, making me cry, humiliating me. I hated the city, especially in winter. I hated Public School Number 13. I hated my skinny flat-chested body, and I envied the black girls who could jump rope so fast that their legs became a blur. They always seemed to be warm while I froze.

There was only one source of beauty and light for me that school year. The only thing I had anticipated at the start of the semester. That was seeing Eugene. In August, Eugene and his

---

1. *El* (ĕl) *Spanish*: the.
2. *salsas* (säl′säs): Latin-American dance music.
3. **the island:** Puerto Rico.
4. **viragoes** (və-rä′gōz): noisy, scolding women.
5. **Sacred Heart:** a picture depicting the physical heart of Jesus Christ. Some Roman Catholics observe a special devotion to the Sacred Heart as a symbol of Christ's love.
6. **spiritist altars:** special areas set up to observe the belief that spirits of the dead communicate with the living.

WORDS
TO
KNOW

abusive (ə-byo͞o′sĭv) *adj.* hurtful
hierarchy (hī′ə-rär′kē) *n.* ranking
martyrs (mär′tərz) *n.* people who are noted for suffering or dying in the upholding of high standards or religious beliefs

295

family had moved into the only house on the block that had a yard and trees. I could see his place from my window in El Building. In fact, if I sat on the fire escape I was literally suspended above Eugene's backyard. It was my favorite spot to read my library books in the summer. Until that August the house had been occupied by an old Jewish couple. Over the years I had become part of their family, without their knowing it, of course. I had a view of their

I was ready for rejection, snobbery, the worst.

kitchen and their backyard, and though I could not hear what they said, I knew when they were arguing, when one of them was sick, and many other things. I knew all this by watching them at mealtimes. I could see their kitchen table, the sink, and the stove. During good times, he sat at the table and read his newspapers while she fixed the meals. If they argued, he would leave and the old woman would sit and stare at nothing for a long time. When one of them was sick, the other would come and get things from the kitchen and carry them out on a tray. The old man had died in June. The last week of school I had not seen him at the table at all. Then one day I saw that there was a crowd in the kitchen. The old woman had finally emerged from the house on the arm of a stocky, middle-aged woman, whom I had seen there a few times before, maybe her daughter. Then a man had

carried out suitcases. The house had stood empty for weeks. I had had to resist the temptation to climb down into the yard and water the flowers the old lady had taken such good care of.

By the time Eugene's family moved in, the yard was a tangled mass of weeds. The father had spent several days mowing, and when he finished, from where I sat, I didn't see the red, yellow, and purple clusters that meant flowers to me. I didn't see this family sit down at the kitchen table together. It was just the mother, a red-headed tall woman who wore a white uniform —a nurse's, I guessed it was; the father was gone before I got up in the morning and was never there at dinner time. I only saw him on weekends when they sometimes sat on lawn chairs under the oak tree, each hidden behind a section of the newspaper; and there was Eugene. He was tall and blond, and he wore glasses. I liked him right away because he sat at the kitchen table and read books for hours. That summer, before we had even spoken one word to each other, I kept him company on my fire escape.

Once school started I looked for him in all my classes, but P.S. 13 was a huge, overpopulated place and it took me days and many discreet questions to discover that Eugene was in honors classes for all his subjects; classes that were not open to me because English was not my first language, though I was a straight A student. After much <u>maneuvering</u>, I managed "to run into him" in the hallway where his locker was—on the other side of the building from mine—and in study hall at the library where he first seemed to notice me, but did not speak; and finally, on the way home after school one day when I decided to approach him directly, though my stomach was doing somersaults.

I was ready for rejection, snobbery, the worst. But when I came up to him, practically panting in my nervousness, and blurted out: "You're

WORDS
TO
KNOW
maneuvering (mə-nōō′və-rĭng) *n.* actions skillfully designed to achieve a goal

In the Province (1920), Charles Demuth. Watercolor over graphite, 23¾" × 19¾", courtesy of Museum of Fine Arts, Boston, anonymous gift in memory of Nathaniel Saltonstall.

Eugene. Right?" he smiled, pushed his glasses up on his nose, and nodded. I saw then that he was blushing deeply. Eugene liked me, but he was shy. I did most of the talking that day. He nodded and smiled a lot. In the weeks that followed, we walked home together. He would linger at the corner of El Building for a few minutes then walk down to his two-story house. It was not until Eugene moved into that house that I noticed that El Building blocked most of the sun, and that the only spot that got a little sunlight during the day was the tiny square of earth the old woman had planted with flowers.

I did not tell Eugene that I could see inside his kitchen from my bedroom. I felt dishonest, but I liked my secret sharing of his evenings, especially now that I knew what he was reading since we chose our books together at the school library.

One day my mother came into my room as I was sitting on the window-sill staring out. In her abrupt way she said: "Elena, you are acting 'moony.'" *Enamorada*[7] was what she really said, that is—like a girl stupidly <u>infatuated</u>. Since I had turned fourteen . . . , my mother had been more vigilant than ever. She acted as if I was going to go crazy or explode or something if she didn't watch me and nag me all the time about being a *señorita*[8] now. She kept talking about virtue, morality, and other subjects that did not interest me in the least. My mother was unhappy in Paterson, but my father had a good

---

7. *Enamorada* (ĕ-nä′mô-rä′dä) *Spanish:* in love.
8. *señorita* (sĕ-nyô-rē′tä) *Spanish:* young lady.

WORDS
TO
KNOW

infatuated (ĭn-făch′ōō-ā′tĭd) *adj.* possessed by an unreasoning love or attraction

job at the bluejeans factory in Passaic and soon, he kept assuring us, we would be moving to our own house there. Every Sunday we drove out to the suburbs of Paterson, Clifton, and Passaic, out to where people mowed grass on Sundays in the summer, and where children made snowmen in the winter from pure white snow, not like the gray slush of Paterson which seemed to fall from the sky in that hue. I had learned to listen to my parents' dreams, which were spoken in Spanish, as fairy tales, like the stories about life in the island paradise of Puerto Rico before I was born. I had been to the island once as a little girl, to grandmother's funera!, and all I remembered was wailing women in black, my mother becoming hysterical and being given a pill that made her sleep two days, and me feeling lost in a crowd of strangers all claiming to be my aunts, uncles, and cousins. I had actually been glad to return to the city. We had not been back there since then, though my parents talked constantly about buying a house on the beach someday, retiring on the island— that was a common topic among the residents of El Building. As for me, I was going to go to college and become a teacher.

But after meeting Eugene I began to think of the present more than of the future. What I wanted now was to enter that house I had watched for so many years. I wanted to see the other rooms where the old people had lived, and where the boy spent his time. Most of all, I wanted to sit at the kitchen table with Eugene like two adults, like the old man and his wife had done, maybe drink some coffee and talk about books. I had started reading *Gone with the Wind*.[9] I was enthralled by it, with the daring and the passion of the beautiful girl living in a mansion, and with her devoted parents and the slaves who did everything for them. I didn't believe such a world had ever really existed, and I wanted to ask Eugene some questions since he and his parents, he had told me, had come up from Georgia, the same place

where the novel was set. His father worked for a company that had transferred him to Paterson. His mother was very unhappy, Eugene said, in his beautiful voice that rose and fell over words in a strange, lilting way. The kids at school called him "the hick" and made fun of the way he talked. I knew I was his only friend so far, and I liked that, though I felt sad for him sometimes. "Skinny Bones" and the "Hick" was what they called us at school when we were seen together.

The day Mr. DePalma came out into the cold and asked us to line up in front of him was the day that President Kennedy was shot. Mr. DePalma, a short, muscular man with slicked-down black

★ ★ ★ ★ ★ ★ ★ ★ ★ ★ ★ ★ ★

"The President is dead, you idiots."

★ ★ ★ ★ ★ ★ ★ ★ ★ ★ ★ ★ ★

hair, was the science teacher, P.E. coach, and disciplinarian at P.S. 13. He was the teacher to whose homeroom you got assigned if you were a troublemaker, and the man called out to break up playground fights, and to escort violently angry teen-agers to the office. And Mr. DePalma was the man who called your parents in for "a conference."

That day, he stood in front of two rows of mostly black and Puerto Rican kids, brittle from their efforts to "keep moving" on a November day that was turning bitter cold. Mr. DePalma, to our complete shock, was crying. Not just silent adult tears, but really sobbing. There were a few titters from the back of the line where I stood shivering.

---

9. *Gone with the Wind:* a 1936 novel by Margaret Mitchell that portrays the South during and immediately after the Civil War.

"Listen," Mr. DePalma raised his arms over his head as if he were about to conduct an orchestra. His voice broke, and he covered his face with his hands. His barrel chest was heaving. Someone giggled behind me.

"Listen," he repeated, "something awful has happened." A strange gurgling came from his throat, and he turned around and spat on the cement behind him.

"Gross," someone said, and there was a lot of laughter.

"The President is dead, you idiots. I should have known that wouldn't mean anything to a bunch of losers like you kids. Go home." He was shrieking now. No one moved for a minute or two, but then a big girl let out a "Yeah!" and ran to get her books piled up with the others against the brick wall of the school building. The others followed in a mad scramble to get to their things before somebody caught on. It was still an hour to the dismissal bell.

A little scared, I headed for El Building. There was an eerie feeling on the streets. I looked into Mario's drugstore, a favorite hangout for the high school crowd, but there were only a couple of old Jewish men at the soda-bar talking with the short order cook in tones that sounded almost angry, but they were keeping their voices low. Even the traffic on one of the busiest intersections in Paterson— Straight Street and Park Avenue—seemed to be moving slower. There were no horns blasting that day. At El Building, the usual little group of unemployed men were not hanging out on the front stoop making it difficult for women to enter the front door. No music spilled out from open doors in the hallway. When I walked into our apartment, I found my mother sitting in front of the grainy picture of the television set.

She looked up at me with a tear-streaked face and just said: "*Dios mio*,"[10] turning back to the

set as if it were pulling at her eyes. I went into my room.

Though I wanted to feel the right thing about President Kennedy's death, I could not fight the feeling of elation that stirred in my chest. Today was the day I was to visit Eugene in his house. He had asked me to come over after school to study for an American history test with him. We had also planned to walk to the public library together. I looked down into his yard. The oak tree was bare of leaves and the ground looked gray with ice. The light through the large kitchen window of his house told me that El Building blocked the sun to such an extent that they had to turn lights on in the middle of the day. I felt ashamed about it. But the white kitchen table with the lamp hanging just above it looked cozy and inviting. I would soon sit there, across from Eugene, and I would tell him about my perch just above his house. Maybe I should.

In the next thirty minutes I changed clothes, put on a little pink lipstick, and got my books together. Then I went in to tell my mother that I was going to a friend's house to study. I did not expect her reaction.

"You are going out *today?*" The way she said "today" sounded as if a storm warning had been issued. It was said in utter disbelief. Before I could answer, she came toward me and held my elbows as I clutched my books.

"*Hija*,[11] the President has been killed. We must show respect. He was a great man. Come to church with me tonight."

She tried to embrace me, but my books were in the way. My first impulse was to comfort her, she seemed so distraught, but I had to meet Eugene in fifteen minutes.

"I have a test to study for, Mama. I will be home by eight."

---

10. **Dios mio** (dyôs mē′ô) *Spanish:* my God.

11. **hija** (ē′hä) *Spanish:* daughter.

WORDS TO KNOW	**elation** (ĭ-lā′shən) *n.* joy **distraught** (dĭ-strôt′) *adj.* deeply upset

Little Girl Reading #3 (1973), Simon Samsonian. Oil on canvas, 42″ × 32″. Private collection, New York.

"You are forgetting who you are, *Niña*.[12] I have seen you staring down at that boy's house. You are heading for humiliation and pain." My mother said this in Spanish and in a <u>resigned</u> tone that surprised me, as if she had no intention of stopping me from "heading for humiliation and pain." I started for the door. She sat in front of the TV holding a white handkerchief to her face.

I walked out to the street and around the chain-link fence that separated El Building from Eugene's house. The yard was neatly edged around the little walk that led to the door. It always amazed me how Paterson, the inner core of the city, had no apparent logic to its architecture. Small, neat, single residences like this one could be found right next to huge, <u>dilapidated</u> apartment buildings like El Building. My guess was that the little houses had been there first, then the immigrants had come in droves, and the monstrosities had been raised for them—the Italians, the Irish, the Jews, and now us, the

12. *niña* (nē′nyä) *Spanish:* girl.

WORDS TO KNOW **resigned** (rǐ-zīnd′) *adj.* accepting some condition or action as inevitable
dilapidated (dǐ-lăp′ǐ-dā′tǐd) *adj.* broken-down and shabby

"You are heading for humiliation and pain."

Puerto Ricans and the blacks. The door was painted a deep green: *verde*, the color of hope, I had heard my mother say it: *Verde-Esperanza*.[13] I knocked softly. A few suspenseful moments later the door opened just a crack. The red, swollen face of a woman appeared. She had a halo of red hair floating over a delicate ivory face—the face of a doll—with freckles on the nose. Her smudged eye make-up made her look unreal to me, like a mannequin seen through a warped store window.

"What do you want?" Her voice was tiny and sweet-sounding, like a little girl's, but her tone was not friendly.

"I'm Eugene's friend. He asked me over. To study." I thrust out my books, a silly gesture that embarrassed me almost immediately.

"You live there?" She pointed up to El Building, which looked particularly ugly, like a gray prison with its many dirty windows and rusty fire escapes. The woman had stepped halfway out and I could see that she wore a white nurse's uniform with St. Joseph's Hospital on the name tag.

"Yes. I do."

She looked intently at me for a couple of heartbeats, then said as if to herself, "I don't know how you people do it." Then directly to me: "Listen. Honey. Eugene doesn't want to study with you. He is a smart boy. Doesn't need help. You understand me. I am truly sorry if he told you you could come over. He cannot study with you. It's nothing personal. You understand? We won't be in this place much longer, no need for him to get close to people— it'll just make it harder for him later. Run back home now."

I couldn't move. I just stood there in shock at hearing these things said to me in such a honey-drenched voice. I had never heard an accent like hers, except for Eugene's softer version. It was as if she were singing me a little song.

"What's wrong? Didn't you hear what I said?" She seemed very angry, and I finally snapped out of my trance. I turned away from the green door, and heard her close it gently.

Our apartment was empty when I got home. My mother was in someone else's kitchen, seeking the <u>solace</u> she needed. Father would come in from his late shift at midnight. I would hear them talking softly in the kitchen for hours that night. They would not discuss their dreams for the future, or life in Puerto Rico, as they often did; that night they would talk sadly about the young widow and her two children, as if they were family. For the next few days, we would observe *luto*[14] in our apartment; that is, we would practice restraint and silence—no loud music or laughter. Some of the women of El Building would wear black for weeks.

That night, I lay in my bed trying to feel the right thing for our dead President. But the tears that came up from a deep source inside me were strictly for me. When my mother came to the door, I pretended to be sleeping. Sometime during the night, I saw from my bed the streetlight come on. It had a pink halo around it. I went to my window and pressed my face to the cool glass. Looking up at the light I could see the white snow falling like a lace veil over its face. I did not look down to see it turning gray as it touched the ground below. ❖

---

13. **Verde-Esperanza** (věr′dě-ĕs′pě-rän′sä) *Spanish:* green hope.
14. **luto** (lōō′tô) *Spanish:* mourning.

WORDS TO KNOW   **solace** (sŏl′ĭs) *n.* comfort in sorrow or misfortune

Connect to the Literature

1. What Do You Think?
What were your thoughts about Elena and her emotions at the end of the story?

Comprehension Check
- Where and on what day does the story take place?
- What attracted Elena to Eugene?
- Why doesn't Elena get to visit Eugene?

Think Critically

2. Why do you think Eugene's mother refuses to let Elena in? Support your answer.

3. Why is getting inside Eugene's house so important to Elena?

 THINK ABOUT
- the contrast she sees between the house and El Building
- her observations of and feelings about the old Jewish couple
- her feelings for Eugene

4. What do you think Elena learns from her experience?

5. | ACTIVE READING | IDENTIFYING SEQUENCE OF EVENTS | Look again at your ▊READER'S NOTEBOOK, where you kept track of both public and private events that were taking place. If the public event of Kennedy's assassination had not occurred, would the private events of the story have turned out differently?

Extend Interpretations

6. Critic's Corner Yahaira Ferreira, one of the members of our student board, commented that she didn't like the fact that Eugene's mother turns Elena away: "I mean, I knew what was going to happen, but it was disappointing. I don't understand how people can act like that." Were you disappointed by Eugene's mother? Were you surprised? Would the story have been better if Eugene's mother had welcomed Elena into the house instead? Why or why not?

7. Connect to Life Do you think an experience such as Elena's could occur in today's society? Support your answer.

Literary Analysis

| PLOT | As a story begins and its **plot** moves forward, a **conflict** is introduced. **Complications** arise, causing difficulties for the main **characters.** This part of the plot is called the **rising action.** As the characters struggle to resolve the conflict, the intensity of the action rises to a peak or **turning point**—usually an event that affects the final outcome. This is also called the **climax** of the story. During the events that occur after the climax, the conflict is resolved and the intensity of the action subsides. This is called the **falling action.**

Cooperative Learning Activity
Use the sequence of events you kept track of in your

▊**READER'S NOTEBOOK**
to create a chart like the one shown. Arrange events in the sequence in which they occur, and group them as **rising action, climax,** and **falling action.**

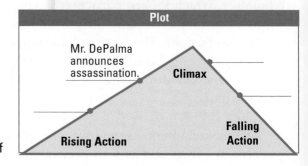

Plot

Mr. DePalma announces assassination.

Climax

Rising Action

Falling Action

Choices & CHALLENGES

Writing Options

1. Thoughtful Poem Write a poem that reflects the narrator's mood at the end of the story, picking up some of its details and imagery.

2. Different Ending Imagine that Eugene's mother decides to allow Elena to study with Eugene after all. Write a different ending to the story.

3. Speculative Essay Look over the important public events that you jotted down earlier. Draft an essay in which you predict which event will still be talked about 50 years from now and why.

Activities & Explorations

1. Story Illustration Imagine that you have been hired to create an illustration for "American History" that will help readers better understand a particular scene in the story. Choose one scene and draw or paint it. ~ **ART**

2. Mood Music Choose two pieces of music for this story, one that evokes the normal life of El Building and one that captures the mood after President Kennedy was killed. Play the music for the class and explain your choices. ~ **MUSIC**

Inquiry & Research

Arriving Immigrants Do a multimedia report on the history of various immigrant groups, including those mentioned in the story (Italians, Irish, Jews, Puerto Ricans, and African Americans). When did each group begin arriving in the United States, and how was it treated? What jobs did immigrants find, and where did they live? Consult encyclopedias as well as the work of Lewis Hine and B.G. Phillips, early photographers of immigrants. If possible, include interviews with immigrants or children of immigrants.

 **More Online: Research Starter** www.mcdougallittell.com

New immigrants gather with suitcases and belongings in front of the Great Hall at Ellis Island, New York, 1900. (by B. G. Phillips)

Vocabulary in Action

EXERCISE: CONTEXT CLUES Write the vocabulary word that best completes each sentence below.

1. A person often acts foolishly when he or she is _____ with someone.
2. Any great national tragedy is likely to leave a person _____.
3. A ringing dismissal bell is usually a time of _____ in students.
4. _____ behavior between people has no place in civilized society.
5. _____ are extreme examples of dedication.
6. We must never be _____ to prejudice.
7. The _____ house failed the safety inspection.
8. _____ from friends can help a person get through a time of sorrow.
9. Deciding whom you want to associate with implies you recognize a _____ of people.
10. To get the attention one wants, a person may need patience or skillful _____.

Building Vocabulary

For an in-depth study of context clues, see page 103.

WORDS TO KNOW				
abusive	distraught	hierarchy	maneuvering	resigned
dilapidated	elation	infatuated	martyrs	solace

Grammar in Context: Complex Sentences

In the following passage, special sentence structures help express relationships between ideas.

> In August, Eugene and his family had moved into the only house on the block that had a yard and trees. I could see his place from my window in El Building. In fact, if I sat on the fire escape I was literally suspended above Eugene's backyard.

The first and last sentences in the passage above are complex sentences. A **complex sentence** consists of one independent clause (a clause that can stand alone as a sentence) and one or more subordinate clauses (clauses that cannot stand by themselves). In the passage above, the subordinate clauses are shown in blue.

WRITING EXERCISE Rewrite each pair of simple sentences as one complex sentence. Add the underlined words in the second sentence to the first sentence at the caret. Omit the words in italics.

Example: *Original* Elena thought about Eugene's mother and her glowing red hair ^. *It was hair* that made her look as if her head were on fire.

Rewritten Elena thought about Eugene's mother and her glowing red hair that made her look as if her head were on fire.

1. El Building was always blaring out music ^. *It sounded* as if it were a giant jukebox.

2. The yard was a tangle of weeds ^. *This was* when Eugene's family moved in.

3. Her mother's voice rumbled ^. *It was* as if Elena's words had generated a storm.

Judith Ortiz Cofer
1952–

Other Works
Terms of Survival
Reaching for the Mainland
Silent Dancing
The Line of the Sun

Two Languages The poems, essays, and fiction of Judith Ortiz Cofer reflect her dual cultural background. Born in Hormigueros, Puerto Rico, she came to the United States as a young child after her father joined the U.S. Navy. As a child, Ortiz Cofer learned Spanish first and was then taught English. She later earned a master of arts degree in English.

Family and Reality Commenting on the autobiographical aspects of her work, especially her poetry, Ortiz Cofer has acknowledged that her family is a major topic and that she has learned more about her life by tracing the life of her family both in the United States and in Puerto Rico. In a 1992 article in *Glamour* magazine, Ortiz Cofer wrote, "With the stories I tell, the dreams and fears I examine in my work, I try to get my audience past the particulars of my skin color, my accent or my clothes."

Wide Recognition Ortiz Cofer has won such honors as a 1989 National Endowment for the Arts fellowship in poetry, the 1990 Pushcart Prize for Nonfiction, and the 1994 O. Henry Award for outstanding American short stories. She now lives in Georgia.

Author Activity

Two Cultures Judith Ortiz Cofer was born in Puerto Rico but lives in the American South. The language she grew up with is Spanish, but her literary language is English. Does Ortiz Cofer consider herself Puerto Rican or American? Find out what she has to say about her identity and about reconciling the two cultures of which she is a part. One place to start looking is the Internet.

More Online: Research Starter
www.mcdougallittell.com

LaserLinks: Background for Reading
Social Studies Connection
Author Background

When Words Don't Mean What They Say

Many of the expressions you use to add color to your language don't make much sense if you interpret the words literally. Read the excerpt on the right and think about the meaning of the highlighted phrases.

You cannot interpret the phrase *beyond its pale* literally, even if you know that *pale* is a word for "fence." The expression has come to mean "beyond its influence." The phrase *touch and go* means "uncertain." Like *beyond its pale*, the phrase is an

> Fashion nearly wrecked my life. I grew up beyond its pale, convinced that this would stunt me in some irreparable way. I don't think it has, but for a long time it was touch and go.
> —Barbara Kingsolver, "Life Without Go-Go Boots"

idiom, an expression whose meaning cannot be determined from the meanings of its individual words. Idioms are "part and parcel" (another idiom) of **informal English,** the language of everyday speaking.

Strategies for Building Vocabulary

In addition to idioms, another type of informal language is **slang**—newly coined words that have special meanings. Although slang terms are colorful, they often have a short life. *Far out* and *groovy* were popular slang expressions in the 1960s but are rarely heard today. Because slang and idioms cannot be interpreted literally, they are sometimes difficult to understand. Here are some strategies for making sense of idioms and slang.

❶ **Look at the Context** Often you can figure out what idioms and slang mean by thinking about the **context** of the passage—that is, the words that surround them. Consider the following example:

> . . . dying patients throw overboard all the following: they don't have to impress you anymore, they do not have to pretend.
> —Elisabeth Kübler-Ross, "Unfinished Business"

The idiom *throw overboard,* means "let go of." This is made clear by the examples that follow it about the things dying patients no longer have to do. Here is another excerpt containing an idiom:

> I'm sitting there putting fuel on the fire and encouraging him to talk. . . . I said, 'I wonder if you're honest enough and have the courage to share that with your sister.'
> —Elisabeth Kübler-Ross, "Unfinished Business"

In this case, the idiom is clarified by the restatement clue *encouraging him to talk* and the example *I wonder if you're honest enough . . . .*

❷ **Use Reference Aids** When you come across an unfamiliar idiom or slang term, you can often use a reference tool to help you determine the meaning. Many dictionaries identify and define idioms and slang terms. Large dictionaries like the *Oxford English Dictionary* list virtually all the formal and the informal uses of a word, along with examples. Other specialized dictionaries are dedicated to identifying and defining slang terms, idioms, and other kinds of informal language.

EXERCISE Use context clues to determine the meaning of the underlined examples of informal language. Then use a dictionary to check your work.

1. She knew nothing about stylish clothes, but her sophisticated friend soon <u>took her in hand</u>.
2. She asked him to <u>keep an eye on us</u>.
3. The little girl has a doll collection <u>to die for</u>.
4. "You're going to a college where you can ski? <u>That's neat</u>."
5. "I can finish this report by Monday. <u>No sweat</u>."

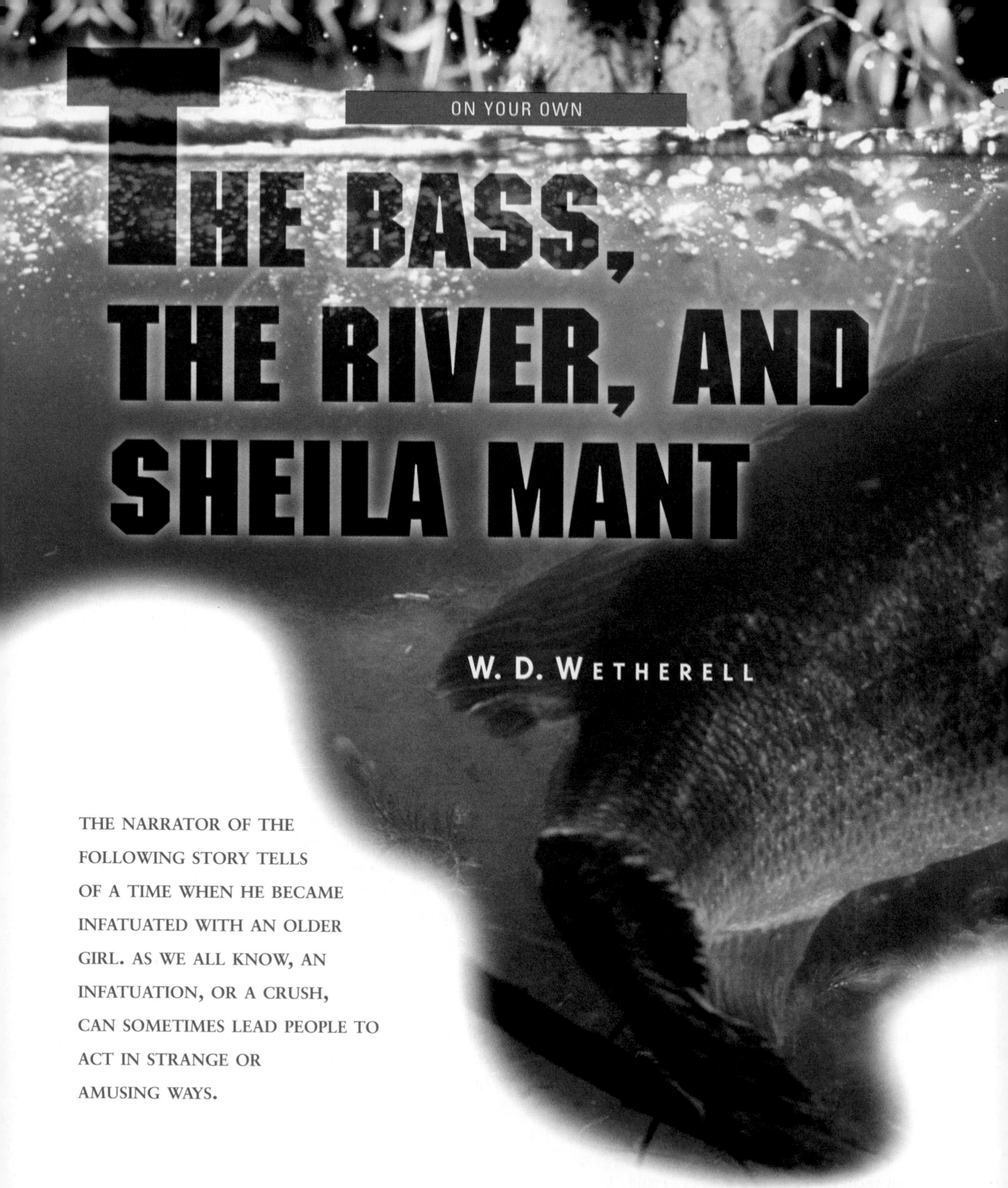

THE BASS, THE RIVER, AND SHEILA MANT

W. D. WETHERELL

THE NARRATOR OF THE
FOLLOWING STORY TELLS
OF A TIME WHEN HE BECAME
INFATUATED WITH AN OLDER
GIRL. AS WE ALL KNOW, AN
INFATUATION, OR A CRUSH,
CAN SOMETIMES LEAD PEOPLE TO
ACT IN STRANGE OR
AMUSING WAYS.

There was a summer in my life when the only creature that seemed lovelier to me than a largemouth bass was Sheila Mant. I was fourteen. The Mants had rented the cottage next to ours on the river; with their parties, their frantic games of softball, their constant comings and goings, they appeared to me denizens[1] of a brilliant existence. "Too noisy by half," my mother quickly decided, but I would have given anything to be invited to one of their parties, and when my parents went to bed I would sneak through the woods to their hedge and stare enchanted at the candlelit swirl of white dresses and bright, paisley skirts.

Sheila was the middle daughter—at seventeen, all but out of reach. She would spend her days sunbathing on a float

1. **denizens** (dĕn′ĭ-zənz): inhabitants.

my Uncle Sierbert had moored in their cove, and before July was over I had learned all her moods. If she lay flat on the diving board with her hand trailing idly in the water, she was pensive, not to be disturbed. On her side, her head propped up by her arm, she was observant, considering those around her with a look that seemed queenly and severe. Sitting up, arms tucked around her long, suntanned legs, she was approachable, but barely, and it was only in those glorious moments when she stretched herself prior to entering the water that her various suitors found the courage to come near.

These were many. The Dartmouth[2] heavyweight crew would scull[3] by her house on their way upriver, and I think all eight of them must have been in love with her at various times during the summer; the coxswain[4] would curse at them through his megaphone but without effect—there was always a pause in their pace when they passed Sheila's float. I suppose to these jaded twenty-year-olds she seemed the incarnation of innocence and youth, while to me she appeared unutterably suave, the epitome of sophistication. I was on the swim team at school, and to win her attention would do endless laps between my house and the Vermont shore, hoping she would notice the beauty of my flutter kick, the power of my crawl. Finishing, I would boost myself up onto our dock and glance casually over toward her, but she was never watching, and the miraculous day she was, I immediately climbed the diving board and did my best tuck and a half for her and continued diving until she had left and the sun went down, and my longing was like a madness and I couldn't stop.

It was late August by the time I got up the nerve to ask her out. The tortured will-I's, won't-I's, the agonized indecision over what to say, the false starts toward her house and embarrassed retreats—the details of these have been seared from my memory, and the only part I remember clearly is emerging from the woods toward dusk while they were playing softball on their lawn, as bashful and frightened as a unicorn.

Sheila was stationed halfway between first and second, well outside the infield. She didn't seem surprised to see me—as a matter of fact, she didn't seem to see me at all.

"If you're playing second base, you should move closer," I said.

She turned—I took the full brunt of her long red hair and well-spaced freckles.

"I'm playing outfield," she said, "I don't like the responsibility of having a base."

"Yeah, I can understand that," I said, though I couldn't. "There's a band in Dixford tomorrow night at nine. Want to go?"

One of her brothers sent the ball sailing over the left fielder's head; she stood and watched it disappear toward the river.

"You have a car?" she said, without looking up.

I played my master stroke. "We'll go by canoe."

I spent all of the following day polishing it. I turned it upside down on our lawn and rubbed every inch with Brillo, hosing off the dirt, wiping it with chamois[5] until it gleamed as bright as aluminum ever gleamed. About five, I slid it into the water, arranging cushions near the bow so Sheila could lean on them if she was in one of her pensive moods, propping up my father's transistor radio by the middle thwart so we could have music when we came back.

---

2. **Dartmouth** (därt'məth): a college located on the Connecticut River in Hanover, New Hampshire.

3. **scull** (skŭl): to move a light and narrow racing boat by means of oars mounted on each side of the craft.

4. **coxswain** (kŏk'sən): the person in a racing boat who steers the boat and directs the crew.

5. **chamois** (shăm'ē): soft leather used as a polishing cloth.

Automatically, without thinking about it, I mounted my Mitchell reel on my Pfleuger spinning rod and stuck it in the stern.

I say automatically, because I never went anywhere that summer without a fishing rod. When I wasn't swimming laps to impress Sheila, I was back in our driveway practicing casts, and when I wasn't practicing casts, I was tying the line to Tosca, our springer spaniel, to test the reel's drag,[6] and when I wasn't doing any of those things, I was fishing the river for bass.

Too nervous to sit at home, I got in the canoe early and started paddling in a huge circle that would get me to Sheila's dock around eight. As automatically as I brought along my rod, I tied on a big Rapala plug, let it down into the water, let out some line and immediately forgot all about it.

It was already dark by the time I glided up to the Mants' dock. Even by day the river was quiet, most of the summer people preferring Sunapee or one of the other nearby lakes, and at night it was a solitude difficult to believe, a corridor of hidden life that ran between banks like a tunnel. Even the stars were part of it. They weren't as sharp anywhere else; they seemed to have chosen the river as a guide on their slow wheel toward morning, and in the course of the summer's fishing, I had learned all their names.

I was there ten minutes before Sheila appeared. I heard the slam of their screen door first, then saw her in the spotlight as she came slowly down the path. As beautiful as she was on the float, she was even lovelier now—her white dress went perfectly with her hair and complimented her figure even more than her swimsuit.

It was her face that bothered me. It had on its delightful fullness a very dubious expression.

"Look," she said. "I can get Dad's car."

"It's faster this way," I lied. "Parking's tense up there. Hey, it's safe. I won't tip it or anything."

She let herself down reluctantly into the bow. I was glad she wasn't facing me. When her eyes were on me, I felt like diving in the river again from agony and joy.

I pried the canoe away from the dock and started paddling upstream. There was an extra paddle in the bow, but Sheila made no move to pick it up. She took her shoes off and dangled her feet over the side.

Ten minutes went by.

"What kind of band?" she said.

"It's sort of like folk music. You'll like it."

"Eric Caswell's going to be there. He strokes number four."[7]

"No kidding?" I said. I had no idea who she meant.

"What's that sound?" she said, pointing toward shore.

"Bass. That splashing sound?"

"Over there."

"Yeah, bass. They come into the shallows at night to chase frogs and moths and things. Big largemouths. *Micropterus salmoides,*"[8] I added, showing off.

"I think fishing's dumb," she said, making a face. "I mean, it's boring and all. Definitely dumb."

Now I have spent a great deal of time in the years since wondering why Sheila Mant should come down so hard on fishing. Was her father a fisherman? Her antipathy toward fishing nothing more than normal filial[9] rebellion? Had she tried it once? A messy encounter with worms? It doesn't matter. What does, is that at that fragile moment in time I would have given anything not to appear dumb in Sheila's severe and unforgiving eyes.

She hadn't seen my equipment yet. What I *should* have done, of course, was push the canoe in closer to shore and carefully slide the rod into some branches where I could pick it up

---

6. **drag:** the pull or tension on a fishing line.

7. **strokes number four:** rows in the fourth position on a sculling crew.

8. *Micropterus salmoides* (mī-krŏp′tə-rəs săl-moi′dēz): the scientific name for the largemouth bass.

9. **filial** (fĭl′ē-əl): relating to a son or daughter.

Early Evening (1978), Ken Danby. Original egg tempera, 24″ × 36″, by permission of the artist and Gallery Moos, Toronto, Canada.

again in the morning. Failing that, I could have surreptitiously dumped the whole outfit overboard, written off the forty or so dollars as love's tribute. What I actually *did* do was gently lean forward and slowly, ever so slowly, push the rod back through my legs toward the stern where it would be less conspicuous.

It must have been just exactly what the bass was waiting for. Fish will trail a lure sometimes, trying to make up their mind whether or not to attack, and the slight pause in the plug's speed caused by my adjustment was tantalizing enough to overcome the bass's inhibitions. My rod, safely out of sight at last, bent double. The line, tightly coiled, peeled off the spool with the

shrill, tearing zip of a high-speed drill.

Four things occurred to me at once. One, that it was a bass. Two, that it was a big bass. Three, that it was the biggest bass I had ever hooked. Four, that Sheila Mant must not know.

"What was that?" she said, turning half around.

"Uh, what was what?"

"That buzzing noise."

"Bats."

She shuddered, quickly drew her feet back into the canoe. Every instinct I had told me to pick up the rod and strike back at the bass, but there was no need to—it was already solidly hooked. Downstream, an awesome distance downstream, it jumped clear of the water, landing with a concussion heavy enough to ripple the entire river. For a moment, I thought it was gone, but then the rod was bending again, the tip dancing into the water. Slowly, not making any motion that might alert Sheila, I reached down to tighten the drag.

While all this was going on, Sheila had begun talking, and it was a few minutes before I was able to catch up with her train of thought.

"I went to a party there. These fraternity men. Katherine says I could get in there if I wanted. I'm thinking more of UVM or Bennington.[10] Somewhere I can ski."

The bass was slanting toward the rocks on the New Hampshire side by the ruins of Donaldson's boathouse. It had to be an old bass—a young one probably wouldn't have known the rocks were there. I brought the canoe back out into the middle of the river, hoping to head it off.

"That's neat," I mumbled. "Skiing. Yeah, I can see that."

"Eric said I have the figure to model, but I thought I should get an education first. I mean, it might be a while before I get started and all. I was thinking of getting my hair styled, more swept back? I mean, Ann-Margret?[11] Like hers, only shorter."

She hesitated. "Are we going backwards?"

We were. I had managed to keep the bass in the middle of the river away from the rocks, but it had plenty of room there and for the first time a chance to exert its full strength. I quickly computed the weight necessary to draw a fully loaded canoe backwards—the thought of it made me feel faint.

"It's just the current," I said hoarsely. "No sweat or anything."

I dug in deeper with my paddle.

Reassured, Sheila began talking about something else, but all my attention was taken up now with the fish. I could feel its desperation as the water grew shallower. I could sense the extra strain on the line, the frantic way it cut back and forth in the water. I could visualize what it looked like—the gape of its mouth, the flared gills and thick, vertical tail. The bass couldn't have encountered many forces in its long life that it wasn't capable of handling, and the unrelenting tug at its mouth must have been a source of great puzzlement and mounting panic.

Me, I had problems of my own. To get to Dixford, I had to paddle up a sluggish stream that came into the river beneath a covered bridge. There was a shallow sandbar at the mouth of this stream—weeds on one side, rocks on the other. Without doubt, this is where I would lose the fish.

"I have to be careful with my complexion. I tan, but in segments. I can't figure out if it's even worth it. I wouldn't even do it probably. I saw Jackie Kennedy[12] in Boston, and she wasn't tan at all."

Taking a deep breath, I paddled as hard as I could for the middle, deepest part of the bar. I could have threaded the eye of a needle with the canoe, but the pull on the stern threw me off and I overcompensated—the canoe veered left and scraped bottom. I pushed the paddle down and shoved. A moment of hesitation . . . a moment more. . . . The canoe shot clear into the deeper water of the stream. I immediately looked down at the rod. It was bent in the same, tight arc—miraculously, the bass was still on.

---

10. **UVM or Bennington:** the University of Vermont or Bennington College in Vermont.

11. **Ann-Margret:** a glamorous movie star, singer, and dancer famous at the time of this story.

12. **Jackie Kennedy:** the wife of President John F. Kennedy. Many people admired Jackie Kennedy's sense of style.

he moon was out now. It was low and full enough that its beam shone directly on Sheila there ahead of me in the canoe, washing her in a creamy, luminous glow. I could see the lithe,[13] easy shape of her figure. I could see the way her hair curled down off her shoulders, the proud, alert tilt of her head, and all these things were as a tug on my heart. Not just Sheila but the aura she carried about her of parties and casual touchings and grace. Behind me, I could feel the strain of the bass, steadier now, growing weaker, and this was another tug on my heart, not just the bass but the beat of the river and the slant of the stars and the smell of the night, until finally it seemed I would be torn apart between longings, split in half. Twenty yards ahead of us was the road, and once I pulled the canoe up on shore, the bass would be gone, irretrievably gone. If instead I stood up, grabbed the rod, and started pumping, I would have it—as tired as the bass was, there was no chance it could get away. I reached down for the rod, hesitated, looked up to where Sheila was stretching herself lazily toward the sky, her small breasts rising beneath the soft fabric of her dress, and the tug was too much for me, and quicker than it takes to write it down, I pulled a penknife from my pocket and cut the line in half.

With a sick, nauseous feeling in my stomach, I saw the rod unbend.

"My legs are sore," Sheila whined. "Are we there yet?"

Through a superhuman effort of self-control, I was able to beach the canoe and help Sheila off. The rest of the night is much foggier. We walked to the fair—there was the smell of popcorn, the sound of guitars. I may have danced once or twice with her, but all I really remember is her coming over to me once the music was done to explain that she would be going home in Eric Caswell's Corvette.

"Okay," I mumbled.

For the first time that night she looked at me, really looked at me.

"You're a funny kid, you know that?"

Funny. Different. Dreamy. Odd. How many times was I to hear that in the years to come, all spoken with the same quizzical, half-accusatory tone Sheila used then. Poor Sheila! Before the month was over, the spell she cast over me was gone, but the memory of that lost bass haunted me all summer and haunts me still. There would be other Sheila Mants in my life, other fish, and though I came close once or twice, it was these secret, hidden tuggings in the night that claimed me, and I never made the same mistake again. ❖

---

13. **lithe** (lĭth): limber; graceful.

SINCE FEELING IS FIRST

E. E. Cummings

since feeling is first
who pays any attention
to the syntax of things
will never wholly kiss you;

5 wholly to be a fool
while Spring is in the world

my blood approves,
and kisses are a better fate
than wisdom
10 lady i swear by all flowers.   Don't cry
—the best gesture of my brain is less than
your eyelids' flutter which says

we are for each other:then
laugh,leaning back in my arms
15 for life's not a paragraph

And death i think is no parenthesis

W. D. Wetherell

1948–

Other Works
Chekhov's Sister
Souvenirs
Vermont River
Hyannis Boat and Other Stories

Many Hats W. D. Wetherell is one of those writers who have taken on a wide variety of jobs in order to buy time to write. He has been a magazine editor, a movie extra, a tour guide, a teacher, and a freelance journalist. He is now a full-time writer who has received considerable acclaim for his novels and short stories. "The Bass, the River, and Sheila Mant" was taken from a collection of short stories, *The Man Who Loved Levittown*, which won the Drue Heinz Literature Prize for short fiction in 1985. The book shows, said one reviewer, that Wetherell has "a sharp, fresh eye and a complicated view of our dislocations, pains, and dreams."

Fish Tales Since fishing is one of Wetherell's interests, it is not surprising that he has published two collections of fly-fishing and nature essays. One of them is *Upland Stream: Notes on the Fishing Passion,* in which he takes up the question, "Why fish?"

Recognition Wetherell has been awarded two fellowships by the National Endowment for the Arts, and his work has appeared in the *New York Times, The Atlantic Monthly,* and various literary magazines. Born in Mineola, New York, he now lives in Lyme, New Hampshire.

Author Activity

Wetherell is becoming known not only for his love of nature but for his praise of simple, lasting pleasures: reading poetry, telling stories, watching the night sky, collecting local folklore, celebrating the first snow. To read some of his little essays on these topics, browse through his *North of Now: A Celebration of Country and the Soon to Be Gone* (Lyons Press, 1998).

Writing Workshop

Sharing your experience. . .

From Reading to Writing Frank McCourt was sick in a hospital bed when his father kissed him for the first time. In *Angela's Ashes,* Frank says this gesture from his father made him so happy he felt like "floating out of the bed." Writing about a strong memory can help you better understand it. A **reflective essay** narrates a personal experience and reveals its significance. Autobiographies, letters, and memoirs often use reflective writing to share important experiences from a writer's life.

For Your Portfolio

WRITING PROMPT Write an essay in which you reflect on an experience that is important to you.

Purpose: To share what an experience means to you

Audience: Your family members or friends

Basics in a Box

Reflective Essay at a Glance

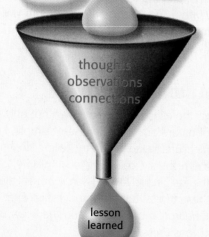

personal experience

thoughts observations connections

lesson learned

RUBRIC Standards for Writing

A successful reflective essay should

- be written in the first-person
- describe an important experience in your life or in the life of someone you admire
- use figurative language, dialogue, sensory details, or other techniques to recreate the experience for the reader
- explain the significance of the event
- make an observation about life based on the experience
- encourage readers to think about the significance of your experience in light of their own lives

Analyzing a Student Model

Bryan Dobkin
Buffalo Grove High School

Running Cross-Country

I never would have guessed something my mother had to force me to do could turn out to be one of the best experiences I had ever had. It was the beginning of the school year, and my mother was determined that I get involved in some clubs or sports.

"Bryan, the discussion is over! You are going to join some school activities this year!"

"But, Mom, I don't like any of the things they have to offer. The only activity that's going on in the fall is cross-country and that's just running. It's got to be so boring!"

"It's only for a couple of months. You might even learn to like it."

"Yeah, whatever."

Before I knew it, I found myself sitting on the ground in a T-shirt and shorts, along with 20 other guys, staring up at my new cross-country coach.

"Okay, everyone, settle down! I'm Mr. Smith, and I'll be your cross-country coach for the next three months. I expect you all to give 150% and to respect me.

"This year we'll be running two miles at our meets. You'll run them hard and fast. Remember, cross-country takes strength, attitude, and endurance. Now I want you all to go outside and do a 30-minute run. No walkers!"

"Hey, Bryan," said one of the guys, "come run with us. Or can't you keep up?"

"I'll keep up just fine, John!" <u>But within a few minutes</u>, I was ready to quit. "Uh, John—is cross-country always like this?"

"You bet. Isn't it great?"

That's when I decided that the next few months were going to be the worst of my life.

Still . . . I didn't want to be embarrassed. So I worked my tail off for the <u>next month and a half</u>. I ran on the weekends and in my free time. Then something strange happened. Running started to be fun instead of work. <u>By the time the meets started</u>, I was faster than most of the other guys in cross-country. Even John. <u>Then one day</u> I overheard some of the guys talking.

"Man, did you see Bryan run in the meet yesterday?"

"Yeah, I did. He got fourth place! I never realized he was such a good runner."

"Who cares?" said John. "Fourth place is nothing. I got third yesterday!"

"Aw, come on, John. He almost beat you!"

"*Almost* is the word that matters. He'll never beat me. I'll make sure!"

① This writer begins by suggesting what the experience means to him.

Other Options:
· Describe the setting.
· Begin with an exciting moment.

② Introduces the first event in the experience, using dialogue

③ Uses transitional words and phrases to make the order of events clear

④ Uses dialogue to show another event in the experience

Other Options:
· Add action to the dialogue.
· Describe the event using figurative language.

I took what John said as a challenge. That night I went to sleep very early so I would have a lot of energy the next day. When I woke up the next morning, I was more nervous than I had ever been in my life. Today was the day I would prove myself to my family and all of my friends. School dragged that day, but finally it was time for the meet.

"Good luck in the race today, John," I said, as we got ready.

"You're the one who's going to need it," John said.

As we waited on the line for the shot, I felt like I was going crazy. My heart started to beat faster and faster, until I could hear the drumming in my ears. I glanced up and the heat from the sun beat on my face. A drop of sweat rolled down my forehead and dropped to the ground. I could feel my palms start to sweat, and my legs were like rubber. Just as I was thinking that I didn't really want to do this, I heard the starting gun fire.

I shot off the starting line like a bullet from a gun and took my place in the middle of the pack. I glanced to my side and saw John moving ahead. But I didn't make my move. No, not just yet. I would save my energy for later. I chose the runner in front of me to keep the pace with. It was someone from another school, and he was especially fast. Some of the runners were dropping back. I was in close competition with two kids from MacArthur School. I could see John about ten seconds ahead of me. He didn't look like he was tiring at all.

Now we were about three-quarters of the way through the race. I had to make my move soon or I would lose. Another runner dropped back with exhaustion. The retention basin was coming up soon, and that would be the perfect opportunity. I picked up my pace, and little by little I caught up to John. Finally, going down the hill, John slowed his pace. As the MacArthur kid and I passed John, I looked over my shoulder and saw John's look of defeat. I almost felt sorry for him. Now I felt a sudden rush of energy and sprinted up the hill. The finish line was coming closer and closer. I dug my toes into the side of the hill and almost climbed up it. I raced with the MacArthur kid until we were neck and neck. With my last ounce of hope, I pulled ahead and ran through the finish line.

I closed my eyes. I had done it. I had won. As I opened my eyes, I saw my family and friends cheering for me. Their pride made me feel good, and that feeling would last a long time. But what lasted even longer was the feeling of pushing myself to try something new. I could have been sitting around the house all fall, but instead I had taken a risk. Now, I even had a first place ribbon to show for it. Who knew what else I could accomplish?

5 Sometimes the writer directly states his feelings.

6 Here, the writer uses sensory details to show, not tell, how he felt.

7 The conclusion emphasizes the significance of the experience.

Writing Your Reflective Essay

❶ Prewriting

I write to find out what I'm thinking about.
Edward Albee, dramatist

Begin by identifying an experience that you want to write about. Try **recalling** past events by looking through a photo album, or listing frightening or funny memories. See the **Idea Bank** in the margin for more suggestions. After you select an event that feels important to you, follow the steps below.

Planning Your Reflective Essay

▶ **1. Replay the experience in your mind.** What happened to you? In what order did the events occur? What will other people find interesting about it?

▶ **2. Picture the specific details.** Where did the experience take place? What did people say? What were they feeling? What did things look, smell, and sound like? What details stand out in your memory?

▶ **3. Reflect on what the experience means to you.** Why did things develop as they did? What is the most obvious meaning you took away from this experience? Talk to others and think about additional or deeper meanings in your experience.

▶ **4. Decide what you want others to think about.** Which of your reflections do you feel are most important to share with readers? How will you help readers understand the significance of these reflections?

❷ Drafting

A reflective essay may combine both "telling" and "showing" to recreate the experience and make clear its deeper meanings for the reader. You may begin writing your essay by describing the events in **chronological order,** starting with the first moment you recall from your experience. Or begin the essay with an intriguing moment that occurred during the middle or end of the experience. Make sure, however, that you fill in the missing pieces and that the order of events is clear.

As you draft, act as an eyewitness, writing down everything you remember. Include **sensory details,** such as sights and sounds, and any **conversations** you recall. For example, *I heard water sloshing and heavy breathing; Willy was catching up to me. "Chump!" he said. Suddenly, I was terrified.*

Ask Your Peer Reader

• Which parts of the essay could you picture most easily?

• Which events confused you?

• Why do you think this incident is important to me?

• What does this essay cause you to think about?

IDEA Bank

1. Your Working Portfolio
Build on one of the **Writing Options** you completed earlier in this unit:
• **Personal Essay,** p. 242
• **Personal Memoir,** p. 256
• **Personal Narrative,** p. 286

2. Life Map
Make a road map of your life listing important events and experiences. Choose one event or experience for your topic.

3. Storytelling
Share family stories with a small group of classmates. Use one of these stories as a starting point.

Have a question?

See the **Writing Handbook**
Narrative Writing, pp. 1153–1154
Elaboration, pp. 1149–1150

While you're writing, additional levels of significance may become clear to you. Continue to reflect on your experience after you draft, as well. Later, you may revise your draft to emphasize the most important meanings of your experience.

❸ Revising

TARGET SKILL ▶ **ADDING DETAILS** Remember that concrete details help readers picture your experience. When adding details, use strong, sensory words that *show* people and events, rather than just telling about them.

Need revising help?

Review the **Rubric,** p. 314

Consider **peer reader** comments

Check **Revision Guidelines,** p. 1143

> *I glanced up and the heat from the sun beat on my face. A drop of sweat rolled down my forehead and dropped to the ground.*
>
> ~~It was hot.~~ I was really nervous. Just as I was thinking that I didn't really want to do this, I heard the starting gun fire.
>
> *I could feel my palms start to sweat and my legs were like rubber.*

❹ Editing and Proofreading

TARGET SKILL ▶ **STRONG VERBS, VERB TENSES** Carefully select your action words, or verbs, to make your writing stronger and more lively. Also note the sequence of verb tenses. Jumping from past to future to present tense can confuse readers.

Stumped by verbs?

See the **Grammar Handbook,** pp. 1183–1185

> Today was the day I would prove myself to my family and all of my friends.
> School ~~went slowly~~ *dragged* that day, but finally it ~~is~~ *was* time for the meet.
>
> "Good luck in the race today, John," I said, as we ~~get~~ *got* ready.
>
> "You're the one who's going to need it," John said.
>
> As we ~~stood~~ *waited* on the line for the shot, I felt like I was going crazy.
> My heart ~~starts to go~~ *started* *beat* faster and faster, until I could hear the drumming in my ears.

Publishing IDEAS

- Submit your essay to a contest with a theme that matches your subject.
- Give copies of your essay to your parents. Mail or e-mail copies to members of your extended family.

More Online: Publishing Options www.mcdougallittell.com

❺ Reflecting

FOR YOUR WORKING PORTFOLIO What did you discover about yourself while completing your essay? How did writing about the experience help you better understand it? Attach your answers to your finished work. Save your essay in your **Working Portfolio.**

Read this paragraph from the first draft of a reflective essay. The underlined sections may include the following kinds of errors:

- **correctly written sentences that should be combined**
- **run-on sentences**
- **capitalization errors**
- **verb tense errors**

For each underlined section, choose the revision that most improves the writing.

<u>My Aunt and Uncle</u> invited me to spend last summer in Alaska with them. <u>I
(1)
didn't know what to expect, I thought it would be interesting.</u> The first place we
(2)
went to was the Imaginarium. I <u>learn</u> a lot about glaciers from the videos and
(3)
exhibits there. After that, I really wanted to see more of Alaska. The three of us

took a trip to the <u>Wrangell-st. elias national park.</u> <u>The Malaspina Glacier is
(4)   (5)
magnificent it attracts people from all over the world.</u> <u>The glacier is 840 square
(6)
miles. It is the largest glacier in North America.</u>

---

1. A. My aunt and Uncle
   B. My aunt and uncle
   C. My Aunt and uncle
   D. Correct as is

2. A. I didn't know what to expect I thought it would be interesting.
   B. I didn't know what to expect, but I thought it would be interesting.
   C. I didn't know what to expect, I thought, it would be interesting.
   D. Correct as is

3. A. learned
   B. will learn
   C. had learned
   D. Correct as is

4. A. Wrangell-St. Elias National park
   B. Wrangell-St. elias national park
   C. Wrangell-St. Elias National Park
   D. Correct as is

5. A. The Malaspina Glacier is magnificent, it attracts people from all over the world.
   B. The Malaspina Glacier is magnificent it attracts people. From all over the world.
   C. The Malaspina Glacier is magnificent, and it attracts people from all over the world.
   D. Correct as is

6. A. The glacier is 840 square miles and the glacier is the largest in North America.
   B. At 840 square miles, this is the largest glacier in North America.
   C. The glacier is 840 square miles and largest.
   D. Correct as is

Need extra help?

See the **Grammar Handbook**

Verb tense, pp. 1184–1185

Correcting Run-on sentences, p. 1197

Capitalization chart, p. 1203

Have there been special milestones in your life—moments when you seemed to step forward, gain new confidence or skill, survive a crisis, and feel more grown-up? Do you look forward to other milestones? Such key transition events are sometimes called rites of passage. They may be public or may be known only to you, but they are all part of living and learning. In this part of Unit Two, you'll read about some milestones of this sort. They may remind you of your own experiences—or give you a glimpse of what might lie ahead.

ACTIVITY

Make a time line showing the important rites of passage in your own life—both those in the past and those to come. Draw a vertical line, marked with a zero at the top and divided into decades for the whole expected length of your life. Then, at various points, put labeled dots to indicate rites of passage. Around year 1, for example, you might write "learned to walk"; at a later point, you might write "got first job." Compare your time line with those of classmates.

*C*haracter development helps readers recognize which characters in a work of fiction are the most important—the ones to watch closely. Think about movies. Some characters are mere extras seen in the background of scenes. Others are minor characters who have only a few lines and whose purpose is to interact with the main characters, helping to move the plot along. Stories work the same way. Characters play different roles and vary in importance and in the level of detail with which they are presented. **Setting** often influences character development because the time and place in which a story's characters live can affect the way they grow and change.

Main and Minor Characters

The most important characters in a story are called **main characters.** Events in the story center on the lives of these characters. Therefore, the writer usually includes many details about their circumstances, appearance, actions, and feelings. The less important characters are called **minor characters.** These characters exist to interact with the main characters and help move the story along.

YOUR TURN Read the passage at the right and try to determine which of the characters mentioned are major characters and which are minor characters. What clues helped you decide?

MAIN AND MINOR CHARACTERS

One flight up Della ran and collected herself, panting. . . .

"Will you buy my hair?" asked Della.

"I buy hair," said Madame. "Take yer hat off and let's have a sight at the looks of it."

Down rippled the brown cascade.

"Twenty dollars," said Madame, lifting the mass with a practiced hand.

"Give it to me quick," said Della.

Oh, and the next two hours tripped by on rosy wings. Forget the hashed metaphor. She was ransacking the stores for Jim's present.

—O. Henry, "The Gift of the Magi"

Protagonist and Antagonist

The **protagonist** of a story is the central character or hero. The protagonist is always a main character, and in most cases he or she is the character with whom the reader identifies. Opposing the protagonist is an **antagonist.** In "The Sniper," for example, the protagonist is the sniper, and the antagonist is his enemy on the other rooftop. Usually an antagonist is another character, but some protagonists are opposed by antagonists of a different sort, like forces of nature or sets of circumstances.

YOUR TURN Identify the protagonist and the antagonist in the passage at the right.

PROTAGONIST AND ANTAGONIST

There were ten youths hidden about the ravine, and they would stage and witness the coming fight. They had tracked the lion to this, his lair, and when the moment came, they would drive him, angered, upon Temas and then would judge his courage and his skill. Good or bad, that judgment would, like a brand mark, cling to him all his life.

But it was Medoto who would watch the closest for a sign, a gesture, a breath of fear in Temas. It was Medoto who would spread the word—Medoto who surely would cry "Coward!" if he could.

—Beryl Markham, "Brothers Are the Same"

Round and Flat Characters

Characters that are complex and fully developed are said to be **round characters.** Round characters tend to display strengths, weaknesses, and a full range of emotions. The writer provides enough detail for the reader to understand their feelings and motives. **Flat characters,** on the other hand, are simple. The writer gives them few emotions. Because minor characters exist mainly to advance the plot or to interact with major characters, they are usually flat characters. They display only the traits needed for their limited roles.

YOUR TURN Read the passage at the right. Is Miss Strangeworth a flat or a round character? Explain the reasons for your decision.

> ## ROUND AND FLAT CHARACTERS
>
> She [Miss Strangeworth] knew everyone in town, of course; she was fond of telling strangers . . . that she had never spent more than a day outside this town in all her long life. She was seventy-one, Miss Strangeworth told the tourists, with a pretty little dimple showing by her lip, and she sometimes found herself thinking that the town belonged to her.
>
> —Shirley Jackson, "The Possibility of Evil"

Dynamic and Static Characters

Generally, one or more of a story's main characters change as a result of the events of the story. A character might grow emotionally, learn a lesson, or alter his or her behavior. Such a character is called a **dynamic character.** A **static character,** in contrast, is one who remains unchanged.

YOUR TURN In the passage at the right, is the sniper a dynamic or a static character? How do you know?

> ## DYNAMIC AND STATIC CHARACTERS
>
> The sniper looked at his enemy falling and he shuddered. The lust of battle died in him. He became bitten by remorse. The sweat stood out in beads on his forehead. . . . His teeth chattered. He began to gibber to himself, cursing the war, cursing himself, cursing everybody.
>
> —Liam O'Flaherty, "The Sniper"

Setting

Often, the **setting** of the story in which a character appears plays an important part in the character's development. Sometimes the setting provides clues to the character's background, beliefs, skills, or lifestyle. Setting can also help explain a character's motives—as when a character works hard to escape an undesirable place, such as a war-torn country. It may also provide hardships or opportunities that allow a character to grow.

YOUR TURN In the passage at the right, what details of setting suggest the social obstacles faced by the narrator?

> ## SETTING
>
> I walked out to the street and around the chain-link fence that separated El Building from Eugene's house. The yard was neatly edged around the little walk that led to the door. It always amazed me how Paterson, the inner core of the city, had no apparent logic to its architecture. Small, neat, single residences like this one could be found right next to huge, dilapidated apartment buildings like El Building. My guess was that the little houses had been there first, then the immigrants had come in droves, and the monstrosities had been raised for them.
>
> —Judith Ortiz Cofer, "American History"

The phrase "reading between the lines" refers to a skill called **making inferences.** You make an inference every time you connect bits of evidence to reach a larger understanding. The process of making inferences about a story is one of developing insights based on the details provided. The strategies explained here can help you make inferences about characters as you read fiction.

Making Inferences

Making inferences about a story involves using the information in the story, as well as your own common sense, to make logical guesses. This skill is especially useful for understanding characters. Writers seldom explain everything about characters' backgrounds, thoughts, and emotions. By making inferences, readers can supply the missing pieces.

1 Strategies for Making Inferences About a Character's Background

- Look for details about the physical environment and about any social, cultural, and moral influences that affect the character.
- **Question** why specific details about the character are included in the story. Which details are clues to the character's inner qualities?
- Think about things you've read or heard that can help you imagine what it would be like to live in the story's setting.
- Consider details about the character in the context of the whole story. For example, in a story set in 1925, it would not be unusual for a character to own a Model T Ford. In a story set in 1995, however, a character's owning such a car might imply that he or she is a wealthy antique-car collector.
- Use a chart like the one shown to help you decide what various details imply about the character.

Facts or Details	What I Know from Reading or Experience	What I Infer About Character
The story is set in 1995. The character has a Model T Ford in the garage.	When Grandpa was a boy, his dad had a Model T. Antiques are expensive.	The character might be a wealthy antique car collector.

2 Strategies for Making Inferences About a Character's Feelings

- **Connect** to what the character is experiencing. Think about similar experiences you have had and the way they made you feel.
- As you read dialogue, stop and imagine how you would say the words if you were in the character's place.
- Reread descriptions of the character's gestures and facial expressions. Close your eyes and **visualize** these. Then think about the emotions you usually associate with the expressions and gestures.

3 Strategies: Making Inferences About a Character's Behavior

- Note any descriptions of dangers or opportunities in the setting. **Question** how they might affect the character's future life.
- Pay attention to the character's responses to conflicts, to setbacks, and to opportunities. Try to see a pattern in the character's behavior—one that can give you an idea of what to expect as the story develops.
- Look for symbols and imagery that may hint at what is to come.

Need More Help?

Remember that active readers use the essential reading strategies explained on page 7: **visualize, predict, clarify, question, connect, evaluate, monitor.**

The Beginning of Something

Short Story by SUE ELLEN BRIDGERS

"She started crying right there on the phone."

Connect to Your Life

Conflicting Feelings Have you ever felt ecstatic about an important event in your life at the same time a person close to you felt awful because something bad happened? Perhaps you can identify with a situation similar to one of the following:

- You won a major award at school, but you learn that your father or mother lost his or her job.
- You made the starting lineup on the basketball team, but your best friend was cut from the team.

In a small group, share similar experiences. Describe your conflict and how you handled it.

Building Background

Funeral Traditions "The Beginning of Something" takes place over the course of a Christian funeral and includes references to a number of Christian funeral traditions. One funeral custom is for neighbors, relatives, and friends to bring food to the family of the deceased or to send flowers to the funeral home. Often the dead person's body is embalmed, or preserved, and displayed in a funeral home the day before the funeral. During a "visitation," people come to pay their respects to the dead person and to express their feelings of sympathy to the family.

WORDS TO KNOW
Vocabulary Preview

bereaved	remorse
infernal	throes
kin	

Focus Your Reading

LITERARY ANALYSIS | **CHARACTER** | The people who participate in the action of a work of fiction are called **characters.** Characters are either **main characters** or **minor characters,** depending upon the extent of their development and on their importance in the story. Main characters are essential to a story; the events of the **plot** are based on what they as characters do, say, think, and feel. As you read this story, decide who you think are the main and minor characters.

ACTIVE READING | **MAKING INFERENCES ABOUT CHARACTER** | When you read fiction, you make **inferences** about the characters. You figure out why they act or think as they do by combining clues in the text with what you already know from your experiences or other reading. In "The Beginning of Something," the **narrator** doesn't tell you everything that is going on in her head. However, there are plenty of clues that a careful reader can use to make inferences. Here is an example of the kind of inference you might make about Roseanne, based on clues she gives you as she tells her story.

What the narrator says	What I know	What I can infer
"Buddy and me stayed all tangled up in the backseat. He can sleep through anything, but I was restless and uneasy."	People are often restless and uneasy when something is troubling them.	Roseanne may be more anxious or upset about Cousin Jessie's death than she lets on.

READER'S NOTEBOOK Several questions have been inserted in the story to help you make inferences about the characters. As you read, take a moment to jot down some brief answers to these questions.

The Beginning of Something

Sue Ellen Bridgers

When Mama said, "We're all going home for Cousin Jessie's funeral," I said, "Not me," but here I am. We rode all night with static blaring off the radio to keep Mama awake so she could nudge Daddy. Nothing keeps him awake except an elbow, not even static. He's so tone-deaf, it sounds like music to him. Buddy and me stayed all tangled up in the backseat. He can sleep through anything, but I was restless and uneasy. It was hot, too.

We left right after supper. Mama already had a chicken stewing for pastry when the phone rang. She started crying right there on the phone, a big wailing sob with her mouth open like she was getting ready for a high note. Mama sings.

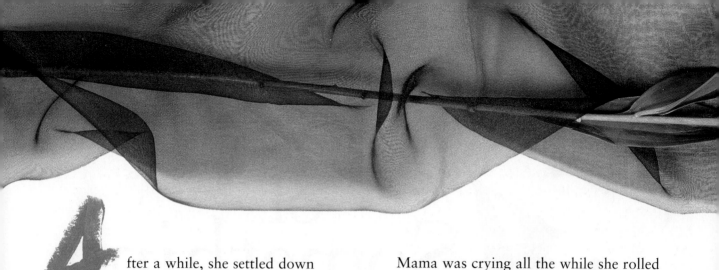

After a while, she settled down enough to find out when the funeral was going to be—Sunday at two o'clock—and she still wanted to get in the car that minute and go. She would have, too, except for the chicken and Daddy's navy blue suit somebody had to get out of the cleaners and having to think of something I could wear. I'm still outgrowing clothes—well, actually, my shape is changing. One day I'm pudgy-looking, and the next I've got this waist that nips in just perfect. Not like Melissa's, of course, who was born with a good body and no brains.

Melissa is Cousin Jessie's daughter. Cousin Jessie was Mama's first cousin and her best friend besides. They grew up together and they've always loved each other the way people do who remember all grades of silliness and mischief between them. I've heard some of the things they used to do, baby stuff like sneaking out after the house was locked and smoking on the front porch. Big deal. Before Cousin Jessie got so sick, the two of them would start giggling and whispering behind their hands and hugging each other. Used to make Melissa and me sick. We've never liked each other all that much, mostly I reckon because we're supposed to. Two weeks at her house every summer, two weeks at mine. The longest month God ever made.

ACTIVE READING

PREDICT What do you think is going to happen between Melissa and the narrator?

Mama was crying all the while she rolled out the dough for the pastry and then the whole time she hunted through the closet for something I could wear. She already had a black dress. People like Mama keep a black dress all the time, just in case. Fourteen-year-old girls don't wear black unless they've got loose morals, except for a T-shirt or something minor like that. Finally Mama found this tacky midnight blue dress I'd pushed to the back of the closet because every time I look at it I about puke, that's how unattractive it is. Mama bought it on sale and anybody can tell it, too. I just about died the one time I wore it. Kept my coat on all through church and it was one of those late winter days that turns out to be positively springlike. Now I've got to wear it to a funeral in July. They might as well lay me out right next to Cousin Jessie.

At this minute I'm sitting here on the porch swing next to Melissa, who won't say a word. I reckon while it's quiet like this, I could tell you what she looks like, and I'm going to try to tell the truth. She's been crying off and on ever since she got up this morning. I think she must of woke up not remembering anything but all of a sudden it came to her because she moaned real loud and pulled the sheet over her head. I could see the sheet trembling like there was a poltergeist[1] under there. I hadn't been asleep

---

1. **poltergeist** (pōl′tər-gīst′): a ghost that manifests itself through noises or other disturbances.

more than two hours and my mouth felt scorched and my eyes wouldn't half open but I couldn't leave her like that so I went over to her bed and put my hand on the jerking sheet. I pressed right on her chest till her breathing slowed down. There wasn't any point in saying anything, was there? She kept on crying, but at least she wasn't wearing herself out with it. Holding on to her like that was like calming a scared animal, but I don't think Melissa would ever think about it that way. She used to want me to rub her back all the time, just a couple of years ago. She expects things like that of people, but it always embarrasses me. Melissa is spoiled.

> # *W*e've never **liked** each other **all that much,** mostly I **reckon** because **we're supposed to.**

She's pretty, though. Even right now with her eyelids swollen and her cheeks puffed up and not a smidgen of lipstick in sight—nothing done to get ready for the world but her teeth and hair brushed—she looks darn near perfect. Like a model. Like she doesn't have to do anything but just *be*. I know you've seen people like that.

I think you ought to consider yourself lucky if you don't know any.

ACTIVE READING

INFER Why is Roseanne surprised at her mother's reaction to the death of cousin Jessie?

So she's sitting here in the morning heat—it's hot down in the flatland at nine o'clock in the morning. There's no haze to burn off so the sun just comes on out at five A.M. and everything's cooking by ten. When Melissa stays with us in the mountains, she sleeps in a double bed with me, and she curls up right tight next to me about daybreak when the air turns as chilly as it's going to get. She sleeps under a blanket every night. I think that's the only part about coming to our house she likes—snuggling under the covers like that. Anyway, we didn't visit this summer because her mama was so sick, hardly walking and needing to be looked after every minute. Cousin Jessie had diabetes[2] from the time she was first married. She gave herself those shots every day and even with doing that, sometimes she'd start shaking and jerking and finally just fall down unconscious. Everybody in the family carried Life Savers around in their pockets. Diabetes is what killed her, Life Savers or no.

When the news came, Mama was brokenhearted. Even knowing Cousin Jessie's time was coming and praying about it and fretting over it, Mama wasn't one bit ready. The look on her face when she was on the telephone was a sight—like she was hearing something terrible and truly unexpected instead of word that Cousin Jessie was at rest.

---

2. **diabetes** (dī′ə-bē′tĭs): a disease capable of producing coma and even death, in which the body produces insufficient insulin to balance sugar levels in the blood. Extra insulin is usually taken by the patient in the form of daily hypodermic shots.

Katie on Sofa (1959), Fairfield Porter. Oil on canvas, 24¼″ × 25¼″, collection of Mr. and Mrs. Edward W. Andrews, Jr.

She looked wild, Mama did, like the time she pulled Buddy out of the path of Mr. Bowdine's car when he reversed by accident. Then there was the time she lost a baby in the bathroom. I didn't even know it was a baby until that summer when I heard Mama and Cousin Jessie going over the details and put two and two together. The point is, that was the look on Mama's face, a look of being ripped apart and so startled she didn't know which was worse, the surprise or the pain.

Diabetes runs in the family. Cousin Jessie's

daddy had it and one of his sisters did, too. Mama's always telling us to watch our blood sugar, although Cousin Jessie's daddy wasn't a blood relative to us, her mama was. So it's Melissa who ought to be watching her blood sugar and I reckon she knows it. There's not an ounce of fat on her. She's wearing white shorts and a pink skinny top that shows everything. Mama didn't even let me bring shorts, even knowing how hot it is here. I've got seersucker slacks and this cotton skirt and that infernal blue dress. Of course, there's nobody to tell Melissa what she ought to be wearing. I mean, who's going to say it? Her daddy is in the throes of grief, so I think Mama's going to end up in charge. Already this morning she's cleaned out the refrigerator to make room for the cold dishes she's expecting. She's cleaned off a pantry shelf on which to put fried chicken, boiled vegetables, and ham. The buffet in the dining room will take care of cakes and pies and, I hope, some brownies. I would die for a brownie right now. And a cold drink. Melissa and I skipped breakfast.

I think she's just going to sit here until one o'clock, when we're supposed to go down to the funeral home and view the body. I told Mama I wasn't going and she said all right, I could take care of Buddy. He's nine and doesn't have any business at a funeral home. Melissa is going, though. She and her daddy are supposed to see if Cousin Jessie looks all right before they let other people view her. It seems to me it ought to be the other way around. Let some objective people get the first look. I think funerals are sick.

"Melissa, let's get something to eat." She's pushing the swing

ACTIVE READING

CLARIFY Why does Roseanne think that objective people should get the first look at Cousin Jessie?

with her bare feet so it trembles a little. She's got the prettiest toenails. I swear it! They curve just perfect and she's put this pink polish on them that turns silvery when the light catches it right. I guess fixing her toenails gave her something to do last night. You can spend hours messing with your nails if you want to. Well, I couldn't, but I bet Melissa can. Her feet are the kind somebody's going to want to kiss. It won't be long either, because Melissa's been going out with boys for a year or more. She's older than me, already sixteen, and there were boys after her when she was twelve. Cousin Jessie was fighting them off with a stick. Mama's never had that trouble with me.

"No, thanks," Melissa says about the food like I'm offering to fix her something. "Jamie's coming over here in a few minutes. He said he would."

That's the boy she's been going out with all summer. He'll be a senior next year, and for their first date he took her to the Junior-Senior Prom this past spring. Their picture's taped smack in the middle of her dresser mirror so you have to look around it to do your face. They're standing in front of a blue curtain with silver stars on it, and she's got her back up against his chest, and he's got his arms around her. I'm going to borrow that dress she's wearing if my figure settles down by next spring. I know Melissa's not intending to wear it again even if it cost one hundred and fifty dollars, which it did. Cousin Jessie told Mama Melissa's got expensive taste. She tried to sound like she was complaining, but I heard the pride in it. Melissa was everything to Cousin Jessie.

"Well, I'm eating something." Mama told me to stay with her. Comfort her, Mama said. "You want me to bring you a sandwich out here?"

WORDS TO KNOW

infernal (ĭn-fûr′nəl) *adj.* awful
throes (thrōz) *n.* a condition of agonizing struggle

We're eating peanut butter and jelly with milk. Melissa nibbles at hers and leaves the milk glass half full on the porch floor. This old tomcat of hers starts nosing around it, trying to get his face down to the milk. She doesn't even notice when he turns it over. I've got to remember to clean up the sticky place when he gets through. Mama wants everything clean, just like Cousin Jessie used to keep the house before she got weak and bloated and the medicine quit doing any good.

"Finished?"

When Melissa nods, I take her half-eaten sandwich and the empty glasses into the house. It's cooler in the house, especially in the living room, because the blinds are shut and it's dark in there. The kitchen's warm, though, and Mama's beading up while she scrubs the counter-tops and the cabinet fronts just like she was home. I think this is nervous energy working because she didn't sleep at all in the car and I don't think she closed her eyes after we got here. She and Cousin Roy sat down together at the kitchen table first thing, and that's where they were this morning when I came down. They'd been talking for hours, Uncle Roy telling Mama step by step what happened. I heard bits and pieces of it and I don't see how anybody remembers everything like that. It's like three days are marked in his brain, minute by minute. Looks like it would all be a blur.

Cousin Roy couldn't have picked a better person to tell it to, because Mama wanted to hear every word of it. I know she wishes she'd been here, but when Cousin Roy first called her to say Cousin Jessie was back in the hospital, practically in a coma, he told her there was no need for her to rush across North Carolina to see her. Cousin Jessie wouldn't know she was there, he said, hoping, I think, to relieve Mama's mind. But she wanted to come, she told Daddy, who agreed with Cousin Roy that she should save her strength for the end. "You can't help Jessie now," Daddy said, "but you can help Roy and Melissa later on if you don't wear yourself out. Jessie'd want them to have plenty of attention."

Mama gave in, but like I say, she fretted about it and prayed and cleaned her own house like we were expecting company ourselves. The older Mama gets, the more nervous she acts. I always thought when you got about forty, nothing much would worry you anymore. I mean, everything ought to be settled by then. But it's not so. Mama's a bundle of nerves under the best of circumstances.

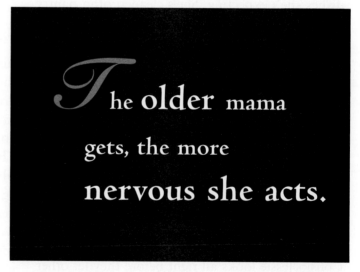

The older mama gets, the more nervous she acts.

Now she's perspiring through the housedress she brought to clean in. "Your daddy's still asleep," she says, aggravated by everything.

"He drove all night," I say in his defense.

"I know it." Mama wishes she weren't mad with Daddy. Her irritation weighs heavy on her, like it's a sin to feel anything but sad. "Your daddy's a fine man," she says, to get rid of her bad feelings. It's what she always does when she catches herself being upset with him. Mama always feels what she calls <u>remorse</u>, which I don't know a thing about unless you call remorse what I felt when Candy Hooper and I got caught copying each other's algebra problems. She'd done half and I'd done half so I don't call that cheating, but Mrs. Siler did and Mama did when Mrs. Siler sent me home from school at ten o'clock with a note saying I was suspended for the rest of the day and for Mama to either come see her or sign the note proving I'd done at least one honorable thing. I think I spent that afternoon in remorse.

"Can I help you do anything?" I ask her, because she's sniffling again. This crying is getting to me. I haven't cried a tear. Not that I don't love Cousin Jessie. She was always more fun than Melissa, but I just don't feel like crying about her. She was real sick and now she's not sick anymore, if you believe what you hear in church. And you're supposed to believe it, aren't you? Preachers talk about faith all the time, but right now I don't see much of it around here.

"Just keep an eye on Melissa," Mama says, scrubbing hard at a spot I could have told her was at least a three-year-old stain. "I haven't had a minute to be with her and I know she's distraught."

"She's sitting on the porch swing waiting for Jamie Fletcher to come see her. He's her boyfriend." I say that harder than I should have. Sometimes I can see where I've got a streak of meanness in me a mile wide.

Mama pauses in her scrubbing to consider the appropriateness of this. Mama's always worrying about what's appropriate.

"Well, maybe it'll do her good," she decides finally. She doesn't have any authority over Melissa anyway. I could have told her that, too.

When I come back to the porch, Jamie Fletcher is here and he's got somebody with him.

"Hey, Roseanne," the other boy says like he knows me, and all of a sudden, I know him! It's Travis, who lives three houses down from Melissa and used to play with us. I haven't seen him in three summers—last summer I didn't come, and the summer before that Travis was at a camp at the beach, where he learned to sail and high-dive and got muscles. Some things I can't describe, not with any amount of trying, and one of them is how Travis Cuthbert looks now that he's filled out and got muscles and a dynamite tan and hair on his legs. He's gorgeous. He's not that tall, blond, golden type like Melissa's Jamie, but he's handsome in a way that suits me better. He's kind of short and tight and his hair is dark and wavy and he's got brown eyes instead of this washed-out blue everybody in our family got stuck with. He's got on cut-off jeans and a green T-shirt from Myrtle Beach and those worn-out looking moccasins that cost a fortune but people never polish so they'll look like they can afford to abuse them. Daddy always polishes my shoes, even if I don't want him to. I hate him doing that.

"How you doing?" Jamie says to Melissa and sits down beside her on the swing. Travis and I are just standing here.

"Fine," Melissa says, but she grabs his hand.

I'm still looking at Travis even though I know I'm making a fool of myself. I'm glad I put my face on.

"How you been, Roseanne?" Travis wants to know. He turns a little away from Melissa and Jamie, like ignoring them will give them privacy in broad daylight.

WORDS TO KNOW   **remorse** (rĭ-môrs´) *n.* bitter regret

take myself over to the steps and plop down on the top one. I can't think of a thing to say. Have you ever been struck dumb like this so you make a fool out of yourself doing absolutely nothing?

"Come sit down," I say when I find my breath. I think my lungs have collapsed on me because no air's going in. I try pushing out and there's a great big sigh like somebody gives to show they're bored, which I definitely am not. "Whatcha' been doing?" I ask when he's sitting next to me.

"The usual. Working at the pool. I earned my senior lifesaver badge so I've got a lifeguarding job."

ACTIVE READING

INFER Why can't Roseanne think of a thing to say when Travis talks to her?

That accounts for the tan. I look pasty beside him, but some people like a delicate look, even in the summertime. I smooth my flowered skirt over my knees and rub my hands down my calves. I've got good calves, tanned or not.

"You've changed a lot," Travis says, noticing my calves. I do baton twirling for a hobby and go to jazz class twice a week. Mama let me take it up when I refused to go to another piano lesson.

"It's been more than two years," I say and wish I hadn't. He'll think I've been keeping track.

"Too bad about the circumstances," he says, nodding toward Melissa, who's got her head resting on Jamie's chest right here on the front porch. Mama's going to have a fit.

"Well, she was real sick," I say like I'm supposed to comfort him or something. "We've got to go to the funeral home at one o'clock and look at her. I'm going with Melissa in case she breaks down over it. She's been so brave." Well, a person can change her mind, can't she?

Travis is looking at me like I'm God's gift to the <u>bereaved</u>. That's the truth. He's got this expression of awe on his face I wish I had a picture of. "Whatcha doing later?" he asks me.

I think to myself, this is how a date gets started. Here I am on Cousin Jessie's porch with her dead in the funeral home and her own child crying on her boyfriend's shirtfront and Mama in the house scrubbing everything in sight and I've got to think of the right thing to say. "Well, there's the visitation . . ." I begin.

"Oh, yeah." I can tell he's disappointed.

"But that's over at nine," I slide in.

"I don't suppose you and Melissa'd want to go somewhere, just out for a ride or to get something to eat," Travis says, brightening up. "Jamie and I were talking about it. Maybe it would do her good to get out of here for a while."

ver since late this morning, I've had this fever. There's a cool dampness inside my clothes but my cheeks are burning. I feel like I've been on fire inside my face all this time but nobody seems to notice. I have a date!

I can't believe Melissa straightened herself up from Jamie Fletcher's arm and went right in the house to her daddy and said to him, "It'll be all right if Roseanne and me ride around awhile after the visitation." Didn't ask him. Told him in that sweet way of hers like her mama had somehow already given her permission, and he just nodded while my mama stared holes through both of us. I kept looking at Mama and after a long minute she sort of half nodded her consent to me, too. She was giving in and her face sagged with it like she was grimacing before the next blow, waiting to be struck down.

I'm burning up. Ever since that minute when Mama gave in, I've been hot under my skin, so I keep thinking about water. About how Travis must look at the pool. I bet during the rest periods he practices his dives. We used to run through the lawn sprinkler spray when it was hot like this and Travis would come over and aggravate us. He'd sit on the jets or chase us with the hose. He'd make Melissa so mad. One time he held the sprinkler on my head so I was surrounded by whirling spray with colors in it, like a crown shooting off diamonds. I remember it like it was yesterday. I have always thought a lot of Travis.

In a few minutes I'm going off with him. I ought to tell you this is my first date in a car. I call riding around a date, don't you? I mean, it's likely we'll go somewhere and get a cola or a soft cone. That would make it official. I believe somebody has to spend some money to make it a date. Craig Watkins comes and sits on our porch sometimes in the evenings after his American Legion baseball practice. He's on his way home and he sees us there and he comes and sits. Sometimes he and Buddy roughhouse or toss a baseball around until it's too dark to see. Most of the time, though, he leans against a porch post and watches the sky with me. It's the only time I like to be still—in that little while between sunset and true dark when the world is closing up and after a while there's nothing to see but our street, the house full of yellow light across the way, and our own porch. The cool smell of night is coming but there are no stars yet. I know just where I am then. Craig Watkins sitting on the porch is not a date.

This afternoon I went with Melissa to view the body, but I didn't look. I went about halfway up there to the casket, which was at one end of a long room lined with vinyl sofas and straight-backed chairs. There were lights in the ceiling along the molding and some plants on end tables that separated the sofas from the chairs. There were flowers on either end of the casket, too. Wreaths of carnations and mums

ACTIVE READING

CONNECT Can you understand how Roseanne might be feeling about her first date?

One time he held the sprinkler on my head so I was surrounded by whirling spray with colors in it, like a crown shooting off diamonds.

Isabella and Lois (1968), Warren Brandt. Oil on canvas, 50″ × 60″, private collection.

and gladioluses. I kept looking at them so I didn't have to look at Cousin Jessie. I don't believe Melissa wanted to look, either, but I reckon she felt like she had to.

"Do you think what she's wearing is all right?" she asked Mama, like clothes were the important thing. Well, they are to Melissa. She's always had everything she wants. You ought to see inside her closet.

"It's fine," Mama said and put her arm around Melissa's shoulder. They were both trembling. You could see their shoulders jumping. Cousin Roy came in with Daddy then, and Mama and Melissa opened a place between them and hugged him, too. Cousin Roy looked weak and sick, not giving his full height, which is more than six feet. I have never liked tall men. Five eight or nine is good enough for me.

By the time we got home, the house was full of people and flowers and food. Melissa wouldn't eat a thing. She wouldn't talk to people either. I don't know what gets into her. I mean, she knows everybody in this town so it's not like anybody expected her to greet strangers. Most of them are unknown to me, however, and I was polite. Even Mama commented on it. I wish I'd brought that mint green top that's cut low in the back. I'd put it on right now if I had it.

Lord, it was hot at the visitation. You'd think a funeral home could keep itself cool, but the place was packed with people, even backed up in the hall, waiting to view Cousin Jessie and pay their respects. Some people were so glad to see Mama they acted like it was a reunion, but Mama held herself back. I heard a woman ask her if she was going to sing something at the funeral. She wanted to hear Mama because it had been such a long time. Mama said she wasn't, but the thought of it brought tears to her eyes. She sang at Cousin Jessie's wedding and was the maid of honor besides.

ACTIVE READING

QUESTION Why can't Roseanne understand why Melissa doesn't feel like talking after visiting her mother in the funeral home?

I feel like I'm going on and on. Diarrhea of the mouth. That's what happens when a person gets feverish. You feel like you've got to get everything said before you pass out of heat exhaustion. My mind's been racing for hours. It's like I've got a top spinning in there, whizzing and making heat. Everywhere I've been it's been so hot and tomorrow I've got to wear that dress. I ought to take some aspirins or something.

When we got home from the visitation it was dark, and Travis and Jamie were waiting on the porch. Mama invited them in to have a piece of cake—we've got six kinds—but they wouldn't. I came upstairs just now to fix my face and see how bad I look. I look flushed and my eyes are shining, just like a person with a fever. There's something pretty about it, though. I mean it's better than looking washed-out and sickly. Melissa, who stayed downstairs with the boys instead of fixing herself, is not as pretty as she used to be. If you saw her baby pictures, you'd think she should have been on the Ivory Snow box.

Now that we're finally riding around, I can tell you that I thought Mama would never let us out of the house, she kept being so social. She's beside herself with worry about every little thing and I could tell she didn't want us out of her sight. Jamie and Melissa are quiet in the backseat. I don't know what they're doing and I don't intend to look. I watch the asphalt running up under us. If you watch the lights on the road long enough, you'll get dizzy and pass out. Travis is a fantastic driver. He's got one hand on the wheel and the other elbow resting out the window. Every now and then he changes hands. Once he put his hand down on the seat between us and I thought to myself, this is it, but then he made a turn. I think we are riding in circles.

I have noticed that Travis likes to talk about himself, which is all right with me. He tells me all about his job, what time he goes to work, when he closes, and the details of several incidents of disciplinary action he's been involved in. Nobody has drowned in his pool. He tells us about the camp he went to. He won lots of certificates and awards. Football practice starts in three weeks. He is first-string running back and ran nine hundred yards for eight touchdowns last year. All this he says in a half whisper so I have to lean a little toward him to hear. If it weren't for my seatbelt I could slip over.

I am absolutely light-headed. The breeze

Boy and Car (1955), David Park. Oil on canvas, 18" × 24", collection of Mrs. Wellington S. Henderson.

gusting past my head is hot and oily like we are trailing in someone's exhaust. The air down here doesn't breathe good like at home. I feel as powdery as used charcoal and every breath I take turns prickly in my throat.

"Let's get some burgers and drinks and go out by the river," Jamie says from the backseat.

He and Melissa are stretching and sighing just like they're waking up. "I could eat a

horse," Melissa says with a little laugh. And we've got all that food at home.

The boys go into a restaurant while Melissa and I wait in the car, so I turn around to talk to her. She's rumpled and relaxed looking. Her lips are puffy and her hair looks tangled in the back. Around her face it's as smooth as silk where she's combed her fingers through it.

"Travis is nice," I say. I have always wanted

to be sitting in a car outside a restaurant waiting for my date to come back. People going in always glance at you and know there's somebody inside getting you something.

"He's all right," Melissa says, sighing. She used to talk a whole lot more than this.

"What's at the river?" I ask.

"Nothing. Just the river bank and trees and stuff. It's where people go to park, Roseanne."

"You mean we're going to park? We can just eat the burgers and talk, can't we?"

"You can do anything you want to," Melissa says.

I think what I'll do is faint.

We rode up here to the church in a black limousine, but there wasn't a thing fun about it. I mean, you ought to be going to a party in a car like that. I rode in front with Melissa. Mama, Daddy, Cousin Roy, and Buddy were in the back. Cousin Roy's family from Wilson was in the car behind and I think his sister Esther is put out about it. After all, she's more <u>kin</u> than we are. Sometimes kin is not what matters, I don't reckon. Cousin Roy knows how it was between Jessie and Mama, so we got to ride in the limousine behind the hearse. The air conditioner was blowing full blast between my legs, but I was hot anyway. We waited in the limo outside the church until they'd slid the casket onto this folding stretcher contraption and rolled it in. Then we got out, and right there I started sweating because the sun could boil water today. This church is not air-conditioned either.

The organ is playing, and we're sitting on the front pews, our backs to everybody. Melissa is between her daddy and my mama. She's wearing blue, but it's a soft color. Soft summery material, too. She looks like an angel, all glittery and shiny, while the rest of us are black and gray and midnight blue. I'm between Daddy and Buddy, but I can see Melissa's hands working a tissue. In a minute she's going to have it torn up, the way she's twisting and squeezing it. Mama has a pocketbook full.

The organ is sending out mournful notes, too draggy to follow. I think we ought to sing. It would be better than sitting here, holding the words in our heads. I'd like to blast right out "j-us-s-t as I am-m-m" so that woman would pick up the beat, but Mama would die. I feel like I'm going to jump out of my skin. I've never been good at waiting. Anybody with eyes can see how I'm fidgeting. My mind won't stop whirring, trying to make sense of all that's in it. Travis Cuthbert kissed me last night! We rode out by the river with me holding the cardboard tray with four drinks and a sack of burgers in my lap. The smell of hot onions and pickles was enough to make a well person sick. I sipped on my drink all the way out there, trying not to throw up, although I am not a person with a weak stomach. Travis parked the car and distributed the food. He kept the switch on so we could listen to the radio. It was dark except for the green dials on the dashboard, so Travis opened the pocket so the little light in there showed. The burger tasted a lot better than I thought it would. When everybody was finished, Travis turned the switch off and shut the pocket so everything was quiet and still and dark around me. I couldn't even see the river, but I could hear it, just this little stirring movement and, now and then, a plopping sound like someone throwing a stone or dipping a cup into the water. Our rivers at home are always moving, rushing and slapping rocks, going somewhere in a hurry. They sound cool and fresh and busy. These rivers down here hardly move at all and the air around them is sticky and sour.

WORDS TO KNOW   **kin** (kĭn) *n.* one's relatives; family

"Let's get out," Travis said. We left Melissa and Jamie in the backseat and walked down to the water. It wasn't any cooler there and mosquitoes were hovering in the grass, but we sat down on a big flat rock right on the water's edge and pulled our feet up.

I didn't get a whole lot of warning. I always thought when I got kissed it was going to be with eye contact, in slow motion, you know, so expecting it would be just as exciting as the kiss itself. It wasn't like that. Travis kissed me hard and flat at first, like it was an attack or something, but right away I knew that wasn't how he meant it. When I didn't pull back, he softened up and we kissed for a while. Little kisses and a couple of big ones. I think he was practicing as much as I was. I felt as weak as water and clammy in my chest and my head was full of light so I just wanted to keep my eyes shut like when you wake up suddenly and the sun's too bright in your room. I didn't want to move or wake up or anything.

We didn't talk much going home. I don't mind admitting I'm tongue-tied in some situations, and Melissa and Jamie were keeping to themselves.

Melissa is not such a bad person. After we got home, she was so quiet and sad looking. I think she'd hoped going out with Jamie would make her feel better but it didn't. Nothing's going to make her feel better for a long time.

We were standing in front of her dresser mirror. She was brushing her hair and I was just looking at myself. I reckon I expected to see some difference but there doesn't seem to be any. Anyway, Melissa and I happened to look at each other in the mirror. It was truly strange because it was like we were seeing each other for the first time. I mean, I think she saw that I was there with her. And I saw—well, I saw that something terrible had happened to her, had been happening most of her life. Her mama had been dying for a long time, and her being pretty and popular hadn't changed that. Melissa knows a lot of things I don't know.

Later on, I could tell she wasn't asleep. I wasn't sleepy either, but I was thinking about Travis, about how a person's life can be changed so quick. I felt good inside, cooled down and calm but excited, too, like some wonderful adventure was just getting started. All the while, Melissa was tossing around, trying to find a comfortable position. Sometimes there's just nothing you can do to stop being miserable. I waited a little bit to see if she'd settle down. When she didn't, I got up and got in bed with her and rubbed her back like she used to want me to do. I wasn't one bit embarrassed.

This preacher is talking about what a good woman Cousin Jessie was. Everything he's saying is the truth. This church feels dark like there's a cloud stopped over it, but I know it's a bright, sunny, July Sunday outside of here. We've got to go to the cemetery next. I'm going to melt out there in this dress, but I'm going to stay as long as Melissa does. I'm going to tell her how sorry I am. I'm going to tell Cousin Roy, too, because I haven't told him yet. But I'm not going to tell anybody except you about Travis Cuthbert kissing me. It's as private as grief but it doesn't need sharing. Just Melissa knows and someday when we're all grown up and married, we'll probably talk about it just like Mama and Cousin Jessie used to talk about things just they knew about.

As soon as I get a chance, I'm going to hug Mama. ❖

ACTIVE READING

INFER Why does Roseanne want to hug her mother?

Oranges

Gary Soto

The first time I walked
With a girl, I was twelve,
Cold, and weighted down
With two oranges in my jacket.
5 December. Frost cracking
Beneath my steps, my breath
Before me, then gone,
As I walked toward
Her house, the one whose
10 Porch light burned yellow
Night and day, in any weather.
A dog barked at me, until
She came out pulling
At her gloves, face bright
15 With rouge. I smiled,
Touched her shoulder, and led
Her down the street, across
A used car lot and a line
Of newly planted trees,
20 Until we were breathing
Before a drugstore. We
Entered, the tiny bell
Bringing a saleslady
Down a narrow aisle of goods.
25 I turned to the candies
Tiered like bleachers,
And asked what she wanted—
Light in her eyes, a smile
Starting at the corners

30 Of her mouth. I fingered
A nickel in my pocket,
And when she lifted a chocolate
That cost a dime,
I didn't say anything.
35 I took the nickel from
My pocket, then an orange,
And set them quietly on
The counter. When I looked up,
The lady's eyes met mine,
40 And held them, knowing
Very well what it was all
About.

Outside,
A few cars hissing past,
45 Fog hanging like old
Coats between the trees.
I took my girl's hand
In mine for two blocks,
Then released it to let
50 Her unwrap the chocolate.
I peeled my orange
That was so bright against
The gray of December
That, from some distance,
55 Someone might have thought
I was making a fire in my hands.

Connect to the Literature

1. **What Do You Think?** How did you react to the narrator as a person? Share your reactions with a classmate.

> **Comprehension Check**
> - How does Roseanne feel about her cousin Melissa at the beginning of the story?
> - What happens to change the narrator's impression of Melissa?
> - Besides hugging her mother, what is Roseanne looking forward to at the end of the story?

Think Critically

2. **ACTIVE READING** | **MAKING INFERENCES ABOUT CHARACTER** Look back at the answers you wrote in your **READER'S NOTEBOOK** for the questions in the story. Now that you have finished the story, what changes would you make in your answers?

3. Why do you think Roseanne's feelings toward Melissa changed?

THINK ABOUT
- how Roseanne feels about herself at different points in the story
- how Roseanne feels after her date with Travis
- what Roseanne realizes when she and Melissa look at each other in the mirror

4. Think about the **title** of the story. What do you think Roseanne's experience is the beginning of?

Extend Interpretations

5. **Critic's Corner** After reading this story, Ruth El-Jamal, a member of our student board, made the following comment: "I loved this selection because Roseanne is telling the story directly to the reader. . . . I felt very involved in her life, like she was talking to me as a friend." How does this response compare with yours? Give your own reason for liking or disliking this story.

6. **Comparing Texts** Both "The Beginning of Something" and the Literary Link poem "Oranges" depict first-time experiences. Compare how the **narrator** of the short story and the **speaker** of the poem deal with an unfamiliar situation in which they want to make a good impression.

7. **Connect to Life** Roseanne says, "I call riding around a date, don't you?" and Gary Soto questions whether walking with a girl is a date. What do you consider the minimum requirements for a date?

Literary Analysis

CHARACTER In addition to **main** and **minor,** characters in a story can be **flat** or **round.** Minor characters, who exist mainly to advance the plot, are usually flat. They display only the traits needed for their limited role. Main characters are usually round. They are well-developed enough to seem like real people. We assume that they have thoughts, feelings, and motivations that we can't see. If they do something surprising, instead of thinking that they are acting "out of character," we try to understand what made them behave that way. Characters can also be described as **static** or **dynamic.** A dynamic character changes as a result of the events in the story. A static character remains unchanged.

Cooperative Learning Activity Divide up the characters in "The Beginning of Something" among several small groups in your class. Each group should trace its assigned character through the story, deciding if he or she is

- a main character or a minor character
- a round character or a flat character
- a static character or a dynamic character

Each group can report its results to the rest of the class, giving examples from the story to support its decisions.

REVIEW **SETTING** The setting of a story is the time and place in which the action occurs. Why do you think the author has this story take place during a family's visit to its hometown for a funeral?

Choices & CHALLENGES

Writing Options

1. First-Date Notes Roseanne's excitement about her first date overshadows everything else. Write preliminary notes for a personal essay explaining why a first date is so often such a nervous and emotional rite of passage.

2. Conflicting-Feelings Poem Think about your discussion for the Connect to Your Life activity on page 324. Write a draft of a poem that describes the conflict you felt in the situation you shared.

Activities & Explorations

1. Mood Concert Choose two songs that convey the different feelings experienced by Melissa and Roseanne. Play the songs for the class and explain why you chose them. ~ **MUSIC/SPEAKING AND LISTENING**

2. Dramatic Reminiscence Imagine that it is 20 years later and Roseanne and Melissa are indeed "all grown up and married" and talking about things "just like Mama and Cousin Jessie." With a partner, take the roles of the two girls and prepare a dramatic re-creation of their reminiscing about the funeral, Roseanne's rite of passage, and their relationship since then. After practicing, you can tape-record your dialogue for presentation or re-create it live for the whole class. ~ **SPEAKING AND LISTENING**

Inquiry & Research

Diabetes Melissa's mother dies of diabetes in middle age. Skim the story and take notes on what Roseanne says about her illness. Then research the symptoms, causes, and treatment of diabetes. Does the information presented early in the story coincide with your findings? Why would the family be carrying candy around in their pockets? Present your findings in an oral report.

Art Connection

Look again at the painting on page 328. Fairfield Porter's *Katie on Sofa* is typical of the domestic scenes he does so well. Why is the young woman staring straight ahead? What might she be thinking about?

Vocabulary in Action

EXERCISE: MEANING CLUES Write the letter of the situation that best demonstrates the meaning of the boldfaced word.

1. bereaved
   a. teenagers at a prom
   b. family at a wedding
   c. relatives at a funeral

2. remorse
   a. you have hurt a friend
   b. you have won a prize
   c. you have helped someone

3. kin
   a. animals in a wildlife refuge
   b. people at a family reunion
   c. students in a classroom

4. infernal
   a. sound of fingernails on a chalkboard
   b. sound of waves lapping the shore
   c. sound of birds singing in a tree

5. throes
   a. a mother with a seriously ill child
   b. a musician playing an instrument
   c. a girl daydreaming about the prom

Building Vocabulary
For an in-depth study of context clues, see page 103.

Grammar in Context: Compound Sentences

In the compound sentence below, Roseanne recounts her brother's ability, and her own inability, to sleep on the long ride to Cousin Jessie's house.

> He can sleep through anything, but I was restless and uneasy.

A **compound sentence** is formed by joining two or more simple sentences. By using compound sentences, a writer can show that ideas are related or equal in importance. Writers also use compound sentences to avoid wordiness and increase sentence variety. Notice that in the example above, Bridgers has combined two simple sentences with a comma and a coordinating conjunction—the word *but.*

Usage Tip: In addition to *and* or *but,* you can use the coordinating conjunction *or, nor,* or *yet* to join sentences.

WRITING EXERCISE Join each pair of sentences to form a compound sentence. Place a comma before the coordinating conjunction.

Example: *Original* Roseanne's mother did not want Roseanne to go out. She gave in.

Rewritten Roseanne's mother did not want Roseanne to go <u>out, but</u> she gave in.

1. Mama and Cousin Jessie grew up together. They've always been best friends.
2. Mama didn't want to tell Melissa what to do. She thought Melissa should stay home.
3. Melissa isn't saying much. She doesn't seem interested in eating, either.
4. Melissa is a pretty girl. Right now, though, her face is swollen.
5. The boys could sit with us on the porch. On the other hand, we could all go inside.

<u>Grammar Handbook</u> The Structure of Sentences, p. 1196

Sue Ellen Bridgers
1942–

Other Works
Home Before Dark
All Together Now
Permanent Connections
Keeping Christina

Family Matters Sue Ellen Bridgers grew up in North Carolina, surrounded by kin. She defines family life "as the core of my writing." The daughter of a farmer, Bridgers was raised in small towns near both her parents' families. Describing her childhood as both happy and difficult, she says, "There were perhaps too many eyes focused on us and yet there was an abundance of concern and well-intentioned affection."

An Early Start While Bridgers was in elementary school, she composed poems that were published by the local newspaper. Her college degree and her writing plans were delayed, however, by marriage and motherhood.

Writing for Teenagers Bridgers did not publish her first novel until she was 34. It won praise for realistically portraying the thoughts, feelings, and actions of young adults. Virtually all her fiction is set in North Carolina, where "the land and the rural way of life are so important" and where she makes her home in the Blue Ridge Mountains. A book reviewer showed gratitude for Bridgers's concentration on teenage audiences and wrote that these readers "deserve their literary giants, too; in Sue Ellen Bridgers, they have one."

Author Activity

Both Sue Ellen Bridgers and Gary Soto are known for writing from the point of view of young people. Find a story, poem, or song—by one of these writers or another you know—that you think shows a good understanding of what the world looks like to someone your age. Present your literary work to the class, along with your explanation of why you chose it.

Young
Poetry by ANNE SEXTON

Hanging Fire
Poetry by AUDRE LORDE

"I am fourteen."

Connect to Your Life

Big Changes Ahead! Think about how your life has changed in the last few years, and about how it is changing now. How do you feel about these changes? With a partner, list a few changes that are normal in the life of someone your age. Using a chart like the one shown, describe the disadvantages of these changes and the immediate or long-term benefits.

Changes Ninth-Graders Have to Face		
Change	Disadvantages	Benefits
Coming to a new school	Not knowing anyone	Making new friends

Build Background

Fun to Be Young? Adults sometimes say that youth is wasted on the young. One reason for that saying might be that the advantages of youth are easier to appreciate when you don't have to deal with any of the disadvantages. While being young can and should be a joyful time, it is also a time of uncertainty, rapid change, and need for understanding from adults. Each of the poems you are about to read deals with this time in a person's life and tries to find words for the strong, sometimes contradictory emotions that come with it.

Focus Your Reading

LITERARY ANALYSIS **SPEAKER** In poetry, the person speaking—the "I" of the poem—is called the **speaker.** The speaker is not necessarily the poet but instead is a dramatic creation of the poet, much like a **character** in a play. As you read these two poems, try to form an impression of the person who is speaking from what she says.

ACTIVE READING **DRAWING CONCLUSIONS** Often, a poet will not state an idea directly but instead will expect the reader to **draw conclusions** based on what is stated and on his or her prior knowledge and experience.

READER'S NOTEBOOK As you read these poems, note places where each poet seems to want the reader to draw a conclusion about the situation being described. Record the conclusions you reach.

Young

ANNE SEXTON

A thousand doors ago
when I was a lonely kid
in a big house with four
garages and it was summer
as long as I could remember,
I lay on the lawn at night,
clover wrinkling under me,
the wise stars bedding over
    me,
my mother's window a funnel
of yellow heat running out,
my father's window, half
    shut,
an eye where sleepers pass,
and the boards of the house
were smooth and white as
    wax

and probably a million leaves
sailed on their strange stalks
as the crickets ticked together
and I, in my brand new body,
which was not a woman's yet,
told the stars my questions
and thought God could really
    see
the heat and the painted light,
elbows, knees, dreams,
    goodnight.

Thinking Through the Literature

1. What image lingers in your mind after reading this poem?

2. **ACTIVE READING** | **DRAWING CONCLUSIONS** | Look back in your
    READER'S NOTEBOOK. What **conclusions** did you draw
   about the situation being described in "Young"? Give evidence
   for your conclusions, referring both to the text and to your own
   experience.

3. How do you think the girl in "Young" feels about where she is
   in her life?

   THINK ABOUT
   - how she perceives her surroundings as she lies
     on the grass
   - why she tells the stars her questions
   - why the poem ends with her falling asleep

Hanging FIRE

AUDRE LORDE

I am fourteen
and my skin has betrayed me
the boy I cannot live without
still sucks his thumb
5　in secret
how come my knees are
always so ashy
what if I die
before morning
10　and momma's in the bedroom
with the door closed.

I have to learn how to dance
in time for the next party
my room is too small for me
15　suppose I die before graduation
they will sing sad melodies
but finally
tell the truth about me
There is nothing I want to do
20　and too much
that has to be done
and momma's in the bedroom
with the door closed.

Nobody even stops to think
25　about my side of it
I should have been on Math Team
my marks were better than his
why do I have to be
the one
30　wearing braces
I have nothing to wear tomorrow
will I live long enough
to grow up
and momma's in the bedroom
35　with the door closed.

By the Gate (1953),
Ernest Crichlow. Oil on
board, 10 ½" × 14 ½",
The Harmon and Harriet
Kelley Collection.

Connect to the Literature

1. **What Do You Think?** Did you feel more or less sympathy with the girl speaking in "Hanging Fire" than with the one speaking in "Young"? Explain your answer.

Think Critically

2. **ACTIVE READING** **DRAWING CONCLUSIONS** Look over the **conclusions** about "Hanging Fire" that you noted in your **READER'S NOTEBOOK.** What conclusions can you draw about the situation described in this poem? Give evidence for your conclusions.

3. Why is the girl in "Hanging Fire" upset about her mother's being in the bedroom with the door closed?

THINK ABOUT {
- the things the girl is worried about
- the things the girl is hopeful about
- what she wants from her mother

4. How would you describe the difference in **tone** between the two poems?

Extend Interpretations

5. **Comparing Texts** How does setting "Young" in the past instead of the present make its impact different from that of "Hanging Fire"?

6. **What If?** How would the situation in "Hanging Fire" change if the girl's mother came out of the bedroom to talk to her?

7. **Connect to Life** Based on your own experiences and your observations about adolescence in general, which of these poems do you think is more true to life?

Literary Analysis

SPEAKER The **speaker** in a poem is the voice that "talks" to the reader. Like the **narrator** in fiction, the speaker is the **character** or person who relates the ideas or story of the poem and from whose point of view the poem is written. When reading a poem, it is usually important to get a sense of who the speaker is in order to fully understand the work.

Cooperative Learning Activity In small groups, discuss what you think are the similarities and differences between the speakers in these two poems. Pay special attention to the relationship in each poem between the speaker and the **main character.**

REVIEW **RHYME SCHEME/ FREE VERSE**
Poems that rhyme are usually arranged in a particular **rhyme scheme**—a pattern of rhymes at the ends of lines that is often repeated in every stanza. Poetry that has no regular pattern of rhyme or **rhythm** is called **free verse**. Free verse may still use repeated sounds (or even entire words) at the ends of lines to create a poetic effect. What repeated sounds can you find in the free-verse poems "Young" and "Hanging Fire"?

Writing Options

Advice Column Imagine that you have an advice column and that the speaker in "Hanging Fire" writes you a letter asking about one or more of her concerns in the poem. Determine what advice you would give. Write both the question from the speaker and your response.

Activities & Explorations

Dramatic Interpretation Select one of the two poems and practice reading it aloud, emphasizing the meaning or emotion of the poem with your voice, facial expression, and gestures. Perform a dramatic interpretation of the poem for the class. ~ **PERFORMING**

Inquiry & Research

Medical Investigation Both Lorde and Sexton had their own battles to fight, Lorde with cancer and Sexton with mental illness. Pick some aspect of either cancer or mental illness and research it. You could look into modern or historical methods of treatment, or note symptoms or methods of prevention. Share the information with the class.

Photograph by Layle Silbert

Audre Lorde
1934–1992

Other Works
Between Our Selves
The Black Unicorn

Overcoming Difficulties Born with severe speech and sight problems, Audre Lorde was insecure and used poetry she had memorized to respond to questions. As she got older, she found that the poems of others did not fully express her feelings, so she began writing her own. Her first poem was published in *Seventeen* magazine while she was a high school student.

Caribbean Roots Lorde's parents were Caribbean immigrants who settled in New York's Harlem district, where Lorde was born. Lorde eventually moved to the Caribbean, spending her last days on the island of St. Croix. In the time between, she held several teaching positions, toured the world as a lecturer, and received numerous awards and honors for her poetry.

Speaking Out Lorde once wrote "I have come to believe. . .that what is most important to me must be spoken, made verbal and shared, even at the risk of having it bruised or misunderstood." Lorde's belief in speaking out took many forms. In addition to her writing, she became active in the civil rights, antiwar, and feminist movements.

Anne Sexton
1928–1974

Other Works
Love Poems
The Book of Folly

Troubled Life Despite having been born into an upper-middle-class Massachusetts family, Anne Sexton led a tragic life. She was plagued by emotional disturbances, attempted suicide several times, and in one year saw her mother die of cancer and her father of a cerebral hemorrhage. However, it was in response to this instability and trauma that her poetry was born. It was after her first suicide attempt that her psychiatrist suggested writing as an outlet.

Growing Acclaim Sexton worked hard at her writing, and it paid off. The quality of her work gained her acceptance into Robert Lowell's graduate writing seminar at Boston University. Her first book of poetry, *To Bedlam and Part Way Back*, an examination of her mental breakdown and recovery, was published in 1960. The autobiographical *All My Pretty Ones* (1962), which takes its title from a passage in Shakespeare's *Macbeth*, is about the deaths of her parents. Her collection *Live or Die* (1967) won her the Pulitzer Prize. Sexton continued to struggle with depression until her tragic death in 1974.

The Seven Ages of Man

Poetry by WILLIAM SHAKESPEARE

"All the world's a stage."

Connect to Your Life

The Stages of Life If you were to divide up the average person's life into segments and identify the different parts, from infancy to old age, where would you draw the lines? What labels would you use to identify the different parts? How would you describe each segment? Create a time line like the one shown below to illustrate how you think of the stages of life. Then circle the stage that you think describes where you are in your life now.

The Stages of Life

Childhood	Adulthood	Old Age

Infancy	Adolescence	Maturity	Death

Build Background

The Melancholy Jaques The speaker in the piece you are about to read is a character named Jaques in Shakespeare's play *As You Like It.* In this romantic comedy, Jaques is a lord living in the Forest of Arden with the banished duke he loyally serves. In strong contrast to the other characters in the play, Jaques is cynical, moody, and philosophical. Others refer to him as "the melancholy Jaques," and we learn of his weeping and moralizing even before he appears on stage. Jaques's gloomy outlook is reflected in his speeches, including this one.

Focus Your Reading

LITERARY ANALYSIS **DRAMATIC MONOLOGUE** A **dramatic monologue** is a kind of poem in which the **speaker** addresses a silent or absent listener, as if engaged in a private conversation. In a dramatic monologue, the speaker often reveals feelings, attitudes, motivations, or personality traits, generally in a moment of high intensity or deep emotion. As you read this poem, notice the feelings and attitudes Jaques expresses and what his speech seems to reveal about his character.

ACTIVE READING **MAIN IDEAS IN POETRY** Jaques's monologue is meant to convey his ideas and opinions about the nature of life. The monologue can be divided into parts, one for each of the "seven ages of man." Just as each paragraph in an **essay** contains a **main idea,** each of the parts of Jaques's monologue contains a main idea that contributes to the message of the speech as a whole.

READER'S NOTEBOOK As you read Shakespeare's poem, jot down briefly in your own words what you see as the main idea of each "age."

The SEVEN AGES OF MAN

from *As You Like It*
WILLIAM SHAKESPEARE

The Ages of Man (17th century), English school. Oil on canvas. Norfolk Museums Service (Norwich Castle Museum), United Kingdom/Bridgeman Art Library, New York.

JAQUES:

All the world's a stage,
And all the men and women merely players:
They have their exits and their entrances;
And one man in his time plays many parts,
His acts being seven ages. At first the infant,
Mewling and puking in the nurse's arms.
And then the whining school-boy, with his satchel,
And shining morning face, creeping like snail
Unwillingly to school. And then the lover,
Sighing like furnace, with a woeful ballad
Made to his mistress' eyebrow. Then a soldier,
Full of strange oaths, and bearded like the pard,
Jealous in honor, sudden and quick in quarrel,
Seeking the bubble reputation
Even in the cannon's mouth. And then the justice,
In fair round belly with good capon lin'd,
With eyes severe, and beard of formal cut,
Full of wise saws and modern instances;
And so he plays his part. The sixth age shifts
Into the lean and slipper'd pantaloon,
With spectacles on nose and pouch on side,
His youthful hose well sav'd, a world too wide
For his shrunk shank; and his big manly voice,
Turning again toward childish treble, pipes
And whistles in his sound. Last scene of all,
That ends this strange eventful history,
Is second childishness and mere oblivion,
Sans teeth, sans eyes, sans taste, sans everything.

6 mewling: whining.

10 woeful ballad (băl′əd): sad, sentimental song.

12 pard: leopard.

16 with . . . lin'd: full of chicken.

18 saws . . . instances: old proverbs and examples that illustrate how they still apply.

20 pantaloon (păn′tə-lōōn′): foolish old man (from the name of a stock character in Italian comedies).

24 treble (trĕb′əl): a high-pitched voice.

27 oblivion (ə-blĭv′ē-ən): complete forgetfulness.

28 sans (sănz): without.

Thinking through the LITERATURE

Connect to the Literature

1. What Do You Think?
Why do you think Jaques is so gloomy?

Comprehension Check
- How is the schoolboy described?
- Where does the soldier try to gain a reputation?
- According to Jaques, what is the last stage of life?

Think Critically

2. [ACTIVE READING] [MAIN IDEAS IN POETRY] Look at the **main ideas** you wrote down in your ▯**READER'S NOTEBOOK** for each part of Jaques's speech. Based on your observations, what do you think is the **theme,** or message, of the speech as a whole?

3. Why do you think Jaques compares life to a theater stage?

- why he says all the men and women are "merely players"
- what he means when he says that "one man in his time plays many parts"
- why he refers to a lifetime as a "strange eventful history"

4. How might a more optimistic person describe some of the stages Jaques talks about?

Extend Interpretations

5. Comparing Texts Do you think Jaques would have anything to teach either of the **speakers** in "Hanging Fire" or "Young"? Would they have anything to teach him? Explain your answer.

6. What If? Imagine that you were one of the people listening to Jaques's speech, but you decided not to be silent. At what point might you break into his monologue? What would you say and how might Jaques respond?

7. Connect to Life Whether or not you share his cynicism, do you agree with Jaques that life is like a play? If you do, explain why it is useful to think of life that way. If you don't, what other comparison for life would you choose and why?

Literary Concept

[DRAMATIC MONOLOGUE] When two **characters** in a play speak to each other, their interaction is called a **dialogue.** But when only one speaks, the speech is called a **monologue.** A **dramatic monologue** is a form of **poetry** in which the **speaker** is like a character in a play addressing another character. Jaques's speech is taken from a play by Shakespeare, but readers have enjoyed it as a free-standing poem for many years, and indeed speeches such as this helped make the dramatic monologue a popular poetic form.

Unlike a **soliloquy,** in which a character on stage is simply thinking out loud, a dramatic monologue is always addressed to someone, even if that person is absent. Although in a poem the reader cannot see or hear the addressee, the speaker can, and sometimes the speaker's reactions to his or her audience become part of the monologue.

Cooperative Learning Activity With a small group of classmates, practice staging Jaques's speech. Choose someone to be Jaques, and let the others be his audience. While "Jaques" makes his speech, the other members of the group should react to his words silently. "Jaques" should show his response to these reactions through his tone, gestures, and movement.

A Language of Their Own

"Could I get your advice about my PC? How many gigabytes of storage should I have on my hard disk? Should I get more RAM or a faster modem?" If you don't know much about computers, these questions may sound like a foreign language. The computer industry has its own specialized vocabulary, as do other professions. Note the technical terms in the passage on the right, written by a surgeon.

By the time he retrieved part of the patient's bowel, Dr. Nolen is saying, the inside of the patient's belly had been contaminated; then he closed the hole in the patient's bowel by stitching it up. The words *cecum, peritoneal cavity,* and *resutured* belong to the language

> By the time we had retrieved the cecum, Mr. Polansky's peritoneal cavity had been contaminated. My self-confidence was shattered. And still George let me continue. True, he all but held my hand as we retied and resutured, but the instruments were in my hand.
>
> —William A. Nolen, *The First Appendectomy*

of medical people, a specialized vocabulary that helps them communicate precisely and avoid misunderstanding.

Strategies for Building Vocabulary

The specialized language of a profession is sometimes called **jargon.** Some technical words become so widely used that they are no longer considered jargon. Such is the case with the verbs *input* and *interface,* computer terms that are now part of everyday language. Most technical terms, however, never enter the mainstream vocabulary. The following strategies will help when you encounter such words.

❶ Use Context Clues Sometimes the surrounding words, or **context,** will provide clues to the meaning of an unfamiliar term. For example, in the sentence "There are five layers of tissue in the abdominal wall: skin, fat, fascia (a tough membranous tissue) . . . ," the term *fascia* is explained by the definition clue in parentheses.

Sometimes the surrounding sentences contain a **description clue** that clarifies the meaning of an unfamiliar term. In the following passage from *The First Appendectomy,* the parenthetical description clarifies the meaning of *purse-string stitch*:

> "'Now,' George directed, 'put in your purse string.' (. . . In an appendectomy the routine procedure is to tie the appendix at its base and cut it off a little beyond the tie. Then the remaining stump is inverted into the cecum and kept there by tying the purse-string stitch.)"

Sometimes you can infer the meaning of a term from the main idea of the passage. Consider this passage: "He plunged a gauze pack into the wound to stop the bleeding. 'Start clamping,' he told me. The nurse handed us hemostats and we applied them to the numerous vessels I had so hastily opened." In this case, the main idea of this passage provides **inference clues** from which you can conclude that *hemostats* refers to instruments clamped on blood vessels to stop bleeding.

❷ Use a Reference Tool Sometimes context clues may not provide you with the precise meaning you need. In such a case, look up the unfamiliar word in a regular dictionary or a dictionary of specialized vocabulary (such as a medical dictionary).

EXERCISE Use context clues to determine the meaning of each underlined term. Then check your definitions in a dictionary.

1. The nurse gave the patient a <u>sedative</u> to help him relax before the operation.
2. Tina used the keyboard to operate her computer because the <u>mouse</u> was broken.
3. A <u>folio</u>, or page number, is put on each page of a book.
4. It was Kowalsky's first <u>hat trick</u>. Never before had the hockey player scored three goals in a game.
5. After posting the $500 <u>bail</u>, he was released from the police station.

The First Appendectomy

William A. Nolen

The road to becoming a doctor is long and full of pressure. After graduating from college, one must complete four years of medical school and then one year of a supervised internship at a hospital. Those who specialize next embark on at least three years of training as a hospital resident. Interns and residents work long hours and gain as much experience as possible. As you read this selection, compare the pressures that you feel with the young doctor's pressure to perform.

The patient, or better, victim, of my first major surgical venture was a man I'll call Mr. Polansky. He was fat, he weighed one hundred and ninety pounds and was five feet eight inches tall. He spoke only broken English. He had had a sore abdomen with all the classical signs and symptoms of appendicitis[1] for twenty-four hours before he came to Bellevue.[2]

After two months of my internship, though I had yet to do anything that could be decently called an "operation," I had had what I thought was a fair amount of operating time. I'd watched the assistant residents work, I'd tied knots, cut sutures[3] and even, in order to remove a skin lesion,[4] made an occasional incision.[5] Frankly, I didn't think that surgery was going to be too damn difficult. I figured I was ready, and I was chomping at the bit to go, so when Mr. Polansky

arrived I greeted him like a long-lost friend. He was overwhelmed at the interest I showed in his case. He probably couldn't understand why any doctor should be so fascinated by a case of appendicitis; wasn't it a common disease? It was just as well that he didn't realize my interest in him was so personal. He might have been frightened, and with good reason.

---

1. **appendicitis** (ə-pĕn′dĭ-sī′tĭs): an illness in which the appendix—a small, wormlike extension of the intestine—becomes inflamed. If an inflamed appendix is not removed, it can burst and cause a fatal infection.
2. **Bellevue** (bĕl′vyōō′): Bellevue Hospital, in New York City.
3. **sutures** (sōō′chərz): stitches closing a wound.
4. **lesion** (lē′zhən): a wound, an injury, or an infected or diseased patch of skin.
5. **incision** (ĭn-sĭzh′ən): a surgical cut.

At any rate, I set some sort of record in preparing Mr. Polansky for surgery. He had arrived on the ward at four o'clock. By six I had examined him, checked his blood and urine, taken his chest x-ray and had him ready for the operating room.

George Walters, the senior resident on call that night, was to "assist" me during the operation. George was older than the rest of us. I was twenty-five at this time and he was thirty-two. He had taken his surgical training in Europe and was spending one year as a senior resident in an American hospital to establish eligibility for the American College of Surgeons. He had had more experience than the other residents and it took a lot to disturb his equanimity in the operating room. As it turned out, this made him the ideal assistant for me.

It was ten o'clock when we wheeled Mr. Polansky to the operating room. At Bellevue, at night, only two operating rooms were kept open—there were six or more going all day—so we had to wait our turn. In the time I had to myself before the operation I had reread the section on appendectomy in the *Atlas of Operative Technique* in our surgical library, and had spent half an hour tying knots on the bedpost in my room. I was, I felt, "ready."

I delivered Mr. Polansky to the operating room and started an intravenous[6] going in his arm. Then I left him to the care of the anesthetist.[7] I had ordered a sedative[8] prior to surgery, so Mr. Polansky was drowsy. The anesthetist, after checking his chart, soon had him sleeping.

Once he was asleep I scrubbed the enormous expanse of Mr. Polansky's abdomen for ten minutes. Then, while George placed the sterile drapes, I scrubbed my own hands for another five, mentally reviewing each step of the operation as I did so. Donning gown and gloves I took my place on the right side of the operating-room table. The nurse handed me the scalpel.[9] I was ready to begin.

Suddenly my entire attitude changed. A split second earlier I had been supremely confident; now, with the knife finally in my hand, I stared down at Mr. Polansky's abdomen and for the life of me could not decide where to make the incision. The "landmarks" had disappeared. There was too much belly.

George waited a few seconds, then looked up at me and said, "Go ahead."

"What?" I asked.

"Make the incision," said George.

"Where?" I asked.

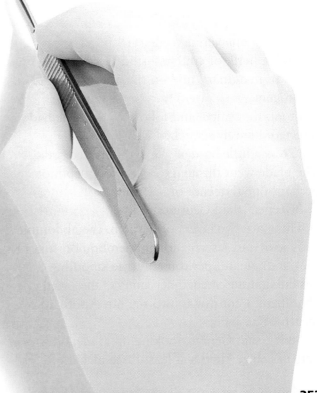

---

6. **intravenous** (ĭn´trə-vē´nəs): a drug or other substance administered into a vein through a needle and tubing.

7. **anesthetist** (ə-nĕs´thĭ-tĭst): a person trained to administer anesthetics, drugs that make a person insensitive to pain.

8. **sedative** (sĕd´ə-tĭv): a drug with a calming effect.

9. **scalpel** (skăl´pəl): a surgical knife.

"Where?"

"Yes," I answered, "where?"

"Why, here, of course," said George and drew an imaginary line on the abdomen with his fingers.

I took the scalpel and followed where he had directed. I barely scratched Mr. Polansky.

"Press a little harder," George directed. I did. The blade went through the skin to a depth of perhaps one sixteenth of an inch.

"Deeper," said George.

There are five layers of tissue in the abdominal wall: skin, fat, fascia (a tough membranous tissue), muscle and peritoneum (the smooth, glistening, transparent inner lining of the abdomen). I cut down into the fat. Another sixteenth of an inch.

"Bill," said George, looking up at me, "this patient is big. There's at least three inches of fat to get through before we even reach the fascia. At the rate you're going, we won't be into the abdomen for another four hours. For God's sake, will you cut?"

I made up my mind not to be hesitant. I pressed down hard on the knife, and suddenly we were not only through the fat but through the fascia as well.

"Not that hard," George shouted, grabbing my right wrist with his left hand while with his other hand he plunged a gauze pack into the wound to stop the bleeding. "Start clamping," he told me.

The nurse handed us hemostats[10] and we applied them to the numerous vessels I had so hastily opened. "All right," George said, "start tying."

---

10. **hemostats** (hē′mə-stătz′): clamplike surgical instruments used to pinch blood vessels and shut off bleeding.

I took the ligature material[11] from the nurse and began to tie off the vessels. Or rather, I tried to tie off the vessels, because suddenly my knot-tying proficiency had melted away. The casual dexterity I had displayed on the bedpost a short hour ago was nowhere in evidence. My fingers, greasy with fat, simply would not perform. My ties slipped off the vessels, the sutures snapped in my fingers, at one point I even managed to tie the end of my rubber glove into the wound. It was, to put it bluntly, a performance in fumbling that would have made Robert Benchley[12] blush.

> At one point I even managed to tie the end of my rubber glove into the wound.

Here I must give my first paean[13] of praise to George. His patience during the entire performance was nothing short of miraculous. The temptation to pick up the catgut and do the tying himself must have been strong. He could have tied off all the vessels in two minutes. It took me twenty.

Finally we were ready to proceed. "Now," George directed, "split the muscle. But gently, please."

I reverted to my earlier tack. Fiber by fiber I spread the muscle which was the last layer but one that kept us from the inside of the abdomen. Each time I separated the fibers and withdrew my clamp, the fibers rolled together again. After five minutes I was no nearer the appendix than I had been at the start.

George could stand it no longer. But he was apparently afraid to suggest I take a more aggressive approach, fearing I would stick the clamp into, or possibly through, the entire abdomen. Instead he suggested that he help me by spreading the muscle in one direction while I spread it in the other. I made my usual infinitesimal attack on the muscle. In one fell swoop George spread the rest.

"Very well done," he complimented me. "Now let's get in."

We each took a clamp and picked up the tissue-paper-thin peritoneum. After two or three hesitant attacks with the scalpel I finally opened it. We were in the abdomen.

"Now," said George, "put your fingers in, feel the cecum [the portion of the bowel to which the appendix is attached] and bring it into the wound."

I stuck my right hand into the abdomen. I felt around—but what was I feeling? I had no idea.

It had always looked so simple when the senior resident did it. Open the abdomen, reach inside, pull up the appendix. Nothing to it. But apparently there was.

Everything felt the same to me. The small intestine, the large intestine, the cecum—how did one tell them apart without seeing them? I grabbed something and pulled it into the wound. Small intestine. No good. Put it back. I grabbed again. This time it was the sigmoid colon.[14] Put it back. On my third try I had the small intestine again.

---

11. **ligature** (lĭg'ə-chŏŏr') **material:** the thread used to make surgical stitches; it may be made of catgut or other material.

12. **Robert Benchley:** an American critic and humorist who made short films in which he played the role of a bumbling person.

13. **paean** (pē'ən): a song of praise or thanks.

14. **sigmoid colon** (sĭg'moid' kō'lən): the part of the colon (which is a section of the large intestine) that is shaped like the letter *s*.

I stuck my right hand into the abdomen. I felt around—but what was I feeling? I had no idea.

"The appendix must be in an abnormal position," I said to George. "I can't seem to find it."

"Mind if I try?" he asked.

"Not at all," I answered. "I wish you would."

Two of his fingers disappeared into the wound. Five seconds later they emerged, cecum between them, with the appendix flopping from it.

"Stuck down a little," he said kindly. "That's probably why you didn't feel it. It's a hot one," he added. "Let's get at it."

The nurse handed me the hemostats, and one by one I applied them to the mesentery of the appendix—the veil of tissue in which the blood vessels run. With George holding the veil between his fingers I had no trouble; I took the ligatures and tied the vessels without a single error. My confidence was coming back.

"Now," George directed, "put in your purse string." (The cecum is a portion of the bowel which has the shape of half a hemisphere. The appendix projects from its surface like a finger. In an appendectomy the routine procedure is to tie the appendix at its base and cut it off a little beyond the tie. Then the remaining stump is inverted into the cecum and kept there by tying the purse-string stitch. This was the stitch I was now going to sew.)

It went horribly. The wall of the cecum is not very thick—perhaps one eighth of an inch. The suture must be placed deeply enough in the wall so that it won't cut through when tied, but not so deep as to pass all the way through the wall. My sutures were alternately too superficial or too deep, but eventually I got the job done.

"All right," said George, "let's get the appendix out of here. Tie off the base."

I did.

"Now cut off the appendix."

At least in this, the definitive act of the operation, I would be decisive. I took the knife and with one quick slash cut through the appendix—too close to the ligature.

"Oh oh, watch it," said George. "That tie is going to slip."

It did. The appendiceal stump lay there, open. I felt faint.

"Don't panic," said George. "We've still got the purse string. I'll push the stump in—you pull up the stitch and tie. That will take care of it."

I picked up the two ends of the suture and put in the first stitch. George shoved the open stump into the cecum. It disappeared as I snugged my tie. Beautiful.

"Two more knots," said George. "Just to be safe."

I tied the first knot and breathed a sigh of relief. The appendiceal stump remained out of sight. On the third knot—for the sake of security—I pulled a little tighter. The stitch broke; the open stump popped up; the cecum disappeared into the abdomen. I broke out in a cold sweat and my knees started to crumble.

Even George momentarily lost his composure. "Bill," he said, grasping desperately for the bowel, "what did you have to do that for?" The low point of the operation had been reached.

By the time we had retrieved the cecum, Mr. Polansky's peritoneal cavity had been contaminated.[15] My self-confidence was shattered. And still George let me continue.

---

15. **peritoneal** (pĕr′ĭ-tn-ē′əl) **cavity had been contaminated:** part of the inside of the abdomen had become infected.

True, he all but held my hand as we retied and resutured, but the instruments were in my hand.

The closure[16] was anticlimactic. Once I had the peritoneum sutured, things went reasonably smoothly. Two hours after we began, the operation was over. "Nice job," George said, doing his best to sound sincere.

"Thanks," I answered, lamely.

The scrub nurse laughed.

Mr. Polansky recovered, I am happy to report, though not without a long and complicated convalescence. His bowel refused to function normally for two weeks and he became enormously distended. He was referred to at our nightly conferences as "Dr. Nolen's pregnant man." Each time the reference was made, it elicited a shudder from me.

During his convalescence I spent every spare moment I could at Mr. Polansky's bedside. My feelings of guilt and responsibility were overwhelming. If he had died I think I would have given up surgery for good. ❖

---

16. **closure** (klō'zhər): the closing up of an opening; here, making sutures to close a surgical incision.

LITERARY LINK

Surgeons must be very careful

Emily Dickinson

Surgeons must be very careful
When they take the knife!
Underneath their fine incisions
Stirs the Culprit—*Life!*

William A. Nolen
1928–1986

Other Works
A Surgeon's World
Healing: A Doctor in Search of a Miracle
A Surgeon's Book of Hope

From Scalpel to Pen William A. Nolen gained national attention in the early 1970s after the publication of his book *The Making of a Surgeon*, from which "The First Appendectomy" is taken. In it he wrote frankly of his experiences as an intern and resident in the 1950s at Bellevue Hospital and of the tremendous pressures doctors work against. One reviewer felt the book was "remarkable for its wit and honesty." Although he acknowledged that some doctors felt he had betrayed the profession, Nolen countered that he didn't "see why there has to be so much mystery to medicine."

On the Other Side of the Knife Nolen became a general surgeon in Minnesota in 1960 and eventually wrote eight books, claiming that writing made him a better doctor by helping him understand the patient's perspective. By 1975 he gained that perspective firsthand, when his own struggle with heart disease led to his having heart bypass surgery.

Under the Knife In an article written for *Esquire* magazine around that time, he wrote, "I . . . have high blood pressure. My father died at 58 of "heart trouble. ". . . [T]he possibility of heart attack threatens my horizon." Following further bypass surgery in 1986, Dr. Nolen died in Minneapolis, ironically at age 58.

LaserLinks: Visual Vocabulary
Historical Connection

Rites of Passage Across Cultures

Brothers Are the Same
Short Story by BERYL MARKHAM

Through the Tunnel
Short Story by DORIS LESSING

What's the Connection?

Sink or Swim! You are about to read two stories that deal with rites of passage—tests or rituals that mark the transition from one stage of life to another. In each story, the rite reveals a young person's passage from childhood to adulthood.

Why are rites of passage important? One reason is that they serve as outward signs of important changes and accomplishments in our lives. Another reason is that they promote values and help maintain standards that are important to a society. Can you think of other reasons?

Points of Comparison

Comparing Rites of Passage Across Cultures In this unit, you have encountered a number of young people confronting first-time experiences and making the transition to adulthood. In the pages that follow, you will analyze and compare two stories in which young men from very different cultures attempt to prove their manhood by performing acts of great courage involving serious personal risk. One rite of passage is "official" ("Brothers Are the Same") and the other "unofficial" ("Through the Tunnel"). Your purpose will be to explore similarities and differences in the rites of passage that they undergo.

Critical Thinking: Analyze and Compare

Identifying Essential Elements The first step in making a comparison is to analyze the elements that make up the whole. To analyze a rite of passage, think about what questions you would ask to learn more about it.

- What is being tested? (courage? loyalty? strength?)

- What are the parts of the test? Who is involved?

- What are the reasons for undergoing the test?

- Who assigns the test and decides the rules?

- How successfully does the individual meet the challenge?

- How does the individual change as a result of the test?

For example, you could analyze the rite of passage in "Brothers Are the Same." Use a chart like the one shown to develop your ideas.

Essential Elements	"Brothers Are the Same"
What is being tested?	*Courage*

📖 **READER'S NOTEBOOK**   If you think of other analysis questions as you read the two selections that follow, add them to your list.

Brothers Are the Same

Short Story by BERYL MARKHAM

"He had not meant to think of her."

Connect to Your Life

Rites of Passage A rite of passage signals a change from one stage of life to another—usually from childhood to adulthood. Rites of passage may be large once-in-a-lifetime occurrences, such as getting your first job or driver's license, or they may be small events that have an enormous impact, like the first time you stood up to someone who frightened you. Think of a rite of passage that you have gone through successfully. With your classmates, discuss what happened and how it changed you.

Build Background

A Warrior People This story is set in the eastern part of Africa, on the vast grassland known as the Serengeti (sĕr'ən-gĕt'ē) Plain. Alongside rises snow-covered Mount Kilimanjaro (kĭl'ə-mən-jär'ō), Africa's tallest peak. The Serengeti is home to many of Africa's most magnificent animals—wildebeests, gazelles, zebras, and lions. The Serengeti is also home to the nomadic, cattle-raising Masai (mä-sī') people. For more than 200 years, the Masai sustained a warrior culture, which allowed them a great degree of independence from the European colonization that rocked Africa. At the time the story is set, one of their greatest enemies was the lion, who threatened their herds of cattle.

WORDS TO KNOW
Vocabulary Preview

improbable   regal
interminable vanquished
malice

Focus Your Reading

LITERARY ANALYSIS   **CHARACTERS IN CONFLICT**   Often, one of the major **conflicts** faced by a **character** in a work of fiction will be the actions or attitudes of another character. For example, in the story you are about to read, Temas is in conflict with Medoto:

> *It was Medoto who would spread the word—Medoto who surely would cry "Coward!" if he could.*

As you read this story, notice the kinds of conflict that Medoto and Temas create for each other and how they are changed by it.

ACTIVE READING   **RECOGNIZING CULTURAL INFLUENCES**
"Brothers Are the Same" takes place among the Masai, a people of eastern Africa. To appreciate a story set in a culture you are not familiar with, you need to interpret events from the perspective of that culture.

READER'S NOTEBOOK As you read this story, note passages in which the Masai culture strikes you as different from your own. Explain briefly how you think these differences might affect the characters or your understanding of them.

Brothers
Are the Same

Beryl Markham

They are tall men, cleanly built and straight as the shafts of the spears they carry, and no one knows their tribal history, but there is some of Egypt in their eyes and the look of ancient Greece about their bodies. They are the Masai.

They are the color of worn copper and, with their graceful women, they live on the Serengeti Plain, which makes a carpet at the feet of high Kilimanjaro. In all of Africa there are today no better husbandmen of cattle.

But once they were warriors and they have not forgotten that, nor have they let tradition die. They go armed, and to keep well-tempered the mettle[1] of their men, each youth among them must, when his hour comes, prove his right to manhood. He must meet in combat the only worthy enemy his people recognize—the destroyer of their cattle, the marauding[2] master of the plains—the lion.

Thus, just before the dawning of a day in what these Masai call the Month of the Little Rains, such a youth with such a test before him lay in a cleft of rock and watched the shadowed outlines of a deep ravine. For at least eight of his sixteen years, this youth, this young Temas,[3] had waited for his moment. He had dreamed of it and lived it in a dozen ways—all of them glorious.

In all of the dreams he had confronted the lion with casual courage, he had presented his spear on the charging enemy with steadiness born of brave contempt[4]—and always he had won the swift duel with half a smile on his lips. Always—in the dreams.

Now it was different. Now as he watched the place where the real lion lay, he had no smile.

He did not fear the beast. He was sure that in his bones and in his blood and in his heart he was not afraid. He was Masai, and legend said that no Masai had ever feared.

Yet in his mind Temas now trembled. Fear of battle was a nonexistent thing—but fear of failure could be real, and was. It was real and living—and kept alive by the nearness of an enemy more formidable than any lion—an enemy with the hated name Medoto.[5]

He thought of Medoto—of that Medoto who lay not far away in the deep grass watching the same ravine. Of that Medoto who, out of hate and jealousy over a mere girl, now hoped in his heart that Temas would flinch at the moment of his trial. That was it. That was the thing that kept the specter[6] of failure dancing in his mind, until already it looked like truth.

There were ten youths hidden about the ravine, and they would stage and witness the coming fight. They had tracked the lion to this, his lair, and when the moment came, they would drive him, angered, upon Temas and then would judge his courage and his skill. Good or bad, that judgment would, like a brand mark, cling to him all his life.

But it was Medoto who would watch the closest for a sign, a gesture, a breath of fear in Temas. It was Medoto who would spread the word—Medoto who surely would cry "Coward!" if he could.

Temas squirmed under the heavy, unwholesome thought, then lifted his head and pierced the dim light with his eyes. To the east, the escarpment[7] stood like a wall against the rising sun. But to the north and to the west and to the south there were no horizons; the grey sky and the grey plain were part and counterpart, and he was himself a shadow in his cleft of rock.

---

1. **mettle:** character; spirit.
2. **marauding:** raiding; taking by force.
3. **Temas** (tĕ′măs).
4. **contempt:** scorn.
5. **Medoto** (mĕ-dō′tō).
6. **specter:** haunting or disturbing image.
7. **escarpment** (ĭ-skärp′mənt): a steep slope or cliff.

He was a long shadow, a lean shadow. The *shuka*[8] that he wore was now bound about his waist, giving freedom to his legs and arms. His necklace and bracelets were of shining copper, drawn fine and finely spiraled, and around each of his slender ankles there was a copper chain.

His long hair, bound by beaded threads, was a chaste black column that lay between his shoulders, and his ears were pierced and hung with gleaming pendants. His nose was straight, with nostrils delicately flanged. The bones of his cheeks were high, the ridges of his jaw were hard, and his eyes were long and dark and a little brooding. He used them now to glance at his weapons, which lay beside him—a spear, a rawhide shield. These, and a short sword at his belt, were his armament.

He lowered his glance to the place he watched.

The ravine was overgrown with a thicket of thorns and the light had not burst through it yet. When it did the lion within it would wake, and the moment would come.

A feeling almost of hopelessness surged through him. It did not seem that he, Temas, could in this great test prove equal to his comrades. All had passed it; all had earned the warrior's title—and none had faltered. Even Medoto—especially Medoto—had proven brave and more than ready for his cloak of manhood. Songs were sung about Medoto. In the evenings in the *manyatta*[9] when the cattle drowsed and the old men drank their honey wine, the girls would gather, and the young men, too, and they

---

8. *shuka* (shōō′kə): *Swahili:* a loose, flowing Masai garment.
9. **manyatta** (măn-yăt′ə) *Swahili:* a Masai camp.

would chant to the heroes of their hearts.

But none chanted to Temas. Not yet. Perhaps they never would—not one of them. Not even . . .

He shook his head in anger. He had not meant to think of her—of Kileghen[10] of the soft, deep-smiling eyes and the reedbuck's grace. Even she, so rightly named after the star Venus, had only last night sung to Medoto, and he to her, laughing the while, as Temas, the yet unproven, had clung to the saving shadows, letting his fury burn. Could she not make up her mind between them? Must it always be first one and then the other?

He saw it all with the eye of his memory—all too clearly. He saw even the sneer of Medoto on the day the elder warrior, the chief of them all, had tendered Temas his spear with the wise words: "Now at last this weapon is your own, but it is only wood and steel and means nothing until it changes to honor, or to shame, within your grasp. Soon we shall know!"

And soon they should! But Medoto had laughed then. Medoto had said, "It seems a heavy spear, my comrade, for one so slight—a big weight for any but a man!" And Temas had made no answer. How could he with Kileghen leaning there against the *boma*[11] as though she heard nothing, yet denying her innocence with that quiet, ever-questing[12] smile? At whom had she smiled? At Medoto for his needless malice— or at Temas for his acceptance of it?

He did not know. He knew only that he had walked away carrying the unstained spear a little awkwardly. And that the joy of having it was quickly dead.

Now he spat on the earth where he rested. He raised a curse against Medoto—a harsh, a bitter curse. But in the midst of it he stiffened and grew tense. Suddenly he lay as still as sleep and watched only the ravine and listened, as to the tone of some familiar silence.

It was the silence of a waking lion, for morning light had breached the thicket, and within his lair the lion was roused.

Within his lair the lion sought wakefulness as suspicion came to him on the cool, unmoving air. Under the bars of sunlight that latticed his flanks and belly, his coat was short and shining. His mane was black and evenly grown. The muscles of his forelegs were not corded, but flat, and the muscles of his shoulders were laminated like sheaths of metal.

Now he smelled men. Now as the sunlight fell in streams upon his sorrel coat and warmed his flanks, his suspicion and then his anger came alive. He had no fear. Whatever lived he judged by strength—or lack of it—and men were puny. And yet the scent of them kindled fire in his brooding eyes and made him contemplate his massive paws.

He arose slowly, without sound—almost without motion—and peered outward through the wall of thorns. The earth was mute, expectant, and he did not break the spell. He only breathed.

The lion breathed and swung his tail in easy, rhythmic arcs and watched the slender figure of a human near him in a cleft of rock.

Temas had risen, too. On one knee now, he waited for the signal of the lifted spears.

Of his ten comrades he could see but two or three—a tuft of warrior's feathers; here and there a gleaming arm. Presently all would leap from the places where they hid, and the Masai battle cry would slash through the silence. And then the lion would act.

---

10. **Kileghen** (kə-lĕg′ən).

11. *boma* (bō′mə) *Swahili:* the wall around a Masai camp.

12. **ever-questing:** always seeking or searching for.

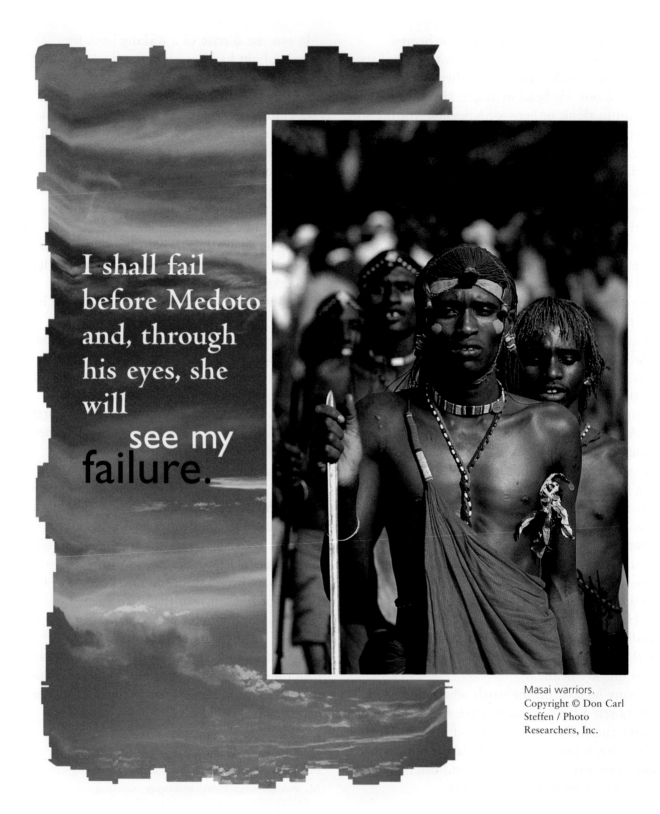

I shall fail before Medoto and, through his eyes, she will **see my failure.**

Masai warriors.
Copyright © Don Carl
Steffen / Photo
Researchers, Inc.

But the silence held. The <u>interminable</u> instant hung like a drop that would not fall, and Temas remembered many of the rules, the laws that governed combat with a lion—but not enough, for stubbornly, wastefully, foolishly, his mind nagged at fear of disgrace—fear of failure. Fear of Medoto's ringing laughter in the *manyatta*—of Kileghen's ever-questing smile.

"I shall fail," he thought. "I shall fail before Medoto and, through his eyes, she will see my failure. I must fail," he said, "because now I see that I am trembling."

And he was. His hand was loose upon the long steel spear—too loose, the arm that held the rawhide shield was hot and too unsteady. If he had ever learned to weep he would have wept—had there been time.

But the instant vanished—and with it, silence. From the deep grass, from the shade of anthills, from clustered rocks, warriors sprang like flames, and as they sprang they hurled upon the waiting lion their shrill arrogant[13] challenge, their scream of battle.

Suddenly the world was small and inescapable. It was an arena whose walls were tall young men that shone like worn gold in the sun, and in this shrunken world there were Temas and the lion.

He did not know when or how he had left the rock. It was as if the battle cry had lifted him from it and placed him where he stood—a dozen paces from the thicket. He did not know when the lion had come forward to the challenge, but the lion was there.

The lion waited. The ring of warriors waited. Temas did not move.

His long Egyptian eyes swept around the circle. All was perfect—too perfect. At every point a warrior stood blocking the lion from <u>improbable</u> retreat—and of these Medoto was one. Medoto stood near—a little behind Temas and to the right. His shield bore proud colors of the proven warrior. He was lean and proud, and upon his level stare he weighed each movement Temas made, though these were hesitant and few.

For the lion did not seek escape, nor want it. His shifting yellow eyes burned with even fire. They held neither fear nor fury—only the hard and <u>regal</u> wrath of the challenged tyrant. The strength of either of his forearms was alone greater than the entire strength of any of these men, his speed in the attack was blinding speed, shattering speed. And with such knowledge, with such sureness of himself, the lion stood in the tawny grass, and stared his scorn while the sun rose higher and warmed the scarcely breathing men.

The lion would charge. He would choose one of the many and charge that one. Yet the choice must not be his to make, for through the generations—centuries, perhaps—the code of the Masai decreed that the challenger must draw the lion upon him. By gesture and by voice it can be done. By movement, by courage.

Temas knew the time for this had come. He straightened where he stood and gripped his heavy spear. He held his shield before him, tight on his arm, and he advanced, step by slow step.

The gaze of the lion did not at once swing to him. But every eye was on him, and the strength of one pair—Medoto's—burned in his back like an unhealed scar.

A kind of anger began to run in Temas's blood. It seemed unjust to him that in this crucial moment, at this first great trial of his courage, his enemy and harshest judge must be a witness. Surely Medoto could see the points of sweat that now rose on his forehead and about his lips as he moved upon the embattled

---

13. **arrogant:** overwhelmingly proud.

WORDS
TO
KNOW

interminable (ĭn-tûr′mə-nə-bəl) *adj.* being or seeming to be without end; endless
improbable (ĭm-prŏb′ə-bəl) *adj.* unlikely to take place or be true
regal (rē′gəl) *adj.* of or pertaining to a monarch; royal

lion. Surely Medoto could see—or sense—the hesitance of his advance—almost hear, perhaps, the pounding of his heart!

He gripped the shaft of his spear until pain stung the muscles of his hand. The lion had crouched and Temas stood suddenly within the radius of his leap. The circle of warriors had drawn closer, tighter, and there was no sound save the sound of their uneven breathing.

The lion crouched against the reddish earth, head forward. The muscles of his massive quarters were taut, his body was a drawn bow. And, as a swordsman unsheaths his blade, so he unsheathed his fangs and chose his man.

It was not Temas.

As if in contempt for this confused and untried youth who paused within his reach, the lion's eyes passed him by and fastened hard upon the stronger figure of another, upon the figure of Casaro,[14] a warrior of many combats and countless victories.

All saw it. Temas saw it, and for an instant—for a shameless breath of time—he felt an overwhelming ease of heart, relief, deliverance, not from danger, but from trial. He swept his glance around the ring. None watched him now. All action, all thought was frozen by the duel of wills between Casaro and the beast.

Slowly the veteran Casaro sank upon one knee and raised his shield. Slowly the lion gathered the power of his body for the leap. And then it happened.

From behind Temas, flung by Medoto's hand, a stone no larger than a grain of maize shot through the air and struck the lion.

No more was needed. The bolt was loosed.

His friends were about to make the kill that must be his.

But not upon Casaro, for if from choice, the regal prowler of the wilderness had first preferred an opponent worthy of *his* worth, he now, under the sting of a hurled pebble, preferred to kill that human whose hand was guilty.

He charged at once, and as he charged, the young Temas was, in a breath, transformed from doubting boy to man. All fear was gone—all fear of fear—and as he took the charge, a light almost of ecstasy burned in his eyes, and the spirit of his people came to him.

Over the rim of his shield he saw fury take form. Light was blotted from his eyes as the dark shape descended upon him—for the lion's last leap carried him above the shield, the spear, the youth, so that, looking upward from his crouch, Temas, for a sliver of time, was intimate[15] with death.

He did not yield. He did not think or feel or consciously react. All was simple. All now happened as in the dreams, and his mind was an observer of his acts.

He saw his own spear rise in a swift arc, his own shield leap on his bended arm, his own eyes seek the vital spot—and miss it.

But he struck. He struck hard, not wildly or too soon, but exactly at the precise, the ripened moment, and saw his point drive full into the shoulder of the beast. It was not enough. In that moment his spear was torn from his grasp, his shield vanished, claws furrowed the flesh of his chest, ripping deep.

---

14. **Casaro** (kă-sä′rō).

15. **intimate:** closely acquainted; familiar.

The weight and the power of the charge overwhelmed him.

He was down. Dust and blood and grass and the pungent lion smell were mingled, blended, and in his ears an enraged, triumphant roar overlaid the shrill, high human cry of his comrades.

His friends were about to make the kill that must be his. Yet his hands were empty, he was caught, he was being dragged. He had scarcely felt the long crescentic teeth close on his thigh, it had been so swift. Time itself could not have moved so fast.

A lion can drag a fallen man, even a fighting man, into thicket or deep grass with incredible ease and with such speed as to outdistance even a hurled spear. But sometimes this urge to plunder first and destroy later is a saving thing. It saved Temas. That and his Masai sword, which now was suddenly in his hand.

Perhaps pain dulled his reason, but reason is a sluggard ally[16] to any on the edge of death. Temas made a cylinder of his slender body and, holding the sword flat against his leg, he whirled, and whirling, felt the fangs tear loose the flesh of his thigh, freeing it, freeing him. And, as he felt it, he lunged.

It was quick. It was impossible, it was mad, but it was Masai madness, and it was done. Dust clothed the tangled bodies of the lion and the youth so that those who clamored close to strike the saving blows saw nothing but this cloud and could not aim into its formless shape. Nor had they need to. Suddenly, as if *En-Gai* himself— God and protector of these men of wilderness— had stilled the scene with a lifted hand, all movement stopped, all sound was dead.

The dust was gone like a <u>vanquished</u> shadow, and the great, rust body of the lion lay quiet on the rust-red earth. Over it, upon it, his sword still tight in his hand, the youth lay breathing, bleeding. And, beyond that, he also smiled.

He could smile because the chant of victory burst now like drumbeats from his comrades' throats—the paeans[17] of praise fell on him where he lay, the sun struck bright through shattered clouds, the dream was true. In a dozen places he was hurt, but these would heal.

And so he smiled. He raised himself and, swaying slightly like any warrior weak in sinew but strong in spirit from his wounds, he stood with pride and took his accolade.[18]

And then his smile left him. It was outdone by the broader, harder smile of another—for Medoto was tall and straight before him, and with his eyes and with his lips Medoto seemed to say: "It is well—this cheering and this honor. But it will pass—and we two have a secret, have we not? We know who threw the stone that brought the lion upon you when you stood hoping in your heart that it would charge another. You stood in fear then, you stood in cowardice. We two know this, and no one else. But there is one who might, if she were told, look not to you but to the earth in shame when you pass by. Is this not so?"

Yes, it was so, and Temas, so lately happy, shrank within himself and swayed again. He saw the young Kileghen's eyes and did not wish to see them. But for Medoto's stone, the spear of Temas would yet be virgin, clean, unproved —a thing of futile vanity.

He straightened. His comrades—the true warriors, of which even now he was not one— had in honor to a fierce and vanquished enemy laid the dead lion on a shield and lifted him. In triumph and with songs of praise (mistaken praise!) for Temas, they were already beginning their march toward the waiting *manyatta*.

---

16. **sluggard ally:** a slow-acting helper.

17. **paeans** (pē′ənz): cheers; joyful exclamations.

18. **accolade** (ăk′ə-lād′): praise or other sign of respect.

It is true
that this, my
enemy, saw
the shame of
my first
fear. He
will tell it
to everyone—
and to her.

Masai maiden.
Copyright © Don Carl Steffen /
Photo Researchers, Inc.

Temas turned from his field of momentary triumph, but Medoto lingered at his side.

And now it will come, Temas thought. Now what he has said with his eyes, he will say with his mouth, and I am forced to listen. He looked into Medoto's face—a calm, unmoving face—and thought: It is true that this, my enemy, saw the shame of my first fear. He will tell it to everyone—and to her. So, since I am lost, it is just as well to strike a blow against him. I am not so hurt that I cannot fight at least once more.

His sword still hung at his side. He grasped it now and said, "We are alone and we are enemies. What you are about to charge me with is true—but, if I was a coward before the lion, I am not a coward before you, and I will not listen to sneering words!"

For a long moment, Medoto's eyes peered into the eyes of Temas. The two youths stood together on the now deserted plain and neither moved. Overhead the sun hung low and red and poured its burning light upon the drying grass, upon the thorn trees that stood in lonely clusters, upon the steepled shrines of dredging ants. There was no sound of birds, no rasping of cicada wings, no whispering of wind.

And into this dearth, into this poverty of sound, Medoto cast his laugh. His lips parted, and the low music of his throat was laughter without mirth, there was sadness in it, a note of incredulity,[19] but not more, not mockery, not challenge.

He stared into the proud unhappy face of Temas. He plunged the shaft of his spear into the earth and slipped the shield from his arm. At last he spoke.

He said, "My comrade, we who are Masai know the saying: 'A man asks not the motives of a friend, but demands reason from his enemy.' It is a just demand. If, until now, I have seemed your enemy, it was because I feared you would be braver than I, for when I fought my lion my knees trembled and my heart was white—until that charge was made. No one knew that, and I am called Medoto, the unflinching, but I flinched. I trembled."

He stepped closer to Temas. He smiled. "It is no good to lie," he said. "I wanted you to fail, but when I saw you hesitate I could not bear it because I remembered my own hour of fear. It was then I threw the stone—not to shame you, but to save you from shame—for I saw that your fear was not fear of death, but fear of failure—and this I understood. You are a greater warrior than I—than any—for who but the bravest would do what you have done?"

Medoto paused and watched a light of wonderment kindle in Temas's eye. The hand of Temas slipped from his sword, his muscles relaxed. Yet, for a moment, he did not speak, and as he looked at Medoto, it was clear to both that the identical thought, the identical vision, had come to each of them. It was the vision that must and always will come to young men everywhere, the vision of a girl.

Now this vision stood between them, and nothing else. But it stood like a barrier, the last barrier.

And Medoto destroyed it. Deliberately, casually, he reached under the folds of his flowing *shuka* and brought from it a slender belt of leather crusted with beads. It was the work and the possession of a girl, and both knew which girl. Kileghen's handiwork was rare enough, but recognized in many places.

"This," said Medoto, "this, I was told to bring, and I was told in these words: 'If in his battle the young Temas proves himself a warrior and a man, make this belt my gift to him so that I may see him wear it when he returns. But if he proves a coward, Medoto, the belt is for you to keep.'"

Medoto looked at the bright gift in his hands. "It is yours, Temas!" He held it out. "I

---

19. **incredulity** (ĭn'krĭ-dōō'lĭ-tē): disbelief.

meant to keep it. I planned ways to cheat you of it, but I do not think a man can cheat the truth. I have seen you fight better than I have ever fought, and now this gift belongs to you. It is her wish and between us you are at last her choice." He laid the belt on the palm of Temas's open hand and reached once more for his shield and spear. "We will return now," Medoto said, "for the people are waiting. She is waiting. I will help you walk."

But Temas did not move. Through the sharp sting of his wounds, above his joy in the promise that now lay in his hands, he felt another thing, a curious, swelling pride in this new friendship. He looked into the face of Medoto and smiled, timidly, then broadly. And then he laughed and drew his sword and cut the beaded belt in half.

"No," he said. "If she has chosen, then she must choose again, for we are brothers now and brothers are the same!"

He entwined one half of the severed belt in the arm band of Medoto, and the other half he hung, as plainly, on himself.

"We begin again," he said, "for we are equal to each other, and this is a truth that she must know. She must make her choice on other things but skill in battle, since only men may judge a warrior for his worth!"

It was not far to the *manyatta* and they walked it arm in arm. They were tall together, and strong and young, and somehow full of song. Temas walked brokenly for he was hurt, and yet he sang:

> *Oi-Konyek of the splendid shield*
> *Has heard the lowing of the kine . . .*

And when they entered the gates of the *manyatta*, there were many of every age to welcome Temas, for his lion had been brought and his story told. They cheered and cried his name and led him past the open doors to the peaceful earthen houses to the *singara*, which is the place reserved for warriors. Medoto did not leave him, nor he Medoto, and it was strange to some to see the enemies transformed and strong in friendship, when yesterday their only bond was hate.

It was strange to one who stood against the *boma* wall, a slender girl of fragile beauty and level, seeking eyes. She was as young as morning, as anticipant. But this anticipation quickly dimmed as she saw the token she had made, one half borne hopefully by Medoto, the other as hopefully carried by Temas!

Both sought her in the gathered crowd, both caught the glance and gave the question with their eyes. Both, in the smug, self-satisfied way of men, swaggered a little.

So the girl paused for an instant and frowned a woman's frown. But then, with musing, lidded eyes, she smiled a woman's smile—and stranger yet, the smile had more of triumph in it, and less of wonder, than it might have had. ❖

> They were tall together, and strong and young, and somehow full of song.

Connect to the Literature

1. **What Do You Think?** How did you react when Temas cut Kileghen's beaded belt in two and gave half to Medoto?

Comprehension Check ······
- Why is Medoto Temas's enemy?
- Why does the lion attack Temas?
- How does Temas escape from the jaws of the lion?
- Why does Temas give half of the belt Kileghen made to Medoto?

Think Critically

2. Why is Temas more afraid of failing than of being hurt or killed by the lion?

3. Why does Temas's victory over the lion enable him and Medoto to put their differences behind them?

THINK ABOUT
- Medoto's own test of manhood
- Medoto's explanation of why he threw the stone at the lion
- what Medoto means when he says, "I do not think a man can cheat the truth"

4. Why do you think Kileghen feels triumphant in the end?

5. What do you think the **title** of the story means? How are brothers the same?

6. **ACTIVE READING** **RECOGNIZING CULTURAL INFLUENCES**
What do you think is the most significant difference between Masai culture and your own? How does this difference affect your understanding of the story? Record your answer in your **READER'S NOTEBOOK.**

Extend Interpretations

7. **What If?** Suppose that Temas had died fighting with the lion. Do you think the Masai would believe he had passed his test of manhood? Would you agree? Give reasons for your answers.

8. **Connect to Life** Do you think rites of passage are easier or harder for young people living in North America than for young people of the Masai? Explain your answer.

9. **Points of Comparison** Revisit the chart you made to analyze a rite of passage on page 358. Create a similar chart for "Brothers Are the Same." Based on your observations, how would you describe the Masai rite of passage described in this story?

Literary Analysis

CHARACTERS IN CONFLICT The **protagonist** is the **main character** or hero in a **narrative** or **drama,** usually the one with whom the reader or audience tends to identify. The **antagonist** is usually the principle character in opposition to the protagonist. In this story, Temas is the protagonist and Medoto is the antagonist.

Cooperative Learning Activity With a group of classmates, go through the story and list ways Temas and Medoto represent **conflict** for each other and ways they help each other find **resolution** or a means of working out their conflict.

Temas Versus Medoto

Conflicts:

Resolutions:

Writing Options

A Story of Friendship Enemies at first, Temas and Medoto become close friends. Think of a time when someone with whom you were in conflict ended up becoming a good friend. Write a narrative describing the transformation.

Writing Handbook
See page 1153: Narrative Writing.

Activities & Explorations

Serengeti Ecosystem Find out what kinds of animals, plants, terrain, and weather conditions exist on the Serengeti Plain. Then construct a model that illustrates how the different parts of the ecosystem—including humans—survive and interact. ~ **SCIENCE**

Vocabulary in Action

EXERCISE: ASSESSMENT PRACTICE For each group of words below, write the letter of the word that is an antonym of the boldfaced Word to Know.

1. **malice:** (a) ease (b) kindness (c) liquid
2. **interminable:** (a) personal (b) unusual (c) limited
3. **improbable:** (a) correct (b) likely (c) enjoyable
4. **regal:** (a) common (b) slow (c) unpleasant
5. **vanquished:** (a) vanished (b) victorious (c) miserable

Building Vocabulary
For an in-depth lesson on such word relationships as antonyms, see page 849.

Beryl Markham
1902–1986

Other Works
The Splendid Outcast: Beryl Markham's African Stories

Writing from Experience Beryl Markham's description of the lion attack that Temas endures did not come solely from her imagination. As a child living in Africa, Markham herself was attacked by a friend's supposedly tame lion. Writing later about that frightening experience, she noted four unforgettable aspects: her own scream, the blow that knocked her to the ground, the feeling of the lion's teeth as they closed on her leg, and—more than anything—the terrifying sound of the lion's roar.

African Childhood Markham's survival of the lion attack is recounted in her autobiography, *West with the Night*, published in 1942. Although born in England, Markham moved with her father to British East Africa (now Kenya) when she was four. She grew up with native children and watched her father turn a wilderness area into a working farm.

A Life of Adventure In the early 1930s Markham worked as a pilot, flying mail, passengers, and supplies to remote African areas. In 1936 she was the first person to fly across the Atlantic Ocean from east to west. She took off from England and landed in Canada, a feat that rivaled the west-to-east Atlantic crossings of Charles Lindbergh and Amelia Earhart. In 1948 she returned to Africa and began raising and training racehorses.

Renewed Popularity Three years before her death in 1986, *West with the Night* was reprinted and soon discovered by a new generation of readers. The renewed interest in her extraordinary life gave rise to new biographies of Markham in the 1990s.

Author Activity

Experience and Imagination In "Brothers Are the Same," Markham's writing is a blend of what she experienced first hand and what she could only imagine. How important do you think it is for a writer to experience everything he or she writes about?

See art on page 384.

"They must all be drowning beneath him."

Through the Tunnel

Short Story by DORIS LESSING

Connect to Your Life

Worth the Risk? Undoubtedly there have been times in your life when you took a risk in order to prove something to yourself or others. For instance, perhaps you risked getting hurt or into trouble in order to accept a dare. Create a balance chart modeled on the one shown. Write down what you did in the triangle, what you risked in one of the boxes, and what you hoped to prove in the other. Then regardless of whether you won or lost, evaluate whether the risk was worth it.

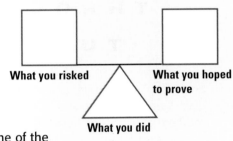

What you risked

What you hoped to prove

What you did

Build Background

A Difference of Geography
The story you are about to read takes place on a European or North African seacoast, perhaps along the Mediterranean Sea at one of the resorts where the British often go on vacation. The coastal setting consists of adjacent but contrasting areas. One is a crowded beach where the swimming is safe. The other is a wild and rocky bay where the swimming is unguarded and involves obvious risk.

WORDS TO KNOW
Vocabulary Preview
beseech   incredulous
contrition   supplication
defiant

Focus Your Reading

LITERARY ANALYSIS   **SYMBOL**   A **symbol** is a thing that stands for something beyond itself. Anything can become a symbol by taking on special meaning for a person. For example, the *Titanic* has become a symbol for many people. In the story you are about to read, Jerry, the main character, becomes fascinated with a "wild and rocky bay" next to the crowded beach where he is vacationing with his mother. As you read this story, look for clues that tell you what the bay and the events that take place there symbolize to Jerry.

ACTIVE READING   **RECOGNIZING CULTURAL INFLUENCES**   In "Brothers Are the Same," Temas has no doubts about what his rite of passage is or what his culture expects of him. In the story you are about to read, things are not so clear-cut. No one tells Jerry what is expected of him. However, he is strongly influenced by his own British culture, by the older boys from a different culture he encounters on vacation, and by his personal ideals.

READER'S NOTEBOOK   As you read this story, make a note of Jerry's important actions and decide which of the three influences noted above you think is affecting him most strongly. Create a chart like the one shown to record your observations.

Influences on Jerry's Actions			
What Jerry Does	British Culture	Older Boys from Different Culture	Jerry's Personal Ideals

THROUGH THE TUNNEL

DORIS LESSING

GOING TO THE SHORE ON THE FIRST MORNING OF THE VACATION, THE YOUNG ENGLISH BOY STOPPED AT A TURNING OF THE PATH AND LOOKED DOWN AT A WILD AND ROCKY BAY, AND THEN OVER TO THE CROWDED BEACH HE KNEW SO WELL FROM OTHER YEARS. HIS MOTHER WALKED ON IN FRONT

of him, carrying a bright striped bag in one hand. Her other arm, swinging loose, was very white in the sun. The boy watched that white, naked arm, and turned his eyes, which had a frown behind them, toward the bay and back again to his mother. When she felt he was not with her, she swung around. "Oh, there you are, Jerry!" she said. She looked impatient, then smiled. "Why, darling, would you rather not come with me? Would you rather—" She frowned, conscientiously worrying over what amusements he might secretly be longing for, which she had been too busy or too careless to imagine. He was very familiar with that anxious, apologetic smile. Contrition sent him running after her. And yet, as he ran, he looked back over his shoulder at the wild bay; and all morning, as he played on the safe beach, he was thinking of it.

Next morning, when it was time for the routine of swimming and sunbathing, his mother said, "Are you tired of the usual beach, Jerry? Would you like to go somewhere else?"

"Oh, no!" he said quickly, smiling at her out of that unfailing impulse of contrition—a sort of chivalry. Yet, walking down the path with her, he blurted out, "I'd like to go and have a look at those rocks down there."

She gave the idea her attention. It was a wild-looking place, and there was no one there; but she said, "Of course, Jerry. When you've had enough, come to the big beach. Or just go straight back to the villa, if you like." She walked away, that bare arm, now slightly reddened from yesterday's sun, swinging. And he almost ran after her again, feeling it unbearable that she should go by herself, but he did not.

WORDS TO KNOW

contrition (kən-trĭsh′ən) *n.* a feeling of regret for doing wrong

She was thinking, Of course he's old enough to be safe without me. Have I been keeping him too close? He mustn't feel he ought to be with me. I must be careful.

He was an only child, eleven years old. She was a widow. She was determined to be neither possessive nor lacking in devotion. She went worrying off to her beach.

As for Jerry, once he saw that his mother had gained her beach, he began the steep descent to the bay. From where he was, high up among red-brown rocks, it was a scoop of moving bluish green fringed with white. As he went lower, he saw that it spread among small promontories[1] and inlets of rough, sharp rock, and the crisping, lapping surface showed stains of purple and darker blue. Finally, as he ran sliding and scraping down the last few yards, he saw an edge of white surf and the shallow, luminous movement of water over white sand, and, beyond that, a solid, heavy blue.

He ran straight into the water and began swimming. He was a good swimmer. He went out fast over the gleaming sand, over a middle region where rocks lay like discolored monsters under the surface, and then he was in the real sea—a warm sea where irregular cold currents from the deep water shocked his limbs.

When he was so far out that he could look back not only on the little bay but past the promontory that was between it and the big beach, he floated on the buoyant surface and looked for his mother. There she was, a speck of yellow under an umbrella that looked like a slice of orange peel. He swam back to

---

1. **promontories** (prŏm′ən-tôr′ēz): high ridges of land or rock jutting out into a body of water.

Balston Beach, Cape Cod (1989), Charles Sovek. Oil on canvas, 16″ × 16″, private collection.

shore, relieved at being sure she was there, but all at once very lonely.

On the edge of a small cape that marked the side of the bay away from the promontory was a loose scatter of rocks. Above them, some boys were stripping off their clothes. They came running, naked, down to the rocks. The English boy swam toward them, but kept his distance at a stone's throw. They were of that coast; all of them were burned smooth dark brown and speaking a language he did not understand. To be with them, of them, was a craving that filled his whole body. He swam a little closer; they turned and watched him with narrowed, alert dark eyes. Then one smiled and waved. It was enough. In a minute, he had swum in and was on the rocks beside them, smiling with a desperate, nervous supplication. They shouted cheerful greetings at him; and then, as he preserved his nervous, uncomprehending smile, they understood that he was a foreigner strayed from his own beach, and they proceeded to forget him. But he was happy. He was with them.

They began diving again and again from a high point into a well of blue sea between rough, pointed rocks. After they had dived and come up, they swam around, hauled themselves up, and waited their turn to dive again. They were big boys—men, to Jerry. He dived, and they watched him; and when he swam around to take his place, they made way for him. He felt he was accepted and he dived again, carefully, proud of himself.

Soon the biggest of the boys poised himself, shot down into the water, and did not come up. The others stood about, watching. Jerry, after waiting for the sleek brown head to appear, let out a yell of warning; they looked at him idly and turned their eyes back toward the water. After a long time, the boy came up on the other side of a big dark rock, letting the air out of his lungs in a sputtering gasp and a shout of triumph. Immediately the rest of them dived in. One moment, the morning seemed full of chattering boys; the next, the air and the surface of the water were empty. But through the heavy blue, dark shapes could be seen moving and groping.

Jerry dived, shot past the school of underwater swimmers, saw a black wall of rock looming at him, touched it, and bobbed up at once to the surface, where the wall was a low barrier he could see across. There was no one visible; under him, in the water, the dim shapes of the swimmers had disappeared. Then one, and then another of the boys came up on the far side of the barrier of rock, and he understood that they had swum through some gap or hole in it. He plunged down again. He could see nothing through the stinging salt water but the blank rock. When he came up the boys were all on the diving rock, preparing to attempt the feat again. And now, in a panic of failure, he yelled up, in English, "Look at me! Look!" and he began splashing and kicking in the water like a foolish dog.

They looked down gravely, frowning. He knew the frown. At moments of failure, when he clowned to claim his mother's attention, it was with just this grave, embarrassed inspection that she rewarded him. Through his hot shame, feeling the pleading grin on his face like a scar that he could never remove, he looked up at the group of big brown boys on the rock and shouted, *"Bonjour! Merci! Au revoir! Monsieur, monsieur!"*[2] while he hooked his fingers round his ears and waggled them.

Water surged into his mouth; he choked, sank, came up. The rock, lately weighted with boys, seemed to rear up out of the water as their weight was removed. They were flying down past him, now, into the water; the air was full of falling bodies. Then the rock was empty in the hot sunlight. He counted one, two, three. . . .

At fifty, he was terrified. They must all be drowning beneath him, in the watery caves of the rock! At a hundred, he stared around him at the empty hillside, wondering if he should yell for help. He counted faster, faster, to hurry them up, to bring them to the surface quickly, to drown them quickly—anything rather than the terror of counting on and on into the blue emptiness of the morning. And then, at a hundred and sixty, the water beyond the rock was full of boys blowing like brown whales. They swam back to the shore without a look at him.

He climbed back to the diving rock and sat down, feeling the hot roughness of it under his thighs. The boys were gathering up their bits of clothing and running off along the shore to another promontory. They were leaving to get away from him. He cried openly, fists in his eyes. There was no one to see him, and he cried himself out.

It seemed to him that a long time had passed, and he swam out to where he could see his mother. Yes, she was still there, a yellow spot under an orange umbrella. He swam back to the big rock, climbed up, and dived into the blue pool among the fanged and angry boulders. Down he went, until he touched the wall of rock again. But the salt was so painful in his eyes that he could not see.

He came to the surface, swam to shore, and went back to the villa to wait for his mother.

---

2. *"Bonjour! Merci! Au revoir! Monsieur, monsieur!"* (bôn-zhōōr′ mĕr-sē′ ō-rə-vwär′ mə-syœ′) *French:* "Good day! Thank you! Goodbye! Sir, sir!"

Soon she walked slowly up the path, swinging her striped bag, the flushed, naked arm dangling beside her. "I want some swimming goggles," he panted, <u>defiant</u> and <u>beseeching</u>.

She gave him a patient, inquisitive look as she said casually, "Well, of course, darling."

But now, now, now! He must have them this minute, and no other time. He nagged and pestered until she went with him to a shop. As soon as she had bought the goggles, he grabbed them from her hand as if she were going to claim them for herself, and was off, running down the steep path to the bay.

Jerry swam out to the big barrier rock, adjusted the goggles, and dived. The impact of the water broke the rubber-enclosed vacuum, and the goggles came loose. He understood that he must swim down to the base of the rock from the surface of the water. He fixed the goggles tight and firm, filled his lungs, and floated, face down, on the water. Now, he could see. It was as if he had eyes of a different kind—fish eyes that showed everything clear and delicate and wavering in the bright water.

Under him, six or seven feet down, was a floor of perfectly clean, shining white sand, rippled firm and hard by the tides. Two grayish shapes steered there, like long, rounded pieces of wood or slate. They were fish. He saw them nose toward each other, poise motionless, make a dart forward, swerve off, and come around again. It was like a water dance. A few inches above them the water sparkled as if sequins were dropping through it. Fish again—myriads of minute fish, the length of his fingernail, were drifting through the water, and in a moment he could feel the innumerable tiny touches of them against his limbs. It was like swimming in flaked silver. The great rock the big boys had swum through rose sheer out of the white sand—black, tufted lightly with greenish weed. He could see no gap in it. He swam down to its base.

Again and again he rose, took a big chestful of air, and went down. Again and again he groped over the surface of the rock, feeling it, almost hugging it in the desperate need to find the entrance. And then, once, while he was clinging to the black wall, his knees came up and he shot his feet out forward and they met no obstacle. He had found the hole.

He gained the surface, clambered about the stones that littered the barrier rock until he found a big one, and, with this in his arms, let himself down over the side of the rock. He dropped, with the weight, straight to the sandy floor. Clinging tight to the anchor of stone, he lay on his side and looked in under the dark shelf at the place where his feet had gone. He could see the hole. It was an irregular, dark gap; but he could not see deep into it. He let go of his anchor, clung with his hands to the edges of the hole, and tried to push himself in.

He got his head in, found his shoulders jammed, moved them in sidewise, and was inside as far as his waist. He could see nothing ahead. Something soft and clammy touched his mouth; he saw a dark frond moving against the grayish rock, and panic filled him. He thought of octopuses, of clinging weed. He pushed himself out backward and caught a glimpse, as he retreated, of a harmless tentacle of seaweed drifting in the mouth of the tunnel.

HE COULD SEE THE HOLE. IT WAS AN IRREGULAR, DARK GAP; BUT HE COULD NOT SEE DEEP INTO IT.

WORDS TO KNOW

defiant (dǐ-fī′ənt) *adj.* boldly resistant of an opposing force or authority
beseech (bǐ-sēch′) *v.* to beg

But it was enough. He reached the sunlight, swam to shore, and lay on the diving rock. He looked down into the blue well of water. He knew he must find his way through that cave, or hole, or tunnel, and out the other side.

First, he thought, he must learn to control his breathing. He let himself down into the water with another big stone in his arms, so that he could lie effortlessly on the bottom of the sea. He counted. One, two, three. He counted steadily. He could hear the movement of blood in his chest. Fifty-one, fifty-two. . . . His chest was hurting. He let go of the rock and went up into the air. He saw that the sun was low. He rushed to the villa and found his mother at her supper. She said only "Did you enjoy yourself?" and he said "Yes."

All night the boy dreamed of the water-filled cave in the rock, and as soon as breakfast was over he went to the bay.

That night, his nose bled badly. For hours he had been underwater, learning to hold his breath, and now he felt weak and dizzy. His mother said, "I shouldn't overdo things, darling, if I were you."

That day and the next, Jerry exercised his lungs as if everything, the whole of his life, all that he would become, depended upon it. Again his nose bled at night, and his mother insisted on his coming with her the next day. It was a torment to him to waste a day of his careful self-training, but he stayed with her on that other beach, which now seemed a place for small children, a place where his mother might lie safe in the sun. It was not his beach.

Ice Blue (1981), Susan Shatter. Oil on canvas, 40″ × 90″, private collection, courtesy of Fischbach Gallery, New York.

He did not ask for permission, on the following day, to go to his beach. He went, before his mother could consider the complicated rights and wrongs of the matter. A day's rest, he discovered, had improved his count by ten. The big boys had made the passage while he counted a hundred and sixty. He had been counting fast, in his fright. Probably now, if he tried, he could get through that long tunnel, but he was not going to try yet. A curious, most unchildlike persistence,

a controlled impatience, made him wait. In the meantime, he lay underwater on the white sand, littered now by stones he had brought down from the upper air, and studied the entrance to the tunnel. He knew every jut and corner of it, as far as it was possible to see. It was as if he already felt its sharpness about his shoulders.

He sat by the clock in the villa, when his mother was not near, and checked his time. He was <u>incredulous</u> and then proud to find he

381

could hold his breath without strain for two minutes. The words "two minutes," authorized by the clock, brought close the adventure that was so necessary to him.

In another four days, his mother said casually one morning, they must go home. On the day before they left, he would do it. He would do it if it killed him, he said defiantly to himself. But two days before they were to leave—a day of triumph when he increased his count by fifteen—his nose bled so badly that he turned dizzy and had to lie limply over the big rock like a bit of seaweed, watching the thick red blood flow on to the rock and trickle slowly down to the sea. He was frightened. Supposing he turned dizzy in the tunnel? Supposing he died there, trapped? Supposing—his head went around, in the hot sun, and he almost gave up. He thought he would return to the house and lie down, and next summer, perhaps, when he had another year's growth in him—*then* he would go through the hole.

But even after he had made the decision, or thought he had, he found himself sitting up on the rock and looking down into the water; and he knew that now, this moment, when his nose had only just stopped bleeding, when his head was still sore and throbbing—this was the moment when he would try. If he did not do it now, he never would. He was trembling with fear that he would not go; and he was trembling with horror at that long, long tunnel under the rock, under the

sea. Even in the open sunlight, the barrier rock seemed very wide and very heavy; tons of rock pressed down on where he would go. If he died there, he would lie until one day—perhaps not before next year—those big boys would swim into it and find it blocked.

He put on his goggles, fitted them tight, tested the vacuum. His hands were shaking. Then he chose the biggest stone he could carry and slipped over the edge of the rock until half of him was in the cool, enclosing water and half in the hot sun. He looked up once at the empty sky, filled his lungs once, twice, and then sank fast to the bottom with the stone. He let it go and began to count. He took the edges of the hole in his hands and drew himself into it, wriggling his shoulders in sidewise as he remembered he must, kicking himself along with his feet.

Soon he was clear inside. He was in a small rock-bound hole filled with yellowish-gray water. The water was pushing him up against the roof. The roof was sharp and pained his back. He pulled himself along with his hands—fast, fast—and used his legs as levers. His head knocked against something; a sharp pain dizzied him. Fifty, fifty-one, fifty-two. . . . He was without light, and the water seemed to press upon him with the weight of rock. Seventy-one, seventy-two. . . . There was no strain on his lungs. He felt like an inflated balloon, his

IF HE DIED THERE, HE WOULD LIE UNTIL ONE DAY...THOSE BIG BOYS WOULD SWIM INTO IT AND FIND IT BLOCKED.

lungs were so light and easy, but his head was pulsing.

He was being continually pressed against the sharp roof, which felt slimy as well as sharp. Again he thought of octopuses, and wondered if the tunnel might be filled with weed that could tangle him. He gave himself a panicky, convulsive kick forward, ducked his head, and swam. His feet and hands moved freely, as if in open water. The hole must have widened out. He thought he must be swimming fast, and he was frightened of banging his head if the tunnel narrowed.

A hundred, a hundred and one. . . . The water paled. Victory filled him. His lungs were beginning to hurt. A few more strokes and he would be out. He was counting wildly; he said a hundred and fifteen, and then, a long time later, a hundred and fifteen again. The water was a clear jewel-green all around him. Then he saw, above his head, a crack running up through the rock. Sunlight was falling through it, showing the clean, dark rock of the tunnel, a single mussel shell, and darkness ahead.

He was at the end of what he could do. He looked up at the crack as if it were filled with air and not water, as if he could put his mouth to it to draw in air. A hundred and fifteen, he heard himself say inside his head—but he had said that long ago. He must go on into the blackness ahead, or he would drown. His head was swelling, his lungs cracking. A hundred and fifteen, a hundred and fifteen pounded through his head, and he feebly clutched at rocks in the dark, pulling himself forward, leaving the brief space of sunlit water behind.

HIS EYES MUST HAVE BURST, HE THOUGHT; THEY WERE FULL OF BLOOD. HE TORE OFF HIS GOGGLES AND A GOUT OF BLOOD WENT INTO THE SEA.

He felt he was dying. He was no longer quite conscious. He struggled on in the darkness between lapses into unconsciousness. An immense, swelling pain filled his head, and then the darkness cracked with an explosion of green light. His hands, groping forward, met nothing; and his feet, kicking back, propelled him out into the open sea.

He drifted to the surface, his face turned up to the air. He was gasping like a fish. He felt he would sink now and drown; he could not swim the few feet back to the rock. Then he was clutching it and pulling himself up onto it. He lay face down, gasping. He could see nothing but a red-veined, clotted dark. His eyes must have burst, he thought; they were full of blood. He tore off his goggles and a gout of blood went into the sea. His nose was bleeding, and the blood had filled the goggles.

He scooped up handfuls of water from the cool, salty sea, to splash on his face, and did not know whether it was blood or salt water he tasted. After a time, his heart quieted, his eyes cleared, and he sat up. He could see the local boys diving and playing half a mile away. He did not want them. He wanted nothing but to get back home and lie down.

In a short while, Jerry swam to shore and climbed slowly up the path to the villa. He flung himself on his bed and slept, waking at the sound of feet on the path outside. His mother was coming back. He rushed to the bathroom, thinking she must not see his face

Reflections (1970), Ken Danby. Original egg tempera, 38″ × 52″, by permission of the artist and Gallery Moos, Toronto, Canada.

with bloodstains, or tearstains, on it. He came out of the bathroom and met her as she walked into the villa, smiling, her eyes lighting up.

"Have a nice morning?" she asked, laying her hand on his warm brown shoulder a moment.

"Oh, yes, thank you," he said.

"You look a bit pale." And then, sharp and anxious, "How did you bang your head?"

"Oh, just banged it," he told her.

She looked at him closely. He was strained; his eyes were glazed-looking. She was worried.

And then she said to herself, Oh, don't fuss! Nothing can happen. He can swim like a fish.

They sat down to lunch together.

"Mummy," he said, "I can stay under water for two minutes—three minutes, at least." It came bursting out of him.

"Can you, darling?" she said. "Well, I shouldn't overdo it. I don't think you ought to swim any more today."

She was ready for a battle of wills, but he gave in at once. It was no longer of the least importance to go to the bay. ❖

Connect to the Literature

1. **What Do You Think?** How did you react to Jerry's swim through the tunnel?

> **Comprehension Check**
> • Where does Jerry go on the second day of his vacation?
> • What makes Jerry feel humiliated in front of the older boys?
> • How does Jerry prepare for his attempt to swim through the tunnel?

Think Critically

2. How does Jerry feel about himself after swimming through the tunnel?

3. How would you describe Jerry's relationship with his mother?

4. Why do you think it is so important to Jerry to take the risk he did?

THINK ABOUT
> • his age and family situation
> • his interactions with the older boys
> • how he reacted when the boys left
> • what he was trying to prove to himself

5. **ACTIVE READING   RECOGNIZING CULTURAL INFLUENCES**
   Look back at the chart you created in your **READER'S NOTEBOOK** showing different influences on Jerry's actions. Based on your observations, is Jerry motivated to swim through the tunnel more by his own culture, by his desire to be like the boys from another culture, or by something strictly personal?

Extend Interpretations

6. **Critic's Corner** One teenage reader of this story claimed that Jerry's success was "a hollow victory." State your reasons for agreeing or disagreeing with this observation.

7. **Connect to Life** As a single parent, Jerry's mother is unsure of how to achieve a balance between concern and control in raising an 11-year-old. From your perspective, discuss what you think is a proper balance.

8. **Points of Comparison** Revisit the chart you made to analyze a rite of passage (see page 358). With a partner, fill in the chart for "Through the Tunnel." Then discuss this question with your classmates: Do you think that because Jerry is the only one who knows about his swim through the tunnel, it is less a rite of passage than that of Temas?

Literary Analysis

SYMBOL A **symbol** is a person, a place, an activity, or an object that stands for something beyond itself. Some symbols are traditional and occur in many works of literature. For example, a dove is a common symbol for peace. Other symbols exist only in a particular work of literature; for example, the tunnel that Jerry swims through could be considered a symbol.

Cooperative Learning Activity What do you think the tunnel could symbolize? Consider the following:
• the danger it puts Jerry in
• its connection to the older boys
• how it looks and feels
• why Jerry keeps it a secret from his mother

Compare your thoughts about the symbolic meaning of the tunnel with those of your classmates. How many different interpretations do you have?

REVIEW   SETTING **Setting** is the time and place of the action of a story. Consider other places in the story besides the tunnel itself; for example, the sheltered beach, the rocky bay, or the rock where Jerry dives with the other boys. With classmates, discuss the significance that these parts of the setting have within the **plot** of the story.

Choices & CHALLENGES

Writing Options

Risk Comparison Look over the chart that you made for the Connect to Your Life. Write a comparison of a risk you've taken and the one that Jerry took. Was your risk as serious as Jerry's? Could it be considered a rite of passage? Place the comparison in your **Working Portfolio.**

Inquiry & Research

Sink and Swim Underwater diving is sometimes considered a dangerous sport. But rules of safety have been developed to make this activity as risk-free as possible. Research ways to reduce the risks involved with underwater diving. Do you think the emphasis on safety makes sports such as these less exciting and enjoyable than they would be if a higher level of risk were involved? Is risk necessary to a rite of passage?

Real World Link Read the list of safe diving practices on page 387–388 before forming your opinion.

Vocabulary in Action

EXERCISE: WORD MEANING For each phrase in the first column, find the phrase in the second column that is closest in meaning. Write the letter of that phrase on your paper.

1. **contrition** due to not locking the barn door
2. **supplication** for the lumberjack to leave
3. **defiant** in swimming among the giant waves
4. **beseech** someone to make breakfast
5. **incredulous** about the road you choose

a. rebels against the swells
b. beg for an egg
c. regret that the goose is loose
d. full of doubt about the route
e. plea to save a tree

Building Vocabulary

Several words to know in this lesson contain suffixes. For an in-depth study of word parts, see page 473.

Doris Lessing
1919–

Other Works
The Grass Is Singing
Going Home
African Stories
The Doris Lessing Reader
African Laughter

African Childhood One of the most respected writers of our day, Doris Lessing was born to British parents in Persia (present-day Iran). She moved with them to Southern Rhodesia (present-day Zimbabwe) in 1924, where her father became a farmer. Lessing lived in Africa until she was 30 and was strongly affected by life there. Years later she wrote, "The fact is, I don't live anywhere; I never have since I left that first home on the kopje

[hill]." Her experiences in colonial Africa made her sensitive to racial and economic exploitation, a subject she has touched upon often in her writing.

England and a Literary Career After the breakup of her second marriage in 1949, Lessing moved with her three-year-old son to England. A year later she published the first of her many books and soon became an acclaimed author. Between 1979 and 1984 she surprised the literary world twice—first, by publishing a series of five science fiction novels, and second, by publishing two novels under the name Jane Somers. Lessing confessed that she was the unknown Jane Somers only after the two books were virtually ignored by critics and buyers. She had wanted to prove the point that today books by new writers have almost no chance of success.

Safe Diving Practices

These guidelines for scuba diving appear in The Skin Diver's Bible. *Think about why both experienced and inexperienced divers need to take the guidelines seriously.*

RULES FOR SAFE DIVING:

❶

1. **NEVER DIVE ALONE.** Always dive with a buddy who is completely familiar with you and your diving practices.

2. **DON'T DIVE BEYOND YOUR LIMITS.** Maintain good mental and physical condition for diving. Only dive when feeling well. Have a regular medical examination for diving. Be sure to exercise regularly, keep well rested, and maintain a well-balanced diet.

3. **AVOID DEPTHS DEEPER THAN 100 FEET.** This is the recommended sport diving limit.

❷

4. **PLAN YOUR DIVE.** Know the area. Establish emergency procedures. Know the limitations of yourself, your buddy, and your equipment. Use the best possible judgment and common sense in planning and setting the limitations of each dive, allowing a margin of safety in order to be prepared for emergencies. Set reasonable limits for depth and time in the water. Always buddy dive—know each other's equipment, use hand signals, and stay in contact.

Reading for Information

In many activities—driving a car, assembling a model airplane, taking a test—people need to follow certain rules, guidelines, or directions. Often, a clear understanding of the guidelines or directions is essential for safety.

COMPLEX GUIDELINES AND DIRECTIONS

Guidelines are rules that apply to particular activities. **Directions** are step-by-step instructions for carrying out activities or processes. "Safe Diving Practices" is a set of guidelines intended to help scuba divers avoid some of the dangers of diving.

YOUR TURN To develop techniques for understanding guidelines, use the questions and activities below.

❶ **Reading Guidelines** Even guidelines that appear toward the end of a list may include important information; overlooking them could lead to problems. Therefore, it is important to read guidelines completely before beginning an activity. What might happen if someone made a dive after reading only the first two guidelines?

❷ **Understanding Purpose** It is sometimes easier to remember what to do if you clarify the purpose of each guideline. Why is it important to plan your dive in advance? Explain the purpose of each of the other guidelines.

5. **USE A DIVER'S FLAG AND FLOAT.** Make sure that your diving area is well-identified to avoid potential hazards from boats in the area.

6. **CANCEL DIVES WHEN WATER AND WEATHER CONDITIONS ARE QUESTIONABLE.** Too many unknowns can happen without aggravating the situation. It is far better to have everything in your favor, which will make emergencies less serious.

7. **BE FAMILIAR WITH THE AREA.** Know your diving location. Avoid dangerous places and poor conditions. Take whatever special precautions are required.

8. **ASCEND PROPERLY.** When surfacing, look up and around, move slowly and listen. Hold your hand up if any possible hazards exist.

9. **DON'T OVEREXTEND YOURSELF.** If you are cold, tired, injured, out of air, or not feeling well, get out of the water. Diving is no longer fun or safe. If any abnormality persists, get medical attention.

10. **AVOID TOUCHING UNKNOWN CREATURES UNDER WATER.** Be especially careful of anything very beautiful or very ugly.

Categorizing Guidelines Remembering related guidelines in groups is easier than trying to memorize a long list covering all the steps of an activity. Group the diving guidelines according to when the actions they apply to would be performed. Make a three-column chart similar to the one shown, entering each guideline in the appropriate column.

Before Diving	During a Dive	When Ending a Dive
• Never dive alone.	• Avoid depths deeper than 100 feet.	• Ascend properly.

Inquiry & Research

Activity Link: "Through the Tunnel," p. 386 Recall that in "Through the Tunnel" Jerry has no equipment for his dives. Now that you've read "Safe Diving Practices," identify two or three tips that might apply to Jerry's experience.

Comparing Literature: Assessment Practice

In writing assessment, you will often be asked to analyze and compare two literary works, such as "Brothers Are the Same" and "Through the Tunnel," that deal with a similar theme or situation. You are now going to practice writing an essay with this kind of focus.

PART 1 Reading the Prompt

Often you will be asked to write in response to a prompt like the one below. First, read through the entire prompt carefully. Then read it again, looking for key words that will help you identify the purpose of the essay and decide how to approach it.

Writing Prompt

"Brothers Are the Same" and "Through the Tunnel" deal with very different cultures, but both stories are about characters who undergo rites of passage on their journey from childhood to adulthood. In an essay, <u>analyze</u> each story's **①** portrayal of this experience and <u>compare</u> the **②** two rites of passage that the stories depict. Cite <u>evidence</u> from the selections to support **③** your opinion.

STRATEGIES IN ACTION

① I have to break the two stories into their component parts.

② I have to show similarities and differences between the selections.

③ I need to include **examples** from the stories.

PART 2 Planning a Comparative Essay

- List the essential elements of the topic being analyzed. These will be your points of comparison. (Refer to the chart you developed on page 358.)
- For each story, analyze the topic by describing each element. (Refer to the Points of Comparison questions on pages 371 and 385.)
- Using the evidence you have gathered under the points of comparison, compare and contrast the rites of passage presented in the two stories.
- Create a graphic like the one shown to organize your ideas.

Rites of Passage Across Cultures			
Elements of a Rite of Passage	"Brothers Are the Same"	"Through the Tunnel"	Similarities and Differences Between Rites of Passage

PART 3 Drafting Your Essay

Introduction Begin by stating your opinion about what the stories have in common and why it makes sense to compare them.

Organization Analyze the rite of passage in each story. Consider each story as a whole or take one element at a time and relate it to both stories.

Conclusion State what you think is in general the basic difference between the rites of passage in the two stories and why this difference is important. Relate your conclusion to cultural differences between the two stories.

Revision Save a little time to review your work at the end for errors in spelling, grammar, and punctuation.

Writing Handbook
See page 1155: Compare and Contrast.

Writing Workshop

Exploring similarities and differences . . .

From Reading to Writing The story "The Beginning of Something" and the poem "Hanging Fire" are told from the first-person point of view and deal with the pain and the challenges of growing up. Their tone, form, and themes differ greatly, however. Comparing these two works—or two other related subjects—can help you understand each of them better. One way to explore such similarities and differences is by writing a **comparison-and-contrast essay.**

For Your Portfolio

WRITING PROMPT Write a comparison-and-contrast essay in which you explore the similarities and differences between two subjects of your choice.

Purpose: To inform, explain, or clarify
Audience: Anyone interested in your subjects

Basics in a Box

Comparison-and-Contrast Essay at a Glance

Body

Introduction
- Identifies the **subjects** being compared
- Tells the **purpose** for the comparison

Subject A only · Both Subjects · Subject B only

Explains similarities and differences

Conclusion
Restates the **main idea** or draws a **conclusion**

RUBRIC Standards for Writing

A successful comparison-and-contrast essay should

- identify the subjects being compared
- establish a clear purpose for the comparison
- include both similarities and differences and support them with specific examples and details

- follow a clear organizational pattern
- use transitional words and phrases to make the relationships among ideas clear
- summarize the comparison in the conclusion

Analyzing a Student Model

Ben Hunter
Lake Forest Country Day

Walkabout and Lord of the Flies

The novels *Lord of the Flies* by William Golding and *Walkabout* by James Vance Marshall are both stories about survival. *Lord of the Flies* traces the struggles of a group of young English school boys who become stranded on a desolate island. In time, the boys' society breaks down and they become savages. In *Walkabout*, a young Australian Aborigine meets a brother and sister who have been stranded in the desert after their plane crashes. While completing his own walkabout, a rite of passage, he helps the boy and girl survive. While the plot, setting, and characters of these two books share some similarities, the themes of the two authors differ significantly.

On the surface, the setting in both books is very similar. Each takes place in a remote area, far away from civilization. *Lord of the Flies* takes place on an uninhabited jungle island. A character named Ralph describes the setting, saying, "We're on an island. We've been on the mountain top and see water all around. . . .We're on an uninhabited island." *Walkabout* also takes place in a desolate area, the Australian outback. The setting is described as "a scene of primeval desolation, mile after hundred mile of desert, sand, and scrub." Both sets of characters must seek out and kill their own food. This is where the major difference between the two settings occurs. While the boys in *Lord of the Flies* have plenty of food and water, the characters in *Walkabout* are stranded in "the vastness of the Australian desert." They have only a few pieces of candy to eat and little water. They have no idea how to find food in this environment. Their chances of survival are not high.

There are also similarities among the characters in these books. All of them are children. They are not yet completely marked by society; their basic instincts are still present. There are similarities between Peter in *Walkabout* and the young children of *Lord of the Flies* known as the "littluns." They are all very young, are vulnerable, and need help from their elders. All are still somewhat influenced by the constraints that were part of their old lives. For example, Piggy in *Lord of the Flies* constantly quotes the warnings and teachings of his "auntie." In *Walkabout,* Mary is shocked by the nakedness of the Aborigine boy and insists that Peter remain "civilized" and keep his clothes on.

There are differences between the characters, however. One important difference is their interaction with their surroundings. In *Lord of the Flies*, the boys' conduct deteriorates quickly when societal restraints are no longer in force. They behave savagely, capable even of murder. In

---

RUBRIC
IN ACTION

❶ Identifies and summarizes the two works being compared and contrasted

❷ Presents a thesis statement that clearly identifies the features being compared

❸ Discusses the first feature—setting

❹ This writer uses a feature-by-feature organization, discussing setting in both works.

Another Option:
• Use a subject-by-subject organization, discussing each feature of the first work and then each feature of the second work.

❺ Begins to examine the second feature—character

Walkabout, Peter and Mary build a relationship with the young Aborigine boy. Because of her upbringing, Mary becomes frightened of him when he performs a wild dance from his culture and when he stares at her as she bathes in a pool. Controlled by fear, she treats him rudely and deeply hurts his feelings. However, because of the Aborigine boy's influence, by the end of the novel Mary is going naked and not feeling self-conscious about it. She and her brother survive in the wilderness because of the Aborigine boy's teachings, and they seem to appreciate his selflessness in saving their lives. Whereas Golding's characters begin to act as though life is cheap, Marshall's characters gain a new respect for life.

> ❻ Uses a transition to signal a comparison

    The most interesting difference between the two books is the way in which the authors use the elements of setting, plot, and characters to express very different views about mankind. William Golding, the author of *Lord of the Flies,* believes that mankind is essentially evil. He demonstrates this belief by testing the boys' behavior in the absence of civilization and rules. He concludes that people will revert to the evil in their nature. In contrast, Marshall believes just the opposite. He shows that people are essentially good. In fact, by suggesting that contact with Peter and Mary is the cause of the Aborigine boy's death, he is suggesting that it is contact with society that leads to evil. In *Lord of the Flies* the boys who become savages, abandoning society and its laws, are mean and destructive. The ones who hold on to the laws are the good ones. In *Walkabout* Mary, the one who has been fully integrated into society, is less kind and generous than the Aborigine boy, who has lived outside civilization. Ironically, it is the "savage," the uncivilized one, who is good. A critic describes Golding's theme as "an attempt to trace the defects of society back to the defects of human nature." In contrast, Marshall's theme is that man is essentially good and it is society that corrupts.

> ❼ Begins to discuss the third feature— theme

> ❽ Supports general statements about theme with evidence—details and examples from each work

    There are many significant similarities between these two novels. The plots are similar. The settings are very much alike, both taking place in desolate places unaffected by the outside world. The characters are the same age with similar upbringings. However, the most important element of each book is its theme. Ultimately the characters, plots, and settings reflect their author's differing views of society. Golding says that mankind is essentially evil. Marshall says that mankind is essentially good. *Lord of the Flies* and *Walkabout* are both very good novels. They both present ideas about the nature of people and society that readers will continue to debate for a long time.

> ❾ This writer concludes by summarizing the major similarities and differences between the works.
>
> **Other Options:**
> • Draw a conclusion.
>
> • Describe something new learned about the works in the process of comparing them.

Writing Your Comparison-and-Contrast Essay

❶ Prewriting

To gather topic ideas for your essay, **brainstorm** about reasons you might compare two things. Do you have to make a choice or decision? Do you want to prove that one product or idea is better than another? Do you need to understand how two subjects are related? See the **Idea Bank** in the margin for more suggestions. After you select two subjects to compare, follow the steps below.

Planning Your Comparison-and-Contrast Essay

▶ **1. Explore the similarities and differences of your subjects.** What are their most important features? Which ones do they share? Which ones are unique? Making a Venn diagram can help you sort out your ideas. If you can't identify several major features, choose two other subjects to compare.

▶ **2. Decide which features to compare and contrast.** Think about the point you are trying to make in your essay. Focus on the similarities and differences that will help you make this point.

▶ **3. Choose an organizational pattern.** There are two basic ways to organize your comparison-and-contrast essay: subject-by-subject or feature-by-feature. You might want to try each organization before deciding which works better for your subject. You might also discuss all your subjects' similarities first and then their differences, or the other way around.

Subject-by-Subject	Feature-by-Feature
Subject A	Feature 1
Feature 1	Subject A
Feature 2	Subject B
Subject B	Feature 2
Feature 1	Subject A
Feature 2	Subject B

IDEABank

1. Your Working Portfolio
Build on this **Writing Option,** which you completed earlier in this unit:

Risk Comparison, p. 386

2. Theme Talk
With classmates, discuss a piece of literature you have read and enjoyed on a compelling theme: love, family, war, or growing up. Choose two works with the same theme to compare and contrast.

3. Get the Picture
Compare a popular television show from the 1970s or '80s with a TV show of today, or compare an original version of a movie with its modern remake.

Need more help with comparison and contrast?

See the **Writing Handbook**

Compare and Contrast, pp. 1155–1156

❷ Drafting

Begin by simply getting your thoughts on paper. You can revise them later. You might start by identifying the subjects you are comparing. As you write your draft, tell what features your essay will compare and contrast, and support the comparisons you make with specific details and examples.

Use **transitional words** to show similarities and differences between ideas. End with a **conclusion** that summarizes your main points.

Ask Your Peer Reader

• Why am I comparing and contrasting these two subjects?

• What is the strongest similarity between my subjects? What is the strongest difference?

• What parts of my essay did you find most and least interesting? Why?

Need revising help?

Review the **Rubric**, p. 390

Consider **peer reader** comments

Check **Revision Guidelines**, p. 1143

Tackling transitions?

See the **Writing Handbook**, p. 1148

❸ Revising

TARGET SKILL ▶ TRANSITIONS In a comparison-and-contrast essay, use transitions to show the logical connections between ideas. Transitions that show comparison include *in the same way*, *also*, *both*, and *similarly*. Transitions that show contrast include *yet*, *while*, *on the other hand*, *in contrast*, and *however*.

> *Both*
> ~~The~~ sets of characters must seek out and kill their own food.
>
> This is where the major difference between the two settings
> *While*
> occurs. ~~T~~he boys in *Lord of the Flies* have plenty of food and
>
> water, ~~and~~ the characters in *Walkabout* are stranded in "the
>
> vastness of the Australian desert."

❹ Editing and Proofreading

TARGET SKILL ▶ PARALLELISM Keeping similar ideas parallel will help you to present your ideas clearly and logically. Parts of a sentence that serve a similar function should be parallel in structure.

> Because of her upbringing Mary becomes frightened of
>
> him when he performs a wild dance from his culture and
> *when he stares*
> ~~is staring~~ at her as she baths *e* in a pool. Controlled by fear,
>
> *deeply hurts*
> she treats him rudely and his feelings ~~are deeply hurt~~.

Publishing IDEAS

• Make a consumer's guide for your classmates or for a general audience.

• Check the Internet for sites on the subjects you have compared. Contribute relevant parts of your essay to discussion groups or Web sites.

More Online: Publishing Options www.mcdougallittell.com

❺ Reflecting

FOR YOUR WORKING PORTFOLIO How did comparing two subjects help you understand them both better? Attach your answer to your finished work. Save your comparison-and-contrast essay in your **Working Portfolio.**

Read this paragraph from the first draft of a comparison-and-contrast essay. The underlined sections may include the following kinds of errors:

- **sentence fragments**
- **lack of parallel structure**
- **incorrect verb forms**
- **incorrect possessive forms**

For each underlined section, choose the revision that most improves the writing.

The character of Kino in <u>John Steinbecks' novel</u> *The Pearl* is transformed
(1)
by greed. At the beginning of the story, Kino is an honest man whose son <u>is</u>
(2)
<u>bited</u> by a scorpion. By the end of the story, he is a jealous killer. Kino begins to
change when he <u>discovers a large pearl and is trying to sell it</u>. The novel shows
(3)
how a <u>wonderful and valuable object</u> can corrupt a good man. The longer Kino
(4)
has the pearl, the greedier he becomes. In the final scene, Kino discovers that
his wife <u>has threw</u> the pearl into the ocean. <u>Now that the pearl is gone. Kino's</u>
(5)   (6)
<u>natural goodness may return</u>.

---

1. A. John Steinbeck's novel

   B. John Steinbecks novel

   C. John Steinbeck novel

   D. Correct as is

2. A. is bitted

   B. is bitten

   C. is bite

   D. Correct as is

3. A. discovers a large pearl and trying to sell it.

   B. discovers a large pearl and tried to sell it.

   C. discovers a large pearl and tries to sell it.

   D. Correct as is

4. A. wonderfully and valuably object

   B. wonderfully and valuable object

   C. wonderful and valuably object

   D. Correct as is

5. A. had thrown

   B. did throw

   C. has thrown

   D. Correct as is

6. A. Now that the pearl is gone, Kino's natural goodness may return.

   B. Kino's natural goodness may return. Now that the pearl is gone.

   C. Now that the pearl is gone; Kino's natural goodness may return.

   D. Correct as is

Need revising help?

See the **Grammar Handbook**

Correcting Fragments, p. 1197

Possessive Nouns, p. 1180

Verb Tense, p. 1184

UNIT TWO *Reflect* and Assess

Passages

How have your ideas about the journey of life changed as a result of reading the selections in this unit? Choose one or more of the options in each of the following sections to help you explore what you've learned.

East Twelfth Street (1946), Ben Shahn. Tempera, 22″ × 30″, collection of Mr. and Mrs. Albert Hackett, New York. Copyright © 1995 Estate of Ben Shahn/Licensed by VAGA, New York.

Reflecting on Theme

> OPTION 1

Judging Impact One person discovers that footwear fashion may matter in the grand scheme of things; another that some of the lessons of American history can be very personal and very painful. Many characters or real people in this unit make surprising discoveries as they experience new things or embark on new challenges. Make a list of these discoveries. Then look back at the "Journeys of Discovery" playing board you designed for the activity on page 232. Which of these discoveries are like ones that you anticipated? Which of them were of a kind you did not anticipate? Write a few paragraphs explaining the difference.

> OPTION 2

Looking Back Going through a rite of passage usually leaves a person permanently changed. For example, after fighting his lion, Temas becomes a Masai warrior and the friend of his old enemy Medoto. Review the selections in Part 2 of this unit; then list the characters who change during their rites of passage, and briefly describe how they change. Now look back at the personal time line you created for the activity on page 320. Write a letter to the characters or people who experience changes that you still have before you, explaining what you have learned by reading about their experiences.

> OPTION 3

Discussing Ideas With a small group of classmates, discuss what you now see as some of the most challenging aspects of growing up or learning to make your way in the world. Use examples from the selections to support your ideas, but be prepared to build on them with examples from your own experience or the experiences of people you know.

Self ASSESSMENT

Reconsider the quotation at the beginning of the unit: "Things do not change; we change." Write a paragraph explaining how reading the selections in this unit has given you a better understanding of the quotation's meaning.

Reviewing Literary Concepts

OPTION 1

Analyzing Nonfiction Several of the selections in this unit are nonfiction. There are many different varieties of nonfiction with different kinds of content, style, purpose, and audience. Make a chart like the one shown, listing selections that are nonfiction and identifying the type of nonfiction—for example, personal essay or memoir—it is. Briefly explain the author's purpose in each selection, the audience to whom it is addressed, and the style in which it is written.

Title	Type of Nonfiction	Purpose	Audience	Style
Life Without Go-Go Boots	Personal Essay	to explain ideas about importance of teen fashion	teenagers and their parents	humorous

OPTION 2

Identifying Types of Character Look back at the selections in this unit and find at least two examples of each of the following types of character: main, minor, round, flat, static, dynamic, protagonist, and antagonist. For each example, give a brief explanation of how the character fits the label.

Building Your Portfolio

- **Writing Options** Several of the Writing Options in this unit asked you to write narratives or essays about important events or times in your life. From your responses, choose the one that you feel best captures the event that helped you to grow or to learn something. Then write a cover note explaining your choice. Attach the note to the response and add both to your **Presentation Portfolio.**

- **Writing Workshops** In this unit you wrote a Reflective Essay about an important event in your life. You also wrote an Informative Expository Essay comparing and contrasting two things. Reread these two essays and decide which you think is a stronger piece of writing. Explain your choice in a note attached to the preferred one. Place the essay in your **Presentation Portfolio.**

- **Additional Activities** Think back to any of the assignments you completed under **Activities & Explorations** and **Inquiry & Research**. Keep a record in your portfolio of any assignments that you especially enjoyed or would like to do further work on in the future.

Self ASSESSMENT

READER'S NOTEBOOK

On a sheet of paper, copy the following literary terms introduced in this unit, but list them in order of difficulty. Write down the concepts you find easiest first, and put at the bottom of the list the concepts you're still not quite sure of.

nonfiction	rising action
personal essay	complication
autobiography	conflict
memoir	suspense
first-person point of view	climax
interview	falling action
biography	setting
autobiographi- cal fiction	character
rhyme scheme	speaker
free verse	dramatic monologue
meter	dialogue
repetition	protagonist
plot	antagonist
	symbol

Self ASSESSMENT

Now that you have some pieces in your **Presentation Portfolio,** notice which kinds of writing demonstrate your strongest work. What other kinds of writing would you like to try as the year goes on?

Setting GOALS

Look back through your portfolio, worksheets, and

READER'S NOTEBOOK.

What did you learn that might help you in your own life? Create a short list of ideas—such as friendship or conflict resolution—that you are interested in learning more about as you complete the next unit.

LITERATURE CONNECTIONS
The Friends

ROSA GUY

When Phyllisia Cathy arrives in New York City from her West Indian homeland, she is ridiculed and reviled by her classmates. Only Edith Jackson tries to befriend her. But Phyllisia wants nothing to do with the untidy, tough-talking girl. As Phyllisia copes with the death of her mother and the demands of her overbearing father, however, she learns the meaning—and the responsibilities—of real friendship.

These thematically related readings are provided along with *The Friends*:

The Refusal to Be Wrecked
BY LILLIAN MORRISON

Adjö Means Goodbye
BY CARRIE A. YOUNG

Drifting Away
BY DIANE COLE

Girls Can We Educate We Dads?
BY JAMES BERRY

The Tropics in New York
BY CLAUDE MCKAY

from **A Grief Observed**
BY C. S. LEWIS

The Long Way Around
BY JEAN MCCORD

And Even *More* . . .

Fallen Angels

WALTER DEAN MEYERS

In brutally realistic terms, Myers presents the experiences—terrifying, numbly routine, and heart-breaking—of a small group of young men who come of age as soldiers during the Vietnam War. The novel's protagonist finds himself in the midst of a war more confusing and traumatic than the life he fled.

Books
O Pioneers!
WILLA CATHER
After her father dies, Alexandra inherits the family farm—over the protests of her brothers. She struggles to overcome tragedy and hardship to keep her family together and forge a living on the hard Nebraska prairie.

Blue Highways: A Journey into America
WILLIAM LEAST HEAT-MOON
The author sets out to discover small-town America by exploring its back roads and talking to the people he meets along the way.

My Ántonia

WILLA CATHER

In this ode to lost childhood, narrator Jim Burden recounts tales of his Nebraska upbringing in the late 1800s. His memories are peopled with the immigrants who settled the Nebraska prairie and tried to carve out a better life for themselves. Above all, Jim tells the story of Bohemian Ántonia Shimerda, whose perseverance and ultimate triumph are at the heart of the novel. In Ántonia, Willa Cather has created one of the memorable women of American literature.

These thematically related readings are provided along with *My Ántonia*:

Prairie Town
BY WILLIAM STAFFORD

If There Be Sorrow
BY MARI EVANS

On the Divide
BY WILLA CATHER

from **The Quilters**
BY NORMA BRADLEY BUFERD

Night on the Prairies
BY WALT WHITMAN

The Chrysanthemums
BY JOHN STEINBECK

That Was Then, This Is Now
S. E. HINTON
This novel provides insight into the changing relationship between two friends who were once inseparable.

A Tree Grows in Brooklyn
BETTY SMITH
A young girl comes of age in early 20th-century Brooklyn.

Living Up the Street: Narrative Recollections
GARY SOTO
In this collection of short prose pieces, the author describes growing up in a Fresno barrio in the 1950s and 1960s.

Other Media

A Christmas Memory
Truman Capote's story about growing up in the rural South is adapted for television.
(VIDEOCASSETTE)

The Chrysanthemums
A brief encounter with a handyman forces a farmer's wife to examine her life and her limitations.
(VIDEOCASSETTE)

The Time, Life and Works of Whitman
Using beautiful visuals and excerpts from Walt Whitman's poetry, this program helps reveal the meaning and relevance of the poet's work.
(CD-ROM)

To Sir, With Love
Sidney Poitier delivers one of his finest performances as a teacher who opens new worlds to students in an inner-city London high school.
(VIDEOCASSETTE)

Reading & Writing for Assessment

Throughout high school, you will be tested on your ability to read and understand many different kinds of reading selections. These tests will assess your basic comprehension of ideas and knowledge of vocabulary. They will also check your ability to analyze and evaluate both the message of the text and the techniques the writer uses in getting that message across.

The following pages will give you test-taking strategies. Practice applying these strategies by working through each of the models provided.

PART 1 How to Read the Test Selection

In many tests, you will read a passage and then answer multiple-choice questions about it. Applying the basic test-taking strategies that follow, taking notes, and highlighting or underscoring passages as you read can help you focus on the information you will need to know.

STRATEGIES FOR READING A TEST SELECTION

▸ **Before you begin reading, skim the questions that follow the passage.** These can help focus your reading.

▸ **Use your active reading strategies such as analyzing, predicting, and questioning.** Make notes in the margin to help you focus your reading. You may do this only if the test directions allow you to mark on the test itself.

▸ **Think about the title.** What does it suggest about the overall message or theme of the selection?

▸ **Look for main ideas.** These are often stated at the beginnings or ends of paragraphs. Sometimes they are implied, not stated. After reading each paragraph, ask, "What was this passage about?"

▸ **Note the literary elements and techniques used by the writer.** For example, be aware of tone (writer's attitude toward the subject), point of view, figurative language, or other elements that catch your attention. Then ask yourself what effect the writer achieves with each choice.

▸ **Unlock word meanings.** Use context clues and word parts to help you unlock the meaning of unfamiliar words.

▸ **Think about the message or theme.** What larger lesson can you draw from the passage? Can you infer anything or make generalizations about other similar situations, human beings, or life in general?

Reading Selection

❶ Her Biggest Test of All
By Lou Carlozo

1   Backstage at Truman College's O'Rourke Performing Arts Center, Gaynell Brewer was recounting her teenage daughter's comeback from bone cancer. Sitting opposite her mother, 14-year-old Shenita Peterson—playwright, high school student, avid reader, admitted gossip, and cancer survivor—listened to her mom describe the tests, the doctors' visits, how her right knee swelled to four times its size.

2   And she giggled.
     Few people would find anything remotely humorous about cancer, let alone an adolescent with cancer. But to Shenita, the image of a knee

3   ballooning to the **❷ size of a cantaloupe** is pretty funny. So are some of the things doctors said as they tried to prepare her for losing her hair to chemotherapy. ("I know how you feel," for starters.)

4   Such incidents provide the fodder for "This Is a Test: One Girl's Fight Against Cancer," a one-act play that will bow Wednesday night at Truman College as part of Pegasus Players' 12th Annual Young Playwrights Festival. And as far as Shenita is concerned, even the story behind her play is worth a wisecrack.

5   "I wasn't inspired to write this, my drama teacher was inspired," said Shenita, now a freshman at Lane Technical High School. "He started talking about writing a book, but I didn't want to write a book. I was too lazy."

6   Though she did get help from teacher Eugene Baldwin and seven other 8th-grade drama students at Washington Irving School, Shenita is not nearly as lazy as she would have people believe. To the astonishment of friends, family, and doctors, she has completely recovered from osteogenic sarcoma, a cancer that mostly strikes young people from 10 to 25. After her surgery two years ago, **❸ she was off crutches and walking in a month—and baffling specialists by climbing steps and running in the months that followed.** . . .

7   Given the heavy nature of cancer as a topic, a healthy dose of humor proves a welcome tonic [in Shenita's play]. "It's not just one hour of really dreary, depressing stuff," said Greg Kolack, the play's director. "It's an incredible story, but I don't know if it would be as enthralling without all the humor."

8   Playing Shenita was [a challenge] for 25-year-old actress Nambi E. Kelley. "It was frustrating because I can never really know what it is she went through," Kelley said. "I can use my imagination; I've watched some videos of children in a cancer research center. And when I was 16, I found a lump in my breast. . . . I was terrified. But I wasn't 13 and going through all that."

❶ Think about the title.

ONE STUDENT'S THOUGHTS
"I wonder what 'her biggest test' was. Also, who is 'she'?"

❷ Note literary elements like use of figurative language.

"The writer compares Shenita's knee to a cantaloupe. Sounds awful, but it shows Shenita's sense of humor."

YOUR TURN
Determine the writer's purpose.

❸ Look for main ideas.

"Walking so soon after that kind of surgery must be pretty unusual. How long does it usually take people to get back on their feet?"

YOUR TURN
Find one or two other key ideas in this selection.

9   ❹ The youngest of three sisters (the other two are 25 and 26), Shenita "was the darling of the family, even as a very young child," said Brewer [Shenita's mother], who lives in North Lawndale and is an assistant principal at Phillips Academy High School. An honor roll student with a flair for writing (but a dislike of grammar), Shenita began her bout with cancer at age 12, in the midst of a typical preteen growth spurt.

10   "She started complaining about her right knee aching in April of '95," Brewer recalled. "We thought it was probably growing pains. But she kept complaining about it, saying she couldn't bend it." . . .

11   A succession of doctor trips followed. Shenita visited a pediatrician, an oncologist, and a bone specialist, and underwent an ❺ MRI scan and biopsy. . . .

12   "When I first found out [about the cancer], I was scared," Shenita said. ❻ "Then I was just mad: Why do I have to go through all of this? Why do I have to go through all that? Blah, blah, blah."

13   Then came eight exhausting rounds of chemotherapy, which drained Shenita of her strength, but not her spirit. In a matter-of-fact way, she decided early on to ignore most of what her doctors told her when it came to possibly losing her leg, or remaining on crutches for a year or longer.

14   Surgery came in October, and it was fraught with sadness and fear. In the days leading up to the surgery, Brewer's uncle died of prostate cancer— and Shenita was still unsure whether the doctors could save her leg.

15   Even after the operation succeeded, Brewer said, "The oncologist told her, 'Your life is going to change. You're going to walk on crutches for a long, long time. You're not going to be able to run. You're not going to be able to dance.' But Shenita decided that she was going to try to do as many of those things as possible."

16   Shenita, who still walks with a limp, holds out hope that she can get fitted for an artificial knee in her early 20s. And the experience had a definite impact on her ambition. "I want to be an oncologist," she said. ❼ "My oncologist was—I don't even know the word—stiff. She just tells you what's going to happen and that's it. 'See you tomorrow. Bye.'"

17   Otherwise, Shenita continues to act like any teenager. Despite her limp, many of her classmates at Lane have no knowledge of her ordeal. And recurrence, it seems, is not in her vocabulary.

❹ **Read actively by asking questions.**

"I wonder how a family is affected when one person becomes seriously ill."

❺ **Use context clues to understand vocabulary.**

"It seems like MRI scans and biopsies must be ways of diagnosing cancer."

❻ **Look for examples of tone.**

"The writer chooses interesting quotes. They really show what Shenita is like."

YOUR TURN

How else does the writer show Shenita's character?

❼ **Skim the questions that follow the passage.**

"There was a question about the oncologist's influence on Shenita. Shenita didn't seem to like her oncologist, so why would she want to become one?"

How To Answer Multiple-Choice Questions

Use the strategies in the box and notes in the side column to help you answer the questions below and on the following pages.

Based on the selection you have just read, choose the best answer for each of the following questions.

1. Why does he include quotations from Shenita and her mother in his article?

   A. because interviews are supposed to include quotations

   B. to make Shenita and her mother more real for his readers

   C. because he liked the way they used language

   D. to prove that he really talked with them

2. In paragraph 12, what does Shenita mean by saying "Blah, blah, blah"?

   A. that she forgot what she said at the time

   B. that she kept saying the same thing over and over because she was angry and afraid

   C. that she thought what she said was stupid

   D. that she used bad language that the newspaper couldn't print

3. What is the writer's tone toward Shenita?

   A. He feels sorry for her.

   B. He is jealous of her.

   C. He looks down on her because she doesn't take her situation seriously enough.

   D. He respects and admires her.

4. In what way did her oncologist influence Shenita's career choice?

   A. She let Shenita watch her operation.

   B. She didn't give Shenita the emotional support cancer patients needed, and Shenita wanted to give it to them.

   C. She gave Shenita books to read and tested her on them.

   D. She offered Shenita a job after she finished high school.

5. How does the title of the article relate to its theme?

   A. It doesn't relate to the theme. The writer is simply reflecting the title of Shenita's play.

   B. The test is whether or not the play is successful.

   C. The cancer tested Shenita's courage and strength of character.

   D. The biggest test is how well Shenita can write a play.

> **Ask questions** that help you eliminate some of the choices.
> **Pay attention to choices** such as "all of the above" or "none of the above." To eliminate them, all you need to find is one answer that doesn't fit.
> **Skim your notes.** Details you noticed as you read may provide answers.

STRATEGIES IN ACTION

Skim your notes.

ONE STUDENT'S THOUGHTS

"He said that the chemotherapy 'drained Shenita of her strength, but not her spirit.' That doesn't seem like he feels sorry for her. *So I can eliminate choice A.*"

YOUR TURN

What other choices can you eliminate?

Ask questions. What makes sense in the real world?

"She might have been nervous about writing a play and wondering whether it would be produced, but why would she include those feelings in her title? *So I can eliminate choices B and D.*"

YOUR TURN

Which other choice doesn't make sense?

How to Respond in Writing

You may also be asked to write answers to questions about a reading passage. **Short-answer questions** usually ask you to answer in a sentence or two. **Essay questions** require a fully developed piece of writing.

Short-Answer Question

STRATEGIES FOR RESPONDING TO SHORT-ANSWER QUESTIONS

▸ **Identify the key words** in the writing prompt that tell you the ideas to discuss. Make sure you know what is meant by each.
▸ **State your response directly** and keep to the point.
▸ **Support your ideas** by using evidence from the selection.
▸ **Use correct grammar.**

Sample Question

Answer the following question in one or two sentences.

What advantages does Lou Carlozo's third-person point of view offer readers of his article? In what ways do you think Shenita could have told her own story more effectively from the first-person point of view?

Essay Question

STRATEGIES FOR ANSWERING ESSAY QUESTIONS

▸ **Look for direction words** in the writing prompt, such as *essay, analyze, describe,* or *compare and contrast,* that tell you how to respond directly to the prompt.
▸ **List the points** you want to make before beginning to write.
▸ **Write an interesting introduction** that presents your main point.
▸ **Develop your ideas** by using evidence from the selection that supports the statements you make. Present the ideas in a logical order.
▸ **Write a conclusion** that summarizes your points.
▸ **Check your work** for correct grammar.

Sample Prompt

According to Shenita Peterson's mother, Shenita "was the darling of the family, even as a very young child." Write an essay in which you analyze how this love and protection may have affected Shenita's ability to deal with her cancer.

STRATEGIES IN ACTION

Identify the key words.

ONE STUDENT'S THOUGHTS

"Key words seem to be *point of view* and *advantages.* I'm supposed to compare the advantages of first- and third-person points of view."

YOUR TURN

What are first-person and third-person points of view?

Look for direction words.

ONE STUDENT'S THOUGHTS

"The important words are *essay* and *analyze.* This means that I'll have to create a fully developed piece of writing that explains the connections between things."

YOUR TURN

What are the main points you will need to cover?

How to Revise, Edit, and Proofread a Test Response

Here is a student's first draft in response to the writing prompt at the bottom of page 404. Read it and answer the multiple-choice questions that follow.

1	Being loved is really important. Not even love can prevent some-
2	one from getting cancer. Even if Shenita had been an orphan, she
3	probably would have gotten cancer anyway.
4	The love of her family may have given her the confidence to be-
5	lieve she could overcome the odds; and fight to regain her health.
6	Knowing that her family loved her no matter what, she was even
7	able to laugh at herself. And as we all know, "Laughter is the best
8	medicine."

> **STRATEGIES** FOR REVISING, EDITING, AND PROOFREADING
>
> ▶ **Read the passage carefully.**
> ▶ **Note the parts that are confusing** or don't make sense. What kinds of errors would that signal?
> ▶ **Look for errors** in grammar, usage, spelling, and capitalization. Common errors include:
> - run-on sentences
> - sentence fragments
> - lack of subject-verb agreement
> - unclear pronoun antecedents
> - lack of transition words

1. What is the BEST way to combine the sentences in lines 1 and 2 ("Being loved . . . getting cancer.")?

   A. Being loved is really important, because not even love can prevent someone from getting cancer.

   B. Not even love can prevent someone from getting cancer, and being loved is really important.

   C. Being loved is really important, but even love can't prevent someone from getting cancer.

   D. Make no change.

2. The best way to make the connection between paragraphs clearer would be to add which of the following sentences to the beginning of line 4 ("The love of her family . . . ")?

   A. Her family's love probably helped her deal with the disease, though.

   B. Her family gave her love, but her mother's uncle died of cancer, too.

   C. She might have been mad at her family because some of them had cancer and may have given it to her, but she loved them anyway.

   D. Make no change.

3. What is the BEST change, if any, to the sentence in lines 4 and 5 ("The love of her family . . . fight to regain her health.")?

   A. Add a colon after *confidence*.

   B. Remove the semicolon after *odds*.

   C. Replace the semicolon after *odds* with a period.

   D. Make no change.

EXPERIENCE

You gain strength,

courage, and

confidence by

every experience

in which you

really stop

to look fear

in the face.

ELEANOR ROOSEVELT

People Flying, Peter Sickles. SuperStock.

S omeone who has "the courage of his or her convictions" not only has strong beliefs but also is willing to stand behind them. The selections in this part of Unit Three portray a number of fictional characters and real people who fit this description. As you read, ask yourself how you would behave in the situations portrayed.

ACTIVITY

With a partner, think of some issues a person your age might want to speak out about but could find hard to address. Discuss the advantages of speaking out about each issue, as well as the disadvantages or obstacles to speaking out. Then decide which of these issues you feel particularly strongly about. Prepare notes for a short speech to deliver to the class.

LEARNING the Language of *Literature*

$\mathcal{D}$rama is any story told in dialogue form and performed by actors for an audience. Since ancient times, people have been entertained and instructed by plays and other types of drama. Today, you experience drama every time you watch a play, a movie, a video, or a story on TV. Yet even though dramas are meant to be performed, they also make good reading. You can create a theater in your mind by visualizing the action and the characters. All dramas share the same elements of **stage direction, plot, character,** and **dialogue.** Use the following passages from *The Devil and Daniel Webster* by Stephen Vincent Benét to learn more about the elements of drama.

Stage Directions

A play usually includes **stage directions,** which are often printed in italic type and separated from the dialogue by parentheses. Stage directions describe

- background on the characters' lives, the historical period, or action that took place before the play begins
- the scenery or setting and the props—the furniture and other objects used on stage
- costumes, lighting, music, and sound effects
- how the actors should look, speak, and behave

YOUR TURN Read the stage directions that begin *The Devil and Daniel Webster.* What scenery and props would be needed to create the setting?

STAGE DIRECTIONS

The scene is the main room of a New Hampshire farmhouse in 1841, a big comfortable room that hasn't yet developed the stuffiness of a front parlor. . . . There is a fireplace, right. Windows, in center, show a glimpse of summer landscape. Most of the furniture has been cleared away for the dance which follows the wedding of Jabez and Mary Stone, but there is a settee or bench by the fireplace, a table, left, with some wedding presents upon it, at least three chairs by the table, and a cider barrel on which the Fiddler sits, in front of the table.

Plot

In drama, as in fiction, the **plot** is a series of events that make up the story. A conflict begins, grows in intensity, reaches a peak, and is finally resolved. The standard elements of plot are **exposition, rising action, climax, falling action,** and **resolution.** (For more on plot, see page 23.) In drama, the action is often divided into scenes, with each scene having a different time or place. In long plays, scenes are grouped into acts.

YOUR TURN In this excerpt Mary and Jabez reveal their deepest feelings. What conflict does this scene suggest?

PLOT

Mary. How proud I am of you. Ever since I was a little girl. Ever since you carried my books. . . .

Jabez (*uncomfortably*). A man can't always be proud of everything, Mary. There's some things a man does, or might do—when he has to make his way.

Mary (*laughing*). I know—terrible things—like being the best farmer in the county and the best State Senator—

Jabez (*quietly*). And a few things, besides. But you remember one thing, Mary, whatever happens. It was all for you. . . . (*He takes both her hands.*) Mary, I've got something to tell you. I should have told you before, but I couldn't seem to bear it.

Characters

In a play, the **main** and **minor** characters are listed in the cast of characters at the beginning of the script, or the written form of the drama. The central character of the play—the one the audience usually identifies with—is called the **protagonist.** The **antagonist** is a character who struggles against the protagonist. Usually the main conflict of the drama involves these two characters. Some characters, acting as **foils,** provide a sharp contrast to the qualities of the main characters. For instance, if the main character is serious, the foil character is light-hearted and funny.

YOUR TURN Read this passage from the play. How does Mary serve as a foil for Daniel Webster? What qualities do the two characters show?

Dialogue

Dialogue, or conversation between characters, is everything in drama. Through dialogue you know each character's thoughts and feelings and learn about every twist and turn of the plot. Benét also uses **dialect,** or regional speech, to emphasize his characters' New England roots (*'lect* instead of *elect*). Playwrights often include stage directions telling actors how to play their parts and describing the action as characters talk.

YOUR TURN

How does Benét use dialogue and stage directions to reveal character and to guide the actors in this scene from *The Devil and Daniel Webster?*

James Craig and Walter Huston in a version of
The Devil and Daniel Webster

CHARACTERS

Mary. Oh, Mr. Webster, can you save [Jabez]? . . .

Webster. I shall do my best, madam. That's all you can ever say till you see what the jury looks like.

Mary. But even you, Mr. Webster—oh, I know you're Secretary of State—I know you're a great man—. . . But it's different—fighting the devil!

Webster (*towering*). I've fought John C. Calhoun, madam. . . . And, by the great shade of Andrew Jackson, I'd fight ten thousand devils to save a New Hampshire man!

Jabez. You hear, Mary?

DIALOGUE

The Crowd. Jabez Stone—Jabez Stone. Where did you get your money, Jabez Stone?

(Scratch [the devil] *grins and taps his collecting box.* Jabez *cannot speak.*)

Jabez. I—I—(*He stops.*)

The Crowd. Jabez Stone—Jabez Stone. What was the price you paid for it, Jabez Stone?

Jabez (*looking around wildly*). Help me, neighbors! Help me!

(*This cracks the built-up tension and sends the Crowd over the edge into fanaticism.*)

A Woman's Voice (*high and hysterical*). He's sold his soul to the devil! (*She points to Jabez.*)

Other Voices. To the devil!

The power of drama comes from its compelling characters, realistic dialogue, detailed setting, and engaging plots. To enjoy drama as literature, you must construct a "theater of the mind" to visualize the play as it unfolds. The reading strategies explained here can help you get the most from each play you read.

Reading Drama

Strategies for Using Your [] READER'S NOTEBOOK

As you read, take notes and
• write down any questions about setting, character, plot, or dialogue
• record any scenes, dialogue, or ideas you find particularly intriguing
• **connect** your personal experiences to what you read about the people, places, and situations in the play

1 Strategies for Visualizing Setting

• Create a sketch like the one below to help you **visualize** the setting described in the stage directions. What props and scenery are included?
• Note how different settings reflect the characters, mood, and plot of the story.

Wings (offstage)	Upstage Right	Upstage Center	Upstage Left	Wings (offstage)
	Right	Center	Left	
	Downstage Right	Downstage Center	Downstage Left	

AUDIENCE

2 Strategies for Examining Plot

• **Question** whether the title, as well as the exposition, offers clues to the main conflict or suggests a conflict to come.
• To **clarify** the main conflict, create a conflict-resolution chart like the one at the right.
• **Evaluate** whether the ending provides a satisfactory resolution to the central conflict.

Conflict → Devil comes to collect on contract

Resolution ← Webster defeats Devil

3 Strategies for Exploring Character

• Read the stage directions to help you **visualize** how the characters might look and act.
• Create a list of main and minor characters. Write down the qualities of each of the main characters.
• Watch for clues to the characters' motives and actions.
• **Evaluate** how the characters change during the story.

4 Strategies for Understanding Dialogue

• Examine the stage directions for clues regarding how the characters might sound when they speak.
• If the vocabulary or dialect is hard for you to understand, ask others to help you with the meaning.
• Read a few lines of dialogue aloud, either by yourself or with others, emphasizing different words to help you understand how actors might perform the play.

Need more help?

Remember that active readers use the essential reading strategies explained on page 7: **visualize, predict, clarify, question, connect, evaluate, monitor.**

The Devil and Daniel Webster

Drama by STEPHEN VINCENT BENÉT

"I never deserted a neighbor in trouble yet."

Connect to Your Life

Counsel for the Defense Have you ever heard any lawyer jokes? Our society enjoys making fun of the legal profession. However, when someone is on trial for his or her life, that person stops making jokes and hires a lawyer right away. Think about the lawyers you have seen interviewed on the news or portrayed in movies and TV shows. Which of them won cases even though the evidence seemed stacked against their clients? Using a cluster diagram like the one shown, list the qualities of a winning lawyer.

well prepared — winning lawyer

Build Background

A Silver-Tongued Lawyer In *The Devil and Daniel Webster,* a New England man asks a famous American statesman for help. Although the play is fictional, Daniel Webster was not. Webster was one of the greatest lawyers and best public speakers of the early and middle 1800s. He argued many important cases before the Supreme Court. As a congressman and a senator, Webster strongly defended the Constitution and the Union. His famous words "Liberty *and* Union, now and forever, one and inseparable!" inspired Northern soldiers during the Civil War.

WORDS TO KNOW
Vocabulary Preview

bias	homage
contemptuously	insinuatingly
discordant	intimidation
fanaticism	oppressor
feigned	placidly

Focus Your Reading

LITERARY ANALYSIS **HISTORICAL DRAMA** A **historical drama** is a play that is set in the past. In all dramas, the **plot** and **characters** are developed through **dialogue** and through action, which is described in the **stage directions.** In this example from the play you are about to read, the dialogue and stage directions work together to reveal that Jabez Stone is nervous about a secret he has kept from his wife:

> Jabez. *I wasn't thinking about Mr. Webster. (He takes both her hands.) Mary, I've got something to tell you. I should have told you before, but I couldn't seem to bear it.*

As you read this play, use both stage directions and lines of dialogue to help you learn about Jabez Stone and Daniel Webster.

ACTIVE READING **VISUALIZING WITH STAGE DIRECTIONS** **Visualizing** is an attempt to imagine what something looks like based on written or spoken information. To visualize while you are reading a play, look for the following in the **stage directions:**

- details about the sets, furniture, props, and lighting
- descriptions of the **characters'** appearance and actions

READER'S NOTEBOOK As you read the stage directions in this play, pause to visualize the scenes that are being described. Draw or sketch the scenes. Then jot down a few words that describe how you might feel if you were in such a scene.

The Devil and Daniel Webster

STEPHEN VINCENT BENÉT

CAST

Jabez Stone   Mary Stone

Daniel Webster
Mr. Scratch
Men and Women of Cross Corners, New Hampshire
Justice Hathorne's Clerk
Justice Hathorne
The Fiddler
King Philip
Walter Butler
Simon Girty
Teach

Scene—Jabez Stone's farmhouse.
Time—1841.

The scene is the main room of a New Hampshire farmhouse in 1841, a big comfortable room that hasn't yet developed the stuffiness of a front parlor. A door, right, leads to the kitchen—a door, left, to the outside. There is a fireplace, right. Windows, in center, show a glimpse of summer landscape. Most of the furniture has been cleared away for the dance which follows the wedding of Jabez and Mary Stone, but there is a settee or bench by the fireplace, a table, left, with some wedding presents upon it, at least three chairs by the table, and a cider barrel on which the Fiddler sits, in front of the table. Near the table, against the sidewall, there is a cupboard where there are glasses and a jug. There is a clock.

A country wedding has been in progress—the wedding of Jabez and Mary Stone. He is a husky young farmer, around twenty-eight or thirty. The bride is in her early twenties. He is dressed in stiff, store clothes but not ridiculously—they are of good quality and he looks important. The bride is in a simple white or cream wedding dress and may carry a small, stiff bouquet of country flowers.

Now the wedding is over and the guests are dancing. The Fiddler is perched on the cider barrel. He plays and calls square-dance figures. The guests include the recognizable types of a small New England town, doctor, lawyer, storekeeper, old maid, schoolteacher, farmer, etc. There is an air of prosperity and hearty country mirth about the whole affair.

At rise, Jabez and Mary are up left center, receiving the congratulations of a few last guests who talk to them and pass on to the dance. The others are dancing. There is a buzz of conversation that follows the tune of the dance music.

First Woman. Right nice wedding.

First Man. Handsome couple.

Second Woman (*passing through crowd with dish of oyster stew*). Oysters for supper!

Second Man (*passing cake*). And layer cake—layer cake—

An Old Man (*hobbling toward cider barrel*). Makes me feel young again! Oh, by jingo!

An Old Woman (*pursuing him*). Henry, Henry, you've been drinking cider!

Fiddler. Set to your partners! Do-si-do![1]

Women. Mary and Jabez.

Men. Jabez and Mary.

A Woman. Where's the State Senator?

A Man. Where's the lucky bride?

(*With cries of "Mary—Jabez—strike it up, fiddler—make room for the bride and groom," the* Crowd *drags Mary and* Jabez, *pleased but embarrassed, into the center of the room and Mary and* Jabez *do a little solo dance, while the* Crowd *claps, applauds and makes various remarks.*)

ACTIVE READING

VISUALIZE Close your eyes and picture the wedding. What do you see?

A Man. Handsome steppers!

A Woman. She's pretty as a picture.

A Second Man. Cut your pigeon-wing, Jabez!

The Old Man. Young again, young again, that's the way I feel! (*He tries to cut a pigeon-wing himself.*)

The Old Woman. Henry, Henry, careful of your rheumatiz!

A Third Woman. Makes me feel all teary—seeing them so happy.

---

1. **Do-si-do** (dō′sē-dō′): a signal to perform the square-dance movement of the same name. Other square-dancing terms follow, such as "cut your pigeon-wing," "scratch for corn," and "left and right—grand chain."

(*The solo dance ends, the music stops for a moment.*)

The Old Man (*gossiping to a neighbor*). Wonder where he got it all—Stones was always poor.

His Neighbor. Ain't poor now—makes you wonder just a mite.

A Third Man. Don't begrudge it to him—but I wonder where he got it.

The Old Man (*starting to whisper*). Let me tell you something—

The Old Woman (*quickly*). Henry, Henry, don't you start to gossip. (*She drags him away.*)

Fiddler (*cutting in*). Set to your partners! Scratch for corn!

(*The dance resumes, but as it does so, the* Crowd *chants back and forth.*)

Women. Gossip's got a sharp tooth.

Men. Gossip's got a mean tooth.

Women. She's a lucky woman. They're a lucky pair.

Men. That's true as gospel. But I wonder where he got it.

Women. Money, land and riches.

Men. Just came out of nowhere.

Women and Men (*together*). Wonder where he got it all.—But that's his business.

Fiddler. Left and right—grand chain!

(*The dance rises to a pitch of ecstasy with the final figure—the fiddle squeaks and stops. The dancers mop their brows.*)

First Man. Whew! Ain't danced like that since I was knee-high to a grasshopper!

Second Man. Play us "The Portland Fancy," fiddler!

Third Man. No, wait a minute, neighbor. Let's hear from the happy pair! Hey, Jabez!

Fourth Man. Let's hear from the State Senator!

(*They crowd around* Jabez *and push him up on the settee.*)

Old Man. Might as well. It's the last time he'll have the last word!

Old Woman. Now, Henry Banks, you ought to be ashamed of yourself!

Old Man. Told you so, Jabez!

The Crowd. Speech!

Jabez (*embarrassed*). Neighbors—friends—I'm not much of a speaker—spite of your 'lecting me to State Senate—

The Crowd. That's the ticket, Jabez. Smart man, Jabez. I voted for ye. Go ahead, Senator, you're doing fine.

Jabez. But we're certainly glad to have you here—me and Mary. And we want to thank you for coming and—

A Voice. Vote the Whig[2] ticket!

Another Voice. Hooray for Daniel Webster!

Jabez. And I'm glad Hi Foster said that, for those are my sentiments, too. Mr. Webster has promised to honor us with his presence here tonight.

The Crowd. Hurray for Dan'l! Hurray for the greatest man in the U.S.!

Jabez. And when he comes, I know we'll give him a real New Hampshire welcome.

The Crowd. Sure we will—Webster forever—and to hell with Henry Clay![3]

Jabez. And meanwhile—well, there's Mary and me (*takes her hand*)—and, if you folks don't have a good time, well, we won't feel right about getting married at all. Because I know I've been lucky—and I hope she feels that way, too. And, well, we're going to be happy or bust a trace!

---

2. **Whig:** a political party founded in the 1830s. Daniel Webster was one of its leaders.

3. **Henry Clay:** a famous American congressman of the time and a rival of Daniel Webster.

(*He wipes his brow to terrific applause. He and* Mary *look at each other.*)

A Woman (*in kitchen doorway*). Come and get the cider, folks!

(*The* Crowd *begins to drift away—a few to the kitchen—a few toward the door that leads to the outside. They furnish a shifting background to the next little scene, where* Mary *and* Jabez *are left alone by the fireplace.*)

Jabez. Mary.

Mary. Mr. Stone.

Jabez. Mary.

Mary. My husband.

Jabez. That's a big word, husband.

Mary. It's a good word.

Jabez. Are you happy, Mary?

Mary. Yes. So happy, I'm afraid.

Jabez. Afraid?

Mary. I suppose it happens to every girl—just for a minute. It's like spring turning into summer. You want it to be summer. But the spring was sweet. (*Dismissing the mood*) I'm sorry. Forgive me. It just came and went, like something cold. As if we'd been too lucky.

Jabez. We can't be too lucky, Mary. Not you and me.

Mary (*rather mischievously*). If you say so, Mr. Stone. But you don't even know what sort of housekeeper I am. And Aunt Hepsy says—

Jabez. Bother your Aunt Hepsy! There's just you and me and that's all that matters in the world.

Mary. And you don't know something else—

Jabez. What's that?

Mary. How proud I am of you. Ever since I was a little girl. Ever since you carried my books. Oh, I'm sorry for women who can't be proud of their men. It must be a lonely feeling.

Jabez (*uncomfortably*). A man can't always be proud of everything, Mary. There's some things a man does, or might do—when he has to make his way.

Mary (*laughing*). I know—terrible things—like being the best farmer in the county and the best State Senator—

Jabez (*quietly*). And a few things, besides. But you remember one thing, Mary, whatever happens. It was all for you. And nothing's going to happen. Because he hasn't come yet—and he would have come if it was wrong.

Mary. But it's wonderful to have Mr. Webster come to us.

Jabez. I wasn't thinking about Mr. Webster. (*He takes both her hands.*) Mary, I've got something to tell you. I should have told you before, but I couldn't seem to bear it. Only, now that it's all right, I can. Ten years ago—

A Voice (*from off stage*). Dan'l! Dan'l Webster!

(Jabez *drops* Mary's *hands and looks around. The* Crowd *begins to mill and gather toward the door. Others rush in from the kitchen.*)

Another Voice. Black Dan'l![4] He's come!

Another Voice. Three cheers for the greatest man in the U.S.!

Another Voice. Three cheers for Daniel Webster!

(*And, to the cheering and applause of the crowd,* Daniel Webster *enters and stands for a moment upstage, in the familiar pose, his head thrown back, his attitude leonine.[5] He stops the cheering of the crowd with a gesture.*)

Webster. Neighbors—old friends—it does me good to hear you. But don't cheer me—I'm not running for President this summer. (*a laugh*

---

4. **Black Dan'l:** a nickname Webster received as a child because of his dark complexion.

5. **leonine** (lē′ə-nīn′): like a lion.

from the Crowd) I'm here on a better errand—to pay my humble respects to a most charming lady and her very fortunate spouse.

(*There is the twang of a fiddlestring breaking.*)

Fiddler. 'Tarnation! Busted a string!

A Voice. He's always bustin' strings.

(Webster *blinks at the interruption but goes on.*)

Webster. We're proud of State Senator Stone in these parts—we know what he's done. Ten years ago he started out with a patch of land that was mostly rocks and mortgages and now—well, you've only to look around you. I don't know that I've ever seen a likelier farm, not even at Marshfield[6]—and I hope, before I die, I'll have the privilege of shaking his hand as Governor of this State. I don't know how he's done it—I couldn't have done it myself. But I know this—Jabez Stone wears no man's collar. (*At this statement there is a discordant squeak from the fiddle, and* Jabez *looks embarrassed.* Webster *knits his brows.*) And what's more, if I know Jabez, he never will. But I didn't come here to talk politics—I came to kiss the bride. (*He does so among great applause. He shakes hands with* Jabez.) Congratulations, Stone—you're a lucky man. And now, if our friend in the corner will give us a tune on his fiddle—

(*The* Crowd *presses forward to meet the great man. He shakes hands with several.*)

A Man. Remember me, Mr. Webster? Saw ye up at the State House at Concord.

Another Man. Glad to see ye, Mr. Webster. I voted for ye ten times.

(Webster *receives their homage politely, but his mind is still on music.*)

Webster (*a trifle irritated*). I said, if our friend in the corner would give us a tune on his fiddle—

Fiddler (*passionately, flinging the fiddle down*). Hell's delight—excuse me, Mr. Webster. But the very devil's got into that fiddle of mine. She was doing all right up to just a minute ago. But now I've tuned her and tuned her and she won't play a note I want.

(*And, at this point, Mr. Scratch makes his appearance. He has entered, unobserved, and mixed with the crowd while all eyes were upon Daniel Webster. He is, of course, the devil—a New England devil, dressed like a rather shabby attorney but with something just a little wrong in clothes and appearance. For one thing, he wears black gloves on his hands. He carries a large black tin box, like a botanist's collecting box, under one arm. Now he slips through the crowd and taps the* Fiddler *on the shoulder.*)

Scratch (*insinuatingly*). Maybe you need some rosin on your bow, fiddler?

Fiddler. Maybe I do and maybe I don't. (*Turns and confronts the stranger*) But who are you? I don't remember seeing you before.

---

6. **Marshfield:** a small town southeast of Boston, where Daniel Webster had a farm.

WORDS	**discordant** (dĭ-skôr′dnt) *adj.* disagreeable in sound; harsh
TO	**homage** (hŏm′ĭj) *n.* special honor or respect shown publicly
KNOW	**insinuatingly** (ĭn-sĭn′yōō-ā′tĭng-lē) *adv.* in a hinting, indirect, or suggestive manner

Scratch. Oh, I'm just a friend—a humble friend of the bridegroom's. (*He walks toward* Jabez. *Apologetically.*) I'm afraid I came in the wrong way, Mr. Stone. You've improved the place so much since I last saw it that I hardly knew the front door. But, I assure you, I came as fast as I could.

Jabez (*obviously shocked*). It—it doesn't matter. (*With a great effort*) Mary—Mr. Webster—this is a—a friend of mine from Boston—a legal friend. I didn't expect him today but—

Scratch. Oh, my dear Mr. Stone—an occasion like this—I wouldn't miss it for the world. (*He bows.*) Charmed, Mrs. Stone. Delighted, Mr. Webster. But—don't let me break up the merriment of the meeting. (*He turns back toward the table and the* Fiddler.)

Fiddler (*with a grudge, to* Scratch). Boston lawyer, eh?

Scratch. You might call me that.

Fiddler (*tapping the tin box with his bow*). And what have you got in that big tin box of yours? Law papers?

Scratch. Oh—curiosities for the most part. I'm a collector, too.

Fiddler. Don't hold much with Boston curiosities, myself. And you know about fiddling, too, do you? Know all about it?

Scratch. Oh—(*a deprecatory shrug*)

Fiddler. Don't shrug your shoulders at me—I ain't no Frenchman. Telling me I needed more rosin!

Mary (*trying to stop the quarrel*). Isaac—please—

Fiddler. Sorry, Mary—Mrs. Stone. But I been playing the fiddle at Cross Corners weddings for twenty-five years. And now here comes a stranger from Boston and tells me I need more rosin!

Scratch. But, my good friend—

Fiddler. Rosin indeed! Here—play it yourself then and see what you can make of it! (*He thrusts the fiddle at* Scratch. *The latter stiffens, slowly lays his black collecting box on the table, and takes the fiddle.*)

Scratch (*with feigned embarrassment*). But really, I— (*He bows toward* Jabez.) Shall I—Mr. Senator? (Jabez *makes a helpless gesture of assent.*)

Mary (*to* Jabez). Mr. Stone—Mr. Stone—are you ill?

Jabez. No—no—but I feel—it's hot—

Webster (*chuckling*). Don't you fret, Mrs. Stone. I've got the right medicine for him. (*He pulls a flask from his pocket.*) Ten-year-old Medford, Stone—I buy it by the keg down at Marshfield. Here—(*He tries to give some of the rum to* Jabez.)

Jabez. No—(*he turns*)—Mary—Mr. Webster—(*But he cannot explain. With a burst.*) Oh, let him play—let him play! Don't you see he's bound to? Don't you see there's nothing we can do?

(*A rustle of discomfort among the guests.* Scratch *draws the bow across the fiddle in a horrible discord.*)

Fiddler (*triumphantly*). I told you so, stranger. The devil's in that fiddle!

Scratch. I'm afraid it needs special tuning. (*Draws the bow in a second discord*) There—that's better (*grinning*). And now for this happy—this very happy occasion—in tribute to the bride and groom—I'll play something appropriate—a song of young love—

Mary. Oh, Jabez—Mr. Webster—stop him! Do you see his hands? He's playing with gloves on his hands.

(Webster *starts forward, but, even as he does so,* Scratch *begins to play, and all freeze as* Scratch *goes on with the extremely inappropriate song that follows. At first his manner is oily and mocking—it is not till he reaches the line "The devil took the words away" that he really becomes terrifying and the crowd starts to be afraid.*)

Scratch (*accompanying himself fantastically*).

Young William was a thriving boy.
(Listen to my doleful tale.)
Young Mary Clark was all his joy.
(Listen to my doleful tale.)

He swore he'd love her all his life.
She swore she'd be his loving wife.
But William found a gambler's den
And drank with livery-stable men.

He played the cards, he played the dice
He would not listen to advice.

And when in church he tried to pray,
The devil took the words away.

(Scratch, *still playing, starts to march across the stage.*)

The devil got him by the toe
And so, alas, he had to go.

"Young Mary Clark, young Mary Clark,
I now must go into the dark."
(*These last two verses have been directed at* Jabez. Scratch *continues, now turning on* Mary.)

Young Mary lay upon her bed.
"Alas my Will-i-am is dead."

He came to her a bleeding ghost—

(*He rushes at* Mary *but* Webster *stands between them.*)

Webster. Stop! Stop! You miserable wretch—can't you see that you're frightening Mrs. Stone? (*He wrenches the fiddle out of* Scratch's *hands and tosses it aside.*) And now, sir—out of this house!

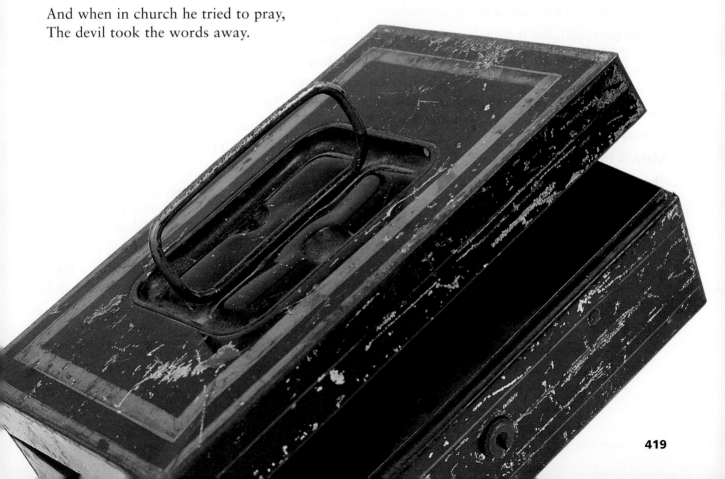

Scratch (*facing him*). You're a bold man, Mr. Webster. Too bold for your own good, perhaps. And anyhow, it wasn't my fiddle. It belonged to—(*He wheels and sees the* Fiddler *tampering with the collecting box that has been left on the table.*) Idiot! What are you doing with my collecting box? (*He rushes for the* Fiddler *and chases him round the table, but the* Fiddler *is just one jump ahead.*)

Fiddler. Boston lawyer, eh? Well, I don't think so. I think you've got something in that box of yours you're afraid to show. And, by jingo—(*He throws open the lid of the box. The lights wink and there is a clap of thunder. All eyes stare upward. Something has flown out of the box. But what?* Fiddler, *with relief.*) Why, 'tain't nothing but a moth.

Mary. A white moth—a flying thing.

Webster. A common moth—telea polyphemus—

The Crowd. A moth—just a moth—a moth—

Fiddler (*terrified*). But it ain't. It ain't no common moth! I seen it! And it's got a death's-head on it! (*He strikes at the invisible object with his bow to drive it away.*)

Voice of the Moth. Help me, neighbors! Help me!

Webster. What's that? It wails like a lost soul.

Mary. A lost soul.

The Crowd. A lost soul—lost—in darkness—in the darkness.

Voice of the Moth. Help me, neighbors!

Fiddler. It sounds like Miser Stevens.

Jabez. Miser Stevens!

The Crowd. The Miser—Miser Stevens—a lost soul—lost.

Fiddler (*frantically*). It sounds like Miser Stevens—and you had him in your box. But it can't be. He ain't dead.

Jabez. He ain't dead—I tell you he ain't dead! He was just as spry and mean as a woodchuck Tuesday.

The Crowd. Miser Stevens—soul of Miser Stevens—but he ain't dead.

Scratch (*dominating them*). Listen!

(*A bell off stage begins to toll a knell, slowly, solemnly.*)

Mary. The bell—the church bell—the bell that rang at my wedding.

Webster. The church bell—the passing bell.

Jabez. The funeral bell.

The Crowd. The bell—the passing bell—Miser Stevens—dead.

Voice of the Moth. Help me, neighbors, help me! I sold my soul to the devil. But I'm not the first or the last. Help me. Help Jabez Stone!

Scratch. Ah, would you! (*He catches the moth in his red bandanna, stuffs it back into his collecting box, and shuts the lid with a snap.*)

Voice of the Moth (*fading*). Lost—lost forever, forever. Lost, like Jabez Stone.

(*The* Crowd *turns on* Jabez. *They read his secret in his face.*)

The Crowd. Jabez Stone—Jabez Stone—answer us—answer us.

Mary. Tell them, dear—answer them—you are good—you are brave—you are innocent.

(*But the* Crowd *is all pointing hands and horrified eyes.*)

The Crowd. Jabez Stone—Jabez Stone. Who's your friend in black, Jabez Stone? (*They point to* Scratch.)

Webster. Answer them, Mr. State Senator.

The Crowd. Jabez Stone—Jabez Stone. Where did you get your money, Jabez Stone?

(Scratch *grins and taps his collecting box,* Jabez *cannot speak.*)

Jabez. I—I—(*He stops.*)

The Crowd. Jabez Stone—Jabez Stone. What was the price you paid for it, Jabez Stone?

Jabez (*looking around wildly*). Help me, neighbors! Help me!

(*This cracks the built-up tension and sends the* Crowd *over the edge into* fanaticism.)

A Woman's Voice (*high and hysterical*). He's sold his soul to the devil! (*She points to* Jabez.)

Other Voices. To the devil!

The Crowd. He's sold his soul to the devil! The devil himself! The devil's playing the fiddle! The devil's come for his own!

Jabez (*appealing*). But, neighbors—I didn't know—I didn't mean—oh, help me!

The Crowd (*inexorably*). He's sold his soul to the devil!

Scratch (*grinning*). To the devil!

The Crowd. He's sold his soul to the devil! There's no help left for him, neighbors! Run, hide, hurry, before we're caught! He's a lost soul—

Jabez Stone—he's the devil's own. Run, hide, hasten! (*They stream across the stage like a flurry of bats, the cannier picking up the wedding presents they have given to take along with them.*)

(Mr. Scratch *drives them out into the night, fiddle in hand, and follows them.* Jabez *and* Mary *are left with* Webster. Jabez *has sunk into a chair, beaten, with his head in his hands.* Mary *is trying to comfort him.* Webster *looks at them for a moment and shakes his head, sadly. As he crosses to exit to the porch, his hand drops for a moment on* Jabez' *shoulder, but* Jabez *makes no sign.* Webster *exits.* Jabez *lifts his head.*)

> **ACTIVE READING**
>
> **CLARIFY** What is the reason that Scratch has come to the wedding?

Mary (*comforting him*). My dear—my dear—

Jabez. I—it's all true, Mary. All true. You must hurry.

Mary. Hurry?

Jabez. Hurry after them—back to the village—back to your folks. Mr. Webster will take you—you'll be safe with Mr. Webster. You see, it's all true and he'll be back in a minute. (*With a shudder*) The other one. (*He groans.*) I've got until twelve o'clock. That's the contract. But there isn't much time.

Mary. Are you telling me to run away from you, Mr. Stone?

Jabez. You don't understand, Mary. It's true.

Mary. We made some promises to each other. Maybe you've forgotten them. But I haven't. I said, it's for better or worse. It's for better or worse. I said, in sickness or in health. Well, that covers the ground, Mr. Stone.

Jabez. But, Mary, you must—I command you.

WORDS
TO
KNOW   **fanaticism** (fə-năt′ĭ-sĭz′əm) *n.* excessive, unreasonable zeal or enthusiasm

My Night Visage (1913), Ludwig Meidner. Marvin and Janet Fishman Collection.

Mary. "For thy people shall be my people and thy God my God." (*Quietly*) That was Ruth, in the Book.[7] I always liked the name of Ruth—always liked the thought of her. I always thought—I'll call a child Ruth, some time. I guess that was just a girl's notion. (*She breaks.*) But, oh, Jabez—why?

Jabez. It started years ago, Mary. I guess I was a youngster then—guess I must have been. A youngster with a lot of ambitions and no way in the world to get there. I wanted city clothes and a big white house—I wanted to be State Senator and have people look up to me. But all I got on the farm was a crop of stones. You could work all day and all night, but that was all you got.

Mary (*softly*). It was pretty—that hill farm, Jabez. You could look all the way across the valley.

Jabez. Pretty? It was fever and ague[8]—it was stones and blight. If I had a horse, he got colic—if I planted garden truck, the woodchucks ate it. I'd lie awake nights and try to figure out a way to get somewhere—but there wasn't any way. And all the time you were growing up, in the town. I couldn't ask you to marry me and take you to a place like that.

Mary. Do you think it's the place makes the difference to a woman? I'd—I'd have kept your house. I'd have stroked the cat and fed the chickens and seen you wiped your shoes on the mat. I wouldn't have asked for more. Oh, Jabez—why didn't you tell me?

Jabez. It happened before I could. Just an average day—you know—just an average day. But there was a mean east wind and a mean small rain. Well, I was plowing, and the share broke clean off on a rock where there hadn't been any rock the day before. I didn't have money for a new one—I didn't have money to get it mended. So I said it and I said loud, "I'll sell my soul for about two cents," I said. (*He stops.* Mary *stares at him.*) Well, that's all there is to it, I guess. He came along that afternoon—that fellow from Boston—and the dog looked at him and ran away. Well, I had to make it more than two cents, but he was agreeable to that. So I pricked my thumb with a pin and signed the paper. It felt hot when you touched it, that paper. I keep remembering that. (*He pauses.*) And it's all come true and he's kept his part of the bargain. I got the riches and I've married you. And, oh, God Almighty, what shall I do?

> **ACTIVE READING**
>
> **EVALUATE** How do you think the author wants you to feel toward Stone?

Mary. Let us run away! Let us creep and hide!

Jabez. You can't run away from the devil—I've seen his horses. Miser Stevens tried to run away.

Mary. Let us pray—let us pray to the God of Mercy that He redeem us.

Jabez. I can't pray, Mary. The words just burn in my heart.

Mary. I won't let you go! I won't! There must be someone who could help us. I'll get the judge and the squire—

Jabez. Who'll take a case against old Scratch? Who'll face the devil himself and do him brown? There isn't a lawyer in the world who'd dare do that.

(Webster *appears in the doorway.*)

Webster. Good evening, neighbors. Did you say something about lawyers—

Mary. Mr. Webster!

---

7. **Ruth, in the Book:** The preceding quote is from the Book of Ruth in the Old Testament of the Bible. When Ruth becomes widowed, she decides to leave her home and go with her mother-in-law, Naomi, to Bethlehem. Her famous words are spoken to Naomi.

8. **ague** (ā′gyōō): a feverish condition.

Jabez. Dan'l Webster! But I thought—

Webster. You'll excuse me for leaving you for a moment. I was just taking a stroll on the porch, in the cool of the evening. Fine summer evening, too.

Jabez. Well, it might be, I guess, but that kind of depends on the circumstances.

Webster. H'm. Yes I happened to overhear a little of your conversation. I gather you're in trouble, Neighbor Stone.

Jabez. Sore trouble.

Webster (*delicately*). Sort of law case, I understand.

Jabez. You might call it that, Mr. Webster. Kind of a mortgage case, in a way.

Mary. Oh, Jabez!

Webster. Mortgage case. Well, I don't generally plead now, except before the Supreme Court, but this case of yours presents some very unusual features, and I never deserted a neighbor in trouble yet. So, if I can be of any assistance—

Mary. Oh, Mr. Webster, will you help him?

Jabez. It's a terrible lot to ask you. But—well, you see, there's Mary. And, if you could see your way to it—

Webster. I will.

Mary (*weeping with relief*). Oh, Mr. Webster!

Webster. There, there, Mrs. Stone. After all, if two New Hampshire men aren't a match for the devil, we might as well give the country back to the Indians. When is he coming, Jabez?

Jabez. Twelve o'clock. The time's getting late.

Webster. Then I'd better refresh my memory. The—er—mortgage was for a definite term of years?

Jabez. Ten years.

Webster. And it falls due—?

Jabez. Tonight. Oh, I can't see how I came to be such a fool!

Webster. No use crying over spilt milk, Stone. We've got to get you out of it, now. But tell me one thing. Did you sign this precious document of your own free will?

Jabez. Yes, it was my own free will. I can't deny that.

Webster. H'm, that's a trifle unfortunate. But we'll see.

Mary. Oh, Mr. Webster, can you save him? Can you?

Webster. I shall do my best, madam. That's all you can ever say till you see what the jury looks like.

Mary. But even you, Mr. Webster—oh, I know you're Secretary of State—I know you're a great man—I know you've done wonderful things. But it's different—fighting the devil!

Webster (*towering*). I've fought John C. Calhoun, madam. And I've fought Henry Clay. And, by the great shade of Andrew Jackson,[9] I'd fight ten thousand devils to save a New Hampshire man!

Jabez. You hear, Mary?

Mary. Yes. And I trust Mr. Webster. But—oh, there must be some way that I can help!

Webster. There is one, madam, and a hard one. As Mr. Stone's counsel, I must formally request your withdrawal.

Mary. No.

---

9. **John C. Calhoun . . . Andrew Jackson:** Calhoun served as vice president from 1825 to 1832. He maintained that states could nullify federal laws, a position that Webster opposed. Andrew Jackson was president from 1829 to 1837. Jackson opposed the Bank of the United States, and Webster supported it.

Webster. Madam, think for a moment. You cannot help Mr. Stone—since you are his wife, your testimony would be prejudiced. And frankly, madam, in a very few minutes this is going to be no place for a lady.

Mary. But I can't—I can't leave him—I can't bear it!

Jabez. You must go, Mary. You must.

Webster. Pray, madam—you can help us with your prayers. Are the prayers of the innocent unavailing?[10]

Mary. Oh, I'll pray—I'll pray. But a woman's more than a praying machine, whatever men think. And how do I know?

Webster. Trust me, Mrs. Stone.

(Mary *turns to go, and, with one hand on* Jabez' *shoulder, as she moves to the door, says the following prayer:*)

Mary.

> Now may there be a blessing and a light betwixt thee and me, forever.
> For, as Ruth unto Naomi, so do I cleave unto thee.
> Set me as a seal upon thy heart, as a seal upon thine arm, for love is strong as death.
> Many waters cannot quench love, neither can the floods drown it.
> As Ruth unto Naomi, so do I cleave unto thee.
> The Lord watch between thee and me when we are absent, one from the other.
> Amen. Amen. (*She goes out.*)

Webster. Amen.

Jabez. Thank you, Mr. Webster. She ought to go. But I couldn't have made her do it.

Webster. Well, Stone—I know ladies—and I wouldn't be surprised if she's still got her ear to the keyhole. But she's best out of this night's business. How long have we got to wait?

Jabez (*beginning to be terrified again*). Not long—not long.

Webster. Then I'll just get out the jug, with your permission, Stone. Somehow or other, waiting's wonderfully shorter with a jug. (*He crosses to the cupboard, gets out jug and glasses, pours himself a drink.*) Ten-year-old Medford. There's nothing like it. I saw an inchworm take a drop of it once, and he stood right up on his hind legs and bit a bee. Come—try a nip.

Jabez. There's no joy in it for me.

Webster. Oh, come, man, come! Just because you've sold your soul to the devil, that needn't make you a teetotaller.[11] (*He laughs and passes the jug to* Jabez, *who tries to pour from it. But at that moment the clock whirs and begins to strike the three-quarters, and* Jabez *spills the liquor.*)

Jabez. Oh, God!

Webster. Never mind—it's a nervous feeling, waiting for a trial to begin. I remember my first case—

Jabez. 'Tain't that. (*He turns to* Webster.) Mr. Webster—Mr. Webster—for God's sake harness your horses and get away from this place as fast as you can!

Webster (*placidly*). You've brought me a long way, neighbor, to tell me you don't like my company.

Jabez. I've brought you the devil's own way. I can see it all, now. He's after both of us—him and his damn collecting box! Well, he can have me, if he likes—I don't say I relish it, but I made

---

10. **unavailing:** not useful or helpful.

11. **teetotaller** (tē′tōt′l-ər): a person who never drinks alcoholic beverages.

Daniel Webster (Black Dan) (1835), Francis Alexander. Oil on canvas, Hood Museum of Art, Dartmouth College, Hanover, New Hampshire, gift of Dr. George C. Shattuck, class of 1803.

the bargain. But you're the whole United States! He can't get you, Mr. Webster—he mustn't get you!

Webster. I'm obliged to you, neighbor Stone. It's kindly thought of. But there's a jug on the table and a case in hand. And I never left a jug or a case half-finished in my life. (*There is a knock at the door.* Jabez *gives a cry.*) Ah, I thought your clock was a trifle slow, neighbor Stone. Come in!

(Scratch *enters from the night.*)

Scratch. Mr. Webster! This is a pleasure!

Webster. Attorney of record for Jabez Stone. Might I ask your name?

Scratch. I've gone by a good many. Perhaps Scratch will do for the evening. I'm often called that in these regions. May I? (*He sits at the table and pours a drink from the jug. The liquor steams as it pours into the glass while* Jabez *watches, terrified.* Scratch *grins, toasting* Webster *and* Jabez *silently in the liquor. Then he becomes businesslike. To* Webster.) And now I call upon you, as a law-abiding citizen, to assist me in taking possession of my property.

Webster. Not so fast, Mr. Scratch. Produce your evidence, if you have it.

(Scratch *takes out a black pocketbook and examines papers.*)

Scratch. Slattery—Stanley—Stone. (*takes out a deed*) There, Mr. Webster. All open and above-board and in due and legal form. Our firm has its reputation to consider—we deal only in the one way.

Webster (*taking deed and looking it over*). H'm. This appears—I say, it appears—to be properly drawn. But, of course, we contest the signature (*tosses it back,* contemptuously).

Scratch (*suddenly turning on* Jabez *and shooting a finger at him*). Is that your signature?

Jabez (*wearily*). You know damn well it is.

Webster (*angrily*). Keep quiet, Stone. (*To* Scratch) But that is a minor matter. This precious document isn't worth the paper it's written on. The law permits no traffic in human flesh.

Scratch. Oh, my dear Mr. Webster! Courts in every State in the Union have held that human flesh is property and recoverable. Read your Fugitive Slave Act.[12] Or, shall I cite Brander versus McRae?

Webster. But, in the case of the State of Maryland versus Four Barrels of Bourbon—

Scratch. That was overruled, as you know, sir. North Carolina versus Jenkins and Co.

Webster (*unwillingly*). You seem to have an excellent acquaintance with the law, sir.

Scratch. Sir, that is no fault of mine. Where I come from, we have always gotten the pick of the Bar.[13]

Webster (*changing his note, heartily*). Well, come now, sir. There's no need to make hay and oats of a trifling matter when we're both sensible men. Surely we can settle this little difficulty out of court. My client is quite prepared to offer a compromise. (Scratch *smiles.*) A very substantial compromise. (Scratch *smiles more broadly, slowly shaking his head.*) Hang it, man, we offer ten thousand dollars! (Scratch *signs "No."*) Twenty thousand—thirty—name your figure! I'll raise it if I have to mortgage Marshfield!

---

12. **Fugitive Slave Act:** law governing the capture and return of runaway slaves.

13. **pick of the Bar:** The best lawyers available. *Bar* means "lawyers considered as a group."

Scratch. Quite useless, Mr. Webster. There is only one thing I want from you—the execution of my contract.

Webster. But this is absurd. Mr. Stone is now a State Senator. The property has greatly increased in value!

Scratch. The principle of caveat emptor[14] still holds, Mr. Webster. (*He yawns and looks at the clock.*) And now, if you have no further arguments to adduce—I'm rather pressed for time—(*He rises briskly as if to take* Jabez *into custody.*)

Webster (*thundering*). Pressed or not, you shall not have this man. Mr. Stone is an American citizen, and no American citizen may be forced into the service of a foreign prince. We fought England for that, in '12,[15] and we'll fight all hell for it again!

Scratch. Foreign? And who calls me a foreigner?

Webster. Well, I never yet heard of the dev—of your claiming American citizenship?

Scratch. And who with better right? When the first wrong was done to the Indian, I was there. When the first slaver put out for the Congo, I stood on her deck. Am I not in your books and stories and beliefs, from the first settlements on? Am I not spoken of, still, in every church in New England? 'Tis true, the North claims me for a Southerner and the South for a Northerner, but I am neither. I am merely an honest American like yourself—and of the best descent—for, to tell the truth, Mr. Webster, though I don't like to boast of it, my name is older in the country than yours.

Webster. Aha! Then I stand on the Constitution! I demand a trial for my client!

Scratch. The case is hardly one for an ordinary jury—and indeed, the lateness of the hour—

Webster. Let it be any court you choose, so it is an American judge and an American jury. Let it be the quick[16] or the dead, I'll abide the issue.

ACTIVE READING

CONNECT How is Daniel Webster like or unlike lawyers of today?

Scratch. The quick or the dead! You have said it! (*He points his finger at the place where the jury is to appear. There is a clap of thunder and a flash of light. The stage blacks out completely. All that can be seen is the face of* Scratch, *lit with a ghastly green light as he recites the invocation that summons the* Jury. *As, one by one, the important* Jurymen *are mentioned, they appear.*)

14. **caveat emptor** (kā′vē-ăt′ ĕmp′tôr′): the principle in commerce that the buyer is responsible for assessing the quality of a purchase before buying. *Caveat emptor* is a Latin phrase that literally means "Let the buyer beware."

15. **in '12:** a reference to the War of 1812, which was caused in part by the British forcing American sailors to serve in the British navy.

16. **quick:** the living.

I summon the jury Mr. Webster demands.
From churchyard mold and gallows grave,
Brimstone pit and burning gulf,
I summon them!
Dastard, liar, scoundrel, knave,
I summon them! Appear!
There's Simon Girty, the renegade,
The haunter of the forest glade
Who joined with Indian and wolf
To hunt the pioneer.
The stains upon his hunting shirt
Are not the blood of the deer.
There's Walter Butler,[17] the loyalist,
Who carried a firebrand in his fist
Of massacre and shame.
King Philip's[18] eye is wild and bright.
They slew him in the great Swamp Fight,
But still, with terror and affright,
The land recalls his name.
Blackbeard Teach, the pirate fell,
Smeet the strangler, hot from hell,
Dale, who broke men on the wheel,
Morton,[19] of the tarnished steel,
I summon them, I summon them
From their tormented flame!

Quick or dead, quick or dead,
Broken heart and bitter head,
True Americans, each one,
Traitor and disloyal son,
Cankered earth and twisted tree,
Outcasts of eternity,
Twelve great sinners, tried and true,
For the work they are to do!
I summon them, I summon them!
Appear, appear, appear!

(*The* Jury *has now taken its place in the jury box—Walter Butler in the place of foreman. They are eerily lit and so made-up as to suggest the*

---

17. **Simon Girty . . . Walter Butler:** Both were white men who fought with Native Americans against white settlers in the late 1700s.

18. **King Philip:** a Wampanoag chief who started an uprising against white settlers in 1675. He was killed in 1676.

19. **Blackbeard Teach . . . Dale . . . Morton:** Edward Teach, known as Blackbeard, was an English pirate who preyed on American ships in the early 1700s. Sir Thomas Dale, governor of the Virginia colony in the early 1600s, was despised for his harsh rule. Thomas Morton of Massachusetts was a free-living Anglican who ridiculed his Puritan neighbors and sold firearms to Native Americans in the 1600s.

unearthly. They sit stiffly in their box. At first, when one moves, all move, in stylized gestures. It is not till the end of Webster's *speech that they begin to show any trace of humanity. They speak rhythmically, and, at first, in low, eerie voices.*)

Jabez (*seeing them, horrified*). A jury of the dead!

Jury. Of the dead!

Jabez. A jury of the damned!

Jury. Of the damned!

Scratch. Are you content with the jury, Mr. Webster?

ACTIVE READING

VISUALIZE Close your eyes and picture the jury. How does their appearance make you feel?

Webster. Quite content. Though I miss General Arnold from the company.

Scratch. Benedict Arnold[20] is engaged upon other business. Ah, you asked for a justice, I believe. (*He points his finger and* Justice Hathorne, *a tall, lean, terrifying Puritan, appears, followed by his* Clerk.) Justice Hathorne is a jurist of experience. He presided at the Salem witch trials. There were others who repented of the business later. But not he, not he!

Hathorne. Repent of such notable wonders and undertakings? Nay, hang them, hang them all! (*He takes his place on the bench.*)

(*The* Clerk, *an ominous little man with clawlike hands, takes his place. The room has now been transformed into a courtroom.*[21])

Clerk (*in a gabble of ritual*). Oyes, oyes, oyes. All ye who have business with this honorable court of special session this night, step forward!

Hathorne (*with gavel*). Call the first case.

Clerk. The World, the Flesh and the Devil versus Jabez Stone.

Hathorne. Who appears for the plaintiff?

Scratch. I, Your Honor.

Hathorne. And for the defendant?

Webster. I.

Jury. The case—the case—he'll have little luck with this case.

Hathorne. The case will proceed.

Webster. Your Honor, I move to dismiss this case on the grounds of improper jurisdiction.

Hathorne. Motion denied.

Webster. On the grounds of insufficient evidence.

Hathorne. Motion denied.

Jury. Motion denied—denied. Motion denied.

Webster. I will take an exception.

Hathorne. There are no exceptions in this court.

Jury. No exceptions—no exceptions in this court. It's a bad case, Daniel Webster—a losing case.

Webster. Your Honor—

Hathorne. The prosecution will proceed—

Scratch. Your Honor—gentlemen of the jury. This is a plain, straightforward case. It need not detain us long.

Jury. Detain us long—it will not detain us long.

Scratch. It concerns one thing alone—the transference, barter and sale of a certain piece of property, to wit, his soul, by Jabez Stone, farmer, of Cross Corners, New Hampshire. That transference, barter or sale is attested by a deed.[22] I offer that deed in evidence and mark it Exhibit A.

---

20. **Benedict Arnold:** an American Revolutionary War general who became a traitor.

21. **courtroom:** In a simple production of this play, a pair of long benches, one higher than the other, are placed at the back of the stage to serve as a jury box. The members of the jury quietly come onstage during the blackout, while Scratch recites his invocation. As he finishes, the light gradually comes up on the jury. The judge now enters and takes his seat on a high bench by the fireplace, with his Clerk sitting on a stool below him. The table, left, becomes the lawyer's table, where Scratch and Webster sit.

22. **attested by a deed:** certified by a signed contract.

Webster. I object.

Hathorne. Objection denied. Mark it Exhibit A.

(Scratch *hands the deed—an ominous and impressive document—to the* Clerk, *who hands it to* Hathorne. Hathorne *hands it back to the* Clerk, *who stamps it. All very fast and with mechanical gestures.*)

Jury. Exhibit A—mark it Exhibit A. (Scratch *takes the deed from the* Clerk *and offers it to the* Jury, *who pass it rapidly among them, hardly looking at it, and hand it back to* Scratch.) We know the deed—the deed—it burns in our fingers—we do not have to see the deed. It's a losing case.

Scratch. It offers incontestable evidence of the truth of the prosecution's claim. I shall now call Jabez Stone to the witness stand.

Jury (*hungrily*). Jabez Stone to the witness stand, Jabez Stone. He's a fine, fat fellow, Jabez Stone. He'll fry like a battercake, once we get him where we want him.

Webster. Your Honor, I move that this jury be discharged for flagrant and open <u>bias</u>!

Hathorne. Motion denied.

Webster. Exception.

Hathorne. Exception denied.

Jury. His motion's always denied. He thinks himself smart and clever—lawyer Webster. But his motion's always denied.

Webster. Your Honor! (*He chokes with anger.*)

Clerk (*advancing*). Jabez Stone to the witness stand!

Jury. Jabez Stone—Jabez Stone.

(Webster *gives* Jabez *an encouraging pat on the back, and* Jabez *takes his place in the witness stand, very scared.*)

Clerk (*offering a black book*). Do you solemnly swear—testify—so help you—and it's no good, for we don't care what you testify?

Jabez. I do.

Scratch. What's your name?

Jabez. Jabez Stone.

Scratch. Occupation?

Jabez. Farmer.

Scratch. Residence?

Jabez. Cross Corners, New Hampshire.

(*These three questions are very fast and mechanical on the part of* Scratch. *He is absolutely sure of victory and just going through a form.*)

Jury. A farmer—he'll farm in hell—we'll see that he farms in hell.

Scratch. Now, Jabez Stone, answer me. You'd better, you know. You haven't got a chance, and there'll be a cooler place by the fire for you.

WORDS
TO
KNOW

bias (bī′əs) *n.* an attitude in which a person is in favor of someone or something without having a good reason for this preference

431

Trial Scene (1860–1863), David Gilmour Blythe. Memorial Art Gallery of the University of Rochester (New York), Marion Stratton Gould Fund.

Webster. I protest! This is <u>intimidation</u>! This mocks all justice!

Hathorne. The process is irrelevant, incompetent and immaterial. We have our own justice. The protest is denied.

Jury. Irrelevant, incompetent and immaterial—we have our own justice—oh, ho, Daniel Webster! (*The* Jury's *eyes fix upon* Webster *for an instant, hungrily.*)

Scratch. Did you or did you not sign this document?

Jabez. Oh, I signed it! You know I signed it. And, if I have to go to hell for it, I'll go!

(*A sigh sweeps over the* Jury.)

Jury. One of us—one of us now—we'll save a place by the fire for you, Jabez Stone.

Scratch. The prosecution rests.

Hathorne. Remove the prisoner.

Webster. But I wish to cross-examine—I wish to prove—

Hathorne. There will be no cross-examination. We have our own justice. You may speak, if you like. But be brief.

Jury. Brief—be very brief—we're weary of earth—incompetent, irrelevant and immaterial—they say he's a smart man, Webster, but he's lost his case tonight—be very brief—we have our own justice here.

(Webster *stares around him like a baited bull. Can't find words.*)

Mary's Voice (*from off stage*). Set me as a seal upon thy heart, as a seal upon thine arm, for love is strong as death—

Jury (*loudly*). A seal!—ha, ha—a burning seal!

Mary's Voice. Love is strong—

Jury (*drowning her out*). Death is stronger than love. Set the seal upon Daniel Webster—the burning seal of the lost. Make him one of us—one of the damned—one with Jabez Stone!

(*The* Jury's *eyes all fix upon* Webster. *The* Clerk *advances as if to take him into custody. But* Webster *silences them all with a great gesture.*)

Webster.

Be still!

I was going to thunder and roar. I shall not do that.

I was going to denounce and defy. I shall not do that.

You have judged this man already with your abominable justice. See that you defend it. For I shall not speak of this man.

You are demons now, but once you were men. I shall speak to every one of you.

Of common things I speak, of small things and common.

The freshness of morning to the young, the taste of food to the hungry, the day's toil, the rest by the fire, the quiet sleep.

These are good things.

But without freedom they sicken, without freedom they are nothing.

Freedom is the bread and the morning and the risen sun.

It was for freedom we came in the boats and the ships. It was for freedom we came.

It has been a long journey, a hard one, a bitter one.

But, out of the wrong and the right, the sufferings and the starvations, there is a new thing, a free thing.

The traitors in their treachery, the wise in their wisdom, the valiant in their courage—all, all have played a part.

It may not be denied in hell nor shall hell prevail against it.

Have you forgotten this? (*He turns to the* Jury.) Have you forgotten the forest?

Girty (*as in a dream*). The forest, the rustle of the forest, the free forest.

Webster (*to* King Philip). Have you forgotten your lost nation?

King Philip. My lost nation—my fires in the wood—my warriors.

Webster (*to* Teach). Have you forgotten the sea and the way of ships?

Teach. The sea—and the swift ships sailing—the blue sea.

Jury. Forgotten—remembered—forgotten yet remembered.

Webster. You were men once. Have you forgotten?

Jury. We were men once. We have not thought of it nor remembered. But we were men.

Webster.

Now here is this man with good and evil in his heart.

Do you know him? He is your brother. Will you take the law of the <u>oppressor</u> and bind him down?

It is not for him that I speak. It is for all of you.

There is sadness in being a man, but it is a proud thing, too.

There is failure and despair on the journey—the endless journey of mankind.

We are tricked and trapped—we stumble into the pit—but, out of the pit, we rise again.

No demon that was ever foaled[23] can know the inwardness of that—only men—bewildered men.

They have broken freedom with their hands and cast her out from the nations—yet shall she live while man lives.

She shall live in the blood and the heart—she shall live in the earth of this country—she shall not be broken.

When the whips of the oppressors are broken and their names forgotten and destroyed,

I see you, mighty, shining, liberty, liberty! I see free men walking and talking under a free star.

God save the United States and the men who have made her free.

The defense rests.

Jury (*exultantly*). We were men—we were free—we were men—we have not forgotten—our children—our children shall follow and be free.

Hathorne (*rapping with gavel*). The jury will retire to consider its verdict.

Butler (*rising*). There is no need. The jury has heard Mr. Webster. We find for the defendant, Jabez Stone!

Jury. Not guilty!

Scratch (*in a screech, rushing forward*). But, Your Honor—

(*But, even as he does so, there is a flash and a thunderclap, the stage blacks out again, and when the lights come on,* Judge *and* Jury *are gone. The yellow light of dawn lights the windows.*)

---

23. **foaled:** given birth to.

WORDS
TO
KNOW

oppressor (ə-prĕs′ər) *n.* one who keeps others down by the cruel use of power

Jabez. They're gone and it's morning—Mary, Mary!

Mary (*in doorway*). My love—my dear. (*She rushes to him.*)

(*Meanwhile* Scratch *has been collecting his papers and trying to sneak out. But* Webster *catches him.*)

Webster. Just a minute, Mr. Scratch. I'll have that paper first, if you please. (*He takes the deed and tears it.*) And, now, sir, I'll have you!

Scratch. Come, come, Mr. Webster. This sort of thing is ridic—ouch—is ridiculous. If you're worried about the costs of the case, naturally, I'd be glad to pay.

Webster. And so you shall! First of all, you'll promise and covenant[24] never to bother Jabez Stone or any other New Hampshire man from now till doomsday. For any hell we want to raise in this State, we can raise ourselves, without any help from you.

Scratch. Ouch! Well, they never did run very big to the barrel but—ouch—I agree!

Webster. See you keep to the bargain! And then—well, I've got a ram named Goliath. He can butt through an iron door. I'd like to turn you loose in his field and see what he could do to you. (Scratch *trembles.*) But that would be hard on the ram. So we'll just call in the neighbors and give you a shivaree.[25]

Scratch. Mr. Webster—please—oh—

Webster. Neighbors! Neighbors! Come in and see what a long-barreled, slab-sided, lantern-jawed, fortune-telling note-shaver I've got by the scruff of the neck! Bring on your kettles and your pans! (*a noise and murmur outside*) Bring on your muskets and your flails!

Jabez. We'll drive him out of New Hampshire!

Mary. We'll drive old Scratch away!

(*The* Crowd *rushes in, with muskets, flails, brooms, etc. They pursue* Scratch *around the stage, chanting.*)

The Crowd.

We'll drive him out of New Hampshire!
We'll drive old Scratch away!
Forever and a day, boys,
Forever and a day!

(*They finally catch* Scratch *between two of them and fling him out of the door, bodily.*)

A Man. Three cheers for Dan'l Webster!

Another Man. Three cheers for Daniel Webster! He's licked the devil!

Webster (*moving to center stage, and joining* Jabez' *hands and* Mary's). And whom God hath joined let no man put asunder. (*He kisses* Mary *and turns, dusting his hands.*) Well, that job's done. I hope there's pie for breakfast, neighbor Stone.

(*And, as some of the women, dancing, bring in pies from the kitchen*)

THE CURTAIN FALLS

---

24. **covenant:** to promise by signing a formal contract.
25. **shivaree** (shĭv′ə-rē′): a noisy mock serenade or celebration for a newly married couple.

Connect to the Literature

1. What Do You Think?
What is your impression of Daniel Webster after finishing the play?

Comprehension Check
- For what did Jabez Stone sell his soul?
- Why does Mr. Scratch come to Jabez Stone's wedding celebration?
- How was the trial rigged against Jabez Stone?

Think Critically

2. If you were sitting on the jury, would Webster's speech persuade you to free Jabez Stone? Explain why or why not.

3. Review the diagram you created in the Connect to Your Life activity on page 412. How well does Daniel Webster fit your idea of a good lawyer? Consider evidence from the **dialogue** and the **stage directions** as you explain your answer.

4. In defending Jabez Stone, Webster fought a number of obstacles. How would you rank these obstacles in order of difficulty?

> **THINK ABOUT**
> - the evidence against Jabez Stone
> - the makeup of the jury
> - the judge's handling of the trial

5. **ACTIVE READING** **VISUALIZING WITH STAGE DIRECTIONS**
Review the sketches of scenes that you recorded in your **READER'S NOTEBOOK**. Compare the way you visualized the wedding dance with the way you visualized the trial. What details in the **stage directions** influenced your visualization of each scene?

6. What do you think Stephen Vincent Benét wanted the audience to think about after they had seen this play? Consider the evidence.

> **THINK ABOUT**
> - the main points in Webster's final speech to the jury
> - the reason the jury gives Stone his freedom
> - the connection drawn between the nation's history and the life of an individual

Extend Interpretations

7. Connect to Life In this play, a lawyer wins freedom for a client who has admitted his guilt. Do you think this is an ethical action? Why or why not? Discuss your opinion with your classmates.

Literary Analysis

HISTORICAL DRAMA A play set in the past is a **historical drama.** In drama, **plot** and **character** are developed through **dialogue** and action. Dialogue, which is written conversation between characters, is the most common way for a writer to reveal character in drama. For example, Webster's line "But don't cheer me—I'm not running for President this summer" shows him to be a politician.

Writers of drama also develop plot and character through **stage directions**—notes included in the script to help performers put on the play or to provide information to the reader. For example, one set of stage directions in this play reveals that Scratch has taken Miser Stevens prisoner. Stage directions can describe sets, costumes, lighting, sound effects, the movement of actors onstage, or the way dialogue should be spoken.

Activity Make a chart like the one below. Use it to record the major points you learned from the dialogue and the stage directions.

	Through dialogue	Through stage directions
What I learned about Stone's character		
What I learned about Webster's character		
What I learned about plot events		

Choices & CHALLENGES

Writing Options

Winning Argument Imagine that you are the lawyer for a modern-day Jabez Stone. Using Webster's final speech as a model, write a summation, which is a concluding argument in a trial, to gain your client's freedom. Include your thoughts on what makes freedom precious to people today. Place the summation in your **Working Portfolio.**

Writing Handbook
See pages 1159–1160: Persuasive Writing.

Activities & Explorations

1. Set Design How would you want the sets to look if you were working on a production of this play? Use details from the stage direction to sketch the set design or to construct a three-dimensional model of the sets. ~ **ART**

2. Advertising Campaign Create a poster advertising a performance of *The Devil and Daniel Webster.* The poster should show the time and place and list main cast members. Cast the play with TV or movie actors of your own choice and make up brief quotations praising the play. ~ **ART**

3. Film Review View a clip from the film version of *The Devil and Daniel Webster.* Then, with classmates, discuss whether the film portrays characters in the same way you visualized them. ~ **VIEWING AND REPRESENTING**

VIDEO Literature in Performance

Inquiry & Research

Rogue's Gallery Using encyclopedias and history books, research one of the notorious figures mentioned in this play, such as Judge Hathorne, Simon Girty, Walter Butler, or Blackbeard the pirate. Then prepare a monologue—a speech in which a character utters thoughts aloud. In the monologue the character should tell something about his or her wicked deeds. Present the monologue to your classmates.

Art Connection

A Strong Presence Lawyers often try to influence juries by appearing to be knowledgeable, powerful, or trustworthy. What do you think a jury would conclude about Webster's character from his appearance, as shown in his portrait by Francis Alexander found on page 426?

Vocabulary in Action

EXERCISE A: CONTEXT CLUES Write the vocabulary word that best completes each sentence below.

1. The defendant pretended to know nothing about the crime, but the jury suspected that his ignorance was _____.

2. The prosecutor made no comment, but she looked _____ at the defendant, suggesting that she knew the man was not telling the truth.

3. The next witness, knowing there was really nothing to worry about, responded _____ to the questions.

4. When the verdict was read, various outcries of disgust, amazement, or relief filled the courtroom with a noisy and _____ clamor.

5. Meanwhile the defendant, furious at the verdict, glared _____ at the jury.

EXERCISE B: WORD MEANING Work in a small group to make up a brief story containing these vocabulary words: *homage, fanaticism, intimidation, oppressor,* and *bias.* The first student should begin by saying a sentence that contains one of the words, the next student should continue the story using another word, and so on. The last student must create an ending for the story as well as use the last vocabulary word.

Building Vocabulary
Several Words to Know in this lesson contain prefixes and suffixes. For an in-depth study of word parts, see page 473.

WORDS TO KNOW				
bias	discordant	feigned	insinuatingly	oppressor
contemptuously	fanaticism	homage	intimidation	placidly

Choices & CHALLENGES

Grammar in Context: Using Contractions

In *The Devil and Daniel Webster,* Benét sometimes uses contractions and sometimes doesn't. How do contractions affect the tone of his writing?

> **The Crowd:** He's sold his soul to the devil! There's no help left for him, neighbors! Run, hide, hurry, before we're caught! He's a lost soul. . . .
>
> **Webster:** . . . It is not for him that I speak. It is for all of you.
> There is sadness in being a man, but it is a proud thing, too.

A **contraction** is formed when two words (often a verb and a pronoun) are joined together, with some letters being replaced by an apostrophe. Writers use contractions when they want to create an informal tone. In the examples above, notice how Benét uses contractions in the frightened speech of the common people but not in Webster's more formal speech. In your writing, you may find that using contractions is helpful when you are creating dialogue.

Usage Tip: Contractions that end in *'d* are considered by some to be more informal than other contractions.

WRITING EXERCISE Rewrite these sentences, replacing contractions with the words from which they were formed.

Example: *Original* If you folks don't have a good time, we won't feel right about getting married.
Rewritten If you folks <u>do not</u> have a good time, we <u>will not</u> feel right about getting married.

1. It doesn't matter what you've decided.
2. Don't you see there's nothing we can do?
3. Maybe you've forgotten the promises we made to each other, but I haven't.
4. There isn't a lawyer in the world who'd dare challenge the devil.

Grammar Handbook Punctuation, p. 1202

Stephen Vincent Benét
1898–1943

Other Works
Johnny Pye and the Fool-Killer
Tales Before Midnight
The Last Circle: Stories and Poems

Rewriting History Combine a poet, historian, short story writer, and patriot, and you have Stephen Vincent Benét. In poetry, fiction, and plays, Benét portrayed some of the most interesting characters and events from the American past. The result is a body of literature that brings history to life.

A Family of Writers The son of an army officer, Benét traveled around the country as his father was transferred from one post to another. His parents encouraged the study of literature and history, and all three of their children became writers. As a 17-year-old student, Benét published his first book of poems. By the time he graduated from Yale University, he had published short stories and several volumes of poetry.

Popular Appeal Benét's poems and stories gained a wide audience. "The Devil and Daniel Webster" began as a short story and was made into an opera, a play, and a film. Benét won Pulitzer prizes for *John Brown's Body,* a long poem about the Civil War, and *Western Star,* a poem about the early colonies. During World War II, Benét wrote for radio and film, and helped to rally the patriotic feelings of Americans. He was only 44 when he died suddenly of heart disease at his home in New York City.

Author Activity

Story v. Play Find a copy of the short story, also by Benét, on which this play is based. Read it to see how it differs from the dramatic version. Then discuss those differences with a classmate.

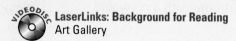

LaserLinks: Background for Reading
Art Gallery

I Have a Dream

Speech by
MARTIN LUTHER KING, JR.

Glory and Hope

Speech by
NELSON MANDELA

"Now is the time to make justice a reality for all of God's children."

> ### Connect to Your Life
>
> **Justice for All** Think about what the word *justice* means. With a partner, consider what justice might mean to a person who is on trial. To a woman who cannot earn enough money to feed her children. To a man who has been denied the right to vote. What does justice mean in your life? After discussing these things, work with your partner to write a definition of justice.

Build Background

Calls for Justice A century after the Emancipation Proclamation had freed enslaved workers in the South, African Americans were still fighting for equality. Many were denied the right to vote, and all faced discrimination and segregation. In August 1963, thousands of Americans marched on Washington, D.C., to urge Congress to pass a bill to counteract those wrongs. Martin Luther King, Jr., delivered his "I Have a Dream" speech to 200,000 of those marchers.

At the same time, in South Africa, Nelson Mandela had been imprisoned because of his fight for racial justice. South Africans lived under a system called apartheid, which means "separateness." Blacks, coloreds (mixed race), and Asians were forced to live apart from whites, mostly in poverty, and suffer discriminatory laws and government oppression. South Africans and others protested until the government finally ended apartheid. In 1994, South Africa held its first election in which all races could vote, and Mandela became president.

WORDS TO KNOW
Vocabulary Preview

amnesty	intimately	pernicious
default	legitimate	reconciliation
discord	mobility	sustain
inextricably		

Focus Your Reading

LITERARY ANALYSIS **SPEECH** A **speech** is the oral presentation of the ideas, beliefs, and proposals of a speaker. For example, Mandela expresses a deep emotional connection with his country when he says in his speech:

> *Each time one of us touches the soil of this land, we feel a sense of personal renewal.*

Speeches are usually prepared in a written form and are sometimes published. As a result, many memorable speeches have become an important part of our literature. As you read the following speeches, try to determine what has made them memorable.

ACTIVE READING **ANALYZING TEXT STRUCTURE** Good readers analyze **text structure** when they evaluate a selection based on the way it is put together. Structure includes the following elements:

- the **order** of the ideas in the text
- **supporting elements,** such as examples or repeated phrases, that draw attention to the main ideas
- **transitions**—the way ideas connect to or build on each other.

Analyze the text of each of the following speeches.

READER'S NOTEBOOK Record elements of text structure as you read. Copy a chart like the one shown for each of the following speeches. Add boxes for additional main ideas.

King's Speech		
First Idea: A century after the Emancipation Proclamation, "the Negro still is not free."	**Supporting Elements:** examples of segregation, discrimination, and poverty	**Transition:** "So we've come here today to dramatize a shameful condition."

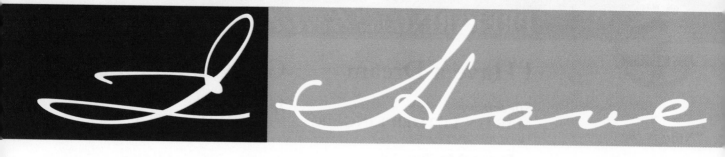

I am happy to join with you today in what will go down in history as the greatest demonstration for freedom in the history of our nation.

Five score[1] years ago, a great American, in whose symbolic shadow we stand today, signed the Emancipation Proclamation.[2] This momentous decree came as a great beacon light of hope to millions of Negro slaves who had been seared in the flames of withering injustice. It came as a joyous daybreak to end the long night of their captivity.

But one hundred years later, the Negro still is not free; one hundred years later, the life of the Negro is still sadly crippled by the manacles of segregation and the chains of discrimination; one hundred years later, the Negro lives on a lonely island of poverty in the midst of a vast ocean of material prosperity; one hundred years later, the Negro is still languishing in the corners of American society and finds himself in exile in his own land.

So we've come here today to dramatize a shameful condition. In a sense we've come to our nation's capital to cash a check. When the architects of our republic wrote the magnificent words of the Constitution and the Declaration of Independence, they were signing a promissory note[3] to which every American was to fall heir. This note was the promise that all men, yes, black men as well as white men, would be guaranteed the unalienable rights of life, liberty, and the pursuit of happiness.

It is obvious today that America has defaulted on this promissory note insofar as her citizens of color are concerned. Instead of honoring this sacred obligation, America has given the Negro people a bad check, a check which has come back marked "insufficient funds." But we refuse to believe that the bank of justice is bankrupt. We refuse to believe that there are insufficient funds in the great vaults of opportunity of this nation. And so we've come to cash this check, a check that will give us upon demand the riches of freedom and the security of justice.

We have also come to this hallowed spot to remind America of the fierce urgency of now. This is no time to engage in the luxury of cooling off or to take the tranquilizing drug of gradualism.[4] Now is the time to make real the promises of democracy; now is the time to rise from the dark and desolate valley of segregation to the sunlit

---

1. **five score:** 100. (The phrasing recalls the beginning of Abraham Lincoln's Gettysburg Address: "Four score and seven years ago . . .")
2. **Emancipation Proclamation** (ĭ-măn′sə-pā′shən prŏk′lə-mā′shən): a document issued by President Abraham Lincoln during the Civil War, declaring that all slaves in states still at war with the Union were free.
3. **promissory** (prŏm′ĭ-sôr′ē) **note:** a written promise to repay a loan.
4. **gradualism:** a policy of seeking to reach a goal slowly, in gradual stages.

WORDS TO KNOW

default (dĭ-fôlt′) *v.* to fail to keep a promise, especially a promise to repay a loan

a Dream

Dr. Martin Luther King, Jr.

path of racial justice; now is the time to lift our nation from the quicksands of racial injustice to the solid rock of brotherhood; now is the time to make justice a reality for all of God's children. It would be fatal for the nation to overlook the urgency of the moment. This sweltering summer of the Negro's <u>legitimate</u> discontent will not pass until there is an invigorating autumn of freedom and equality.

Nineteen sixty-three is not an end, but a beginning. And those who hope that the Negro needed to blow off steam and will now be content will have a rude awakening if the nation returns to business as usual. There will be neither rest nor tranquility in America until the Negro is granted his citizenship rights. The whirlwinds of revolt will continue to shake the foundations of our nation until the bright day of justice emerges.

But there is something that I must say to my people, who stand on the worn threshold which leads into the palace of justice. In the process of gaining our rightful place, we must not be guilty of wrongful deeds. Let us not seek to satisfy our thirst for freedom by drinking from the cup of bitterness and hatred. We must forever conduct our struggle on the high plain of dignity and discipline. We must not allow our creative

protests to degenerate[5] into physical violence. Again and again we must rise to the majestic heights of meeting physical force with soul force. The marvelous new militancy,[6] which has engulfed the Negro community, must not lead us to a distrust of all white people. For many of our white brothers, as evidenced by their presence here today, have come to realize that their destiny is tied up with our destiny. And they have come to realize that their freedom is <u>inextricably</u> bound to our freedom. We cannot walk alone. And as we walk, we must make the pledge that we shall always march ahead. We cannot turn back.

There are those who are asking the devotees[7] of civil rights, "When will you be satisfied?" We can never be satisfied as long as the Negro is the victim of the unspeakable horrors of police brutality; we can never be satisfied as long as our bodies, heavy with the fatigue of travel, cannot gain lodging in the motels of the highways and the hotels of the cities; we cannot be satisfied as

---

5. **degenerate** (dĭ-jĕn′ə-rāt′): descend; decline.

6. **militancy:** aggressiveness in pursuing a goal.

7. **devotees:** people devoted to something.

National Museum of American History, Smithsonian Institution, Washington, D.C.

MARCH ON WASHINGTON FOR JOBS & FREEDOM AUGUST 28, 1963 AFL-CIO LOCAL 66 UNION MADE

long as the Negro's basic <u>mobility</u> is from a smaller ghetto to a larger one; we can never be satisfied as long as our children are stripped of their selfhood and robbed of their dignity by signs stating For Whites Only; we cannot be satisfied as long as the Negro in Mississippi cannot vote and a Negro in New York believes he has nothing for which to vote. No! No, we are not satisfied, and we will not be satisfied until "justice rolls down like waters and righteousness like a mighty stream."

I am not unmindful that some of you have come here out of great trials and tribulations. Some of you have come fresh from narrow jail cells. Some of you have come from areas where your quest for freedom left you battered by the storms of persecution and staggered by the winds of police brutality. You have been the veterans of creative suffering. Continue to work with the faith that unearned suffering is redemptive.[8] Go back to Mississippi. Go back to Alabama. Go back to South Carolina. Go back to Georgia. Go back to Louisiana. Go back to the slums and ghettos of our Northern cities, knowing that somehow this situation can

and will be changed. Let us not wallow in the valley of despair.

I say to you today, my friends, even though we face the difficulties of today and tomorrow, I still have a dream. It is a dream deeply rooted in the American dream. I have a dream that one day this nation will rise up and live out the true meaning of its creed, "We hold these truths to be self-evident; that all men are created equal." I have a dream that one day on the red hills of Georgia, sons of former slaves and the sons of former slave owners will be able to sit down together at the table of brotherhood. I have a dream that one day even the state of Mississippi, a state sweltering with the heat of injustice, sweltering with the heat of oppression, will be transformed into an oasis of freedom and justice. I have a dream that my four little children will one day live in a nation where they will not be judged by the color of their skin, but by the content of their character.

I have a dream today!

I have a dream that one day down in

---

8. **is redemptive:** is a way of earning freedom or salvation.

Alabama—with its vicious racists, with its Governor having his lips dripping with the words of interposition and nullification[9]—one day right there in Alabama, little black boys and black girls will be able to join hands with little white boys and white girls as sisters and brothers.

I have a dream today!

I have a dream that one day every valley shall be exalted,[10] and every hill and mountain shall be made low. The rough places will be plain and the crooked places will be made straight, "and the glory of the Lord shall be revealed, and all flesh shall see it together."

This is our hope. This is the faith that I go back to the South with. With this faith we will be able to hew[11] out of the mountain of despair a stone of hope. With this faith we will be able to transform the jangling <u>discords</u> of our nation into a beautiful symphony of brotherhood. With this faith we will be able to work together, to pray together, to struggle together, to go to jail together, to stand up for freedom together, knowing that we will be free one day. And this will be the day. This will be the day when all of God's children will be able to sing with new meaning, "My country 'tis of thee, sweet land of liberty, of thee I sing. Land where my fathers died, land of the pilgrims' pride, from every mountainside, let freedom ring." And if America is to be a great nation, this must become true.

So let freedom ring from the prodigious[12]

hilltops of New Hampshire; let freedom ring from the mighty mountains of New York; let freedom ring from the heightening Alleghenies of Pennsylvania; let freedom ring from the snowcapped Rockies of Colorado; let freedom ring from the curvaceous slopes of California. But not only that. Let freedom ring from Stone Mountain of Georgia; let freedom ring from Lookout Mountain of Tennessee; let freedom ring from every hill and molehill of Mississippi. "From every mountainside, let freedom ring."

And when this happens, and when we allow freedom to ring, when we let it ring from every village and every hamlet, from every state and every city, we will be able to speed up that day when all of God's children—black men and white men, Jews and Gentiles, Protestants and Catholics—will be able to join hands and sing in the words of the old Negro spiritual, "Free at last. Free at last. Thank God Almighty, we are free at last." ❖

---

9. **Governor . . . interposition** (ĭn′tər-pə-zĭsh′ən) **and nullification:** When ordered by the federal government to allow the integration of the University of Alabama, Governor George Wallace claimed that the principle of nullification (a state's alleged right to refuse to accept a federal law) allowed him to resist the federal government's "interposition," or interference in state affairs.

10. **exalted:** raised up.

11. **hew:** hack.

12. **prodigious** (prə-dĭj′əs): magnificent.

Thinking Through the Literature

1. What words or phrases from King's speech stand out in your mind?

2. Do you think that King's dream at the end of this speech offers a solution for the problems outlined at the beginning of the speech? Explain why or why not.

3. Why do you think King quotes from the Declaration of Independence and the patriotic song "My Country 'Tis of Thee" in his speech?

WORDS TO KNOW

discord (dĭs′kôrd′) *n.* a harsh mixture of sounds; conflict

Glory & Hope

BY NELSON MANDELA

Your majesties, your royal highnesses, distinguished guests, comrades and friends: Today, all of us do, by our presence here, and by our celebrations in other parts of our country and the world, confer glory and hope to newborn liberty.

Out of the experience of an extraordinary human disaster[1] that lasted too long must be born a society of which all humanity will be proud.

Our daily deeds as ordinary South Africans must produce an actual South African reality that will reinforce humanity's belief in justice, strengthen its confidence in the nobility of the human soul and sustain all our hopes for a glorious life for all.

All this we owe both to ourselves and to the peoples of the world who are so well represented here today.

To my compatriots, I have no hesitation in saying that each one of us is as intimately attached to the soil of this beautiful country as are the famous jacaranda trees of Pretoria[2] and the mimosa trees of the bushveld.[3]

Each time one of us touches the soil of this land, we feel a sense of personal renewal. The national mood changes as the seasons change.

We are moved by a sense of joy and exhilaration when the grass turns green and the flowers bloom.

That spiritual and physical oneness we all share with this common homeland explains the depth of the pain we all carried in our hearts as we saw our country tear itself apart in terrible conflict, and as we saw it spurned, outlawed and isolated by the peoples of the world, precisely because it has become the universal base of the pernicious ideology and practice of racism and racial oppression.

We, the people of South Africa, feel fulfilled that humanity has taken us back into its bosom, that we, who were outlaws not so long ago, have today been given the rare privilege to be host to the nations of the world on our own soil.

We thank all our distinguished international guests for having come to take possession with the people of our country of what is, after all, a common victory for justice, for peace, for human dignity.

---

1. **an extraordinary human disaster:** apartheid—the official policy of racial segregation formerly practiced in South Africa.
2. **Pretoria:** the capital of South Africa.
3. **bushveld:** a region of grassland in northern South Africa.

WORDS TO KNOW
sustain (sə-stān') *v.* to keep alive; support
intimately (ĭn'tə-mĭt-lē) *adv.* closely
pernicious (pər-nĭsh'əs) *adj.* deadly; harmful

We trust that you will continue to stand by us as we tackle the challenges of building peace, prosperity, nonsexism, nonracialism and democracy.

We deeply appreciate the role that the masses of our people and their democratic, religious, women, youth, business, traditional and other leaders have played to bring about this conclusion. Not least among them is my Second Deputy President, the Honorable F. W. de Klerk.[4]

We would also like to pay tribute to our security forces, in all their ranks, for the distinguished role they have played in securing our first democratic elections and the transition to democracy, from bloodthirsty forces which still refuse to see the light.

The time for the healing of the wounds has come.

The moment to bridge the chasms that divide us has come.

The time to build is upon us.

We have, at last, achieved our political emancipation. We pledge ourselves to liberate all our people from the continuing bondage of poverty, deprivation,[5] suffering, gender and other discrimination.

We succeeded to take our last steps to freedom in conditions of relative peace. We commit ourselves to the construction of a complete, just and lasting peace.

We have triumphed in the effort to implant hope in the breasts of the millions of our people. We enter into a covenant[6] that we shall build the society in which all South Africans, both black and white, will be able to walk tall, without any fear in their hearts, assured of their inalienable right to human dignity—a rainbow nation at peace with itself and the world.

As a token of its commitment to the renewal of our country, the new Interim[7] Government of National Unity will, as a matter of urgency, address the issue of amnesty for various categories of our people who are currently serving terms of imprisonment.

We dedicate this day to all the heroes and heroines in this country and the rest of the world who sacrificed in many ways and surrendered their lives so that we could be free.

Their dreams have become reality. Freedom is their reward.

We are both humbled and elevated by the honor and privilege that you, the people of South Africa, have bestowed on us, as the first President of a united, democratic, nonracial and nonsexist South Africa, to lead our country out of the valley of darkness.

We understand it still that there is no easy road to freedom.

We know it well that none of us acting alone can achieve success.

We must therefore act together as a united people, for national reconciliation, for nation building, for the birth of a new world.

Let there be justice for all.

Let there be peace for all.

Let there be work, bread, water and salt for all.

Let each know that for each the body, the mind and the soul have been freed to fulfill themselves.

Never, never and never again shall it be that this beautiful land will again experience the oppression of one by another and suffer the indignity of being the skunk of the world.

The sun shall never set on so glorious a human achievement!

Let freedom reign. God bless Africa! ❖

---

4. **F. W. de Klerk:** the president of South Africa who preceded Mandela, holding office from 1989 to 1994.

5. **deprivation** (dĕp′rə-vā′shən): a lack of the necessities or comforts of life.

6. **covenant** (kŭv′ə-nənt): solemn agreement.

7. **interim:** temporary.

WORDS
TO
KNOW

amnesty (ăm′nĭ-stē) *n.* a general pardon, especially one granted by a government to people who have committed political offenses
reconciliation (rĕk′ən-sĭl′ē-ā′shən) *n.* a return to a state of friendship or harmony

Connect to the Literature

1. What Do You Think? What parts of Mandela's speech do you remember most clearly?

> **Comprehension Check**
> - What goals do King and Mandela share?
> - What examples of racial injustice does King describe?
> - What gives Mandela hope for the future of South Africa?

Think Critically

2. What challenges do you think Mandela expects as the first black president of South Africa? Consider the evidence in Mandela's speech.

THINK ABOUT
> - his references to South Africa's past problems
> - his goals for South Africa's future
> - people or conditions that might prevent him from reaching those goals

3. Review the definition of justice that you wrote with your classmate. What would you add to that definition now that you have read King's and Mandela's speeches?

4. Both King and Mandela use **metaphors**—figures of speech that make comparisons without using the words *like* or *as.* Identify a metaphor from either speech and explain what it adds to the speech's meaning.

5. Do you think King and Mandela were speaking only to the audiences gathered before them? Identify each **author's purpose** for his speech and how that relates to audience.

6. ` ACTIVE READING ` ` ANALYZING TEXT STRUCTURE ` Review the chart you made in your 📖 **READER'S NOTEBOOK** about the **structure** of the two speeches. Compare and contrast the ways that King and Mandela order their ideas, cite supporting examples, and use repeated words and phrases. How did each author use structure to achieve his purpose for his speech?

Extend Interpretations

7. Comparing Texts In your opinion, which is the better speech—"I Have a Dream" or "Glory and Hope"? Discuss similarities and differences in the two speeches as you explain your answer.

8. Connect to Life Do you think Martin Luther King's dream has come true? Why or why not? Share your opinion in class.

Literary Analysis

` SPEECH ` A **speech** is meant to be heard. The oral presentation of a speech allows the listener to hear the speaker's emotions, as well as his or her opinions and proposals. Good speakers must consider the following points when preparing to deliver a speech:

- their **purpose** for giving the speech—for example, to entertain, to inform, or to persuade
- the **main idea** they want to emphasize
- the words and phrases to stress
- the emotions they wish to convey

Paired Activity Working with a partner, imagine that you are either King or Mandela. Go back through your speech, and jot down thoughts about the following: your purpose for the speech, the main idea, words and phrases to emphasize, and the emotions to convey. Then, keeping these components in mind, take turns reading the speech aloud. Be ready to give reasons for your method of delivery.

Title of Speech:
1. Purpose of Speech:
2. Main Idea:
3. Words or Phrases to Emphasize:
4. Emotions to Convey:

Choices & CHALLENGES

Writing Options

"Dream" Speech Think about a social or political issue that is important to you. Write some notes about what you would say in your own "I Have a Dream" speech on this topic. Jot down examples that might persuade others to share your opinion. Place your notes in your **Working Portfolio.**

My own
"I have a dream"
speech

Activities & Explorations

Video Review Watch the video recording of one or both speeches. Then discuss with classmates the following question: What does the speaker's delivery add to the impact of the speech?

~ VIEWING AND REPRESENTING

VIDEO Literature in Performance

Inquiry & Research

Apartheid Means Separateness Nelson Mandela fought against the apartheid that once existed in South Africa. With a group of classmates, use encyclopedias or world history books to learn about apartheid. Find out about specific apartheid regulations and how they affected various groups of South Africans. Also learn about how South Africa has changed since the end of apartheid.

 Real World Link As part of your research, read "The End of Separateness" on page 451.

Vocabulary in Action

EXERCISE: MEANING CLUES On your paper, write the Word to Know that is most clearly related to the situation described in each sentence below. Use each word only once.

1. Because people of different races live and work in the same communities, their lives are woven together in ways that cannot be unraveled without harming society as a whole.

2. Although one woman was African American and the other was white, they knew each other as well as if they had been sisters.

3. The man had been imprisoned for his role in antigovernment demonstrations, but the new president ordered him set free, with all charges dismissed.

4. The severe poverty of the South African townships affected the health and well-being of those forced to live in them under apartheid.

5. The inspiring words of their leaders encouraged civil rights workers to keep their spirits up.

6. Some state governments failed to keep their promise to uphold the law when African-American citizens were denied the right to vote.

7. Over a period of 30 years, my family worked hard to overcome poverty and become part of the middle class.

8. With the end of apartheid came a renewal of good relations between South Africa and nations around the world.

9. During the 1960s, clashing views on civil rights led to angry protests.

10. The changes proposed by the civil rights leader were reasonable, logical, and sound.

Building Vocabulary
For an in-depth lesson on how to build your vocabulary, see page 572.

WORDS TO KNOW	amnesty default	discord inextricably	intimately legitimate	mobility pernicious	reconciliation sustain

Grammar in Context: Verb Tenses

Although Martin Luther King, Jr., refers to the past in his famous address, he focuses primarily on the present and the future.

> **I have a dream that one day this nation will rise up and live out the true meaning of its creed.**

Tenses are verb forms that show time. As long as the actions they describe take place at the same time or nearly the same time, writers usually do not change from one tense to another. They shift tenses only when describing actions that occur at different times. King uses the present tense to talk about his dream for a better world ("I *have* a dream") and the future tense to describe what that world will be like ("this nation *will rise* up and *live* out"). You can switch verb tenses in your own writing to show relationships between ideas and to clarify the sequence of events.

WRITING EXERCISE Rewrite these sentences, correcting incorrect shifts in verb tense. If a sentence needs no correction, write *Correct.*

Example: *Original* As television drew attention to the issue, President Kennedy proposes a civil rights bill.
Rewritten As television drew attention to the issue, President Kennedy <u>proposed</u> a civil rights bill.

1. King and Coretta Scott, whom he had met at Boston University, were married in June 1953.
2. King studied the teachings of Mohandas K. Gandhi and develops a deep understanding of nonviolent civil disobedience.
3. It is in 1964 that *Time* magazine named Martin Luther King, Jr., its "man of the year."
4. Nelson Mandela spent many years in prison before he becomes president of South Africa.

Grammar Handbook Verb Tense, p. 1184

Martin Luther King, Jr.
1929–1968

Other Works
Stride Toward Freedom
Why We Can't Wait
The Trumpet of Conscience

Hero Martin Luther King, Jr., one of the most famous civil rights leaders in American history, championed the rights of African Americans and led nonviolent protests against racial injustice. In 1964, he was awarded the Nobel Prize for peace.

Violent End Although King taught nonviolence, his opponents often responded violently. They pelted him with rocks, they bombed his home, and one woman stabbed him. In 1968, at age 39, King was shot and killed. His tombstone reads: "Free at last, free at last, thank God Almighty, I'm free at last."

Nelson Mandela
1918–

Other Works
No Easy Walk to Freedom
I Am Prepared to Die
Long Walk to Freedom

Life Choices The son of a tribal chief, Nelson Mandela was born in the South African village of Umtata. Mandela gave up the right to become a tribal chief and studied law instead. In 1944, he became a leader in the African National Congress (ANC), a political party that called for racial equality.

Prison In 1964, Mandela, who had advocated acts of sabotage against the government, was sentenced to life in prison, where he became an international symbol of South Africa's struggle against apartheid. After his release, Mandela agreed to work peacefully for racial justice. In 1993, Mandela was awarded the Nobel Peace Prize, and a year later he became president of South Africa.

THE END OF SEPARATENESS

Waiting to vote, we were all—at last—together
by André Brink

*On April 27, 1994, South Africa held its first presidential
election in which black South Africans were allowed to vote.
André Brink, a South African journalist, described this
historic day and its impact on him in the following essay. As
you read, notice details about the writer's personal
background as well as his reactions to the event.*

What perversity drives one to travel 10,000 kilometers to
cast a vote? I was wondering this during the long day of
April 27, as I stood in a queue
in pouring rain, for six hours,
to enter the polling booth. The
ranks of the waiting had been
swollen by busloads of people
from the black township of
Khayelitsha, where no ballot
papers had arrived—part of the
confusion that characterized
South Africa's first democratic
elections. There were, indeed,
moments when the whole
enterprise seemed mad.

Nelson Mandela casts his ballot in
South Africa's first democratic election.

I had been teaching in
France before the elections. It
was perfectly possible to vote
in Paris. But that would not
have been the same. Many
years before, at the end of 1968, I had given up the dream
of settling in France to return to my troubled country in the
belief that I could assume my full responsibility as a writer
only by being on the spot. Other writers in exile were not, at
the time, allowed this choice: the fact that I could choose
made it imperative for me to come back—even if it involved
the absurdity of an escaped prisoner choosing to return to his
prison. This time the choice was of course less dramatic; but
it was still linked to that original decision: to return, to be
here. How could I not be present at the decisive turn from

Reading for Information

André Brink's essay reveals details
about his personal ties to South
Africa as well as his feelings about
the elections. Sometimes the topic
of an article and the author's
feelings and attitude about the
topic are closely related.

AUTHOR'S PERSPECTIVE

The **author's perspective** is the
way an author treats his or her
subject. The perspective can be the
result of a political viewpoint, an
attitude, a belief, or a feeling about
a topic or issue. An author's
perspective is not necessarily good
or bad; rather, it simply reflects the
author's feelings or beliefs.

YOUR TURN Use the questions and
activities below to explore André
Brink's perspective.

① **Identifying the Author's
Perspective** Authors bring their
background and personal
experiences to their writing.
Brink writes, "I had been
teaching in France before the
elections." He goes on to
describe his situation of living in
exile. Find other examples in
this passage that focus on
Brink's past. What details reveal
his feelings about his return?

the nightmare of the past to a future with a range of more human possibilities?

Possibilities; not certainties. One's only certainty lies in knowing that being there is better than being absent. The interaction of innumerable presences is the condition of history. And certainly April 27 was one of those occasions when one is aware of history, not as a great impersonal force sweeping past but as a collective expression of the wills, hopes, urgencies, fears, and wishes of individual women, men, and children.

On the morning of the 27th we woke up to the news of a bomb attack; it was followed by several more. Was this to be the outcome of all the years of waiting and hoping? Then came that six-hour queue in the rain—one of the most moving and exhilarating experiences of my life. There we were, thousands upon thousands of us, representing every race and group and section of South Africa: rich and poor, powerful and socially insignificant, galvanized by the knowledge that each one was of equal importance, every vote of equal weight in deciding our shared future. Everybody was talking to everybody else not about politics, but about our daily lives, our jobs, our friends, our children.

It had all been worthwhile; that much one could read on the beaming faces of the people emerging from the hall after they had cast their votes—exhausted, aching in every limb, but ecstatic that at last their human worth had been recognized. We were there, said the faces, and our being there together has made a difference. For six hours whole lifetimes of separateness had been suspended. We had discovered, in the simplest and most basic way imaginable, and in the smallest of everyday actions—a shared umbrella, a mug of coffee passed from hand to hand, communal laughter, hands touching in the throng—the grounds of our common South Africanness and our common humanity. That brief experience has marked us for life. In achieving, for a few hours, what had seemed for so long impossible, we had caught a glimpse of the possible.

❷ Author's perspective includes an author's **tone,** the attitude he or she has toward the subject. In this section of the essay, Brink describes the big event—election day. What words does he use to describe what it was like to wait in the *queue,* or line? How would you describe his tone in this passage?

❸ Brink describes what "being there together" meant to the South Africans. How does this passage add to your understanding of the author's perspective in this article? In your opinion, could Brink have written about this event as powerfully if he had not been South African?

Inquiry & Research

Activity Link: "Glory and Hope," p. 449 Organize the material you found on apartheid after reading "Glory and Hope." In a group, share your findings and discuss South Africa after the election in 1994.

The United States vs. Susan B. Anthony

Biography by MARGARET TRUMAN

"My natural rights, my civil rights, my political rights, are all alike ignored."

Connect to Your Life

Cast Your Ballot In a few years, you will be old enough to vote in city, state, and national elections. But what if you, as an adult citizen, were not allowed to vote simply because of your sex or your race? Think about the right to vote. Name three reasons why a citizen's right to vote is important. Share your reasons with a classmate.

Build Background

Born in the USA In most areas of the early United States, only white males were considered citizens with suffrage—the right to vote. In 1868, as a way to protect formerly enslaved African Americans, the 14th Amendment to the Constitution was ratified. It made "all persons" born in the United States citizens with full citizenship "privileges." Although the amendment did not mention gender, its authors intended it to apply only to males. A woman named Susan B. Anthony, a reformer who fought for women's rights, had other ideas. This **biography** describes how in 1873 she tried to force the courts to recognize that the 14th Amendment granted women the right to vote.

WORDS TO KNOW
Vocabulary Preview

adamant	fortitude
blatant	inadvertently
competent	oratory
concur	retrospect
denunciation	tirade

LaserLinks: Background for Reading
Historical Connection

Focus Your Reading

LITERARY ANALYSIS **BIOGRAPHY** A **biography** is an account of a person's life, written by someone else. Biographies present many facts about their subjects. In this selection, the following sentence gives basic information about Susan B. Anthony.

> *She joined the woman's suffrage movement in 1852, when she was thirty-two years old.*

As you read this biography, look for other factual details.

ACTIVE READING **SPECIALIZED VOCABULARY** Many professions use **specialized vocabulary,** or terms that have specific meaning for the people in that profession. This **biography** contains many legal terms that may be unfamiliar to you. The chart below defines two of the most important ones. Other specialized terms are defined in footnotes.

READER'S NOTEBOOK Copy the chart into your notebook. As you read this biography, add to the chart the legal terms and definitions that you find in the footnotes. Especially note terms that relate to citizens' rights.

Legal Term	Definition
draw up a *bill of indictment* (ĭn-dīt'mənt)	write a description of the crime a person is accused of committing
convene a *grand jury*	gather a private session of 12 to 23 people who decide if there is enough evidence to issue an indictment, or formally charge a person with a crime

THE UNITED STATES

vs.

SUSAN B. ANTHONY

Margaret

Truman

Susan B. Anthony (*right*), her sister Mary (*center*), and her friend Elizabeth Miller (*left*)

Susan B. Anthony has never been one of my favorite characters. Stern-eyed and grim-lipped, she seemed utterly devoid of warmth and humor and much too quick to dominate the women she worked with. I always thought her personality could be summed up in one word: battle-ax.[1] On top of that drawback, she was a fanatic. She joined the woman's suffrage movement in 1852, when she was thirty-two years old. From then until her death in 1906, she could think of little else.

The fanatics of one generation have a habit of turning into the heroes and heroines of the next, as Susan B. Anthony proved. And since I've been making a study of heroines, I decided to give

Miss Anthony a second look. I have to report that my original assessment of her character was much too harsh. . . .

Susan B. Anthony was a stern and single-minded woman. Like most crusaders for causes—especially unpopular causes—she had little time for fun and games. But I have a sneaky feeling that behind her severe manner and unremitting devotion to duty, she may actually have had a sense of humor. Let me tell you about my favorite episode in Susan B. Anthony's career, and perhaps you'll agree.

---

1. **battle-ax:** derogatory slang for a woman who is harsh and domineering.

It began on Friday morning, November 1, 1872. Susan was reading the morning paper at her home in Rochester. There, at the top of the editorial page of the *Democrat and Chronicle,* was an exhortation[2] to the city's residents:

Now register! Today and tomorrow are the only remaining opportunities. If you were not permitted to vote, you would fight for the right, undergo all privations[3] for it, face death for it. You have it now at the cost of five minutes' time to be spent in seeking your place of registration and having your name entered. And yet, on election day, less than a week hence, hundreds of you are likely to lose your votes because you have not thought it worth while to give the five minutes. Today and tomorrow are your only opportunities. Register now!

Susan B. Anthony read the editorial again. Just as she thought, it said nothing about being addressed to men only. With a gleam in her eye, she put down the paper and summoned her sister Guelma, with whom she lived. The two women donned their hats and cloaks and went off to call on two other Anthony sisters who lived nearby. Together, the four women headed for the barbershop on West Street, where voters from the Eighth Ward were being registered.

For some time, Susan B. Anthony had been looking for an opportunity to test the Fourteenth Amendment to the Constitution as a weapon to win the vote for women. Adopted in 1870,[4] the amendment had been designed to protect the civil rights—especially the voting rights—of recently freed slaves. It stated that:

All persons born or naturalized in the United States, and subject to the jurisdiction thereof, are citizens of the United States and of the state wherein they reside. No state shall make or enforce any law which shall abridge[5] the privileges or immunities of citizens of the United States, nor shall any state deprive any person of life, liberty, or property without due process of law, nor deny to any person within its jurisdiction the equal protection of the laws.

The amendment did not say that "persons" meant only males, nor did it spell out "the privileges or immunities of citizens." Susan B. Anthony felt perfectly justified in concluding that the right to vote was among the privileges of citizenship and that it extended to women as well as men. I'm sure she must have also seen the humor of outwitting the supposedly superior males who wrote the amendment.

It was bad enough for a bunch of women to barge into one sacred male precinct[6]—the barbershop—but to insist on being admitted to another holy of holies—the voting booth—was absolutely outrageous. Moustaches twitched; throats were cleared; a whispered conference was held in the corner.

Susan had brought along a copy of the Fourteenth Amendment. She read it aloud, carefully pointing out to the men in charge of registration that the document failed to state that the privilege of voting extended only to males.

Only one man in the barbershop had the nerve to refuse the Anthony sisters the right to register. The rest buckled under Susan's determined <u>oratory</u> and allowed them to sign

---

2. **exhortation** (ĕg′zôr-tā′shən): an urgent call to action.

3. **privations** (prī-vā′shənz): shortages of the basic necessities or comforts of life.

4. **1870:** This date is incorrect. The 14th Amendment was passed in 1868.

5. **abridge:** to cut short.

6. **precinct** (prē′sĭngkt′): a place marked off by definite limits, such as walls.

the huge, leather-bound voter registration book. If the men in the barbershop thought they were getting rid of a little band of crackpots the easy way, they were wrong. Susan urged all her followers in Rochester to register. The next day, a dozen women invaded the Eighth Ward barbershop, and another thirty-five appeared at registration sites elsewhere in the city. The *Democrat and Chronicle,* which had <u>inadvertently</u> prompted the registrations, expressed no editorial opinion on the phenomenon, but its rival, the *Union and Advertiser,* denounced the women. If they were allowed to vote, the paper declared, the poll inspectors[7] "should be prosecuted to the full extent of the law."

The following Tuesday, November 5, was Election Day. Most of the poll inspectors in Rochester had read the editorial in the *Union and Advertiser* and were too intimidated to allow any of the women who had registered to vote. Only in the Eighth Ward did the males weaken. Maybe the inspectors were *Democrat and Chronicle* readers, or perhaps they were more afraid of Susan B. Anthony than they were of the law. Whatever the reason, when Susan and her sisters showed up at the polls shortly after 7 A.M., there was only a minimum of fuss. A couple of inspectors were hesitant about letting the women vote, but when Susan assured them that she would pay all their legal expenses if they were prosecuted, the men relented, and one by one, the women took their ballots and stepped into the voting booth. There were no insults or sneers, no rude remarks. They marked their ballots, dropped them into the ballot box, and returned to their homes.

Susan B. Anthony's feat quickly became the talk of the country. She was applauded in some circles, vilified[8] in others. But the day of reckoning was not long in arriving. On November 28, Deputy U.S. Marshal E. J.

Keeney appeared at her door with a warrant[9] for her arrest. She had violated Section 19 of the Enforcement Act of the Fourteenth Amendment, which held that anyone who voted illegally was to be arrested and tried on criminal charges.

Susan B. Anthony was a great believer in planning ahead. The day after she registered, she decided to get a legal opinion on whether or not she should attempt to vote. A number of lawyers turned her away, but she finally found one who agreed to consider the case. He was Henry R. Selden, a former judge of the court of appeals, now a partner in one of Rochester's most prestigious law firms.

On the Monday before Election Day, Henry Selden informed his new client that he agreed with her interpretation of the Fourteenth Amendment and that in his opinion, she had every right to cast her ballot. The U.S. commissioner of elections in Rochester, William C. Storrs, did not <u>concur</u>.

E. J. Keeney, the marshal dispatched to arrest Susan B. Anthony, was not at all happy with his assignment. He nervously twirled his tall felt hat while waiting for her to come to the front door. When she finally appeared, he blushed and stammered, shifted uncomfortably from one foot to the other, and finally blurted out, "The commissioner wishes to arrest you."

---

7. **poll inspectors:** officials who make sure that votes are cast according to the law.
8. **vilified:** spoken of viciously
9. **warrant:** a legal document authorizing an officer to make an arrest, a search, or a seizure.

New York suffragists advertise a meeting at which governors of states with woman suffrage were scheduled to speak. The Bettmann Archive.

COME LE COME HI
TRU 5 GOVER

WORDS TO KNOW	**inadvertently** (ĭn′əd-vûr′tnt-lē) *adv.* without intending to; not on purpose **concur** (kən-kûr′) *v.* to agree

usan couldn't help being amused at Keeney's embarrassment. "Is this your usual method of serving a warrant?" she asked calmly. With that, the marshal recovered his official dignity, presented her with the warrant, and told her that he had come to escort her to the office of the commissioner of elections.

When Susan asked if she could change into a more suitable dress, the marshal saw his opportunity to escape. "Of course," he said, turning to leave. "Just come down to the commissioner's office whenever you're ready."

"I'll do no such thing," Susan informed him curtly. "You were sent here to arrest me and take me to court. It's your duty to do so."

Keeney had no choice but to wait while his prisoner went upstairs and put on a more appropriate outfit. When she returned, she thrust out her wrists and said, "Don't you want to handcuff me, too?"

"I assure you, madam," Marshal Keeney stuttered, "it isn't at all necessary."

With the U.S. marshal at her side, Susan was brought before the federal commissioner of elections, William C. Storrs. Her arrest was recorded, and she was ordered to appear the next day for a hearing. It was conducted by U.S. District Attorney Richard Crowley and his assistant, John E. Pound.

Susan answered District Attorney Crowley's questions politely. She said that she thought the Fourteenth Amendment gave her the right to vote. She admitted that she had consulted an attorney on the question but said that she would have voted even if he had not advised her to do so. When Crowley asked if she had voted deliberately to test the law, she said, "Yes, sir. I have been determined for three years to vote the first time I happened to be at home for the required thirty days before an election."

The district attorney's next step was to convene a grand jury to draw up a bill of indictment. He and his assistant fell to wrangling over a suitable trial date. Susan interrupted them. "I have lecture dates that will take me to central Ohio," she said. "I won't be available until December 10."

"But you're supposed to be in custody[10] until the hearing," Crowley informed her.

"Is that so?" said Susan coolly. "I didn't know that."

---

10. **in custody:** held under guard.

The district attorney backed down without an argument and scheduled the grand jury session for December 23.

Sixteen women had voted in Rochester. All sixteen were arrested and taken before the grand jury, but Susan alone was brought to trial. The district attorney had decided to single her out as a test case.[11] The three poll inspectors who had allowed the women to vote were also arrested. The grand jury indicted them too, set bail[12] at five hundred dollars each, and ordered their trial set for the summer term of the U.S. district court.

Susan Anthony's case now involved nineteen other men and women. All of them—including Susan—were liable to go to prison if they were found guilty and the judge was in a sentencing mood. Prison in the 1870s was a very unpleasant place. There were no minimum security setups where a benevolent government allowed corrupt politicians, crooked labor leaders, and political agitators to rest and rehabilitate, as we do today. Prison meant a cold cell, wretched food, the company of thieves and murderers.

For a while it looked as if Susan might be behind bars even before the trial. She refused to post a bond[13] for her five-hundred-dollar bail. Henry Selden paid the money for her. "I could not see a lady I respected put in jail," he said.

It must be agonizing to sweat out the weeks before a trial. There is time to look ahead and brood about the possibility of an unfavorable verdict and time to look back, perhaps with regret, at the decision that placed you in the hands of the law. But Susan B. Anthony had no regrets. Nor did she appear to have any anxieties about her trial. She had already proven her fortitude by devoting twenty years of her life to fighting for the right to vote. If she won her case, the struggle would be over. But even if she lost, Susan was not ready to give up the fight. . . .

The trial of *The United States* vs. *Susan B. Anthony* opened on the afternoon of June 17, 1873, with the tolling of the Canandaigua Courthouse bell. The presiding justice was Ward Hunt, a prim, pale man, who owed his judgeship to the good offices of Senator Roscoe Conkling, the Republican boss of New York State. Conkling was a fierce foe of woman suffrage, and Hunt, who had no wish to offend his powerful patron, had written his decision before the trial started.

District Attorney Crowley opened the arguments for the prosecution.[14] They didn't make much sense at the time, and in retrospect, they sound nothing short of ridiculous. The district attorney mentioned that Susan B. Anthony was a woman and therefore she had no right to vote. His principal witness was an inspector of elections for the Eighth Ward, who swore that on November 5 he had seen Miss Anthony put her ballot in the ballot box. To back up his testimony, the inspector produced the voter registration book with Susan B. Anthony's signature in it.

Henry Selden's reply for the defense was equally simple. He contended that Susan Anthony had registered and voted in good faith, believing that it was her constitutional right to do so. When he attempted to call his client to the stand, however, District Attorney Crowley announced that she was not competent to testify in her own behalf. Judge Hunt agreed, and the only thing Henry Selden could do was read excerpts from the testimony Susan had given at her previous hearings when presumably she was

---

11. **test case:** a legal action chosen specifically for the example or standard that its outcome may establish.

12. **bail:** a sum of money for which a court agrees to release an arrested person. It serves as a guarantee that the person will appear for trial.

13. **bond:** money paid as bail.

14. **prosecution:** in a court case, the lawyers who represent the government.

WORDS
TO
KNOW

fortitude (fôr′tĭ-tōōd′) *n.* the strength of mind required to withstand hardship
retrospect (rĕt′rə-spĕkt′) *n.* a review of things in the past
competent (kŏm′pĭ-tənt) *adj.* in law, mentally fit to participate

Susan B. Anthony in front of her Rochester home, now a national historical monument.
Reproduced from the Collections of the Library of Congress.

The Susan B. Anthony dollar, the first U.S. coin in general circulation to honor a famous American woman

no less incompetent than she was right now.

Henry Selden tried to make up for this gross injustice by making his closing argument a dramatic, three-hour speech on behalf of woman suffrage. District Attorney Crowley replied with a two-hour rehash of the original charge.

By the afternoon of June 18, the case of *The United States* vs. *Susan B. Anthony* was ready to go to the jury. It was impossible to predict what their verdict might be, so Judge Hunt, determined to make it the verdict he and Roscoe Conkling wanted, took matters into his own hands. "Gentlemen of the jury," he said, "I direct that you find the defendant guilty."

Henry Selden leaped to his feet. "I object, Your Honor," he thundered. "The court has no power to direct the jury in a criminal case."

Judge Hunt ignored him. "Take the verdict, Mr. Clerk," he said.

The clerk of the court must have been another Conkling man. "Gentlemen of the jury," he intoned as if the whole proceeding was perfectly normal, "hearken to the verdict as the court hath recorded it. You say you find the defendant guilty of the offense charged. So say you all."

The twelve jurymen looked stunned. They had not even met to discuss the case, much less agree on a verdict. When Henry Selden asked if the clerk could at least poll the jury, Judge Hunt rapped his gavel sharply and declared, "That cannot be allowed. Gentlemen of the jury, you are discharged."

An enraged Henry Selden lost no time in introducing a motion for a new trial on the grounds that his client had been denied the right to a jury verdict. Judge Hunt denied the motion. He turned to Susan B. Anthony and said, "The prisoner will stand up. Has the prisoner anything to say why sentence shall not be pronounced?"

Thus far in the trial, Susan B. Anthony had remained silent. Now, she rose to her feet and said slowly, "Yes, Your Honor, I have many things to say."

Without further preliminaries, she launched into a scathing <u>denunciation</u> of Judge Hunt's conduct of her trial. ". . . In your ordered verdict of guilty," she said, "you have trampled underfoot every vital principle of our government. My natural rights, my civil rights, my political rights, are all alike ignored. Robbed of the fundamental privilege of citizenship, I am degraded from the status of a citizen to that of a subject; and not only myself individually, but all of my sex, are, by Your Honor's verdict, doomed to political subjection under this so-called Republican government."

Judge Hunt reached for his gavel, but Susan B. Anthony refused to be silent.

"May it please Your Honor," she continued. "Your denial of my citizen's right to vote is the denial of my right to a trial by a jury of my peers as an offender against law, therefore, the denial of my sacred rights to life, liberty, property, and—"

"The court cannot allow the prisoner to go on," Judge Hunt cried out.

Susan ignored him and continued her impassioned <u>tirade</u> against the court. Hunt frantically rapped his gavel and ordered her to sit down and be quiet. But Susan, who must have been taking delight in his consternation, kept on talking. She deplored the fact that she had been denied the right to a fair trial. Even if she had been given such a trial, she insisted, it would not have been by her peers. Jury, judges, and lawyers were not her equals, but her superiors, because they could vote and she could not. Susan was <u>adamant</u> about the fact that she had been denied the justice guaranteed in the Constitution to every citizen of the United States.

Judge Hunt was sufficiently cowed by now to try to defend himself. "The prisoner has been tried according to the established forms of law," he sputtered.

"Yes, Your Honor," retorted Susan, overlooking his <u>blatant</u> lie, "but by forms of law all made by men, interpreted by men, administered by men, in favor of men, and against women; and hence Your Honor's ordered verdict of guilty, against a United States citizen for the exercise of that citizen's right to vote, simply because that citizen was a woman and not a man. But yesterday, the same manmade forms of law declared it a crime punishable with a one-thousand-dollar fine and six months imprisonment, for you, or me, or any of us, to give a cup of cold water, a crust of bread, or a night's shelter to a panting fugitive while he was tracking his way to Canada. And every man or woman in whose veins coursed a drop of human sympathy violated that wicked law, reckless of consequences, and was justified in so doing. As, then, the slaves who got their freedom must take it over, or under, or through the unjust forms of law, precisely so now must women, to get their right to a voice in this government, take it, and I have taken mine and mean to take it at every opportunity."

Judge Hunt flailed his gavel and gave the by now futile order for the prisoner to sit down and be quiet. Susan kept right on talking.

"When I was brought before Your Honor for trial," she said, "I hoped for a broad and liberal interpretation of the Constitution and its recent amendments. One that would declare all United States citizens under its protection. But failing to get this justice—failing, even, to get a trial by a jury *not* of my peers—I ask not leniency at your hands—but to take the full rigors of the law."

With that Susan finally obeyed Judge Hunt's orders and sat down. Now he had to reverse himself and order her to stand up so he could impose sentence. As soon as he pronounced the sentence—a fine of one hundred dollars plus the costs of prosecuting the trial—Susan spoke up again. "May it please Your Honor," she said, "I shall never pay a dollar of your unjust penalty. All the stock in trade[15] I possess is a ten-thousand-dollar debt, incurred by publishing my paper—*The Revolution*—four years ago, the sole object of which was to educate all women to do precisely as I have done, rebel against your manmade, unjust, unconstitutional forms of law, that tax, fine, imprison, and hang women, while they deny them the right of representation in the government; and I shall work on with might and main to pay every dollar of that honest debt, but not a penny shall go to this unjust claim. And I shall earnestly and persistently continue to urge all women to the practical recognition of the old Revolutionary maxim, that 'Resistance to tyranny is obedience to God.'"

Judge Hunt must have had strict orders not only to see that the defendant was convicted, but to do everything he could to prevent the case from going on to a higher court. He allowed Susan to walk out of the courtroom without imposing a prison sentence in lieu of[16] her unpaid fine. If he had sent her to prison, she could have been released on a writ of habeas corpus[17] and would have had the right to appeal.[18] As it was, the case was closed.

Although she was disappointed that her case would not go to the Supreme Court as she had originally hoped, Susan knew that she had struck an important blow for woman's suffrage. Henry Selden's arguments and her own speech at the end of the trial were widely publicized, and Judge Hunt's conduct of the trial stood as proof that women were treated unjustly before the law.

Susan did not forget the election inspectors who had allowed her to cast her ballot. The men were fined twenty-five dollars each and sent to jail when they refused to pay. In all, they spent about a week behind bars before Susan, through the influence of friends in Washington, obtained presidential pardons for each of them. In the meantime, her followers, who included some of the best cooks in Rochester, saw to it that the men were supplied with delicious hot meals and home-baked pies.

True to her promise, Susan paid the legal expenses for the three inspectors. With the help of contributions from sympathetic admirers, she paid the costs of her own trial. But she never paid that one-hundred-dollar fine. Susan B. Anthony was a woman of her word as well as a woman of courage. ❖

---

15. **stock in trade:** resources available in a given situation.

16. **in lieu (lōō) of:** in place of.

17. **writ of habeas corpus** (hā′bē-əs kôr′pəs): a legal document requesting that a person appear in court—the document is used to gain the release of a person being held illegally.

18. **appeal:** transfer a case to a higher court for rehearing.

Thinking *through the* LITERATURE

Connect to the Literature

1. What Do You Think? Describe your impressions of Susan B. Anthony before, during, and after her trial.

Comprehension Check
- What sparks Anthony's decision to register to vote?
- What happens to her as a result of her vote?
- Who decides the verdict in Anthony's trial?
- How does Anthony protest what she called an "unjust penalty"?

Think Critically

2. What, if anything, do you think was wrong about this trial? Explain your reasoning.

- what the 14th Amendment says
- how the verdict was arrived at
- how Anthony was treated in the courtroom

3. What do you think was the biggest obstacle that Anthony faced—male attitudes in general, specific men in power, or laws of the day? Support your answer.

4. Reread the first three paragraphs of this selection to learn how the author's opinion of Anthony's **character** changed. Which of Truman's opinions do you agree with more? Consider the evidence presented in this biography as you explain why.

5. **ACTIVE READING** **SPECIALIZED VOCABULARY** Which of the terms you listed in your **READER'S NOTEBOOK** relate to citizens' rights? Explain how these rights influenced the outcome of Anthony's case.

Extend Interpretations

6. Comparing Texts Both *The Devil and Daniel Webster* and this biography portray trials. How do the fictional and real-life trials compare in terms of the fairness of the proceedings? Support your answer with details from the two selections.

7. Connect to Life Review your list of reasons for why the right to vote is important. If you had lived in Anthony's time, would you have joined her in speaking out for women's suffrage? Why or why not?

Literary Analysis

BIOGRAPHY A **biography** is the true story of a person's life told by someone else. The writer, or biographer, interviews the subject if possible and/or researches the person's life. Biographers often focus on remarkable or admirable aspects of their subjects, such as Susan B. Anthony's courageous willingness to go to jail in the fight for women's suffrage. Although biographers often present their subject in a favorable way, they also strive for a balance between fact and interpretation.

Paired Activity With a partner, evaluate how objective Truman's portrayal of Susan B. Anthony is. Make a chart like the one shown, listing objective statements of fact and subjective statements of opinion from the selection. Then decide whether fact or opinion is more dominant in this biography.

Statements of Fact	Statements of Opinion
•	•
•	•
•	•

Writing Options

1. Persuasive Pamphlet Create a small pamphlet that Anthony might have used to persuade people that women should vote. Place the pamphlet in your **Working Portfolio.**

2. Critical Commentary If women were denied the right to vote in the 1800s, what does that imply about society's attitudes toward women at the time? What did you learn about society's attitudes from this biography? Write a brief commentary on the subject.

Writing Handbook

See page 1157: Analysis.

3. Amendment Draft What right do you think U.S. citizens should have today that they do not have? Write a draft of a proposed amendment to the Constitution stating this right.

Activities & Explorations

1. Anthony Monologue Assuming the character of Susan B. Anthony, present a dramatic monologue to the class. Try to imitate her as closely as possible. To prepare, use a **cluster diagram** like the one below to list the characteristics that made her distinctive and then practice portraying those characteristics. ~ **SPEAKING AND LISTENING**

```
        ( )        ( )
          \        /
         Appearance
              |
    Anthony's
    Characteristics
      /            \
  Style of      Gestures and
  Speech          Actions
     |           /        \
    ( )        ( )        ( )
```

2. Political Cartoon The newspapers of 1872 and 1873 published political cartoons about Anthony's efforts to gain the vote for women. Draw your own cartoon about Anthony's actions. Remember that the cartoon should be clearly for or against women's suffrage. ~ **ART**

Inquiry & Research

Reforming Woman Susan B. Anthony did not only promote women's rights. She also fought in the temperance (anti-alcohol) and abolition (anti-slavery) movements. How did she try to get those reforms passed? Learn about Anthony's efforts to promote temperance or abolition. Share your findings in class.

INTERNET **More Online:**
Research Starter
www.mcdougallittell.com

Vocabulary in Action

EXERCISE: MEANING CLUES Write the word that each rhyme illustrates.

1. I have words at my command that give my speech the upper hand.
2. The stubborn lawyer stood his ground, certain that his case was sound.
3. With fists waving and nostrils flaring, I state my case with rage and daring.
4. The judge expressed his condemnation of the lawyer's lack of preparation.
5. The defendant was quite sane and able as she calmly sat at her lawyer's table.
6. The judge's bias was open and clear; he gave the defendant good reason to fear.
7. This defendant shows the inner strength to survive the trial, regardless of length.
8. The trial showed for all to see that the defendant is innocent—so we agree.
9. A look to the past can help us see that some old laws weren't meant to be.
10. The witness proclaimed 'twas an accident: "Don't send her to jail for what was not meant."

Building Vocabulary

For an in-depth lesson on analyzing the roots of words, see page 191.

WORDS TO KNOW					
	adamant	competent	denunciation	inadvertently	retrospect
	blatant	concur	fortitude	oratory	tirade

Grammar in Context: Using Action Verbs

In "The United States vs. Susan B. Anthony," Margaret Truman chooses verbs that show Anthony's strong, persuasive character. She uses **action verbs** like *summoned, urged, assured, informed, interrupted, refused, insisted,* and *deplored* to describe Anthony's actions.

> **Without further preliminaries, she launched into a scathing denunciation of Judge Hunt's conduct of her trial.**

Try substituting *began* or *started* for *launched into.* You can see that Truman's wording is more dramatic and helps to bring alive the scene at the trial.

Usage Tip: Be sure subjects and verbs agree in number.

WRITING EXERCISE Replace the underlined words with vivid action verbs.

Example: ***Original*** The suffragists' determined efforts got women the right to vote.
Rewritten The suffragists' determined efforts won women the right to vote.

1. A newspaper editorial caused Susan B. Anthony to try to vote.
2. The men were surprised to see the four sisters go into the barbershop.
3. Susan B. Anthony decided not to post a bond for her bail.
4. The district attorney said that because Anthony was a woman, she had no right to vote.
5. Even though Anthony lost her case, she had given a powerful message to the government.

Grammar Handbook Subject-Verb Agreement, p. 1198

Margaret Truman
1924–

Other Works
Harry S Truman
Bess W. Truman
Murder in the White House
Murder on the Potomac

First Daughter When Franklin Delano Roosevelt died suddenly on April 12, 1945, Harry S. Truman became President of the United States. He moved into the White House with his wife, Bess, and his 21-year-old daughter, Margaret. The Trumans were a close, devoted family with a strong sense of privacy. In her autobiography, Margaret Truman comments on that time: "As a family, we had a code, which was to do the right thing, do it the best we could, never complain and never take advantage. When my father became President, our code did not change."

Thumbs Down After graduating from George Washington University in 1946, Truman sang professionally in operas, acted, and worked in radio and television. For seven years, as a President's daughter, Truman had a tough time.

She was sometimes the object of ridicule and harsh reviews from critics—particularly over her singing.

Insider Accounts In 1954 she gave up her performing career and two years later published her first book—an autobiographical work called *Souvenir.* She later wrote biographies of her parents and a collection of biographies, *Women of Courage,* from which this selection comes. Truman has also drawn on her knowledge of political life in the nation's capital to write 15 murder mysteries. These mysteries all center around famous sites in Washington, D.C. Truman's biographies and mysteries have been bestsellers.

Author Activity

Find out about the presidency of Margaret Truman's father. Then discuss with your classmates what effect her father's career might have had on Margaret Truman. Do you think it shaped her writing?

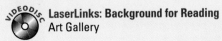

LaserLinks: Background for Reading
Art Gallery

Theme for English B

Poetry by LANGSTON HUGHES

The Writer

Poetry by RICHARD WILBUR

"It's not easy to know what is true for you or me."

Connect to Your Life

Write Away How do you feel when you have to write a paper for school? Each of the two poems you are about to read focuses on the struggle of a young writer. Since you are a writer, too, think about your own experiences with the writing process—both its difficulties and its pleasures. Describe one or two of these experiences and your reactions to them to a classmate.

Build Background

Inspiration v. Perspiration Even professional writers can struggle with the process of writing. Sometimes, if they're very lucky, they are struck by inspiration and the writing comes easily. Langston Hughes once wrote, "There are seldom many changes in my poems, once they're down." At other times, writers struggle to find just the right word or to figure out the point of what they're trying to say. Richard Wilbur has said that he sometimes spends years writing one poem. In the poems that follow, Hughes and Wilbur both describe someone who is writing and the creative struggle that the writer experiences.

Focus Your Reading

LITERARY ANALYSIS **THEME IN POETRY** A **theme** is the central idea or message in a work of literature. (This should not be confused with the use of the word *theme* in the poem's title, where it means "an essay.") Sometimes a work will contain direct statements that give clues to the theme, as in this line from "Theme for English B":

Let that page come out of you.

Clues to theme can also be found in **description, figurative language,** and action. As you read the poems, look for clues to help you understand their messages about how writing relates to life.

ACTIVE READING **MAKING GENERALIZATIONS** A **generalization** is a broad statement about a group or about a process. To make a generalization, look for patterns in the group or in the process you want to describe. Sometimes, generalizations are too broad to be true. For example, the statement *It always snows in winter* is not true for much of the United States. It would be more accurate to say *In the north, it usually snows in winter.*

READER'S NOTEBOOK As you read the poems, pay attention to the way each one portrays the experience of writing. On a chart like the one shown, record statements about writing, descriptions of the process, and comparisons that appear in each poem. Then use those details to make a generalization about the ease or difficulty of the writing process.

	Details About Writing
"Theme for English B"	
"The Writer"	

Theme
for English B

Langston Hughes

The instructor said,

    Go home and write
    a page tonight.
    And let that page come out of you—
5   Then, it will be true.

I wonder if it's that simple?

I am twenty-two, colored, born in Winston-Salem.
I went to school there, then Durham,[1] then here
to this college on the hill above Harlem.[2]
10 I am the only colored student in my class.

---

1. **Winston-Salem . . . Durham:** cities in North Carolina.

2. **this college on the hill above Harlem:** Columbia University in New York City. Harlem, a district in upper Manhattan, is home to an important African-American community.

The steps from the hill lead down into
    Harlem,
through a park, then I cross St. Nicholas,
Eighth Avenue, Seventh, and I come to the Y,
the Harlem Branch Y, where I take the
    elevator
15 up to my room, sit down, and write this
    page:

It's not easy to know what is true for you or
    me
at twenty-two, my age. But I guess I'm what
I feel and see and hear. Harlem, I hear you:
hear you, hear me—we two—you, me talk on
    this page.
20 (I hear New York, too.) Me—who?

Well, I like to eat, sleep, drink, and be in love.
I like to work, read, learn, and understand
    life.
I like a pipe for a Christmas present,
or records—Bessie, bop, or Bach.[3]

25 I guess being colored doesn't make me not
    like
the same things other folks like who are
    other races.
So will my page be colored that I write?
Being me, it will not be white.
But it will be
30 a part of you, instructor.
You are white—
yet a part of me, as I am a part of you.
That's American.
Sometimes perhaps you don't want to be a
    part of me.
35 Nor do I often want to be a part of you.
But we are, that's true!
As I learn from you,
I guess you learn from me—
although you're older—and white—
40 and somewhat more free.

This is my page for English B.

---

3. **Bessie, bop, or Bach:** Bessie Smith was a leading jazz and
   blues singer of the 1920s and early 1930s. Bop is a style
   of jazz that became popular in the 1940s. Johann
   Sebastian Bach was an 18th-century German composer
   of classical music.

Thinking Through the Literature

1. **Comprehension Check** What are some of the things that the speaker likes?
2. What is your impression of the **speaker?** Refer to lines in the poem that support your ideas.
3. Do you think that the poem is "true" in the sense that the instructor meant? Consider the evidence.

   THINK ABOUT
   - the instructions "And let that page come out of you" (line 4)
   - the personal information that the speaker reveals

4. Do you agree that the speaker and the instructor are part of each other, whether they want to be or not? Explain the reasons for your opinion.

The Writer

Richard Wilbur

Painted pottery typewriter, Adrían Luis González. Photo by David Lavender.

In her room at the prow[1] of the house
Where light breaks, and the windows are tossed with linden,[2]
My daughter is writing a story.

I pause in the stairwell, hearing
5 From her shut door a commotion of typewriter-keys
Like a chain hauled over a gunwale.[3]

Young as she is, the stuff
Of her life is a great cargo, and some of it heavy:
I wish her a lucky passage.

10 But now it is she who pauses,
As if to reject my thought and its easy figure.[4]
A stillness greatens, in which

The whole house seems to be thinking,
And then she is at it again with a bunched clamor
15 Of strokes, and again is silent.

---

1. **prow:** the forward part of a ship.
2. **linden:** a shade tree with heart-shaped leaves.
3. **gunwale** (gŭn'əl): the upper edge of the side of a ship.
4. **figure:** figure of speech (such as a simile or metaphor).

I remember the dazed starling
Which was trapped in that very room, two years ago;
How we stole in, lifted a sash

And retreated, not to affright[5] it;
20 And how for a helpless hour, through the crack of the door,
We watched the sleek, wild, dark

And iridescent creature
Batter against the brilliance, drop like a glove
To the hard floor, or the desk-top,

25 And wait then, humped and bloody,
For the wits to try it again; and how our spirits
Rose when, suddenly sure,

It lifted off from a chair-back,
Beating a smooth course for the right window
30 And clearing the sill of the world.

It is always a matter, my darling,
Of life or death, as I had forgotten. I wish
What I wished you before, but harder.

---

5. **affright:** scare.

The Artist
A Chinese Fable
Isabelle C. Chang

There was once a king who loved the graceful curves of the rooster. He asked the court artist to paint a picture of a rooster for him. For one year he waited, and still this order was not fulfilled. In a rage, he stomped into the artist's studio and demanded to see the artist.

Quickly the artist brought out paper, paint, and brush. In five minutes a perfect picture of a rooster emerged from his skillful brush. The king turned purple with anger, saying, "If you can paint a perfect picture of a rooster in five minutes, why did you keep me waiting for over a year?"

"Come with me," begged the artist. He led the king to his storage room. Paper was piled from the floor to the ceiling. On every sheet was a painting of a rooster.

"Your Majesty," explained the artist, "it took me more than a year to learn how to paint a perfect rooster in five minutes."

Life is short, art is long.

Thinking through the LITERATURE

Connect to the Literature

1. What Do You Think?
How did you react to "The Writer"? Share your reaction with your classmates.

Comprehension Check
- In "The Writer," what is the speaker's daughter trying to write?
- What does the speaker wish for the daughter?

Think Critically

2. Why do you think the **speaker** is reminded of the trapped starling as the daughter writes? Consider the evidence.

THINK ABOUT
- how the daughter resembles the starling
- how the speaker feels toward the daughter and the starling
- what is the matter of "life or death" that the speaker refers to

3. "The Writer" is written is **stanzas**—groupings of two or more lines. Do you think the stanzas help to organize the ideas in the poem? Explain your response.

4. **ACTIVE READING** **MAKING GENERALIZATIONS** What is it like to write about one's own life? Make a generalization that broadly describes the process.

THINK ABOUT
- the discussion you had with a classmate in the Connect to Your Life activity on page 466 about your experiences in writing
- the chart you filled out in your **📖 READER'S NOTEBOOK** about how "Theme for English B" and "The Writer" portray the experience of writing

Extend Interpretations

5. Comparing Texts What similar ideas about the creative struggle do you find in "The Writer" and "The Artist" on page 470?

6. Connect to Life Whose creative process most closely resembles your own—the student in "Theme for English B," the daughter in "The Writer," or the painter in "The Artist"? Explain your thinking.

Literary Analysis

THEME IN POETRY The **theme** of a literary work is the message that the writer presents to the reader. Theme should not be confused with subject. Each of these poems is about the subject of writing, but the theme is the message that the poem delivers about writing.

Themes are rarely stated directly, so readers have to figure them out. In "Theme for English B," the instructor says, "let that page come out of you— / Then, it will be true." The speaker answers, "It's not easy to know what is true" and "You are white— / yet a part of me, as I am a part of you. / That's American." These lines indicate one theme of this poem: Portraying a person's place in society is an important part of writing about his or her life.

Cooperative Learning Activity Go back through the poems, looking for words and lines that hint at theme. Then get together with a small group to compare what you have found. Discuss what each poem seems to reveal about writing and its relationship to life.

EXTENDED METAPHOR An **extended metaphor** is a figure of speech that compares two things at some length and in several ways. The speaker in the poem "The Writer" uses two extended metaphors to describe the daughter's writing. Identify one of these extended metaphors and explain how the thing described is like writing.

Choices & CHALLENGES

Writing Options

1. Report Card Imagine you are the instructor in "Theme for English B." Give a grade for and make comments about the speaker's theme.

2. Parent's Diary In a diary entry, have the speaker of "The Writer" record the incident that was recounted in the poem. Have the speaker conclude by making a generalization about how parents should respond to their children's struggles.

Activities & Explorations

1. Illustrated Poem Create a drawing, painting, or collage inspired by your reading of these poems. Entitle it "The Struggling Writer" and display it for your class. ~ **ART**

2. Public Poll Conduct a poll of your classmates to find out what kind of writing environment they like best. Do they prefer to write where it's quiet or where there is background noise? What room at school or at home is their favorite place to write? Convert your results to percentages using a worksheet and then present them on a pie graph. ~ **MATH**

3. Dramatic Reading Choose one of the poems or the fable "The Artist" to perform before the class. Practice your reading several times until you can express the emotion of the selection. Consider playing instrumental background music as you perform. Present your reading to the class. ~ **PERFORMING**

Langston Hughes
1902–1967

Other Works
The Weary Blues
The Big Sea: An Autobiography
The Best of Simple

A Struggling Poet Hughes was born in Joplin, Missouri. His parents separated shortly after he was born, and Hughes led a lonely childhood, moving often with his mother. After briefly attending a university in New York City, he worked at odd jobs while writing poetry and enjoying the music of Harlem. While working as a busboy, Hughes left three of his poems at a table where a well-known poet was dining. The poet was impressed with Hughes's work and introduced it to the public.

Sharing His Success For the rest of his life, Hughes traveled widely and wrote prolifically. He gave readings of his poetry to overflowing audiences and founded theaters in several cities. He also wrote a weekly newspaper column that featured stories about a black laborer and folk philosopher named Simple. After he became successful, Hughes often helped young writers who came to him for advice.

Richard Wilbur
1921–

Other Works
Things of This World
New and Collected Poems

His Grandfather's Footsteps Richard Wilbur had an early interest in painting. His decision to take up writing as a career was sparked by his mother's father and grandfather, both of whom were newspaper editors. In high school Wilbur began writing for his school newspaper, and in college he wrote for the student magazine. After graduation, Wilbur served with the U. S. forces in Europe during World War II. Around this time he became serious about writing poetry as a way of coping with the wartime disorder and confusion.

Word Crazy Unlike many other contemporary poets, Wilbur is known for his lack of experimentation and his optimistic viewpoint. His poetry displays a wide and varied vocabulary, which is not surprising for a man who describes himself as "crazy about words."

 LaserLinks: Background for Reading
Author Background
Geographical Connection

Creating Meaning from Word Parts

Have you ever opened a watch or a clock to see how it works? Like machines, words can be taken apart and analyzed to understand how they "work." Read the excerpt on the right, noting the highlighted words. Try to construct their meanings by analyzing their parts.

The word *urgency* is formed from the base word *urgent*, meaning "needing immediate attention," and the affix *-cy*, meaning "a state of." An **affix** is a word part added to a base word or a root to change its meaning. *Urgency* therefore means "a state of needing immediate attention." (Notice that the *t* is dropped from *urgent* when the affix is added, to avoid a hard-to-pronounce combination of letters.)

> It would be fatal for the nation to overlook the urgency of the moment. This sweltering summer of the Negro's legitimate discontent will not pass until there is an invigorating autumn of freedom and equality.
> —Martin Luther King, Jr., "I Have a Dream"

The word *discontent* can be analyzed in a similar way. The affix *dis-*, meaning "the opposite of," has been added to the base word *content*, meaning "satisfaction," to form a word meaning "a lack of satisfaction."

Strategies for Building Vocabulary

There are two kinds of affixes: **prefixes,** which go at the beginnings of words; and **suffixes,** which go at the ends of words. Knowing the meanings of affixes can help you figure out word meanings.

❶ Take the Word Apart When you encounter an unfamiliar word, see if you can recognize the meanings of its parts. Try to put the meanings together and think about the word in the context of the sentence. Consider the following example:

> We trust that you will continue to stand by us as we tackle the challenges of building peace, prosperity, nonsexism. . . .
> —Nelson Mandela, "Glory and Hope"

The word *nonsexism* can be broken into three distinct parts:

Prefix	Root	Suffix
non-	*sex*	*-ism*
"not"	"gender"	"prejudice based on"

By considering the meanings of the word parts and the word's context, you can infer that Mandela is referring to an elimination of prejudice based on people's gender.

❷ Learn the Meanings of Prefixes and Suffixes Study the following charts to help you learn the meanings of some common prefixes and suffixes.

Prefix	Meaning	Example
counter-	against	counteract
dis-	the opposite of	disconnect
extra-	outside, beyond	extracurricular
in-	not	ineffective
pre-	before	prewar
re-	again, back	reread
trans-	across, beyond	transatlantic

Suffix	Meaning	Example
-ant	one who	claimant
-cy	a state of	vacancy
-er	one who, a person associated with	reporter
-ion	an act or state of	completion
-ize	to become, to cause to be	familiarize, dramatize
-less	without	effortless
-ment	an act or state of	commitment
-ward	toward	skyward

EXERCISE Break each word into its parts and give a definition of the word. If necessary, use a dictionary to help you find the meanings of the word parts.

1. reexamination   3. selfless   5. restlessness
2. disbeliever   4. decontamination

Poets often use extended metaphors, which compare two things at some length and in several ways. As you read the poems that follow, see if you can identify what Blake compares to a poison tree and what Lowell compares to fireworks.

A poison Tree

william Blake

I was angry with my friend;
I told my wrath, my wrath did end.
I was angry with my foe:
I told it not, my wrath did grow.

5 And I watered it in fears,
Night & morning with my tears:
And I sunnéd it with smiles,
And with soft deceitful wiles.

And it grew both day and night.
10 Till it bore an apple bright.
And my foe beheld it shine,
And he knew that it was mine.

And into my garden stole,
When the night had veiled the pole;
15 In the morning glad I see;
My foe outstretched beneath the tree.

William Blake
1757–1827

Other Works
Songs of Innocence
Songs of Experience
The Marriage of Heaven and Hell
Jerusalem

An Early Start Born in London, William Blake began his artistic career at the age of 14. His first work was produced not as a poet, but as a painter and engraver, working in the shop of a well-known master. It soon became clear, however, that Blake's creativity was not limited to the visual arts, and at

26, he published his first book of poetry. It was written in the bold, simple style that would mark all of his later work.

Artist of the Spirit The other hallmark of Blake's art and life was his unusual spirituality. Once, a visitor came upon Blake in his studio, looking intently at a point not far from him and then back to the pad where he was drawing. He looked and drew, alternately, until the visitor commented on it. Blake explained that Lot—the only survivor of the Biblical destruction of Sodom and Gomorrah—was sitting for his portrait!

fireworks

A m y   L o w e l l

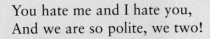

You hate me and I hate you,
And we are so polite, we two!

But whenever I see you, I burst apart
And scatter the sky with my blazing heart.
5 It spits and sparkles in stars and balls,
Buds into roses—and flares, and falls.

Scarlet buttons, and pale green disks,
Silver spirals and asterisks,
Shoot and tremble in a mist
10 Peppered with mauve and amethyst.

I shine in the windows and light up the trees,
And all because I hate you, if you please.

And when you meet me, you rend asunder
And go up in a flaming wonder
15 Of saffron cubes, and crimson moons,
And wheels all amaranths and maroons.

Golden lozenges and spades,
Arrows of malachites and jades,
Patens of copper, azure sheaves.
20 As you mount, you flash in the glossy leaves.

Such fireworks as we make, we two!
Because you hate me and I hate you.

Amy Lowell
1874–1925

Other Works
Sword Blades and Poppy Seed
Pictures of the Floating World
What's O'Clock

Daughter of a Distinguished Family Amy Lowell was a member of the prestigious New England family that also produced the earlier poet James Russell Lowell and the later poet Robert Lowell. A large, energetic, quick-witted woman, Amy Lowell was known for her black cigars, her troupe of dogs, and her arrogant manner. She was almost 30 years old when she decided to write poetry, and she worked at it for eight years before publishing a single poem.

Championing a Revolution In 1913, Lowell read some poems from the imagist movement. This group of poets was rebelling against traditional poetry by concentrating on images rather than ideas. Lowell began to experiment with imagist poetry herself, and she used her considerable resources to publicize the new literary school. Her premature death in 1925 cut short a career devoted to promoting modern poetry.

Author Study
MAYA ANGELOU

> "Maya Angelou . . .
> confronts her own life
> with such moving
> wonder, such a
> luminous dignity."
>
> —*James Baldwin*

1928–

A Full and Varied Life

Beset by poverty and trouble as a child, Maya Angelou overcame adversity to pursue several different careers. Although her writings are largely based on her experiences as an African American, she expresses universal human feelings, ideas, and struggles. Angelou has achieved both critical respect and tremendous public popularity. Read on to learn about a woman who turned her self-discovery into powerful literature.

EARLY PAIN AND CHALLENGES Maya Angelou was born Marguerite Johnson on April 4, 1928, in St. Louis, Missouri. When her parents divorced three years later, they sent Maya and her older brother, Bailey, to live with their grandmother, Annie Henderson, in Stamps, Arkansas. The South of the 1930s was rigidly segregated. "Black Stamps," where Angelou's grandmother lived, was a world apart from "White Stamps." Annie Henderson ran the only African-American–owned general store in town. In that store and in the local church, Angelou discovered a loving African-American community.

1928
Is born in
St. Louis on
April 4

1931
Moves to
Stamps,
Arkansas

HER LIFE
HER TIMES

1925   **1930**   **1935**

1929
Great
Depression
begins.

1933
FDR
launches
the New
Deal.

When Angelou was seven, she and her brother returned to their mother in St. Louis. A few months later, one of her mother's friends abused Angelou. Shaken by the assault and the trial that followed, Angelou stopped speaking. Shortly afterward, her mother sent Angelou and her brother back to their grandmother. Angelou maintained nearly complete silence for five years. With the help of sympathetic family members and friends, she finally overcame her fear of speaking.

STUDY AND STRUGGLE In 1940, Bailey and Angelou went to live with their mother in San Francisco. While attending high school, Angelou also studied dance and drama at night. She graduated from high school at age 16 and went on to become the first female and first African-American streetcar conductor in San Francisco. She also gave birth to a son, Guy.

Angelou struggled to support herself and her son during the 1940s and early 1950s. During this period, she was married for five years to a former sailor named Tosh Angelos. She eventually got a job as a calypso dancer in San Francisco. For her stage name, she chose Maya, from Bailey's childhood habit of calling her "mya sister" and Angelou, a variation of her former husband's surname. Angelou soon moved to New York, where she performed as a singer, dancer, and dramatic actress. She also began to attend meetings of the Harlem Writers Guild with writers such as James Baldwin.

1940 **Moves to San Francisco**	1944 **Graduates from high school in San Francisco**		1954–55 **Tours Europe and Africa in *Porgy and Bess***

1940   **1945**   **1950**   **1955**

1941 **United States enters World War II.**	1945 **United States drops the atomic bomb on Japan.**	1947 **Jackie Robinson breaks the color barrier in major league baseball.**	1954 ***Brown v. Board of Education* ruling orders desegregation of public schools.**

Author Study: MAYA ANGELOU

FINDING A VOICE The late 1950s and early 1960s was a time when the civil rights movement was leading a highly publicized campaign against segregation in public places. After hearing Martin Luther King, Jr., speak, Angelou committed herself to the cause of African-American rights. In 1960, she wrote and co-produced a musical revue, *Cabaret for Freedom*, to raise funds for the Southern Christian Leadership Conference (SCLC), a civil rights organization. Impressed with her abilities, the SCLC leaders asked her to become northern coordinator of the organization in 1961.

Later that year, Angelou's life took another turn when she moved to Egypt, remarried, and became a reporter. The 1960s was an exciting time to be in Africa. Egypt was trying to modernize and had begun construction of the Aswan Dam. In addition, dozens of African nations had recently gained independence from the European countries that had colonized them. Many African Americans, such as Angelou, responded to these events by taking a growing interest in their African heritage.

Angelou's marriage ended in 1963, and she moved to Ghana, where her son was a university student. There she continued working as a reporter and became a teacher and an administrator at the School of Music and Drama of the University of Ghana. She also continued performing.

In 1966, Angelou returned to the United States. She reestablished her stage career and wrote a ten-part series for television, *Black, Blues, Black*, about the role of African culture in American life. At a party one night, Angelou fascinated the other guests by telling the story of her life. The famous novelist James Baldwin and other literary friends began to urge her to capture that story on paper.

Eventually, Angelou wrote *I Know Why the Caged Bird Sings* about her life up to the age of 16. The book was published in 1970 and became an immediate critical and popular success. "Not since the days of my childhood, when the

Angelou's autobiographical work *I Know Why the Caged Bird Sings* (1970) chronicles her early years in Stamps, Arkansas.

people in books were more real than the people one saw every day, have I found myself so moved," said James Baldwin of her autobiography.

1961	1963	1968	1970	1976
Appears in controversial play *The Blacks*; moves to Egypt	Works as writer, editor, university teacher, and administrator in Ghana	*Black, Blues, Black* produced by National Educational Television	*I Know Why the Caged Bird Sings* is published.	Writes two television specials, "The Legacy" and "The Inheritors"

1960　　　　　**1965**　　　　　**1970**　　　　　**1975**

1963	1965	1968	1973
200,000 people take part in the March on Washington.	Voting Rights bill is passed.	Martin Luther King, Jr., and Robert Kennedy are assassinated.	U.S. direct involvement in Vietnam War ends.

478　UNIT THREE　AUTHOR STUDY: MAYA ANGELOU

REACHING OUT Since 1970, Angelou has published four other volumes of autobiography and eight of poetry. A professor at Wake Forest University, Angelou lectures and gives poetry readings nationwide. She has also continued to act, write plays and screenplays, and direct. Angelou once said, "I always feel that I've just started. The work to be, the work that's yet to come: that's the one loyalty I can count on. Loyalty—not mine to the work, but of the work to me."

Of her various endeavors, Angelou says, "All my work is meant to say, 'You may encounter many defeats, but you must not be defeated.' In fact, the encountering may be the very experience which creates the vitality and the power to endure." In writing about her own life, Angelou has captured the human experience in a way that speaks to millions of readers.

 More Online: Author Link
www.mcdougallittell.com

Poet of the President

When Bill Clinton asked Maya Angelou to compose a poem to commemorate his swearing in as president, she became only the second poet to be invited to speak at a presidential inauguration. (Robert Frost had spoken at John Kennedy's inauguration.) The poem Angelou wrote, "On the Pulse of Morning," calls for unity in the diverse American nation. As a literary work, it received mixed reviews. Angelou told talk show host Oprah Winfrey that although she thinks it is a good celebratory or public poem, it is not one of her best pieces. In fact, she plans to rework her material. Her public, however, loved the poem and the way she read it. According to novelist Louise Erdrich, "Her presence was so powerful and momentous, she made a statement that I was personally longing to see and hear."

Angelou reading "On the Pulse of Morning" at Bill Clinton's inauguration, 1993

1977
Acts in television miniseries *Roots*

Maya Angelou and Cicely Tyson in *Roots*

1981
Is appointed Reynolds Professor of American Studies at Wake Forest University

1986
***All God's Children Need Traveling Shoes* is published.**

1994
Receives Grammy Award for Best Spoken Word or Non-Musical Album

1980　　**1985**　　**1990**　　**1995**

1979
Camp David Accords are signed by Israel and Egypt.

1984
South African bishop Desmond Tutu receives the Nobel Peace Prize.

1989
Germans dismantle the Berlin Wall.

1993
White minority rule ends in South Africa.

from I Know Why the Caged Bird Sings

Autobiography by MAYA ANGELOU

See art on page 482.

Connect to Your Life

Thanks to You Think of someone you admire because of his or her influence on your life. Perhaps it was a teacher, a neighbor, a grandparent, or a coach. How did that person change your life? Did he or she make you feel less alone? help you get out of trouble? prove you could do more than you thought you could? Describe that person and his or her influence to a classmate.

Build Background

A Friend in Need In *I Know Why the Caged Bird Sings,* Maya Angelou tells about her childhood in the 1930s in the small, segregated town of Stamps, Arkansas. Angelou and her brother, Bailey, lived with their grandmother, whom they called Momma. Momma owned a general store in the part of town referred to as Black Stamps. After being abused by a family friend in St. Louis when she was eight, Angelou withdrew into herself and barely spoke for five years. This recollection tells about a person she greatly admired, who helped her to find her voice.

WORDS TO KNOW
Vocabulary Preview

aristocrat	illiteracy
aura	incessantly
cascading	infuse
essence	sacrilegious
familiarity	sophistication

Focus Your Reading

LITERARY ANALYSIS **AUTOBIOGRAPHY** An **autobiography** is the story of a person's life written by that person. In this excerpt from her autobiography, Angelou (referred to as Marguerite) not only describes events but also relates her feelings and thoughts about the person she admired:

> *I don't think I ever saw Mrs. Flowers laugh, but she smiled often. A slow widening of her thin black lips to show even, small white teeth, then the slow, effortless closing. When she chose to smile on me, I always wanted to thank her.*

As you read, look for other details that show how Mrs. Flowers influenced Maya Angelou's life.

ACTIVE READING **UNDERSTANDING POINT OF VIEW** Most autobiographies are written from the **first-person point of view,** which means that the narrator tells everything in his or her own words. However, autobiographies often reflect the viewpoints of two people—the writer as he or she experienced events, and the writer writing about the events years later. When Maya Angelou writes "I picked up the groceries and went out to wait in the hot sunshine," she is speaking from her viewpoint as a child. When she says, "Childhood's logic never asks to be proved," she is commenting on her experience from her adult viewpoint.

READER'S NOTEBOOK In a table like the one at the right, record Angelou's observations about Mrs. Flowers from both her child and adult viewpoints.

Observations About Mrs. Flowers	
Child's Viewpoint	**Adult's Viewpoint**
Why on earth did she insist on calling her Sister Flowers? Shame made me want to hide my face.	She was one of the few gentlewomen I have ever known, and has remained throughout my life the measure of what a human being can be.

For nearly a year, I sopped around the house, the Store, the school and the church, like an old biscuit, dirty and inedible. Then I met, or rather got to know, the lady who threw me my first life line.

Mrs. Bertha Flowers was the aristocrat of Black Stamps. She had the grace of control to appear warm in the coldest weather, and on the Arkansas summer days it seemed she had a private breeze which swirled around, cooling her. She was thin without the taut look of wiry people, and her printed voile dresses and flowered hats were as right for her as denim overalls for a farmer. She was our side's answer to the richest white woman in town.

Her skin was a rich black that would have peeled like a plum if snagged, but then no one would have thought of getting close enough to Mrs. Flowers to ruffle her dress, let alone snag her skin. She didn't encourage familiarity. She wore gloves too.

from

I KNOW WHY THE CAGED BIRD SINGS

MAYA ANGELOU

I don't think I ever saw Mrs. Flowers laugh, but she smiled often. A slow widening of her thin black lips to show even, small white teeth, then the slow, effortless closing. When she chose to smile on me, I always wanted to thank her. The action was so graceful and inclusively benign.[1]

She was one of the few gentlewomen I have ever known, and has remained throughout my life the measure of what a human being can be.

Momma had a strange relationship with her. Most often when she passed on the road in front of the Store, she spoke to Momma in that soft yet carrying voice, "Good day, Mrs. Henderson." Momma responded with "How you, Sister Flowers?"

Mrs. Flowers didn't belong to our church, nor was she Momma's familiar.[2] Why on earth did she insist on calling her Sister Flowers? Shame made me want to hide my face. Mrs. Flowers deserved

---

1. **inclusively benign** (bǐ-nīn′): good-natured and kindly in a way that takes others in.
2. **familiar:** a close friend or associate.

Portrait of Dorothy Porter, Librarian (1952), James Porter. Oil on canvas, National Portrait Gallery, Smithsonian Institution/Art Resource, New York.

better than to be called Sister. Then, Momma left out the verb. Why not ask, "How *are* you, *Mrs.* Flowers?" With the unbalanced passion of the young, I hated her for showing her ignorance to Mrs. Flowers. It didn't occur to me for many years that they were as alike as sisters, separated only by formal education.

Although I was upset, neither of the women was in the least shaken by what I thought an unceremonious greeting. Mrs. Flowers would continue her easy gait up the hill to her little bungalow,[3] and Momma kept on shelling peas or doing whatever had brought her to the front porch.

Occasionally, though, Mrs. Flowers would drift off the road and down to the Store and Momma would say to me, "Sister, you go on and play." As I left I would hear the beginning of an intimate conversation. Momma persistently using the wrong verb, or none at all.

"Brother and Sister Wilcox is sho'ly the meanest—" "Is," Momma? "Is"? Oh, please, not "is," Momma, for two or more. But they talked, and from the side of the building where I waited for the ground to open up and swallow me, I heard the soft-voiced Mrs. Flowers and the textured voice of my grandmother merging and melting. They were interrupted from time to time by giggles that must have come from Mrs. Flowers (Momma never giggled in her life). Then she was gone.

She appealed to me because she was like people I had never met personally. Like women in English novels who walked the moors[4] (whatever they were) with their loyal dogs racing at a respectful distance. Like the women who sat in front of roaring fireplaces, drinking tea incessantly from silver trays full of scones and crumpets.[5] Women who walked over the "heath"[6] and read morocco-bound[7] books and had two last names divided by a hyphen. It would be safe to say that she made me proud to be Negro, just by being herself.

She acted just as refined as whitefolks in the movies and books and she was more beautiful, for none of them could have come near that warm color without looking gray by comparison.

It was fortunate that I never saw her in the company of powhitefolks. For since they tend to think of their whiteness as an evenizer, I'm certain that I would have had to hear her spoken to commonly as Bertha, and my image of her would have been shattered like the unmendable Humpty-Dumpty.

One summer afternoon, sweet-milk fresh in my memory, she stopped at the Store to buy provisions. Another Negro woman of her health and age would have been expected to carry the paper sacks home in one hand, but Momma said, "Sister Flowers, I'll send Bailey up to your house with these things."

She smiled that slow dragging smile, "Thank you, Mrs. Henderson. I'd prefer Marguerite, though." My name was beautiful when she said it. "I've been meaning to talk to her, anyway." They gave each other age-group looks.

Momma said, "Well, that's all right then. Sister, go and change your dress. You going to Sister Flowers's."

The chifforobe[8] was a maze. What on earth did one put on to go to Mrs. Flowers's house? I knew I shouldn't put on a Sunday dress. It might be sacrilegious. Certainly not a house

---

3. **bungalow** (bŭng′gə-lō): a small, one-story house or cottage.
4. **moors:** broad areas of open land with patches of low shrubs and marshes.
5. **scones** (skōnz) **and crumpets** (krŭm′pĭts):   s are small, sweet biscuits; crumpets are rolls s   to English muffins.
6. **heath** (hēth): a moor.
7. **morocco-bound** (mə-rŏk′ō): bound, or covered, in soft leather.
8. **chifforobe** (shĭf′ə-rōb′): a chest of drawers combined with a small closet for storing clothes.

---

dress, since I was already wearing a fresh one. I chose a school dress, naturally. It was formal without suggesting that going to Mrs. Flowers's house was equivalent to attending church.

I trusted myself back into the Store.

"Now, don't you look nice." I had chosen the right thing, for once.

"Mrs. Henderson, you make most of the children's clothes, don't you?"

"Yes, ma'am. Sure do. Store-bought clothes ain't hardly worth the thread it take to stitch them."

"I'll say you do a lovely job, though, so neat. That dress looks professional."

Momma was enjoying the seldom-received compliments. Since everyone we knew (except Mrs. Flowers, of course) could sew competently, praise was rarely handed out for the commonly practiced craft.

"I try, with the help of the Lord, Sister Flowers, to finish the inside just like I does the outside. Come here, Sister."

I had buttoned up the collar and tied the belt, apronlike, in back. Momma told me to turn around. With one hand she pulled the strings and the belt fell free at both sides of my waist. Then her large hands were at my neck, opening the button loops. I was terrified. What was happening?

"Take it off, Sister." She had her hands on the hem of the dress.

"I don't need to see the inside, Mrs. Henderson, I can tell . . ." But the dress was over my head and my arms were stuck in the sleeves. Momma said, "That'll do. See here, Sister Flowers, I French-seams around the armholes." Through the cloth film, I saw the shadow approach. "That makes it last longer. Children these days would bust out of sheet-metal clothes. They so rough."

"That is a very good job, Mrs. Henderson. You should be proud. You can put your dress back on, Marguerite."

"No ma'am. Pride is a sin. And 'cording to the Good Book, it goeth before a fall."

"That's right. So the Bible says. It's a good thing to keep in mind."

I wouldn't look at either of them. Momma hadn't thought that taking off my dress in front of Mrs. Flowers would kill me stone dead. If I had refused, she would have thought I was trying to be "womanish." Mrs. Flowers had known that I would be embarrassed and that was even worse. I picked up the groceries and went out to wait in the hot sunshine. It would be fitting if I got a sunstroke and died before they came outside. Just dropped dead on the slanting porch.

There was a little path beside the rocky road, and Mrs. Flowers walked in front swinging her arms and picking her way over the stones.

She said, without turning her head, to me, "I hear you're doing very good school work, Marguerite, but that it's all written. The teachers report that they have trouble getting you to talk in class." We passed the triangular farm on our left, and the path widened to allow us to walk together. I hung back in the separate unasked and unanswerable questions.

"Come and walk along with me, Marguerite." I couldn't have refused even if I wanted to. She pronounced my name so nicely. Or more correctly, she spoke each word with such clarity that I was certain a foreigner who didn't understand English could have understood her.

"Now no one is going to make you talk—possibly no one can. But bear in mind, language is man's way of communicating with his fellow man, and it is language alone which separates him from the lower animals." That was a totally new idea to me, and I would need time to think about it.

Back Street (1983), LaVere Hutchings. Watercolor, 11″ × 15″, collection of the artist.

"Your grandmother says you read a lot. Every chance you get. That's good, but not good enough. Words mean more than what is set down on paper. It takes the human voice to <u>infuse</u> them with the shades of deeper meaning."

I memorized the part about the human voice infusing words. It seemed so valid and poetic.

She said she was going to give me some books and that I not only must read them, I must read them aloud. She suggested that I try to make a sentence sound in as many different ways as possible.

"I'll accept no excuse if you return a book to me that has been badly handled." My imagination boggled at the punishment I would deserve if in fact I did abuse a book of Mrs. Flowers's. Death would be too kind and brief.

The odors in the house surprised me. Somehow I had never connected Mrs. Flowers with food or eating or any other common experience of common people. There must have been an outhouse, too, but my mind never recorded it.

The sweet scent of vanilla had met us as she opened the door.

485

"I made tea cookies this morning. You see, I had planned to invite you for cookies and lemonade so we could have this little chat. The lemonade is in the icebox."

It followed that Mrs. Flowers would have ice on an ordinary day, when most families in our town bought ice late on Saturdays only a few times during the summer to be used in the wooden ice-cream freezers.

She took the bags from me and disappeared through the kitchen door. I looked around the room that I had never in my wildest fantasies imagined I would see. Browned photographs leered or threatened from the walls, and the white, freshly done curtains pushed against themselves and against the wind. I wanted to gobble up the room entire and take it to Bailey, who would help me analyze and enjoy it.

"Have a seat, Marguerite. Over there by the table." She carried a platter covered with a tea towel. Although she warned that she hadn't tried her hand at baking sweets for some time, I was certain that like everything else about her the cookies would be perfect.

They were flat, round wafers, slightly browned on the edges and butter-yellow in the center. With the cold lemonade they were sufficient for childhood's lifelong diet. Remembering my manners, I took nice little lady-like bites off the edges. She said she had made them expressly for me and that she had a few in the kitchen that I could take home to my brother. So I jammed one whole cake in my mouth, and the rough crumbs scratched the insides of my jaws, and if I hadn't had to swallow, it would have been a dream come true.

As I ate she began the first of what we later called "my lessons in living." She said that I must always be intolerant of ignorance but understanding of illiteracy. That some people, unable to go to school, were more educated and even more intelligent than college professors. She encouraged me to listen carefully to what country people called mother wit. That in those homely sayings was couched the collective wisdom of generations.

When I finished the cookies she brushed off the table and brought a thick, small book from the bookcase. I had read *A Tale of Two Cities*

> *S*ome people, unable to go to school, were more educated and even more intelligent than college professors.

WORDS
TO
KNOW
illiteracy (ĭ-lĭt′ər-ə-sē) *n.* a lack of ability to read and write

and found it up to my standards as a romantic novel. She opened the first page and I heard poetry for the first time in my life.

"It was the best of times and the worst of times . . ."[9] Her voice slid in and curved down through and over the words. She was nearly singing. I wanted to look at the pages. Were they the same that I had read? Or were there notes, music, lined on the pages, as in a hymn book? Her sounds began cascading gently. I knew from listening to a thousand preachers that she was nearing the end of her reading, and I hadn't really heard, heard to understand, a single word.

"How do you like that?"

It occurred to me that she expected a response. The sweet vanilla flavor was still on my tongue, and her reading was a wonder in my ears. I had to speak.

I said, "Yes, ma'am." It was the least I could do, but it was the most also.

"There's one more thing. Take this book of poems and memorize one for me. Next time you pay me a visit, I want you to recite."

I have tried often to search behind the sophistication of years for the enchantment I so easily found in those gifts. The essence escapes but its aura remains. To be allowed, no, invited, into the private lives of strangers, and to share their joys and fears, was a chance to exchange the Southern bitter wormwood for a cup of mead with Beowulf or a hot cup of tea and milk with Oliver Twist.[10] When I said aloud, "It is a far, far better thing that I do, than I have ever done . . ."[11] tears of love filled my eyes at my selflessness.

On that first day, I ran down the hill and into the road (few cars ever came along it) and had the good sense to stop running before I reached the Store.

I was liked, and what a difference it made. I was respected not as Mrs. Henderson's grandchild or Bailey's sister but for just being Marguerite Johnson.

Childhood's logic never asks to be proved (all conclusions are absolute). I didn't question why Mrs. Flowers had singled me out for attention, nor did it occur to me that Momma might have asked her to give me a little talking to. All I cared about was that she had made tea cookies for *me* and read to *me* from her favorite book. It was enough to prove that she liked me. ❖

---

9. **"It was . . . worst of times . . .":** This opening sentence of Charles Dickens's novel *A Tale of Two Cities* is famous for its apparent contradictions. The novel is set in Paris and London during the French Revolution (1789–1799).

10. **a chance to exchange . . . with Oliver Twist:** Angelou here compares her existence as a black child in the bigoted South to wormwood, a bitter herb. She hopes to escape this bitterness by turning instead to mead, a sweet drink, or tea with milk, common beverages to such characters as Beowulf and Oliver Twist from English literature.

11. **"It is a far . . . have ever done . . .":** a quotation from the very end of *A Tale of Two Cities*. It is spoken by a man who nobly sacrifices his own life to save that of another.

WORDS TO KNOW	**cascading** (kă-skā′dǐng) *v.* falling or flowing, like a waterfall
	sophistication (sə-fǐs′tǐ-kā′shən) *n.* the state of being experienced; maturity
	essence (ĕs′əns) *n.* the basic or most important quality
	aura (ôr′ə) *n.* the unique but undefinable atmosphere that surrounds a person, an object, or an event

CAGED BIRD

MAYA ANGELOU

A free bird leaps
on the back of the wind
and floats downstream
till the current ends
5   and dips his wing
in the orange sun rays
and dares to claim the sky.

But a bird that stalks
down his narrow cage
10   can seldom see through
his bars of rage
his wings are clipped and
his feet are tied
so he opens his throat to sing.

15   The caged bird sings
with a fearful trill
of things unknown
but longed for still
and his tune is heard
20   on the distant hill
for the caged bird
sings of freedom.

The free bird thinks of another breeze
and the trade winds soft through the sighing trees
25   and the fat worms waiting on a dawn-bright lawn
and he names the sky his own

16 trill: a quivering musical sound; warble.

24 trade winds: winds that blow steadily in one direction in tropical areas.

Mahoning (1956), Franz Kline.
Oil on canvas, 80" x 100".
The Whitney Museum of
American Art, New York. Gift
of the Friends of the Whitney
Museum of American Art
(57.10).

But a caged bird stands on the grave of dreams
his shadow shouts on a nightmare scream
his wings are clipped and his feet are tied
30 so he opens his throat to sing.

The caged bird sings
with a fearful trill
of things unknown
but longed for still
35 and his tune is heard
on the distant hill
for the caged bird
sings of freedom.

Thinking through the LITERATURE

Connect to the Literature

1. **What Do You Think?** What do you think of Marguerite's admiration for Mrs. Flowers? Share your thoughts with the class.

   > **Comprehension Check**
   > • What is Mrs. Flowers's feeling about language?
   > • What does Marguerite think is the reason that Mrs. Flowers likes her?

Think Critically

2. Why do you think Marguerite admires Mrs. Flowers so much?

3. In what ways does Mrs. Flowers help young Marguerite? Think about the obvious gifts that Mrs. Flowers offers her as well as the less obvious ones.

4. What do you think motivates Mrs. Flowers to help Marguerite?

   THINK ABOUT
   - Mrs. Flowers's social and economic position in Black Stamps
   - her relationship with Momma
   - Marguerite's performance in school
   - what Mrs. Flowers might gain from the relationship

5. **ACTIVE READING** | **UNDERSTANDING POINT OF VIEW** | Review the chart that you kept in your **READER'S NOTEBOOK.** How does Angelou's adult viewpoint help you to understand the long-range effect that Mrs. Flowers had on her life?

Extend Interpretations

6. **Comparing Texts** Reread the paragraph that begins "Mrs. Bertha Flowers was the aristocrat of Black Stamps" on page 481 and the poem on page 488. Look for examples of **imagery,** descriptive language that appeals to the five senses. Which of these two writing samples do you find has the more appealing imagery?

7. **Connect to Life** The young Marguerite is embarrassed by her grandmother's way of speaking. How important is a person's use of language to the way people react to him or her? Discuss your opinions in class.

Literary Analysis

AUTOBIOGRAPHY An **auto-biography** is an account of a person's life written by that person and usually told from the **first-person point of view.** Autobiographies are based upon the writer's memories and sometimes upon records such as diaries and letters. An autobiography is generally more subjective than a **biography,** which is an account of a person's life written by someone else and based upon research and interviews.

Cooperative Learning Activity In a small group, go back through the selection and look for details that might have been omitted if this had been written by someone other than Angelou. Then discuss what information a biographer might have included that Angelou did not. Share your ideas with the class.

ALLUSION An **allusion** is a reference to another literary work or to a famous person, place, or event. The title *I Know Why the Caged Bird Sings* is an allusion to the poem "Sympathy" by the African-American writer Paul Laurence Dunbar (1872–1906). The last stanza reads:

> *I know why the caged bird sings,*
>   *ah me,*
> *When his wing is bruised and his*
>   *bosom sore,—*
> *When he beats his bars and he*
>   *would be free;*
> *It is not a carol of joy or glee,*
> *But a prayer that he sends from*
>   *his heart's deep core,*
> *But a plea, that upward to Heaven*
>   *he flings—*
> *I know why the caged bird sings!*

Why do you think Angelou refers to that poem in the title of her autobiography?

Choices & CHALLENGES

Writing Options

1. Story of Influence Think about the discussion you had in Connect to Your Life on page 480 about a person you admire. Describe an incident that shows how that person influenced you. A graphic like the one shown might help you plan your anecdote.

```
Description of the person
        ↓
What the person did to influence me
        ↓
How I responded at the time
        ↓
How I feel about the person now
```

Writing Handbook
See pages 1153–1154: Narrative Writing.

2. Discussion of Angelou's Poem Imagine that Angelou has shared her poem "Caged Bird" with Mrs. Flowers. Write a dialogue in which the two discuss the poem.

Activities & Explorations

1. Dramatic Monologue Create a monologue in which Mrs. Flowers presents her version of the events in this excerpt. Find clues in the autobiography about how Mrs. Flowers moves, speaks, and dresses. Perform your monologue for the class. ~ **SPEAKING AND LISTENING**

2. Film Review Rent a copy of the videotape of *I Know Why the Caged Bird Sings*. With a partner, discuss how the filmmaker's portrayal of the setting and the characters compares with the way you visualized them. ~ **VIEWING AND REPRESENTING**

Inquiry & Research

A Tale of Two Writers In this excerpt, Angelou refers to two novels by the British writer Charles Dickens: *A Tale of Two Cities* and *Oliver Twist*. Investigate why Dickens and his work might have appealed to Marguerite. Read an excerpt of one of the novels or view a film version on videotape. You could use a biography, a literature text, or an encyclopedia to learn about Dickens's life. How did the hardships of his youth influence his writing? Which of his novels are considered autobiographical? Share your findings with the class.

Scene from *Oliver!* the musical version of *Oliver Twist*

Vocabulary in Action

EXERCISE: ANALOGIES Complete the analogies below by determining the relationship between the first pair of words and then deciding which vocabulary word best completes the second part of the analogy. Write the word on your paper.

1. *Glow* is to *radiance* as _____ is to *atmosphere*.
2. *Beauty* is to *ugliness* as _____ is to *inexperience*.
3. *Drifting* is to *snow* as _____ is to *water*.
4. *Disease* is to *medicine* as _____ is to *education*.
5. *Democrat* is to *democracy* as _____ is to *aristocracy*.
6. *Toxic* is to *environment* as _____ is to *religion*.
7. *Quickly* is to *slowly* as _____ is to *occasionally*.
8. *Affection* is to *love* as _____ is to *know*.
9. *Care* is to *careful* as _____ is to *essential*.
10. *Help* is to *assist* as _____ is to *inject*.

Building Vocabulary
For an in-depth study on analogies, see page 641.

WORDS TO KNOW				
aristocrat	cascading	familiarity	incessantly	sacrilegious
aura	essence	illiteracy	infuse	sophistication

From an
Interview
with

Maya

Build Background

In 1990, George Plimpton, editor in chief of *The Paris Review,* interviewed Maya Angelou as part of his magazine's on-going series on writers. At one point, Plimpton asked Angelou how she decided to write her autobiography. Angelou responded that it was when an editor at Random House publishers heard that she had been telling friends stories about her life. He called her a few times about the stories, and each time Angelou resisted the offer to write them out. It was not until the editor challenged her with the difficulty of writing autobiography "as literature" that she said she'd do it. At this point, Plimpton turned to the many books of autobiography that Angelou has now written.

Focus Your Reading

PRIMARY SOURCES **INTERVIEWS** Primary sources are works that offer firsthand information. These sources include letters, stories, essays, poems, and speeches by a writer as well as interviews. As you read an interview, notice the kinds of questions the interviewer asks and how he or she uses the subject's responses as the basis for additional questions. Also note the values, personality, and tone that the subject's answers reveal.

Do you select a dominant theme for each book?

I try to remember times in my life, incidents in which there was the dominating theme of cruelty, or kindness, or generosity, or envy, or happiness, glee . . . perhaps four incidents in the period I'm going to write about. Then I select the one which lends itself best to my device and which I can write as drama without falling into melodrama.

Did you write for a particular audience?

I thought early on if I could write a book for black girls it would be good, because there were so few books for a black girl to read that said "This is how it is to grow up." Then, I thought, "I'd better, you know, enlarge that group, the market group, that I'm trying to reach." I decided to write for black boys, and then white girls, and then white boys.

But what I try to keep in mind mostly is my craft. That's what I really try for; I try to allow myself to be impelled by my art—if that doesn't sound too pompous and weird—accept the impulse, and then try my best to have a command of the craft. If I'm feeling depressed, and losing my control, then I think about the reader. But that is very rare—to think about the reader when the work is going on.

Angelou

by
George Plimpton

So you don't keep a particular reader in mind when you sit down in that hotel room and begin to compose or write. It's yourself. It's myself . . . and my reader. I would be a liar, a hypocrite, or a fool—and I'm not any of those—to say that I don't write for the reader. I do. But for the reader who hears, who really will work at it, going behind what I seem to say. So I write for myself and that reader who will pay the dues. There's a phrase in West Africa, in Ghana; it's called "deep talk." For instance, there's a saying: "The trouble for the thief is not how to steal the chief's bugle, but where to blow it." Now, on the face of it, one understands that. But when you really think about it, it takes you deeper. In West Africa they call that "deep talk." I'd like to think I write "deep talk." When you read me, you should be able to say, "Gosh, that's pretty. That's lovely. That's nice. Maybe there's something else? Better read it again."

Thinking Through the Literature

1. What insights into Maya Angelou did you gain from reading this **interview?**

2. What do you think Angelou means by "deep talk," and how does it relate to her writing?

THINK ABOUT
- the last sentence of the interview, in which she describes a reader's response
- the kind of reader she says she writes for
- the African proverb she quotes and what she says about it

3. How does Angelou balance an awareness of her **audience** with a concern for her craft as a writer?

New Directions

Essay by MAYA ANGELOU

See art on page 495.

(Connect to Your Life)

Success! People often have to work very hard to achieve their goals. What sacrifices have successful people you know had to make? What difficulties might you have to face in achieving your own goals? What personal qualities do you think will help you be successful? Share your answers to these questions in class.

Build Background

Pursuing Economic Success
Mrs. Annie Johnson in "New Directions" is Maya Angelou's grandmother—the same person called Momma and Mrs. Henderson in *I Know Why the Caged Bird Sings.* In this essay, Angelou explains how her grandmother pursued the goal of providing for her sons. At the turn of the century, economic success was not easy for an African-American woman. In many parts of the country, discrimination kept African Americans from obtaining education or high-paying jobs. In addition, women were considered men's inferiors and were excluded from the best jobs. Many African-American women could find work only as domestic servants, such as cooks or maids. Annie Johnson, however, was determined to overcome those obstacles.

Focus Your Reading

LITERARY ANALYSIS **THEME** The **theme** is the major idea or message of a literary work. It is an insight about life or human nature that goes beyond the subject of the work. The theme can be directly stated or merely implied in the text. Sometimes, the **title** of a work provides clues to its theme. As you read this essay, ask yourself what message Maya Angelou is trying to convey about new directions.

ACTIVE READING **DRAWING CONCLUSIONS** **Drawing conclusions** involves connecting pieces of information in a text with your own prior knowledge and making summary statements after reading. For example, Angelou writes of her grandmother's scheme to sell meat pies:

She made her plans meticulously and in secret.

Some readers might already know that in the early 1900s it was hard for African Americans to start their own businesses. This could explain why Annie Johnson kept her plans secret. In addition, the word *meticulously* means "with great care." By connecting prior knowledge and details in the text, a reader can conclude that Annie Johnson was focused and determined.

READER'S NOTEBOOK As you read this essay, use a chart like the one shown to draw conclusions about Angelou's grandmother. Record Annie Johnson's actions. Use your prior knowledge to decide what those actions imply about Annie's character. Also, record any character traits that Angelou states directly.

Annie Johnson's Actions	Character Traits Implied by Those Actions	Character Traits Stated Directly by Angelou
made plans in secret	determined not to be stopped by people who oppose African-American progress	meticulous

NEW DIRECTIONS

MAYA ANGELOU

"In many places, because of the war, food had doubled in price," panel 11 from *The Migration Series* (1940–1941), Jacob Lawrence. Tempera on masonite, 18″ × 12″. The Phillips Collection, Washington, D.C. Acquired 1942.

IN 1903 THE LATE MRS. ANNIE JOHNSON OF ARKANSAS FOUND HERSELF WITH TWO TODDLING SONS, VERY LITTLE MONEY, A SLIGHT ABILITY TO READ AND ADD SIMPLE NUMBERS. TO THIS PICTURE ADD A DISASTROUS MARRIAGE AND THE BURDENSOME FACT THAT MRS. JOHNSON WAS A NEGRO.

When she told her husband, Mr. William Johnson, of her dissatisfaction with their marriage, he conceded that he too found it to be less than he expected, and had been secretly hoping to leave and study religion. He added that he thought God was calling him not only to preach but to do so in Enid, Oklahoma. He did not tell her that he knew a minister in Enid with whom he could study and who had

"... I decided to step off the road and cut me a new path."

a friendly, unmarried daughter. They parted amicably, Annie keeping the one-room house and William taking most of the cash to carry himself to Oklahoma.

Annie, over six feet tall, big-boned, decided that she would not go to work as a domestic and leave her "precious babes" to anyone else's care. There was no possibility of being hired at the town's cotton gin[1] or lumber mill, but maybe there was a way to make the two factories work for her. In her words, "I looked up the road I was going and back the way I come, and since I wasn't satisfied, I decided to step off the road and cut me a new path." She told herself that she wasn't a fancy cook but that she could "mix groceries well enough to scare hungry away and from starving a man."

She made her plans meticulously[2] and in secret. One early evening to see if she was ready, she placed stones in two five-gallon pails and carried them three miles to the cotton gin. She rested a little, and then, discarding some rocks, she walked in the darkness to the saw

mill five miles farther along the dirt road. On her way back to her little house and her babies, she dumped the remaining rocks along the path.

That same night she worked into the early hours boiling chicken and frying ham. She made dough and filled the rolled-out pastry with meat. At last she went to sleep.

The next morning she left her house carrying the meat pies, lard, an iron brazier,[3] and coals for a fire. Just before lunch she appeared in an empty lot behind the cotton gin. As the dinner noon bell rang, she dropped the savors[4] into boiling fat and the aroma rose and floated over to the workers who spilled out of the gin, covered with white lint, looking like specters.[5]

Most workers had brought their lunches of pinto beans and biscuits or crackers, onions and cans of sardines, but they were tempted by the hot meat pies which Annie ladled out of the fat. She wrapped them in newspapers, which soaked up the grease, and offered them for sale at a nickel each. Although business was slow, those first days Annie was determined. She balanced her appearances between the two hours of activity.

So, on Monday if she offered hot fresh pies at the cotton gin and sold the remaining cooled-down pies at the lumber mill for three cents, then on Tuesday she went first to the lumber mill presenting fresh, just-cooked pies as the lumbermen covered in sawdust emerged from the mill.

1. **cotton gin:** a factory in which seeds and other foreign matter are removed from cotton.
2. **meticulously** (mǐ-tǐk′yə-ləs-lē): very carefully and precisely.
3. **brazier** (brā′zhər): a device for cooking food over burning coals.
4. **savors:** tasty items of food.
5. **specters:** ghosts.

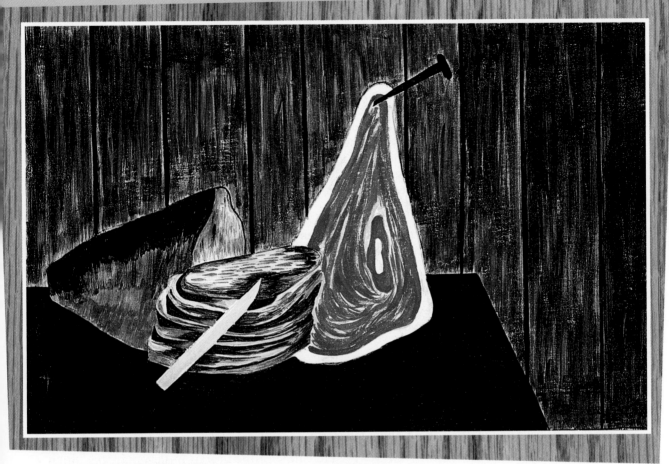

"But living conditions were better in the North," panel 44 from *The Migration Series* (1940–1941; text and title revised by the artist, 1993), Jacob Lawrence. Tempera on gesso on composition board, 12″ × 18″. The Museum of Modern Art, New York. Gift of Mrs. David M. Levy. Photograph copyright © 2000 The Museum of Modern Art.

For the next few years, on balmy spring days, blistering summer noons, and cold, wet, and wintry middays, Annie never disappointed her customers, who could count on seeing the tall, brown-skin woman bent over her brazier, carefully turning the meat pies. When she felt certain that the workers had become dependent on her, she built a stall between the two hives of industry and let the men run to her for their lunchtime provisions.

She had indeed stepped from the road which seemed to have been chosen for her and cut herself a brand-new path. In years that stall became a store where customers could buy cheese, meal, syrup, cookies, candy, writing tablets, pickles, canned goods, fresh fruit, soft drinks, coal, oil, and leather soles for worn-out shoes.

Each of us has the right and the responsibility to assess the roads which lie ahead, and those over which we have traveled, and if the future road looms ominous[6] or unpromising, and the roads back uninviting, then we need to gather our resolve and, carrying only the necessary baggage, step off that road into another direction. If the new choice is also unpalatable,[7] without embarrassment, we must be ready to change that as well. ❖

---

6. **ominous** (ŏm′ə-nəs): threatening.

7. **unpalatable** (ŭn-păl′ə-tə-bəl): unpleasant; disagreeable.

Connect to the Literature

1. **What Do You Think?** What reaction did you have to Annie Johnson's story? Share your thoughts with a classmate.

   Comprehension Check
   - Why didn't Annie Johnson want to work as a domestic?
   - How did Annie build up her business of selling meat pies?
   - When did Annie stop traveling to the factories and open her stall halfway between the two?

Think Critically

2. How did Annie Johnson step "from the road which seemed to have been chosen for her and cut herself a brand-new path"?

   THINK ABOUT
   - the limits placed on her as an African-American woman in 1903
   - her response to the knowledge that neither of the town's factories would hire her
   - her resources and her skills

3. What was Annie Johnson's goal? Did she achieve it? Explain your answer by citing details from the essay.

4. **ACTIVE READING** **DRAWING CONCLUSIONS** What conclusions have you reached about Annie Johnson's character? Consider evidence from the essay and from the chart in your 📖 **READER'S NOTEBOOK.**

5. What can you **infer** from this essay about Maya Angelou's values?

   THINK ABOUT
   - which of her grandmother's character traits Angelou most seems to admire
   - what Angelou says in the last paragraph of the essay

Extend Interpretations

6. **What If?** What do you think Annie Johnson would have done if the factory workers had not come to her stall after she opened it? Explain your answer.

7. **Comparing Texts** Maya Angelou portrays her grandmother in both "New Directions" and *I Know Why the Caged Bird Sings.* How are the portrayals similar? How do they differ?

8. **Connect to Life** Think about a personal goal that you would like to achieve. What can you learn from Annie Johnson's story about how to reach your goal?

Literary Analysis

THEME One of the reasons that Maya Angelou is so popular with her readers is that she often writes about uplifting or encouraging **themes.** A theme is the central idea or message in a work of literature. Theme should not be confused with subject. Rather, theme is a perception about life or humanity that a writer expresses about a subject. For example, much of Angelou's writing recounts painful experiences, yet the message those experiences convey is usually a positive one.

Paired Activity With a partner, go back through the essay and look for Angelou's overall message. Consider what she is conveying through the **title,** through her grandmother's example, and through direct statements. You may want to fill out a diagram like the one shown.

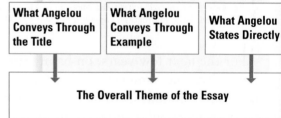

Writing Options

1. Help Wanted Ad Write an advertisement for a person to start up a small food-service business such as Annie Johnson's. Using Annie as the role model, describe the type of person who should apply for the position in the ad.

2. Loan Application Suppose that in order to build her stall, Annie Johnson needed a loan from the bank. As part of the loan application, she would have to explain what service her business would provide, who her customers would be, and why she believed that her business would succeed. Using Annie's voice, write a paragraph explaining those things.

Writing Handbook
See pages 1157–1158: Analysis.

3. Inspirational Poem Choose one of Angelou's phrases, such as "cut herself a brand-new path" or "step off that road into another direction," as the starting point for an inspirational poem. Before writing, jot down ideas and images you associate with the phrase you have chosen. Then write your poem.

Activities & Explorations

1. Meat Pie Poster Create a poster that Annie Johnson could use to advertise her meat pies. Use both art and slogans to make the pies sound appetizing. Show your poster in class. ~ **ART**

2. Map the Area Locate Stamps on a map of Arkansas. Find out what terrain is typical for that area of the state and decide whether Annie Johnson most likely had to travel on flat roads or hilly roads as she walked to the factories. Create a map showing the road to the factories and indicating both distance and terrain. ~ **GEOGRAPHY**

Inquiry & Research

Arkansas History For much of her childhood, Angelou lived in a segregated section of Stamps, Arkansas. In her work, she often mentions the limits faced by African Americans there. Use reference books or history books to research the history of African Americans in Arkansas.

Was Arkansas a state where slavery was legal before the Civil War? For what side did Arkansas fight during the Civil War? Did any significant events of the civil rights campaign take place in Arkansas? Have other well-known African Americans come from Arkansas?

Use your findings to create a bulletin board about African Americans in Arkansas.

Photo shows Elizabeth Eckford, one of the nine African-American students whose admission to Little Rock's Central High School was ordered by a federal court following legal action by NAACP Legal Defense Fund attorneys.

Martin Luther King Jr.

Black Heritage USA 13c

Encounter with Martin Luther King, Jr.

Autobiography by MAYA ANGELOU

Connect to Your Life

The Person Behind the Fame Think about a celebrity whom you would like to meet. What interests you about that person? If you did meet a celebrity, would you want that person to fit his or her public image exactly? Or would you rather discover a more private side? With a classmate, discuss the differences between the public image and the private life of a famous person.

Build Background

Civil Rights Hero Today Martin Luther King, Jr., is honored as a hero who died for the cause of civil rights. When Maya Angelou met King, he was just becoming famous—and he was a controversial figure in American life. Some people thought he was stirring up trouble between the races and that he should be more patient about waiting for discrimination to end.

Angelou met King while she was working for the Southern Christian Leadership Conference (SCLC), which he headed. The SCLC promoted nonviolent protest as a means of gaining civil rights for African Americans. Its members campaigned for desegregation, staged demonstrations supporting civil rights legislation, and coordinated voter registration drives.

Focus Your Reading

LITERARY ANALYSIS   CHARACTER STUDY   A **character study** is a piece of **nonfiction** whose purpose is to provide insight into the personality of a contemporary figure. A writer of a character study usually provides extensive details about the subject's speech, actions, and facial expressions. In addition, the writer may record the reactions of other people to the subject—including the writer's own reactions, if the character study is a **first-person account.** As you read Angelou's first-person account of her encounter with Martin Luther King, Jr., notice the details that give insight into King's character.

ACTIVE READING   SUMMARIZING   A **summary** is a short restatement of the main ideas and important points of what you've read. In preparation for summarizing the main ideas of a character study, you should keep track of the most important things you learn about the subject—in this case, Martin Luther King, Jr.

READER'S NOTEBOOK   Before you read, think about what you already know about King. Then, as you read "Encounter with Martin Luther King, Jr.," use a chart like the one shown to record important details.

What I Know About King Before Reading	What Angelou Expected King to Be Like	What Angelou Learned About King During the Encounter

Encounter with
MARTIN LUTHER KING, JR.

Maya Angelou

I returned from lunch. In the outer office Millie Jordan was working over a table of papers. Hazel was busy on the telephone. I walked into my office and a man sitting at my desk, with his back turned, spun around, stood up and smiled. Martin Luther King said, "Good afternoon, Miss Angelou. You are right on time."

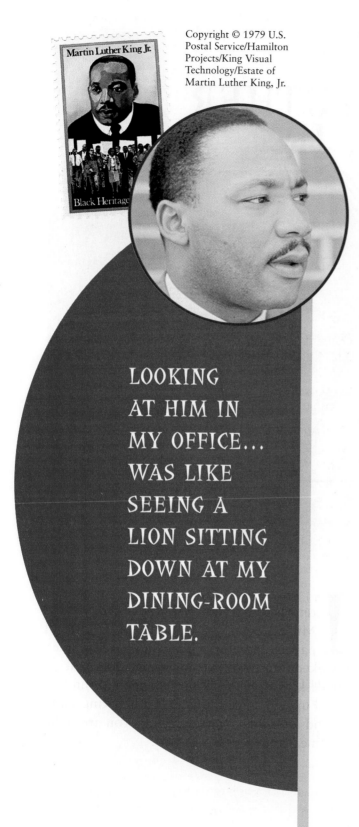

LOOKING AT HIM IN MY OFFICE... WAS LIKE SEEING A LION SITTING DOWN AT MY DINING-ROOM TABLE.

The surprise was so total that it took me a moment to react to his outstretched hand.

I had worked two months for the SCLC,[1] sent out tens of thousands of letters and invitations signed by Rev. King, made hundreds of statements in his name, but I had never seen him up close. He was shorter than I expected and so young. He had an easy friendliness, which was unsettling. Looking at him in my office, alone, was like seeing a lion sitting down at my dining-room table eating a plate of mustard greens.

"We're so grateful for the job you all are doing up here. It's a confirmation for us down on the firing line.[2]"

I was finally able to say how glad I was to meet him.

"Come on, take your seat back and tell me about yourself."

I settled gratefully into the chair and he sat on the arm of the old sofa across the room.

"Stanley says you're a Southern girl. Where are you from?" His voice had lost the church way of talking and he had become just a young man asking a question of a young woman. I looked at him and thought about the good-looking... school athlete, who was invariably the boyfriend of the high-yellow cheerleader.

I said, "Stamps, Arkansas. Twenty-five miles from Texarkana."

He knew Texarkana and Pine Bluff, and, of course, Little Rock. He asked me the size and population of Stamps and if my people were farmers. I said no and started to explain about Mamma and my crippled uncle who raised me. As I talked he nodded as if he knew them personally. When I described the dirt roads and shanties and the little schoolhouse on top

---

1. **SCLC:** Southern Christian Leadership Conference—an organization established in 1957 by Dr. Martin Luther King, Jr., and others to support the struggle for equal rights for African Americans.

2. **a confirmation . . . line:** a comfort to those of us in the midst of the struggle.

of the hill, he smiled in recognition. When I mentioned my brother Bailey, he asked what he was doing now.

The question stopped me. He was friendly and understanding, but if I told him my brother was in prison, I couldn't be sure how long his understanding would last. I could lose my job. Even more important, I might lose his respect. Birds of a feather and all that, but I took a chance and told him Bailey was in Sing Sing.[3]

He dropped his head and looked at his hands.

"It wasn't a crime against a human being." I had to explain. I loved my brother and although he was in jail, I wanted Martin Luther King to think he was an uncommon criminal. "He was a fence. Selling stolen goods. That's all."

He looked up. "How old is he?"

"Thirty-three and very bright. Bailey is not a bad person. Really."

"I understand. Disappointment drives our young men to some desperate lengths." Sympathy and sadness kept his voice low. "That's why we must fight and win. We must save the Baileys of the world. And Maya, never stop loving him. Never give up on him. Never deny him. And remember, he is freer than those who hold him behind bars."

Redemptive[4] suffering had always been the part of Martin's argument which I found difficult to accept. I had seen distress fester souls and bend peoples' bodies out of shape, but I had yet to see anyone redeemed from pain, by pain.

There was a knock at the door and Stanley Levison entered.

"Good afternoon, Maya. Hello, Martin. We're about ready."

Martin stood and the personal tenderness disappeared. He became the fighting preacher, armed and ready for the public fray.

He came over to my desk. "Please accept my thanks. And remember, we are not alone. There are a lot of good people in this nation. White people who love right and are willing to stand up and be counted." His voice had changed back to the mellifluous Baptist cadence[5] raised for the common good.

We shook hands and I wondered if his statement on the existence of good whites had been made for Stanley's benefit.

At the door, he turned. "But we cannot relax, because for every fair-minded white American, there is a Bull Connor[6] waiting with his shotgun and attack dogs."

I was sitting, mulling over the experience, when Hazel and Millie walked in smiling.

"Caught you that time, didn't we?"

I asked her if she had set up the surprise. She had not. She said when Martin came in he asked to meet me. He was told that I was due back from lunch and that I was fanatically punctual.[7] He offered to play a joke by waiting alone in my office.

Millie chuckled. "He's got a sense of humor. You never hear about that, do you?"

Hazel said, "It makes him more human somehow. I like a serious man to be able to laugh. Rounds out the personality."

Martin King had been a hero and a leader to me since the time when Godfrey and I heard him speak and had been carried to glory on his wings of hope. However, the personal sadness he showed when I spoke of my brother put my heart in his keeping forever, and made me thrust away the small constant worry which my mother had given me as a part of an early parting gift: Black folks can't change because white folks won't change. ❖

---

3. **Sing Sing:** a prison in New York State.

4. **redemptive:** earning freedom or salvation.

5. **mellifluous** (mə-lĭf′lōō-əs) **Baptist cadence** (kād′ns): smooth speaking rhythms characteristic of Baptist preachers.

6. **Bull Connor:** a Birmingham, Alabama, official who ordered police officers to use fire hoses and police dogs to break up a civil rights demonstration in 1963.

7. **fanatically punctual:** extremely concerned with being on time.

Connect to the Literature

1. **What Do You Think?**
What is your reaction to the encounter between Angelou and King? Share your response in class.

Comprehension Check
- What joke did King play on Angelou?
- What questions did King ask Angelou?
- How did King win a place in Angelou's heart?

Think Critically

2. Why do you think Angelou's encounter with King enabled her to "thrust away the small constant worry" that her mother had given her? Consider the evidence in the selection.

THINK ABOUT
- her mother's belief that "Black folks can't change because white folks won't change"
- how the conversation with King might have calmed that worry

3. **ACTIVE READING** **SUMMARIZING** Review the chart that you kept in your **READER'S NOTEBOOK.** Then summarize the new insights that you gained into the character of Martin Luther King, Jr., from reading this selection.

4. Judging from what you read in this selection, how would you describe the difference between the public image and the private side of King?

5. Which side of King—public or private—do you think meant the most to Angelou? Explain your answer.

6. From what viewpoint does Angelou relate this encounter? Does she recount only her thoughts and feelings of the time, or does she include the viewpoint of an older self? Cite details to support your answer.

Extend Interpretations

7. **What If?** If Maya Angelou had recorded the same conversation with a less famous individual, how would the impact of the selection be different?

8. **Connect to Life** This conversation between King and Angelou took place in the early 1960s. What can people today learn from the things King had to say?

Literary Analysis

CHARACTER STUDY A **character study** is a nonfiction account that provides insight into the character or personality of a contemporary figure. The writer of a character study often uses the same methods that a fiction writer uses in **characterization:**
- describing the subject's physical appearance
- reporting the subject's speech and actions
- reporting the feelings that other people have about the subject
- making direct comments about the subject

Unlike a fiction writer, a writer of a character study cannot report the inner thoughts and feelings of the person he or she is describing. However, the writer can provide clues to those thoughts and feelings by describing speech, gestures, and facial expressions.

Activity Go back through the selection and note which techniques Angelou uses to portray King's character. Record your findings on a chart like the one shown.

Describing King's Physical Appearance	
Reporting King's Speech and Actions	
Reporting Feelings About King	
Making Direct Comments About King	

THE AUTHOR'S STYLE
Angelou's Vivid Portrayals

As Maya Angelou stated in her interview, she uses incidents from her life to "dramatize" her themes. At the heart of those incidents are the people involved. Angelou's particular genius lies in portraying those people so vividly that they step right off the page and into readers' memories.

Key Aspects of Angelou's Style

- uses **language** creatively, often coining new words
- varies **sentence structure** to achieve a flowing and rhythmic effect
- creates vivid descriptions through the use of **imagery** and **figurative language,** especially striking **similes**
- uses **dialect** and realistic **dialogue** to portray characters and set the scene

---

Analysis of Style

At the right are four excerpts from Maya Angelou's writings. Look closely at the list of characteristics of her style. Then read each excerpt carefully. Complete the following activities.

- Identify examples of each of Angelou's stylistic devices in the excerpts.
- Think about how each element of style helps to make the people she describes memorable.
- Choose another excerpt from one of the selections in this Author Study. Working with a partner, identify the stylistic devices Angelou uses and discuss their impact.

Applications

1. Imitating Style Jot down the details of a memorable incident in your life. Then write about the incident, incorporating elements of Angelou's style.

2. Speaking and Listening With a partner, choose an excerpt of Angelou's writing to read aloud. Take turns practicing your oral reading and commenting on each other's performance. Choose appropriate volumes, phrasings, pitches, and gestures to convey the emotions of the piece.

3. Representing Style Choose a descriptive passage from one of the selections and make a collage to represent it. Consider the colors and shapes that people, the setting, and the action bring to mind. You might use symbolic representations based on either Angelou's figurative language or ideas of your own.

---

from I Know Why the Caged Bird Sings

It was fortunate that I never saw her in the company of powhitefolks. For since they tend to think of their whiteness as an evenizer, I'm certain that I would have had to hear her spoken to commonly as Bertha, and my image of her would have been shattered like the unmendable Humpty-Dumpty.

from I Know Why the Caged Bird Sings

"Brother and Sister Wilcox is sho'ly the meanest—" "Is," Momma? "Is"? Oh, please, not "is," Momma, for two or more. But they talked, and from the side of the building where I waited for the ground to open up and swallow me, I heard the soft-voiced Mrs. Flowers and the textured voice of my grandmother merging and melting.

from "New Directions"

Annie, over six feet tall, big-boned, decided that she would not go to work as a domestic and leave her "precious babes" to anyone else's care. There was no possibility of being hired at the town's cotton gin or lumber mill, but maybe there was a way to make the two factories work for her. In her words, "I looked up the road I was going and back the way I come, and since I wasn't satisfied, I decided to step off the road and cut me a new path."

from "Encounter with Martin Luther King, Jr."

He was shorter than I expected and so young. He had an easy friendliness, which was unsettling. Looking at him in my office, alone, was like seeing a lion sitting down at my dining-room table eating a plate of mustard greens.

Writing Options

1. Comparing Influences Write a brief comparison-contrast essay that discusses the influence on Angelou of Mrs. Flowers in *I Know Why the Caged Bird Sings* and of Martin Luther King, Jr. Use a Venn diagram like the one shown to organize your ideas.

Mrs. Flowers — Similarities — Martin Luther King, Jr.

Writing Handbook
See page 1155: Compare and Contrast.

2. Sermon on Family King was a minister as well as a civil rights worker. Imagine that he is going to preach a sermon to persuade people not to give up on family members who make mistakes, just as he urged Angelou not to give up on Bailey. Write the outline for such a sermon. Place the outline in your **Working Portfolio.**

Activities & Explorations

1. Character-Study Collage Create a collage of images and words that convey your impression of King's character. Display your finished product in class. **~ ART**

2. Panel Discussion Review Angelou's comments about "deep talk" on page 493. Then look for evidence of deep talk in "New Directions" or "Encounter with Martin Luther King, Jr." With a small group, present a panel discussion of the general concept of deep talk and the specific instances you found.
~ SPEAKING AND LISTENING

Inquiry & Research

The SCLC Find out about the work of the SCLC. What protests did it lead in the late 1950s and the 1960s? What laws did it succeed in getting passed or overturned? Where did it meet with failure? Present your findings in a time line.

Maya Angelou

Author Study Project
MAPPING ANGELOU'S LIFE

Work with a small group to present a map-based visual biography of Maya Angelou. Start by reviewing the Life and Times on pages 476–479 and the autobiographical excerpts in this Author Study. Note the many places where Angelou lived and the years that she lived in each one. Locate those places on a large map of the world. Then create a visual biography by illustrating historical and cultural events that Angelou witnessed or participated in. You might use photographs, art from the time, art of your own creation, or newspaper headlines. Connect the images to the map and write captions. Use the following suggestions to research what was happening in each of the places that Angelou lived.

History and Travel Books Use these resources to find out important events that occurred in the places she lived. Also, look for important landmarks or cultural spots that she would have known. Think about how you might represent these visually.

Newspapers and Magazines Look in these resources for news photos and headlines of the time. In addition, look for articles about cultural events. Particularly focus on the art forms in which Angelou worked—poetry, drama, and dance.

Web Sites Search for Web sites about topics related to Angelou's life. For example, you might look for information on the civil rights movement, on Egypt, and on Ghana. Especially search for sites that offer historical information.

 More Online: Research Starter
www.mcdougallittell.com

Communication Workshop

Speaking out to persuade others

From Reading to Writing Martin Luther King, Jr.'s, powerful "I Have a Dream" speech helped convince Congress to pass landmark civil rights legislation. It also continues to influence people of all ages to believe in and work to achieve their personal dreams. **Persuasive speeches** such as Dr. King's can move listeners to tears and inspire them to move mountains. Politicians, advertisers, and businesspeople—and those students who want more input into school policy, later curfews, or a bigger allowance—all use persuasive speeches to help them reach their goals.

For Your Portfolio

WRITING PROMPT Write and deliver a persuasive speech about an issue that is important to you.

Purpose: To convince others to agree with you

Audience: Anyone who can help you achieve your goal or whose views you want to change

---

Basics in a Box

GUIDELINES & STANDARDS | Persuasive Speech

Content
A successful persuasive speech should

- open with a clear statement of the issue and your opinion
- be geared to the audience you're trying to persuade
- provide facts, examples, statistics, and reasons to support your opinion
- answer opposing views

- show clear reasoning
- include strategies such as frequent summaries to help listeners remember your message
- end with a strong restatement of your opinion or a call to action

Delivery
An effective speaker should

- convey enthusiasm and confidence
- stand with good, but relaxed, posture and make eye contact with the audience

- include gestures and body language to enhance the presentation
- incorporate visual aids effectively

Analyzing a Student Model

Alex Mehta
McKinley High School

Should Our Community Council Impose a Curfew?

In the story "Cinderella," a magical world disintegrates at the stroke of midnight. If our community council has its way, everyone under 18 will have even more reason to fear 12:00 A.M. The council is proposing a curfew that would require teens to be off the street by midnight or be subject to arrest. I'm sure the council believes this curfew will reduce crime and vandalism, but I don't agree. A curfew threatens our basic rights as Americans—and this is no fairy tale.

You'll see on this chart the three major reasons I believe the way I do. First, curfew laws don't work. Some police officers, like Joe Bovaconti of Maryland Heights, Missouri, say that the laws protect juveniles. "Anything juveniles are doing after midnight is probably getting them in trouble," he maintains. On the other hand, Nadine Strossen of the American Civil Liberties Union (ACLU) speaks from a nationwide perspective. She states that there is no evidence that most crimes either by or against juveniles are committed after curfews. In fact, the Justice Policy Institute in California reported a slight increase in youth crime following the institution of a curfew there.

Second, in addition to the fact that curfews are ineffective, they are not cost-effective. The community will either have to hire more police officers to enforce the curfew or overburden the officers it has. What would these choices mean for the community? In the first case, more money, which spells higher taxes. In the second case, a loss of police morale, and possibly, less effective protection. I don't think either cost is one we want to pay.

GUIDELINES
IN ACTION

❶ Captures listeners' attention with his enthusiasm and with direct eye contact, and states the issue and his position with a striking analogy

CURFEW LAWS...
• DON'T WORK
• CAUSE TAX HIKES
• VIOLATE BASIC RIGHTS

❷ Uses visual aids to help listeners follow his points

❸ Presents and answers an opposing view

So we've already determined that curfew laws don't work and that their cost may be too high. A more important issue, however—and my third reason for opposing a curfew—is that it puts America's guaranteed rights and freedoms at risk. These rights include freedom from <u>a) age discrimination, b) invasion of privacy, and c) arrest without good cause.</u>

A curfew would violate each of these rights. I'll discuss them in order.

a) Freedom from age discrimination. If our grandparents can't be fired just because they've reached a certain age, teenagers should not be harassed just because they have not reached a certain age.

b) Freedom from invasion of privacy. A person of any age who is on the street without bothering anyone or doing anything illegal should have the right to be left alone.

c) Freedom from unjust arrest. Being under 18 isn't a crime, and it isn't a good enough reason for arresting an American citizen.

In addition to endangering those three basic rights, a curfew would also damage our community values. It would give adults a reason to mistrust teens and teens a reason to mistrust the police.

In summary, a curfew would not only be ineffective, but it also would violate the rights of every citizen under 18. And rights denied to a few Americans could soon be denied to all Americans. Therefore, I urge each of you, no matter what your age, to protect your basic rights. Speak out against a curfew law—now.

❹ Summarizes the points made to help the audience remember them

❺ Supports position with reasons and examples

❻ Restates position strongly and makes a call to action, using gestures for emphasis

1. Your Working Portfolio
Look for ideas in the **Writing Options** you completed earlier in this unit:

- **Winning Argument**, p. 437
- **"Dream" Speech**, p. 449
- **Persuasive Pamphlet**, p. 464
- **Sermon on Family**, p. 506

2. Monitor the Airwaves
As you listen to the radio or watch television, be alert for programs on controversial issues that you feel strongly about.

3. Complete the Thought
Jot down as many ways as you can to complete the following sentence: "What our community needs is_____." Choose one of these issues to develop into a speech.

Writing and Delivering Your Persuasive Speech

❶ Planning and Drafting

To find a topic for your speech, **make a list** of things you feel strongly about. You might also **brainstorm** with friends about issues that you often debate. See the **Idea Bank** in the margin for more suggestions. After you find a topic that you'd like to develop into a speech, follow the steps below.

Steps for Planning and Drafting Your Speech

▶ 1. **Clarify your position.** How do you feel about the issue and why?

▶ 2. **Find support for your position.** What research will you have to do to back up your case? Where can you find that information? Which evidence will help you make your point most effectively?

▶ 3. **Identify your audience.** What do your listeners already know about the issue? What is their stand on it?

▶ 4. **Consider how to grab your listeners' attention.** What startling statistic, amusing anecdote, or intriguing question can you use to hook your audience at the beginning of your speech?

▶ 5. **Decide how to present your arguments.** How can you organize your arguments so they have the greatest impact? Do you want to begin with the argument your audience will probably agree with and move to more controversial points? Would starting with your strongest argument—or ending with it—work better?

Think about how you will present your speech. Will your audience respond best to a straightforward, scholarly approach, or would humor be more effective? What verbal and nonverbal techniques will work best to capture and maintain your audience's interest and attention?

❷ Practicing and Delivering

The best way to practice your speech is to present it aloud—again and again. Try speaking in front of a mirror so you can evaluate and improve your posture, gestures, eye contact, and use of visual aids. You might tape-record a practice session so you can critique your voice quality and effectiveness.

Steps for Delivering Your Speech

▶ **1. Use your voice effectively.** Speak loudly enough to be heard, but vary your pitch and tone to avoid boring your audience.

▶ **2. Maintain eye contact.** Look directly at a member of the audience while you speak, moving your eyes from person to person.

▶ **3. Incorporate gestures and facial expressions.** Let your emotions show in your face—particularly in your eyes and mouth.

▶ **4. Use visual aids.** Organize your information into charts, graphs, or drawings that will reinforce your message. Make sure your materials are large enough and clear enough that everyone in the audience can read them.

❸ Revising

TARGET SKILL ▶ RESPONDING TO AUDIENCE FEEDBACK A persuasive speech is successful only if it convinces your audience. Here are some comments peer reviewers might make and ways you can respond.

- **I couldn't remember the points you made.** Include frequent summaries and reminders such as "I've just shown that you should believe X for reason A. My second reason for believing X is . . . ."

- **I couldn't hear you.** Speak loudly, but don't shout. Be sure to vary your volume and tone. Try to speak clearly and not too quickly.

- **Your evidence didn't convince me.** Gather additional expert opinions, facts, statistics, and examples; reorganize your arguments; check your reasoning.

- **I was bored.** Include an interesting quotation or personal anecdote; change the pace and volume of your voice; move around the room.

Ask Your Peer Reviewer

- What argument was most convincing?
- Which points do you disagree with and why?
- What aspects of my delivery were most effective?
- What aspects of my delivery do I need to improve?

❹ Reflecting

FOR YOUR WORKING PORTFOLIO What did you learn about your issue from writing and delivering your speech? Attach your answer to your speech. Save your speech in your **Working Portfolio.**

Need revising help?

Review the **Rubric,** p. 507

Consider **peer reader** comments

Check **Revision Guidelines,** p. 1143

Publishing IDEAS

- Record yourself delivering your speech on either audiotape or videotape.
- Set up a soapbox event with several other classmates and take turns delivering your speeches.
- Deliver your speech to your family.

More Online: Publishing Options www.mcdougallittell.com

Read this paragraph from the first draft of a persuasive speech. The underlined sections may include the following kinds of errors:

- **incorrect verb forms**
- **double negatives**
- **comma errors**
- **correctly written sentences that should be combined**

For each underlined section, choose the revision that most improves the writing.

> For years, the Riverdale community <u>had needed</u> to clean up the riverfront.
> (1)
> The river's edge in our town <u>has become</u> overgrown and dangerous. <u>Our</u>
> (2)   (3)
> <u>community can work on this together. We can clean up the riverfront. We can</u>
> <u>restore the riverfront.</u> There <u>aren't no</u> easily accessible public parks along the
> (4)
> river. We can use our <u>resources both human and financial, to</u> renew this area.
> (5)
> Imagine a riverfront walk that could be used by bicyclists, skaters, and
> walkers. <u>This park would benefit residents. This park would attract visitors.</u>
> (6)

1. **A.** has need
   B. has needed
   C. had need
   D. Correct as is

2. **A.** had became
   B. have become
   C. becomes
   D. Correct as is

3. **A.** Our community can work together, but we can clean up and restore the riverfront.
   B. Our community can work together, we can clean up and restore the riverfront.
   C. Our community can work together to clean up and restore the riverfront.
   D. Correct as is

4. **A.** aren't any
   B. are none
   C. aren't hardly
   D. Correct as is

5. **A.** resources both human and financial to
   B. resources both, human and financial, to
   C. resources, both human and financial, to
   D. Correct as is

6. **A.** This park would benefit residents, attract visitors.
   B. This park would benefit residents and attract visitors.
   C. This park would benefit residents and attract them.
   D. Correct as is

Need extra help?

See the **Grammar Handbook**

Double Negatives, p. 1188

Punctuation Chart, pp. 1201–1202

Verb Tense, p. 1184

You may have heard the old saying "Fools rush in where angels fear to tread." While we admire people who face a challenge with courage and determination, a wise person understands the limits of his or her power to act in a particular situation. The fictional characters and real people in this part of Unit Three face different kinds of limits—personal or common to everyone, external or internal, chosen freely or imposed on them by fate. As you read, ask yourself what you would do in the situations these individuals face.

ACTIVITY

With a small group of classmates, brainstorm a list of limits that you think apply to all people. For example, you might list facts about how long human beings can go without air, water, or food. Then make a second list of limits volunteered by particular classmates about themselves that are more specific to them as individuals. For example, one classmate might be good enough at track to place at the state level, but not at the national. Another might, like Indiana Jones, be willing to fight an entire army but still be afraid of snakes. Discuss the impact that personal limits can have on a person's life.

LEARNING the Language of *Literature*

$\mathcal{S}$tyle in the fashion world makes some celebrities instantly recognizable. In literature, **style** works much the same way. Style refers to the particular way that a piece of literature is written—not *what* is said, but *how* it is said. Every writer has a unique style, which is made up of many different elements. **Word choice, tone, sentence structure** and **variety**, devices such as **repetition** and **parallelism**, and **imagery** all contribute to a writer's style.

Word Choice and Tone

Word choice, or **diction,** involves a writer's selection of language. Many writers use **informal diction,** or words that sound like everyday speech, to help the reader relate to characters. In "The Beginning of Something," Sue Ellen Bridgers uses informal diction, such as "Mama wasn't one bit ready," to portray a teenage narrator. Writers often use **formal diction**—difficult, sometimes abstract language—to write about serious subjects. In "I Have a Dream," Martin Luther King, Jr., says, "We have also come to this hallowed spot to remind America of the fierce urgency of now." This example shows that diction often reveals a writer's **tone,** or attitude toward a subject.

YOUR TURN Decide whether the passage here has formal or informal diction. What words or phrases support your decision?

> ### WORD CHOICE
>
> First, a gorgeous breakfast: just everything you can imagine—from flapjacks and fried squirrel to hominy grits and honey-in-the-comb. Which puts everyone in a good humor except my friend and me. Frankly, we're so impatient to get at the presents we can't eat a mouthful.
>
> Well, I'm disappointed. Who wouldn't be? With socks, a Sunday school shirt, some handkerchiefs, a hand-me-down sweater, and a year's subscription to a religious magazine for children, *The Little Shepherd.* It makes me boil. It really does.
>
> —Truman Capote, "A Christmas Memory"

Sentence Structure and Variety

Sentence structure is an important element of any writer's style. Some writers are famous for writing long, complex sentences, while others prefer short, simple sentences. However, most writers use a **variety** of sentence structures. Writers often use short sentences to convey action or strong emotion. In "A Christmas Memory," Truman Capote conveys anger with short, choppy phrases: "Enter: two relatives. Very angry. Potent with eyes that scold, tongues that scald." Long sentences are often used to discuss complicated ideas, as in the excerpt at the right.

YOUR TURN In the passage here, what does the combination of all the phrases into one long sentence convey about the nature of King's dream?

> ### SENTENCE STRUCTURE
>
> And when this happens, and when we allow freedom to ring, when we let it ring from every village and every hamlet, from every state and every city, we will be able to speed up that day when all of God's children—black men and white men, Jews and Gentiles, Protestants and Catholics—will be able to join hands and sing in the words of the old Negro spiritual, "Free at last. Free at last. Thank God Almighty, we are free at last."
>
> —Martin Luther King, Jr., "I Have a Dream"

Repetition and Parallelism

When a writer uses the same word or phrase more than once, it is called **repetition.** Speechwriters often use repetition to help the audience follow a speech. In "Hope and Glory," Nelson Mandela uses repetition when he says, "Let there be justice for all. Let there be peace for all. Let there be work, bread, water and salt for all." **Parallelism** is the use of similar grammatical structures, sentence patterns, or figures of speech to express ideas that are equal or similar.

YOUR TURN Read the passage at the right. Identify examples of repetition and parallelism.

REPETITION AND PARALLELISM

I have a dream that one day this nation will rise up and live out the true meaning of its creed, "We hold these truths to be self-evident; that all men are created equal." I have a dream that one day on the red hills of Georgia, sons of former slaves and the sons of former slave owners will be able to sit down together at the table of brotherhood. I have a dream that one day even the state of Mississippi, a state sweltering with the heat of injustice, . . . will be transformed into an oasis of freedom and justice.

—Martin Luther King, Jr., "I Have a Dream"

Imagery

The use of **imagery,** or words and phrases that appeal to the reader's senses, can also contribute to style. In this excerpt from Maya Angelou's *I Know Why the Caged Bird Sings,* Angelou helps the reader *see* the "slow widening of her thin black lips" when Mrs. Flowers smiles and *smell* "the sweet scent of vanilla" in Mrs. Flowers's house.

YOUR TURN Which of the five senses does Angelou appeal to in the passage quoted at the right?

IMAGERY

They were flat, round wafers, slightly browned on the edges and butter-yellow in the center. With the cold lemonade they were sufficient for childhood's lifelong diet. . . . So I jammed one whole cake in my mouth, and the rough crumbs scratched the insides of my jaws, and if I hadn't had to swallow, it would have been a dream come true.

—Maya Angelou, *I Know Why the Caged Bird Sings*

Style at Work

Study the following example to see how Martin Luther King, Jr., combines sentence structure, imagery, and repetition to create his inspiring style.

The main idea is stated simply and briefly.

It is followed by long sentences containing vivid imagery that emphasizes the main idea.

The repetition of "Now is the time" helps structure the passage and make it memorable.

STYLE AT WORK

Now is the time to make real the promises of democracy; now is the time to rise from the dark and desolate valley of segregation to the sunlit path of racial justice; now is the time to lift our nation from the quicksands of racial injustice to the solid rock of brotherhood; now is the time to make justice a reality for all of God's children.

—Martin Luther King, Jr., "I Have a Dream"

The Active Reader: Skills and Strategies

Has a friend ever described what happened at a party or in another class? If so, you might have imagined the people or events that your friend described. When you did so, you were visualizing. Visualizing is a skill that you can also use as you read. The strategies described here will help you to visualize setting, characters, and imagery.

Visualizing

The process of forming a mental picture from a written or verbal description is called **visualizing.** As you read a story, you constantly use details supplied by the writer to help you picture settings, characters, and events. In addition, writers frequently use imagery—language that appeals to the five senses. One purpose of imagery is to create vivid mental images in a reader's mind.

1 Strategies for Visualizing Setting
- Note specific details about the setting. For outdoor settings, look for descriptions of weather, landscape, and buildings. For indoor settings, pay attention to details about rooms, furniture, and decor.
- **Connect** to the setting by asking yourself if the description reminds you of any place you have visited or seen in a movie.
- **Question** what it would be like to be a character in such a setting. Ask yourself if it would be easy or difficult to live in the place described.
- If the setting is confined to a small area, picture it as the set for a play. Think about how you would design the backdrop and where you would place props. Try drawing a sketch of how you think it would look.

2 Strategies for Visualizing Character
- Note details about the characters' age, coloring, height, weight, and distinguishing features. **Connect** to what you read by thinking of people you know or actors who remind you of the characters.
- Imagine you are actually seeing the action, watching the characters move and speak. Try to hear their words in your mind.
- Pay attention to descriptions of the characters' expressions and gestures. Write down key phrases that help you see the emotion on their faces.
- Pretend you are a movie director. Think about how you would film this selection. Create a list, like the one shown, of the shots you would use—for example, close-ups, medium shots, or long shots.

Filming "A Christmas Memory"
- Long shot showing "a spreading old house in a country town"
- Camera moves in toward the window of the house.
- Close-up of the face of an old woman looking out the window
- Cut to interior of kitchen.
- Medium shot of the old woman being joined by a young boy

3 Strategies for Visualizing Imagery
- Look for details that appeal to the five senses. Especially notice words and phrases that appeal to the sense of sight.
- Pay particular attention to adjectives that describe size, shape, color, and position.
- Read a passage. Then try drawing sketches of what is being described.

Need more help?

Remember that active readers use the essential reading strategies explained on page 7: **visualize, predict, clarify, question, connect, evaluate, monitor.**

To Build a Fire

Short Story by JACK LONDON

"When it is seventy-five below zero, a man must not fail in his first attempt to build a fire."

Connect to Your Life

Daring Adventures A lone hiker treks through the wilderness, 60 miles from civilization. A young woman crosses the Pacific Ocean alone in a small sailboat. A cyclist sets off across the desert. How would a person prepare for such risky adventures? Choose an adventure that you find interesting and think about how to prepare for it. Use a chart like the one shown and jot down your ideas. Then discuss your suggestions with your classmates.

Prepare for Adventure	
Type of Adventure:	
Skills to Acquire:	
Sources to Consult:	
Equipment to Obtain:	
Other Preparations:	

Build Background

"I Struck Gold!" Throughout history, the discovery of gold has fueled people's desires for wealth and has lured people to leave their homes in a quest for the precious ore. Seeking riches and adventure, Jack London joined a gold rush to the Yukon Territory in 1897. He found no gold, but his experiences provided him with the **setting** and **characters** for many of his stories, including "To Build a Fire."

The Yukon Territory is a region in far northwestern Canada. In parts of this territory, the sun doesn't shine for several days in the winter. As a result, winters are long and cold. Temperatures can fall as low as 80 degrees below zero, creating conditions that challenge the most well-prepared adventurer.

WORDS TO KNOW
Vocabulary Preview

anesthetic	extremity
apathetically	intangible
appeasingly	smite
appendage	undulation
ensue	

Focus Your Reading

LITERARY ANALYSIS **IMAGERY** **Imagery** consists of descriptive words and phrases that appeal to one or more of the five senses. Notice how the writer appeals to the senses of sight and hearing in this description from the story you are about to read:

> *There was the fire, snapping and crackling and promising life with every dancing flame.*

As you read the story, look for other examples of imagery that add to your appreciation of the setting and the plot.

ACTIVE READING **VISUALIZING** Many examples of imagery are visual—that is, they appeal to your sense of sight. The process of forming a mental picture from a written description is called **visualizing.**

READER'S NOTEBOOK As you read "To Build a Fire," practice your visualizing skills. Jot down a few descriptions that help you to picture the setting, characters, or action. If you wish, you may draw sketches instead.

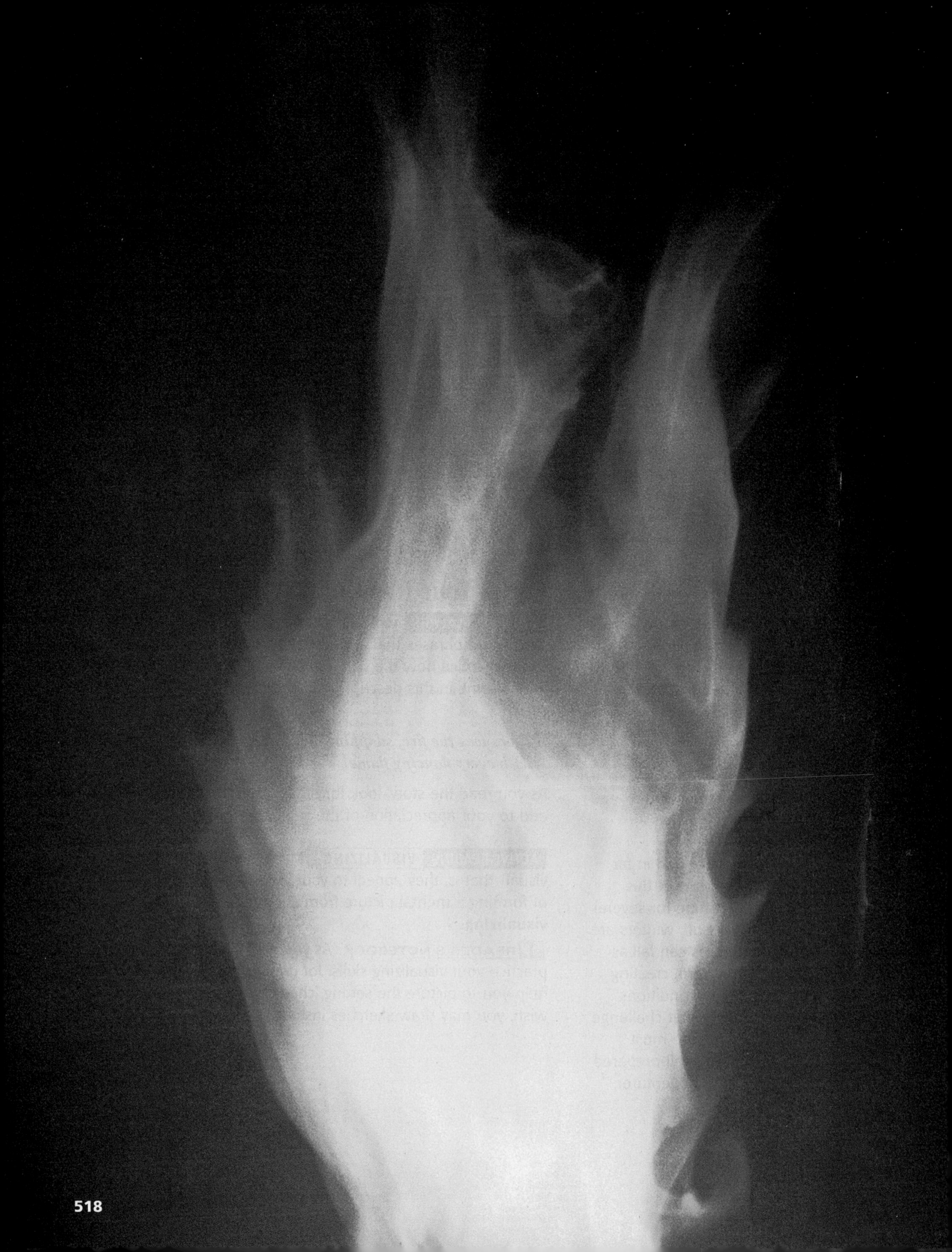

Jack London — To Build a Fire

Day had broken cold and gray, exceedingly cold and gray, when the man turned aside from the main Yukon trail and climbed the high earth-bank, where a dim and little-travelled trail led eastward through the fat spruce timberland. It was a steep bank, and he paused for breath at the top, excusing the act to himself by looking at his watch. It was nine o'clock. There was no sun nor hint of sun, though there was not a cloud in the sky. It was a clear day, and yet there seemed an intangible pall over the face of things, a subtle gloom that made the day dark, and that was due to the absence of sun. This fact did not worry the man. He was used to the lack of sun. It had been days since he had seen the sun, and he knew that a few more days must pass before that cheerful orb,[1] due south, would just peep above the sky line and dip immediately from view.

The man flung a look back along the way he had come. The Yukon lay a mile wide and hidden under three feet of ice. On top of this ice were as many feet of snow. It was all pure white, rolling in gentle undulations where the ice jams of the freeze-up had formed. North and south, as far as his eye could see, it was unbroken white, save for a dark hairline that curved and twisted from around the spruce-covered island to the south, and that curved and twisted away into the north, where it disappeared behind another spruce-covered island. This dark hairline was the trail—the main trail—that led south five hundred miles to the Chilcoot Pass, Dyea, and salt water; and that led north seventy miles to Dawson, and still on to the north a thousand miles to Nulato, and finally to St. Michael, on Bering Sea, a thousand miles and half a thousand more.

But all this—this mysterious, far-reaching hairline trail, the absence of sun from the sky, the tremendous cold, and the strangeness and weirdness of it all—made no impression on the man. It was not because he was long used to it. He was a newcomer in the land, a *chechaquo*, and this was his first winter. The trouble with him was that he was without imagination. He was quick and alert in the things of life, but only in the things, and not in the significances.

---

1. **orb:** globe.

519

Fifty degrees below zero was to him just precisely fifty degrees below zero.

ACTIVE READING

EVALUATE What do you think are the man's strengths and weaknesses?

Fifty degrees below zero meant eighty-odd degrees of frost. Such fact impressed him as being cold and uncomfortable, and that was all. It did not lead him to meditate upon his frailty as a creature of temperature, and upon man's frailty in general, able only to live within certain narrow limits of heat and cold; and from there on it did not lead him to the conjectural[2] field of immortality and man's place in the universe. Fifty degrees below zero stood for a bite of frost that hurt and that must be guarded against by the use of mittens, ear flaps, warm moccasins, and thick socks. Fifty degrees below zero was to him just precisely fifty degrees below zero. That there should be anything more to it than that was a thought that never entered his head.

As he turned to go, he spat speculatively.[3] There was a sharp, explosive crackle that startled him. He spat again. And again, in the air, before it could fall to the snow, the spittle crackled. He knew that at fifty below spittle crackled on the snow, but this spittle had crackled in the air. Undoubtedly it was colder than fifty below—how much colder he did not know. But the temperature did not matter. He was bound for the old claim[4] on the left fork of Henderson Creek, where the boys were already. They had come over across the divide from the Indian Creek country, while he had come the roundabout way to take a look at the possibilities of getting out logs in the spring from the islands in the Yukon. He would be in to camp by six o'clock; a bit after dark, it was true, but the boys would be there, a fire would be going, and a hot supper would be ready. As for lunch, he

---

2. **conjectural** (kən-jĕk′chə-rəl): involving guesswork.
3. **speculatively** (spĕk′yə-lə-tĭv-lē): out of curiosity.
4. **claim**: a tract of public land claimed by a miner.

pressed his hand against the protruding bundle under his jacket. It was also under his shirt, wrapped up in a handkerchief and lying against the naked skin. It was the only way to keep the biscuits from freezing. He smiled agreeably to himself as he thought of those biscuits, each cut open and sopped in bacon grease, and each enclosing a generous slice of fried bacon.

He plunged in among the big spruce trees. The trail was faint. A foot of snow had fallen since the last sled had passed over, and he was glad he was without a sled, travelling light. In fact, he carried nothing but the lunch wrapped in the handkerchief. He was surprised, however, at the cold. It certainly was cold, he concluded, as he rubbed his numb nose and cheekbones with his mittened hand. He was a warm-whiskered man, but the hair on his face did not protect the high cheek-bones and the eager nose that thrust itself aggressively into the frosty air.

At the man's heels trotted a dog, a big native husky, the proper wolf dog, gray-coated and without any visible or temperamental[5] difference from its brother, the wild wolf. The animal was depressed by the tremendous cold. It knew that it was no time for travelling. Its instinct told it a truer tale than was told to the man by the man's judgment. In reality, it was not merely colder than fifty below zero; it was colder than sixty below, than seventy below. It was seventy-five below zero. Since the freezing point is thirty-two above zero, it meant that one hundred and seven degrees of frost obtained.[6] The dog did not know anything about thermometers. Possibly in its brain there was no sharp consciousness of a condition of very cold such as was in the man's brain. But the brute had its instinct. It experienced a vague but menacing apprehension that subdued it and made it slink along at the man's heels, and that made it question eagerly every unwonted[7] movement of the man as if expecting him to go into camp or to seek shelter somewhere and build a fire. The dog had learned fire, and it wanted fire, or else to burrow under the snow and cuddle its warmth away from the air.

The frozen moisture of its breathing had settled on its fur in a fine powder of frost, and especially were its jowls, muzzle and eyelashes whitened by its crystalled breath. The man's red beard and mustache were likewise frosted, but more solidly, the deposit taking the form of ice and increasing with every warm, moist breath he exhaled. Also, the man was chewing tobacco, and the muzzle of ice held his lips so rigidly that he was unable to clear his chin when he expelled the juice. The result was that a crystal beard of the color and solidity of amber[8] was increasing its length on his chin. If he fell down it would shatter itself, like glass, into brittle fragments. But he did not mind the appendage. It was the penalty all tobacco chewers paid in that country, and he had been out before in two cold snaps. They had not been so cold as this, but by the spirit thermometer[9] at Sixty Mile he knew that they had been registered at fifty below and at fifty-five.

He held on through the level stretch of woods for several miles, crossed a wide flat . . . and dropped down a bank to the frozen bed of a small stream. This was Henderson Creek, and

---

5. **temperamental:** involving a characteristic way of behaving.
6. **obtained:** existed.
7. **unwonted:** unusual.
8. **amber:** a clear yellow gemstone consisting of fossilized tree sap.
9. **spirit thermometer:** a thermometer in which temperature is indicated by the height of a column of colored alcohol.

WORDS
TO
KNOW
   appendage (ə-pĕn′dĭj) *n.* something attached to a larger object

he knew he was ten miles from the forks. He looked at his watch. It was ten o'clock. He was making four miles an hour, and he calculated that he would arrive at the forks at half-past twelve. He decided to celebrate that event by eating his lunch there.

The dog dropped in again at his heels, with a tail drooping discouragement, as the man swung along the creek bed. The furrow of the old sled trail was plainly visible, but a dozen inches of snow covered the marks of the last runners. In a month no man had come up or down that silent creek. The man held steadily on. He was not much given to thinking, and just then particularly he had nothing to think about save that he would eat lunch at the forks and that at six o'clock he would be in camp with the boys. There was nobody to talk to; and, had there been, speech would have been impossible because of the ice muzzle on his mouth. So he continued monotonously to chew tobacco and to increase the length of his amber beard.

ACTIVE READING

PREDICT Do you think the man will make it safely to the camp?

Once in a while the thought reiterated[10] itself that it was very cold and that he had never experienced such cold. As he walked along he rubbed his cheekbones and nose with the back of his mittened hand. He did this automatically, now and again changing hands. But, rub as he would, the instant he stopped his cheekbones went numb, and the following instant the end of his nose went numb. He was sure to frost his cheeks; he knew that, and experienced a pang of regret that he had not devised a nose strap of the sort Bud wore in cold snaps. Such a strap passed across the cheeks, as well, and saved them. But it didn't matter much, after all. What were frosted cheeks? A bit painful, that was all; they were never serious.

Empty as the man's mind was of thoughts, he was keenly observant, and he noticed the changes in the creek, the curves and bends and timber jams,[11] and always he sharply noted where he placed his feet. Once, coming around a bend he shied abruptly, like a startled horse, curved away from the place where he had been walking, and retreated several paces back along the trail. The creek he knew was frozen clear to the bottom—no creek could contain water in that arctic winter—but he knew also that there were springs that bubbled out from the hillsides and ran along under the snow and on top the ice of the creek. He knew that the coldest snaps never froze these springs, and he knew likewise their danger. They were traps. They hid pools of water under the snow that might be three inches deep, or three feet. Sometimes a skin of ice half an inch thick covered them, and in turn was covered by the snow. Sometimes there were

---

10. **reiterated** (rē-ĭt′ə-rā′tĭd): repeated.
11. **timber jams:** piled-up masses of floating logs and branches.

Once clear of the danger, he took a fresh chew of tobacco and swung along at his four-mile gait.[12]

In the course of the next two hours he came upon several similar traps. Usually the snow above the hidden pools had a sunken, candied appearance that advertised the danger. Once again, however, he had a close call; and once, suspecting danger, he compelled the dog to go on in front. The dog did not want to go. It hung back until the man shoved it forward, and then it went quickly across the white, unbroken surface. Suddenly it broke through, floundered to one side, and got away to firmer footing. It had wet its forefeet and legs, and almost immediately the water that clung to it turned to ice. It made quick efforts to lick the ice off its legs, then dropped down in the snow and began to bite out the ice that had formed between the toes. This was a matter of instinct. To permit the ice to remain would mean sore feet. It did not know this. It merely obeyed the mysterious prompting that arose from the deep crypts[13] of its being. But the man knew, having achieved a judgment on the subject, and he removed the mitten from his right hand and helped tear out the ice particles. He did not expose his fingers more than a minute, and was astonished at the swift numbness that <u>smote</u> them. It certainly was cold. He pulled on the mitten hastily, and beat the hand savagely across his chest.

At twelve o'clock the day was at its brightest. Yet the sun was too far south on its winter journey to clear the horizon. The bulge of the earth intervened between it and Henderson Creek, where the man walked under a clear sky at noon and cast no shadow. At half-past twelve, to the minute, he arrived at the forks of the creek. He was pleased at the speed he had made. If he kept it up, he would certainly be

alternate layers of water and ice skin, so that when one broke through he kept on breaking through for a while, sometimes wetting himself to the waist.

That was why he had shied in such panic. He had felt the give under his feet and heard the crackle of a snow-hidden ice skin. And to get his feet wet in such a temperature meant trouble and danger. At the very least it meant delay, for he would be forced to stop and build a fire, and under its protection to bare his feet while he dried his socks and moccasins. He stood and studied the creek bed and its banks, and decided that the flow of water came from his right. He reflected awhile, rubbing his nose and cheeks, then skirted to the left, stepping gingerly and testing the footing for each step.

ACTIVE READING

CONNECT What do you think should be the relationship between humans and dogs? Compare that to the relationship in this story.

---

12. **four-mile gait:** walking pace of four miles per hour.
13. **crypts:** underground chambers; hidden places.

WORDS
TO
KNOW
smite (smīt) *v.* to strike; *past tense—***smote** (smōt)

523

with the boys by six. He unbuttoned his jacket and shirt and drew forth his lunch. The action consumed no more than a quarter of a minute, yet in that brief moment the numbness laid hold of the exposed fingers. He did not put the mitten on, but, instead, struck the fingers a dozen sharp smashes against his leg. Then he sat down on a snow-covered log to eat. The sting that followed upon the striking of his fingers against his leg ceased so quickly that he was startled. He had had no chance to take a bite of biscuit. He struck the fingers repeatedly and returned them to the mitten, baring the other hand for the purpose of eating. He tried to take a mouthful, but the ice muzzle prevented. He had forgotten to build a fire and thaw out. He chuckled at his foolishness, and as he chuckled he noted the numbness creeping into the exposed fingers. Also, he noted that the stinging which had first come to his toes when he sat down was already passing away. He wondered whether the toes were warm or numb. He moved them inside the moccasins and decided that they were numb.

He pulled the mitten on hurriedly and stood up. He was a bit frightened. He stamped up and down until the stinging returned into the feet. It certainly was cold, was his thought. That man from Sulphur Creek had spoken the truth when telling how cold it sometimes got in the country. And he had laughed at him at the time! That showed one must not be too sure of things. There was no mistake about it, it *was* cold. He strode up and down, stamping his feet and threshing his arms, until reassured by the returning warmth. Then he got out matches and proceeded to make a fire. From the undergrowth, where high water of the previous spring had lodged a supply of seasoned twigs, he got his firewood. Working carefully from a small beginning, he soon had a roaring fire, over which he thawed the ice from his face and in the protection of which he ate his biscuits.

For the moment the cold of space was outwitted. The dog took satisfaction in the fire, stretching out close enough for warmth and far enough away to escape being singed.

When the man had finished, he filled his pipe and took his comfortable time over a smoke, then he pulled on his mittens, settled the ear flaps of his cap firmly about his ears, and took the creek trail up the left fork. The dog was disappointed and yearned back towards the fire. This man did not know cold. Possibly all the generations of his ancestry had been ignorant of cold, of real cold, of cold one hundred and seven degrees below freezing point. But the dog knew; all its ancestry knew, and it had inherited the knowledge. And it knew that it was not good to walk abroad in such fearful cold. It was the time to lie snug in a hole in the snow and wait for a curtain of cloud to be drawn across the face of outer space whence this cold came. On the other hand, there was no keen intimacy between the dog and the man. The one was the toil slave[14] of the other, and the only caresses it had ever received were the caresses of the whip lash and of harsh and menacing throat sounds that threatened the whip lash. So the dog made no effort to communicate its apprehension to the man. It was not concerned in the welfare of the man; it was for its own sake that it yearned back toward the fire. But the man whistled, and spoke to it with the sound of whip lashes, and the dog swung in at the man's heels and followed after.

The man took a chew of tobacco and proceeded to start a new amber beard. Also, his moist breath quickly powdered with white his mustache, eyebrows, and lashes. There did not seem to be so many springs on the left fork of the Henderson, and for half an hour the man saw no signs of any. And then it happened. At

---

14. **toil slave:** slave who performs hard labor.

a place where there were no signs, where the soft, unbroken snow seemed to advertise solidity beneath, the man broke through. It was not deep. He wet himself halfway to the knees before he floundered out to the firm crust. He was angry, and cursed his luck aloud. He had hoped to get into camp with the boys at six o'clock, and this would delay him an hour, for he would have to build a fire and dry out his footgear. This was imperative[15] at that low temperature—he knew that much; and he turned aside to the bank, which he climbed. On top, tangled in the underbrush about the trunks of several small spruce trees, was a high-water deposit[16] of dry firewood—sticks and twigs, principally, but also larger portions of seasoned branches and fine, dry, last year's grasses. He threw down several large pieces on top of the snow. This served for a foundation and prevented the young flame from drowning itself in the snow it otherwise would melt. The flame he got by touching a match to a small shred of birch bark that he took from his pocket. This burned even more readily than paper. Placing it on the foundation, he fed the young flame with wisps of dry grass and with the tiniest dry twigs.

He worked slowly and carefully, keenly aware of his danger. Gradually, as the flame grew stronger, he increased the size of the twigs with which he fed it. He squatted in the snow, pulling the twigs out from their entanglement in the brush and feeding directly to the flame. He knew there must be no failure. When it is seventy-five below zero, a man must not fail in his first attempt to build a fire—that is, if his feet are wet. If his feet are dry, and he fails, he can run along the trail for half a mile and restore his circulation. But the circulation of wet and freezing feet cannot be restored by running when it is seventy-five below. No matter how fast he runs, the wet feet will freeze the harder.

All this the man knew. The old-timer on Sulphur Creek had told him about it the previous fall, and now he was appreciating the advice. Already all sensation had gone out of his feet. To build the fire he had been forced to remove his mittens, and the fingers had quickly gone numb. His pace of four miles an hour had kept his heart pumping blood to the surface of his body and to all the extremities. But the instant he stopped, the action of the pump eased down. The cold of space smote the unprotected tip of the planet, and he, being on that unprotected tip, received the full force of the blow. The blood of his body recoiled before it. The blood was alive, like the dog, and like the dog it wanted to hide away and cover itself up from the fearful cold. So long as he walked four miles an hour, he pumped the blood, willy-nilly,[17] to the surface; but now it ebbed away and sank down into the recesses of his body. The extremities were the first to feel its absence. His wet feet froze the faster, and his exposed fingers numbed the faster, though they had not yet begun to freeze. Nose and cheeks were already freezing, while the skin of all his body chilled as it lost its blood.

But he was safe. Toes and nose and cheeks would be only touched by the frost, for the fire was beginning to burn with strength. He was feeding it with twigs the size of his finger. In another minute he would be able to feed it with branches the size of his wrist, and then he could remove his wet footgear, and, while it dried, he could keep his naked feet warm by the fire, rubbing them at first, of course, with snow. The fire was a success. He was safe. He remembered

---

15. **imperative** (ĭm-pĕr′ə-tĭv): urgently necessary.
16. **high-water deposit:** debris left on the bank of a stream as the water recedes from its highest level.
17. **willy-nilly:** unavoidably.

WORDS TO KNOW **extremity** (ĭk-strĕm′ĭ-tē) *n.* a hand or a foot

the advice of the old-timer on Sulphur Creek, and smiled. The old-timer had been very serious in laying down the law that no man must travel alone in the Klondike after fifty below. Well, here he was; he had had the accident; he was alone; and he had saved himself. Those old-timers were rather womanish, some of them, he thought. All a man had to do was to keep his head, and he was all right. Any man who was a man could travel alone. But it was surprising, the rapidity with which his cheeks and nose were freezing. And he had not thought his fingers could go lifeless in so short a time. Lifeless they were, for he could scarcely make them move together to grip a twig, and they seemed remote from his body and from him. When he touched a twig, he had to look and see whether or not he had hold of it. The wires were pretty well down between him and his finger ends.

All of which counted for little. There was the fire, snapping and crackling and promising life with every dancing flame. He started to untie his moccasins. They were coated with ice; the thick German socks were like sheaths of iron halfway to the knees; and the moccasin strings were like rods of steel all twisted and knotted as by some conflagration.[18] For a moment he tugged with his numb fingers, then, realizing the folly of it, he drew his sheath knife.

But before he could cut the strings, it happened. It was his own fault or, rather, his mistake. He should not have built the fire under the spruce tree. He should have built it in the open. But it had been easier to pull the twigs from the brush and drop them directly on the fire. Now the tree under which he had done this carried a weight of snow on its boughs. No wind had blown for weeks, and each bough was full freighted. Each time he had pulled a twig he had communicated a slight agitation[19] to the tree—an imperceptible agitation, so far as he was concerned, but an agitation sufficient to bring about the disaster. High up in the tree

one bough capsized[20] its load of snow. This fell on the boughs beneath, capsizing them. This process continued, spreading out and involving the whole tree. It grew like an avalanche, and it descended upon the man and the fire, and the fire was blotted out! Where it had burned was a mantle of fresh and disordered snow.

ACTIVE READING

VISUALIZE Picture the events that cause the fire to go out. What words or phrases help you imagine them?

The man was shocked. It was as though he had just heard his own sentence of death. For a moment he sat and stared at the spot where the fire had been. Then he grew very calm.

Perhaps the old-timer on Sulphur Creek was right. If he had only had a trail mate he would have been in no danger now. The trail mate could have built the fire. Well, it was up to him to build the fire over again, and this second time there must be no failure. Even if he succeeded, he would most likely lose some toes. His feet must be badly frozen by now, and there would be some time before the second fire was ready.

Such were his thoughts, but he did not sit and think them. He was busy all the time they were passing through his mind. He made a new foundation for a fire, this time in the open, where no treacherous tree could blot it out. Next he gathered dry grasses and tiny twigs from the high-water flotsam.[21] He could not bring his fingers together to pull them out, but he was able to gather them by the handful. In this way he got many rotten twigs and bits of green moss that were undesirable, but it was the best he could do. He worked methodically, even collecting an armful of the larger branches to be used later when the fire gathered strength. And

---

18. **conflagration** (kŏn′flə-grā′shən): large, destructive fire.

19. **agitation:** disturbance.

20. **capsized:** overturned.

21. **flotsam** (flŏt′səm): debris.

all the while the dog sat and watched him, a certain wistfulness in its eyes, for it looked upon him as the fire provider, and the fire was slow in coming.

When all was ready, the man reached in his pocket for a second piece of birch bark. He knew the bark was there, and though he could not feel it with his fingers, he could hear its crisp rustling as he fumbled for it. Try as he would, he could not clutch hold of it. And all the time, in his consciousness, was the knowledge that each instant his feet were freezing. This thought tended to put him in a panic, but he fought against it and kept calm. He pulled on his mittens with his teeth, and threshed his arms back and forth, beating his hands with all his might against his sides. He did this sitting down, and he stood up to do it; and all the while the dog sat in the snow, its wolf brush of a tail curled around warmly over its forefeet, its sharp wolf ears pricked forward intently as it watched the man. And the man, as he beat and threshed with his arms and hands, felt a great surge of envy as he regarded the creature that was warm and secure in its natural covering.

...all the while the dog sat in the snow, its wolf brush of a tail curled around warmly over its forefeet...

After a time he was aware of the first faraway signals of sensations in his beaten fingers. The faint tingling grew stronger till it evolved into a stinging ache that was excruciating, but which the man hailed with satisfaction. He stripped the mitten from his right hand and fetched forth the birch bark. The exposed fingers were quickly going numb again. Next he brought out his bunch of sulphur matches. But the tremendous cold had already driven the life out of his fingers. In his effort to separate one match from the others, the whole bunch fell into the snow. He tried to pick it out of the snow, but failed. The dead fingers could neither clutch nor touch. He was very careful. He drove the thought of his freezing feet, and nose, and cheeks, out of his mind, devoting his whole soul to the matches. He watched, using the sense of vision in place of that of touch, and when he saw his fingers on each side the bunch, he closed them—that is, he willed to close them, for the wires were down, and the fingers did not obey. He pulled the mitten on the right hand, and beat it fiercely against his knee. Then, with both mittened hands, he scooped the bunch of matches, along with much snow, into his lap. Yet he was no better off.

ACTIVE READING

CLARIFY Why is the man having difficulty rebuilding his fire?

After some manipulation he managed to get the bunch between the heels of his mittened hands. In this fashion he carried it to his mouth. The ice crackled and snapped when by a violent effort he opened his mouth. He drew the lower jaw in, curled the upper lip out of the way and scraped the bunch with his upper teeth in order to separate a match. He succeeded in getting one, which he dropped on his lap. He was no

better off. He could not pick it up. Then he devised a way. He picked it up in his teeth and scratched it on his leg. Twenty times he scratched before he succeeded in lighting it. As it flamed he held it with his teeth to the birch bark. But the burning brimstone[22] went up his nostrils and into his lungs, causing him to cough spasmodically. The match fell into the snow and went out.

The old-timer on Sulphur Creek was right, he thought in the moment of controlled despair that <u>ensued</u>: after fifty below, a man should travel with a partner. He beat his hands, but failed in exciting any sensation. Suddenly he bared both hands, removing the mittens with his teeth. He caught the whole bunch between the heels of his hands. His arm muscles not being frozen enabled him to press the hand heels tightly against the matches. Then he scratched the bunch along his leg. It flared into flame, seventy sulphur matches at once! There was no wind to blow them out. He kept his head to one side to escape the strangling fumes, and held the blazing bunch to the birch bark. As he so held it, he became aware of sensation in his hand. His flesh was burning. He could smell it. Deep down below the surface he could feel it. The sensation developed into pain that grew acute. And still he endured it, holding the flame of the matches clumsily to the bark that would not light readily because his own burning hands were in the way, absorbing most of the flame.

At last, when he could endure no more, he jerked his hands apart. The blazing matches fell sizzling into the snow, but the birch bark was alight. He began laying dry grasses and the tiniest twigs on the flame. He could not pick and choose, for he had to lift the fuel between the heels of his hands. Small pieces of rotten

---

22. **brimstone:** sulfur—a chemical used in match heads.

WORDS
TO
KNOW
ensue (ĕn-sōō') v. to occur as a result; follow

wood and green moss clung to the twigs, and he bit them off as well as he could with his teeth. He cherished[23] the flame carefully and awkwardly. It meant life, and it must not perish. The withdrawal of blood from the surface of his body now made him begin to shiver, and he grew more awkward. A large piece of green moss fell squarely on the little fire. He tried to poke it out with his fingers, but his shivering frame made him poke too far, and he disrupted the nucleus of the little fire, the burning grasses and the tiny twigs separating and scattering. He tried to poke them together again, but in spite of the tenseness of the effort, his shivering got away with him, and the twigs were hopelessly scattered. Each twig gushed a puff of smoke and went out. The fire provider had failed. As he looked <u>apathetically</u> about him, his eyes chanced on the dog, sitting across the ruins of the fire from him, in the snow, making restless, hunching movements, slightly lifting one forefoot and then the other, shifting its weight back and forth on them with wistful eagerness.

The sight of the dog put a wild idea into his head. He remembered the tale of the man, caught in a blizzard, who killed a steer and crawled inside the carcass, and so was saved. He would kill the dog and bury his hands in the warm body until the numbness went out of

---

23. **cherished:** tended; guarded.

WORDS
TO
KNOW

apathetically (ăp′ə-thĕt′ĭ-klē) *adv.* with little interest or emotion

them. Then he could build another fire. He spoke to the dog, calling it to him; but in his voice was a strange note of fear that frightened the animal, who had never known the man to speak in such a way before. Something was the matter, and its suspicious nature sensed danger—it knew not what danger, but somewhere, somehow, in its brain arose an apprehension of the man. It flattened its ears down at the sound of the man's voice, and its restless, hunching movements and the liftings and shiftings of its forefeet became more pronounced; but it would not come to the man. He got on his hands and knees and crawled toward the dog. This unusual posture again excited suspicion, and the animal sidled mincingly[24] away.

The man sat up in the snow for a moment and struggled for calmness. Then he pulled on his mittens, by means of his teeth, and got upon his feet. He glanced down at first in order to assure himself that he was really standing up, for the absence of sensation in his feet left him unrelated to the earth. His erect position in itself started to drive the webs of suspicion from the dog's mind; and when he spoke <u>peremptorily</u>, with the sound of whip lashes in his voice, the dog rendered its customary allegiance and came to him. As it came within reaching distance, the man lost his control. His arms flashed out to the dog, and he experienced genuine surprise when he discovered that his hands could not clutch, that there was neither bend nor feeling in his fingers. He had forgotten for the moment that they were frozen and that they were freezing more and more. All this happened quickly, and before the animal could get away, he encircled its body with his arms. He sat down in the snow, and in this fashion held the dog, while it snarled and whined and struggled.

He would kill the dog and bury his hands in the warm body until the numbness went out of them.

---

24. **sidled** (sīd'ld) **mincingly:** moved sideways with small steps.

WORDS TO KNOW

peremptorily (pə-rĕmp'tə-rĭ-lē) *adv.* in a commanding manner

But it was all he could do, hold its body encircled in his arms and sit there. He realized that he could not kill the dog. There was no way to do it. With his helpless hands he could neither draw nor hold his sheath knife nor throttle the animal. He released it, and it plunged wildly away, with tail between its legs, and still snarling. It halted forty feet away and surveyed him curiously, with ears sharply pricked forward.

The man looked down at his hands in order to locate them, and found them hanging on the ends of his arms. It struck him as curious that one should have to use his eyes in order to find out where his hands were. He began threshing his arms back and forth, beating the mittened hands against his sides. He did this for five minutes, violently, and his heart pumped enough blood up to the surface to put a stop to his shivering. But no sensation was aroused in the hands. He had an impression that they hung like weights on the ends of his arms, but when he tried to run the impression down, he could not find it.

A certain fear of death, dull and oppressive, came to him. This fear quickly became poignant[25] as he realized that it was no longer a mere matter of freezing his fingers and toes, or of losing his hands and feet, but that it was a matter of life and death with the chances against him. This threw him into a panic, and he turned and ran along the old, dim trail. The dog joined in behind and kept up with him. He ran blindly, without intention, in fear such as he had never known in his life. Slowly, as he plowed and floundered through the snow, he began to see things again— the banks of the creek, the old timber jams, the leafless aspens, and the sky. The running made him feel better. He did not shiver. Maybe, if he ran on, his feet would thaw out; and, anyway, if he ran far enough, he would reach camp and the boys. Without doubt he would lose some fingers and toes and some of his face; but the boys

would take care of him, and save the rest of him when he got there. And at the same time there was another thought in his mind that said he would never get to the camp and the boys; that he would soon be stiff and dead. This thought he kept in the background and refused to consider. Sometimes it pushed itself forward and demanded to be heard, but he thrust it back and strove[26] to think of other things.

It struck him as curious that he could run at all on feet so frozen that he could not feel them when they struck the earth and took the weight of his body. He seemed to himself to skim along above the surface, and to have no connection with the earth. Somewhere he had once seen a winged Mercury,[27] and he wondered if Mercury felt as he felt when skimming over the earth.

His theory of running until he reached camp and the boys had one flaw in it: he lacked the endurance. Several times he stumbled, and finally he tottered, crumpled up, and fell. When he tried to rise, he failed. He must sit and rest, he decided, and next time he would merely walk and keep on going. As he sat and regained his breath, he noted that he was feeling quite warm and comfortable. He was not shivering, and it even seemed that a warm glow had come to his chest and trunk. And yet, when he touched his nose or cheeks, there was no sensation. Running would not thaw them out. Nor would it thaw out his hands and feet. Then the thought came to him that the frozen portions of his body must be extending. He tried to keep this thought down, to forget it, to think of something else; he was aware of the panicky feeling that it caused, and he was afraid of the panic. But the thought asserted itself, and persisted, until it produced a

---

25. **poignant** (poin′yənt): painful; distressing.
26. **strove**: tried hard; struggled.
27. **Mercury**: the messenger of the gods in Roman mythology, who flew about by means of wings on his helmet and sandals.

vision of his body totally frozen. This was too much, and he made another wild run along the trail. Once he slowed down to a walk, but the thought of the freezing extending itself made him run again.

And all the time the dog ran with him, at his heels. When he fell down a second time, it curled its tail over its forefeet and sat in front of him, facing him, curiously eager and intent. The warmth and security of the animal angered him, and he cursed it till it flattened down its ears appeasingly. This time the shivering came more quickly upon the man. He was losing in his battle with the frost. It was creeping into his body from all sides. The thought of it drove him on, but he ran no more than a hundred feet, when he staggered and pitched headlong. It was his last panic. When he had recovered his breath and control, he sat up and entertained in his mind the conception of meeting death with dignity. However, the conception did not come to him in such terms. His idea of it was that he had been making a fool of himself, running around like a chicken with its head cut off— such was the simile that occurred to him. Well, he was bound to freeze anyway, and he might as well take it decently. With this newfound peace of mind came the first glimmerings of drowsiness. A good idea, he thought, to sleep off to death. It was like taking an anesthetic. Freezing was not so bad as people thought. There were lots worse ways to die.

He pictured the boys finding his body the next day. Suddenly he found himself with them, coming along the trail and looking for himself. And, still with them, he came around a turn in the trail and found himself lying in the snow. He did not belong with himself any more, for even then he was out of himself, standing with the boys and looking at himself in the snow. It certainly was cold, was his thought. When he

As he sat and regained his breath, he noted that he was feeling quite warm and comfortable.

got back to the States he could tell the folks what real cold was. He drifted on from this to a vision of the old-timer on Sulphur Creek. He could see him quite clearly, warm and comfortable, and smoking a pipe.

"You were right, old hoss;[28] you were right," the man mumbled to the old-timer of Sulphur Creek.

Then the man drowsed off into what seemed to him the most comfortable and satisfying sleep he had ever known. The dog sat facing him and waiting. The brief day drew to a close in a long, slow twilight. There were no signs of a fire to be made, and, besides, never in the dog's experience had it known a man to sit like that in the snow and make no fire. As the twilight drew on, its eager yearning for the fire mastered it, and with a great lifting and shifting of forefeet, it whined softly, then flattened its ears down in anticipation of being chidden[29] by the man. But the man remained silent. Later the dog whined loudly. And still later it crept close to the man and caught the scent of death. This made the animal bristle and back away. A little longer it delayed, howling under the stars that leaped and danced and shone brightly in the cold sky. Then it turned and trotted up the trail in the direction of the camp it knew, where there were other food providers and fire providers. ❖

---

28. **old hoss:** old horse—here used as an affectionate term of address.

29. **chidden:** scolded.

Connect to the Literature

1. **What Do You Think?** What was your first thought when the snow put out the fire?

Comprehension Check
- What different problems does the man in the story face?
- Describe the man's relationship with the dog.
- Why is the man forced to try to rebuild his fire?
- Why does he have difficulty rebuilding the fire?

Think Critically

2. Would you want the man in this story to be your partner on an adventure? Explain what aspects of his **character** influenced your decision.

THINK ABOUT

- the statement that "he was quick and alert in the things of life" but "not in the significances"
- how he responds to the advice of the old-timer on Sulphur Creek
- his reactions to the cold temperatures
- his relationship with the dog

3. What do you blame most for the man's death—the harsh Yukon **setting** or the man's own decisions and actions? Consider the evidence in the story as you explain your answer.

4. Does the man's attitude toward death surprise you? Why or why not?

5. **ACTIVE READING VISUALIZING** Look back at your **READER'S NOTEBOOK.** Decide which of the descriptions you recorded creates the most vivid picture in your mind. What phrases help you to visualize the scene?

Extend Interpretations

6. **Critic's Corner** One critic has said that at the end of the story, the man "achieves a kind of heroic stature." Do you agree? Explain your answer.

7. **What If?** If his relationship with the dog had been different, do you think the man might have survived? Cite evidence for your opinion.

8. **Connect to Life** Review the chart you prepared in Connect to Your Life on page 517. If you were setting off today on the same daring adventure described in this story, what skills and equipment would you want?

Literary Analysis

IMAGERY Writers use **imagery** to create a picture in the reader's mind or to remind the reader of a familiar sensation. Imagery is language that appeals to one or more of the five senses—sight, smell, hearing, taste, and touch. Although much imagery is visual, an image can appeal to any of the five senses or to a combination of them.

Cooperative Learning Activity
Make a chart like the one shown. Then, working with a partner, go back through the story. Look for words and phrases that appeal to each of the five senses, listing as many different kinds of images as you can find. When you are done, discuss the following question with a larger group: How important is the author's use of imagery to the story?

Imagery in "To Build a Fire"	
Sight	
Smell	
Hearing	
Taste	
Touch	

MOOD The imagery in a story often contributes to the **mood.** Mood is the feeling or atmosphere that a writer creates for the reader. How would you describe the mood in "To Build a Fire"? What imagery helps create this mood? Share your thoughts with your classmates.

Writing Options

1. Yukon News Report Write a news report for a Yukon newspaper that reports the man's death, the discovery of his body, and the reaction of his comrades. Include a quote from the old-timer on Sulphur Creek.

2. Fire-Building Instructions Using the information in the story, write instructions for the process of building a fire in winter. Be sure to list any necessary equipment. Place the instructions in your **Working Portfolio.**

Writing Handbook
See page 1157: Analysis.

3. Man v. Beast Paragraph Think about differences between the man and the dog. Consider their

- natural abilities
- behavior toward each other
- relationship to the environment

Write a paragraph or create a chart in which you highlight the differences between the two.

Writing Handbook
See page 1155: Compare and Contrast.

Activities & Explorations

1. Story Illustration Create a drawing or painting that illustrates one scene from this story. Share your work with classmates. ~ **ART**

2. Solar Demonstration Demonstrate for classmates how the position of the sun and earth causes sunless days during the Yukon winter. Consult a science book if necessary, and use a diagram, globe, or other objects for your demonstration. ~ **SCIENCE**

Inquiry & Research

Cold Hard Facts Does it have to be as cold as 75 degrees below zero for weather to be dangerous? Use an encyclopedia or medical book to answer the following questions: What degree of coldness is life-threatening? What are the symptoms of frostbite and hypothermia? How are those conditions treated? Use your findings to create a safety poster.

Vocabulary in Action

EXERCISE A: IDIOMS On your paper, write the Word to Know suggested by each set of idioms.

1. couldn't care less, don't give a hoot
2. neither here nor there, hard to fathom
3. leader of the pack, king of the hill
4. smooth things over, mend fences
5. out like a light, feeling no pain

Building Vocabulary
For an in-depth lesson on idioms, see page 305.

EXERCISE B: RELATED WORDS On your paper, write the letter of the word that does not belong in each group.

1. (a) undulation, (b) stream, (c) ripple, (d) wave
2. (a) hand, (b) foot, (c) extremity, (d) heart
3. (a) follow, (b) ensue, (c) involve, (d) succeed
4. (a) cower, (b) kick, (c) strike, (d) smite
5. (a) attachment, (b) addition, (c) appendage, (d) abrasion

WORDS TO KNOW				
anesthetic	appeasingly	ensue	intangible	smite
apathetically	appendage	extremity	peremptorily	undulation

Grammar in Context: Participles

In "To Build a Fire," Jack London uses participles to add detail and lively descriptions to nouns.

> He kept his head to one side to escape the strangling fumes, and held the blazing bunch to the birch bark.

> The moccasin strings were like rods of steel all twisted and knotted. . . .

A **participle** is a verb form that functions as an adjective. A present participle is formed by adding *-ing* to the present-tense form of a verb. The past participle of a regular verb is formed by adding *-d* or *-ed* to the present-tense form of the verb. The following diagram shows how two of the participles in the examples above were formed.

VERB: *strangle* → PRESENT PARTICIPLE: *strangling* → PARTICIPLE + NOUN: *strangling fumes*

VERB: *twist* → PAST PARTICIPLE: *twisted* → NOUN + PARTICIPLE: *steel (all) twisted*

WRITING EXERCISE Add a participle to modify each underlined noun.

Punctuation Tip: Use commas after participles that begin sentences.

> **Example:** _____, the dog continued to follow the man.
> Discouraged, the dog continued to follow the man.

1. He hunched over to protect himself from the _____ wind.
2. The dog moved closer to the _____ fire.
3. The _____ cold drained the man's energy.
4. _____, the traveler seemed to have lost his way.
5. The dog howled at the stars _____ in the night sky.

Connect to the Literature Reread the paragraph beginning at the bottom of page 529 ("At last, when he could endure no more . . .") and find the participles in it. Remember that not all words ending in *-ing* and *-ed* are participles. To be a participle, a word must act as an adjective, modifying a noun or pronoun.

Grammar Handbook Verbals, p. 1194

Jack London
1876–1916

Other Works
The Sea-Wolf
The Call of the Wild
White Fang

Unhappy Childhood Growing up in California, Jack London lived in what he later described as poverty. To help his family, he began doing odd jobs at age nine, and after eighth grade he quit school to work full-time in a pickle cannery. Lonely most of the time, London turned to books for companionship and claimed to have received much of his education in the public library.

Pirate to Hobo London is as famous for his risky adventures as for his writing. At age 15, he became an oyster pirate, illegally raiding commercial oyster beds along the California coast. He later joined the crew of a seal-hunting vessel. While still a teenager, London roamed across the country and was arrested in New York for being a hobo. After a sobering 30 days in jail, he returned home and completed his high school studies. He then entered the University of California but had no money and was forced to quit after only one semester.

Rags to Riches His 1897 trip to the Yukon Territory in search of gold was a turning point in his life. It inspired the young man to write adventure stories, which the public loved. Within a few years, he was an internationally famous author and a self-made millionaire. Unfortunately, tropical ailments acquired during a sailing trip damaged his health severely. He was only 40 when he died. In just 20 years, however, London had produced 200 short stories, 400 essays and articles, and 50 books.

from **Into Thin Air**

Eyewitness Account by JON KRAKAUER

"Ten minutes later all my oxygen was gone."

Connect to Your Life

Risk Takers What do you think is the most dangerous sport—white-water rafting, skydiving, or something else? With a classmate, choose a sport that is extremely risky and list the dangers it involves. As you read this selection, compare those risks with the risks involved in climbing Mount Everest.

Build Background

Gasping for Breath With an altitude of 29,028 feet, Mount Everest is the highest peak on earth. Mountain climbers call the region above 26,000 feet the Death Zone because the air is too thin for humans. At that altitude, brain cells die, the blood grows thick, the heart speeds up, and the brain can swell—leading to death.

In spite of those risks, reaching the top of Everest has become a status symbol. By the 1990s, even people with little experience and poor physical conditioning were climbing Everest.

Jon Krakauer was one of those climbers. A journalist, he was hired by *Outside* magazine to write about the trend of unskilled climbers buying their way onto Everest. The selection opens with Krakauer on top of the mountain and the hardest part still to come. He had been warned that "any idiot can get up this hill. The trick is to get back down alive."

WORDS TO KNOW
Vocabulary Preview

cognizant	initiative
compulsively	meander
critical	obscuring
escalate	obstinacy
hindsight	supplemental

Focus Your Reading

LITERARY ANALYSIS **WORD CHOICE** Writers use language to express their particular thoughts and feelings. To do this well, they must choose exactly the right words. In one passage, Jon Krakauer describes a delay that occurred as he was climbing down Everest with a low oxygen supply:

> *I encountered a clot of climbers chuffing up the single strand of rope.*

The word *clot* can also mean a lump that obstructs blood flow. By choosing this word, Krakauer conveys not only the obstacle to his descent but also his sense of danger. As you read, notice how the word choices Krakauer makes reveal his feelings about his subject.

ACTIVE READING **DETERMINING A WRITER'S MOTIVES** Many different motives, or reasons, prompt people to write. Possible motives for writers of eyewitness accounts include:

- to record the facts for history
- to analyze mistakes in order to prevent future problems
- to explain their own behavior
- to explain the behavior of others

When choosing which events and people to include in their accounts, writers must decide which material will best serve their purpose. For example, Krakauer records a blinded climber's response to his offer of help:

> *"Thanks anyway,"* Beck said. *"I think I'll just wait for Mike. He's got a rope."*

Krakauer includes this exchange to explain why he left Beck alone on the mountain—an act that endangered Beck's life.

READER'S NOTEBOOK As you read this account, look for clues to Krakauer's motives for writing. You may want to add other motives to the list above.

Into Thin Air

JON KRAKAUER

In my backpack was a banner from *Outside* magazine, a small pennant emblazoned with a whimsical lizard that Linda, my wife, had sewn, and some other mementos with which I'd intended to pose for a series of triumphant photos. Cognizant of my dwindling oxygen reserves, however, I left everything in my pack and stayed on top of the world just long enough to fire off four quick shots of Andy Harris and Anatoli Boukreev posing in front of the summit survey marker. Then I turned to descend. About twenty yards below the summit I passed Neal Beidleman and a client of Fischer's named Martin Adams[1] on their way up. After exchanging a high five with Neal, I grabbed a handful of small stones from a wind-scoured patch of exposed shale, zipped the souvenirs into the pocket of my down suit, and hastened down the ridge.

539

A moment earlier I'd noticed that wispy clouds now filled the valleys to the south, <u>obscuring</u> all but the highest peaks. Adams—a small, pugnacious[2] Texan who'd gotten rich selling bonds during the booming 1980s—is an experienced airplane pilot who'd spent many hours gazing down on the tops of clouds; later he told me that he recognized these innocent-looking puffs of water vapor to be the crowns of robust thunderheads immediately after reaching the top. "When you see a thunderhead in an airplane," he explained, "your first reaction is to get . . . out of there. So that's what I did."

But unlike Adams, I was unaccustomed to peering down at cumulonimbus cells from 29,000 feet, and I therefore remained ignorant of the storm that was even then bearing down. My concerns revolved instead around the diminishing supply of oxygen in my tank.

Fifteen minutes after leaving the summit I reached the top of the Hillary Step,[3] where I encountered a clot of climbers chuffing up the single strand of rope, and my descent came to an enforced halt. As I waited for the crowd to pass, Andy arrived on his way down. "Jon," he asked, "I don't seem to be getting enough air. Can you tell if the intake valve to my mask is iced up?"

A quick check revealed a fist-sized chunk of frozen drool blocking the rubber valve that admitted ambient[4] air into the mask from the atmosphere. I chipped it off with the pick of my ice ax, then asked Andy to return the favor by turning off my regulator in order to conserve my gas until the Step cleared. He mistakenly opened the valve instead of closing it, however, and ten minutes later all my oxygen was gone. My cognitive functions,[5] which had been marginal before, instantly went into a nosedive. I felt like I'd been slipped an overdose of a powerful sedative.

I fuzzily remember Sandy Pittman climbing past as I waited, bound for the summit, followed an indeterminate time later by Charlotte Fox and then Lopsang Jangbu. Yasuko materialized next, just below my precarious stance, but was flummoxed[6] by the last and steepest portion of the Step. I watched helplessly for fifteen minutes as she struggled to haul herself up the uppermost brow of rock, too exhausted to manage it. Finally Tim Madsen, who was waiting impatiently directly below her, . . . pushed her to the top.

Rob Hall[7] appeared not long after that. Disguising my rising panic, I thanked him for getting me to the top of Everest. "Yeah, it's turned out to be a pretty good expedition," he replied, then mentioned that Frank Fischbeck, Beck Weathers, Lou Kasischke, Stuart Hutchison, and John Taske had all turned back. Even in my state of hypoxic imbecility,[8] it was obvious Hall was profoundly disappointed that five of his eight

---

1. **Andy Harris . . . Martin Adams:** Harris, Boukreev, and Beidleman were professional guides; Adams was a client of another guide, Scott Fischer.

2. **pugnacious** (pŭg-nā′shəs): aggressive and tough.

3. **Hillary** (hĭl′ə-rē) **Step:** a steep, smooth wall of rock that is one of the most difficult obstacles in a climb of Everest.

4. **ambient** (ăm′bē-ənt): surrounding.

5. **cognitive functions:** thought processes.

6. **flummoxed** (flŭm′əkst): frustrated; baffled.

7. **Rob Hall:** the guide who organized and led Krakauer's expedition. Hall was competing with expedition leader Scott Fischer.

8. **hypoxic imbecility** (hī-pŏk′sĭk ĭm′bə-sĭl′ĭ-tə): mental slowness caused by a lack of oxygen.

clients had packed it in—a sentiment that I suspected was heightened by the fact that Fischer's entire crew appeared to be plugging toward the summit. "I only wish we could have gotten more clients to the top," Rob lamented before continuing on his way.

Soon thereafter, Adams and Boukreev arrived on their way down, stopping immediately above me to wait for the traffic to clear. A minute later the overcrowding atop the Step intensified further as Makalu Gau, Ang Dorje, and several other Sherpas[9] came up the rope, followed by Doug Hansen and Scott Fischer. Then, finally, the Hillary Step was clear—but only after I'd spent more than an hour at 28,900 feet without supplemental oxygen.

By that point, entire sectors of my cerebral cortex[10] seemed to have shut down altogether. Dizzy, fearing that I would black out, I was frantic to reach the South Summit, where my third bottle was waiting. I started tenuously down the fixed lines, stiff with dread. Just below the step, Anatoli and Martin scooted around me and hurried down. Exercising extreme caution, I continued descending the tightrope of the ridge, but fifty feet above the oxygen cache the rope ended, and I balked at going farther without gas.

Over at the South Summit, I could see Andy Harris sorting through a pile of orange oxygen bottles. "Yo, Harold!"[11] I yelled, "Could you bring me a fresh bottle?"

"There's no oxygen here!" the guide shouted back. "These bottles are all empty!" This was disturbing news. My brain screamed for oxygen. I didn't know what to do. Just then, Mike Groom caught up to me on his way down from the summit. Mike had climbed Everest in 1993 without gas, and he wasn't overly concerned about going without. He gave me his oxygen bottle, and we quickly scrambled over to the South Summit.

When we got there, an examination of the oxygen cache immediately revealed that there were at least six full bottles. Andy, however, refused to believe it. He kept insisting that they were all empty, and nothing Mike or I said could convince him otherwise.

The only way to know how much gas is in a canister is to attach it to your regulator and read the gauge; presumably this is how Andy had checked the bottles at the South Summit. After the expedition, Neal Beidleman pointed out that if Andy's regulator had become fouled with ice, the gauge might have registered empty even though the canisters were full, which would explain his bizarre obstinacy. And if his regulator was perhaps on the fritz and not delivering oxygen to his mask, that would also explain Andy's apparent lack of lucidity.[12]

This possibility—which now seems so self-evident—didn't occur to either Mike or me at the time, however. In hindsight, Andy was acting irrationally and had plainly slipped well beyond routine hypoxia, but I was so mentally impeded[13] myself that it simply didn't register.

My inability to discern the obvious was exacerbated to some degree by the guide-client protocol. Andy and I were very similar in terms of physical ability and technical expertise; had we been climbing together in a nonguided situation as equal partners, it's inconceivable to me that I would have neglected to recognize his plight. But on this expedition he had been cast in the role of

---

9. **Sherpas** (shûr′pəz): members of a native people of the Himalayas, who have traditionally worked as guides and porters on Everest expeditions.

10. **cerebral** (sĕr′ə-brəl) **cortex:** the outer layer of the brain, responsible for higher brain functions, such as thought, reasoning, and memory.

11. **Harold:** Andy Harris's nickname.

12. **lucidity** (loo-sĭd′ĭ-tē): mental clarity.

13. **impeded** (ĭm-pē′dĭd): hampered.

WORDS
TO
KNOW

obstinacy (ŏb′stə-nə-sē) *n.* stubbornness
hindsight (hīnd′sīt′) *n.* a full knowledge of events after they have occurred

Andy Harris, professional guide

Rob Hall, organizer of Krakauer's expedition

immediately descended into a dense layer of clouds. Light snow started to fall. I could scarcely tell where the mountain ended and where the sky began in the flat, diminishing light; it would have been very easy to blunder off the edge of the ridge and never be heard from again. And the conditions only worsened as I moved down the peak.

At the bottom of the rock steps on the Southeast Ridge I stopped with Mike to wait for Yasuko, who was having difficulty negotiating the fixed ropes.[15] He attempted to call Rob on the radio, but Mike's transmitter was working only intermittently and he couldn't raise anybody. With Mike looking after Yasuko, and both Rob and Andy accompanying Doug Hansen—the only other client still above us—I assumed the situation was under control. So as Yasuko caught up to us, I asked Mike's permission to continue down alone. "Fine," he replied. "Just don't walk off any cornices."[16]

About 4:45 p.m., when I reached the Balcony—the promontory[17] at 27,600 feet on the Southeast Ridge where I'd sat watching the sunrise with Ang Dorje—I was shocked to encounter Beck Weathers, standing alone in the snow, shivering violently. I'd assumed that he'd descended to Camp Four hours earlier. "Beck!" I exclaimed, "what . . . are you still doing up here?"

invincible guide, there to look after me and the other clients; we had been specifically indoctrinated not to question our guides' judgment. The thought never entered my crippled mind that Andy might in fact be in terrible straits—that a guide might urgently need help from me.

As Andy continued to assert that there were no full bottles at the South Summit, Mike looked at me quizzically. I looked back and shrugged. Turning to Andy, I said, "No big deal, Harold. Much ado about nothing."[14] Then I grabbed a new oxygen canister, screwed it onto my regulator, and headed down the mountain. Given what unfolded over the hours that followed, the ease with which I abdicated responsibility—my utter failure to consider that Andy might have been in serious trouble—was a lapse that's likely to haunt me for the rest of my life.

Around 3:30 p.m. I left the South Summit ahead of Mike, Yasuko, and Andy, and almost

---

14. **Much ado about nothing:** a lot of fuss for no reason.

15. **fixed ropes:** guide ropes anchored to rock, marking the best trail.

16. **cornices** (kôr′nĭs-əz): masses of snow extending beyond the edges of ridges.

17. **promontory** (prŏm′ən-tôr′ē): a projecting mass of land.

Years earlier, Beck had undergone a radial keratotomy[18] to correct his vision. A side effect of the surgery, he discovered early in the Everest climb, was that the low barometric pressure that exists at high altitude caused his eyesight to fail. The higher he climbed, the lower the barometric pressure fell, and the worse his vision became.

The previous afternoon as he was ascending from Camp Three to Camp Four, Beck later confessed to me, "my vision had gotten so bad that I couldn't see more than a few feet. So I just tucked right behind John Taske and when he'd lift a foot I'd place my foot right in his bootprint."

Beck had spoken openly of his vision problem earlier, but with the summit in reach he neglected to mention its increasing severity to Rob or anyone else. His bad eyes notwithstanding, he was climbing well and feeling stronger than he had since the beginning of the expedition, and, he explained, "I didn't want to bail out prematurely."

Climbing above the South Col through the night, Beck managed to keep up with the group by employing the same strategy he'd used the previous afternoon—stepping in the footsteps of the person directly in front of him. But by the time he reached the Balcony and the sun came up, he realized his vision was worse than ever. In addition, he'd inadvertently rubbed some ice crystals into his eyes, lacerating both corneas.

"At that point," Beck revealed, "one eye was completely blurred over, I could barely see out of the other, and I'd lost all depth perception. I felt that I couldn't see well enough to climb higher without being a danger to myself or a burden to someone else, so I told Rob what was going on."

"Sorry pal," Rob immediately announced, "you're going down. I'll send one of the Sherpas down with you." But Beck wasn't quite ready to give up his summit hopes: "I explained to Rob that I thought there was a pretty good chance my vision would improve once the sun got higher and my pupils contracted. I said I wanted to wait a little while, and then boogie on up after everybody else if I started seeing more clearly."

Rob considered Beck's proposal, then decreed, "O.K., fair enough. I'll give you half an hour to find out. But I can't have you going down to Camp Four on your own. If your vision isn't better in thirty minutes I want you to stay here so I know exactly where you are until I come back from the summit, then we can go down together. I'm very serious about this: either you go down right now, or you promise me you'll sit right here until I return."

"So I crossed my heart and hoped to die," Beck told me good-naturedly as we stood in the blowing snow and waning light. "And I've kept my word. Which is why I'm still standing here."

Shortly after noon, Stuart Hutchison, John Taske, and Lou Kasischke had gone past on their way down with Lhakpa and Kami, but Weathers elected not to accompany them. "The weather was still good," he explains, "and I saw no reason to break my promise to Rob at that point."

Now, however, it was getting dark and conditions were turning grim. "Come down with me," I implored. "It will be at least another two or three hours before Rob shows up. I'll be your eyes. I'll get you down, no problem." Beck was nearly persuaded to descend with me when I made the mistake of mentioning that Mike Groom was on his way down with Yasuko, a few minutes behind me. In a day of many mistakes, this would turn out to be one of the larger ones.

"Thanks anyway," Beck said. "I think I'll just wait for Mike. He's got a rope; he'll be able to short-rope[19] me down."

"O.K., Beck," I replied. "It's your call. I guess I'll see you in camp, then." Secretly, I was relieved that I wouldn't have to deal with getting Beck down the problematic slopes to come, most of which were not protected by fixed lines. Daylight was waning, the weather was worsening, my

---

18. **radial keratotomy** (rā′dē-əl kĕr′ə-tŏt′ə-mē): a surgical procedure to correct nearsightedness.

19. **short-rope:** to pull a weaker climber along by means of a rope attached to a stronger climber.

reserves of strength were nearly gone. Yet I still didn't have any sense that calamity[20] was around the corner. Indeed, after talking with Beck I even took the time to find a spent oxygen canister that I'd stashed in the snow on the way up some ten hours earlier. Wanting to remove all my trash from the mountain, I stuffed it into my pack with my other two bottles (one empty, one partially full) and then hurried toward the South Col, 1,600 feet below.

From the Balcony I descended a few hundred feet down a broad, gentle snow gully without incident, but then things began to get sketchy. The route meandered through outcroppings of broken shale blanketed with six inches of fresh snow. Negotiating the puzzling, infirm terrain demanded unceasing concentration, an all-but-impossible feat in my punch-drunk state.

Because the wind had erased the tracks of the climbers who'd gone down before me, I had difficulty determining the correct route. In 1993, Mike Groom's partner—Lopsang Tshering Bhutia, a skilled Himalayan climber who was a nephew of Tenzing Norgay's[21]—had taken a wrong turn in this area and fallen to his death. Fighting to maintain a grip on reality, I started talking to myself out loud. "Keep it together, keep it together, keep it together," I chanted over and over, mantra-like. " . . . This is way serious. Keep it together."

I sat down to rest on a broad, sloping ledge, but after a few minutes a deafening boom! frightened me back to my feet. Enough new snow had accumulated that I feared a massive slab avalanche had released on the slopes above, but when I spun around to look I saw nothing. Then there was another boom!, accompanied by a flash that momentarily lit up the sky, and I realized I was hearing the crash of thunder.

In the morning, on the way up, I'd made a point of continually studying the route on this part of the mountain, frequently looking down to pick out landmarks that would be helpful on the descent, compulsively memorizing the terrain:

"Remember to turn left at the buttress[22] that looks like a ship's prow. Then follow that skinny line of snow until it curves sharply to the right." This was something I'd trained myself to do many years earlier, a drill I forced myself to go through every time I climbed, and on Everest it may have saved my life. By 6:00 p.m., as the storm escalated into a full-scale blizzard with driving snow and winds gusting in excess of 60 knots,[23] I came upon the rope that had been fixed by the Montenegrins on the snow slope 600 feet above the Col. Sobered by the force of the rising tempest, I realized that I'd gotten down the trickiest ground just in the nick of time.

Wrapping the fixed line around my arms to rappel,[24] I continued down through the blizzard. Some minutes later I was overwhelmed by a disturbingly familiar feeling of suffocation, and I realized that my oxygen had once again run out. Three hours earlier when I'd attached my regulator to my third and last oxygen canister, I'd noticed that the gauge indicated that the bottle was only half full. I'd figured that would be enough to get me most of the way down, though, so I hadn't bothered exchanging it for a full one. And now the gas was gone.

I pulled the mask from my face, left it hanging around my neck, and pressed onward, surprisingly unconcerned. However, without supplemental oxygen, I moved more slowly, and I had to stop and rest more often.

The literature of Everest is rife with accounts of hallucinatory experiences attributable to hypoxia and fatigue. In 1933, the noted English climber Frank Smythe observed "two curious looking

---

20. **calamity** (kə-lăm′ĭ-tē): disaster.

21. **a nephew of Tenzing Norgay's:** a nephew of the Sherpa who, along with Edmund Hillary, first reached the summit of Everest.

22. **buttress:** projecting mass of rock.

23. **60 knots:** a knot is about 1.15 miles per hour.

24. **rappel** (ră-pĕl′): to descend the face of a cliff by sliding down a rope while using one's feet to push off the rock.

WORDS TO KNOW

meander (mē-ăn′dər) v. to follow a winding path
compulsively (kəm-pŭl′sĭv-lē) adv. in obedience to an irresistible impulse
escalate (ĕs′kə-lāt′) v. to increase in intensity
supplemental (sŭp′lə-mĕn′tl) adj. extra; additional

objects floating in the sky" directly above him at 27,000 feet: "[One] possessed what appeared to be squat underdeveloped wings, and the other a protuberance[25] suggestive of a beak. They hovered motionless but seemed slowly to pulsate." In 1980, during his solo ascent, Reinhold Messner imagined that an invisible companion was climbing beside him. Gradually, I became aware that my mind had gone haywire in a similar fashion, and I observed my own slide from reality with a blend of fascination and horror.

I was so far beyond ordinary exhaustion that I experienced a queer detachment from my body, as if I were observing my descent from a few feet overhead. I imagined that I was dressed in a green cardigan and wingtips.[26] And although the gale was generating a windchill in excess of seventy below zero Fahrenheit, I felt strangely, disturbingly warm.

At 6:30, as the last of the daylight seeped from the sky, I'd descended to within 200 vertical feet of Camp Four. Only one obstacle now stood between me and safety: a bulging incline of hard, glassy ice that I would have to descend without a rope. Snow pellets borne by 70-knot gusts stung my face; any exposed flesh was instantly frozen. The tents, no more than 650 horizontal feet away, were only intermittently[27] visible through the whiteout. There was no margin for error. Worried about making a <u>critical</u> blunder, I sat down to marshal my energy before descending further.

Once I was off my feet, inertia[28] took hold. It was so much easier to remain at rest than to summon the <u>initiative</u> to tackle the dangerous ice slope; so I just sat there as the storm roared around me, letting my mind drift, doing nothing for perhaps forty-five minutes.

I'd tightened the drawstrings on my hood until only a tiny opening remained around my eyes, and I was removing the useless, frozen oxygen mask from beneath my chin when Andy Harris suddenly appeared out of the gloom beside me.

I imagined that I was dressed in a green cardigan and wingtips.

Shining my head-lamp in his direction, I reflexively recoiled when I saw the appalling condition of his face. His cheeks were coated with an armor of frost, one eye was frozen shut, and he was slurring his words badly. He looked in serious trouble. "Which way to the tents?" Andy blurted, frantic to reach shelter.

I pointed in the direction of Camp Four, then warned him about the ice just below us. "It's steeper than it looks!" I yelled, straining to make myself heard over the tempest. "Maybe I should go down first and get a rope from camp—" As I was in midsentence, Andy abruptly turned away and moved over the lip of the ice slope, leaving me sitting there dumbfounded.[29]

Scooting on his butt, he started down the steepest part of the incline. "Andy," I shouted

---

25. **protuberance** (prō-tōō′bər-əns): something sticking out.
26. **cardigan and wingtips:** vestlike sweater and dress shoes.
27. **intermittently:** occasionally.
28. **inertia** (ĭ-nûr′shə): the tendency of an object at rest to remain at rest.
29. **dumbfounded:** speechless with surprise.

after him, "it's crazy to try it like that! You're going to blow it for sure!" He yelled something back, but his words were carried off by the screaming wind. A second later he lost his purchase, flipped . . . over . . . , and was suddenly rocketing headfirst down the ice.

Two hundred feet below, I could just make out Andy's motionless form slumped at the foot of the incline. I was sure he'd broken at least a leg, maybe his neck. But then, incredibly, he stood up, waved that he was O.K., and started lurching toward Camp Four, which at the moment was in plain sight, 500 feet beyond.

I could see the shadowy forms of three or four people standing outside the tents; their headlamps flickered through curtains of blowing snow. I watched Harris walk toward them across the flats, a distance he covered in less than ten minutes. When the clouds closed in a moment later, cutting off my view, he was within sixty feet of the tents, maybe closer. I didn't see him again after that, but I was certain that he'd reached the security of camp, where Chuldum and Arita would doubtless be waiting with hot tea. Sitting out in the storm, with the ice bulge still standing between me and the tents, I felt a pang of envy. I was angry that my guide hadn't waited for me.

My backpack held little more than three empty oxygen canisters and a pint of frozen lemonade; it probably weighed no more than sixteen or eighteen pounds. But I was tired, and worried about getting down the incline without breaking a leg, so I tossed the pack over the edge and hoped it would come to rest where I could retrieve it. Then I stood up and started down the ice, which was as smooth and hard as the surface of a bowling ball.

Fifteen minutes of dicey, fatiguing crampon[30] work brought me safely to the bottom of the incline, where I easily located my pack, and another ten minutes after that I was in camp myself. I lunged into my tent with my crampons still on, zipped the door tight, and sprawled across the frost-covered floor too tired to even sit upright. For the first time I had a sense of how wasted I really was: I was more exhausted than I'd ever been in my life. But I was safe. Andy was safe.[31] The others would be coming into camp soon. We'd . . . done it. We'd climbed Everest. It had been a little sketchy there for a while, but in the end everything had turned out great.

It would be many hours before I learned that everything had not in fact turned out great— that nineteen men and women were stranded up on the mountain by the storm, caught in a desperate struggle for their lives. ❖

---

30. **crampon work:** climbing with steel spikes attached to one's boots to prevent slipping on ice.

31. **Andy was safe:** Confused by the lack of oxygen, Krakauer thought he had seen Andy Harris reach safety, but the man he had talked to and watched was actually Martin Adams. He later learned that Harris had died farther up the mountain while trying to save others.

1. What Do You Think?
How did you feel about the final revelation that 19 people were trapped on the mountain? Share your reaction with the class.

Comprehension Check
- How did crowds cause a problem for Krakauer?
- Why did Krakauer and Andy Harris have difficulty thinking clearly?
- Why was Beck Weathers unable to get down by himself?

Think Critically

2. Do you think Krakauer should blame himself for his failures to help Andy Harris and Beck Weathers? Consider the evidence from the account.

THINK ABOUT

- the effect that lack of oxygen had on Krakauer
- how he responded to Harris and Weathers when they met
- Krakauer's own opinion of his actions

3. How does Krakauer use **description** to convey what it is like on Mount Everest? Cite a passage that helped you to imagine the **setting.**

4. **ACTIVE READING** **DETERMINING A WRITER'S MOTIVES**
Judging from this excerpt, what do you think was Krakauer's main **motive** for writing his book? Refer back to the chart you made in your **READER'S NOTEBOOK** of clues to his motives.

5. Which do you consider more risky—climbing Mount Everest or the sport you discussed on page 538 before you read the selection? Explain your response.

Extend Interpretations

6. Critic's Corner Anatoli Boukreev, one of the guides who was on Everest in 1996, said this about Krakauer: "I believe his lack of proximity to certain events and limited experience at high altitude may have gotten in the way of his ability to objectively evaluate the events of summit day." How might those two factors have affected Krakauer's reporting?

7. Connect to Life Why do you think people risk injury and death to climb Everest? Discuss your ideas in class.

Literary Analysis

WORD CHOICE AND TONE

Word choice involves a writer's selection of the proper language—words, phrases, figures of speech—to best express particular thoughts, feelings, and perceptions. Word choice often reveals a writer's **tone,** or attitude toward his or her subject. For example, Krakauer wrote

. . . the ease with which I abdicated responsibility—my utter failure to consider that Andy might have been in serious trouble—was a lapse that's likely to haunt me for the rest of my life.

The word *abdicated* means gave up, *utter failure* means total failure, and *lapse* means error. Through careful word choices, Krakauer reveals his attitude, or tone, toward his actions on that day. He sits in judgment of his behavior, and he both criticizes and regrets his decisions.

Paired Activity With a partner, choose a passage of two or three paragraphs that conveys the author's attitude about what happened on Everest. You may determine that his tone is one of judgment, regret, anger, or something else. On a chart like the one shown, list the words or phrases that convey that tone. Share your findings with the class.

	Tone of Passage	Words that convey that tone
Student 1	judgment regret	abdicated utter failure lapse haunt
Student 2		

Choices & CHALLENGES

Writing Options

1. Safety Memo Write a memo to a company that leads Everest expeditions. Describe one of the major problems that occurred in this account. Then recommend a solution and explain how it would help to solve that problem.

Writing Handbook
See page 1157: Problem-Solution.

2. Medical Definition Write a definition of hypoxia that might appear in a medical textbook. Describe its effects using examples from this account.

3. Ode to Everest Write a poem expressing your feelings about Mount Everest. Before composing the poem, use a cluster diagram like the one shown to explore your thoughts and impressions.

Activities & Explorations

1. Everest Poster Create a poster to help a grade school student understand how high Everest is. Convert the height of Everest from feet into miles, football-field lengths, or some other large measurement. Illustrate this information on your poster.
~ MATH

2. Persuasive Speech Prepare a speech stating your opinion about whether people should be allowed to pursue high-risk sports. After practicing, deliver your speech in class. **~ SPEAKING AND LISTENING**

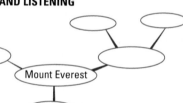

Mount Everest

Inquiry & Research

Hazards of Everest Why is climbing Mount Everest so hazardous? How do climbers prepare for this adventure? What factors—both human and in nature—make the climb such a challenge?

 Real World Link Read the feature article on page 550 and use the text and graphic information it provides to learn the answers to these questions.

Vocabulary in Action

EXERCISE: CONTEXT CLUES On your paper, write *correct* or *incorrect* to indicate whether the boldfaced word in each sentence is used correctly or incorrectly. If the word is used incorrectly, write a sentence in which it is used correctly.

1. The discovery of much-needed oxygen supplies helped to **escalate** the climbers' fears.

2. A mountain climber is often faced with **critical** decisions that may mean the difference between life and death.

3. Knowing my **obstinacy,** they realized that it would be impossible to change my mind.

4. Fear and **initiative** can keep even the strongest climber from reaching the summit.

5. To lighten her pack, she took out everything except what was **supplemental.**

6. The snow continued to fall, completely **obscuring** the climbers' path.

7. He failed to bring extra oxygen because he was **cognizant** of the need for it.

8. Thanks to **hindsight,** they understood the danger of their situation and took the steps necessary to avoid disaster.

9. Fearing that the only other choice was to freeze, they walked **compulsively** all through the night.

10. The slope was so steep and icy that we decided to sit down and **meander** straight to the bottom.

WORDS TO KNOW				
cognizant	critical	hindsight	meander	obstinacy
compulsively	escalate	initiative	obscuring	supplemental

Grammar in Context: Choosing Precise Verbs

Jon Krakauer's use of precise verbs helps him create chillingly realistic descriptions. Notice the verbs he uses in describing his descent from Everest.

> My brain screamed for oxygen.
>
> Snow pellets borne by 70-knot gusts stung my face. . . .
>
> I lunged into my tent with my crampons still on . . . and sprawled across the frost-covered floor. . . .

By using precise verbs, writers can eliminate unnecessary adverbs and make their writing clearer. If Krakauer had chosen *badly needed* instead of *screamed for* and *went quickly* instead of *lunged,* how would the tone of his writing have changed?

WRITING EXERCISE Replace the underlined words with precise verbs.

Example: *Original* Heading down from the summit, he suddenly saw Andy.
Rewritten Heading down from the summit, he spotted Andy.

1. A lack of oxygen negatively affected Krakauer's thinking ability.
2. Andy said confidently that all the bottles of oxygen were empty.
3. Storm clouds came steadily up the side of the mountain.
4. Krakauer watched in shock as the man fell awkwardly down the icy incline.
5. Krakauer used his crampons to move slowly down the slope.

Jon Krakauer
1954–

Other Works
Eiger Dreams
Into the Wild

Dreaming of Everest When Jon Krakauer was nine years old, Willi Unsoeld and another man reached the top of Everest by a difficult route that no one had ever used. Krakauer knew Unsoeld personally. The climber was a friend of Krakauer's father and had accompanied the Krakauers when Jon reached the top of his first mountain, a 10,000-foot peak. Inspired by Unsoeld, Krakauer dreamed of climbing Mount Everest himself.

Living to Climb By the time Krakauer was in his 20s, he "lived to climb." He would work as a carpenter or a commercial fisherman just long enough to finance his next expedition. Climbing fascinated Krakauer because, "unlike most of life, what you do really matters. . . . Your actions have real consequences." However, he gave up the idea of Everest because he'd heard that the route wasn't challenging enough.

Nature Writer In the 1970s, Krakauer wrote a couple of articles about his exploits. Then a friend suggested that he try writing full-time, so in 1983 he quit carpentry and launched a new career. Many of his articles have to do with the outdoors, although he also writes on other subjects. When *Outside* magazine asked Krakauer to do an article on Everest, his childhood dream flamed up again. He agreed to take the assignment, but only if he could try to summit the world's highest peak himself instead of just reporting on others' attempts. Krakauer still goes mountain climbing but says, "I won't go back to Everest; I'm afraid of that."

Author Activity

Expedition Outcome What happened to the 19 people trapped on the mountain at the end of this account? Find out by investigating Krakauer's entire book *Into Thin Air,* his September 1996 article from *Outside* magazine, or a newspaper from May 1996 that ran an article on the expedition.

The Summit: Next Stop for Those on Everest
by Tim Friend/USA TODAY

As a reporter with the Everest Extreme Expedition, Tim Friend wrote the following article about the challenges climbers face tackling the world's highest mountain. Before reading the article, read the right-hand column up through the first item.

EVEREST BASE CAMP—The push to the summit of Mount Everest has begun for at least 16 men and women here on the south side of the mountain. The climbers, representing five expeditions, left their camps at 26,000 feet shortly after 11 PM Monday and began the grueling 10- to 12-hour march to Everest's 29,028-foot-high peak.

Wearing headlights to illuminate their ways and crampons on their boots to bite into the ice and snow, the climbers—who have not slept since Sunday night—face perhaps the longest day of their lives. The first of the climbers could begin arriving at the summit as early as 9 AM today. Among those on their way to the summit: three climbers representing the 1998 American Everest Expedition; four members of the first Iranian Everest climbing team; four members of the first Singapore team; and a solo climber from Denmark.

Mount Everest
Summit: 29,028 feet

Camp 4
26,300 feet

Camp 3
23,000 feet

Camp 2
21,300 feet

Camp 1
19,500 feet

Base camp
17,500 feet

Reading for Information

News accounts of risky events offer readers the thrill of adventure. Such accounts can also overwhelm readers with an avalanche of details. When you research the Everest climb, skimming and scanning can help you find the details you need.

SKIMMING, SCANNING, AND UNDERSTANDING GRAPHICS

To find key information quickly in a newspaper article, try skimming and scanning.
- **Skimming** is reading quickly to get the main idea or an overview of a work.
- **Scanning** is searching through writing for a particular fact or piece of information. Look for **key words** that relate to your topic.

❶ **Skimming** When you skim, read the headline, the first and last paragraphs, the first sentence of other paragraphs, and any graphics. Before you begin reading this article, **skim** the headlines and the map. What do you know about climbing Mount Everest at this point? Now go on to read the article.

YOUR TURN Use the questions and activities below to help you get the most from both the text and the graphic.

❷ **Understanding Graphics** On the map shown here, trace the path from the base camp to the summit. Discuss changes in elevation and the possible hazards that climbers could encounter.

Meanwhile, on the north side of Everest in Tibet, 19 people reportedly reached the summit Monday. A growing number of expeditions are being conducted from Tibet because the costs are much less than from Nepal. But the southern route is still the most popular. It is the same route taken by Sir Edmund Hillary, who in 1953 was the first person to climb Everest, the world's highest peak.

Pemba Sherpa, a Nepalese climber with a commercial group called Himalayan Kingdoms, suffered a fractured femur Monday. He was ascending a steep slope just below Camp 3 when he was struck by a large piece of falling ice. At least two doctors, including emergency physician Chuck Huss of Iowa City, Iowa, treated the climber on the scene. He will be brought to base camp today from Camp 3 after Nepalese climbers ascend with a stretcher. Taking wounded climbers down through the Khumbu ice fall is extremely dangerous.

Two Western climbers reported by radio over the weekend that they were suffering from snow blindness, a sunburn of the cornea that is temporary but extremely painful. Both climbers apparently have recovered and will continue their summit attempts.

A second round of summit attempts is planned for Wednesday, although those climbers may be in a race against heavy snows that are predicted to reach Everest by 5 PM that day. At least 30 people spent Monday night at Camp 3 and positioned themselves for their push today.

Base camp, meanwhile, is practically a ghost town. Most of its residents left over the weekend in a long line, resembling pilgrims to Mecca, and began making their ways to Camps 2 and 3. About half the members of our group—the Everest Extreme Expedition, which has been conducting telemedicine experiments—are making their ways back down to thicker air and warmer temperatures.

Seven of us from the original 13 members of that expedition are still here, monitoring the climbers' progress. We've all been at high altitude now for 24 days and at base camp's 17,500 feet for two weeks. The adventure has been priceless, but we miss our loved ones, as well as food, flushing toilets, beds and hot showers.

All of us are ready to go home.

❸ Comparing Texts Both Jon Krakauer, author of *Into Thin Air,* and Tim Friend describe the physical problems and injuries climbers experience. How is Friend's account of climbing Everest different from Krakauer's? **Scan** the article by sweeping your eyes across the page to look for key words that may lead you to essential information.

❹ Many climbers were inspired by the same challenge that Edmund Hillary met in 1953. Considering the technological advances made since then and expertise that climbers have developed, do you think it is safer to climb Everest today than it was in Hillary's time? Give reasons for your answer.

Inquiry & Research

Activity Link: *from* **Into Thin Air, p. 548**

Using information from this article and what you recall from reading the excerpt from *Into Thin Air,* devise a web about Everest similar to the one shown below. Discuss your responses with a classmate.

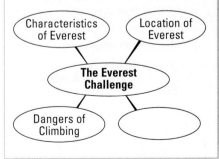

The Sharks

Poetry *by* DENISE LEVERTOV

A narrow Fellow in the Grass

Poetry *by* EMILY DICKINSON

*"It was sundown
when they came"*

Connect to Your Life

Emotional Responses to Animals Different animals in nature evoke different responses from people. For example, many people find the koala bear to be cute and lovable. In contrast, people often see the crocodile as frightening or dangerous. Copy the list shown and fill in your own opinions. Then, with a classmate, discuss your choices.

Responses to Animals
An animal that I find beautiful:
An animal that inspires me:
An animal that makes me laugh:
An animal that is dangerous:
An animal that seems mean:

Build Background

The Balance of Nature Very few animals are either completely beneficial or completely harmful to humans. For instance, spiders frighten some people because they crawl, bite, and are sometimes poisonous. On the positive side, spiders prey on many insects, such as flies, that humans find bothersome. This helps to maintain the balance of nature. As you read the two poems, keep in mind that humans can perceive animals both positively and negatively.

LaserLinks:
Background for Reading
Ecology Connection

Focus Your Reading

LITERARY ANALYSIS | **MOOD** | When you say to a friend, "That movie was really creepy," you're talking about **mood.** Stories and poems also have mood, which is the feeling or atmosphere that a writer creates for the reader. As you read the following poems, notice the feelings they produce in you. See if you can identify why they make you feel that way.

ACTIVE READING | **ANALYZING WORD CHOICE** | The **mood** of a literary work is often created through the writer's choice of words. Denise Levertov makes an unusual **word choice** in the following line from "Sharks":

Dark fins appear, innocent as if in fair warning.

Some readers might expect a poem about sharks to create a feeling of danger. Although the word *dark* fits that expectation, the word *innocent* does not. Careful readers consider all of a writer's words to determine mood.

Use the suggestions that follow to help you analyze word choice in "The Sharks" and "A narrow Fellow in the Grass":

• Read each poem several times, both silently and aloud.
• Pay close attention to the poet's word choice. Which nouns, adverbs, verbs, and adjectives create emotions in you as a reader? What are those emotions?
• Are there any words or phrases you find surprising or unexpected? Ask yourself why the poet might have used them and what they add to the meaning of the poem.

READER'S NOTEBOOK As you read each poem, jot down the words and phrases that make a strong impression on you as a reader.

THE Sharks

Denise Levertov

Well then, the last day the sharks appeared.
Dark fins appear, innocent
as if in fair warning. The sea becomes
sinister, are they everywhere?
5   I tell you, they break six feet of water.
Isn't it the same sea, and won't we
play in it any more?
I liked it clear and not
too calm, enough waves
10   to fly in on. For the first time
I dared to swim out of my depth.
It was sundown when they came, the time
when a sheen of copper stills the sea,
not dark enough for moonlight, clear enough
15   to see them easily. Dark
the sharp lift of the fins.

4 sinister (sĭn′ĭ-stər): threatening harm, evil, or misfortune.

5 they break . . . water: The sharks can enter water as shallow as six feet, posing a danger to swimmers.

13 sheen: brightness; shininess.

Thinking Through the Literature

1. Who do you picture the **speaker** to be? Consider the evidence in the poem about the speaker's age and situation. Remember that the speaker and the poet are not necessarily the same.

2. Line 1 suggests this is the last day of the speaker's vacation at the seashore. How does the presence of the sharks change the way the speaker perceives the sea?

   THINK ABOUT
   - the description of the speaker's activities in lines 6–11
   - the words used to describe the sea when the sharks are sighted

3. Do you think the sharks in the poem are evil? Explain your answer, citing details from the poem.

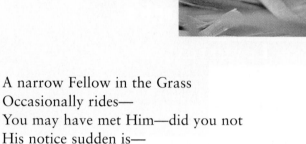

A narrow Fellow in the Grass

Emily Dickinson

A narrow Fellow in the Grass
Occasionally rides—
You may have met Him—did you not
His notice sudden is—

5   The Grass divides as with a Comb—
A spotted shaft is seen—
And then it closes at your feet
And opens further on—

He likes a Boggy Acre
10 A Floor too cool for Corn—
Yet when a Boy, and Barefoot—
I more than once at Noon
Have passed, I thought, a Whip lash
Unbraiding in the Sun
15 When stopping to secure it
It wrinkled, and was gone—

Several of Nature's People
I know, and they know me—
I feel for them a transport
20 Of cordiality—

But never met this Fellow
Attended, or alone
Without a tighter breathing
And Zero at the Bone—

Connect to the Literature

1. **What Do You Think?**
   What are your impressions of the speaker of this poem? Share them with the class.

   ┌─ **Comprehension Check**
   │ • What are two places where the "narrow fellow" can be found?
   │ • To what does the speaker compare the grass dividing?

Think Critically

2. In addition to the photograph, what clues helped you figure out what animal the narrow fellow is?

   THINK ABOUT

   • the description of what the "narrow Fellow" looks like in lines 6 and 13–14
   • the description of the way it moves through the grass in lines 5-8
   • the details of where it lives in lines 9–10

3. Reread the last two stanzas of the poem. How would you describe the speaker's reaction to the narrow fellow?

4. Contrast the speaker's feelings toward other living things with his feelings toward the narrow fellow. Consider the evidence in the poem as you explain your answer.

5. **ACTIVE READING** **ANALYZING WORD CHOICE** Look at the words and phrases you jotted down in your **READER'S NOTEBOOK**. Pick one and explain why you think the poet chose it. What effect did the poet want to produce?

Extend Interpretations

6. **Comparing Texts** Which poem do you think presents a more positive view of the animal it describes? Why?

7. **What If?** How would your reaction to either poem change if the time of day had been different—for example, if the sharks had come at noon or the boy had encountered the narrow fellow at night?

8. **Connect to Life** Review your chart of responses to animals and decide where you would list sharks and the narrow fellow. How do your responses to those animals compare with those of the speakers?

Literary Analysis

MOOD AND WORD CHOICE

In a literary work, the feeling or atmosphere that the writer creates for the reader is called **mood.** Writers—especially poets—create mood by the words they choose and the sound and **rhythm** of the language they use.

When examining the role that word choice plays in creating mood, consider the following points:
   • *Denotation* is the literal, "dictionary" meaning of a word.
   • *Connotation* is the emotional response evoked by a word.

In the first line of "The Sharks," the phrase *last day* literally means the final day *of vacation* but the poet chose not to add those two words. Perhaps this is because some people use the phrase *last days* to mean the end of time or the end of a person's life. Therefore, the phrase *last day* has a more ominous connotation than just the end of a vacation—a connotation of doom that hints at the threat posed by sharks.

Paired Activity Working with a partner, identify specific words in each poem that you think evoke a certain emotion. Then rewrite a stanza of one of the poems, substituting different words to change the mood. Share your rewritten stanza in class.

Choices & CHALLENGES

Writing Options

1. Animal Poem Write a short poem about an encounter you have had with an animal. Share your finished poem with classmates.

2. Essay on Mystery Both Levertov and Dickinson have reputations for writing poems that explore the element of mystery in everyday occurrences. Choose one of the poems and write a brief essay in which you discuss whether that poem fits this description.

Activities & Explorations

Animal Collage Create a collage to illustrate one of these poems. Assemble photos, drawings, or other pictures that portray the animal or capture the mood of the poem. Display your work in class.
~ **ART**

Inquiry & Research

Animal Pros and Cons Each of these poems describes an animal that is often considered dangerous to humans. Find out more about one of these two animals. What positive roles does it play in nature? To locate information, use an encyclopedia, a science textbook, or a nature guide. Report back to your classmates.

Denise Levertov
1923–1997

Other Works
The Jacob's Ladder
Relearning the Alphabet
Breathing the Water

Childhood in England Born in 1923, Denise Levertov grew up in England. Her father, a Russian Jew who converted to Christianity, became an Anglican minister who filled the house with thousands of books and interesting people like artists and writers. Her mother read classics to the family. Although Levertov never attended school, her family educated her through reading, traveling, studying nature, and going to museums.

Becoming an American Voice Levertov published her first collection of poetry when she was 23. Her second volume did not appear until ten years later. By then, she had moved to New York and evolved into a thoroughly American poet. Her poetry has covered many subjects, including the Vietnam War, the Gulf War, pollution, and the threat of nuclear weapons.

Emily Dickinson
1830–1886

Other Works
The Complete Poems of
Emily Dickinson
The Letters of Emily Dickinson

Close to Home Except for a year at school, Emily Dickinson lived her entire life in Amherst, Massachusetts with her family. Neither Dickinson nor her sister ever married. In her 30s, Dickinson began to dress only in white and to refuse to leave her home. Some people think an unhappy love affair caused her retreat. Others believe that she chose to live quietly to protect her artistic talent.

A Secret Poet Dickinson spent long hours in her room, secretly writing poems on scraps of paper. Of her 1,775 poems, only seven were published during her life. Dickinson experimented with punctuation, capitalization, and rhyme. Although she used simple words and short stanzas, she expressed original insights. Today, she is considered one of the most popular and influential of American poets.

My Wonder Horse/Mi Caballo Mago

Short Story by SABINE R. ULIBARRÍ (ōō′lē-bä-rē′)

"Although I had never seen the Wonder Horse, he filled my imagination and fired my ambition."

Connect to Your Life

Wild for Animals! What is your favorite wild animal? Perhaps it's the dolphin, the wolf, the snow leopard—or maybe an animal that you've seen in films or only heard about. On a piece of paper, make a sketch of this animal, or if you prefer, write a description of the animal. Share your sketch or your description with a classmate.

Build Background

A Legendary Horse "My Wonder Horse" is set in the mountains of northern New Mexico. In this and other areas of the West, wild horses, also called mustangs, have lived for hundreds of years, and they survive to the present day. These horses live in bands consisting of a single stallion and his mares, which the stallion guards fiercely. Since the early 1800s, stories have been told in the West of a white stallion, sometimes known as the Pacing White Mustang, remarkable for his beauty, speed, grace, intelligence, and elusiveness. In Native American legends, the white stallion is considered a ghost horse. "My Wonder Horse" builds on this tradition of the legendary white stallion.

WORDS TO KNOW
Vocabulary Preview

evoke	mystic
indignity	transcendent
indomitable	ultimate
lethargy	vigil
mandate	wane

Focus Your Reading

LITERARY ANALYSIS **STYLE** Style is the way that a work of literature is written. Every writer has a unique style. For example, one element of Ulibarrí's style is variety in sentence length. This can be seen in the **description** that opens the story you are about to read:

He was white. White as memories lost. He was free. Free as happiness is. He was fantasy, liberty, and excitement. He filled and dominated the mountain valleys and surrounding plains. He was a white horse that flooded my youth with dreams and poetry.

As you read this story, pay attention to the style in which it is written. Look for passages whose style you especially like.

ACTIVE READING **INFERENCES ABOUT CHARACTER CHANGE** An **inference** is a logical guess or a conclusion based on facts. Making an inference is like "reading between the lines." Readers infer by combining clues in the text with what they already know in order to reach a conclusion that goes beyond what the words say.

Making inferences is useful for understanding **characters.** Often, a writer will not tell you everything that is going on inside a character. You might have to use clues in the story to figure out what the character is thinking or feeling. An example of such an inference is shown in the chart below.

READER'S NOTEBOOK Use a chart like the one shown to record clues about the **narrator's** thoughts and feelings and then to make inferences about them. Pay special attention to how the narrator's thoughts and feelings change as the story develops.

What the narrator says	What I know from experience	What I can infer
I used to listen open-mouthed as my father and the ranch hands talked about the phantom horse.	People's mouths often drop open when they are surprised or impressed.	The narrator is impressed by the stories of the phantom horse.

MY WONDER HORSE

Sabine R. Ulibarrí

MI CABALLO MAGO

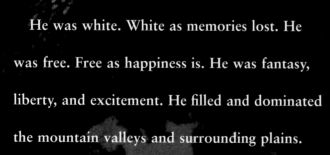

He was white. White as memories lost. He was free. Free as happiness is. He was fantasy, liberty, and excitement. He filled and dominated the mountain valleys and surrounding plains.

Era blanco. Blanco como el olvido. Era libre. Libre como la alegría. Era la ilusión, la libertad y la emoción. Poblaba y dominaba las serranías y las llanuras de las cercanías. Era un caballo

Around the campfires of the country and in the sunny patios of the town, the ranch hands talked about him with enthusiasm and admiration. But gradually their eyes would become hazy and blurred with dreaming. The lively talk would die down. All thoughts fixed on the vision <u>evoked</u> by the horse. Myth of the animal kingdom. Poem of the world of men.

White and mysterious, he paraded his harem through the summer forests with lordly rejoicing. Winter sent him to the plains and sheltered hillsides for the protection of his females. He spent the summer like an Oriental potentate[1] in his woodland gardens. The winter he passed like an illustrious warrior celebrating a well-earned victory.

He was a legend. The stories told of the Wonder Horse were endless. Some true, others fabricated. So many traps, so many snares, so many searching parties, and all in vain. The horse always escaped, always mocked his pursuers, always rose above the control of man. Many a valiant cowboy swore to put his halter and his brand on the animal. But always he had to confess later that the <u>mystic</u> horse was more of a man than he.

I was fifteen years old. Although I had never seen the Wonder Horse, he filled my imagination and fired my ambition. I used to listen open-mouthed as my father and the ranch hands talked about the phantom horse who turned into mist and air and nothingness when he was trapped. I joined in the universal obsession—like the hope of winning the lottery—of putting my lasso on him some day, of capturing him and showing him off on Sunday afternoons when the girls of the town strolled through the streets.

It was high summer. The forests were fresh, green, and gay. The cattle moved slowly, fat and sleek in the August sun and shadow. Listless and drowsy in the <u>lethargy</u> of late afternoon, I was dozing on my horse. It was time to round up the herd and go back to the good bread of the cowboy camp. Already my comrades would be sitting around the campfire, playing the guitar, telling stories of past or present, or surrendering to the languor[2] of the late afternoon. The sun was setting behind me in a riot of streaks and colors. Deep, harmonious silence.

I sit drowsily still, forgetting the cattle in the glade. Suddenly the forest falls silent, a deafening quiet. The afternoon comes to a standstill. The breeze stops blowing, but it vibrates. The sun flares hotly. The planet, life, and time itself have stopped in an inexplicable way. For a moment, I don't understand what is happening.

Then my eyes focus. There he is! The Wonder Horse! At the end of the glade, on high ground surrounded by summer green. He is a statue. He is an engraving. Line and form and white stain on a green background. Pride, prestige, and art incarnate in animal flesh. A picture of burning beauty and virile[3] freedom. An ideal, pure and invincible, rising from the eternal dreams of humanity. Even today my being thrills when I remember him.

A sharp neigh. A far-reaching challenge that soars on high, ripping the virginal fabric of the rosy clouds. Ears at the point. Eyes flashing. Tail waving active defiance. Hoofs glossy and destructive. Arrogant ruler of the countryside.

The moment is never-ending, a momentary eternity. It no longer exists, but it will always live. . . . There must have been mares. I did not see them. The cattle went on their indifferent way. My horse followed them, and I came slowly back from the land of dreams to the world of toil. But life could no longer be what it was before.

---

1. **Oriental potentate** (pōt′n-tāt′): Asian king.
2. **languor** (lăng′gər): a dreamy, lazy mood or quality.
3. **virile** (vîr′əl): masculine, strong, vigorous, and powerful.

WORDS
TO
KNOW

evoke (ĭ-vōk′) *v.* to call to mind
mystic (mĭs′tĭk) *adj.* inspiring a sense of mystery and wonder
lethargy (lĕth′ər-jē) *n.* a state of drowsiness, inactivity, and lack of energy

Alrededor de las fogatas del campo y en las resolanas del pueblo los vaqueros de esas tierras hablaban de él con entusiasmo y admiración. Y la mirada se volvía turbia y borrosa de ensueño. La animada charla se apagaba. Todos atentos a la visión evocada. Mito del reino animal. Poema del mundo viril.

Blanco y arcano. Paseaba su harén por el bosque de verano en regocijo imperial. El invierno decretaba el llano y la ladera para sus hembras. Veraneaba como rey de oriente en su jardín silvestre. Invernaba como guerrero ilustre que celebra la victoria ganada.

Era leyenda. Eran sin fin las historias que se contaban del caballo brujo. Unas verdad, otras invención. Tantas trampas, tantas redes, tantas expediciones. Todas venidas a menos. El caballo siempre se escapaba, siempre se burlaba, siempre se alzaba por encima del dominio de los hombres. ¡Cuánto valedor no juró ponerle su jáquima y su marca para confesar después que el brujo había sido más hombre que él!

Yo tenía quince años. Y sin haberlo visto nunca el brujo me llenaba ya la imaginación y la esperanza. Escuchaba embobado a mi padre y a sus vaqueros hablar del caballo fantasma que al atraparlo se volvía espuma y aire y nada. Participaba de la obsesión de todos, ambición de lotería, de algún día ponerle yo mi lazo, de hacerlo mío, y lucirlo los domingos por la tarde cuando las muchachas salen a paseo por la calle.

Pleno el verano. Los bosques verdes, frescos

y alegres. Las reses lentas, gordas y luminosas en la sombra y en el sol de agosto. Dormitaba yo en un caballo brioso, lánguido y sutil en el sopor del atardecer. Era hora ya de acercarse a la majada, al buen pan y al rancho del rodeo. Ya los compañeros estarían alrededor de la

That night under the stars I didn't sleep. I dreamed. How much I dreamed awake and how much I dreamed asleep, I do not know. I only know that a white horse occupied my dreams and filled them with vibrant sound, and light, and turmoil.

Summer passed and winter came. Green grass gave place to white snow. The herds descended from the mountains to the valleys and the hollows. And in the town they kept saying that the Wonder Horse was roaming through this or that secluded area. I inquired everywhere for his whereabouts. Every day he became for me more of an ideal, more of an idol, more of a mystery.

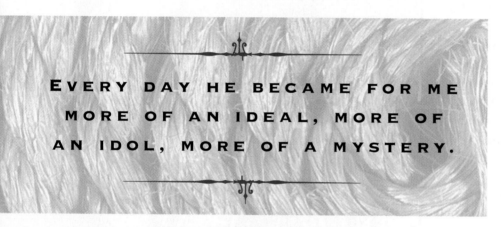

EVERY DAY HE BECAME FOR ME MORE OF AN IDEAL, MORE OF AN IDOL, MORE OF A MYSTERY.

It was Sunday. The sun had barely risen above the snowy mountains. My breath was a white cloud. My horse was trembling with cold and fear like me. I left without going to mass. Without any breakfast. Without the usual bread and sardines in my saddlebags. I had slept badly but had kept the <u>vigil</u> well. I was going in search of the white light that galloped through my dreams.

On leaving the town for the open country, the roads disappear. There are no tracks, human or animal. Only a silence, deep, white, and sparkling. My horse breaks trail with his chest and leaves an unending wake, an open rift, in the white sea. My trained, concentrated gaze covers the landscape from horizon to horizon, searching for the noble silhouette of the talismanic[4] horse.

It must have been midday. I don't know. Time had lost its meaning. I found him! On a slope stained with sunlight. We saw one another at the same time. Together, we turned to stone. Motionless, absorbed, and panting, I gazed at his beauty, his pride, his nobility. As still as sculptured marble, he allowed himself to be admired.

A sudden, violent scream breaks the silence. A glove hurled into my face.[5] A challenge and a <u>mandate</u>. Then something surprising happens. The horse that in summer takes his stand between any threat and his herd, swinging back and forth from left to right, now plunges into the snow. Stronger than they, he is breaking trail for his mares. They follow him. His flight is slow in order to conserve his strength.

I follow. Slowly. Quivering. Thinking about his intelligence. Admiring his courage. Understanding his courtesy. The afternoon advances. My horse is taking it easy.

One by one the mares become weary. One by one, they drop out of the trail. Alone! He and I. My inner ferment[6] bubbles to my lips. I speak to him. He listens and is quiet.

---

4. **talismanic** (tăl´ĭs-măn´ĭk): possessing or believed to possess magic power.

5. **A glove . . . face:** a defiant challenge. Historically, one man challenged another to a duel by throwing down a glove, or gauntlet.

6. **ferment:** agitation or excitement.

hoguera agitando la guitarra, contando cuentos del pasado o de hoy o entregándose al cansancio de la tarde. El sol se ponía ya, detrás de mí, en escándalos de rayo y color. Silencio orgánico y denso.

Sigo insensible a las reses al abra. De pronto el bosque se calla. El silencio enmudece. La tarde se detiene. La brisa deja de respirar, pero tiembla. El sol se excita. El planeta, la vida y el tiempo se han detenido de una manera inexplicable. Por un instante no sé lo que pasa.

Luego mis ojos aciertan. ¡Allí está! ¡El caballo mago! Al extremo del abra, en un promontorio, rodeado de verde. Hecho estatua, hecho estampa. Línea y forma y mancha blanca en fondo verde. Orgullo, fama y arte en carne animal. Cuadro de belleza encendida y libertad varonil. Ideal invicto y limpio de la eterna ilusión humana. Hoy palpito todo aún al recordarlo.

Silbido. Reto trascendental que sube y rompe la tela virginal de las nubes rojas. Orejas lanzas. Ojos rayos. Cola viva y ondulante, desafío movedizo. Pezuña tersa y destructiva. Arrogante majestad de los campos.

El momento es eterno. La eternidad momentanea. Ya no está, pero siempre estará. Debió de haber yeguas. Yo no las vi. Las reses siguen indiferentes. Mi caballo las sigue y yo vuelvo lentamente del mundo del sueño a la tierra del sudor. Pero ya la vida no volverá a ser lo que antes fue.

Aquella noche bajo las estrellas no dormí. Soñé. Cuánto soñé despierto y cuánto soñé dormido yo no sé. Sólo sé que un caballo blanco pobló mis sueños y los llenó de resonancia y de luz y de violencia.

Pasó el verano y entró el invierno. El verde pasto dió lugar a la blanca nieve. Las manadas bajaron de las sierras a los valles y cañadas. Y en el pueblo se comentaba que el brujo andaba por este o aquel rincón. Yo indagaba por todas partes su paradero. Cada día se me hacía más ideal, más imagen, más misterio.

Domingo. Apenas rayaba el sol de la sierra nevada. Aliento vaporoso. Caballo tembloroso de frío y de ansias. Como yo. Salí sin ir a misa. Sin desayunarme siquiera. Sin pan y sardinas en las alforjas. Había dormido mal y velado bien. Iba en busca de la blanca luz que galopaba en mis sueños.

Al salir del pueblo al campo libre desaparecen los caminos. No hay rastro humano o animal. Silencio blanco, hondo y rutilante. Mi caballo corta el camino con el pecho y deja estela eterna, grieta abierta, en la mar cana. La mirada diestra y atenta puebla el paisaje hasta cada horizonte buscando el noble perfil del caballo místico.

Sería medio día. No sé. El tiempo había perdido su rigor. Di con él. En una ladera contaminada de sol. Nos vimos al mismo tiempo. Juntos nos hicimos piedra. Inmóvil, absorto y jadeante contemplé su belleza, su arrogancia, su nobleza. Esculpido en mármol, se dejó admirar.

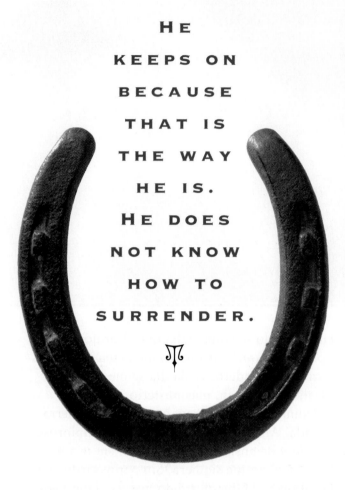

HE KEEPS ON BECAUSE THAT IS THE WAY HE IS. HE DOES NOT KNOW HOW TO SURRENDER.

He still opens the way, and I follow in the path he leaves me. Behind us a long, deep trench crosses the white plain. My horse, which has eaten grain and good hay, is still strong. Undernourished as the Wonder Horse is, his strength is waning. But he keeps on because that is the way he is. He does not know how to surrender.

I now see black stains over his body. Sweat and the wet snow have revealed the black skin beneath the white hair. Snorting breath, turned to steam, tears the air. White spume[7] above white snow. Sweat, spume, and steam. Uneasiness.

I felt like an executioner. But there was no turning back. The distance between us was growing relentlessly shorter. God and Nature watched indifferently.

I feel sure of myself at last. I untie the rope. I open the lasso and pull the reins tight. Every nerve, every muscle is tense. My heart is in my mouth. Spurs pressed against trembling flanks. The horse leaps. I whirl the rope and throw the obedient lasso.

A frenzy of fury and rage. Whirlpools of light and fans of transparent snow. A rope that whistles and burns the saddletree. Smoking, fighting gloves. Eyes burning in their sockets. Mouth parched. Fevered forehead. The whole earth shakes and shudders. The long, white trench ends in a wide, white pool.

Deep, gasping quiet. The Wonder Horse is mine! Both still trembling, we look at one another squarely for a long time. Intelligent and realistic, he stops struggling and even takes a hesitant step toward me. I speak to him. As I talk, I approach him. At first, he flinches and recoils. Then he waits for me. The two horses greet one another in their own way. Finally, I succeed in stroking his mane. I tell him many things, and he seems to understand.

Ahead of me, along the trail already made, I drove him toward the town. Triumphant. Exultant. Childish laughter gathered in my throat. With my newfound manliness, I controlled it. I wanted to sing, but I fought down the desire. I wanted to shout, but I kept quiet. It was the ultimate in happiness. It was the pride of the male adolescent. I felt myself a conqueror.

Occasionally the Wonder Horse made a try for his liberty, snatching me abruptly from my thoughts. For a few moments, the struggle was renewed. Then we went on.

---

7. **spume** (spyo͞om): foam or froth.

Silbido violento que rompe el silencio. Guante arrojado a la cara. Desafío y decreto a la vez. Asombro nuevo. El caballo que en verano se coloca entre la amenaza y la manada, oscilando a distancia de diestra a siniestra, ahora se lanza a la nieve. Más fuerte que ellas, abre la vereda a las yeguas. Y ellas lo siguen. Su fuga es lenta para conservar sus fuerzas.

Sigo. Despacio. Palpitante. Pensando en su inteligencia. Admirando su valentía. Apreciando su cortesía. La tarde se alarga. Mi caballo cebado a sus anchas.

Una a una las yeguas se van cansando. Una a una se van quedando a un lado. ¡Solos! El y yo. La agitación interna reboza a los labios. Le hablo. Me escucha y calla.

El abre el camino y yo sigo por la vereda que me deja. Detrás de nosotros una larga y honda zanja blanca que cruza la llanura. El caballo que ha comido grano y buen pasto sigue fuerte. A él, mal nutrido, se la han agotado las fuerzas. Pero sigue porque es él y porque no sabe ceder.

Encuentro negro y manchas negras por el cuerpo. La nieve y el sudor han revelado la piel negra bajo el pelo. Mecheros violentos de vapor rompen el aire. Espumarajos blancos sobre la blanca nieve. Sudor, espuma y vapor. Ansia.

Me sentí verdugo. Pero ya no había retorno. La distancia entre nosotros se acortaba impla- cablemente. Dios y la naturaleza indiferentes.

Me siento seguro. Desato el cabestro. Abro el lazo. Las riendas tirantes. Cada nervio, cada músculo alerta y el alma en la boca. Espuelas tensas en ijares temblorosos. Arranca el caballo. Remolineo el cabestro y lanzo el lazo obediente.

Vértigo de furia y rabia. Remolinos de luz y abanicos de transparente nieve. Cabestro que silba y quema en la teja de la silla. Guantes violentos que humean. Ojos ardientes en sus pozos. Boca seca. Frente caliente. Y el mundo se sacude y se estremece. Y se acaba la larga zanja blanca en un ancho charco blanco.

Sosiego jadeante y denso. El caballo mago es

mío. Temblorosos ambos, nos miramos de hito en hito por un largo rato. Inteligente y realista, deja de forcejear y hasta toma un paso hacia mí. Yo le hablo. Hablándole me acerco. Primero recula. Luego me espera. Hasta que los dos caballos se saludan a la manera suya. Y por fin llego a alisarle la crin. Le digo muchas cosas, y parece que me entiende.

Por delante y por las huellas de antes lo dirigí hacia el pueblo. Triunfante. Exaltado. Una risa infantil me brotaba. Yo, varonil, la dominaba. Quería cantar y pronto me olvidaba. Quería gritar pero callaba. Era un manojo de alegría. Era el orgullo del hombre adolescente. Me sentí conquistador.

El Mago ensayaba la libertad una y otra vez, arrancándome de mis meditaciones abruptamente. Por unos instantes se armaba la lucha otra vez. Luego seguíamos.

Fue necesario pasar por el pueblo. No había remedio. Sol poniente. Calles de hielo y gente en los portales. El Mago lleno de terror y pánico por primera vez. Huía y mi caballo herrado lo detenía. Se resbalaba y caía de costalazo. Yo lloré por él. La indignidad. La humillación. La alteza venida a menos. Le rogaba que no forcejeara, que se dejara llevar. ¡Cómo me dolió que lo vieran así los otros!

Por fin llegamos a la casa. "¿Qué hacer con- tigo, Mago? Si te meto en el establo o en el corral, de seguro te haces daño. Además sería un insulto. No eres esclavo. No eres criado. Ni siquiera eres animal." Decidí soltarlo en el potrero. Allí podría el Mago irse acostum- brando poco a poco a mi amistad y compañía. De ese potrero no se había escapado nunca un animal.

Mi padre me vió llegar y me esperó sin hablar. En la cara le jugaba una sonrisa y en los ojos le bailaba una chispa. Me vió quitarle el cabestro al Mago y los dos lo vimos alejarse, pensativos. Me estrechó la mano un poco más fuerte que de ordinario y me dijo: "Esos son

It was necessary to go through the town. There was no other way. The sun was setting. Icy streets and people on the porches. The Wonder Horse full of terror and panic for the first time. He ran, and my well-shod horse stopped him. He slipped and fell on his side. I suffered for him. The indignity. The humiliation. Majesty degraded. I begged him not to struggle, to let himself be led. How it hurt me that other people should see him like that!

Finally we reached home.

"What shall I do with you, Mago?"[8] If I put you into the stable or the corral, you are sure to hurt yourself. Besides, it would be an insult. You aren't a slave. You aren't a servant. You aren't even an animal."

I decided to turn him loose in the fenced pasture. There, little by little, Mago would become accustomed to my friendship and my company. No animal had ever escaped from that pasture.

My father saw me coming and waited for me without a word. A smile played over his face, and a spark danced in his eyes. He watched me take the rope from Mago, and the two of us thoughtfully observed him move away. My father clasped my hand a little more firmly than usual and said, "That was a man's job." That was all. Nothing more was needed. We understood one another very well. I was playing the role of a real man, but the childish laughter and shouting that bubbled up inside me almost destroyed the impression I wanted to create.

That night I slept little, and when I slept, I did not know that I was asleep. For dreaming is the same when one really dreams, asleep or awake. I was up at dawn. I had to go to see my Wonder Horse. As soon as it was light, I went out into the cold to look for him.

The pasture was large. It contained a grove of trees and a small gully. The Wonder Horse was not visible anywhere, but I was not worried. I walked slowly, my head full of the events of yesterday and my plans for the future. Suddenly I realized that I had walked a long way. I quicken my steps. I look apprehensively around me. I begin to be afraid. Without knowing it, I begin to run. Faster and faster.

He is not there. The Wonder Horse has escaped. I search every corner where he could be hidden. I follow his tracks. I see that during the night he walked incessantly, sniffing, searching for a way out. He did not find one. He made one for himself.

I followed the track that led straight to the fence. And I saw that the trail did not stop but continued on the other side. It was a barbed-wire fence. There was white hair on the wire. There was blood on the barbs. There were red stains on the snow and little red drops in the hoofprints on the other side of the fence.

I stopped there. I did not go any farther. The rays of the morning sun on my face. Eyes clouded and yet filled with light. Childish tears on the cheeks of a man. A cry stifled in my throat. Slow, silent sobs.

Standing there, I forgot myself and the world and time. I cannot explain it, but my sorrow was mixed with pleasure. I was weeping with happiness. No matter how much it hurt me, I was rejoicing over the flight and the freedom of the Wonder Horse, the dimensions of his indomitable spirit. Now he would always be fantasy, freedom, and excitement. The Wonder Horse was transcendent. He had enriched my life forever.

My father found me there. He came close without a word and laid his arm across my shoulders. We stood looking at the white trench with its flecks of red that led into the rising sun.

Translated by Thelma Campbell Nason

---

8. **Mago** (mä′gô) *Spanish:* magician; wizard.

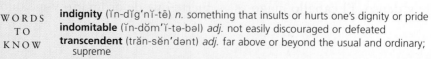

WORDS TO KNOW
indignity (ĭn-dĭg′nĭ-tē) *n.* something that insults or hurts one's dignity or pride
indomitable (ĭn-dŏm′ĭ-tə-bəl) *adj.* not easily discouraged or defeated
transcendent (trăn-sĕn′dənt) *adj.* far above or beyond the usual and ordinary; supreme

hombres." Nada más. Ni hacía falta. Nos entendíamos mi padre y yo muy bien. Yo hacía el papel de *muy hombre* pero aquella risa infantil y aquel grito que me andaban por dentro por poco estropean la impresión que yo quería dar.

Aquella noche casi no dormí y cuando dormí no supe que dormía. Pues el soñar es igual, cuando se sueña de veras, dormido o despierto. Al amanecer yo ya estaba de pie. Tenía que ir a ver al Mago. En cuanto aclaró salí al frío a buscarlo.

El potrero era grande. Tenía un bosque y una cañada. No se veía el Mago en ninguna parte pero yo me sentía seguro. Caminaba despacio, la cabeza toda llena de los acontecimientos de ayer y de los proyectos de mañana. De pronto me di cuenta que había andado mucho. Aprieto el paso. Miro aprensivo a todos lados. Empieza a entrarme el miedo. Sin saber voy corriendo. Cada vez más rápido.

No está. El Mago se ha escapado. Recorro cada rincón donde pudiera haberse agazapado. Sigo la huella. Veo que durante toda la noche el Mago anduvo sin cesar buscando, olfateando, una salida. No la encontró. La inventó.

Seguí la huella que se dirigía directamente a la cerca. Y vi como el rastro no se detenía sino continuaba del otro lado. El alambre era de púa. Y había pelos blancos en el alambre. Había sangre en las púas. Había manchas rojas en la nieve y gotitas rojas en las huellas del otro lado de la cerca.

Allí me detuve. No fui más allá. Sol rayante en la cara. Ojos nublados y llenos de luz. Lágrimas infantiles en mejillas varoniles. Grito hecho nudo en la garganta. Sollozos despaciosos y silenciosos.

Allí me quedé y me olvidé de mí y del mundo y del tiempo. No sé cómo estuvo, pero mi tristeza era gusto. Lloraba de alegría. Estaba celebrando, por mucho que me dolía, la fuga y la libertad del Mago, la transcendencia de ese espíritu indomable. Ahora seguiría siendo el ideal, la ilusión y la emoción. El Mago era un absoluto. A mí me había enriquecido la vida para siempre.

Allí me halló mi padre. Se acercó sin decir nada y me puso el brazo sobre el hombro. Nos quedamos mirando la zanja blanca con flecos de rojo que se dirigía al sol rayante. ❖

FABLE FOR WHEN THERE'S NO WAY OUT

MAY SWENSON

Grown too big for his skin,
and it grown hard,

without a sea and atmosphere—
he's drunk it all up—

5 his strength's inside him now,
but there's no room to stretch.

He pecks at the top
but his beak's too soft;

though instinct and ambition shoves,
10 he can't get through.

Barely old enough to bleed
and already bruised!

In a case this tough
what's the use

15 if you break your head
instead of the lid?

Despair tempts him
to just go limp:

20 Maybe the cell's
already a tomb,

and beginning end
in this round room.

Still, stupidly he pecks
and pecks, as if from under

25 his own skull—
yet makes no crack . . .

No crack until
he finally cracks,

and kicks and stomps.
30 What a thrill

and shock to feel
his little gaff[1] poke

through the floor!
A way he hadn't known or meant.

35 Rage works if reason won't.
When locked up, bear down.

---

1. **gaff:** a hook attached to a handle.

Thinking through the LITERATURE

Connect to the Literature

1. What Do You Think? How did you explain the boy's tears and joy at the end of the story?

Comprehension Check
- How does the boy hear about the wonder horse?
- Why does the boy admire the horse?
- In what season does the boy capture the horse?
- How does the boy lose the horse?

Think Critically

2. What do you think the boy learns through his experience with the wonder horse?

THINK ABOUT
- his age and stage in life
- what the horse represents for him
- what he hopes to achieve by capturing and owning the horse
- why he weeps with happiness at the end

3. ACTIVE READING INFERENCES ABOUT CHARACTER CHANGE Review the chart of inferences you made in your READER'S NOTEBOOK. Which of the inferences that you recorded helped you to understand how the **narrator** changes through the story?

4. What do you think the wonder horse **symbolizes,** or represents? Refer to details from the story as you explain your answer.

Extend Interpretations

5. Comparing Texts Read the poem "Fable for When There's No Way Out" on page 568. Does the situation described in the poem remind you more of the predicament of the boy or the horse in "My Wonder Horse"? Why?

6. What If? What if the horse had not escaped? What might the narrator have lost in owning him?

7. Connect to Life Do you think it is acceptable to capture wild animals and raise them as pets? Explain your reasoning.

Literary Analysis

STYLE **Style** refers to the special way in which a writer expresses ideas. It describes not the ideas themselves but rather how they are presented. Every writer has a unique style. Some elements that make up a writer's style are **sentence length, word choice,** use of **descriptive language,** and **tone.** One of the distinctive elements of Ulibarrí's style is his variety of sentence length, as in the following excerpt:

Then my eyes focus. There he is! The Wonder Horse! At the end of the glade, on high ground surrounded by summer green. He is a statue. He is an engraving.

The use of so many short sentences and sentence fragments in the passage creates an abrupt feeling that helps convey the unexpectedness of seeing the horse.

Cooperative Learning Activity With a small group, take turns sharing a paragraph from the story whose style you found interesting. For each paragraph, list the variety of sentence lengths. Discuss how the variety of sentence lengths might reflect the emotional content or the action in the passage. Decide which paragraph is the best example of style reflecting content. Then share your findings with the class.

Choices & CHALLENGES

Writing Options

1. Story Outline Use this story as a model for one of your own about your favorite wild animal. Write an outline of the story. Remember to begin with an attention-getting event that introduces conflict.

2. Dream Letter Write a letter to a friend describing a dream that you have had, just as the narrator dreamed of capturing the white horse. Use sensory details or descriptions to help your friend understand why your dream is important to you.

Writing Handbook
See page 1149: Elaboration.

Activities & Explorations

1. Bilingual Book on Tape If possible, form a team of an English-speaking student and a Spanish-speaking student (either a native speaker or someone learning it in school). Use the English and Spanish versions of the story provided in this text to create an audio book excerpt. Decide whether you want to alternate passages in each language, or to record all of one language, then all of the other. ~ **SPEAKING AND LISTENING/SPANISH**

Inquiry & Research

Save the Mustangs Find out more about the wild horses, or mustangs, of the West. Use reference materials or other books to learn about their numbers, their location, and threats to their continued existence. In an oral report, share your findings with the class.

Vocabulary in Action

EXERCISE A: CONTEXT CLUES On your paper, fill in each blank with the word that best completes the sentence.

1. The story "My Wonder Horse" will _____, in some readers, memories about other remarkable animals.

2. A horse named Clever Hans that could solve math problems was, perhaps, the _____ "wonder horse" of all time.

3. Since Clever Hans's behavior was not the result of trickery, people were amazed by his strange, _____ performances.

4. An _____ psychologist, O. Pfungst, refused to accept this and eventually discovered that Clever Hans responded to clues from members of the audience.

5. As this news spread, the public's intense interest in Clever Hans began to _____.

EXERCISE B: MEANING CLUES Answer the following questions.

1. Would a person show **lethargy** by yawning, sobbing, or shuddering?

2. Does someone who gives a **mandate** have wealth, wit, or power?

3. Does a person who is keeping a **vigil** most need to be alert, sympathetic, or relaxed?

4. Would you expect a person with **transcendent** ability to win a first-place ribbon, honorable mention, or a booby prize?

5. Would a proud person be most likely to respond to an **indignity** by saying "Thank you!" "How dare you!" or "I deserved that"?

Building Vocabulary

Several Words to Know in this lesson have interesting origins. For an in-depth lesson on word origins, see page 973.

WORDS TO KNOW				
evoke	indomitable	mandate	transcendent	vigil
indignity	lethargy	mystic	ultimate	wane

Choices & CHALLENGES

Grammar in Context: Changing Tenses for Dramatic Effect

"My Wonder Horse" is narrated in the past tense, except when the horse is the center of the action. Then the narrator switches to the present tense, highlighting the drama and excitement of the horse's appearance. In the following passage, the past-tense verb is in blue type and the present-tense verbs are in red type.

> The sun **was setting** behind me in a riot of streaks and colors. Deep, harmonious silence.
> I **sit** drowsily still, forgetting the cattle in the glade. Suddenly the forest **falls** silent. . . . For a moment, I **don't understand** what **is happening.**
> Then my eyes **focus. There he is!** The Wonder Horse!

Usage Tip: Shift tenses only when you have a good reason and when the shift won't confuse the reader.

WRITING EXERCISE Rewrite the following passage so that it is similar to the example at the left. Begin by deciding at which point in the paragraph you will switch to the present tense. Later in the paragraph, switch back to the past tense.

It was a muggy evening in early July. My horse and I were covered with sweat when I pulled off the trail to make camp. I unsaddled the horse and let him graze, but I felt too weary to eat anything myself. Tucking my bedroll under my head, I drifted off into a deep sleep. Suddenly my eyes flew open! The sky was filled with a million colored lights! My heart leapt into my throat. I didn't understand what was happening. Was the world coming to an end? Caught up in the magnificent beauty of the event, I almost didn't care. Gradually, of course, I realized what I was seeing. It was a Fourth of July celebration in a nearby town. Even though the fireworks inevitably ended, their afterglow remained. I carried that summer night's gift with me long after my years on the trail.

Sabine R. Ulibarrí
1919–

Other Works
Tierra Amarilla: Stories of New Mexico

Write What You Know Sabine Ulibarrí's family is part of an established Hispanic heritage in northern New Mexico that pre-dates by three centuries the formation of the United States. Ulibarrí was born in a town in the mountain foothills of the region, rode the range on his father's cattle ranch there, and as a child listened to stories of a legendary white horse.

Going Public Ulibarrí was a constant reader even before reaching school age. While still an adolescent, he organized a literary club among students his age and led debates on various topics. After finishing his schooling, he taught Spanish for many years at the University of New Mexico.

However, Ulibarrí was 42 years old before he published his first writings. "This business of publishing is frightening because . . . one is confessing whether one has talent or not," he once said in an interview.

Preserving the Past Recording the history of Hispanics of northern New Mexico is the focus of Ulibarrí's short stories. He feels that the Hispanic world of his childhood is becoming lost, and so his stories "attempt to document the *historia sentimental,* the essence of that culture before it completely disappears." In the United States, most of his writings appear in bilingual editions because he writes entirely in Spanish.

Author Activity

Hispanic Heritage Use an encyclopedia to learn what two countries controlled the territory of present-day New Mexico before the United States did. How does this background relate to Ulibarrí's reason for writing?

Close Encounters with Unfamiliar Words

What strategies do you know for figuring out the meanings of unfamiliar words that you encounter in your reading? For example, how would you determine the meaning of *sensations* in the excerpt on the right?

The word *sensations* might make you think of related words like *sense* and *sensitive*. These words share the Latin root *sens*, meaning "feel" or "perceive," and therefore have related meanings. You might also consider the context of the passage, which is about a man getting feeling (sensations) back in his fingers.

> After a time he was aware of the first faraway signals of sensations in his beaten fingers. The faint tingling grew stronger till it evolved into a stinging ache. . . .
> —Jack London, *To Build a Fire*

Thinking of related words and finding context clues are two good ways of determining the meanings of words.

Strategies for Building Vocabulary

Here is a review of four strategies for learning new words. The fifth strategy suggests a way for you to remember the words you learn.

❶ Use Context Clues Context clues can help you understand unfamiliar words like *immortality*. Read the sentences in box 1 of the chart on the right, and notice how the contrast clue *death* following *immortality* helps to clarify its meaning.

❷ Think of Related Words When you come across a new word, think of words you know that have a similar root or base word. For example, *mortal* ("subject to death") and *mortality* ("a state of being subject to death") are related to *immortality*. If you know the meanings of related words, you can often figure out the meaning of the new word.

❸ Analyze Word Parts The parts of a word can sometimes reveal its meaning. *Immortality* has four parts: *im-, mort, -al,* and *-ity*. If you know that the prefix *im-* means "not," the Latin root *mort* means "death," the suffix *-al* means "characterized by," and the suffix *-ity* means "a state of," then you can put together a meaning for *immortality*—"a state of not being subject to death."

❹ Consult a Dictionary If the first three strategies fail you, look up the word in a dictionary. A dictionary entry will also give you the word's origin, or etymology. Be sure to note the word's origin because it can often help you remember the word's meaning.

❺ Record and Use New Words When you encounter an interesting new word, record its definition, its root, and related words in your **📖 READER'S NOTEBOOK.** Also, put the word to work right away—say it aloud and use it in your writing. That will help you make the word a permanent part of your vocabulary.

1 Context Clues	2 Related Words
Most mountain climbers don't indulge in feelings of immortality. They know that one wrong move can cause their <u>death</u>.	*mortal, mortality*

immortality

3 Word Parts	4 Dictionary
im- ("not") + *mort* ("death") + *-al* ("characterized by") + *-ity* ("a state of")	**immortality:** the condition of not being subject to death; endless existence. [From Latin root *mort*, death.]

ACTIVITY Choose five Words to Know from the selections you have read in this unit. For each word, complete a graphic organizer like the one above.

On Being Seventeen, Bright— and Unable to Read

David Raymond

Think of all the things that you read daily, such as the television guide, food labels, and street signs, as well as school texts. Imagine what it would be like to have trouble recognizing the simplest words. That is the plight of David Raymond, the author of this essay. Raymond has dyslexia, a type of learning disability that makes it difficult to read and write.

ne day a substitute teacher picked me to read aloud from the textbook. When I told her "No, thank you," she came unhinged. She thought I was acting smart and told me so. I kept calm, and that got her madder and madder. We must have spent 10 minutes trying to solve the problem, and finally she got so red in the face I thought she'd blow up: She told me she'd see me after class.

Maybe someone like me was a new thing for that teacher. But she wasn't new to me. I've been through scenes like that all my life. You see, even though I'm 17 and a junior in high school, I can't read because I have dyslexia. I'm told I read "at a fourth-grade level," but from where I sit, that's not reading. You can't know what that means unless you've been there. It's not easy to tell how it feels when you can't read your homework assignments or the newspaper or a menu in a restaurant or even notes from your own friends.

My family began to suspect I was having problems almost from the first day I started school. My father says my early years in school were the worst years of his life. They weren't so good for me, either. As I look back on it now, I can't find the words to express how bad it really was. I wanted to die. I'd come home from school screaming, "I'm dumb. I'm dumb—I wish I were dead!"

I guess I couldn't read anything at all then—not even my own name—and they tell me I didn't talk as good as other kids. But what I remember about those days is that I couldn't throw a ball where it was supposed to go, I couldn't learn to swim, and I wouldn't learn to ride a bike, because no matter what anyone told me, I knew I'd fail.

Sometimes my teachers would try to be encouraging. When I couldn't read the words on the board they'd say, "Come on, David, you know that word." Only I didn't. And it was embarrassing. I just felt dumb. And dumb was how the kids treated me. They'd make fun of me every chance they got, asking me to spell "cat" or something like that. Even if I knew how to spell it, I wouldn't; they'd only give me another word. Anyway, it was awful, because more than anything I wanted friends. On my birthday when I blew out the candles I didn't wish I could learn to read; what I wished for was that the kids would like me.

With the bad reports coming from school and with me moaning about wanting to die and how everybody hated me, my parents began looking for help. That's when the testing started. The school tested me, the child-guidance center tested me, private psychiatrists tested me. Everybody

LIVING WITH DYSLEXIA

Most people with dyslexia have average or above-average intelligence; they simply cannot learn to read the way most people learn. Dyslexia often causes people to make mistakes in one or more of the following areas:

1. Recognizing and remembering printed words and numbers.
2. Reading and writing letters and numerals. Some dyslexics reverse letters and numerals, for example, mistaking the letter *b* for *d* or *p*.
3. Reading a word as it is written. Some dyslexics reverse the order of the letters when they read, such as seeing the word *saw* as *was*.
4. Reading a sentence as it is written, without leaving out or adding words.
5. Interpreting sounds correctly. Sometimes dyslexics confuse vowel sounds or substitute one consonant for another.

Research on dyslexia has resulted in techniques and programs that help most dyslexics manage their disability.

The passage below is from *Moby-Dick* as it might look to one dyslexic child on a particular day. Problems differ from day to day and child to child.

> It is a thiug uot nucommouly happeuiug to the whale-doats iu those swarmiug seas; the sharks at timesaqqareutly followiug them iu the same qrescieut way that vnltnres hover over the dauuers of marchiug regimeuts in the east.

---

knew something was wrong—especially me.

It didn't help much when they stuck a fancy name onto it. I couldn't pronounce it then—I was only in second grade—and I was ashamed to talk about it. Now it rolls off my tongue, because I've been living with it for a lot of years—dyslexia.

All through elementary school it wasn't easy. I was always having to do things that were "different," things the other kids didn't have to do. I had to go to a child psychiatrist, for instance.

One summer my family forced me to go to a camp for children with reading problems. I hated the idea, but the camp turned out pretty good, and I had a good time. I met a lot of kids who couldn't read, and somehow that helped. The director of the camp said I had a higher I.Q. than 90 percent of the population. I didn't believe him.

About the worst thing I had to do in fifth and sixth grade was go to a special education class in another school in our town. A bus picked me up, and I didn't like that at all. The bus also picked up emotionally disturbed kids and retarded kids. It was like going to a school for the retarded. I always worried that someone I knew would see me on that bus. It was a relief to go to the regular junior high school.

Life began to change a little for me then, because I began to feel better about myself. I found the teachers cared; they had meetings about me, and I worked harder for them for a while. I began to work on the potter's wheel, making vases and pots that the teachers said were pretty good. Also, I got a letter for being on the track team. I could always run pretty fast.

At high school the teachers are good, and everyone is trying to help me. I've gotten honors some marking periods, and I've won a letter on the cross country team. Next quarter I think the school might hold a show of my pottery. I've got some friends. But there are still some embarrassing times. For instance, every time there is writing in the class, I get up and go to the special education room. Kids ask me where I go all the time. Sometimes I say, "to Mars."

Homework is a real problem. During free periods in school I go into the special ed room, and staff members read assignments to me. When I get home my mother reads to me. Sometimes she reads an assignment into a tape recorder, and then I go into my room and listen to it. If we have a novel or something like that to read, she reads it out loud to me. Then I sit down with her, and we do the assignment. She'll write, while I talk my answers to her. Lately I've taken to dictating into a tape recorder, and then someone—my father, a private tutor, or my mother—types up what I've dictated. Whatever homework I do takes someone else's time, too. That makes me feel bad.

We had a big meeting in school the other day— eight of us: four from the guidance department, my private tutor, my parents, and me. The subject was me. I said I wanted to go to college, and they told me about colleges that have facilities and staff to handle people like me. That's nice to hear.

As for what happens after college, I don't know, and I'm worried about that. How can I make a living if I can't read? Who will hire me? How will I fill out the application form? The only thing that gives me any courage is the fact that I've learned about well-known people who couldn't read or had other problems and still made it. Like Albert Einstein, who didn't talk until he was 4 and flunked math. Like Leonardo da Vinci, who everyone seems to think had dyslexia.

I've told this story because maybe some teacher will read it and go easy on a kid in the classroom who has what I've got. Or, maybe some parent will stop nagging his kid and stop calling him lazy. Maybe he's not lazy or dumb. Maybe he just can't read and doesn't know what's wrong. Maybe he's scared, like I was. ❖

David Raymond
1958–

Overcoming Disability David Raymond was born in Norwalk, Connecticut. He attended Curry College in Massachusetts in a special program for students with learning disabilities. Listening to lectures and books on tape enabled him to complete his assignments. He graduated cum laude (with honor) in 1981 with a B.A. in business management.

Building His Future After graduation, Raymond lived in Connecticut, where he was in business for himself—owning and managing rental properties and being involved in the building and carpentry field. He also returned to school to study architecture.

Writing Workshop

Telling how something works . . .

From Reading to Writing In "To Build a Fire," Jack London's meticulous description of the steps needed to build a fire in the Arctic gives the reader a keen awareness of what a traveler must do to survive. In everyday life, you frequently rely on **process descriptions** to figure out how something works or to learn how to do something. You use them to get from your home to an unfamiliar destination, to cook dinner, or to assemble furniture, for instance. If you are given a wrong step or if a step is left out, you may become painfully aware of how important a good process description can be.

For Your Portfolio

WRITING PROMPT Write an essay that tells how to do something or how something works.

Purpose: To inform and explain
Audience: Someone who has a special interest in your subject

Basics in a Box

Process Description at a Glance

Part 1

Presents purpose and topic, provides background information, and lists necessary equipment or materials

Part 2

Describes all steps in the process in logical order using transitional words and phrases

Part 3

Summarizes the process and describes the end result or final product

RUBRIC Standards for Writing

A successful process description should

- begin with a clear statement of the topic and your purpose
- explain to readers how to do something or how something works
- present the steps of the process in a logical order
- define any unfamiliar words or phrases and provide background information that is essential to the reader's understanding
- use precise language and transitional words to describe each step clearly

Analyzing a Professional Model

John Caldwell
Author

From *Cross-Country Skiing Today*

Pictures of a cross-country skier in full flight—limbs crossed in a perfect diagonal, with a happy, confident expression—make you think, "That looks as easy as walking!" But if you ever try to duplicate these movements, you will find that full diagonal flight isn't so simple after all. Here are some steps to help you develop a powerful yet relaxing diagonal stride that eventually will feel as natural as it looks in pictures.

Step One: The Double-Pole

Are you ready to go? I will assume that your equipment is ready and your skis work—that is, they are waxed correctly or are waxless skis that work in given conditions. I will also assume that you are skiing in tracks, packed out especially for cross-country skiing.

The first exercise takes place on the flat or on a very gradual downhill. It's called double-poling, and you simply reach forward slightly and place both poles in the snow at enough of an angle so that, when you push down on them, the force will propel you forward along the tracks. Keep your elbows close to your body.

You may find you don't have enough strength to do this. If so, you'll have to train your arms gradually and build them up. Meanwhile, you can try this exercise on a slightly steeper downgrade where you can coast without pushing on the poles. Begin coasting, then give a push with the poles to get the feel of it. After a few times you'll have the ability to go back to the flatter—i.e., less steep—downhill.

Step Two: Single-Poling

Here comes a really good builder of coordination and strength. In it you propel yourself along the track using just one arm at a time, alternately, while you keep your skis steady, like a sled's runners.

Place each pole at an angle so the force will propel you forward as you push down and back on it. In this poling motion you should begin to think about pushing each arm far enough to the rear so that your hand passes by your thigh.

Again it will be easier to start on a gentle downgrade. If you progress so you can do this on the flats, then on gradual uphills, you will have developed excellent strength and coordination, both of which will come in handy doing the diagonal stride. However, it's not necessary to be able to do this exercise uphill before proceeding to the next step.

RUBRIC
IN ACTION

❶ Begins with a strong introduction, which includes a clear statement of the topic and purpose

❷ Headings identify each step and make the sequence clear.

Another Option:
• Introduce the steps by describing them in chronological order in separate paragraphs.

❸ Shows awareness of readers by using second person and by suggesting solutions to possible problems

Other Options:
• Include photos or other visuals to help readers.
• Remind readers of any benefits involved with learning this process.

Step Three: One-Step Double-Pole

In this exercise you reach forward with both arms simultaneously, as in the double-pole, and at the same time, slide one ski forward. Then push with the arms.

Practice so that you can slide either leg forward, and pole, using both arms forcefully. A good drill is to alternate your legs. Start with the left ski sliding ahead, pole, then coast a bit; slide the right leg ahead, double-pole, and coast, then continue.

At this point you may begin using your legs for some power. As you double-pole, give a little push, or bounce (here called a *kick*), off the leg you did not slide forward. If you push too hard off this more stationary leg, your ski will slip back. If this happens, don't push back so hard with the rear leg. Instead, try pushing (kicking) *downward* more.

Review of 1 through 3

A review is a good idea at this time. Make sure you can do the three preceding exercises fairly well. Pay attention to your arm-swing, so it is relaxed as it goes forward and there is enough extension beyond your hip as the arms push to the rear. I ask my skiers to continue pushing back with the arms, whether they are using them one or two at a time, so that I can see some daylight between their arms and hips.

Step Four: The Diagonal Itself

To do the diagonal, simply reach forward with your right arm and at the same time slide your left leg ahead; pole with your right arm and give a little push off your right leg. Then reach forward with your left arm, slide the right ski ahead, and push with your left leg.

It's like walking. You alternate: right arm and left leg ahead, left arm and right leg behind.

If you've followed the sequence leading up to the diagonal, you haven't concentrated much on using your legs. But you ought to begin now. As you pole, give a slight push down and back with the more stationary leg—which has completed its glide and is ready to extend behind you—just as I suggested you do in the one-step double-pole.

When everything goes well you will glide a bit on the forward ski, then reach forward with the other arm and slide its opposite leg ahead simultaneously, pole, and push off the stationary leg, and soon you've got it. After a while you will gain some rhythm and will be able to glide along in near effortless fashion.

4 Uses transitional words to show order of actions

5 Uses clear, concrete descriptions to explain how to stand correctly

6 This writer waited to describe the main step until readers had reviewed their skills.

7 Concludes by restating what readers will be able to do after practicing this process

Writing Your Process Description

Write what you care about and understand.

Richard North Patterson, novelist

❶ Prewriting

One way to find an interesting process to describe is simply to observe people. Watch someone cook a dish you like, or study an athlete, artist, or family member in action. You may want to consider describing something you already know how to do well. See the **Idea Bank** in the margin for other suggestions. After you choose a process you want to describe, follow the steps below.

Planning Your Process Description

▶ **1. Know your audience.** How much will they already know? What information will be most helpful? What special terms might they need to know? Consider whether a humorous or more serious tone best suits your audience.

▶ **2. Gather information.** What do you need to know to describe your process clearly and completely? Also, consider whether you or your readers will need background information or certain skills or materials before beginning.

▶ **3. Organize your information.** You might make a numbered list of the steps in chronological order before you begin writing.

❷ Drafting

Begin by explaining why the process is important or useful. Tell your readers what you will be describing and why. Use the following strategies to make your description clear and interesting.

- **Details**: Include all the steps, described in enough detail for the readers to carry out each part of the process themselves. Also, list any equipment or materials readers might need.

- **Definitions**: Explain any words or phrases your readers might not know.

- **Illustrations**: Use maps, charts, graphs, diagrams, or other illustrations when they will help your readers better understand the process.

- **Transitions**: Use words such as *first, next, before, after,* or *during* to help readers know when each step occurs.

If possible, set your draft aside for a few hours or a day before you begin to revise it.

IDEABank

1. Your Working Portfolio 📁
Build on this **Writing Option,** which you completed earlier in this unit:

- **Fire-Building Instructions,** p. 536

2. Fill in the Blank
Make a list of as many ideas as you can think of to complete this sentence: *How does (did) _____ work?*

For example, *How does a radio work?*

3. Everyday Activities
With a small group of students, take turns naming a daily chore or activity and describing the steps involved in completing it.

Have a question?

See the **Writing Handbook**
Transitions, p. 1148
Analysis, p. 1157

Ask Your Peer Reader

- What are the main steps in my description?

- What was the most helpful part of the process for you?

- Where did you run into problems trying to follow my directions?

- What parts of my description aren't really necessary?

Need revising help?

Review the **Rubric**, p. 576

Consider **peer reader** comments

Check **Revision Guidelines**, p. 1143

❸ Revising

TARGET SKILL ▶ **CLARIFYING MEANING** Vague phrases or words in your process description may leave readers uncertain of what to do. For instance, telling readers to *move* their legs could mean you want them to *kick, bend,* or *run.* Including specific words and details will help make your process description easier for readers to follow.

> A skate stride ~~is useful sometimes~~. ^can help you pick up speed.^ To use this technique, ~~you~~ ^glide forward^ ~~simply move,~~ while kicking out to the side and back as if you're ^with one ski^ ^with your other ski^ ice-skating. Try to ~~use~~ ^plant^ both poles ^into the snow^ at the same time, then use this leverage to push forward.

Stumped by verb tenses?

See the **Grammar Handbook**, p. 1184

❹ Editing and Proofreading

TARGET SKILL ▶ **VERB TENSES** Using the wrong tenses in your writing can cause confusion when you are giving directions. Check to see that your verb tenses—past, present, or future—are consistent and make sense when you edit your work.

> First, to get comfortable standing up in cross-country skis, plant a pole into the snow on either side of you. ~~You have made~~ ^Make^ sure your poles ~~were~~ ^are^ parallel to each other. Next, ~~you will~~ slide your left foot so it ~~will be~~ ^is^ even with your right foot. Remember to leave some space—perhaps a few inches—between your skis, depending on what ~~felt~~ ^feels^ most natural to you.

Publishing IDEAS

- Demonstrate the process to an audience.
- Prepare a videotape of someone performing the process described in your essay.

More Online: Publishing Options www.mcdougallittell.com

❺ Reflecting

TARGET SKILL ▶ **FOR YOUR WORKING PORTFOLIO** What did you learn about your process or subject by writing a process description? What did you find was most difficult about writing the description? Attach your answers to your finished work. Save your process description in your **Working Portfolio.**

Read this paragraph from the first draft of a process description. The underlined sections may include the following kinds of errors:

- **lack of pronoun-antecedent agreement**
- **run-on sentences**
- **verb tense errors**
- **incorrect suffixes**

For each underlined section, choose the revision that most improves the writing.

All hikers and outdoor travelers should know how to treat snake bites. <u>Many people think that they should try to suck out the venom, this belief is not true.</u> (1)

Hikers and travelers may rely on <u>his or her memory</u> of such folklore—with (2)

possibly fatal results. Trying to suction the venom out <u>often caused</u> more harm (3)

than good. To effectively treat a snake bite, first place the bitten area below the

level of the heart. Then wash <u>them</u> thoroughly with soap and water. <u>Looselly</u> (4) (5)

cover the bite with clean bandages. Do not apply a tourniquet or cut into the bite.

Most importantly, <u>get</u> medical help immediately. (6)

---

1. A. Many people think that they should try to suck out the venom. This belief is not true.

   B. Many people think that they should try to suck out the venom this belief is not true.

   C. Many people think that you should try to suck out the venom, it's not true.

   D. Correct as is

2. A. one's memory

   B. their memories

   C. his memory

   D. Correct as is

3. A. often causing

   B. often did cause

   C. often causes

   D. Correct as is

4. A. one

   B. theirs

   C. it

   D. Correct as is

5. A. Loosely

   B. Loosly

   C. Loosefully

   D. Correct as is

6. A. have gotten

   B. gets

   C. getting

   D. Correct as is

Need extra help?

See the **Grammar Handbook**

Pronoun Agreement, p. 1181

Verb Tense, p. 1184

Correcting Run-on Sentences, p. 1197

Voices of Experience

The selections in this unit deal with a variety of situations that turn out to be learning experiences. Based on your reading, what would you say it means to learn from experience? Explore this question by completing one or more of the options in each of the following sections.

People Flying, Peter Sickles. SuperStock.

Reflecting on Theme

OPTION 1

Analyzing Costs and Benefits Many of the fictional characters and real people depicted in Part 1 of this unit pay a price or take a risk in order to speak out. Create a chart to analyze the costs and the benefits of their actions. List the action taken in the first column, the costs (or risks) in the second, and the benefits in the third. In the fourth column, explain why the benefit was or was not worth the cost. Finally, look back at the list of topics that you brainstormed for the activity on page 408. What have you learned about the value of speaking out from your readings in this unit?

OPTION 2

Learning from Limits One person misjudges the danger of the cold and pays with his life. Another finds that though she is generally fond of animals, there are certain exceptions. In different ways, the fictional characters and real people in Part 2 of this unit struggle with limitations upon their ability to act, think, or feel. Make a list of these limits. Write *P* or *A* after the limit to indicate whether it is a personal one or one that is true of all people. If the limit is external (like the danger of cold), underline it; if it is internal (like a fear of snakes), draw a circle around it. Then compare this list with the one you made for the activity on page 513. Do you see any similarities?

OPTION 3

Evaluating Reading Experiences Discuss the following questions with your classmates: What selections did you learn the most from in this unit and why? How does reading literature compare with real-life experience as a way to learn? Support your opinions with examples from the selections.

Self ASSESSMENT

📖 **READER'S NOTEBOOK**

Reconsider the quotation at the beginning of the unit: "You gain strength, courage, and confidence by every experience in which you really stop to look fear in the face." Write a paragraph explaining how reading the selections in this unit has led you to agree or disagree with this statement.

Reviewing Literary Concepts

OPTION 1

Analyzing Style Choose two or three selections from this unit that you think have an interesting style. For each, create a chart like the one shown. List elements of style that give the selection its unique flavor. Then give an example of the element from the selection and explain briefly how it contributes to the style.

LANGSTON HUGHES—"THEME FOR ENGLISH B"		
Elements of Style	**Example**	**Contribution**
Tone—playful, gently mocking	*"The instructor said, Go home and write a page tonight."*	*Sounds like he's having a conversation with the teacher—questioning the assignment, but also taking it seriously.*

OPTION 2

Connecting Characterization and Genre Often, the genre of a work influences the writer's methods of characterization. For example, in a drama the playwright cannot comment about a character directly but has many opportunities to develop character through dialogue. For each of the genres represented in this unit, give an example of a method of characterization that the writer uses.

📁 Building Your Portfolio

- **Writing Options** Several of the Writing Options in this unit asked you to develop and present your opinions about important public issues. Choose the one that you feel is most successful at conveying your opinion. Write a cover note explaining the reasons for your choice. Then attach the note to the assignment and place it in your **Presentation Portfolio.** 📁

- **Writing Workshops** In this unit you wrote a Persuasive Speech. You also wrote an informative Expository Essay describing the steps in a process. Reread these two pieces and decide which you think does a better job of showing your strengths as a writer. Explain your choice on a cover page, attach it to the piece you have selected, and place it in your **Presentation Portfolio.** 📁

- **Additional Activities** Think back to any of the assignments you completed under **Activities & Explorations** and **Inquiry & Research**. Keep a record in your portfolio of any assignments that you especially enjoyed, found helpful, or would like to do further work on in the future.

Self ASSESSMENT

📖 READER'S NOTEBOOK

Copy down the following literary terms introduced or reviewed in this unit. Put a question mark next to each term that you do not fully understand. Consult the **Glossary of Literary Terms** (page 1126) to clarify the meanings of the terms you've marked.

historical drama	imagery
biography	mood
theme	word choice
extended metaphor	denotation
	connotation
autobiography	tone
first-person point of view	style
	speech
character study	

Self ASSESSMENT

Check to see whether there is enough variety in your **Presentation Portfolio.** 📁 Have you included an example of creative writing? Do you have a piece of expository writing, such as an essay? Is there a record of an activity? Throughout the year, look for opportunities to add diversity to your portfolio.

Setting GOALS

As you work through the next unit, think of ways you'd like to challenge yourself—perhaps by volunteering to be part of a performance, giving an oral reading of a selection, or doing research to find out more about a subject and sharing your findings with the class.

LITERATURE CONNECTIONS
The Miracle Worker

WILLIAM GIBSON

This play tells the true story of Annie Sullivan's struggle to release Helen Keller from the prison of her dark and silent world. When Annie first arrives at the Keller home, the young teacher realizes the near impossibility of the task before her. Helen is spoiled, willful, and wild. But she is also very bright. Convinced that she can give Helen the gift of language, Annie applies herself to her task with fanatical dedication.

These thematically related readings are provided along with *The Miracle Worker*:

from **Three Days to See**
BY HELEN KELLER

Darkness at Noon
BY HAROLD KRENTS

And Sarah Laughed
BY JOANNE GREENBERG

The Game
BY JUDITH ORTIZ COFER

Miss Awful
BY ARTHUR CAVANAUGH

A Man
BY NINA CASSIAN, TRANSLATED BY ROY MACGREGOR-HASTIE

from **Seeing**
BY ANNIE DILLARD

And Even *More* . . .

I Know Why the Caged Bird Sings

MAYA ANGELOU

Read the entire book from which our excerpt on page 480 is taken. With a poet's gift for language, Angelou recounts her girlhood in the Depression-era South and her efforts as a young woman to break racial barriers.

Books
Barrio Boy
ERNESTO GALARZA
In this autobiography, Galarza describes his childhood in a barrio in Sacramento, California.

Story of My Life
HELEN KELLER
In this memoir, Helen Keller recalls the patience of her teacher, Annie Sullivan, and her own exhilaration when she learned to communicate.

from **Animal Farm**

GEORGE ORWELL

After realizing their desire for freedom, the animals of Manor Farm chase Mr. Jones off his property and take control. As they struggle to create an equal community, however, some animals come to believe that they are more equal than others. Presented in the form of a fable, *Animal Farm* satirizes the events of the Russian Revolution and the years following, from 1917 to 1943. It is also a prophecy that points to a frightening future life—a life in which the boundaries between friends and foes are not clear.

These thematically related readings are provided along with *Animal Farm*:

from **The Rise and Fall of the Soviet Union**
BY MICHAEL KORT

The Stalin Epigram
BY OSIP MANDELSTAM

The Rebellion of the Magical Rabbits
BY ARIEL DORFMAN

Crow Song
BY MARGARET ATWOOD

Harrison Bergeron
BY KURT VONNEGUT, JR.

The Birds
BY DAPHNE DU MAURIER

The Call of the Wild
JACK LONDON
London's classic novel tells the story of Buck, a domesticated dog stolen from his home and made to work as a sled dog during the Alaskan gold rush.

The Other Side of the Mountain
EVANS G. VALENS
Valens tells the inspiring true story of Olympic skier Jill Kinmont, who found a way to reshape her life after a crippling accident.

Other Media
The Devil and Daniel Webster
In this film version of Stephen Vincent Benét's play, the great lawyer and statesman tries to wrest a young farmer's soul from the devil.
(VIDEOCASSETTE)

Cry, the Beloved Country
This film adaptation of Alan Paton's novel tells the story of a Zulu pastor and his son as they struggle to survive in apartheid South Africa.
(VIDEOCASSETTE)

Maya Angelou
Poet, writer, and civil rights activist, Maya Angelou talks about personal challenges and social progress.
(AUDIOCASSETTES)

The Miracle Worker
Anne Bancroft and Patty Duke star in this powerful dramatization of Gibson's play.
(VIDEOCASSETTE)

All in the Family

Call it a clan,

call it a network,

call it a tribe,

call it a family.

Whatever you call it,

whoever you are,

you need one.

Jane Howard
Journalist and lecturer

hen we speak of ties that bind us to other people, we mean emotions like love and friendship. But the idea of being tied to another person can also be unpleasant. Family ties are some of the strongest connections that can exist between human beings, but they can sometimes feel constricting. Anyone who has a sibling understands the complicated feelings of love and annoyance one can have. As you read this part of Unit Four, you'll learn that you're not alone in sometimes feeling that family ties can be a mixed blessing.

LEARNING *the Language of* *Literature*

*T*heme is the central idea in a work of literature. It is an observation about life or human nature that the writer shares with a reader. A theme is similar to the moral tacked on to the end of an Aesop fable. For example, in the fable "The Lion and the Mouse," the lion reluctantly lets a mouse go after the mouse promises to do him a favor some day. When the lion is captured by hunters a few days later, the mouse shows up to bite through the ropes, thus freeing the lion. The moral of the story: "Even a small friend may be a great friend." Most themes are not as directly stated as Aesop's morals, however. You have to infer themes from the combined elements of a story.

Distinguishing Between Subject and Theme

Theme should not be confused with the subject of a story, or what the story is about. Rather, **theme** is an observation that a writer expresses about a **subject.** For example, the subject of "My Wonder Horse" (page 557) is a boy's capture of a legendary wild horse. The theme of the story is rooted in the boy's recognition that the horse should remain free. The boy realizes that the horse would die or become just another horse if it remained in captivity.

YOUR TURN Read the passage at the right, taken from the end of the story after the horse escapes. Why is the boy so happy at the horse's escape? How would you state the theme of the story?

> **THEME**
>
> No matter how much it hurt me, I was rejoicing over the flight and the freedom of the Wonder Horse, the dimensions of his indomitable spirit. Now he would always be fantasy, freedom, and excitement. The Wonder Horse was transcendent. He had enriched my life forever.
>
> —Sabine R. Ulibarrí, "My Wonder Horse"

Identifying Theme from Elements in a Story

The theme of a story usually doesn't come into focus until after you've finished reading. But you can look for clues to theme as you read by closely observing the key elements of title, character, setting, and plot.

TITLE The title of a story is often a good clue to theme. The title of "To Build a Fire" (page 517), for example, emphasizes the most important feature of human survival in the arctic. Fire is something that humans can create, and according to the narrator, it can momentarily "outwit" the cold.

In "To Build a Fire," a dog senses what a man eventually learns—the power of nature.

CHARACTER The way characters are presented and developed can also point toward theme. "To Build a Fire" only has one character—called simply "the man"—and refers to "an old-timer on Sulphur Creek" whose advice the man consistently ignores. Early in the story, the narrator gives important information about the man that not only hints at what eventually happens to him but also helps explain why.

YOUR TURN Read the passage at the right. Find ideas in the passage that point to the theme of the story.

SETTING AND PLOT The cold, arctic setting is so important in "To Build a Fire" that it functions as the **antagonist** opposing the man. Alone in the cold, the man has only a fire to protect him: "When it is seventy-five below zero, a man must not fail in his first attempt to build a fire—that is, if his feet are wet." A few things go wrong for the man—he gets his feet wet and loses his second fire. But in such a harsh setting, there is no margin for error.

YOUR TURN Read the passage at the right that describes the **climax** of the story. How does this development in the plot confirm the dangers that have been given throughout the story? What can you infer about the theme from this passage?

> ### CHARACTER CLUES
>
> The trouble with him was that he was without imagination. He was quick and alert in the things of life, but only in the things, and not in the significances. Fifty degrees below zero meant eighty-odd degrees of frost. Such fact impressed him as being cold and uncomfortable, and that was all. It did not lead him to meditate upon his frailty as a creature of temperature, and upon man's frailty in general, able only to live within certain narrow limits of heat and cold.
>
> —Jack London, "To Build a Fire"

> ### SETTING AND PLOT CLUES
>
> High up in the tree one bough capsized its load of snow. . . . It grew like an avalanche, and it descended upon the man and the fire, and the fire was blotted out! Where it had burned was a mantle of fresh and disordered snow.
>
> The man was shocked. It was as though he had just heard his own sentence of death. . . . Perhaps the old-timer on Sulphur Creek was right. If he had only had a trail mate he would have been in no danger now. The trail mate could have built the fire.
>
> —Jack London, "To Build a Fire"

Putting It All Together

Study the chart at the right for specific ways to look for themes in fiction. Then, using clues provided by the title, as well as the above excerpts on character, setting, and plot of "To Build a Fire," write a sentence stating the theme as you interpret it.

Identifying Themes	
Key Elements	**Clues**
Title	• What idea the title emphasizes
Character	• How characters act alone and with each other
	• What the narrator says directly about the characters
	• How a character changes or what he or she learns
Setting	• How setting affects characters, plot, and/or mood
Plot	• How conflicts arise
	• How conflicts are resolved

When you're scolded for not doing your homework, you probably can guess—or conclude— that it's not a good time to ask to go to a concert that evening. **Drawing conclusions** is a natural part of your daily life, even in your reading. Use the strategies on this page to help you draw conclusions about what you read.

Drawing Conclusions

Drawing conclusions is a special kind of inference that involves not reading *between* the lines but reading *beyond* the lines. You combine what you already know with information from the text. You can draw a conclusion from stated facts or facts you infer, and then combine all the facts to support your conclusion. Use the strategies below to help you draw conclusions about fiction. For each literary element, organize details in a chart like this one. Then draw conclusions based on that information.

Plot, Character, Setting, or Theme	Stated Facts	Inferred Facts

Conclusions:_____
_____

1 Strategies for Drawing Conclusions About Plot
- Record important facts related to the plot. For example, in "To Build a Fire," you might record the fact that the man's feet get wet.
- Identify the conflict and the resolution of the conflict.
- **Question** how the climax impacts the outcome of the action.

2 Strategies for Drawing Conclusions About Character
- Record important facts related to character. In "To Build a Fire," you might note that the man did not fully imagine the possible dangers of his situation.
- **Evaluate** a character's thoughts, motivations, and actions.
- Pay close attention to any comments about a character made by the narrator or other characters.

3 Strategies for Drawing Conclusions About Setting
- Record important facts related to setting. Look at the notebook at the right for one student's notes on setting in "To Build a Fire."
- Note how the setting affects the plot.

4 Strategies for Drawing Conclusions About Theme
- Record your ideas related to the theme of a story. For example, one theme for "To Build a Fire" might be the frailty of humans in the face of nature.
- Pay close attention to any messages the writer may be conveying about the human condition.

"To Build a Fire"
Dangers:
— the extreme cold
— underground streams

Need More Help?

Remember that active readers use the essential reading strategies explained on page 7: **visualize, predict, clarify, question, connect, evaluate, monitor.**

"Doodle was just about the craziest brother a boy ever had."

The Scarlet Ibis

Short Story by JAMES HURST

Connect to Your Life

What People Expect Expectations are ideas about what a person is capable of doing or becoming. The narrator of this story has high expectations of his younger brother. Think about the expectations that others have of you. Do some people expect great things of you? Do you expect great things of yourself? For each of the following groups of people, assign a number from one to five, with five being the highest, to indicate the level of expectation they have for you: parents, siblings, friends, teachers and coaches, and yourself. Whose expectations are the highest?

Build Background

Southern Setting "The Scarlet Ibis" is set on a cotton farm in the South around the time of World War I—a setting much like the one in which the author, James Hurst, grew up. Hurst refers to a number of trees and flowers by the local names that he learned as a boy. For example, the "bleeding tree" is a type of pine from which white sap runs like blood when the bark is cut. "Graveyard flowers" are sweet-smelling gardenias, which, because they bloom year after year, are often planted in cemeteries. The frayed twigs of the "toothbrush tree" were once used by people to clean their teeth after eating.

WORDS TO KNOW
Vocabulary Preview

careen	infallibility
doggedness	invalid
exotic	iridescent
heresy	precariously
imminent	reiterate

LaserLinks:
Background for Reading
Historical Connection
Visual Vocabulary

Focus Your Reading

LITERARY ANALYSIS **THEME** A **theme** is the central idea or message in a work of fiction. It is a perception about life or human nature that the writer shares with the reader. Remember that a theme is not the same as the subject of a story—for example, "love" or "jealousy." A theme is an insight *about* the subject—a statement you might make, such as "Jealousy can be very destructive."

A story may have more than one theme. A good way to find a theme is to pay attention to the main character of a story. Does that person go through some sort of change? What does he or she learn? This might be an insight that the writer wants to share with the reader.

As you read "The Scarlet Ibis," think about the experiences that the main characters go through and about what they come to realize by the end of the story.

ACTIVE READING **DRAWING CONCLUSIONS ABOUT THE NARRATOR** When you look at a number of details and make a logical guess about what they mean, you are making an **inference.** You might also combine inferences with what you already know and **draw a conclusion.** For example, if a friend shows up with torn clothes and a black eye, you infer he has met with some trouble. When you remember how angry he was at someone, you conclude he probably got into a fight. As an active reader of **fiction,** you constantly make inferences and conclusions about what the **characters** are doing or thinking and about what motivates them.

READER'S NOTEBOOK As you read this story, jot down two or three things you can infer about its **narrator,** as well as any conclusions you come to about him. This may help you discover a **theme.**

The *Scarlet Ibis*

James Hurst

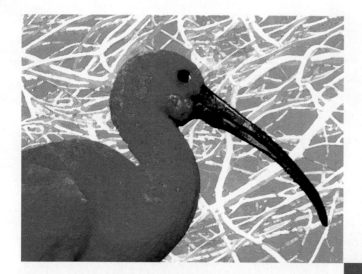

It was in the clove[1] of seasons, summer was dead but autumn had not yet been born, that the ibis lit in the bleeding tree. The flower garden was stained with rotting brown magnolia petals and ironweeds grew rank[2] amid the purple phlox. The five o'clocks by the chimney still marked time, but the oriole nest in the elm was untenanted and rocked back and forth like an empty cradle. The last graveyard flowers were blooming, and their smell drifted across the cotton field and through every room of our house, speaking softly the names of our dead.

---

1. **clove:** a separation or split.
2. **rank:** growing wildly and vigorously.

It's strange that all this is still so clear to me, now that that summer has long since fled and time has had its way. A grindstone stands where the bleeding tree stood, just outside the kitchen door, and now if an oriole sings in the elm, its song seems to die up in the leaves, a silvery dust. The flower garden is prim, the house a gleaming white, and the pale fence across the yard stands straight and spruce. But sometimes (like right now), as I sit in the cool, green-draped parlor, the grindstone begins to turn, and time with all its changes is ground away—and I remember Doodle.

Doodle was just about the craziest brother a boy ever had. Of course, he wasn't a crazy crazy like old Miss Leedie, who was in love with President Wilson and wrote him a letter every day, but was a nice crazy, like someone you meet in your dreams. He was born when I was six and was, from the outset, a disappointment. He seemed all head, with a tiny body which was red and shriveled like an old man's. Everybody thought he was going to die—everybody except Aunt Nicey, who had delivered him. She said he would live because he was born in a caul,[3] and cauls were made from Jesus' nightgown. Daddy had Mr. Heath, the carpenter, build a little mahogany coffin for him. But he didn't die, and when he was three months old, Mama and Daddy decided they might as well name him. They named him William Armstrong, which was like tying a big tail on a small kite. Such a name sounds good only on a tombstone.

I thought myself pretty smart at many things, like holding my breath, running, jumping, or climbing the vines in Old Woman Swamp, and I wanted more than anything else someone to race to Horsehead Landing, someone to box with, and someone to perch

with in the top fork of the great pine behind the barn, where across the fields and swamps you could see the sea. I wanted a brother. But Mama, crying, told me that even if William Armstrong lived, he would never do these things with me. He might not, she sobbed, even be "all there." He might, as long as he lived, lie on the rubber sheet in the center of the bed in the front bedroom where the white marquisette curtains billowed out in the afternoon sea breeze, rustling like palmetto fronds.[4]

It was bad enough having an <u>invalid</u> brother, but having one who possibly was not all there was unbearable, so I began to make plans to kill him by smothering him with a pillow. However, one afternoon as I watched him, my head poked between the iron posts of the foot of the bed, he looked straight at me and grinned. I skipped through the rooms, down the echoing halls, shouting, "Mama, he smiled. He's all there! He's all there!" and he was.

When he was two, if you laid him on his stomach, he began to move himself, straining terribly. The doctor said that with his weak heart this strain would probably kill him, but it didn't. Trembling, he'd push himself up, turning first red, then a soft purple, and finally collapse back onto the bed like an old worn-out doll. I can still see Mama watching him, her hand pressed tight across her mouth, her eyes wide and unblinking. But he learned to crawl (it was his third winter), and we brought him out of the front bedroom, putting him on the rug before the fireplace. For the first time he became one of us.

---

3. **caul** (kôl): a thin membrane that covers the head of some babies at birth.

4. **palmetto fronds**: the fanlike leaves of a kind of palm tree.

As long as he lay all the time in bed, we called him William Armstrong, even though it was formal and sounded as if we were referring to one of our ancestors, but with his creeping around on the deerskin rug and beginning to talk, something had to be done about his name. It was I who renamed him. When he crawled, he crawled backward, as if he were in reverse and couldn't change gears. If you called him, he'd turn around as if he were going in the other direction, then he'd back right up to you to be picked up. Crawling backward made him look like a doodlebug, so I began to call him Doodle, and in time even Mama and Daddy thought it was a better name than William Armstrong. Only Aunt Nicey disagreed. She said caul babies should be treated with special respect since they might turn out to be saints. Renaming my brother was perhaps the kindest thing I ever did for him, because nobody expects much from someone called Doodle.

Although Doodle learned to crawl, he showed no signs of walking, but he wasn't idle. He talked so much that we all quit listening to what he said. It was about this time that Daddy built him a go-cart and I had to pull him around. At first I just paraded him up and down the piazza,[5] but then he started crying to be taken out into the yard, and it ended up by my having to lug him wherever I went. If I so much as picked up my cap, he'd start crying to go with me, and Mama would call from wherever she was, "Take Doodle with you."

. . .nobody expects much from someone called Doodle.

He was a burden in many ways. The doctor had said that he mustn't get too excited, too hot, too cold, or too tired and that he must always be treated gently. A long list of don'ts went with him, all of which I ignored once we got out of the house. To discourage his coming with me, I'd run with him across the ends of the cotton rows and careen him around corners on two wheels. Sometimes I accidentally turned him over, but he never told Mama. His skin was very sensitive, and he had to wear a big straw hat whenever he went out.

When the going got rough and he had to cling to the sides of the go-cart, the hat slipped all the way down over his ears. He was a sight. Finally, I could see I was licked. Doodle was my brother and he was going to cling to me forever, no matter what I did, so I dragged him across the burning cotton field to share with him the only beauty I knew, Old Woman Swamp. I pulled the go-cart through the sawtooth fern, down into the green dimness where the palmetto fronds whispered by the stream. I lifted him out and set him down in the soft rubber grass beside a tall pine. His eyes were round with wonder as he gazed about him, and his little hands began to stroke the rubber grass. Then he began to cry.

"For heaven's sake, what's the matter?" I asked, annoyed.

ACTIVE READING

CONNECT As a child, how would you have felt about having to take a brother like Doodle with you everywhere?

---

5. **piazza** (pē-ăz′ə): a large covered porch.

WORDS TO KNOW

careen (kə-rēn′) v. to rush carelessly

Richard at Age Five (1944), Alice Neel. Oil on canvas, 26″ × 14″, courtesy of Robert Miller Gallery, New York. Copyright © Estate of Alice Neel.

beyond the touch of the everyday world. Then when the slanted rays of the sun burned orange in the tops of the pines, we'd drop our jewels into the stream and watch them float away toward the sea.

There is within me (and with sadness I have watched it in others) a knot of cruelty borne by the stream of love, much as our blood sometimes bears the seed of our destruction, and at times I was mean to Doodle. One day I took him up to the barn loft and showed him his casket, telling him how we all had believed he would die. It was covered with a film of Paris green[6] sprinkled to kill the rats, and screech owls had built a nest inside it.

Doodle studied the mahogany box for a long time, then said, "It's not mine."

"It is," I said. "And before I'll help you down from the loft, you're going to have to touch it."

"I won't touch it," he said sullenly.

"Then I'll leave you here by yourself," I threatened, and made as if I were going down.

Doodle was frightened of being left. "Don't go leave me, Brother," he cried, and he leaned toward the coffin. His hand, trembling, reached out, and when he touched the casket he screamed. A screech owl flapped out of the box into our faces, scaring us and covering us with Paris green.[6] Doodle was paralyzed, so I put him on my shoulder and carried him down the ladder, and even when we were outside in the bright sunshine, he clung to me, crying, "Don't leave me. Don't leave me."

When Doodle was five years old, I was embarrassed at having a brother of that age who couldn't walk, so I set out to teach him. We were down in Old Woman Swamp and it was spring and the sick-sweet smell of bay flowers hung everywhere like a mournful song. "I'm going to teach you to walk, Doodle," I said.

"It's so pretty," he said. "So pretty, pretty, pretty."

After that day Doodle and I often went down into Old Woman Swamp. I would gather wildflowers, wild violets, honeysuckle, yellow jasmine, snakeflowers, and water lilies, and with wire grass we'd weave them into necklaces and crowns. We'd bedeck ourselves with our handiwork and loll about thus beautified,

---

6. **Paris green:** a poisonous green powder used to kill pests.

He was sitting comfortably on the soft grass, leaning back against the pine. "Why?" he asked.

I hadn't expected such an answer. "So I won't have to haul you around all the time."

"I can't walk, Brother," he said.

"Who says so?" I demanded.

"Mama, the doctor—everybody."

"Oh, you can walk," I said, and I took him by the arms and stood him up. He collapsed onto the grass like a half-empty flour sack. It was as if he had no bones in his little legs.

"Don't hurt me, Brother," he warned.

"Shut up. I'm not going to hurt you. I'm going to teach you to walk." I heaved him up again, and again he collapsed.

This time he did not lift his face up out of the rubber grass. "I just can't do it. Let's make honeysuckle wreaths."

"Oh yes you can, Doodle," I said. "All you got to do is try. Now come on," and I hauled him up once more.

It seemed so hopeless from the beginning that it's a miracle I didn't give up. But all of us must have something or someone to be proud of, and Doodle had become mine. I did not know then that pride is a wonderful, terrible thing, a seed that bears two vines, life and death. Every day that summer we went to the pine beside the stream of Old Woman Swamp, and I put him on his feet at least a hundred times each afternoon. Occasionally I too became discouraged because it didn't seem as if he was trying, and I would say, "Doodle, don't you *want* to learn to walk?"

He'd nod his head, and I'd say, "Well, if you don't keep trying, you'll never learn." Then I'd paint for him a picture of us as old men, white-haired, him with a long white beard and me still pulling him around in the go-cart. This never failed to make him try again.

Finally one day, after many weeks of practicing, he stood alone for a few seconds. When he fell, I grabbed him in my arms and hugged him, our laughter pealing through the swamp like a ringing bell. Now we knew it could be done. Hope no longer hid in the dark palmetto thicket but perched like a cardinal in the lacy toothbrush tree, brilliantly visible.

"Yes, yes," I cried, and he cried it too, and the grass beneath us was soft and the smell of the swamp was sweet.

With success so <u>imminent</u>, we decided not to tell anyone until he could actually walk. Each day, barring rain, we sneaked into Old Woman Swamp, and by cotton-picking time Doodle was ready to show what he could do. He still wasn't able to walk far, but we could wait no longer. Keeping a nice secret is very hard to do, like holding your breath. We chose to reveal all on October eighth, Doodle's sixth birthday, and for weeks ahead we mooned around the house, promising everybody a most spectacular surprise. Aunt Nicey said that, after so much talk, if we produced anything less tremendous than the Resurrection,[7] she was going to be disappointed.

At breakfast on our chosen day, when Mama, Daddy, and Aunt Nicey were in the dining room, I brought Doodle to the door in the go-cart just as usual and had them turn their backs, making them cross their hearts and hope to die if they peeked. I helped Doodle up, and when he was standing alone I let them look. There wasn't a sound as Doodle walked slowly across the room and sat down at his place at the table. Then Mama began to cry and ran over to him, hugging him and kissing him. Daddy hugged him too, so I went to Aunt Nicey, who was thanks praying in

ACTIVE READING

PREDICT Do you think Doodle will be able to walk?

---

7. **the Resurrection:** the rising of Jesus Christ from the dead after his burial.

WORDS
TO
KNOW

imminent (ĭm′ə-nənt) *adj.* about to occur

the doorway, and began to waltz her around. We danced together quite well until she came down on my big toe with her brogans,[8] hurting me so badly I thought I was crippled for life.

Doodle told them it was I who had taught him to walk, so everyone wanted to hug me, and I began to cry.

"What are you crying for?" asked Daddy, but I couldn't answer. They did not know that I did it for myself; that pride, whose slave I was, spoke to me louder than all their voices, and that Doodle walked only because I was ashamed of having a crippled brother.

ACTIVE READING

DRAW CONCLUSIONS

Notice how the narrator's expectations of Doodle are tied to his own feelings. Do you judge the narrator for his pride as much as he judges himself?

Within a few months Doodle had learned to walk well and his go-cart was put up in the barn loft (it's still there) beside his little mahogany coffin. Now, when we roamed off together, resting often, we never turned back until our destination had been reached, and to help pass the time, we took up lying.[9] From the beginning Doodle was a terrible liar and he got me in the habit. Had anyone stopped to listen to us, we would have been sent off to Dix Hill.

My lies were scary, involved, and usually pointless, but Doodle's were twice as crazy. People in his stories all had wings and flew wherever they wanted to go. His favorite lie was about a boy named Peter who had a pet peacock with a ten-foot tail. Peter wore a golden robe that glittered so brightly that when he walked through the sunflowers they turned away from the sun to face him. When Peter was ready to go to sleep, the peacock spread his magnificent tail, enfolding the boy gently like a closing go-to-sleep flower, burying him in the gloriously iridescent, rustling vortex.[10] Yes, I must admit it. Doodle could beat me lying.

Doodle and I spent lots of time thinking about our future. We decided that when we were grown we'd live in Old Woman Swamp and pick dog-tongue for a living. Beside the stream, he planned, we'd build us a house of whispering leaves and the swamp birds would be our chickens. All day long (when we weren't gathering dog-tongue) we'd swing through the cypresses on the rope vines, and if it rained we'd huddle beneath an umbrella tree and play stickfrog. Mama and Daddy could come and live with us if they wanted to. He even came up with the idea that he could marry Mama and I could marry Daddy. Of course, I was old enough to know this wouldn't work out, but the picture he painted was so beautiful and serene that all I could do was whisper Yes, yes.

Once I had succeeded in teaching Doodle to walk, I began to believe in my own infallibility, and I prepared a terrific development program for him, unknown to Mama and Daddy, of course. I would teach him to run, to swim, to climb trees, and to fight. He, too, now believed in my infallibility, so we set the deadline for these accomplishments less than a year away, when, it had been decided, Doodle could start to school.

That winter we didn't make much progress, for I was in school and Doodle suffered from one bad cold after another. But when spring came, rich and warm, we raised our sights again. Success lay at the end of summer like a pot of gold, and our campaign got off to a good start. On hot days, Doodle and I went down to Horsehead Landing, and I gave him swimming lessons or showed him how to row a boat.

---

8. **brogans** (brō'gənz): heavy, ankle-high work shoes.

9. **lying:** here used to refer to the telling of tall tales, not untruths intended to deceive.

10. **vortex:** a whirlpool or whirlwind; here, a reference to the funnel-shaped covering of feathers.

WORDS TO KNOW

iridescent (ĭr'ĭ-dĕs'ənt) *adj.* shining with shifting rainbow colors
infallibility (ĭn-făl'ə-bĭl'ĭ-tē) *n.* an inability to make errors

Doodle and I spent lots of time thinking about our future. We decided that when we were grown we'd live in Old Woman Swamp . . .

Sometimes we descended into the cool greenness of Old Woman Swamp and climbed the rope vines or boxed scientifically beneath the pine where he had learned to walk. Promise hung about us like the leaves, and wherever we looked, ferns unfurled and birds broke into song.

That summer, the summer of 1918, was blighted. In May and June there was no rain and the crops withered, curled up, then died under the thirsty sun. One morning in July a hurricane came out of the east, tipping over the oaks in the yard and splitting the limbs of the elm trees. That afternoon it roared back out of the west, blew the fallen oaks around, snapping their roots and tearing them out of the earth like a hawk at the entrails[11] of a chicken. Cotton bolls were wrenched from the stalks and lay like green walnuts in the valleys between the rows, while the cornfield leaned over uniformly so that the tassels touched the ground. Doodle and I followed Daddy out into the cotton field, where he stood, shoulders sagging, surveying the ruin. When his chin sank down onto his chest, we were frightened, and Doodle slipped his hand into mine. Suddenly Daddy straightened his shoulders, raised a giant knuckly fist, and with a voice that seemed to rumble out of the earth itself began cursing heaven, hell, the weather, and the Republican Party.[12] Doodle and I, prodding each other and giggling, went back to the house, knowing that everything would be all right.

And during that summer, strange names were heard through the house: Château-Thierry, Amiens, Soissons, and in her blessing at the supper table, Mama once said, "And bless the Pearsons, whose boy Joe was lost at Belleau Wood."[13]

---

11. **entrails:** internal organs.

12. **Republican Party:** In 1918, most Southerners were Democrats.

13. **Château-Thierry** (shä-tō-tyĕ-rē′), **Amiens** (ä-myăɴ′), **Soissons** (swä-sôɴ′) . . . **Belleau** (bĕ-lō′) **Wood:** places in France where famous battles were fought near the end of World War I.

So we came to that clove of seasons. School was only a few weeks away, and Doodle was far behind schedule. He could barely clear the ground when climbing up the rope vines, and his swimming was certainly not passable. We decided to double our efforts, to make that last drive and reach our pot of gold. I made him swim until he turned blue and row until he couldn't lift an oar. Wherever we went, I purposely walked fast, and although he kept up, his face turned red and his eyes became glazed. Once, he could go no further, so he collapsed on the ground and began to cry.

"Aw, come on, Doodle," I urged. "You can do it. Do you want to be different from everybody else when you start school?"

"Does it make any difference?"

"It certainly does," I said. "Now, come on," and I helped him up.

As we slipped through dog days,[14] Doodle began to look feverish, and Mama felt his forehead, asking him if he felt ill. At night he didn't sleep well, and sometimes he had nightmares, crying out until I touched him and said, "Wake up, Doodle. Wake up."

It was Saturday noon, just a few days before school was to start. I should have already admitted defeat, but my pride wouldn't let me. The excitement of our program had now been gone for weeks, but still we kept on with a tired doggedness. It was too late to turn back, for we had both wandered too far into a net of expectations and had left no crumbs behind.

Daddy, Mama, Doodle, and I were seated at the dining-room table having lunch. It was a hot day, with all the windows and doors open in case a breeze should come. In the kitchen Aunt Nicey was humming softly. After a long silence, Daddy spoke. "It's so calm, I wouldn't be surprised if we had a storm this afternoon."

"I haven't heard a rain frog," said Mama, who believed in signs, as she served the bread around the table.

"I did," declared Doodle. "Down in the swamp."

"He didn't," I said contrarily.

"You did, eh?" said Daddy, ignoring my denial.

"I certainly did," Doodle reiterated, scowling at me over the top of his iced-tea glass, and we were quiet again.

Suddenly, from out in the yard, came a strange croaking noise. Doodle stopped eating, with a piece of bread poised ready for his mouth, his eyes popped round like two blue buttons. "What's that?" he whispered.

I jumped up, knocking over my chair, and had reached the door when Mama called, "Pick up the chair, sit down again, and say excuse me."

By the time I had done this, Doodle had excused himself and had slipped out into the yard. He was looking up into the bleeding tree. "It's a great big red bird!" he called.

The bird croaked loudly again, and Mama and Daddy came out into the yard. We shaded our eyes with our hands against the hazy glare of the sun and peered up through the still leaves. On the topmost branch a bird the size of a chicken, with scarlet feathers and long legs, was perched precariously. Its wings hung down loosely, and as we watched, a feather dropped away and floated slowly down through the green leaves.

"It's not even frightened of us," Mama said.

ACTIVE READING

CLARIFY Why can't the two boys give up their program?

14. **dog days:** the hot, uncomfortable days between early July and early September (named after the Dog Star, Sirius, which rises and sets with the sun at that time).

WORDS
TO
KNOW

doggedness (dô'gĭd-nĭs) *n.* persistence; stubbornness
reiterate (rē-ĭt'ə-rāt') *v.* to repeat
precariously (prĭ-kâr'ē-əs-lē) *adv.* insecurely; in a dangerous way

Down Home (1992), Tony Couch. Watercolor, 22″ × 30″, private collection. Copyright © Tony Couch, from *Tony Couch's Keys to Successful Painting*, published by North Light Books, 1992.

"It looks tired," Daddy added. "Or maybe sick."

Doodle's hands were clasped at his throat, and I had never seen him stand still so long. "What is it?" he asked.

Daddy shook his head. "I don't know, maybe it's—"

At that moment the bird began to flutter, but the wings were uncoordinated, and amid much flapping and a spray of flying feathers, it tumbled down, bumping through the limbs of the bleeding tree and landing at our feet with a thud. Its long, graceful neck jerked twice into an S, then straightened out, and the bird was still. A white veil came over the eyes and the long white beak unhinged. Its legs were crossed and its clawlike feet were delicately curved at rest. Even death did not mar its grace, for it lay on the earth like a broken vase of red flowers, and we stood around it, awed by its <u>exotic</u> beauty.

"It's dead," Mama said.

"What is it?" Doodle repeated.

"Go bring me the bird book," said Daddy.

I ran into the house and brought back the bird book. As we watched, Daddy thumbed through its pages. "It's a scarlet ibis," he said, pointing to a picture. "It lives in the tropics— South America to Florida. A storm must have brought it here."

Sadly, we all looked back at the bird. A scarlet ibis! How many miles it had traveled to die like this, in *our* yard, beneath the bleeding tree.

"Let's finish lunch," Mama said, nudging us back toward the dining room.

"I'm not hungry," said Doodle, and he knelt down beside the ibis.

"We've got peach cobbler for dessert," Mama tempted from the doorway.

Doodle remained kneeling. "I'm going to bury him."

"Don't you dare touch him," Mama warned. "There's no telling what disease he might have had."

"All right," said Doodle. "I won't."

Daddy, Mama, and I went back to the dining-room table, but we watched Doodle through the open door. He took out a piece of string from his pocket and, without touching the ibis, looped one end around its neck. Slowly, while singing softly "Shall We Gather at the River," he carried the bird around to the front yard and dug a hole in the flower garden,

WORDS TO KNOW

exotic (ĭg-zŏt′ĭk) *adj.* excitingly strange

"Go wash your hands, and then you can have some peach cobbler," said Mama.

"I'm not hungry," he said.

"Dead birds is bad luck," said Aunt Nicey, poking her head from the kitchen door. "Specially *red* dead birds!"

As soon as I had finished eating, Doodle and I hurried off to Horsehead Landing. Time was short, and Doodle still had a long way to go if he was going to keep up with the other boys when he started school. The sun, gilded with the yellow cast of autumn, still burned fiercely, but the dark green woods through which we passed were shady and cool. When we reached the landing, Doodle said he was too tired to swim, so we got into a skiff and floated down the creek with the tide. Far off in the marsh a rail was scolding, and over on the beach locusts were singing in the myrtle trees. Doodle did not speak and kept his head turned away, letting one hand trail limply in the water.

After we had drifted a long way, I put the oars in place and made Doodle row back against the tide. Black clouds began to gather in the southwest, and he kept watching them, trying to pull the oars a little faster. When we reached Horsehead Landing, lightning was playing across half the sky and thunder roared out, hiding even the sound of the sea. The sun disappeared and darkness descended, almost like night. Flocks of marsh crows flew by, heading inland to their roosting trees; and two egrets, squawking, arose from the oyster-rock shallows and careened away.

Doodle was both tired and frightened, and when he stepped from the skiff he collapsed onto the mud, sending an armada of fiddler crabs rustling off into the marsh grass. I helped him up, and as he wiped the mud off his trousers, he smiled at me ashamedly. He had

next to the petunia bed. Now we were watching him through the front window, but he didn't know it. His awkwardness at digging the hole

ACTIVE READING

QUESTION Why do you think Doodle is so moved by the scarlet ibis?

with a shovel whose handle was twice as long as he was made us laugh, and we covered our mouths with our hands so he wouldn't hear.

When Doodle came into the dining room, he found us seriously eating our cobbler. He was pale and lingered just inside the screen door. "Did you get the scarlet ibis buried?" asked Daddy.

Doodle didn't speak but nodded his head.

failed and we both knew it, so we started back home, racing the storm. We never spoke (What are the words that can solder[15] cracked pride?), but I knew he was watching me, watching for a sign of mercy. The lightning was near now, and from fear he walked so close behind me he kept stepping on my heels. The faster I walked, the faster he walked, so I began to run. The rain was coming, roaring through the pines, and then, like a bursting Roman candle, a gum tree ahead of us was shattered by a bolt of lightning. When the deafening peal of thunder had died, and in the moment before the rain arrived, I heard Doodle, who had fallen behind, cry out, "Brother, Brother, don't leave me! Don't leave me!"

The knowledge that Doodle's and my plans had come to naught[16] was bitter, and that streak of cruelty within me awakened. I ran as fast as I could, leaving him far behind with a wall of rain dividing us. The drops stung my face like nettles,[17] and the wind flared the wet glistening leaves of the bordering trees. Soon I could hear his voice no more.

I hadn't run too far before I became tired, and the flood of childish spite evanesced[18] as well. I stopped and waited for Doodle. The sound of rain was everywhere, but the wind had died and it fell straight down in parallel paths like ropes hanging from the sky. As I waited, I peered through the downpour, but no one came. Finally I went back and found him huddled beneath a red nightshade bush beside the road. He was sitting on the ground, his face buried in his arms, which were resting on his drawn-up knees. "Let's go, Doodle," I said.

He didn't answer, so I placed my hand on his forehead and lifted his head. Limply, he fell backward onto the earth. He had been bleeding from the mouth, and his neck and the front of his shirt were stained a brilliant red.

"Doodle! Doodle!" I cried, shaking him, but there was no answer but the ropy rain. He lay very awkwardly, with his head thrown far back, making his vermilion[19] neck appear unusually long and slim. His little legs, bent sharply at the knees, had never before seemed so fragile, so thin.

I began to weep, and the tear-blurred vision in red before me looked very familiar. "Doodle!" I screamed above the pounding storm and threw my body to the earth above his. For a long long time, it seemed forever, I lay there crying, sheltering my fallen scarlet ibis from the heresy of rain. ❖

---

15. **solder** (sŏd'ər): to join or bond together.
16. **naught:** nothing.
17. **nettles:** weeds covered with stinging hairs.
18. **evanesced** (ĕv'ə-nĕst'): disappeared; vanished.
19. **vermilion** (vər-mĭl'yən): bright red or scarlet.

Woman with Flower
Naomi Long Madgett

I wouldn't coax the plant if I were you.
Such watchful nurturing may do it harm.
Let the soil rest from so much digging
And wait until it's dry before you water it.
5 The leaf's inclined to find its own direction;
Give it a chance to seek the sunlight
    for itself.

Much growth is stunted by too careful prodding,
10 Too eager tenderness.
The things we love we have to learn to
    leave alone.

WORDS TO KNOW   **heresy** (hĕr'ĭ-sē) *n.* an action or opinion contrary to what is generally thought of as right

Thinking through the LITERATURE

Connect to the Literature

1. What Do You Think? What was your reaction to the narrator's treatment of Doodle at the end of the story? Share your thoughts.

Comprehension Check
- How is Doodle different from other children?
- How does the narrator try to help Doodle?
- What are the narrator's motives for working with Doodle?

Think Critically

2. ACTIVE READING **DRAWING CONCLUSIONS ABOUT NARRATOR**
Look back at what you jotted down in your READER'S NOTEBOOK. What **inferences** or **conclusions** can you draw about the **narrator's** state of mind as it changes during the course of the story?

3. What is your judgment of the narrator's treatment of Doodle?

THINK ABOUT
- which of his actions seem cruel
- the reasons he gives for his actions
- the effect of his actions on Doodle

4. What is your opinion of Doodle's **character**?

THINK ABOUT
- his strengths and weaknesses
- why his brother has such a powerful influence on him
- what his "lies" may reveal about him

5. As you look back at the story, what hints or clues do you see that **foreshadow** what eventually happens?

Extend Interpretations

6. Critic's Corner In his biography on page 607, Hurst comments that the **setting** of this story is one of the **characters.** What do you think he means?

7. Comparing Texts What advice does the poem "Woman with Flower" on page 604 seem to offer the narrator of "The Scarlet Ibis"? What is your opinion of the message of this poem?

8. Connect to Life The narrator says, "There is within me . . . a knot of cruelty borne by the stream of love." Think about your relationships with people you love, especially in your family. Can love and cruelty exist at the same time? Why or why not?

Literary Analysis

THEME The **theme** of a story may not be stated, but it is a central insight about life or human nature that the story illustrates. Different readers may find different themes in the same story. Here are some ways to look for a theme in a story:

- Review what happens to the main **character.** Does he or she change during the story? What does he or she learn about life?
- Skim the story for key phrases and sentences that say something about life or people in general.
- Think about the **title** of the story. Does it have a meaning that could lead you to a major theme?
- Remember that a story may have more than one theme.

Paired Activity Make a chart like the one shown. With a partner, go back through the story and list whatever statements you can find under the three headings. Remember that a theme should be expressed as a complete sentence, and that you may find more than one theme.

What Narrator Learns	Key Passages	Importance of Title

REVIEW **SYMBOL** A **symbol** is a person, an animal, a place, an activity, or an object that stands for something beyond itself. For example, a flag is a colored piece of cloth, but it also symbolizes a nation. Symbols can communicate complicated, emotionally rich ideas. Look for an obvious symbol in "The Scarlet Ibis." What does it have in common with what it symbolizes? How might this help suggest the **theme**?

Choices&CHALLENGES

Writing Options

1. Response to Narrator Write a letter to the narrator of the story, describing your feelings about the day of Doodle's death. Offer insights to the narrator about how he may come to feel in the future, based on your own perspective. Place your letter in your **Working Portfolio**.

2. Official Interview Analyze the narrator's relationship with Doodle from another character's point of view. Write up your analysis as an interview between your character and a police officer investigating the case.

3. Interpretive Essay Write an interpretation of Doodle's favorite lie, the one about the boy named Peter. Explain what you think it means.

Activities & Explorations

1. Thoughtful Soliloquy Imagine that at the end of the story Doodle is only unconscious and that he later recovers. How might this affect the narrator, and what might he think to do next? Present his thoughts in a soliloquy, a speech in which a character reveals his or her thoughts when alone.
~ SPEAKING AND LISTENING

2. Homestead Map Use the descriptions in the story to create a map of Doodle's small world, with the house in the center and roads and paths leading away from it. Show where you imagine Horsehead Landing and the creek, Old Woman Swamp, the garden, the corn and cotton fields, the barn, and the bleeding tree to be located. Compare your map with those of your classmates. ~ **ART**

Inquiry & Research

Odd Birds Use Internet databases to do some research on ibises, which are little known in the United States outside of Florida. What are the basic characteristics of these birds? What kinds of ibises are there? How do they differ from one another?

 More Online: Research Starter www.mcdougallittell.com

Art Connection

The portrait of a five-year-old boy on page 597 is one of several portraits Alice Neel (1900–1984) made of children. This boy, Richard, is posed naturally. What qualities of Doodle do you find reflected in Neel's painting?

Vocabulary in Action

EXERCISE A: ASSESSMENT PRACTICE For each group of words below, write the letter of the word that is an antonym of the boldfaced word.

1. **exotic:** (a) ordinary, (b) frightening, (c) indirect
2. **careen:** (a) crawl, (b) hide, (c) race
3. **heresy:** (a) conflict, (b) conformity, (c) distance
4. **reiterate:** (a) cease, (b) lose, (c) originate
5. **precariously:** (a) firmly, (b) cleverly, (c) thoughtlessly

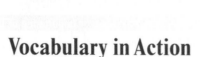

For an in-depth lesson on word relationships such as synonyms and antonyms, see page 849.

6. **doggedness:** (a) intelligence, (b) kindness, (c) casualness
7. **invalid:** (a) large, (b) healthy, (c) probable
8. **infallibility:** (a) respectability, (b) inaccuracy, (c) absence
9. **iridescent:** (a) obvious, (b) charming, (c) dull
10. **imminent:** (a) distant, (b) native, (c) unknown

EXERCISE B With a small group of classmates, act out five of the vocabulary words, having the rest of the class try to guess the words.

Grammar in Context: Prepositional Phrases

In the first three sentences of "The Scarlet Ibis," James Hurst uses a number of prepositional phrases that help to establish the setting *(in the clove of seasons, in the bleeding tree, amid the purple phlox, by the chimney, in the elm).* The next sentence contains more prepositional phrases.

> "The last graveyard flowers were blooming, and their smell drifted across the cotton field and through every room of our house, speaking softly the names of our dead."

You may recall that a **prepositional phrase** consists of a preposition, its object, and any modifiers of its object. In the excerpt above, the prepositional phrases allow the reader to follow the drifting scent of the flowers and to imagine what it said.

Usage Tip Be sure to position propositional phrases close to the words that they modify. Misplaced prepositional phrases can cause confusion

WRITING EXERCISE Rewrite these sentences, adding a prepositional phrase to modify each underlined noun, verb, or adjective. The prepositional phrase should answer the question in parentheses.

Example: *Original* We scattered flowers (where?) and made ourselves giddy (how?).
Rewritten We scattered flowers onto our pillows and made ourselves giddy with laughter.

1. Momma put the baby (where?), and he crawled (how?).
2. I looked at the baby (where?) and wondered (what?).
3. When he took his first steps (how?), my brother laughed (how?).
4. My brother and I roamed (where?)
5. My brother found it difficult to keep up (where?) (when?).

Connect to the Literature Look at the sentence beginning "Even death did not mar . . ." in the first column on page 602. How would leaving out the prepositional phrases change the meaning?

Grammar Handbook Phrases, p. 1193.

James Hurst
1922–

Musical Beginning James Hurst grew up in North Carolina on a farm near the sea. After attending North Carolina State College and serving in the United States Army during World War II, he studied singing at the famous Juilliard School of Music in New York. Hoping for an operatic career, Hurst went to Italy for additional study, but he soon abandoned his musical ambitions. In 1951, he began a 34-year career in the international department of a large New York bank.

Literary Breakthrough During his early years, Hurst wrote and published short stories and a play.

"The Scarlet Ibis" was first published in *The Atlantic Monthly* in July 1960 and won the "Atlantic First" award that year. Quickly recognized as a classic, the story has appeared in virtually every high-school literature textbook series published since the late 1960s.

His Own View Today, Hurst lives not far from the place in North Carolina where he was born. Hurst says that there are three "characters" in the story— Doodle, the narrator, and the setting, which comments on the inner action. When asked about the meaning of the story, Hurst once replied, "I hesitate to respond, since authors seldom understand what they write. That is why we have critics. I venture to say, however, that it comments on the tenacity and the splendor of the human spirit."

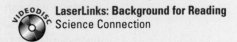
LaserLinks: Background for Reading
Science Connection

Lineage
Poetry by
MARGARET WALKER

The Courage That My Mother Had
Poetry by
EDNA ST. VINCENT MILLAY

Connect to Your Life

Your Own Tree How much do you know about your ancestors—the people you are descended from? To explore your lineage, or ancestry, draw a family tree based on the model shown here. Fill in your family members' names where possible, and extend the tree, if you can, with great-grandparents. After completing the diagram, identify the qualities that made these ancestors special in the lives of those younger than they. Then share your thoughts with the rest of the class.

Grandfather | Grandmother | Grandfather | Grandmother

Father | Mother

You

Build Background

Family Women In the poems you are about to read, the speakers describe their ancestors. Although the poets are from different backgrounds, both appreciated the admirable qualities of their own female ancestors. Margaret Walker, who was born in Alabama, grew up listening to stories her grandmother told about her family history during the years of slavery. Edna St. Vincent Millay grew up in Maine. Her mother was a singer and practical nurse who raised her three children alone after divorcing her husband.

Focus Your Reading

LITERARY ANALYSIS SOUND DEVICES Part of the power of poetry comes from the poet's use of sound devices. These include not only **rhyme** and **rhythm** but other techniques as well. **Alliteration** is the repetition of consonant sounds at the beginnings of words, as in the phrase "light lingers." **Repetition** is a repeated use of words or phrases for effect or emphasis, as in the phrase "over and over." **Assonance** is the repetition of vowel sounds within nonrhyming words. *Sea* and *free* are words that rhyme. *Sea* and *heat* are an example of assonance.

Look for examples of these sound devices in the poems you are about to read.

ACTIVE READING DRAWING CONCLUSIONS ABOUT THE SPEAKER When you read a story, you **draw conclusions** about its characters. Likewise, when you read a poem whose **speaker** tells his or her thoughts in the **first person,** you try to get an idea of who that person is. You make **inferences** based on what you read, and then you draw some kind of conclusion if you can.

READER'S NOTEBOOK As you read these two poems, jot down anything you can conclude about the speakers, such as their values, feelings, or sense of identity. Remember that the speaker of a poem is not necessarily the same as the poet.

Lineage

Margaret Walker

The Way They Live (1879), Thomas Pollock Anshutz. Oil on canvas, 24″ × 17″, The Metropolitan Museum of Art, Morris K. Jesup Fund, 1940 (40.40). Copyright © 1985 The Metropolitan Museum of Art.

My grandmothers were strong.
They followed plows and bent to toil.
They moved through fields sowing seed.
They touched earth and grain grew.
5 They were full of sturdiness and singing.
My grandmothers were strong.

My grandmothers are full of memories
Smelling of soap and onions and wet clay
With veins rolling roughly over quick hands
10 They have many clean words to say.
My grandmothers were strong.
Why am I not as they?

Thinking Through the Literature

1. What image of the speaker's grandmothers does the poem leave in your mind?

2. In line 10 the speaker says, "They have many clean words to say." What do you think this means?

   THINK ABOUT
   - the line "Smelling of soap and onions and wet clay"
   - other characteristics of the grandmothers

3. How does the last line affect your interpretation of the poem?

The Courage That My Mother Had

Edna St. Vincent Millay

The courage that my mother had
Went with her, and is with her still:
Rock from New England quarried;
Now granite in a granite hill.

5   The golden brooch my mother wore
She left behind for me to wear;
I have no thing I treasure more:
Yet, it is something I could spare.

Oh, if instead she'd left to me
10   The thing she took into the grave!—
That courage like a rock, which she
Has no more need of, and I have.

Connect to the Literature

1. **What Do You Think?** What image of the speaker's mother do you get from "The Courage That My Mother Had"? List words and phrases that come to mind.

Comprehension Check

- In "Lineage," where did the grandmothers work?
- What quality of her ancestors does the speaker feel she lacks?
- In "The Courage That My Mother Had," what did the mother leave her daughter?
- What does the daughter wish her mother had left her?

Think Critically

2. **ACTIVE READING** **DRAWING CONCLUSIONS ABOUT SPEAKER**
Look back at the notes you took in your **READER'S NOTEBOOK.** What does this poem suggest to you about the **speaker's** values and priorities?

3. In what way has the daughter received mixed blessings from her mother?

Extend Interpretations

4. **Comparing Texts** What do the **speakers** in "Lineage" and "The Courage That My Mother Had" have in common? What similarities are there between the grandmothers in the Walker poem and the mother in the Millay poem?

5. **Different Perspectives** If the two poets had written about grandfathers or fathers, how might the **imagery** of these poems have been different?

6. **Connect to Life** Compare the feelings that the speakers of these poems have toward their ancestors with the feelings you had after you drew your family tree in Connect to Your Life on page 608.

7. **Connect to Life** Do you feel that your ancestors were more courageous or stronger than you are? Explain your opinion by giving examples, just as the poets did.

Literary Analysis

SOUND DEVICES Poetry commonly makes effective use of repeated sounds. **Rhyme** is one example of this technique. Another example is **alliteration,** the repetition of consonant sounds at the beginning of words. An example would be "the sounds of summer." **Repetition** as a sound device consists of repeated words or phrases, as in "forever and ever." Still another sound device is **assonance,** the repetition of internal vowels in words that don't rhyme: "late rain" or "glorious morning."

Cooperative Learning Activity With a small group, read carefully through each of these poems, looking for examples of the repetition of sounds. You might take turns having one person slowly read the lines aloud, as the others listen. You will probably find most of your examples in Walker's poem. Use a chart like the one below to keep track of your findings. Two examples have already been filled in.

Alliteration	Repetition	Assonance
went with	with her/with her	

Writing Options

1. Last Will Imagine that people can write wills in which they leave personal qualities to their descendants. Choose one of the ancestors from these poems—or one of your own ancestors—and write such a will.

2. Ancestor Poem Look over your family tree that you completed in Connect to Your Life on page 608. Write a poem about one of your ancestors. Use specific images to help readers see why the person commands your respect. Consider following the format of Walker's poem:

My _____ was _____ .
He/she . . .

Activities & Explorations

1. Musical Settings Set the two poems to music, either as songs or as dramatic readings with musical backgrounds, and present them to the class. ~ **PERFORMING**

2. Art Accompaniment Create a work of art to accompany each poem. You might choose to make a collage, a mobile, a sculpture, a carving, a mural, or a painting. ~ **ART**

Inquiry & Research

Family Interviews Interview your parents or grandparents and find out what they know about their parents. What were the parents' lives like? What qualities or values did they pass on? Make a tape-recorded or written family record of what you learn.

Margaret Walker
1915–1998

Other Works
Prophets for a New Day
How I Wrote Jubilee
This Is My Century: New and Collected Poems

Words and Music Margaret Walker grew up with books. Her father was a well-educated, scholarly Methodist minister, and her mother was a music teacher. Her father shared with her his great love of literature, and her mother played ragtime music and read poetry to her daughter.

Poetry and History Early in life, Walker decided to write poetry. She won the Yale University Younger Poets Award in 1942 for her first collection of poems, *For My People*. The title poem portrays the experiences of African Americans and is written in the rhythm of a preacher's sermon. One of Walker's most famous works is a novel, *Jubilee*. It tells the story of her great-grandmother, a slave in Georgia during the time of the Civil War. Walker used the traditional form of the slave narrative to create her historical novel. During the 30 years it took her to write this novel, she also raised four children, taught school, and earned a doctorate.

Edna St. Vincent Millay
1892–1950

Other Works
Renascence and Other Poems
A Few Figs from Thistles
Collected Sonnets

Youthful Rebel Edna St. Vincent Millay was considered by many to be the voice of the rebellious youth of her time. A Pulitzer Prize-winning poet and a feminist, she reflected in her work many of the social changes that swept through the United States during the first half of the 20th century.

The Artistic Life After graduating, Millay became a part of New York City's Greenwich Village scene. From the 1920s through the 1940s, this area's reputation as a center for artists and writers grew. Millay created some of her most successful writing while living there in the early 1920s. Her works often shocked the older generation while voicing the views of her liberated contemporaries during the decade that became known as the Roaring Twenties. In all, Millay wrote more than 20 volumes of poetry, plays, and essays, as well as an opera. She also directed and acted in plays.

My Papa's Waltz

Poetry by
THEODORE ROETHKE

Grape Sherbet

Poetry by
RITA DOVE

"Everyone agrees —

it's wonderful."

Connect to Your Life

Fathers and Children In the two poems you are about to read, the speakers describe childhood memories of their fathers. Before you read the poems, think about your image of an ideal father. Using a chart like the one shown, jot down your thoughts about an ideal father's role in a family, his behavior, his activities, and the way his children should regard him. As you read, compare your image of an ideal father with the father described in each poem.

An Ideal Father	
Role in Family	
Behavior	
Activities	
How His Children Regard Him	

Build Background

Childhood Memories Both Theodore Roethke and Rita Dove have written several poems about their fathers. Roethke's father, Otto, was a stern man who demanded that his son work hard in the family's floral business. Roethke made his father the subject of "My Papa's Waltz" and another poem titled simply "Otto." Dove has said that her thoughts about how she got to be where she is today always lead to reflections on her childhood. She describes childhood memories of her father in quite a few poems, including "My Father's Telescope," "Roses," and "Grape Sherbet."

Focus Your Reading

LITERARY ANALYSIS **IMAGERY** The **imagery** in a poem consists of descriptive words and phrases that re-create sensory experiences for the reader. An image usually appeals to one or more of the five senses—sight, hearing, smell, taste, and touch. For example, the following lines from "My Papa's Waltz" appeal to both sight and hearing as you imagine the pans sliding and crashing to the floor:

> *We romped until the pans*
> *Slid from the kitchen shelf;*

As you read the following poems, notice how many different senses they call to mind.

ACTIVE READING **ANALYZING SENSORY DETAILS** The words and phrases that re-create sensory experience for the reader are often referred to as **sensory details.** Sensory details help the reader experience a poem to its fullest.

READER'S NOTEBOOK As you read "My Papa's Waltz" and "Grape Sherbet," jot down any sensory details that seem particularly striking.

MY PAPA'S WALTZ

Theodore Roethke

The whiskey on your breath
Could make a small boy dizzy;
But I hung on like death:
Such waltzing was not easy.

5   We romped until the pans
Slid from the kitchen shelf;
My mother's countenance[1]
Could not unfrown itself.

The hand that held my wrist
10   Was battered on one knuckle;
At every step you missed
My right ear scraped a buckle.

You beat time on my head
With a palm caked hard by dirt,
15   Then waltzed me off to bed
Still clinging to your shirt.

---

1. **countenance:** face or facial expression.

Thinking Through the Literature

1. **Comprehension Check** What is happening in this poem?

2. How would you describe the father's behavior in this poem? Cite specific lines to support your statements.

3. How do you think the boy feels about being waltzed by his father?

    THINK ABOUT
   • the way he holds on to his father
   • the physical experiences he describes
   • the title of the poem

Rita Dove

GRAPE SHERBET

The day? Memorial.
After the grill
Dad appears with his masterpiece—
swirled snow, gelled light.
5 We cheer. The recipe's
a secret and he fights
a smile, his cap turned up
so the bib resembles a duck.

That morning we galloped
10 through the grassed-over mounds
and named each stone
for a lost milk tooth. Each dollop
of sherbet, later,
is a miracle,
15 like salt on a melon that makes it sweeter.

Everyone agrees—it's wonderful!
It's just how we imagined lavender
would taste. The diabetic grandmother
stares from the porch,
20 a torch
of pure refusal.

We thought no one was lying
there under our feet,
we thought it
25 was a joke. I've been trying
to remember the taste,
but it doesn't exist.
Now I see why
you bothered,
30 father.

Thinking *through the* LITERATURE

Connect to the Literature

1. **What Do You Think?**
Describe the setting of "Grape Sherbet" as you visualized it.

   Comprehension Check
   - On what day are these events taking place?
   - Where are they taking place?
   - Who made the grape sherbet?

Think Critically

2. How were the speaker's reactions as a child different from what they might be now?

   - lines 9–12 and 22–25
   - the description of the children's play that morning

3. Why do you think the father "bothered"?

   - the time and the place
   - what he might hope would be remembered

4. **ACTIVE READING** **ANALYZING SENSORY DETAILS** Look back over the list of particularly striking sensory details that you noted in your 📖 **READER'S NOTEBOOK**. With another classmate, discuss why you chose these particular details from the two poems.

Extend Interpretations

5. **Comparing Texts** Do you think the speakers in the two poems share the same kinds of feelings toward their fathers? Give reasons to support your answer.

6. **Critic's Corner** In writing about "My Papa's Waltz," one critic remarked that Roethke reveals "something of his own joy, and bafflement, as the victim of his father's exuberant energy." Do you consider victim too harsh a word to describe the boy's part in the evening waltz? Why or why not?

7. **Connect to Life** How do the portraits of the fathers in these two poems compare with the image of a father that you described in Connect to Your Life on page 613?

Literary Analysis

IMAGERY **Imagery** is language that appeals to any of the senses. A poet uses imagery to help bring a poem "inside" the reader, to help the reader see, hear, feel, smell, and taste what's being described. The imagery in a poem can also help the reader understand the **tone,** or the speaker's attitude, in the poem.

Cooperative Learning Activity With a partner, create a chart like the one shown, listing the five senses: sight, hearing, smell, taste, and touch. Then write down as many examples of imagery as you can find in each of the two poems. Two are already listed.

Senses	Images in "My Papa's Waltz"	Images in "Grape Sherbet"
Sight	mother's frown	
Hearing	pans falling	
Smell		
Taste		
Touch		

LITERARY ANALYSIS **TONE** **Tone** is the attitude a writer takes toward a subject. People often speak in a particular tone of voice, such as sarcastic or amused, but tone comes out in writing, too. For example, the tone of a poem might be sentimental, angry, playful, or sarcastic. How would you describe the tone of each of these poems?

Writing Options

1. Memories in Verse Write your own poem about a memorable incident that happened when you were much younger. Try to capture your reactions at the time, as well as some of the sensory details of that experience.

2. Mother's Diary The speaker in "My Papa's Waltz" mentions the expression on his mother's face during the waltz. Imagine that you are the speaker's mother. Write the diary entry she might have recorded to describe her thoughts about the incident described in the poem.

Activities & Explorations

Artistic Response Create a piece of artwork that conveys your response to one or both of the poems. You might assemble a collage of drawings or photographs portraying different images of father-child relationships. ~ **ART**

Theodore Roethke
1908–1963

Other Works
Words for the Wind: The Collected Verse of Theodore Roethke
The Far Field

Rita Dove
1952–

Other Works
Thomas and Beulah
Fifth Sunday
Grace Notes

Tennis and Writing The son of German immigrants, Theodore Roethke grew up in Saginaw, Michigan. Although shy and sickly as a child, Roethke became fairly good at both tennis and writing during high school. During his freshman year, a speech that he composed on the Junior Red Cross was published in 26 languages and distributed internationally. His interest in writing continued into college, where he earned both a bachelor's and a master's degree in literature.

Popular Instructor Roethke taught English and coached tennis at a number of colleges and universities. He was an extremely popular teacher and inspired several of his students to become poets. A large man, standing over six feet tall and weighing close to 200 pounds, he brought a unique intensity to the classroom.

Fame and Misfortune Roethke suffered from alcoholism and mental illness during much of his adult life. However, in spite of frequent hospitalizations, he composed many collections of poetry for both adults and young children. He also won many awards, including the Pulitzer Prize.

Budding Author Born to well-educated parents in Akron, Ohio, Rita Dove acquired an early love of books. From the time she first learned to read, Dove tackled every book she could get her hands on, checking out stacks at a time from the public library. Her first attempt as a writer came early, too. In third or fourth grade she composed a science-fiction novel containing 43 chapters based on her classroom spelling lists!

Literary Careers In addition to her writing career, Dove is a professor of English, teaching most recently at the University of Virginia. She is also a poetry editor for several magazines. As an African American, she occasionally touches upon issues of race in her writing. However, she does not focus on that topic alone, claiming that her "poems are about humanity."

Prizes and Prestige In 1987, Dove won the Pulitzer Prize for *Thomas and Beulah,* a collection of 44 poems based on the history of her maternal grandparents. In 1993, she was further honored by being named Poet Laureate of the United States. The first African American to receive this title, Dove served as Poet Laureate until 1995.

"I crouched in the hallway around the corner from the kitchen and listened as long as I dared."

Marine Corps Issue

Short Story by DAVID McLEAN

Connect to Your Life

War's Aftermath The impact of war often extends far beyond the battlefield. In this story, the lingering effects of the Vietnam War on one U.S. soldier are dramatically portrayed. From books, movies, newspapers, magazines, and perhaps personal experience, you probably already have impressions about the aftermath of war. How do you think war affects those who fight—and relatives who stay at home? In a small group, brainstorm a list of the effects of war on returning soldiers and their families. Then record your list in a diagram like the one shown.

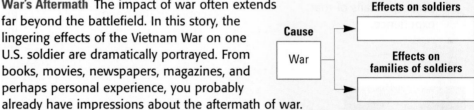

Build Background

A Cruel Struggle The war between North Vietnam and South Vietnam lasted from 1957 to 1975, though U.S. troops fought in it (alongside South Vietnamese troops) only from 1965 to 1973. This war is particularly notable for being the first one in which the United States ever failed in its mission—in this case, to prevent a Communist takeover of South Vietnam. The effects of this war were devastating for many soldiers and their families. The fighting took the lives of about 58,000 Americans and left another 365,000 wounded. Many U.S. servicemen, especially the wounded and the hundreds who had been held prisoner by the North Vietnamese, returned from the war with both physical and psychological scars.

> WORDS TO KNOW **Vocabulary Preview**
>
> | | | |
> |---|---|---|
> | agitated | devoid | intrigue |
> | animosity | disjunction | trepidation |
> | demeanor | grotesque | vulnerability |
> | deprivation | | |

LaserLinks: Background for Reading
Historical Connection
Art Gallery

Focus Your Reading

LITERARY ANALYSIS **FLASHBACK** A **flashback** is an account of a conversation, an episode, or an event that happened before the beginning of a story. In "Marine Corps Issue," the narrator's memory flashes back to several different experiences in his childhood, all involving his father:

> *My father used to keep three wooden locker boxes stacked in the tool shed behind our garage.*

As you read, pay attention to when each event in the story actually takes place.

ACTIVE READING **RECOGNIZING CAUSE AND EFFECT**
Sometimes two events are related as cause and effect—that is, one event actually brings about the other. The first event in time is the **cause;** the second event is the **effect.** For example, in this story, the father, a Vietnam veteran, has disabled hands (a cause). This condition forces him to retire from the Marines (an effect). His son is puzzled by the lingering effects of the war on his father because he does not understand what caused them.

READER'S NOTEBOOK As you read this story, jot down the effects that the war seems to have on the narrator's father. Also note the effect that the war has on the family.

MARINE CORPS ISSUE

David McLean

My father used to keep three wooden locker boxes stacked in the tool shed behind our garage. This was at our house in southern Illinois, where I grew up. The boxes, big heavy chests with an iron handle on each end, were fatigue green but had splintered in places. Chips of paint and wood had broken off during the miles of travel, and a shiny splayed pine showed underneath. Each box was padlocked with an oily bronze lock, the keys to which my father kept on his key ring, along with his house keys and car keys. I knew that because I saw him open the top box once, when a friend of his came to visit. My father lifted the lid of the top chest and then a tray within and pulled out an album or a yearbook of some kind, something to do with the war. The visitor was an old Marine Corps buddy, still active and in uniform. They laughed over photographs and drank whiskey, a whole bottle. I crouched in the hallway around the corner from the kitchen and listened as long as I dared. I don't remember much of the talk, names and places I had never heard of, but I do recall the man's calling my father "gunny,"[1] and commenting on his hands. My father had damaged hands. "Look at your hands, gunny— look at them!" And I think they cried, or maybe it was just drunken giggles. I don't know. That was the only time I ever saw my father drink. That was 1974. I was ten years old.

My original name was Charles Michael, and for the first ten months of my life, my mother tells me, I was called Charlie. I had no father then—that is, he had never seen me. But when he returned from Vietnam the first time, in early 1965, within a week he began the legal proceedings to change my name. Soon after, I was Jonathan Allen; I still am. I learned all this from my mother when I was twenty and needed my birth certificate for a passport application. My father was three months dead then, when my mother explained to me about Charlie[2] and how I had been renamed for a dead corporal from a small town in Georgia.

I see my father most often in two ways: playing handball or, years later, sitting on the edge of our elevated garden, black ashes from a distant fire falling lightly like snow around him. As I said, my father had damaged hands—a degenerative arthritis,[3] we were told. They were large, leprous[4] hands, thick with scar tissue and slightly curled. He could neither make a fist nor straighten them completely. Normally they hung limp at his sides or were stashed in his pockets. To grip things he had to use a lot of

wrist movement, giving him a grotesque bird-on-a-perch appearance. He rarely touched anyone with them, though he did hit me once, a well-deserved blow I know now and knew even then in the vague way of an innocent.

My older brother, Joe, and I would watch him from the walkway above and behind the handball courts while our mother waited outside. I was six years old but can still see him clearly, playing alone, as always. He wears olive-green shorts, plain white canvas shoes and long white socks, a gray sweatshirt, the neck ripped loose down the front, and a fatigue-green headband wrapped tightly around his bony forehead. Black thinning hair dipped in gray rises up like tufts of crabgrass around the headband. He wears dirty white leather gloves. He swings at the hard black ball forcefully, as though he held paddles of thick oak. I hear the amplified slap of his hand and then a huge explosion booming through the court as the ball ricochets back. He runs after it, catches up to it, and slaps it again, driving it powerfully into the corner. His tall, thin figure jerks across the court and off the wall, his slaps alternating with the hollow explosions, his shoes squeaking, his

---

1. **gunny:** a nickname for a gunnery sergeant in the U.S. Marine Corps.

2. **Charlie:** a slang term for the Vietcong—Communist-trained South Vietnamese soldiers against whom the United States fought.

3. **degenerative arthritis:** a condition in which the cartilage in joints breaks down, so that bones rub together painfully.

4. **leprous:** having an appearance like that caused by the disease leprosy.

controlled breaths bursting out of him as he tries, it seems to me, to break the ball or maybe rid himself of it forever.

But it always returns, somehow, even dribbling, to the center of the court. Exhausted, he sits against the wall, breathing heavily, his court gone suddenly quiet, though the booming echoes from nearby courts can still be heard. He watches the ball bounce off its final wall and then slowly roll to a stop. I watch it with him, until it again becomes an inert black ball on the wooden floor.

I said that my father had hit me once; it was at our second meeting. The first had been on that six-month home leave when he changed my name. I remember nothing of that, of course. I do remember his second return home, though, when I was five years old. To my new consciousness, Daddy was simply a figure in a photograph, a steely, strong-looking man in dress blues.[5] I remember the disjunction I felt upon seeing him for the first time, how I had trouble believing that this man was the same man as in the photograph. He was thin and gaunt and silent, with deeper eyes and a higher forehead than I had expected to see. He looked at me strangely. He hadn't seen me grow up. I could have been any child, an adopted son, were it not for my resemblance to him.

What I learned shortly after that first real meeting was the necessity of being a noisy child. Noise alerted him to my presence and prevented his being surprised and reacting on instinct. I began to knock on the walls or shuffle my feet or sing to myself as I walked through the house.

I discovered this survival technique one Saturday morning shortly after his return. I had awakened early and had rolled off the lower bunk, my blanket under my arms, a sleepy animal child going to look for his mother. I walked down the hall and into the living room, where my father sat reading. He had not heard

me come in. I wanted to play a game. I crept around an end table near his chair, suppressing a giggle, and watched him for a minute. I looked at the back of his head, smelled his sharp after-shave smell, stared freely, for the first time, at his gnarled left hand holding the book in that rolled-wrist way, and then I leaped out from the table and shouted *Boo!*

I saw a white flash—I was airborne, backwards, on my shoulders and over my head. I landed hard on my face and knees, bleeding from the nose and mouth. I looked up and saw him crouched and rigid, eyes on fire, palms flat, fingers as stiff as he could make them.

Then he melted, right there before me, his body slumping down like warm wax, and he began shouting, and crying, "Diane! come and get this child away from me!" He wouldn't look at me. His hands were in his pockets. He walked out of the house and into the back yard. I didn't see him again until breakfast the following morning. My mother arrived and swooped me into her arms. Only then did I begin to cry.

My mother's life intrigues me. Her strength, well hidden when I was younger, becomes obvious upon reflection. I spend a lot of time reading about the Marine Corps and Vietnam; it is a way of knowing my father. And yet I often find my mother in the books. I cannot read of Khe Sanh or Da Nang[6] without imagining my mother at home with two children under the age of seven and a husband across the world fighting in a war, what I think of as a stupid war at that. She has never spoken about that time, not even about the four continuous years of my father's absence, when,

---

5. **dress blues:** the dress uniform of the Marine Corps.
6. **Khe Sanh** (kā sän′) . . . **Da Nang** (də năng′): South Vietnamese towns near the North Vietnamese border—sites of U.S. military bases during the Vietnam War.

The Mighty Hand (1885), Auguste Rodin. Bronze, 18″ × 11½″ × 7½″, collection of the First National Bank of Chicago.

my grandmother told me, she would spend at least two hours every night weeping alone, the children already asleep, and when she could hardly sleep herself. Even after my father's return tension and distance continued for some time. Our family was different from others. I can best describe it as being composed of opposing camps—not camps at war with each other but survival camps: my mother and I in one, my father and Joe in the other. We had no open <u>animosity</u> toward each other, only distance.

My father was in the Marine Corps for seventeen years before beginning his second career in the offices of the Stone City Steel Mill. He was a decorated soldier, a career man forced to retire disabled because of his hands. He had been a drill instructor, a fact that always widens the eyes of those I tell. I can see them reassessing me as soon as I say it—Marine Corps drill instructor—and they look at me in a shifted way that is hard to define. A pity, perhaps, sometimes a fear. I do have a temper comparable to my father's, which usually shows itself in short, explosive bursts of expletives that roll out of my mouth naturally, as if I were a polyglot[7] switching tongues. The violence is verbal only, though I can still see my father, if I make the effort, at my brother's throat. Joe has been caught smoking in the garage a second time. He is fourteen and has been warned. He is pinned to the wall of the garage by my father's crooked paw, his feet dangling, toes groping for solid ground as though he will fall upward and off the earth if he can't find a grip. His eyes are wide and swollen with tears. My father's voice is a slow burn, his nostrils wide. He finishes speaking, drops Joe onto the concrete floor, and strides quickly away.

---

7. **polyglot:** a person who speaks or writes many languages.

WORDS
TO
KNOW

animosity (ăn′ə-mŏs′ĭ-tē) *n.* a feeling of strong dislike or hatred

Despite my father's years of service, our house was devoid of memorabilia.[8] A visitor would have no idea about my father's military career were it not evident in his walk and demeanor. Civilians might miss even these clues. Our house was not a family museum like other houses. We had few family photographs; the decor consisted chiefly of landscape paintings and small ceramic collectibles, dolls and Norman Rockwell scenes and wooden elephants from around the world.

t sixteen I saw the movie *Apocalypse Now*.[9] I had no interest in Vietnam then; I knew nothing of it. The film left me enthralled and fascinated, even a little horrified in an abstract way. I came home agitated but still had not made any connection. The epiphany[10] came when I walked in the front door. My father was sitting quietly in his recliner, sipping coffee and watching the Cardinals play the Reds on television. My mother sat on the couch crocheting under a lamp, humming a hymn to herself, our Labrador, Casey, resting on the floor at her feet. I stared at them for a long twenty seconds before my father snapped the spell. "Hey, Johnny," he said, "come in here and watch the game. Redbirds are up five to three in the seventh."

"Yeah?" I moved into the room and turned to face the television.

"What'd you go see, hon?" my mother asked.

"What?"

"What movie'd you see?"

I lied. I quickly named some comedy that was showing in the same complex. "It was awful," I added, to cut off the questioning.

I saw the movie again a few days later, and I saw it anew. My father was in there somewhere, dug into a bunker, behind a wall of foliage, there amid the ragged poor and the dripping trees and the sounds of gunfire and explosions. And when I returned home from the movie that night, he was reading a John Le Carré novel, sipping coffee, the silky voice of Jack Buck in the background describing the Cardinals game in Atlanta. The evening was hot and dry. It would be a hard summer of drought in southern Illinois.

The next day I walked to the library and borrowed three books about the Vietnam War. My summer project would be to learn about the war and my father's place there. Under a hot midmorning sun I skimmed the thinnest of the three on the way home, anxious, as though poised to turn the knob of a mysterious door. At home I hid two of the books in my safest place, above the loose tiles of the lowered ceiling in my bedroom, and took the third book and my copy of *The Pickwick Papers*[11] into the back yard.

We had a large yard behind the house, enclosed by a fence of pointed wooden slats five feet high. Against the back fence stood a terraced flower garden, built long before by a previous owner. It ran the length of the fence and was fronted by a red brick wall about two feet high. The three levels were separated by stacked railroad ties. My parents loved the garden and would labor all summer to keep it lush. Even that summer of drought, as the grass was browning under a merciless sun, my parents kept the garden well watered. From April to September we had cut flowers on the dinner table every night.

---

8. **memorabilia:** objects valued for their connection with important events; souvenirs.

9. *Apocalypse Now:* a 1979 film about the Vietnam War in which battles are dramatically re-created.

10. **epiphany:** a sudden insight into the meaning of something.

11. *The Pickwick Papers:* a classic 19th-century novel by Charles Dickens.

WORDS TO KNOW
devoid (dĭ-void´) *adj.* completely without; empty
demeanor (dĭ-mē´nər) *n.* outward behavior; conduct
agitated (ăj´ĭ-tā´tĭd) *adj.* emotionally excited or disturbed **agitate** *v.*

I kept a private place in the upper left corner of the garden. It was known to everyone; if I was nowhere to be found, my family would always check to see if I was there reading. Before watering, my parents would always shout a warning lest I be rained on. Although known, it was still quiet and just isolated enough. I would lie down on the ground behind a thick

IT TOOK HIM SO LONG TO FORGET ALL OF THAT. DON'T ASK HIM TO START REMEMBERING AGAIN.

wall of day lilies, my back against the fence, and read or think while staring up at the sky.

That is where I learned about the Vietnam War. I lay on my side and read for at least three hours every day, softly repeating the names of places and operations, marking pages with thin weeds. If called or found, I would rise from the flowers with *The Pickwick Papers* in hand, leaving the history book in a plastic bag among the day lilies, to be collected later. In the evenings, while listening to baseball games, I transferred notes from the weed-marked pages into a notebook that I kept hidden in my sock-and-underwear drawer.

Within two weeks I had finished those first three books. Upon completion of the third I emerged from the day lilies feeling expert. My knowledge of the war—dates, places, names—had zoomed up from zero. I was ready to ask my mother some questions. I approached her one afternoon before my father had returned from work. She was peeling potatoes over the kitchen sink when I padded in nervously. "Mom?"

"Yes, Johnny?"

"Mom, where was Dad stationed in Vietnam?" My throat was dry. I had never before uttered the word to my parents. My mother stopped working and turned to face me, potato peeler held upright in her hand. She looked puzzled.

"I don't remember, Johnny. Lord, that was over ten years ago. I don't remember those funny foreign names. He was stationed in more than one place anyway. Why?"

I felt ashamed, flushed. "Just curious. We learned a little about it at school, and I was just curious. That's all."

"I wish I could tell you, but I don't remember. You know me. I have trouble remembering what I did last week." She laughed an unhumorous laugh.

"Should I ask Dad?"

She suddenly looked very tired and thoughtful. "Oh, Johnny, please don't," she whispered. "Don't bring it up with him. It took him so long to forget all of that. Don't ask him to start remembering again." Then she looked directly at me, and I could see that she was pleading with me, and I thought that she was going to cry. But she turned back to the sink and ran her hands and a potato under the tap. She began working again.

"Okay, Momma. I won't. I'm sorry."

"Don't be sorry, honey. You've a right to be curious."

The next day I was with Joe. We were returning from the shopping mall in Fairview

Art and Artie (1989), Connie Hayes. Oil on paper, 27″ × 27″, collection of the artist. Copyright © Connie Hayes.

Heights, twenty miles away. We were in the old pickup truck he used on construction jobs, trying to cool ourselves with wide-open windows, though even the rushing air was warm and uncomfortable. Joe was eighteen then and worked nearly every day. I was enjoying the trip all the more because he allowed himself so few days off.

We were speeding down an empty two-lane road through the farmland south of Stone City. It was sickening to see. The corn, usually head high by the end of June, was barely up to my waist. The ground was cracked and broken in places. Some farmers had recently given up. You could see by the dry brown stalks, standing packed closely together, that they had stopped watering.

"Look at it," Joe said, shaking his head and poking his thumb out the window. He had to shout to be heard over the sound of rushing air. "I've never seen anything like this before. Even Grandma says it's the worst she's seen." I nodded and looked around at the dying fields.

"What'd you buy?" he shouted, pointing at my bag. I pulled out *Great Expectations*[12] and showed it to him. He gave it only half a look and a nod. Then he shouted, "What's the other?" pointing again at the bag. I hesitated but pulled out *Dispatches,* by Michael Herr.[13] Joe grabbed it and began reading the back cover, completely ignoring the road. We began to drift across the center line into the oncoming lane. I reached over and gave the wheel a slight pull to the right. Joe looked up and grinned. He continued reading, now flicking his eyes up every few seconds.

"Vietnam?" he shouted. "What'd you buy this for?" I shrugged. Joe rolled up his window and motioned for me to do the same. The cab was suddenly very quiet. I looked over and watched a red-winged blackbird light upon a fence post. Joe nearly whispered, "What'd you buy this for?"

"Just curious. I've been reading some history of the war."

"Does Dad know?"

"No."

"Mom?"

"Only a little. Not about my reading." Joe looked down the road. We were already baking in the closed, quiet cabin.

"Just watch out. Keep it to yourself." He threw the book into my lap.

"What do you remember about the war?"

"Not much. I remember Dad coming home, hands all screwed up. Quiet, but I hadn't seen him in so long that I don't remember him being different or anything. Maybe quieter. I don't know. I was only seven. And I remember the POW-MIA sticker.[14] Never understood that until I was in high school. We had a bumper sticker on the old green Impala. Remember?"

"No."

"Well, that's all I remember, really. I never took too much interest. I figured he'd tell us if he wanted to."

"Weren't you ever curious?"

"No, not too much. It seemed all bad and ancient history. Water under the bridge and all that. I got to roll this window down!"

I considered asking Joe what he thought about my plan but didn't. I had decided after talking to my mother that I was going to get into the locker boxes, though I had yet to figure out how. My father was in the garden nearly every day after work and saw the boxes while getting tools or the hose. Obviously, I needed the keys.

I examined the boxes the next morning. They were stacked in a corner next to a small worktable. Coffee cans full of paintbrushes and nails and loose nuts and bolts stood on top of them. As far as I knew, they hadn't been opened in six years. Spider webs were constructed with a confident permanence between the sides of the boxes and the shed walls. I gave a cursory tug at the three locks, each of which had been scratched with a number.

The locks were the common hardware-store variety that always come with two keys. I began searching for the extras in the drawers in the tool shed. In the days that followed, I rummaged through boxes and cleaned the attic over the garage. I carefully went through my father's dresser, with no luck. I did find one loose key at the bottom of a toolbox and raced out to the

---

12. *Great Expectations*: another classic novel by Charles Dickens.

13. *Dispatches,* **by Michael Herr:** a book consisting of impressions of the Vietnam War by an on-the-scene reporter—considered by many to be the best account of the war.

14. **POW-MIA sticker:** a bumper sticker directing public attention to the U.S. servicemen who were prisoners of war (POW's) or missing in action (MIA) in Vietnam and whose deaths were unaccounted for at the time.

shed to try it, but it wouldn't even slide into the core of the locks. I would have to take the risky route for the operation. The useless old key would help.

I spent three scorching days in the garden reading *Dispatches* and an oral history of the war while I looked for the courage necessary to put the plan into effect. The plan was simple, but I wasn't certain it was safe. I would switch the old key I'd found for one from the key ring, rummage a box and switch the key for a second the following day, and then switch the one after that, for a three-day operation.

The next morning I rose as early as my father, much to his and my mother's surprise. My mother was in the kitchen scrambling eggs, and my father was in the shower, as I'd hoped. I slipped into their bedroom and with nervous, fumbling fingers forced the key numbered one off the key ring, replacing it with my found key. The key ring was tight, and I slipped in my haste, gouging my index finger in doing so. I left the bedroom with my slightly bleeding finger in my mouth, jamming it into my pocket as I passed my mother in the kitchen.

Later, quietly, with an archaeologist's caution, I moved the coffee cans from the top box and set them on the worktable. I then slipped in the key and flicked open the lock. Despite the heat, I felt a shiver through my back and shoulders, my body reminding me that I was crossing some line of knowledge, transgressing some boundary of my father's. My hands shook and I held my breath as I lifted the lid.

The first thing I saw was a yellowed newspaper clipping: the death of James Dean,[15] carefully cut to keep the date intact. I read the whole article with interest. I knew nothing of his death. Then I saw my mother's high school diploma, class of 1955. Stacks of old photographs. Family snapshots, black and white with wavy white borders. I found my old

report cards from early grade school and all of my brother's report cards up to the sixth grade. I found a baked-clay saucer with a tiny handprint pressed into it and "Johnny 1968" scratched on the back. It was all interesting but not my reason for the risk, so I lifted out the tray full of family memorabilia and set it to one side.

Underneath I found uniforms. Dress blues neatly pressed and folded. A shoeshine kit. A drill instructor's Smokey the Bear hat. Little plastic bags full of Marine Corps emblem pins like the one on the hat. A tan uniform. And the yearbook my father had pulled out six years before for his visitor. It was a thin platoon book dated 1964, San Diego. I flipped slowly through the black-and-white photos, looking for pictures of my father. The photos were mostly head shots of similar-looking boys in dress blues and white hats. I found action shots of boot training, of the mess hall, of track-and-field competitions. I saw my father here and there, leading a parade, demonstrating a hand-to-hand hold. He was still youthful and very muscular, stern-looking but not weary. The picture of him in his dress blues was the same I'd learned to call Daddy before I'd met him. His hands looked normal in the photographs, the vulnerability gone, his arms strong and well shaped, like solid tree limbs. Upon looking through again, I noticed small notations next to a few of the photos: "KIA,"[16] followed by a date. I was looking at dead men. I didn't know it then, but I would go back years later and find a picture of my namesake, Jonathan Allen Whitney, of Hinesville, Georgia, in that book.

But that was all, and it amounted to little. I replaced the tray and closed the lid, reconstructing the tool shed as well as I could.

---

15. **James Dean:** young American movie star who died in an automobile accident in 1955, at the age of 24.

16. **KIA:** military shorthand for *killed in action*.

That night at dinner I waited for the explosion, the accusation, my father holding up the key ring, his tight voice burning through me. I saw it all, but it never came. Later, in my room, I sorted through what I'd seen and made notes in my journal. I hadn't learned much, except that my mother loved James Dean and was a curator[17] of her young sons' lives. As for my father, I'd found little new except the images of a younger, stronger man.

I opened the second box with less <u>trepidation</u>, half expecting to see my mother's junior-prom dress folded neatly inside, a dry corsage still pinned to the front. Instead, I found the memorabilia that probably should have been hanging on the walls inside the house.

---

17. **curator:** one who manages or has care over something, often a museum or library.

© Donald J. Weber

628

In the top tray were three wooden plaques commemorating different things my father had done, all before the war. They were homely little plaques given to him by platoons or friends. His dog tags[18] lay wrapped in a green handkerchief underneath the plaques, "Joseph D Bowen" pressed into the thin aluminum. The tags read "Methodist," which surprised me, since he never went to church. I found a pile of old letters written by my mother which had been mailed to an address in San Francisco. I couldn't bring myself to read them. I did, however, find three letters dated shortly after my birthday and opened them. One contained the expected photograph, the usual hideous newborn, with the words "Hi, Daddy! Love, Charlie" written on the back. There was another photo, of my mother with Joe and me. Joe was two, and I was just weeks old. The picture was taken at my grandmother's house and dated June 30, 1964.

Beneath the tray I found more uniforms. Khakis this time, combat-style fatigues with "Bowen" stenciled onto them. There was also a pair of worn black boots, a canteen, two thick belts, and a cigar box full of uniform ribbons and their matching medals. Vietnam service, the crossed rifles for marksmanship, and others. There was an unexpected find: a Purple Heart.[19] He'd been wounded. I wondered where. His hands, perhaps, or the fairly large scar on his left thigh—a childhood farming accident, he'd told us. I was staring at the medal, trying to open my imagination, when I heard the back door of the house swing out and bang against the siding. I threw the medal back into the box, and the box into the locker, and hurriedly shoved everything else inside. I pushed on the lock as the footsteps left the patio, and heaved the first box back on top. I was arranging the coffee cans when Joe walked in. "Hey, what are you doing?" he said. I was sweating but felt a twitching relief that it was only Joe.

"Looking for a nut. I need one for my bicycle." I dumped one can over and began sifting through the dirty nuts and bolts. Joe walked around me, glanced down at the wall, and began sifting through the pile with me. "I need one for the seat," I told him. He quickly handed me a nut.

"That'll do it," he said and then added, "Hear what happened?"

"What?"

"Some old farmer set his fields on fire this morning. Acres and acres are burning."

"Where?"

"Just east of town, off one-eleven. You can see smoke from the front yard. I thought we could drive out and see it."

"Why'd he do it?"

"I don't know. Just mad, probably. Wasn't doing him any good, dying there in front of him."

It wasn't much to see, really. The flames weren't huge, just crawling slowly across the field of dry stalks, crackling softly. Large glowing leaves swirled into the sky and became flocks of black birds in erratic flight. A few other people had pulled over to watch from the highway before a patrolman came slowly by and moved them along. Joe asked him if the fire department would put it out, and he said no,

---

18. **dog tags:** metal identification tags worn on a neck chain by members of the armed forces.

19. **Purple Heart:** a U.S. military decoration showing George Washington in profile, awarded to personnel who have been wounded in action.

that it was no real danger, though the farmer would be fined or something. He said it would burn itself out in a day or so. We saw a man near the farmhouse, about a hundred yards from the road. He was old, wearing a red baseball cap, sitting on a tractor watching the wall of black smoke rise from the field. "Probably him," Joe said.

hat night my father came home with two tickets to a Cardinals game against the Mets. "Box seats," he said, dropping them onto the table. He was as excited as we ever saw him, shining eyes and a slight smile, nothing showy or too expressive. "Let's go, Johnny."

From the car I watched the thin sheet of black smoke rising harmlessly like a veil on the horizon, not the ominous black plume that comes from a single house burning. I told my father about Joe and me driving out to see the fire and about the old man on the tractor. My father just shook his head. We were driving by his office at the steel mill, a different kind of fire and smoke shooting from the stacks. "Poor old man" was all he said.

I kept looking at the keys hanging from the steering column, expecting a wave of recognition to light up his face any second. I couldn't imagine how he would react, though I considered anger to be the best guess. What I was doing was wrong; I knew that and felt bad about it, especially since he was in such a good mood. His face was relaxed and peaceful, and he was smiling. He'd fought in a war; he'd been wounded in some unknown place; his hands gripped the steering wheel like arthritic talons; his friends had been killed, and his sons had grown without him. I imagined him weathering bitter nights; he was driving us to a baseball game, sliding easily

through traffic. I kept glancing at his profile, the thinning hair touched with gray, the deep circles under his eyes, the rounded nose—my nose. We were crossing the Mississippi River on the Poplar Street Bridge. The Arch was a bright filament in the afternoon sun. The river was remarkably low, looking as though you could simply wade across the once unswimmable, strong-currented distance. I considered telling my father everything right then. I was consumed by guilt, tapping my fingers on my leg. "What happened to your finger?" he asked.

"Nothing. Caught it on a nail in the tool shed. I was looking for a key to my old bike lock." I'd had that excuse saved for two days. I couldn't look at him. I watched people in the streets. He began talking baseball. It had always been the bridge between us. There had always been the gap and one bridge, a love of the game.

The game that night was exciting, a pitchers' duel with outstanding defensive plays. We had never sat together in box seats before, and we marveled at seeing everything so close up, how quickly the game really moves. We talked baseball all night. I kept score; I marked every pitch on the card, like a memory. The game went into extra innings. I didn't want it to end. I knew even then that this was the first time I had ever felt really close to my father. We shared a soul that night, and then, in the bottom of the twelfth, the game ended suddenly with one swing by Ted Simmons, a crack, and a long home run disappearing over the left-field wall. We drove home happy, though quiet from fatigue.

Strangely, he passed our exit and continued around town to the east. "You missed our exit," I said.

"I didn't miss it" was all he said. He was pensive. I was puzzled, but only for a few minutes. We turned onto Route 111 and headed south on the dark highway. Suddenly the land to our left was a glowing pile of embers. We

Illustration by Jim Dietz.

could see little smoke, but the field was alive with orange fires, flickering and rising like fireflies. My father clicked on his hazard lights and pulled onto the shoulder. He stepped out of the car and walked across the still road, with me trailing behind. The unseen smoke was too thick. I coughed and my eyes burned. "I just wanted to see it," he said quietly, and we stood in silence watching for ten minutes before driving home.

I didn't notice the ashes falling until after I'd changed the second key for the third. I was walking back through the kitchen when I saw, out of the corner of my eye, a leaf fall against the window screen, break into pieces, and then disappear. I looked up and out the window. The wind had shifted in the night, and the ashes from the corn field were swirling above like elm leaves in autumn, some falling gently to earth like a light November flurry, except that the flakes were black. In the back yard I held out my hand to catch one, and it disintegrated in my grasp. The temperature was already over ninety degrees. It was a wonderful and hellish sight. Ashes blew across the patio and collected in the corner against the house.

After my father left for work, I went into the garden to read. Ashes drifted down, breaking between the pages of my book and landing in the day lilies and roses along the fence. I felt strangely uninterested in the third box. The previous night had left me content with my knowledge of my father's past. A new understanding had come to our relationship.

I felt guilty opening the third box, as though I were breaking some new agreement between us.

The top tray contained nothing of interest. I found shoe polish, dried and cracked, two more plaques, socks, two dungaree hats. I sifted through these things mechanically and quickly, wanting to be done with it all. The compartment beneath was only half full. A musty smell rose

I WAS A LITTLE AFRAID TO GO FURTHER, BUT I PICKED UP THE SMALL PAPERBOARD BOX, FELT IT RATTLE, AND OPENED IT.

out of the box. It came from the clothing—an old khaki uniform tattered and worn, filthy but neatly folded—that lay on top of the items inside. Also within sight was an old pair of combat boots, unpolished and ragged. They, too, smelled musty. I lifted out the uniform and found a small box made of dried palm fronds. It was poorly woven around narrow sticks with an ill-fitting lid on top. Inside it were yellow newspaper clippings

folded up into squares and a small paper ring box. I unfolded one of the clippings carefully, so as not to tear its tightly creased edges. The headline read "LOCAL PRISONER OF WAR TO COME HOME," and was accompanied by that same photograph of my father in his dress blues. The clipping was dated July 13, 1969. I read the article slowly, trying not to miss any details. It explained that my father had been a prisoner for just over three years, that he was to be released July 30, and that he would be returning to the base in San Diego within days. He was being held in a prison camp in the North, just above the DMZ,[20] and had been captured while on patrol near Khe Sanh in 1966. It gave details about the family in Stone City.

I set the clipping aside and quickly unfolded the others. They all told the same story. One was from the Stone City paper, dated the day of his release. I read them all twice, almost uncomprehendingly, before carefully folding them and returning them to the homemade box. I was a little afraid to go further, but I picked up the small paperboard box, felt it rattle, and opened it. Inside were teeth, all molars, yellowed and with black spots in places. I picked one up. On closer inspection the black blemishes became legible: painted on the side of the molar in tiny letters was "N.V. 3.3.66." I picked up a second. It read "N.V. 5.12.66." All six of them had dates, three from March third, one each from three other days. I was breathing through my nose in a deep, mechanical way, sweating heavily in the hot late morning. I put the teeth back in the box and set the box aside. I was shaking and didn't want to

---

20. **DMZ:** military shorthand for *demilitarized zone*—a term used to describe a buffer area between opposing armies, in which military forces and operations are prohibited.

Solitary Confinement: Insects Witness My Agony (1982), Theodore Gostas.
Collection of the U.S. Air Force, Washington, D.C.

continue. There was more to see, a few letters, some folders, a small book.

The book was a paperback, a Marine Corps field manual bound with a manila cover. It was titled *Escape and Torture*. I began flicking through the pages. There were some small, meaningless diagrams, a dull text about techniques for escaping from some generalized prison camp. Then there was a section on Vietnamese torture techniques. I began reading the clinical, distant descriptions of various forms of torture. Naked men in small, cold concrete cells, sleep <u>deprivation</u>, swelling legs, tied hands, beatings. A few pages into the text the notations began. They were written in black ink, always the single word "this" in the margin next to an underlined passage. The first, as I recall, described something with the feet. Then beating on the legs, "this." Then the hands. "This" was bamboo splinters under the nails. "This" was a beating of the knuckles. "This" was being strung up by the wrists. I felt my stomach go hollow and my comprehension numb as I stared at that awkward, childlike scrawl in the margin of each page.

I didn't hear my father walk into the tool shed. He appeared suddenly, as though he'd sprung from the ground. I felt a presence and turned to see him standing there in the doorway of the shed, holding his key ring in his right hand and my useless bronze key in his left. I have never seen such confusion on a man's face. He was startlingly angry, I could see, his body stiff, his nostrils flared, his breathing heavy, his jaw muscles rolling beneath his skin. But his eyes were weary, even desperate. We stared at each other while he decided what to do. I didn't move. I said nothing, only watching him. His eyes welled, and bright molten tears ran down his cheeks. Then he dropped the single key and walked away.

I rose and walked out of the dark shed into the hot sun and falling ashes. He was sitting on the edge of the garden with his head down and his eyes closed as if in prayer, his hands lying loose and unattached in his lap. He then moved them to his sides and began clawing at the dry dirt in the garden until he had dug two holes and half buried each hand under the loose dirt. He sat as still as a memorial statue, and I realized that I didn't belong there. I left him with his head down and eyes closed and walked into the house. I see him there every day.

In the four years that he lived beyond that moment he told me a little about the war. It was a topic I could never raise. On occasion, if we were alone, he would begin talking about some aspect of the war or of his service. These were heavily guarded moments, slow monologues as he groped for the correct words to tell me. It is another way I remember him, speaking the things that he knew he wasn't capable of saying. This is how I love him the most, this great man. Semper Fi.[21] ❖

---

21. **Semper Fi** (sĕm′pər fī′): a shortened version of *Semper Fidelis (Latin* for "Always Faithful"), the Marine Corps motto.

WORDS
TO
KNOW

deprivation (dĕp′rə-vā′shən) *n.* a state of being forced to do without

ON WRITING "MARINE CORPS ISSUE"

David McLean

The origin of "Marine Corps Issue" is in the book mentioned at the end of the story. My father was a Marine. While I was growing up, this field manual, *Escape and Torture,* was sitting on a dusty bookshelf. Unlike the house in the story, our house contained a lot of Marine Corps memorabilia on display. I had always been interested in my father's career, but only after I had moved away did I think it strange to have had this kind of book on my shelves as a teenager. I grew up very near the Vietnam War—my father had been there twice and afterwards, from 1969 to 1972, was a drill instructor training men for the war. My brothers and sisters and I used to watch him parade his recruits as each platoon graduated, never realizing that they were young men on their way to war. So, despite this nearness to the war, I was completely unaware of it. I knew nothing about it until I was in college.

These elements—a war, a book, a father, and a son—caused me to think of a story. I thought of what a son might learn about his father if he found *Escape and Torture* locked away in a box. The idea began there. The rest of the story grew from that little picture of a boy secretly reading the book. The story was difficult to write at first, getting the voice and the details right, but at one point—the scene with the two brothers driving in the truck—something magical happened and the story began to tell itself, as though I had reached the top of a hill and could coast down the other side. These little moments of magic are what keep writers at their desks.

U.S. Soldiers serving in Vietnam met with little support upon their return home.
© Donald J. Weber

Thinking through the LITERATURE

Connect to the Literature

1. What Do You Think?
At the end of the story, what were your thoughts about the character of the father?

> **Comprehension Check**
> - What is the father's attitude about his war experiences?
> - How does the boy try to find out more about his father's past?
> - What does he learn?

Think Critically

2. **ACTIVE READING** **RECOGNIZING CAUSE AND EFFECT** Look back at the **cause-effect** relationships you jotted in your **READER'S NOTEBOK**. How would you sum up the effects of the Vietnam War on this family?

3. How does the secret that Johnny learns about his father help explain the way his father has behaved?

THINK ABOUT
- the **cause** of his father's injuries
- the **effects** of his father's experience as a prisoner of war

4. Why do you think the father has kept his war experience a secret from his sons?

5. Does Johnny have a right to know everything about his father's war experience—and to use any method to learn about it? Explain your reasoning.

6. Do you think Johnny is better off for having learned the truth about his father? Explain why or why not.

Extend Interpretations

7. Critic's Corner Peter Lum and Michael Little, members of our student advisory board, had different reactions to the way the story ended. Peter was disappointed that the story "did not have a very happy ending." Michael, however, felt the ending "had a nice touch." What do you think about the ending? Support your opinion.

8. Comparing Texts How does the Literary Link on page 635 add to your understanding of the story? Explain your answer.

9. Connect to Life In general, do you think it is better to talk about a terrible experience or to remain silent about it, as the father in this story mostly does? Explain.

Literary Analysis

FLASHBACK Not all stories are told in strict chronological order. A writer may use **flashback**—an account of a conversation, an episode, or an event that happened before the beginning of a story. At the beginning of "Marine Corps Issue," the **narrator** is a grown man. He tells the story in a series of flashbacks to different times in his life.

Cooperative Learning Activity Go back through the story, identify the flashbacks, and discuss with your classmates why you think the author chose to tell his story in this way.

REVIEW **SUSPENSE** The gradual unfolding of the story through flashbacks helps build **suspense,** the excitement or tension that readers feel as they become involved in a story and eager to know the outcome. What places in the story do you think are suspenseful? Discuss these places with your classmates.

Choices & CHALLENGES

Writing Options

1. Personal Response Write a letter to Johnny's mother describing your response to her plight of raising two young sons while her husband was away at war. Use your own experiences or memories to imagine what life was like for her. Save your writing for your **Working Portfolio.**

2. Field Manual The manual *Escape and Torture* prepared military personnel for prison camp. Write a chapter for a follow-up field manual, called *Return and Adjustment,* to help former POWs take up civilian life again. Offer the kinds of tips you think Johnny's father could have used.

Writing Handbook
See page 1155: Explanatory Writing.

Activities & Explorations

Quick Sketch The narrator describes two vivid images—one of his father on the handball court and the other of his father sitting like a statue at the edge of the garden. In a sketch or painting, capture the image of the father that you found most vivid in this story. ~ **ART**

Inquiry & Research

Wars always have serious effects upon those who fight them, but each war leaves its own particular aftermath. What lasting effects do you think the Vietnam War had on U.S. soldiers? How might these effects be different from the effects of other wars, such as World War II?

Real World Link Read the article on pages 639-640 before forming your opinion.

Art Connection

Look again at the painting on page 633. Solitary confinement is an especially agonizing form of imprisonment in which a prisoner is shut off from contact with other prisoners. What aspects of the story can you find in the painting? From 1968 to 1973 the artist, Theodore Gostas, was himself a prisoner of war in North Vietnam. Explain how aspects of the painting might reflect Gostas's experience.

See art on p. 633.

Vocabulary in Action

EXERCISE A: ASSESSMENT PRACTICE Write the letter of the word that is a synonym of each boldfaced vocabulary word below.

1. **vulnerability:** (a) charm, (b) sensitivity, (c) immunity
2. **demeanor:** (a) behavior, (b) rudeness, (c) intelligence
3. **deprivation:** (a) hardship, (b) publicity, (c) bravery
4. **grotesque:** (a) huge, (b) mean, (c) deformed
5. **agitated:** (a) puzzled, (b) humble, (c) jumpy
6. **devoid:** (a) empty, (b) roomy, (c) scarce
7. **trepidation:** (a) anxiety, (b) loyalty, (c) shock
8. **animosity:** (a) cruelty (b) jealousy, (c) hostility
9. **disjunction:** (a) collision, (b) disconnection, (c) loneliness
10. **intrigue:** (a) worry, (b) fascinate, (c) affect

EXERCISE B Work with a partner to act out the meaning of *disjunction, agitated, animosity, vulnerability,* or *deprivation* while another pair of students tries to guess the word. Then switch, with you and your partner trying to guess which word the other pair is acting out. Keep playing this game of charades until all the words are used.

Building Vocabulary
For an in-depth lesson on word relationships such as synonyms and antonyms, see page 849.

Grammar in Context: Appositive Phrases

In "Marine Corps Issue," appositive phrases help the reader understand one of the story's characters.

> He was a decorated soldier, a career man forced to retire disabled because of his hands.

> This is how I love him the most, this great man.

An **appositive phrase** consists of a noun and its modifiers and serves to explain or add information about another noun or a pronoun in a sentence. In the first sentence above, the appositive phrase tells why the narrator's father is no longer a Marine ("a career man forced to retire . . ."). In the second sentence, the appositive phrase sums up the son's attitude toward his father ("this great man").

WRITING EXERCISE Rewrite each sentence, adding an appositive phrase to provide more information about the underlined noun or pronoun.

Usage Tip: Appositive phrases can come before or after the words they modify. They are usually set off with commas.

Example: *Original* His dog tags reflected the sun's piercing light.

Rewritten His dog tags, those metal labels that described him so poorly, reflected the sun's piercing light.

1. I don't remember much about my father before I was five years old.
2. He never spoke about his past.
3. My brother and I knew little about the war.
4. I was always curious about the boxes.

Grammar Handbook Phrases, p. 1193

David McLean
1964–

Background David McLean was a 1994 winner of the O. Henry Award for short stories. He has provided the following information about his life:

"I was born and grew up in Granite City, Illinois, a town very much like the Stone City of 'Marine Corps Issue.' My father was a career Marine, and my brothers, sisters, and I moved a number of times. He retired when I was 11, and we settled permanently in Granite City.

"In 1987, I graduated from Bradley University in Peoria, Illinois, where I studied biology as well as English. I knew when I was in high school that I wanted to be a writer, but it was at Bradley that I first began to think seriously about it. I spent one year of college in London, England, and then attended graduate school at Boston University, where I obtained a master's degree in English."

Traveling and Teaching "Not many people can make a living solely as a writer, especially during the years when you are learning your craft. After finishing graduate school, I worked in a bookstore in Boston for about 3½ years before traveling to Slovakia. The revolutions in Eastern Europe had occurred in 1989, and I was curious to see what life was like there. I love to travel and wanted to teach, so in January 1992 I went to Slovakia (then still part of Czechoslovakia) and spent seven months teaching English to high school students."

Writing at a Distance "I was in Slovakia when I wrote 'Marine Corps Issue.' I have found during my years of writing that I often write better about a place when I'm living somewhere else. I think the distance forces the imagination to work harder, to recall or invent details of a place that is a disorganized jumble of memories. As a result, Stone City in the story resembles my hometown but has taken on an existence all its own. I have a picture of it in my mind, and it is not exactly my hometown but is like a lot of similar towns in the Midwest. It is like an actual place for me. I visit there often and write stories about others who 'live' there."

Vietnam Warfare Breeding Ground for Post-traumatic Stress Disorder

by Dennis McEaneney

As you know, the United States was involved in the war between North Vietnam and South Vietnam from 1965 to 1973. This article details the psychological effects of the conflict on its veterans and describes how the basic approach to warfare differed from that of World War II (1941–1945). As you read, discover how the two wars have affected those who served in them.

❶ AKRON, Ohio—World War II circled the globe. Vietnam was fought in a country the size of the Florida peninsula.

More than 16.3 million men and women served in U.S. military forces from 1941 to 1945. In Vietnam, 3.5 million Americans were sent to fight a 10-year war that began in 1965.

In World War II, the Army's 79th Infantry Division spent 172 days in combat after D-Day and the invasion of Normandy. The fiercest and most widespread battle of the Vietnam War, the Tet Offensive of 1968, lasted a month.

So in which war were military personnel at greater risk for post-traumatic stress disorder, a paralyzing psychological and physical reaction to combat experiences?

"Vietnam—no question about it," said psychologist Edgardo Paden, chief of PTSD (post-traumatic stress disorder) therapy at the Veterans Affairs Medical Center in Brecksville, Ohio.

❷ One of the main differences is the kind of warfare the troops encountered, Paden said. World War II was a conventional war in which soldiers generally fought across front lines. Danger was ahead, safety to the rear. Engagements in World War II sometimes began with infantry troops 500 yards apart. Vietnam was a guerrilla war in which there were no front lines. Danger was all around; safety was difficult to imagine. Engagements in Vietnam most often began at distances of 50 yards or less.

"Guerrilla war increases the risk of PTSD," Paden said.

Another major difference was the purpose of the two wars.

❸ World War II was "the good war," and its fighters were rewarded with parades, the GI Bill to pay for college, housing assistance, and job training.

Reading for Information

This article focuses on two critical time periods in American history. The writer has structured the information so that readers can see differences between these two periods. Being aware of comparisons and contrasts can help readers sort through facts, which can lead to insights into historical events.

COMPARING AND CONTRASTING

To compare or contrast, writers usually organize the writing to point out similarities and differences between two or more things.

- **Comparing** is examining how events, people, and ideas are alike.
- **Contrasting** is examining how events, people, and ideas are different.

YOUR TURN Use the activities that follow to help you compare and contrast some details of two major events.

❶ The writer makes his first comparison within the first paragraph. For each paragraph, identify the points on which World War II and the Vietnam War are compared.

❷ In your own words, explain why guerrilla warfare led to PTSD more frequently than did conventional warfare.

❸ Writers also make comparisons across paragraphs. Notice the aspect of World War II that McEaneney focuses on in this paragraph. Watch for his comments later in the article on the same issue in the Vietnam War.

"They could reason they did the things they did to make the world a better place," Paden said. "That was not the case with Vietnam."

Vietnam was a political war fought for reasons that remain obscure to many who served there. "It was not a war to defend the homeland," Paden said.

After World War II, military leaders blamed PTSD on the length of time that individuals had been spent in combat— many from the time they arrived in Europe and the Pacific until the war was over.

So during Vietnam, military commanders decided that troops would be limited to 12 months of duty in Vietnam, 13 months for Marines.

But gone was the camaraderie that came from going as a unit and staying there. Individuals were replaced as tours of duty expired.

After the first units were sent to Vietnam in 1965, the remainder of the troops sent to the war zone "went there alone and came home alone," Paden said.

"Strong camaraderie was quickly made and quickly severed. There was very little debriefing, very little counseling, very little work done to reacclimate them when they returned to America."

4 When Vietnam veterans came home, they found an America that was polarized. "They found hawks vs. doves, blacks vs. whites, men vs. women, young vs. old," Paden said. "They were forgotten or horribly treated in terms of the respect and the gratitude they expected for what they had done.

"What they got instead was hearing that what they had done was terribly wrong and that they had been pawns of the government—which was true," said Paden, who was a helicopter pilot in Vietnam.

"So, there was a very strong bitterness. They realized they had been used and abused by having been made to serve other interests" besides honor, American values and morality and love of country.

"Among Vietnam vets, almost all of them who have or had PTSD will tell you they hated the government," Paden said. Other factors contributed to PTSD, Paden said.

Body count—measuring the success of the war in the number of enemy dead instead of how much land had been freed—also contributed to the stress.

"Body count produced a cynicism among the officer corps," Paden said. "Men didn't trust their officers, whose first responsibility was to protect their men." Patrols were sent out as decoys to lure the enemy into fighting. The patrols were lost, but the body count made up for it.

"To me, PTSD is about inner conflict. When you're presented with a problem you cannot solve, it stays in your head."

4 Notice how the comparison across paragraphs continues. How did the treatment of Vietnam veterans differ from the treatment of veterans of World War II?

Devising a Graphic A chart can help readers see the points of comparison more easily. Review the article to find points of comparison or contrast. Enter this information in a chart like the one shown.

Wars in Contrast		
Categories	**WW II**	**Vietnam**
Type of Warfare		
Purpose of War		
U.S. Support		
Length of Service		
Homecoming		

Inquiry & Research

Activity Link: "Marine Corps Issue," p. 637 How well did Vietnam War veterans fare after the war compared with veterans of World War II? Use the chart as well as what you read in "Marine Corps Issue" to support your views in a class discussion.

Kinds of Comparisons

You make comparisons every day. Whether in choosing between two foods or in describing a sunset, comparison is essential. It is especially so to poets. Consider the excerpts on the right.

In "Grape Sherbet," Dove compares the staring grandmother to a torch. In "The Courage That My Mother Had," Millay compares her mother's courage to New England granite. Through the comparisons, the poets suggest thought-provoking similarities and evoke powerful images. Comparisons like these are sometimes called **analogies.**

> . . . The diabetic grandmother
> stares from the porch,
> a torch
> of pure refusal.
> —Rita Dove, "Grape Sherbet"
>
> The courage that my mother had
> Went with her, and is with her still:
> Rock from New England quarried;
> Now granite in a granite hill.
> —Edna St. Vincent Millay,
>   "The Courage That My Mother Had"

Strategies for Building Vocabulary

You may encounter analogies on tests as well as in literature. Like literary analogies, test analogies involve relationships between pairs of words and ideas. Some analogy problems are expressed this way:

> Determine the relationship between the capitalized words. Then decide which of the choices best completes the analogy.
>
> LOVE : HATE :: war : _____
> (A) soldier, (B) peace,
> (C) battle, (D) disagreement

This problem may be restated as "*Love* is to *hate* as *war* is to ___?___." Solving such a problem requires logical thinking and a knowledge of the meanings of words. Here are some strategies to help you solve analogy problems.

❶ Determine Word Relationships To complete an analogy, you first need to figure out the relationship between the capitalized words. In the example above, *love* and *hate* are antonyms—words with opposite meanings. Therefore, you must find a word that is an antonym of *war*. The best answer is *peace.* The other three choices may be related to the idea of war, but they are not antonyms of the word *war.*

❷ Learn Relationship Types The word pairs in analogy problems express various kinds of relationships. The more familiar you are with these types of relationships, the better you will be able to solve the problems. Here are some common types.

Common Types of Analogies		
Type	**Example**	**Relationship**
Part to Whole	SYLLABLE : WORD	is a part of
Synonyms	NICE : PLEASANT	means the same as
Antonyms	SICK : HEALTHY	means the opposite of
Cause to Effect	VIRUS : COLD	results in or leads to
Worker to Tool	WEAVER : LOOM	works with
Degree of Intensity	DISLIKE : HATRED	is less (or more) intense than
Grammar	ACCUSE : ACCUSATION	is grammatically related to
Item to Category	PAINTING : ARTWORK	is a type or example of

EXERCISE Complete each analogy by choosing a word from the list below. Identify the relationship on which the analogy is based.

hammer   penmanship   carpentry   exhausted
temporary   momentary   building   tall
legibility   city

1. VULNERABLE : VULNERABILITY :: legible : ___?___
2. IDLE : BUSY :: permanent : ___?___
3. ODD : BIZARRE :: tired : ___?___
4. DRESSER : FURNITURE :: skyscraper : ___?___
5. WRITER : PEN :: carpenter : ___?___

MY FATHER'S SONG

SIMON J. ORTIZ

SOMETIMES A

PARTICULAR MEMORY

CAN SUMMON UP

EVERYTHING WE KNOW,

EVERYTHING WE LOVED,

ABOUT SOMEONE WHO

HAS LEFT US. HERE IS A

POEM THAT CAPTURES

SUCH A MEMORY.

Wanting to say things,
I miss my father tonight.
His voice, the slight catch,
the depth from his thin chest,
5 the tremble of emotion
in something he has just said
to his son, his song:

We planted corn one Spring at Acu[1]—
we planted several times
10 but this one particular time
I remember the soft damp sand
in my hand.

My father had stopped at one point
to show me an overturned furrow;[2]
15 the plowshare[3] had unearthed
the burrow nest of a mouse
in the soft moist sand.

Very gently, he scooped tiny pink animals
into the palm of his hand
20 and told me to touch them.
We took them to the edge
of the field and put them in the shade
of a sand moist clod.

I remember the very softness
25 of cool and warm sand and tiny alive mice
and my father saying things.

---

1. **Acu** (ä′kōō): the Acoma people's name for the Acoma pueblo.
2. **furrow:** a long, shallow trench made in the ground by a plow.
3. **plowshare:** the cutting blade of a plow.

Simon J. Ortiz
1941–

Other Works
Going for the Rain
Woven Stone
Fightin'
Howbah Indians

His Beginnings Simon J. Ortiz was born in Albuquerque, New Mexico, and raised in the Acoma Pueblo community about 65 miles to the west. He attended Bureau of Indian Affairs and Roman Catholic elementary schools and a public high school, continuing his education at the University of New Mexico and the University of Iowa. Although best known as a poet, he has also written short stories and essays and has edited anthologies of Native American writing.

His Father's Voice Ortiz, who has worked as a baker's helper, a clerk, a laborer, a soldier in the U. S. Army, and a university professor, had his first poem published when he was in the fifth grade. In part, he attributes his love of words to his father, who sang and talked to his son as he worked. Ortiz told an interviewer that his father "was a good singer in Acoman, in English, in Spanish, and in other languages like Zuni and some Navajo. He had a beautiful voice. He was an inspiration to me."

His Heritage Ortiz also traces his love of words to his Native American heritage. He once commented, "The voices of the stories, poems, songs are as old as Acu, which is my home. What I do is listen and watch as carefully as I am able and then tell what happens. The source of my writing comes from my community and people."

Writing Workshop

Reacting to a literary work. . .

From Reading to Writing Stories such as "The Scarlet Ibis" by James Hurst and poems such as "My Papa's Waltz" by Theodore Roethke evoke strong emotional responses in many readers. Readers' own memories and experiences often affect their responses to stories and poems. Analyzing your personal **response to literature** can generate valuable insights about your own life and the world around you. One way to share these insights is to talk about them. Another is to write about them. Writers often share their responses to music, movies, and plays as well as to literature.

For Your Portfolio

WRITING PROMPT Write a personal response to a short story or a poem.

Purpose: To express yourself and to inform others

Audience: Anyone interested in the literature you are responding to

---

Basics in a Box

Response to Literature at a Glance

Introduction
Introduces the literary work and includes a clear thesis statement that introduces the response

Body
Supports the response with evidence from the literary work

- Explanation
- Evidence
- Evidence
- Evidence

Conclusion
Summarizes the response

RUBRIC Standards for Writing

A successful response to literature should

- include an introduction that identifies the literary work and clearly states your overall response to it
- tell enough about the literary work so that readers can understand your response
- contain clearly described, specific reactions and responses to the literary work
- support your statements with quotations and details
- use language and details that are appropriate for your audience

---

Analyzing a Student Model

Jessica Ross
Lake Forest Country Day School

Personal Response to "The Scarlet Ibis"

In his short story "The Scarlet Ibis," James Hurst presents a theme centered around pride. This story is seen through the eyes of a boy with an invalid younger brother, Doodle. When Doodle was born, no one expected him to survive more than a couple of weeks, but despite the predictions, Doodle lived and eventually began to crawl. As Doodle grew older, he begged to tag along with his older brother and soon became a burden. The narrator came to realize that Doodle, as his brother, would always tag along, so he might as well attempt to teach him how to walk. With hard work and support from his brother, Doodle reached the goal that no one thought possible. The narrator's expectations only grew from there and his pride would not let him admit defeat, although soon it became evident that the goal of running, jumping, and climbing was still, after a year, far out of reach. One afternoon the two were caught in a storm and because his brother was so caught up in Doodle's failure, he ran ahead leaving Doodle behind in the cold rain. He came back to find Doodle huddled beneath a red nightshade bush, his body limp and lifeless.

Pride, Hurst suggests, has two facets. One is remarkable, motivating humankind to achieve great things in life. But pride also has a darker side that can push too hard and expect too much, driving one to strive for unreachable goals. When I first read the passage about Doodle's brother teaching him to walk because he felt ashamed, I was disturbed that he did it for himself, not to help his disabled brother. How could the narrator, as a brother, not want the achievement of this goal for Doodle, but for himself? Isn't that what brotherly and unconditional love is all about? In this story Hurst forces us to question ourselves about the actions we take. Do we act out of selflessness and pure love or because we feel ashamed or embarrassed with the way someone is and feel we must change the person to satisfy ourselves?

RUBRIC
IN ACTION

❶ Identifies the title, author, and main characters of the literary work in the introduction

❷ Tells enough about the story to make the personal response understandable

❸ Describes the personal response to a specific event in the story

As a result of his brother's pride, Doodle achieves goals once viewed as impossible. But in the end, that same pride pushes too hard and expects too much of Doodle, leading to his death. As the brother says, "I did not know then that pride is a wonderful, terrible thing, a seed that bears two vines, life and death."

Goals achieved because of pride may appear admirable from the outside, but sometimes the underlying motivation is immoral. Doodle's brother realizes that he did not teach Doodle how to walk out of selfless love, as he would like to believe: "They did not know that I did it for myself; that pride, whose slave I was, spoke to me louder than all their voices, and that Doodle walked only because I was ashamed of having a crippled brother."

He taught Doodle because he was ashamed, and his pride was damaged knowing that he would never have a normal brother.

Hurst's theme concerning the two sides of pride caused me to reflect on my own life and how pride has affected my actions toward others. Although my first reaction was anger when I read the passage about the narrator reaching the goal for his own purposes, when I reread it, I began thinking how I have been in similar situations and have chosen to take the same path. This story made me question how I would respond if I had a sibling who was an invalid. Would I feel ashamed and embarrassed, or would my love overpower my pride? If I became a parent, would I be able to encourage my child with selfless love to strive for whatever he found enjoyable even if it hurt my pride when he did not choose what I preferred? Hurst has presented his readers with the uncomfortable task of exploring their own motivations to find the answer to a difficult question. Is pride made up of selfish or pure love; or is there such a thing as pure love at all?

④ Supports the personal response with quotations and details exploring the theme of the story

⑤ Clearly describes a specific personal response to the literature

⑥ This writer concludes by describing some thoughts about life and self generated by the story.

Other Options:
- Summarize the overall response to the story.
- Explain how the response changed after careful consideration of the story.

Writing Your Response to Literature

❶ Prewriting

Originality does not consist in saying what no one has ever said before,
but in saying exactly what you think yourself.

Sir James F. Stephen, British journalist and judge

In selecting a poem or story for your response, recall **characters** with whom you identify. Consider **themes** that make you think about your own life. Focus on **settings** that stimulated your imagination. Remember a **plot** that surprised or pleased you. See the **Idea Bank** in the margin for more suggestions. After you select a piece of literature for your response, follow the steps below.

Planning Your Response to Literature

▶ **1. Carefully read the piece of literature.** Take notes on passages that affect you. Include page numbers for your future reference.

▶ **2. Freewrite about your responses.** How did you respond to the characters? theme? plot? setting? style? Identify your reactions to the literature, such as sad, angry, excited, curious, happy, confused.

▶ **3. Consider how your own memories and experiences affected your responses.** Have you had a similar experience? Does the story's theme coincide or clash with beliefs of your own? Do you know people like the story's characters?

▶ **4. Identify your audience.** How familiar is your audience with the work you are discussing? What will they need to know in order to understand your response?

❷ Drafting

Begin writing even if you have not decided on everything you want to say.

• Write an **introduction** that includes the title and author of the work and summarizes important information such as characters, plot, and setting.

• Begin the **body** by stating your general response to the piece of literature. Then explain why you felt as you did.

• **Elaborate** on your response by quoting or summarizing specific passages. You also may mention personal experiences that affected your reading.

• **Summarize** your response in the conclusion of your essay.

Ask Your Peer Reader

• How would you describe my overall response to this piece of literature?

• Where did you need additional quotes or references to the literature?

• What other points should I include to clarify my response?

IDEABank

1. Your Working Portfolio
Look for ideas in the **Writing Options** you completed earlier in this unit:

• **Response to Narrator,** p. 606

• **Personal Response,** p. 637

2. Literary Journal
Keep a journal of your responses to literature that you read both in and out of school. Write about a piece to which you responded strongly.

3. Literary Challenge
Choose a piece of literature that you find difficult to understand or one that others have reacted to differently than you.

Need revising help?

Review the **Rubric**, p. 644

Consider **peer reader** comments

Check **Revision Guidelines**, p. 1143

❸ Revising

TARGET SKILL ▶ USING ACTIVE VOICE To make your responses to the literary work clear, use active voice whenever possible. A sentence is in the active voice when the subject performs the action: *Jake threw the ball.* In the passive voice, the subject receives the action: *The ball was thrown by Jake.* You may sometimes use passive voice for variety or when you don't know the doer of the action. However, frequent use of the active voice makes your writing stronger, livelier, and less wordy.

> In the short story "The Scarlet Ibis" ~~by~~ James Hurst ∧ *presents* a theme
>
> centered around pride ~~is presented.~~ This story is seen through
>
> the eyes of a boy with an invalid younger brother, Doodle.

❹ Editing and Proofreading

Distracted by misplaced modifiers?

See the **Grammar Handbook**

Phrases, p. 1204

TARGET SKILL ▶ MISPLACED MODIFIERS Express your ideas clearly by using modifiers correctly. Always place a modifier as close as possible to the word it modifies. A misplaced modifier may leave readers with an unclear description or imply a meaning that doesn't make sense. For instance, *In the street, Bob heard a bus* implies Bob was in the street. Moving the modifying phrase changes the sentence's meaning. *Bob heard a bus in the street* clarifies that the bus was in the street.

> When first reading the passage, Doodle's brother ~~was~~ *about*
>
> teaching him to walk because he felt ashamed. I was
>
> disturbed that he did it for himself, not to help his disabled
>
> brother. How could the narrator, as a brother, want the
>
> achievement not for Doodle but for himself ~~(of this goal)~~?

Publishing IDEAS

• Meet with classmates who wrote a response to the same work. Compare your classmates' responses to your own.

• Post excerpts from the responses to literature on a school or class Web site.

More Online: Publishing Options www.mcdougallittell.com

❺ Reflecting

FOR YOUR WORKING PORTFOLIO How did writing about a piece of literature help you understand it? Which elements in the literature had the greatest effect on your response? Attach your reflections to your finished work. Save your response to literature in your **Working Portfolio.**

Read this passage from the first draft of a personal response to literature. The underlined sections may include the following kinds of errors:

- **comma errors**
- **misplaced modifiers**
- **incorrect possessive forms**
- **lack of parallel structure**

For each underlined section, choose the revision that most improves the writing.

In "My <u>Papas'</u> Waltz," Theodore Roethke describes a childhood moment
(1)
with his father. <u>The father is sharing a special time with his young son and</u>
(2)
<u>dances him around the room.</u> You can tell that the poet loves his father a lot
just because he remembers the experience. Some of <u>Roethke's words, details</u>
<u>and images</u> describe physical pain or danger. They bring out the <u>boy's</u> fear of
(3)   (4)
his father. <u>The boy says his fathers breath made him "dizzy"</u> and that
(5)
he "hung on like death." In the third stanza, he says that his "right ear scraped
a buckle," and goes on to say in the fourth that "You beat time on my head."
<u>I think Roethke is saying that love can be dangerous in this poem</u>.
(6)

---

1. **A.** Papa's
　　B. Papas
　　C. Papas's
　　D. Correct as is

2. **A.** The father shares a special time with his young son and had danced him around the room.
　　B. The father is sharing a special time with his young son and danced him around the room.
　　C. The father is sharing a special time with his young son and is dancing him around the room.
　　D. Correct as is

3. **A.** Roethke's words, details, and images
　　B. Roethke's words details and images
　　C. Roethke's words, details, and, images
　　D. Correct as is

4. **A.** boys
　　B. boys'
　　C. boy'
　　D. Correct as is

5. **A.** The boy say's his fathers breath made him "dizzy"
　　B. The boy says his father's breath made him "dizzy"
　　C. The boy says his fathers' breath made him "dizzy"
　　D. Correct as is

6. **A.** I think Roethke is saying that love in this poem can be dangerous.
　　B. I think Roethke is saying in this poem that love can be dangerous.
　　C. I think Roethke is in this poem saying that love can be dangerous.
　　D. Correct as is

Need extra help?

See the **Grammar Handbook**

Active and Passive Voice, p. 1185

Phrases, p. 1204

Modifiers, p 1206

Possessive Nouns, p. 1180

PART 2 — Declarations of Independence

When an older brother or sister wants you to do something one way and you want to do it another, what do you do? If your friends decide to go to a movie that you've already seen, do you go anyway? Sometimes you have to do things your way—to declare your independence—even if doing so may make you unpopular. As you read this part of Unit Four, see how the fictional characters and real people in the selections try to declare their independence within their families.

ACTIVITY

With a small group of classmates, role-play a situation in which a person has to resist pressure from others in order to declare his or her independence. For example, a person's friends might try to convince him or her to ostracize someone, stay out past curfew, or go to a party instead of studying for a test. Choose a member of the group to try to resist the persuasions of the others. Share the results of your group's experience with the rest of the class, performing your role-playing for them if you like.

LEARNING the Language of *Literature*

*A*uthor's Perspective is the way an author

looks at the world—it is a blending of the ideas, attitudes, feelings, values, and beliefs that are often reflected in his or her works. You know that where you stand physically affects what you see: you can see farther from the top of a building than from the ground, but you miss some details. Likewise, where people "stand" mentally—what they think, feel, or believe—will affect how they see the world around them and how they write about it.

Author's Perspective in Nonfiction

An author's perspective is usually more important, and more obvious, in a work of nonfiction than in one of fiction. For example, essayists generally want you to know their opinions; so they often state their **biases**—their preferences and prejudices—up front. Margaret Truman opens her biographical essay, "The United States *vs.* Susan B. Anthony" (page 453), by stating, "Susan B. Anthony has never been one of my favorite characters." But the rest of her essay demonstrates why she changed her mind about Anthony and possibly even convinces readers to change their minds as well.

PORTRAYAL OF INDIVIDUALS In most narrative nonfiction, such as autobiographies and biographies, an author's perspective can also be revealed through the presentation of an important person in the author's life. In the excerpt from *I Know Why the Caged Bird Sings* (page 480), Maya Angelou describes Mrs. Flowers in the glowing terms of a girl's admiration, but she also reveals the more lasting impact Mrs. Flowers had on her life.

YOUR TURN Read the two passages at the right, taken from different places in the excerpt. Which passage gives you insight into Maya Angelou's own adult beliefs and values? How would you describe her perspective?

PORTRAYAL OF INDIVIDUALS

1 Mrs. Bertha Flowers was the aristocrat of Black Stamps. She had the grace of control to appear warm in the coldest weather, and on the Arkansas summer days it seemed she had a private breeze which swirled around, cooling her.

2 As I ate she began the first of what we later called "my lessons in living." She said that I must always be intolerant of ignorance but understanding of illiteracy. That some people, unable to go to school, were more educated and even more intelligent than college professors. She encouraged me to listen carefully to what country people called mother wit. That in those homely sayings was couched the collective wisdom of generations.

—Maya Angelou, *from* I Know Why the Caged Bird Sings

Author's Perspective at a Glance	
In nonfiction, look at:	**In fiction, look at:**
• direct statements • portrayals of important individuals • cultural context • tone	• themes • characters • plot • setting or cultural context • tone

TONE A writer's attitude toward a subject is referred to as **tone.** Just as a friend's attitude toward something can tell you how he or she feels, so can an author's tone give you insight into his or her perspective. The tone of a work can vary greatly, ranging from a serious tone, as in "On Being Seventeen, Bright, and Unable to Read" (page 573), to a humorous tone, as in "Life Without Go-Go Boots" (page 236).

THE IMPACT OF CULTURE The behavior, beliefs, institutions, art, and values of a community or time period make up a culture. For some writers, the culture in which they live or come from is the major influence on their lives. This is true for Richard Wright, who grew up in the segregated South a generation before Maya Angelou. In the excerpt from *Black Boy* (page 654), he explains how his desire to be a writer brought him into conflict with his family and the laws and customs that were meant to keep him down.

YOUR TURN What does the passage at the right tell you about the culture of Wright's boyhood? What is his tone, or attitude, in the passage?

> ### TONE AND CULTURE
>
> I was building up in me a dream which the entire educational system of the South had been rigged to stifle. I was feeling the very thing that the state of Mississippi had spent millions of dollars to make sure that I would never feel; . . . I was acting on impulses that southern senators in the nation's capital had striven to keep out of Negro life; I was beginning to dream the dreams that the state had said were wrong, that the schools had said were taboo.
>
> —Richard Wright, *from* Black Boy

Author's Perspective in Fiction

Fiction writers don't usually state their personal opinions in their works. Their perspectives are given directly only in interviews, in nonfiction they write themselves, or in articles about them written by someone else. Still, readers often try to infer an author's perspective from elements in a story—such as plot, character, and theme—and from the tone and cultural context of a story.

THEME The **theme,** or central idea, in a work of fiction is usually the best expression of an author's perspective. In "The Scarlet Ibis," the drama between the two brothers helps illustrate the theme that excessive pride, although seemingly beneficial in the short run, proves destructive in the end.

YOUR TURN The passage at the right is one of several in which the narrator in "The Scarlet Ibis" addresses his selfish pride. Do you think the author, James Hurst, agrees with the narrator's comments or not? Explain how you infer Hurst's perspective.

> ### THEME
>
> "What are you crying for?" asked Daddy, but I couldn't answer. They did not know that I did it for myself; that pride, whose slave I was, spoke to me louder than all their voices, and that Doodle walked only because I was ashamed of having a crippled brother.
>
> —James Hurst, *from* "The Scarlet Ibis"

Purposes for Writing

Does this sound familiar? A friend tells you a story. You laugh hysterically. Your friend then gives you a withering look and says, "Hey, I wasn't trying to be funny." You cringe.

Recognizing an author's or speaker's **purpose** will help you understand and evaluate his or her ideas.

1 Determining Author's Purpose

Author's purpose refers to the reasons an author has for writing something. Usually, an author has one of these four basic purposes in mind: to entertain; to inform or explain; to persuade or influence; to express emotions, thoughts, or ideas.

Most writing, however, is complex enough to have more than one purpose. For example, Jon Krakauer's *Into Thin Air* (p. 538) is exciting and entertaining, but it also is informative about the process of climbing Mount Everest. Why is understanding the author's purpose important?

- First of all, it helps you to understand the author's message. If an author writes a story about prejudice, for example, you will have missed something critical if you read it only at a surface level.
- Second, being aware of an author's purpose sometimes tells you *how* to read—if you realize that an author is trying to persuade you, you will read with a much more critical eye, watching for persuasive techniques used.

Strategies for Determining Purpose

Look for direct statements of purpose in the introduction. (In nonfiction, the purpose is often part of the **thesis statement**.) Or, you may have to **infer** the purpose from the theme, from what you already know about the genre or the author, or from your own response to the writing.

Monitor your own reaction to a piece of writing. Are you entertained? Are you learning something? Are you being persuaded to believe something or to take action?

Analyze any facts in the piece. How are they used—to explain, to support an argument, to add realism to a story?

2 Evaluating What You Read

Once you have determined the author's purpose, part of your job as a reader is to **evaluate** how well the author achieves that purpose. Ask yourself the following questions, and be prepared to support your opinion with evidence:

- If the purpose was to entertain, did I enjoy the selection? Was the language appropriate to the purpose, and were effective literary techniques used?
- If the purpose was to explain, did I understand the subject? Was the information presented thoroughly and logically?
- If the author was trying to persuade, was I convinced? Did I feel that the opinion was supported with sound reasons and sufficient evidence?
- If the purpose was to create a certain mood or share personal experiences, beliefs, or feelings, did I understand why the author felt as he or she did?

Need More Help?

Remember that active readers use the essential reading strategies explained on page 7: **visualize, predict, clarify, question, connect, evaluate, monitor.**

from Black Boy

Autobiography by RICHARD WRIGHT

"I'm going to offer you something more valuable than money."

Connect to Your Life

Aspirations The selection you are about to read is an excerpt from the autobiography of Richard Wright, a well-known African-American writer. In the excerpt, Wright tells about an aspiration—a strong desire to achieve something—that he had when he was 15 years old, trying to succeed on his own terms. Think about your own aspirations. What do you dream of achieving in your life? Share one of your aspirations with a classmate.

Build Background

Discrimination In *Black Boy,* Wright tells about his life between the ages of 4 and 19. At the time described in this excerpt, Wright was living in Jackson, Mississippi, with his mother, his grandmother, and other relatives. In the South during the early 1900s, when Wright was growing up, discrimination against African Americans was legally enforced through what were called Jim Crow laws. In many parts of the southern United States, laws required separate public facilities, including schools, for blacks and whites. Through these discriminatory practices, whites attempted to restrict the lives and aspirations of African Americans. Blacks received less schooling than whites or were given only vocational education. Blacks who fought such discrimination were often beaten or killed.

WORDS TO KNOW
Vocabulary Preview

alien	mode
articulate	naive
hedge	relent
heedless	speculate
intuitively	stifle

LaserLinks: Background for Reading
Historical Connection

Focus Your Reading

LITERARY ANALYSIS **DIALOGUE** Conversation between two or more characters in a work of literature is called **dialogue.** Well-written dialogue not only moves a story forward but helps the writer with **characterization** by revealing the personalities of the speakers. As you read this excerpt from *Black Boy,* notice passages of dialogue that strike you as particularly effective and think about what they tell you about the characters.

ACTIVE READING **MAKING INFERENCES** Even though *Black Boy* is an autobiography—a kind of nonfiction—the author, Richard Wright, often does not directly state his opinion about the people he describes. Instead, he communicates indirectly through the choices he makes—choices about which events to recount, what methods of **characterization** to use, and what ways to structure the story. In order to understand the **author's perspective** toward these people, you must **make inferences** based on what is stated in the text and on your own common sense.

READER'S NOTEBOOK As you read this selection, pay special attention to the dialogue between young Richard and each of the people he encounters. For each person, jot down one or two things the dialogue reveals about him or her. Then state briefly what you can conclude about the author's perspective toward the people he describes. Make charts like the one shown to record your ideas.

Young Richard		
What He Says	**What This Reveals About Him**	**Author's Perspective**

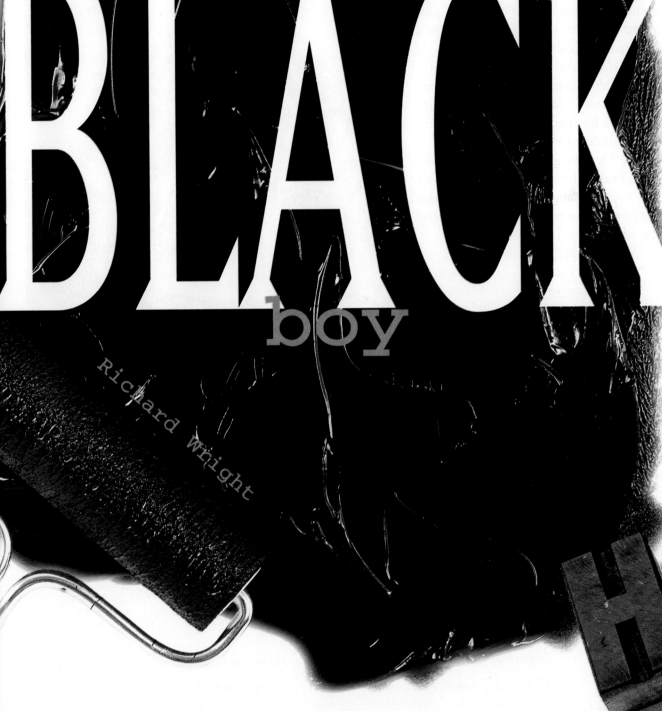

from

BLACK
boy

Richard Wright

The eighth grade days flowed in their hungry path, and I grew more conscious of myself; I sat in classes, bored, wondering, dreaming. One long dry afternoon I took out my composition book and told myself that I would write a story; it was sheer idleness that led me to it. What would the story be about? It resolved itself into a plot about a villain who wanted a widow's home, and I called it *The Voodoo of Hell's Half-Acre*. It was crudely atmospheric, emotional, <u>intuitively</u> psychological, and stemmed from pure feeling. I finished it in three days and then wondered what to do with it.

The local Negro newspaper! That's it . . . I sailed into the office and shoved my ragged composition book under the nose of the man who called himself the editor.

"What's that?" he asked.

"A story," I said.

"A news story?"

"No, fiction."

"All right. I'll read it," he said.

He pushed my composition book back on his desk and looked at me curiously, sucking at his pipe.

"But I want you to read it *now*," I said.

He blinked. I had no idea how newspapers were run. I thought that one took a story to an editor, and he sat down then and there and read it and said yes or no.

"I'll read this and let you know about it tomorrow," he said.

I was disappointed; I had taken time to write it, and he seemed distant and uninterested.

"Give me the story," I said, reaching for it.

He turned from me, took up the book, and read ten pages or more.

Brown Boy, (1935), Lois Mailou Jones. Watercolor, private collection.

"Won't you come in tomorrow?" he asked. "I'll have it finished then."

I honestly <u>relented</u>.

ACTIVE READING

PREDICT What do you think will happen when Richard comes back tomorrow?

"All right," I said. "I'll stop in tomorrow."

I left with the conviction that he would not read it. Now, where else could I take it after he had turned it down? The next afternoon, en route to my job, I stepped into the newspaper office.

"Where's my story?" I asked.

"It's in galleys," he said.

WORDS
TO
KNOW

intuitively (ĭn-tōō′ĭ-tĭv-lē) *adv.* in a way that involves knowing something without having consciously learned it

relent (rĭ-lĕnt′) *v.* to become less harsh, strict, or stubborn

"What's that?" I asked; I did not know what galleys were.

"It's set up in type," he said. "We're publishing it."

"How much money will I get?" I asked, excited.

"We can't pay for manuscript," he said.

"But you sell your papers for money," I said with logic.

"Yes, but we're young in business," he explained.

"But you're asking me to *give* you my story, but you don't *give* your papers away," I said.

He laughed.

"Look, you're just starting. This story will put your name before our readers. Now, that's something," he said.

"But if the story is good enough to sell to your readers, then you ought to give me some of the money you get from it," I insisted.

He laughed again, and I sensed that I was amusing him.

"I'm going to offer you something more valuable than money," he said. "I'll give you a chance to learn to write."

I was pleased, but I still thought he was taking advantage of me.

"When will you publish my story?"

ACTIVE READING

INFER What do you think this dialogue shows about Richard's character?

"I'm dividing it into three installments," he said. "The first installment appears this week. But the main thing is this: Will you get news for me on a space rate basis?"[1]

"I work mornings and evenings for three dollars a week," I said.

"Oh," he said. "Then you better keep that. But what are you doing this summer?"

"Nothing."

"Then come to see me before you take another job," he said. "And write some more stories."

A few days later my classmates came to me with baffled eyes, holding copies of the *Southern Register* in their hands.

"Did you really write that story?" they asked me.

"Yes."

"Why?"

"Because I wanted to."

"Where did you get it from?"

"I made it up."

"You didn't. You copied it out of a book."

"If I had, no one would publish it."

"But what are they publishing it for?"

"So people can read it."

"Who told you to do that?"

"Nobody."

"Then why did you do it?"

"Because I wanted to," I said again.

They were convinced that I had not told them the truth. We had never had any instruction in literary matters at school; the literature of the nation or the Negro had never been mentioned. My schoolmates could not understand why anyone would want to write a story; and, above all, they could not understand why I had called it *The Voodoo of Hell's Half-Acre*. The mood out of which a story was written was the most <u>alien</u> thing conceivable to them. They looked at me with new eyes, and a distance, a suspiciousness, came between us. If I had thought anything in writing the story, I had thought that perhaps it would make me more acceptable to them, and now it was cutting me off from them more completely than ever.

At home the effects were no less disturbing. Granny came into my room early one morning and sat on the edge of my bed.

"Richard, what is this you're putting in the papers?" she asked.

---

1. **space rate basis:** a system of payment based on the length of the articles.

WORDS
TO
KNOW   **alien** (āʹlē-ən) *adj.* foreign; strange; unfamiliar

Portrait of My Father (about 1921), Archibald J. Motley, Jr.
Collection of Archie Motley and Valerie Gerrard Browne,
Chicago Historical Society.

"A story," I said.

"About what?"

"It's just a story, Granny."

"But they tell me it's been in three times."

"It's the same story. It's in three parts."

"But what is it about?" she insisted.

I hedged, fearful of getting into a religious argument.

"It's just a story I made up," I said.

"Then it's a lie," she said.

"Granny, please . . . I'm sorry," I pleaded. "But it's hard to tell you about the story. You see, Granny, everybody knows that the story isn't true, but . . ."

"Then why write it?" she asked.

"Because people might want to read it."

"That's the Devil's work," she said and left.

My mother also was worried.

"Son, you ought to be more serious," she said. "You're growing up now, and you won't be able to get jobs if you let people think that you're weak-minded. Suppose the superintendent of schools would ask you to teach here in Jackson, and he found out that you had been writing stories?"

I could not answer her.

"I'll be all right, Mama," I said.

Uncle Tom, though surprised, was highly critical and contemptuous. The story had no point, he said. And whoever heard of a story by the title of *The Voodoo of Hell's Half-Acre?* Aunt Addie said that it was a sin for anyone to use the word "hell" and that what was wrong with me was that I had nobody to guide me. She blamed the whole thing upon my upbringing.

In the end I was so angry that I refused to talk about the story. From no quarter,[2] with the exception of the Negro newspaper editor, had there come a single encouraging word. It was rumored that the principal wanted to know why I had used the word "hell." I felt that I had committed a crime. Had I been conscious of the full

ACTIVE READING

INFER Why do the reactions he gets from people end up making Richard angry?

_____

2. **quarter:** direction.

WORDS
TO
KNOW

hedge (hĕj) *v.* to avoid giving a direct answer

extent to which I was pushing against the current of my environment, I would have been frightened altogether out of my attempts at writing. But my reactions were limited to the attitude of the people about me, and I did not speculate or generalize.

I dreamed of going north and writing books, novels. The North symbolized to me all that I had not felt and seen; it had no relation whatever to what actually existed. Yet, by imagining a place where everything was possible, I kept hope alive in me. But where had I got this notion of doing something in the future, of going away from home and accomplishing something that would be recognized by others? I had, of course, read my Horatio Alger stories, my pulp stories, and I knew my Get-Rich-Quick Wallingford series[3] from cover to cover, though I had sense enough not to hope to get rich; even to my naive imagination that possibility was too remote. I knew that I lived in a country in which the aspirations of black people were limited, marked off. Yet I felt that I had to go somewhere and do something to redeem my being alive.

I was building up in me a dream which the entire educational system of the South had been rigged to stifle. I was feeling the very thing that the state of Mississippi had spent millions of dollars to make sure that I would never feel; I was becoming aware of the thing that the Jim Crow laws had been drafted and passed to keep out of my consciousness; I was acting on impulses that southern senators in the nation's capital had striven to keep out of Negro life; I

was beginning to dream the dreams that the state had said were wrong, that the schools had said were taboo.[4]

Had I been articulate about my ultimate aspirations, no doubt someone would have told me what I was bargaining for; but nobody seemed to know, and least of all did I. My classmates felt that I was doing something that was vaguely wrong, but they did not know how to express it. As the outside world grew more meaningful, I became more concerned, tense; and my classmates and my teachers would say: "Why do you ask so many questions?" Or: "Keep quiet."

I was in my fifteenth year; in terms of schooling I was far behind the average youth of the nation, but I did not know that. In me was shaping a yearning for a kind of consciousness, a mode of being that the way of life about me had said could not be, must not be, and upon which the penalty of death had been placed. Somewhere in the dead of the southern night my life had switched onto the wrong track, and, without my knowing it, the locomotive of my heart was rushing down a dangerously steep slope, heading for a collision, heedless of the warning red lights that blinked all about me, the sirens and the bells and the screams that filled the air. ❖

ACTIVE READING

EVALUATE Do you think the author is justified in comparing his yearning for a better life to a train switching "onto the wrong track"?

---

3. **Horatio Alger stories . . . Wallingford series:** works of popular fiction about achieving wealth through hard work or cleverness.

4. **taboo:** forbidden.

WORDS
TO
KNOW

speculate (spĕk′yə-lāt′) v. to guess
naive (nä-ēv′) adj. simple in a natural and perhaps foolish way; unsophisticated
stifle (stī′fəl) v. to smother; hold back
articulate (är-tĭk′yə-lĭt) adj. clear and effective in speech
mode (mōd) n. a manner or way
heedless (hēd′lĭs) adj. unmindful; careless; unaware

Connect to the Literature

1. What Do You Think?
What do you think
of the ways in
which people
reacted to Wright's
writing? Explain.

Comprehension Check
• When did Wright write his first
story, and where was it published?
• How did his friends and family
respond to his story?
• How did Wright respond to
everyone's criticism?

Think Critically

2. **ACTIVE READING** **MAKING INFERENCES** Look back at your
 READER'S NOTEBOOK. What do you think is the
author's perspective on publishing his first story as a boy?

3. Why do you think Wright's family and classmates reacted as
they did?

> **THINK ABOUT**
>
> • their unfamiliarity with teenagers who wrote
>   stories
> • their attitudes toward **fiction** and imaginative
>   writing
> • the limitations imposed upon African
>   Americans at the time

4. Why do you think Wright clung to his aspirations despite the
lack of support from people around him?

Extend Interpretations

5. Different Perspectives If Richard had grown up in a family
that encouraged writing, how might his first publication
experience have been different?

6. What If? What do you think you would do if you met with
the kind of resistance Wright encountered?

7. Connect to Life Do you think the aspirations of African
Americans and other minorities are still limited by society?
Give evidence to support your answer.

Literary Analysis

DIALOGUE **Dialogue** is written
conversation between two or more
characters. It is a way of making
characters and events seem real.
Dialogue is used in all forms of
literature, but it is most common in
drama. In a play, the story is
developed primarily through
dialogue. In an **autobiography,**
dialogue is a way of "dramatizing"
experiences that the author thinks
are important.

Cooperative Learning Activity With
a small group of classmates, reread
one of the three primary dialogues
in this selection—either one of the
two conversations Richard has with
the editor or the one he has with
Granny. Discuss what you think the
author conveys in the dialogue.
Then decide how the lines should
be spoken to show the **author's
perspective.** Present your dialogue
to the class.

REVIEW **EXTENDED METAPHOR**
At the end of this excerpt, Wright
compares his life to a train in
several ways, creating an **extended
metaphor.** Examine the details of
this metaphor. Why does it seem
appropriate? In what ways does
Wright's life resemble a train?

Choices & CHALLENGES

Writing Options

1. Letter of Recommendation
Write an imaginary letter of recommendation for Wright to the college of his choice, concentrating on his character traits. The letter could come from you or from a character in the selection. Place your draft in your **Working Portfolio.**

2. Inner Dialogue Write the thoughts that might have gone through the newspaper editor's mind as he talked to Wright and read his story.

Activities & Explorations

1. Black Boy Skit In a small group, present this excerpt as a skit to the rest of the class.
~ PERFORMING

2. Musical Expression Find or compose a blues or rap song that expresses Wright's feelings. Play your song for the class.
~ MUSIC

See art on p. 656.

Art Connection

Look again at the painting on page 656. The painter of *Brown Boy,* Lois Mailou Jones, was born in Boston in 1905. She taught art in North Carolina before becoming a professor of watercolor painting at Howard University in Washington, D.C. (1930–1977).

She is considered the first major African-American woman artist. What is your impression of the subject of the painting and how does it compare to your impression of the young Richard Wright?

Vocabulary in Action

EXERCISE: CONTEXT CLUES Write the vocabulary word that best completes each of the following sentences.

1. When Wright took his story to the newspaper, he was _____ of the difficulties he might face.

2. Although the newspaper editor laughed at him, Wright somehow knew _____ that the man was amused, not scornful.

3. Wright did not know what galleys were, because the world of publishing was _____ to him.

4. Even though Wright argued with him, the editor did not _____ and agree to pay Wright for the story.

5. Wright knew that it would have been _____ of him to believe that his writing would gain him quick wealth.

6. It seemed, at least at first, that more people wanted to _____ Wright's creativity than wanted to encourage it.

7. It was not completely truthful of Wright to _____ when his grandmother asked him questions about his story.

8. Some of Wright's relatives were upset by words he used in his writing and began to _____ about what was wrong with him.

9. Wright's classmates were not _____ enough to express clearly what they thought was wrong with what he was doing.

10. Wright thought that if he moved to the North, he might find a _____ of existence that was more to his liking.

Building Vocabulary
For an in-depth study of context clues, see page 103.

WORDS TO KNOW				
alien	hedge	intuitively	naive	speculate
articulate	heedless	mode	relent	stifle

Grammar in Context: Gerund Phrases

In *Black Boy*, Richard Wright's use of gerund phrases provides a sense of ongoing action and adds sentence variety. A **gerund phrase** consists of a **gerund**—a verb form that ends in *-ing* and functions as a noun—along with its modifiers and complements.

> But where had I got this notion of doing something in the future, of going away from home and accomplishing something . . . ?

What if Wright had written "But where had I got this notion of *future action,* of *life away from home* and *accomplishment?*" Not only would the sentence have lost its feeling of ongoing action; it would also have lost the rhythm of the repeated *-ing* of the gerunds (*doing, going, accomplishing*). The rhythm emphasizes the author's dreams.

WRITING EXERCISE Rewrite each sentence, changing one of the elements into a gerund phrase. Underline the gerund phrase.

Usage Tip: You can use a gerund phrase as a subject, as the object of a verb, or as the object of a preposition.

> **Example: *Original*** One reason I wrote stories was for my family's entertainment.
>
> ***Rewritten*** <u>Entertaining my family</u> was one reason I wrote stories.

1. When I demanded to see the newspaper editor, it was a very bold act.
2. I enjoyed myself as I watched him read my story.
3. He read about ten pages, and it seemed to take him forever.
4. I wanted to write books; that was my dream.

Grammar Handbook Verbals, p. 1194

Richard Wright
1908–1960

Other Works
Twelve Million Black Voices
The Outsider
Black Power
White Man, Listen!

A Hard Beginning The son of a sharecropper and a teacher, Richard Wright grew up in poverty in the South. *Black Boy* contains frequent references to the hunger that he had to endure while he was growing up. Wright's father deserted the family when Wright was young, and his mother worked as a cook to support her two sons. Because the family moved often and his mother became ill, Wright attended school irregularly.

Public Recognition After he left school, Wright worked at menial jobs, reading widely in his spare time. While living in Chicago and New York City, he began to get his stories and articles published in magazines. Recognition came to him with his first published book, *Uncle Tom's Children*, which consists of four long short stories. He then won a Guggenheim Fellowship and completed the novel *Native Son.* Considered by many to be a classic work of American literature, *Native Son* was a great success, and in 1941 Wright received the Spingarn Medal from the NAACP for his achievement. Later, in *American Hunger,* Wright continued the autobiography he had begun with *Black Boy.*

French Citizenship In 1947, Wright and his family moved to Paris, where he felt greater acceptance and freedom than in the United States. Wright became a French citizen, and though he traveled widely, France remained his home until his death.

Author Activity

Read another excerpt from one of Wright's autobiographical works (either *Black Boy* or *American Hunger*). In a brief oral report, explain to your classmates how the section you have read contributes to or changes the image of the author that you get in this excerpt.

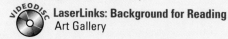

LaserLinks: Background for Reading
Art Gallery

Daughter of Invention

Short Story by JULIA ALVAREZ

"We wanted to become Americans and my father— and my mother, at first—would have none of it."

Connect to Your Life

Culture Shock You may have had the experience of moving to a new town or going to a new school, and you know or can imagine the sorts of changes to expect in such a situation. Can you imagine, however, what it would be like to move to a new country with a very different culture? What kinds of problems do you think immigrants to the United States face? What are some possible solutions to these problems, and what advantages or disadvantages might these solutions have? Share your thoughts or personal experiences in a small group.

Build Background

Immigrant Story A version of the story "Daughter of Invention" appears in Julia Alvarez's novel *How the García Girls Lost Their Accents.* In this novel, the García family settles in New York City after fleeing from the Dominican Republic. They leave their homeland to escape the harsh rule of the dictator, Generalissimo Trujillo (trōō-hē′yō), and the brutal vengeance of his secret police, the SIM. Although the Garcías are fictional, Trujillo is not. During his rule (1930–1961), many families sought refuge and a new life in the United States.

WORDS TO KNOW
Vocabulary Preview

antibiotic	mortified
idiom	plagiarized
inhospitable	provoke
innumerable	reconcile
insubordinate	tentative

Focus Your Reading

LITERARY ANALYSIS **AUTHOR'S PERSPECTIVE AND CHARACTERIZATION**

An **author's perspective** is the viewpoint he or she expresses in a piece of literature. In fiction, an author's perspective is often disclosed in part through **characterization.** For example, consider the following description of the mother in the story you are about to read:

> *She did not want to go back to the old country where she was only a wife and a mother (and a failed one at that, since she had never had the required son).*

By suggesting that the mother might feel like a failure for giving birth only to girls, the author may be expressing a critical view of the "old country" and its values. As you read the story, look for clues in the characterization that may help you understand the author's perspective on different events and issues.

ACTIVE READING **UNDERSTANDING CHARACTERIZATION** Writers can use four types of **characterization,** or techniques to develop a character. They can: (1) describe the character's physical appearance; (2) describe how the character speaks, thinks, feels, or acts; (3) describe what others say, think, or feel and how they act toward the character; and (4) let the narrator make direct comments about the character. As you read this story, notice how the author uses these different techniques to bring the characters to life.

READER'S NOTEBOOK Write down one or two examples of each technique used by the author to create the character of the mother.

Daughter of Invention

Julia Alvarez

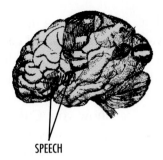

SPEECH

She wanted to invent something, my mother. There was a period after we arrived in this country, until five or so years later, when my mother was inventing. They were never pressing, global needs she was addressing with her pencil and pad. She would have said that was for men to do, rockets and engines that ran on gasoline and turned the wheels of the world. She was just fussing with little house things, don't mind her.

She always invented at night, after settling her house down. On his side of the bed my father would be conked out for an hour already, his Spanish newspaper draped over his chest, his glasses, propped up on his bedside table, looking out eerily at the darkened room like a disembodied guard. But in her lighted corner, like some devoted scholar burning the midnight oil, my mother was inventing, sheets pulled to her lap, pillows propped up behind her, her reading glasses riding the bridge of her nose like a schoolmarm's. On her lap lay one of those <u>innumerable</u> pads of paper my father always brought home from his office, compliments of some pharmaceutical company, advertising tranquilizers or <u>antibiotics</u> or skin cream; in her other hand, my mother held a pencil that looked like a pen with a little cylinder of lead inside. She would work on a sketch of something familiar, but drawn at such close range so she could attach a special nozzle or handier handle, the thing looked peculiar. Once, I mistook the spiral of a corkscrew for a nautilus shell, but it could just as well have been a galaxy forming.

It was the only time all day we'd catch her sitting down, for she herself was living proof of the *perpetuum mobile*[1] machine so many inventors had sought over the ages. My sisters and I would seek her out now when she seemed to have a moment to talk to us: We were having trouble at school or we wanted her to persuade my father to give us permission to go into the city or to a shopping mall or a movie—in broad daylight! My mother would wave us out of her room. "The problem with you girls. . ." I can tell you right now what the problem always boiled down to: We wanted to become Americans and my father—and my mother, at first—would have none of it.

"You girls are going to drive me crazy!" She always threatened if we kept nagging. "When I end up in Bellevue,[2] you'll be safely sorry!"

She spoke in English when she argued

---

1. *perpetuum mobile* (pĕr-pĕt′oo-əm mō′bĭ-lĕ) *Latin:* perpetual motion; operating continuously without a sustained source of energy.

2. **Bellevue** (bĕl′vyoo′): a large hospital in New York City with a well-known psychiatric ward.

WORDS TO KNOW

innumerable (ĭ-noo′mər-ə-bəl) *adj.* too many to count
antibiotic (ăn′tĭ-bī-ŏt′ĭk) *n.* a drug used to treat infectious diseases

665

with us, even though, in a matter of months, her daughters were the fluent ones. Her English was much better than my father's, but it was still a mishmash of mixed-up <u>idioms</u> and sayings that showed she was "green behind the ears," as she called it.

If my sisters and I tried to get her to talk in Spanish, she'd snap, "When in Rome, do unto the Romans . . ."

I had become the spokesman for my sisters, and I would stand my ground in that bedroom. "We're not going to that school anymore, Mami!"

"You have to." Her eyes would widen with worry. "In this country, it is against the law not to go to school. You want us to get thrown out?"

"You want us to get killed? Those kids were throwing stones today!"

"Sticks and stones don't break bones . . ." she chanted. I could tell, though, by the look on her face, it was as if one of those stones the kids had aimed at us had hit her. But she always pretended we were at fault. "What did you do to <u>provoke</u> them? It takes two to tangle, you know."

"Thanks, thanks a lot, Mom!" I'd storm out of that room and into mine. I never called her Mom except when I wanted her to feel how much she had failed us in this country. She was a good enough Mami, fussing and scolding and giving advice, but a terrible girlfriend parent, a real failure of a Mom.

Back she'd go to her pencil and pad, scribbling and tsking and tearing off paper, finally giving up,

and taking up her *New York Times.* Some nights, though, she'd get a good idea, and she'd rush into my room, a flushed look on her face, her tablet of paper in her hand, a cursory[3] knock on the door she'd just thrown open: "Do I have something to show you, Cukita!"

This was my time to myself, after I'd finished my homework, while my sisters were still downstairs watching TV in the basement. Hunched over my small desk, the overhead light turned off, my lamp shining poignantly on my paper, the rest of the room in warm, soft, uncreated darkness, I wrote my secret poems in my new language. "You're going to ruin your eyes!" My mother would storm into my room, turning on the overly bright overhead light, scaring off whatever shy passion I had just begun coaxing out of a labyrinth[4] of feelings with the blue thread of my writing. "Oh Mami!" I'd cry out, my eyes blinking up at her. "I'm writing."

"Ay, Cukita." That was her communal pet name for whoever was in her favor. "Cukita, when I make a million, I'll buy you your very own typewriter." (I'd been nagging my mother for one just like the one father had bought her to do his order forms at home.) "Gravy on the turkey" was what she called it when someone was buttering her up. She'd butter and pour. "I'll hire you your very own typist."

Down she'd plop on my bed and hold out her pad to me. "Take a guess, Cukita?" I'd study her

"You girls are going to drive me crazy!"

---

3. **cursory** (kûr′sə-rē): hasty; careless.
4. **labyrinth** (lăb′ə-rĭnth′): a maze.

WORDS
TO
KNOW

idiom (ĭd′ē-əm) *n.* an expression whose meaning is different from that of the individual words taken together
provoke (prə-vōk′) *v.* to make angry

rough sketch a moment: soap sprayed from the nozzle head of a shower when you turned the knob a certain way? Coffee with creamer already mixed in? Time-released water capsules for your plants when you were away? A key chain with a timer that would go off when your parking meter was about to expire? (The ticking would help you find your keys easily if you mislaid them.) The famous one, famous only in hindsight, was the stick person dragging a square by a rope—a suitcase with wheels? "Oh, of course," we'd humor her. "What every household needs: a shower like a car wash, keys ticking like a bomb, luggage on a leash!" By now, as you can see, it'd become something of a family joke, our Thomas Edison Mami, our Benjamin Franklin Mom.

Her face would fall. "Come on now! Use your head." One more wrong guess, and she'd tell me, pressing with her pencil point the different highlights of this incredible new wonder. "Remember that time we took the car to Bear Mountain,[5] and we re-ah-lized that we had forgotten to pack an opener with our pick-a-nick?" (We kept correcting her, but she insisted this is how it should be said.) "When we were ready to eat we didn't have any way to open the refreshments cans?" (This before fliptop lids, which she claimed had crossed her mind.) "You know what this is now?" A shake of my head. "Is a car bumper, but see this part is a removable can opener. So simple and yet so necessary, no?"

"Yeah, Mami. You should patent[6] it." I'd shrug. She'd tear off the scratch paper and fold it, carefully, corner to corner, as if she were going to save it. But then, she'd toss it in the wastebasket on her way out of the room and give a little laugh like a disclaimer.[7] "It's half of one or two dozen of another . . ."

I suppose none of her daughters was very encouraging. We resented her spending time on those dumb inventions. Here, we were trying to fit in America among Americans; we needed help figuring out who we were, why these Irish kids whose grandparents were micks two generations ago, why they were calling us spics.[8] Why had we come to the country in the first place? Important, crucial, final things, you see, and here was our own mother, who didn't have a second to help us puzzle any of this out, inventing gadgets to make life easier for American moms. Why, it seemed as if she were arming our own enemy against us!

One time, she did have a moment of triumph. Every night, she liked to read *The New York Times* in bed before turning off her light, to see what the Americans were up to. One night, she let out a yelp to wake up my father beside her, bolt upright, reaching for his glasses which, in his haste, he knocked across the room. "*Que pasa? Que pasa?*" What is wrong? There was terror in his voice, fear she'd seen in his eyes in the Dominican Republic before we left. We were being watched there; he was being followed; he and mother had often exchanged those looks. They could not talk, of course, though they must have whispered to each other in fear at night in the dark bed. Now in America, he was safe, a success even; his Centro Medico[9] in Brooklyn was thronged with the sick and the homesick. But in dreams, he went back to those awful days and long nights, and my mother's screams

---

5. **Bear Mountain:** a mountain and state park on the Hudson River in upstate New York.

6. **patent:** to apply for a government grant for the economic rights to an idea or invention.

7. **disclaimer:** an abandonment of interest or responsibility.

8. **micks . . . spics:** *Micks* is a derogatory term for people of Irish descent; *spics* is a derogatory term for people of Hispanic descent.

9. **Centro Medico** (sĕn′trô mĕ′dē-kô) *Spanish*: a medical center.

confirmed his secret fear: we had not gotten away after all; they had come for us at last.

"Ay, Papi, I'm sorry. Go back to sleep, Cukito. It's nothing, nothing really." My mother held up the *Times* for him to squint at the small print, back page headline, one hand tapping all over the top of the bedside table for his glasses, the other rubbing his eyes to wakefulness.

"Remember, remember how I showed you that suitcase with little wheels so we would not have to carry those heavy bags when we traveled? Someone stole my idea and made a million!" She shook the paper in his face. She shook the paper in all our faces that night. "See! See! This man was no bobo! He didn't put all his pokers on a back burner. I kept telling you, one of these days my ship would pass me by in the night!" She wagged her finger at my sisters and my father and me, laughing all the while, one of those eerie laughs crazy people in movies laugh. We had congregated in her room to hear the good news she'd been yelling down the stairs, and now we eyed her and each other. I suppose we were all thinking the same thing: Wouldn't it be weird and sad if Mami did end up in Bellevue as she'd always threatened she might?

"Ya, ya! Enough!" She waved us out of her room at last. "There is no use trying to drink spilt milk, that's for sure."

It was the suitcase rollers that stopped my mother's hand; she had weather vaned[10] a minor brainstorm. She would have to start taking herself seriously. That blocked the free play of her ingenuity. Besides, she had also begun working at my father's office, and at night, she was too tired and busy filling in columns with how much money they had made that day to be fooling with gadgets!

She did take up her pencil and pad one last time to help me out. In ninth grade, I was chosen

Primavera (1995), Michael Bergt. Egg tempera on gesso panel. DC Moore Gallery, New York.

by my English teacher, Sister Mary Joseph, to deliver the teacher's day address at the school assembly. Back in the Dominican Republic, I was a terrible student. No one could ever get me to sit down to a book. But in New York, I needed to settle somewhere, and the natives were unfriendly, the country inhospitable, so I took root in the language. By high school, the nuns were reading my stories and compositions out loud to my classmates as examples of imagination at work.

This time my imagination jammed. At first I didn't want and then I couldn't seem to write that speech. I suppose I should have thought of it as a "great honor," as my father called it. But I was mortified. I still had a pronounced lilt to my accent, and I did not like to speak in public, subjecting myself to my classmates' ridicule. Recently, they had begun to warm toward my sisters and me, and it took no great figuring to see that to deliver a eulogy[11] for a convent full of crazy, old overweight nuns was no way to endear myself to the members of my class.

But I didn't know how to get out of it. Week after week, I'd sit down, hoping to polish off some quick, noncommittal little speech. I couldn't get anything down.

The weekend before our Monday morning assembly I went into a panic. My mother would just have to call in and say I was in the hospital, in a coma. I was in the Dominican Republic. Yeah, that was it! Recently, my father had been talking about going back home to live.

---

10. **weather vaned:** pointed to; helped create.
11. **eulogy** (yo͞o′lə-jē): a speech giving praise.

My mother tried to calm me down. "Just remember how Mister Lincoln couldn't think of anything to say at the Gettysburg, but then, Bang! 'Four score and once upon a time ago,'"[12] she began reciting. Her version of history was half invention and half truths and whatever else she needed to prove a point. "Something is going to come if you just relax. You'll see, like the Americans say, 'Necessity is the daughter of invention.' I'll help you."

All weekend, she kept coming into my room with help. "Please, Mami, just leave me alone, please," I pleaded with her. But I'd get rid of the goose only to have to contend with the gander. My father kept poking his head in the door just to see if I had "fulfilled my obligations," a phrase he'd used when we were a little younger, and he'd check to see whether we had gone to the bathroom before a car trip. Several times that weekend around the supper table, he'd recite his valedictorian speech from when he graduated from high school. He'd give me pointers on delivery, on the great orators and their tricks. (Humbleness and praise and falling silent with great emotion were his favorites.)

My mother sat across the table, the only one who seemed to be listening to him. My sisters and I were forgetting a lot of our Spanish, and my father's formal, florid diction[13] was even harder to understand. But my mother smiled softly to herself, and turned the Lazy Susan at the center of the table around and around as if it were the prime mover, the first gear of attention.

That Sunday evening, I was reading some poetry to get myself inspired: Whitman[14] in an old book with an engraved cover my father had picked up in a thrift shop next to his office a few weeks back. "I celebrate myself and sing myself. . ." "He most honors my style who learns under it to destroy the teacher." The poet's words shocked and thrilled me. I had gotten used to the nuns, a literature of

appropriate sentiments, poems with a message, expurgated[15] texts. But here was a flesh and blood man, belching and laughing and sweating in poems. "Who touches this book touches a man."

That night, at last, I started to write, recklessly, three, five pages, looking up once only to see my father passing by the hall on tiptoe. When I was done, I read over my words, and my eyes filled. I finally sounded like myself in English!

As soon as I had finished that first draft, I called my mother to my room. She listened attentively, as she had to my father's speech, and in the end, her eyes were glistening too. Her face was soft and warm and proud. "That is a beautiful, beautiful speech, Cukita. I want for your father to hear it before he goes to sleep. Then I will type it for you, all right?"

Down the hall we went, the two of us, faces flushed with accomplishment. Into the master bedroom where my father was propped up on his pillows, still awake, reading the Dominican papers, already days old. He had become interested in his country's fate again. The dictatorship had been toppled. The interim government was going to hold the first free elections in thirty years. There was still some question in his mind whether or not we might want to move back. History was in the making, freedom and hope were in the air again! But my mother had gotten used to the life here. She did

---

12. **Gettysburg . . . *ago:*** At Gettysburg, Pennsylvania, the site of a decisive and bloody Union victory in the U.S. Civil War, President Abraham Lincoln gave his famous speech known as the Gettysburg Address, which began "Four score and seven years ago, . . ."

13. **florid** (flôr′ĭd) **diction:** speech characterized by long, fancy words.

14. **Whitman:** Walt Whitman, the 19th-century U.S. writer whose famous book of poetry *Leaves of Grass* celebrates individualism and democracy.

15. **expurgated** (ĕk′spər-gā′tĭd): edited to remove sections thought to be vulgar or immoral.

not want to go back to the old country where she was only a wife and a mother (and a failed one at that, since she had never had the required son). She did not come straight out and disagree with my father's plans. Instead, she fussed with him about reading the papers in bed, soiling those sheets with those poorly printed, foreign tabloids. "The *Times* is not that bad!" she'd claim if my father tried to humor her by saying they shared the same dirty habit.

The minute my father saw my mother and me, filing in, he put his paper down, and his face brightened as if at long last his wife had delivered a son, and that was the news we were bringing him. His teeth were already grinning from the glass of water next to his bedside lamp, so he lisped when he said, "Eh-speech, eh-speech!"

"It is so beautiful, Papi," my mother previewed him, turning the sound off on his TV. She sat down at the foot of the bed. I stood before both of them, blocking their view of the soldiers in helicopters landing amid silenced gun reports[16] and explosions. A few weeks ago it had been the shores of the Dominican Republic. Now it was the jungles of Southeast Asia they were saving. My mother gave me the nod to begin reading.

I didn't need much encouragement. I put my nose to the fire, as my mother would have said, and read from start to finish without looking up. When I was done, I was a little embarrassed at my pride in my own words. I pretended to quibble[17] with a phrase or two I was sure I'd be talked out

I finally sounded like myself in English!

of changing. I looked questioningly to my mother. Her face was radiant. She turned to share her pride with my father.

But the expression on his face shocked us both. His toothless mouth had collapsed into a dark zero. His eyes glared at me, then shifted to my mother, accusingly. In barely audible Spanish, as if secret microphones or informers were all about, he whispered, "You will permit her to read *that?*"

My mother's eyebrows shot up, her mouth fell open. In the old country, any whisper of a challenge to authority could bring the secret police in their black V.W.'s. But this was America. People could say what they thought. "What is wrong with her speech?" my mother questioned him. "What ees wrrrong with her eh-speech?" My father wagged his head at her. His anger was always more frightening in his broken English. As if he had mutilated the language in his fury—and now there was nothing to stand between us and his raw, dumb anger. "What is wrong? I will tell you what is wrong. It shows no gratitude. It is boastful. 'I celebrate myself'? 'The best student learns to destroy the teacher'?" He mocked my plagiarized words. "That is insubordinate. It is improper. It is disrespecting of her teachers—" In his anger he had forgotten his fear of lurking spies: Each wrong he voiced was a decibel higher than the last outrage. Finally, he was yelling at me, "As your father, I forbid you to say that eh-speech!"

My mother leapt to her feet, a sign always that she was about to make a speech or deliver an

---

16. **reports:** explosive noises.
17. **quibble:** find small faults with.

ultimatum.[18] She was a small woman, and she spoke all her pronouncements standing up, either for more protection or as a carry-over from her girlhood in convent schools where one asked for, and literally took, the floor in order to speak. She stood by my side, shoulder to shoulder; we looked down at my father. "That is no tone of voice, Eduardo—" she began.

By now, my father was truly furious. I suppose it was bad enough I was rebelling, but here was my mother joining forces with me. Soon he would be surrounded by a house full of independent American women. He too leapt from his bed, throwing off his covers. The Spanish newspapers flew across the room. He snatched my speech out of my hands, held it before my panicked eyes, a vengeful, mad look in his own, and then once, twice, three, four, countless times, he tore my prize into shreds.

"Are you crazy?" My mother lunged at him. "Have you gone mad? That is her speech for tomorrow you have torn up!"

"Have *you* gone mad?" He shook her away. "You were going to let her read that . . . that insult to her teachers?"

"Insult to her teachers!" My mother's face had crumpled up like a piece of paper. On it was written a love note to my father. Ever since they had come to this country, their life together was a constant war. "This is America, Papi, America!" she reminded him now. "You are not in a savage country any more!"

I was on my knees, weeping wildly, collecting all the little pieces of my speech, hoping that I could put it back together before the assembly tomorrow morning. But not even a sibyl[19] could have made sense of all those scattered pieces of paper. All hope was lost. "He broke it, he broke it," I moaned as I picked up a handful of pieces.

Probably, if I had thought a moment about it, I would not have done what I did next. I would have realized my father had lost brothers and comrades to the dictator Trujillo.[20] For the rest of his life, he would be haunted by blood in the streets and late night disappearances. Even after he had been in the states for years, he jumped if a black Volkswagen passed him on the street. He feared anyone in uniform: the meter maid giving out parking tickets, a museum guard approaching to tell him not to touch his favorite Goya[21] at the Metropolitan.

I took a handful of the scraps I had gathered, stood up, and hurled them in his face. "Chapita!" I said in a low, ugly whisper. "You're just another Chapita!"

It took my father only a moment to register the hated nickname of our dictator, and he was after me. Down the halls we raced, but I was quicker than he and made it to my room just in time to lock the door as my father threw his weight against it. He called down curses on my head, ordered me on his authority as my father to open that door this very instant! He throttled that doorknob, but all to no avail. My mother's love of gadgets saved my hide that night. She had hired a locksmith to install good locks on all the bedroom doors after our house had been broken into while we were away the previous summer. In case burglars broke in again, and we were in the house, they'd have a second round of locks to contend with before they got to us.

"Eduardo," she tried to calm him down. "Don't you ruin my new locks."

He finally did calm down, his anger spent. I

---

18. **ultimatum** (ŭl′tə-mā′təm): a statement of final requirements.

19. **sibyl** (sĭb′əl): a female prophet.

20. **Trujillo**: Rafael Trujillo (rä-fä-yĕl′ trōō-hē′yō), dictator of the Dominican Republic from 1930 until his assassination in 1961.

21. **his favorite Goya** (goi′ə): a work by the Spanish painter Francisco Goya, whose art reflected the political struggles of the late 1700s and early 1800s.

heard their footsteps retreating down the hall. I heard their door close, the clicking of their lock. Then, muffled voices, my mother's peaking in anger, in persuasion, my father's deep murmurs of explanation and of self-defense. At last, the house fell silent, before I heard, far off, the gun blasts and explosions, the serious, self-important voices of newscasters reporting their TV war.

A little while later, there was a quiet knock at my door, followed by a <u>tentative</u> attempt at the doorknob. "Cukita?" my mother whispered. "Open up, Cukita."

"Go away," I wailed, but we both knew I was glad she was there, and I needed only a moment's protest to save face before opening that door.

What we ended up doing that night was putting together a speech at the last moment. Two brief pages of stale compliments and the polite commonplaces[22] on teachers, wrought by necessity without much invention by mother for daughter late into the night in the basement on the pad of

Pedro Mañach (1901), Pablo Picasso. Oil on linen, 41 ½″ × 27 ½″. Chester Dale Collection, National Gallery of Art, Washington, D.C. Copyright © 1998 Board of Trustees of the National Gallery of Art.

---

22. **commonplaces:** overused remarks; clichés.

paper and with the same pencil she had once used for her own inventions, for I was too upset to compose the speech myself. After it was drafted, she typed it up while I stood by, correcting her misnomers[23] and mis-sayings.

She was so very proud of herself when I came home the next day with the success story of the assembly. The nuns had been flattered, the audience had stood up and given "our devoted teachers a standing ovation," what my mother had suggested they do at the end of my speech.

She clapped her hands together as I recreated the moment for her. "I stole that from your father's speech, remember? Remember how he put that in at the end?" She quoted him in Spanish, then translated for me into English.

That night, I watched him from the upstairs hall window where I'd retreated the minute I heard his car pull up in front of our house. Slowly, my father came up the driveway, a grim expression on his face as he grappled with a large, heavy cardboard box. At the front door, he set the package down carefully and patted all his pockets for his house keys—precisely why my mother had invented her ticking key chain. I heard the snapping open of the locks downstairs. Heard as he struggled to maneuver the box through the narrow doorway. Then, he called my name several times. But I would not answer him.

"My daughter, your father, he love you very much," he explained from the bottom of the stairs. "He just want to protect you." Finally, my mother came up and pleaded with me to go down and reconcile with him. "Your father did not mean to harm. You must pardon him. Always it is better to let bygones be forgotten, no?"

I guess she was right. Downstairs, I found him setting up a brand new electric typewriter on the kitchen table. It was even better than the one I'd been begging to get like my mother's. My father had outdone himself with all the extra features: a plastic carrying case with my initials, in decals, below the handle, a brace to lift the paper upright while I typed, an erase cartridge, an automatic margin tab, a plastic hood like a toaster cover to keep the dust away. Not even my mother, I think, could have invented such a machine!

But her inventing days were over just as mine were starting up with my schoolwide success. That's why I've always thought of that speech my mother wrote for me as her last invention rather than the suitcase rollers everyone else in the family remembers. It was as if she had passed on to me her pencil and pad and said, "Okay, Cukita, here's the buck. You give it a shot." ❖

_____

23. **misnomers** (mĭs-nō′mərz): wrong names.

WORDS
TO
KNOW

reconcile (rĕk′ən-sīl′) *v.* to reestablish a close relationship

674

Metaphor
Eve Merriam

Morning is
a new sheet of paper
for you to write on.

Whatever you want to say,
5 all day,
until night
folds it up
and files it away.

The bright words and the dark words
10 are gone
until dawn
and a new day
to write on.

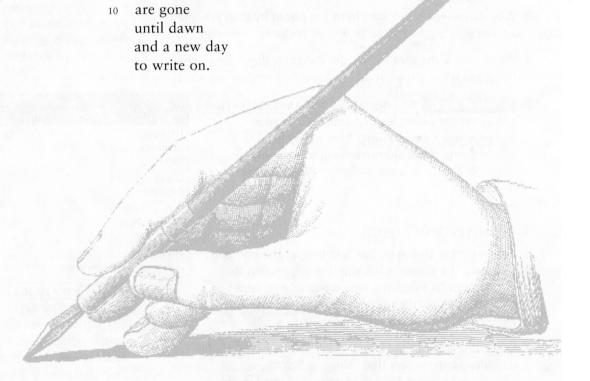

Thinking through the LITERATURE

Connect to the Literature

1. What Do You Think?
What thoughts do you have about the individual family members in this story?

> **Comprehension Check**
> - Why do the mother's inventions annoy her daughters?
> - How does the narrator's father react to his daughter's speech?
> - How does the mother help her daughter with the speech?
> - What does the father do at the end of the story?

Think Critically

2. How would you explain the father's reaction to the speech?

 THINK ABOUT
- his life in the Dominican Republic
- the cultural differences between his homeland and America
- his concerns about his daughter

3. Why do you think the lines from the **poem** by Walt Whitman inspire the daughter to write a speech she feels proud of?

4. Do you think the mother lets the daughter down when she helps her write a speech that is more flattering to the nuns?

5. **ACTIVE READING** **UNDERSTANDING CHARACTERIZATION**
Look over the examples that you cited in your **READER'S NOTEBOOK.** Based on your observations about **characterization** techniques, what do you think is the author's opinion of the mother?

Extend Interpretations

6. Critic's Corner One critic has said that, at the end of this story, the reader is left with the impression that the narrator "is living in a new world where even the old obstacles of culture can be overcome." Do you agree? Explain your answer.

7. Comparing Texts In the Literary Link "Metaphor" on page 675, Eve Merriam says that "Morning is a new sheet of paper for you to write on." How might the characters in "Mother of Invention" respond to this quotation?

8. Connect to Life At one point in the story the narrator describes her mother as "a good enough Mami . . . but a terrible girlfriend parent, a real failure of a Mom." Do you think a mother should be a "girlfriend parent" ? Explain.

Literary Analysis

AUTHOR'S PERSPECTIVE AND CHARACTERIZATION

In fiction, writers often express their own personal beliefs and feelings about life through their **characters.** While a particular fictional character may have strong opinions and attitudes, the author may portray those attitudes in such a way that suggests that his or her own viewpoint is very different.

Cooperative Learning Activity
Make a chart like the one shown below. With a partner, go back through the story and look for clues in the characterizations that reveal the author's perspective on each issue. Then describe what you think the author's perspective is. Compare your opinions with those of other classmates.

Issue	Clues in Characterizations	Author's Perspective
Life in the Dominican Republic		
Life in America		
Parent-Child Relationships		
The Role of Women		

REVIEW **DIALOGUE** **Dialogue—** written conversation between two or more characters—is one of a writer's most important tools in character development. What traits of the main characters in this story are developed primarily through dialogue?

Choices & CHALLENGES

Writing Options

1. Persuasive Letter Write a letter to the narrator's father, persuading him to let her give the original version of her speech. Include your interpretation of the lines from Walt Whitman that inspired the speech.

Writing Handbook
See page 1159: Persuasive Writing.

2. Comparison Paragraph In what ways are the narrator and her mother alike? How do they differ? Write a paragraph in which you point out the similarities and differences between the two

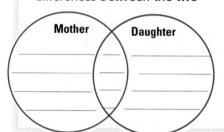

characters. You could use a Venn diagram to organize your thoughts.

3. Wacky-Character Sketch Write a description of a person you have known who was both odd and amusing, as the mother is in "Daughter of Invention." Place the sketch in your **Working Portfolio.**

Activities & Explorations

Untangling Sayings In the story, the mother uses "a mishmash of mixed-up idioms and sayings," for example, "Necessity is the daughter of invention." Find the correct wordings for this and other mixed-up sayings in the story. You may need to use a book of

proverbs or idioms. Then share your ideas about what the sayings mean. ~ **SPEAKING AND LISTENING**

Inquiry & Research

1. Comparing Cultures Using details from the story as well as information from encyclopedias or other sources, learn more about the geography, history, and culture of the Dominican Republic. Share your findings.

2. Whose Invention? In the story, the mother invents a suitcase on wheels, a product that is eventually designed and sold by someone else. Research how the mother could have profited from her ideas.

Real World Link Read the selection on page 679 as part of your research.

Vocabulary in Action

EXERCISE: CONTEXT CLUES Choose the word in parentheses that best completes each sentence.

1. Always full of clever ideas, the narrator's mother has sketched (insubordinate, innumerable) inventions.

2. She jots down her ideas on a pad of paper advertising an (antibiotic, insubordinate) or some other medicine.

3. With her unreliable grasp of English, she usually makes a mistake when trying to use an (idiom, antibiotic), such as "It takes two to tango."

4. Because the narrator finds New York so unfriendly and (innumerable, inhospitable), she spends her time writing stories and compositions.

5. She doesn't mean for her speech to (provoke, reconcile) her father, but he becomes enraged when he hears it.

6. Sure that he knows what is right, he is not at all (inhospitable, tentative) in his response to his daughter's speech.

7. He objects to some of his daughter's (innumerable, plagiarized) words not because he thinks they are stolen but because he thinks they are disrespectful.

8. In the Dominican Republic, people had been killed for expressing views the government regarded as (tentative, insubordinate).

9. When the narrator is finally ready to present her polite but insincere speech at school, her parents are full of pride, but she is probably (mortified, plagiarized).

10. After their fight, her father wants to make amends and (reconcile, provoke) with her.

WORDS TO KNOW	antibiotic	inhospitable	insubordinate	plagiarized	reconcile
	idiom	innumerable	mortified	provoke	tentative

Grammar in Context: Participial Phrases

In the following excerpts from "Daughter of Invention," Julia Alvarez uses participial phrases to create pictures of characters and in some cases to give a sense of ongoing action.

past participial phrase
Hunched over my small desk, . . . I wrote my secret poems in my new language.

present participial phrase
Week after week, I'd sit down, hoping to polish off some quick, noncommittal little speech.

A **participial phrase** consists of a participle—a verb form used as an adjective—along with its modifiers and complements. Besides using them to add details, writers use participial phrases as a way of varying their sentences. Without the participial phrases, the sentences above might sound monotonous: "I sat hunched over my small desk. . . . I wrote my secret poems. . . ." "Week after week, I'd sit down. I hoped to polish off . . ."

WRITING EXERCISE Combine each pair of sentences by changing one of them into a participial phrase. Underline the participial phrase.

Punctuation Tip: Participial phrases are usually set off with commas.

Example: *Original* The students marveled at the echo in the auditorium. They raised their voices even more.

Rewritten Marveling at the echo in the auditorium, the students raised their voices even more.

1. My mother worked on her inventions night after night. She bent over her drawings.
2. I studied hard at school. I hoped the other kids would like me.
3. Day after day I sat down to write. I was trying to think of something to say.
4. My mother listened to my speech. She beamed with pride.
5. My father chased me down the hall. He shouted that I was ungrateful and stupid.

Grammar Handbook Verbals, p. 1194

Julia Alvarez
1950–

Other Works
In the Time of the Butterflies
Homecoming

Immigrant Experience In 1960, when she was just ten years old, Julia Alvarez was forced to leave her homeland. Like the characters in "Daughter of Invention," she and her family emigrated to the United States from the Dominican Republic. Adapting to a new culture was difficult. In the Dominican Republic, Alvarez was an outgoing child and had many friends. As a new immigrant in New York City, she felt out of place and was sometimes the victim of insensitive name-calling. It was at this time that Alvarez began to write, finding comfort as she wrote down memories of her old life in the Dominican Republic.

College Experience Alvarez studied writing and literature in college and received a bachelor's degree from Middlebury College in Vermont and a master's degree from Syracuse University in New York. Later, she taught those same subjects at several different universities, including the University of Illinois and Middlebury College.

Literary Success Alvarez has won many awards for her writing, which includes novels and poetry as well as short stories. Her fiction often centers around the grim political history of the Dominican Republic as well as the experiences of Hispanic immigrants in New York City. Both her poetry and short stories have appeared in numerous magazines and anthologies.

If You Build It...

by Debra Phillips and Cynthia E. Griffin

Youth is not necessarily an impediment to inventing success—if anything, it may actually be an advantage. That's what Thomas Edison discovered. So, too, did Alexander Graham Bell. This month, we focus on young inventors and the road they took to build a better mousetrap.

YOU'RE NEVER TOO YOUNG

Suppose you're 10 years old and invent a spill-proof bowl. Can you get a patent? No problem, according to the U.S. Patent and Trademark Office, which places no limitation on how old a patent holder must be.

While there are no official limitations, 17-year-old Alexia Abernathy found there can be practical barriers. When she was a fifth grader, Abernathy created the Oops! Proof No-Spill Feeding Bowl for an Invent Iowa contest for young inventors. As the Cedar Rapids teen swept local, district, and regional competitions, she was encouraged to market her bowl.

"My dad talked to a friend who was a patent attorney because we both thought the next step would be to get a patent," says Abernathy.

The friend advised otherwise, saying it would cost several thousand dollars to complete the patent process. Instead, he suggested writing to companies to see if there was any interest in marketing the product. Abernathy wrote to 12 companies and eventually scored with Little Kids, Inc., an East Providence, Rhode Island, children's products man-ufacturer that wanted to market the bowl.

"We worked with them for close to a year, then applied for a joint patent," says Abernathy. "They paid for it and put my name on it. After about a year, we got a licensing agreement."

This is just one way young inventors can get a patent. You can also get a joint patent with a parent or get one in your own name.

ype a plus sign (+) inside this box → ☐

Under the Paperwork Reduction Act of 1995, no persons are required to respond to a collection of information unless it contains a valid OMB control number.

PTO/SB/01 (12-97)
Approved for use through 9/30/00. OMB 0651-0032
Patent and Trademark Office; U.S. DEPARTMENT OF COMMERCE

ECLARATION — Utility or Design Patent Application

laim the benefit under 35 U.S.C. 120 of any United States application(s), or 365(c) of any PCT international application designating the ates of America, listed below and, insofar as the subject matter of each of the claims of this application is not disclosed in the prior tes or PCT International application in the manner provided by the first paragraph of 35 U.S.C. 112, I acknowledge the duty to disclose which is material to patentability as defined in 37 CFR 1.56 which became available between the filing date of the prior application tional or PCT international filing date of this application.

U.S. Parent Application or PCT Parent Number	Parent Filing Date (MM/DD/YYYY)	Parent Patent Number (if applicable)

Reading for Information

Often you will be asked to do research on a specific topic and to report to others what you've learned. You might write a lengthy research report or oral presentation, or a brief review of the important information—a summary.

SUMMARIZING

A **summary** is a shortened version of a text and includes only the most important information.

YOUR TURN Use the questions and activities below to help you explore this article.

❶ Watch for facts and information that might express the main idea of the article. What important details about the patent process are included in this passage?

❷ **Inferring the Main Idea** In order to summarize what you read, you may need to state the main idea. Sometimes you have to infer (or make logical guesses about) that main idea from the whole text. What is the main idea of this article?

Summarizing Write a short summary of this article. Be sure to use your own words when explaining the main idea and supporting details.

Inquiry & Research

Activity Link: "Daughter of Invention," p. 677 After reading this article, what have you learned about the process of obtaining a patent? If you want to know more about the patent process, consult reference sources, including the Internet.

A Voice
Poetry by PAT MORA

The Journey
Poetry by MARY OLIVER

See art on page 682.

"One day you finally knew / what you had to do."

Connect to Your Life

Moment of Insight Part of growing up is recognizing that people whose job it is to take care of us—parents, teachers, and other adults in authority—are human, just as we are, and have experienced the same kinds of difficulties that we have. Think about a time when you had a moment of insight into the life of an adult close to you. Perhaps you felt sympathy with that person because of something he or she had gone through. Maybe you heard a story about something that had happened to this person when he or she was younger. Share this moment of insight with a classmate.

Build Background

Different Kinds of Learning
Young people frequently learn from the successes of those who are older and more experienced. However, we don't usually think of learning from their failures or from the times when they could not face a challenge. Both of the poems you are about to read are unusual in that they insist there is something to be learned from—and even admired in—an adult's *in*ability to face a particular situation. These poems suggest that there are other ways of thinking about courage, about success, and about how we learn from others.

Focus Your Reading

LITERARY ANALYSIS **AUTHOR'S PERSPECTIVE AND DICTION** A writer's **diction** or choice of words is an important clue to his or her own personal perspective. For example, in the first poem you are about to read, the poet uses the word *unrelenting* to describe lights on a stage. By choosing this word, she reveals an attitude toward the experience being described and toward the person having the experience. As you read these poems, notice what words the poets have chosen and think about what the choices reveal about each **author's perspective.**

ACTIVE READING **UNDERSTANDING DICTION** To gain a better understanding of a writer's use of **diction,** notice any words or phrases that strike you as vivid, unusual, or surprising or that have strong associations with particular experiences, situations, or feelings you've encountered in your own life.

READER'S NOTEBOOK For each poem, jot down at least three interesting word choices. Use a word web like the one shown to explore the word's meanings and associations.

A VOICE

Pat Mora

Even the lights on the stage unrelenting
as the desert sun couldn't hide the other
students, their eyes also unrelenting,
students who spoke English every night

5   as they ate their meat, potatoes, gravy.
Not you. In your house that smelled like
rose powder, you spoke Spanish formal
as your father, the judge without a courtroom

in the country he floated to in the dark
10 on a flatbed truck. He walked slow
as a hot river down the narrow hall
of your house. You never dared to race past him,

to say, "Please move," in the language
you learned effortlessly, as you learned to run,
15 the language forbidden at home, though your mother
said you learned it to fight with the neighbors.

You liked winning with words. You liked
writing speeches about patriotism and democracy.
You liked all the faces looking at you, all those eyes.
20 "How did I do it?" you ask me now. "How did I do it

when my parents didn't understand?"
The family story says your voice is the voice
of an aunt in Mexico, spunky as a peacock.
Family stories sing of what lives in the blood.

25 You told me only once about the time you went
to the state capitol, your family proud as if
you'd been named governor. But when you looked
around, the only Mexican in the auditorium,
you wanted to hide from those strange faces.

30 Their eyes were pinpricks, and you faked
hoarseness. You, who are never at a loss
for words, felt your breath stick in your throat

like an ice-cube. "I can't," you whispered.
"I can't." Yet you did. Not that day but years later.
35 You taught the four of us to speak up.
This is America, Mom. The undo-able is done

in the next generation. Your breath moves
through the family like the wind
moves through the trees.

Thinking Through the Literature

1. **Comprehension Check** What happens when the mother goes to the state capitol to give her speech?

2. Why does the mother suddenly become self-conscious about giving her speech at the State Capitol, when she usually likes "winning with words" and being looked at?

3. Why does the daughter interpret her mother's failure as a success and credit her with teaching her to speak up?

4. How do you interpret the speaker's statement that her mother's breath "moves / through the family like the wind / moves through the trees"?

Girls from Guadalupita, New Mexico, Miguel Martinez. Oil pastel on paper, 30″ × 40″. Contemporary Southwest Galleries, Sante Fe, New Mexico.

THE JOURNEY

Mary Oliver

One day you finally knew
what you had to do, and began,
though the voices around you
kept shouting
5 their bad advice—
though the whole house
began to tremble
and you felt the old tug
at your ankles.
10 "Mend my life!"
each voice cried.
But you didn't stop.
You knew what you had to do,
though the wind pried
15 with its stiff fingers
at the very foundations,
though their melancholy
was terrible.
It was already late
20 enough, and a wild night,
and the road full of fallen
branches and stones.
But little by little,
as you left their voices behind,
25 the stars began to burn
through the sheets of clouds,
and there was a new voice
which you slowly
recognized as your own,
30 that kept you company

as you strode deeper and deeper
into the world,
determined to do
the only thing you could do—
35 determined to save
the only life you could save.

17 melancholy (mĕl′ən-kŏl′ē):
great sadness; depression.

Connect to the Literature

1. **What Do You Think?**
   What is your reaction to what the "you" does in this poem?

   Comprehension Check
   • What keeps the "you" company in the poem?

Think Critically

2. Why must the "you" in the poem run away from the voices of others crying for help in order to find her own voice?

   THINK ABOUT
   • who tugs at her ankles crying, "Mend my life!"
   • why it takes her a while to recognize the new voice as her own
   • why her life is the only life she can save

3. **ACTIVE READING** **UNDERSTANDING DICTION** Look back at your **READER'S NOTEBOOK** to see what words you thought were particularly interesting. What effect do the words *strode* and *determined* have on your understanding of the poem?

4. Why does the **speaker** in the poem think that the "you" made the right decision to put herself first?

Extend Interpretations

5. **Comparing Texts** What personal qualities are being praised in "The Journey"? Compare these qualities to those being praised in "A Voice."

6. **Different Perspectives** Would it change the **theme** of "The Journey" if the speaker in the poem were a daughter talking to her mother, as in "A Voice"?

7. **Connect to Life** Is running away ever the most courageous response to a difficult situation? Explain your answer.

Literary Analysis

AUTHOR'S PERSPECTIVE AND DICTION

An **author's perspective** is the viewpoint he or she expresses in a piece of literature. In poetry, this perspective is often disclosed, in part, through **diction.** Diction is a writer's specific choice of words and the way those words are arranged in a sentence.

Paired Activity With a partner, review one of the poems and list several word choices that seem to you to be particularly effective. For each word, write down the definition or definitions of the word, other words the poet might have chosen instead, and the associations (or **connotations**) that the word has for you. Then, with a larger group, discuss what each word choice might reveal about the author's perspective.

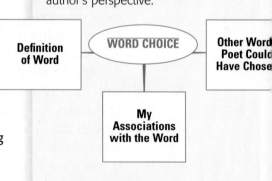

Definition of Word — **WORD CHOICE** — **Other Words Poet Could Have Chosen**

My Associations with the Word

Building Vocabulary
For an in-depth lesson on connotation and denotation, see page 686.

Choices & CHALLENGES

Writing Options

1. Letter of Praise Think back to the person you identified in the Connect to Your Life on page 680. Write a short letter to this person explaining your appreciation of him or her.

Dear Grandma,

2. Personal Narrative Write a short narrative about a time when you or someone you know "froze" while delivering a speech or performing in front of others. Use sensory details to capture the experience.

Activities & Explorations

Spiritual Map Both "A Voice" and "The Journey" deal with journeys that are psychological or emotional as well as physical. Draw a map that represents the path of your own journey of the spirit, either as it is or as you would like it to be. Think about the type of road, the destination, and the geography that you will include in your map. Include a key to explain what different things on your map represent. **~ VIEWING AND REPRESENTING**

Pat Mora
1942–

Other Works
Borders
Agua Santa/Holy Water
House of Houses

Bilingual Beginnings Pat Mora grew up in El Paso, Texas. When she was young, she spoke Spanish at home with her grandmother and aunt. She now feels fortunate to have belonged to a bilingual household, but as a girl she sometimes tried to keep her classmates from finding out that she spoke Spanish.

Writing Out of a Heritage Mora's poetry reflects her ethnic heritage and her feeling for the Southwestern landscape. She thinks it is important for her as a Mexican-American woman to contribute to the diversity of American literature. "I also write," she says, "because I am fascinated by the pleasure and power of words."

Mary Oliver
1935–

Other Works
American Primitive
New and Selected Poems
Blue Pastures

Befriending the Poets When Mary Oliver was growing up in Ohio in the 1950s, she felt isolated from the mainstream culture around her. She came to feel that some of her closest friends were the poets she read, especially Walt Whitman. She learned from Whitman that "the poem was made not just to exist, but to speak—to be company."

Award-Winning Writing Oliver has won major awards for her poetry, including the Pulitzer Prize and the National Book Award. In addition to writing, she has taught poetry at various colleges. Critics often praise her intensely lyrical voice. Many of her poems are inspired by her observations of nature in Ohio and New England, where she has lived for much of her adult life.

Understanding Careful Word Choice

Good writers choose their words carefully. They think about words' literal meanings, of course, but they also consider the implied meanings and associations that words have. Read the sentence on the right and think about why Julia Alvarez used *thronged* instead of some other word.

Alvarez could have chosen the word *filled* or *crowded* instead of *thronged*, but her description would have been less precise. *Thronged* implies a

> Now in America, he was safe, a success even; his Centro Medico in Brooklyn was **thronged** with the sick and the homesick.
> —Julia Alvarez, "Daughter of Invention"

crowd of people pressing in, conveying just the right image in the context of the description.

Strategies for Building Vocabulary

A word's literal meaning or definition is called its **denotation.** A word may also have an implied meaning, an association that evokes a particular emotion. This is the word's **connotation.** Synonyms have similar denotations, but their connotations may differ. By being aware of the connotations of words, you can improve your understanding of literature and enhance your writing.

❶ **Look Beyond the Literal** Some words have an attitude. Writers use them to evoke their positive or negative connotations. Read the following example, noting the use of the word *concocted*:

> There was no way we could tell Mom we'd broken her prized vase. So we **concocted** a story about the doorbell ringing and the dog jumping up and knocking over the table.

The word *concocted* is a good choice because its negative association with scheming and lying perfectly fits the situation.

❷ **Consider Connotations** When you are writing, think about the connotations of the words you use. Consider whether particular words have positive associations or negative associations. The chart below shows some examples.

Positive Connotation	Negative Connotation
gaze	gape
modest	severe

The verbs *gaze* and *gape* both mean "to look intently." *Gaze,* however, has a positive connotation of looking at something with wonder, whereas *gape* connotes a look that is open-mouthed and stupid. In a similar way, *modest* connotes an absence of showiness, but *severe* has a negative connotation, implying an extreme plainness. If you are not sure about words' connotations, a dictionary of synonyms, a thesaurus, or a standard English dictionary can help you.

EXERCISE Think about the difference in connotation between the words in each pair below. (A dictionary may help you to clarify the difference.) Then write a sentence containing each word, making sure that the sentence reflects the word's connotation. Compare your sentences with a partner's and discuss the words' connotations.

1. innocent/naive
2. quibble/argue
3. observe/snoop
4. brash/brazen
5. deliberate/slow

POWDER

TOBIAS WOLFF

Although Tobias Wolff did not base the story on actual events, "Powder" was inspired by his father. As Wolff says, "My own father has been dead some 30 years now. . . . This story is a way, my only way, of having him back for a while in all his outlaw charm and maddening, tragic irresponsibility."

J ust before Christmas my father took me skiing at Mount Baker.[1] He'd had to fight for the privilege of my company, because my mother was still angry with him for sneaking me into a nightclub during his last visit, to see Thelonious Monk.[2]

He wouldn't give up. He promised, hand on heart, to take good care of me and have me home for dinner on Christmas Eve, and she relented. But as we were checking out of the lodge that morning it began to snow, and in this snow he observed some rare quality that made it necessary for us to get in one last run. We got in several last runs. He was indifferent to my fretting. Snow whirled around us in bitter, blinding squalls, hissing like sand, and still we skied. As the lift bore us to the peak yet again, my father looked at his watch and said, "Criminy. This'll have to be a fast one."

By now I couldn't see the trail. There was no point in trying. I stuck to him like white on rice and did what he did and somehow made it to the bottom without sailing off a cliff. We returned our skis and my father put chains on the Austin-Healey[3] while I swayed from foot to foot, clapping my mittens and wishing I was home. I could see everything. The green tablecloth, the plates with the holly pattern, the red candles waiting to be lit.

We passed a diner on our way out. "You want some soup?" my father asked. I shook my head. "Buck up," he said. "I'll get you there. Right, doctor?"

I was supposed to say, "Right, doctor," but I didn't say anything.

A state trooper waved us down outside the resort. A pair of sawhorses were blocking the road. The trooper came up to our car and bent down to my father's window. His face was bleached by the cold. Snowflakes clung to his eyebrows and to the fur trim of his jacket and cap.

"Don't tell me," my father said.

The trooper told him. The road was closed. It might get cleared, it might not. Storm took everyone by surprise. So much, so fast. Hard to get people moving. Christmas Eve. What can you do.

My father said, "Look. We're talking about five, six inches. I've taken this car through worse than that."

The trooper straightened up. His face was out of sight but I could hear him. "The road is closed."

My father sat with both hands on the wheel, rubbing the wood with his thumbs. He looked at the barricade for a long time. He seemed to be trying to master the idea of it. Then he thanked the trooper, and with a weird, old-maidy show of caution turned the car around. "Your mother will never forgive me for this," he said.

"We should have left before," I said. "Doctor."

He didn't speak to me again until we were in a booth at the diner, waiting for our burgers. "She won't forgive me," he said. "Do you understand? Never."

"I guess," I said, but no guesswork was required; she wouldn't forgive him.

"I can't let that happen." He bent toward me. "I'll tell you what I want. I want us all to be together again. Is that what you want?"

"Yes, sir."

He bumped my chin with his knuckles. "That's all I needed to hear."

When we finished eating he went to the pay phone in the back of the diner, then joined me

---

1. **Mount Baker:** a mountain in northern Washington State.
2. **Thelonious Monk** (thə-lō′nē-əs mŭngk): American jazz pianist whose unique style made him one of the most influential modern jazz musicians.
3. **Austin-Healy:** an English sports car.

"YOUR MOTHER WILL NEVER FORGIVE ME FOR THIS," HE SAID.

in the booth again. I figured he'd called my mother, but he didn't give a report. He sipped at his coffee and stared out the window at the empty road. "Come on, come on," he said, though not to me. A little while later he said it again. When the trooper's car went past, lights flashing, he got up and dropped some money on the check. "Okay. *Vamanos.*"[4]

The wind had died. The snow was falling straight down, less of it now and lighter. We drove away from the resort, right up to the barricade. "Move it," my father told me. When I looked at him he said, "What are you waiting for?" I got out and dragged one of the sawhorses aside, then put it back after he drove through. He pushed the door open for me. "Now you're an accomplice," he said. "We go down together." He put the car into gear and gave me a look. "Joke, son."

Down the first long stretch I watched the road behind us, to see if the trooper was on our tail. The barricade vanished. Then there was nothing but snow: snow on the road, snow kicking up from the chains, snow on the trees, snow in the sky; and our trail in the snow. Then I faced forward and had a shock. The lay of the road behind us had been marked by our own tracks, but there were no tracks ahead of us. My father was breaking virgin snow between a line of tall trees. He was humming

"Stars Fell on Alabama." I felt snow brush along the floorboards under my feet. To keep my hands from shaking I clamped them between my knees.

My father grunted in a thoughtful way and said, "Don't ever try this yourself."

"I won't."

"That's what you say now, but someday you'll get your license and then you'll think you can do anything. Only you won't be able to do this. You need, I don't know—a certain instinct."

"Maybe I have it."

"You don't. You have your strong points, but not this. I only mention it because I don't want you to get the idea this is something just anybody can do. I'm a great driver. That's not a virtue, okay? It's just a fact, and one you should be aware of. Of course you have to give the old heap some credit, too. There aren't many cars I'd try this with. Listen!"

I did listen. I heard the slap of the chains, the stiff, jerky rasp of the wipers, the purr of the engine. It really did purr. The old heap was almost new. My father couldn't afford it, and kept promising to sell it, but here it was.

I said, "Where do you think that policeman went to?"

"Are you warm enough?" He reached over and cranked up the blower. Then he turned off the wipers. We didn't need them. The clouds had brightened. A few sparse, feathery flakes

---

4. **Vámanos** (vä′mô-nôs) *Spanish:* Let's go. Proper spelling is vámonos.

drifted into our slipstream[5] and were swept away. We left the trees and entered a broad field of snow that ran level for a while and then tilted sharply downward. Orange stakes had been planted at intervals in two parallel lines and my father steered a course between them, though they were far enough apart to leave considerable doubt in my mind as to exactly where the road lay. He was humming again, doing little scat riffs[6] around the melody.

"Okay then. What are my strong points?"

"Don't get me started," he said. "It'd take all day."

"Oh, right. Name one."

"Easy. You always think ahead."

True. I always thought ahead. I was a boy who kept his clothes on numbered hangers to insure proper rotation. I bothered my teachers for homework assignments far ahead of their due dates so I could draw up schedules. I thought ahead, and that was why I knew that there would be other troopers waiting for us at the end of our ride, if we even got there. What I did not know was that my father would wheedle and plead his way past them—he didn't sing "O Tannenbaum," but just about—and get me home for dinner, buying a little more time before my mother decided to make the split final. I knew we'd

get caught; I was resigned to it. And maybe for this reason I stopped moping and began to enjoy myself.

Why not? This was one for the books. Like being in a speedboat, only better. You can't go downhill in a boat. And it was all ours. And it kept coming, the laden trees, the unbroken surface of snow, the sudden white vistas. Here and there I saw hints of the road, ditches, fences, stakes, but not so many that I could have found my way. But then I didn't have to. My father was driving. My father in his forty-eighth year, rumpled, kind, bankrupt of honor, flushed with certainty. He was a great driver. All persuasion, no coercion.[7] Such subtlety at the wheel, such tactful pedalwork. I actually trusted him. And the best was yet to come—switchbacks and hairpins[8] impossible to describe. Except maybe to say this: if you haven't driven fresh powder, you haven't driven.

---

5. **slipstream:** the area of reduced air pressure and forward suction behind a fast-moving vehicle.

6. **scat riffs:** jazz singing in which improvised, meaningless syllables are sung to short, rhythmic melodies.

7. **coercion** (kō-ûr′zhən): force.

8. **switchbacks and hairpins:** zigzags and sharp turns.

Tobias Wolff
1945—

Other Works
The Night in Question
The Barracks Thief
This Boy's Life

Early Years When Tobias Wolff was five years old, his parents divorced. Wolff, who remained with his mother, lost contact with his father and his brother Geoffrey (who also became a writer). Wolff's mother remarried, and Wolff did not get along

with his stepfather. His troubles at home led him to drop out of high school. He later wrote about this period in his memoir *This Boy's Life,* which was the basis for a film starring Robert De Niro and Leonardo DiCaprio.

Literary Career Wolff is best known for his short stories, which have appeared in many anthologies and have won major awards. He says that his stories usually come from unexpected places: The original idea for the story is most often a kind of cocoon in which the real story develops. Wolff teaches English at Stanford University.

Author Study
Sandra Cisneros

"Her work is sensitive, alert, nuanceful . . . rich with music and picture."

—*Gwendolyn Brooks*

1954–

The Voice of a Latina Writer

Inspired by the people from the Spanish-speaking neighborhood in her native Chicago, Sandra Cisneros (sĭs-nĕr′ōs) *was one of the first Chicana writers to chronicle life in the barrio, or neighborhood. Her award-winning work of fiction* The House on Mango Street *(1984) brings to life the many different voices of that community. Learn more about this contemporary Mexican-American writer whose work speaks for those who have been silenced because of their gender, class, or race.*

"A HOUSE ALL MY OWN" Sandra Cisneros was born in Chicago, Illinois, on December 20, 1954. The daughter of a Mexican father, Alfredo, and a Mexican-American mother, Elvira Cordero, she grew up poor in a family with six brothers. Because of her father's homesickness, Cisneros's family moved frequently between Mexico City and Chicago when she was a young girl. She never remained in one place long enough to make close friends, and she longed for a "perfect" house like the ones she read about and saw on TV. In 1966 the Cisneros

1954
Is born Dec. 20 in Chicago, Illinois

HER LIFE
HER TIMES

1955

1960

1954
USSR opens the world's first nuclear power station.

1959
First U.S. casualties in Vietnam War

LITERARY Contributions

A versatile writer, Cisneros has published poems and essays as well as fiction. Since her groundbreaking work, *The House on Mango Street,* first appeared in 1984, she has continued to focus on the experiences of Hispanic women in contemporary American society.

Poetry Many of Cisneros's poems stretch the boundaries of poetry by incorporating elements of fiction. Her poetry collections include the following:

> *Bad Boys* (1980)
> *The Rodrigo Poems* (1985)
> *My Wicked Wicked Ways* (1987)

Fiction A poetic quality is evident in these works of fiction:

> *The House on Mango Street* (1984)
> *Woman Hollering Creek and Other Stories* (1991)

Essays In addition to "Only Daughter" and "On Writing *The House on Mango Street,*" her essays include the following:

> **"Straw into Gold: The Metamorphosis of the Everyday"** (1987)
> **"An Offering to the Power of Language"** (1997)
> **"The Genius of Creative Flexibility"** (1998)

family did move into their first house. However, like the house described in her book *The House on Mango Street,* it was not the dream house that Cisneros had imagined.

"MY OWN QUIET WAR" Growing up in a male-dominated household where her father and six brothers were the figures of authority, Cisneros quietly rebelled against the traditional role she was expected to play as a Mexican-American female. She wrote secretly at home and openly expressed her creativity in high school only in her editing of the literary magazine. Determined to get an education, she attended Loyola University in Chicago, where she took her first creative writing class in 1974. After graduating from college in 1976, Cisneros enrolled in the master of fine arts program at the University of Iowa. Her discovery in graduate school that she was different from others in her writing classes helped her find her literary voice—a voice that reflected her own unique ethnic and cultural background.

"I LIKE TO TELL STORIES" What Cisneros wrote first was *The House on Mango Street,* a series of 44 related prose vignettes—short literary sketches—narrated by Esperanza Cordero, a young girl growing up in a Chicago barrio. Cisneros spent the next several years working as an administrative assistant at Loyola University, a teacher to high school dropouts at Chicago's Latino Youth Alternative High School, a poet-in-residence at schools, and a visiting writer at colleges.

1966
Cisneros family moves to a Puerto Rican neighborhood in Chicago.

1976
Receives B.A. in English from Loyola University

1978
Earns M.F.A. from the University of Iowa's Writers' Workshop; begins teaching

1982
Receives National Endowment for the Arts fellowship for poetry

1965 — **1970** — **1975** — **1980**

1965
Cesar Chavez launches nationwide boycott of California grapes.

1970
Texan José Angel Gutiérrez forms *La Raza Unida.*

1973
U.S. troops withdraw from Vietnam.

1980
Ronald Reagan is elected president.

In 1986 Cisneros relocated to Texas, where she was able to write full time with a Dobie-Paisano fellowship. After the fellowship was finished, she struggled to make a living. She passed out flyers in supermarkets and laundromats to advertise her writing workshop but could not generate enough responses. Fortunately, a second National Endowment for the Arts fellowship eased her financial troubles and afforded her the time to continue writing.

In 1991 Cisneros became the first Chicana writer to earn a major publishing contract. In that same year she published *Woman Hollering Creek and Other Stories*, a collection of stories about the lives of Hispanic women on both sides of the Texas-Mexico border.

Considered one of the foremost Chicana writers today, Cisneros continues to speak for the powerless—the poor, the oppressed, those who do not feel they are a part of mainstream American culture. According to Cisneros, "The meaning of literary success is that I could change the way someone thinks about my community, or my gender, or my class."

More Online: Author Link
www.mcdougallittell.com

LaserLinks: Background for Reading
Author Background

Cisneros outside her home in San Antonio. Photo copyright © Bryce Harper.

House Rules

Like Esperanza, the narrator in *The House on Mango Street*, Cisneros desperately longed for a house of her own when she was a young girl. Ironically, in 1997 she caused a public stir after having her Victorian home in the historic King William district of San Antonio, Texas, painted bright purple. Appearing at a hearing of the historic review board, Cisneros failed to defend her color choice but was instead given permission to paint her house bright pink, another traditional Texas color. For Cisneros, however, the battle was not over. She said, "This is not about a capricious woman who wanted to paint her house purple. This is about Mexican history counting in this part of the world."

1985	1987	1988	1991	1995	1997
Wins Before Columbus American Book Award; publishes *The Rodrigo Poems*	Publishes a third collection of poems, *My Wicked Wicked Ways*	Receives National Endowment for the Arts fellowship	Publishes *Woman Hollering Creek and Other Stories*, which wins the *L.A. Times* Book Award	Wins MacArthur Foundation Fellowship	Her father, Alfredo, dies.

1985   **1990**   **1995**   **2000**

1984	1989	1992	1994
Geraldine Ferraro is the first woman to run for the vice presidency on a major party's ticket.	Communist governments fall in Czechoslovakia, East Germany, and Hungary.	Bill Clinton is elected president.	Peasants in southern Mexican state of Chiapas rebel against national government.

"I am the only daughter in a family of six sons. That explains everything."

Only Daughter

Personal Essay by SANDRA CISNEROS

Connect to Your Life

Gender Roles During the 1960s, the women's movement reawakened in the United States. Since then, ideas about the proper roles of males and females have changed dramatically. For example, people have grown more accustomed to girls' being athletic and participating in traditionally all-male sports such as basketball, soccer, and field hockey. In a class discussion, share your thoughts about the roles of males and females today. Discuss gender roles at school, at home, in the workplace, and in the community.

Build Background

Traditional Values In her personal essay "Only Daughter," Cisneros describes her father's ideas about the proper role of females. Coming from the culture of old Mexico, Cisneros's father holds the patriarchal beliefs of many traditional cultures—that is, he considers men the heads of families and the leaders of society. According to the values of the culture in which Cisneros's father was raised, a woman needs only to "become someone's wife" and devote herself to her home and family.

WORDS TO KNOW
Vocabulary Preview
anthology
embroider
fulfill
nostalgia
trauma

Focus Your Reading

LITERARY ANALYSIS **THEME** The **theme** of a work of literature is the central idea or message. Theme should not be confused with subject, or what the work is about. Rather, theme is a perception about life or human nature. As you read this personal essay, think about the perceptions Cisneros shares with you. Keep in mind that the central message she conveys in the essay is drawn from her own unique perspective as a woman, as a Mexican American, and as an only daughter in a family of six sons.

ACTIVE READING **UNDERSTANDING GENERALIZATIONS** A **generalization** is a broad statement about a number of people or things. Valid generalizations are based on a wide range of evidence. "Edgar Allan Poe's short stories rarely contain humor," for instance, is a valid generalization when made by someone who has read many of Poe's stories. Notice, moreover, that the word *rarely* qualifies the statement, so that it is not claiming to be universally true. On the other hand, the statement "Dogs are better pets than cats" is an example of a faulty generalization. Generalizations can be faulty if they are

- overgeneralized, lack the support of backup evidence, or contain the words *all, one, every,* or *never*
- stereotyped, or based on fixed, unfair ideas about all members of ethnic, racial, or other groups

READER'S NOTEBOOK As you read this selection, use a chart like the one shown here to judge the accuracy of the generalizations you find about females and their roles. Write each generalization in the first column, then put a check in one of the other columns to classify it.

Generalization	Valid	Overgeneralized	Stereotyped

Only Daughter

Sandra Cisneros

Once, several years ago, when I was just starting out my writing career, I was asked to write my own contributor's note for an anthology I was part of. I wrote: "I am the only daughter in a family of six sons. *That* explains everything."

Well, I've thought about that ever since, and yes, it explains a lot to me, but for the reader's sake I should have written: "I am the only daughter in a *Mexican* family of six sons." Or even: "I am the only daughter of a Mexican farmer and a Mexican-American mother." Or: "I am the only daughter of a working-class family of nine." All of these had everything to do with who I am today.

I was/am the only daughter and *only* a daughter. Being an only daughter in a family of six sons forced me by circumstance to spend a lot of time by myself because my brothers felt it beneath them to play with a *girl* in public. But that aloneness, that loneliness, was good for a would-be writer— it allowed me time to think and think, to imagine, to read and prepare myself.

Being only a daughter for my father meant my destiny would

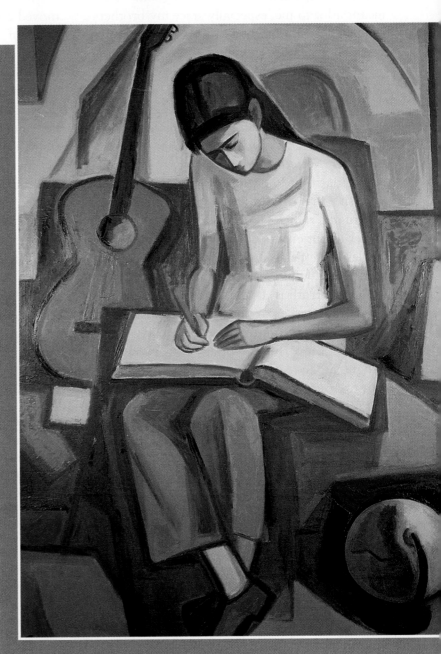

Student with Guitar (1975), Simon Samsonian. Oil on canvas, 52″ × 37″, private collection, New York.

lead me to become someone's wife. That's what he believed. But when I was in the fifth grade and shared my plans for college with him, I was sure he understood. I remember my father saying, *"Que bueno, mi'ja,*[1] that's good." That meant a lot to me, especially since my brothers thought the idea hilarious. What I didn't realize was that my father thought college was good for girls—good for finding a husband. After four years in college and two more in graduate school and still no husband, my father shakes his head even now and says I wasted all that education.

In retrospect, I'm lucky my father believed daughters were meant for husbands. It meant it didn't matter if I majored in something silly like English. After all, I'd find a nice professional eventually, right? This allowed me the liberty to putter about <u>embroidering</u> my little poems and stories without my father interrupting with so much as a "What's that you're writing?"

But the truth is, I wanted him to interrupt. I wanted my father to understand what it was I was scribbling, to introduce me as "My only daughter, the writer." Not as "This is only my daughter. She teaches." *Es maestra*[2]—teacher. Not even *profesora.*[3]

In a sense, everything I have ever written has been for him, to win his approval even though I know my father can't read English words, even though my father's only reading includes the brown-ink *Esto* sports magazines from Mexico City and the bloody ¡*Alarma!* magazines that feature yet another sighting of *La Virgen de Guadalupe*[4] on a tortilla or a wife's revenge on her philandering[5] husband by bashing his skull in with a *molcajete*[6] (a kitchen mortar[7] made of volcanic rock). Or the *fotonovelas,*[8] the little picture paperbacks with tragedy and <u>trauma</u> erupting from the characters' mouths in bubbles.

My father represents, then, the public majority. A public who is disinterested in reading, and yet one whom I am writing about and for and privately trying to woo.

When we were growing up in Chicago, we moved a lot because of my father. He suffered bouts of <u>nostalgia</u>. Then we'd have to let go our flat, store the furniture with mother's relatives, load the station wagon with baggage and bologna sandwiches, and head south. To Mexico City.

We came back, of course. To yet another Chicago flat, another Chicago neighborhood, another Catholic school. Each time, my father would seek out the parish priest in order to get a tuition break and complain or boast: "I have seven sons."

He meant *siete hijos,*[9] seven children, but he translated it as "sons." "I have seven sons." To anyone who would listen. The Sears Roebuck employee who sold us the washing machine. The short-order cook where my father ate his ham-and-eggs breakfasts. "I have seven sons." As if he deserved a medal from the state.

My papa. He didn't mean anything by that mistranslation, I'm sure. But somehow I could feel myself being erased. I'd tug my father's sleeve and whisper: "Not seven sons. Six! and *one daughter.*"

---

1. *Que bueno, mi'ja* (kĕ bwĕ'nô mē'hä) *Spanish:* That's good, my daughter. (*Mi'ja* is a shortened form of *mi hija.*)
2. *Es maestra* (ĕs mä-ĕs'trä) *Spanish:* She is a teacher.
3. *profesora* (prô-fĕ-sô'rä) *Spanish:* professor.
4. *La Virgen de Guadalupe* (lä vēr'hĕn dĕ gwä-dä-lōō'pĕ) *Spanish:* the Virgin of Guadalupe. According to legend, a vision of Mary, the virgin mother of Jesus, appeared on a hill outside Mexico City in 1531.
5. **philandering:** engaging in many casual love affairs.
6. *molcajete* (môl-kä-hĕ'tĕ) *Spanish.*
7. **mortar:** a bowl for grinding up grain.
8. *fotonovelas* (fô-tô-nô-vĕ'läs) *Spanish.*
9. *siete hijos* (syĕ'tĕ ē'hôs) *Spanish.* (*Hijos* can mean either "children" or "sons.")

WORDS TO KNOW
embroider (ĕm-broi'dər) *v.* to add imaginative details to; ornament
trauma (trou'mə) *n.* a serious physical or emotional shock or injury
nostalgia (nŏ-stăl'jə) *n.* a bittersweet longing for something or someone in the past

When my oldest brother graduated from medical school, he <u>fulfilled</u> my father's dream that we study hard and use this—our heads, instead of this—our hands. Even now my father's hands are thick and yellow, stubbed by a history of hammer and nails and twine and coils and springs. "Use this," my father said, tapping his head, "and not this," showing us those hands. He always looked tired when he said it.

Wasn't college an investment? And hadn't I spent all those years in college? And if I didn't marry, what was it all for? Why would anyone go to college and then choose to be poor? Especially someone who had always been poor.

Last year, after ten years of writing professionally, the financial rewards started to trickle in. My second National Endowment for the Arts Fellowship.[10] A guest professorship at the University of California, Berkeley. My book, which sold to a major New York publishing house.

At Christmas, I flew home to Chicago. The house was throbbing, same as always; hot *tamales*[11] and sweet *tamales* hissing in my mother's pressure cooker, and everybody—my mother, six brothers, wives, babies, aunts, cousins—talking too loud and at the same time, like in a Fellini[12] film, because that's just how we are.

I went upstairs to my father's room. One of my stories had just been translated into Spanish and published in an anthology of Chicano[13] writing, and I wanted to show it to him. Ever since he recovered from a stroke two years ago, my father likes to spend his leisure hours horizontally. And that's how I found him, watching a Pedro Infante[14] movie on Galavisión[15] and eating rice pudding.

There was a glass filmed with milk on the bedside table. There were several vials of pills and balled Kleenex. And on the floor, one black sock and a plastic urinal that I didn't want to look at but looked at anyway. Pedro Infante was about to burst into song, and my father was laughing.

I'm not sure if it was because my story was translated into Spanish or because it was published in Mexico or perhaps because the story dealt with Tepeyac,[16] the *colonia* my father was raised in and the house he grew up in, but at any rate, my father punched the mute button on his remote control and read my story.

I sat on the bed next to my father and waited. He read it very slowly. As if he were reading each line over and over. He laughed at all the right places and read lines he liked out loud. He pointed and asked questions: "Is this So-and-so?"

"Yes," I said. He kept reading.

When he was finally finished, after what seemed like hours, my father looked up and asked: "Where can we get more copies of this for the relatives?"

Of all the wonderful things that happened to me last year, that was the most wonderful. ❖

---

10. **National Endowment for the Arts Fellowship:** The National Endowment for the Arts (NEA)—a U.S. government agency—awards money in the form of fellowships to artists and writers.

11. *tamales* (tä-mä′lĕs) *Spanish:* rolls of cornmeal dough filled with meat and peppers and steamed in cornhusk wrappings.

12. **Fellini:** the Italian movie director Federico Fellini (1920–1994), famous for his noisy, energetic films.

13. **Chicano:** Mexican-American.

14. **Pedro Infante:** a popular Mexican film star.

15. **Galavisión:** a cable TV network that features movies and programs in Spanish.

16. **Tepeyac** (tĕ-pĕ-yäk′): a district of Mexico City.

WORDS TO KNOW **fulfill** (fo͝ol-fĭl′) *v.* to achieve; make a reality

The Dream Tree, Daniel Nevins. Private Collection/SuperStock.

Sandra Cisneros

If you are a poet, you will see clearly that there is a cloud floating in this sheet of paper.
—*Thich Nhat Hanh*

Before you became a cloud, you were an ocean, roiled and murmuring like a mouth. You were the shadow of a cloud crossing over a field of tulips. You were the tears of a man who cried into a plaid handkerchief. You were a sky without a hat. Your heart puffed and flowered like sheets drying on a line.

And when you were a tree, you listened to trees and the tree things trees told you. You were the wind in the wheels of a red bicycle. You were the spidery *María* tattooed on the hairless arm of a boy in downtown Houston. You were the rain rolling off the waxy leaves of a magnolia tree. A lock of straw-colored hair wedged between the mottled pages of a Victor Hugo novel. A crescent of soap. A spider the color of a fingernail. The black nets beneath the sea of olive trees. A skein of blue wool. A tea saucer wrapped in newspaper. An empty cracker tin. A bowl of blueberries in heavy cream. White wine in a green-stemmed glass.

And when you opened your wings to wind, across the punched-tin sky above a prison courtyard, those condemned to death and those condemned to life watched how smooth and sweet a white cloud glides.

1. What Do You Think? How did this selection affect your thoughts about gender roles?

Comprehension Check
- Why does Cisneros's father say she "wasted" her education?
- What does Cisneros's father typically read?
- How does Cisneros's father react as he reads his daughter's translated work of fiction?

Think Critically

2. **ACTIVE READING** **UNDERSTANDING GENERALIZATIONS**
Look over the chart of generalizations that you made in your **READER'S NOTEBOOK.** How might those generalizations have affected Cisneros as she was growing up?

3. How would you describe Cisneros's relationship with her father?

4. Why do you think Cisneros says that everything she has ever written has been written to win her father's approval?

THINK ABOUT {
- her role in her home as she was growing up
- her father's attitude toward her and her writing

5. In what ways do you think Cisneros lived her life on her own terms?

Extend Interpretations

6. Different Perspectives What if Cisneros's father were to write his own "Only Daughter" essay, on the subject of his daughter's upbringing? How might his viewpoint differ from his daughter's?

7. Comparing Texts How would you compare Cisneros's father's reactions to her aspirations with the ways in which Richard Wright's family reacts to his aspirations in the excerpt from *Black Boy* (page 654)?

8. Connect to Life Think about Cisneros's essay "Only Daughter" and the poem "Cloud." Which of these two would you say relates more to your life? Explain.

Literary Analysis

THEME A story's **theme** is the central idea or ideas the writer wishes to share with the reader. The idea may be a lesson about life or about people and their actions that the story conveys. Although "Only Daughter" is a work of nonfiction, it is still a story that Sandra Cisneros tells and has a theme that she wishes to share with her readers.

Sometimes the theme of a work of literature is directly stated; at other times it is implied, and the reader must infer the theme. One way to discover the theme is to think about what happens to the central characters or people. The importance of those events, stated in terms that apply to all human beings, is often the theme.

Activity What idea about life do you think Cisneros wants the reader to understand? In one or two sentences, state what you feel the theme of "Only Daughter" is, and share your statement with the class.

Choices & CHALLENGES

Writing Options

1. Five-minute Dialogue Imagine that you are the young Cisneros and your father has just bragged to a salesclerk that he has seven sons. Write a short dialogue between you and your father, in which you politely but forcefully correct him.

2. A Prose Poem The poem "Cloud" is written in free verse. Using this poem as a model, create your own poem that describes what it is like for Cisneros to be the only daughter.

3. A Stamp of Approval Write a proverb—a short, wise saying that expresses a basic truth—about a kind of approval that children seek from their parents.

Activities & Explorations

1. Family Interview Interview any older relatives to find out the ideas about gender roles that were common when they were growing up. Share with your classmates how ideas have changed in one or two generations. ~ **SPEAKING AND LISTENING**

2. Gender Roles With a small group of classmates, investigate differences in gender roles in different cultures of the world. For example, you might consider Japan, India, and Saudi Arabia. Concentrate on two or three differences and list these on a chart that you will present to class. ~ **VIEWING AND REPRESENTING**

3. Genealogical Diagram Cisneros has six brothers and is the only daughter in her family. Create a family tree, for yourself or a friend, that includes the following: parents, siblings, grandparents, aunts, uncles, and cousins. ~ **VIEWING AND REPRESENTING**

Inquiry & Research

Mexican-American Culture Find out more about the Mexican-American culture that Cisneros writes about. What are some of its values, traditions, and customs? To find information, interview a Mexican-American classmate, or use print resources such as periodicals and encyclopedias or nonprint resources such as the internet and databases. Then present your findings to the class in an oral report.

 More Online: Research Starter
www.mcdougallittell.com

Vocabulary in Action

EXERCISE: MEANING CLUES Review the Words to Know at the bottom of the selection pages. Then read each book title below and write the vocabulary word that you would expect to find in that book.

1. *A Stitch in Time*
2. *You Can Make Your Dreams Come True*
3. *First Aid on the Battlefield*
4. *The Best Short Stories of the Nineties*
5. *The Good Old Days and Why We Miss Them*

WORDS TO KNOW	anthology	fulfill	trauma
	embroider	nostalgia	

from **The House on Mango Street**

Fiction by SANDRA CISNEROS

"I knew then I had to have a house. A real house. One I could point to. But this isn't it."

Connect to Your Life

Home Sweet Home The narrator of this selection describes her home on Mango Street—the house itself and the members of her family who live there. Think about your own home. What are some of its features? What words or phrases describe your home and your neighborhood? Draw a word web with the word *home* in the center. Fill in the ovals with as many specific words and phrases as you can about your home.

Build Background

The Setting of Mango Street
From the age of 11, Cisneros and her family lived in a modest bungalow in Humboldt Park, a poor Puerto Rican *barrio* on Chicago's West Side. In her first book of fiction, *The House on Mango Street,* Cisneros paints a memorable portrait of this neighborhood and its people. Having experienced a childhood marked by frequent moves, she once explained that living "in a neighborhood, a real one, with plenty of friends and neighbors" was extremely important to her as a writer. This selection offers a glimpse into Cisneros's life in the Chicago *barrio* as seen through the eyes of the young narrator, Esperanza Cordero.

Focus Your Reading

LITERARY ANALYSIS **VIGNETTE** *The House on Mango Street* consists of a series of 46 related vignettes. A **vignette** is a short, descriptive literary sketch that may stand alone or may be part of a larger work. Like a short story, a vignette is a work of fiction that can be read in one sitting; however, its plot and characterization are less fully developed than that of a short story. As you read these vignettes, think about how each is similar to and different from short stories you have read.

ACTIVE READING **DRAWING CONCLUSIONS** When you read fiction, you may have to **draw conclusions** about characters, events, setting, and other aspects of a story that have not been directly stated. To draw a conclusion, follow these steps:
- Notice details from the story.
- Consider your own experience and knowledge.
- Make a logical guess about the meaning of the story details.

As you read this excerpt from *The House on Mango Street,* draw conclusions about the main character, Esperanza. What kind of person is she? How old is she? What experiences has she had? What are her hopes and dreams for the future?

READER'S NOTEBOOK Create a diagram like the one shown. In the first box, write facts and details about Esperanza from the text. In the second box, jot down your thoughts based on your own experiences and prior knowledge. Then use information from the diagram to draw conclusions about Esperanza.

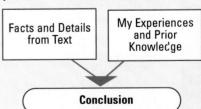

from
The House On
Sandra Cisneros
Mango Street

The House on Mango Street

We didn't always live on Mango Street. Before that we lived on Loomis on the third floor, and before that we lived on Keeler. Before Keeler it was Paulina, and before that I can't remember. But what I remember most is moving a lot. Each time it seemed there'd be one more of us. By the time we got to Mango Street we were six—Mama, Papa, Carlos, Kiki, my sister Nenny and me.

The house on Mango Street is ours, and we don't have to pay rent to anybody, or share the yard with the people downstairs, or be careful not to make too much noise, and there isn't a landlord banging on the ceiling with a broom. But even so, it's not the house we'd thought we'd get.

We had to leave the flat[1] on Loomis quick. The water pipes broke and the landlord wouldn't fix them because the house was too old. We had to leave fast. We were using the washroom next door and carrying water over in empty milk gallons. That's why Mama and Papa looked for a house, and that's why we moved into the house on Mango Street, far away, on the other side of town.

They always told us that one day we would move into a house, a real house that would be ours for always so we wouldn't have to move each year. And our house would have running water and pipes that worked. And inside it would have real stairs, not hallway stairs, but stairs inside like the houses on TV. And we'd have a basement and at least three washrooms so when we took a bath we wouldn't have to tell everybody. Our house would be white with trees around it, a great big yard and grass growing without a fence. This was the house Papa talked about when he held a lottery ticket and this was the house Mama dreamed up in the stories she told us before we went to bed.

But the house on Mango Street is not the way they told it at all. It's small and red with tight steps in front and windows so small you'd think they were holding their breath. Bricks are crumbling in places, and the front door is so swollen you have to push hard to get in. There is no front yard, only four little elms the city planted by the curb. Out back is a small garage for the car we don't own yet and a small yard that looks smaller between the two buildings on either side. There are stairs in our house, but they're ordinary hallway stairs, and the house has only one washroom. Everybody has to share a bedroom—Mama and Papa, Carlos and Kiki, me and Nenny.

Once when we were living on Loomis, a nun from my school passed by and saw me playing out front. The laundromat downstairs had been boarded up because it had been robbed two days before and the owner had painted on the wood YES WE'RE OPEN so as not to lose business.

Where do you live? she asked.

There, I said pointing up to the third floor.

You live *there?*

There. I had to look to where she pointed—the third floor, the paint peeling, wooden bars Papa had nailed on the windows so we wouldn't fall out. You live *there?* The way she said it made me feel like nothing. *There.* I lived *there.* I nodded.

I knew then I had to have a house.

---

1. **flat:** an apartment on one floor of a building.

Waverly Place, Andrew F. Engel. Courtesy of the artist.

A real house. One I could point to. But this isn't it. The house on Mango Street isn't it. For the time being, Mama says. Temporary, says Papa. But I know how those things go. 🏠

My Name

In English my name means hope. In Spanish it means too many letters. It means sadness, it means waiting. It is like the number nine. A muddy color. It is the Mexican records my father plays on Sunday mornings when he is shaving, songs like sobbing.

It was my great-grandmother's name and now it is mine. She was a horse woman too, born like me in the Chinese year of the horse[2]—which is supposed to be bad luck if you're born female— but I think this is a Chinese lie because the Chinese, like the Mexicans, don't like their women strong.

My great-grandmother. I would've liked to have known her, a wild horse of a woman, so wild she wouldn't marry. Until my great-grandfather threw a sack over her head and carried her off. Just like that, as if she were a fancy chandelier. That's the way he did it.

And the story goes she never forgave him. She looked out the window her whole life, the way so many women sit their sadness on an elbow. I wonder if she made the best with what she got or was she sorry because she couldn't be all the things she wanted to be. Esperanza. I have inherited her name, but I don't want to inherit her place by the window.

In English my name means hope. In Spanish it means too many letters.

---

2. **Chinese year of the horse:** The traditional Chinese calendar names each year after one of a series of twelve animals: rat, ox, tiger, hare, dragon, snake, horse, sheep, monkey, fowl, dog, and pig. People born in years named after the same animal are believed to share certain traits. Horse people are active and energetic, quick-witted and cunning. The horse is an individual who depends only on his wits and his labor to get what he wants.

I have

never

seen my

Papa cry

and don't

know what

to do.

At school they say my name funny as if the syllables were made out of tin and hurt the roof of your mouth. But in Spanish my name is made out of a softer something, like silver, not quite as thick as sister's name—Magdalena—which is uglier than mine. Magdalena who at least can come home and become Nenny. But I am always Esperanza.

I would like to baptize myself under a new name, a name more like the real me, the one nobody sees. Esperanza as Lisandra or Maritza or Zeze the X. Yes. Something like Zeze the X will do. ✗

Papa Who Wakes Up Tired in the Dark

Your *abuelito*[3] is dead, Papa says early one morning in my room. *Está muerto,*[4] and then as if he just heard the news himself, crumples like a coat and cries, my brave Papa cries. I have never seen my Papa cry and don't know what to do.

I know he will have to go away, that he will take a plane to Mexico, all the uncles and aunts will be there, and they will have a black-and-white photo taken in front of the tomb with flowers shaped like spears in a white vase because this is how they send the dead away in that country.

Because I am the oldest, my father has told me first, and now it is my turn to tell the others. I will have to explain why we can't play. I will have to tell them to be quiet today.

My Papa, his thick hands and thick shoes, who wakes up tired in the dark, who combs his hair with water, drinks his coffee, and is gone before we wake, today is sitting on my bed.

And I think if my own Papa died what would I do. I hold my Papa in my arms. I hold and hold and hold him. ✂

---

3. *abuelito* (ä-bwe-lē′tô) *Spanish:* grandfather.
4. *Está muerto* (ĕs-tä′ mwĕr′tô) *Spanish:* He is dead.

A Smart Cookie

I could've been somebody, you know? my mother says and sighs. She has lived in this city her whole life. She can speak two languages. She can sing an opera. She knows how to fix a T.V. But she doesn't know which subway train to take to get downtown. I hold her hand very tight while we wait for the right train to arrive.

She used to draw when she had time. Now she draws with a needle and thread, little knotted rosebuds, tulips made of silk thread. Someday she would like to go to the ballet. Someday she would like to see a play. She borrows opera records from the public library and sings with velvety lungs powerful as morning glories.

Today while cooking oatmeal she is Madame Butterfly[5] until she sighs and points the wooden spoon at me. I could've been somebody, you know? Esperanza, you go to school. Study hard. That Madame Butterfly was a fool. She stirs the oatmeal. Look at my *comadres*.[6] She means Izaura whose husband left and Yolanda whose husband is dead. Got to take care all your own, she says shaking her head.

Then out of nowhere:

Shame is a bad thing, you know. It keeps you down. You want to know why I quit school? Because I didn't have nice clothes. No clothes, but I had brains.

Yup, she says disgusted, stirring again. I was a smart cookie then.

Mango Says Goodbye Sometimes

I like to tell stories. I tell them inside my head. I tell them after the mailman says, Here's your mail. Here's your mail he said.

I make a story for my life, for each step my brown shoe takes. I say, "And so she trudged up the wooden stairs, her sad brown shoes taking her to the house she never liked."

I like to tell stories. I am going to tell you a story about a girl who didn't want to belong.

We didn't always live on Mango Street. Before that we lived on Loomis on the third floor, and before that we lived on Keeler. Before Keeler it was Paulina, but what I remember most is Mango Street, sad red house, the house I belong but do not belong to.

I put it down on paper and then the ghost does not ache so much. I write it down and Mango says goodbye sometimes. She does not hold me with both arms. She sets me free.

One day I will pack my bags of books and paper. One day I will say goodbye to Mango. I am too strong for her to keep me here forever. One day I will go away.

Friends and neighbors will say, What happened to that Esperanza? Where did she go with all those books and paper? Why did she march so far away?

They will not know I have gone away to come back. For the ones I left behind. For the ones who cannot out.

---

5. **Madame Butterfly:** the main character in an opera by Giacomo Puccini. She is a Japanese woman who kills herself when she discovers that her fiancé has abandoned her and married a woman from the United States.

6. *comadres* (kô·mä′drĕs) *Spanish:* women friends.

Connect to the Literature

1. What Do You Think?
What are your impressions of life on Mango Street?

> **Comprehension Check**
> • What does Esperanza's name mean in English?
> • Why does Esperanza's father cry?
> • What three things does Esperanza's mother know how to do?

Think Critically

2. How would you describe Esperanza's family?

THINK ABOUT
- • her descriptions of life on Mango Street
- • her descriptions of her mother and father
- • the story she tells about her great-grandmother in "My Name"

3. **ACTIVE READING** **DRAWING CONCLUSIONS** Refer to the diagram you made in your **READER'S NOTEBOOK**. What **conclusions** can you draw about Esperanza after reading about her?

4. Which of these **vignettes** do you think best illustrates the role that a Mexican-American female is expected to play? Support your opinion with evidence from the vignette.

5. Consider the economic and cultural challenges that Esperanza faces. Do you think she will be able to break free from Mango Street? Why or why not?

Extend Interpretations

6. Comparing Texts How would you compare the childhood experiences that Cisneros includes in her essay "Only Daughter" (page 694) with those of her fictional narrator, Esperanza, in these vignettes?

7. Critic's Corner Many literary critics question whether Cisneros's work is poetry or prose because it has elements of both types of literature. How would you characterize the vignettes you have read? Are they poetry or prose? Explain your response.

8. Connect to Life *The House on Mango Street* portrays the experiences of a young girl growing up in a Chicago barrio. Which of the experiences described in this selection remind you of experiences you've had in your own home or neighborhood?

Literary Analysis

VIGNETTE A **vignette** is a short, descriptive sketch that may stand alone or may be part of a larger work of fiction. According to Cisneros, the vignettes in *The House on Mango Street* "tell one big story, each story contributing to the whole—like beads in a necklace."

Activity Refer to the word web you created for Connect to Your Life on page 701. Then write a **vignette** either describing the physical features of your home or creating sketches of family members or people who live in your neighborhood. Share your vignette with classmates.

TONE **Tone** is the attitude a writer takes toward his or her subject. For example, a writer's tone may be angry or amused, serious or humorous, positive or negative. To identify a writer's tone, consider his or her choice of words.

Cooperative Learning Activity With a small group of classmates, analyze the tone of the vignettes. Create a word web like this one. List specific words, phrases, and details from the vignettes that convey Cisneros's attitude toward herself, toward her cultural and ethnic heritage, and toward her writing, as revealed through the thoughts, feelings, and experiences of her narrator, Esperanza.

Cisneros's attitude toward herself, her culture, and her writing.

Writing Options

1. Critic's Essay Look back at the vignettes you've read. Select one that you would rank high or low on a scale of one to five. Write an evaluation of the vignette explaining your rating. You might want to focus on the message, the narrator's attitude toward her community and life in general, or the stylistic devices that Cisneros uses.

2. Dialogue Imagine that you are the adult Esperanza who comes back to Mango Street. Write a **dialogue** between you and a friend or neighbor in which you discuss your life since leaving Mango Street.

Activities & Explorations

1. Opera Recording In "A Smart Cookie," you learn that Esperanza's mother enjoys opera. With a small group of classmates, find and listen to a recording of an opera such as Madame Butterfly by Giacomo Puccini. Then discuss what Esperanza's mother's love of opera reveals about her as a character.
~ SPEAKING AND LISTENING/ MUSIC

2. Vignette Illustration Draw a picture to illustrate one of the vignettes you read. For example, you might make an architectural sketch of Esperanza's house or a portrait of one of her family members. Display your artwork.
~ ART

Grammar in Context: Infinitive Phrases

In the following sentences from *The House on Mango Street,* Sandra Cisneros uses infinitive phrases to specify the wishes of the narrator's mother.

> Someday she would like to go to the ballet.
> Someday she would like to see a play.

An infinitive phrase consists of an infinitive (*to* + a verb) along with its modifiers and complements. Infinitive phrases are versatile; they can be used to add details to nouns, verbs, adverbs, and adjectives. They also offer writers a concise and rhythmic way to describe the actions of characters or objects ("to go to the ballet," "to see a play").
Punctuation Tip: When combining two infinitive phrases with the word *and* or *or,* do not use a comma after the first infinitive phrase.

WRITING EXERCISE Rewrite each sentence, using an infinitive phrase to express what is expressed by the underlined words.

Example: *Original* Singing professionally on the stage is what she wanted.
Rewritten She wanted to sing professionally on the stage.

1. We asked my mother if she would talk our father into letting us go to the mall.
2. My parents promised that they would buy a new house someday.
3. My mother rarely had a chance when she could spend time with us or talk with us.

Grammar Handbook Verbals, p. 1193

The House On **MANGO STREET**

A LOCAL UNIVERSE Book Review by Jenny Uglow

Build Background

After the U.S. publisher Random House took over publication of *The House on Mango Street* in 1991, Cisneros began to receive international as well as national attention. Following the British publication of *The House on Mango Street,* this review of the book appeared in a weekly British periodical, the *Times Literary Supplement,* on May 15, 1992.

Sandra Cisneros

The House on Mango Street

"Sandra Cisneros is one of the most brilliant of today's young writers. Her work is sensitive, alert, nuanceful... rich with music and picture."—Gwendolyn Brooks

This small book puts on no airs, but after a handful of its forty-six vignettes, you feel you've always known the people of Mango Street. More remarkable still, you begin to care about them with the narrator, Esperanza: about her mother, stirring soup and singing *Madama Butterfly;* her father, weeping for his dead father in Mexico; her sister, Nenny . . . and many more.

Here are the white socks, hidden gardens and borrowed high heels of many childhood novels, and the familiar *rites de passage:* . . . the first encounters with violence, loneliness and death; the inevitable gulf between brothers and sisters: "The boys in their universe and we in ours." But Mango Street (clearly based on the Puerto Rican district of Chicago where Sandra Cisneros grew up) is also unfamiliar, a universe in itself. Its families are always moving, but never quite arrive: "Before that we lived on Loomis on the third floor, and before that we lived on Keeler. Before Keeler it was Paulina, and before that I can't remember."

When the Latinos move in, others move out—the neighborhood is getting bad. Strangers shiver and think of shiny knives. But it's the Mango Street folk who are really scared. Outside their all-brown area, their knees go "shakity-shake," their car windows get rolled up tight and their eyes look straight ahead.

For many, like Mamacita, who speaks no English and cries for her pink house in the sun . . . America means broken dreams. The people at home will "wonder, shrug, remember, Geraldo—he went north . . . we never heard from him again." The reality of Hispanic life (as opposed to those shiny knives), rarely enters mainstream American writing. Cisneros sets out to fill the blank page and let her people speak. There's much sadness here, but, paradoxically, the "naivety" of her narrator is a bar to sentiment; the sharp child's eye sees even a dying aunt as a figure of fun, mystery or awe, no more. And her prose, with its Spanish rhythms and lush, tumbling imagery, stays artfully this side of overripe.

Esperanza—"hope"—is the girl who doesn't fit, who learns "The Walrus and the Carpenter" by heart. She tells stories. Her favorite film stars are cruel and beautiful and know their own power. So does she: "I have begun my own quiet war. Sure. Simple. I am the one who leaves the table like a man, without putting back the chair or picking up the plate." But when she does escape, taking her books and papers, she knows she will return to find "the ones who cannot out." *The House on Mango Street,* loving, playful and powerful, is alive with the people that Esperanza—and Cisneros—left behind.

The Times Literary Supplement, May 15, 1992

On *Writing* The House on Mango Street

Author's Introduction by SANDRA CISNEROS

"I knew I wanted to tell . . . a series of stories . . . contributing to the whole—like beads in a necklace."

Connect to Your Life

Discovering "Otherness" In this selection, Cisneros states, "At one time or another, we all have felt other." Think about a time when you discovered your "otherness"—when you realized how you differed from your friends, family, neighbors, classmates, or people in your community. Jot down words and phrases that help define who you are.

Build Background

Author's Introduction The following selection is the introduction that appeared in the tenth-anniversary edition of Cisneros's *The House on Mango Street* in 1994. In this introduction essay, Cisneros traces the evolution of her first work of fiction, beginning when she was a graduate student studying creative writing at the University of Iowa's Writers' Workshop in Iowa City, Iowa. She not only provides a historical account of the book's development in this essay, but she also explores other major influences that helped shape her as a writer.

> WORDS TO KNOW
> **Vocabulary Preview**
> affirmation   ingest
> evolve   presumption
> inception

Focus Your Reading

LITERARY ANALYSIS **VOICE**   The term **voice** refers to a writer's unique use of the language that allows a reader to "hear" a human personality in his or her writing. Cisneros writes:

> *The conversation, I remember, was about the house of memory—the attic, the stairwells, the cellar. Attic? My family lived in third-floor flats. . . . Stairwells reeked of Pine Sol. . . . Basements were filled with urban fauna.*

The use of vivid images, concrete words, and a friendly, conversational tone all contribute to create Cisneros's voice. As you read this essay, think about other qualities that give Cisneros her distinct voice.

ACTIVE READING **MAIN IDEA AND SUMMARIZING**   When you read a work of nonfiction, you will better understand the **topic**—what the selection is about—if you look for main ideas. The **main idea** is the writer's most important, or central, idea. Sometimes the main idea is stated directly in a topic sentence, or it may be implied, or suggested, by the details the writer gives. To understand an implied main idea, you must make an inference based on the details.

A **summary** is a short restatement or retelling of written or spoken material. When you summarize, you use your own words to restate the main points and important details of what you have learned.

READER'S NOTEBOOK   As you read this essay, use a chart to list important details that relate to the topic of the essay. Then identify the main idea, using your own words to restate the main points and important details.

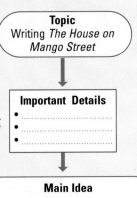

Topic
Writing *The House on Mango Street*

Important Details
• ....
• ....
• ....

Main Idea

The House On
MANGO ST

Sandra Cisneros

It's been ten years since *The House on Mango Street* was first published. I began writing it in graduate school, the spring of 1977, in Iowa City. I was twenty-two years old.

I'm thirty-eight now, far from that time and place, but the questions from readers remain, Are these stories true? Are you Esperanza? When I began *The House on Mango Street*, I thought I was writing a memoir. By the time I finished it, my memoir was no longer memoir, no longer autobiographical. It had evolved into a collective story peopled with several lives from my past and present, placed in one fictional time and neighborhood—Mango Street.

A story is like a Giacometti[1] sculpture. The farther away it is from you, the clearer you can see it. In Iowa City, I was undergoing several changes of identity. For the first time I was living alone, in a community very different in class and culture from the one where I was raised. This caused so much unrest I could barely speak, let alone write about it. The story I was living at twenty-two would have to wait, but I could take the story of an earlier place, an earlier voice, and record that on paper.

The voice of *Mango Street* and all my work was born at one moment, when I realized I was different. This sounds absurd and simple, but until Iowa City, I assumed the world was like Chicago, made up of people of many cultures all living together—albeit[2] not happily at times but still coexisting. In Iowa, I was suddenly aware of feeling odd when I spoke, as if *I* were a foreigner. But this was my land too. This is not to say I hadn't felt this "otherness" before in Chicago, but I hadn't felt it quite as keenly as I did in graduate school. I couldn't articulate what it was that was happening, except I knew I felt ashamed when I spoke in class, so I chose not to speak.

I can say my political consciousness[3] began the moment I recognized my otherness. I was in a graduate seminar on memory and the imagination. The books required were Vladimir Nabokov's *Speak Memory*, Isak Dinesen's *Out of Africa*, and Gaston Bachelard's *Poetics of Space*.[4] I had enjoyed the first two, but as usual I said nothing, just listened to the dialogue around me, too afraid to speak. The third book, though, left me baffled. I assumed I just didn't get it because I wasn't as smart as everyone else, and if I didn't

---

1. **Giacometti** (jä-kə-mĕt′ē): Alberto Giacometti, a Swiss sculptor of the 1900s known for his extremely thin, stalklike sculptures.

2. **albeit** (ôl-bē′ĭt): although.

3. **political consciousness:** awareness of the relationships among groups within a society.

4. **Vladimir . . . *Space:*** Vladimir Nabokov (nə-bô′kəf): Russian-born U.S. novelist who describes his youth in the autobiographical work *Speak, Memory*; Isak Dinesen (dē′nĭ-sən): Danish writer who lived for 17 years in Kenya, a country in eastern Africa, and wrote about that period of her life in her memoir *Out of Africa*; Gaston Bachelard (bäsh-lär′): French writer and philosopher whose *Poetics of Space* deals with his theory that daydreaming and fantasizing are the highest functions of the mind, and that the human experience is revealed most fully through the imagination.

WORDS
TO
KNOW

evolve (ĭ-vŏlv′) *v.* to develop gradually

say anything, maybe no one would notice. The conversation, I remember, was about the house of memory—the attic, the stairwells, the cellar. Attic? My family lived in third-floor flats for the most part, because noise traveled down. Stairwells reeked of Pine Sol from the Saturday scrubbing. We shared them with the people downstairs; they were public zones no one except us thought to clean. We mopped them all right, but not without resentment for cleaning up some other people's trash. And as for cellars, we had a basement, but who'd want to hide in there? Basements were filled with urban fauna[5]. Everyone was scared to go in there including the meter reader and the landlord. What was this guy Bachelard talking about when he mentioned the familiar and comforting house of memory? It was obvious he never had to clean one or pay the landlord rent for one like ours.

Then it occurred to me that none of the books in this class or in any of my classes, in all the years of my education, had ever discussed a house like mine. Not in books or magazines or films. My classmates had come from real houses, real neighborhoods, ones they could point to, but what did I know?

When I went home that evening and realized my education had been a lie—had made <u>presumptions</u> about what was "normal," what was American, what was valuable—I wanted to quit school right then and there, but I didn't. Instead, I got angry, and anger when it is used to act, when it is used nonviolently, has power. I asked myself what I could write about that my classmates could not. I didn't know what I wanted exactly, but I did have enough sense to know what I *didn't* want. I didn't want to sound like my classmates; I didn't want to keep imitating the writers I had been reading. Their voices were right for *them* but not for *me*.

---

5. **fauna** (fô′nə): animals.

for the "ugliest" subjects I could find...

Instead, I searched for the "ugliest" subjects I could find, the most un-"poetic"—slang, monologues in which waitresses or kids talked their own lives. I was trying as best I could to write the kind of book I had *never* seen in a library or in a school, the kind of book not even my professors could write. Each week I ingested the class readings and then went off and did the opposite. It was a quiet revolution, perhaps a reaction taken to extremes, but it was out of this negative experience that I found something positive: my own voice.

The language in *Mango Street* is based on speech. It's very much an antiacademic voice—a child's voice, a girl's voice, a poor girl's voice, a spoken voice, the voice of an American-Mexican. It's in this rebellious realm of antipoetics[6] that I tried to create a poetic text with the most unofficial language I could find. I did it neither ingenuously nor naturally. It was as clear to me as if I were tossing a Molotov.[7]

At one time or another, we all have felt other. When I teach writing. I tell the story of the moment of discovering and naming my otherness. It is not enough simply to sense it; it has to be named, and then written about from there. Once I could name it, I ceased being ashamed and silent. I could speak up and celebrate my otherness as a woman, as a working-class person, as an American of Mexican descent. When I recognized the places where I departed from my neighbors, my classmates, my family, my town, my brothers, when I discovered what I knew that no one else in the room knew, and then spoke it in a voice that was my voice, the voice I used when I was sitting in the kitchen, dressed in my pajamas,

talking over a table littered with cups and dishes, when I could give myself permission to speak from that intimate space, then I could talk and sound like myself, not like me trying to sound like someone I wasn't. Then I could speak, shout, laugh from a place that was uniquely mine, that was no one else's in the history of the universe, that would never be anyone else's, ever.

I wrote these stories that way, guided by my heart and by my ear. I was writing a novel and didn't know I was writing a novel; if I had, I probably couldn't have done it. I knew I wanted to tell a story made up of a series of stories that would make sense if read alone, or that could be read all together to tell one big story, each story contributing to the whole—like beads in a necklace. I hadn't seen a book like this before. After finishing my book, I would discover these novels later: Gwendolyn Brooks' *Maud Martha*, Nellie Campobello's *Cartucho*, Ermilo Abreu Gómez's *Canek*, and Tomás Rivera's *Y no se lo tragó la tierra*.[8]

---

6. **antipoetics** (ăn´tĭ-pō-ĕt´ĭks): poetry that rejects traditional poetic techniques.

7. **Molotov** (mŏl´ə-tôf´): Molotov cocktail; a handmade bomb that is set on fire and thrown. It was named for the Soviet politician Vyacheslav Molotov, who ordered the production of such bombs during World War II.

8. **Gwendolyn . . . *tierra*:** Gwendolyn Brooks: American poet and novelist whose novel *Maud Martha* depicts an African-American girl growing up in Chicago; Nellie Campobello: Mexican writer whose work *Cartucho: Relatos de la lucha en el norte de México (Tales of the Struggle in Northern Mexico)* depicts the period of the Mexican Revolution, which she lived through as a child; Ermilo Abreu Gómez: Mexican writer whose work *Canek* is one of three sections of a larger work, *Mayan Heroes*, and depicts an event in Mayan history; Tomás Rivera: American writer who wrote *Y no se lo tragó la tierra* (ē nō sĕ lō trä-gō´ lä tyĕ´rä) *(And the Earth Did Not Devour Him)*, a bilingual collection of short stories.

When I was writing *Mango Street*, I remember reading Nicanor Parra's[9] *Antipoems* and delighting in their irreverence to "Poetry," just as I had been delighted by Carl Sandburg's[10] wise-guy, working-class voice and Gwendolyn Brooks' *Bronzeville* poems.[11] I remember I was trying to write something that was a cross between fiction and poetry—like Jorge Luis Borges'[12] *Dream Tigers*, a book whose stories read like fables, but with the lyricism and succinctness of poetry.

I finished writing my book in November 1982, miles from the Iowa cornfields. I had traveled a great distance both physically and mentally from the book's <u>inception</u>. And in the meantime, lots of things happened to me. I taught Latino high-school dropouts and counseled Latina students. Because I often felt helpless as a teacher and counselor to alter their lives, their stories began to surface in my "memoir"; then *Mango Street* ceased to be my story. I arranged and diminished events on Mango Street to speak a message, to take from different parts of other people's lives and create a story like a collage. I merged characters from my twenties with characters from my teens and childhood. I edited, changed, shifted the past to fit the present. I asked questions I didn't know to ask when I was an adolescent. But best of all, writing in a younger voice allowed me to name that thing without a name, that shame of being poor, of being female, of being not quite good enough, and examine where it had come from and why, so I could exchange shame for celebration.

I had never been trained to think of poems or stories as something that could change someone's life. I had been trained to think about where a line ended or how best to work a metaphor. It was always the "how" and not the "what" we talked about in class. Even while I was teaching in the Chicago community, the two halves of my life were at odds with each other—the half that wanted to roll up my sleeves and do something for the community, and the half that wanted to retreat to my kitchen and write. I still believed my writing couldn't save anyone's life but my own.

In the ten years since *Mango Street* has been published those two halves of my life have met and merged. I believe this because I've witnessed families buying my book for themselves and for family members, families for whom spending money on a book can be a sacrifice. Often they bring a mother, father, sibling, or cousin along to my readings, or I am introduced to someone who says their son or daughter read my book in a class and brought it home for them. And there are the letters from readers of all ages and colors who write to say I have written their story. The raggedy state of my books that some readers and educators hand me to sign is the best compliment of all. These are my <u>affirmations</u> and blessings. ❖

---

9. **Nicanor Parra** (pä´rä): Chilean poet who in his *Poems and Antipoems* attempts to reach ordinary people by using simple, direct language and by writing about everyday problems, often from a humorous or ironic point of view.

10. **Carl Sandburg:** popular Midwestern U.S. poet and writer, whose best-known works include the poems "Chicago" and "Fog," and a six-volume biography of Abraham Lincoln that was awarded the Pulitzer Prize in 1939.

11. ***Bronzeville* poems:** *A Street in Bronzeville*, Brooks's first published collection of poetry, in which she reveals the extraordinary in the everyday lives of her neighbors.

12. **Jorge Luis Borges** (bôr´hĕs): Argentine poet and short story writer whose work helped bring Latin American literature to the attention of readers throughout the Western world.

WORDS TO KNOW

inception (ĭn-sĕp´shən) *n.* the beginning

affirmation (ăf´ər-mā´shən) *n.* something that supports the validity or truth of something else

Thinking through the LITERATURE

Connect to the Literature

1. **What Do You Think?** What insights about Cisneros did you gain from reading this essay?

> **Comprehension Check**
> • When did Cisneros begin to write *The House on Mango Street?*
> • What characteristics does Cisneros use to define her "otherness"?
> • How does Cisneros describe the voice of the narrator of *The House on Mango Street?*

Think Critically

2. **ACTIVE READING MAIN IDEA AND SUMMARIZING** Refer to the chart you made in your **READER'S NOTEBOOK.** In your own words, summarize this essay based on the main idea and the supporting details.

3. Do you think Cisneros's graduate school experience was mostly positive or mostly negative? Explain your response.

> **THINK ABOUT**
> • the identity changes she experiences while in graduate school
> • her feelings of "otherness" because of her class and culture
> • the birth of her writer's voice

4. Based on this essay, what advice do you think Cisneros might give to younger writers?

Extend Interpretations

5. **What If?** How might *The House on Mango Street* have been different if Cisneros had not discovered and named her "otherness" while she was in graduate school?

6. **Comparing Texts** Think about the selections you have read—the two personal **essays** by Cisneros and the **vignettes** from *The House on Mango Street.* Which of these selections do you think best addresses the issues of poverty, race, and gender? Explain.

7. **Connect to Life** Cisneros describes the positive effects of discovering and naming her "otherness" in this essay. Refer to the notes you made for Connect to Your Life on page 711. How would you compare your own experience of "otherness" with that of Cisneros?

Literary Analysis

VOICE A writer's unique way of using language to convey his or her personality through the writing is referred to as the writer's **voice.** In "On Writing *The House on Mango Street*," Cisneros uses a personal, informal, and conversational voice.

The elements that contribute to a writer's voice are sentence structure, word choice, and tone. For example, some writers rely on short, simple sentences, while others make use of long, complicated ones. Certain writers use concrete words; others prefer abstract terms. A writer's tone, or attitude toward the subject—for example, sarcastic, passionate, or humorous—also gives meaning to the term *voice.*

Activity Choose another passage from one of the selections in this Author Study and analyze its sentence length, word choice, and tone. Create a chart like the one shown, adding appropriate details in each column. Then choose a passage by another writer from the unit. Analyze it, and record your findings on a second chart. Discuss how Cisneros's voice differs from this other writer's.

Cisneros's Voice

Sentence Length	Word Choice	Tone

PERSONAL ESSAY A **personal essay** is a short work of nonfiction that expresses a writer's thoughts, feelings, and opinions about a subject. This type of essay reflects the writer's feelings and personality and provides an opportunity to explore the meaning of events and issues in his or her life.

THE AUTHOR'S STYLE
Cisneros's Poetic Prose

Cisneros acknowledges, "I wanted to write stories that were a cross between poetry and fiction . . . compact and lyrical and ending with a reverberation." Here are some of the features that make Cisneros's work so distinctive:

Key Aspects of Cisneros's Style

- simple, conversational language oftentimes characterized by the use of idioms
- loosely structured, lyrical sentences
- blending of Spanish and English to enrich the text
- vivid sensory imagery that speaks of the Mexican-American experience
- convincing, true-to-life characters in search of self-identity, cultural acceptance, and independence

Analysis of Style

At the right are excerpts from vignettes in *The House on Mango Street.* Study the chart above, and then read each excerpt carefully. Then complete the following activities:

- Find examples of Cisneros's key stylistic devices in the excerpts. Think about the effect that is created by each device and how it enriches the text.
- Find examples of other devices you see at work in the excerpts.
- Review the other reading selections in this Author Study. Choose one, and discuss with others the stylistic devices that Cisneros has used in it.

Applications

1. **Changing Style** Work with a partner to rewrite one of these excerpts using a very different style. For example, you might write complex, tightly structured sentences using conventional punctuation and word order. Then with a classmate, discuss how altering Cisneros's style changes her writing voice.

2. **Imitating Style** Using elements of Cisneros's style in *The House on Mango Street,* write another Mango Street vignette about Esperanza and her family.

3. **Speaking and Listening** Working alone or with a small group of classmates, read each excerpt aloud to emphasize the different aspects of Cisneros's style. Discuss any additional stylistic devices that you hear at work in these excerpts.

---

from **"A Smart Cookie"**

She used to draw when she had time. Now she draws with a needle and thread, little knotted rosebuds, tulips made of silk thread. Someday she would like to go to the ballet. Someday she would like to see a play. She borrows opera records from the public library and sings with velvety lungs powerful as morning glories.

---

from **"Papa Who Wakes Up Tired in the Dark"**

Your *abuelito* is dead, Papa says early one morning in my room. *Está muerto*, and then as if he just heard the news himself, crumples like a coat and cries, my brave Papa cries. I have never seen my Papa cry and don't know what to do.

---

from **"Mango Says Goodbye Sometimes"**

Friends and neighbors will say, What happened to that Esperanza? Where did she go with all those books and paper? Why did she march so far away?

They will not know I have gone away to come back. For the ones I left behind. For the ones who cannot out.

Choices & CHALLENGES

Writing Options

Character Sketch Create a character sketch of Esperanza or another character from Mango Street.

Activities & Explorations

Inspirational Poster Work with a group of classmates to create a poster that celebrates "otherness"—either your own or Cisneros's. Include quotes from the writer's work that convey pride and self-respect. ~ **ART**

Inquiry & Research

Inspiring Models Cisneros refers to writers who influenced her writing. With a classmate, find four or five poems from *Complete Poems* by Carl Sandburg or *A Street in Bronzeville* by Gwendolyn Brooks. Then discuss the connections you see among the poems and Cisneros's *The House on Mango Street.*

Vocabulary in Action

EXERCISE: CONTEXT CLUES Write the Word to Know that best completes each sentence.

1. In graduate school, Cisneros realized that she had made an incorrect _____ about what was a "normal" childhood.

2. She realized that none of the books she had read were about people like her, and this discovery marked the _____ of her career as a writer.

3. For Cisneros, Gwendolyn Brooks's poems about ordinary people were an _____ of her own experiences.

4. Cisneros saw her writing ability _____ as she slowly gained self-confidence.

5. Cisneros believes that the truths people _____ as they read can change them.

WORDS	affirmation	ingest
TO	evolve	presumption
KNOW	inception	

Building Vocabulary

All of the Words to Know in this lesson contain affixes. For an in-depth lesson on these word parts, see page 473.

Sandra Cisneros

Author Study Project

Creating a Dramatic Skit

With a small group of classmates, write and perform a dramatic skit inspired by one of the selections. The following suggestions can help you create and present your skit.

Choose a Dramatic Scene First, review the selections by Cisneros to find a situation that you would like to dramatize. Then discuss ideas as a group and choose one situation.

Write a Script As a group, discuss ways in which you can bring this situation to life. What events and characters from Cisneros's works will be part of your dramatic skit? Brainstorm ideas. After you finish making decisions about how to dramatize the situation, prepare a script. Include the following elements:

- setting
- characters' dialogue
- stage directions

Rehearse the Skit Once you have completed the script, have members of your group decide which of these roles they will play— the director, characters in the script, members of the stage crew, and so on. Then read through the script, making any changes that members of your group feel are needed to improve it.

Perform the Skit Before you begin the skit, you should analyze your audience to give an appropriate presentation. Performers should speak clearly, using a suitable pitch and tone of voice, make eye contact with the audience, use facial expressions, and pace the performance according to the dialogue of the script. You may want to videotape the reading for future audiences.

Writing Workshop

Creating a portrait with words . . .

From Reading to Writing Mary Oliver captures the nature of a person in her poem "The Journey." In the story "Powder," Tobias Wolff draws a more leisurely portrait of a man "in his forty-eighth year, rumpled, kind, bankrupt of honor, flushed with certainty." A good **character sketch** captures the personality and appearance of a person and can be part of almost any writing genre, from poetry to fictional narratives to biography to news stories.

For Your Portfolio

WRITING PROMPT Write a character sketch of someone you know or admire.

Purpose: To reveal the key elements of an individual's personality

Audience: Classmates, family, or general readers

Basics in a Box

Character Sketch at a Glance

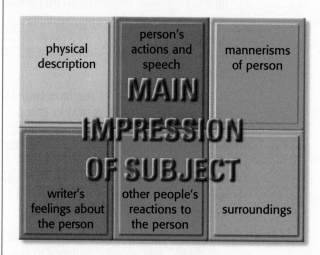

physical description

person's actions and speech

mannerisms of person

MAIN IMPRESSION OF SUBJECT

writer's feelings about the person

other people's reactions to the person

surroundings

RUBRIC Standards for Writing

A successful character sketch should

- present a vivid picture of the personality and physical appearance of a person
- establish a dominant, or main, impression of the person
- reveal the writer's response to the person
- include dialogue, mannerisms, descriptions, and other devices that show rather than tell what the character is like
- place the character in a context that contributes to the reader's understanding of the character
- have a clear organizational structure and a strong conclusion

Analyzing a Student Model

Hannah Barker
Evanston Township High School

The "Bear"

When my grandfather walks into a room, everyone looks up. The bright, cheesy smile on his huge, creased face drags an internal groan from everyone: here we go again. Sure enough, he begins to sing in a warbling, cracked voice, "Do you knooooooooow Kokomo Joooooooooooe? Do you knooooooooooow Kokomo Joooooooooooe? Do you knooooooooooow Kokomo Jooooe? Kokomo Joooooooooooe, he's an old hoboooooooooo." As he sings, he shuffles his feet as if dancing, a surprisingly graceful step for one so huge and bearlike. His faded slippers flap on the floor. "So, what do you want to do this evening? Do you want to watch some golf on TV or play cards?"

"Gin!" I shout at once. Being clobbered at gin by my grandpa is one of my great passions in life. He produces a pack of cards from the pocket of his loose sweat pants. His thick, leathery fingers flick the cards with expert speed and grace. Slap, slap, slap, slap. Each card lands right on top of the last in a fairly neat pile. He sweeps up his cards with an elegant gesture, frowning mockingly over his hand. He hunches his shoulders and bends his head, revealing the thin gray hair combed carefully over his pink scalp. He mutters softly and unintelligibly to himself, obviously trying to annoy me. His clumsy fingers gently tap the table as he ponders the cards.

Finally, the fingers grip a card and lay it on the table: queen of spades. That is not what I want, so I draw from the pile and discard a useless jack. He looks at me in hurt shock. "A jack! What did you put that down for? I can't use a jack! See if you can't do a little better next time." Turn follows breathless turn, my thoughtful silence punctuated by relentless commentary from the other side of the table describing my awful choices of discard cards.

Finally, the grumbling bear on the other side of the table exhales. "Gin!" He slaps down his cards: three eights, a king, queen, and jack of clubs, and four threes. I only have one set of cards: four tens. I am left with two kings in my hand, so I would have lost even if he had not gotten gin first. "You got to stop collecting those Rembrandts!" he says. It's very bad to get stuck with face cards because they cost a lot of points in gin. Rembrandts are very expensive pictures, and keeping those picture cards around really cost me. "Play again," I say. "This time I'll win."

① Captures interest early with a strong title and image

② This writer focuses on the character's words, mannerisms, and physical appearance to show rather than tell what the character is like.

Another Option:
• Tell what others say about the character.

③ Places the character in a context that helps to reveal the character's personality

④ Repeats the "bear" image introduced in the first paragraph

Once again Grandpa deals the cards with graceful ease. As the new game progresses, he suddenly says, "Tell me about your school. What classes are you in now?" I begin to describe my high school, each class in turn, starting with first period and moving towards ninth. The time flows gently along as we play together. Sometimes he interrupts our game to ask me questions about home: what kinds of stuff do I do after school, what are my friends like, what do I want to be when I grow up, do I have a boyfriend, why not, what do I think about college, how is everyone in my family, and what kinds of things are they doing now? In return I ask about his life, what he does now and what school was like when he was a kid. I especially love his stories about my dad when he was a kid.

Occasionally, my grandmother joins us. In the wake of her cheerful, friendly bustle, the bear on the opposite side of the table suddenly seems ludicrous, constantly cracking puns and bad jokes. Finally, she retreats to the study to watch golf and my grandfather says, "I have something to show you." We finish the game (he wins, as usual) and descend into the cool basement.

> **❺** Introduces contrast to show the character from another point of view

From a shelf in the basement, Grandpa produces two boxes and gently opens them. Several old, crumbling books lie inside. One is a cookbook, another is an early science fiction story, a third is a book of poetry, and another is a humorous book of history. "Some of these belonged to your Grandma LaRue," Grandpa says. He no longer speaks in the grinning, smooth-guy voice he uses to kid around or the deep, muttering voice he uses to complain, but uses a normal, serious voice. Grandma LaRue was his first wife. She died in a car crash many years before I was born, so I do not know very much about her. I'm interested in the books because of their age, but this is also an excuse to learn something new about Grandma LaRue. However, he says very little and Grandpa and I end by packing the books safely for the plane ride home.

> **❻** Shows a change in the character's actions and manner of speaking in order to present another dimension of the character

Over a pasta dinner cooked by my Italian step-grandma, Grandpa returns to grumpy-old-bear-trying-to-be-funny mode. His eyes twinkle as we groan at his fake guffaw. When Grandma mockingly scolds him for jokes made in bad taste, his tone turns injured. "Who, me? Would I tell a stupid joke like that? No. I am the soul of tact. You doubt me? Would I lie? My middle name is Honesty." At last I go down to bed, the warmth of his huge bear hug still lingering in my mind.

> **❼** Ends with an image that reinforces the writer's affection for the character

Writing Your Character Sketch

❶ Prewriting

A writer must learn to deepen characters, trim writing, intensify scenes.
Richard North Patterson

Whom do you want to write about? Usually it is easier to write about someone you know well. Consider an interesting relative, a special teacher, or a remarkable friend. Another approach is to write about someone you have only casually observed but whose actions are particularly revealing—a person on the bus or an eccentric neighbor. See the **Idea Bank** in the margin for more suggestions. You might also look for character sketches presented in magazine and newspaper articles to use as writing models. Think about how the writers portray their subjects.

Planning your Character Sketch

▶ **1. Explore your feelings.** How do you feel about the person? What tone will you use to convey your feelings—detached, admiring, humorous, serious?

▶ **2. Create mental images of the person.** Mentally replay scenes in which your character speaks, moves, and interacts with others. Which details stand out? Record those details using a chart like the one below.

How character looks	What character says	What character does	How others react

▶ **3. Place your character in a setting.** Describe the person in a time and place that will reveal his or her personality. Which setting will best show how your character interacts with others? Which setting will reveal your character's inner self?

▶ **4. Create a dominant impression.** What is the main impression you want to give? What descriptions and incidents involving the character will best create this impression?

❷ Drafting

The best part of writing a character sketch is that you can start anywhere. Just begin drafting and let the person emerge as you write. You can rework the details when you revise and edit.

Show rather than tell.

Good character sketches let readers draw conclusions. Use anecdotes, dialogue, or any other device that will show rather than tell what your character is like. Instead of telling your readers that your character is angry, describe what the character did that showed he was angry, such as slammed a door.

IDEABank

1. Your Working Portfolio
Build on one of the **Writing Options** you completed earlier in this unit:

- **Letter of Recommendation**, p. 661
- **Wacky-Character Sketch**, p. 677

2. Photographs
Look at photographs at home or at school to identify people you might want to write about.

3. Key Words
Make a list of words that describe personality traits, such as *funny, warm, brave, sad*. Then think of a person who matches each word.

Grab attention early but save the best for last.

Draw in your audience by starting with an interest tickler—a funny incident or a bizarre detail about your character's appearance. As you develop your character, save the best for last. That is, plan your ending so that it leaves your readers with a powerful impression of who this character is and how you feel about him or her.

Ask Your Peer Reader

- How do you think I feel about this person?
- How would you describe the character's personality?
- What details help you picture the character?
- How does the setting help your understanding of the character?

Need revising help?

Review the **Rubric**, p. 720

Consider **peer reader** comments

Check **Revision Guidelines**, p. 1143

❸ Revising

TARGET SKILL ▶ **WORD CHOICE** In a character sketch, carefully chosen words add clarity and vigor to description. Specific verbs can bring the action to life. Specific modifiers can paint vivid pictures of how things look, smell, sound, taste, and feel.

> *breathless thoughtful punctuated relentless*
> Turn follows ^ turn, my ^ silence ~~interrupted~~ by ^ commentary
>
> from the other side of the table describing my awful choices
>
> of discard cards.

❹ Editing and Proofreading

TARGET SKILL ▶ **PERSONAL PRONOUNS** Pronouns help present ideas clearly and help prevent unnecessary repetition. Make sure your pronouns agree with their antecedents in number (singular or plural) and gender (masculine, feminine, or neuter) and are the right case (nominative, objective, or possessive).

> From a shelf in the basement, Grandpa produces two small
> *them*
> boxes and gently opens ~~it~~. . . . However, ~~Grandpa~~ *he* says
>
> very little and Grandpa and ~~me~~ ^ end by packing the books
>
> safely for the plane ride home.

Publishing IDEAS

- Make a collection of character sketches written by your classmates and submit them to a student-writing Web site.
- Use audiotape or videotape to record a reading of your character sketch for your friends or a general audience.

More Online: Publishing Options www.mcdougallittell.com

❺ Reflecting

FOR YOUR WORKING PORTFOLIO What did you discover about your subject while you were completing your character sketch? What did you learn about yourself? Attach your reflections to your finished character sketch. Save your character sketch in your **Working Portfolio.**

Read this paragraph from the first draft of a character sketch. The underlined sections may include the following kinds of errors:

- **lack of subject-verb agreement**
- **run-on sentences**
- **incorrect personal pronouns**
- **sentence fragments**

For each underlined section, choose the revision that most improves the writing.

Zack is the smartest kid I know. He always <u>carry</u> a dictionary and at least

(1)
two other books with him. Last month, <u>Zack, my brother, and us</u> went to see a

(2)
movie. <u>We</u> like movies a lot and <u>has seen</u> all the action ones this year. In this

(3)   (4)
movie, one of the characters used the word *dichotomy*. I asked Zack what it
meant. <u>He pulled out his dictionary and handed it to me. A little pocket</u>

(5)
<u>flashlight, too.</u> <u>He told me I should look up the word myself, maybe someday I</u>

(6)
<u>can be as smart as he is</u>.

---

1. A. carried
   B. carries
   C. carrying
   D. Correct as is

2. A. Zack, my brother, and we
   B. Zack, my brother, and me
   C. Zack, my brother, and I
   D. Correct as is

3. A. Us
   B. Them
   C. Me and them
   D. Correct as is

4. A. has saw
   B. have seen
   C. was seeing
   D. Correct as is

5. A. He pulled out his dictionary and handed it to me, along with a little pocket flashlight.
   B. He pulled out his dictionary and handed it to me, a little pocket flashlight, too.
   C. He pulled out his dictionary, handed me a little pocket flashlight.
   D. Correct as is

6. A. He told me I should look up the word myself maybe someday I can be as smart as he is.
   B. He told me I should look up the word myself maybe, someday, I can be as smart as he is.
   C. He told me I should look up the word myself. Maybe someday I can be as smart as he is.
   D. Correct as is

Need extra help?

See the **Grammar Handbook**

Correcting Fragments, p. 1197

Correcting Run-on Sentences, p. 1197

Personal Pronouns, p. 1181

Subject-Verb Agreement, p. 1198–1199

All in the Family

The selections in this unit deal with a variety of family relationships and situations. To explore the new understanding of family that you may have gained, complete one or more of the options in each of the following sections.

Family (1992), Varnette P. Honeywood. Collage, Copyright © 1992 Varnette P. Honeywood.

Reflecting on Theme

OPTION 1

Resolving Conflict In many of the selections in this unit, family conflicts don't get fully resolved. For example, even though the narrator of "Marine Corps Issue" finds out about his father's injury, the two of them still cannot really talk about the war. With a small group of classmates, discuss some of the unresolved family conflicts in the selections. Decide which conflicts you think should—or even *can*—be resolved, then propose ways to resolve them or otherwise ease the tensions in the situations. If possible, use or adapt some of the solutions you discussed for the activity on page 588.

OPTION 2

Assessing Steps Toward Independence Which of the "declarations of independence" in this unit do you admire the most? Make a list of the characters or real people who make these declarations, noting the methods they use to deal with resistance from friends and family. Then decide on the method that impresses you most, and write a paragraph explaining how you could apply it to the situation you role-played for the activity on page 650.

OPTION 3

Evaluating Writing About the Family Imagine that you have been asked to compile an anthology—a collection of writings—about the family for teenage readers. What selections from this unit would you include? What title would you give the anthology? Pick four or five selections and create a table of contents, listing their titles in the order you want the works to be read. Then write an introduction to your anthology, explaining why you chose the selections.

Self ASSESSMENT

📓 **READER'S NOTEBOOK**

Think for a moment about the quotation at the beginning of the unit: "Call it a clan, call it a network, call it a tribe, call it a family. Whatever you call it, whoever you are, you need one." Now that you have read the selections in this unit, do you tend to agree or disagree with this statement? Write a paragraph explaining your opinion.

Reviewing Literary Concepts

Identifying Themes Most themes are not stated directly but only implied. Write down several themes that you can find in this unit's readings, expressing each theme as a statement, as if you were writing an ad for a movie. Remember that a work can have more than one theme and that there can be more than one good way of stating a theme.

NOW PLAYING!

Black Boy

Even if nobody but you believes in your dream, be persistent and you may get somewhere.

Understanding Author's Perspective In nonfiction, the author usually tries to make his or her perspective clear to the reader. In fiction, the author focuses on developing a story and his or her perspective must be inferred. Look back through the selections in this unit and choose two works that interest you—one fiction and one nonfiction. For each, write a paragraph explaining what you think the author's perspective is and giving evidence for your conclusions.

Self ASSESSMENT

READER'S NOTEBOOK

Copy down the following literary terms introduced or reviewed in this unit. Then look back through the unit and find at least one example of each concept. Jot down a passage from the text or a brief description that illustrates the term, noting the page number for later reference.

theme	dialogue
symbol	extended metaphor
sound devices	
rhyme	author's perspective
rhythm	
alliteration	characteri- zation
repetition	diction
assonance	vignette
imagery	tone
flashback	voice
suspense	personal essay

Building Your Portfolio

- **Writing Options** Several of the Writing Options in this unit asked you to develop and present your opinions about family issues. From your responses, choose the one that you think expresses your ideas most effectively. Explain the reasons for your evaluation in a cover note, attach it to the assignment, and place them together in your **Presentation Portfolio.**

- **Writing Workshops** In this unit you wrote a Personal Response to a literary work. You also wrote a Character Sketch. Reread these two essays and decide which you think is a more successful piece of writing. Explain your choice on a cover sheet, attach it to the piece you have selected, and place it in your **Presentation Portfolio.**

- **Additional Activities** Think back to any of the assignments you completed under **Activities & Explorations** and **Inquiry & Research**. Keep a record in your portfolio of any assignments that you especially enjoyed, found helpful, or would like to do further work on.

Self ASSESSMENT

Look over the writing pieces and records of activities in your portfolio. Do you see improvement in your work? Would you like to replace any of your earlier choices?

Setting GOALS

Now that you are more than halfway through this book, what expectations do you have for the remaining lessons? What are some things you can do that will help you to polish your writing skills and improve your skill in interpreting literary works?

LITERATURE CONNECTIONS
The Chosen

CHAIM POTOK

Danny Saunders and Reuven Malter live blocks apart in Brooklyn but belong to different worlds. Danny's father, a stern Hasidic rabbi, expects his son to become a spiritual leader. Reuven's father, though a devout Jewish scholar, embraces modern ways and gives his son more freedom. The two boys, both gifted students, become best friends. Reuven, the narrator, slowly comes to understand Danny's Hasidic world and the unusual silence that separates him from his father.

These thematically related readings are provided along with *The Chosen*:

from Somewhere a Master
BY ELIE WIESEL

from In My Father's Court
BY ISAAC BASHEVIS SINGER

I Never Saw a Moor
BY EMILY DICKINSON

The Three Hermits
BY LEO TOLSTOY

from The Way to Rainy Mountain
BY N. SCOTT MOMADAY

from Fifth Chinese Daughter
BY JADE SNOW WONG

New African
BY ANDREA LEE

And Even *More* . . .

One Writer's Beginnings

EUDORA WELTY

In this memoir, Welty brings to life her family, her younger self, and the American South in the early 1900s. She also conveys her love for stories—those she found in books as well as those she heard on long, hot summer afternoons.

Books
How the García Girls Lost Their Accents
JULIA ALVAREZ
After the four García girls leave the Dominican Republic, they eagerly embrace American culture, often to the dismay of their old-world parents.

A Yellow Raft in Blue Water
MICHAEL DORRIS
Dorris's novel tells the story of three generations of Native American women.

The Promise
CHAIM POTOK
In this sequel to *The Chosen,* Potok writes about the continuing relationship between Danny and Reuven as they become men.

Picture Bride

YOSHIKO UCHIDA

Yoshiko Uchida tells the story of Hana Omiya, a Japanese woman who comes to the United States as a "picture bride"—a woman whose marriage is arranged by family members through an exchange of photographs. The novel follows Hana's experiences, beginning with her arrival in San Francisco in 1917 and continuing through her family's relocation to a Japanese internment camp in Utah in 1943. As her expectations change, Hana learns to adapt to America on her own terms.

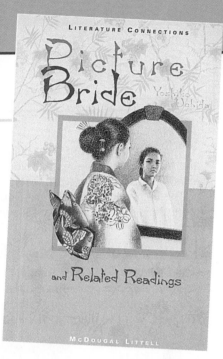

These thematically related readings are provided along with *Picture Bride*:

from **City in the Sun**
BY PAUL BAILEY

from **Farewell to Manzanar**
BY JEANNE WAKATSUKI HOUSTON AND JAMES D. HOUSTON

No Speak English
BY SANDRA CISNEROS

A Migration Created by Burden of Suspicion
BY DIRK JOHNSON

Selected Poems
BY JANICE MIRIKITANI

Clothes
BY CHITRA BANERJEE DIVAKARUNI

The Heart of a Woman
BY GEORGIA DOUGLAS JOHNSON

A Raisin in the Sun
LORRAINE HANSBERRY
This three-act play explores the struggles of an African-American family to achieve the American dream. This book is also part of the *Literature Connections* series published by McDougal Littell.

This Boy's Life
TOBIAS WOLFF
Wolff recounts growing up in the 1950s with the mother he loved and the stepfather he hated.

Other Media
Brighton Beach Memoirs
Neil Simon's semi-autobiographical play is brought to life in this film about a boy growing up in a crowded Jewish home.
(VIDEOCASSETTE)

Richard Wright: Black Boy
This documentary focuses on Wright's life while interweaving historical, social, and cultural images of the 20th century. PBS Video.
(VIDEOCASSETTE)

The Road to Freedom (The Vernon Johns Story)
The Reverend Vernon Johns was one of the earliest voices in the civil rights movement.
(VIDEOCASSETTE)

The House on Mango Street
Sandra Cisneros reads the stories she wrote about Esperanza and life on Mango Street.
(AUDIOCASSETTE)

Reading & Writing for Assessment

When you studied the test-taking strategies on pages 400–405, you learned and practiced techniques that you can apply in taking end-of-course examinations, standardized tests, and many other types of assessments.

The following pages will give you more practice using these strategies. Read the explanatory material that follows and then work through each of the models.

PART 1 How to Read a Test Selection

Listed below are the basic reading strategies you studied earlier along with several new ones geared to a different type of reading selection. By applying these strategies, by taking notes, and by highlighting or underscoring passages as you read, you can identify the information you need in answering test questions.

STRATEGIES FOR READING A TEST SELECTION

▶ **Before you begin reading, skim the questions that follow the passage.** These can help focus your reading.

▶ **Think about the title.** What does it suggest about the overall message and tone of the passage?

▶ **Use active reading strategies** such as analyzing, predicting, and questioning. If the test directions allow you to mark on the test itself, make notes in the margin as you read.

▶ **Look for main ideas.** These are often stated at the beginnings or ends of paragraphs. Sometimes they are implied, not stated. After reading each paragraph, ask "What was this passage about?"

▶ **Note the literary elements and techniques used by the writer.** Consider the tone (the writer's attitude toward the subject), the mood (the overall feeling or atmosphere the writer creates), and the use of techniques like comparison and contrast. Then ask yourself why the writer chose a particular technique.

▶ **Examine the sequence of ideas.** Are the ideas developed in chronological order, presented in order of importance, or organized in some other way? What does the sequence of ideas suggest about the writer's message?

▶ **Look for expert testimony.** What sources of information does the writer use? Why are these sources appropriate to the subject?

▶ **Think about the message and the writer's purpose.** What questions does the selection answer? What new questions or generalizations does it imply?

Reading Selection

❶ The Magic of Paper
Jon R. Luoma

1   Ever since the Cro-Magnons began painting bison and mammoths on the walls of caves, humans have been searching for the ideal surface on which to record ideas. The ancient Chinese carved pictographs in bone. Greeks scribbled on parchment made from animal skin. The Maya painted hieroglyphs on beaten mulberry bark. The ancient Egyptians made papyrus, the writing material that one day would lend paper its name, by pressing together wet layers of Nile sedge. ❷But real paper proved cheaper than parchment to make and could be produced in great quantities. And paper was better than papyrus or tree bark for printing.

2   ❸The first papermaker, according to legend, was Ts'ai Lun, who created paper from hemp, tree bark, rags, and fishnets in A.D. 105, perhaps to fulfill Chinese calligraphists' desire for a more practical writing material than silk or bamboo strips. The Chinese have loved paper ever since. Centuries before Gutenberg, they invented movable type. They were the first to make paper money, toilet paper, and paper books. It was forbidden even to step on a piece of paper with writing on it.

3   "Lovely and precious is this material," wrote Fu Hsien, a scholar in the third century. "Luxury but at a small price; / Matter immaculate and pure in its nature / Embodied in beauty with elegance incarnate, / Truly it pleases men of letters." ❹

4   When papermaking reached Europe in the 12th century, it set the stage for the first information revolution, which began three centuries later with Gutenberg's printing press. "It was mass printing that was responsible for the big spreading of ideas," says Peter Tschudin, president of the International Association of Paper Historians. "And there is no doubt at all that the arrival of paper was the real advent of the printed word."

5   In the Gutenberg era, printers used paper made of hemp and linen rags. The purity and strength of these papers ensured the survival of great works for hundreds of years. Jesse Munn, a paper conservator at the Library of Congress in Washington, D.C., treated me to such a work, Saint Augustine's *City of God,* printed in 1473. It looked as handsome today as it did when new: The thick pages were the color of Devonshire cream, the lettering was ornate and filigreed, with each drop initial carefully hand-colored.

STRATEGIES IN ACTION

❶ **Think about the title.**

ONE STUDENT'S THOUGHTS

"I wonder why the writer thinks paper is so magical? It seems pretty ordinary to me."

❷ **Skim the questions that follow the passage.**

"There's a question about pictographs and hieroglyphs. The selection says those were types of writing used before paper was invented."

YOUR TURN

Why does the writer mention these types of writing, since they had nothing to do with paper?

❸ **Examine the sequence of ideas.**

"The writer's starting at the beginning. He's probably presenting the history of paper in chronological order."

YOUR TURN

Why do you think the writer chose to use chronological order?

❹ **Read actively— analyze.**

"Fu Hsien talks about paper as if it were a treasure. That's not true today." What makes paper less precious now?

YOUR TURN

Look for evidence in the selection to answer this question.

6   Jumping ahead a few hundred years, we then examined a cantata in the hand of Johann Sebastian Bach: "Feast of the Visitation: My Soul Doth Magnify the Lord." Slashing, slanting sixteenth notes, and sometimes excess drips of ink, rushed along the page.

7   But while I marveled at Bach's energy, Munn only nodded distractedly at the cheap, dull paper Bach bought, apparently because he couldn't afford anything better. "He really used poor papers," she said, shaking her head. At least one of his compositions appears to have been committed to a sheet he got from the fishmonger.

8   ❺ Yet even the maestro's paper was in better shape than the yellowing pages of books I bought only 20 years ago. Why are some of my books slowly turning to dust?

9   The problem stems from the increased demand for paper during the 19th century, when papermakers turned to fiber from trees for their raw material because it was cheaper and more abundant than rags. Unlike cotton, which is almost pure cellulose, tree fibers are cemented together with a natural substance called lignin, which eventually oxidizes and turns the paper brown. An acid sizing added to the paper made the problem worse. Over time, the paper turned as brittle as a dead leaf.

10   In the U.S. today the majority of the books published are printed on nonacidic paper to better preserve them, but what about most of the books published since 1900? ❻ Conservators rescue some damaged pages by bathing them in solutions that neutralize the acids. But the Library of Congress, which houses some 20 million volumes, has only a handful of conservators to save its treasures. It is also scrambling to store its collection on microfilm or in computerized form, but with the books decaying at an alarming rate, it expects to record only a fraction.

STRATEGIES
IN ACTION

❺ Note the writer's use of comparison and contrast.

"The writer says a book printed hundreds of years ago lasted longer than one only 20 years old. What did paper-makers know then that modern ones don't?"

YOUR TURN
How does this comparison contribute to the writer's message?

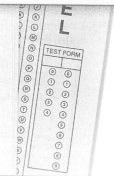

❻ Determine the writer's tone.

"The writer seems to value paper and books very much. In the title, he even called paper 'magic.'"

How to Answer Multiple-Choice Questions

Use the strategies in the box and notes in the side column to help you answer the questions below and on the following pages.

Based on the selection you have just read, choose the best answer for each of the following questions.

1. Why do you think the essay is titled "The Magic of Paper"?
   A. Ideas written on paper can survive for centuries.
   B. Paper is much more plentiful than papyrus or bark.
   C. Paper doesn't look anything like the materials out of which it is made.
   D. Some kinds of paper last for centuries while others crumble after only a few years.

2. What main idea does the writer support by mentioning pictographs and hieroglyphs?
   A. Life was difficult before the invention of paper.
   B. Paper fills a need humans have had since prehistoric times.
   C. Compared to using a computer, writing on paper is like drawing hieroglyphs.
   D. The quality of paper has improved over time.

3. In paragraph 2, why do you think that the writer notes that in ancient China, people were forbidden to step on a piece of paper with writing on it?
   A. He wants readers to know how precious paper was.
   B. He wants readers to handle paper with care.
   C. He is explaining why Chinese paper lasted so long.
   D. All of the above

4. Why do you think the writer tells an anecdote about seeing an original musical score by Johann Sebastian Bach?
   A. He wants to prove that he used original sources in his research.
   B. He wants to show that Bach's work would be even better preserved if the composer had used better paper.
   C. He wants to show that without good quality paper, treasures like the original Bach work would be lost.
   D. He wants to point out how poor Bach was.

5. How does the writer change his tone in paragraph 8?
   A. His attitude toward books changes from respectful to contemptuous.
   B. He stops quoting experts and expresses his own opinion.
   C. He stops comparing and contrasting types of papers.
   D. He stops speaking neutrally and expresses concern and puzzlement.

STRATEGIES FOR ANSWERING MULTIPLE-CHOICE QUESTIONS

▸ **Ask questions** that help you eliminate some of the choices.
▸ **Pay attention to choices such as "all of the above" or "none of the above."** To eliminate them, all you need to find is one answer that doesn't fit.
▸ **Choose the one best answer.** More than one choice may be true, but only one will be true and answer the question completely.

STRATEGIES IN ACTION

Choose the one best answer.

ONE STUDENT'S THOUGHTS

"All of these choices may be true, but this essay doesn't deal with life before the invention of paper. So I can eliminate choice A."

YOUR TURN
What other choices can you eliminate?

Pay attention to choices such as "all of the above."

ONE STUDENT'S THOUGHTS

"Not stepping on paper doesn't explain why paper lasted so long. *So I can eliminate choice C. That means that choice D—all of the above—can't be right either.*"

YOUR TURN
Which of the remaining choices makes the most sense?

PART 3 | How to Respond in Writing

You may also be asked to write answers to questions about a reading passage. **Short-answer questions** usually ask you to answer in a sentence or two. **Essay questions** require a fully developed piece of writing.

Short-Answer Questions

> **STRATEGIES** FOR RESPONDING TO SHORT-ANSWER QUESTIONS
>
> ▶ **Identify the key words** in the writing prompt that tell you the ideas to discuss. Make sure you know what each word means.
> ▶ **State your response directly** and to the point.
> ▶ **Support your ideas** by using evidence from the selection.
> ▶ **Use correct grammar.**
>
> > **Sample Question**
> > Answer the following question in one or two sentences.
> >
> > > Explain what you think the writer's purpose was in researching and reporting on the history of paper.

Identify the key words.

ONE STUDENT'S THOUGHTS

"The key words are *explain* and *purpose*. This means that I'll have to decide why the writer did this article and tell why I think that way."

YOUR TURN

What clues to the writer's purpose can you find in the selection?

Essay Question

> **STRATEGIES** FOR ANSWERING ESSAY QUESTIONS
>
> ▶ **Look for direction words** in the writing prompt that tell you what to write and what to do, such as *essay, analyze, describe,* or *compare and contrast.*
> ▶ **List the points** you want to make before beginning to write.
> ▶ **Write an interesting introduction** that presents your main point.
> ▶ **Develop your ideas** by using evidence from the selection that supports the statements you make. Present the ideas in a logical order.
> ▶ **Write a conclusion** that summarizes your points.
> ▶ **Check your work** for correct grammar.
>
> > **Sample Prompt**
> >
> > The writer of this selection sees paper as a magical material that has played a major role in human history. Write an essay in which you summarize how the composition and uses of paper have changed over time.

Identify direction words.

ONE STUDENT'S THOUGHTS

"The key direction words are *essay* and *summarize*. This means that I'll have to discuss the steps in the development of paper in a fully developed piece of writing."

YOUR TURN

What important points will you have to include in your essay?

PART 4

How to Revise, Edit, and Proofread a Test Selection

Here is a student's first draft in response to the writing prompt at the bottom of page 734. Read it and answer the multiple-choice questions that follow.

1	The earliest papermakers lived in the first century in China.
2	Paper was not made in Europe until the 12th century. Chinese
3	papermakers used hemp and linen rags. Later, European
4	papermakers also made paper out of hemp and linen rags. Paper
5	made this way was thick and lasted for a long time. In the 19th
6	century, papermakers began using tree fiber. Because more and
7	more people wanted paper. Tree fiber cost less and there was
8	more of it than linen. The new paper decayed rapidly, however.
9	Today, paper is still made out of tree fiber, but books are printed
10	on nonacidic paper so that it will last longer.

▸ **Read the passage carefully.**

▸ **Notice parts that are confusing.** What types of errors might cause that confusion?

▸ **Look for errors** in grammar, usage, spelling, and capitalization. Common errors include:
- sentence fragments
- lack of subject-verb agreement
- pronoun antecedent problems
- lack of transition words

1. What is the BEST way to combine the sentences in lines 2–4? ("Chinese papermakers . . . linen rags.")

   A. Hemp and linen rags were used by both Chinese, and later European, papermakers to make paper.

   B. Both Chinese and, later, European papermakers made paper out of hemp and linen rags.

   C. Chinese papermakers used hemp and linen rags to make paper and European papermakers did too.

   D. Make no change.

2. What is the BEST way to revise the sentences in lines 5–7? ("In the 19th . . . wanted paper.")

   A. In the 19th century, papermakers began using tree fiber; because more and more people wanted paper.

   B. In the 19th century, papermakers began using tree fiber because more and more people wanted it.

   C. In the 19th century, papermakers began using tree fiber because more and more people wanted paper.

   D. Make no change.

3. What is the BEST way to revise the sentence in lines 9–10? ("Today . . . will last longer.")

   A. Today, paper is still made out of tree fiber, but books are printed on nonacidic paper so that they will last longer.

   B. Today, paper is still made out of tree fiber: but books are printed on nonacidic paper so that it will last longer.

   C. Today, paper is still made out of tree fiber, but they print books on nonacidic paper so that they will last longer.

   D. Make no change.

A World of Mysteries

A lie hides the truth.

A story tries to find it.

Paula Fox
Writer and professor

Voice I (1963), George Tooker. Egg tempera on gesso panel, 19½″ × 17½″, private collection, courtesy DC Moore Gallery, New York.

When we say that people have "criminal minds," we are not talking about how they *behave*, but how they *think*. Often we mean not only that they are likely to break the law but also that they are capable of doing so in a way that is especially devious or clever. The criminal mind has fascinated writers for centuries, and in this part of Unit Five you will meet a number of interesting examples.

ACTIVITY

Think of some famous villains from real life, literature, movies, or television. With a small group of classmates, pick one or two of these figures and discuss the following questions: What motivates this criminal mind? Is this person evil by nature or has something happened to turn him or her to criminal activity? What in this person's behavior serves as clues to his or her personality? Do you feel any sympathy or understanding for this person?

The Detective Story

is a specific type of mystery. Most people love a good mystery story, whether it's one that scares the wits out of them or just intrigues them with a curious crime. Detective stories share the traits listed here. Most mystery fans feel that if any of the traits is altered—if there is no detective, for example, or if the identity of the murderer is known early on, then a story is a mystery story, not a detective story.

> **Traits of Detective Stories**
> - a detective who is either a police investigator or a private detective hired by an ordinary citizen
> - a crime, usually a murder, committed by an unknown person
> - a set of clues that let the detective—and the reader—logically determine who the criminal is
> - use of literary devices, such as **suspense**, **irony**, and **surprise endings**, to weave interesting and perplexing cases

Suspense

Suspense is a key element of detective fiction because it gets the reader involved in trying to crack the case right along with the detective. For this reason, the crime usually occurs early in a detective story. The writer wants to move quickly beyond the **exposition** and start building suspense. Detective writers also sometimes introduce a clue called a "red herring"—something that seems important but that leads to a wrong conclusion or a dead end. On the other hand, an important clue may at first appear insignificant. These are all tricks that detective writers play to sustain suspense so that the reader stays involved.

YOUR TURN In the paragraph at the right, where does the author introduce an element of tension? What words or phrases help to build this feeling?

Irony

Dramatic irony occurs when the reader knows something that a character does not. In detective stories, the detective and the reader may be aware of information or clues that are not known to the other characters. Dramatic irony is often used to increase suspense. As you read, you wonder whether the other characters will learn what you know and, if they do, what effect their knowledge will have on the plot.

Situational irony is the contrast between what the character expects to happen and what actually happens. Writers of detective stories may use situational irony to enliven readers' interest or to deepen the mystery by making readers wonder why things are not as they should be.

SUSPENSE

A bright red Porsche was bearing down on her in the fast lane. I adjusted my speed, making room for her, sensing that she meant to cut in front of me. A navy blue pickup truck was coming up on my right, each of us jockeying for position as the late afternoon sun washed down out of a cloudless California spring sky. I had glanced in my rearview mirror, checking traffic behind me, when I heard a loud popping noise. I snapped my attention back to the road in front of me. The white compact veered abruptly back into the fast lane, clipped the rear of the red Porsche, then hit the center divider and careened directly into my path. I slammed on my brakes, adrenaline shooting through me as I fought to control [my car's] fishtailing rear end.

—Sue Grafton, "Full Circle"

Famous Detectives in Fiction

Nancy Drew Courageous and smart teenage detective whose father's law cases inspire her investigations

Kinsey Millhone No-nonsense ex-cop who specializes in uncovering insurance fraud

Hardy Boys Teenage sleuths who often help their detective father

Miss Marple The quiet yet incomparable sleuth uses her intuitive understanding of criminal behavior to solve a crime.

Sherlock Holmes *Clever, unerring, scientific, mastermind* . . . are all words that describe the most famous of all fictional detectives.

The Rules of the Game

Piecing together the solution to a crime means answering the basic question *who:* Whodunit? Who committed the crime? Traditional detective stories usually follow a few ground rules:

- The crime must be significant enough to hold readers' interest.
- The reader must get the same clues that the detective gets.
- The culprit must be someone who has been known of throughout the story.

Surprise Ending

Detective stories often have surprise endings in which an unexpected event or a revealing explanation completely changes the expected outcome of the story. Usually the detective unmasks the person who committed the crime and provides an explanation of how the crime was committed. The detective will also describe how, through clever observation and careful deduction, he or she solved the mystery. Once the explanation has been given, it should fit perfectly with all the clues presented in the story.

The Active Reader: Skills and Strategies

Reading Detective Stories

In a detective story, the reader tries to predict the solution to the crime—the who, why, and how—before the writer reveals it. This kind of prediction requires strong powers of observation, as well as the ability to make inferences based on the evidence. Both the detective and the reader must analyze clues and draw conclusions about what the clues mean.

1 Strategies for Making Inferences from Clues

- **Question** the nature of the crime. Write down all the information you have—even information that seems unconnected—on a chart like the one below. As you read, add your inferences to the chart.

Investigating a Crime		
Clues	**Initial Information**	**Inferences About Crime**
What happened?		
When?		
Where?		
How?		
Why?		
Other Clues		

- Make a list of all possible suspects, their motives, and their alibis.
- **Evaluate** what all the characters say. Be suspicious. Any one of them may be lying to hide guilt or to cover for someone else.

2 Strategies for Analyzing Clues

- Keep track of all clues and evidence but distinguish between them. A clue is not necessarily evidence against someone.
- Beware of red herrings—clues that point a bit too obviously to one character. Solving the crime is usually not going to be that easy or obvious.
- **Predict** which clues will turn out to be the most valuable.
- Compare the detective's methods with police methods. What does the detective find that the police ignore or miss?

3 Strategies for Drawing Conclusions

- **Connect** the crime in this detective story with what you know from reading other detective stories. Does your knowledge of other stories provide clues to the solution of the crime in this story?
- Review the chart you've created to devise your solution to the crime. Go back through the story and see how well the text supports your solution.
- Evaluate the quality of the detective story. Did the detective's methods make sense? If there was a surprise ending, did it seem believable? If you were to read more detective stories, could you apply lessons you've learned from this story to help solve a new crime?

Need More Help?

Remember that active readers use the essential reading strategies explained on page 7: **visualize, predict, clarify, question, connect, evaluate.**

"The accident seemed to happen in slow motion . . . one of those stop-action sequences that seem to go on forever."

Full Circle

Short Story by SUE GRAFTON

Connect to Your Life

Mysterious Attraction Think about the mystery stories you have read or seen. What do you think causes readers and viewers to enjoy stories of mystery and deception? Create a cluster diagram in which you explore what draws people to mystery stories.

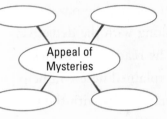

Appeal of Mysteries

Build Background

A Detective in Her Element Like other Sue Grafton mystery stories, this one features a private investigator named Kinsey Millhone and is set in a fictional California town called Santa Teresa. Santa Teresa is based on the actual town of Santa Barbara, where Grafton lives. Santa Barbara is a little more than an hour's drive northwest of Los Angeles. Along with two nearby cities, it forms a metropolitan area with a population of about 370,000. The University of California has a large campus about ten miles northwest of Santa Barbara. Appropriately enough for a city near Los Angeles, much of the action in this mystery occurs on a freeway.

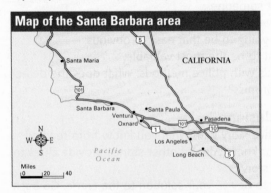

Map of the Santa Barbara area

WORDS TO KNOW	Vocabulary Preview		
brevity	egotistical	inexplicable	sullen
despondently	enigmatic	skewed	wary
dispel	harass		

Focus Your Reading

LITERARY ANALYSIS **PLOT** A **plot** is the chain of related events that take place in a story, usually as part of a **conflict,** or struggle. Problems and complications make up the **rising action,** which builds toward a **climax** or turning point. Meanwhile, **exposition** provides background, such as information about **characters** and **setting.** The **falling action** consists of events that occur after the climax. In the story you are about to read, the rising action begins in the very first paragraph, which also includes important exposition about the main character.

ACTIVE READING **PREDICTING** As **suspense** builds during the rising action of a story, the reader makes **predictions,** or logical guesses about what will happen next. Part of the fun in a mystery or detective story is to try to figure out the solution to the crime and then to find out if you were right.

READER'S NOTEBOOK As you read "Full Circle," jot down your predictions as well as answers to Active Reading questions that are placed within the selection. Base your predictions on information in the story, prior knowledge, logic, and even what seems most unexpected.

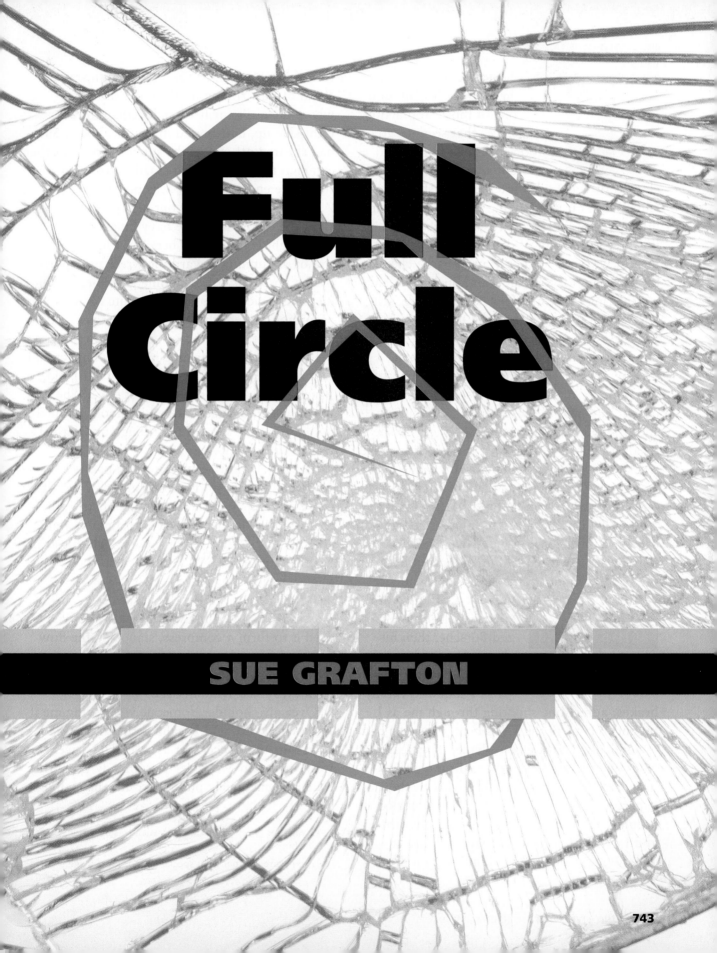

Full Circle

SUE GRAFTON

The accident seemed to happen in slow motion . . . one of those stop-action sequences that seem to go on forever though in truth no more than a few seconds have elapsed. It was Friday afternoon, rush hour, Santa Teresa traffic moving at a lively pace, my little VW holding its own despite the fact that it's fifteen years out of date. I was feeling good. I'd just wrapped up a case and I had a check in my handbag for four thousand bucks, not bad considering that I'm a female private eye, self-employed, and subject to the feast-or-famine vagaries[1] of any other free-lance work.

I glanced to my left as a young woman, driving a white compact, appeared in my side view mirror. A bright red Porsche was bearing down on her in the fast lane. I adjusted my speed, making room for her, sensing that she meant to cut in front of me. A navy blue pickup truck was coming up on my right, each of us jockeying for position as the late afternoon sun washed down out of a cloudless California spring sky. I had glanced in my rearview mirror, checking traffic behind me, when I heard a loud popping noise. I snapped my attention back to the road in front of me. The white compact veered abruptly back into the fast lane, clipped the rear of the red Porsche, then hit the center divider and careened directly into my path. I slammed on my brakes, adrenaline shooting through me as I fought to control the VW's fishtailing rear end.

Suddenly a dark green Mercedes appeared from out of nowhere and caught the girl's car broadside, flipping the vehicle with all the expertise[2] of a movie stunt. Brakes squealed all around me like a chorus of squawking birds and I could hear the successive thumps of colliding cars piling up behind me in a drum

ACTIVE READING

QUESTION What might the loud popping noise be?

roll of destruction. It was over in an instant, a cloud of dust roiling up from the shoulder where the girl's car had finally come to rest, right side up, half-buried in the shrubbery. She had sheared off one of the support posts for the exit sign that now leaned crazily across her car roof. The ensuing silence was profound.

I pulled over and was out of my car like a shot, the fellow from the navy blue pickup truck right behind me. There must have been five of us running toward the wreckage, spurred by the possibility of exploding gasoline, which mercifully did not ignite. The white car was accordion-folded, the door on the driver's side jammed shut. Steam billowed out from under the hood with an alarming hiss. The impact had rammed the girl headfirst into the windshield, which had cracked in a starburst effect. She was unconscious, her face bathed in blood. I willed myself to move toward her though my instinct was to turn away in horror.

The guy from the pickup truck nearly wrenched the car door off its hinges in one of those emergency-generated bursts of strength that can't be duplicated under ordinary circumstances. As he reached for her, I caught his arm.

"Don't move her," I said. "Let the paramedics handle this."

He gave me a startled look but drew back as he was told. I shed my windbreaker and we used it to form a compress, stanching the flow of blood from the worst of her cuts. The guy was in his twenties, with dark curly hair and dark eyes filled with anxiety.

Over my shoulder, someone was asking me if I knew first aid, and I realized that others had been hurt in the accident as well. The driver from the green Mercedes was already using the roadside emergency phone, presumably calling

---

1. **vagaries** (vā′gə-rēz): odd or erratic ideas or actions; whims.

2. **expertise** (ĕk′spûr-tēz′): special skill or knowledge.

police and ambulance. I looked back at the guy from the pickup truck, who was pressing the girl's neck, looking for a pulse.

"Is she alive?" I asked.

"Looks like it."

I jerked my head at the people on the berm[3] behind me. "Let me see what I can do down there until the ambulance comes," I said. "Holler if you need me."

He nodded in reply.

I left him with the girl and moved along the shoulder toward a writhing man whose leg was visibly broken. A woman was sobbing hysterically somewhere close by and her cries added an eerie counterpoint to the moans of those in pain. The fellow from the red Porsche simply stood there numb, immobilized by shock.

Meanwhile, traffic had slowed to a crawl and commuters were rubbernecking as if freeway accidents were some sort of spectator sport and this was the main event. Sirens approached. The next hour was a blur of police and emergency vehicles. I spotted my friend John Birkett, a photographer from the local paper, who'd reached the scene moments behind the paramedics. I remember marveling at the speed with which news of the pileup had spread. I watched as the girl was loaded into the ambulance. While flashbulbs went off, several of us gave our accounts of the accident to the highway patrol officer, conferring with one another compulsively as if repetition might relieve us of tension and distress. I didn't get home until nearly seven and my hands were still shaking. The jumble of images made sleep a torment of sudden awakenings, my foot jerking

in a dream sequence as I slammed on my brakes again and again.

When I read in the morning paper that the girl had died, I felt sick with regret. The article was brief. Caroline Spurrier was twenty-two, a senior psychology major at the University of California, Santa Teresa. She was a native of Denver, Colorado, just two months short of graduation at the time of her death. The photograph showed shoulder-length blond hair, bright eyes, and an impish grin.

According to the paper, six other people had suffered injuries, none fatal. The weight of the young woman's death settled in my chest like a cold I couldn't shake.

My office in town was being repainted, so I worked at home that next week, catching up on reports. On Thursday, when the knock came, I'd just broken for lunch. I opened the door. At first glance, I thought the dead girl was miraculously alive, restored to health, and standing on my doorstep with all the solemnity of a ghost. The illusion was dispelled. A close look showed a blond woman in her midforties, her face etched with weariness.

"I'm Michelle Spurrier," she said. "I understand you were a witness to my daughter's accident."

I stepped back. "Please come in. I'm sorry for your loss, Mrs. Spurrier. That was terrible."

She moved past me like a sleepwalker as I closed the door.

A WOMAN WAS SOBBING HYSTERICALLY.

---

3. **berm:** the edge or shoulder of a road.

Untitled (Green Volkswagen) (1971), Don Eddy. Acrylic on canvas, 66″ × 95″, courtesy of Nancy Hoffman Gallery, New York.

"Please sit down. Can I get you anything?"

She shook her head, looking around with bewilderment as if she couldn't quite remember what had brought her here. She set her purse aside and sank down on my couch, placing her cupped hands across her nose and mouth like an oxygen mask.

I sat down beside her, watching as she breathed deeply, struggling to speak. "Take your time," I said.

When the words came, her voice was so low I had to lean closely to hear her. "The police examined Caroline's car at the impound lot and found a bullet hole in the window on the passenger side. My daughter was shot." She burst into tears.

ACTIVE READING

CLARIFY What was the loud popping noise?

I sat beside her while she poured out a grief tinged with rage and frustration. I brought her a glass of water and a fistful of tissues, small comfort, but all I could think to do. "What are the police telling you?" I asked when she'd composed herself.

She blew her nose and then took another deep breath. "The case has been transferred from traffic detail to homicide. The officer I talked to this morning says it looks like a random freeway shooting, but I don't believe it."

"God knows they've had enough of those down in Los Angeles," I remarked.

"Well, I can't accept that. For one thing,

what was she doing speeding down the highway at that hour of the day? She was supposed to be at work, but they tell me she left abruptly without a word to anyone."

"Where was she employed?"

"A restaurant out in Colgate. She'd been waiting tables there for a year. The shift manager told me a man had been <u>harassing</u> her. He thinks she might have left to try to get away from him."

"Did he know who the guy was?"

She shook her head. "He wasn't sure. Some fellow she'd been dating. Apparently, he kept stopping by the restaurant, calling her at all hours, making a terrible pest of himself. Lieutenant Dolan tells me you're a private

detective, which is why I'm here. I want you to find out who's responsible for this."

"Mrs. Spurrier, the police here are very competent. I'm sure they're doing everything possible."

"Skip the public relations message," she said with bitterness. "I have to fly back to Denver. Caroline's stepfather is very ill and I need to get home, but I can't go unless I know someone here is looking into this. Please."

I thought about it briefly, but it didn't take much to persuade me. As a witness to the accident, I felt more than a professional interest in the case. "I'll need the names of her friends," I said.

I made a note of Mrs. Spurrier's address and phone number, along with the name of Caroline's roommate and the restaurant where she'd worked. I drew up a standard contract, waiving the advance. I'd bill her later for whatever time I put in. Ordinarily I bypass police business in an attempt to stay out of Lieutenant Dolan's way. As the officer in charge of homicide, he's not crazy about private eyes. Though he's fairly tolerant of me, I couldn't imagine what she'd had to threaten to warrant the referral.[4]

As soon as she left, I grabbed a jacket and my handbag and drove over to the police station, where I paid six dollars for a copy of the police report. Lieutenant Dolan wasn't in, but I spent a few minutes chatting with Emerald, the clerk in Identification and Records. She's a heavy black woman in her fifties, usually <u>wary</u> of my questions but a sucker for gossip.

"I hear Jasper's wife caught him with Rowena Hairston," I said, throwing out some bait. Jasper Sax is one of Emerald's interdepartmental foes.

---

4. **warrant the referral:** be a good reason for sending Mrs. Spurrier to the narrator for help.

747

"Why tell me?" she said. She was pretending disinterest, but I could tell the rumor cheered her. Jasper, from the crime lab, is forever lifting files from Emerald's desk, which only gets her in trouble when Lieutenant Dolan comes around.

"I was hoping you'd fill me in on the Spurrier accident. I know you've memorized all the paperwork."

She grumbled something about flattery that implied she felt flattered, so I pressed for specifics. "Anybody see where the shot was fired from?" I asked.

"No ma'am."

I thought about the fellow in the red Porsche. He'd been in the lane to my left, just a few yards ahead of me when the accident occurred. The man in the pickup might be a help as well. "What about the other witnesses? There must have been half a dozen of us at the scene. Who's been interviewed?"

Emerald gave me an indignant look. "What's the matter with you? You know I'm not allowed to give out information like that!"

"Worth a try," I said equably.[5] "What about the girl's professors from the university? Has Dolan talked to them?"

"Check it out yourself if you're so interested," she snapped.

"Come on, Emerald. Dolan knows I'm doing this. He was the one who told Mrs. Spurrier about me in the first place. I'll make it easy for you. Just one name."

She squinted at me suspiciously. "Which one's that?"

I took a flier,[6] describing the guy in the pickup, figuring she could identify him from the list by age. Grudgingly, she checked the list and her expression changed.

"Uh-oh," she said. "I might know you'd zero in on this one. Fellow in the pickup gave a phony name and address. Benny Seco was the name, but he must have made that up. Telephone was a fake, too. Looks like he took off and nobody's seen him since. Might have been a warrant out against him he was trying to duck."

"How about the guy in the Porsche?"

I heard a voice behind me. "Well, well, well. Kinsey Millhone. Hard at work, I see."

Emerald faded into the background with all the practice of a spy. I turned to find Lieutenant Dolan standing in the hallway in his habitual pose: hands shoved down in his pants pockets, rocking on his heels. He'd recently celebrated a birthday, his baggy face reflecting every one of his sixty years.

I folded the police report and tucked it in my bag. "Mrs. Spurrier got in touch with me and asked me to follow up on this business of her daughter's death. I feel bad about the girl."

His manner shifted. "I do, too," he said.

"What's the story on the missing witness?"

Dolan shrugged. "He must have had some reason to give out a phony name. Did you talk to him at the scene?"

"Just briefly, but I'd know him if I saw him again. Do you think he could be of help?"

Dolan ran a hand across his balding pate.[7] "I'd sure like to hear what the fellow has to say. Nobody else was aware that the girl was shot. I gather

"ANYBODY SEE WHERE THE SHOT WAS FIRED FROM?"

---

5. **equably** (ĕk'wə-blē): calmly.

6. **took a flier:** took a chance; did something risky.

7. **pate** (pāt): the top of the head.

he was close enough to have done it himself."

"There's gotta be a way to track him down, don't you think?"

"Maybe," he said. "No one remembers much about the man except the truck he drove. Toyota, dark blue, maybe four or five years old from what they say."

ACTIVE READING

PREDICT Do you think the guy in the blue pickup is a suspect?

"Would you object if I checked back with the other witnesses? I might get more out of them since I was there."

He studied me for a moment, then reached over to the file and removed the list of witnesses, which he handed to me without a word.

"Don't you need this?" I said, surprised.

"I have a copy."

"Thanks. This is great. I'll let you know what I find out."

Dolan pointed a finger. "Keep in touch with the department. I don't want you going off half-cocked."

I drove out to the campus area to the restaurant where Caroline Spurrier had worked. The place had changed hands recently, the decor downgraded from real plants to fake as the nationality of the food changed from Mexican to Thai. The shift manager, David Cole, was just a kid himself, barely twenty-two, tall, skinny, with a nose that belonged on a much larger face.

I introduced myself and told him I was looking into Caroline's death.

"Oh, yeah, that was awful. I talked to her mom."

"She says you mentioned some guy who'd been bugging her. What else can you tell me?"

"That's about all I know. I mean, I never saw the guy myself. She was working nights for the last couple months and just switched back to days to see if she could get away from him."

"She ever mention his name?"

"Terry something, I think. She said he used to follow her around in this green van he drove. She really thought the dude was bent."

"Bent?"

"You know . . . twisted." He twiddled an index finger beside his head to indicate his craziness.

"Why'd she go out with him?"

"She said he seemed like a real nice guy at first, but then he got real possessive, all jealous and like that. In the end, I guess he was totally nuts. He must have showed up on Friday, which is why she took off."

ACTIVE READING

PREDICT This guy has a motive. Could he be the guy in the blue pickup?

I quizzed him, but couldn't glean much more from his account. I thanked him and drove over to the block of university housing where Caroline had lived. The apartment was typical of student digs;[8] faintly shabby, furnished with mismatched items that had probably been languishing in someone's garage. Her roommate was a young woman named Judy Layton, who chatted despondently as she emptied kitchen cabinets and packed assorted cardboard boxes. I kept the questions light at first, asking her about herself as she wrapped some dinner plates in newspaper, shoving each in a box. She was twenty-two, a senior English major with family living in town.

"How long did you know Caroline?"

"About a year," she said. "I had another roommate, but Alice graduated last year. Caroline and I connected up through one of those roommate referral services."

"How come you're moving out?"

She shrugged. "Going back to my folks'. It's too late in the school year to find someone else and I can't afford this place on my own. My brother's on his way over to help me move."

---

8. **digs:** a slang term for apartment or lodgings.

WORDS TO KNOW	**despondently** (dǐ-spŏn′dənt-lē) *adv.* in a very discouraged or depressed manner

According to her, Caroline was a "party-hearty" who somehow managed to keep her grades up and still have a good time.

"Did she have a boyfriend?"

"She dated lots of guys."

"But no one in particular?"

She shook her head, intent on her work.

I tried again. "She told her mom about some guy harassing her at work. Apparently she'd dated him and they'd just broken up. Do you have any idea who she might have been talking about?"

"Not really. I didn't keep track of the guys in her life."

"She must have mentioned this guy if he was causing such a fuss."

"Look. She and I were not close. We were roommates and that was it. She went her way and I went mine. If some guy was bugging her, she didn't say a word to me."

"She wasn't in any trouble that you knew about?"

"No."

Her manner seemed <u>sullen</u> and it was getting on my nerves. I stared at her. "Judy, I could use a little help. People get murdered for a reason. It might seem stupid or insignificant to the rest of us, but there was *something* going on. What gives?"

ACTIVE READING

EVALUATE Do you think Judy Layton is telling the truth?

"You don't know it was murder. The policeman I talked to said it might have been some bozo in a passing car."

"Her mother disagrees."

"Well, I can't help you. I already told you everything I know."

I nailed her with a look and let a silence fall, hoping her discomfort would generate further comment. No such luck. If she knew more, she was determined to keep it to herself. I left a business card, asking her to phone me if she remembered anything.

I spent the next two days talking to Caroline Spurrier's professors and friends. From the portrait that emerged, she seemed like a likable kid, funny, good-natured, popular, and sweet. She'd complained of the harassment to a couple of classmates without giving any indication who the fellow was. I went back to the list of witnesses at the scene of the accident, talking to each in turn. I was still tantalized[9] by the guy in the pickup. What reason could he have to falsify his identity?

I'd clipped out the news account of Caroline Spurrier's death, pinning her picture on the bulletin board above my desk. She looked down at me with a smile that seemed more <u>enigmatic</u> with the passing days. I couldn't bear the idea of having to tell her mother my investigation was at an impasse,[10] but I knew I owed her a report.

I was sitting at my typewriter when an idea came to me, quite literally, in a flash. I was staring at the newspaper picture of the wreckage when I spotted the photo credit. I suddenly remembered John Birkett at the scene, his flash going off as he shot pictures of the wreck. If he'd inadvertently snapped one of the guy in the pickup, at least I'd have something to show the cops. Maybe we could get a lead on the fellow that way. I gave Birkett a call. Twenty minutes later, I was in his cubbyhole at the Santa Teresa *Dispatch*, our heads bent together while we scanned the contact sheets.

"No good," John said. "This one's not bad, but the focus is off. I never really got a clear shot of him."

"What about the truck?"

John pulled out another contact sheet that showed various views of the wrecked compact, the pickup visible on the berm behind. "Well,

---

9. **tantalized:** tempted; enticed; provoked.

10. **impasse** (ĭm′păs′): a difficulty without a solution; a standstill.

WORDS TO KNOW

sullen (sŭl′ən) *adj.* showing irritation or unhappiness by a gloomy silence; moody
enigmatic (ĕn′ĭg-măt′ĭk) *adj.* mysterious; puzzling

you can see it in the background, if that's any help."

"Can we get an enlargement?"

"You looking for anything in particular?"

"The license plate," I said.

The California plate bore a seven-place combination of numbers and letters that we finally discerned[11] in the grainy haze of the two blowups. I should have called Lieutenant Dolan and had him run the license number, but I confess to an <u>egotistical</u> streak that sometimes overrides common sense. I didn't want to give the lead back to him just yet. I called a pal of mine at the Department of Motor Vehicles and asked him to check it out instead.

The license plate was registered to a 1984 Toyota pickup, navy blue, the owner listed as Ron Cagle with an address on McClatchy Way.

The house was stucco, dark gray, with the trim done in white. My heart was pounding as I rang the bell. The fellow's face was printed so indelibly in my memory that when the door was finally opened, I just stood there and stared. Wrong man. This guy was probably six foot seven, over two hundred pounds, with a strong chin, ruddy complexion, blue eyes, auburn hair, red moustache. "Yes?"

"I'm looking for Ron Cagle."

"I'm Ron Cagle."

"You are?" My voice broke in astonishment like a kid reaching puberty. "You're the owner of a navy blue Toyota pickup?" I read off the number of the license plate.

He looked at me quizzically. "Yes. Is something wrong?"

"Well, I don't know. Has someone else been driving it?"

"Not for the last six months."

"Are you sure?"

He half laughed. "See for yourself. It's sitting on the parking pad just behind the house."

He pulled the door shut behind him, leading

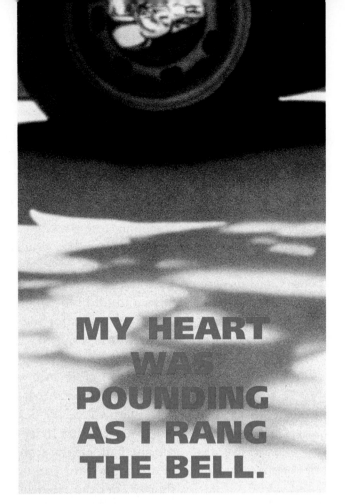

MY HEART WAS POUNDING AS I RANG THE BELL.

the way as the two of us moved off the porch and down the driveway to the rear. There sat the navy blue Toyota pickup, without wheels, up on blocks. The hood was open and there was empty space where the engine should have been. "What's going on?" he asked.

"That's what I'm about to ask you. This truck was at the scene of a recent accident where a girl was killed."

"Not this one," he said. "This has been right here."

Without another word, I pulled out the photographs. "Isn't that your license plate?"

He studied the photos with a frown. "Well, yes, but the truck isn't mine. It couldn't be." He

---

11. **discerned** (dĭ-sûrnd'): perceived; recognized.

751

glanced back at his pickup, spotting the discrepancy.[12] "There's the problem . . ." He pointed to the license. The plate on the truck was an altogether different set of numbers.

It took me about thirty seconds before the light finally dawned. "Somebody must have lifted your plates and substituted these."

"What would be the point?"

I shrugged. "Maybe someone stole a navy blue Toyota truck and wanted plates that would clear a license check if he was stopped by the cops. Can I use your telephone?"

I called Lieutenant Dolan and told him what I'd found. He ran a check on the plates for the pickup sitting in the drive that turned out to match the numbers on a vehicle reported stolen two weeks before. An APB[13] was issued for the truck with Cagle's plates. Dolan's guess was that the guy had left the state, or abandoned the pickup shortly after the accident. It was also possible that even if we found the guy, he might not have any real connection with the shooting death. Somehow I doubted it.

ACTIVE READING

PREDICT What do you think? Will the guy in the blue pickup turn out to be the murderer?

A week passed with no results. The silence was discouraging. I was right back where I started from with no appreciable progress. If a case is going to break, it usually happens fast, and the chances of cracking this one were diminishing with every passing day. Caroline Spurrier's photograph was still pinned to the bulletin board above my desk, her smile nearly mocking as the days went by. In situations like this, all I know to do is go back to the beginning and start again.

Doggedly[14] I went through the list of witnesses, calling everybody on the list. Most tried to be helpful, but there was really nothing new to add. I drove back to the campus to look for Caroline's roommate. Judy Layton had to know something more than she'd told me at first. Maybe I could find a way to worm some information out of her.

The apartment was locked, and a quick peek in the front window showed that all the furniture was gone. I picked up her forwarding address from the manager on the premises and headed over to her parents' house in Colgate, the little suburb to the north.

The house was pleasant, a story and a half of stucco and frame, an attached three-car garage visible at the right. I rang the bell and waited, idly scanning the neighborhood from my vantage point on the porch. It was a nice street, wide and tree-lined, with a grassy divider down the center planted with pink and white flowering shrubs. I rang the bell again. Apparently no one was home.

I went down the porch steps and paused in the driveway, intending to return to my car, which was parked at the curb. I hesitated where I stood. There are times in this business when a hunch is a hunch . . . when a little voice in your gut tells you something's amiss. I turned with curiosity toward the three-car garage at the rear. I cupped my hands, shading my eyes so I could peer through the side window. In the shadowy interior, I saw a pickup, stripped of paint.

I tried the garage's side entrance. The door was unlocked and I pushed my way in. The space smelled of dust, motor oil, and primer. The pickup's license plates were gone. This had to be the same truck, though I couldn't think why it hadn't been dumped. Maybe it was too perilous[15] to attempt at this point. Heart thumping, I did a quick search of the cab's

---

12. **discrepancy** (dĭ-skrĕp′ən-sē): difference or disagreement between facts.
13. **APB:** all points bulletin: a radio message for all police officers.
14. **doggedly:** with stubborn determination.
15. **perilous:** dangerous; risky.

interior. Under the front seat, on the driver's side, I saw a handgun, a .45. I left it where it was, eased the cab door shut, and backed away from the truck. Clearly, someone in the Layton household had been at the murder scene.

ACTIVE READING

PREDICT What do you think now? Who's the murderer?

I left the garage at a quick clip, trotting toward the street. I had to find a telephone and call the cops. I had just started my car, shoving it into gear, when I saw a dark green VW van pass on the far side of the divider and circle back in my direction, headed toward the Layton's drive. The fellow driving was the man I'd seen at the accident. Judy's brother? The similarities were obvious, now that I thought of it. No wonder she'd been unwilling to tell me what was going on! He slowed for the turn, and that's when he spotted me.

If I'd had any doubts about his guilt, they vanished the minute he and I locked eyes. His surprise was replaced by panic, and he gunned his engine, taking off. I peeled after him, flooring it. At the corner he skidded sideways and recovered, speeding out of sight. I went after him, zigzagging crazily through a residential area that was laid out like a maze. I could almost chart his course ahead of me by the whine of his transmission. He was heading toward the freeway.

At the overpass, I caught a glimpse of him in the southbound lane. He wasn't hard to track, the boxy shape of the van clearly visible as we tore toward town. The traffic began to slow, massing in one of those inexplicable logjams on the road. I couldn't tell if the problem was a fender-bender in the northbound lane, or a bottleneck in ours, but it gave me the advantage I needed. I was catching him.

As I eased up on his left, I saw him lean on the accelerator, cutting to his right. He hit the shoulder of the road, his tires spewing out gravel as he widened the gap between us. He was bypassing stalled cars, hugging the shrubbery as he flew down the berm. I was right behind him, keeping as close to him as I dared. My car wasn't very swift, but then neither was his van. I jammed my accelerator to the floor and pinned myself to his tail. He was watching me steadily in his rearview mirror, our eyes meeting in a deadlock of determination and grit.

I spotted the maintenance crew just seconds before he did; guys in bright orange vests working with a crane that was parked squarely in his path. There was no way for him to slow in time and no place else to go. His van plowed into the rear of the crane with a crash that made my blood freeze as I slammed on my brakes. I was luckier than he. My VW came to a stop just a kiss away from death.

Like a nightmare, we repeated all the horror of the first wreck. Police and paramedics, the wailing of the ambulance. When I finally stopped shaking, I realized where I was. The road crew was replacing the big green highway sign sheared in half when Caroline Spurrier's car had smashed into it. Terry Layton died at the very spot where he killed her.

Caroline's smile has shifted back to impishness in the photograph above my desk. I keep it there as a reminder, but of what I couldn't say. The brevity of life, perhaps, the finality of death . . . the irony of events that sometimes connect the two. We live in a world in which justice is skewed. ❖

WORDS TO KNOW
inexplicable (ĭn-ĕkʹsplĭ-kə-bəl) *adj.* difficult or impossible to explain
brevity (brĕvʹĭ-tē) *n.* the quality of being brief in time; shortness
skewed (skyōōd) *adj.* distorted or slanted in a particular direction; unbalanced
skew *v.*

Thinking through the LITERATURE

Connect to the Literature

1. What Do You Think? What is **ironic** about the ending of this story? Share your thoughts with your classmates.

> **Comprehension Check**
> - How does Caroline Spurrier die?
> - Why are the police looking for the man in the pickup?
> - How does Kinsey find out the identity of the killer?

Think Critically

2. **ACTIVE READING** **PREDICTING** Look over the predictions you made in your **READER'S NOTEBOOK**. At what point in the story did you predict the solution to the crime?

3. This story ends with the narrator's statement, "We live in a world in which justice is skewed." Explain what you think this statement of **theme** means and how the story illustrates it.

4. Do you think "Full Circle" is an appropriate **title** for this story? Explain why or why not.

5. Think about the beginning of the story. Why do you think Terry Layton stopped at the accident scene and went to Caroline Spurrier's car? Explain your interpretation.

Extend Interpretations

6. Critic's Corner One critic says the reason for Kinsey Millhone's popularity is that she qualifies as a traditional detective hero: someone who is "the best man in his world, and a good enough man for any world. Gender aside, Kinsey fills that prescription perfectly." Compare and contrast Kinsey Millhone with male detectives you may be familiar with from books, films, or television.

7. Connect to Life Do you agree with the narrator that justice in this world is "skewed"? Give examples that support your opinion.

>
> THINK ABOUT { • examples within the legal or judicial system
> • examples from your own experience

Literary Analysis

PLOT The sequence of events in a story is called the **plot.** Generally built around a **conflict,** the plot usually includes these elements:

- **Exposition** gives background about characters, conflict, and setting.
- The **rising action** introduces and develops the conflict, causing **suspense** to build.
- The **climax** is the turning point or peak of the action, the decisive moment when the outcome of the conflict becomes clear.
- The **falling action,** sometimes called the **resolution,** consists of the events after the climax as the story winds down.

Cooperative Learning Activity With a small group, outline the plot stages in "Full Circle." Use a diagram like the one shown. Then discuss the following questions: What does the exposition tell you? What point would you identify as the climax? What do you find out in the falling action?

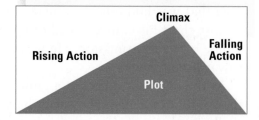

Choices & CHALLENGES

Writing Options

1. Alternative Ending A common device in detective stories is to include one or more misleading clues, or "red herrings," to divert readers from the identity of the real killer. Imagine that Terry Layton did not kill Caroline Spurrier. Draft a different ending to the story. Provide clues leading to the identify of the real killer. Place the draft in your **Working Portfolio.**

2. Mystery Outline Many mystery writers plan their stories by starting with the ending—that is, they first decide on the who, what, why, and how. Then they build a story that will intrigue readers and lead them up to the ending. Try this method and write a plot outline for a mystery story.

Writing Handbook
See page 1153: Narrative Writing.

Activities & Explorations

Clue Cards With a small group, write these names on separate index cards: Michelle Spurrier, Emerald, Lt. Dolan, D. Cole, Judy Layton, J. Birkett, R. Cagle. On each card, list the clues to the crime that person provides. Then, taking away a card at a time, try to solve the case with the remaining clues. Are any clues unimportant?
~ SPEAKING AND LISTENING

An investigator holds a Polaroid snapshot of a fingerprint taken by police

Inquiry & Research

Alternative Crime-Solving Methods Police and special investigators are most often the first group of people involved in the solution of a crime. But sometimes the police are stumped, or their explanation of a crime fails to satisfy family members or other interested parties. Investigate alternate methods of crime solving. What help can nonprofessionals be? What steps can parents take to protect their children from harm?

 Real World Link Read "'Who Killed My Daughter?': Lois Duncan Searches for an Answer" on pages 757–758 to help you answer these questions.

Vocabulary in Action

EXERCISE A: ASSESSMENT PRACTICE For each group of words below, write the letter of the word that is the best antonym for the boldfaced word.

1. **egotistical** (a) secure, (b) modest, (c) dull
2. **harass** (a) protect, (b) discourage, (c) scorn
3. **brevity** (a) sadness, (b) courage, (c) permanence
4. **enigmatic** (a) common, (b) important, (c) understandable
5. **skewed** (a) balanced, (b) loyal, (c) fortunate

EXERCISE B For each phrase in the first column, write the letter of the synonymous phrase from the second column.

1. a **sullen** visitor
2. **despondently** separated
3. an **inexplicable** increase
4. **wary** of Larry
5. **dispel** the smell

a. get rid of the odor
b. distrustful of Lawrence
c. a depressed guest
d. downheartedly parted
e. an unexplainable gain

Building Vocabulary

For an in-depth lesson on synonyms, antonyms, and other relationships among words, see page 849.

Grammar in Context: Using Adjective Clauses to Combine Sentences

In the following sentence from "Full Circle," Sue Grafton uses an adjective clause to help her convey several facts about a character in one sentence.

> I spotted my friend John Birkett, a photographer from the local paper, who'd reached the scene moments behind the paramedics.

An **adjective clause** is a group of words that contains a subject and a predicate and that modifies a noun or pronoun. Such a clause usually begins with *who, whom, whose, that,* or *which.* If Grafton had not used an adjective clause in the sentence above, she would have had to use two or more sentences to say the same thing: "I spotted my friend John Birkett, a photographer from the local paper. He'd reached the scene moments behind the paramedics." The combined sentence conveys rapid action better.

WRITING EXERCISE Combine each pair of sentences into a single sentence containing an adjective clause. Underline the adjective clause.

Example: *Original* The green Mercedes had caused the accident. It didn't have a scratch on it.
Rewritten The green Mercedes that had caused the accident didn't have a scratch on it.

1. My old VW could still keep up in traffic. The car suited my needs just fine.
2. In the next lane over was a young man. His pickup truck had seen better days.
3. In the other lane was a young woman. She seemed lost in thought.
4. I'm a detective. That fact makes me notice such details.
5. Others want explanations. I'm a person they rely on for them.

<u>Grammar Handbook</u> Clauses, p. 1195

Sue Grafton
1940–

Other Works
"A" Is for Alibi
"B" Is for Burglar
"C" Is for Corpse

Looking for Answers Someone once asked the award-winning mystery writer Sue Grafton what themes are in her books. Her answer was that she is interested in why people do what they do. "Why do we kill each other?" she said. "Why can't we be happy? I'm looking for answers, trying to figure it out."

Leading Two Lives Grafton's novels feature the California private investigator Kinsey Millhone, a tough, independent, sassy heroine. With the popular Millhone, Grafton firmly established a female hero as a detective, a role that was traditionally male. Grafton compared herself to Kinsey Millhone in an interview in *Armchair Detective:* "She's the person I would have been

had I not married young and had children. She'll always be thinner and younger and braver, the lucky so-and-so. Her biography is different, but our sensibilities are identical. At the core, we're the same. . . . Because of Kinsey, I get to lead two lives—hers and mine. Sometimes I'm not sure which I prefer."

Branching Out Besides mysteries, Grafton has written screenplays and television scripts, sometimes collaborating with her husband. She is the editor of *The Best American Mystery Stories 1998* and *Writing Mysteries: A Handbook by the Mystery Writers of America.*

Author Activity

What Comes After "Z"? Since 1982, Sue Grafton has been turning out Kinsey Millhone novels based on letters of the alphabet, starting with *"A" Is for Alibi.* Check a list of books in print and find out what letter she is up to now and what titles she came up with for the other letters not listed on this page.

"Who Killed My *Daughter?*"

Lois Duncan Searches for an Answer

When her 18-year-old daughter was murdered in 1989, Lois Duncan, a popular author of young adult (YA) mystery and crime novels, suffered the tragedy of having one of her plots become reality. The following article by Maria Simson appeared in the "Book News" section of Publisher's Weekly just prior to the release of Who Killed My Daughter?, Duncan's 1992 book.

"*Don't Look Behind You* was a book about a teenage girl who was chased by a hitman in a Camaro," says Lois Duncan of her 1989 YA novel. "Later that year, my eldest daughter, who was the model for the girl, was chased by a hitman driving a Camaro." The difference is that in real life, 18-year-old Kaitlyn Arquette was shot and killed. Since then, Duncan, who has 39 novels to her credit, has written only one book—*Who Killed My Daughter?: The True Story of a Mother's Search for Her Daughter's Murderer.*

Had Kaitlyn's death been the random killing that the police labeled it, there would have been no need for a search. But while settling her daughter's affairs, Duncan discovered from a telephone bill that calls had been made from Kaitlyn's apartment to an unlisted California number minutes after her death. Other discrepancies, too, led Duncan to suspect that her daughter's death was no accident.

"Soon after the murder I began having memory blackouts," says Duncan. "As I didn't want to misremember anything, I began taking daily notes"—notes that quickly began developing into a book. "It helped keep me sane. I would sit down and write a chapter in real time, but I never knew what was going to happen next."

Duncan, who used to teach journalism at the University of New Mexico, spent the next two years following up leads. When these cooled, she turned, with some skepticism, to psychic investigators who helped her pick up the trail. But these leads, too, petered out. Duncan decided that "the only way to find out the missing information was to make the story public."

Reading for Information

When you complete an essay or report for school, you write with specific goals or aims. This is true of all writers whether they're writing a book, a newspaper feature, or a magazine article.

AUTHOR'S PURPOSE

Author's purpose refers to the reasons the writer has for writing. Authors write for a variety of reasons, including to persuade, to inform, to entertain, or to express an opinion. Often there is more than one purpose for a particular piece of writing. In this case, Maria Simson's purpose is to promote Duncan's book to the publishing field. The article appears in a trade magazine that covers news in the book and publishing industry.

YOUR TURN Use the questions and activities below to evaluate the nature of the author's purpose in this article.

❶ In this lengthy passage, Simson gives information about Duncan and explains why she has written this book. What would you say is Simson's purpose in this part of the article?

This January, on what would have been Kaitlyn's 21st birthday, she mailed the manuscript to her agent, Claire Smith, who in turn sent it on to both Dell/Delacorte publisher Carole Baron and Books for Young Readers division publisher George Nicholson. "We had done a lot of business with Lois through the Books for Young Readers department, so it was natural we would see it," says Baron. Even though she did not know Duncan personally, she was well aware of her daughter's death, having been in Albuquerque at the time of the killing.

Baron hopes that the book will travel beyond the normal true-crime audience to interest any parent who is concerned about the increasing violence against children: "It doesn't matter who you are—all kids can get hurt," she says. According to associate publicity director Judy Westerman, the mainstream media, including major talk shows, have already expressed considerable interest in the book, which will no doubt bolster[1] Duncan on her first-ever author tour.

But Delacorte sees yet another audience as well, among Duncan's original readers—young adults. "Booksellers who know her from her novels are very interested in this project, and our sales force is tapping into that," says Baron. "Young adults will have no difficulty reading the book." Everyone connected with the book remarks upon its similarities to Duncan's YA stories of murder and mystery. And when Duncan visits the American Library Association and the Canadian Library Association this year, she will be participating both as an adult author and as a YA author.

There is, however, one other audience and that is the one Duncan is most desperate to reach. "We've found out so much [about Kaitlyn's death] but there are still holes. We're hoping that someone out there will be able to help fill a few of those holes." With that in mind, *Who Killed My Daughter?* opens with a list of possible scenarios[2] and unanswered questions, along with addresses for Duncan and for the New Mexico attorney general, in the hope that some reader will come forward with information that answers the question in Duncan's title.

---

1. **bolster:** support or strengthen.
2. **scenarios:** outlines or models of a supposed sequence of events.

❷ In these two paragraphs, Simson includes comments about Duncan's book from people in the publishing industry. What reasons does Carole Baron give for publishing the book? What do you think Simson's purpose is in these two paragraphs? What other information could she have included that would have helped her purpose?

❸ Why do you think Simson includes this paragraph in a promotional piece for the publishing industry? Does she want to inform, to persuade, to entertain, or to express an opinion? Explain.

Inquiry & Research

Activity Link: "Full Circle," p. 755 Now that you've read an article about a real person trying to solve a loved one's murder, how would you compare Duncan's effort to those of the narrator in "Full Circle"?

Wasps' Nest

Short Story by AGATHA CHRISTIE

See art on p. 764.

Connect to Your Life

A Good Detective Imagine that you are the chief of police and that you need a detective to investigate a murder. What kind of person would you want for the job? Think about any fictional detectives that you have encountered in stories, movies, or television shows. What qualities do they possess? Think about the qualities you would look for in a good detective. With your classmates, discuss which qualities seem to be the most important, as well as traits that would not be desirable.

Build Background

Setting a Challenge For almost 60 years, Agatha Christie created mystery plots to challenge her famous fictional detective, Hercule Poirot. In 33 books and 56 short stories, including "Wasps' Nest," this somewhat eccentric little man solves crimes by using what he calls his "little gray cells"— that is, his brain. Poirot's method is to look beyond obvious clues to the psychology of a crime, using hunches and his "gray cells" to establish motives and hunt down murderers.

WORDS TO KNOW
Vocabulary Preview

absurd	languorous
fathom	lull
foreboding	resolutely
hospitable	slacken
impersonally	suitor

Focus Your Reading

LITERARY ANALYSIS BUILDING SUSPENSE Mystery and detective writers work hard to develop **suspense** in their stories. They use a variety of techniques to make the reader uncertain about the outcome of the plot. For example, a key character might disappear, or an innocent person might look guilty for a while. Writers may also use **foreshadowing,** supplying hints or clues about what might occur later. These techniques build suspense at the same time that they prepare the reader for what is to come.

As you read "Wasps' Nest," look for foreshadowing and other techniques that build tension. Try to predict what will happen, keeping in mind that a writer of a detective story wants to keep you off balance.

ACTIVE READING QUESTIONING To get the most out of a story, be a reading detective. Think about questions you would like to ask the author or a character. **Questioning** can help you become more involved in what you're reading. Make a mental note of confusing or mysterious statements, motives, or behavior and then see if further reading makes them clear. For example, read this sentence from "Wasps' Nest":

> *The detective was looking straight at him and again there was something so unusual in his glance that Harrison hardly knew how to proceed.*

At this point you might ask questions such as: "What is so unusual about the detective's glance?" or "Why is he looking at him that way?"

READER'S NOTEBOOK As you read this story, jot down any questions that come to your mind about the characters or plot.

WASPS' NEST

Agatha Christie

OUT OF THE HOUSE CAME JOHN HARRISON AND STOOD A MOMENT ON THE TERRACE LOOKING OUT OVER THE GARDEN. HE WAS A BIG MAN WITH A LEAN, CADAVEROUS[1] FACE. HIS ASPECT WAS USUALLY SOMEWHAT GRIM BUT WHEN, AS NOW, THE RUGGED FEATURES SOFTENED INTO A SMILE, THERE WAS SOMETHING VERY ATTRACTIVE ABOUT HIM.

John Harrison loved his garden, and it had never looked better than it did on this August evening, summery and languorous. The rambler roses were still beautiful; sweet peas scented the air.

A well-known creaking sound made Harrison turn his head sharply. Who was coming in through the garden gate? In another minute, an expression of utter astonishment came over his face, for the dandified[2] figure coming up the path was the last he expected to see in this part of the world.

"By all that's wonderful," cried Harrison. "Monsieur Poirot!"

It was, indeed, the famous Hercule Poirot whose renown as a detective had spread over the whole world.

"Yes," he said, "it is I. You said to me once: 'If you are ever in this part of the world, come and see me.' I take you at your word. I arrive."

"And I'm delighted," said Harrison heartily. "Sit down and have a drink."

With a hospitable hand, he indicated a table on the veranda bearing assorted bottles.

"I thank you," said Poirot, sinking down into a basket chair. "You have, I suppose, no *sirop*?[3] No, no, I thought not. A little plain soda water then—no whisky." And he added in a feeling voice as the other placed the glass beside him: "Alas, my moustaches are limp. It is this heat!"

"And what brings you into this quiet spot?" asked Harrison as he dropped into another chair. "Pleasure?"

"No, *mon ami*,[4] business."

1. cadaverous (kə-dăv′ər-əs): thin and bony.
2. dandified (dăn′də-fīd′): carefully and elegantly dressed.
3. sirop (sē-rō′) *French:* fruit syrup.
4. mon ami (môn ä-mē′) *French:* my friend.

WORDS TO KNOW
languorous (lăng′gər-əs) *adj.* creating a dreamy, lazy mood
hospitable (hŏs′pĭ-tə-bəl) *adj.* welcoming; cordial

"Business? In this out-of-the-way place?"

Poirot nodded gravely. "But yes, my friend, all crimes are not committed in crowds, you know?"

The other laughed. "I suppose that was rather an idiotic remark of mine. But what particular crime are you investigating down here, or is that a thing I mustn't ask?"

"You may ask," said the detective. "Indeed, I would prefer that you asked."

Harrison looked at him curiously. He sensed something a little unusual in the other's manner. "You are investigating a crime, you say?" he advanced rather hesitatingly. "A serious crime?"

"A crime of the most serious there is."

"You mean . . ."

"Murder."

So gravely did Hercule Poirot say that word that Harrison was quite taken aback. The detective was looking straight at him and again there was something so unusual in his glance that Harrison hardly knew how to proceed. At last, he said: "But I have heard of no murder."

"No," said Poirot, "you would not have heard of it."

"Who has been murdered?"

"As yet," said Hercule Poirot, "nobody."

"What?"

"That is why I said you would not have heard of it. I am investigating a crime that has not yet taken place."

"But look here, that is nonsense."

"Not at all. If one can investigate a murder before it has happened, surely that is very much better than afterwards. One might even—a little idea—prevent it."

Harrison stared at him. "You are not serious, Monsieur Poirot."

"But yes, I am serious."

"You really believe that a murder is going to be committed? Oh, it's absurd!"

Hercule Poirot finished the first part of the sentence without taking any notice of the exclamation.

"Unless we can manage to prevent it. Yes, *mon ami,* that is what I mean."

"We?"

"I said we. I shall need your co-operation."

"Is that why you came down here?"

Again Poirot looked at him, and again an indefinable something made Harrison uneasy.

"I came here, Monsieur Harrison, because I—well—like you."

And then he added in an entirely different voice: "I see, Monsieur Harrison, that you have a wasps' nest there. You should destroy it."

The change of subject made Harrison frown in a puzzled way. He followed Poirot's glance and said in rather a bewildered voice:

"As a matter of fact, I'm going to. Or rather, young Langton is. You remember Claude Langton? He was at that same dinner where I met you. He's coming over this evening to take the nest. Rather fancies himself at the job."[5]

"Ah!" said Poirot. "And how is he going to do it?"

"Petrol[6] and the garden syringe.[7] He's bringing his own syringe over; it's a more convenient size than mine."

"There is another way, is there not?" asked Poirot. "With cyanide of potassium?"

"You really believe that a murder is going to be committed?"

---

5. **fancies himself at the job:** thinks he's good at the task.

6. **petrol** (pĕt′rəl): gasoline.

7. **syringe** (sə-rĭnj′): sprayer.

WORDS TO KNOW   **absurd** (əb-sûrd′) *adj.* ridiculous; nonsensical

Harrison looked a little surprised. "Yes, but that's rather dangerous stuff. Always a risk having it about the place."

Poirot nodded gravely. "Yes, it is deadly poison." He waited a minute and then repeated in a grave voice: "Deadly poison."

"Useful if you want to do away with your mother-in-law, eh?" said Harrison with a laugh.

But Hercule Poirot remained grave. "And you are quite sure, Monsieur Harrison, that it is with petrol that Monsieur Langton is going to destroy your wasps' nest?"

"Quite sure. Why?"

"I wondered. I was at the chemist's[8] in Barchester this afternoon. For one of my purchases I had to sign the poison book. I saw the last entry. It was for cyanide of potassium and it was signed for by Claude Langton."

Harrison stared. "That's odd," he said. "Langton told me the other day that he'd never dream of using the stuff; in fact, he said it oughtn't to be sold for the purpose."

Poirot looked out over the roses. His voice was very quiet as he asked a question. "Do you like Langton?"

The other started. The question somehow seemed to find him quite unprepared. "I—I—well, I mean—of course, I like him. Why shouldn't I?"

"I only wondered," said Poirot placidly, "whether you did."

And as the other did not answer, he went on. "I also wondered if he liked you?"

"What are you getting at, Monsieur Poirot? There's something in your mind I can't <u>fathom</u>."

"I am going to be very frank. You are engaged to be married, Monsieur Harrison. I know Miss Molly Deane. She is a very charming, a very beautiful girl. Before she was engaged to you, she was engaged to Claude Langton. She threw him over for you."

Harrison nodded.

"I do not ask what her reasons were; she may have been justified. But I tell you this, it is not too much to suppose that Langton has not forgotten or forgiven."

"You're wrong, Monsieur Poirot. I swear you're wrong. Langton's been a sportsman;[9] he's taken things like a man. He's been amazingly decent to me—gone out of his way to be friendly."

"And that does not strike you as unusual? You use the word 'amazingly,' but you do not seem to be amazed."

"What do you mean, Monsieur Poirot?"

"I mean," said Poirot, and his voice had a new note in it, "that a man may conceal his hate till the proper time comes."

"Hate?" Harrison shook his head and laughed.

"The English are very stupid," said Poirot. "They think that they can deceive anyone but that no one can deceive them. The sportsman—the good fellow—never will they believe evil of him. And because they are brave, but stupid, sometimes they die when they need not die."

"You are warning me," said Harrison in a low voice. "I see it now—what has puzzled me all along. You are warning me against Claude Langton. You came here today to warn me . . ."

Poirot nodded. Harrison sprang up suddenly. "But you are mad, Monsieur Poirot. This is England. Things don't happen like that here. Disappointed <u>suitors</u> don't go about stabbing people in the back and poisoning them. And you're wrong about Langton. That chap wouldn't hurt a fly."

"The lives of flies are not my concern," said Poirot placidly. "And although you say Monsieur Langton would not take the life of one, yet you forget that he is even now preparing to take the lives of several thousand wasps."

---

8. **chemist's:** pharmacy.

9. **sportsman:** good sport.

WORDS TO KNOW	**fathom** (făth′əm) v. to understand; comprehend **suitor** (sōō′tər) n. a man courting a woman

763

The Garden in the rue Cortot, Montmartre (1876), Pierre-Auguste Renoir. Oil on canvas, 59¾″ × 38⅜″. Carnegie Museum of Art, Pittsburgh, Pennsylvania. Acquired through the generosity of Mrs. Alan M. Scaife (65.35). Photograph by Peter Harholdt.

Harrison did not at once reply. The little detective in his turn sprang to his feet. He advanced to his friend and laid a hand on his shoulder. So agitated was he that he almost shook the big man, and, as he did so, he hissed into his ear: "Rouse yourself, my friend; rouse yourself. And look—look where I am pointing. There on the bank, close by that tree root. See you, the wasps returning home, placid at the end of the day? In a little hour, there will be destruction, and they know it not. There is no one to tell them. They have not, it seems, a Hercule Poirot. I tell you, Monsieur Harrison, I am down here on business. Murder is my business. And it is my business before it has happened as well as afterwards. At what time does Monsieur Langton come to take this wasps' nest?"

"Langton would never . . ."

"At what time?"

"At nine o'clock. But I tell you, you're all wrong. Langton would never . . ."

"These English!" cried Poirot in a passion. He caught up his hat and stick and moved down the path, pausing to speak over his shoulder. "I do not stay to argue with you. I should only enrage myself. But you understand, I return at nine o'clock?"

Harrison opened his mouth to speak, but Poirot did not give him the chance. "I know what you would say: 'Langton would never,' et cetera. Ah, Langton would never! But all the same I return at nine o'clock. But, yes, it will amuse me—put it like that—it will amuse me to see the taking of a wasps' nest. Another of your English sports!"

He waited for no reply but passed rapidly down the path and out through the door that creaked. Once outside on the road, his pace slackened. His vivacity[10] died down, his face became grave and troubled. Once he drew his watch from his pocket and consulted it. The hands pointed to ten minutes past eight. "Over three quarters of an hour," he murmured. "I wonder if I should have waited."

His footsteps slackened; he almost seemed on the point of returning. Some vague foreboding seemed to assail him. He shook it off resolutely, however, and continued to walk in the direction of the village. But his face was still troubled, and once or twice he shook his head like a man only partly satisfied.

It was still some minutes of nine when he once more approached the garden door. It was a clear, still evening; hardly a breeze stirred the leaves. There was, perhaps, something a little sinister in the stillness, like the lull before a storm.

Poirot's footsteps quickened ever so slightly. He was suddenly alarmed—and uncertain. He feared he knew not what.

And at that moment the garden door opened and Claude Langton stepped quickly out into the road. He started when he saw Poirot.

"Oh—er—good evening."

"Good evening, Monsieur Langton. You are early."

Langton stared at him. "I don't know what you mean."

"You have taken the wasps' nest?"

"As a matter of fact, I didn't."

"Oh!" said Poirot softly. "So you did not take the wasps' nest. What did you do then?"

"Oh, just sat and yarned[11] a bit with old Harrison. I really must hurry along now, Monsieur Poirot. I'd no idea you were remaining in this part of the world."

"I had business here, you see."

"Oh! Well, you'll find Harrison on the terrace. Sorry I can't stop."

---

10. **vivacity** (vĭ-văs′ĭ-tē): liveliness.

11. **yarned:** chatted.

He hurried away. Poirot looked after him. A nervous young fellow, good-looking, with a weak mouth!

"So I shall find Harrison on the terrace," murmured Poirot. "I wonder." He went in through the garden door and up the path. Harrison was sitting in a chair by the table. He sat motionless and did not even turn his head as Poirot came up to him.

"Ah! *Mon ami,*" said Poirot. "You are all right, eh?"

There was a long pause and then Harrison said in a queer, dazed voice, "What did you say?"

"I said—are you all right?"

"All right? Yes, I'm all right. Why not?"

"You feel no ill effects? That is good."

"Ill effects? From what?"

"Washing soda."[12]

Harrison roused himself suddenly. "Washing soda? What do you mean?"

Poirot made an apologetic gesture. "I infinitely regret the necessity, but I put some in your pocket."

"You put some in my pocket? What on earth for?"

Harrison stared at him. Poirot spoke quietly and <u>impersonally</u> like a lecturer coming down to the level of a small child.

"You see, one of the advantages, or disadvantages, of being a detective is that it brings you into contact with the criminal classes. And the criminal classes, they can teach you some very interesting and curious things. There was a pickpocket once—I interested myself in him because for once in a way he has not done what they say he has done—and so I get him off. And because he is grateful he pays me in the only way he can think of—which is to show me the tricks of his trade.

"And so it happens that I can pick a man's pocket if I choose without his ever suspecting the fact. I lay one hand on his shoulder, I excite myself, and he feels nothing. But all the same I have managed to transfer what is in his pocket to my pocket and leave washing soda in its place.

"You see," continued Poirot dreamily, "if a man wants to get at some poison quickly to put in a glass, unobserved, he positively must keep it in his right-hand coat pocket; there is nowhere else. I knew it would be there."

He dropped his hand into his pocket and brought out a few white, lumpy crystals. "Exceedingly dangerous," he murmured, "to carry it like that—loose."

Calmly and without hurrying himself, he took from another pocket a wide-mouthed bottle. He slipped in the crystals, stepped to the table and filled up the bottle with plain water. Then carefully corking it, he shook it until all the crystals were dissolved. Harrison watched him as though fascinated.

Satisfied with his solution, Poirot stepped across to the nest. He uncorked the bottle, turned his head aside, and poured the solution into the wasps' nest, then stood back a pace or two watching.

Some wasps that were returning alighted, quivered a little and then lay still. Other wasps crawled out of the hole only to die. Poirot watched for a minute or two and then nodded his head and came back to the veranda.

"A quick death," he said. "A very quick death."

Harrison found his voice. "How much do you know?"

Poirot looked straight ahead. "As I told you, I saw Claude Langton's name in the book. What I did not tell you was that almost immediately afterwards, I happened to meet him. He told me he had been buying cyanide of potassium at your request—to take a wasps' nest. That struck me as

---

12. **washing soda:** sodium carbonate, a nonpoisonous chemical once commonly used as a cleaning agent.

WORDS
TO
KNOW

impersonally (ĭm-pûr′sə-nə-lē) *adv.* in an emotionally distant manner

a little odd, my friend, because I remember that at that dinner of which you spoke, you held forth[13] on the superior merits of petrol and denounced the buying of cyanide as dangerous and unnecessary."

"Go on."

"I knew something else. I had seen Claude Langton and Molly Deane together when they thought no one saw them. I do not know what lovers' quarrel it was that originally parted them and drove her into your arms, but I realized that misunderstandings were over and that Miss Deane was drifting back to her love."

"Go on."

"I knew something more, my friend. I was in Harley Street the other day, and I saw you come out of a certain doctor's house. I know that doctor and for what disease one consults him, and I read the expression on your face. I have seen it only once or twice in my lifetime, but it is not easily mistaken. It was the face of a man under sentence of death. I am right, am I not?"

"Quite right. He gave me two months."

"You did not see me, my friend, for you had other things to think about. I saw something else on your face—the thing that I told you this afternoon men try to conceal. I saw hate there, my friend. You did not trouble to conceal it, because you thought there were none to observe."

"Go on," said Harrison.

"There is not much more to say. I came down here, saw Langton's name by accident in the poison book as I tell you, met him, and came here to you. I laid traps for you. You denied having asked Langton to get cyanide, or rather you expressed surprise at his having done so.

You were taken aback at first at my appearance, but presently you saw how well it would fit in and you encouraged my suspicions. I knew from Langton himself that he was coming at half-past eight. You told me nine o'clock, thinking I should come and find everything over. And so I knew everything."

"Why did you come?" cried Harrison. "If only you hadn't come!"

Poirot drew himself up. "I told you," he said, "murder is my business."

"Murder? Suicide, you mean."

"No." Poirot's voice rang out sharply and clearly. "I mean murder. Your death was to be quick and easy, but the death you planned for Langton was the worst death any man can die. He bought the poison; he comes to see you, and he is alone with you. You die suddenly, and the cyanide is found in your glass, and Claude Langton hangs. That was your plan."

Again Harrison moaned.

"Why did you come? Why did you come?"

"I have told you, but there is another reason. I liked you. Listen, *mon ami,* you are a dying man; you have lost the girl you loved, but there is one thing that you are not: you are not a murderer. Tell me now: are you glad or sorry that I came?"

There was a moment's pause and Harrison drew himself up. There was a new dignity in his face—the look of a man who has conquered his own baser self.[14] He stretched out his hand across the table.

"Thank goodness you came," he cried. "Oh, thank goodness you came." ❖

---

13. **held forth:** talked at great length; lectured.

14. **his own baser** (bā′sər) **self:** the worst part of his character

Connect to the Literature

1. **What Do You Think?** What is your opinion of the "Hercule Poirot" method of detective work? Explain.

Comprehension Check
- What warning does Hercule Poirot give John Harrison?
- What "murder" plot does Poirot actually prevent?
- How does he prevent it?

Think Critically

2. How seriously do you think Harrison takes Poirot's warning about Claude Langton? Explain your answer.

3. Poirot knows about the real murder plan when he first visits Harrison. What is his **motivation** for making up a story about Langton instead of accusing Harrison right away?

THINK ABOUT

- Harrison's state of mind
- Poirot's reason for substituting the washing soda for the cyanide
- Harrison's final words

4. Why do you think Poirot gets so excited when trying to convince Harrison that Langton is capable of murder?

5. **ACTIVE READING   QUESTIONING**   Look at the **questions** you jotted down in your **READER'S NOTEBOOK** while reading the story. What questions were eventually answered by the story? What questions, if any, remained unanswered? Discuss them with classmates.

Extend Interpretations

6. **Critic's Corner** Critics often mention "Christie's technique of trickery." How does the author use trickery in this story? Who is the victim of this trickery?

7. **Connect to Life** Think about the way Poirot gathers evidence, approaches his suspect, and goes about getting a confession of guilt. How do the methods of this **character** compare with those of real-life detectives or even other fictional detectives as portrayed in films and television shows?

Literary Analysis

SURPRISE ENDING   A **surprise ending** is an unexpected twist in the **plot** at the end of a story. The surprise may be a sudden turn in the action or a piece of information that forces the reader to view the entire story in a new way. Especially in mystery and detective fiction, the idea is to surprise the reader, even though important clues have been planted. From the very beginning of this story, Christie cleverly directs the plot to a surprise ending. This raises two questions: Why is the ending unexpected? Do any details prepare the reader for the ending?

Paired Activity With a partner, see if you can agree on why the ending is a surprise. Then start at the beginning of the story and look for hints that all is not what it seems or that Harrison, rather than Langton, is actually the murder suspect. Look for clues in the words and actions of both Poirot and Harrison. In a chart like the one shown, jot down any clues that you find. Then decide whether they are obvious enough, when put together, to prepare the reader for the surprise ending. Share your clues, and discuss your thoughts with other classmates.

Clues to Surprise Ending		
Character	Words	Actions
Hercule Poirot		
John Harrison		

Choices & CHALLENGES

Writing Options

Diary Entry An important character in the story who does not appear is Molly Deane. Write one or two diary entries she might have composed during this story. Place your draft in your **Working Portfolio.**

Inquiry & Research

Nest Builders Using encyclopedias or the Internet, find out more about the nests built by wasps, yellow jackets, or hornets. How

dangerous are these insects? What should you do about a nest? Share your findings in an oral report to classmates.

More Online: Research Starter
www.mcdougallittell.com

Vocabulary in Action

EXERCISE: CONTEXT CLUES On your paper, write the Word to Know that best replaces the italicized word or phrase in each sentence below.

1. The suspect's *gracious and pleasant* manner masked her fear.
2. She seemed relaxed and even *drowsy.*
3. She spoke *in a detached way* about the victim.
4. "Was the victim ever a *boyfriend* of yours?" the detective asked.
5. "Oh, no," she said. "I didn't like him, but I still can't *conceive* why anyone would want to

harm him."

6. During a *pause* in the conversation, the detective studied his notes.
7. He knew it would be *foolish* to believe anything she told him.
8. He also had an *uneasy suspicion* that she would not tell him the truth.
9. I'm going to get to the bottom of this, he thought *with tenacity.*
10. Once he began a case, the detective didn't *let up* until the case was solved.

WORDS TO KNOW					
	absurd	foreboding	impersonally	lull	slacken
	fathom	hospitable	languorous	resolutely	suitor

Building Vocabulary
For an in-depth lesson on context clues, see page 103.

Agatha Christie
1890–1976

Other Works
Murder on the Orient Express
The Murder of Roger Ackroyd
The A.B.C. Murders
Ten Little Indians
The Mousetrap

Self-Starter Agatha Christie never attended school. Her mother believed that girls should not receive a formal education and should not learn to read before the age of eight. However, Christie learned to read earlier by asking the names of stores in the town of Torquay, England, where she was raised.

From Poirot to Marple When Christie was in her 20s, her sister dared her to write a detective story. As a result of this challenge, she created Hercule Poirot for her first novel, *The Mysterious Affair at*

Styles. Six publishers rejected it, but the book was finally published in 1920. In the 1930s, Christie created another crime-solver, Miss Jane Marple, who became as famous as Poirot. She solves murders through hunches, gossip, and a "nose for evil."

Dame Agatha In 1971, Queen Elizabeth of England honored Christie for her achievements by giving her the honorary British title *Dame.* Christie has been called "the most successful mystery writer the world has known." Over 2 billion copies of her books have already been sold, and approximately 25 million more are sold each year.

Author Activity

Poirot in Movies Find out which of Agatha Christie's works have been made into films and what actors have played the part of Poirot.

Trifles

Drama by SUSAN GLASPELL

"She was rockin' back and forth. She had her apron in her hand and was kind of— pleating it."

Connect to Your Life

Weighing Evidence *Trifles* is a short play about a murder in an isolated farmhouse. The word *trifle* means something of little importance or significance. Think about murder investigations that you have read or heard about and the kinds of rules or procedures that police follow when examining a crime scene. What kind of physical evidence do you think they consider most crucial, and what evidence might be overlooked or thought unimportant? What kinds of clues do you think women might notice more than men? Discuss these questions with your classmates.

Build Background

Life in a Lonely Place This play has an unusual setting for a murder—a Midwestern farm in the early 1900s. Farm life at that time was very different from what it is today. Few farmers owned cars or tractors. Some farmers had telephones, but most did not. Neither television nor radio had been invented yet. In fact, some farmhouses had no electricity until many years later. These conditions often created a sense of isolation, especially among farm women. Local church organizations, such as the Ladies' Aid, sponsored occasional social events that brought people together. Still, relief from the isolation and the loneliness of farm life was temporary at best.

> WORDS TO KNOW
> **Vocabulary Preview**
> abashed   facetiously
> comprehension   preoccupied
> covert

Focus Your Reading

LITERARY ANALYSIS | **DRAMATIC IRONY** | While watching a movie or a play, sometimes we see or know things that the characters themselves do not. This contrast between what a character is aware of and what the reader or audience knows is called **dramatic irony.**

For example, in a play we might see a phone ringing in an empty room—but the hero has just left, missing an important call. In a television program, we might observe a killer prowling a deserted house—and hope he doesn't find the frightened woman hiding in the closet. In each case, we experience a sense of dramatic irony.

ACTIVE READING | **MAKING INFERENCES** | **Inferences** are logical guesses based on facts. You often need to draw inferences to make sense of what you read or see. In *Trifles,* characters notice clues that allow them to make inferences. These clues are often isolated and seemingly unimportant. When put together, however, they form the basis for inferences about the circumstances of the murder, leading to a reconstruction of the crime and the revelation of the killer.

READER'S NOTEBOOK
As you read the play, jot down details that might turn out to be clues to the murderer.

Clues to the Murderer in Trifles
1. a half-wiped table
2.
3.

TRIFLES

Susan
Glaspell

CAST OF CHARACTERS

George Henderson, **County Attorney**
Henry Peters, **Sheriff**
Lewis **Hale,** a neighboring farmer

Mrs. Peters
Mrs. Hale

SCENE: *The kitchen in the now abandoned farmhouse of John Wright, a gloomy kitchen, and left without having been put in order—the walls covered with a faded wallpaper. Downstage right is a door leading to the parlor. On the right wall above this door is a built-in kitchen cupboard with shelves in the upper portion and drawers below. In the rear wall at right, up two steps, is a door opening onto stairs leading to the second floor. In the rear wall at left is a door to the shed and from there to the outside. Between these two doors is an old-fashioned black iron stove. Running along the left wall from the shed door is an old iron sink and sink shelf, in which is set a hand pump. Downstage of the sink is an uncurtained window. Near the window is an old wooden rocker. Center stage is an unpainted wooden kitchen table with straight chairs on either side. There is a small chair downstage right. Unwashed pans under the sink, a loaf of bread outside the breadbox, a dish towel on the table—other signs of incompleted work. At the rear the shed door opens and the* Sheriff *comes in followed by the* County Attorney *and* Hale. *The* Sheriff *and* Hale *are men in middle life, the* County Attorney *is a young man; all are much bundled up and go at once to the stove. They are followed by the two women—the* Sheriff's *wife,* Mrs. Peters, *first; she is a slight wiry woman, a thin nervous face.* Mrs. Hale *is larger and would ordinarily be called more comfortable-looking, but she is disturbed now and looks fearfully about as she enters. The women have come in slowly, and stand close together near the door.*

County Attorney (*at stove rubbing his hands*). This feels good. Come up to the fire, ladies.

Mrs. Peters (*after taking a step forward*). I'm not—cold.

Sheriff (*unbuttoning his overcoat and stepping away from the stove to right of table as if to mark the beginning of official business*). Now, Mr. Hale, before we move things about, you explain to Mr. Henderson just what you saw when you came here yesterday morning.

County Attorney (*crossing down to left of the table*). By the way, has anything been moved? Are things just as you left them yesterday?

Sheriff (*looking about*). It's just the same. When it dropped below zero last night, I thought I'd better send Frank out this morning to make a fire for us—(*sits right of center table*) no use getting pneumonia with a big case on, but I told him not to touch anything except the stove—and you know Frank.

County Attorney. Somebody should have been left here yesterday.

Sheriff. Oh—yesterday. When I had to send Frank to Morris Center for that man who went crazy—I want you to know I had my hands full yesterday. I knew you could get back from Omaha by today and as long as I went over everything here myself—

County Attorney. Well, Mr. Hale, tell just what happened when you came here yesterday morning.

Hale (*crossing down to above table*). Harry and I had started to town with a load of potatoes. We came along the road from my place and as I got here I said, "I'm going to see if I can't get John Wright to go in with me on a party telephone."[1] I spoke to Wright about it once before and he put me off, saying folks talked too much anyway, and all he asked was peace and quiet—I guess you know about how much he talked himself; but I thought maybe if I went to the house and talked about it before his wife, though I said to Harry that I didn't know as what his wife wanted made much difference to John—

County Attorney. Let's talk about that later, Mr. Hale. I do want to talk about that, but tell now just what happened when you got to the house.

Hale. I didn't hear or see anything; I knocked at the door, and still it was all quiet inside. I knew they must be up, it was past eight o'clock. So I knocked again, and I thought I heard somebody say, "Come in." I wasn't sure, I'm not sure yet, but I opened the door—this door (*indicating the door by which the two women are still standing*) and there in that rocker—(*pointing to it*) sat Mrs. Wright. (*They all look at the rocker downstage left.*)

County Attorney. What—was she doing?

Hale. She was rockin' back and forth. She had her apron in her hand and was kind of—pleating it.

County Attorney. And how did she—look?

Hale. Well, she looked queer.

County Attorney. How do you mean—queer?

Hale. Well, as if she didn't know what she was going to do next. And kind of done up.

County Attorney (*takes out notebook and pencil and sits left of center table*). How did she seem to feel about your coming?

Hale. Why, I don't think she minded—one way or other. She didn't pay much attention. I said, "How do, Mrs. Wright, it's cold, ain't it?" And she said, "Is it?"—and went on kind of pleating at her apron. Well, I was surprised; she didn't ask me to come up to the stove, or to set down, but just sat there, not even looking at me, so I said, "I want to see John." And then she—laughed. I guess you would call it a laugh. I thought of Harry and the team outside, so I said a little sharp: "Can't I see John?" "No,"

---

1. **party telephone:** A form of telephone circuit in which the telephone users—referred to as parties by the telephone company—within a particular community had to share the same phone line.

Room After Room (1967), Andrew Wyeth. Tempera on panel, collection of Mr. and Mrs. Andrew Wyeth.
Copyright © 1995 Andrew Wyeth.

she says, kind o' dull like. "Ain't he home?" says I. "Yes," says she, "he's home." "Then why can't I see him?" I asked her, out of patience. "'Cause he's dead," says she. "Dead?" says I. She just nodded her head, not getting a bit excited, but rockin' back and forth. "Why—where is he?" says I, not knowing what to say. She just pointed upstairs—like that (*himself pointing to the room above*). I started for the stairs, with the idea of going up there. I walked from there to here—then I says, "Why, what did he die of?" "He died of a rope round his neck," says she, and just went on pleatin' at her apron. Well, I went out and called Harry. I thought I might—need help. We went upstairs and there he was lyin'—

County Attorney. I think I'd rather have you go into that upstairs, where you can point it all out. Just go on now with the rest of the story.

Hale. Well, my first thought was to get that rope off. It looked . . . (*Stops. His face twitches.*) . . . but Harry, he went up to him, and he said, "No, he's dead all right, and we'd better not touch anything." So we went back downstairs. She was still sitting that same way. "Has anybody been notified?" I asked. "No," says she, unconcerned. "Who did this, Mrs. Wright?" said Harry. He said it businesslike—and she stopped pleatin' of her apron. "I don't know," she says. "You don't *know?*" says Harry. "No," says she. "Weren't you sleepin' in the bed with him?" says Harry. "Yes," says she, "but I was on the inside." "Somebody slipped a rope round his neck and strangled him and you didn't wake up?" says Harry. "I didn't wake up," she said after him. We must 'a' looked as if we didn't see how that could be, for after a minute she said, "I sleep sound." Harry was going to ask her more questions but I said maybe we ought to let her tell her story first to the coroner, or the sheriff, so Harry went fast as he could to Rivers' place, where there's a telephone.

County Attorney. And what did Mrs. Wright do when she knew that you had gone for the coroner?

Hale. She moved from the rocker to that chair over there (*pointing to a small chair in the downstage right corner*) and just sat there with her hands held together and looking down. I got a feeling that I ought to make some conversation, so I said I had come in to see if John wanted to put in a telephone, and at that she started to laugh, and then she stopped and looked at me—scared. (*The County Attorney, who has had his notebook out, makes a note.*) I dunno, maybe it wasn't scared. I wouldn't like to say it was. Soon Harry got back, and then Dr. Lloyd came, and you, Mr. Peters, and so I guess that's all I know that you don't.

County Attorney (*rising and looking around*). I guess we'll go upstairs first—and then out to the barn and around there. (*To the* Sheriff) You're convinced that there was nothing important here—nothing that would point to any motive?

Sheriff. Nothing here but kitchen things. (*The County Attorney, after again looking around the kitchen, opens the door of a cupboard closet in right wall. He brings a small chair from right—gets up on it and looks on a shelf. Pulls his hand away, sticky.*)

County Attorney. Here's a nice mess. (*The women draw nearer upstage center.*)

Mrs. Peters (*to the other woman*). Oh, her fruit; it did freeze. (*To the* Lawyer) She worried about that when it turned so cold. She said the fire'd go out and her jars would break.

Sheriff (*rises*). Well, can you beat the women! Held for murder and worryin' about her preserves.

County Attorney (*getting down from chair*). I guess before we're through she may have something more serious than preserves to worry about. (*crosses down right center*)

Hale. Well, women are used to worrying over trifles.

(*The two women move a little closer together.*)

County Attorney (*with the gallantry of a young politician*). And yet, for all their worries, what would we do without the ladies? (*The women do not unbend. He goes below the center table to the sink, takes a dipperful of water from the pail and, pouring it into a basin, washes his hands. While he is doing this, the* Sheriff *and* Hale *cross to cupboard, which they inspect. The* County Attorney *starts to wipe his hands on the roller towel, turns it for a cleaner place.*) Dirty towels! (*Kicks his foot against the pans under the sink.*) Not much of a housekeeper, would you say, ladies?

Mrs. Hale (*stiffly*). There's a great deal of work to be done on a farm.

County Attorney. To be sure. And yet (*with a little bow to her*) I know there are some Dickson County farmhouses which do not have such roller towels. (*He gives it a pull to expose its full length again.*)

Mrs. Hale. Those towels get dirty awful quick. Men's hands aren't always as clean as they might be.

County Attorney. Ah, loyal to your sex, I see. But you and Mrs. Wright were neighbors. I suppose you were friends, too.

Mrs. Hale (*shaking her head*). I've not seen much of her of late years. I've not been in this house—it's more than a year.

County Attorney (*crossing to women upstage center*). And why was that? You didn't like her?

Mrs. Hale. I liked her all well enough. Farmers' wives have their hands full, Mr. Henderson. And then—

County Attorney. Yes—?

Mrs. Hale (*looking about*). It never seemed a very cheerful place.

County Attorney. No—it's not cheerful. I shouldn't say she had the homemaking instinct.

Mrs. Hale. Well, I don't know as Wright had, either.

County Attorney. You mean that they didn't get on very well?

Mrs. Hale. No, I don't mean anything. But I don't think a place'd be any cheerfuller for John Wright's being in it.

County Attorney. I'd like to talk more of that a little later. I want to get the lay of things upstairs now. (*He goes past the women to upstage right where steps lead to a stair door.*)

Sheriff. I suppose anything Mrs. Peters does'll be all right. She was to take in some clothes for her, you know, and a few little things. We left in such a hurry yesterday.

County Attorney. Yes, but I would like to see what you take, Mrs. Peters, and keep an eye out for anything that might be of use to us.

Mrs. Peters. Yes, Mr. Henderson. (*The men leave by upstage right door to stairs. The women listen to the men's steps on the stairs, then look about the kitchen.*)

Mrs. Hale (*crossing left to sink*). I'd hate to have men coming into my kitchen, snooping around and criticizing. (*She arranges the pans under sink which the lawyer had shoved out of place.*)

Mrs. Peters. Of course it's no more than their duty. (*crosses to cupboard upstage right*)

Mrs. Hale. Duty's all right, but I guess that deputy sheriff that came out to make the fire might have got a little of this on. (*Gives the roller towel a pull.*) Wish I'd thought of that sooner. Seems mean to talk about her for not having things slicked up when she had to come away in such a hurry. (*Crosses right to Mrs. Peters at cupboard.*)

Mrs. Peters (*who has been looking through cupboard, lifts one end of a towel that covers a pan*). She had bread set. (*Stands still.*)

Mrs. Hale (*eyes fixed on a loaf of bread beside the breadbox, which is on a low shelf of the cupboard*). She was going to put this in there. (*Picks up loaf, then abruptly drops it. In a manner of returning to familiar things.*) It's a

The Pantry, Art Gore.

shame about her fruit. I wonder if it's all gone. (*Gets up on the chair and looks.*) I think there's some here that's all right, Mrs. Peters. Yes—here; (*holding it toward the window*) this is cherries, too. (*looking again*) I declare I believe that's the only one. (*Gets down, jar in her hand. Goes to the sink and wipes it off on the outside.*) She'll feel awful bad after all her hard work in the hot weather. I remember the afternoon I put up my cherries last summer. (*She puts the jar on the big kitchen table, center of the room. With a sigh, is about to sit down in the rocking chair. Before she is seated realizes what chair it is; with a slow look at it, steps back. The chair which she has touched rocks back and forth. Mrs. Peters moves to center table and they both watch the chair rock for a moment or two.*)

Mrs. Peters (*shaking off the mood which the empty rocking chair has evoked; now in a businesslike manner she speaks*). Well, I must get those things from the front room closet. (*She goes to the door at the right, but, after looking into the other room, steps back*). You coming with me, Mrs. Hale? You could help me carry them. (*They go in the other room; reappear,* Mrs. Peters *carrying a dress, petticoat and skirt,* Mrs. Hale *following with a pair of shoes.*) My, it's cold in there. (*She puts the clothes on the big table, and hurries to the stove.*)

Mrs. Hale (*right of center table examining the skirt*). Wright was close.[2] I think maybe that's why she kept so much to herself. She didn't even belong to the Ladies' Aid. I suppose she felt she couldn't do her part, and then you don't enjoy things when you feel shabby. I heard she used to wear pretty clothes and be lively, when she was Minnie Foster, one of the town girls singing in the choir. But that—oh, that was thirty years ago. This all you was to take in?

Mrs. Peters. She said she wanted an apron. Funny thing to want, for there isn't much to get you dirty in jail, goodness knows. But I suppose just to make her feel more natural. (*crosses to cupboard.*) She said they was in the top drawer in this cupboard. Yes, here. And then her little shawl that always hung behind the door. (*Opens stair door and looks.*) Yes, here it is. (*Quickly shuts door leading upstairs.*)

Mrs. Hale (*abruptly moving toward her*). Mrs. Peters?

Mrs. Peters. Yes, Mrs. Hale? (*At upstage right door.*)

Mrs. Hale. Do you think she did it?

Mrs. Peters (*in a frightened voice*). Oh, I don't know.

Mrs. Hale. Well, I don't think she did. Asking for an apron and her little shawl. Worrying about her fruit.

Mrs. Peters (*Starts to speak, glances up, where footsteps are heard in the room above. In a low voice*). Mr. Peters says it looks bad for her. Mr. Henderson is awful sarcastic in a speech and he'll make fun of her sayin' she didn't wake up.

Mrs. Hale. Well, I guess John Wright didn't wake when they was slipping that rope under his neck.

Mrs. Peters (*crossing slowly to table and placing shawl and apron on table with other clothing*). No, it's strange. It must have been done awful crafty and still. They say it was such a—funny way to kill a man, rigging it all up like that.

Mrs. Hale (*crossing to left of* Mrs. Peters *at table*). That's just what Mr. Hale said. There was a gun in the house. He says that's what he can't understand.

Mrs. Peters. Mr. Henderson said coming out that what was needed for the case was a motive; something to show anger, or—sudden feeling.

Mrs. Hale (*who is standing by the table*). Well, I don't see any signs of anger around here. (*She puts her hand on the dishtowel which lies on the table, stands looking down at table, one-half of which is clean, the other half messy.*) It's wiped to here. (*Makes a move as if to finish work, then turns and looks at loaf of bread outside the breadbox. Drops towel. In that voice of coming back to familiar things.*) Wonder how they are finding things upstairs. (*Crossing below table to downstage right*) I hope she had it a little more readied-up[3] up there. You know, it seems kind of sneaking. Locking her up in town and then coming out here and trying to get her own house to turn against her!

Mrs. Peters. But, Mrs. Hale, the law is the law.

Mrs. Hale. I s'pose 'tis. (*unbuttoning her coat*) Better loosen up your things, Mrs. Peters. You won't feel them when you go out. (Mrs. Peters *takes off her fur tippet,[4] goes to hang it on chair back left of table, stands looking at the work basket on floor near downstage left window.*)

---

2. **close:** giving or spending reluctantly; stingy.

3. **readied-up:** *dialect,* made ready; straightened up.

4. **tippet:** a scarflike or shawllike garment.

Mrs. Peters. She was piecing a quilt. (*She brings the large sewing basket to the center table and they look at the bright pieces,* Mrs. Hale *above the table and* Mrs. Peters *left of it.*)

Mrs. Hale. It's a log cabin pattern.[5] Pretty, isn't it? I wonder if she was goin' to quilt it or just knot it?[6] (*Footsteps have been heard coming down the stairs. The* Sheriff *enters followed by* Hale *and the* County Attorney.)

Sheriff. They wonder if she was going to quilt it or just knot it! (*The men laugh, the women look* abashed.)

County Attorney (*rubbing his hands over the stove*). Frank's fire didn't do much up there, did it? Well, let's go out to the barn and get that cleared up. (*The men go outside by upstage left door.*)

Mrs. Hale (*resentfully*). I don't know as there's anything so strange, our takin' up our time with little things while we're waiting for them to get the evidence. (*She sits in chair right of table smoothing out a block with decision.*) I don't see as it's anything to laugh about.

Mrs. Peters (*apologetically*). Of course they've got awful important things on their minds. (*Pulls up a chair and joins* Mrs. Hale *at the left of the table.*)

Mrs. Hale (*examining another block*). Mrs. Peters, look at this one. Here, this is the one she was working on, and look at the sewing! All the rest of it has been so nice and even. And look at this! It's all over the place! Why, it looks as if she didn't know what she was about! (*After she has said this they look at each other, then start to glance back at the door. After an instant* Mrs. Hale *has pulled at a knot and ripped the sewing.*)

Mrs. Peters. Oh, what are you doing, Mrs. Hale?

Mrs. Hale (*mildly*). Just pulling out a stitch or two that's not sewed very good. (*threading a needle*) Bad sewing always made me fidgety.

Mrs. Peters (*with a glance at door, nervously*). I don't think we ought to touch things.

Mrs. Hale. I'll just finish up this end. (*suddenly stopping and leaning forward*) Mrs. Peters?

Mrs. Peters. Yes, Mrs. Hale?

Mrs. Hale. What do you suppose she was so nervous about?

Mrs. Peters. Oh—I don't know, I don't know as she was nervous. I sometimes sew awful queer when I'm just tired. (Mrs. Hale *starts to say something, looks at* Mrs. Peters, *then goes on sewing.*) Well, I must get these things wrapped up. They may be through sooner than we think. (*Putting apron and other things together*) I wonder where I can find a piece of paper, and string. (*Rises.*)

Mrs. Hale. In that cupboard, maybe.

Mrs. Peters (*crosses right looking in cupboard*). Why, here's a birdcage. (*Holds it up.*) Did she have a bird, Mrs. Hale?

Mrs. Hale. Why, I don't know whether she did or not—I've not been here for so long. There was a man around last year selling canaries cheap, but I don't know as she took one; maybe she did. She used to sing real pretty herself.

Mrs. Peters (*glancing around*). Seems funny to think of a bird here. But she must have had one, or why would she have a cage? I wonder what happened to it?

Mrs. Hale. I s'pose maybe the cat got it.

Mrs. Peters. No, she didn't have a cat. She's got that feeling some people have about cats—being afraid of them. My cat got in her room and she was real upset and asked me to take it out.

---

5. **log cabin pattern:** a common pattern for a quilt.

6. **quilt it or just knot it:** the bottom and top layers of a quilt are either quilted—sewn together—or knotted—held together with yarn tied into knots. Knotting is a much simpler and faster method.

Mrs. Hale. My sister Bessie was like that. Queer, ain't it?

Mrs. Peters (*examining the cage*). Why, look at this door. It's broke. One hinge is pulled apart. (*Takes a step down to* Mrs. Hale's *right.*)

Mrs. Hale (*looking too*). Looks as if someone must have been rough with it.

Mrs. Peters. Why, yes. (*She brings the cage forward and puts it on the table.*)

Mrs. Hale (*glancing toward upstage left door*). I wish if they're going to find any evidence they'd be about it. I don't like this place.

Mrs. Peters. But I'm awful glad you came with me, Mrs. Hale. It would be lonesome for me sitting here alone.

Mrs. Hale. It would, wouldn't it? (*dropping her sewing*) But I tell you what I do wish, Mrs. Peters. I wish I had come over sometimes when she was here. I—(*looking around the room*)—wish I had.

Mrs. Peters. But of course you were awful busy, Mrs. Hale—your house and your children.

Mrs. Hale (*rises and crosses left*). I could've come. I stayed away because it weren't cheerful—and that's why I ought to have come. I—(*looking out left window*)—I've never liked this place. Maybe because it's down in a hollow and you don't see the road. I dunno what it is, but it's a lonesome place and always was. I wish I had come over to see Minnie Foster sometimes. I can see now—(*shakes her head*)

Mrs. Peters (*left of table and above it*). Well, you mustn't reproach yourself, Mrs. Hale. Somehow we just don't see how it is with other folks until—something turns up.

Mrs. Hale. Not having children makes less work—but it makes a quiet house, and Wright out to work all day, and no company when he did come in. (*turning from window*) Did you know John Wright, Mrs. Peters?

Mrs. Peters. Not to know him; I've seen him in town. They say he was a good man.

Mrs. Hale. Yes—good; he didn't drink, and kept his word as well as most, I guess, and paid his debts. But he was a hard man, Mrs. Peters. Just to pass the time of day with him—(*shivers*) Like a raw wind that gets to the bone. (*pauses, her eye falling on the cage*) I should think she would 'a' wanted a bird. But what do you suppose went with it?

Mrs. Peters. I don't know, unless it got sick and died. (*She reaches over and swings the broken door, swings it again, both women watch it.*)

Mrs. Hale. You weren't raised round here, were you? (Mrs. Peters *shakes her head.*) You didn't know—her?

Mrs. Peters. Not till they brought her yesterday.

Mrs. Hale. She—come to think of it, she was kind of like a bird herself—real sweet and pretty, but kind of timid and—fluttery. How—she—did—change. (*Silence; then as if struck by a happy thought and relieved to get back to everyday things, crosses right above* Mrs. Peters *to cupboard, replaces small chair used to stand on to its original place downstage right.*) Tell you what, Mrs. Peters, why don't you take the quilt in with you? It might take up her mind.

Mrs. Peters. Why, I think that's a real nice idea, Mrs. Hale. There couldn't possibly be any objection to it, could there? Now, just what would I take? I wonder if her patches are in here—and her things. (*They look in the sewing basket.*)

Mrs. Hale (*crosses to right of table*). Here's some red. I expect this has got sewing things in it. (*Brings out a fancy box.*) What a pretty box. Looks like something somebody would give you. Maybe her scissors are in here. (*Opens box. Suddenly puts her hand to her nose.*) Why— (Mrs. Peters *bends nearer, then turns her face away.*) There's something wrapped up in this piece of silk.

Mrs. Peters. Why, this isn't her scissors.

Mrs. Hale (*lifting the silk*). Oh, Mrs. Peters—it's— (Mrs. Peters *bends closer.*)

Mrs. Peters. It's the bird.

Mrs. Hale. But, Mrs. Peters—look at it! Its neck! Look at its neck! It's all—other side *to*.[7]

Mrs. Peters. Somebody—wrung—its—neck. (*Their eyes meet. A look of growing comprehension, of horror. Steps are heard outside, Mrs. Hale slips box under quilt pieces, and sinks into her chair. Enter* Sheriff *and* County Attorney. *Mrs. Peters steps downstage left and stands looking out of window.*)

County Attorney (*as one turning from serious things to little pleasantries*). Well, ladies, have you decided whether she was going to quilt it or knot it? (*Crosses to center above table.*)

Mrs. Peters. We think she was going to—knot it. (Sheriff *crosses to right of stove, lifts stove lid and glances at fire, then stands warming hands at stove.*)

County Attorney. Well, that's interesting, I'm sure. (*Seeing the birdcage.*) Has the bird flown?

Mrs. Hale (*putting more quilt pieces over the box*). We think the—cat got it.

County Attorney (*preoccupied*). Is there a cat? (Mrs. Hale *glances in a quick covert way at* Mrs. Peters.)

Mrs. Peters (*turning from window takes a step in*). Well, not *now*. They're superstitious, you know. They leave.

County Attorney (*to* Sheriff Peters, *continuing an interrupted conversation*). No sign at all of anyone having come from the outside. Their own rope. Now let's go up again and go over it piece by piece. (*They start upstairs.*) It would have to have been someone who knew just the— (Mrs. Peters *sits down left of table. The two women sit there not looking at one another, but as if peering into something and at the same time holding back. When they talk now it is in the manner of feeling their way*

over strange ground, as if afraid of what they are saying, but as if they cannot help saying it.)

Mrs. Hale (*hesitantly and in hushed voice*). She liked the bird. She was going to bury it in that pretty box.

Mrs. Peters (*in a whisper*). When I was a girl—my kitten—there was a boy took a hatchet, and before my eyes—and before I could get there— (*covers her face an instant*) If they hadn't held me back I would have—(*catches herself, looks upstairs where steps are heard, falters weakly*)—hurt him.

Mrs. Hale (*with a slow look around her*). I wonder how it would seem never to have had any children around. (*pause*) No, Wright wouldn't like the bird—a thing that sang. She used to sing. He killed that, too.

Mrs. Peters (*moving uneasily*). We don't know who killed the bird.

Mrs. Hale. I knew John Wright.

Mrs. Peters. It was an awful thing was done in this house that night, Mrs. Hale. Killing a man while he slept, slipping a rope around his neck that choked the life out of him.

Mrs. Hale. His neck. Choked the life out of him. (*Her hand goes out and rests on the birdcage.*)

Mrs. Peters (*with rising voice*). We don't know who killed him. We don't *know*.

Mrs. Hale (*her own feeling not interrupted*). If there'd been years and years of nothing, then a bird to sing to you, it would be awful—still, after the bird was still.

Mrs. Peters (*something within her speaking*). I know what stillness is. When we homesteaded[8]

---

7. **other side *to*:** back side forward. The bird's head was facing the wrong way.

8. **homesteaded:** settled and farmed on land that was given to settlers by the U.S. government following the 1862 Homestead Act; ownership was granted after the settler had lived on the land for five years.

WORDS TO KNOW	**comprehension** (kŏm′prĭ-hĕn′shən) *n.* awareness and understanding.
	preoccupied (prē-ŏk′yə-pīd′) *adj.* absorbed in other thoughts.
	covert (kō′vərt) *adj.* concealed; secretive.

The Gilded Cage, Art Gore.

in Dakota, and my first baby died—after he was two years old, and me with no other then—

Mrs. Hale (*moving*). How soon do you suppose they'll be through looking for the evidence?

Mrs. Peters. I know what stillness is. (*pulling herself back*) The law has got to punish crime, Mrs. Hale.

Mrs. Hale (*not as if answering that*). I wish you'd seen Minnie Foster when she wore a white

dress with blue ribbons and stood up there in the choir and sang. (*a look around the room*) Oh, I *wish* I'd come over here once in a while! That was a crime! That was a crime! Who's going to punish that?

Mrs. Peters (*looking upstairs*). We mustn't—take on.

Mrs. Hale. I might have known she needed help! I know how things can be—for women. I tell you, it's queer, Mrs. Peters. We live close together and we live far apart. We all go through the same things—it's all just a different kind of the same thing. (*Brushes her eyes. Noticing the jar of fruit, reaches out for it.*) If I was you I wouldn't tell her her fruit was gone. Tell her it *ain't*. Tell her it's all right. Take this in to prove it to her. She—she may never know whether it was broke or not.

Mrs. Peters (*takes the jar, looks about for something to wrap it in; takes petticoat from the clothes brought from the other room, very nervously begins winding this around the jar; in a false voice*). My, it's a good thing the men couldn't hear us. Wouldn't they just laugh! Getting all stirred up over a little thing like a—dead canary. As if that could have anything to do with—with—wouldn't they *laugh!* (*The men are heard coming downstairs.*)

Mrs. Hale (*under her breath*). Maybe they would—maybe they wouldn't.

County Attorney. No, Peters, it's all perfectly clear except a reason for doing it. But you know juries when it comes to women. If there was some definite thing. (*Crosses slowly to above table. Sheriff crosses downstage right. Mrs. Hale and Mrs. Peters remain seated at either side of table.*) Something to show—something to make a story about—a thing that would connect up with this strange way of doing it—(*The women's eyes meet for an instant. Enter Hale from outer door.*)

Hale (*remaining upstage left by door*). Well, I've got the team around. Pretty cold out there.

County Attorney. I'm going to stay awhile by myself. (*To the* Sheriff) You can send Frank out for me, can't you? I want to go over everything. I'm not satisfied that we can't do better.

Sheriff. Do you want to see what Mrs. Peters is going to take in? (*The* Lawyer *picks up the apron, laughs.*)

County Attorney. Oh, I guess they're not very dangerous things the ladies have picked out. (*Moves a few things about, disturbing the quilt pieces which cover the box. Steps back.*) No, Mrs. Peters doesn't need supervising. For that matter a sheriff's wife is married to the law. Ever think of it that way, Mrs. Peters?

Mrs. Peters. Not—just that way.

Sheriff (*chuckling*). Married to the law. (*Moves to downstage right door to the other room.*) I just want you to come in here a minute, George. We ought to take a look at these windows.

County Attorney (*scoffingly*). Oh, windows!

Sheriff. We'll be right out, Mr. Hale. (*Hale goes outside. The* Sheriff *follows the* County Attorney *into the other room. Then* Mrs. Hale *rises, hands tight together, looking intensely at* Mrs. Peters, *whose eyes make a slow turn, finally meeting* Mrs. Hale's. *A moment* Mrs. Hale *holds her, then her own eyes point the way to where the box is concealed. Suddenly* Mrs. Peters *throws back quilt pieces and tries to put the box in the bag she is carrying. It is too big. She opens box, starts to take bird out, cannot touch it, goes to pieces, stands there helpless. Sound of a knob turning in the other room,* Mrs. Hale *snatches the box and puts it in the pocket of her big coat. Enter* County Attorney *and* Sheriff, *who remains downstage right.*)

County Attorney (*crosses to upstage left door facetiously*). Well, Henry, at least we found out that she was not going to quilt it. She was going to—what is it you call it, ladies?

Mrs. Hale (*standing center below table facing front, her hand against her pocket*). We call it—knot it, Mr. Henderson.

Curtain

WORDS TO KNOW

facetiously (fə-sē′shəs-lē) *adv.* in a manner not meant to be taken seriously; humorously.

1. What Do You Think? What is your reaction to the behavior of Mrs. Hale and Mrs. Peters at the end of the story? Share your thoughts with classmates.

Comprehension Check
- What sort of man was John Wright?
- What apparently happened to Mrs. Wright's bird?
- What does Mrs. Hale regret not having done?

Think Critically

2. **ACTIVE READING** **MAKING INFERENCES** Look back at the chart you created in your **READER'S NOTEBOOK** as you read the play. Based on the **inferences** you made, reconstruct the crime as you think it happened. With a partner, dramatize the events leading up to and following the murder.

3. The county attorney feels he needs a clear "reason," or motive, for the murder because "you know juries when it comes to women." What do you think he means by this remark?

4. Why do you think the **characters** Mrs. Hale and Mrs. Peters are sympathetic toward the murder suspect, Mrs. Wright, and are willing to deceive the men about their discoveries?

THINK ABOUT
- the life that Mrs. Hale leads
- their view of the Wrights' married life
- the men's attitude toward the women

Extend Interpretations

5. The Writer's Style *Trifles* is the first play by Susan Glaspell to display what was to become her signature trademark: the nonappearance on stage of a **drama's** central character—in this case, Minnie Wright. Explain the way in which Glaspell makes this unseen woman the play's central character.

6. Comparing Texts A murder is central to both *Trifles* and "Full Circle." Beyond that, how are the two selections similar and different? Refer to the Learning the Language of Literature article on page 739. Would you call *Trifles* a dramatized version of a mystery story or of a detective story? Defend your choice.

7. Connect to Life Do you think women are generally more observant and intuitive than men? Explain your opinion.

Literary Analysis

DRAMATIC IRONY **Dramatic irony** occurs when the reader or viewer of a story or play is aware of information but a **character** is not aware of it. In *Trifles*, the reader is aware of certain clues that the women have uncovered, but the men do not notice this evidence.

Paired Activity Make a chart like the one shown below. Working with a partner, go back through the play and find several pieces of evidence that the women know about but the men do not. Indicate what **inference** might be drawn from each clue. With a larger group discuss the question of how this dramatic irony can help you interpret Mrs. Hale's final statement about knots.

What the women know	What they infer
Careless sewing	

REVIEW **SYMBOL** A **symbol** is a person, a place, an event, or an object that stands for something beyond itself. The bird cage and the dead canary in this play are important symbols that stand for something beyond themselves. Think about the characters in the play and explain what these symbols stand for.

Choices & CHALLENGES

Writing Options

1. Crime Report List the main facts you think that Sheriff Peters will have on his crime report. The facts should be those that he has gathered from his observations and from Mr. Hale.

2. News Story Imagine that you are a local reporter covering the Wright murder. Write a news account of the murder and the investigation. Include quotations from characters in the play that hint at concealed evidence.

Activities & Explorations

1. Mock Trial As a class, stage the trial of Minnie Wright. One group can prepare the county attorney's case, which will try to prove guilt. Another can act as the defense attorney, trying for a verdict of not guilty based on lack of evidence. Other groups can act as the judge, the jury, and the play's characters who are witnesses. ~ **SPEAKING AND LISTENING**

2. Crime Scene Diagrams Create two diagrams, one of the Wrights' kitchen—the setting for *Trifles*—and one of the crime scene, with X marking the spot where the body was found. Include the clues from the play in your diagrams. ~ **VIEWING AND REPRESENTING**

3. Production Plan In a group, make a model of the set for *Trifles* and create a list of props and costumes that might be required in a production of the play. You will need to find out where you can acquire some of the period pieces. If time permits, join with other groups to stage the play. ~ **DRAMA**

Room After Room (1967), Andrew Wyeth. Tempera on panel, collection of Mr. and Mrs. Andrew Wyeth. Copyright © 1995 Andrew Wyeth.

Art Connection

Room After Room The painting on page 774 is by the American artist Andrew Wyeth, who is praised for capturing "the essence of a particular moment in a specific place," such as "the simple dignity of an aging farmhouse." Of this painting Wyeth said that "it's the succession of rooms that makes the impact." What elements of *Trifles* do you feel are found in this painting?

Vocabulary in Action

EXERCISE: CONTEXT CLUES On your paper, write the vocabulary word that best completes each sentence.

1. Trifles are those small details that we tend not to notice when we're _____ with more important things.

2. However, what seem at first to be trifles may be clues that reveal _____ problems and tensions.

3. The women take what they discover quite seriously, although the men speak _____ about it.

4. Because they cannot see the importance of small details, the men lack any real _____ of Minnie Wright's motives.

5. Can you imagine the men's _____ reaction if they had discovered that there were important clues in the kitchen?

Building Vocabulary

For an in-depth study of context clues, see page 103.

WORDS TO KNOW		
abashed	covert	preoccupied
comprehension	facetiously	

Grammar in Context: Using Adverb Clauses to Add Details About Events

In *Trifles,* Susan Glaspell uses adverb clauses to draw out details about the time frame of a murder.

> **County Attorney.** Well, Mr. Hale, tell just what happened when you came here yesterday morning.

An **adverb clause** is a group of words that contains a subject and a predicate and that functions as an adverb. Conjunctions that can introduce adverb clauses include *after, before, because, when, as, until, so that, while,* and *although.* By using such clauses, writers can shift backward and forward in time without confusing their readers. In the example above, the adverb clause clarifies the sequence of events as the murder scene is reconstructed.

WRITING EXERCISE Rewrite each sentence, adding an adverb clause that conveys the information in parentheses. Underline the adverb clause.

Punctuation Tip: Adverb clauses at the beginning or in the middle of sentences should be set off with commas. Usually no comma is necessary before an adverb clause that comes at the end of a sentence.

Example: *Original* The sheriff unbuttons his overcoat. (He comes into the house.)

Rewritten As he comes into the house, the sheriff unbuttons his overcoat.

1. Mr. Hale stopped in to visit the Wrights. (He wanted to talk about sharing a telephone line.)
2. He found Mrs. Wright but not Mr. Wright. (He came into the kitchen.)
3. She was just sitting in the rocking chair. (The kitchen chores were only half done.)

Grammar Handbook Punctuation, p. 1201

Susan Glaspell
1882–1948

Other Works
Suppressed Desires
The Outside
Bernice
Lifted Masks

Surprise Request A year after Susan Glaspell and her husband, George Cook, founded an experimental Massachusetts theater group, The Provincetown Players, in 1915, they found themselves in need of new scripts. Cook told his wife, "Now, Susan, I have announced a play of yours for the next bill." A shocked Glaspell protested that she had no play, to which Cook responded that she would have to write one.

The Birth of *Trifles* As Glaspell sat down in front of the theater group's stage the next day, she reflected on her days as a newspaper reporter in her home state of Iowa. Glaspell had once covered a murder trial and had never forgotten how she felt in the kitchen of the woman who sat in jail, accused of murdering her husband. Glaspell had wanted to turn the event into a short story one day, but after a time, sitting there, the bare stage became a kitchen. As Glaspell put it, the stage took the story "for its own," and ten days later *Trifles* was born, becoming Glaspell's most popular play.

Plays and Novels For the Provincetown Players, Glaspell wrote, directed, and sometimes acted in nine more plays between 1917 and 1922. Then, following the sudden death of George Cook in Greece in 1924, Glaspell wrote *The Road to the Temple,* a moving memorial to her husband. Later she wrote her most acclaimed play, *Alison's House,* which is loosely based on the life of Emily Dickinson. *Alison's House* won the 1931 Pulitzer Prize, but Glaspell wrote only one play afterward, instead concentrating on writing novels. Most of her writing features strong women characters dealing with psychological conflicts often caused by roles they are expected to play in society.

 **LaserLinks: Background for Reading**
Literary Connection

The Great Taos Bank Robbery

Essay by TONY HILLERMAN

"She told the city editor that the Taos bank would be robbed that morning."

Connect to Your Life

Small-Town Living What is your image of life in a small town? How is the way of life different from that in large cities and suburbs? What are the people like? With a group of classmates, brainstorm a list of characteristics of small-town life.

Build Background

It Really Happened This selection tells about actual events that occurred in 1957 in Taos, New Mexico. Taos is a small town today, with a population of about 4,000, but at the time of this story it was even smaller—about 1,850. The town lies north of Santa Fe in north-central New Mexico. Situated on a high plateau amid the Sangre de Cristo Mountains, Taos has a unique beauty that has attracted many artists and writers to the area. The town also has an interesting mixture of three cultures: Native American, Mexican American, and Anglo-American.

Map of New Mexico

- Taos
- Santa Fe
- Albuquerque

TEXAS

Rio Grande

NEW MEXICO

N W E S

Miles 0 60 120

WORDS TO KNOW **Vocabulary Preview**

affront	dissenting	irreverence
authenticity	fiasco	tolerant
conformity	impeccable	
depreciate	influx	

Focus Your Reading

LITERARY ANALYSIS **HUMOR** **Humor**—what makes you laugh or smile—is difficult to define, but it always seems to involve the element of **surprise.** Thus humor is related to **irony,** since irony also involves the unexpected. In the following story you will come across two kinds of ironic humor:

- **verbal irony,** when what is said is not what is meant. This can include sarcasm, exaggeration, puns, and **understatement.** In this selection, we are told that suspects urged to wait for the police "took a dissenting position" and drove away.
- **irony of situation,** when something happens that is very different from what is expected. In literature, **plot** and **character** can produce situational humor. In what you are about to read, bank robbers wait politely in line at the teller window.

ACTIVE READING **VISUALIZING** The process of forming a mental picture from a written description is called **visualizing.** As you read a story, you constantly use details supplied by the writer to help you picture settings, characters, and events. In this selection, the author presents details that create a picture of a small town—a picture that can be enlivened by a reader who visualizes the **characters, setting,** and **action.**

READER'S NOTEBOOK To imagine the setting and action of this story, follow what is happening as if it were a movie. Jot down key phrases about the images you picture in your mind as you go. Also sketch a map of the town of Taos as you imagine it from the descriptions of the "robbery," "chase scene," and "manhunt."

TONY HILLERMAN

THE GREAT TAOS BANK ROBBERY

Taos Today (1934), Ward Lockwood. Oil on panel, Spencer Museum of Art, University of Kansas, gift of the Ward and Clyde Lockwood Collection.

The newsroom of *The New Mexican* first got word of the incident about ten minutes after nine the morning of November 12, 1957. Mrs. Ruth Fish, who had served for many years as manager of the Taos Chamber of Commerce and almost as many as Taos correspondent for the Santa Fe newspaper, called collect and asked for the city editor.

She told the city editor that the Taos bank would be robbed that morning. She said that she would walk over to the bank and watch this operation. She promised to call in an eyewitness account before the first edition deadline at 11:00 A.M.

The city editor asked how Mrs. Fish knew the bank was to be robbed. Mrs. Fish, in a hurry to get off the telephone and become an eyewitness, explained very briefly that one of her lady friends had stopped in her office and told her so. The lady was now waiting so that they could walk down together and watch.

But, the city editor insisted, how did the lady friend know the bank was to be robbed that morning?

Because, Mrs. Fish explained with patience, the two bank robbers were standing in line at this very moment waiting their turn at the teller's cage.

But, persisted the city editor, how was it possible to predict that these two persons intended to rob the bank?

This presumption seemed safe, Mrs. Fish said, because one of the two men was disguised as a woman and because he was holding a pistol under his purse. Whereupon she said good-bye and hung up.

While astonished by the foregoing, the city editor recalled later that he had no doubt at all that the bank would indeed be robbed in the fashion described. If the reader feels less sure at this point, it is because the city editor had two advantages. First, he knew Mrs. Fish. An elderly woman of dignity, charm, and grandmotherly appearance, she possessed a flawless reputation for accuracy. Second, he knew Taos. While bank robbers probably wouldn't stand politely in line with the paying customers in Omaha or Atlanta, there was no reason to believe they wouldn't in this peculiar little town.

As a matter of fact they were doing exactly this, and their courtliness was about to cause them trouble. The chain of events that followed did not reach its semifinal anticlimax[1] until sixty hours later and was not officially ended until the following February, when the federal grand jury met sixty-five miles south in Santa Fe. By then the affair was being called The Great Taos Bank Robbery.

Lest the reader be misled by this title, he should be warned that Taos also lists in its litany[2] of notable events The Great Flood of 1935. If the reader can accept the fact that Taos managed a Great Flood without a river and with the very modest amount of water available in its arid climate, he is prepared to hear more about what happened on November 12, 1957.

After the city editor collected his wits, he placed a long-distance call to the bank. The secretary who answered didn't know anything about any bank robbery, but she referred the call to a higher ranking official. The city editor asked this gentleman if his bank had been robbed. Certainly not, said the banker. How in the world did such rumors get started?

A few minutes later Mrs. Fish called back, slightly breathless. She reported that she and her friend had walked through the alley behind the Safeway store and arrived at the bank just as two men with drawn pistols dashed from the front door. One of the men was dressed as a woman, as previously reported. He ran awkwardly in his high heels. The two jumped into a green pickup truck parked in the alley and drove away. From what she had learned from spectators fortunate enough to arrive earlier, the two men had not taken any money from the bank. She would investigate further and call back. Mrs. Fish, a woman of impeccable courtesy, hung up without a word of reproach to the city editor for causing her to be late for the event.

The city editor now placed another call to the banker. He asked the banker if he was sure his bank hadn't been robbed, or something. The bank official now was less confident. He was sure nobody had taken any money but he was also sure that something funny had been going on. He had been hearing something about a man dressed as a woman, and two men running wildly out of the bank lobby, and other confusing stories.

Meanwhile, the police reporter had called the Taos police department and said he was checking on a rumor that there had been a bank robbery. The policeman who answered said no, there hadn't been one and he guessed the police would be the first to hear about it if there was one, wouldn't they? The reporter said yes, he guessed that was true. Actually, the police would be approximately the last to hear about it, being informed only after the pastor of the local United Brethren Church entered the picture.

By then Mrs. Fish had made her third call and provided the city editor with a detailed account of what had happened in the bank lobby. The two men had arrived just as the bank opened its doors at 9:00 A.M. They found a crowd of Taos businessmen waiting to

---

1. **anticlimax:** something low-key or commonplace that concludes a series of exciting or significant events.

2. **litany:** in this case, something often referred to or repeated.

check out funds to fuel their cash registers for the day. The suspects joined the rush to the tellers' cages but were outdistanced, perhaps because of the high heels, and were stuck well back in the line. Customers quickly noticed that the line-stander clad as a woman had a full day's growth of dark stubble bristling through his pancake makeup and that the nylons encased an unseemly growth of leg hair. They also noticed that this person's costume was remarkably chic for Taos, which is one of the few places where a man can still feel adequately dressed downtown in bib overalls. All this was enough to cause a modest amount of buzzing in the lobby, but probably not much. Taos is a <u>tolerant</u> village, well accustomed to whimsy. It has been said that if the late James Thurber had been raised here he would never have celebrated the antics of his family in print, since what seems outlandish in Columbus, Ohio, seems fairly normal in Taos. It is also said that if Sinclair Lewis had been a Taoseño, Babbitt would have had a common-law wife and worn sandals.[3] In Taos a certain amount of eccentricity is required for <u>conformity</u>.

Interest among the spectators quickened, however, when some of them saw—or thought they saw—a pistol in the hand of the pseudo-[4] woman. The fleet-footed ones, who had beaten the rush to the tellers' windows and therefore left early, spread the news of this unusual sight around Taos Plaza. Thus did Mrs. Fish receive the word, and thus were many curious townfolks drawn to the bank to watch the spectacle.

Several days later, one of the two suspects was to complain to federal agents that some among this growing crowd of spectators began giggling. Whether or not Taos residents were guilty of such churlishness,[5] the two young men soon began suffering from stage fright. Embarrassed by the scrutiny of the crowd, they fled from the bank just as Mrs. Fish and her friend were arriving.

It was definitely established finally that both men were armed with loaded pistols. Although they were not to use these weapons until later, and then only when cruelly provoked, these revolvers are important because they lend an air of reality to The Great Taos Bank Robbery. It was much the same with The Great Flood of 1935. While it wasn't a flood in the usual definition, people actually did get wet and Taoseños defend this historic event from scoffers by pointing out that Governor Clyde Tingley declared an emergency and scores of families were evacuated to the National Guard Armory.

These facts seem persuasive unless one knows that this Great Flood was actually an epidemic of leaking roofs—the combined effect of a freakishly slow and persistent rain and the traditional Taos habit of roofing flat-topped adobe buildings with

---

3. **Sinclair Lewis . . . sandals:** In a novel by Lewis, Babbitt is a businessman who conforms blindly to his small town's conservative ethics and standards. The suggestion is that the people of Taos tend to have a freer and more permissive lifestyle.

4. **pseudo-** (sōō′dō): false; pretend.

5. **churlishness:** bad-tempered, rude behavior.

WORDS TO KNOW

tolerant (tŏl′ər-ənt) *adj.* having or showing understanding and respect for others' customs or beliefs

conformity (kən-for′mĭ-tē) *n.* the state of being in agreement with rules, customs, or popular opinion

hard-packed adobe clay. This roofing material is usually as effective as it is inexpensive, since Taos rainstorms are commonly brief, noisy, and productive of very little moisture. Taos learned in 1935 that when an Eastern-style three-day drizzle happens, such economical roofs tend to dissolve and pour through the ceilings. Residents, Taos-like, persist in using dirt roofs and profited from the experience only by the legends of bravery, charity, and outrageous discomfort that it created.

Today Taoseños rely on the two loaded pistols to lend <u>authenticity</u> to their Great Taos Bank Robbery just as they drag out the governor's unlocking of the armory when an outsider <u>depreciates</u> their flood. But before these pistols started going off, a couple of things had to happen.

As Mrs. Fish reported, the two suspects roared away from the scene of their <u>fiasco</u> in a pickup truck. Their rush may have been prompted by the erroneous notion that some-one would call the police, or perhaps by sheer embarrassment. Whatever the cause, the two ran a stop sign and sideswiped a car driven by the United Brethren minister. The minister was not in the mood that morning to turn the other fender. He insisted that the accident be reported to the police and that neither vehicle be moved until an officer arrived. The suspects took a <u>dissenting</u> position and insisted on driving away. The reader is aware that they had good reason for this rudeness but the pastor at the moment was not. Neither could he know that the man in the pickup who wore lipstick and face powder had gotten himself up as a female for the relatively innocent purpose of misleading bank personnel. It is safe to guess that the minister suspected a darker purpose, since Taos has long been known as a place of confusion concerning gender. At any rate, when the two men drove away, the minister gave chase.

Taos is a small community and its streets are few, narrow, crooked, and short. It is a

WORDS TO KNOW

authenticity (ô'thĕn-tĭs'ĭ-tē) *n.* genuineness
depreciate (dĭ-prē'shē-āt') *v.* to make something seem unimportant; belittle
fiasco (fē-ăs'kō) *n.* a complete failure; especially, a project whose great plans end in ridiculous failure
dissenting (dĭ-sĕn'tĭng) *adj.* disagreeing; having a different opinion **dissent** *v.*

completely inappropriate setting for a high-speed automobile chase and offers limited opportunity for the chasees to elude the chaser. After two or three times around the village the two suspects must have faced the fact that there was no hope of shaking off their pursuer. They began firing their pistols at the minister's car. Thus discouraged, the minister stopped at a telephone and the police, at long last, learned that something was amiss in Taos. . . .

Once the police were belatedly informed of the doings of November 12, at the bank and elsewhere, they reacted with vigor. A search began immediately for the two suspects. The State Police were notified and the Federal Bureau of Investigation was told of the apparent <u>affront</u> to the Federal Banking Act. By noon, the population of Taos—normally about 1,850—had been swollen by the <u>influx</u> of various types of officers. In addition to the genuine gendarmes[6] representing federal, state, county, and village governments, volunteer organizations such as the Mounted Patrol and Sheriff's Posse were mobilized.

Authorities soon had the escape vehicle. It was driven into the midst of a swarm of lawmen by Jose T. Cardenas. Mr. Cardenas, when he collected himself from the shock of having guns pointed at him, explained that he had lent his truck to a friend the previous day and that it had been left at his house that morning bearing signs of collision damage. Mr. Cardenas was at that moment in search of this friend to demand an explanation.

The reader might well pause here and recollect that it is traditional among robbers to steal escape vehicles, not to borrow them from friends. Borrowing, while more polite, leads to speedy identification when the car is recovered. Mr. Cardenas was able to tell police that he had loaned his truck to a man I shall call Joe Gomez, a thirty-three-year-old Taos native, and

---

6. **gendarmes** (zhän′därmz′) *French:* police officers.

that Mr. Gomez was accompanied by Frederick Smith, a twenty-three-year-old resident of Maine who had been visiting in the village.

Police also quickly received a hint of why the two had borrowed the truck a day early. Witnesses were found who had seen them at the entrance of the bank the previous morning—the morning of November 11. The witnesses remembered this because they thought it odd to see a man dressed as a woman trying to get into the bank on Veterans' Day. If any doubts remained on the subject, this should have proved that the two were not professional bank bandits, since professionals presumably would know about national bank holidays.

At this point, the authorities appeared to be in an unusually happy position. They knew the identities of both men they sought. They had excellent descriptions of the suspects. They were confident both were afoot in Taos. The village is small, the lawmen were numerous, and there was every reason for confidence that the two culprits would be in custody in a very few minutes. The officers fanned out from the plaza to press their search.

This proved to be a mistake, because Gomez and Smith had decided to walk down to the plaza to try to borrow some money. While the federal, state, county, and city officers and their volunteer posses manned roadblocks and poked around in the outlying areas, the two fugitives were making a door-to-door canvass of downtown bars soliciting loans from the bartenders. Not unnaturally, the barkeeps considered the two as poor credit risks at the moment. By the time it occurred to someone to inform the law of this activity, Gomez and Smith had become

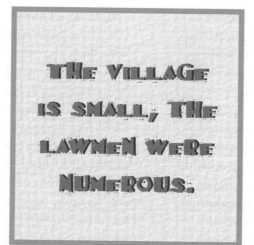

THE VILLAGE IS SMALL, THE LAWMEN WERE NUMEROUS.

discouraged and wandered off.

By the time the sun dipped behind the Conejos Mountains, the lawmen had found Gomez's female attire abandoned in an outdoor toilet but the fugitives were still at large. The hunt continued through the night, brightening the frosty November darkness with flashlights and electric lanterns. Considering the number of officers involved and the modest dimensions of Taos it is safe to guess that at least one policeman looked almost everywhere at least once, except in the deserted house where the two had chosen to sleep. When the sun rose over the Taos Mountains the morning of November 13, Gomez and Smith were still at large. There was some talk now of sending for Sam, the New Mexico bloodhound, but the motion apparently died for lack of a second. Perhaps this was because the only time Sam was used in Taos County he immediately became disoriented, strayed, and was lost for two days.

November 13 passed with a methodical and fruitless combing of the village. There was a brief flurry of excitement when officers learned in some roundabout manner that Gomez and Smith had again appeared on the plaza, renewing their futile attempts to float a loan. Police now discovered, twelve hours too late to do them any good, where Gomez and Smith had spent the previous night. They discovered that a neighborhood householder had happened by their hideout, had seen the fugitives, had stopped to chat with them about the excitement they had caused and had then left to buy them some groceries. The reader by now will not be surprised to know that this good neighbor did not bother to notify the police. But he did play a little joke on the culprits when he returned with the food, telling them that they had critically wounded the minister and that officers had orders to get them dead or alive. This unnerving bit of misinformation drove the two to make their second return to the plaza the next morning to renew the attempt to borrow traveling money. While one can imagine that their pleas were eloquent, the bartenders remained adamant. Gomez told a reporter two days later that by now he and Smith were "feeling mighty blue."

f the fugitives were depressed by November 13, it is reasonable to bet that those involved in the search for them shared this feeling. Taos does not lend itself to extended manhunts, since the posse members soon run out of places to look. To make matters worse, the press had taken the matter lightly from the first and the newspaper irreverence increased as the search dragged. When November 14 wore on without a sign of the fugitives, those in charge of the hunt must have been casting about for a dignified excuse to call off the whole affair. Their ordeal, however, was almost over.

That night, a Taos resident named Nat Flores was lying on his bed reading the evening paper when he heard a tapping on his window. Outside he saw two young men whom he recognized as Gomez and Smith. The two inquired if he might provide them with a meal and Flores, with typical "my house is your house" Taos hospitality, invited his visitors in for supper. During the meal, Flores and Joe V. Montoya, a brother-in-law who had stopped in for a chat, found Gomez and Smith in a gloomy mood. The two said they had spent the previous night in frostbitten discomfort in Kit Carson Park, a small recreation area not far from Taos Plaza. One of the possemen, Smith complained, had almost stepped on his finger.

Flores and Montoya, after a lengthy argument in which Flores recalled quoting passages from the Bible, persuaded the two that they should accept a ride down to the sheriff's office after supper and turn themselves in.

The final footnote on The Great Taos Bank Robbery was not written until February 4, 1958. After the surrender, officers found the two refreshingly frank about their activities. In due course, Joe Gomez and Frederick Smith were accused by the U.S. District Attorney of conspiring to violate the provisions of the Federal Banking Act and their case was placed on the winter docket for consideration by the Federal Grand Jury. Unfortunately, grand jury proceedings are secret so we will never know exactly what happened when the case was presented. We do know that the jury returned a "no bill," which indicates—at the very least—that the jurors could not be convinced that Gomez and Smith took their pistols into the Taos bank with felonious[7] intentions. If the jurors were not familiar with Taos, they may have suspected the FBI imagined the whole unlikely episode.

Thus The Great Bank Robbery was denied the official federal imprimatur[8] of indictments and was left as the sort of thing Alice's Mad Hatter might call an Unfelonious Unrobbery.

Still, if you happen to be in Taos on Veterans' Day and the man on the next barstool happens to be an Old Taos Hand, you're likely to hear something like this:

"You know, tomorrow is the anniversary of our Big Bank Robbery."

Or maybe he'll tell you about The Great Flood of 1935. ❖

---

7. **felonious** (fə-lō′nē-əs): of or like a major crime; criminal.

8. **imprimatur** (ĭm′prə-mä′tŏŏr) **of indictments**: official approval of statements formally charging a person with a crime.

Connect to the Literature

1. **What Do You Think?** What advice would you give to the would-be robbers? Share your advice with a classmate.

> **Comprehension Check**
> - After the attempt, how did Gomez and Smith try to get money?
> - What was the reaction of the United Brethren minister?
> - What was the legal outcome of the incident?

Think Critically

2. Do you agree with the grand jury's decision? Would you have decided to indict the would-be robbers? Explain why or why not.

3. **ACTIVE READING** **VISUALIZING** Look back at the notes and the map you made in your 📖 **READER'S NOTEBOOK.** Compare your image of a small town with the one portrayed by Tony Hillerman. How does Taos fit your idea of a small town? How is it different?

4. Do you find this **nonfiction** selection believable? Why or why not?

THINK ABOUT

- the way the robbers acted
- the way the witnesses and other townspeople acted
- what the author says about the eccentricities of Taoseños

5. In what ways is the Great Taos Bank Robbery similar to the town's Great Flood of 1935?

Extend Interpretations

6. **Comparing Texts** How would you compare the **tone** of this selection with the tone of any one of the following: "Full Circle," "Wasps' Nest," or *Trifles?*

7. **Connect to Life** Would you want to live in a small town like Taos? Why or why not?

Literary Analysis

HUMOR **Humor** is what makes people laugh. While sometimes we laugh at something that seems out of place, such as a very ugly person's being a contestant in a beauty pageant, other times we are amused by word play and witty remarks, such as a clever saying or song lyric. Other humor is related to the ironic. Humor and **irony** have an element in common: they both involve the unexpected. One form of irony is **situational.** For instance, a man in a top hat makes a pompous remark—then slips on a banana peel. There is also the humor of **verbal irony.** This occurs when someone knowingly exaggerates or says one thing and means another. For example, you're disgusted when your favorite team loses nine games in a row, so you say, "There's a little room for them to improve." If you decide to use **understatement,** you might say, "It's somewhat regrettable."

Cooperative Learning Activity
Working in a group, go back through the story and find any passages that seem humorous to you. In each instance, decide whether it is an example of verbal or situational irony. Use a chart like the one below to place it in one category or the other. Identify any examples of understatement.

Situational Irony	Verbal Irony
Bank robbers stand in line to wait their turn	

Writing Options

1. Interview Questions Which person in this selection would you most like to interview about the events of "The Great Taos Bank Robbery" or about life in Taos in general? Imagine that you have an appointment to talk with this person. Write a list of questions you would ask.

2. Prisoner's Confession Draft the confession that Gomez or Smith might have given the authorities after they turned themselves in. Write the confession as a dialogue in which the suspect is interviewed by an FBI agent.

Activities & Explorations

Taos Comics Choose a scene from this selection and present it in the form of a cartoon or comic strip. ~ **ART**

Art Connection

Look again at the painting on pages 788–789 by Ward Lockwood, who lived most of his life in the vicinity of Taos. What aspects of the artwork hint at Taos's unique, easygoing lifestyle?

Taos Today (1934), Ward Lockwood. Oil on panel. Spencer Museum of Art, University of Kansas, gift of the Ward and Clyde Lockwood Collection.

Vocabulary in Action

EXERCISE: ASSESSMENT PRACTICE For each group of words below, write the letter of the word that is the best antonym of the boldfaced word.

1. **irreverence** (a) honor, (b) connection, (c) wit
2. **fiasco** (a) control, (b) success, (c) honesty
3. **tolerant** (a) foolish, (b) unfriendly, (c) narrow-minded
4. **impeccable** (a) cheap, (b) faulty, (c) critical
5. **depreciate** (a) praise, (b) consider, (c) ignore
6. **affront** (a) decrease, (b) pleasantness, (c) outrage
7. **authenticity** (a) restlessness, (b) kindness, (c) falseness
8. **conformity** (a) pain, (b) creation, (c) opposition
9. **influx** (a) departure, (b) memory, (c) panic
10. **dissenting** (a) cooperative, (b) humble, (c) senseless

Building Vocabulary

For an in-depth lesson on antonyms and the relationship among words, see page 849.

Tony Hillerman
1925–

Other Works
Leaphorn and Chee: Three Classic Mysteries
Indian Country: America's Sacred Land

Navajo Mystery Writer A long-time resident of New Mexico, Tony Hillerman is noted for his detective novels featuring two Navajo police officers. One critic called him "one of the nation's most convincing and authentic interpreters of Navajo culture, as well as one of our best and most innovative mystery writers."

Restless Reporter Hillerman grew up in Oklahoma, but at the time of the Great Taos Bank Robbery, he was working as a reporter for *The New Mexican*. Several years later, at age 38, he wanted a change. He quit his job, got a master's degree in English, and began teaching and writing books. Since 1970, he has published more than 25 titles, mostly novels.

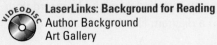

LaserLinks: Background for Reading
Author Background
Art Gallery

Building Vocabulary | Investigating Meanings in Figurative Language

Go Figurative

When you describe something to others, do you use comparisons to help your hearers mentally picture what you're describing? If so, you are using **figurative language**—language that expresses more than can be gathered from the literal meanings of its words. Look at how Sue Grafton uses figurative language in the excerpt on the right.

In this passage, Grafton compares a car accident to a movie stunt, the sound of brakes to a chorus of squawking birds, and the sound of crashing cars to a drum roll. These figurative comparisons help to make her description vivid and powerful.

> Suddenly a dark green Mercedes appeared from out of nowhere and caught the girl's car broadside, flipping the vehicle with all the expertise of a movie stunt. Brakes squealed all around me like a chorus of squawking birds and I could hear the successive thumps of colliding cars piling up behind me in a drum roll of destruction.
> —Sue Grafton, "Full Circle"

Strategies for Building Vocabulary

Two of the most common types of figurative language are similes and metaphors. In a **simile** the word *like* or *as* is used in comparing two things. In a **metaphor** one thing is said to *be* another thing. Such comparisons, in addition to helping you write stronger descriptions, can also help you figure out the meanings of unfamiliar words, as the following strategies illustrate.

❶ **Look for Context Clues** When you encounter a word you don't know, look at its **context**—the words that surround it—to try to find clues to its meaning. Consider, for example, the following sentence. How does the metaphor help to clarify the meaning of the word *emblem?*

> My scars were the emblem and symbol of our love.
> —Ray Bradbury, "The Utterly Perfect Murder"

The metaphor likening scars to an emblem and symbol of love provides a **comparison clue.** The comparison indicates that an emblem must be similar to a scar and a symbol. Therefore, if you know the words *scar* and *symbol,* you can guess that *emblem* must mean something like "a visible sign."

❷ **Use Graphic Organizers** When investigating the meaning of an unfamiliar word in a simile or metaphor, you may find it helpful to record your thinking in a diagram like the one above on the right.

1 Simile or Metaphor

The concussion from the blast hit him like a punch in the face.

2 Unfamiliar Word

concussion

3 Context Clue

"like a punch in the face"

4 Inferred Meaning

a shock or force

5 Dictionary Definition

a violent jarring

EXERCISE Use the context of each sentence to help you determine the meaning of the underlined word. Then write a definition of the word.

1. The scene of the robbery was more enigmatic than a broken stone inscribed with a forgotten language.
2. The investigation turned into a labyrinth as detectives followed twisting leads to dead ends.
3. The sight of the ransacked room and empty safe made him recoil as if he'd been hit.
4. The events surrounding the disappearance of the diamonds were dark clouds that couldn't be dispelled by the investigation.
5. Like a dam bursting, the impasse was finally broken when the police found several new clues.

Revenge—the settling of old scores—is a common theme in literature. The revenge planned in "The Utterly Perfect Murder" is a
response to the hurts in childhood that have haunted Doug
Spaulding for nearly 40 years. What does he have planned for the
bully Ralph Underwood? Will Doug come to terms with the past?

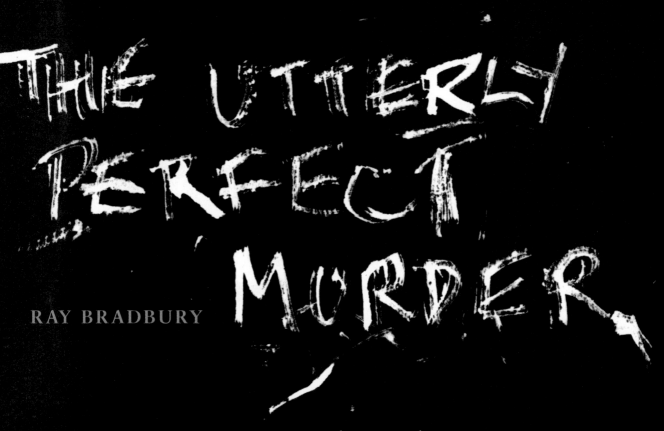

THE UTTERLY PERFECT MURDER

RAY BRADBURY

It was such an utterly
perfect, such an incredibly
delightful idea for murder,
that I was half out of my mind
all across America.

Drawing of a Face from the Rilke Portfolio (1968), Ben Shahn. Copyright © 1995 Estate of Ben Shahn. Licensed by VAGA, New York.

The idea had come to me for some reason on my forty-eighth birthday. Why it hadn't come to me when I was thirty or forty, I cannot say. Perhaps those were good years and I sailed through them unaware of time and clocks and the gathering of frost at my temples or the look of the lion about my eyes. . . .

Anyway, on my forty-eighth birthday, lying in bed that night beside my wife, with my children sleeping through all the other quiet moonlit rooms of my house, I thought:

I will arise and go now and kill Ralph Underhill.

Ralph Underhill! I cried, who is *he*?

Thirty-six years later, kill him? For *what*?

Why, I thought, for what he did to me when I was twelve.

My wife woke, an hour later, hearing a noise.

"Doug?" she called. "What are you doing?"

"Packing," I said. "For a journey."

"Oh," she murmured, and rolled over and went to sleep.

"Board! All aboard!" the porter's cries went down the train platform.

The train shuddered and banged.

"See you!" I cried, leaping up the steps.

"Someday," called my wife, "I wish you'd *fly!*"

Fly? I thought, and spoil thinking about murder all across the plains? Spoil oiling the pistol and loading it and thinking of Ralph Underhill's face when I show up thirty-six years late to settle old scores? Fly? Why, I would rather pack cross-country on foot, pausing by night to build fires and fry my bile and sour spit and eat again my old, mummified but still-living antagonisms and touch those bruises which have never healed. Fly?!

The train moved. My wife was gone.

I rode off into the Past.

Crossing Kansas the second night, we hit a beaut of a thunderstorm. I stayed up until four in the morning, listening to the rave of winds and thunders. At the height of the storm, I saw my face, a darkroom negative-print on the cold window glass, and thought:

Where is that fool going?

To kill Ralph Underhill!

Why? Because!

Remember how he hit my arm? Bruises. I was covered with bruises, both arms; dark blue, mottled black, strange yellow bruises. Hit and run, that was Ralph, hit and run—

And yet . . . you loved him?

Yes, as boys love boys when boys are eight, ten, twelve, and the world is innocent and boys are evil beyond evil because they know not what they do, but do it anyway.

So, on some secret level, I *had* to be hurt. We dear fine friends needed each other. I to be hit. He to strike. My scars were the emblem and symbol of our love.

What else makes you want to murder Ralph so late in time?

The train whistle shrieked. Night country rolled by.

And I recalled one spring when I came to school in a new tweed knicker suit and Ralph knocking me down, rolling me in snow and fresh brown mud. And Ralph laughing and me going home, shamefaced, covered with slime, afraid of a beating, to put on fresh dry clothes.

Yes! And what *else?*

Remember those toy clay statues you longed to collect from the Tarzan radio show? Statues of Tarzan and Kala the Ape and Numa the Lion,[1] for just twenty-five cents?! Yes, yes! Beautiful! Even now, in memory, O the sound of the Ape man swinging through green jungles far away, ululating![2] But who had twenty-five cents in the middle of the Great Depression?[3] No one.

Except Ralph Underhill.

And one day Ralph asked you if you wanted one of the statues.

Wanted! you cried. Yes! Yes!

That was the same week your brother in a strange seizure of love mixed with contempt gave you his old, but expensive, baseball-catcher's mitt.

"Well," said Ralph, "I'll give you my extra Tarzan statue if you'll give me that catcher's mitt."

Fool! I thought. The statue's worth twenty-five cents. The glove cost two dollars! No fair! Don't!

But I raced back to Ralph's house with the glove and gave it to him and he, smiling a worse contempt than my brother's, handed me the Tarzan statue and, bursting with joy, I ran home.

My brother didn't find out about his catcher's mitt and the statue for two weeks, and when he did he ditched me when we hiked out in farm country and left me lost because I was such a

---

1. **Tarzan . . . Numa the Lion:** These characters are from the radio show *Tarzan*, which was based on the stories of Edgar Rice Burroughs and broadcast from 1932 to 1935 and from 1951 to 1952. In the stories, Tarzan, a young boy stranded in Africa, is raised by an ape and befriends other African animals.

2. **ululating** (ŭl′yə-lā′tĭng): wailing or yelling loudly.

3. **Great Depression:** the worldwide economic slump of the 1930s, during which many people lost their jobs and many banks and businesses closed.

sap. "Tarzan statues! Baseball mitts!" he cried. "That's the last thing I *ever* give you!"

And somewhere on a country road I just lay down and wept and wanted to die but didn't know how to give up the final vomit that was my miserable ghost.

The thunder murmured.

The rain fell on the cold Pullman-car[4] windows.

What *else?* Is that the list?

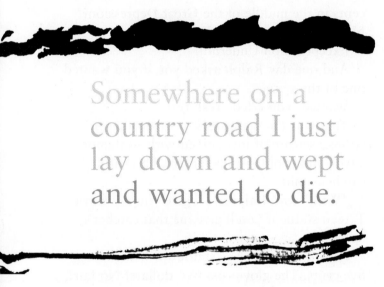

> Somewhere on a country road I just lay down and wept and wanted to die.

No. One final thing, more terrible than all the rest.

In all the years you went to Ralph's house to toss up small bits of gravel on his Fourth of July six-in-the-morning fresh dewy window or to call him forth for the arrival of dawn circuses in the cold fresh blue railroad stations in late June or late August, in all those years, never once did Ralph run to your house.

Never once in all the years did he, or anyone else, prove their friendship by coming by. The door never knocked. The window of your bedroom never faintly clattered and belled with a high-tossed confetti of small dusts and rocks.

And you always knew that the day you stopped going to Ralph's house, calling up in the morn, that would be the day your friendship ended.

You tested it once. You stayed away for a whole week. Ralph never called. It was as if you had died, and no one came to your funeral.

When you saw Ralph at school, there was no surprise, no query, not even the faintest lint of curiosity to be picked off your coat. Where *were* you, Doug? I need someone to beat. Where you *been,* Doug, I got no one to *pinch!*

Add all the sins up. But especially think on the last:

He never came to my house. He never sang up to my early-morning bed or tossed a wedding rice of gravel on the clear panes to call me down to joy and summer days.

And for this last thing, Ralph Underhill, I thought, sitting in the train at four in the morning, as the storm faded, and I found tears in my eyes, for this last and final thing, for that I shall kill you tomorrow night.

Murder, I thought, after thirty-six years. Why, you're madder than Ahab.[5]

The train wailed. We ran crosscountry like a mechanical Greek Fate[6] carried by a black metal Roman Fury.[7]

They say you can't go home again.[8]

That is a lie.

If you are lucky and time it right, you arrive at sunset when the old town is filled with yellow light.

I got off the train and walked up through Green Town and looked at the courthouse, burning with sunset light. Every tree was hung

---

4. **Pullman-car:** a railroad parlor car or sleeping car.

5. **Ahab** (ā′hăb′): in Herman Melville's *Moby-Dick,* the ship captain who is obsessed with killing a white whale.

6. **Greek Fate:** In Greek and Roman mythology, the Fates were three goddesses who controlled people's lives.

7. **Roman Fury:** In Greek and Roman mythology, the Furies were three goddesses of vengeance, or revenge.

8. **you can't go home again:** A saying taken from the title of a novel by Thomas Wolfe, *You Can't Go Home Again.* The main character in the novel revisits his hometown and is disappointed by the changes he sees.

Bolton Junction, Eccleshill (1956), David Hockney. Oil on board, 48″ × 40″, Copyright © David Hockney.

Finally, at eight-thirty on this cool October night, I walked across town, past the ravine.

I never doubted Ralph would still be there.

People do, after all, move away. . . .

I turned down Park Street and walked two hundred yards to a single streetlamp and looked across. Ralph Underhill's white two-story Victorian house waited for me.

And I could feel him *in* it. He was there, forty-eight years old, even as I felt myself here, forty-eight, and full of an old and tired and self-devouring spirit.

I stepped out of the light, opened my suitcase, put the pistol in my right-hand coat pocket, shut the case, and hid it in the bushes where, later, I would grab it and walk down into the ravine and across town to the train.

with gold doubloons[9] of color. Every roof and coping[10] and bit of gingerbread was purest brass and ancient gold.

I sat in the courthouse square with dogs and old men until the sun had set and Green Town was dark. I wanted to savor Ralph Underhill's death.

No one in history had ever done a crime like this.

I would stay, kill, depart, a stranger among strangers.

How would anyone dare to say, finding Ralph Underhill's body on his doorstep, that a boy aged twelve, arriving on a kind of Time Machine train, traveled out of hideous self-contempt, had gunned down the Past? It was beyond all reason. I was safe in my pure insanity.

I walked across the street and stood before his house and it was the same house I had stood before thirty-six years ago. There were the windows upon which I had hurled those spring bouquets of rock in love and total giving. There were the sidewalks, spotted with firecracker burn marks from ancient July Fourths when Ralph and I had just blown up the whole damned world, shrieking celebrations.

I walked up on the porch and saw on the mailbox in small letters: UNDERHILL.

---

9. **doubloons** (dŭ-blo͞onz′): gold coins formerly used in Spain and Spanish America.

10. **coping** (kō′pǐng): the top layer or course of a stone or brick wall, usually having a slanting upper surface to shed water.

What if his wife answers?

No, I thought, he himself, with absolute Greek-tragic perfection, will open the door and take the wound and almost gladly die for old crimes and minor sins somehow grown to crimes.

I rang the bell.

Will he know me, I wondered, after all this time? In the instant before the first shot, *tell* him your name. He must know who it is.

Silence.

I rang the bell again.

The doorknob rattled.

I touched the pistol in my pocket, my heart hammering, but did not take it out.

The door opened.

Ralph Underhill stood there.

He blinked, gazing out at me.

"Ralph?" I said.

"Yes—?" he said.

We stood there, riven, for what could not have been more than five seconds. But many things happened in those five swift seconds.

I saw Ralph Underhill.

I saw him clearly.

And I had not seen him since I was twelve.

Then, he had towered over me to pummel and beat and scream.

Now he was a little old man.

I am five foot eleven.

But Ralph Underhill had not grown much from his twelfth year on.

The man who stood before me was no more than five feet two inches tall.

I *towered* over him.

I gasped. I stared. I saw more.

I was forty-eight years old.

But Ralph Underhill, forty-eight, had lost most of his hair, and what remained was threadbare gray, black and white. He looked sixty or sixty-five.

I was in good health.

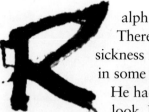alph Underhill was waxen pale. There was a knowledge of sickness in his face. He had traveled in some sunless land.

He had a ravaged and sunken look. His breath smelled of funeral flowers.

All this, perceived, was like the storm of the night before, gathering all its lightnings and thunders into one bright concussion. We stood in the explosion.

So this is what I came for? I thought. This, then, is the truth. This dreadful instant in time. Not to pull out the weapon. *Not* to kill. No, no. But simply—

To see Ralph Underhill as he *is* in this hour.

That's all.

Just to be here, stand here, and look at him as he has become.

Ralph Underhill lifted one hand in a kind of gesturing wonder. His lips trembled. His eyes flew up and down my body, his mind measured this giant who shadowed his door. At last his voice, so small, so frail, blurted out:

"Doug—?"

I recoiled.

"Doug?" he gasped, "is that *you?*"

I hadn't expected that. People don't remember! They can't! Across the years? Why would he know, bother, summon up, recognize, call?

I had a wild thought that what had happened to Ralph Underhill was that after I left town, half of his life had collapsed. I had been the center of his world, someone to attack, beat, pummel, bruise. His whole life had cracked by my simple act of walking away thirty-six years ago.

Nonsense! Yet, some small crazed mouse of wisdom scuttered about my brain and screeched what it knew: You needed Ralph, but, *more!* he needed *you!* And you did the only unforgivable, the wounding, thing! You vanished.

"Doug?" he said again, for I was silent there on the porch with my hands at my sides. "Is that you?"

This was the moment I had come for.

At some secret blood level, I had always known I would not use the weapon. I had brought it with me, yes, but Time had gotten here before me, and age, and smaller, more terrible deaths. . . .

Bang.

Six shots through the heart.

But I didn't use the pistol. I only whispered the sound of the shots with my mouth. With each whisper, Ralph Underhill's face aged another ten years. By the time I reached the last shot he was one hundred and ten years old.

"Bang," I whispered. "Bang. Bang. Bang. Bang. Bang."

His body shook with the impact.

"You're dead. Oh, God, Ralph, you're dead."

I turned and walked down the steps and reached the street before he called:

"Doug, is that *you?*"

I did not answer, walking.

"Answer me?" he cried, weakly. "Doug! Doug Spaulding, is that you? Who is that? Who are you?"

I got my suitcase and walked down into the cricket night and darkness of the ravine and across the bridge and up the stairs, going away.

"Who is that?" I heard his voice wail a last time.

A long way off, I looked back.

All the lights were on all over Ralph Underhill's house. It was as if he had gone around and put them all on after I left.

On the other side of the ravine I stopped on the lawn in front of the house where I had been born.

Then I picked up a few bits of gravel and did the thing that had never been done, ever in my life.

I tossed the few bits of gravel up to tap that window where I had lain every morning of my first twelve years. I called my own name. I called me down in friendship to play in some long summer that no longer was.

I stood waiting just long enough for my other young self to come down to join me.

Then swiftly, fleeing ahead of the dawn, we ran out of Green Town and back, thank you, dear Christ, back toward Now and Today for the rest of my life. ❖

Ray Bradbury
1920–

Other Works
The Illustrated Man
Dandelion Wine
I Sing the Body Electric!

Classic Science Fiction Known primarily for such classic works of science fiction as *The Martian Chronicles* and *Fahrenheit 451,* Ray Bradbury has written a wide range of short stories, novels, poems, plays, and nonfiction. According to one critic, Bradbury "writes less about strange things happening to people than about strange imaginings of the human mind." Bradbury says that his own imagination was fueled by reading a variety of material.

The Early Years Born in Waukegan, Illinois, Bradbury spent his boyhood in the Midwest. By the time he had moved to Los Angeles as a teenager, he was already writing. At the age of 12, he wrote his own sequel to a novel about Martians because he couldn't wait for the next book to come out. Besides, he said, "I couldn't afford to buy it." In high school, he saved part of his lunch money to buy a ten-dollar typewriter so that he could write for the school newspaper. Starting at the age of 19, in addition to writing, he sold newspapers until he was able to make enough money on his writing alone, three years later.

"Teller of Tales" Bradbury's writing is aided, he says, by having a memory that gives him total recall of every book he's ever read and every movie he's ever seen. His interests in technology and childhood imaginings combine to create an optimistic brand of fantasy. Bradbury says he would like the following to be written on his tombstone: "Here's a teller of tales who wrote about everything with a great sense of expectancy and joy, who wanted to celebrate things . . . even the dark things because they have meaning."

LaserLinks: Background for Reading
Art Gallery

Writing Workshop

Telling a fictional story . . .

From Reading to Writing Questions keep readers in suspense as they read "Full Circle" by Sue Grafton and "The Utterly Perfect Murder" by Ray Bradbury. Like most stories, these are meant to entertain, but stories may also explore ideas and emotions, expose a truth about life, or inform their audience about specific facts. As a **short story** writer, you are free to explore other worlds and other minds besides your own. No wonder we find intriguing stories everywhere we look, from magazines and movies to music videos.

For Your Portfolio

WRITING PROMPT Write a short story based on a mystery or on a compelling conflict.

Purpose: To entertain
Audience: Your classmates and friends

Basics in a Box

Short Story at a Glance

Introduction	Body	Conclusion
Sets the stage by • introducing the **characters** • describing the **setting**	**Develops the plot by** • introducing the **conflict** • telling a sequence of **events** • developing **main characters** • building toward a **climax**	**Finishes the story by** • resolving the **conflict** • telling the **last event**

RUBRIC Standards for Writing

A successful short story should
- use the elements of character, setting, and plot to create a convincing world
- use techniques such as vivid sensory language, concrete details, and dialogue to create believable characters and setting
- develop and resolve a central conflict
- present a clear sequence of events
- maintain a consistent point of view

Analyzing a Student Model

Susan Frank
Arapahoe High School

The Intruder

Thunder crashed violently, vibrating the very foundations of the house. Even before the grumbling finished rolling across the night sky, another jagged bolt of lightning ripped through the rain. Brilliant light illuminated the room, momentarily revealing the figure of a young girl cowering across the hall. Her sudden appearance startled <u>me</u>, and <u>I</u> froze to avoid detection. In the flash of brightness, I saw her delicate hand cover her small mouth, muffling a scream. The room fell into blackness again, but I had seen her. She must have heard the crash of the vase I had knocked off the table only moments earlier. I crouched down, knowing that if she caught me it would mean trouble.

Melting back into the shadows, I glanced over at the open window through which I had entered the house. Now the rain dripped on to the carpet, blurring my muddied footprints. I slipped into the next room, scanning the space for a hiding place. Cautious footsteps creaked across the entry way; the girl was trying to walk silently. I wondered how she would react if she saw me. I could tell from her whimper that she had seen the open window.

I flattened myself behind a chair and watched her creep into the room. The girl sniffled, and as she turned her head I saw tears on her face. She knew I was in the house. The girl backed into a corner, her eyes darting around the room. Her hands hung limply at her sides, although every few minutes she wrung them frantically. She made no further move to continue her search for me.

I shifted slightly, and she jumped at the sound. "MOMMY! DADDY!" she screamed at the top of her lungs. Cursing my luck, I darted through the shadows into a study. My heart pounded against my ribcage as I slid between two bookcases. The girl was too small to inflict any harm upon me, but I had to move cautiously. Her scream had probably awakened the entire household. Perhaps they would all come searching for me. I winced at the thought and shoved myself a little farther into hiding. If someone came in, they would be able to corner me. I considered hiding in a different location, but I eventually relaxed in the unbroken silence of the house.

<u>Lightning flashed outside</u> the tall window directly across from me, and the <u>roar of thunder was less than a moment behind.</u> As the <u>room lit up</u> momentarily, <u>a movement in the far corner caught my eye.</u> Another door I

RUBRIC
IN ACTION

❶ Opens with a vivid description that sets the scene

❷ This writer uses first-person point of view: the narrator is an active participant in the story.
Another Option:
• Use a third-person omniscient narrator who tells what is going on in several characters' minds.

❸ Uses description of the setting to set a scary mood

❹ Keeps the sequence clear throughout

had not noticed earlier was opening slowly, as if of its own accord. The room plunged into darkness once more, and I strained my eyes through the inky blackness to find the person whom I knew to be entering the study.

The floor creaked softly, and a fleeting shadow swept across the wooden panels to my right. Stiffening, I lifted my head slightly, beginning to suspect the other person in the room was not the girl. The mysterious shadow loomed threateningly; the owner of the shadow was obviously much larger than the girl. I found myself unable to shake the idea of my punishment. Heat rose under my skin until I felt as if searing flames were threatening to engulf my whole body. Panicked rage began to take the place of my fear. Enclosed by the four walls, I had allowed myself to become trapped. The unending seconds ticked by until my anxiety and anger rose to an intolerable level. No longer able to contain the white heat racking my nerves, I attacked. I sprang from concealment and smacked into the dark form shuffling across the carpet. A man shouted as he crashed to the floor under my weight. Less than a moment later, the overhead lamp came on. At the door of the room stood a slightly disheveled woman staring at me in open-mouthed disbelief.

"How did you get in here?!" she shrieked. "Bad, bad dog!"

Looking down, I saw my master pinned underneath my paws. I slunk across the room, punishment hanging over me. Careful to keep my tail tucked between my legs, I glanced back at the couple. The girl appeared in the doorway, as well. She frowned and waggled her finger at me, her own fear forgotten. "Bad dog," she emphasized, imitating her mother's reprimand. The man picked himself up off the floor and, grabbing my collar, dragged me toward the back door.

"Let's go, Houdini," he growled at me. "And this time I'm going to chain you to the doghouse."

⑤ Uses concrete details to increase suspense

⑥ Uses dialogue to expose the surprise identity of the narrator

⑦ Resolves events of plot clearly

Writing Your Short Story

❶ Prewriting

> *With me, a story usually begins with a single idea*
> *or memory or mental picture.*
> **William Faulkner, American writer**

Find a "seed" for your story in one of the following ways. Elaborate on an interesting **daydream**. Contemplate recent **news stories** that you find intriguing. Recall **unusual events** experienced by yourself or others. Ask a **"What-if"** question with fictional potential. See the **Idea Bank** in the margin for more suggestions. After you select an idea for your short story, follow the steps below.

Planning Your Short Story

▶ **1. Develop your story's key elements.**
  - **Characters** Who is the main character? What supporting characters are necessary?
  - **Setting** Where and when does the story take place? Does the setting affect the characters or plot in any way?
  - **Plot** What background information is necessary at the beginning of your story? What are the main events? What is the conflict? Will the conflict be resolved? Use a timeline like the following to decide what will happen at the beginning, middle, and end of the story:

| Background | ➡ | Event 1 | ➡ | Event 2 | ➡ | Event 3 | ➡ | Climax/Resolution |

▶ **2. Choose a point of view.** Will the story work best told in first person by the main character? Or is a third-person omniscient narrator necessary to get into the minds of several characters? Another option is a third-person limited narrator who can tell what is going on in one character's mind.

▶ **3. Create a mood.** What general emotional quality, or atmosphere, do you wish to create with your characters, setting, and plot? Will your story be dramatic, sad, scary, serious, or funny?

❷ Drafting

Your story may begin with an incident that sets the plot in motion, with background information, or with an incident that happens later in the story. Begin writing and see where the story takes you. Then elaborate on your story in the following ways.

Dialogue

Have your characters talk to "show" instead of "tell" your story. You may use slang, dialect, and various shades of formal and informal language to show what your characters are like.

IDEABank

1. Your Working Portfolio 📁
Look for ideas in the **Writing Options** you completed earlier in this unit:
- **Alternative Ending,** p. 755
- **Diary Entry,** p. 769

2. Fascinating Characters
Use your imagination to get into the mind of a sports hero, historical character, small child, or elderly person. Write your story about one of these people.

3. Eavesdropping
Build a story around a line of dialogue overheard on a bus, in a mall, or in a restaurant.

Need help organizing your short story?

See the **Writing Handbook**

Narrative Writing, pp. 1153–1154

Description

Description also helps you "show" your story. Describing a broken window and a carpet with muddy footprints is more effective than saying, "Someone had broken into the house." Use images that appeal to the senses and figurative language to describe characters, setting, and events in a compelling way.

Flashbacks and Foreshadowing

If you begin with an event from the middle of your story, you may want to go back in time—*flashback*—to an earlier event that is significant to the conflict. You may also want to give hints—*foreshadowing*—as to how the conflict will be resolved.

Ask Your Peer Reader

- Which actions and dialogue were most convincing? Which were least convincing?
- What key elements of the plot were most interesting? Which ones need to be clearer?
- How would you define the mood of the story?

Need revising help?

Review the **Rubric**, p. 806

Consider **peer reader** comments

Check **Revision Guidelines**, p. 1143

❸ Revising

TARGET SKILL ▶ FIGURATIVE LANGUAGE Figurative language such as **simile** and **metaphor** helps readers see the world in a new way by comparing two unlike things. A simile uses the word *like* or *as:* "My headache felt like a bass drum pounding in my head." A metaphor is an implied comparison: "A bass drum pounded in my head."

> *as if searing flames were threatening to engulf my whole body.*
> Heat rose under my skin until I felt ~~hot all over~~. No longer able
> *contain the white heat, racking my nerves,*
> to ~~stand the stress~~, I attacked.

❹ Editing and Proofreading

TARGET SKILL ▶ PUNCTUATING CLAUSES Keep your story line clear by punctuating clauses correctly. Use a comma before the conjunction that joins the two independent clauses of a compound sentence. Also use commas to set off non-essential, or nonrestrictive, clauses. Do not set off an essential clause with commas.

> The room fell into blackness again, but I had seen her. She must
>   *a*
> have herd the crash of the vase, that I had knocked off the table,
> only moments earlier.

Publishing IDEAS

- Illustrate your story and combine it with your classmates' stories in a one-volume collection.
- Record a reading of your story with an audio-recorder. Lend the tape to friends and family members.

More Online: Publishing Options www.mcdougallittell.com

❺ Reflecting

FOR YOUR WORKING PORTFOLIO Which aspects of short stories do you need to work on most? How has writing a short story changed your view of short fiction? Attach your reflections to your finished work. Save your short story in your **Working Portfolio.**

Read this paragraph from the first draft of a short story. The underlined sections may include the following kinds of errors:

- **spelling errors**
- **comma errors**
- **incorrectly used modifiers: adverbs**
- **verb-tense errors**

For each underlined section, choose the revision that most improves the writing.

After <u>scaning</u> the horizon for any sign of human life, Derek sat down and
<u>(1)</u>
thought about his predicament. Things looked <u>real bad</u>. He <u>had been stranded</u>
<u>(2)</u>   <u>(3)</u>
in the wilderness for two days. Would it be wiser to stay put and hope for
rescue or to try to find shelter? It bothered him that he couldn't make up his
mind. He usually <u>handled crises good</u>. <u>Fortunately, he had quite a bit of food in</u>
<u>(4)</u>   <u>(5)</u>
<u>his pack and, his feet were still dry inside his boots</u>. After eating a handful of
granola and some dried fruit, he decided to push on. He put on his pack and
<u>begins</u> walking across the featureless snow.
(6)

---

1. **A.** skanning
   B. skaning
   C. scanning
   D. Correct as is

2. **A.** really bad
   B. real badly
   C. really badly
   D. Correct as is

3. **A.** stranded
   B. have been stranded
   C. has been stranded
   D. Correct as is

4. **A.** handled crises very good
   B. handled crises well
   C. handled crises awful well
   D. Correct as is

5. **A.** Fortunately, he had quite a bit of food in his pack, and his feet were still dry inside his boots.
   B. Fortunately, he had quite a bit of food, in his pack, and his feet were still dry inside his boots.
   C. Fortunately, he had quite a bit of food in his pack, and, his feet were still dry inside his boots.
   D. Correct as is

6. **A.** has begun
   B. began
   C. had begun
   D. Correct as is

Need extra help?

See the **Grammar Handbook**
Modifiers, pp. 1186–1187
Punctuation Chart, pp. 1201-1202
Verb Tense, pp. 1184–1185

Have you ever watched an old horror movie in which a small creature, such as a lizard or a spider, is made through trick photography to look as large as a house? What we see affects what we believe, but what we believe also affects how we see things. If we believe the lizard is as far away as the house, when in fact it is right in front of the camera, the lizard will—logically—appear to be a monster. The relationship between illusion and reality can be a complex one. Writers of imaginative literature often enjoy exploring this relationship, as you'll discover in this part of Unit Five.

ACTIVITY

All fiction, because it describes imaginary events as if they really occurred, is a kind of illusion. Yet most people want their fiction, even fantasy and science fiction, to be told in a way that makes it come to life— that makes it *seem* real, vivid, and believable. With a partner, think of some works of fiction you have read or seen performed that impressed you as having these qualities. For each work, jot down one or two techniques that the writer or director used to achieve this effect.

How Writers Make Works of Fiction Come to Life

The Wizard of Oz
1. Good explanations— how Dorothy gets to Oz
2. Lots of detail— what Dorothy sees in Oz

LEARNING *the Language of Literature*

*P*oint of View refers to the vantage point from which a story is told. Think of it as the lens that a writer chooses for his or her readers to look through. Point of view determines much about a story, from its overall tone to our opinion of its characters and how much we learn about them. The following passages and the chart on this page demonstrate the three that writers use most.

First-Person Point of View

When a story is narrated by one of its characters, the writer is using the **first-person point of view.** The first-person narrator is often, but not always, the main character. A first-person narrator tells the story as he or she experienced it. One advantage of this is that the narrator can vividly describe his or her own thoughts, feelings, and observations. This helps the reader feel close to the narrator or to the action. One disadvantage is that the narrator does not have direct access to the thoughts and feelings of other characters. In addition, the narrator cannot relate events that happen when he or she is not present. Therefore, the reader cannot learn about those events until the narrator learns of them.

YOUR TURN Read the passage at the right. How does this narrative point of view affect the way you picture the action? Explain.

> **FIRST-PERSON POINT OF VIEW**
>
> If I'd had any doubts about his guilt, they vanished the minute he and I locked eyes. His surprise was replaced by panic, and he gunned his engine, taking off. I peeled after him, flooring it. At the corner he skidded sideways and recovered, speeding out of sight. I went after him, zigzagging crazily through a residential area that was laid out like a maze. I could almost chart his course ahead of me by the whine of his transmission. He was heading toward the freeway.
>
> —Sue Grafton, "Full Circle"

Point of View		
1st-Person	**3rd-Person Limited**	**3rd-Person Omniscient**
Narrator is a character in the story.	Narrator does not participate in action of story.	Narrator does not participate in action of story.
Narrator uses first-person pronouns *I, me, my, we, us, our* to refer to himself or herself.	Narrator does not refer to himself or herself.	Narrator does not refer to himself or herself.
Narrator knows the thoughts and feelings of one character and speaks directly to reader.	Narrator knows the thoughts and feelings of one character, but readers are able to maintain some emotional distance from that character.	Narrator knows the thoughts and feelings of all characters; readers get insight into several characters.

Third-Person Point of View

When a story is told by a narrator who does not participate in the action, the writer is using the **third-person point of view.** The two types are **third-person limited point of view** and **third-person omniscient point of view.**

THIRD-PERSON OMNISCIENT POINT OF VIEW An **omniscient,** or all-knowing, narrator has access to the thoughts, feelings, motives, and experiences of all the characters. Using such a narrator, the writer can shift attention from place to place, from time to time, and from character to character. The omniscient narrator can describe aspects of the characters that they themselves do not know or cannot see, such as their facial expressions. Omniscient narrators are also able to comment on what the events in a story mean.

YOUR TURN Read the passage at the right. If third-person omniscient point of view had not been used, what would you not have learned about the man and the dog?

THIRD-PERSON LIMITED POINT OF VIEW With **third-person limited point of view,** the narrator tells only what one character thinks, feels, and observes. The narrator does not reach into the mind of any other character. Other characters' thoughts and experiences can be revealed to the reader only through indirect means, such as dialogue. Third-person limited point of view often allows writers to add an extra dimension to their stories. For example, third-person limited point of view is useful for surprise endings, in which the reader learns crucial information only at the story's end.

YOUR TURN Read the passage at the right. How would your sense of suspense be different if you also knew the thoughts of the sniper's enemy?

THIRD-PERSON OMNISCIENT

The sight of the dog put a wild idea into his head. He remembered the tale of the man, caught in a blizzard, who killed a steer and crawled inside the carcass, and so was saved. He would kill the dog and bury his hands in the warm body until the numbness went out of them. Then he could build another fire. He spoke to the dog, calling it to him; but in his voice was a strange note of fear that frightened the animal, who had never known the man to speak in such a way before. Something was the matter, and its suspicious nature sensed danger.

—Jack London, "To Build a Fire"

THIRD-PERSON LIMITED

Morning must not find him wounded on the roof. The enemy on the opposite roof covered his escape. He must kill that enemy and he could not use his rifle. He had only a revolver to do it. Then he thought of a plan.

Taking off his cap, he placed it over the muzzle of his rifle. Then he pushed the rifle slowly upwards over the parapet, until the cap was visible from the opposite side of the street. Almost immediately there was a report, and a bullet pierced the center of the cap. The sniper slanted the rifle forward. The cap slipped down into the street.

—Liam O'Flaherty, "The Sniper"

Part of growing up involves learning to make judgments—what books to read, which friends to hang out with, how long to study for a test. Active readers also make judgments about what they read. The strategies explained on this page can help you develop your own literary judgment.

Making Judgments

When you judge a literary work, you probably evaluate it in light of a few generally accepted standards of what a good work should contain. These standards, or **criteria**, can reflect your own views and interests, but should also be specific to the subject you are judging. For example, if you choose your favorite movie based only on its high-profile stars, you may be overlooking the twistings of the plot or the impact of the special effects.

Judging a Literary Work The same thing holds true for judging a piece of literature. You may have read many horror tales and developed your own standards for what makes a horror tale effective. But if you only judge the tales by the creepiness of the monsters, you might miss the eeriness of the setting or the heart-pounding action. All elements of fiction, then, usually need to work together for a story to hold your interest. A good plot isn't enough to engage a reader if the characters are not well developed, the setting is boring, and the theme doesn't seem important.

1 Strategies for Using a Graphic to Make Judgments

- Finalize your list of criteria, making sure that they are both specific enough and complete enough for the work you are judging. Enter the criteria on a chart like the one begun here for "The Cask of Amontillado."
  - Try to find examples from the selection that meet the criteria. Record your ratings on the chart.
  - On the chart, rank your criteria in order of their importance in making your judgment.
- Look closely at the criteria you've established and the ratings you've made. Make a judgment about the work that is based on your evaluation.

Selection Criteria				
Criteria	Meets	Neutral	Doesn't meet	Order of importance
The setting is scary.	✓			4
The ending is spine-tingling.	✓			2
Judgment:				

2 Strategies for Making Judgments About Fiction and Nonfiction

As you develop your own criteria for judging a work, consider these questions:
- Does the plot seem realistic? Are the characters believable?
- Is the theme, or central message, of a story one that conveys something important about the human condition?
- In biography and autobiography, are the subjects and events portrayed in an engaging way?
- In historical writing, is the information presented accurate?
- In an essay, are the opinions convincing or objective?
- In news reporting, what elements give the impression of credibility?

Need More Help?

Remember that active readers use the essential reading strategies explained on page 7: **visualize, predict, clarify, question, connect, evaluate, monitor.**

The Open Window

Short Story by SAKI

"Her great tragedy happened just three years ago."

Connect to Your Life

Social Settings Recall a time when you were in a new social situation and had to present yourself to one or more strangers. For instance, you may have been at a new school, at an interview, or at a party. Were you self-possessed—in other words, calm and composed? Explain to a partner how you felt at the time. Then read this story about a meeting between strangers and notice the degree to which each character is self-possessed.

Build Background

Upper-Class Traditions "The Open Window" depicts the world of the British upper class at the turn of the century. Saki, himself a member of the upper class, often poked fun at the traditions of society. One tradition was the importance of proper manners; for example, people were expected to present formal letters of introduction when visiting strangers. In "The Open Window," Framton Nuttel presents himself in this formal fashion. Another tradition or custom is the "nerve cure," a trip to a rural place to treat nervous exhaustion and irritability. Only people of a certain financial and social standing would be able to afford such a treatment. Today a person who is suffering from high levels of stress might be under a doctor's care and, in extreme cases, might even be sent to a clinic or hospital for treatment.

Focus Your Reading

LITERARY ANALYSIS | **POINT OF VIEW** The perspective from which events in a story are told is called **point of view.** The **third-person omniscient point of view** allows the story to be told by an all-knowing narrator, who can comment on the thoughts and actions of all the characters in a short story or a novel. The third-person omniscient narrator in the story you are about to read tells you information about Mr. Nuttel, his sister, his responses to Vera, and the reactions of Vera and Mrs. Sappleton to him. As you read, pay particular attention to the information the narrator gives you about both Mr. Nuttel and Vera.

ACTIVE READING | **MAKING JUDGMENTS** When you evaluate a character, an event, a topic, an author, or a selection, you are using the skill of **making judgments.** You can give reasons for why you like or dislike something, agree or disagree with a statement or issue, or place a value on an action or outcome. The key to doing a good job in making judgments is to develop a set of criteria, or rules against which something is evaluated.

READER'S NOTEBOOK As you read, pay attention to Vera's actions in "The Open Window." Jot down your thoughts about the kind of person she is.

Saki

The Open Window

Detail, *Girl by the Window*, Harry Morley. Christie's, London/SuperStock.

"My aunt will be down presently, Mr. Nuttel," said a very self-possessed young lady of fifteen; "in the mean-time you must try and put up with me."

Framton Nuttel endeavored to say the correct something that should duly flatter the niece of the moment without unduly discounting the aunt that was to come. Privately he doubted more than ever whether these formal visits on a succession of total strangers would do much toward helping the nerve cure[1] which he was supposed to be undergoing.

---

1 **nerve cure:** treatment for nervousness or anxiety.

"I know how it will be," his sister had said when he was preparing to migrate to this rural retreat; "you will bury yourself down there and not speak to a living soul, and your nerves will be worse than ever from moping. I shall just give you letters of introduction to all the people I know there. Some of them, as far as I can remember, were quite nice."

Framton wondered whether Mrs. Sappleton, the lady to whom he was presenting one of the letters of introduction, came into the nice division.

"Do you know many of the people round here?" asked the niece, when she judged that they had had sufficient silent communion.

"Hardly a soul," said Framton. "My sister was staying here, at the rectory[2], you know, some four years ago, and she gave me letters of introduction to some of the people here."

He made the last statement in a tone of distinct regret.

"Then you know practically nothing about my aunt?" pursued the self-possessed young lady.

"Only her name and address," admitted the caller. He was wondering whether Mrs. Sappleton was in the married or widowed state. An undefinable something about the room seemed to suggest masculine habitation.[3]

"Her great tragedy happened just three years ago," said the child; "that would be since your sister's time."

"Her tragedy?" asked Framton; somehow in this restful country spot tragedies seemed out of place.

"You may wonder why we keep that window wide open on an October afternoon," said the niece, indicating a large French window[4] that opened on to a lawn.

"It is quite warm for the time of the year," said Framton; "but has that window got anything to do with the tragedy?"

"Out through that window, three years ago to a day, her husband and her two young brothers went off for their day's shooting. They never came back. In crossing the moor to their favorite snipe[5]-shooting ground they were all three engulfed by a treacherous piece of bog. It had been that dreadful wet summer, you know, and places that were safe in other years gave way suddenly without warning. Their bodies were never recovered. That was the dreadful part of it." Here the child's voice lost its self-possessed note and became falteringly human. "Poor aunt always thinks that they will come back some day, they and the little brown spaniel that was lost with them, and walk in that window just as they used to do. That is why the window is kept open every evening till it is quite dusk. Poor dear aunt, she has often told me how they went out, her husband with his white waterproof coat over his arm, and Ronnie, her youngest brother, singing 'Bertie, why do you bound?' as he always did to tease her, because she said it got on her nerves. Do you know, sometimes on still, quiet evenings like this, I almost get a creepy feeling that they will all walk in through that window—"

She broke off with a little shudder. It was a relief to Framton when the aunt bustled into the room with a whirl of apologies for being late in making her appearance.

"I hope Vera has been amusing you?" she said.

"She has been very interesting," said Framton.

"I hope you don't mind the open window," said Mrs. Sappleton briskly; "my husband and brothers will be home directly from shooting, and they always come in this way. They've

---

2. **the rectory** (rĕk′tə-rē): the parish priest's house.

3. **masculine habitation** (măs′kyə-lĭn hăb′ĭ-tā′shən): that men lived there.

4. **French window:** a pair of windows that extend to the floor and open like doors.

5. **snipe:** a long-billed bird found in marshy areas.

Girl by the Window, Harry Morley. Christie's, London/SuperStock.

been out for snipe in the marshes today, so they'll make a fine mess over my poor carpets. So like you menfolk, isn't it?"

She rattled on cheerfully about the shooting and the scarcity of birds, and the prospects[6] for duck in the winter. To Framton it was all purely horrible. He made a desperate but only partially successful effort to turn the talk on to a less ghastly topic; he was conscious that his hostess was giving him only a fragment of her attention, and her eyes were constantly straying past him to the open window and the lawn beyond. It was certainly an unfortunate coincidence that he should have paid his visit on this tragic anniversary.

"The doctors agree in ordering me complete rest, an absence of mental excitement, and avoidance of anything in the nature of violent physical exercise," announced Framton, who labored under the tolerably widespread delusion that total strangers and chance acquaintances are hungry for the least detail of one's ailments and infirmities, their cause and cure. "On the matter of diet they are not so much in agreement," he continued.

"No?" said Mrs. Sappleton, in a voice which only replaced a yawn at the last moment. Then she suddenly brightened into alert attention—but not to what Framton was saying.

"Here they are at last!" she cried. "Just in time for tea, and don't they look as if they were muddy up to the eyes!"

Framton shivered slightly, and turned toward the niece with a look intended to convey sympathetic comprehension. The child was staring out through the open window with dazed horror in her eyes. In a chill shock of nameless fear Framton swung round in his seat and looked in the same direction.

In the deepening twilight three figures were walking across the lawn toward the window; they all carried guns under their arms, and one of them was additionally burdened with a white coat hung over his shoulders. A tired brown spaniel kept close at their heels. Noiselessly they neared the house, and then a hoarse young voice chanted out of the dusk:

"I said, Bertie, why do you bound?"

Framton grabbed wildly at his stick and hat; the hall door, the gravel drive, and the front gate were dimly noted stages in his headlong retreat. A cyclist coming along the road had to run into the hedge to avoid imminent[7] collision.

"Here we are, my dear," said the bearer of the white mackintosh, coming in through the window; "fairly muddy, but most of it's dry. Who was that who bolted out as we came up?"

"A most extraordinary man, a Mr. Nuttel," said Mrs. Sappleton; "could only talk about his illnesses, and dashed off without a word of goodbye or apology when you arrived. One would think he had seen a ghost."

"I expect it was the spaniel," said the niece calmly; "he told me he had a horror of dogs. He was once hunted into a cemetery somewhere on the banks of the Ganges[8] by a pack of pariah dogs[9], and had to spend the night in a newly dug grave with the creatures snarling and grinning and foaming just above him. Enough to make anyone lose his nerve."

Romance[10] at short notice was her specialty. ❖

---

6. **prospects:** expectations.

7. **imminent** (ĭm′ə-nənt): about to occur.

8. **Ganges** (găn′jēz′): a large river in northern India.

9. **pariah** (pə-rī′ə) **dogs:** dogs that have escaped from their owners and become wild.

10. **romance:** highly imaginative fiction.

1. What Do You Think? How did you respond to the last sentence of the story? Share your reaction with the class.

Comprehension Check
- What tragedy in the Sappleton family has Vera explained to Mr. Nuttel?
- Why, according to Vera, is the window left open?
- Why does Nuttel leave in such a hurry?
- How does Vera explain Nuttel's hurried departure?

Think Critically

2. How does Saki's **characterization** of Vera set the reader up for the **surprise ending**?

THINK ABOUT
- the description of Vera as "self-possessed"
- Vera's treatment of Nuttel
- the last line of the story

3. **ACTIVE READING** **MAKING JUDGMENTS** Look back at the notes you made in your **READER'S NOTEBOOK**. How would you evaluate Vera as a hostess? as a niece? as a potential friend? What criteria would you use in each of these cases?

4. Is Vera's "practical joke" funny or cruel? Explain.

5. What is Saki's attitude toward Mr. Nuttel?

THINK ABOUT
- the character's name
- the way he is described by the narrator and Mrs. Sappleton
- the amount of sympathy you feel for him

6. Is Mrs. Sappleton aware of her niece's deception? Give reasons for your opinion.

Extend Interpretations

7. What If? Imagine that Mr. Nuttel learns the truth about the Sappleton tragedy. How might he respond to the news?

8. Comparing Texts In what ways is Lizabeth's relationship to Miss Lottie in "Marigolds" similar to or different from Vera's relationship with Mr. Nuttel?

9. Connect to Life Based on your own experiences in new social situations, what advice or consolation could you offer Nuttel?

Literary Analysis

POINT OF VIEW **Point of view** refers to the perspective from which events in a story are told. The two main types of point of view are first-person and third-person. Saki uses a **third-person omniscient narrator** in "The Open Window." A narrator outside the action describes events and characters. The reader has access to the thoughts and feelings of all the characters and to events that may be occurring simultaneously.

Paired Activity With a partner, review the story, looking for information that the narrator gives about the thoughts and feelings of Nuttel, Vera, and Mrs. Sappleton. On a chart like the one shown, list details from the story about each of the characters. Then circle any of the details that a reader couldn't know had the narrator been one of the characters instead of being omniscient.

What the Narrator Tells Us	
About Nuttel	He is not sure this visit is a good idea.
About Vera	She is self-possessed.
About Vera's aunt	

Writing Options

1. Defining Paragraph Saki describes Vera as self-possessed. Write a paragraph defining the term for someone who has never met or read about Vera.

2. Letter of Introduction Imagine that your best friend is moving to a new school. Write a modern letter of introduction, telling your friend's new classmates about him or her.

3. Cause-and-Effect Paragraph Did Vera's imaginative storytelling cause Mr. Nuttel's hasty departure, or did Mr. Nuttel's nervousness cause Vera's mischievous storytelling? In a paragraph or two, write about the relationship between the events in "The Open Window." Place your draft in your **Working Portfolio.**

Activities & Explorations

1. Film Review View a clip from the film version of "The Open Window." Then, with classmates, discuss whether or not the film version is true to the tone of Saki's story. ~ **VIEWING AND REPRESENTING**

 Literature in Performance

2. Humorous Monologue Plan a humorous monologue in which Nuttel explains to his sister what happened to him at the Sappletons'. After practicing, deliver your monologue in class. ~ **SPEAKING AND LISTENING**

Inquiry & Research

Period Furnishings Do research in art and architectural magazines or by speaking with a salesperson in a furniture store to find out what kind of furnishings would have been common in an English country house in the early 1900s. Create a diorama or a sketch of the setting of "The Open Window" and display your work for the class.

Saki
1870–1916

Other Works
Reginald in Russia, and Other Sketches
The Chronicles of Clovis
Beasts and Super-Beasts

Early Years Saki is the pseudonym of H. H. Munro, a British writer of short stories and novels. Munro was born in Burma to well-to-do parents. His father was a colonel in the British military police there. Two years later, the family returned to Britain, where Munro's mother died suddenly. He was then raised by two aunts in rural England, while his father returned to his duties in Burma. At 23, Munro himself joined the military police in Burma. He enjoyed the exotic animals and even kept a pet tiger cub. Munro remained in Burma for only one year, returning to England after being stricken with malaria.

The Writing Life Back in England, Munro decided to become a writer and adopted the pseudonym Saki, which he borrowed from the cupbearer to the gods, a character in Edward FitzGerald's *Rubáiyát of Omar Khayyám.* He later became a foreign correspondent. He covered a war in the Balkans and traveled throughout Europe. In 1909, he returned to England to devote himself to writing fiction. When World War I broke out, Munro enlisted almost immediately. During a night march in 1916, he was shot and killed by a German sniper.

Author Activity

Common Elements Read another of Saki's short stories. Compare the setting and the characters with those in this story and discuss your observations with your classmates.

PREPARING to *Read*

Sorry, Right Number

Screenplay by STEPHEN KING

"Polly? Is that you? What's wrong?"

Connect to Your Life

Can You Believe? Because Stephen King is the author of the next selection, it should come as no surprise to you that the story will contain at least one supernatural event. Supernatural events play a part in many stories of fantasy, mystery, and horror. Think of as many supernatural occurrences as you can that come from stories and movies you are familiar with. Jot them down. Then compare your list with those of your classmates.

Build Background

Writing for Television The following selection is a **screenplay,** a script for a story to be filmed as a movie. To be more exact, *Sorry, Right Number* is a **teleplay,** since King wrote the script for a television series of supernatural stories. **Stage directions,** as found in regular plays, are replaced here by **camera directions,** which let the reader know exactly what is filling the screen. Mixed in with the camera directions, however, is King's own voice. He acts as both author and narrator of the story, frequently talking to the audience. He also points out things he wants his reader to know and comments on situations. For example, when the characters Dennis and Connie torment their younger brother, Jeff, and get him visibly upset, King's narration points out that the two of them are pleased, "in the grand tradition of older brothers and sisters." Further, King explains the abbreviations he uses in a unique personal note at the beginning.

> WORDS TO KNOW
> **Vocabulary Preview**
> bleakly   interim   prone
> chasm   intuition

Focus Your Reading

LITERARY ANALYSIS   FORESHADOWING   **Foreshadowing** is a writer's use of hints or clues to indicate events and situations that will occur later in a plot. For example, in *Sorry, Right Number,* a mysterious caller pleads for help. Although we don't find out until later in the play what the call is about, we understand immediately that something somewhere is wrong, and our expectation is that we will eventually learn the details. Foreshadowing is one of the ways writers create suspense. As you read this screenplay, notice passages in which the author hints at future plot developments.

ACTIVE READING   VISUALIZING A SCREENPLAY   Reading a **screenplay** is different from reading a script for a stage play. Your mind's eye will be challenged to **visualize** what the camera is focusing on. For example, a camera can take you much closer to the action. In *Sorry, Right Number,* when a camera direction calls for an "extreme close-up" and then takes you inside a telephone receiver, you have to imagine not only how this looks but also what effect it creates. In addition, in a screenplay, you don't have to wait for official scene changes to have changes in setting, as you do in a script for a stage play. You can be instantly thrown from one setting to the next, even from one time period to another, by a camera direction that reads "slam cut to."

READER'S NOTEBOOK   Before you read, study the author's note to familiarize yourself with common screenplay terms. As you read, use your experience in watching TV and movies to help you visualize what the camera wants you to see. List any information from the camera directions (in italics) that hint at foreshadowing or at supernatural events. Put a letter *F* in front of those items that are foreshadowing and a letter *S* for those that seem supernatural.

SORRY, NUMBER

CAST OF CHARACTERS

Katie Weiderman

Jeff Weiderman

Connie Weiderman

Dennis Weiderman

Bill Weiderman

Polly Weiderman

Operator

Dawn

Minister

Groundskeeper

Hank

RIGHT

STEPHEN KING

Author's note: Screenplay abbreviations are simple and exist, in this author's opinion, mostly to make those who write screenplays feel like lodge brothers.[1] In any case, you should be aware that *CU* means *close-up; ECU* means *extreme close-up; INT.* means *interior; EXT.* means *exterior; B.G.* means *background; POV* means *point of view.* Probably most of you knew all that stuff to begin with, right?

ACT 1

(*Fade in on* Katie Weiderman's *mouth, ECU*)
(*She's speaking into the telephone. Pretty mouth; in a few seconds we'll see that the rest of her is just as pretty.*)

Katie. Bill? Oh, he says he doesn't feel very well, but he's always like that between books . . . can't sleep, thinks every headache is the first symptom of

---

1. **lodge brothers:** members of the same men's social organization. Lodges sometimes have special rituals or vocabularies that may seem mysterious to outsiders.

a brain tumor . . . once he gets going on something new, he'll be fine.

(*Sound, B.G.: the television*)

(*The camera draws back.* Katie *is sitting in the kitchen phone nook, having a good gab with her sister while she idles through some catalogues. We should notice one not-quite-ordinary thing about the phone she's on: it's the sort with two lines. There are lighted buttons to show which ones are engaged. Right now only one—Katie's —is. As* Katie *continues her conversation, the camera swings away from her, tracks[2] across the kitchen, and through the arched doorway that leads into the family room.*)

Katie (*voice, fading*). Oh, I saw Janie Charlton today . . . yes! Big as a *house!* . . .

(*She fades. The TV gets louder. There are three kids:* Jeff, *eight,* Connie, *ten, and* Dennis, *thirteen. Wheel of Fortune is on, but they're not watching. Instead they're engaged in that great pastime, Fighting About What Comes On Later.*)

Jeff. Come *onnn!* It was his first *book!*

Connie. His first *gross* book.

Dennis. We're gonna watch *Cheers* and *Wings,* just like we do every week, Jeff.

(Dennis *speaks with the utter finality only a big brother can manage. "Wanna talk about it some more and see how much pain I can inflict on your scrawny body, Jeff?" his face says.*)

Jeff. Could we at least tape it?

Connie. We're taping CNN[3] for Mom. She said she might be on the phone with Aunt Lois for quite a while.

Jeff. How can you tape CNN, for God's sake? It *never* stops!

Dennis. That's what she likes about it.

Connie. And don't say God's sake, Jeffie—you're not old enough to talk about God except in church.

Jeff. Then don't call me Jeffie.

Connie. Jeffie, Jeffie, Jeffie.

(Jeff *gets up, walks to the window, and looks out into the dark. He's really upset.* Dennis *and* Connie, *in the grand tradition of older brothers and sisters, are delighted to see it.*)

Dennis. Poor Jeffie.

Connie. I think he's gonna commit suicide.

Jeff (*turns to them*). It was his *first* book! Don't you guys even *care?*

Connie. Rent it down at the Video Stop tomorrow, if you want to see it so bad.

Jeff. They don't rent R-rated pictures to little kids and you know it!

Connie (*dreamily*). Shut up, it's Vanna! I *love* Vanna!

Jeff. Dennis—

Dennis. Go ask Dad to tape it on the VCR in his office and quit being such a totally annoying little booger.

(Jeff *crosses the room, poking his tongue out at Vanna White as he goes. The camera follows as he goes into the kitchen.*)

Katie. . . . so when he asked me if *Polly* had tested strep[4] positive, I had to remind him she's away at prep school[5] . . . Lois, I miss her . . .

(Jeff *is just passing through, on his way to the stairs.*)

Katie. Will you kids *please* be quiet?

Jeff (*glum*). They'll be quiet. *Now.*

(*He goes up the stairs, a little dejected.* Katie *looks after him for a moment, loving and worried.*)

Katie. They're squabbling again. Polly used to keep them in line, but now that she's away at school

---

2. **tracks:** moves smoothly.
3. **CNN:** abbreviation for Cable News Network.
4. **strep:** strep throat, an infection caused by a bacteria called streptococcus.
5. **prep school:** a private high school that prepares students for entering college.

. . . I don't know . . . maybe sending her to Bolton wasn't such a hot idea. Sometimes when she calls home she sounds so unhappy . . .

(INT. *Bela Lugosi[6] as Dracula, CU*)

(*Drac's standing at the door of his Transylvanian castle. Someone has pasted a comic-balloon coming out of his mouth which reads: "Listen! My children of the night! What music they make!" The poster is on a door but we only see this as Jeff opens it and goes into his father's study.*)

(INT. *a photograph of* Katie, CU)

(*The camera holds, then pans[7] slowly right. We pass another photo, this one of Polly, the daughter away at school. She's a lovely girl of sixteen or so. Past Polly is Dennis . . . then Connie . . . then Jeff.*)

(*The camera continues to pan and also widens out so we can see* Bill Weiderman, *a man of about forty-four. He looks tired. He's peering into the word processor on his desk, but his mental crystal ball must be taking the night off, because the screen is blank. On the walls we see framed book covers. All of them are spooky. One of the titles is* Ghost Kiss.)

(Jeff *comes up quietly behind his dad. The carpet muffles his feet. Bill sighs and shuts off the word-cruncher. A moment later Jeff claps his hands on his father's shoulders.*)

Jeff. BOOGA-BOOGA!

Bill. Hi, Jeffie.

(*He turns in his chair to look at his son, who is disappointed.*)

Jeff. How come you didn't get scared?

---

6. **Bela Lugosi** (bĕl′ə lōō-gō′sē): American actor known for portraying monsters in a number of films of the 1930s and 1940s.

7. **pans:** moves horizontally to reveal a series of images representing a continuous scene.

Bill. Scaring is my business. I'm case-hardened. Something wrong?

Jeff. Daddy, can I watch the first hour of *Ghost Kiss* and you tape the rest? Dennis and Connie are hogging *everything*.

(Bill *swivels to look at the bookjacket, bemused.*)

Bill. You sure you want to watch *that*, champ? It's pretty—

Jeff. *Yes!*

(*INT.* Katie, *in the phone nook*)

(*In this shot, we clearly see the stairs leading to her husband's study behind her.*)

Katie. I *really* think Jeff needs the orthodontic work but you know Bill—

(*The other line rings. The other light stutters.*)

Katie. That's just the other line, Bill will—

(*But now we see* Bill *and* Jeff *coming downstairs behind her.*)

Bill. Honey, where're the blank videotapes? I can't find any in the study and—

Katie (*to Bill*). *Wait!*

(*to Lois*). Gonna put you on hold a sec, Lo.

(*She does. Now both lines are blinking. She pushes the top one, where the new call has just come in.*)

Katie. Hello, Weiderman residence.

(*Sound: desperate sobbing*)

Sobbing voice (*filter*).[8] Take . . . please take . . . t-t-

Katie. Polly? Is that you? What's wrong?

(*Sound: sobbing. It's awful, heartbreaking.*)

Sobbing voice (filter). Please—*quick*—

(*Sound: sobbing . . . Then, click! A broken connection.*)

Katie. Polly, calm down! Whatever it is can't be that b—

(*hum of an open line*)

(Jeff *has wandered toward the TV room, hoping to find a blank tape.*)

Bill. Who was that?

(*Without looking at her husband or answering him,* Katie *slams the lower button in again.*)

Katie. Lois? Listen, I'll call you back. That was Polly, and she sounded very upset. No . . . she hung up. Yes. I will. Thanks.

(*She hangs up.*)

Bill (*concerned*). It was Polly?

Katie. Crying her head off. It sounded like she was trying to say "Please take me home" . . . I knew that school was bumming her out . . . Why I ever let you talk me into it . . .

(*She's rummaging frantically on her little phone desk. Catalogues go slithering to the floor around her stool.*)

Katie. *Connie did you take my address book?*

Connie (*voice*). No, Mom.

(Bill *pulls a battered book out of his back pocket and pages through it.*)

Bill. I got it. Except—

Katie. I know, damn dorm phone is always busy. Give it to me.

Bill. Honey, calm down.

Katie. I'll calm down after I talk to her. She is sixteen, Bill. Sixteen-year-old girls are prone to depressive interludes. Sometimes they even k . . . just give me the number!

Bill. 617-555-8641.

(*As she punches the numbers, the camera slides in to CU.*)

Katie. Come on, come on . . . don't be busy . . . just this once . . .

---

8. **filter:** The caller's voice is processed through an electronic filter to make it sound as if it is coming over the telephone line.

WORDS TO KNOW **prone** (prōn) *adj.* having a tendency; inclined

(*Sound: clicks. A pause. Then . . . the phone starts ringing.*)

Katie (*eyes closed*). Thank You, God.

Voice (*filter*). Hartshorn Hall, this is Frieda.

Katie. Could you call Polly to the phone? Polly Weiderman? This is Kate Weiderman. Her mother.

Voice (*filter*). Hang on, please, Mrs. Weiderman.

(*Sound: the phone clunks down.*)

Voice (*filter, and very faint*). Polly? Pol? . . . Phone call! . . . It's your mother!

(*INT. a wider angle on the phone nook, with Bill*)

Bill. Well?

Katie. Somebody's getting her. I hope.

(*Jeff comes back in with a tape.*)

Jeff. I found one, Dad. Dennis hid 'em. As usual.

Bill. In a minute, Jeff. Go watch the tube.

Jeff. But—

Bill. I won't forget. Now go *on*.

(*Jeff goes.*)

Katie. Come on, come on, come on . . .

Bill. Calm down, Katie.

Katie (*snaps*). If you'd heard her, you wouldn't tell me to calm down! She sounded—

Polly (*filter, cheery voice*). Hi, Mom!

Katie. Pol? Honey? Are you all right?

Polly (*happy, bubbling voice*). Am I *all right*? I aced my bio exam, got a B on my French Conversational Essay, and Ronnie Hansen asked me to the Harvest Ball. I'm so all right that if one more good thing happens to me today, I'll probably blow up like the Hindenburg.[9]

Katie. You didn't just call me up, crying your head off?

(*We see by* Kate's *face that she already knows the answer to this question.*)

Polly (*filter*). Heck no!

Katie. I'm glad about your test and your date, honey. I guess it was someone else. I'll call you back, okay?

Polly (*filter*). 'Kay. Say hi to Dad!

Katie. I will.

(*INT. the phone nook, wider*)

Bill. She okay?

Katie. Fine. I could have *sworn* it was Polly, but . . . *she's* walking on air.

Bill. So it was a prank. Or someone who was crying so hard she dialed a wrong number . . . "through a shimmering film of tears," as we veteran hacks[10] like to say.

Katie. It was not a prank and it was not a wrong number! It was someone in *my family*!

Bill. Honey, you can't know that.

Katie. No? If Jeffie called up, just crying, would you know it was him?

Bill (*struck by this*). Yeah, maybe. I guess I might.

(*She's not listening. She's punching numbers, fast.*)

Bill. Who you calling?

(*She doesn't answer him. Sound: phone rings twice. Then:*)

Older Female Voice (*filter*). Hello?

Katie. Mom? Are you . . . (*She pauses.*) Did you call just a few seconds ago?

Voice (*filter*). No, dear . . . why?

Katie. Oh . . . you know these phones. I was talking to Lois and I lost the other call.

Voice (*filter*). Well, it wasn't me. Kate, I saw the *prettiest* dress in La Boutique today, and—

Katie. We'll talk about it later, Mom, okay?

Voice (*filter*). Kate, are you all right?

---

9. *Hindenburg:* an airship that exploded, crashed, and burned spectacularly in 1937.

10. **veteran hacks:** writers whose books sell well but are not great, or even good, literature. "Through a shimmering film of tears" is Bill's example of the sort of unimaginative, overused phrases such writers turn out.

Katie. I have . . . Mom, I think maybe I've got diarrhea. I have to go. 'Bye.

(*She hangs up.* Bill *hangs on until she does; then he bursts into wild donkey-brays of laughter.*)

Bill. Oh boy . . . diarrhea . . . I gotta remember that the next time my agent calls . . . oh Katie, that was so cool—

Katie (*almost screaming*). *This is not funny!*

(Bill *stops laughing.*)
  (INT. *the TV room*)
  (Jeff *and* Dennis *have been tussling. They stop. All three kids look toward the kitchen.*)
  (INT. *the phone nook, with* Bill *and* Katie)

Katie. *I tell you it was someone in my family and she sounded—*oh, you don't understand. I *knew* that voice.

Bill. But if Polly's okay and your mom's okay . . .

Katie (*positive*). It's Dawn.

Bill. Come on, hon, a minute ago you were sure it was Polly.

Katie. It *had* to be Dawn. I was on the phone with Lois and Mom's okay, so Dawn's the only other one it *could* have been. She's the youngest . . . I could have mistaken her for Polly . . . and she's out there in that farmhouse alone with the baby!

Bill (*startled*). What do you mean, alone?

Katie. Jerry's in Burlington! It's Dawn! *Something's happened to Dawn!*

(Connie *comes into the kitchen, worried.*)

Connie. Mom? Is Aunt Dawn okay?

Bill. So far as we know, she's fine. Take it easy, doll. Bad to buy trouble before you know it's on sale.

(Katie *punches numbers and listens. Sound: the dah-dah-dah of a busy signal.* Katie *hangs up.* Bill *looks a question at her with raised eyebrows.*)

Katie. Busy.

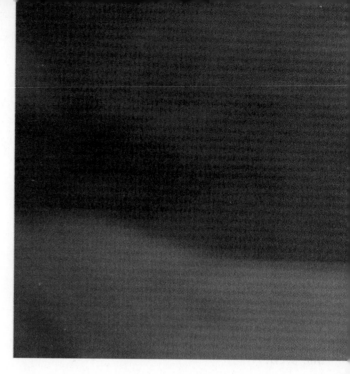

Bill. Katie, are you sure—

Katie. She's the only one left—it had to be her. Bill, I'm scared. Will you drive me out there?

(Bill *takes the phone from her.*)

Bill. What's her number?

Katie. 555-6169.

(Bill *dials. Gets a busy. Hangs up and punches* 0.)

Operator (*filter*). Operator.

Bill. I'm trying to reach my sister-in-law, operator. The line is busy. I suspect there may be a problem. Can you break into the call, please?

(INT. *the door to the TV room*)
  (All three kids are standing there, silent and worried.*)
  (INT. *the phone nook, with* Bill *and* Katie)

Operator (*filter*). What is your name, sir?

Bill. William Weiderman. My number is—

Operator (*filter*). Not the William Weiderman that wrote *Spider Doom?!*

Bill. Yes, that was mine. If—

Operator (*filter*). Oh . . . , I just *loved* that book! I love *all* your books! I—

Bill. I'm delighted you do. But right now my wife is very worried about her sister. If it's possible for you to—

Operator (*filter*). Yes, I can do that. Please give me your number, Mr. Weiderman, for the records. (*She giggles.*) I *promise* not to give it out.

Bill. It's 555-4408.

Operator (*filter*). And the call number?

Bill (*looks at* Katie). Uh . . .

Katie. 555-6169.

Bill. 555-6169.

Operator (*filter*). Just a moment, Mr. Weiderman . . . *Night of the Beast* was also great, by the way. Hold on.

(*Sound: telephonic clicks and clacks.*)

Katie. Is she—

Bill. Yes. Just . . .

(*There's one final click.*)

Operator (*filter*). I'm sorry, Mr. Weiderman, but that line is not busy. It's off the hook. I wonder if I sent you my copy of *Spider Doom*—

(Bill *hangs up the phone.*)

Katie. Why did you hang up?

Bill. She can't break in. Phone's not busy. It's off the hook.

(*They stare at each other* bleakly.)
 (*EXT. A low-slung sports car passes the camera. Night.*)
 (*INT. the car, with* Katie *and* Bill)
 (Katie's *scared.* Bill, *at the wheel, doesn't look exactly calm.*)

Katie. Hey, Bill—tell me she's all right.

Bill. She's all right.

Katie. Now tell me what you really think.

Bill. Jeff snuck up behind me tonight and put the old booga-booga on me. He was disappointed as hell when I didn't jump. I told him I was case-hardened. (*pause*) I lied.

Katie. Why did Jerry have to move out there when he's gone half the time? Just her and that little tiny baby? *Why?*

Bill. Shh, Kate. We're almost there.

Katie. Go faster.

(*INT. the car*)

   (*He does. That car is smokin'.*)

   (*INT. the Weiderman TV room*)

   (*The tube's still on and the kids are still there, but the horsing around has stopped.*)

Connie. Dennis, do you think Aunt Dawn's okay?

Dennis (*thinks she's dead, decapitated[11] by a maniac*). Yeah. Sure she is.

(*INT. the phone, POV from the TV room*)

   (*just sitting there on the wall in the phone nook, lights dark, looking like a snake ready to strike*)

   (*Fade out*)

(*EXT. an isolated farmhouse*)

   (*A long driveway leads up to it. There's one light on in the living room. Car lights sweep up the driveway. The Weiderman car pulls up close to the garage and stops.*)

(*INT. the car, with* Bill *and* Katie)

Katie. I'm scared.

(Bill *bends down, reaches under his seat, and brings out a pistol.*)

Bill (*solemnly*). Booga-booga.

Katie (*total surprise*). How long have you had that?

Bill. Since last year. I didn't want to scare you or the kids. I've got a license to carry. Come on.

(*EXT.* Bill *and* Katie)

   (*They get out.* Katie *stands by the front of the car while* Bill *goes to the garage and peers in.*)

Bill. Her car's here.

(*The camera tracks with them to the front door. Now we can hear the TV, playing loud.* Bill *pushes the doorbell. We hear it inside. They wait.* Katie *pushes it. Still no answer. She pushes it again and doesn't take her finger off.* Bill *looks down at:*)

(*EXT. the lock,* Bill's *POV*)

   (*Big scratches on it.*)

(*EXT.* Bill *and* Katie)

Bill (*low*). The lock's been tampered with.

(Katie *looks, and whimpers.* Bill *tries the door. It opens. The TV is louder.*)

Bill. Stay behind me. Be ready to run if something happens. . . . I wish I'd left you home, Kate.

(*He starts in.* Katie *comes after him, terrified, near tears.*)

   (*INT. Dawn and Jerry's living room*)

   (*From this angle we see only a small section of the room. The TV is much louder.* Bill *enters the room, gun up. He looks to the right . . . and suddenly all the tension goes out of him. He lowers the gun.*)

Katie (*draws up beside him*). Bill . . . what . . .

(*He points.*)

   (*INT. the living room, wide,* Bill *and* Katie's *POV*)

   (*The place looks like a cyclone hit it . . . but it wasn't robbery and murder that caused this mess; only a healthy eighteen-month-old baby. After a strenuous day of trashing the living room, Baby got tired and Mommy got tired and they fell asleep on the couch together. The baby is in* Dawn's *lap. There is a pair of Walkman earphones on her head. There are toys—tough plastic Sesame Street and PlaySkool stuff, for the most part—scattered hell to breakfast. The baby has also pulled most of the books out of the bookcase. Had a good munch on one of them, too, by the look.* Bill *goes over and picks it up. It is* Ghost Kiss.)

Bill. I've had people say they just eat my books up, but this is ridiculous.

(*He's amused.* Katie *isn't. She walks over to her sister, ready to be mad . . . but she sees how really exhausted* Dawn *looks and softens.*)

   (*INT.* Dawn *and the baby,* Katie's *POV*)

---

11. **decapitated:** beheaded.

(*Fast asleep and breathing easily, like a Raphael painting of Madonna and Child. The camera pans down to: the Walkman. We can hear the faint strains of Huey Lewis and the News. The camera pans a bit further to a Princess telephone on the table by the chair. It's off the cradle. Not much; just enough to break the connection and scare people to death.*)

(*INT.* Katie)

(*She sighs, bends down, and replaces the phone. Then she pushes the stop button on the Walkman.*)

(*INT.* Dawn, Bill, *and* Katie)

(Dawn *wakes up when the music stops. Looks at* Bill *and* Katie, *puzzled.*)

Dawn (*fuzzed out*). Well . . . hi.

(*She realizes she's got the Walkman phones on and removes them.*)

Bill. Hi, Dawn.

Dawn (*still half asleep*). Shoulda called, guys. Place is a mess.

(*She smiles. She's radiant when she smiles.*)

Katie. We *tried.* The operator told Bill the phone was off the hook. I thought something was wrong. How can you sleep with that music blasting?

Dawn. It's restful. (*Sees the gnawed book Bill's holding*) Oh . . . Bill, I'm sorry! Justin's teething and—

Bill. There are critics who'd say he picked just the right thing to teethe on. I don't want to scare you, beautiful, but somebody's been at your front door lock with a screwdriver or something. Whoever it was forced it.

Dawn. Gosh, no! That was Jerry, last week. I locked us out by mistake and he didn't have his key and the spare wasn't over the door like it's supposed to be. He was mad because he had to take a whiz real bad and so he took the screwdriver to it. It didn't work, either—that's one tough lock. (*pause*) By the time I found

my key he'd already gone in the bushes.

Bill. If it wasn't forced, how come I could just open the door and walk in?

Dawn (*guiltily*). Well . . . sometimes I forget to lock it.

Katie. You didn't call me tonight, Dawn?

Dawn. Gee, no! I didn't call *anyone!* I was too busy chasing Justin around! He kept wanting to eat the fabric softener! Then he got sleepy and I sat down here and thought I'd listen to some tunes while I waited for your movie to come on, Bill, and I fell asleep—

(*At the mention of the movie* Bill *starts visibly and looks at the book. Then he glances at his watch.*)

Bill. I promised to tape it for Jeff. Come on, Katie, we've got time to get back.

Katie. Just a second.

(*She picks up the phone and dials.*)

Dawn. Gee, Bill, do you think Jeffie's old enough to watch something like that?

Bill. It's network. They take out the blood-bags.

Dawn (*confused but amiable*). Oh. That's good.

(*INT.* Katie, *CU*)

Dennis (*filter*). Hello?

Katie. Just thought you'd like to know your Aunt Dawn's fine.

Dennis (*filter*). Oh! Cool. Thanks, Mom.

(*INT. the phone nook, with* Dennis *and the others*)
(*He looks very relieved.*)

Dennis. Aunt Dawn's okay.

(*INT. the car, with* Bill *and* Katie)

(*They drive in silence for a while.*)

Katie. You think I'm a hysterical idiot, don't you?

Bill (*genuinely surprised*). No! I was scared, too.

Katie. You sure you're not mad?

Bill. I'm too relieved. (*laughs*) She's sort of a scatterbrain, old Dawn, but I love her.

Katie (*leans over and kisses him*). I love *you*. You're a sweet man.

Bill. I'm the *boogeyman!*

Katie. I am not fooled, sweetheart.

(*EXT. the car*)
  (*Passes the camera and we dissolve[12] to:*)
  (*INT. Jeff, in bed*)
  (*His room is dark. The covers are pulled up to his chin.*)

Jeff. You promise to tape the rest?

(*Camera widens out so we can see* Bill, *sitting on the bed.*)

Bill. I promise.

Jeff. I especially liked the part where the dead guy ripped off the punk rocker's head.

Bill. Well . . . they *used* to take out all the blood-bags.

Jeff. What, Dad?

Bill. Nothing. I love you, Jeffie.

Jeff. I love you, too. So does Rambo.

(Jeff *holds up a stuffed dragon of decidedly unmilitant aspect.[13]* Bill *kisses the dragon, then* Jeff.)

Bill. 'Night.

Jeff. 'Night. (*As* Bill *reaches his door*) Glad Aunt Dawn was okay.

Bill. Me too.

(*He goes out.*)
  (*INT. TV, CU*)
  (*A guy who looks like he died in a car crash about two weeks prior to filming [and has since been subjected to a lot of hot weather] is staggering out of a crypt.[14] The camera widens to show* Bill, *releasing the VCR pause button.*)

Katie (*voice*). Booga-booga.

(Bill *looks around companionably. The camera widens out more to show* Katie, *wearing a . . . nightgown.*)

Bill. Same to you. I missed the first forty seconds or so after the break. I had to kiss Rambo.

Katie. You sure you're not mad at me, Bill?

(*He goes to her and kisses her.*)

Bill. Not even a smidge.

Katie. It's just that I could have sworn it was one of mine. You know what I mean? One of mine?

Bill. Yes.

Katie. I can still hear those sobs. So lost . . . so heartbroken.

Bill. Kate, have you ever thought you recognized someone on the street, and called her, and when she finally turned around it was a total stranger?

Katie. Yes, once. In Seattle. I was in a mall and I thought I saw my old roommate. I . . . oh. I see what you're saying.

Bill. Sure. There are sound-alikes as well as look-alikes.

Katie. But . . . *you know your own.* At least I thought so until tonight.

(*She puts her cheek on his shoulder, looking troubled.*)

Katie. I was so *positive* it was Polly . . .

Bill. Because you've been worried about her getting her feet under her at the new school . . . but judging from the stuff she told you tonight, I'd say she's doing just fine in that department. Wouldn't you?

Katie. Yes . . . I guess I would.

Bill. Let it go, hon.

Katie (*looks at him closely*). I hate to see you looking so tired. Hurry up and have an idea, you.

Bill. Well, I'm trying.

Katie. You coming to bed?

Bill. Soon as I finish taping this for Jeff.

---

12. **dissolve:** This is a film technique for shifting scenes in which one scene fades out while the next appears and grows clearer.

13. **unmilitant aspect:** nonaggressive appearance.

14. **crypt:** underground burial chamber.

Katie (*amused*). Bill, that machine was made by Japanese technicians who think of near everything. It'll run on its own.

Bill. Yeah, but it's been a long time since I've seen this one, and . . .

Katie. Okay. Enjoy. I think I'll be awake for a little while. . . .

(*She starts out, . . . then turns in the doorway as something else strikes her.*)

Katie. If they show the part where the punk's head gets—

Bill (*guiltily*). I'll edit it.

Katie. 'Night. And thanks again. For everything.

(*She leaves.* Bill *sits in his chair.*)

(*INT. TV, CU*)

(*A couple is necking in a car. Suddenly the passenger door is ripped open by the dead guy and we dissolve to:*)

(*INT. Katie, in bed*)

(*It's dark. She's asleep. She wakes up . . . sort of.*)

Katie (*sleepy*). Hey, big guy—

(*She feels for him, but his side of the bed is empty, the coverlet still pulled up. She sits up. Looks at:*)

(*INT. A clock on the night table, Katie's POV*)

(*It says 2:03 a.m. Then it flashes to 2:04.*)

(*INT. Katie*)

(*Fully awake now. And concerned. She gets up, puts on her robe, and leaves the bedroom.*)

(*INT. The TV screen, CU*)

(*snow*)

Katie (*voice, approaching*). Bill? Honey? You okay? Bill? Bi—

(*INT. Katie, in Bill's study*)

(*She's frozen, wide-eyed with horror.*)

(*INT. Bill, in his chair*)

(*He's slumped to one side, eyes closed, hand inside his shirt. Dawn* was *sleeping. Bill* is *not.*)

(*EXT. A coffin, being lowered into a grave*)

Minister (*voice*). And so we commit the earthly remains of William Weiderman to the ground, confident of his spirit and soul. "Be ye not cast down, brethren . . ."

(*EXT. graveside*)

(*All the Weidermans are ranged here. Katie and Polly* wear identical black dresses and veils. Connie *wears a black skirt and white blouse.* Dennis *and* Jeff *wear black suits.* Jeff *is crying. He has Rambo the Dragon under his arm for a little extra comfort.*)

(*Camera moves in on* Katie. *Tears course slowly down her cheeks. She bends and gets a handful of earth. Tosses it into the grave.*)

Katie. Love you, big guy.

(*EXT.* Jeff)

(*weeping*)

(*EXT. looking down into the grave*)

(*scattered earth on top of the coffin*)

(*Dissolve to:*)

(*EXT. the grave*)

(*A groundskeeper pats the last sod into place.*)

Groundskeeper. My wife says she wishes you'd written a couple more before you had your heart attack, mister. (*pause*) I like Westerns, m'self.

(*The groundskeeper* walks away, whistling.)

(*Dissolve to:*)

(*EXT. A church. Day.*)

(*Title card: five years later*)

(*The Wedding March is playing.* Polly, *older and radiant with joy, emerges into a pelting shower of rice. She's in a wedding gown, her new husband by her side.*)

(*Celebrants throwing rice line either side of the path. From behind the bride and groom come others. Among them are* Katie, Dennis, Connie, *and* Jeff . . . *all five years older. With* Katie *is another man. This is* Hank. *In the* <u>interim</u>, Katie *has also taken a husband.*)

(Polly *turns and her mother is there.*)

Polly. Thank you, Mom.

Katie (*crying*). Oh doll, you're so welcome.

(*They embrace. After a moment* Polly *draws away and looks at* Hank. *There is a brief moment of tension, and then* Polly *embraces* Hank, *too.*)

Polly. Thank you too, Hank. I'm sorry I was such a creep for so long . . .

Hank (*easily*). You were never a creep, Pol. A girl only has one father.

Connie. Throw it! Throw it!

(*After a moment,* Polly *throws her bouquet.*)
(*EXT. The bouquet, CU, slow motion.*)
(*turning and turning through the air*)

(*Dissolves to:*)
(*INT. The study, with* Katie. *Night.*)
(*The word processor has been replaced by a wide lamp looming over a stack of blueprints. The book jackets have been replaced by photos of buildings. Ones that have first been built in* Hank's *mind, presumably.*)
(*Katie is looking at the desk, thoughtful and a little sad.*)

Hank (*voice*). Coming to bed, Kate?

(*She turns and the camera widens out to give us* Hank. *He's wearing a robe over pajamas. She comes to him and gives him a little hug, smiling. Maybe we notice a few streaks of gray in her hair; her pretty pony has done its fair share of running since Bill died.*)

Katie. In a little while. A woman doesn't see her first one get married every day, you know.

Hank. I know.

(*The camera follows as they walk from the work area of the study to the more informal area. This is much the same as it was in the old days, with a coffee table, stereo, TV, couch, and Bill's old easy chair. She looks at this.*)

Hank. You still miss him, don't you?

Katie. Some days more than others. You didn't know, and Polly didn't remember.

Hank (*gently*). Remember what, doll?

Katie. Polly got married on the five-year anniversary of Bill's death.

Hank (*hugs her*). Come on to bed, why don't you?

Katie. In a little while.

Hank. Okay. Maybe I'll still be awake.

(*He kisses her, then leaves, closing the door behind him. Katie sits in Bill's old chair. Close by, on the coffee table, is a remote control for the TV and an extension phone. Katie looks at the blank TV, and the camera moves in on her face. One tear rims one eye, sparkling like a sapphire.*)

Katie. I *do* still miss you, big guy. Lots and lots. Every day. And you know what? It hurts.

(*The tear falls. She picks up the TV remote and pushes the on button.*)

(*INT. TV, Katie's POV*)

(*An ad for Ginsu Knives comes to an end and is replaced by a star logo.*)

Announcer (*voice*). Now back to Channel 63's Thursday night Star Time Movie . . . *Ghost Kiss.*

(*The logo dissolves into a guy who looks like he died in a car crash about two weeks ago and has since been subjected to a lot of hot weather. He comes staggering out of the same old crypt.*)

(*INT. Katie*)

(*Terribly startled—almost horrified. She hits the off button on the remote control. The TV blinks off.*)

(*Katie's face begins to work. She struggles against the impending emotional storm, but the coincidence of the movie is just one thing too many on what must have already been one of the most emotionally trying days of her life. The dam breaks and she begins to sob . . . terrible, heartbroken sobs. She reaches out for the little table by the chair, meaning to put the remote control on it, and knocks the phone onto the floor.*)

(*Sound: the hum of an open line*)

(*Her tear-stained face grows suddenly still as she looks at the telephone. Something begins to fill it . . . an idea? an* intuition? *Hard to tell. And maybe it doesn't matter.*)

(*INT. the telephone, Katie's POV*)

(*The camera moves in to ECU . . . moves in until the dots in the off-the-hook receiver look like* chasms.)

(*Sound of open-line buzz up to loud.*)

(*We go into the black . . . and hear*)

Bill (*voice*). Who are you calling? Who do you *want* to call? Who *would* you call, if it wasn't too late?

(*INT. Katie*)

(*There is now a strange hypnotized look on her face. She reaches down, scoops the telephone up, and punches in numbers, seemingly at random.*)

(*Sound: ringing phone*)

(*Katie continues to look hypnotized. The look holds until the phone is answered . . . and she hears herself on the other end of the line.*)

Katie (*voice; filter*). Hello, Weiderman residence.

(*Katie—our present-day Katie with the streaks of gray in her hair—goes on sobbing, yet an expression of desperate hope is trying to be born on her face. On some level she understands that the*

W O R D S
T O
K N O W

intuition (ĭn'tōō-ĭsh'ən) *n.* a piece of knowledge or a sense of something that is gained without the use of logical reasoning

chasm (kăz'əm) *n.* a deep hole, as in the earth's surface

depth of her grief has allowed a kind of telephonic time travel. She's trying to talk, to force the words out.)

Katie (*sobbing*). Take . . . please take . . . t-t-

(*INT. Katie, in the phone nook, reprise*)[15]

(*It's five years ago, Bill is standing beside her, looking concerned. Jeff is wandering off to look for a blank tape in the other room.*)

Katie. Polly? What's wrong?

(*INT. Katie, in the study*)

Katie (*sobbing*). Please—quick—

(*Sound: click of a broken connection*)

Katie (*screaming*). Take him to the hospital! If you want him to live, take him to the hospital! He's going to have a heart attack! He—

(*Sound: hum of an open line*)

(*Slowly, very slowly, Katie hangs up the telephone. Then, after a moment, she picks it up*

again. She speaks aloud with no self-consciousness whatever. Probably doesn't even know she's doing it.)

Katie. I dialed the old number. I dialed—

(*Slam cut*[16] *to:*)

(*INT. Bill, in the phone nook with Katie beside him*)

(*He's just taken the phone from Katie and is speaking to the operator.*)

Operator (*filter, giggles*). I *promise* not to give it out.

Bill. It's 555-

(*Slam cut to:*)

(*INT. Katie, in Bill's old chair, CU*)

Katie (*finishes*) -4408.

(*INT. the phone, CU*)

(*Katie's trembling finger carefully picks out*

---

15. **reprise:** to repeat something that happened earlier.
16. **slam cut:** a sudden, sharp change of scene.

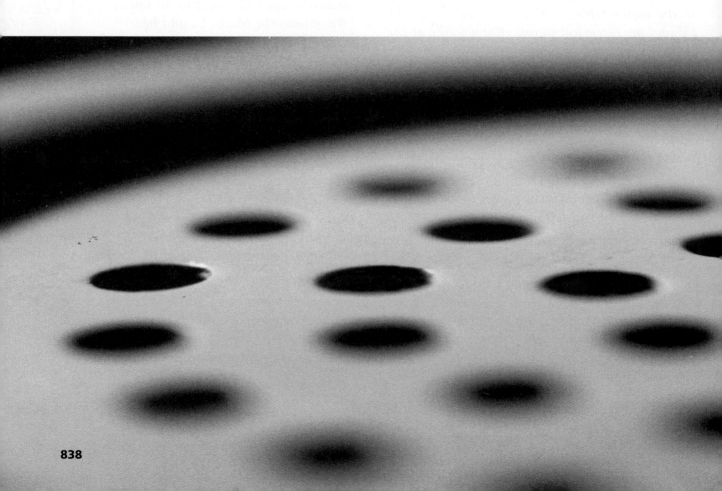

the number, and we hear the corresponding tones: 555-4408.)

(INT. Katie, in Bill's old chair, CU)

(She closes her eyes as the phone begins to ring. Her face is filled with an agonizing mixture of hope and fear. If only she can have one more chance to pass the vital message on, it says . . . just one more chance.)

Katie (*low*). Please . . . please . . .

Recorded voice (*filter*). You have reached a non-working number. Please hang up and dial again. If you need assistance—

(Katie hangs up again. Tears stream down her cheeks. The camera pans away and down to the telephone.)

(INT. The phone nook, with Katie and Bill, reprise)

Bill. So it was a prank. Or someone who was crying so hard she dialed a wrong number . . .

"through a shimmering film of tears," as we veteran hacks like to say.

Katie. It was not a prank and it was not a wrong number! It was someone in *my family!*

(INT. Katie [present day] in Bill's study)

Katie. Yes. Someone in *my family*. Someone very close. (*pause*) Me.

(She suddenly throws the phone across the room. Then she begins to sob again and puts her hands over her face. The camera holds on her for a moment, then dollies[17] across to:)

(INT. the phone)

(It lies on the carpet, looking both bland and somehow ominous. Camera moves in to ECU— the holes in the receiver once more look like huge dark chasms. We hold, then)

(Fade to black.)

---

17. **dollies:** moves smoothly.

Thinking through the LITERATURE

Connect to the Literature

1. What Do You Think?
How did you react to the last spoken word in the screenplay? Share your reaction with a classmate.

> **Comprehension Check**
> - Who does Katie believe is the crying phone caller?
> - Why do Katie and Bill drive out to check on Katie's sister Dawn?
> - Why doesn't Bill return to bed after watching the movie?
> - What does Katie see when she turns on the television on the fifth anniversary of Bill's death?

Think Critically

2. **ACTIVE READING** **VISUALIZING A SCREENPLAY** Look back at your notes in your **READER'S NOTEBOOK.** What clues does the camera give you for interpreting the play's supernatural occurrence?

3. Give your interpretation of the story's supernatural occurrence. Did you have anything similar to it on the list you created for the Connect to Your Life activity on page 823?

4. How would you explain the vague understanding—the "desperate hope . . . trying to be born"—that comes to Katie after she hears her own voice on the phone (page 837)?

5. Do you have sympathy for Katie? Why or why not?

> **THINK ABOUT**
> - the interactions between Katie and her children
> - the relationship between Katie and Bill
> - the relationship between Katie and Hank

Extend Interpretations

6. Comparing Texts What common fear or fears do you think *Sorry, Right Number* and "The Open Window" play on?

7. Connect to Life What do you think attracts readers to tales of the supernatural such as the ones that Stephen King writes?

Literary Analysis

> **FORESHADOWING**

Foreshadowing, or hints of events to come, can deepen the mood of suspense in a story. In *Sorry, Right Number,* the author builds suspense by hinting that something dreadful is going to happen.

Activity Look again at your **READER'S NOTEBOOK.** Review the list of camera directions that you marked with the letter *F* to indicate the **foreshadowing** of later developments in the play. Add to or delete from your list now that you know how the story turns out.

Camera Directions in *Sorry, Right Number*

the phone has two lights on it — F

Katie hears herself on the other end of the line — S

Choices & CHALLENGES

Writing Options

1. Alternate Ending What would you imagine as the outcome of King's story if Katie's phone call at the end had accomplished its purpose? Write an outline for an alternate ending of the teleplay based on this development.

2. "Scientific" Explanation Use your imagination and, in a paragraph or two, write a "scientific" explanation of how telephonic time travel works. Frame your explanation within a cause-and-effect organization. Place the outline in your **Working Portfolio.**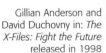

Writing Handbook
See page 1155: Explanatory Writing.

Gillian Anderson and David Duchovny in: *The X-Files: Fight the Future* released in 1998

Activities & Explorations

1. Stage Script Conversion In a small group, work out the ending of the teleplay as a straight stage production. Begin at the point where Katie turns on the TV set. Decide what elements of the teleplay you could not transfer to a stage production, and figure out how to convey that information to a live audience. When you are comfortable with your solution, present the scene to the rest of your class.
~ PERFORMING

2. Radio Review Tales of the supernatural and the unexplained are frequently told in the form of television shows, such as *The X-Files,* or movies, such as *The Shining.* Select a movie or a television show that deals with time travel, telepathy, or other supernatural occurrences and compose a radio review of it. Think about your audience and your purpose for reviewing. Discuss your review for the class or audiotape it. **~ SPEAKING AND LISTENING**

3. Magazine Cover Suppose that *Sorry, Right Number* were being featured on the cover of a magazine that lists and describes TV shows. Design the art for this cover and display it for the class. **~ VIEWING AND REPRESENTING/ART**

Inquiry & Research

Paranormal Phenomena Is there any scientific confirmation for the existence of paranormal phenomena such as telepathy?

Real World Link Read the article on cheatproof telepathy testing on page 843–844 before forming your opinion.

Vocabulary in Action

ACTIVITY: MEANING CLUES Answer the questions that follow.

1. What is another name for an **interim** between classes—a hallway, a break, or a competition?

2. Would a person who was **prone** to illness be sickly, healthy, or a good nurse?

3. Would a person who had an **intuition** about something have learned it, guessed it, or forgotten it?

4. Which is a famous **chasm**—the Washington Monument, Niagara Falls, or the Grand Canyon?

5. Would a child be most likely to look out the window **bleakly** at warm sunshine, dripping rain, or freshly fallen snow?

Building Vocabulary
For an in-depth lesson on how to build your vocabulary, see page 572.

Grammar in Context: Using Adverb Clauses to Direct the Reader's Attention

In *Sorry, Right Number,* Stephen King includes adverb clauses in some of the camera directions that describe what the audience should see.

> Katie *is sitting in the kitchen phone nook, having a good gab with her sister while she idles through some catalogues.*

> Katie *continues to look hypnotized. The look holds until the phone is answered.*

In the first sentence above, the adverb clause tells what the actor should be doing while talking on the phone. The second sentence indicates the sequence of events that should be followed in the scene. When writing various kinds of instructions and directions, writers often use adverb clauses to direct their readers' attention to important information.

WRITING EXERCISE Rewrite each sentence, adding an adverb clause to direct the reader's attention to the action in parentheses. Underline the adverb clause.

Example: *Original* Katie is talking to her sister on the phone. (Another call interrupts.)
Rewritten Katie is talking to her sister on the phone when another call interrupts.

1. She listens carefully. (The camera moves in for a close-up.)
2. The camera turns to the arched doorway that leads to the family room. (Katie continues talking.)
3. The camera pans slowly right. (We see Bill Weiderman at his computer.)
4. Katie and Hank walk through the house. (The camera follows them from room to room.)
5. Katie believes she can warn her younger self. (She sees the telephone on the table.)

Grammar Handbook Clauses, p. 1195

Stephen King
1947–

Other Works
The Shining
The Stand
The Dead Zone
Firestarter

One-Man Entertainment Industry Stephen King, a former English teacher, nearly threw away his writing career before it began. He originally dumped his manuscript for *Carrie* into the trash, but his wife retrieved it and urged him to continue working on it. Later, after *Carrie* became a hit movie, King went on to become a best-selling author and the first writer to have five titles on the *New York Times'* bestseller lists at the same time. Credited with reviving the market for both horror fiction and horror films, King has been called a "one-man entertainment industry."

A Devoted Writer Born in Portland, Maine, King began writing as a child and published his first story, "I Was a Teenage Grave Robber," in *Comics Review* when he was 18. A prolific and compulsive writer, King works every day except the Fourth of July, his birthday, and Christmas.

From Brain to Screen King has written that the idea for *Sorry, Right Number* came to him "one night on my way home from buying a pair of shoes." He wrote the script in two sittings and about a week later submitted it to a friend who had a TV series called *Tales from the Darkside.* The friend bought the teleplay the day he read it, had it in production a week or two later, and a month after that, telecast it—"one of the fastest turns from in-the-head to on-the-screen that I've ever heard of," King commented.

Author Activity

Movie Versions Many of Stephen King's stories have been made into movies—for example, *Carrie, Pet Sematary, The Dead Zone, Cujo,* and *The Shining.* Compare one of these films with the book from which it was made and present your findings to your classmates.

❶ # PHYSICISTS TEST TELEPATHY IN A "CHEAT-PROOF" SETTING

By Boyce Rensberger, *The New York Times*

❷ Scientists at the Stanford Research Institute who conducted experiments with a number of persons, including Uri Geller, the magician and purported psychic, report that Mr. Geller, and probably most people, have an ability to send and receive information by some "as yet unidentified perceptual modality."

Despite the publicity that has been given to Mr. Geller's contention that he has the ability to bend metal or move objects by mental power alone, the researchers said in the generally conservative journal *Nature* that they were unable to confirm the authenticity of such feats under conditions that eliminated the possibility of deception.

Although several professional magicians have duplicated many of Mr. Geller's feats by using sleight-of-hand techniques, the S.R.I. scientists said in a telephone interview that their current report was based on experiments in which trickery would seem to be unlikely. The scientists said they had consulted professional magicians in designing their experiments to be as "cheat proof" as possible. Mr. Geller was seated in a room with metal walls capable of insulating it from external sights, sounds, and radio waves, the scientists said.

Random Selection

Outside that room, the researchers opened a dictionary at random, looked down the list of entries for the first word that could be depicted graphically, and then drew a picture corresponding to the word. Mr. Geller's task was to draw a similar picture. The researchers said he was never told who would select the picture or how it would be done.

In nine such experiments, Mr. Geller produced seven drawings or sets of drawings. All of Mr. Geller's responses, which were published in the *Nature* article alongside the researchers' drawings, showed some degree of correspondence to the target pictures. Most showed remarkable similarity.

In the two instances in which Mr. Geller did not produce a drawing, he had been fitted with brain wave recording electrodes that, he said, interfered with his ability.

In a 10th experiment, the drawing was placed in the sealed room before Mr. Geller's arrival.

Uri Geller's ability to bend metal objects with "mind power" has been challenged for years.

Reading for Information

When reading news or feature articles that cover topics of a special nature, you need to be a critical reader. In cases like these, it is necessary to question the text as you read.

ANALYZING TEXT CHARACTERISTICS

In analyzing a text such as a news article, it is helpful to first establish standards, or **criteria,** to judge the work. Think of the elements that make a good news article, some of which are shown on this graphic.

Criteria	Meets Criteria	Neutral	Doesn't Meet Criteria
The article's intended audience is evident.			
The structure of the article is clear and easy to follow.			
The word choice is appropriate to the subject.			
The article uses credible information sources.			

YOUR TURN Fill in the graphic as you examine this article.

❶ **Audience** This article was published in the *New York Times,* a daily newspaper that is distributed nationally. Think about the scientific nature of the article's headline and what it might reveal about the audience's interest in telepathy. Who would you identify as the intended audience?

❷ **Structure** Note that the article uses an overall pattern of organization in which a generalization at the beginning is supported by specific facts. Then the article draws a specific conclusion. Identify the generalization, and list a few of the facts used to support it.

Later, when asked to reproduce the drawing he was unable to do so.

In three additional experiments, images that could be displayed by computer were stored in the machine's memory, known only to the programmer. Mr. Geller, in the sealed room during the selection and programming of the image, produced drawings that all bore some degree of similarity.

From these experiments, among others, the scientists, Russell Targ and Dr. Harold Puthoff, concluded that Mr. Geller did indeed possess telepathic ability.

❸ Publication of the report by the British scientific magazine *Nature,* one of the most respected international science journals, represents something of a first for parapsychology.[1] Research in the field is almost always reported only in journals that circulate within the specialty.

❹ The editors of *Nature,* aware of the controversy that the article, included in the October 18 issue, might arouse, then published an editorial explaining why they had chosen to print the article despite the objections of some article "referees." According to the editorial, consultants said that the report was "weak in design and presentation" and that details of precautions against conscious or unconscious fraud were "uncomfortably vague." Nonetheless, the editors said, the report represented a legitimate attempt by bona fide scientists to verify existence of a purported phenomenon that scientists frequently debated privately.

Abilities Held Common

"Perhaps the most important issue raised by the circumstances surrounding the publication of this paper is whether science has yet developed the competence to confront claims of the paranormal," the editorial said.

The scientists, both physicists who have long studied parapsychology as an avocation,[2] experimented with Mr. Geller as part of a continuing study of telepathic abilities that, they contend, are relatively common.

"We feel we have a repeatable phenomenon that doesn't depend on Geller," Mr. Targ said in a telephone interview from S.R.I. offices in Menlo Park, California. Mr. Targ said he felt the phenomenon was not "extrasensory at all but one that depended on an unknown, seldom exercised sensory capability possessed by many, perhaps all, persons." He said that experiments with a number of persons who were unaware of any telepathic ability, "including some skeptics," had suggested that the phenomenon might be common.

---

1. **parapsychology:** the study of the evidence for psychological phenomena, such as telepathy.

2. **avocation:** hobby.

❸ **Credibility** It is an accepted practice for journalists to present sources for the information that they report. What effect do the details about the scientists and the magazine that reported on the test have on your opinion of the **credibility,** or believability, of the article? How reliable do you think the information is from those sources?

❹ **Diction or Word Choice** Sometimes a writer qualifies a statement—or chooses words carefully to indicate that the statement is open to interpretation. Words such as *alleged, reportedly,* and *might* are used to qualify a writer's statements. List a few of the words or phrases used to qualify statements in the article. How does the writer's **diction** affect your reaction to the article?

Inquiry & Research

Activity Link: "Sorry, Right Number," p. 841 Now that you've read this article, do you think that telepathy exists? If so, do you think that all people have this capability, or just a few? Write an essay explaining whether you think telepathy exists. Include facts that support your views.

Beware: Do Not Read This Poem

Poetry by ISHMAEL REED

"do not resist this poem"

Connect to Your Life

Warning! Keep Out! Do Not Enter! Beware of Dog! No Trespassing! Enter at Your Own Risk! You probably see warning signs like these posted in your neighborhood or community every day. How do you react to them? What thoughts go through your mind when you read a warning sign? Explore your thinking with a cluster diagram like the one shown.

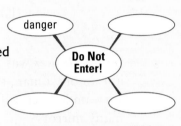

Build Background

Doing Things Reed's Way In his writing, Ishmael Reed has challenged writers and other artists to find their own way, to do what works best for them, and to ignore those who say there is only one way to do something. Reed has certainly followed his own advice and dared to be different. In both his prose and his poetry, he blends many styles. He also introduces a few new ones and often ignores those who insist that good literature must follow the rules of proper English. Reed's poetry is full of surprises, so you may want to ignore the poet's warning and READ this poem.

Focus Your Reading

LITERARY ANALYSIS **POETIC FORM** The way a poem looks and is arranged on a page is its **poetic form.** Some poems follow certain standard conventions. They may contain complete sentences, which are arranged in consistent stanzas throughout the poem, and follow standard patterns of spelling and grammar. Other poems, however, break these conventions and deliberately flout tradition by using sentence fragments, irregular stanza forms, and invented spelling or punctuation. Ishmael Reed sometimes writes in the kind of shorthand used in this line from "Beware: Do Not Read This Poem":

> *relax now & go w/ this poem*

As you read the poem, think about its form and how it differs from other poetry you have read.

ACTIVE READING **AUTHOR'S PURPOSE** In poetry, as in other types of literature, the poet usually has a purpose for writing. An **author's purpose** may be simply to entertain, or it might be to inform, to express an opinion, or to persuade. An author might also combine several purposes for writing in one piece of literature.

READER'S NOTEBOOK As you read the poem, keep a list of your responses to the poem. Later you will use your responses as a basis for figuring out what the author's purposes for writing the poem might have been.

beware: do not read this poem

Ishmael Reed

Fate #17 (1984), Bruce Charlesworth. SuperStock.

tonite, *thriller* was
abt an ol woman, so vain she
surrounded her self w/
many mirrors

5   It got so bad that finally she
locked herself indoors & her
whole life became the
mirrors

one day the villagers broke
10 into her house, but she was too
swift for them. she disappeared
   into a mirror
each tenant who bought the house
after that, lost a loved one to
15   the ol woman in the mirror:
   first a little girl
   then a young woman
   then the young woman/s husband

the hunger of this poem is legendary
20 it has taken in many victims
back off from this poem
it has drawn in yr feet
back off from this poem
it has drawn in yr legs
25 back off from this poem
it is a greedy mirror
you are into this poem. from
the waist down
nobody can hear you can they?
30 this poem has had you up to here
   belch

this poem aint got no manners
you cant call out frm this poem
relax now & go w/ this poem
35 move & roll on to this poem

do not resist this poem
this poem has yr eyes
this poem has his head
this poem has his arms
40 this poem has his fingers
this poem has his fingertips

this poem is the reader & the
reader this poem

statistic: the us bureau of missing persons
   reports
45 that in 1968 over 100,000 people
   disappeared
leaving no solid clues
   nor trace only
a space in the lives of their friends

Thinking through the LITERATURE

Connect to the Literature

1. What Do You Think? Did you like this poem? Why or why not?

> **Comprehension Check**
> - What story does the poem tell in the first three stanzas?
> - What has claimed "many victims"?

Think Critically

2. What do you think are the most striking **images** in the poem?

3. Why does the speaker tell the story about the "ol woman"?

 THINK ABOUT { • your reaction to the story
• the line, "it is a greedy mirror"

4. How does the poem's suggestion that you "not resist this poem" relate to the poem's **theme?**

5. **ACTIVE READING** **AUTHOR'S PURPOSE** Look back at the notes you made in your **READER'S NOTEBOOK.** Use your responses to **infer** the author's purposes for writing the poem, and compare your interpretation with those of your classmates.

Extend Interpretations

6. Different Perspectives If the title of this poem had been "The Woman and the Mirror" or "Go w/ This Poem," how would your reaction to the poem have been different? Explain your answer.

7. Connect to Life The speaker says this poem has "taken in many victims." Think about your own reading habits. What attracts you to certain stories, books, or magazines? How do you become a "victim" of the written word? Share your thoughts with a partner.

Literary Analysis

POETIC FORM In this poem, Ishmael Reed does not use a standard **poetic form,** or way of arranging words on a page. Instead, he invents his own arrangement of lines and stanzas and follows his own rules for capitalization and punctuation. He also introduces some creative spellings and a few graphic symbols.

Cooperative Learning Activity With a partner, reread the poem and study its form. In a chart like the one shown, list some of the spellings and graphic symbols used, and describe the author's use of capitalization and punctuation. Then decide what overall effect these features have on the poem. Share your ideas with other classmates as you discuss these questions: Why did the poet choose this poetic form? Is the form of the poem connected to the author's purposes for writing the poem?

Poetic Form in "Beware: Do Not Read This Poem"

Spellings:
abt
yr

Symbols:

Capitalization:

Punctuation:

Writing Options

1. Letter to Ishmael Write a letter to the poet, stating your opinion of his poem. Explain your thoughts about his title, his subject matter, his use of form, and any specific lines you choose to comment about.

Writing Handbook
See page 1155: Explanatory Writing.

2. Do-It-Yourself Poetry Follow Reed's lead and write your own poem, using an original poetic form. Arrange your words on the page in a way that expresses the ideas or emotions of your poem.

Activities & Explorations

1. Oral Interpretation With a partner, prepare an oral interpretation of Reed's poem, in which you alternate reciting lines or stanzas. Decide who will read what sections. Then practice aloud, using your voices to create suspense or other emotions. Concentrate on volume, tone, and speed. Finally, present your polished reading to your classmates. ~ **SPEAKING AND LISTENING**

2. Poetic Poster Design a poster to publicize a public reading of Reed's poem. Select an image to represent the message of the poem and make a sketch, a painting, or a collage to grab attention. Include details of date, time, and place on the poster. ~ **ART**

Inquiry & Research

Thrillers The first line of the poem suggests that the story about the woman and the mirrors was the plot in a thriller—perhaps a suspenseful movie or television show. Consult television or movie guides for plot summaries that mention mirrors. Compile a list of titles for a class listing of recommended thrillers.

Ishmael Reed
1938–

Other Works
Conjure
Chattanooga
A Secretary to the Spirits

Early Activism Ishmael Reed was born in Chattanooga, Tennessee. At the age of four, he moved with his family to Buffalo, New York, where he spent the next 20 years. Reed attended the State University of New York at Buffalo, where professors recognized and encouraged his ability to write. However, he dropped out during his junior year because of financial problems and because he felt that the university environment did not provide a true picture of the gaps between America's social classes. In 1960, he moved into a low-income housing project to judge for himself how the poor really lived.

Literary Careers Although writing is his primary profession, Reed has also worked as a reporter, an editor, a publisher, and an actor. He has taught and lectured at Dartmouth, Harvard, Yale, and the University of California at Berkeley. In 1961, while working as a newspaper reporter in Buffalo, he co-hosted a local radio talk show. The show was canceled after Reed interviewed the controversial civil rights leader Malcolm X.

Outspoken Critic Reed believes strongly in freedom of speech and is an outspoken critic of political and social injustices. He criticizes those who think things are fine just as they are, and he uses his poetry and prose to point out the faults of well-known individuals from all corners of society—from politicians and dictators to actors and authors. Although he has made enemies with some of his criticism, he has also won many admirers and many awards for his writing.

Understanding Relationships Between Words

Words can be related in various ways. Some are **synonyms,** words with similar meanings; some are **antonyms,** words with opposite meanings. Others are related as **homonyms,** words with the same spelling and pronunciation but with different meanings. See if you can find a pair of antonyms in the excerpt on the right.

Did you recognize that the words *treacherous* and *safe* in the passage are antonyms?

> In crossing the moor to their favorite snipe-shooting ground they were all three engulfed by a treacherous piece of bog. It had been that dreadful wet summer, you know, and places that were safe in other years gave way suddenly without warning.
> —Saki, "The Open Window"

Strategies for Building Vocabulary

By increasing your knowledge of synonyms, antonyms, and homonyms, you can broaden your understanding of words and thus become a more skillful reader and writer.

❶ **Collect Synonyms** If you know many synonyms, you will be better able to choose the most appropriate words to use in your writing. Dictionaries and thesauruses are invaluable aids for finding and learning synonyms. Note this dictionary excerpt, in which synonyms of the word *recover* are listed and their connotations are explained:

> SYNONYMS: . . . *Regain* suggests success in recovering something that has been taken from one. . . . To *recoup* is to get back the equivalent of something lost. . . . *Retrieve* pertains to the effortful recovery of something. . . .
> —*The American Heritage Dictionary of the English Language*

❷ **Learn Antonyms** Antonyms are especially useful when you want to express contrasts. Dictionaries of synonyms and antonyms, as well as some thesauruses, can help you find antonyms of a word. If you don't have such references at hand, try adding the prefixes *anti-, in-, un-,* and *ex-* to the word to explore opposites. Also, look up the word's definition in a standard dictionary, and then guess what words might have opposite meanings. Check your guesses by looking them up in the dictionary.

❸ **Understand Homonyms** Because homonyms are spelled and pronounced the same but have different meanings, they sometimes plague readers.

In most cases, though, the context reveals which of a set of homonyms is being used. In a sentence containing the word *row,* for example, the context will most likely make it clear whether the meaning is "a line of objects" or "to use oars to propel a boat." For some homonyms, you may need to check a dictionary to determine which meaning is intended. The chart below gives some examples of homonyms.

Homonyms	Meanings
pole	a stick
pole	an end of the earth's axis
bark	the outer covering of a tree
bark	the sound of a dog
bark	a sailing ship
sage	a wise person
sage	an herb
grouse	a game bird
grouse	to grumble; complain

EXERCISE For each word, write a related word of the type indicated in parentheses. (Include definitions for the homonyms.) Then write a sentence containing the given word and the related word.

1. *grandeur* (synonym)
2. *frail* (antonym)
3. *shore* (homonym)
4. *motionless* (synonym)
5. *disperse* (antonym)

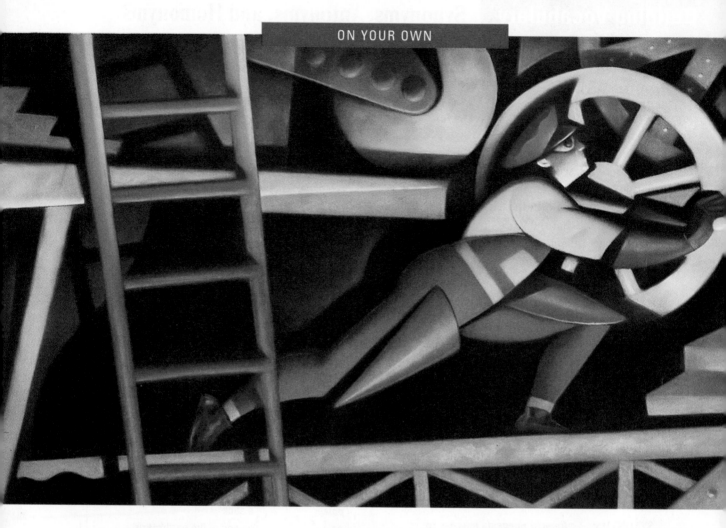

THE CULTURAL WORKER

Sue Doro

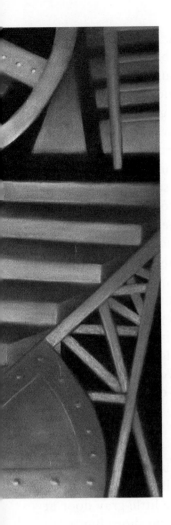

"The Cultural Worker" introduces us to a female factory worker on a late-night shift. In telling the story, the author relies heavily on personification, a figure of speech in which human qualities are attributed to an object, an animal, or an idea. She presents the poem in the story not only as a living thing, but as one of the main characters. As you read, notice the way the worker and the poem relate to each other and think about what the author wants to say about the creative process.

The poem waited for her outside the wheel-shop door. Waited, as if it were one of the leaning train wheels stacked against each other, like round brown five-hundred-pound dominoes. Train wheels waiting to be hauled inside the factory, machined to order, then mounted on shiny steel axles and rolled out the door into the Menomonee Valley[1] train yard.

So too, the poem waited. It had been waiting for her to finish work since 3:30 that afternoon. Now it was midnight. Soon she would step out of second shift into the dark of the going-home night.

Hours ago in the early evening, the summer sun hung low and rosy over old freight cars in the yard. The poem had gone to the window nearest the machine the woman was operating that night. The poem thought that the sunset would surely get her attention. But not tonight. She was measuring a train axle with a micrometer,[2] straining on her tiptoes to reach around its diameter. The poem could see she was too busy to be thinking poem words, so it did what it knew how to do.

It waited. Measuring minutes against the sun's shadows on the dirty cream-colored brick wall. It waited, as 5 o'clock break time came. It waited and watched through a different window as the woman ate half of her sandwich sitting at the lunch table by the men's locker room, sharing a newspaper and talking with some of the guys. She was the only woman in the shop. There used to be two others, but they got laid off. Now she was the only one of her kind left, and sometimes she was lonely. But tonight the poem saw that she was having a good time, joking with her "buddies."

It was an hour and a half later when the poem looked in again. The woman was standing with the micrometer in her hand, listening to a short elderly man with gray-brown whiskers. He wore a work-worn green hardhat, low over his eyes. His hands glistened with dark brown dirty train-bearing grease. In one, he held a red-handled putty scraper. In the other,

---

1. **Menomonee** (mə-nŏm′ə-nē) **Valley:** a river valley in the vicinity of Milwaukee, Wisconsin.
2. **micrometer** (mī-krŏm′ĭ-tər): a device for measuring small distances, objects, or angles.

by their cuffs, a pair of oily rubber gloves. The ring finger was missing on that hand. A cigarette bobbed up and down from his mouth as he talked. Its ashes dusting the man's brown shirt every so often. The poem could catch only a few of the man's words . . . "wife . . . divorce . . . still love her . . . the kids don't . . ." The woman was intent on listening to the man. The poem went back to wait at the door until dinner break.

In summer it was still light at 8 in the evening, and the poem knew that the woman would come outside to sit on the long bench against the building. Most of the men would go out for dinner to the tavern up the hill, so she would usually be alone. Sometimes she would take a walk by the railroad tracks, heading under the freeway. There was a river to watch and listen to, and wild flowers to pick. In the early spring, there were little green onions and asparagus hidden in the tall grasses. Sometimes she would read or write in her journal. But tonight she had no pad of paper, no pencil or pen. She was sitting on the bench, but she was leaning forward a bit, holding a book. A union agreement. And she was not alone. She and some other workers were talking words like "lost jobs . . . bankruptcy . . . layoffs beginning in July . . . the company can't . . . illegal . . . they'll try . . . four guys fired . . ." The poem saw it was useless to try to get into her head. Then the factory whistle blew, and a foreman appeared in the doorway, motioning the woman and the men back to work.

The poem stayed outside.

At 10 o'clock the poem went to look in the window by the woman again. She was staring out into the blackness of the night, but she didn't notice the poem. Her eyes were taking in the silhouettes of axles and wheels and oil drums. Watching black birds fly in front of the huge pink streetlights on tall poles that illuminated the train yard. Her face was feeling a good west wind blowing in. She wasn't thinking poem thoughts. She was thinking of going home and wishing the night would hurry so she could get there. "A few more axles," is what she was thinking, as she turned away from the warm starry night. A night smelling of Menomonee Valley city wilderness, and NOT the stockyards, thanks to the west wind. Away from the window she turned. Away from the poem looking in the window, and back to her job.

And finally it was midnight. The moon was high over the factory roof. The yard was a watercolored wash of moonlight and pink from the lights in the valley. The moon was a white ball with a golden ring. The poem waited with the moon, holding its breath. The pink lights shone down over the top of the building, casting shadows on the path next to the tracks.

The woman would be the first ready to leave. Usually she waited for the guys by the little gray door at the far end of the shop. But tonight she had told them she was in a hurry. She stepped alone into the night as the midnight whistle blew. She was short, but her shadow was ten feet tall. She carried a paper sack of dirty work clothes in her arms. The poem was with her like her shadow, walking quickly. The farther away from the building, the taller her shadow grew, from the pink lights and the moon on her shoulders. Little rocks and pebbles at her feet crunched under her shoes. Each pebble had its own shadow, like pink moon rocks under her feet. She smiled to herself, enjoying the moment.

A cat meowed and scampered under a parked freight car. Night birds called. Now her shadow split in two, growing taller, taller,

taller. Catching pink lights on more poles in the train yard. She stepped carefully across one, two, three sets of tracks. Past stacks of unmachined main axles and rows of wheels. Past lines of mounted wheels and axles waiting to be shipped out. A lone black bird cawed at her from a telephone wire. Something stirred in her brain. Some disjointed words seemed to come together. She laughed aloud, and the crow cawed again, leaving its perch to fly over her head into the blackness beyond the realm of pink lights. Then suddenly the woman threw her head back and yelled up into the pink and black sky. "HEY . . . I'm a midnight rider. A cat's eye glider. I'm a second shift lady goin' home!"

She laughed again. And surprised and delighted, the poem jumped INSIDE HER like a fetus kicking in the ninth month. She hurried along, faster now, almost running the last few yards past the guard shanty.

She was at her car in the parking lot now. She unlocked its door, opened it and flung her sack of dirty clothes in the back seat. Getting in, she started the car up and aimed it out of the lot, waving to other workers that were now crossing the tracks behind her. Finally she would have time for herself. She felt the uneasy urgency she'd had all night go from her in a deep earth-moving sigh, as she drove past the guard shanty and turned up the road to the ramp leading from the valley.

And a poem was born, comfortable as a well-fitting work shoe, and satisfying as the end of the workday. The poem. The woman. The machinist. All became one. And she sang to the hum of her car:

I'm a midnight rider
A cat's eye glider
I'm a second shift woman goin' home

I'm a moon rock walker
A night bird stalker
I'm a short tall shadow headin' home

I'm a cool old river
A seasoned survivor
I'm a factory workin' poet goin' home

Sue Doro
1936–

Other Works
Of Birds and Factories
Heart, Home, and Hard Hats

Blue-Collar Writer Sue Doro has impressive credentials both as a writer and a tradeswoman. She started writing in her late 20s, choosing labor and feminist topics. Meanwhile, she worked as a railway machinist in Milwaukee, Wisconsin, for 13 years—and raised five children. A social activist, Doro aims to bring "worker writing"—literature written by and about blue-collar workers—into the mainstream of American culture. Her book

Blue Collar Goodbyes is based on her experiences at the railway factory around the time of its closing. The selections in the book capture "the hearts of survivors / that corporate minds will never know."

Career Combination After the railway plant closed down, Doro moved to Oakland, California. For two and a half years, she served as the executive director of Tradeswomen, Inc., a national organization for women in blue-collar jobs. She currently works as an affirmative-action compliance officer for the U.S. Department of Labor. She is also poetry editor for *Tradeswoman Magazine*.

LaserLinks: Background for Reading
Sociological Connection
Art Gallery

POETRY

Pablo Neruda

And it was at that age . . . poetry
    arrived
in search of me. I don't know, I don't
    know where
it came from, from winter or a river.
I don't know how or when,
5 no, they were not voices, they were not
words, not silence,
but from a street it called me,
from the branches of night,
abruptly from the others,
10 among raging fires
or returning alone,
there it was, without a face,
and it touched me.

I didn't know what to say, my mouth
15 had no way
with names,
my eyes were blind.
Something knocked in my soul,
fever or forgotten wings,
20 and I made my own way,
deciphering[1]
that fire,
and I wrote the first, faint line,
faint, without substance, pure

25 nonsense,
pure wisdom
of someone who knows nothing;
and suddenly I saw
the heavens
30 unfastened
and open,
planets,
palpitating[2] plantations,
the darkness perforated,[3]
35 riddled[4]
with arrows, fire, and flowers,
the overpowering night, the universe.

And I, tiny being,
drunk with the great starry
40 void,
likeness, image of
mystery,
felt myself a pure part
of the abyss.[5]
45 I wheeled with the stars.
My heart broke loose with the wind.

---

1. **deciphering** (dĭ-sī′fər-ĭng): interpreting.
2. **palpitating** (păl′pĭ-tā′tĭng): beating rapidly, throbbing.
3. **perforated** (pûr′fə-rā′tĭd): punctured.
4. **riddled**: pierced many times.
5. **abyss** (ə-bĭs′): a huge empty space or depth.

Comparing Literature

Magical Realism

In the Family
Short Story by MARÍA ELENA LLANO

A Very Old Man with Enormous Wings
Short Story by GABRIEL GARCÍA MÁRQUEZ

What's the Connection?

Impossible! You are about to read two stories that focus on events that are not possible in the world as we know it. One story deals with a mirror that reflects some deceased family members and the other with the mysterious appearance of an old man with wings. Both stories are examples of **magical realism,** a kind of storytelling popular with Hispanic writers in which fantastic events take place in a realistic setting.

Why might authors enjoy writing—or readers reading—realistic stories that contain a strong element of fantasy? One reason is that this way of storytelling allows the writer to show characters dealing with new challenges and novel situations. Another is that such stories provide powerful, highly imaginative metaphors that give us some insight into very real aspects of our own lives. As you read, you may think of other reasons.

The False Mirror [Le Faux Miroir] (1928), René Magritte. Oil on canvas, 21¼″ × 31⅞″. The Museum of Modern Art, New York. Purchase. Photograph copyright © 1998 The Museum of Modern Art.

Points of Comparison

Analyzing Magical Realism Stories In this unit, you have read stories involving mysterious or supernatural events. In the pages that follow, you will analyze two selections, noting how each matches the characteristics of magical realism and developing your understanding of and appreciation for this type of literature.

Critical Thinking: Establishing a Basis for Analysis
To analyze two works of literature, you need to decide which characteristics you will examine. The chart shown will help you focus on details of four aspects of each story—the characters, the setting, the plot, and the theme—that can serve as your basis for analysis.

📖 READER'S NOTEBOOK As you read the two stories that follow, fill in the chart with details.

Elements of Magical Realism	Story Title
Details of Plot What kind of fantastic action occurs? Are there any elements of surprise?	
Details of Setting How realistic is the world of the story? Does the author make use of time shifts?	
Details of Character How do the different characters react to the occurrence of something fantastic? Are there elements of unusual humor?	
Details of Theme What do the characters or the reader learn from the fantastic event? How does the presence of the unexplainable change the meaning of the story?	

In the Family

Short Story by MARÍA ELENA LLANO

*"We kept the
secret to ourselves
since, after all,
it was nobody
else's business."*

Connect to Your Life

Fantasy or Reality Have you ever had an experience where you questioned whether or not you saw what you think you saw? Perhaps you've awakened to wonder about the feeling of reality you had about events in a dream. Maybe you've caught a glimpse of a person that couldn't possibly be who you thought it was. The mind can play strange tricks on you, leading to a blurring of what's real and what is not. With a partner, share an experience when your mind played such a trick.

Build Background

Popular Form of Literature María Elena Llano uses a form of fiction that has become popular among authors from Latin American countries such as Argentina, Chile, Brazil, Colombia, and Cuba. It is a style of writing that blends fantasy with reality. Since the 1950s, there has been a growing trend among Hispanic, or Spanish-speaking, authors to weave the folklore, myths, and superstitions of their native culture into stories that otherwise describe ordinary people and events. "In the Family" is one example of this mix of fantasy and reality.

> WORDS TO KNOW
> **Vocabulary Preview**
>
> bolster   indolent
> contemplation   oversight
> grievously

Focus Your Reading

LITERARY ANALYSIS   **MAGICAL REALISM**   **Magical realism** is the term used to describe a style of writing that combines fantasy and reality so that unnatural, or magical, events occur in a natural setting. Even though some events of the story may be supernatural or fantastic, the characters accept those events as believable. In magical realism, the boundary between fantasy and reality becomes blurred or hard to recognize, as in this passage from "In the Family."

> *At any rate, some time went by before each one of us would feel absolutely comfortable about sitting down in our favorite chair and learning that, in the mirror, that same chair was occupied by somebody else.*

As you read the story, look for examples of magical realism, and see whether you can identify what is real and what is magical from your perspective.

ACTIVE READING   **READING FOR DETAILS**   Stories that are written in the style of magical realism include two kinds of **details,** magical and realistic. **Magical details** are those that describe a fantasy world of people or events that most readers would consider unreal. **Realistic details** are those that describe an everyday world of seemingly normal people and events. Both types of details are used in descriptions of **character, setting,** and **plot,** and both types of detail appear in stories told by first-person and third-person narrators.

📖 **READER'S NOTEBOOK**   As you read "In the Family," create a chart like the one on page 855 to record details of character, setting, and plot.

In the Family

María Elena Llano

When my mother found out that the large mirror in the living room was inhabited, we all gradually went from disbelief to astonishment, and from this to a state of <u>contemplation</u>, ending up by accepting it as an everyday thing.

The fact that the old, spotted mirror reflected the dear departed in the family was not enough to upset our life style. Following the old saying of "let the house burn as long as no one sees the smoke," we kept the secret to ourselves since, after all, it was nobody else's business.

At any rate, some time went by before each one of us would feel absolutely comfortable about sitting down in our favorite chair and learning that, in the mirror, that same chair was occupied by somebody else. For example, it could be Aurelia, my grandmother's sister (1939), and even if cousin Natalie would be on my side of the room, across from her would be the almost forgotten Uncle Nicholas (1927). As could have been expected, our departed reflected in the mirror presented the image of a family gathering almost identical to our own, since nothing, absolutely nothing in the living-room—the furniture and its

arrangement, the light, etc.—was changed in the mirror. The only difference was that on the other side it was them instead of us.

I don't know about the others, but I sometimes felt that, more than a vision in the mirror, I was watching an old worn-out movie, already clouded. The deceaseds' efforts to copy our gestures were slower, restrained, as if the mirror were not truly showing a direct image but the reflection of some other reflection.

From the very beginning I knew that everything would get more complicated as soon as my cousin Clara got back from vacation. Because of her boldness and determination, Clara had long given me the impression that she had blundered into our family by mistake. This suspicion had been somewhat <u>bolstered</u> by her being one of the first women dentists in the country. However, the idea that she might have been with us by mistake went away as soon as my cousin hung up her diploma and started to embroider sheets beside my grandmother, aunts and other cousins, waiting

La Voix du Silence [The Voice of Silence] (1928), Rene Magritte. Oil on canvas, 54 × 73 cm. Galerie Christine et Isy Brachot, Brussels, Belgium. Copyright © 1998 Artists Rights Society (ARS), New York.

for a suitor who actually did show up but was found lacking in one respect or another—nobody ever really found out why.

Once she graduated, Clara became the family oracle,[1] even though she never practiced her profession. She would prescribe painkillers and was the arbiter[2] of fashion; she would choose the theater shows and rule on whether the punch had the right amount of liquor at each social gathering. In view of all this, it was fitting that she take one month off every year to go to the beach.

That summer when Clara returned from her vacation and learned about my mother's discovery, she remained pensive for a while, as if weighing the symptoms before issuing a diagnosis. Afterwards, without batting an eye, she leaned over the mirror, saw for herself that it was true, and then tossed her head, seemingly accepting the situation. She immediately sat by the bookcase and craned her neck to see who was sitting in the chair on the other side. "Gosh, look at Gus," was all she said. There in the very same chair the mirror showed us Gus, some sort of godson of Dad, who after a flood in his hometown came to live with us and had remained there in the somewhat ambiguous[3] character of adoptive poor relation. Clara greeted him amiably with a wave of the hand, but he seemed busy, for the moment, with something like a radio tube[4] and did not pay attention to her. Undoubtedly, the mirror people weren't going out of their way to be sociable. This must have wounded Clara's self-esteem, although she did not let it on.

Naturally, the idea of moving the mirror to the dining-room was hers. And so was its sequel: to bring the mirror near the big table, so we could all sit together for meals.

In spite of my mother's fears that the mirror people would run away or get annoyed because of the fuss, everything went fine. I must admit it was comforting to sit every day at the table and see so many familiar faces, although some of those from the other side were distant relatives, and others, due to their lengthy—although unintentional—absence, were almost strangers. There were about twenty of us sitting at the table every day, and even if their gestures and movements seemed more remote than ours and their meals a little washed-out, we generally gave the impression of being a large family that got along well.

At the boundary between the real table and the other one, on this side, sat Clara and her brother Julius. On the other side was Eulalia (1949), the second wife of Uncle Daniel, aloof and indolent in life, and now the most distant of anyone on the other side. Across from her sat my godfather Sylvester (1952), who even though he was not a blood relative was always a soul relation. I was sad to see that Sylvester had lost his ruddiness, for he now looked like a faded mannequin, although his full face seemed to suggest perfect health. This pallor did not suit the robust Asturian,[5] who undoubtedly felt a bit ridiculous in these circumstances.

For a while we ate all together, without further incidents or problems. We mustn't forget Clara, however, who we had allowed to sit at the frontier between the two tables, the equator separating what was from what was not. Although we paid

---

1. **oracle** (ôr′ə-kəl): a person serving as a source of wise advice.
2. **arbiter** (är′bĭ-tər): decision-maker; judge.
3. **ambiguous** (ăm-bĭg′yōō-əs): unclear; uncertain.
4. **radio tube:** one of the glass, bulblike devices formerly used in radios to serve the purposes now served by transistors.
5. **Asturian** (ăs-tōōr′ē-ən): a person from Asturias, a region in northwestern Spain.

WORDS TO KNOW   **indolent** (ĭn′də-lənt) adj. lazy

no attention to the situation, we should have. Compounding our regrettable oversight was the fact that lethargic[6] Eulalia sat across from her so that one night, with the same cordiality with which she had addressed Gus, Clara asked Eulalia to pass the salad. Eulalia affected the haughty disdain of offended royalty as she passed the spectral[7] salad bowl, filled with dull lettuce and grayish semi-transparent tomatoes which Clara gobbled up, smiling mischievously at the novelty of it all. She watched us with the same defiance in her eyes that she had on the day she enrolled in a man's subject. There was no time to act. We just watched her grow pale, then her smile faded away until finally Clara collapsed against the mirror.

Once the funeral business was over and we sat back down at the table again, we saw that Clara had taken a place on the other side. She was between cousin Baltazar (1940) and a great-uncle whom we simply called "Ito."

This *faux pas*[8] dampened our conviviality[9] somewhat. In a way, we felt betrayed; we felt that they had grievously abused our hospitality. However, we ended up divided over the question of who was really whose guest. It was also plain that our carelessness and Clara's irrepressible inquisitiveness had contributed to the mishap. In fact, a short time later we realized that there wasn't a great deal of difference between what Clara did before and what she was doing now, and so we decided to overlook the incident and get on with things. Nevertheless, each day we became less and less sure about which side was life and which its reflection, and as one bad step leads to another, I ended up taking Clara's empty place.

I am now much closer to them. I can almost hear the distant rustle of the folding and unfolding of napkins, the slight clinking of glasses and cutlery, the movement of chairs. The fact is that I can't tell if these sounds come from them or from us. I'm obviously not worried about clearing that up. What really troubles me, though, is that Clara doesn't seem to behave properly, with either the solemnity or with the opacity[10] owed to her new position; I don't know how to put it. Even worse, the problem is that I—more than anybody else in the family—may become the target of Clara's machinations,[11] since we were always joined by a very special affection, perhaps because we were the same age and had shared the same children's games and the first anxieties of adolescence. . .

As it happens, she is doing her best to get my attention, and ever since last Monday she has been waiting for me to slip up so she can pass me a pineapple this big, admittedly a little bleached-out, but just right for making juice and also a bit sour, just as she knows I like it. ❖

For a while we ate all together...

---

6. **lethargic** (lə-thär′jĭk): sluggish; inactive.
7. **spectral** (spĕk′trəl): ghostly.
8. **faux pas** (fI pä′): social blunder.
9. **conviviality** (kən-vĭv′ē-ăl′ĭ-tē): friendly togetherness.
10. **opacity** (ō-păs′ĭ-tē): a quality of being difficult to understand or interpret.
11. **machinations** (măk′ə-nā′shənz): crafty schemes.

WORDS TO KNOW

oversight (ō′vər-sīt′) *n.* an unintentional mistake
grievously (grē′vəs-lē) *adv.* severely

860

Thinking through the LITERATURE

Connect to the Literature

1. What Do You Think?
What do you predict will happen to the narrator based on how the story ends? Share your thoughts with other classmates.

Comprehension Check
- What is unusual about the "old, spotted mirror"?
- Where does the "spectral salad bowl" come from?
- What two things happen to Clara after she eats the salad?
- What is the narrator concerned about at the end of the story?

Think Critically

2. How do you think the family's attitude toward the "mirror people" changes during the course of the story? Explain.

3. In your opinion, does the character of Clara make the story more or less believable?

- her educational achievements
- her status in the family
- her reaction to the mirror people

4. How would you describe the narrator's **tone,** or attitude, in this story?

5. The narrator talks about the "boundary between the real table and the other one" and "the frontier between the two tables." Why do you think the author chose the words *boundary* and *frontier?*

6. **ACTIVE READING** **READING FOR DETAILS** Look back at the chart of magical and realistic details in your **READER'S NOTEBOOK.** Was it ever difficult for you to decide whether a detail was magical or realistic? Use examples to support your answer.

Extend Interpretations

7. Connect to Life The family in this story accepts the fact that their dead ancestors visit them through an old mirror. Different people, cultures, and religions have a variety of concepts of death and and beliefs about what happens to people when they die. What different beliefs about death or the relationships between the dead and the living are familiar to you? Share this information with your classmates.

8. **Points of Comparison** Look again at the chart in your **READER'S NOTEBOOK.** Now that you have analyzed one story, how has your appreciation or understanding of any of the elements changed?

Literary Analysis

MAGICAL REALISM | **Magical realism** is a form of fiction that skillfully blends elements of fantasy and the real world. In addition to the mixture of reality and fantasy, its characteristics include:
- the element of surprise
- unusual humor
- the use of time shifts
- the presence of the unexplainable

Paired Activity With a partner, discuss the five characteristics of magical realism and decide which of these characteristics can be found in "In the Family."

REVIEW **POINT OF VIEW**
The **point of view** in a story is the perspective from which events are told. In this story, the point of view is **first-person,** meaning that the narrator is a character within the story. Why do you think the author uses the first-person point of view in "In the Family"? What do you get from a first-person narrator in this story?

ACTIVE READING **REVIEW AUTHOR'S PURPOSE**
The most common purposes for writing are to entertain, to inform or explain, to express an opinion, and to persuade. Which of these purposes do you think the author María Elena Llano might have had in writing "In The Family" in the style of magical realism?

Writing Options

Family Dialogue Imagine a conversation that might take place between Clara and the narrator, between Clara and Eulalia, or between Eulalia and Gus. Write the dialogue for a brief chat between any two of the family members.

Activities & Explorations

Two Worlds Pantomime Perform a pantomime for the class of the events described in this story. Devise your own method of creating the "boundary" between living family members and mirror people.

Art Connection

Look again at the painting by René Magritte on page 858. Magritte created this painting with the deliberate intentions of playing with logic and of creating questions in the mind of the viewer. What questions would you like to ask about the painting? How is Magritte's divided room like or unlike the room in "In the Family"?

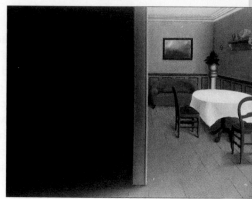

Detail of La Voix du Silence [The Voice of Silence] (1928), René Magritte. Oil on canvas, 54 × 73 cm. Galerie Christine et Isy Brachot, Brussels, Belgium. Copyright © 1998 Artists Rights Society (ARS), New York.

Vocabulary in Action

EXERCISE: MEANING CLUES On your paper, write the Word to Know suggested by each sentence below.

1. The girl gazed at the photograph of her great-grandmother.
2. Uncle Edgar never worked a day in his life.
3. We had forgotten to set a place for Cousin Sara.
4. We all complimented the cook to build her confidence.
5. Mother was deeply offended by Aunt Patricia's unkind remark.

Building Vocabulary

Most of the Words to Know in this lesson come from Latin. For an in-depth study of word origins, see page 973.

WORDS TO KNOW			
	bolster contemplation	grievously indolent	oversight

María Elena Llano
1936–

Other Works
La reja (The Plowshare)

Journalist by Trade Born in Cuba, María Elena Llano is a journalist who has won many awards for her writing. Among her award-winning works are stories that she has written for both radio and television shows. Llano has been recognized for the humor she interjects into some of her journalism, which she practices in the cultural department of a news agency in Havana called the Latin Press.

Range of Writing Llano writes in Spanish, but her stories have been translated into several other languages, including English. They occasionally appear in anthologies with stories by other Hispanic authors. In 1966, she published her first collection of short stories, *La reja (The Plowshare)*. Since then Llano has written a second book of stories and a collection of poems. She also writes scripts for stage plays and art reviews.

A Very Old Man with Enormous Wings

Short Story by GABRIEL GARCÍA MÁRQUEZ

"His huge buzzard wings, dirty and half-plucked, were forever entangled in the mud."

Connect to Your Life

Mysterious Creatures Throughout the world, thousands of people have reported seeing strange creatures that are unlike any animal known to science. There have been sightings of cats with wings, monstrous snakes, wolf-like men, and hairy half-human animals. What is your reaction to the reported sightings of these mysterious creatures? Do you think creatures of this type are real or imaginary? Discuss your thoughts with other classmates.

Build Background

A Special Kind of Storytelling In his stories, Gabriel García Márquez draws upon the folktales and superstitions of the townspeople he knew as a child in Colombia, a Spanish-speaking country in South America. He weaves those tales of mysterious creatures and superstitions into a special kind of story, a tale of **magical realism,** which blends fantasy with reality and often uses exaggeration. One example of that kind of exaggeration is reporting that *someone cried so much that she flooded the first floor of the house in which she lived.* In some cultures around the world, people accept this blend of fantasy and reality as a normal part of everyday life. Even the title of García Márquez's story suggests that this blending will be demonstrated in "A Very Old Man with Enormous Wings."

WORDS TO KNOW
Vocabulary Preview
conjecture   proliferate
disperse   ungainly
magnanimous

Focus Your Reading

LITERARY ANALYSIS **STYLE** The particular way in which a piece of literature is written is called **style.** Many elements contribute to a writer's style, including word choice, tone, use of dialogue, sentence length, use of figurative language and point of view. Among many Latin American writers, **magical realism** is a special type of style. The elements of word choice, tone, and use of figurative language are particularly important in magical realism. As you read "A Very Old Man with Enormous Wings," look for the use of these elements.

ACTIVE READING **READING FOR DETAILS** Just as you did with "In the Family," pay attention to magical and realistic details about character, setting, and plot. Notice that García Márquez tells his story through the use of a third-person narrator.

READER'S NOTEBOOK As you read, add a column for this story to the chart that you began on page 855.

A Very Old Man With Enormous Wings

Gabriel García Márquez

On the third day of rain they had killed so many crabs inside the house that Pelayo had to cross his drenched courtyard and throw them into the sea, because the newborn child had a temperature all night and they thought it was due to the stench. The world had been sad since Tuesday. Sea and sky were a single ash-gray thing and the sands of the beach, which on March nights glimmered like powdered light, had become a stew of mud and rotten shellfish. The light was so weak at noon that when Pelayo was coming back to the house after throwing away the crabs, it was hard for him to see what it was that was moving and groaning in the rear of the courtyard. He had to go very close to see that it was an old man, a very old man, lying face down in the mud, who, in spite of his tremendous efforts, couldn't get up, impeded by his enormous wings.

Frightened by that nightmare, Pelayo ran to get Elisenda, his wife, who was putting compresses on the sick child, and he took her to the rear of the courtyard. They both looked at the fallen body with mute stupor.[1] He was dressed like a ragpicker.[2] There were only a few faded hairs left on his bald skull and very few teeth in his mouth, and his pitiful condition of a drenched great-grandfather had taken away any sense of grandeur he might have had. His huge buzzard wings, dirty and half-plucked, were forever entangled in the mud. They looked at him so long and so closely that Pelayo and Elisenda very soon overcame their surprise and in the end found him familiar. Then they dared speak to him, and he answered in an incomprehensible dialect with a strong sailor's voice. That was how they skipped over the inconvenience of the wings and quite intelligently concluded that he was a lonely castaway from some foreign ship wrecked by the storm. And yet, they called in a neighbor woman who knew everything about life and death to see him, and all she needed was one look to show them their mistake.

"He's an angel," she told them. "He must have been coming for the child, but the poor fellow is so old that the rain knocked him down."

On the following day everyone knew that a flesh-and-blood angel was held captive in Pelayo's house. Against the judgment of the wise neighbor woman, for whom angels in those times were the fugitive survivors of a celestial[3] conspiracy, they did not have the heart to club him to death. Pelayo watched over him all afternoon from the kitchen, armed with his bailiff's club,[4] and before going to bed he dragged him out of the mud and locked him up with the hens in the wire chicken coop. In the middle of the night, when the rain stopped,

Pelayo and Elisenda were still killing crabs. A short time afterward the child woke up without a fever and with a desire to eat. Then they felt magnanimous and decided to put the angel on a raft with fresh water and provisions for three days and leave him to his fate on the high seas. But when they went out into the courtyard with the first light of dawn, they found the whole neighborhood in front of the chicken coop having fun with the angel, without the slightest reverence, tossing him things to eat through the openings in the wire as if he weren't a supernatural creature but a circus animal.

Father Gonzaga arrived before seven o'clock, alarmed at the strange news. By that time onlookers less frivolous than those at dawn had already arrived and they were making all kinds of conjectures concerning the captive's future. The simplest among them thought that he should be named mayor of the world. Others of sterner mind felt that he should be promoted to the rank of five-star general in order to win all wars. Some visionaries hoped that he could be put to stud[5] in order to implant on earth a race of winged wise men who could take charge of the universe. But Father Gonzaga, before becoming a priest, had been a robust woodcutter. Standing by the wire, he reviewed his catechism[6] in an instant and asked them to open the door so that he could take a close look at that pitiful man who looked more like a huge decrepit hen among the fascinated chickens. He was lying in a corner drying his open wings in the sunlight among the fruit peels and breakfast

---

1. **with mute stupor:** in a speechless daze.
2. **ragpicker:** a person who makes a living by collecting rags and other rubbish.
3. **celestial** (sə-lĕs′chəl): heavenly.
4. **bailiff's club:** a weapon like a policeman's nightstick.
5. **put to stud:** used for breeding.
6. **catechism** (kăt′ĭ-kĭz′əm): a summary of the basic principles of Christianity.

WORDS
TO
KNOW

magnanimous (măg-năn′ə-məs) *adj.* generous and noble
conjecture (kən-jĕk′chər) *n.* an inference or guess

The Old Guitarist (1903), Pablo Picasso. Oil on panel, 122.9 cm. × 82.6 cm. The Art Institute of Chicago, Helen Birch Bartlett Memorial Collection (1926.253). Copyright © 1999 Estate of Pablo Picasso/Artists Rights Society (ARS), New York.

leftovers that the early risers had thrown him. Alien to the impertinences of the world, he only lifted his antiquarian eyes and murmured something in his dialect when Father Gonzaga went into the chicken coop and said good morning to him in Latin. The parish priest had his first suspicion of an imposter when he saw that he did not understand the language of God or know how to greet His ministers. Then he noticed that seen close up he was much too human: he had an unbearable smell of the out-doors, the back side of his wings was strewn with parasites and his main feathers had been mistreated by terrestrial winds, and nothing about him measured up to the proud dignity of angels. Then he came out of the chicken coop and in a brief sermon warned the curious against the risks of being ingenuous. He re-minded them that the devil had the bad habit of making use of carnival tricks in order to confuse the unwary. He argued that if wings were not the essential element in determining the difference between a hawk and an airplane, they were even less so in the recognition of angels. Nevertheless, he promised to write a letter to his bishop so that the latter would write to his primate[7] so that the latter would write to the Supreme Pontiff[8] in order to get the final verdict from the highest courts.

His prudence fell on sterile hearts. The news of the captive angel spread with such rapidity that after a few hours the courtyard had the bustle of a marketplace and they had to call in troops with fixed bayonets to <u>disperse</u> the mob that was about to knock the house down. Elisenda, her spine all twisted from sweeping up so much marketplace trash, then got the idea of fencing in the yard and charging five cents admission to see the angel.

The curious came from far away. A traveling carnival arrived with a flying acrobat who buzzed over the crowd several times, but no one paid any attention to him because his wings were not those of an angel but, rather, those of a sidereal[9] bat. The most unfortunate invalids on earth came in search of health: a poor woman who since childhood had been counting her heartbeats and had run out of numbers; a Portuguese man who couldn't sleep because the noise of the stars disturbed him; a sleepwalker who got up at night to undo the things he had done while awake; and many others with less serious ailments. In the midst of that shipwreck disorder that made the earth tremble, Pelayo and Elisenda were happy with fatigue, for in less than a week they had crammed their rooms with money and the line of pilgrims waiting their turn to enter still reached beyond the horizon.

The angel was the only one who took no part in his own act. He spent his time trying to get comfortable in his borrowed nest, befuddled by the hellish heat of the oil lamps and sacramental candles that had been placed along the wire. At first they tried to make him eat some mothballs, which, according to the wisdom of the wise neighbor woman, were the food prescribed for angels. But he turned them down, just as he turned down the papal lunches that the penitents brought him, and they never found out whether it was because he was an angel or because he was an old man that in the end he ate nothing but eggplant mush. His only supernatural virtue seemed to be patience. Especially during the first days, when the hens pecked at him, searching for the stellar parasites that <u>proliferated</u> in his wings, and the cripples pulled out feathers to touch their defective parts with, and even the most merciful threw stones at him, trying to get him to rise so

---

7. **primate** (prī'mĭt): the highest-ranking bishop in a country.
8. **Supreme Pontiff:** the pope.
9. **sidereal** (sī-dîr'ē-əl): from the stars.

WORDS
TO
KNOW

disperse (dĭ-spûrs') v. to scatter
proliferate (prə-lĭf'ə-rāt') v. to multiply or spread rapidly

they could see him standing. The only time they succeeded in arousing him was when they burned his side with an iron for branding steers, for he had been motionless for so many hours that they thought he was dead. He awoke with a start, ranting in his hermetic[10] language and with tears in his eyes, and he flapped his wings a couple of times, which brought on a whirlwind of chicken dung and lunar dust and a gale of panic that did not seem to be of this world. Although many thought that his reaction had been one not of rage but of pain, from then on they were careful not to annoy him, because the majority understood that his passivity was not that of a hero taking his ease but that of a cataclysm[11] in repose.

Father Gonzaga held back the crowd's frivolity with formulas of maidservant inspiration[12] while awaiting the arrival of a final judgment on the nature of the captive. But the mail from Rome showed no sense of urgency.

They spent their time finding out if the prisoner had a navel, if his dialect had any connection with Aramaic,[13] how many times he could fit on the head of a pin, or whether he wasn't just a Norwegian with wings. Those meager letters might have come and gone until the end of time if a providential[14] event had not put an end to the priest's tribulations.

It so happened that during those days, among so many other carnival attractions, there arrived in town the traveling show of the woman who had been changed into a spider for having disobeyed her parents. The admission to see her was not only less than the admission to see the angel, but people were permitted to ask her all manner of questions about her absurd state and to examine her up and down so that no one would ever doubt the truth of her horror. She was a frightful tarantula the size of a ram and with the head of a sad maiden. What was most heart-rending, however, was not her outlandish shape but the sincere affliction with which she recounted the details of her misfortune. While still practically a child she had sneaked out of her parents' house to go to a dance, and while she was coming back through the woods after having danced all night without permission, a fearful thunderclap rent the sky in two and through the crack came the lightning bolt of brimstone[15] that changed her into a spider. Her only nourishment came from the meatballs that charitable souls chose to toss into her mouth. A spectacle like that, full of so much human truth and with such a fearful lesson, was bound to defeat without even trying that of a haughty angel who scarcely deigned to look at mortals. Besides, the few miracles attributed to the angel showed a certain mental disorder, like the blind man who didn't recover his sight but grew three new teeth, or the paralytic who didn't get to walk but almost won the lottery, and the leper whose sores sprouted sunflowers. Those consolation miracles, which were more like mocking fun, had already ruined

They spent their time finding out if the prisoner had a navel...

---

10. **hermetic** (hər-mĕt′ĭk): mysterious.

11. **a cataclysm** (kăt′ə-klĭz′əm) **in repose:** a destructive force that is resting.

12. **formulas of maidservant inspiration:** pious notions characteristic of uneducated people.

13. **Aramaic** (ăr′ə-mā′ĭk): a language spoken in the Middle East at the time of Christ.

14. **providential** (prŏv′ĭ-dĕn′shəl): fortunate.

15. **brimstone:** hellfire.

the angel's reputation when the woman who had been changed into a spider finally crushed him completely. That was how Father Gonzaga was cured forever of his insomnia and Pelayo's courtyard went back to being as empty as during the time it had rained for three days and crabs walked through the bedrooms.

The owners of the house had no reason to lament. With the money they saved they built a two-story mansion with balconies and gardens and high netting so that crabs wouldn't get in during the winter, and with iron bars on the windows so that angels wouldn't get in. Pelayo also set up a rabbit warren close to town and gave up his job as bailiff for good, and Elisenda bought some satin pumps with high heels and many dresses of iridescent silk, the kind worn on Sunday by the most desirable women in those times. The chicken coop was the only thing that didn't receive any attention. If they washed it down with creolin[16] and burned tears of myrrh[17] inside it every so often, it was not in homage to the angel but to drive away the dungheap stench that still hung everywhere like a ghost and was turning the new house into an old one. At first, when the child learned to walk, they were careful that he not get too close to the chicken coop. But then they began to lose their fears and got used to the smell, and before the child got his second teeth he'd gone inside the chicken coop to play, where the wires were falling apart. The angel was no less standoffish with him than with other mortals, but he tolerated the most ingenious infamies[18] with the patience of a dog who had no illusions. They both came down with chicken pox at the same time. The doctor who took care of the child couldn't resist the temptation to listen to the angel's heart, and he found so much whistling in the heart and so many sounds in his kidneys that it seemed impossible for him to be alive. What surprised him most, however, was the logic of his wings. They seemed so natural on that completely human organism that he couldn't understand why other men didn't have them too.

*W*hen the child began school it had been some time since the sun and rain had caused the collapse of the chicken coop. The angel went dragging himself about here and there like a stray dying man. They would drive him out of the bedroom with a broom and a moment later find him in the kitchen. He seemed to be in so many places at the same time that they grew to think that he'd been duplicated, that he was reproducing himself all through the house, and the exasperated and unhinged Elisenda shouted that it was awful living in that hell full of angels. He could scarcely eat and his antiquarian eyes had also become so foggy that he went about bumping into posts. All he had left were the bare cannulae[19] of his last feathers. Pelayo threw a blanket over him and extended him the charity of letting him sleep in the shed, and only then did they notice that he had a temperature at night, and was delirious with the tongue twisters of an old Norwegian. That was one of the few times they became alarmed, for they thought he was going to die and not even the wise neighbor woman had been able to tell them what to do with dead angels.

---

16. **creolin** (krē′ə-lĭn′): a disinfectant.

17. **tears of myrrh** (mûr): lumps of hardened tree sap used as incense.

18. **ingenious infamies** (ĭn′fə-mēz): clever acts of wickedness.

19. **cannulae** (kăn′yə-lē′): central shafts; quills.

And yet he not only survived his worst winter, but seemed improved with the first sunny days. He remained motionless for several days in the farthest corner of the courtyard, where no one would see him, and at the beginning of December some large, stiff feathers began to grow on his wings, the feathers of a scarecrow, which looked more like another misfortune of decrepitude.[20] But he must have known the reason for those changes, for he was quite careful that no one should notice them, that no one should hear the sea chanteys[21] that he sometimes sang under the stars. One morning Elisenda was cutting some bunches of onions for lunch when a wind that seemed to come from the high seas blew into the kitchen. Then she went to the window and caught the angel in his first attempts at flight. They were so clumsy that his finger-nails opened a furrow in the vegetable patch and he was on the point of knocking the shed down with the ungainly flapping that slipped on the light and couldn't get a grip on the air. But he did manage to gain altitude. Elisenda let out a sigh of relief, for herself and for him, when she saw him pass over the last houses, holding himself up in some way with the risky flapping of a senile vulture. She kept watching him even when she was through cutting the onions and she kept watching until it was no longer possible for her to see him, because then he was no longer an annoyance in her life but an imaginary dot on the horizon of the sea. ❖

Copyright © Kamil Vojnar/Photonica.

20. **decrepitude** (dĭ-krĕpʹĭ-tōōdʹ): weakness from age or illness.
21. **sea chanteys** (shănʹtēz): sailors' work songs.

Thinking through the LITERATURE

Connect to the Literature

1. What Do You Think? What thoughts do you have about Pelayo, Elisenda, and Father Gonzaga at the end of the story?

Comprehension Check
- Where does Pelayo find the winged man?
- What kind of creature do the neighbors think Pelayo has found?
- How is the winged man treated?
- What eventually happens to him?

Think Critically

2. What do you think the **theme** of this story is? What is the author saying about human nature?

3. What is your theory about who the mysterious creature is and why he appears in Pelayo's yard?

THINK ABOUT

- the explanations considered by Pelayo and his wife, the neighbor woman, and Father Gonzaga
- the winged man's physical appearance and abilities
- the miracles attributed to the winged man
- the changes that occur in Pelayo's household

4. What is your reaction to the way Pelayo and his wife treat their visitor?

5. **ACTIVE READING** **READING FOR DETAILS** Look back at the chart of **details** about **character, setting,** and **plot** in your **READER'S NOTEBOOK.** In your opinion, what details in this story are most realistic? Which are most magical?

Extend Interpretations

6. Critic's Corner One critic has said that magical realism usually portrays a positive or "hopeful vision of life." Do you agree? Cite details from the story to support your answer.

7. Connect to Life Do the reactions of the crowds and onlookers in this story surprise you, or do you think they are typical of human nature? Explain your answer.

8. **Points of Comparison** Again review the chart in your **READER'S NOTEBOOK.** Compare the information that you recorded for "In the Family" and "A Very Old Man with Enormous Wings." What do you think are the most important differences between the two stories? What elements of **magical realism** do the two stories have in common?

Literary Analysis

STYLE **Style** is a particular way of writing a piece of literature. Style is not what is said, but how it is said—the words, tone, and sentence construction. The writer's use of dialogue, the point of view of the narrator, and the kind of figurative language all contribute to defining a writer's style. Style may be formal or informal, wordy or spare, filled with exaggeration or just the facts. Look at the opening sentence of "A Very Old Man with Enormous Wings."

On the third day of rain they had killed so many crabs inside the house that Pelayo had to cross his drenched courtyard and throw them into the sea because the newborn child had a temperature all night and they thought it was due to the stench.

The vividly detailed, complex sentence is characteristic of the García Márquez style.

Cooperative Learning Activity With a small group, take turns sharing a paragraph from the story whose style you found interesting. Discuss how the author used word choice, tone, sentence length, or exaggeration in the passage. Select the most interesting passage to share with the whole class.

REVIEW **MAGICAL REALISM** One particular style of writing is magical realism, in which elements of fantasy and the real world are mixed together. What details of the story seem most fantastic to you?

*Choices&*CHALLENGES

Writing Options

1. Winged Man's Diary Imagine that the winged man has been keeping a hidden diary. Write one entry that he might have recorded.

2. Late-Breaking News Story Write a news story that might have appeared in a local paper after Pelayo's discovery of the winged man. Include comments from townspeople and a suitable headline.

Inquiry & Research

Bigfoot Since the 1950s, thousands of people in North America have reported seeing a large, hairy, half-human creature they call Bigfoot, or Sasquatch. With classmates, prepare a chart about Bigfoot with information from encyclopedias and library books. Discuss whether Bigfoot is more or less realistic than the winged man in the story.

Vocabulary in Action

EXERCISE: CONTEXT CLUES Read each newspaper heading below. Then, on your paper, write the Word to Know that would most likely appear in the article introduced by each heading.

1. Awkward Angel Trapped
2. Angel's Identity Anyone's Guess
3. Angel Showered with Gifts
4. Angel Watchers on the Rise
5. Priest's Warning Scatters Watchers

WORDS TO KNOW	conjecture	proliferate
	disperse	ungainly
	magnanimous	

Building Vocabulary
For an in-depth lesson on context clues, see page 103.

Gabriel García Márquez
1928–

Other Works
One Hundred Years of Solitude
Love in the Time of Cholera
Strange Pilgrims: Twelve Stories

Law Student Gabriel García Márquez was born in Aracataca, Colombia. He attended high school on a scholarship and then enrolled in law school, first at the National University in Bogotá and then at the University of Cartagena. In 1948, he interrupted his law studies to take a job writing for a Cartagena newspaper.

Controversial Journalist Although he is best known today as a novelist and short-story writer, García Márquez thinks of himself primarily as a journalist. He became a highly respected news correspondent in Colombia during the 1950s and, over the years, has worked as a journalist in many cities, including London, Paris, New York, and Mexico City. As a journalist, he often criticizes Latin American politics and governments. After writing about the illegal activities of his own government, he eventually decided to move his family out of Colombia. They lived in a variety of places, including Paris, Rome, and Mexico City. In the 1980s, the government of Chile burned nearly 15,000 copies of a book in which García Márquez criticized the Chilean dictator, Augusto Pinochet.

Popular Author Although García Márquez writes in Spanish, his works are popular worldwide. Whenever he publishes a new book, it is immediately translated into many other languages. Critics have called his novel *One Hundred Years of Solitude* a masterpiece. One critic has suggested that it "should be required reading for the entire human race." In 1982, García Márquez was awarded the Nobel Prize for Literature.

Comparing Literature: Assessment Practice

In writing assessments, you will often be asked to analyze literary works like "In the Family" and "A Very Old Man with Enormous Wings." You are now going to practice writing an essay with this kind of focus.

PART 1 · Reading the Prompt

You will often be asked to write in response to a prompt like the one below. Your first step should be to read through the entire prompt carefully. Then you should read it again, looking for key words that will help you identify the purpose of the essay and decide how to approach it.

Writing Prompt

In "In the Family," a mirror reflects deceased relatives of the members of the household. In "A Very Old Man with Enormous Wings," a creature like an angel falls from the sky. Both stories are examples of "magical realism"—they take place in the "real world," yet they are based on events that are fantastic. In an essay, analyze the authors' use of magical realism. Discuss the authors' use of the elements of the short story. Cite evidence from the stories to support your analysis. ❶ ❷ ❸

STRATEGIES IN ACTION

❶ I have to explain how these two stories fit the definition of magical realism.

❷ I have to base my analysis on the elements of **plot, setting, characterization,** and **theme** of the two stories.

❸ I need to include **examples** or **quotations** from the stories.

PART 2 · Planning an Analytical Essay

- Identify the basis of comparison. (Refer to the chart on page 855.)
- Create a graphic like the one shown to help in planning your analysis.
- Determine how the stories are alike and different. (Review the information on the charts you completed for both stories.)
- State similarities and differences as simply as possible.

Elements of Magical Realism	Examples from Selection 1	Examples from Selection 2
Plot		
Setting		
Character		
Theme		

PART 3 · Drafting Your Essay

Introduction Begin by introducing your topic and identifying the focus of your analysis. Clearly state the subject and its individual parts.

Organization Use a specific organizing structure to provide a logical flow of information. Include the important characteristics of magical realism. Use examples from the stories.

Conclusion Conclude your analysis by returning to your thesis statement and restating it in different words.

Revision Allow a little time after you've finished to review and revise your draft. Make sure your points are clear and well-supported. Proofread for errors.

Writing Handbook
See page 1157: Analysis

Writing Workshop

Explaining why something happened . . .

From Reading to Writing In Stephen King's teleplay *Sorry, Right Number,* a mysterious phone call sets off a chain of events. Not until the end of the story does King reveal the cause of the call itself. Examining causes and effects is one way to make sense of the world, and you can explore and share your understanding by writing a **cause-and-effect essay.** You can use this type of writing to show why something happens, how events are linked, or the consequences of an action.

For Your Portfolio

WRITING PROMPT Write a cause-and-effect essay examining why a real or imagined event happens or what consequences it has.

    Purpose: To inform and explain
    Audience: Your classmates or anyone interested in your subject

---

Basics in a Box

Cause-and-Effect Essay at a Glance

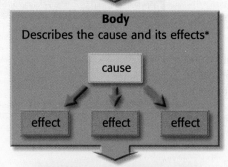

Introduction
Introduces the subject

Body
Describes the cause and its effects*

cause

effect   effect   effect

Conclusion
Summary

*or may present an effect and then analyze the causes

RUBRIC Standards for Writing

A successful cause-and-effect essay should

- clearly state the cause-and-effect relationship being examined
- provide any necessary background information
- make the relationship between causes and effects clear
- arrange details logically and include transitions to show relationships between effects and causes
- summarize the cause-and-effect relationship in the conclusion

---

Analyzing a Professional Model

George M. Mahawinney
Columnist, *Philadelphia Inquirer*

Excerpt from "An Invasion from the Planet Mars"
November 1, 1938

Terror struck at the hearts of hundreds of thousands of persons in the length and breadth of the United States last night. Out of the heavens, they learned, objects at first believed to be meteors crashed down near Trenton, killing many. Then out of the "meteors" came monsters, spreading destruction with torch and poison gas. It was all just a radio dramatization, but the result was nationwide hysteria.

In reality there was no danger. The broadcast was merely a Halloween program in which Orson Welles, actor-director of the Mercury Theater on the Air, related, as though he were one of the few human survivors of the catastrophe, an adaptation of H. G. Wells' *The War of the Worlds*. The circumstances of the story were unbelievable enough, but the manner of its presentation apparently was convincing to hundreds of thousands of persons—despite the fact that the program was interrupted thrice for an announcement that it was fiction, and fiction only.

The realism of the broadcast, especially for those who had tuned in after it had started, brought effects which none—not the directors of the Federal Radio Theater Project, which sponsored it, not the Columbia Broadcasting Company, which carried it over a coast-to-coast chain of 151 stations, nor Station WCAU, which broadcast it locally—could foresee.

Within a few minutes, newspaper offices, radio stations, and police departments everywhere were flooded with anxious telephone calls. Station WCAU received more than four thousand calls and eventually interrupted a later program to make an elaborate explanation that death had not actually descended on New Jersey, and that monsters were not actually invading the world.

But calm did not come readily to the frightened radio listeners of the country. The hysteria reached such proportions that the New York City Department of Health called up a newspaper and wanted advice on offering its facilities for the protection of the populace. Nurses and physicians were among the telephone callers everywhere. They were ready to offer their assistance to the injured or maimed.

In scores of New Jersey towns, women in their homes fainted as the horror of the broadcast fell on their ears. A weeping lady stopped Motorcycle Patrolman Lawrence Treger and asked where she should go to escape the "attack." A terrified motorist asked the patrolman the way to Route 24. "All creation's busted loose. I'm getting out of Jersey," he screamed.

RUBRIC IN ACTION

❶ Captures reader's attention with a startling statement

❷ Identifies the cause of the events

❸ Identifies the first effect—initial panic

❹ Presents the second effect—growing hysteria

"Grovers Mill, New Jersey," was mentioned as a scene of destruction. At Princeton University, women members of the geology faculty, equipped with flashlights and hammers, started for Grovers Corners. Dozens of cars were driven to the hamlet by curious motorists. A score of university students were phoned by their parents and told to come home.

5 Discusses third effect— people flocking to the "disaster" area

The Trenton police and fire telephone board bore the brunt of the nation's calls, because of its geographical location close to the presumed scene of catastrophe. On that board were received calls from Wilmington, Washington, Philadelphia, Jersey City, and Newark.

Many New Yorkers seized personal effects and raced out of their apartments, some jumping into their automobiles and heading for the wide-open spaces. Police in the vicinity at first regarded the excitement as a joke, but they were soon hard-pressed in controlling the swarms in the streets. A man entered the Wadsworth Avenue station uptown and said he heard "planes had bombed Jersey and were headed for Times Square." A rumor spread over Washington Heights that a war was on.

6 Explores fourth effect— people fleeing the area

Reactions as strange, or stranger, occurred in other parts of the country. In Indianapolis, Indiana, a woman ran screaming into a church.

"New York is destroyed; it's the end of the world," she cried. "You might as well go home to die."

At Brevard College, North Carolina, five boys in dormitories fainted on hearing the broadcast. In Birmingham, Alabama, men and women gathered in groups and prayed. Throughout Atlanta was a wide-spread belief that a "planet" had struck New Jersey, killing from forty to seven thousand persons.

New Jersey state police sent out a teletype message to its various stations and barracks, containing explanations and instructions to police officers on how to handle the hysteria. The radio stations and the Columbia Broadcasting Company spent much of the remainder of the evening clearing up the situation. Again and again they explained the whole thing was nothing more than a dramatization.

7 This writer concludes with a summary of how the event ended.
Other Options:
• State the significance of the cause-effect relationship.
• Make a prediction.

In the long run, however, calm was restored in the myriad American homes which had been momentarily threatened by interplanetary invasion. Fear of the monsters from Mars eventually subsided. There was no reason for being afraid of them, anyway. Even the bulletins of the radio broadcast explained they all soon died. They couldn't stand the earth's atmosphere and perished of pneumonia.

Writing Your Cause-and-Effect Essay

❶ Prewriting

Find out the cause of this effect.

William Shakespeare, playwright and poet

One way to find writing ideas is to **brainstorm** with friends about things that cause you to ask "Why does that happen?" (for example, Why does exercising give you energy?) or "What happens after that?" (for example, What effects does television violence have on young children?). Make sure you find a topic that really interests you and that you want to dig into. See the **Idea Bank** in the margin for more suggestions. Once you have decided on a topic, follow the steps below.

Planning Your Cause-and-Effect Essay

▶ **1. Think about the relationship between events.** Are they really linked by cause and effect? Just because one event follows another in time doesn't necessarily mean that the first event caused the second.

▶ **2. Explore causes and effects.** Does a single cause have one effect or many? Is an effect the result of multiple causes or only one? Is there a causal chain in which a cause produces an effect, which becomes the cause of another effect, and so on?

▶ **3. Identify your audience.** What do they already know about the events you're describing? What background information or explanation of terms will you need to include in your essay?

▶ **4. Gather supporting information.** What details will support your analysis of causes and effects? What sources of information can you draw on—observation, research, or your own imagination and reflection?

❷ Drafting

Use drafting as a way to explore and figure out causes and effects. As you draft, concentrate on just getting your ideas down on paper. Don't worry about getting everything right the first time. If you realize that you need to stop and gather more information as you write, do so. At some point, though, be sure to write a **clear statement of the cause-and-effect relationship** you are examining.

Ask Your Peer Reader

- How would you summarize the cause-and-effect relationships that I wrote about?
- What did you like best about my essay? Why?
- What parts were unclear?
- What do you disagree with or want to know more about?

IDEABank

1. Your Working Portfolio
Build on the **Writing Option** you completed earlier in this unit:

- "Scientific" Explanation, p. 841

2. The Pages of History
Think about an important historical event, such as the Great Depression. What were the causes of the event? What were its effects?

3. Something New
Make a quick list of modern inventions. Choose one and examine the effects the invention has had on people's lives.

Include details to support your statements and eventually organize your ideas into a coherent pattern. You might show a single cause leading to multiple effects or multiple causes leading to a single effect.

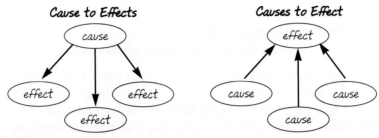

❸ Revising

TARGET SKILL ▶ USING TRANSITIONAL WORDS AND PHRASES
Transitional words and phrases can help you clearly explain the relationships between causes and effects. Choose from words such as *before, after, therefore, consequently, because, since, as a result* and *for this reason.*

> The fictional broadcast was quite convincing. *After hearing it,* People all over the region fled for their lives. *In reality,* They did not need to be afraid *because* It was only a story.

❹ Editing and Proofreading

TARGET SKILL ▶ CLAUSES AS FRAGMENTS A cause-and-effect essay should clarify ideas. However, using clauses that are not complete sentences can confuse your readers. Many times, you can fix a fragment by joining it to another sentence.

> There is the danger that pandemonium can result. *W*hen people think fiction is reality. Producers want ~~they're~~ *their* shows to be convincing, *but* ~~Although~~ they have a responsibility to let everyone know what is true and what is not.

❺ Reflecting

FOR YOUR WORKING PORTFOLIO What did you learn about your subject in writing your cause-and-effect essay? What would you do differently next time? Attach your reflections to your finished essay. Save your essay in your **Working Portfolio.**

Need revising help?

Review the **Rubric**, p. 874

Consider **peer reader** comments

Check **Revision Guidelines**, p. 1143

Publishing IDEAS

- Submit your essay to your school or community newspaper.
- Present your essay orally to your history or science class.

More Online: Publishing Options www.mcdougallittell.com

Read this paragraph from the first draft of a cause-and-effect essay. The underlined sections may include the following kinds of errors:

- **lack of parallel structure**
- **sentence fragments**
- **incorrect comparative forms**
- **double negatives**

For each underlined section, choose the revision that most improves the writing.

Ever since a dam was built on the White River. The tourist population of
<u>(1)</u>
Lake Parker has declined greatly. After the dam was built, the water level of

the lake fell by more than 15 feet. <u>That isn't nothing to ignore.</u> The lake is now
<u>(2)</u>

shallower and heats up <u>more quicker.</u> <u>The water's average temperature has</u>
<u>(3)</u> <u>(4)</u>

<u>risen. An increase of about 8°F.</u> Many native fish <u>cannot hardly</u> tolerate the
<u>(5)</u>

higher temperature. Green algae now covers the surface of the lake. Tourists

who came to the lake for <u>fishing, swimming, and to go out in boats</u> can no
<u>(6)</u>

longer enjoy these activities.

---

1. A. Ever since a dam was built on the White River and the tourist population of Lake Parker has greatly decreased.
   B. Ever since a dam was built on the White River, the tourist population of Lake Parker has declined greatly.
   C. A dam was built on the White River. The tourist population of Lake Parker has declined greatly.
   D. Correct as is

2. A. That is anything to ignore.
   B. That is nothing that shouldn't be ignored.
   C. That isn't something to ignore.
   D. Correct as is

3. A. quickest
   B. more quickly
   C. more quick
   D. Correct as is

4. A. The water's average temperature has risen about 8°F.
   B. The water's average temperature has risen: about 8°F.
   C. The water's average temperature rise, about 8°F.
   D. Correct as is

5. A. can't hardly
   B. cannot barely
   C. cannot
   D. Correct as is

6. A. fishing, swimming, and out in boats
   B. fishing, swimming, and boating
   C. swim, fish, and to go out in boats
   D. Correct as is

Need extra help?

See the **Grammar Handbook**

Comparison of Modifiers, pp. 1186–1187

Correcting Fragments, p. 1197

Double Negatives, p. 1188

Regular and Irregular Comparisons, p. 1187

A World of Mysteries

The word *mystery* has multiple meanings. It can refer to something that is not known or understood. It can also mean something that inspires wonder and arouses curiosity. Has reading about the mysteries in this unit given you any new ideas or insights that you can apply in your everyday life? Complete one or more of the following options to help you explore this question.

Voice I (1963), George Tooker. Egg tempera on gesso panel, 19½″ × 17½″, private collection, courtesy of DC Moore Gallery, New York.

Reflecting on the Unit

OPTION 1

Analyzing Motives With a partner, make a list of the "criminal minds" you have encountered in this unit. For each person, jot down motivations for his or her actions. Some motivations you will find stated directly in the text; others you will be able to infer from the situation or from the person's behavior. Based on the motivations you have noted, decide if you feel sympathetic or unsympathetic toward this person. Then arrange your gallery of rogues in order from *most sympathetic* to *least sympathetic*. Include in your ranking the "criminal minds" you analyzed for the activity on page 738. How does your ranking compare with those of your classmates?

OPTION 2

Distinguishing Illusion and Reality Create a chart with two columns, one headed *Could Happen* and the other *Could Not Happen*. In the first column, place selections from Part 2 of this unit that describe events you think *could happen* in the real world. In the second column, place the selections that describe events that *could not happen*. Now go through both columns and circle the selections in which the illusion of being real and believable was strong for you. Draw a line through titles of selections you did *not* find very convincing. Compare your chart with those of your classmates and discuss what you learned from making them.

OPTION 3

Presenting Mysterious Characters To survey the range of interesting and unusual characters in this unit, get together with a small group of classmates and play a mystery game. Take turns acting out characters for the other members of the group to identify. You might use distinctive gestures or pantomime emotions to reveal aspects of the character. Continue playing the game until your group has acted out all the characters.

Self ASSESSMENT

READER'S NOTEBOOK

Consider once again the quotation at the beginning of the unit: "A lie hides the truth. A story tries to find it." Write a few paragraphs in which you explain how reading the selections in this unit has given you a better understanding of this definition of fiction.

Reviewing Literary Concepts

OPTION 1

Understanding Climax The climax, or turning point, of a story is the key event that the earlier events build up to. Choose several stories from this unit. In a chart, identify the climax of each story and explain how a character or situation is changed by the climax.

Story	Climax	What Changes
"The Open Window"	Framton Nuttel runs away.	Vera Sappleton makes Framton think he sees ghosts and pushes his fragile nerves to the breaking point.

OPTION 2

Evaluating Point of View Some of the selections in this unit are written from the first-person point of view. Others are written from the third-person point of view. To survey the different points of view in the selections, make two lists. First list the titles of all the selections told from the first-person point of view. Then list the titles of all the selections told from the third-person point of view. Circle the titles of the selections in which you think the choice of point of view had a major influence on your understanding and enjoyment.

Self ASSESSMENT

📖 READER'S NOTEBOOK

In addition to *climax,* the following literary terms introduced or reviewed in this unit are also used in analyzing the plot of a story: *conflict, rising action, exposition, falling action, resolution, suspense, foreshadowing,* and *surprise ending.* Working with a partner, choose one story from this unit and use it to identify examples of each of these plot elements.

🗂 Portfolio Building

- **Writing Options** Several of the Writing Options in this unit asked you to build on situations or characters introduced in works of fiction. From these assignments, choose the one that you think was most successful at entering into the spirit of the story. Explain the reasons for your evaluation on a cover page, attach it to the assignment, and place them together in your **Presentation Portfolio.** 🗂

- **Writing Workshops** In this unit you wrote a Short Story based on a mystery or on a compelling conflict. You also wrote a Cause-and-Effect Essay examining why a real or imagined event happens or what consequences it has. Reread these two assignments and decide which you think is a more effective piece of writing. Explain your choice in a cover note, attach it to the piece you have selected, and place both in your **Presentation Portfolio.** 🗂

- **Additional Activities** Think back to any of the assignments you completed under **Activities & Explorations** and **Inquiry & Research.** Keep a record in your portfolio of any assignments that you especially enjoyed, found helpful, or would like to do further work on in the future.

Self ASSESSMENT

Presentation Portfolio 🗂
Now that you have several pieces of writing in your portfolio, look back over them. Which ones reflect improvements in your writing skills? Are you gaining more confidence in your ability to organize and express your thoughts?

Setting GOALS

Have the mystery stories in this unit sharpened your skills of observation, analysis, and inference? Use these skills as you try to understand the personalities and motivations of the famous characters in the next unit.

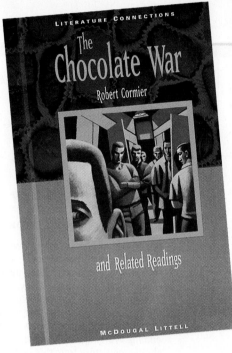

LITERATURE CONNECTIONS
The Chocolate War

ROBERT CORMIER

Freshman Jerry Renault is trying to make his way at Trinity High, a boys' prep school run by two despots: Brother Leon, the acting headmaster, and Archie Costello, the leader of a secret society called The Vigils. When Jerry finds himself in a struggle between the two leaders on an unlikely battlefield—the school's annual chocolate sale—the consequences are shocking. More than 20 years after its publication, Robert Cormier's award-winning novel is still controversial.

These thematically related readings are provided along with *The Chocolate War:*

I took my Power in my Hand
By EMILY DICKINSON

Some Opposites of Good
By LESLIE NORRIS

It's Fun Being in Power
By MARIA HINOJOSA

Breaking Bones
By PHILIP CIOFFARI

White Places
By MARY FLANAGAN

Bad Company
By REBECCA BARRY

And Even *More* . . .

Fahrenheit 451

RAY BRADBURY

This classic science fiction novel depicts a terrifying future in which reading is banned and the job of firemen is to burn books. A searing attack on censorship, the book is also fiercely critical of the dehumanizing effects of mass media, commercialism, and modern technology.

Books
And Then There Were None
AGATHA CHRISTIE
Considered one of Christie's best mysteries, *And Then There Were None* tells the story of ten strangers lured to an island from which there is no escape.

The Blessing Way
TONY HILLERMAN
Navajo detective Lieutenant Joe Leaphorn follows the trail of a killer who some claim is not human.

Mary Reilly
VALERIE MARTIN
This novel retells the classic Jekyll and Hyde story from the point of view of the doctor's young housemaid.

1984

GEORGE ORWELL

This novel sounded a warning and left its mark on the language. The terms *Orwellian* and *Big Brother* convey the chilling vision of a future totalitarian society, a world where the government can control individual thought and even reality itself. *1984*, a modern classic and the culminating work in Orwell's life as a novelist, remains timely and continues to stir the imagination while asking fascinating questions about human nature.

These thematically related readings are provided along with *1984*:

What Can They
By JULIA HARTWIG

End Game
By J. G. BALLARD

The Spy
By BERTOLT BRECHT

from **Politics and the English Language**
By GEORGE ORWELL

No One Died in Tiananmen Square
By WILLIAM LUTZ

The Invasion of Privacy
By REED KARAIM

The IWM 1000
By ALICIA YÁÑEZ COSSIO

Thumbprint
By EVE MERRIAM

The Daughter of Time
JOSEPHINE TEY
In this popular mystery novel, Inspector Alan Grant of Scotland Yard uses historical clues to investigate Richard III's supposed murder of his own nephews.

Slaughterhouse Five
KURT VONNEGUT, JR.
In Vonnegut's famous antiwar novel, American prisoner of war Billy Pilgrim travels through time on a search for life's meaning after witnessing the firebombing of Dresden.

Other Media
Holmes: Hound of the Baskervilles
Jeremy Brett stars as Sherlock Holmes in this version of Arthur Conan Doyle's classic mystery about a supernatural hound. PBS Video.
(VIDEOCASSETTE)

Myst
This popular game begins on the strange and beautiful island of Myst. A series of puzzles and clues helps the player proceed and discover the purpose of the quest.
(CD-ROM)

1984
Starring John Hurt, this film version of Orwell's attack on totalitarianism faithfully re-creates the novel.
(VIDEOCASSETTE)

Ray Bradbury Tales of Fantasy
Ray Bradbury reads some of his best-known stories, including "The Illustrated Man," "The Veldt," and "The Pedestrian."
(AUDIOCASSETTES)

THE
CLASSIC
TRADITION

When you reread
a classic you
do not see more
in the book than
you did before;
you see more
in *you* than
there was before.

CLIFTON FADIMAN

Winged Victory, Victor Higgins. Oil on canvas, 40″ × 43¼″.
Collection of the Museum of Fine Arts, Museum of New
Mexico, Gift of Joan Higgins Reed. Photo by Blair Clark.

PART 1 | The Odyssey

Y ou are about to meet Odysseus, one of the most famous heroes of all time. You will follow him on a legendary journey as he battles monsters, explores the unknown, and overcomes incredible hazards. Think about the qualities that you usually associate with a hero. Can someone be heroic and human at the same time, with human flaws and weaknesses?

ACTIVITY

Get together with a partner to brainstorm a word web like the one shown. On the left side, jot down qualities that you think would be helpful to a hero, such as physical strength. Then, on the right side, jot down qualities that you think might hinder a person from being an effective hero. Keep these qualities in mind as you read this part of the *Odyssey*.

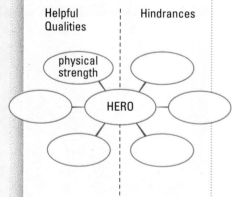

Helpful Qualities | Hindrances

physical strength

HERO

HOMER'S WORLD

*E*XAMINING THE HOMERIC EPICS

Composed in Greece around 800 B.C., Homer's two related epics—the *Iliad* and the *Odyssey*—are perhaps the greatest masterpieces of the epic form, a long narrative poem about a hero's adventures. Both stories were first told orally, perhaps even sung, and it may not have been until several generations later that they were set down in writing. Partly because of this delay, scholars disagree over the authorship of the epics. A blind poet named Homer usually gets the credit, but many think that the epics are actually the combined work of several poets. Although there have been many translations of these poems into English, Robert Fitzgerald's verse renderings are considered among the best at capturing the high drama and intense emotions of the epics. Three important elements of their plots are the Trojan War, the heroism of Odysseus, and the interference of the gods.

THE TROJAN WAR The *Iliad* presents an episode of the Trojan War, which may have occurred around 1200 B.C. According to legend, this war began after Paris, a prince of Troy, kidnapped Helen—the most beautiful woman in the world—from her husband, Menelaus (mĕn´ə-lā´əs), the king of Sparta. Menelaus then recruited kings and soldiers from all over Greece to help him avenge his honor and recover his wife. Odysseus, the king of the island of Ithaca (ĭth´ə-kə), was one of many Greeks who sailed to Troy and besieged the walled city. For ten long years the Greeks battled the Trojans without succeeding in conquering them. To break this stalemate, Odysseus, "the master strategist," thought of a plan to deceive the Trojans into thinking that the Greeks had abandoned the struggle. He ordered that a giant wooden horse be built and left at the gates of Troy at night. The Trojans, waking to find it there—and not a Greek in sight—assumed that their enemy had fled and left them a peace offering. They took the horse inside the city, only to discover, too late, that it was filled with Greek soldiers and that Troy was doomed.

THE HEROIC STORY OF ODYSSEUS The *Odyssey* deals with Odysseus' adventures as he makes his way home from Troy and with events that take place on Ithaca just before and after his return. The first excerpts that you will read depict some of the wanderings of Odysseus after his departure from Troy with a fleet of 12 ships carrying about 720 men. This time his opponents are not military ones. Instead, he encounters various monsters who try to devour him and enchanting women who try to keep him from his wife, Penelope (pə-nĕl´ə-pē). The final excerpts describe Odysseus' homecoming and his reunion with his wife and son, Telemachus. In addition to great strength and courage, what sets Odysseus apart from others is a special quality that has been called his craft or his guile: the ingenious tricks he uses to get himself out of difficult situations.

THE INTERVENTION OF THE GODS AND GODDESSES Adding another dimension to the human struggles recounted in Homer's epics are the conflicts among the gods and goddesses on Mount Olympus (ə-lĭm´pəs). In Homer's time, most Greeks believed that the gods not only took an active interest in human affairs but also behaved in recognizably human ways, often engaging in their own trivial quarrels and petty jealousies. For example, Athena (ə-thē´nə), the goddess of war and practical wisdom, supported the Greek cause in the Trojan War and championed Odysseus, while Aphrodite (ăf´rə-dī´tē), the goddess of love, sided with Paris and his fellow Trojans. The story of Odysseus' return from Troy contains some notable instances of divine interference. Odysseus has Athena on his side, but he has displeased the gods who were on the side of Troy. Furthermore, as you will see, he angers another god during one of his first adventures and still another one later. As a result, he is forced to suffer many hardships before he manages to return home.

To Homer's audience, the *Odyssey,* with its interfering gods and goddesses, its strange lands and creatures, must have seemed as full of mystery and danger as science fiction and fantasy adventures seem to people today. Just as we can imagine aliens in the next galaxy or creatures created in a laboratory, the ancient Greeks could imagine monsters living just beyond the boundaries of their known world. It was not necessary for them to believe that creatures such as one-eyed giants did exist, but only that they might.

PEOPLE AND PLACES OF THE ODYSSEY

You will find it helpful to become familiar with important people and places in the *Odyssey* before you begin reading. The map identifies real places mentioned in the poem—such as Troy, Sparta, and Ithaca. It also shows where later readers have thought that some of the imaginary lands visited by Odysseus—such as Aeaea, Ogygia, and the islands of Aeolus and the Sirens—could have been located, after applying actual Mediterranean area geography to Homer's descriptions. The chart identifies important characters and places and tells you how to pronounce their names.

IMPORTANT CHARACTERS IN THE ODYSSEY

(in order of mention)

Book 9

Calypso (kə-lĭp′sō)—a sea goddess who lives on the island of **Ogygia** (ō-gĭj′yə)

Alcinous (ăl-sĭn′ō-əs)—the king of the **Phaeacians** (fē-ā′shənz)

Laertes (lā-ûr′tēz)—Odysseus' father

Circe (sûr′sē)—a goddess and enchantress who lives on the island of **Aeaea** (ē-ē′ə)

Zeus (zōōs)—the chief of the Greek gods and goddesses; father of Athena and Apollo

Cicones (sĭ-kō′nēz)—allies of the Trojans, who live at **Ismarus** (ĭs-mär′əs)

Lotus Eaters (lō′təs-ē′tərz)—inhabitants of a land Odysseus visits

Cyclopes (sī-klō′pēz)—a race of one-eyed giants; an individual member of the race is a **Cyclops** (sī′klŏps)

Apollo (ə-pŏl′ō)—the god of music, poetry, prophecy, and medicine

Poseidon (pō-sīd′n)—the god of the sea, earthquakes, and horses; father of the Cyclops who battles Odysseus

Book 10

Aeolus (ē′ə-ləs)—the guardian of the winds

Laestrygones (lĕs′trĭ-gō′nēz)—cannibal inhabitants of a distant land

Eurylochus (yŏŏ-rĭl′ə-kəs)—a trusted officer of Odysseus'

Hermes (hûr′mēz)—the god of invention, commerce, and cunning; messenger of the gods

Persephone (pər-sĕf′ə-nē)—the wife of the ruler of the underworld

Tiresias (tī-rēs′yəs) of Thebes (thēbz)—a blind prophet whose spirit Odysseus visits in the underworld

Book 12

Sirens (sī′rənz)—creatures, part woman and part bird, whose songs lure sailors to their death

Scylla (sĭl′ə)—a six-headed sea monster who devours sailors

Charybdis (kə-rĭb′dĭs)—a dangerous whirlpool personified as a female sea monster

Helios (hē′lē-ŏs′)—the sun god, who pastures his cattle on the island of Thrinacia (thrĭ-nā′shə)

Books 21–23

Antinous (ăn-tĭn′ō-əs) a suitor of Penelope's

Eurymachus (yŏŏ-rĭm′ə-kəs)—a suitor of Penelope's

Telemachus (tə-lĕm′ə-kəs)—Odysseus' son

Eumaeus (yŏŏ-mē′əs)—a servant in Odysseus' household

Philoetius (fĭ-lē′shəs)—a servant in Odysseus' household

Eurycleia (yŏŏr′ĭ-klē′ə)—an old female servant, still loyal to Odysseus

The Epic is a long, narrative poem that tells about the adventures of a hero who reflects the ideals and values of a nation or race. Although epics are often based on legends that contain a kernel of truth, they are not works of history but works of the imagination. The epic portrays the past, but it is an imaginary past—a time supposedly better than the time in which the epic is created. The *Iliad* and the *Odyssey* were composed sometime between 800 B.C. and 600 B.C. by a Greek poet known as Homer, but they tell about events happening long before Homer's time. Still, the values and beliefs that come through are those of Homer's world—including its sense of the heroic.

The Heroic Tradition

The heroic tradition set standards on the value of man's honor. How important was honor? Consider this story. A king's wife is kidnapped, and he starts a war to avenge this act. A great hero refuses to fight in this war because he too feels dishonored in a dispute over a woman. Then the hero's dear friend borrows the hero's armor and is himself killed in the war. Now the hero, full of rage, must avenge this death. Afterward he must finally overcome his anger and return the body of his slain enemy to his enemy's father. Peace must be made. Honor must be restored. These events make up the story of the great tragic poem the *Iliad.* The war is the Trojan War. The hero's name is Achilles.

The *Odyssey,* taking up where the *Iliad* leaves off, brings us a different kind of hero. This is Odysseus, that craftiest of Greeks, who has masterminded the end of the war, using a trick wooden horse, and now wants to go home, perhaps seeing a bit of the world on the way. How can Odysseus get back to his wife and son—and keep his honor in the process? That is the story of the *Odyssey.*

Mosaic of a mask discovered in Pompeii. Leaves, fruit, and festoon used for detail.

Epic Hero

As much as anything, then, an epic is about its hero, and about how he becomes heroic. An **epic hero** is a larger-than-life figure, usually male, who embodies the ideals of a nation or race. Epic heroes take part in long, dangerous adventures and accomplish great deeds that require courage and superhuman strength. You will see that Odysseus is an epic hero who displays some of the qualities that were honored in Greek society. Yet because he is human, Odysseus also displays some human faults.

YOUR TURN In the excerpt at the right, Odysseus has been offered a meal by Circe, an enchantress who has turned a group of his men into pigs. What do you learn about Odysseus from these lines? What values does he represent?

> **EPIC HERO**
>
> "Circe regarded me, as there I sat
> disconsolate, and never touched a crust.
> Then she stood over me and chided me:
> 'Why sit at table mute, Odysseus? . . . '
> I turned to her at once, and said:
>
>   'Circe,
> where is the captain who could bear to touch
> this banquet, in my place? A decent man
> would see his company before him first.
> Put heart in me to eat and drink—you may,
> by freeing my companions. I must see them.'"
>
> —Book 10, lines 81–93

The Craft of the Epic

The *Odyssey* was not a written story that the Greeks would sit down and read. Rather it was a *performance* by a master storyteller, a poet with a golden voice, singing or reciting his great tale in verse, crafting many of the details as he went. Two of the techniques that he used are the **epic simile** and the **epithet.**

EPIC SIMILE As you know, a simile is a comparison between two things that uses the word *like* or *as.* Oftentimes, Homer develops a simile at great length and detail, going on for several lines. This is known as the **epic simile,** an elaborate, more involved version of a regular simile. Homer uses epic similes for emphasis, whether he's describing a character's thoughts and feelings or the magnitude of a battle between two armies.

YOUR TURN In the excerpt at the right, Odysseus is watching the performance of a bard, a minstrel like Homer himself. Suddenly he finds himself listening to the story of the fall of Troy and of his own part in it. What is his reaction? Notice the two things that are being compared. What does the comparison help to emphasize?

EPITHETS A bard telling his story is like a jazz musician who plays a melody a little differently each time. The musician, improvising around a known theme, has standard little riffs— handy musical phrases he or she can throw in when needed. The Homeric bard did the same with **epithets**— brief, descriptive phrases that helped to characterize a particular person or thing, and that had the right meter or number of syllables to fill out a line. In the *Odyssey,* Odysseus is referred to as "master mariner" or "old contender." The hero of the *Iliad* is often called "swift-footed" Achilles. Again and again, the dawn comes up "with fingertips of rose." The ocean becomes the "winedark sea."

YOUR TURN In the passage at the right, Odysseus, who has been spending time with Circe, "the loveliest of goddesses," now begs her to help him get home. Her advice is not something he wants to hear. What epithets, or descriptive phrases, can you find in this passage?

EPIC SIMILE

And Odysseus
let the bright molten tears run down his cheeks,
weeping [like] the way a wife mourns for her lord
on the lost field where he has gone down fighting
the day of wrath that came upon his children.
At sight of the man panting and dying there,
she slips down to enfold him, crying out;
then feels the spears, prodding her back and shoulders,
and goes bound into slavery and grief.
Piteous weeping wears away her cheeks:
but no more piteous than Odysseus' tears,
cloaked as they were, now, from the company.

—Book 8, lines 560–571

EPITHET

"'Son of Laertes and the gods of old,
Odysseus, master mariner and soldier,
you shall not stay here longer against your will;
but home you may not go
unless you take a strange way round and come
to the cold homes of Death and pale Persephone.
You shall hear prophecy from the rapt shade
of blind Tiresias of Thebes, forever
charged with reason even among the dead;
to him alone, of all the flitting ghosts,
Persephone has given a mind undarkened.'"

—Book 10, lines 200–210

Imagine an evening long ago. A traveling story-teller is about to perform. You can't read or write, but you like a good story. This bard will tell the latest news from afar and then spin tales of the heroes of old—their adventures with monsters and gods and goddesses. The epic you're about to read is much like what you might have heard that night. The strategies explained here can help you appreciate the craft of the epic.

Reading the Epic

Strategies for Using your 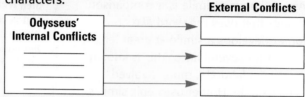 READER'S NOTEBOOK

As you read, take notes to
• help you keep track of the epic as a story
• record memorable poetic images and sound effects
• analyze and understand the epic hero

1 Strategies for Reading the Epic as Narrative

• Look for signs of conflict in the story. Try using a simple graphic like this one to identify external and internal conflicts among characters.

Odysseus' Internal Conflicts → **External Conflicts**

• Track the events of the plot, and try to **predict** the outcome.
• Identify the main and minor characters and **question** what motivates them.
• **Visualize** the time and place of the setting.
• **Clarify** the overall theme of the epic.
• When possible, **connect** the story to your personal experiences.

2 Strategies for Reading the Epic as Poetry

• Read the lines for their sense, just as you would read prose. Follow the punctuation, and remember that the end of a line does not always mean the end of a thought.
• Try reading the lines aloud, the way the epic was originally heard.
• Listen for sound effects, such as alliteration, assonance, consonance, and rhyme, that the poet has created.
• Read difficult passages more than once. You can also read ahead to keep track of the plot.
• Notice how figurative language, such as the epic simile, can **clarify** the meaning of the epic.

3 Strategies for Understanding the Epic Hero

• Decide what ideals and values the hero represents and what his goals are.
• Determine what the hero does to preserve his honor and fame.
• **Evaluate** the hero's role in any conflicts. How does he resolve them? Does he ever, through a character flaw, make them worse?
• Identify any changes or development in the hero's character.

Need More Help?

Remember that active readers use the essential reading strategies explained on page 7: **visualize, predict, clarify, question, connect, evaluate, monitor.**

PREPARING to *Read*

from the Odyssey

Epic Poetry by HOMER

Translated by ROBERT FITZGERALD

"I am Laertes'
son, Odysseus.
Men hold me
formidable for
guile in peace
and war."

Connect to Your Life

Heroic Adversaries Who is your favorite monster? What science fiction or horror creature do you think is the most unusual or frightening? Using a chart like the one shown, list the characteristics of this creature. Then briefly explain why you think it is the best—or perhaps the worst—monster ever created.

In Books 9–12 of the *Odyssey,* the poem's hero, Odysseus (ō-dĭs'ē-əs), runs into several kinds of monsters. How he deals with them is part of what makes him a hero. After you read each episode, list the characteristics of any new monsters Odysseus encounters. Think of what heroic qualities Odysseus shows as he battles each of them.

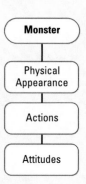

Build Background

The *Iliad* and the *Odyssey* contain timeless portraits of several heroes, including Odysseus, king of Ithaca, and they present plots, characters, and themes that have been echoing throughout Western literature ever since. Although these epics are an artful blend of mythology and legend, they are based on an event that may actually have happened. This was a war waged by the combined forces of a number of Greek city-states against the walled city of Troy. For centuries Troy was thought to be imaginary. In 1871, however, an archaeologist began unearthing the remains of nine ancient cities—each built on the ruins of the last—in northwestern Turkey, near where the *Iliad* places Troy. One of those cities may have been the legendary city of the Trojan War.

LaserLinks:
Background for
Reading
Historical
Connection

WORDS TO KNOW
Vocabulary Preview

adversary   formidable
appalled   guile
avenge   indifferent
disdain   ponderous
entreat   whim

Focus Your Reading

LITERARY ANALYSIS EPIC HERO The **hero** of an **epic** is a larger-than-life figure who embodies the ideals of a nation or race. Epic heroes take part in long, dangerous adventures and accomplish great deeds that require extraordinary courage and superhuman strength. Odysseus is such a hero, and the *Odyssey,* as its opening lines announce, is his story:

> *the story*
> *of that man skilled in all ways of contending,*
> *the wanderer, harried for years on end,*
> *after he plundered the stronghold*
> *on the proud height of Troy.*

As you read the episodes that follow, consider what qualities the Greeks seemed to regard as heroic. Ask yourself how well Odysseus lived up to these standards.

ACTIVE READING PREDICTING **Predicting** is the skill that helps you use clues in a text, along with your prior knowledge and experience, to make reasonable guesses about what will happen later in a story. Good readers make and revise predictions almost unconsciously as they read.

READER'S NOTEBOOK As you follow Odysseus' adventures, look for clues that seem to **foreshadow** future events. These might be remarks that hint at things to come, or they could be decisions that Odysseus makes at crucial moments. Jot down the clues, together with your predictions.

THE WANDERINGS OF ODYSSEUS

from

THE ODYSSEY

HOMER

Translated by Robert Fitzgerald

Sing in me, Muse, and through me tell the story
of that man skilled in all ways of contending,
the wanderer, harried for years on end,
after he plundered the stronghold
5   on the proud height of Troy.

                          He saw the townlands
and learned the minds of many distant men,
and weathered many bitter nights and days
in his deep heart at sea, while he fought only
10   to save his life, to bring his shipmates home.
But not by will nor valor could he save them,
for their own recklessness destroyed them all—
children and fools, they killed and feasted on
the cattle of Lord Helios, the Sun,
15   and he who moves all day through heaven
took from their eyes the dawn of their return.
Of these adventures, Muse, daughter of Zeus,
tell us in our time, lift the great song again.

IN THESE OPENING LINES *of the* Odyssey, *the poet invokes or calls upon the Muse—the goddess of poetry—to give him inspiration in telling the story of Odysseus. During seven of Odysseus' ten years on the Mediterranean Sea, he is held captive by the goddess Calypso. With Athena's help, Odysseus finally persuades Calypso to let him go, and she helps him build a raft to leave her island. After Odysseus sails away, his raft is destroyed by storms.*

Alone and exhausted, Odysseus is washed up on the land of the Phaeacians, where Alcinous is king. Alcinous gives a banquet in honor of Odysseus and asks him to reveal who he is and where he came from. Odysseus relates to the king his adventures up to that time. His account makes up Books 9–12 of the Odyssey.

BOOK

NEW COASTS AND POSEIDON'S SON

NINE

Guide for Reading

        "What shall I
say first? What shall I keep until the end?
The gods have tried me in a thousand ways.

3 tried: tested.

But first my name: let that be known to you,
5 and if I pull away from pitiless death,
friendship will bind us, though my land lies far.

I am Laertes' son, Odysseus.
          Men hold me

7 hold: regard.

<u>formidable</u> for <u>guile</u> in peace and war:
this fame has gone abroad to the sky's rim.
10 My home is on the peaked sea-mark of Ithaca
under Mount Neion's wind-blown robe of leaves,
in sight of other islands—Dulichium,
Same, wooded Zacynthus—Ithaca
being most lofty in that coastal sea,
15 and northwest, while the rest lie east and south.
A rocky isle, but good for a boy's training;
I shall not see on earth a place more dear,
though I have been detained long by Calypso,

11–13 Mount Neion's (nē'ŏnz') . . .
Dulichium (dōō-lĭk'ē-əm) . . . **Same**
(sä'mē) . . . **Zacynthus** (zə-sĭn'thəs).

> WORDS
> TO
> KNOW
>
> **formidable** (fôr'mĭ-də-bəl) *adj.* inspiring admiration, awe, or fear
> **guile** (gīl) *n.* skillful slyness; craftiness

896

loveliest among goddesses, who held me
20 in her smooth caves, to be her heart's delight,
as Circe of Aeaea, the enchantress,
desired me, and detained me in her hall.
But in my heart I never gave consent.
Where shall a man find sweetness to surpass
25 his own home and his parents? In far lands
he shall not, though he find a house of gold.

What of my sailing, then, from Troy?
                          What of those years
of rough adventure, weathered under Zeus?"

18–22 Odysseus refers to two beautiful goddesses, Calypso and Circe, who have delayed him on their islands. (Details about Circe appear in Book 10.) Notice, however, that Odysseus seems nostalgic for his own family and homeland. At this point in the story, Odysseus has been away from home for more than 18 years—10 of them spent in the war at Troy.

28 weathered: survived.

SOON AFTER LEAVING TROY, *Odysseus and his crew land near Ismarus, the city of the Cicones. The Cicones are allies of the Trojans and therefore enemies of Odysseus. Odysseus and his crew raid the Cicones, robbing and killing people, until the Ciconian army kills 72 of Odysseus' men and drives the rest out to sea. Delayed by a storm for two days, Odysseus and his remaining companions continue their journey.*

"I might have made it safely home, that time,
30 but as I came round Malea the current
took me out to sea, and from the north
a fresh gale drove me on, past Cythera.
Nine days I drifted on the teeming sea
before dangerous high winds. Upon the tenth
35 we came to the coastline of the Lotus Eaters,
who live upon that flower. We landed there
to take on water. All ships' companies
mustered alongside for the mid-day meal.
Then I sent out two picked men and a runner
40 to learn what race of men that land sustained.
They fell in, soon enough, with Lotus Eaters,
who showed no will to do us harm, only
offering the sweet Lotus to our friends—
but those who ate this honeyed plant, the Lotus,
45 never cared to report, nor to return:
they longed to stay forever, browsing on
that native bloom, forgetful of their homeland.

38 mustered: assembled; gathered.

41–47 How are the Lotus Eaters a threat to Odysseus and his men?

I drove them, all three wailing, to the ships,
tied them down under their rowing benches,
50   called the rest: 'All hands aboard;
come, clear the beach and no one taste
the Lotus, or you lose your hope of home.'
Filing in to their places by the rowlocks
my oarsmen dipped their long oars in the surf,
55   and we moved out again on our sea faring.

In the next land we found were Cyclopes,
giants, louts, without a law to bless them.
In ignorance leaving the fruitage of the earth in mystery
to the immortal gods, they neither plow
60   nor sow by hand, nor till the ground, though grain—
wild wheat and barley—grows untended, and
wine-grapes, in clusters, ripen in heaven's rain.
Cyclopes have no muster and no meeting,
no consultation or old tribal ways,
65   but each one dwells in his own mountain cave
dealing out rough justice to wife and child,
<u>indifferent</u> to what the others do."

57 louts: clumsy, stupid people.

58–67 Why doesn't Odysseus respect the Cyclopes?

ACROSS THE BAY *from the land of the Cyclopes is a lush, deserted island.*
Odysseus and his crew land on the island in a dense fog and spend several days feasting
on wine and wild goats and observing the mainland, where the Cyclopes live. On the third
day, Odysseus and his company of men set out to learn if the Cyclopes are friends or foes.

"When the young Dawn with fingertips of rose
came in the east, I called my men together
70   and made a speech to them:

                    'Old shipmates, friends,
the rest of you stand by; I'll make the crossing
in my own ship, with my own company,
and find out what the mainland natives are—
for they may be wild savages, and lawless,
75   or hospitable and god-fearing men.'

68 This use of "with fingertips of rose" to describe the personified Dawn is a famous epithet—a descriptive phrase that presents a trait of a person or thing. Watch for reappearances of this epithet in the poem, and be on the lookout for other epithets.

WORDS
TO
KNOW
indifferent (ĭn-dĭf′ər-ənt) *adj.* having no interest in or concern for

At this I went aboard, and gave the word
to cast off by the stern. My oarsmen followed,
filing in to their benches by the rowlocks,
and all in line dipped oars in the gray sea.

77 stern: the rear end of a ship.

80   As we rowed on, and nearer to the mainland,
at one end of the bay, we saw a cavern
yawning above the water, screened with laurel,
and many rams and goats about the place
inside a sheepfold—made from slabs of stone
85   earthfast between tall trunks of pine and rugged
towering oak trees.

82 screened with laurel: partially hidden by laurel trees.
84 sheepfold: a pen for sheep.

                              A prodigious man
slept in this cave alone, and took his flocks
to graze afield—remote from all companions,
knowing none but savage ways, a brute
90   so huge, he seemed no man at all of those
who eat good wheaten bread; but he seemed rather
a shaggy mountain reared in solitude.
We beached there, and I told the crew
to stand by and keep watch over the ship;
95   as for myself I took my twelve best fighters
and went ahead. I had a goatskin full
of that sweet liquor that Euanthes' son,
Maron, had given me. He kept Apollo's
holy grove at Ismarus; for kindness
100   we showed him there, and showed his wife and child,
he gave me seven shining golden talents
perfectly formed, a solid silver winebowl,
and then this liquor—twelve two-handled jars
of brandy, pure and fiery. Not a slave
105   in Maron's household knew this drink; only
he, his wife and the storeroom mistress knew;
and they would put one cupful—ruby-colored,
honey-smooth—in twenty more of water,
but still the sweet scent hovered like a fume
110   over the winebowl. No man turned away
when cups of this came round.

86 prodigious (prə-dĭj′əs): enormous, huge.

91–92 What does Odysseus' metaphor imply about the Cyclops?

97–98 Euanthes' (yōō-ăn′thēz) . . . **Maron** (mâr′ŏn′).

101 talents: bars of gold or silver of a specified weight, used as money in ancient Greece.

                              A wineskin full
I brought along, and victuals in a bag,
for in my bones I knew some towering brute
would be upon us soon—all outward power,

112 victuals (vĭt′lz): food.

115   a wild man, ignorant of civility.

We climbed, then, briskly to the cave. But Cyclops
had gone afield, to pasture his fat sheep,
so we looked round at everything inside:
a drying rack that sagged with cheeses, pens
120   crowded with lambs and kids, each in its class:
firstlings apart from middlings, and the 'dewdrops,'
or newborn lambkins, penned apart from both.
And vessels full of whey were brimming there—
bowls of earthenware and pails for milking.
125   My men came pressing round me, pleading:

                                              'Why not
Take these cheeses, get them stowed, come back,
throw open all the pens, and make a run for it?
We'll drive the kids and lambs aboard. We say
put out again on good salt water!'

                                              Ah,
130   how sound that was! Yet I refused. I wished
to see the caveman, what he had to offer—
no pretty sight, it turned out, for my friends.
We lit a fire, burnt an offering,
and took some cheese to eat; then sat in silence
135   around the embers, waiting. When he came
he had a load of dry boughs on his shoulder
to stoke his fire at suppertime. He dumped it
with a great crash into that hollow cave,
and we all scattered fast to the far wall.
140   Then over the broad cavern floor he ushered
the ewes he meant to milk. He left his rams
and he-goats in the yard outside, and swung
high overhead a slab of solid rock
to close the cave. Two dozen four-wheeled wagons,
145   with heaving wagon teams, could not have stirred
the tonnage of that rock from where he wedged it
over the doorsill. Next he took his seat
and milked his bleating ewes. A practiced job
he made of it, giving each ewe her suckling;
150   thickened his milk, then, into curds and whey,
sieved out the curds to drip in withy baskets,
and poured the whey to stand in bowls
cooling until he drank it for his supper.

115 civility: polite behavior.

120 kids: young goats.

121–122 The Cyclops has separated his lambs into three age groups.

123 whey: the watery part of milk, which separates from the curds, or solid part, during the making of cheese.

129 good salt water: the open sea. (The men want to rob the Cyclops and quickly sail away.)

130–132 Why does Odysseus refuse his men's "sound" request?

133 burnt an offering: burned a portion of the food as an offering to secure the gods' goodwill. (Such offerings were frequently performed by Greek sailors during difficult journeys.)

137 stoke: build up; feed.

144–147 Notice the size of the rock that closes the entrance of the Cyclops' cave.

THE WANDERINGS OF ODYSSEUS **901**

When all these chores were done, he poked the fire,
155 heaping on brushwood. In the glare he saw us.

'Strangers,' he said, 'who are you? And where from?
What brings you here by sea ways—a fair traffic?
Or are you wandering rogues, who cast your lives
like dice, and ravage other folk by sea?'

160 We felt a pressure on our hearts, in dread
of that deep rumble and that mighty man.
But all the same I spoke up in reply:

'We are from Troy, Achaeans, blown off course
by shifting gales on the Great South Sea;
165 homeward bound, but taking routes and ways
uncommon; so the will of Zeus would have it.
We served under Agamemnon, son of Atreus—
the whole world knows what city
he laid waste, what armies he destroyed.
170 It was our luck to come here; here we stand,
beholden for your help, or any gifts
you give—as custom is to honor strangers.
We would <u>entreat</u> you, great Sir, have a care
for the gods' courtesy; Zeus will <u>avenge</u>
175 the unoffending guest.'

He answered this
from his brute chest, unmoved:

'You are a ninny,
or else you come from the other end of nowhere,
telling me, mind the gods! We Cyclopes
care not a whistle for your thundering Zeus
180 or all the gods in bliss; we have more force by far.
I would not let you go for fear of Zeus—
you or your friends—unless I had a <u>whim</u> to.
Tell me, where was it, now, you left your ship—
around the point, or down the shore, I wonder?'

185 He thought he'd find out, but I saw through this,
and answered with a ready lie:

157–159 The Cyclops asks whether the seafaring men are here for honest trading ("fair traffic") or are dishonest people ("rogues") who steal from ("ravage") those they meet.

163 Achaeans (ə-kē'ənz): Greeks.

167 Agamemnon (ăg'ə-mĕm'nŏn'): the Greek king (Menelaus' brother) who led the war against the Trojans; **Atreus** (ā'trē-əs).

172–175 It was a sacred Greek custom to honor strangers with food and gifts. Odysseus is warning the Cyclops that Zeus will punish anyone who mistreats a guest.

176 ninny: fool.

178–182 What is the Cyclops' attitude toward the gods?

185–190 Why do you think Odysseus lies about his ship?

WORDS
TO
KNOW

entreat (ĕn-trēt') *v.* to ask earnestly; beg
avenge (ə-vĕnj') *v.* to take revenge on behalf of
whim (hwĭm) *n.* a sudden impulse or notion; fancy

'My ship?

Poseidon Lord, who sets the earth a-tremble,
broke it up on the rocks at your land's end.
A wind from seaward served him, drove us there.
190 We are survivors, these good men and I.'

Neither reply nor pity came from him,
but in one stride he clutched at my companions
and caught two in his hands like squirming puppies
to beat their brains out, spattering the floor.
195 Then he dismembered them and made his meal,
gaping and crunching like a mountain lion—
everything: innards, flesh, and marrow bones.
We cried aloud, lifting our hands to Zeus,
powerless, looking on at this, <u>appalled</u>;
200 but Cyclops went on filling up his belly
with manflesh and great gulps of whey,
then lay down like a mast among his sheep.
My heart beat high now at the chance of action,
and drawing the sharp sword from my hip I went
205 along his flank to stab him where the midriff
holds the liver. I had touched the spot
when sudden fear stayed me: if I killed him
we perished there as well, for we could never
move his <u>ponderous</u> doorway slab aside.
210 So we were left to groan and wait for morning.

When the young Dawn with fingertips of rose
lit up the world, the Cyclops built a fire
and milked his handsome ewes, all in due order,
putting the sucklings to the mothers. Then,
215 his chores being all dispatched, he caught
another brace of men to make his breakfast,
and whisked away his great door slab
to let his sheep go through—but he, behind,
reset the stone as one would cap a quiver.
220 There was a din of whistling as the Cyclops
rounded his flock to higher ground, then stillness.
And now I pondered how to hurt him worst,
if but Athena granted what I prayed for.
Here are the means I thought would serve my turn:

193–196 The two similes in this passage emphasize the helplessness of the men ("like squirming puppies") and the savagery of the Cyclops ("gaping and crunching like a mountain lion").

203–210 Why doesn't Odysseus kill the Cyclops at this time?

215 dispatched: completed.

216 brace: pair.

218–219 The Cyclops reseals the cave with the massive rock as easily as an ordinary human places the cap on a container of arrows.

223 Odysseus calls on his protector, the goddess Athena, for help as he forms a plan.

WORDS TO KNOW **appalled** (ə-pôld′) *adj.* filled with dismay; horrified **appall** v.
ponderous (pŏn′dər-əs) *adj.* heavy in a clumsy way; bulky

225　a club, or staff, lay there along the fold—
　　　an olive tree, felled green and left to season
　　　for Cyclops' hand. And it was like a mast
　　　a lugger of twenty oars, broad in the beam—
　　　a deep-sea-going craft—might carry:

228 lugger: a small, wide sailing ship.

230　so long, so big around, it seemed. Now I
　　　chopped out a six-foot section of this pole
　　　and set it down before my men, who scraped it;
　　　and when they had it smooth, I hewed again
　　　to make a stake with pointed end. I held this

233 hewed: chopped.

235　in the fire's heart and turned it, toughening it,
　　　then hid it, well back in the cavern, under
　　　one of the dung piles in profusion there.
　　　Now came the time to toss for it: who ventured
　　　along with me? whose hand could bear to thrust

237 profusion: abundance.

238–243 What does Odysseus plan to do to the Cyclops?

240　and grind that spike in Cyclops' eye, when mild
　　　sleep had mastered him? As luck would have it,
　　　the men I would have chosen won the toss—
　　　four strong men, and I made five as captain.

　　　At evening came the shepherd with his flock,
245　his woolly flock. The rams as well, this time,
　　　entered the cave: by some sheep-herding whim—
　　　or a god's bidding—none were left outside.
　　　He hefted his great boulder into place
　　　and sat him down to milk the bleating ewes
250　in proper order, put the lambs to suck,
　　　and swiftly ran through all his evening chores.
　　　Then he caught two more men and feasted on them.
　　　My moment was at hand, and I went forward
　　　holding an ivy bowl of my dark drink,
255　looking up, saying:

　　　　　　　　　　　'Cyclops, try some wine.
　　　Here's liquor to wash down your scraps of men.
　　　Taste it, and see the kind of drink we carried
　　　under our planks. I meant it for an offering
　　　if you would help us home. But you are mad,
260　unbearable, a bloody monster! After this,
　　　will any other traveler come to see you?'

255–261 Why does Odysseus offer the Cyclops the liquor he brought from the ship?

　　　He seized and drained the bowl, and it went down
　　　so fiery and smooth he called for more:

'Give me another, thank you kindly. Tell me,
how are you called? I'll make a gift will please you.
Even Cyclopes know the wine-grapes grow
out of grassland and loam in heaven's rain,
but here's a bit of nectar and ambrosia!'

Three bowls I brought him, and he poured them down.
I saw the fuddle and flush come over him,
then I sang out in cordial tones:

                                    'Cyclops,
you ask my honorable name? Remember
the gift you promised me, and I shall tell you.
My name is Nohbdy: mother, father, and friends,
everyone calls me Nohbdy.'

                        And he said:
'Nohbdy's my meat, then, after I eat his friends.
Others come first. There's a noble gift, now.'

Even as he spoke, he reeled and tumbled backward,
his great head lolling to one side: and sleep
took him like any creature. Drunk, hiccupping,
he dribbled streams of liquor and bits of men.

Now, by the gods, I drove my big hand spike
deep in the embers, charring it again,
and cheered my men along with battle talk
to keep their courage up: no quitting now.
The pike of olive, green though it had been,
reddened and glowed as if about to catch.
I drew it from the coals and my four fellows
gave me a hand, lugging it near the Cyclops
as more than natural force nerved them; straight
forward they sprinted, lifted it, and rammed it
deep in his crater eye, and I leaned on it
turning it as a shipwright turns a drill
in planking, having men below to swing
the two-handled strap that spins it in the groove.
So with our brand we bored that great eye socket
while blood ran out around the red hot bar.
Eyelid and lash were seared; the pierced ball
hissed broiling, and the roots popped.

265
270
275
280
285
290
295

268 **nectar** (nĕk'tər) **and ambrosia**
(ăm-brō'zhə): the drink and food of
the gods.

270 **fuddle and flush**: the state of
confusion and redness of the face
caused by drinking alcohol.

274–275 Say the name *Nohbdy* out
loud and listen to what it sounds
like. What might Odysseus be
planning?

286 **the pike**: the pointed stake.

292–295 Odysseus compares the
way he stabs the Cyclops in the eye
to the way a shipbuilder drills a
hole in a board.

In a smithy
300   one sees a white-hot axehead or an adze
plunged and wrung in a cold tub, screeching steam—
the way they make soft iron hale and hard—:
just so that eyeball hissed around the spike.
The Cyclops bellowed and the rock roared round him,
305   and we fell back in fear. Clawing his face
he tugged the bloody spike out of his eye,
threw it away, and his wild hands went groping;
then he set up a howl for Cyclopes
who lived in caves on windy peaks nearby.
310   Some heard him; and they came by divers ways
to clump around outside and call:

'What ails you,
Polyphemus? Why do you cry so sore
in the starry night? You will not let us sleep.
Sure no man's driving off your flock? No man
315   has tricked you, ruined you?'

Out of the cave
the mammoth Polyphemus roared in answer:

'Nohbdy, Nohbdy's tricked me, Nohbdy's ruined me!'

To this rough shout they made a sage reply:

'Ah well, if nobody has played you foul
320   there in your lonely bed, we are no use in pain
given by great Zeus. Let it be your father,
Poseidon Lord, to whom you pray.'

So saying
they trailed away. And I was filled with laughter
to see how like a charm the name deceived them.
325   Now Cyclops, wheezing as the pain came on him,
fumbled to wrench away the great doorstone
and squatted in the breach with arms thrown wide
for any silly beast or man who bolted—
hoping somehow I might be such a fool.
330   But I kept thinking how to win the game:
death sat there huge; how could we slip away?
I drew on all my wits, and ran through tactics,
reasoning as a man will for dear life,

299 smithy: blacksmith's shop.

300 adze (ădz): an axlike tool with a curved blade.

310 divers: various.

312 Polyphemus (pŏl'ə-fē'məs): the name of the Cyclops.

318 sage: wise.

319–322 Odysseus' lie about his name has paid off. What do the other Cyclopes assume to be the source of Polyphemus' pain?

327 breach: opening.

330–334 Notice Odysseus' great mental struggle and, as you read on, the clever plan he has managed to come up with on the spot.

until a trick came—and it pleased me well.
335 The Cyclops' rams were handsome, fat, with heavy
fleeces, a dark violet.

                        Three abreast
I tied them silently together, twining
cords of willow from the ogre's bed;
then slung a man under each middle one
340 to ride there safely, shielded left and right.
So three sheep could convey each man. I took
the woolliest ram, the choicest of the flock,
and hung myself under his kinky belly,
pulled up tight, with fingers twisted deep
345 in sheepskin ringlets for an iron grip.
So, breathing hard, we waited until morning.

When Dawn spread out her fingertips of rose
the rams began to stir, moving for pasture,
and peals of bleating echoed round the pens
350 where dams with udders full called for a milking.
Blinded, and sick with pain from his head wound,
the master stroked each ram, then let it pass,
but my men riding on the pectoral fleece
the giant's blind hands blundering never found.
355 Last of them all my ram, the leader, came,
weighted by wool and me with my meditations.
The Cyclops patted him, and then he said:

'Sweet cousin ram, why lag behind the rest
in the night cave? You never linger so,
360 but graze before them all, and go afar
to crop sweet grass, and take your stately way
leading along the streams, until at evening
you run to be the first one in the fold.
Why, now, so far behind? Can you be grieving
365 over your Master's eye? That carrion rogue
and his accurst companions burnt it out
when he had conquered all my wits with wine.
Nohbdy will not get out alive, I swear.
Oh, had you brain and voice to tell
370 where he may be now, dodging all my fury!
Bashed by this hand and bashed on this rock wall

353 pectoral fleece: the wool covering a sheep's chest.

his brains would strew the floor, and I should have
rest from the outrage Nohbdy worked upon me.'

He sent us into the open, then. Close by,
375 I dropped and rolled clear of the ram's belly,
going this way and that to untie the men.
With many glances back, we rounded up
his fat, stiff-legged sheep to take aboard,
and drove them down to where the good ship lay.
380 We saw, as we came near, our fellows' faces
shining; then we saw them turn to grief
tallying those who had not fled from death.
I hushed them, jerking head and eyebrows up,
and in a low voice told them: 'Load this herd;
385 move fast, and put the ship's head toward the breakers.'
They all pitched in at loading, then embarked
and struck their oars into the sea. Far out,
as far off shore as shouted words would carry,
I sent a few back to the <u>adversary</u>:

385 put . . . the breakers: turn the
ship around so that it is heading
toward the open sea.

390 'O Cyclops! Would you feast on my companions?
Puny, am I, in a Caveman's hands?
How do you like the beating that we gave you,
you damned cannibal? Eater of guests
under your roof! Zeus and the gods have paid you!'

390–394 Notice that Odysseus
assumes that the gods are on
his side.

395 The blind thing in his doubled fury broke
a hilltop in his hands and heaved it after us.
Ahead of our black prow it struck and sank
whelmed in a spuming geyser, a giant wave
that washed the ship stern foremost back to shore.
400 I got the longest boathook out and stood
fending us off, with furious nods to all
to put their backs into a racing stroke—
row, row, or perish. So the long oars bent
kicking the foam sternward, making head
405 until we drew away, and twice as far.
Now when I cupped my hands I heard the crew
in low voices protesting:

                      'Godsake, Captain!

395–403 The hilltop thrown by
Polyphemus lands in front of the
ship, causing a huge wave that
carries the ship back to the shore.
Odysseus uses a long pole to push
the boat away from the land.

WORDS
TO   **adversary** (ăd′vər-sĕr′ē) *n.* an opponent; enemy
KNOW

Why bait the beast again? Let him alone!'

'That tidal wave he made on the first throw
410 all but beached us.'

'All but stove us in!'

'Give him our bearing with your trumpeting,
he'll get the range and lob a boulder.'

'Aye
he'll smash our timbers and our heads together!'

I would not heed them in my glorying spirit,
415 but let my anger flare and yelled:

'Cyclops,
if ever mortal man inquire
how you were put to shame and blinded, tell him
Odysseus, raider of cities, took your eye:
Laertes' son, whose home's on Ithaca!'

420 At this he gave a mighty sob and rumbled:

'Now comes the weird upon me, spoken of old.
A wizard, grand and wondrous, lived here—Telemus,
a son of Eurymus; great length of days
he had in wizardry among the Cyclopes,
425 and these things he foretold for time to come:
my great eye lost, and at Odysseus' hands.
Always I had in mind some giant, armed
in giant force, would come against me here.
But this, but you—small, pitiful and twiggy—
430 you put me down with wine, you blinded me.
Come back, Odysseus, and I'll treat you well,
praying the god of earthquake to befriend you—
his son I am, for he by his avowal
fathered me, and, if he will, he may
435 heal me of this black wound—he and no other
of all the happy gods or mortal men.'

Few words I shouted in reply to him:

407–413 The near disaster of Odysseus' boast has frightened the crew. As earlier, in the cave, the men make reasonable appeals.

415–419 Odysseus uses the warlike epithet "raider of cities" in his second boast to the Cyclops. Why do you think he reveals so much about himself?

421 Now comes . . . of old: Now I recall the destiny predicted long ago.

422 Telemus (tĕl'ə-məs): a magician who could predict the future for the Cyclopes.

427–430 Polyphemus is not blind to the irony of being beaten by someone only about one-eighth his size.

432 the god of earthquake: Poseidon.

433 avowal: honest admission.

'If I could take your life I would and take
your time away, and hurl you down to hell!
440   The god of earthquake could not heal you there!'

At this he stretched his hands out in his darkness
toward the sky of stars, and prayed Poseidon:

'O hear me, lord, blue girdler of the islands,
if I am thine indeed, and thou art father:
445   grant that Odysseus, raider of cities, never
see his home: Laertes' son, I mean,
who kept his hall on Ithaca. Should destiny
intend that he shall see his roof again
among his family in his father land,
450   far be that day, and dark the years between.
Let him lose all companions, and return
under strange sail to bitter days at home.'

In these words he prayed, and the god heard him.
Now he laid hands upon a bigger stone
455   and wheeled around, titanic for the cast,
to let it fly in the black-prowed vessel's track.
But it fell short, just aft the steering oar,
and whelming seas rose giant above the stone
to bear us onward toward the island.
                                                    There
460   as we ran in we saw the squadron waiting,
the trim ships drawn up side by side, and all
our troubled friends who waited, looking seaward.
We beached her, grinding keel in the soft sand,
and waded in, ourselves, on the sandy beach.
465   Then we unloaded all the Cyclops' flock
to make division, share and share alike,
only my fighters voted that my ram,
the prize of all, should go to me. I slew him
by the seaside and burnt his long thighbones
470   to Zeus beyond the stormcloud, Cronus' son,
who rules the world. But Zeus disdained my offering;
destruction for my ships he had in store
and death for those who sailed them, my companions.
Now all day long until the sun went down

443–452 Note the details of
Polyphemus' curse on Odysseus.
As you read on, you'll find out
whether the curse comes true.

455 titanic for the cast: drawing
on all his enormous strength in
preparing to throw.

457 aft: behind.

459 the island: the deserted island
where most of Odysseus' men had
stayed behind.

WORDS
TO   **disdain** (dĭs-dān') v. to refuse or reject scornfully
KNOW

912

475   we made our feast on mutton and sweet wine,
till after sunset in the gathering dark
we went to sleep above the wash of ripples.

When the young Dawn with fingertips of rose
touched the world, I roused the men, gave orders
480   to man the ships, cast off the mooring lines;
and filing in to sit beside the rowlocks
oarsmen in line dipped oars in the gray sea.
So we moved out, sad in the vast offing,
having our precious lives, but not our friends."

483 in the vast offing: toward the open sea.

Connect to the Literature

1. **What Do You Think?**
   What is your general impression of Odysseus, based on his adventures with the Cyclopes?

   Comprehension Check
   • What is Odysseus' ultimate destination?
   • What does Odysseus think of the way the Cyclopes live?
   • How does Odysseus injure Polyphemus?

Think Critically

2. **ACTIVE READING** **PREDICTING** What **predictions** did you make in your **READER'S NOTEBOOK** as you read this episode? Discuss with a classmate the clues that prompted your predictions.

3. What positive and negative qualities of Odysseus' **character** are revealed by his behavior in the land of the Cyclopes?

   THINK ABOUT
   • why he insists on seeing the Cyclops in the first place
   • how he defeats Polyphemus
   • why he taunts Polyphemus and reveals his real name as he sails away

4. Do you consider Polyphemus a **villain**? Do Odysseus' actions toward him seem justified? Explain.

5. From the **characterization** of Polyphemus, what **conclusions** can you draw about the qualities that ancient Greek society considered barbaric or monstrous? Use specific examples from the excerpt to support your ideas.

Extend Interpretations

6. **Critic's Corner** Odysseus tells King Alcinous of his fame "for guile." According to critic Bernard Knox, Odysseus tries to preserve his reputation for "successful courage and intelligence." These are "values for which he stands, and to which he must be true." From what you have read about Odysseus so far, do you think this reputation is deserved? Support your opinion.

7. **Connect to Life** What qualities do people in today's society consider barbaric or monstrous? What qualities do we think of as civilized?

8. **Connect to Life** Look over the characteristics of your favorite monster that you recorded for the chart on page 893. How does Polyphemus compare with your monster?

Literary Analysis

EPIC HERO The larger-than-life central figure or "superhero" of an epic is known as the **epic hero.** Usually a male figure, he is a person of imposing stature who stands for the ideals of a nation or race. He performs deeds of great valor that require superhuman courage. Sometimes he is assisted by supernatural forces.

Paired Activity With a partner, create a two-column chart to evaluate the extent to which Odysseus acts like an epic hero in Book 9. In the first column, list the larger-than-life qualities and actions that show Odysseus to be an epic hero. In the second column, list Odysseus' human weaknesses and unwise actions that do not seem to fit the ideal of an epic hero. After you complete your chart, discuss with your partner the ways in which you think Odysseus' character needs improvement. As you read more of the *Odyssey,* you'll be able to decide whether Odysseus changes for the better.

Heroic Qualities of Odysseus	Weaknesses of Odysseus

Choices & CHALLENGES

Writing Options

1. Diary Entries Write one or two diary entries in which one of Odysseus' crew describes the events of this episode.

2. Cyclops' Story How might the Cyclops have viewed the events? Experiment with writing a draft of the episode as Polyphemus might tell it.

Writing Handbook
See page 1153: Narrative Writing.

Activities & Explorations

1. Dramatized Scenes With the class divided into small groups, act out scenes from Book 9 of the *Odyssey*. (Scenes could include Odysseus and his crew in the land of the Lotus Eaters, the attack on the Cyclops, the escape from the Cyclops' cave, and the departure from the land of the Cyclopes.) Focus on portraying the character of Odysseus.
~ PERFORMING

2. Escape Plan If Polyphemus had not brought the rams into the cave, how might Odysseus and his men have escaped? With a partner, devise an escape plan and explain it to your classmates.
~ SPEAKING AND LISTENING

Inquiry & Research

Classical Influences The lasting effects of classical Greek culture extend beyond literature. In a small group, find out more about ancient Greek civilization and its impact upon later cultures of the world. Each group member may want to research a different aspect of the subject, such as religion, the arts, government, or technology.

More Online: Research Starter
www.mcdougallittell.com

LaserLinks: Background for Reading
Art Gallery

Art Connection

Look again at the image on page 910. This painting from a 6th-century krater—a wide-necked, two-handled jar used as a mixing bowl by the ancient Greeks—depicts Odysseus hidden beneath the Cyclops' largest ram. How successful is this painting at illustrating the difficulty of Odysseus' feat?

Vocabulary in Action

EXERCISE A: ASSESSMENT PRACTICE For each group of words below, write the letter of the word that is an antonym of the boldfaced word.

1. **ponderous:** (a) dainty, (b) careless, (c) intelligent
2. **adversary:** (a) partner, (b) guarantee, (c) obstacle
3. **avenge:** (a) dare, (b) resist, (c) forgive
4. **disdain:** (a) stop, (b) accept, (c) scorn
5. **formidable:** (a) shapeless, (b) unimpressive, (c) likely

EXERCISE B: ANALOGIES Write the letter of the word pair that expresses the relationship most similar to that expressed by the capitalized pair.

1. GUILE : FOX ::
   (a) loyalty : squirrel   (c) timidity : mouse
   (b) wisdom : sparrow   (d) courage : sheep
2. WHIM : NOTION ::
   (a) request : plea   (c) letter : invitation
   (b) idea : emotion   (d) separation : link

3. ENTREAT : RESPOND ::
   (a) speak : shout   (c) reject : refuse
   (b) throw : catch   (d) suggest : recommend
4. APPALLED : AWFUL ::
   (a) bored : amusing   (c) tortured : helpful
   (b) surprised : predicted (d) interested : fascinating
5. INDIFFERENT : SHRUG ::
   (a) rebellious : nod   (c) enthusiastic : sigh
   (b) sleepy : yawn   (d) startled : groan

Building Vocabulary
For an in-depth lesson on analogies, see page 641.

Read On
As you read the next adventure, pay attention to Odysseus' weaknesses as well as his strengths. Compare him with his loyal but cautious officer Eurylochus.

B O O K

THE GRACE OF THE WITCH

T E N

ODYSSEUS AND HIS MEN *next land on the island of Aeolus, the wind*

king, and stay with him a month. To extend his hospitality, Aeolus gives Odysseus two

parting gifts, a fair west wind blowing the ships toward Ithaca and a great bag holding

all the unfavorable, stormy winds. Within sight of home, and while Odysseus is sleeping,

the men open the bag, thinking it contains gold and silver. The bad winds thus escape

and blow the ships back to Aeolus' island. The king refuses to help them again,

believing now that their voyage has been cursed by the gods.

The discouraged mariners next stop briefly in the land of the Laestrygones, fierce

cannibals, who bombard their ships with boulders. Only Odysseus, his ship, and its

crew of 45 survive the shower of boulders. The lone ship then sails to Aeaea, home of

the goddess Circe, considered by many to be a witch. There, Odysseus divides his men

into two groups. Eurylochus leads one platoon to explore the island, while Odysseus

stays behind on the ship with the remaining crew.

"In the wild wood they found an open glade,
around a smooth stone house—the hall of Circe—
and wolves and mountain lions lay there, mild
in her soft spell, fed on her drug of evil.
5   None would attack—oh, it was strange, I tell you—
but switching their long tails they faced our men
like hounds, who look up when their master comes
with tidbits for them—as he will—from table.
Humbly those wolves and lions with mighty paws
10 fawned on our men—who met their yellow eyes
and feared them.

                          In the entrance way they stayed
to listen there: inside her quiet house
they heard the goddess Circe.

                                        Low she sang
in her beguiling voice, while on her loom
15 she wove ambrosial fabric sheer and bright,
by that craft known to the goddesses of heaven.
No one would speak, until Polites—most
faithful and likable of my officers, said:

'Dear friends, no need for stealth: here's a young weaver
20 singing a pretty song to set the air
a-tingle on these lawns and paven courts.
Goddess she is, or lady. Shall we greet her?'

So reassured, they all cried out together,
and she came swiftly to the shining doors
25 to call them in. All but Eurylochus—
who feared a snare—the innocents went after her.
On thrones she seated them, and lounging chairs,
while she prepared a meal of cheese and barley
and amber honey mixed with Pramnian wine,
30 adding her own vile pinch, to make them lose
desire or thought of our dear father land.
Scarce had they drunk when she flew after them
with her long stick and shut them in a pigsty—
bodies, voices, heads, and bristles, all
35 swinish now, though minds were still unchanged.
So, squealing, in they went. And Circe tossed them

Guide for Reading

1–11 What is unusual about Circe's hall?

10 fawned on: showed affection for

15 ambrosial: fit for the gods.

17 Polites (pə-lī′tēz).

23–26 If you were among this group, whom would you follow—Polites or Eurylochus? Why?

27–36 What happens to the men after they drink Circe's magic potion?

WORDS
TO
KNOW

beguiling (bǐ-gī′lǐng) *adj.* charming; pleasing   **beguile** *v.*
stealth (stĕlth) *n.* quiet, secret, or sneaky behavior
snare (snâr) *n.* a trap
vile (vīl) *adj.* evil; disgusting

acorns, mast, and cornel berries—fodder
for hogs who rut and slumber on the earth.

Down to the ship Eurylochus came running
40   to cry alarm, foul magic doomed his men!
But working with dry lips to speak a word
he could not, being so shaken; blinding tears
welled in his eyes; foreboding filled his heart.
When we were frantic questioning him, at last
45   we heard the tale: our friends were gone."

43 foreboding: a sense of approaching evil.

EURYLOCHUS TELLS ODYSSEUS *what has happened and begs his captain to sail away from Circe's island. Against Eurylochus' advice, however, Odysseus rushes to save his men from the enchantress. On the way, he meets the god Hermes, who gives him a magical plant—called moly—to protect him from Circe's power. Still, Hermes warns, Odysseus must make the goddess swear that she will play no "witches' tricks." Armed with the moly and Hermes' warning, Odysseus arrives at Circe's palace. Circe welcomes him and leads him to a magnificent silver-studded chair.*

"The lady Circe
mixed me a golden cup of honeyed wine,
adding in mischief her unholy drug.
I drank, and the drink failed. But she came forward
50   aiming a stroke with her long stick, and whispered:

'Down in the sty and snore among the rest!'

Without a word, I drew my sharpened sword
and in one bound held it against her throat.
She cried out, then slid under to take my knees,
55   catching her breath to say, in her distress:

'What champion, of what country, can you be?
Where are your kinsmen and your city?
Are you not sluggish with my wine? Ah, wonder!
Never a mortal man that drank this cup

60 but when it passed his lips he had <u>succumbed</u>.
    Hale must your heart be and your tempered will.
    Odysseus then you are, O great <u>contender</u>,
    of whom the glittering god with golden wand
    spoke to me ever, and foretold
65 the black swift ship would carry you from Troy.
    Put up your weapon in the sheath. We two
    shall mingle and make love upon our bed.
    So mutual trust may come of play and love.'

    To this I said:

                                    'Circe, am I a boy,
70 that you should make me soft and doting now?
    Here in this house you turned my men to swine;
    now it is I myself you hold, <u>enticing</u>
    into your chamber, to your dangerous bed,
    to take my manhood when you have me stripped.
75 I mount no bed of love with you upon it.
    Or swear me first a great oath, if I do,
    you'll work no more enchantment to my harm.'

    She swore at once, outright, as I demanded,
    and after she had sworn, and bound herself,
80 I entered Circe's flawless bed of love."

Circe's maidens bathe Odysseus *and offer him a tempting meal, yet his mind remains on his captive men.*

    "Circe regarded me, as there I sat
    <u>disconsolate</u>, and never touched a crust.
    Then she stood over me and <u>chided</u> me:

    'Why sit at table mute, Odysseus?
85 Are you mistrustful of my bread and drink?
    Can it be treachery that you fear again,
    after the gods' great oath I swore for you?'

    I turned to her at once, and said:

61 tempered: strengthened and hardened, like steel.

63 The "glittering god with golden wand" is Hermes.

70 doting: fond; loving.

75–78 How does Odysseus protect himself from Circe?

81–106 Why does Circe free Odysseus' men from her spell?

WORDS
TO
KNOW
succumb (sə-kŭm') *v.* to be overpowered; surrender
contender (kən-tĕn'dər) *n.* a fighter
enticing (ĕn-tī'sĭng) *adj.* luring; tempting **entice** *v.*
disconsolate (dĭs-kŏn'sə-lĭt) *adj.* extremely sad
chide (chīd) *v.* to scold mildly

'Circe,

where is the captain who could bear to touch
90 this banquet, in my place? A decent man
would see his company before him first.
Put heart in me to eat and drink—you may,
by freeing my companions. I must see them.'

But Circe had already turned away.
95 Her long staff in her hand, she left the hall
and opened up the sty. I saw her enter,
driving those men turned swine to stand before me.
She stroked them, each in turn, with some new chrism;
and then, behold! their bristles fell away,
100 the coarse pelt grown upon them by her drug
melted away, and they were men again,
younger, more handsome, taller than before.
Their eyes upon me, each one took my hands,
and wild regret and longing pierced them through,
105 so the room rang with sobs, and even Circe
pitied that transformation. Exquisite
the goddess looked as she stood near me, saying:

'Son of Laertes and the gods of old,
Odysseus, master mariner and soldier,
110 go to the sea beach and sea-breasting ship;
drag it ashore, full length upon the land;
stow gear and stores in rock-holes under cover;
return; be quick; bring all your dear companions.'

Now, being a man, I could not help consenting.
115 So I went down to the sea beach and the ship,
where I found all my other men on board,
weeping, in despair along the benches.
Sometimes in farmyards when the cows return
well-fed from pasture to the barn, one sees
120 the pens give way before the calves in tumult,
breaking through to cluster about their mothers,
bumping together, bawling. Just that way
my crew poured round me when they saw me come—
their faces wet with tears as if they saw
125 their homeland, and the crags of Ithaca,
even the very town where they were born.
And weeping still they all cried out in greeting:

98 chrism (krĭz´əm): ointment.

108–110 Notice these epithets, which Circe will use repeatedly in addressing Odysseus.

114 Odysseus says that "being a man," he had to go along with Circe's request. What do you think he means by this statement?

118–126 What two things are compared in this epic simile? How does the simile help you picture the scene that Odysseus is describing?

'Prince, what joy this is, your safe return!
Now Ithaca seems here, and we in Ithaca!
130 But tell us now, what death befell our friends?'

And, speaking gently, I replied:

'First we must get the ship high on the shingle,   **132 shingle:** pebbly beach.
and stow our gear and stores in clefts of rock   **133 clefts:** openings; cracks.
for cover. Then come follow me, to see
135 your shipmates in the magic house of Circe
eating and drinking, endlessly regaled.'

They turned back, as commanded, to this work;
only one lagged, and tried to hold the others:
Eurylochus it was, who blurted out:

140 'Where now, poor remnants? Is it devil's work   **140 remnants:** a small group of
survivors.

you long for? Will you go to Circe's hall?
Swine, wolves, and lions she will make us all,
beasts of her courtyard, bound by her enchantment.
Remember those the Cyclops held, remember
145 shipmates who made that visit with Odysseus!
The daring man! They died for his foolishness!'

When I heard this I had a mind to draw
the blade that swung against my side and chop him,
bowling his head upon the ground—kinsman
150 or no kinsman, close to me though he was.
But others came between, saying, to stop me,

'Prince, we can leave him, if you say the word;
let him stay here on guard. As for ourselves,
show us the way to Circe's magic hall.'

155 So all turned inland, leaving shore and ship,
and Eurylochus—he, too, came on behind,
fearing the rough edge of my tongue. Meanwhile
at Circe's hands the rest were gently bathed,
anointed with sweet oil, and dressed afresh
160 in tunics and new cloaks with fleecy linings.
We found them all at supper when we came.
But greeting their old friends once more, the crew
could not hold back their tears; and now again
the rooms rang with sobs. Then Circe, loveliest
165 of all immortals, came to counsel me:

'Son of Laertes and the gods of old,
Odysseus, master mariner and soldier,
enough of weeping fits. I know—I, too—
what you endured upon the inhuman sea,
170 what odds you met on land from hostile men.
Remain with me, and share my meat and wine;
restore behind your ribs those gallant hearts
that served you in the old days, when you sailed
from stony Ithaca. Now parched and spent,
175 your cruel wandering is all you think of,
never of joy, after so many blows.'

As we were men we could not help consenting.
So day by day we lingered, feasting long

140–146 Do you think Eurylochus is right in his harsh criticism of Odysseus? Why or why not?

174 parched and spent: thirsty and worn out.

on roasts and wine, until a year grew fat.
180 But when the passing months and wheeling seasons
brought the long summery days, the pause of summer,
my shipmates one day summoned me and said:

'Captain, shake off this trance, and think of home—
if home indeed awaits us,
                                                              if we shall ever see
185 your own well-timbered hall on Ithaca.'

They made me feel a pang, and I agreed.
That day, and all day long, from dawn to sundown,
we feasted on roast meat and ruddy wine,
and after sunset when the dusk came on
190 my men slept in the shadowy hall, but I
went through the dark to Circe's flawless bed
and took the goddess' knees in supplication,
urging, as she bent to hear:

                                                              'O Circe,
now you must keep your promise; it is time.
195 Help me make sail for home. Day after day
my longing quickens, and my company
give me no peace, but wear my heart away
pleading when you are not at hand to hear.'

The loveliest of goddesses replied:

200 'Son of Laertes and the gods of old,
Odysseus, master mariner and soldier,
you shall not stay here longer against your will;
but home you may not go
unless you take a strange way round and come
205 to the cold homes of Death and pale Persephone.
You shall hear prophecy from the rapt shade
of blind Tiresias of Thebes, forever
charged with reason even among the dead;
to him alone, of all the flitting ghosts,
210 Persephone has given a mind undarkened.'

At this I felt a weight like stone within me,
and, moaning, pressed my length against the bed,
with no desire to see the daylight more.''

180–185 Notice that Odysseus' men have to remind him of home.

185 well-timbered: well-constructed.

186 pang: a sharp feeling of emotional distress. What emotion do you think Odysseus is feeling?

192 supplication: humble request or prayer.

200–213 Circe tells Odysseus that he must go to the underworld, the land of the dead. The god of the underworld is Hades (hā′dēz), referred to here as Death; Persephone is his wife. One of the spirits—or "shades"—in the underworld is that of Tiresias, a blind prophet who has been allowed to keep his mental powers. He will give Odysseus instructions about returning home. What is Odysseus' reaction upon hearing all of this?

Thinking through the LITERATURE

Connect to the Literature

1. **What Do You Think?** What new impressions of Odysseus did you get from the episode with Circe?

Comprehension Check

- What happens to Eurylochus' men after they drink Circe's wine?
- How is Odysseus able to withstand Circe's magic?
- After a year of Circe's hospitality, who convinces Odysseus that it is time to depart?
- Where does Circe tell Odysseus he must go before he can return home?

Think Critically

2. In what ways is Circe a danger to Odysseus and his men? Is she more dangerous or less dangerous than the Cyclops? Support your opinion with evidence from the epic.

3. Eurylochus' **character** contrasts sharply with that of Odysseus in this episode. Analyze the aspects of Odysseus' character that are revealed through this contrast.

> **THINK ABOUT**
>
> - how each feels about Circe
> - what each wants to do after Circe has transformed the first group of men
> - how Eurylochus criticizes Odysseus
> - how Odysseus reacts to Eurylochus' criticism

4. What heroic qualities does Odysseus reveal in this episode?

5. **ACTIVE READING** **PREDICTING** Look back at your **READER'S NOTEBOOK.** Which, if any, of your **predictions** have been correct? Do you want to change any of the predictions you have made so far?

Extend Interpretations

6. **Connect to Life** A major **theme** in the literature of the ancient Greeks concerns the roles of fate (the nonhuman power that determines the outcome of events) and free will (the power that humans have to control the events) in human life. Which of Odysseus' actions determine the destiny of his men? When are Odysseus and his men at the mercy of geography, of acts of the gods, and of other things beyond their control? What can you conclude about Homer's view of the ability of human beings to control their own lives? How does his view compare with your own?

7. **Connect to Life** In what ways can romantic attraction become a trap? Give several examples.

Literary Analysis

EPITHETS AND EPIC SIMILES

Epithets and epic similes are two descriptive techniques commonly found in Homeric epics. An **epithet** is a descriptive phrase that presents a particular trait of a person or thing. It can be a quick aid to **characterization.** For example, Odysseus is called "raider of cities" in Book 9. Throughout the poem, dawn is frequently pictured "with fingertips of rose." This, too, is an epithet.

A **simile** is a comparison between two things that are actually unlike yet have something in common. An **epic simile,** also called a **Homeric simile,** is an elaborate comparison that continues for a number of lines. Epic similes contain words such as *like, as, so,* or *just as.* Two such similes, involving a shipwright and a blacksmith's shop, convey the blinding of Polyphemus in Book 9 (lines 293–295 and lines 299–303).

Paired Activity Working with a partner, go back through Book 10 and identify at least one epic simile. Then find several epithets that are used to describe Odysseus and Circe.

Choices & CHALLENGES

Writing Options

1. Tabloid News Story Describe Circe's capturing of Odysseus' men in a news story that might appear in a tabloid newspaper at the supermarket.

2. Epic Similes Compose an epic simile that conveys Circe's appeal for Odysseus and his men and the way she helps them. Then write another epic simile that conveys the threat she poses to them.

3. Descriptive Epithets Make up new epithets to describe several of the characters, including Circe and Odysseus.

Activities & Explorations

Oral Reading Imagine that you are Odysseus, describing your adventures to King Alcinous. Prepare an oral reading of this episode, keeping in mind your purpose, your audience, and the occasion for your tale. Practice reading with the appropriate tone of voice, pauses, and changes in pitch and volume. Make a recording of your reading and play it for your class.
~ **SPEAKING AND LISTENING**

Inquiry & Research

Ship Model Notice the references to ships in the parts of the *Odyssey* you have read. Consult encyclopedias, online databases, and other print or nonprint resources to find out about the kinds of ships used by the Greeks in Homeric times. (You might investigate the work of the navigator-adventurer Tim Severin.) Use your findings to make a model of Odysseus' ship.

 LaserLinks: Background for Reading
Art Gallery

Art Connection

Look again at the image on page 920. This painting, from the 5th-century B.C., portrays two of Odysseus' men transformed into swine. These creatures have pigs' heads and human bodies. Why do you think the artist represented the creatures as part swine and part man?

Vocabulary in Action

EXERCISE: WORD MEANING Answer the following questions.

1. Whom would you expect to act with **stealth**—a spy, a surgeon, or a firefighter?

2. If you're feeling **disconsolate,** are you happy, sad, or angry?

3. Is a **vile** deed a wicked deed, a brave deed, or an impractical deed?

4. Would a **beguiling** person disgust other people, attract other people, or bore other people?

5. Which is meant to be **enticing** to a fish—a hook, a worm, or a net?

6. Who is most likely to use a **snare** at work—a beautician, a doctor, or a dogcatcher?

7. Would you be most likely to **chide** someone for being cruel, for being mischievous, or for being heroic?

8. Does someone ready to **succumb** in a struggle say "Charge," "Take that," or "I give up"?

9. If you were **regaled** with a performance, would you applaud, yawn, or stomp out?

10. Would you expect someone known as a **contender** to compete, to surrender, or to cooperate?

Building Vocabulary
For an in-depth lesson on how to build your vocabulary, see page 572.

> **Read On**
> In his next adventures, Odysseus faces more challenges. As you read, evaluate his handling of each new situation.

BOOK

SEA PERILS AND DEFEAT

TWELVE

IN BOOK 11, *Odysseus and his men visit the underworld, where the shades, or*
spirits of the dead, reside. During Odysseus' visit there, the spirit of the prophet Tiresias
warns him that death and destruction will follow unless he and his crew act with restraint
and control. Tiresias then reveals what Odysseus must do on his return to Ithaca.
Odysseus also speaks with the spirit of his mother, who died of grief because Odysseus
was away for so long.

  Odysseus and his men then leave the underworld and return to Circe's island. While
his men sleep, Circe takes Odysseus aside to hear about the underworld and to offer advice.

"Then said the Lady Circe:

'So: all those trials are over.

                              Listen with care
to this, now, and a god will arm your mind.
Square in your ship's path are Sirens, crying

Guide for Reading

2–3 In Circe, Odysseus has found a
valuable ally. In the next hundred
lines, she describes in detail each
danger that he and his men will
meet on their way home.

5   beauty to bewitch men coasting by;
woe to the innocent who hears that sound!
He will not see his lady nor his children
in joy, crowding about him, home from sea;
the Sirens will sing his mind away

10   on their sweet meadow lolling. There are bones
of dead men rotting in a pile beside them
and flayed skins shrivel around the spot.

                            Steer wide;

keep well to seaward; plug your oarsmen's ears
with beeswax kneaded soft; none of the rest

15   should hear that song.

                        But if you wish to listen,
let the men tie you in the lugger, hand
and foot, back to the mast, lashed to the mast,
so you may hear those harpies' thrilling voices;
shout as you will, begging to be untied,

20   your crew must only twist more line around you
and keep their stroke up, till the singers fade.
What then? One of two courses you may take,
and you yourself must weigh them. I shall not
plan the whole action for you now, but only

25   tell you of both.

                     Ahead are beetling rocks
and dark blue glancing Amphitrite, surging,
roars around them. Prowling Rocks, or Drifters,
the gods in bliss have named them—named them well.
Not even birds can pass them by.

30   A second course
lies between headlands. One is a sharp mountain
piercing the sky, with stormcloud round the peak
dissolving never, not in the brightest summer,
to show heaven's azure there, nor in the fall.

35   No mortal man could scale it, nor so much
as land there, not with twenty hands and feet,
so sheer the cliffs are—as of polished stone.
Midway that height, a cavern full of mist
opens toward Erebus and evening. Skirting

40   this in the lugger, great Odysseus,
your master bowman, shooting from the deck,
would come short of the cavemouth with his shaft;

12 flayed: torn off; stripped.

14 kneaded (nē′dĭd): squeezed and pressed.

15–21 Circe suggests a way for Odysseus to hear the Sirens safely. Do you think he will follow her suggestion?

18 those harpies' thrilling voices: the delightful voices of those evil females.

25 beetling: jutting or over-hanging.

26 glancing Amphitrite (ăm′fĭ-trī′tē): sparkling seawater. (Amphitrite is the goddess of the sea and the wife of Poseidon. Here, Circe uses the name to refer to the sea itself.)

31 headlands: points of land jutting out into the sea; promontories.

34 heaven's azure (ăzh′ər): the blue sky.

39 Erebus (ĕr′ə-bəs): a land of darkness beneath the earth.

but that is the den of Scylla, where she yaps
abominably, a newborn whelp's cry,
45 though she is huge and monstrous. God or man,
no one could look on her in joy. Her legs—
and there are twelve—are like great tentacles,
unjointed, and upon her serpent necks
are borne six heads like nightmares of ferocity,
50 with triple serried rows of fangs and deep
gullets of black death. Half her length, she sways
her head in air, outside her horrid cleft,
hunting the sea around that promontory
for dolphins, dogfish, or what bigger game
55 thundering Amphitrite feeds in thousands.
And no ship's company can claim
to have passed her without loss and grief; she takes,
from every ship, one man for every gullet.

The opposite point seems more a tongue of land
60 you'd touch with a good bowshot, at the narrows.
A great wild fig, a shaggy mass of leaves,
grows on it, and Charybdis lurks below
to swallow down the dark sea tide. Three times
from dawn to dusk she spews it up
65 and sucks it down again three times, a whirling
maelstrom; if you come upon her then
the god who makes earth tremble could not save you.
No, hug the cliff of Scylla, take your ship
through on a racing stroke. Better to mourn
70 six men than lose them all, and the ship, too.'

So her advice ran; but I faced her, saying:

'Only instruct me, goddess, if you will,
how, if possible, can I pass Charybdis,
or fight off Scylla when she raids my crew?'

75 Swiftly that loveliest goddess answered me:

'Must you have battle in your heart forever?
The bloody toil of combat? Old contender,
will you not yield to the immortal gods?

43–55 Circe presents a very unpleasant image of Scylla. To get a better idea of what Odysseus and his crew will be up against, try using this detailed description to draw a picture of Scylla.

66 maelstrom (māl′strəm): a large, violent whirlpool.

68–70 What is Circe's advice for dealing with Charybdis?

72–85 Notice this exchange between Odysseus and Circe. What does Circe caution Odysseus against doing, and why?

WORDS TO KNOW

abominably (ə-bŏm′ə-nə-blē) *adv.* in a hateful way; horribly
lurk (lûrk) *v.* to lie hidden, ready to ambush

That nightmare cannot die, being eternal
80 evil itself—horror, and pain, and <u>chaos</u>;
there is no fighting her, no power can fight her,
all that avails is flight.

                   Lose headway there
along that rockface while you break out arms,
and she'll swoop over you, I fear, once more,
85 taking one man again for every gullet.
No, no, put all your backs into it, row on;
invoke Blind Force, that bore this <u>scourge</u> of men,
to keep her from a second strike against you.

Then you will coast Thrinacia, the island
90 where Helios' cattle graze, fine herds, and flocks
of goodly sheep. The herds and flocks are seven,
with fifty beasts in each.

               No lambs are dropped,
or calves, and these fat cattle never die.
Immortal, too, their cowherds are—their shepherds—
95 Phaethusa and Lampetia, sweetly braided
nymphs that divine Neaera bore
to the overlord of high noon, Helios.
These nymphs their gentle mother bred and placed
upon Thrinacia, the distant land,
100 in care of flocks and cattle for their father.

Now give those kine a wide berth, keep your thoughts
intent upon your course for home,
and hard seafaring brings you all to Ithaca.
But if you raid the beeves, I see destruction
105 for ship and crew.

                 Rough years then lie between
you and your homecoming, alone and old,
the one survivor, all companions lost.'"

82 all . . . flight: all you can do is flee.

87 invoke . . . men: pray to the goddess of blind force, who gave birth to Scylla.

89 coast: sail along the coast of.

95–96 Phaethusa (fā′ə-thoo′sə) . . . **Lampetia** (lăm-pē′shə) . . . **Neaera** (nē-ē′rə).

101–105 Circe warns Odysseus not to steal Helios' fine cattle (also called kine and beeves) because Helios will take revenge.

A T   D A W N , *Odysseus and his men continue their journey. Odysseus decides to tell the men only of Circe's warnings about the Sirens, whom they will soon encounter. He is fairly sure that they can survive this peril if he keeps their spirits up. Suddenly, the wind stops.*

932

          "The crew were on their feet
briskly, to furl the sail, and stow it; then,
110 each in place, they poised the smooth oar blades
and sent the white foam scudding by. I carved
a massive cake of beeswax into bits
and rolled them in my hands until they softened—
no long task, for a burning heat came down
115 from Helios, lord of high noon. Going forward
I carried wax along the line, and laid it
thick on their ears. They tied me up, then, plumb
amidships, back to the mast, lashed to the mast,
and took themselves again to rowing. Soon,
120 as we came smartly within hailing distance,
the two Sirens, noting our fast ship
off their point, made ready, and they sang.

117–118 plumb amidships: exactly in the center of the ship.

The lovely voices in ardor appealing over the water
made me crave to listen, and I tried to say
125 'Untie me!' to the crew, jerking my brows;
but they bent steady to the oars. Then Perimedes
got to his feet, he and Eurylochus,
and passed more line about, to hold me still.
So all rowed on, until the Sirens
130 dropped under the sea rim, and their singing
<u>dwindled</u> away.

               My faithful company
rested on their oars now, peeling off
the wax that I had laid thick on their ears;
then set me free.

               But scarcely had that island
135 faded in blue air than I saw smoke
and white water, with sound of waves in tumult—
a sound the men heard, and it terrified them.
Oars flew from their hands; the blades went knocking
wild alongside till the ship lost way,
140 with no oarblades to drive her through the water.

Well, I walked up and down from bow to stern,
trying to put heart into them, standing over
every oarsman, saying gently,

123 ardor: passion.

126 Perimedes (pĕr'ĭ-mē'dēz).

134–159 The men panic when they hear the thundering surf. How does Odysseus help them overcome their fear and thus regain control of the ship?

WORDS
TO   **dwindle** (dwĭn'dl) *v.* to become gradually less; diminish
KNOW

933

                           'Friends,
have we never been in danger before this?
145   More fearsome, is it now, than when the Cyclops
penned us in his cave? What power he had!
Did I not keep my nerve, and use my wits
to find a way out for us?

                              Now I say
by hook or crook this <u>peril</u> too shall be
150   something that we remember.

WORDS
TO   **peril** (pĕr′əl) *n.* danger; risk
KNOW

934

<blockquote>

　　　　　　　　Heads up, lads!
We must obey the orders as I give them.
Get the oarshafts in your hands, and lay back
hard on your benches; hit these breaking seas.
Zeus help us pull away before we founder.
You at the tiller, listen, and take in
all that I say—the rudders are your duty;
keep her out of the combers and the smoke;
steer for that headland; watch the drift, or we
fetch up in the smother, and you drown us.'

</blockquote>

155

154 founder: sink.

157 combers: breaking waves.

158–159 watch . . . smother: keep
the ship on course, or it will be
crushed in the rough water.

160 That was all, and it brought them round to action.
But as I sent them on toward Scylla, I
told them nothing, as they could do nothing.
They would have dropped their oars again, in panic,
to roll for cover under the decking. Circe's
165 bidding against arms had slipped my mind,
so I tied on my cuirass and took up
two heavy spears, then made my way along
to the foredeck—thinking to see her first from there,
the monster of the gray rock, harboring
170 torment for my friends. I strained my eyes
upon that cliffside veiled in cloud, but nowhere
could I catch sight of her.

And all this time,
in travail, sobbing, gaining on the current,
we rowed into the strait—Scylla to port
175 and on our starboard beam Charybdis, dire
gorge of the salt sea tide. By heaven! when she
vomited, all the sea was like a cauldron
seething over intense fire, when the mixture
suddenly heaves and rises.

The shot spume
180 soared to the landside heights, and fell like rain.

But when she swallowed the sea water down
we saw the funnel of the maelstrom, heard
the rock bellowing all around, and dark
sand raged on the bottom far below.
185 My men all blanched against the gloom, our eyes
were fixed upon that yawning mouth in fear
of being devoured.

Then Scylla made her strike,
whisking six of my best men from the ship.
I happened to glance aft at ship and oarsmen
190 and caught sight of their arms and legs, dangling
high overhead. Voices came down to me
in anguish, calling my name for the last time.

A man surfcasting on a point of rock
for bass or mackerel, whipping his long rod

161–168 Odysseus doesn't tell his men that several of them will be killed. Moreover, forgetting Circe's warning against trying to fight Scylla, he takes up his body armor (cuirass) and spears. What do you think will happen?

176 gorge: throat; gullet.

179 shot spume: flying foam.

185 blanched: became pale.

189 aft: toward the rear of the ship.

WORDS   **travail** (trə-vāl´) *n.* painful effort
TO   **dire** (dīr) *adj.* dreadful; terrible
KNOW   **anguish** (ăng´gwĭsh) *n.* great physical or mental suffering; agony

195 to drop the sinker and the bait far out,
will hook a fish and rip it from the surface
to dangle wriggling through the air:

so these

were borne aloft in spasms toward the cliff.

She ate them as they shrieked there, in her den,
200 in the dire grapple, reaching still for me—
and deathly pity ran me through
at that sight—far the worst I ever suffered,
<u>questing</u> the passes of the strange sea.

We rowed on.

The Rocks were now behind; Charybdis, too,
205 and Scylla dropped astern."

198 borne aloft in spasms: lifted high while struggling violently.

200 grapple: grasp.

ODYSSEUS TRIES TO PERSUADE *his men to bypass Thrinacia, the island of the sun god Helios, but they insist on landing. Driven by hunger, they ignore Odysseus' warning not to feast on Helios' cattle. This disobedience angers the sun god, who threatens to stop shining if payment is not made for the loss of his cattle. To appease Helios, Zeus sends down a thunderbolt to sink Odysseus' ship. Odysseus alone survives. He eventually drifts to Ogygia, the home of Calypso, who keeps him on her island for seven years. With this episode, Odysseus ends the telling of his tale to King Alcinous.*

WORDS TO KNOW   **questing** (kwĕs'tĭng) *adj.* journeying over; exploring   **quest** *v.*

SIREN SONG

MARGARET ATWOOD

This is the one song everyone
would like to learn: the song
that is irresistible:

the song that forces men
5   to leap overboard in squadrons[1]
even though they see the beached skulls

the song nobody knows
because anyone who has heard it
is dead, and the others can't remember.

10   Shall I tell you the secret
and if I do, will you get me
out of this bird suit?

I don't enjoy it here
squatting on this island
15   looking picturesque[2] and mythical

with these two feathery maniacs,
I don't enjoy singing
this trio, fatal and valuable.

I will tell the secret to you,
20   to you, only to you.
Come closer. This song

is a cry for help: Help me!
Only you, only you can,
you are unique

25   at last. Alas
it is a boring song
but it works every time.

---

1. **in squadrons** (skwŏd´rənz): in great numbers.
2. **picturesque** (pĭk´chə-rĕsk´): having a wild, natural beauty.

The Sirens (1990), Shlomo Katz, Courtesy of Strictly Limited Editions, San Francisco.

Thinking through the LITERATURE

Connect to the Literature

1. What Do You Think?
How would you rank Odysseus' adventures in this section as compared to his adventures with the Cyclops and Circe?

Comprehension Check
- At the beginning of this episode, where have Odysseus and his men been?
- How does Odysseus manage to hear the Sirens safely?
- What does Circe tell Odysseus to do about Scylla and Charybdis?
- How do Odysseus' men anger the sun god?

Think Critically

2. Odysseus chooses to tell his crew only part of what Circe reveals about the dangers ahead. Do you think this is a wise decision? Why or why not?

3. Do you think Odysseus has improved as a leader and a **hero** over the course of his adventures? Support your opinion.

THINK ABOUT
- the chart that you completed on page 914
- Tiresias' warning to Odysseus about acting with restraint and control
- Odysseus' power over Circe and his later obedience to her
- Odysseus' treatment of his crew

4. Of all the monsters and perils that Odysseus and his crew face during their wanderings, which do you think is the most terrifying? Why? Refer to the chart on monsters that you made before you began reading Book 9.

5. **ACTIVE READING** **PREDICTING** Look at the clues and predictions you jotted in your **READER'S NOTEBOOK.** Using text evidence and your own experience, discuss with a classmate how successful you think Odysseus' efforts to get home will be.

Extend Interpretations

6. Comparing Texts Consider the nature of the appeal the Siren makes in Atwood's poem on page 938. From what you know about Odysseus, how do you think he would respond?

7. Connect to Life Imagine Odysseus in our society today—as a guest in your home, for example. How would you treat him? What would you tell him about the dangers and the pleasures of our world? Suggest some jobs you think he might be suited for and a place you think he might want to live.

Literary Analysis

THEME Recall that a story's **theme** is an important idea that the story conveys to the reader. In his **epics,** Homer passed on lessons about life and human nature that were important to the Greeks of his time and that have remained important in our own time. A long **narrative** like the *Odyssey* usually has several themes.

Cooperative Learning Activity One of the *Odyssey*'s themes concerns what it means to be a hero—an idea you've already been discussing. Think about other meaningful ideas or lessons about life that you found in these episodes. For example, what do Odysseus' experiences tell you about pride, about power and self-control, about the importance of home and family, and about responsibility to others? Discuss these ideas with a small group of classmates. Then work with your group to write a statement explaining a theme that you've identified. If possible, use a quotation from the epic to support your choice of a theme. Share your statement with the rest of the class.

Choices & CHALLENGES

Writing Options

1. Encyclopedia Entries Write short informative articles about two of the creatures Odysseus and his crew encounter. Begin with a definition, and then provide additional information from the *Odyssey* and from your own imagination. Place your reports in your **Working Portfolio**.

2. Character Sketch Draft a description of Odysseus, based on the episodes you have read. Include details about his appearance, attitudes, and heroic acts.

Activities & Explorations

1. Follow the Leader? If you had been a member of Odysseus'

crew, would you have followed his leadership? With the class divided into opposing teams, debate Odysseus' worthiness as a leader. Cite examples of his decisions and actions in Books 9–12. If your team declares Odysseus unworthy, explain how you think he should have acted.
~ SPEAKING AND LISTENING

2. Board Game Create a game based on the travels and adventures of Odysseus. To get ideas, review each adventure and study the map on page 889. Read the rules of a familiar game to get tips on writing the rules for your game. Decide whether players' moves will be determined by choosing cards, spinning a wheel, or rolling dice.
~ VIEWING AND REPRESENTING

Inquiry & Research

Trail of a Wanderer Trace or redraw the map on page 889. Then, on the basis of the episodes you have read, draw lines on the map to represent Odysseus' wanderings from Troy to the imaginary land of the Phaeacians—where he tells of his adventures—and then home to Ithaca. (Leave out the voyage to Hades.) Estimate, in miles or kilometers, the distance he travels. Finally, consult an atlas or encyclopedia and label the places on your map with their modern names.

LaserLinks: Background for Reading
Art Gallery

Vocabulary in Action

EXERCISE A: WORD MEANING For each phrase in the first column, write the letter of the rhyming phrase in the second column that has a similar meaning.

1. **lurk** on the left
2. traveling in one's dreams
3. designed to **dwindle**
4. a terrifying blaze
5. mental **anguish**

   a. a **dire** fire
   b. made to fade
   c. **questing** while resting
   d. brain pain
   e. hide on one side

EXERCISE B Write the vocabulary word, not used in Exercise A, described by each sentence below.

1. People wear seat belts, hardhats, and safety goggles to protect themselves against this.
2. Odysseus goes through a lot of this on his homeward journey, and the truth is, it isn't easy.

3. An example of this might be the Black Death of the Middle Ages, Scylla in Odysseus' day, or war in any time or place.
4. How terrible is unbearable? It's how Scylla expresses herself and how the men she captures die.
5. When Scylla is yapping, Charybdis is spewing up the sea, and Odysseus' men are losing their oars, this word pretty accurately describes the scene.

Building Vocabulary
For an in-depth lesson on using a dictionary to explore word origins, see page 973.

> **Read On**
> The next adventures will see Odysseus home at last, but facing greater challenges than ever. As you read, evaluate how well he rises to these challenges.

WORDS TO KNOW				
abominably	chaos	dwindle	peril	scourge
anguish	dire	lurk	questing	travail

PREPARING to *Read*

from the **Odyssey** (continued)

Epic Poetry by HOMER

Translated by ROBERT FITZGERALD

"Now watch me hit a target that no man has hit before, if I can make this shot. Help me, Apollo."

(Connect to Your Life)

Is It Really You? The following excerpts from the *Odyssey* present the hero's homecoming: Odysseus returns to Ithaca and is reunited with his wife and son after an absence of nearly 20 years. If you had not seen a close relative–a grandparent, a parent, or a sibling–for a long time, how would you react when you were reunited with him or her? What thoughts, feelings, and problems do you think you might have? Imagine such a reunion and share with a partner the reactions you might have.

Build Background

My House Is Your House In ancient Greece, rules of hospitality governed the behavior of hosts and guests. The Greek social code required people to take strangers in and feed them without question. Remember that King Alcinous, a model king, hosted a banquet for Odysseus without knowing who he was, whereas the barbaric Cyclops not only refused to give Odysseus and his men food and drink but started to eat them instead. After allowing a stranger to stay as long as he wished, a host also had to give him a gift when he left. These obligations were enforced by Zeus, the king of the gods and also the god of hospitality.

Guests as well as hosts could violate the code of hospitality. In this part of the *Odyssey,* you'll meet the suitors who, believing that Odysseus is dead, want to marry his wife, Penelope, and take over his lands and fortune. Because Penelope still hopes for a reunion with her husband, she delays making a choice–but the suitors remain.

 LaserLinks: Background for Reading
Literary Connection
Storyteller

Focus Your Reading

LITERARY ANALYSIS **EPIC** A major feature of the **epic** is its scope. Epics are large. They tend to have long and involved plots, multiple conflicts, larger-than-life heroes, large-scale settings, and themes of universal significance. They have much to tell. Book 9 of the *Odyssey* begins:

> *"What shall I say first? What shall I keep until the end? The gods have tried me in a thousand ways."*

As you read the episodes of Odysseus' homecoming, think of some of the ways he has been tried and what he has learned. Decide what themes of universal significance you think this epic is intended to tell.

ACTIVE READING **IDENTIFYING CONFLICTS** Just as **conflict** is part of life and central in any narrative, it is basic to the epic. Epic plots center around the way various conflicts are faced, evaded, or resolved. To identify conflict as you read, ask yourself the following:

- What opposing persons or forces, external or internal, are in conflict?
- How would you describe the conflict?
- Is the conflict resolved? If so, how?
- What insights does the conflict reveal to you?

READER'S NOTEBOOK As you read the story of Odysseus' homecoming, jot down specific examples of conflict and the answer to questions about conflict raised above.

THE HOMECOMING
from
THE ODYSSEY
HOMER

Translated by Robert Fitzgerald

WITH THE HELP *of King Alcinous, Odysseus finally returns home to the shores of Ithaca, where he is met by the goddess Athena. She warns him that his palace is overrun by more than 100 suitors who, believing Odysseus is dead, want to marry Penelope and take over his fortune. Following her advice, Odysseus disguises himself as a beggar and visits the palace. There he sees that two suitors in particular, Antinous and Eurymachus, are rude and demanding. Odysseus has a tearful reunion with his son, Telemachus, and together they discuss how to avenge their family honor. In the meantime, Penelope—who knows nothing of this and has given up hope for Odysseus' return—proposes an archery contest to the suitors, with marriage to her as the prize. She enters the storeroom and takes down the heavy bow that Odysseus left behind.*

BOOK

THE TEST OF THE BOW

TWENTY-ONE

Now Penelope
sank down, holding the weapon on her knees,
and drew her husband's great bow out, and sobbed
and bit her lip and let the salt tears flow.
5 Then back she went to face the crowded hall,
tremendous bow in hand, and on her shoulder hung
the quiver spiked with coughing death. Behind her
maids bore a basket full of axeheads, bronze
and iron implements for the master's game.
10 Thus in her beauty she approached the suitors,
and near a pillar of the solid roof
she paused, her shining veil across her cheeks,
her maids on either hand and still,
then spoke to the banqueters:

"My lords, hear me:
15 suitors indeed, you <u>commandeered</u> this house
to feast and drink in, day and night, my husband
being long gone, long out of mind. You found
no <u>justification</u> for yourselves—none
except your lust to marry me. Stand up, then:

Guide for Reading

1–4 Notice that Penelope still grieves for Odysseus, even after 20 years.

7 quiver (kwĭv′ər): a case in which arrows are carried. What do you think is meant by "the quiver spiked with coughing death"?

8–9 axeheads . . . game: metal heads of axes (without handles) that Odysseus used to employ in a display of archery skill.

WORDS
TO
KNOW

commandeer (kŏm′ən-dîr′) v. to take control of by force
justification (jŭs′tə-fĭ-kā′shən) n. an explanation or excuse for an action

944

20 we now declare a contest for that prize.
Here is my lord Odysseus' hunting bow.
Bend and string it if you can. Who sends an arrow
through iron axe-helve sockets, twelve in line?
I join my life with his, and leave this place, my home,
25 my rich and beautiful bridal house, forever
to be remembered, though I dream it only."

Then to Eumaeus:

"Carry the bow forward.
Carry the blades."

Tears came to the swineherd's eyes
as he reached out for the big bow. He laid it
30 down at the suitors' feet. Across the room
the cowherd sobbed, knowing the master's weapon.
Antinous growled, with a glance at both:

"Clods.

They go to pieces over nothing.

You two, there,
why are you sniveling? To upset the woman
35 even more? Has she not pain enough
over her lost husband? *Sit down*.
Get on with dinner quietly, or cry about it
outside, if you must. Leave us the bow.
A clean-cut game, it looks to me.
40 Nobody bends that bowstave easily
in this company. Is there a man here
made like Odysseus? I remember him
from childhood: I can see him even now."

That was the way he played it, hoping inwardly
45 to span the great horn bow with corded gut
and drill the iron with his shot—he, Antinous,
destined to be the first of all to savor
blood from a biting arrow at his throat,
a shaft drawn by the fingers of Odysseus
50 whom he had mocked and <u>plundered</u>, leading on
the rest, his boon companions.

946

Despite heating and greasing the bow, the lesser suitors prove unable to string it. The most able suitors, Antinous and Eurymachus, hold off. While the suitors are busy with the bow, Odysseus—still disguised as an old beggar—goes to enlist the aid of two of his trusted servants, Eumaeus the swineherd and Philoetius the cowherd.

Two men had meanwhile left the hall:
swineherd and cowherd, in companionship,
one downcast as the other. But Odysseus
55 followed them outdoors, outside the court,
and coming up said gently:

      "You, herdsman,
and you, too, swineherd, I could say a thing to you,
or should I keep it dark?

        No, no; speak,
my heart tells me. Would you be men enough
60 to stand by Odysseus if he came back?
Suppose he dropped out of a clear sky, as I did?
Suppose some god should bring him?
Would you bear arms for him, or for the suitors?"

The cowherd said:

      "Ah, let the master come!
65 Father Zeus, grant our old wish! Some courier
guide him back! Then judge what stuff is in me
and how I manage arms!"

      Likewise Eumaeus
fell to praying all heaven for his return,
so that Odysseus, sure at least of these,
70 told them:

     "I am at home, for I am he.
I bore adversities, but in the twentieth year
I am ashore in my own land. I find
the two of you, alone among my people,
longed for my coming. Prayers I never heard
75 except your own that I might come again.
So now what is in store for you I'll tell you:

72–75 What is the quality that Odysseus values so highly in these two servants?

If Zeus brings down the suitors by my hand
I promise marriages to both, and cattle,
and houses built near mine. And you shall be
80 brothers-in-arms of my Telemachus.
Here, let me show you something else, a sign
that I am he, that you can trust me, look:
this old scar from the tusk wound that I got
boar hunting on Parnassus—
85 Autolycus' sons and I."

84 Parnassus (pär-năs'əs): a
mountain in central Greece.

85 Autolycus' (ô-tŏl'ĭ-kəs) **sons**:
Odysseus' uncles. (Autolycus was
Odysseus' grandfather on his
mother's side.)

Shifting his rags
he bared the long gash. Both men looked, and knew,
and threw their arms around the old soldier, weeping,
kissing his head and shoulders. He as well
took each man's head and hands to kiss, then said—
90 to cut it short, else they might weep till dark—

"Break off, no more of this.
Anyone at the door could see and tell them.
Drift back in, but separately at intervals
after me.
Now listen to your orders:
95 when the time comes, those gentlemen, to a man,
will be dead against giving me bow or quiver.
Defy them. Eumaeus, bring the bow
and put it in my hands there at the door.
Tell the women to lock their own door tight.
100 Tell them if someone hears the shock of arms
or groans of men, in hall or court, not one
must show her face, but keep still at her weaving.
Philoetius, run to the outer gate and lock it.
Throw the cross bar and lash it."

He turned back
105 into the courtyard and the beautiful house
and took the stool he had before. They followed
one by one, the two hands loyal to him.

Eurymachus had now picked up the bow.
He turned it round, and turned it round
110 before the licking flame to warm it up,
but could not, even so, put stress upon it

*94–104 Odysseus has a plan but
reveals to the servants only the
details they must take care of.* On
the basis of the orders he gives,
what do you think Odysseus is
planning?

to jam the loop over the tip
              though his heart groaned to bursting.
Then he said grimly:

                      "Curse this day.
What gloom I feel, not for myself alone,
115 and not only because we lose that bride.
Women are not lacking in Achaea,
in other towns, or on Ithaca. No, the worst
is humiliation—to be shown up for children
measured against Odysseus—we who cannot
120 even hitch the string over his bow.
What shame to be repeated of us, after us!"

113–121 Since most of the suitors have already tried the challenge and failed, Eurymachus here speaks for all of them when he expresses his shame and embarrassment. Is the suitors' concern about their reputation for physical strength similar to attitudes men have today?

116 Achaea (ə-kē′ə): the Greek mainland.

Then spoke Odysseus, all craft and <u>gall</u>:

"My lords, contenders for the queen, permit me:
a passion in me moves me to speak out.
125 I put it to Eurymachus above all
and to that brilliant prince, Antinous. . . .
But let me try my hand at the smooth bow!
Let me test my fingers and my pull
to see if any of the oldtime kick is there,
130 or if thin fare and roving took it out of me."

Now irritation beyond reason swept them all,
since they were nagged by fear that he could string it.
Antinous answered, coldly and at length:

"You bleary vagabond, no rag of sense is left you.
135 Are you not coddled here enough, at table
taking meat with gentlemen, your betters,
denied nothing, and listening to our talk?
When have we let a tramp hear all our talk?
The sweet goad of wine has made you rave!"

🔲 🔲 🔲

140 At this the watchful queen Penelope
interposed:

"Antinous, discourtesy
to a guest of Telemachus—whatever guest—
that is not handsome. What are you afraid of?
Suppose this exile put his back into it
145 and drew the great bow of Odysseus—
could he then take me home to be his bride?
You know he does not imagine that! No one
need let that prospect weigh upon his dinner!
How very, very improbable it seems."

122–130 Remember that Odysseus is disguised as an old beggar. Think about the effect of an old beggar's request to try the challenge just after the finest princes in the land have failed so miserably.

130 thin fare and roving: poor food and hard travel.

134–139 How does Antinous react to the beggar's request?

140–149 The epithet "watchful queen" characterizes Penelope as patient and observant. Here she scolds the suitors for their lack of courtesy and hospitality—values they consistently ignore—and urges them to give the stranger a chance.

AT TELEMACHUS' REQUEST, *Penelope leaves the men to settle the question of the bow among themselves.*

WORDS
TO   **gall** (gôl) *n.* scornful boldness
KNOW

951

150 The swineherd had the horned bow in his hands
moving toward Odysseus, when the crowd
in the banquet hall broke into an ugly din,
shouts rising from the flushed young men:

                                    "Ho! Where
do you think you are taking that, you smutty slave?"

153–157 How would you describe the way the suitors treat the old swineherd?

155 "What is this dithering?"

                          "We'll toss you back alone
among the pigs, for your own dogs to eat,
if bright Apollo nods and the gods are kind!"

He faltered, all at once put down the bow, and stood
in panic, buffeted by waves of cries,
160 hearing Telemachus from another quarter
shout:

"Go on, take him the bow!

                          Do you obey this pack?
You will be stoned back to your hills! Young as I am
my power is over you! I wish to God
165 I had as much the upper hand of these!
There would be suitors pitched like dead rats
through our gate, for the evil plotted here!"

162–172 As Penelope did earlier, Telemachus stands up to the suitors. He wishes that he had as much power over them as he has, despite his youth, over the servant Eumaeus. The suitors just laugh at Telemachus, but as they do, Eumaeus is able to deliver the bow safely to Odysseus.

Telemachus' frenzy struck someone as funny,
and soon the whole room roared with laughter at him,
170 so that all tension passed. Eumaeus picked up
bow and quiver, making for the door,
and there he placed them in Odysseus' hands.
Calling Eurycleia to his side he said:

                                    "Telemachus
trusts you to take care of the women's doorway.
175 Lock it tight. If anyone inside
should hear the shock of arms or groans of men
in hall or court, not one must show her face,
but go on with her weaving."

173–178 Eumaeus orders Eurycleia to lock the women's room. Why does he say that the orders came from Telemachus rather than from Odysseus?

                                    The old woman
nodded and kept still. She disappeared

WORDS
TO
KNOW
dithering (dĭth′ər-ĭng) *n.* acting in a nervous or uncertain way **dither** *v.*
frenzy (frĕn′zē) *n.* a wildly excited state of mind

952

180　into the women's hall, bolting the door behind her.
　　Philoetius left the house now at one bound,
　　catlike, running to bolt the courtyard gate.
　　A coil of deck-rope of papyrus fiber
　　lay in the gateway; this he used for lashing,
185　and ran back to the same stool as before,
　　fastening his eyes upon Odysseus.

　　　　　　　　　　And Odysseus took his time,
　　turning the bow, tapping it, every inch,
　　for borings that termites might have made
　　while the master of the weapon was abroad.
190　The suitors were now watching him, and some
　　jested among themselves:

　　　　　　　　　　　　　"A bow lover!"

"Dealer in old bows!"

　　　　　　　　　　"Maybe he has one like it
at home!"

　　　　　　　"Or has an itch to make one for himself."

"See how he handles it, the sly old buzzard!"

195　And one disdainful suitor added this:

"May his fortune grow an inch for every inch he bends it!"

　　But the man skilled in all ways of contending,
　　satisfied by the great bow's look and heft,
　　like a musician, like a harper, when
200　with quiet hand upon his instrument
　　he draws between his thumb and forefinger
　　a sweet new string upon a peg: so effortlessly
　　Odysseus in one motion strung the bow.
　　Then slid his right hand down the cord and plucked it,
205　so the taut gut vibrating hummed and sang
　　a swallow's note.
　　　　　　　　　　In the hushed hall it smote the suitors
　　and all their faces changed. Then Zeus thundered
　　overhead, one loud crack for a sign.
　　And Odysseus laughed within him that the son

198 heft: weight.

199–203 In this epic simile Odysseus' stringing of the bow is compared to the stringing of a harp. What qualities of Odysseus does this comparison emphasize?

206 smote: struck; affected sharply.

207–208 The thunder, a sign from Zeus, indicates that the gods are on Odysseus' side.

210 of crooked-minded Cronus had flung that <u>omen</u> down.
He picked one ready arrow from his table
where it lay bare: the rest were waiting still
in the quiver for the young men's turn to come.
He nocked it, let it rest across the handgrip,
215 and drew the string and grooved butt of the arrow,
aiming from where he sat upon the stool.

                             Now flashed
arrow from twanging bow clean as a whistle
through every socket ring, and grazed not one,
to thud with heavy brazen head beyond.

                            Then quietly
220 Odysseus said:

                    "Telemachus, the stranger
you welcomed in your hall has not disgraced you.
I did not miss, neither did I take all day
stringing the bow. My hand and eye are sound,
not so <u>contemptible</u> as the young men say.
225 The hour has come to cook their lordships' mutton—
supper by daylight. Other amusements later,
with song and harping that adorn a feast."

He dropped his eyes and nodded, and the prince
Telemachus, true son of King Odysseus,
230 belted his sword on, clapped hand to his spear,
and with a clink and glitter of keen bronze
stood by his chair, in the forefront near his father.

210 Cronus (krō′nəs): Zeus' father.

214 nocked it: placed the arrow's feathered end against the bow-string.

219 brazen: made of brass.

228–232 Book 21 ends with the image of father and son standing side by side facing more than 100 enemies.

WORDS
TO
KNOW
omen (ō′mən) *n.* an event thought to foretell good or evil; sign
contemptible (kən-tĕmp′tə-bəl) *adj.* deserving of scorn or disdain; worthless

BOOK

DEATH IN THE GREAT HALL

TWENTY-TWO

Now shrugging off his rags the <u>wiliest</u> fighter of the islands
leapt and stood on the broad door sill, his own bow in his
   hand.
235 He poured out at his feet a rain of arrows from the quiver
and spoke to the crowd:

         "So much for that. Your clean-cut game is over.
Now watch me hit a target that no man has hit before,
if I can make this shot. Help me, Apollo."

He drew to his fist the cruel head of an arrow for Antinous
240 just as the young man leaned to lift his beautiful drinking
   cup,
embossed, two-handled, golden: the cup was in his fingers:
the wine was even at his lips: and did he dream of death?
How could he? In that <u>revelry</u> amid his <u>throng</u> of friends
who would imagine a single foe—though a strong foe
   indeed—
245 could dare to bring death's pain on him and darkness on
   his eyes?
Odysseus' arrow hit him under the chin
and punched up to the feathers through his throat.

233 The epithet "wiliest fighter of
the islands" emphasizes Odysseus'
cleverness and skill at this important point in the story.

238 The god Apollo was, among
other things, the supporter and
protector of archers. The bow was
his sacred weapon.

239–252 Why does Odysseus kill
Antinous first? Why does he do it
in such a sudden, terrible way?

WORDS	**wiliest** (wī′lē-ĭst) *adj.* most crafty or sly; trickiest
TO	**revelry** (rĕv′əl-rē) *n.* noisy merrymaking; festivity
KNOW	**throng** (thrông) *n.* a large gathering; crowd

Backward and down he went, letting the winecup fall
from his shocked hand. Like pipes his nostrils jetted
250 crimson runnels, a river of mortal red,
and one last kick upset his table
knocking the bread and meat to soak in dusty blood.

Now as they craned to see their champion where he lay
the suitors jostled in uproar down the hall,
255 everyone on his feet. Wildly they turned and scanned
the walls in the long room for arms; but not a shield,
not a good ashen spear was there for a man to take and
      throw.
All they could do was yell in outrage at Odysseus:

"Foul! to shoot at a man! That was your last shot!"

260 "Your own throat will be slit for this!"

                              "Our finest lad is down!
You killed the best on Ithaca."

250 runnels: streams.

255–257 Earlier, in preparation for this confrontation, Odysseus and Telemachus removed all the weapons and shields that were hanging on the walls.

"Buzzards will tear your eyes out!"

For they imagined as they wished—that it was a wild
    shot,
an unintended killing—fools, not to comprehend
they were already in the grip of death.

265   But glaring under his brows Odysseus answered:

"You yellow dogs, you thought I'd never make it
home from the land of Troy. You took my house to plunder,
twisted my maids to serve your beds. You dared
bid for my wife while I was still alive.

270   Contempt was all you had for the gods who rule wide
    heaven,
contempt for what men say of you hereafter.
Your last hour has come. You die in blood."

As they all took this in, sickly green fear
pulled at their entrails, and their eyes flickered

275   looking for some hatch or hideaway from death.

266–272 At last Odysseus reveals his true identity and announces that he plans to kill all the suitors. What reasons does he give for killing them?

274 entrails: internal organs.

Eurymachus alone could speak. He said:

"If you are Odysseus of Ithaca come back,
all that you say these men have done is true.
Rash actions, many here, more in the countryside.
280 But here he lies, the man who caused them all.
Antinoüs was the ringleader; he whipped us on
to do these things. He cared less for a marriage
than for the power Cronion has denied him
as king of Ithaca. For that
285 he tried to trap your son and would have killed him.
He is dead now and has his portion. Spare
your own people. As for ourselves, we'll make
restitution of wine and meat consumed,
and add, each one, a tithe of twenty oxen
290 with gifts of bronze and gold to warm your heart.
Meanwhile we cannot blame you for your anger."

Odysseus glowered under his black brows
and said:

                    "Not for the whole treasure of your fathers,
all you enjoy, lands, flocks, or any gold
295 put up by others, would I hold my hand.
There will be killing till the score is paid.
You forced yourselves upon this house. Fight your way
    out,
or run for it, if you think you'll escape death.
I doubt one man of you skins by."

300 They felt their knees fail, and their hearts—but heard
Eurymachus for the last time rallying them.

"Friends," he said, "the man is implacable.
Now that he's got his hands on bow and quiver
he'll shoot from the big door stone there
305 until he kills us to the last man.
                                   Fight, I say,
let's remember the joy of it. Swords out!
Hold up your tables to deflect his arrows.
After me, everyone: rush him where he stands.
If we can budge him from the door, if we can pass

276–291 What is Eurymachus'
strategy here? How does he hope
to save himself and the remaining
suitors?

279 rash: foolish; thoughtless.

283 Cronion (krō′nē-ŏn′): Zeus, the
son of Cronus.

289 tithe: payment.

293–299 Why do you think
Odysseus rejects Eurymachus'
explanation and offer of
restitution?

299 skins by: sneaks away.

WORDS
TO
KNOW

restitution (rĕs′tĭ-tōō′shən) n. a making good for loss or damage; repayment
implacable (ĭm-plăk′ə-bəl) adj. impossible to soothe; unforgiving

958

310 into the town, we'll call out men to chase him.
This fellow with his bow will shoot no more."

He drew his own sword as he spoke, a broadsword of fine
     bronze,
honed like a razor on either edge. Then crying hoarse and
     loud
he hurled himself at Odysseus. But the kingly man let fly
315 an arrow at that instant, and the quivering feathered butt
sprang to the nipple of his breast as the barb stuck in his
     liver.
The bright broadsword clanged down. He lurched and fell
     aside,
pitching across his table. His cup, his bread and meat,
were spilt and scattered far and wide, and his head
     slammed on the ground.
320 Revulsion, anguish in his heart, with both feet kicking out,
he downed his chair, while the shrouding wave of mist
     closed on his eyes.

Amphinomus now came running at Odysseus,
broadsword naked in his hand. He thought to make
the great soldier give way at the door.
325 But with a spear throw from behind Telemachus hit him
between the shoulders, and the lancehead drove
clear through his chest. He left his feet and fell
forward, thudding, forehead against the ground.
Telemachus swerved around him, leaving the long dark spear
330 planted in Amphinomus. If he paused to yank it out
someone might jump him from behind or cut him down
     with a sword
at the moment he bent over. So he ran—ran from the tables
to his father's side and halted, panting, saying:

"Father let me bring you a shield and spear,
335 a pair of spears, a helmet.
I can arm on the run myself; I'll give
outfits to Eumaeus and this cowherd.
Better to have equipment."

                              Said Odysseus:

"Run then, while I hold them off with arrows

320 **revulsion** (rĭ-vŭl′shən): a sudden feeling of disgust.

320–321 Eurymachus' death is physically painful, but he also has "revulsion, anguish in his heart." What do you think causes this emotional pain?

322 **Amphinomus** (ăm-fĭn′ə-məs): one of the suitors.

325–332 Telemachus proves to be a valuable help to his father.

340 as long as the arrows last. When all are gone
if I'm alone they can dislodge me."

Quick

upon his father's word Telemachus
ran to the room where spears and armor lay.
He caught up four light shields, four pairs of spears,
345 four helms of war high-plumed with flowing manes,
and ran back, loaded down, to his father's side.
He was the first to pull a helmet on
and slide his bare arm in a buckler strap.
The servants armed themselves, and all three took their
    stand
350 beside the master of battle.

While he had arrows

he aimed and shot, and every shot brought down
one of his huddling enemies.
But when all barbs had flown from the bowman's fist,
he leaned his bow in the bright entry way
355 beside the door, and armed: a four-ply shield
hard on his shoulder, and a crested helm,
horsetailed, nodding stormy upon his head,
then took his tough and bronze-shod spears.

345 helms: helmets.

353–358 Notice this depiction of Odysseus as a warrior. Try drawing a sketch of him armed for battle to get the full impact.

T H E S U I T O R S M A K E V A R I O U S *unsuccessful attempts to expel Odysseus from his post at the door. Athena urges Odysseus on to battle, yet holds back her fullest aid, waiting for Odysseus and Telemachus to prove themselves. Six of the suitors attempt an attack on Odysseus, but Athena deflects their arrows. Odysseus and his men seize this opportunity to launch their own attack, and the suitors begin to fall. At last Athena's presence becomes known to all, as the shape of her shield becomes visible above the hall. The suitors, recognizing the intervention of the gods on Odysseus' behalf, are frantic to escape but to no avail. Odysseus and his men are compared to falcons who show no mercy to the flocks of birds they pursue and capture. Soon the room is reeking with blood. Thus the battle with the suitors comes to an end, and Odysseus prepares himself to meet Penelope.*

BOOK

THE TRUNK OF THE OLIVE TREE

TWENTY-THREE

Greathearted Odysseus, home at last,
360 was being bathed now by Eurynome
and rubbed with golden oil, and clothed again
in a fresh tunic and a cloak. Athena
lent him beauty, head to foot. She made him
taller, and massive, too, with crisping hair
365 in curls like petals of wild hyacinth
but all red-golden. Think of gold infused
on silver by a craftsman, whose fine art
Hephaestus taught him, or Athena: one
whose work moves to delight: just so she lavished
370 beauty over Odysseus' head and shoulders.
He sat then in the same chair by the pillar,
facing his silent wife, and said:

                                "Strange woman,
the immortals of Olympus made you hard,
harder than any. Who else in the world
375 would keep <u>aloof</u> as you do from her husband
if he returned to her from years of trouble,
cast on his own land in the twentieth year?

360 Eurynome (yo͝o-rĭn′ə-mē): a
female servant.

368 Hephaestus (hĭ-fĕs′təs): the
god of metalworking.

369 lavished: showered.

373 immortals of Olympus: the
gods, who live on Mount Olympus.

WORDS
TO
KNOW

aloof (ə-lo͞of′) *adj.* distant; remote; standoffish

961

Nurse, make up a bed for me to sleep on.
Her heart is iron in her breast."

                                Penelope

380   spoke to Odysseus now. She said:

                          "Strange man,
if man you are . . . This is no pride on my part
nor scorn for you—not even wonder, merely.
I know so well how you—how he—appeared
boarding the ship for Troy. But all the same . . .

385   Make up his bed for him, Eurycleia.
Place it outside the bedchamber my lord
built with his own hands. Pile the big bed
with fleeces, rugs, and sheets of purest linen."

With this she tried him to the breaking point,
390   and he turned on her in a flash raging:

"Woman, by heaven you've stung me now!
Who dared to move my bed?
No builder had the skill for that—unless
a god came down to turn the trick. No mortal
395   in his best days could budge it with a crowbar.
There is our pact and pledge, our secret sign,
built into that bed—my handiwork
and no one else's!

                       An old trunk of olive
grew like a pillar on the building plot,
400   and I laid out our bedroom round that tree,
lined up the stone walls, built the walls and roof,
gave it a doorway and smooth-fitting doors.
Then I lopped off the silvery leaves and branches,
hewed and shaped that stump from the roots up
405   into a bedpost, drilled it, let it serve
as model for the rest. I planed them all,
inlaid them all with silver, gold and ivory,
and stretched a bed between—a pliant web
of oxhide thongs dyed crimson.
                         There's our sign!
410   I know no more. Could someone else's hand
have sawn that trunk and dragged the frame away?"

380–384 Think about why Penelope might hold herself aloof from a man who claims to be the husband she hasn't seen in 20 years and who has just killed more than 100 men in her banquet hall. Note the doubt she expresses in "if man you are."

385–411 The bed symbolizes the lasting love between Odysseus and Penelope, and the way it was built is a secret only they know. Because one of the bedposts is the trunk of an olive tree still rooted in the ground, the bed is unmovable. Why do you think Penelope asks the servant to move a bed that she knows cannot be moved?

408–409 a pliant web . . . crimson: a network of ox-hide straps, dyed red, stretched between the sides of the bed to form a springy base for the bedding.

Their secret! as she heard it told, her knees
grew tremulous and weak, her heart failed her.
With eyes brimming tears she ran to him,
415 throwing her arms around his neck and kissed him,
murmuring:

                              "Do not rage at me, Odysseus!
No one ever matched your caution! Think
what difficulty the gods gave: they denied us
life together in our prime and flowering years,
420 kept us from crossing into age together.
Forgive me, don't be angry. I could not
welcome you with love on sight! I armed myself
long ago against the frauds of men,
impostors who might come—and all those many
425 whose underhanded ways bring evil on!
Helen of Argos, daughter of Zeus and Leda,
would she have joined the stranger, lain with him,
if she had known her destiny? known the Achaeans
in arms would bring her back to her own country?
430 Surely a goddess moved her to adultery,
her blood unchilled by war and evil coming,
the years, the desolation; ours, too.
But here and now, what sign could be so clear
as this of our own bed?
435 No other man has ever laid eyes on it—
only my own slave, Actoris, that my father
sent with me as a gift—she kept our door.
You make my stiff heart know that I am yours."

Now from his breast into his eyes the ache
440 of longing mounted, and he wept at last,
his dear wife, clear and faithful, in his arms,
longed for
        as the sunwarmed earth is longed for by a swimmer
spent in rough water where his ship went down
under Poseidon's blows, gale winds and tons of sea.
445 Few men can keep alive through a big surf
to crawl, clotted with brine, on kindly beaches
in joy, in joy, knowing the abyss behind:
and so she too rejoiced, her gaze upon her husband,
her white arms round him pressed as though forever.

413 tremulous: trembling; quivering.

421–425 Like Odysseus, Penelope proves to be an able trickster. Her explanation here gives insight into the troubles that she's had to endure during Odysseus' long absence.

426 Argos (är′gŏs) . . . **Leda** (lē′də).

426–432 Penelope contrasts her faithfulness with Helen's adultery, which caused the Trojan War and therefore the long separation between Penelope and Odysseus.

436 Actoris (ăk-tôr′ĭs).

442–449 In this epic simile, Odysseus is compared to a person who has suffered a shipwreck, swum through rough seas, and finally crawled ashore, covered with sea salt ("clotted with brine") but rejoicing to have survived the ordeal.

WORDS
TO
KNOW   **desolation** (dĕs′ə-lā′shən) *n.* lonely grief; misery

Thinking through the LITERATURE

Connect to the Literature

1. **What Do You Think?**
What was your reaction to the reunion of Odysseus and Penelope? Jot down your impressions and share them in class.

Comprehension Check
- What does Penelope arrange for the suitors who want to marry her?
- Why isn't Odysseus recognized when he first arrives?
- Who helps Odysseus fight the suitors?
- Why does Penelope test Odysseus?

Think Critically

2. **ACTIVE READING** **IDENTIFYING CONFLICT** Of the conflicts you noted in your **READER'S NOTEBOOK**, which seems the most significant for Odysseus? With a classmate, discuss your reaction to how it was resolved.

3. Whose pain and suffering do you think has been greater—Odysseus' or Penelope's? Defend your choice.

   THINK ABOUT
   - the obstacles that Odysseus has faced during his 20-year absence
   - the uncertainty that Penelope has lived with, as expressed in lines 416–425

4. Do you think Odysseus is right to kill all the suitors? Why or why not?

5. Why do you think Penelope devises the contest with the bow? What does this contest reveal about her **character**?

6. Do Odysseus' actions in these excerpts seem consistent with what you have come to expect of him as an **epic hero**? Explain your opinion.

Extend Interpretations

7. **Critic's Corner** One critic says that although Odysseus loves Penelope, his motivation is not romantic. Rather, "she is part of his home and hearth. . . . It is his father and his land that give Odysseus status and substance . . . and these are his overt reasons for wanting to return home." Do you agree or disagree? State your reasons.

8. **Connect to Life** Assume that Odysseus represents the ancient Greeks' ideal of a man and that Penelope represents their ideal of a woman. In what ways are the characters similar to and different from the ideal man and woman of today?

Literary Analysis

EPIC There is nothing small about an **epic**. Instead, it is known for the scope and magnitude of its plot, character, setting, and theme. **Epic heroes** are "larger than life" and usually of noble birth and legendary importance, with superhuman strength and boundless courage. **Epic plots** have large spans, complicated by supernatural beings or events, and may involve long and dangerous journeys through foreign lands. **Epic settings** can be huge in scale, usually involving more than one nation. **Epic themes** reflect time-less concerns such as courage and honor, good and evil, life and death.

Cooperative Learning Activity In a discussion with classmates, speculate about why the *Odyssey* is still considered a classic more than 2,500 years after it was written. Examine such aspects of the work as **character, suspense, description,** and **theme**. Present your group's analysis of the epic's appeal to the rest of the class.

Choices & CHALLENGES

Writing Options

1. Plot Outline Think of a modern-day equivalent of the suitors—a serious one, such as a group of terrorists or a street gang, or a humorous one, such as a carload of unwelcome relatives. Then, working alone or with a partner, create a plot outline for a story of epic proportions, relating how you, as an epic hero or heroine, get rid of the intruders.

2. Press Conference Now that he is home and the dust has settled, Odysseus must face reporters who want him to tell about his adventures and defend his actions. Write the questions and answers that you think would be heard at such a press conference.

Activities & Explorations

Translation Report The *Odyssey* has been translated, both in verse and in prose, by many writers throughout the ages. To appreciate how much a translation reflects the translator's personal style, compare the following words of Penelope in Fitzgerald's translation (lines 416-420) and in two other modern translations. Explain which one you like best in an oral report to the class.

> *"Do not rage at me, Odysseus! / No one ever matched your caution! Think / what difficulty the gods gave: they denied us / life together in our prime and flowering years, / kept us from crossing into age together."*
> —Robert Fitzgerald

> *"Do not be angry with me, Odysseus, since, beyond other men, / you have the most understanding. The gods granted us misery, / in jealousy over the thought that we two, always together, / should enjoy our youth, and then come to the threshold of old age."*
> —Richmond Lattimore

> *"Do not scowl at me, Odysseus, since in everything else / You have been the wisest of men. The gods have given us woe / Who begrudged it to us that, staying with one another, / We should enjoy our vigor and reach the threshold of age."*
> —Albert Cook

~ **SPEAKING AND LISTENING**

Inquiry & Research

In many ways a classic is timeless, but every new generation of readers may see it in a fresh light. From your own standpoint, what do you think makes for a good translation of a classical work?

 Real World Link Read the book review on page 968 to help you form your opinion.

Vocabulary in Action

EXERCISE: ASSESSMENT PRACTICE For each numbered word, write the letter of the best synonym.

1. **wiliest**	9. **implacable**	a. seize	i. sneakiest
2. **frenzy**	10. **revelry**	b. disgusting	j. unsociable
3. **commandeer**	11. **throng**	c. nerve	k. repayment
4. **aloof**	12. **gall**	d. raid	l. bumbling
5. **desolation**	13. **restitution**	e. forewarning	m. celebration
6. **plunder**	14. **justification**	f. fit	n. unforgiving
7. **omen**	15. **dithering**	g. sadness	o. mob
8. **contemptible**		h. grounds	

Building Vocabulary

For an in-depth lesson on word relationships such as synonyms and antonyms, see page 849.

Grammar in Context: Sentence Closers

In these excerpts from the *Odyssey,* notice how the translator ends a sentence about Polyphemus and a sentence about Circe.

> **We felt a pressure on our hearts, in dread**
> **of that deep rumble and that mighty man.**
> (prepositional phrase)
>
>   **Low she sang**
> **in her beguiling voice, while on her loom**
> **she wove ambrosial fabric sheer and bright,**
> **by that craft known to the goddesses of heaven.**
> (adverb clause)

A **sentence closer** is a word, phrase, or clause that follows the main idea of a sentence. Each of the sentences above begins with an independent clause that contains the main idea. The sentence closers, shown in blue, add additional details. (The grammatical structure of each closer is indicated in parentheses.) You can use sentence closers in your writing to add descriptive details and to increase the variety of your sentences.

WRITING EXERCISE Follow the directions in parentheses to rewrite each sentence, adding a sentence closer to it.

Punctuation Tip: Most sentence closers should be preceded by commas.

   Example: *Original* Odysseus and his men leave Polyphemus behind. (Add a participle describing Polyphemus' condition.)
Rewritten Odysseus and his men leave Polyphemus behind, <u>blinded</u>.

1. The men sit eating the lotus. (Add an adjective phrase describing how the men felt.)
2. Odysseus approaches the Cyclops' cavern. (Add a prepositional phrase indicating what Odysseus did not know about the Cyclops.)
3. Circe feeds some of Odysseus' men a special meal. (Add a participial phrase indicating what the meal did to the men.)
4. The Sirens' song makes Odysseus want to leave the ship. (Add an adverb clause beginning with the word *although.*)

Homer

Shadowy Figure Although the ancient Greeks credited a man named Homer with composing the *Iliad* and the *Odyssey,* scholars have long debated whether Homer really existed. There are many theories about who Homer may have been and when and where he may have lived. According to ancient accounts, he lived sometime between 900 and 700 B.C., possibly on the island of Chios in the eastern Aegean Sea, and he was blind. Most modern scholars agree that the Homeric poems are the work of one or more exceptionally talented bards— singers who make up their verses as they sing.

Oral History Homer's epics are all that remains of a series of poems that told the whole story of the Trojan War. In later centuries, the *Iliad* and the *Odyssey* were memorized by professional reciters, who performed them at religious festivals throughout Greece. They were also the first works read by Greek schoolchildren. By 300 B.C. many slightly different versions of the poems existed, and scholars began to work at restoring them to their original form.

Models for the Ages Homer's epics became models for many later writers, including the Roman poet Virgil and the English poet John Milton. Moreover, by helping to shape classical Greek culture, they have contributed to the development of all later Western ideas and values.

The Odyssey:

A Book Review by Stephen Goode

❶ The classics are back, if indeed they've ever been gone. Jane Austen's *Emma, Pride and Prejudice,* and *Sense and Sensibility* have been made into popular films. The same is true for Shakespeare's plays and the novels of Henry James, Edith Wharton, and E. M. Forster.

Now add Homer's the *Odyssey,* created before 700 B.C., to this group of masterworks enjoying a revival. The epic poem has been republished in a splendid, vigorous translation by Princeton professor and poet Robert Fagles and made into a Hallmark Entertainment miniseries. . . .

❷ Everyone knows the story told in the *Odyssey,* or at least parts of it. The great warrior Odysseus has left Troy, victorious after 10 years of war. He's eager to return home, where his son Telemachus, a small child when Odysseus left, and his wife, Penelope, wait for him.

But Odysseus has angered the god Poseidon, who arranges for the great warrior to wander the Earth for 10 years before the goddess Athena intercedes and allows him to return to Ithaca. During his decade-long journey, Odysseus encounters the temptress Circe, the one-eyed giant Polyphemus, and undergoes many other adventures. He's sorely tested, as is the long-suffering Penelope, pursued by very eager suitors. At the great poem's conclusion, the family is reunited.

❸ Fagles's translation is fast-paced and written in contemporary American idiom—without once stooping to slang or cliché. "When young Dawn with her rose-red fingers shone once more," Fagles writes, translating the end of Book 3, "they yoked their pair again, mounted the blazoned car and out through the gates and echoing colonnade they whipped the team to a run and on they flew, holding nothing back . . . so fast those purebred stallions raced them on as the sun sank and the roads of the world grew dark."

"Homer was a performer; he was a ventriloquist capable of speaking in each of the voices of his many characters, an artist of many effects," Fagles tells Insight. "He was a man

Reading for Information

Before you go to a movie or read a book, do you ever wonder if you're going to like it? Many readers and viewers rely on reviews to help them make worthwhile choices.

ANALYZING A BOOK REVIEW

A book review is an essay in which a person writes his or her opinion about a book. A successful review usually includes these elements:

- identification of the work
- enough information to describe the story without giving away the plot
- a clear and convincing opinion of the work followed by supporting examples

YOUR TURN Use the questions and activities below to analyze Stephen Goode's review of the *Odyssey.*

❶ A good review quickly identifies its subject and presents an interesting angle on it. What is the subject of the review? How does Goode attempt to interest readers in the subject?

❷ Reviewers should always assume that their readers know nothing about the subject matter. Imagine that you know nothing about the *Odyssey,* and then reread the section in which Goode has described the book. Do you think he has explained enough about the book without giving away the story? Explain.

with a wealth of experience that he could call up at will. He was a person with the breadth of imagination of Shakespeare."

Fagles, who also has translated the *Iliad,* Homer's epic poem about the siege of Troy, has a theory about the unlikely popularity of the *Odyssey.* "It's a case of getting back to first things," he says, "and this poem is where we began, 2,700 years ago." Indeed, the *Odyssey* has something for everyone. It's a coming-of-age story as Telemachus grows into manhood. It's a tale about growing into middle age as Odysseus and Penelope are reunited after their 20-year separation. It's a story, too, about old Laertes, Odysseus' father, and "his return to life" when his son comes home.

❹ Fagles's translation is hard to put down, conveying the dramatic energy that must have excited Homer's listeners— who heard him declaim his long poem (it wasn't written down until much later). Audiotapes of Fagles's complete *Odyssey* have been recorded by English actor Ian McKellen.

❸ A writer must clearly present his or her opinion. Goode states, "[Robert] Fagles's translation is fast-paced and written in contemporary American idiom—without once stooping to slang or cliché." Does Goode provide examples that support this opinion? Are there enough examples to convince you that his opinion is valid? Explain.

❹ Goode ends his review by saying, "Fagles's translation is hard to put down, conveying the dramatic energy that must have excited Homer's listeners. . . ." Does Goode's review inspire you to read the book? Why or why not?

Odysseus, bound to the mast, is enchanted by the Sirens' song, as his crew "dashed their oars in the gray sea" away from the Sirens' lure.

Inquiry & Research
Activity Link: *from the* **Odyssey, p. 966** Reexamine your answers for what makes a good translation of a classical work. Now, using the criteria for a successful book review, discuss your opinions of the translation of the *Odyssey* that's in your textbook.

Through the centuries, the *Odyssey* has appealed to the imagination of many other writers. Its story and characters continue to inspire countless works of literature. In "Penelope," for example, Dorothy Parker wonders what might have been in the mind of the woman who waited behind, all that time. In "Ithaka," Greek poet C. P. Cavafy prays that our road to Ithaca will be a long one. Each of these poems helps us to see the *Odyssey* itself a little more clearly.

Penelope DOROTHY PARKER

In the pathway of the sun,
   In the footsteps of a breeze,
Where the world and sky are one,
   He shall ride the silver seas,
5   He shall cut the glittering wave.
I shall sit at home, and rock;
Rise, to heed a neighbor's knock;
Brew my tea, and snip my thread;
Bleach the linen for my bed.
10   They will call him brave.

Dorothy Parker
1893-1967

Other Works
Enough Rope
Sunset Gun
Death and Taxes
Laments for the Living
After Such Pleasures

Humor with an Edge Considered one of the wittiest women in America, Dorothy Parker was regularly quoted by newspaper columnists during her lifetime. In 1933, upon hearing that former President Calvin Coolidge, a solemn man of few words, had died, Parker remarked, "How could they tell?" Although her best known poetry is light verse on the subject of romantic love (she coined the often-quoted "Men seldom make passes/At girls who wear glasses"), she also wrote poems centering on lonely love. Many of them deal with women abandoned by their loved ones—as one critic put it, "smarting from the sense of unworthiness and the pain of rejection, trying to cope with her dismay and despair."

Stories of Her Time Parker also achieved critical acclaim for her well-crafted short stories, portraying the shallow lives of wealthy women of the 1920s and early 1930s. For a time, Parker herself was a wealthy woman, living a lavish life among the rich and famous in New York during the Roaring Twenties. But in her later life, she was plagued by financial difficulties and alcoholism. After her death, a friend described her as being "at war with herself all her life."

Penelope (1990) by Shlomo Katz.
Courtesy of Strictly Limited
Editions, San Francisco, CA.

Ithaka C.P. CAVAFY

As you set out for Ithaka
hope the voyage is a long one,
full of adventure, full of discovery.
Laistrygonians and Cyclops,
5   angry Poseidon—don't be afraid of them:
you'll never find things like that on your way
as long as you keep your thoughts raised high,
as long as a rare excitement
stirs your spirit and your body.
10 Laistrygonians and Cyclops,
wild Poseidon—you won't encounter them
unless you bring them along inside your soul,
unless your soul sets them up in front of you.

Hope the voyage is a long one.
15 May there be many a summer morning when,
with what pleasure, what joy,
you come into the harbors seen for the first time;
may you stop at Phoenician trading stations
to buy fine things,

4 Laistrygonians (līs′trĭ-gō′nē-ənz):
the Laestrygones (see the map on
page 889).

18 Phoenician (fĭ-nĭsh′ən) **trading
centers:** port cities of the
Phoenicians, an ancient people of
the Near East who were famous as
seafaring traders.

20   mother of pearl and coral, amber and ebony,
sensual perfume of every kind—
as many sensual perfumes as you can;
and may you visit many Egyptian cities
to gather stores of knowledge from their scholars.

25   Keep Ithaka always in your mind.
Arriving there is what you are destined for.
But do not hurry the journey at all.
Better if it lasts for years,
so you are old by the time you reach the island,
30   wealthy with all you have gained on the way,
not expecting Ithaka to make you rich.

Ithaka gave you the marvelous journey,
Without her you would not have set out.
She has nothing left to give you now.

35   And if you find her poor, Ithaka won't have fooled you.
Wise as you will have become, so full of experience,
you will have understood by then what these Ithakas mean.

20 mother of pearl and coral, amber: natural materials used in making jewelry and other decorative items; **ebony:** a hard, black, valuable wood.

C. P. Cavafy
1863–1933

Other Works
Artificial Flowers
"Candles"
"Thermopylae"
"Trojans"
"Waiting for the Barbarians"

International Citizen Although his background was Greek, Constantine P. Cavafy was born in Alexandria, Egypt, where his father ran a business. Both of his parents came from the Greek community in Constantinople (now Istanbul), Turkey. When Cavafy was 7 his father died. His mother moved the family to Britain, where he lived for nearly a decade, also spending three years in Constantinople. At the age of 22, he returned to Alexandria and spent most of the rest of his life there.

Greek Heritage Cavafy's time in Britain made him comfortable with the English tongue, but when creating poetry he wrote in Greek, using a combination of the spoken and more literary forms of that language. From his Greek heritage he also drew much of the content of his poetry, often finding inspiration in ancient Greek myths and legends. He was extremely self-critical and destroyed far more poems than he saved. As a result he left behind only about 200 poems, though in his lifetime he probably wrote thousands of others. He was reluctant to publish his own work, often preferring to circulate it privately among friends.

Spreading Fame Cavafy first won widespread attention when British author E. M. Forster, after working in Alexandria during World War I, described him in a 1923 book about Egypt. Cavafy's complete poems did not appear in English translation until nearly two decades after his death.

Exploring the Roots of Meaning

Researching the history of a word is like researching your family tree—both explorations involve tracing a trail of ancestors back through time. The ancestry of most English words can be traced to Old English (the earliest form of the language) or to Latin or Greek. Consider, for example, the passage on the right, from Robert Fitzgerald's translation of Homer's *Odyssey*. The word *chaos* in the excerpt comes from a Greek word meaning, among other things, "infinite darkness." *Eternal, horror, power,* and *avails* have their roots in Latin, and *evil* and *nightmare* have ancestors in Old English.

> That **nightmare cannot die, being** eternal
> evil **itself**—horror, **and pain, and** chaos;
> **there is no fighting her, no** power **can fight her,**
> **all that** avails **is flight.**
> —*Odyssey,* Book 12, lines 79–82

Strategies for Building Vocabulary

Researching a word's **etymology**—that is, its history and origin—can give you insight into the word's meaning and help you remember it. It can also help you figure out the meanings of related words. Use the strategies that follow to boost your etymological IQ.

❶ Begin with a Dictionary One easy way to learn a word's etymology is to look the word up in an unabridged or college dictionary. Information about the word's origin will appear near the beginning or end of the dictionary entry, as in the highlighted part of this entry for *epic*.

> **ep•ic** (ĕp′ĭk) *adj.* **1.** having the characteristics of an epic. **2.** beyond the usual in size or scope. [From Latin *epicus,* from Greek *epikos,* from *epos,* word, poem, song]

The etymology of *epic* reveals that the word can ultimately be traced to the Greek word *epos.* It also implies that epics were originally recited or sung. In fact, epic tales like the *Odyssey* were part of peoples' oral traditions for many centuries.

❷ Note How Words Are Created As you research etymologies, you may discover that some words evolved in interesting ways. **Compound words,** like *homeland* and *earthquake,* were formed by combining existing words. Other words, called **eponyms,** derive from the names of people and places. The word *boycott,* for example, comes from the name of Charles C. Boycott, a 19th-century Irish land agent who was shunned by people because he refused to lower rents.

❸ Recognize Word Families Words with the same origin are likely to have related meanings. Consider the words *ponder, ponderous,* and *preponderance,* which are part of a family of words that can be traced to the Latin word *pondus,* meaning "weight." As the chart below shows, the idea of weight is still present in these words.

Words Derived from Latin *Pondus*	
ponder	to weigh in one's mind
ponderous	weighty or massive; labored or dull
preponderance	a superiority in weight, strength, or power

Knowing the etymology of one member of a word family can help you guess at the meanings of other words in the family.

EXERCISE With the help of a dictionary, summarize the etymology of each word.

Example:
> *thousand:* from Old English *thûsend,* "thousand"

1. geyser
2. cavern
3. azure
4. navigate
5. ambrosia
6. tentacle
7. rudder
8. shepherd
9. survive
10. succumb

Writing Workshop

Exploring a topic in depth . . .

From Reading to Writing The *Odyssey* often raises questions in readers' minds: Was Odysseus a real person? Were the places mentioned in the poem real or fictional? Who was Homer? Questions like these could be the starting point for a short **research report**, a written report in which you investigate an idea or a question by doing research. Research skills can help you find and make use of the information you need—whether you're looking for the best pair of inline skates or a part-time job, or you just want to satisfy your curiosity.

For Your Portfolio

WRITING PROMPT Write a short research report about a literary topic or another topic that interests you.

Purpose: To share information and draw a conclusion about your topic

Audience: Your classmates, teacher, or anyone who shares your interest in the topic

---

Basics in a Box

Research Report at a Glance

THESIS

INTRODUCTION
Presents the thesis statement

BODY
Presents evidence that **supports** the thesis statement

CONCLUSION
Restates the thesis

WORKS CITED
Lists the sources of information

RESEARCH

RUBRIC Standards for Writing

A successful research report should

- include a strong introduction with a clear thesis statement
- use evidence from primary and secondary sources to develop and support ideas
- credit sources of information

- follow a logical pattern of organization, using transitions between ideas
- summarize ideas in a satisfying conclusion
- provide a correctly formatted Works Cited list at the end of the paper

Analyzing a Student Model

Jonas Moss
English I
Mr. Cramer
April 11

Moss 1

The Odyssey: Fact or Fiction?

The adventures described in *The Odyssey* have amazed readers for centuries. Odysseus outwitted the Cyclops, avoided Circe's trap, and navigated through the dangers of Scylla and Charybdis among many other episodes in his ten-year journey. Were these events just stories and legends? Or did they really happen in real places? A final answer to these questions may not be possible, but an explanation of the issue can lead to a greater understanding of *The Odyssey*. Some scholars believe *The Odyssey* is entirely fictional; some insist it tells of real adventures and real places; others say that it is fictional but is based on real places (Connolly 61).

The debate has been going on at least since the fifth century B.C. At that time, Thucydides, the first great historian, mentioned the legendary Cyclops. Even today, if you visit the Sicilian town of Acireale, local guides will point out the rocks that Polyphemos hurled at Odysseus's ship (Lattimore 26). On the other side of the argument, it isn't easy to believe that a creature like the Cyclops existed, and no one can prove that there ever was a man named Odysseus. But while some of the more fantastic parts of *The Odyssey* are certainly fictional, there's considerable evidence that at least some of these stories are based on actual places and events.

What do we know? First of all, we know that there was a Troy just where Homer says it was. The city was discovered and excavated by Heinrich Schliemann in the 19th century (Bradford ix). The details that Homer gives about the places Odysseus visits have elements that are both fantastic and real. This is how he describes Charybdis, for example (Book 12, lines 62–66):

> Charybdis lurks below
> to swallow down the dark sea tide. Three times
> from dawn to dusk she spews it up
> and sucks it down again three times, a whirling
> maelstrom

❶ This writer begins with a series of questions that lead to his thesis statement.
Other Options:
• Open with a strong quotation.
• Begin with an interesting anecdote.

❷ Uses transitional phrases to show how ideas are related

❸ Uses evidence from a primary source to support his ideas

Moss 2

Thucydides, Greek historian from the 5th century B.C., wrote, "The Strait in question is the sea that lies between Rhegium (Reggio) and Messana (Messina). . . . This is the so-called Charybdis through which Odysseus is said to have sailed. It has naturally become accounted dangerous because of the narrowness and of the currents caused by the inrush of the Tyrrhenian sea" (Bradford 144).

Although the place in question does not have an actual whirlpool today, it does have inrushing tides that swirl around in the narrow strait. This action of the sea may be the inspiration for Homer's story of Charybdis (Bradford 144).

Many scholars use Homer's descriptions to argue that *The Odyssey* may be based on fact but is still the product of Homer's imagination. There is no question that Homer was a great storyteller, and he was probably also a very good listener who learned about many foreign places and worked them into his tales. For example, he gives a detailed and fairly accurate description of Ithaca, Odysseus's home, but he doesn't give its true location. At the beginning of Book 9, he describes Ithaca as being very

❹ Credits the secondary source where the quote is found

❺ This writer paraphrases a source and credits it.
Another Option:
• Present and credit a direct quotation from the work.

Works Cited

Bradford, Ernle. Ulysses Found. New York: Harcourt, 1963.

Connolly, Peter. The Legend of Odysseus. New York: Oxford UP, 1986.

DeHaven, Angela. "Homer." Greek Civilization Home Page. Portland State U. 2 April 1998 <http://www-adm.pdx.edu/user/sinq/greekciv/arts/greeklit/homer.htm>.

Homer. The Odyssey. Trans. Robert Fitzgerald. New York: Vintage, 1990.

Lacarriere, Jacques. "The Trials of Ulysses." UNESCO Courier, Dec. 1997: 18–21.

Lattimore, Richmond. "Introduction to The Odyssey of Homer." Twentieth Century Interpretations of The Odyssey. Ed. Howard W. Clarke. Englewood Cliffs: Prentice, 1983. 13–37.

"Odyssey." Benét's Reader's Encyclopedia. 3rd ed. 1987.

Pillot, Gilbert. The Secret Code of the Odyssey. Trans. Francis E. Albert. New York: Abelard, 1972.

Works Cited
• Identifies sources of information used in researching the paper
• Alphabetizes entries by author's last name or article title
• Gives complete publication information
• Punctuates entries correctly
• Double spaces entire list
• Follows a preferred style

Need help with Works Cited?

See pages 1165–1166 in the **Writing Handbook**.

Writing Your Research Report

Writing to me is a voyage, an odyssey, a discovery,
because I'm never certain of precisely what I will find.
Gabriel Fielding, British physician and novelist

❶ Prewriting and Exploring

The first step in writing a research report is to find a topic that really interests you. Even if your subject has been assigned, you can still find some aspect of it that will make it exciting to you. Try creating a **knowledge inventory**. List everything you know about the assigned subject or about another subject you'd like to explore. Underline topics that interest you and make a list of questions you have about those topics. See the **Idea Bank** in the margin for more suggestions. Once you've chosen a subject, follow the suggestions below to develop your idea.

Planning Your Research Report

▶ **1. Focus your topic.** How much information is available on your topic? Is there too much to cover adequately in a short research paper? Is there too little to make the report worthwhile? To either expand or narrow your topic, try making a cluster diagram like this.

▶ **2. Set your goals.** What do you want to accomplish in your report? Do you want to entertain your readers, convince them of something, or share information that you learn about your topic? You may want to include a combination of these goals in your report.

▶ **3. Identify your audience.** Who will read your report? What will interest them most about your topic? What do they already know about it? What background information will you need to provide?

▶ **4. Consider your purpose.** What will be the focus of your report? Identifying your purpose by writing it in a single sentence will guide your research and give you direction as you work. Later on, you can revise this sentence to become your thesis statement.

❷ Researching

To gather the information for your report, you will need to do research using reliable sources. Begin by reading one or two general articles on your topic, such as those found in encyclopedias or other reference materials. Then write a list of questions you want to answer about the topic and look for the answers to those questions as you continue your research.

There are two types of sources—primary and secondary. **Primary sources** offer first-hand information. They include letters, original literary works, diaries, journals, and historical documents. **Secondary sources** provide interpretations,

IDEABank

1. Your Working Portfolio
Look for ideas in the **Writing Option** you completed in this unit:
• **Encyclopedia Entries** p. 940

2. Sharing Ideas
Meet with a group of classmates to discuss what you know and what you want to know about your favorite subjects or issues.

3. Questioning
Make a list of questions about things that interest you. Asking "what if?" questions might lead to an interesting report topic.

Need help with your research report?

See pages 1161–1166 in the **Writing Handbook**.

RESEARCHTIP

Secondary sources can help you explain ideas and interpret information. Use primary sources to give examples of the points you make.

More Online: Research Starter
www.mcdougallittell.com

explanations, and comments on material from other sources. Encyclopedias, newspapers, magazines, and many books are examples of secondary sources.

Evaluate Your Sources

Not all sources of information are equally valuable. The following questions can help you evaluate and choose the best sources.

- **Is the source up-to-date?** Fields such as technology, science, and medicine change especially quickly. Use the most recent information you can find.

- **Is the source reliable?** Look for sources whose authors are from respected universities, businesses, or other institutions.

- **What are the author's viewpoint and biases?** Identify the author's gender, ethnic background, and political beliefs. Ask yourself how these factors influence his or her presentation of information. Be sure to read material from several different viewpoints.

Make Source Cards

Using index cards, create a source card for each source you use. Number the cards sequentially so you can easily refer to them when you take notes and prepare your Works Cited list. For library books, include the call number so you can locate the book again if necessary. Follow the formats shown on the right.

Take Notes

Record on index cards the information you gather from your sources. Write just one piece of information on each card so you can easily rearrange the cards in various organizations as you draft your report. Label each card with the number of the source card and the page number of the information.

Book ①

Bradford, Ernle. *Ulysses Found*.
New York: Harcourt Brace, 1963.
910.4B727u

Periodical ②

Lacarriere, Jacques.
"The Trials of Ulysses."
UNESCO Courier December 1997:
18-21.

Encyclopedia ③

"Odyssey." *Benét's Reader's
Encyclopedia*, 3rd ed. 1987.

Internet ④

DeHaven, Angela. "Homer." *Greek
Civilization Home Page*.
Portland State University, 2 April 1998
<http://www-admpdxedu/user/sing/
greekciv/arts/greeklit/homer.htm

Troy ①

Troy is a real place. Found by Heinrich
Schliemann who was 19th-century German
archeologist. "Taking the works of Homer
as his guide, he set out and found the
ancient city–in exactly the place where
classical authorities had once stated that
it used to exist." ix
Paraphrase and quotation

Page Number.

Source Number.

Paraphrase. Restate ideas in your own words to summarize them and to avoid plagiarism, which is using someone else's material without permission.

Quotation. Write the quote exactly as it appears in the source and enclose it in quotation marks. Quote material for emphasis or when the author's words are especially clear and powerful.

Organize Your Material

One way to organize your research notes is to group your note cards by main ideas. Then think about the order in which you want to discuss those ideas. Consider **chronological**, **cause-and-effect**, **comparison-and-contrast**, **problem-solution**, or a mix of organizations to see which one works best for your material. Then create an outline, using your main ideas as the main heads. Next, subdivide the groups of note cards into smaller groups. These will become subheads in your outline. Remember that your outline is just meant to guide your writing. You can change it at any time as you draft.

Need help organizing your material?

See the **Writing Handbook,** p. 1163.

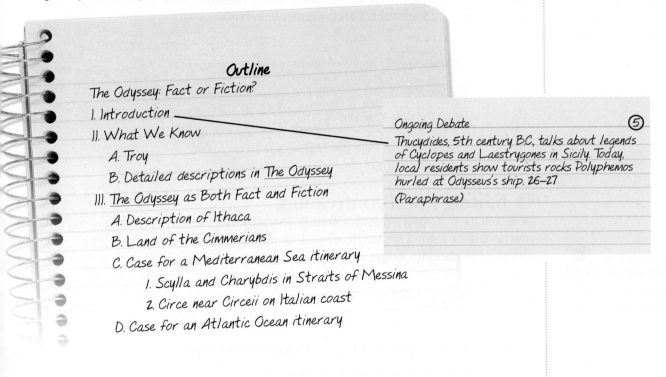

Outline

The Odyssey: Fact or Fiction?

I. Introduction

II. What We Know
   A. Troy
   B. Detailed descriptions in The Odyssey

III. The Odyssey as Both Fact and Fiction
   A. Description of Ithaca
   B. Land of the Cimmerians
   C. Case for a Mediterranean Sea itinerary
      1. Scylla and Charybdis in Straits of Messina
      2. Circe near Circeii on Italian coast
   D. Case for an Atlantic Ocean itinerary

Ongoing Debate   ⑤

Thucydides, 5th century BC, talks about legends of Cyclopes and Laestrygones in Sicily. Today, local residents show tourists rocks Polyphemos hurled at Odysseus's ship. 26–27

(Paraphrase)

❸ Drafting

Using your outline as a guide, begin drafting your report. Remember that your main goal is to get your ideas down on paper. Your draft doesn't have to be perfect; you can revise it as much as you want later. At some point, you should write a thesis statement that expresses the main idea of your report. State your thesis clearly in the introduction of your report.

The body of your report should **support your thesis**. To do this, develop the main ideas of your outline using examples, facts, statistics, anecdotes, and quotations from your sources. **Analyze, interpret, synthesize, make inferences**, and **draw conclusions** about the information as you work it into your report. Do more research as necessary. **Summarize your thesis** in the conclusion. To **avoid plagiarism**, be sure to indicate the source of the information you use. After each paraphrased or quoted statement, write in parentheses the author's name (or the title of the source if no author is given) and the page number.

As you **review your draft,** ask yourself how you can make your thesis statement clearer and your support stronger. Make sure your sources are cited correctly, and look for ways to tighten your organization.

DRAFTINGTIP

Consider beginning with a startling fact, an anecdote, or a quotation to quickly capture your readers' interest.

Ask Your Peer Reader

- What part of my report was most interesting?
- What do you want or need to know more about?
- What parts were confusing?
- What did you learn about my topic?

Need revising help?

Review the **Rubric**, p. 974

Consider **peer reader** comments

Check **Revision Guidelines**, p. 1143

❹ Revising

TARGET SKILL ► **ELABORATING WITH FACTS AND STATISTICS**

Facts and statistics can provide strong support for your statements. A fact is a statement that can be proved either by the use of reference materials or by first-hand observation. Statistics are facts expressed in numbers.

> Although there is no way to know exactly what Odysseus' ship was like, it was probably like the Greek warships used during the time of Homer. *about 750 B.C. There were two kinds of ships, one with room for 20 oars and the other with room for 50.*

❺ Editing and Proofreading

TARGET SKILL ► **COMBINING SENTENCES** You can add interest to your writing by varying the length of your sentences. Try combining some shorter sentences into longer, more interesting ones.

Confused by sentence structure?

See the **Grammar Handbook**, p. 1196

> Ody~~s~~seus sailed around Cape Malea. ~~It is~~ a dangerous point of land sticking out into the Mediterranean Sea. A storm struck his ship there. *and* ~~It~~ blew his fleet out to sea. Ancient sailors did not have compasses. *so* ~~I~~f they were blown out of sight of land, they would not know which way to sail.

❻ Making a Works Cited list

When you have finished revising and editing your report, make a **Works Cited** list and attach it to the end of your paper. See pages 1165–1166 in the **Writing Handbook** for the correct format.

❼ Reflecting

FOR YOUR WORKING PORTFOLIO What else would you like to learn about the topic of your report? Make a list of questions you have about your topic for further study. Keep your list of questions with your research report in your **Working Portfolio.**

Publishing IDEAS

- Present your research report as an oral report to the class.
- Post your report on an Internet site that focuses on your topic.

More Online: Publishing Options www.mcdougallittell.com

Read this paragraph from the first draft of a research report. The underlined sections may include the following kinds of errors:

- **sentence fragments**
- **comma errors**
- **lack of subject-verb agreement**
- **correctly written sentences that should be combined**

For each underlined section, choose the revision that most improves the writing.

The heat of the earth's core can be useful to people. This energy <u>source called geothermal energy, is powerful</u> and renewable. <u>To harness geothermal energy water is pumped underground.</u> Massive rocks lie below the earth's surface. They <u>give</u> off a great deal of heat. The intense heat and pressure <u>turns</u> the water into high-pressured steam. <u>The steam can be used for power. It powers an engine. The engine produces electricity.</u> <u>Excess hot water is carried away. To heat people's homes.</u>

(1) source called geothermal energy, is powerful
(2) To harness geothermal energy water is pumped underground
(3) give
(4) turns
(5) The steam can be used for power. It powers an engine. The engine produces electricity.
(6) Excess hot water is carried away. To heat people's homes.

---

1. A. source, called geothermal energy, is powerful
    B. source called geothermal energy is powerful
    C. source, called geothermal energy is powerful
    D. Correct as is

2. A. To harness geothermal energy; water is pumped underground.
    B. To harness geothermal energy. Water is pumped underground.
    C. To harness geothermal energy, water is pumped underground.
    D. Correct as is

3. A. gave
    B. gives
    C. have given
    D. Correct as is

4. A. turned
    B. turn
    C. has turned
    D. Correct as is

5. A. The steam can be used to power an engine. It produces electricity.
    B. The steam can be used to power an engine; producing electricity.
    C. The steam can be used to power an engine that produces electricity.
    D. Correct as is

6. A. Excess hot water is carried away, to heat people's homes.
    B. Excess hot water is carried away to heat people's homes.
    C. Excess, hot water is carried away to heat. People's homes.
    D. Correct as is

Need extra help?

See the **Grammar Handbook**

Correcting Fragments, p. 1197

Subject-Verb Agreement, p. 1198

Punctuation Chart, pp. 1201–1202

PART 2   Romeo and Juliet

What do you know about Shakespeare and Shakespearean theater? How familiar are you with the story of Romeo and Juliet? You have probably heard this famous line:

O Romeo, Romeo! wherefore art thou Romeo?

But did you know that the meaning of the line is not "*Where* are you, Romeo?" but "*Why* are you Romeo?" As you read this well-known play, find out how Juliet's question relates to Shakespeare's central theme.

ACTIVITY

With a small group of classmates, discuss your knowledge, assumptions, or even guesses about Shakespearean theater. Don't worry at this point about getting your facts exactly straight. Instead, concentrate more on becoming aware of your own and other classmates' expectations—good and bad. After all members of the group have had a chance to share their thoughts and feelings, choose someone to present a summary of the group's expectations to the rest of the class.

SHAKESPEARE'S WORLD

ENGLAND IN SHAKESPEARE'S DAY

William Shakespeare is widely considered to be the greatest writer in the English language and the greatest playwright of all time. His plays have been produced more often and in more countries than those of any other author. Shakespeare lived in England during the flowering of intellectual activity known as the Renaissance. The European Renaissance was marked by a renewed interest in science, commerce, philosophy, and the arts. Basic to Renaissance thinking was a new emphasis on the individual and on freedom of choice. The Renaissance movement began in 14th-century Italy and gradually moved north and west toward England, where it reached its peak during the reign of Queen Elizabeth I. Shakespeare started his literary career during Elizabeth's reign, a period that lasted from 1558 to 1603 and is often called the Elizabethan Age.

Elizabeth was the last member of England's royal house of Tudor, which began with her grandfather, King Henry VII. Henry VII had brought stability and prosperity to his kingdom, and it was during his reign that Renaissance ideas began taking hold in England. However, political and religious problems surfaced during the reign of Elizabeth's father, Henry VIII, and continued into the early years of Elizabeth's own reign. Luckily, Elizabeth proved to be a strong monarch, able to guide England along a more moderate and prosperous course. It was a course that most Elizabethans, including William Shakespeare, seem to have appreciated.

Elizabeth I

Like her grandfather and father before her, Elizabeth I was a strong supporter of English culture. As a result, artists of all types—including playwrights, poets, painters, sculptors, musicians, and architects—were held in high esteem. Taking the cue from their monarch, members of England's upper class often became patrons, or financial sponsors, of the arts. In the early 1590s, Shakespeare began acting in and writing plays for a theater company sponsored by two men who had both held the office of England's Lord Chamberlain, a high-ranking position in Elizabeth's court. The company was called the Lord Chamberlain's Men, and Elizabeth herself attended some of its productions.

THEATER IN SHAKESPEARE'S DAY

Though acting companies toured throughout England, London was the center of the Elizabethan stage. In 1576, well before Shakespeare became affiliated with the Lord Chamberlain's Men, the

company built England's first theater in the suburbs of London; by the end of the 1590s, London boasted more theaters than any other European capital. One reason the London theaters did so well was that they attracted an audience of rich and poor alike. In fact, the Elizabethan theater was one of the few forms of entertainment available to working-class people of the day, and one of the few places where the working class and educated upper class could mix. Shakespeare appealed to English audience members of all classes by including a great deal of variety in his plays: poetic speeches, exciting action, fast-paced humor, vivid character portrayals, and wise

Top, photo of the stage at the New Globe Theatre. Above, a model of what scholars believe the old Globe Theatre looked like.

observations about human nature and universal human concerns. Thus, while he was respected by the rich and powerful people of his day, he also became very popular with the common people.

Actors in *Henry V* at the New Globe

In 1599, Shakespeare and the other shareholders, or part owners, of the Lord Chamberlain's Men became joint owners of the company's new home. The theater company settled into the Globe Theatre, on the banks of the River Thames (tĕmz) in central London. The Globe was a three-story wooden structure with an open-air courtyard in the center. Actors performed on a raised platform stage within the courtyard. The theater could hold as many as three thousand spectators, many of whom stood in the part of the courtyard near the stage known as the pit. These customers, called groundlings, paid the lowest admission charge, usually just a penny. Richer theatergoers paid more and sat in the partially enclosed galleries, or inner balconies, which surrounded most of the courtyard. Audiences became emotionally involved in performances, openly showing their pleasure or their disappointment. They cheered, booed, hissed, and sometimes threw rotten vegetables. They applauded agile sword fighting and dramatic sound effects, such as blares of trumpets, drum rolls, and claps of thunder.

Elizabethan theater relied heavily on the audience's imagination. Most theaters had no curtains, no artificial lighting, and very little scenery. Instead, props, sound effects, and sometimes lines of dialogue let the audience know when and where a scene took place. However, while the staging was simple, it was hardly dull. Swords, shields, brightly colored banners, and elegant costumes often added to the spectacle. The costumes also helped audiences imagine that women were playing the female roles, which in fact were played by young male actors. In Shakespeare's day, no women belonged to English acting companies, for it was considered improper for women to appear on stage. The boys who played female roles underwent rigorous training in acting, singing, and dancing. Before they could play a role such as Juliet in a first-rate company, they had to learn to move gracefully and speak convincingly.

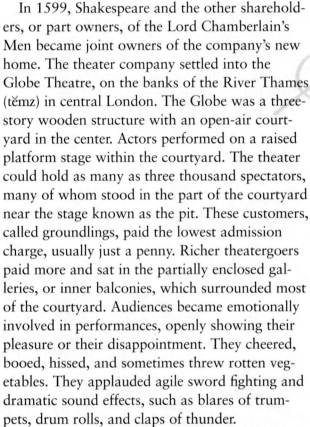

SHAKESPEARE'S IMPACT ON THE ENGLISH LANGUAGE

Shakespeare was a master of dramatic language and a great experimenter with spoken English. He was clever and imaginative, playing with words and their meanings and creating striking images that, once heard or read, are rarely forgotten.

Shakespeare contributed more words, phrases, and expressions to the English language than any other writer. Some of these words were his own invention, including *assassination, bump,* and *lonely.* Other expressions might have been part of the everyday speech of Elizabethan England, but Shakespeare was the first to use them in writing, and their inclusion in his plays gave them a permanent place in the language.

Many of these phrases and expressions have become so common that people use them without realizing that they are quoting Shakespeare. In fact, the expressions have become "household words"—a term first used in Shakespeare's historical play *Henry V.* Other expressions that have become part of the language include "dead as a doornail" (*Henry VI,* Part 2), "laughing-stock" (*The Merry Wives of Windsor*), "the green-eyed monster" (*Othello*), and "for goodness' sake" (*Henry VIII*). Shakespeare's fine ear for the English language prompted the British writer George Orwell to call him a "word musician."

Shakespearean drama, the 37 plays written

by Shakespeare, includes histories—plays about historical figures—comedies, and tragedies. These plays explore many aspects of human experience. Most of the dialogue in Shakespearean drama is written in **blank verse,** a form of unrhymed poetry. Shakespeare makes use of certain conventions of drama, including **foil characters, soliloquies,** and **asides.** He also often uses **allusions** to enrich the meaning of his work. Looking at some passages from *Romeo and Juliet,* his first romantic tragedy, will help you better understand these aspects of Shakespearean drama.

Tragedy

A **tragedy** is a drama that ends in catastrophe—most often death—for the main character and often for several other important characters as well. In Shakespearean tragedy, the main character, or **tragic hero,** is usually someone who is nobly born and who may have great influence in his or her society. This character also has, however, one or more fatal character flaws—a weakness or a serious error in judgment—that leads to his or her downfall. Although the events in a tragedy are often set in motion by an action of the tragic hero, fate may also seem to play a role in the course that the events take.

Comic Relief

In his tragedies Shakespeare often includes **comic relief,** a humorous scene, incident, or speech that relieves the overall emotional intensity. By providing contrast, comic relief helps the audience to absorb the earlier events in the plot and get ready for the ones to come. Shakespeare also had a practical reason for including comedy in his tragedies. Theater companies in his day liked to use all of their star performers in each play, including those who specialized in comedy roles.

Allusion

An **allusion** is a brief reference, within a work, to something outside the work that the reader or audience is expected to know. For example, the writer might allude to a historical or current event or to a line from another work of literature. Shakespeare's plays often contain allusions to ancient Greek and Roman mythology and to the Bible.

YOUR TURN The lines at the right are spoken by Romeo's friend Mercutio. Do you recognize any of the allusions? If so, discuss them with a classmate.

ALLUSION

Mercutio. . . . Speak to my gossip **Venus** one fair word,
One nickname for her purblind son and heir,
Young **Adam Cupid,** he that shot so trim
When **King Cophetua** loved the beggar maid!

—Act Two, Scene 1, lines 13–16

Foil

A **foil** is a character whose personality or attitudes are in sharp contrast to those of another character in the same work. By using a foil, the writer highlights the other character's traits or attitude. The kind behavior of one character, for example, will be made clearer when it is presented in sharp contrast to another character who is not at all kind.

YOUR TURN What are some opposing personality types that you think might make good character foils?

Soliloquy and Aside

Like all playwrights, Shakespeare makes use of what are called **dramatic conventions,** devices that theater audiences accept as realistic even though they do not necessarily reflect the way real-life people behave.

- A **soliloquy** is a speech that a character gives when he or she is alone on stage. Its purpose is to let the audience know what the character is thinking.
- An **aside** is a character's remark, either to the audience or to another character, that others on stage are not supposed to hear. Its purpose, too, is to reveal the character's private thoughts. A stage direction, usually in brackets or parentheses, indicates when an aside is being made. Asides are spoken to the audience unless the stage directions say otherwise.

YOUR TURN The passage at the right is from a soliloquy spoken by Juliet in Act Three of *Romeo and Juliet.* What can the audience learn about Juliet and her feelings for Romeo from these lines?

> **SOLILOQUY**
>
> [Enter Juliet alone.]
> **Juliet.** . . . Come, gentle night; come, loving, black-browed night;
> Give me my Romeo; and, when he shall die,
> Take him and cut him out in little stars,
> And he will make the face of heaven so fine
> That all the world will be in love with night
> And pay no worship to the garish sun. . . .
>
> —Act Three, Scene 2, lines 20–26

Blank Verse

Shakespeare's plays are written largely in **blank verse,** a form of poetry that uses unrhymed lines of **iambic pentameter,** lines that ideally have five unstressed syllables, each followed by a stressed syllable. However, the pattern is not perfect; sometimes there are breaks in the pattern.

YOUR TURN Where is the pattern of perfect iambic pentameter broken in the lines at the right?

> **BLANK VERSE**
>
> **Romeo.** . . . But soft! What light through yonder window breaks?
> It is the East, and Juliet is the sun!
> Arise, fair sun, and kill the envious moon,
> Who is already sick and pale with grief
> That thou her maid art far more fair than she.
>
> —Act Two, Scene 2, lines 2–6

The Active Reader: Skills and Strategies

The plays of Shakespeare are still greatly enjoyed by audiences and readers today. But because Shakespeare lived centuries ago, his use of language sometimes takes some getting used to. The reading strategies explained here can help you understand difficult passages and enable you to make the most of the characters and events you meet.

Reading Shakespearean Drama

Strategies for Using Your 📖 READER'S NOTEBOOK

As you read, take notes in which you
- keep track of characters and their relationships
- record any dialogues, soliloquies, and asides that interest you
- write down any words or terms that you don't understand

1 Strategies for Reading Drama
- Study the opening cast of characters.
- Read any stage directions at the start of an act or scene, and try to **visualize** the setting from any details provided.
- Pay attention to stage directions that tell how a character should speak or move.
- To get a sense of how the dialogue might sound, read some of it aloud, either alone or in a small group.

2 Strategies for Reading Shakespearean Tragedy
- Identify the main characters and note how they are related to one another. **Evaluate** each character's speech and actions to try to determine his or her attitudes, personality, and motives. You may want to use a chart like the one shown here to organize your ideas.

Character:	
Attitudes	Speech and Actions:
Personality	Speech and Actions:
Motives	Speech and Actions:

- **Evaluate** the strengths and weaknesses of the tragic hero. Look especially for a tragic flaw.
- Look for cause-and-effect relationships between events. Try to **predict** what each major event might lead to.
- Look for stage directions that indicate a soliloquy or an aside. Try to **visualize** how an actor might speak and move when delivering these lines.

3 Strategies for Understanding Shakespeare's Language
- Use the sidenotes and, if necessary, a dictionary, to help you figure out the meaning of unfamiliar words, grammatical structures, and word order. Paraphrase difficult passages to clarify the meaning.
- Be on the lookout for puns (jokes that play with multiple meanings of a particular word or phrase) and allusions. Use the sidenotes and dictionaries or other reference works to track down obscure passages.

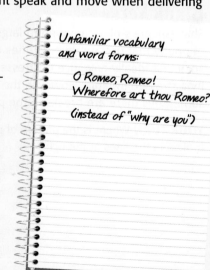

Unfamiliar vocabulary
and word forms:

O Romeo, Romeo!
Wherefore art thou Romeo?

(instead of "why are you")

Need More Help?

Remember that active readers use the essential reading strategies explained on page 7: **visualize, predict, clarify, question, connect, evaluate, monitor.**

The Tragedy of Romeo and Juliet

Drama by WILLIAM SHAKESPEARE

"For never was a story of more woe / Than this of Juliet and her Romeo."

Connect to Your Life

A Little Romance Recall love stories that you have read about in books or seen in movies and on TV. Did the couple's love seem real to you? Did the romance end happily? Whether a romance ends happily or not, a writer has to provide some obstacles to the couple's love to keep the story going until the end. With your classmates, discuss the following questions: What were the complications in your favorite romances? Were the obstacles caused by the couple themselves, or by social factors or other outside forces beyond the couple's control?

Build Background

Love and Marriage *Romeo and Juliet* is one of the world's most famous love stories. Based on a 16th-century English poem, the play takes place in the Italian city of Verona in the 14th century, when Italy was not a unified nation but a group of separate city-states. Each city-state was ruled by a different hereditary ruler, usually called a prince or a duke. At the time when the play takes place, most European marriages, especially among the upper classes, were arranged by families for social and economic reasons. Because life spans were shorter than they are today, marriages took place at a younger age, and parents often made marriage plans for children long before the actual wedding ceremonies occurred. Romantic love was recognized as a powerful force, but society did not generally view it as the basis of a sound marriage.

Focus Your Reading

LITERARY ANALYSIS **BLANK VERSE** Shakespeare wrote his plays almost entirely in **blank verse**—unrhymed lines of **iambic pentameter,** in which a line generally has five unstressed syllables each followed by a stressed syllable:

Mŏre líght, yŏu knáves! ănd túrn thĕ tábles úp,

Ănd quénch thĕ fíre, thĕ róom ĭs grówn tŏo hót.

Sometimes, however, he has characters speak in prose, and sometimes he uses rhymed lines, especially two rhymed lines in a row, called a **couplet.**

Lĕt twó mŏre súmmĕrs wíthĕr ín theĭr príde

Ĕre wé măy thínk hĕr rípe tŏ bé ă bríde.

As you read, speak some of the lines aloud to hear the rhythm and to listen for any effect that sound may have on meaning. Note variations in the rhythmic pattern. Watch for passages written in prose and in couplets.

ACTIVE READING **READING SHAKESPEAREAN DRAMA** Reading a Shakespearean play for the first time is not easy. Most modern editions of the plays include notes to explain allusions and unfamiliar language. The sidenotes for *Romeo and Juliet* in this book also include questions to help guide you through the play. Refer to the sidenotes and think about the questions to help you understand the actions, characters, and dialogue more clearly.

Keeping track of events can also make the play easier to follow. The events in *Romeo and Juliet* all take place in six days, beginning on a Sunday.

📖 **READER'S NOTEBOOK** As you read the play, fill in a graphic like the one shown to keep track of how the plot develops and how the characters relate to one another.

Sunday	Monday	Tuesday	Wednesday	Thursday	Friday
street brawl					

The Montagues

Lord Montague (män'tə-gyōō)

Lady Montague

Romeo, son of Montague

Benvolio (bĕn-vō'lē-ō), nephew of Montague and friend of Romeo

Balthasar (bäl'thə-sär'), servant to Romeo

Abram, servant to Montague

THE TRAGEDY OF ROMEO +

OTHERS

Prince Escalus (ĕs'kə-ləs), ruler of Verona

Mercutio (mĕr-kyōō'shō), kinsman of the Prince and friend of Romeo

Friar Laurence, a Franciscan priest

Friar John, another Franciscan priest

Count Paris, a young nobleman, kinsman of the Prince

Apothecary (ə-päth'ə-kĕr'ē)

Page to Paris

Chief Watchman

Three Musicians

An Officer

Citizens of Verona, Gentlemen and Gentlewomen of both houses, Maskers, Torchbearers, Pages, Guards, Watchmen, Servants, and Attendants.

TIME

The 14th century

PLACE

Verona (və-rō'nə); Mantua (măn'chōō-ə) in northern Italy

The Capulets

Lord Capulet (kăp'yōō-lĕt')

Lady Capulet

Juliet, daughter of Capulet

Tybalt (tĭb'əlt), nephew of Lady Capulet

Nurse to Juliet

Peter, servant to Juliet's Nurse

Sampson

Gregory

An old man of the Capulet family

Above left: From Franco Zeffirelli's 1968 interpretation of *Romeo and Juliet* starring Leonard Whiting and Olivia Hussey.

Left: From Baz Luhrmann's 1996 interpretation of *Romeo and Juliet* starring Claire Danes and Leonardo DiCaprio.

The *Prologue*

Act One, The Prologue. The feud between the Capulets and the Montagues will end in tragedy. (Zeffirelli, 1968)

The CHORUS is one actor who serves as a narrator. He enters from the back of the stage to introduce and explain the theme of the play. His job is to "hook" the audience's interest by telling them just enough to quiet them down and make them eager for more. In this prologue, or preview, the narrator explains that the play will be about a feud between two families (the Capulets and the Montagues). In addition, the narrator says that the feud will end in tragedy. As you read the prologue, determine what the tragedy will be.

[*Enter* Chorus.]

Chorus. Two households, both alike in dignity,
    In fair Verona, where we lay our scene,
    From ancient grudge break to new mutiny,
    Where civil blood makes civil hands unclean.
5   From forth the fatal loins of these two foes,
    A pair of star-crossed lovers take their life,
    Whose misadventured piteous overthrows
    Doth with their death bury their parents' strife.
    The fearful passage of their death-marked love,
10   And the continuance of their parents' rage,
    Which, but their children's end, naught could remove,
    Is now the two hours' traffic of our stage,
    The which if you with patient ears attend,
    What here shall miss, our toil shall strive to mend.

[*Exit.*]

3–4 ancient . . . unclean: A new outbreak of fighting (**mutiny**) between families has caused the citizens of Verona to have one another's blood on their hands.

6 star-crossed: doomed. The position of the stars when the lovers were born was not favorable. In Shakespeare's day, people took astrology and horoscopes very seriously.

11 but: except for; **naught:** nothing.

12 two hours' . . . stage: the action that will take place on the stage during the next two hours.

14 What . . . mend: We will fill in the details that have been left out of the prologue.

ACT *One*

SCENE 1 *A public square in Verona.*

As the scene opens, two young Capulet servants swagger across the stage joking and bragging. When they happen to meet servants from the rival house of Montague, a quarrel begins that grows into an ugly street fight. Finally the ruler of Verona, Prince Escalus, appears. He is angry about the violence in his city and warns that the next offenders will receive the death penalty. The crowd fades away and the stage is set for the entrance of Romeo, heir of the Montague family. Romeo, lovesick and miserable, can talk of nothing but his love for Rosaline and her cruelty in refusing to love him back.

[*Enter* Sampson *and* Gregory, *servants of the house of* Capulet, *armed with swords and bucklers (shields).*]

Sampson. Gregory, on my word, we'll not carry coals.

Gregory. No, for then we should be colliers.

Sampson. I mean, an we be in choler, we'll draw.

Gregory. Ay, while you live, draw your neck out of
5   collar.

Sampson. I strike quickly, being moved.

Gregory. But thou art not quickly moved to strike.

Sampson. A dog of the house of Montague moves me.

Gregory. To move is to stir, and to be valiant is
10   to stand. Therefore, if thou art moved, thou runnest
    away.

Sampson. A dog of that house shall move me to stand
    I will take the wall of any man or maid of
    Montague's.

15 **Gregory.** That shows thee a weak slave, for the weakest
    goes to the wall.

Sampson. 'Tis true; and therefore women, being the
    weaker vessels, are ever thrust to the wall. Therefore
    push I will Montague's men from the wall and thrust
20   his maids to the wall.

Gregory. The quarrel is between our masters and us
    their men.

1–5 we'll not carry coals: We won't stand to be insulted. (Those involved in the dirty work of hauling coal were often the targets of jokes and insults.) Here the comic characters Gregory and Sampson are bragging about how brave they are. Their boasts include several bad jokes based on words that sound alike: **collier** means "coal dealer"; **in choler** means "angry"; **collar** refers to a hangman's noose.

13 take the wall: walk nearest to the wall. People of higher rank had the privilege of walking closer to the wall, to avoid any water or garbage that might be in the street. What claim is Sampson making about himself and anyone from the rival house of Montague?

17–28 Sampson's tough talk includes boasts about his ability to overpower women.

Sampson. 'Tis all one. I will show myself a tyrant.
When I have fought with the men, I will be cruel
25 with the maids: I will cut off their heads.

Gregory. The heads of the maids?

Sampson. Ay, the heads of the maids, or their
maidenheads. Take it in what sense thou wilt.

Gregory. They must take it in sense that feel it.

30 **Sampson.** Me they shall feel while I am able to stand;
and 'tis known I am a pretty piece of flesh.

Gregory. 'Tis well thou art not fish; if thou hadst, thou
hadst been poor-John. Draw thy tool! Here comes
two of the house of Montagues.

[*Enter* Abram *and* Balthasar, *servants to the* Montagues.]

35 **Sampson.** My naked weapon is out. Quarrel! I will
back thee.

Gregory. How? turn thy back and run?

Sampson. Fear me not.

Gregory. No, marry. I fear thee!

40 **Sampson.** Let us take the law of our sides; let them
begin.

Gregory. I will frown as I pass by, and let them take it
as they list.

Sampson. Nay, as they dare. I will bite my thumb at
45 them; which is disgrace to them, if they bear it.

Abram. Do you bite your thumb at us, sir?

Sampson. I do bite my thumb, sir.

Abram. Do you bite your thumb at us, sir?

Sampson. [*Aside to* Gregory] Is the law of our side if
50 I say ay?

Gregory. [*Aside to* Sampson] No.

Sampson. No, sir, I do not bite my thumb at you, sir;
but I bite my thumb, sir.

Gregory. Do you quarrel, sir?

55 **Abram.** Quarrel, sir? No, sir.

Sampson. But if you do, sir, I am for you. I serve as good
a man as you.

Abram. No better.

Sampson. Well, sir.

33 poor-John: a salted fish, considered
fit only for poor people to eat.

35 During the next few speeches in this
comic scene, watch what happens when
the foolish, boastful servants actually
meet their rivals face to face.

39 marry: a short form of "by the Virgin
Mary" and so a mild swear word.

40–51 Gregory and Sampson decide to
pick a fight by insulting the Montague
servants with a rude gesture (**bite my
thumb**). To appreciate the humor in this
scene, think about what the servants say
openly, what they say in asides, and what
they actually do

49 Aside: privately, in a way that keeps
the other characters from hearing what is
said. Think of it as a whisper that the
audience happens to overhear.

Act One, Scene 1. A fight breaks out among members of both families. (Zeffirelli, 1968)

[*Enter* Benvolio, *nephew of* Montague *and first cousin of* Romeo.]

60 **Gregory.** [*Aside to* Sampson] Say "better." Here comes one of my master's kinsmen.

Sampson. Yes, better, sir.

Abram. You lie.

Sampson. Draw, if you be men. Gregory, remember
65 thy swashing blow.

[*They fight.*]

Benvolio. Part, fools! [*Beats down their swords.*] Put up your swords. You know not what you do.

[*Enter* Tybalt, *hot-headed nephew of* Lady Capulet *and first cousin of Juliet.*]

Tybalt. What, art thou drawn among these heartless hinds?
Turn thee, Benvolio! look upon thy death.

70 **Benvolio.** I do but keep the peace. Put up thy sword,
Or manage it to part these men with me.

Tybalt. What, drawn, and talk of peace? I hate the word
As I hate hell, all Montagues, and thee.
Have at thee, coward!

[*They fight.*]

60–65 From the corner of his eye, Gregory can see Tybalt, a Capulet, arriving on the scene. With help on the way, his interest in fighting suddenly returns. He reminds Sampson to use **swashing,** or smashing, blows.

66 As you read the next few lines, think about the different attitudes shown by Benvolio and Tybalt. How would you describe the contrast between them?

68–74 Tybalt misunderstands that Benvolio is trying to stop the fight. He challenges Benvolio.

68 heartless hinds: cowardly servants.

72 drawn . . . peace: You have your sword out, and yet you have the nerve to talk of peace?
74 Have at thee: Defend yourself.

[*Enter several of both houses, who join the fray; then enter* Citizens *and* Peace Officers, *with clubs.*]

75 **Officer.** Clubs, bills, and partisans! Strike! beat them down!

Citizens. Down with the Capulets! Down with the Montagues!

[*Enter old* Capulet *and* Lady Capulet.]

Capulet. What noise is this? Give me my long sword,
80   ho!

Lady Capulet. A crutch, a crutch! Why call you for a sword?

Capulet. My sword, I say! Old Montague is come
      And flourishes his blade in spite of me.

[*Enter old* Montague *and* Lady Montague.]

85 **Montague.** Thou villain Capulet!—Hold me not, let me go.

Lady Montague. Thou shalt not stir one foot to seek a foe.

[*Enter Prince Escalus, with attendants. At first no one hears him.*]

Prince. Rebellious subjects, enemies to peace,
90   Profaners of this neighbor-stained steel—
      Will they not hear? What, ho! you men, you beasts,
      That quench the fire of your pernicious rage
      With purple fountains issuing from your veins!
      On pain of torture, from those bloody hands
95   Throw your mistempered weapons to the ground
      And hear the sentence of your moved prince.
      Three civil brawls, bred of an airy word
      By thee, old Capulet, and Montague,
      Have thrice disturbed the quiet of our streets
100   And made Verona's ancient citizens
      Cast by their grave beseeming ornaments
      To wield old partisans, in hands as old,
      Cankered with peace, to part your cankered hate.
      If ever you disturb our streets again,
105   Your lives shall pay the forfeit of the peace.
      For this time all the rest depart away.

75 bills and partisans: spears.

81–88 A crutch . . . sword: You need a crutch more than a sword. How do both wives respond to their husbands' "fighting words"?

89–96 The Prince is furious about the street fighting caused by the feud. He commands all the men to put down their weapons and pay attention.
92 pernicious: destructive.

97–103 Three . . . hate: The Prince holds Capulet and Montague responsible for three recent street fights, probably started by an offhand remark or insult **(airy word)**. He warns the old men that they will be put to death if any more fights occur.

You, Capulet, shall go along with me;
And, Montague, come you this afternoon,
To know our farther pleasure in this case,
110   To old Freetown, our common judgment place.
Once more, on pain of death, all men depart.

[Exeunt all but Montague, Lady Montague, *and* Benvolio.*]*

Montague. Who set this ancient quarrel new abroach?
Speak, nephew, were you by when it began?

Benvolio. Here were the servants of your adversary
115   And yours, close fighting ere I did approach.
I drew to part them. In the instant came
The fiery Tybalt, with his sword prepared;
Which, as he breathed defiance to my ears,
He swung about his head and cut the winds,
120   Who, nothing hurt withal, hissed him in scorn.
While we were interchanging thrusts and blows,
Came more and more, and fought on part and part,
Till the Prince came, who parted either part.

Lady Montague. O, where is Romeo? Saw you him today?
125   Right glad I am he was not at this fray.

Benvolio. Madam, an hour before the worshiped sun
Peered forth the golden window of the East,
A troubled mind drave me to walk abroad,
Where, underneath the grove of sycamore
130   That westward rooteth from the city's side,
So early walking did I see your son.
Towards him I made, but he was ware of me
And stole into the covert of the wood.
I—measuring his affections by my own,
135   Which then most sought where most might not be
found,
Being one too many by my weary self—
Pursued my humor, not pursuing his,
And gladly shunned who gladly fled from me.

Montague. Many a morning hath he there been seen,
140   With tears augmenting the fresh morning's dew,
Adding to clouds more clouds with his deep sighs;
But all so soon as the all-cheering sun
Should in the farthest East begin to draw

Exeunt *(Latin):* they leave. When one person leaves the stage, the direction is Exit.

112 Who . . . abroach: Who reopened this old argument?

114 adversary: enemy.

115 ere: before.

114–123 According to Benvolio, what kind of person is Tybalt? How might Tybalt be likely to act if he meets Benvolio again?

120 withal: by this.

122 on part and part: some on one side, some on the other.

125 fray: fight.

128 drave: drove.

130 rooteth: grows.

132–138 made: moved; **covert:** covering. Romeo saw Benvolio coming toward him and hid in the woods. Benvolio decided to respect Romeo's privacy and went away. What does this action tell you about Benvolio?

139–150 Romeo has been wandering through the woods at night, often in tears. At daybreak he returns home and locks himself in his darkened room. Montague is deeply concerned about his son's behavior and feels he needs guidance.

The shady curtains from Aurora's bed,
145 Away from light steals home my heavy son
And private in his chamber pens himself,
Shuts up his windows, locks fair daylight out,
And makes himself an artificial night.
Black and portentous must this humor prove
150 Unless good counsel may the cause remove.

Benvolio. My noble uncle, do you know the cause?

Montague. I neither know it nor can learn of him.

Benvolio. Have you importuned him by any means?

Montague. Both by myself and many other friends;
155 But he, his own affections' counselor,
Is to himself—I will not say how true—
But to himself so secret and so close,
So far from sounding and discovery,
As is the bud bit with an envious worm
160 Ere he can spread his sweet leaves to the air
Or dedicate his beauty to the sun.
Could we but learn from whence his sorrows grow,
We would as willingly give cure as know.

[*Enter* Romeo *lost in thought.*]

Benvolio. See, where he comes. So please you step aside,
165 I'll know his grievance, or be much denied.

Montague. I would thou wert so happy by thy stay
To hear true shrift. Come, madam, let's away.

[*Exeunt* Montague *and* Lady.]

Benvolio. Good morrow, cousin.

Romeo.   Is the day so young?

170 **Benvolio.** But new struck nine.

Romeo.   Ay me! sad hours seem long.
Was that my father that went hence so fast?

Benvolio. It was. What sadness lengthens Romeo's hours?

Romeo. Not having that which having makes them short.

175 **Benvolio.** In love?

Romeo. Out—

Benvolio. Of love?

---

153 importuned: demanded.

155 his own affections' counselor:
Romeo keeps to himself.

158–163 So far from . . . know:
Finding out what Romeo is thinking is
nearly impossible. Montague compares his
son to a young bud destroyed by the bite
of an envious worm. He wants to find out
what is bothering Romeo so he can help
him.

167 shrift: confession.

168 cousin: any relative or close friend.
The informal version is **coz.**

174–180 Why has Romeo been so
depressed?

Romeo. Out of her favor where I am in love.

Benvolio. Alas that love, so gentle in his view,
180 Should be so tyrannous and rough in proof!

Romeo. Alas that love, whose view is muffled still,
Should without eyes see pathways to his will!
Where shall we dine?—O me! What fray was
    here?—
Yet tell me not, for I have heard it all.
185 Here's much to do with hate, but more with love.
Why then, O brawling love! O loving hate!
O anything, of nothing first create!
O heavy lightness! serious vanity!
Misshapen chaos of well-seeming forms!
190 Feather of lead, bright smoke, cold fire, sick health!
Still-waking sleep, that is not what it is!
This love feel I, that feel no love in this.
Dost thou not laugh?

Benvolio.   No, coz, I rather weep.

195 **Romeo.** Good heart, at what?

Benvolio.   At thy good heart's oppression.

Romeo. Why, such is love's transgression.
Griefs of mine own lie heavy in my breast,
Which thou wilt propagate, to have it prest
200 With more of thine. This love that thou hast shown
Doth add more grief to too much of mine own.
Love is a smoke raised with the fume of sighs;
Being purged, a fire sparkling in lovers' eyes;
Being vexed, a sea nourished with lovers' tears.
205 What is it else? A madness most discreet,
A choking gall, and a preserving sweet.
Farewell, my coz.

Benvolio.   Soft! I will go along.
An if you leave me so, you do me wrong.

210 **Romeo.** Tut! I have lost myself; I am not here:
This is not Romeo, he's some other where.

Benvolio. Tell me in sadness, who is that you love?

Romeo. What, shall I groan and tell thee?

Benvolio.   Groan? Why, no;
215 But sadly tell me who.

179–182 love: refers to Cupid, the god of love. Cupid is pictured as a blind boy with wings and a bow and arrow. Anyone hit by one of his arrows falls in love instantly. Since he is blind, love is blind. He looks gentle, but in reality he can be a harsh master.

185–193 Romeo, confused and upset, tries to describe his feelings about love in phrases like "loving hate." Look for other expressions in this speech made up of pairs of words that contradict each other. Has love ever made you feel this way?

194–201 Benvolio expresses his sympathy for Romeo. Romeo replies that this is one more problem caused by love. He now feels worse than before because he must carry the weight of Benvolio's sympathy along with his own grief.

203 purged: cleansed (of the smoke).
204 vexed: troubled.

208 Soft: Wait a minute.

212 sadness: seriousness

Romeo. Bid a sick man in sadness make his will.
Ah, word ill urged to one that is so ill!
In sadness, cousin, I do love a woman.

Benvolio. I aimed so near when I supposed you loved.

220 **Romeo.** A right good markman! And she's fair I love.

Benvolio. A right fair mark, fair coz, is soonest hit.

Romeo. Well, in that hit you miss. She'll not be hit
With Cupid's arrow. She hath Dian's wit,
And, in strong proof of chastity well armed,
225 From Love's weak childish bow she lives unharmed.
She will not stay the siege of loving terms,
Nor bide the encounter of assailing eyes,
Nor ope her lap to saint-seducing gold.
O, she is rich in beauty; only poor
230 That, when she dies, with beauty dies her store.

Benvolio. Then she hath sworn that she will still live
chaste?

Romeo. She hath, and in that sparing makes huge waste;
For beauty, starved with her severity,
235 Cuts beauty off from all posterity.
She is too fair, too wise, wisely too fair,
To merit bliss by making me despair.
She hath forsworn to love, and in that vow
Do I live dead that live to tell it now.

240 **Benvolio.** Be ruled by me: forget to think of her.

Romeo. O, teach me how I should forget to think!

Benvolio. By giving liberty unto thine eyes:
Examine other beauties.

Romeo.   'Tis the way
245 To call hers (exquisite) in question more.
These happy masks that kiss fair ladies' brows,
Being black, puts us in mind they hide the fair.
He that is strucken blind cannot forget
The precious treasure of his eyesight lost.
250 Show me a mistress that is passing fair,
What doth her beauty serve but as a note
Where I may read who passed that passing fair?
Farewell. Thou canst not teach me to forget.

Benvolio. I'll pay that doctrine, or else die in debt.

[*Exeunt.*]

218–219 Romeo seems unaware of how foolish his dramatic confession sounds. Benvolio responds with appropriate but gentle sarcasm.

219–222 Romeo and Benvolio talk of love in terms of archery, another reference to Cupid and his love arrows.

222–225 She'll . . . unharmed: The girl isn't interested in falling in love. She is like Diana, the goddess of chastity, the moon, and the hunt, who avoided Cupid's arrows.

226–228 She is unmoved by Romeo's declaration of love, his adoring looks, and his wealth.

231–235 Since she has vowed to remain chaste, she will die without children, and her beauty will not be passed on to future generations (**posterity**).

237–238 To merit . . . despair: The girl will reach heaven (**bliss**) by being chaste, which causes Romeo **despair,** or hopelessness. **forsworn to:** sworn not to.

242–243 What is Benvolio's advice?

244–245 'Tis . . . more: That would only make me appreciate my own love's beauty more.

246 Masks were worn by Elizabethan women to protect their complexions from the sun.

254 I'll pay . . . debt: I'll convince you you're wrong, or die trying.

SCENE 2 *A street near the Capulet house.*

This scene opens with Count Paris, a young nobleman, asking Capulet for permission to marry his daughter, Juliet. Capulet says that Juliet is too young but gives Paris permission to court her and try to win her favor. He also invites Paris to a party he is giving that night.

Romeo finds out about the party and discovers that Rosaline, the girl who rejected him, will be present. Benvolio urges Romeo to go to the party to see how Rosaline compares with the other women.

[*Enter* Capulet *with* Paris, *a kinsman of the* Prince, *and* Servant.]

Capulet. But Montague is bound as well as I,
    In penalty alike; and 'tis not hard, I think,
    For men so old as we to keep the peace.

Paris. Of honorable reckoning are you both,
5   And pity 'tis you lived at odds so long.
    But now, my lord, what say you to my suit?

Capulet. But saying o'er what I have said before:
    My child is yet a stranger in the world,
    She hath not seen the change of fourteen years;
10   Let two more summers wither in their pride
    Ere we may think her ripe to be a bride.

Paris. Younger than she are happy mothers made.

Capulet. And too soon marred are those so early made.
    The earth hath swallowed all my hopes but she;
15   She is the hopeful lady of my earth.
    But woo her, gentle Paris, get her heart;
    My will to her consent is but a part.
    An she agree, within her scope of choice
    Lies my consent and fair according voice.
20   This night I hold an old accustomed feast,
    Whereto I have invited many a guest,
    Such as I love, and you among the store,
    One more, most welcome, makes my number more.
    At my poor house look to behold this night
25   Earth-treading stars that make dark heaven light.
    Such comfort as do lusty young men feel
    When well-appareled April on the heel
    Of limping Winter treads, even such delight
    Among fresh female buds shall you this night

1 bound: obligated.

4 reckoning: reputation.

6 what say . . . suit: Paris is asking for Capulet's response to his proposal to marry Juliet.

8–13 My child . . . made: Capulet repeats his claim that Juliet, still thirteen, is too young for marriage. He further argues that girls are hurt by becoming mothers too soon.

14 The earth . . . she: All my children are dead except Juliet.

16 woo her: try to win her affection.

18–19 An . . . voice: I will give my approval to the one she chooses.

20 old accustomed feast: a traditional or annual party.

30 Inherit at my house. Hear all, all see,
And like her most whose merit most shall be;
Which, on more view of many, mine, being one,
May stand in number, though in reck'ning none.
Come, go with me. [*To Servant, giving him a paper.*]
35   Go, sirrah, trudge about
Through fair Verona; find those persons out
Whose names are written there, and to them say,
My house and welcome on their pleasure stay.

[*Exeunt* Capulet *and* Paris.]

Servant. Find them out whose names are written here!
40   It is written that the shoemaker should meddle with
his yard and the tailor with his last, the fisher with
his pencil and the painter with his nets; but I am
sent to find those persons whose names are here
writ, and can never find what names the writing
45   person hath here writ. I must to the learned. In
good time!

[*Enter* Benvolio *and* Romeo.]

Benvolio. Tut, man, one fire burns out another's
burning;
One pain is lessened by another's anguish;
50   Turn giddy, and be holp by backward turning;
One desperate grief cures with another's languish.
Take thou some new infection to thy eye,
And the rank poison of the old will die.

Romeo. Your plantain leaf is excellent for that.

55 **Benvolio.** For what, I pray thee?

Romeo.   For your broken shin.

Benvolio. Why, Romeo, art thou mad?

Romeo. Not mad, but bound more than a madman is;
Shut up in prison, kept without my food,
60   Whipped and tormented and—God-den, good
fellow.

Servant. God gi' go-den. I pray, sir, can you read?

Romeo. Ay, mine own fortune in my misery.

Servant. Perhaps you have learned it without book.
65   But I pray, can you read anything you see?

Romeo. Ay, if I know the letters and the language.

29–33 Among . . . none: Tonight at the party you will witness (**inherit**) the loveliest young girls in Verona, including Juliet. When you see all of them together, your opinion of Juliet may change.

35 sirrah: a term used to address a servant.

38 My house . . . stay: My house and my welcome wait for their pleasure. What does Capulet send the servant to do?

39–42 The servant is bewildered and frustrated because he has been asked to read—a skill he does not have. He confuses the craftsmen and their tools, tapping a typical source of humor for Elizabethan clowns, then goes off to seek help.

45–46 In good time: What luck; he is referring to the arrival of Romeo and Benvolio, who look like men who can read.

47–53 Tut, man . . . die: Benvolio is still trying to convince Romeo that the best way he can be helped (**holp**) in his love for Rosaline is to find someone else. Notice that he compares love to a disease that can only be cured by another disease.

58–61 Romeo is giving Benvolio a dismal picture of how he feels when he is interrupted by Capulet's servant. **God-den:** good evening.

62 God gi' go-den: God give you a good evening.

Act One, Scene 2. Romeo learns of the party at the Capulets'. (Zeffirelli, 1968)

Servant. Ye say honestly. Rest you merry!

[*Romeo's* joking goes over the clown's head. He concludes *that* Romeo *cannot read and prepares to seek someone who can.*]

Romeo. Stay, fellow; I can read.   [*He reads.*]
 "Signior Martino and his wife and daughters;
70   County Anselmo and his beauteous sisters;
   The lady widow of Vitruvio;
   Signior Placentio and his lovely nieces;
   Mercutio and his brother Valentine;
   Mine uncle Capulet, his wife, and daughters;
75   My fair niece Rosaline and Livia;
   Signior Valentio and his cousin Tybalt;
   Lucio and the lively Helena."

67 Rest you merry: Stay happy; a polite form of *goodbye*.

75 Notice that Romeo's beloved Rosaline, a Capulet, is invited to the party. (This is the first time in the play that her name is mentioned.) Mercutio, a friend of both Romeo and the Capulets, is also invited.

[*Gives back the paper.*]

  A fair assembly. Whither should they come?

Servant. Up.

80 **Romeo.** Whither?

Servant. To supper, to our house.

Romeo. Whose house?

Servant. My master's.

Romeo. Indeed I should have asked you that before.

85 **Servant.** Now I'll tell you without asking. My master is
  the great rich Capulet; and if you be not of the house
  of Montagues, I pray come and crush a cup of wine.
  Rest you merry!

[*Exit.*]

Benvolio. At this same ancient feast of Capulet's
90   Sups the fair Rosaline whom thou so lovest,
  With all the admired beauties of Verona.
  Go thither, and with unattainted eye
  Compare her face with some that I shall show,
  And I will make thee think thy swan a crow.

95 **Romeo.** When the devout religion of mine eye
  Maintains such falsehood, then turn tears to fires;
  And these, who, often drowned, could never die,
  Transparent heretics, be burnt for liars!
  One fairer than my love? The all-seeing sun
100   Ne'er saw her match since first the world begun.

Benvolio. Tut! you saw her fair, none else being by,
  Herself poised with herself in either eye;
  But in that crystal scales let there be weighed
  Your lady's love against some other maid
105   That I will show you shining at this feast,
  And she shall scant show well that now shows best.

Romeo. I'll go along, no such sight to be shown,
  But to rejoice in splendor of mine own.

[*Exeunt.*]

78 **Whither:** where.

87–88 **crush a cup of wine:** slang for "drink some wine."

92–94 **Go . . . crow:** Go to the party and, with unbiased eyes, compare Rosaline with the other beautiful girls.

95–98 **When . . . liars:** If the love I have for Rosaline, which is like a religion, changes because of such lies (that others could be more beautiful), let my tears be turned to fire and my eyes be burned. To what does Romeo compare Rosaline's beauty?

101–106 **Tut . . . best:** You've seen Rosaline alone; now compare her with some other woman. How does Benvolio think Rosaline will stack up against the other girls?

107–108 Romeo agrees to go to the party, but only to see Rosaline.

SCENE 3 *Capulet's house.*

In this scene, you will meet Juliet, her mother, and her nurse. The Nurse, a merry and slightly crude servant, has been in charge of Juliet since her birth. Once she starts talking, she can't stop. Just before the party, Juliet's mother asks if Juliet has thought about getting married. Lady Capulet is matchmaking, trying to convince her daughter that Paris would make a good husband. Juliet responds just as you might if your parents set up a blind date for you—without much enthusiasm.

[*Enter* Lady Capulet *and* Nurse.]

Lady Capulet. Nurse, where's my daughter? Call her forth
  to me.

Nurse. Now, by my maidenhead at twelve year old,
  I bade her come. What, lamb! what, ladybird!
5 God forbid! Where's this girl? What, Juliet!

[*Enter* Juliet.]

Juliet. How now? Who calls?

Nurse. Your mother.

Juliet. Madam, I am here. What is your will?

Lady Capulet. This is the matter—Nurse, give leave
10 awhile,
  We must talk in secret. Nurse, come back again;
  I have remembered me, thou's hear our counsel.
  Thou knowest my daughter's of a pretty age.

Nurse. Faith, I can tell her age unto an hour.

15 **Lady Capulet.** She's not fourteen.

Nurse.   I'll lay fourteen of my teeth—
  And yet, to my teen be it spoken, I have but four—
  She's not fourteen. How long is it now
  To Lammastide?

20 **Lady Capulet.** A fortnight and odd days.

Nurse. Even or odd, of all days in the year,
  Come Lammas Eve at night shall she be fourteen.
  Susan and she (God rest all Christian souls!)
  Were of an age. Well, Susan is with God;
25 She was too good for me. But, as I said,
  On Lammas Eve at night shall she be fourteen;

4–5 What: a call like "Hey, where are you?"

9–12 give leave . . . counsel: Lady Capulet seems flustered or nervous. First she tells the Nurse to leave, then she remembers that the Nurse knows Juliet as well as anyone and asks her to stay and listen. **of a pretty age:** of an attractive age, ready for marriage.

17 teen: sorrow.

19 Lammastide: August 1, a religious feast day and the day after Juliet's birthday. The feast day is now a little more than two weeks (**a fortnight**) away.

21–54 The Nurse now begins to babble on about various memories of Juliet's childhood. She talks of her dead daughter, Susan, who was the same age as Juliet. Susan probably died in infancy, allowing for the Nurse to become a wet nurse to (breast-feed) Juliet. She remembers an earthquake that happened on the day she stopped breast-feeding Juliet (**she was weaned**).

That shall she, marry; I remember it well.
'Tis since the earthquake now eleven years;
And she was weaned (I never shall forget it),
30 Of all the days of the year, upon that day.
For I had then laid wormwood to my dug,
Sitting in the sun under the dovehouse wall.
My lord and you were then at Mantua—
Nay, I do bear a brain—But, as I said,
35 When it did taste the wormwood on the nipple
Of my dug and felt it bitter, pretty fool,
To see it tetchy and fall out with the dug!
Shake, quoth the dovehouse! 'Twas no need, I trow,
To bid me trudge.
40 And since that time it is eleven years,
For then she could stand alone; nay, by the rood,
She could have run and waddled all about;
For even the day before, she broke her brow;
And then my husband (God be with his soul!
45 'A was a merry man) took up the child.
"Yea," quoth he, "dost thou fall upon thy face?
Thou wilt fall backward when thou has more wit,
Wilt thou not, Jule?" And, by my holidam,
The pretty wretch left crying, and said "Ay."
50 To see now how a jest shall come about!
I warrant, an I should live a thousand years,
I never should forget it. "Wilt thou not, Jule?"
     quoth he,
And, pretty fool, it stinted, and said "Ay."

55 **Lady Capulet.** Enough of this. I pray thee hold thy peace.

Nurse. Yes, madam. Yet I cannot choose but laugh
To think it should leave crying and say "Ay."
And yet, I warrant, it had upon its brow
A bump as big as a young cock'rel's stone;
60 A perilous knock; and it cried bitterly.
"Yea," quoth my husband, "fallst upon thy face?
Thou wilt fall backward when thou comest to age,
Wilt thou not, Jule?" It stinted, and said "Ay."

Juliet. And stint thou too, I pray thee, nurse, say I.

65 **Nurse.** Peace, I have done. God mark thee to his grace!
Thou wast the prettiest babe that e'er I nursed.
An I might live to see thee married once,
I have my wish.

31 applied wormwood, a plant with a bitter taste, to her breast in order to discourage the child from breast-feeding.

37 tetchy: touchy; cranky.

38–39 shake . . . trudge: When the dovehouse shook, I knew enough to leave.

41 by the rood: The rood is the cross on which Christ was crucified. The expression means something like "by God."
43 broke her brow: cut her forehead.

46–54 "Yea" . . . "Ay": To quiet Juliet after her fall, the Nurse's husband makes a crude joke, asking the baby whether she'll fall the other way (on her back) when she's older. Although at three Juliet doesn't understand the question, she stops crying (stinted) and innocently answers, "Yes." The Nurse finds this story so funny, she can't stop retelling it.

66 e'er: ever.

Act One, Scene 3. Lady Capulet speaks to Juliet about marriage to Paris. (Zeffirelli, 1968)

Lady Capulet. Marry, that "marry" is the very theme
70   I came to talk of. Tell me, daughter Juliet,
    How stands your disposition to be married?

Juliet. It is an honor that I dream not of.

Nurse. An honor? Were not I thine only nurse,
    I would say thou hadst sucked wisdom from thy teat.

75 **Lady Capulet.** Well, think of marriage now. Younger
      than you,
    Here in Verona, ladies of esteem,
    Are made already mothers. By my count,
    I was your mother much upon these years
80   That you are now a maid. Thus then in brief:
    The valiant Paris seeks you for his love.

Nurse. A man, young lady! lady, such a man
    As all the world—why he's a man of wax.

Lady Capulet. Verona's summer hath not such a
85   flower.

Nurse. Nay, he's a flower, in faith—a very flower.

69 Lady Capulet uses the word **marry** in two different senses. The first **marry** means "by the Virgin Mary"; the second means "to wed."

79–80 I was . . . maid: I was your mother at about your age, yet you are still unmarried.

83 a man of wax: a man so perfect he could be a wax statue. Sculptors used to use wax figures as models for their works.

Lady Capulet. What say you? Can you love the
    gentleman?
    This night you shall behold him at our feast.
90   Read o'er the volume of young Paris' face,
    And find delight writ there with beauty's pen;
    Examine every several lineament,
    And see how one another lends content;
    And what obscured in this fair volume lies
95   Find written in the margent of his eyes.
    This precious book of love, this unbound lover,
    To beautify him only lacks a cover.
    The fish lives in the sea, and 'tis much pride
    For fair without the fair within to hide.
100   That book in many's eyes doth share the glory,
    That in gold clasps locks in the golden story;
    So shall you share all that he doth possess,
    By having him making yourself no less.

Nurse. No less? Nay, bigger! Women grow by men.

105 **Lady Capulet.** Speak briefly, can you like of Paris' love?

Juliet. I'll look to like, if looking liking move;
    But no more deep will I endart mine eye
    Than your consent gives strength to make it fly.

[*Enter a* Servingman.]

Servingman. Madam, the guests are come, supper served
110   up, you called, my young lady asked for, the nurse
    cursed in the pantry, and everything in extremity. I
    must hence to wait. I beseech you follow straight.

Lady Capulet. We follow thee. [*Exit* Servingman.]
    Juliet, the County stays.

115 **Nurse.** Go, girl, seek happy nights to happy days.
    [*Exeunt.*]

90–97 Read . . . cover: Lady Capulet uses an extended metaphor that compares Paris to a book that Juliet should read. Look for the similarities she points out.

92 several lineament: separate feature. Lady Capulet points out how each of Paris' features makes the others look even better.

95 margent . . . eyes: She compares Paris' eyes to the margin of the page of a book where notes are written that explain the content.

96–99 This . . . hide: This beautiful book (Paris) only needs a cover (wife) to become even better. He may be hiding even more wonderful qualities inside.

104 The Nurse can't resist one of her earthy comments. She notes that women get bigger (pregnant) when they marry.

106 I'll look . . . move: Juliet's playful answer means "I'll look at him with the intention of liking him, if simply looking can make me like him."

111 extremity: confusion. The servant is upset because everything is happening at once, and he can't handle it. **straight:** immediately.

114 the County stays: Count Paris is waiting for you.

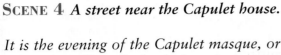

SCENE 4 *A street near the Capulet house.*

It is the evening of the Capulet masque, or costume ball. Imagine the guests proceeding through the darkened streets with torches to light the way.

Romeo and his two friends, Mercutio and Benvolio, join the procession. Their masks will prevent them from being recognized as Montagues. Mercutio and Benvolio are in a playful, partying mood, but Romeo is still depressed by his unanswered love for Rosaline. Romeo has also had a dream that warned him of the harmful consequences of this party. He senses trouble.

[*Enter* Romeo, Mercutio, Benvolio, *with five or six other* Maskers; Torchbearers.]

Romeo. What, shall this speech be spoke for our excuse?
  Or shall we on without apology?

Benvolio. The date is out of such prolixity.
  We'll have no Cupid hoodwinked with a scarf,
5 Bearing a Tartar's painted bow of lath,
  Scaring the ladies like a crowkeeper;
  Nor no without-book prologue, faintly spoke
  After the prompter, for our entrance;
  But let them measure us by what they will,
10 We'll measure them a measure, and be gone.

Romeo. Give me a torch. I am not for this ambling;
  Being but heavy, I will bear the light.

Mercutio. Nay, gentle Romeo, we must have you dance.

Romeo. Not I, believe me. You have dancing shoes
15 With nimble soles; I have a soul of lead
  So stakes me to the ground I cannot move.

Mercutio. You are a lover. Borrow Cupid's wings
  And soar with them above a common bound.

Romeo. I am too sore enpierced with his shaft
20 To soar with his light feathers, and so bound
  I cannot bound a pitch above dull woe.
  Under love's heavy burden do I sink.

Mercutio. And, to sink in it, should you burden love—
  Too great oppression for a tender thing.

25 **Romeo.** Is love a tender thing? It is too rough,
  Too rude, too boist'rous, and it pricks like thorn.

Mercutio. If love be rough with you, be rough with love.
  Prick love for pricking, and you beat love down.

1–10 shall this . . . be gone: Romeo asks whether they should send a messenger announcing their arrival at the party. Benvolio replies that this custom is out of date. He then lists all the things they won't use to make such an announcement. For example, **We'll have . . . crowkeeper:** We won't send someone dressed as a blindfolded Cupid, carrying a bow and looking like a scarecrow. Let them think what they want. We'll **measure them a measure** (dance one dance with them) and go.

12 heavy: sad. In spite of his mood, Romeo makes a joke based on the meanings of **heavy** and **light**.

13–32 As you read these lines, try to visualize each man. Romeo is overcome with sadness because of his lovestruck condition. Mercutio is determined to cheer him up. He is making fun of Romeo, but he is doing it in a friendly way.

Give me a case to put my visage in.

30 A visor for a visor! What care I
What curious eye doth quote deformities?
Here are the beetle brows shall blush for me.

Benvolio. Come, knock and enter, and no sooner in
But every man betake him to his legs.

35 **Romeo.** A torch for me! Let wantons light of heart
Tickle the senseless rushes with their heels;
For I am proverbed with a grandsire phrase,
I'll be a candle-holder and look on;
The game was ne'er so fair, and I am done.

40 **Mercutio.** Tut, dun's the mouse, the constable's own
word!
If thou art Dun, we'll draw thee from the mire
Of, save your reverence, love, wherein thou stickst
Up to the ears. Come, we burn daylight, ho!

45 **Romeo.** Nay, that's not so.

Mercutio. I mean, sir, in delay
We waste our lights in vain, like lamps by day.
Take our good meaning, for our judgment sits
Five times in that ere once in our five wits.

50 **Romeo.** And we mean well in going to this masque;
But 'tis no wit to go.

Mercutio. Why, may one ask?

Romeo. I dreamt a dream tonight.

Mercutio. And so did I.

55 **Romeo.** Well, what was yours?

Mercutio. That dreamers often lie.

Romeo. In bed asleep, while they do dream things true.

Mercutio. O, then I see Queen Mab hath been with you.
She is the fairies' midwife, and she comes
60 In shape no bigger than an agate stone
On the forefinger of an alderman,
Drawn with a team of little atomies
Athwart men's noses as they lie asleep;
Her wagon spokes made of long spinners' legs,
65 The cover, of the wings of grasshoppers;
Her traces, of the smallest spider's web;
Her collars, of the moonshine's wat'ry beams;
Her whip, of cricket's bone; the lash, of film;
Her wagoner, a small grey-coated gnat,

29–32 Give . . . for me: Give me a mask for an ugly face. I don't care if people notice my ugliness. Here, look at my heavy eyebrows.

34 betake . . . legs: dance.

35–38 Let . . . look on: Let playful people tickle the grass (**rushes**) on the floor with their dancing. I'll stick with the old saying (**grandsire phrase**) and hold a candle and watch the dancers.

40–44 Tut . . . daylight: Mercutio jokes using various meanings of the word **dun,** which sounds like Romeo's last word, **done.** He concludes by saying they should not waste time (**burn daylight**).

58–100 In this famous speech Mercutio tries to cheer up Romeo by spinning a tale about how Queen Mab brings dreams to people. Queen Mab, queen of the fairies, was a folktale character well known to Shakespeare's audience. Mercutio is a born storyteller. He dominates the stage with his vivid descriptions, puns, and satires of people and professions. Don't worry about understanding everything in the speech. Read it instead for the language Mercutio uses and the dreamlike scene he creates.

60 agate stone: jewel for a ring.

62 atomies: tiny creatures. Note the description of Mab's tiny and delicate carriage.

64 spinners' legs: spiders' legs.

66 traces: harness.

70 Not half so big as a round little worm
    Pricked from the lazy finger of a maid;
    Her chariot is an empty hazelnut,
    Made by the joiner squirrel or old grub,
    Time out o' mind the fairies' coachmakers.
75 And in this state she gallops night by night
    Through lovers' brains, and then they dream of love;
    O'er courtiers' knees, that dream on curtsies straight;
    O'er lawyers' fingers, who straight dream on fees;
    O'er ladies' lips, who straight on kisses dream,
80 Which oft the angry Mab with blisters plagues,
    Because their breaths with sweetmeats tainted are.
    Sometime she gallops o'er a courtier's nose,
    And then dreams he of smelling out a suit,
    And sometime comes she with a tithe-pig's tail
85 Tickling a parson's nose as 'a lies asleep,
    Then dreams he of another benefice.
    Sometime she driveth o'er a soldier's neck,
    And then dreams he of cutting foreign throats,
    Of breaches, ambuscadoes, Spanish blades,
90 Of healths five fathom deep; and then anon
    Drums in his ear, at which he starts and wakes,
    And being thus frighted, swears a prayer or two
    And sleeps again. This is that very Mab
    That plaits the manes of horses in the night
95 And bakes the elflocks in foul sluttish hairs,
    Which once untangled much misfortune bodes.
    This is the hag, when maids lie on their backs,
    That presses them and learns them first to bear,
    Making them women of good carriage.
100 This is she—

Romeo.   Peace, peace, Mercutio, peace!
    Thou talkst of nothing.

Mercutio.   True, I talk of dreams;
    Which are the children of an idle brain,
105 Begot of nothing but vain fantasy;
    Which is as thin of substance as the air,
    And more inconstant than the wind, who woos
    Even now the frozen bosom of the North
    And, being angered, puffs away from thence,
110 Turning his face to the dew-dropping South.

Benvolio. This wind you talk of blows us from
        ourselves.

73 **joiner:** carpenter.

78–80 What does Mab make lawyers and ladies dream of?

82–83 **Sometime she . . . suit:** Sometimes Mab makes a member of the king's court dream of receiving the king's special favors.

86 **benefice:** well-paying position for a church parson.

89 **ambuscadoes:** ambushes; **Spanish blades:** high-quality Spanish swords.

94 **plaits:** braids.

103–110 **True . . . South:** Mercutio is trying to keep Romeo from taking his dreams too seriously.

Supper is done, and we shall come too late.

Romeo. I fear, too early; for my mind misgives
115 Some consequence, yet hanging in the stars,
Shall bitterly begin his fearful date
With this night's revels and expire the term
Of a despised life, closed in my breast,
By some vile forfeit of untimely death.
120 But he that hath the steerage of my course
Direct my sail! On, lusty gentlemen!

Benvolio. Strike, drum.

[*Exeunt.*]

114–119 my mind . . . death: Romeo will not be cheered. He fears that some terrible event, caused by the stars, will begin at the party. Remember the phrase "star-crossed lovers" from the prologue of this act.

SCENE 5 *A hall in Capulet's house; the scene of the party.*

This is the scene of the party at which Romeo and Juliet finally meet. Romeo and his friends, disguised in their masks, arrive as uninvited guests. As he watches the dancers, Romeo suddenly sees Juliet and falls in love at first sight. At the same time, Tybalt recognizes Romeo's voice and knows he is a Montague. He alerts Capulet and threatens to kill Romeo. Capulet, however, insists that Tybalt behave himself and act like a gentleman. Promising revenge, Tybalt leaves. Romeo and Juliet meet and kiss in the middle of the dance floor. Only after they part do they learn each other's identity.

[Servingmen *come forth with napkins.*]

First Servingman. Where's Potpan, that he helps not to take away? He shift a trencher! he scrape a trencher!

Second Servingman. When good manners shall lie all in one or two men's hands, and they unwashed too,
5 'tis a foul thing.

First Servingman. Away with the joint-stools, remove the court-cupboard, look to the plate. Good thou, save me a piece of marchpane and, as thou lovest me, let the porter let in Susan Grindstone and Nell.
10 Anthony, and Potpan!

Second Servingman. Ay, boy, ready.

First Servingman. You are looked for and called for, asked for and sought for, in the great chamber.

Third Servingman. We cannot be here and there too.

1–16 The opening lines of the scene are a comic conversation among three servants as they do their work.

2 trencher: wooden plate.

7–8 plate: silverware and plates.
marchpane: marzipan, a sweet made from almond paste.

15　Cheerly, boys! Be brisk awhile, and the longer liver
　　　take all.

[*Exeunt.*]

[Maskers *appear with* Capulet, Lady Capulet, Juliet, *all the*
Guests, *and* Servants.]

Capulet. Welcome, gentlemen! Ladies that have their
　　　toes
　　　Unplagued with corns will have a bout with you.
20　Ah ha, my mistresses! which of you all
　　　Will now deny to dance? She that makes dainty,
　　　She I'll swear hath corns. Am I come near ye now?
　　　Welcome, gentlemen! I have seen the day
　　　That I have worn a visor and could tell
25　A whispering tale in a fair lady's ear,
　　　Such as would please. 'Tis gone, 'tis gone, 'tis gone!
　　　You are welcome, gentlemen! Come, musicians, play.
　　　A hall, a hall! give room! and foot it, girls.

[*Music plays and they dance.*]

　　　More light, you knaves! and turn the tables up,
30　And quench the fire, the room is grown too hot.
　　　Ah, sirrah, this unlooked-for sport comes well.
　　　Nay, sit, nay, sit, good cousin Capulet,
　　　For you and I are past our dancing days.
　　　How long is't now since last yourself and I
35　Were in a mask?

Second Capulet. By'r Lady, thirty years.

Capulet. What, man? 'Tis not so much, 'tis not so
　　　much!
　　　'Tis since the nuptial of Lucentio,
40　Come Pentecost as quickly as it will,
　　　Some five-and-twenty years, and then we masked.

Second Capulet. 'Tis more, 'tis more! His son is elder, sir;
　　　His son is thirty.

Capulet.　　　　　Will you tell me that?
45　His son was but a ward two years ago.

Romeo. [*To a* Servingman] What lady's that, which doth
　　　enrich the hand of yonder knight?

Servant. I know not, sir.

Romeo. O, she doth teach the torches to burn bright!
50　It seems she hangs upon the cheek of night

17–31 Capulet is welcoming his guests and inviting them all to dance. At the same time, like a good host, he is trying to get the party going. He alternates talking with his guests and telling the servants what to do.

21–22 She that . . . corns: Any woman too shy to dance will be assumed to have **corns,** ugly and painful growths on the toes.

24 visor: mask.

31–45 The dancing has begun, and Capulet and his relative are watching as they talk about days gone. Although the two old men are speaking, whom do you think the audience is watching?

46–47 Romeo has spotted Juliet across the dance hall, and he is immediately hypnotized by her beauty.

Act One, Scene 5. Romeo sees Juliet for the first time. (Zeffirelli, 1968)

Like a rich jewel in an Ethiop's ear—
Beauty too rich for use, for earth too dear!
So shows a snowy dove trooping with crows
As yonder lady o'er her fellows shows.
55 The measure done, I'll watch her place of stand
And, touching hers, make blessed my rude hand.
Did my heart love till now? Forswear it, sight!
For I ne'er saw true beauty till this night.

Tybalt. This, by his voice, should be a Montague.
60 Fetch me my rapier, boy. What, dares the slave
Come hither, covered with an antic face,
To fleer and scorn at our solemnity?
Now, by the stock and honor of my kin,
To strike him dead I hold it not a sin.

51–52 Ethiop's ear: the ear of an Ethiopian (African). **for earth too dear:** too precious for this world.

55–58 The measure . . . night: When the dance is over, Romeo will "bless" his hand by touching that of this beautiful woman. He swears that he has never loved before this moment because he's never seen true beauty before. What seems to be Romeo's standard for falling in love?

59–64 Tybalt recognizes Romeo's voice and tells his servant to get his sword **(rapier).** He thinks Romeo has come to mock **(fleer)** their party. What does Tybalt want to do to Romeo?

Capulet. Why, how now, kinsman? Wherefore storm
    you so?

65

Tybalt. Uncle, this is a Montague, our foe;
    A villain, that is hither come in spite
    To scorn at our solemnity this night.

Capulet. Young Romeo is it?

70

Tybalt.   'Tis he, that villain Romeo.

Capulet. Content thee, gentle coz, let him alone.
    'A bears him like a portly gentleman,
    And, to say truth, Verona brags of him
    To be a virtuous and well-governed youth.
    I would not for the wealth of all this town
    Here in my house do him disparagement.
    Therefore be patient, take no note of him.
    It is my will; the which if thou respect,
    Show a fair presence and put off these frowns,
    An ill-beseeming semblance for a feast.

75

80

72–101 Capulet is not concerned about Romeo's presence and notes that the boy has a reputation for being well-mannered. He insists that Tybalt calm down and enjoy the party.

Tybalt. It fits when such a villain is a guest.
    I'll not endure him.

Capulet.   He shall be endured.
    What, goodman boy? I say he shall. Go to!
    Am I the master here, or you? Go to!
    You'll not endure him? God shall mend my soul!
    You'll make a mutiny among my guests!
    You will set cock-a-hoop! You'll be the man.

85

85 goodman boy: a term used to address an inferior. In an angrier tone Capulet tells Tybalt that he's acting childishly and in an ungentlemanly manner.
Go to: Stop, that's enough!

89 set cock-a-hoop: cause everything to be upset.

Tybalt. Why, uncle, 'tis a shame.

90

Capulet.   Go to, go to!
    You are a saucy boy. Is't so, indeed?
    This trick may chance to scathe you. I know what.
    You must contrary me! Marry, 'tis time.—
    Well said, my hearts!—You are a princox—go!
    Be quiet, or—More light, more light!—For shame!
    I'll make you quiet; what!—Cheerly, my hearts!

95

93–94 scathe: harm; **what:** what I'm doing. You dare to challenge my authority?

95–97 Capulet interrupts his angry speech with concerned comments to his guests and servants.

Tybalt. Patience perforce with willful choler meeting
    Makes my flesh tremble in their different greeting.
    I will withdraw; but this intrusion shall,
    Now seeming sweet, convert to bitter gall.

100

98–101 Patience . . . gall: Tybalt says he will restrain himself, being forced to; but his suppressed anger (**choler**) makes his body shake. What do you think he might do about his anger?

[*Exit.*]

Romeo. If I profane with my unworthiest hand
This holy shrine, the gentle fine is this:
My lips, two blushing pilgrims, ready stand
105   To smooth that rough touch with a tender kiss.

Juliet. Good pilgrim, you do wrong your hand too much,
Which mannerly devotion shows in this;
For saints have hands that pilgrims' hands do touch,
110   And palm to palm is holy palmers' kiss.

Romeo. Have not saints lips, and holy palmers too?

Juliet. Ay, pilgrim, lips that they must use in prayer.

Romeo. O, then, dear saint, let lips do what hands do!
They pray; grant thou, lest faith turn to despair.

115   **Juliet.** Saints do not move, though grant for prayers' sake.

Romeo. Then move not while my prayer's effect I take.
Thus from my lips, by thine my sin is purged.

[*Kisses her.*]

Juliet. Then have my lips the sin that they have took.

120   **Romeo.** Sin from my lips? O trespass sweetly urged! Give me my sin again.

[*Kisses her.*]

Juliet. You kiss by the book.

Nurse. Madam, your mother craves a word with you.

Romeo. What is her mother?

125   **Nurse.**   Marry, bachelor,
Her mother is the lady of the house.
And a good lady, and a wise and virtuous.
I nursed her daughter that you talked withal.
I tell you, he that can lay hold of her
130   Shall have the chinks.

Romeo.   Is she a Capulet?
O dear account! my life is my foe's debt.

Benvolio. Away, be gone, the sport is at the best.

Romeo. Ay, so I fear; the more is my unrest.

135   **Capulet.** Nay, gentlemen, prepare not to be gone;
We have a trifling foolish banquet towards.

102–121 Think of this part of the scene as a close-up involving only Romeo and Juliet. With the party going on around them, Romeo and Juliet are at center stage, ignoring everyone else. They touch the palms of their hands together. Their conversation revolves around Romeo's comparison of his lips to pilgrims (**palmers**) who have traveled to visit a holy shrine, Juliet. Juliet goes along with his comparison because she feels the same way he does.

118 In the midst of the dancers, Romeo kisses Juliet.

122 kiss by the book: Juliet could mean "You kiss like an expert, someone who has studied the correct method." Or she could be teasing Romeo, meaning "You kiss coldly, as though you had learned it by reading a book."

123–130 Because of the Nurse's message from Lady Capulet, Juliet leaves, and Romeo is left to talk with the Nurse. She informs him that Juliet is Capulet's daughter and a good catch—whoever wins her shall become rich (**have the chinks**).

132 my life . . . debt: my life belongs to my enemy. How does Romeo react when he learns that Juliet is Capulet's daughter?

136 towards: coming up.

VIEW AND COMPARE

(Zeffirelli, 1968)

Which of these images better captures the emotions of Romeo and Juliet when they first meet?

(Luhrmann, 1996)

[They whisper in his ear.]

Is it e'en so? Why then, I thank you all.
I thank you, honest gentlemen. Good night.
More torches here! *[Exeunt* Maskers.] Come on then,
   let's to bed.
140   Ah, sirrah, by my fay, it waxes late;
I'll to my rest.

[Exeunt all but Juliet *and* Nurse.]

Juliet. Come hither, nurse. What is yond gentleman?

Nurse. The son and heir of old Tiberio.

145   **Juliet.** What's he that now is going out of door?

Nurse. Marry, that, I think, be young Petruchio.

Juliet. What's he that follows there, that would not
   dance?

Nurse. I know not.

150   **Juliet.** Go ask his name.—If he be married,
My grave is like to be my wedding bed.

Nurse. His name is Romeo, and a Montague,
The only son of your great enemy.

Juliet. My only love, sprung from my only hate!
155   Too early seen unknown, and known too late!
Prodigious birth of love it is to me
That I must love a loathed enemy.

Nurse. What's this? what's this?

Juliet.   A rhyme I learnt even now
160   Of one I danced withal.

[One calls within, "Juliet."]

Nurse. Anon, anon!
Come, let's away; the strangers all are gone.

[Exeunt.]

143–148 Juliet asks the Nurse to identify various guests as they leave the house. What does she really want to know?

151 In this line Juliet tells her own fortune, although she doesn't know it.

155–156 Too early . . . too late: I fell in love with him before I learned who he is. **Prodigious:** abnormal, unlucky.

157 How does Juliet feel about the fact that she's fallen in love with the son of her father's enemy?

Connect to the Literature

1. **What Do You Think?** Which character in Act One appealed to you the most? Why?

> **Comprehension Check**
> - What warning does the Prince issue to the Capulets and Montagues?
> - What agreement is reached between Paris and Juliet's father?
> - Why does Romeo go to the party?

Think Critically

2. How would you describe Romeo and his attitude toward love?

3. In your opinion, how might Juliet be changed by meeting Romeo?

THINK ABOUT
- her reaction when Lady Capulet tells her of Paris's proposal
- her response to Romeo at the party
- what the speech beginning "My only love, sprung from my only hate!" indicates about her understanding of the circumstances

4. A **foil** is a character that highlights, through sharp contrast, another character's personality or attitudes. Identify two characters in Act One who are foils for each other. What do you learn about each character by seeing them in this way?

5. **ACTIVE READING** | **READING SHAKESPEAREAN DRAMA**
Look at the graphic that you are working on in your **READER'S NOTEBOOK.** As you review the events that have occurred in Act One, which ones seem the most important in setting up **conflicts** in the **plot?** Explain.

Extend Interpretations

6. **Critic's Corner** William Hazlitt, a well-known 19th-century British writer, had the following praise for Shakespeare's ability to create **characters:** "By an art like that of the ventriloquist, he throws his imagination out of himself, and makes every word appear to proceed from the mouth of the person in whose name it is given." Based on what you have read so far, do you agree with this assessment? Support your opinion with evidence.

7. **Connect to Life** The feud between the Montagues and Capulets has continued for a long time. What sorts of longstanding disputes exist today in communities and nations? Why do you think these conflicts are so hard to resolve?

Literary Analysis

BLANK VERSE | **Blank verse** consists of unrhymed lines of **iambic pentameter,** in which a typical line has five unstressed syllables each followed by a stressed syllable. The rhythms of blank verse are closest to those of natural speech, and because of this, blank verse is particularly suited for drama.

> *Mў líps, twŏ blúshĭng pílgrĭms, réadў stánd*
> (Act One, Scene 5, line 104)

Lines of blank verse can also contain variations—a change in the order of stressed and unstressed syllables, an extra syllable added, or one left out. For example, in this line spoken by Lord Capulet, there is an extra syllable:

> *Whĕretŏ Ĭ háve ĭnvítĕd mánў ă guést*
> (Act One, Scene 2, line 21)

Such variations contribute to giving the lines the flow and sound of spoken English.

Shakespeare also sometimes has characters speak in prose and sometimes in rhymed lines—usually couplets.

Paired Activity With a partner, find and copy four lines of blank verse from Act One of *Romeo and Juliet.* Mark the unstressed (ˇ) and stressed (´) syllables in each line. Are there any variations in the rhythmic pattern? Discuss how well you think the passage captures the sound of spoken English and how this sound affects meaning.

Act Two, Scene 1. Juliet thinks about her beloved Romeo. (Luhrmann, 1996)

The *Prologue*

In a sonnet the CHORUS summarizes what has happened so far in the play. He reviews how Romeo and Juliet have fallen in love and suggests both the problems and delights they now face. He also includes hints about what will result from the events of Act One.

[*Enter* Chorus.]

Chorus. Now old desire doth in his deathbed lie,
    And young affection gapes to be his heir.
    That fair for which love groaned for and would die,
    With tender Juliet matched, is now not fair.
5   Now Romeo is beloved, and loves again,
    Alike bewitched by the charm of looks;
    But to his foe supposed he must complain,
    And she steal love's sweet bait from fearful hooks.
    Being held a foe, he may not have access
10 To breathe such vows as lovers use to swear,
    And she as much in love, her means much less
    To meet her new beloved anywhere;
    But passion lends them power, time means, to meet,
    Temp'ring extremities with extreme sweet.

[*Exit.*]

1–4 old . . . heir: Romeo's love for Rosaline (**old desire**) is now dead. His new love (**young affection**) replaces the old. Compared to Juliet, Rosaline no longer seems so lovely.

6 What attracted Romeo and Juliet to each other?

7 But . . . complain: Juliet, a Capulet, is Romeo's enemy; yet she is the one to whom he must plead (**complain**) his love.

9–12 What problem now faces Romeo and Juliet?

14 Temp'ring . . . sweet: moderating great difficulties with extreme delights.

ACT *Two*

SCENE 1 *A lane by the wall of Capulet's orchard.*

Later in the evening of the party, Romeo returns alone to the Capulet home, hoping for another glimpse of Juliet. He climbs the wall and hides outside, in the orchard. Meanwhile, Benvolio and Mercutio come looking for him, but he remains hidden behind the wall. Mercutio makes fun of Romeo and his lovesick condition. Keep in mind that Mercutio and Benvolio think Romeo is still in love with Rosaline, since they know nothing about his meeting with Juliet.

[*Enter* Romeo *alone.*]

Romeo. Can I go forward when my heart is here?
　　Turn back, dull earth, and find thy center out.

[*Climbs the wall and leaps down within it.*]

[*Enter* Benvolio *with* Mercutio.]

Benvolio. Romeo! my cousin Romeo! Romeo!

Mercutio. He is wise,
5　　And, on my life, hath stol'n him home to bed.

Benvolio. He ran this way, and leapt this orchard wall.
　　Call, good Mercutio.

Mercutio. 　　　　　　　Nay, I'll conjure too.
　　Romeo! humors! madman! passion! lover!
10　　Appear thou in the likeness of a sigh;
　　Speak but one rhyme, and I am satisfied!
　　Cry but "Ay me!" pronounce but "love" and "dove";
　　Speak to my gossip Venus one fair word,
　　One nickname for her purblind son and heir,
15　　Young Adam Cupid, he that shot so trim
　　When King Cophetua loved the beggar maid!
　　He heareth not, he stirreth not, he moveth not;
　　The ape is dead, and I must conjure him.
　　I conjure thee by Rosaline's bright eyes,
20　　By her high forehead and her scarlet lip,
　　By her fine foot, straight leg, and quivering thigh,

1–2 Can . . . out: How can I leave when Juliet is still here? My body **(dull earth)** has to find its heart **(center).**

8 conjure: use magic to call him.

10–23 Appear . . . us: Mercutio makes a series of loud jokes about Romeo's lovesickness. He tries to make Romeo appear by teasing him and suggestively naming parts of Rosaline's body. **demesnes:** areas.

And the demesnes that there adjacent lie,
That in thy likeness thou appear to us!

Benvolio. An if he hear thee, thou wilt anger him.

25 **Mercutio.** This cannot anger him. 'Twould anger him
To raise a spirit in his mistress' circle
Of some strange nature, letting it there stand
Till she had laid it and conjured it down.
That were some spite; my invocation
30 Is fair and honest and in his mistress' name
I conjure only but to raise up him.

Benvolio. Come, he hath hid himself among these trees
To be consorted with the humorous night.
Blind is his love, and best befits the dark.

35 **Mercutio.** If love be blind, love cannot hit the mark.
Now will he sit under a medlar tree
And wish his mistress were that kind of fruit
As maids call medlars when they laugh alone.
Oh, Romeo, that she were, O, that she were
40 An open et cetera, thou a pop'rin pear!
Romeo, good night. I'll to my truckle bed;
This field-bed is too cold for me to sleep.
Come, shall we go?

Benvolio.   Go then, for 'tis in vain
45 To seek him here that means not to be found.

[*Exeunt.*]

25–31 'Twould . . . raise up him: It would anger him if I called a stranger to join his lover (**mistress**), but I'm only calling Romeo to join her.

33 To be . . . night: to join with the night, which is as gloomy as Romeo is.

36 medlar: a fruit that looks like a small, brown apple.

41–45 Romeo . . . found: Mercutio jokes that he will go to his child's bed (**truckle bed**) since he is so "innocent."

Scene 2 *Capulet's orchard.*

The following is one of the most famous scenes in all literature. The speeches contain some of the most beautiful poetry Shakespeare ever wrote.
Juliet appears on the balcony outside her room. She cannot see Romeo, who stands in the garden just below. At the beginning of the scene, both characters are speaking private thoughts to themselves. Romeo, however, can hear Juliet as she expresses her love for him despite his family name. Eventually, he speaks directly to her, and they declare their love for each other. Just before dawn Romeo leaves to make plans for their wedding.

[*Enter* Romeo.]

Romeo. He jests at scars that never felt a wound.

[*Enter* Juliet *above at a window.*]

1 He jests: Mercutio makes jokes. What is Romeo saying about Mercutio?

But soft! What light through yonder window breaks?
It is the East, and Juliet is the sun!
Arise, fair sun, and kill the envious moon,
5   Who is already sick and pale with grief
That thou her maid art far more fair than she.
Be not her maid, since she is envious;
Her vestal livery is but sick and green,
And none but fools do wear it; cast it off.
10   It is my lady; O, it is my love!
O that she knew she were!
She speaks, yet she says nothing. What of that?
Her eye discourses; I will answer it.
I am too bold; 'tis not to me she speaks.
15   Two of the fairest stars in all the heaven,
Having some business, do entreat her eyes
To twinkle in their spheres till they return.
What if her eyes were there, they in her head?
The brightness of her cheek would shame those stars
20   As daylight doth a lamp; her eyes in heaven
Would through the airy region stream so bright
That birds would sing and think it were not night.
See how she leans her cheek upon her hand!
O that I were a glove upon that hand,
25   That I might touch that cheek!

Juliet.   Ay me!

Romeo. She speaks.
O, speak again, bright angel! for thou art
As glorious to this night, being o'er my head,
30   As is a winged messenger of heaven
Unto the white-upturned wond'ring eyes
Of mortals that fall back to gaze on him
When he bestrides the lazy-pacing clouds
And sails upon the bosom of the air.

35   **Juliet.** O Romeo, Romeo! wherefore art thou Romeo?
Deny thy father and refuse thy name!
Or, if thou wilt not, be but sworn my love,
And I'll no longer be a Capulet.

Romeo. [*Aside*] Shall I hear more, or shall I speak at
40   this?

Juliet. 'Tis but thy name that is my enemy.
Thou art thyself, though not a Montague.
What's Montague? It is nor hand, nor foot,

2–9 But soft . . . cast it off: Romeo sees Juliet at her window. For a moment he is speechless (**But soft:** be still), but then he describes her beauty in glowing images of light and the heavenly bodies. He compares Juliet's beauty to the sun and says the moon looks sick and green because it is jealous of her.

11–14 O that . . . speaks: Romeo shifts back and forth between wanting to speak to Juliet and being afraid. Why is he reluctant to let her know he is in the garden?

15–22 Two of . . . not night: Romeo compares Juliet's eyes to stars in the sky.

26 Remember that Juliet does not know that Romeo is listening.

28–34 thou art . . . of the air: He compares Juliet to an angel (**winged messenger of heaven**) who stands over (**bestrides**) the clouds.

35–38 wherefore: why. Juliet asks why the man she loves is named Montague, a name that she is supposed to hate. What does she ask him to do? What does she promise to do?

Nor arm, nor face, nor any other part
45   Belonging to a man. O, be some other name!
What's in a name? That which we call a rose
By any other name would smell as sweet.
So Romeo would, were he not Romeo called,
Retain that dear perfection which he owes
50   Without that title. Romeo, doff thy name;
And for that name, which is no part of thee,
Take all myself.

Romeo.   I take thee at thy word.
Call me but love, and I'll be new baptized;
55   Henceforth I never will be Romeo.

Juliet. What man art thou that, thus bescreened in night,
So stumblest on my counsel?

Romeo.   By a name
60   I know not how to tell thee who I am.
My name, dear saint, is hateful to myself,
Because it is an enemy to thee.
Had I it written, I would tear the word.

Juliet. My ears have yet not drunk a hundred words
65   Of that tongue's utterance, yet I know the sound.
Art thou not Romeo, and a Montague?

Romeo. Neither, fair saint, if either thee dislike.

Juliet. How camest thou hither, tell me, and
wherefore?
70   The orchard walls are high and hard to climb,
And the place death, considering who thou art,
If any of my kinsmen find thee here.

Romeo. With love's light wings did I o'erperch these
walls;
75   For stony limits cannot hold love out,
And what love can do, that dares love attempt.
Therefore thy kinsmen are no let to me.

Juliet. If they do see thee, they will murder thee.

Romeo. Alack, there lies more peril in thine eye
80   Than twenty of their swords! Look thou but sweet,
And I am proof against their enmity.

Juliet. I would not for the world they saw thee here.

Romeo. I have night's cloak to hide me from their
sight;

46–52 Juliet tries to convince herself that a name is just a meaningless word that has nothing to do with the person. She asks Romeo to get rid of **(doff)** his name.

53–55 Romeo startles Juliet by speaking aloud.

56–58 How dare you, hiding **(bescreened)**, listen to my private thoughts **(counsel)?**

68–69 How . . . wherefore: How did you get here, and why did you come?

73–78 With . . . thee: Love helped me climb **(o'erperch)** the walls. Neither walls nor your relatives are a hindrance **(let)** to my love. (Romeo is carried away with emotion, but Juliet is more realistic.) What warning does she give?

80–81 Look . . . enmity: Smile on me, and I will be defended against your family's hatred **(enmity).**

Act Two, Scene 2. Romeo joins Juliet on the balcony to profess his love. (Zeffirelli, 1968)

85 And but thou love me, let them find me here.
My life were better ended by their hate
Than death prorogued, wanting of thy love.

Juliet. By whose direction foundst thou out this place?

Romeo. By love, that first did prompt me to enquire.
90 He lent me counsel, and I lent him eyes.
I am no pilot, yet, wert thou as far
As that vast shore washed with the farthest sea,
I would adventure for such merchandise.

Juliet. Thou knowest the mask of night is on my face;
95 Else would a maiden blush bepaint my cheek
For that which thou hast heard me speak tonight.
Fain would I dwell on form—fain, fain deny
What I have spoke; but farewell compliment!
Dost thou love me? I know thou wilt say "Ay";
100 And I will take thy word. Yet, if thou swearst,
Thou mayst prove false. At lovers' perjuries,
They say Jove laughs. O gentle Romeo,
If thou dost love, pronounce it faithfully.

86–87 My life . . . love: I'd rather die from their hatred than have my death postponed **(prorogued)** if you don't love me.

94–98 Thou . . . compliment: Had I known you were listening, I would have gladly **(fain)** behaved more properly, but now it's too late for good manners **(farewell compliment).** Why is Juliet embarrassed that Romeo overheard her?

101–102 At . . . laughs: Jove (the king of the gods) laughs at lovers who lie to each other. Why is Juliet worried?

Or if thou thinkst I am too quickly won,
105   I'll frown, and be perverse, and say thee nay,
So thou wilt woo; but else, not for the world.
In truth, fair Montague, I am too fond,
And therefore thou mayst think my 'havior light;
But trust me, gentleman, I'll prove more true
110   Than those that have more cunning to be strange.
I should have been more strange, I must confess,
But that thou overheardst, ere I was ware,
My true love's passion. Therefore pardon me,
And not impute this yielding to light love,
115   Which the dark night hath so discovered.

Romeo. Lady, by yonder blessed moon I swear,
  That tips with silver all these fruit-tree tops—

Juliet. O, swear not by the moon, the inconstant moon,
  That monthly changes in her circled orb,
120   Lest that thy love prove likewise variable.

Romeo. What shall I swear by?

Juliet.   Do not swear at all;
  Or if thou wilt, swear by thy gracious self,
  Which is the god of my idolatry,
125   And I'll believe thee.

Romeo.   If my heart's dear love—

Juliet. Well, do not swear. Although I joy in thee,
  I have no joy of this contract tonight.
  It is too rash, too unadvised, too sudden;
130   Too like the lightning, which doth cease to be
Ere one can say "It lightens." Sweet, good night!
This bud of love, by summer's ripening breath,
May prove a beauteous flow'r when next we meet.
Good night, good night! As sweet repose and rest
135   Come to thy heart as that within my breast!

Romeo. O, wilt thou leave me so unsatisfied?

Juliet. What satisfaction canst thou have tonight?

Romeo. The exchange of thy love's faithful vow for
    mine.

140 **Juliet.** I gave thee mine before thou didst request it;
  And yet I would it were to give again.

Romeo. Wouldst thou withdraw it? For what purpose,
    love?

104–110 if . . . strange: You might think I've fallen in love too easily and that I am too forward. But I'll be truer to you than those who hide their feelings **(be strange)** and play romantic games.

118–120 swear . . . variable: Why doesn't Juliet want Romeo to swear by the moon?

128–131 I have . . . lightens: Juliet is worried about their love **(contract)**, which has happened as quickly as lightning and could be gone as fast. What is Juliet's attitude at this point? Do you agree with her feelings about the relationship?

Juliet. But to be frank and give it thee again.
145   And yet I wish but for the thing I have.
   My bounty is as boundless as the sea,
   My love as deep; the more I give to thee,
   The more I have, for both are infinite.
   I hear some noise within. Dear love, adieu!

[Nurse *calls within.*]

150   Anon, good nurse! Sweet Montague, be true.
   Stay but a little, I will come again.

[*Exit.*]

Romeo. O blessed, blessed night! I am afeard,
   Being in night, all this is but a dream,
   Too flattering-sweet to be substantial.

[*Re-enter* Juliet, *above.*]

155 **Juliet.** Three words, dear Romeo, and good night
     indeed.
   If that thy bent of love be honorable,
   Thy purpose marriage, send me word tomorrow,
   By one that I'll procure to come to thee,
160   Where and what time thou wilt perform the rite;
   And all my fortunes at thy foot I'll lay
   And follow thee my lord throughout the world.

Nurse. [*Within*] Madam!

Juliet. I come, anon.—But if thou meanst not well,
165   I do beseech thee—

Nurse. [*Within*]   Madam!

Juliet. By-and-by I come.—
   To cease thy suit and leave me to my grief.
   Tomorrow will I send.

170 **Romeo.**   So thrive my soul—

Juliet. A thousand times good night! [*Exit.*]

Romeo. A thousand times the worse, to want thy light!
   Love goes toward love as schoolboys from their books;
   But love from love, towards school with heavy looks.

[*Enter* Juliet *again, above.*]

175 **Juliet.** Hist! Romeo, hist! O for a falc'ner's voice
   To lure this tassel-gentle back again!

150–151 Anon: Right away! Juliet calls to her nurse but meanwhile asks Romeo to wait till she returns. The Nurse's repeated calls begin to create urgency and tension.

157–160 If that . . . rite: I'll send a messenger to you tomorrow. If your intention is to marry me, tell the messenger where and when the ceremony will be. Although in love, Juliet continues to be practical and wants proof that Romeo's intentions are serious.

173–174 Love . . . looks: The simile means that lovers meet as eagerly as schoolboys leave their books; lovers separate with the sadness of boys going to school.

Bondage is hoarse and may not speak aloud;
Else would I tear the cave where Echo lies,
And make her airy tongue more hoarse than mine
180 With repetition of my Romeo's name.
Romeo!

Romeo. It is my soul that calls upon my name.
How silver-sweet sound lovers' tongues by night,
Like softest music to attending ears!

185 **Juliet.** Romeo!

Romeo.   My sweet?

Juliet. What o'clock tomorrow
Shall I send to thee?

Romeo.   By the hour of nine.

190 **Juliet.** I will not fail. 'Tis twenty years till then.
I have forgot why I did call thee back.

Romeo. Let me stand here till thou remember it.

Juliet. I shall forget, to have thee still stand there,
Rememb'ring how I love thy company.

195 **Romeo.** And I'll still stay, to have thee still forget,
Forgetting any other home but this.

Juliet. 'Tis almost morning. I would have thee gone—
And yet no farther than a wanton's bird,
That lets it hop a little from her hand,
200 Like a poor prisoner in his twisted gyves,
And with a silk thread plucks it back again,
So loving-jealous of his liberty.

Romeo. I would I were thy bird.

Juliet.   Sweet, so would I.
205 Yet I should kill thee with much cherishing.
Good night, good night! Parting is such sweet
sorrow,
That I shall say good night till it be morrow.

[*Exit.*]

Romeo. Sleep dwell upon thine eyes, peace in thy
210 breast!
Would I were sleep and peace, so sweet to rest!
Hence will I to my ghostly father's cell,
His help to crave and my dear hap to tell.

[*Exit.*]

175–181 Hist . . . name: Listen, Romeo, I wish I could speak your name as loudly as a falconer calls his falcon (**tassel-gentle**), but because of my parents, I must whisper. Echo was a nymph in Greek mythology whose unreturned love for Narcissus caused her to waste away until only her voice was left.

187–188 The ever-practical Juliet asks for details.

197–202 I would . . . liberty: I know you must go, but I want you close to me like a pet bird that a thoughtless child (**wanton**) keeps on a string.

212–213 ghostly father: spiritual advisor or priest. **dear hap:** good fortune.

Friar Laurence's cell in the monastery.

Romeo goes from Capulet's garden to the monastery where Friar Laurence lives. The friar knows Romeo well and often gives him advice. As the scene begins, Friar Laurence is gathering herbs in the early morning. He talks of good and bad uses for herbs. Keep this in mind, since Friar Laurence's skill at mixing herbs becomes important later in the play. Romeo tells the friar that he loves Juliet and wants to marry her. The friar is amazed that Romeo has forgotten about Rosaline so easily and suggests that Romeo might be acting in haste. Eventually, however, he agrees to marry Romeo and Juliet, hoping that the marriage might end the feud between their families.

[*Enter* Friar Laurence *alone, with a basket.*]

Friar Laurence. The grey-eyed morn smiles on the
   frowning night,
   Chequ'ring the Eastern clouds with streaks of light;
   And flecked darkness like a drunkard reels
5 From forth day's path and Titan's fiery wheels.
   Now, ere the sun advance his burning eye
   The day to cheer and night's dank dew to dry,
   I must upfill this osier cage of ours
   With baleful weeds and precious-juiced flowers.
10 The earth that's nature's mother is her tomb,
   What is her burying grave, that is her womb;
   And from her womb children of divers kind
   We sucking on her natural bosom find;
   Many for many virtues excellent,
15 None but for some, and yet all different.
   O, mickle is the powerful grace that lies
   In plants, herbs, stones, and their true qualities;
   For naught so vile that on the earth doth live
   But to the earth some special good doth give;
20 Nor aught so good but, strained from that fair use,
   Revolts from true birth, stumbling on abuse.
   Virtue itself turns vice, being misapplied,
   And vice sometime's by action dignified.
   Within the infant rind of this small flower
25 Poison hath residence, and medicine power;
   For this, being smelt, with that part cheers each part;
   Being tasted, slays all senses with the heart.
   Two such opposed kings encamp them still
   In man as well as herbs—grace and rude will;
30 And where the worser is predominant,
   Full soon the canker death eats up that plant.

1–31 Friar Laurence begins his speech by describing how night changes into day. He then speaks of the herbs he is collecting. The friar is particularly fascinated with the idea that in herbs as well as man both good and evil can exist.

5 Titan is the god whose chariot pulls the sun into the sky each morning.

8 osier cage: willow basket.

10–11 The earth . . . womb: The same earth that acts as a tomb, or burial ground, is also the womb, or birthplace, of useful plants.

16–19 mickle: great. The Friar says that nothing from the earth is so evil that it doesn't do some good.

24–27 Within . . . heart: He holds a flower that can be used either as a poison or a medicine. If the flower is smelled, its fragrance can improve health in each part of the body; if eaten, it causes death.

29 grace and rude will: good and evil. Both exist in people as well as in plants.

[*Enter* Romeo.]

Romeo. Good morrow, father.

Friar Laurence.   Benedicite!
What early tongue so sweet saluteth me?
35   Young son, it argues a distempered head
So soon to bid good morrow to thy bed.
Care keeps his watch in every old man's eye,
And where care lodges sleep will never lie;
But where unbruised youth with unstuffed brain
40   Doth couch his limbs, there golden sleep doth reign.
Therefore thy earliness doth me assure
Thou art uproused with some distemp'rature;
Or if not so, then here I hit it right—
Our Romeo hath not been in bed tonight.

45   **Romeo.** That last is true, the sweeter rest was mine.

Friar Laurence. God pardon sin! Wast thou with
       Rosaline?

Romeo. With Rosaline, my ghostly father? No.
I have forgot that name, and that name's woe.

50   **Friar Laurence.** That's my good son! But where hast
       thou been then?

Romeo. I'll tell thee ere thou ask it me again.
I have been feasting with mine enemy,
Where on a sudden one hath wounded me
55   That's by me wounded. Both our remedies
Within thy help and holy physic lies.
I bear no hatred, blessed man, for, lo,
My intercession likewise steads my foe.

Friar Laurence. Be plain, good son, and homely in thy
60   drift.
Riddling confession finds but riddling shrift.

Romeo. Then plainly know my heart's dear love is set
On the fair daughter of rich Capulet;
As mine on hers, so hers is set on mine,
65   And all combined, save what thou must combine
By holy marriage. When, and where, and how
We met, we wooed, and made exchange of vow,
I'll tell thee as we pass; but this I pray,
That thou consent to marry us today.

33 Benedicite (bā′nā-dē′chĭ-tā′): God bless you.

35–44 it argues . . . tonight: Only a disturbed (**distempered**) mind could make you get up so early. Old people may have trouble sleeping, but it is not normal for someone as young as you. Or were you up all night?

46–47 God . . . Rosaline: The Friar is shocked that Romeo has not been to bed yet. Where does he think Romeo has been?

52–61 Romeo tries to explain the situation and asks for help for both himself and his enemy (Juliet). In his excitement, Romeo talks in riddles, which confuse the Friar. The Friar tells Romeo to talk clearly.

70 **Friar Laurence.** Holy Saint Francis! What a change
　　　　is here!
　　　Is Rosaline, that thou didst love so dear,
　　　So soon forsaken? Young men's love then lies
　　　Not truly in their hearts, but in their eyes.
75 　Jesu Maria! What a deal of brine
　　　Hath washed thy sallow cheeks for Rosaline!
　　　How much salt water thrown away in waste,
　　　To season love, that of it doth not taste!
　　　The sun not yet thy sighs from heaven clears,
80 　Thy old groans ring yet in mine ancient ears.
　　　Lo, here upon thy cheek the stain doth sit
　　　Of an old tear that is not washed off yet.
　　　If e'er thou wast thyself, and these woes thine,
　　　Thou and these woes were all for Rosaline.
85 　And art thou changed? Pronounce this sentence then:
　　　Women may fall when there's no strength in men.

　　Romeo. Thou chidst me oft for loving Rosaline.

　　Friar Laurence. For doting, not for loving, pupil mine.

　　Romeo. And badest me bury love.

90 **Friar Laurence.**　　　　　　　　Not in a grave
　　　To lay one in, another ought to have.

　　Romeo. I pray thee chide not. She whom I love now
　　　Doth grace for grace and love for love allow.
　　　The other did not so.

95 **Friar Laurence.**　　　　　O, she knew well
　　　Thy love did read by rote, that could not spell.
　　　But come, young waverer, come go with me.
　　　In one respect I'll thy assistant be;
　　　For this alliance may so happy prove
100　To turn your households' rancor to pure love.

　　Romeo. O, let us hence! I stand on sudden haste.

　　Friar Laurence. Wisely, and slow. They stumble that
　　　run fast.

　　[*Exeunt.*]

73–74 Young . . . eyes: How would you paraphrase this sentence?

75–85 brine: salt water. The Friar is referring to the tears Romeo has been shedding for Rosaline. What is his opinion of Romeo's rapid change of affections from one girl to another?

86 Women . . . men: If men are so weak, women may be forgiven for sinning.

87–88 chidst: scolded. The Friar replies that he scolded Romeo for being lovesick, not for loving.

92–96 She whom . . . spell: Romeo says that the woman he loves feels the same way about him. That wasn't true of Rosaline. The Friar replies that Rosaline knew that he didn't know what real love is.

99–100 This marriage may work out well and turn the feud between your families into love.

102–103 How is the Friar's warning similar to Juliet's fears in the previous scene?

SCENE 4   *A street.*

Several hours after his meeting with Friar Laurence, Romeo meets Benvolio and Mercutio in the street. He is excited and happy; his mood is key to the comic nature of this scene, which includes much talk of swordplay and many suggestive jokes. Mercutio makes fun of Tybalt and teases Romeo. The Nurse comes to carry a message from Romeo to Juliet. Romeo tells her that Juliet should meet him at Friar Laurence's cell for their secret marriage ceremony.

[*Enter* Benvolio *and* Mercutio.]

Mercutio. Where the devil should this Romeo be?
　　Came he not home tonight?

Benvolio. Not to his father's. I spoke with his man.

3 man: servant.

Mercutio. Why, that same pale hard-hearted wench,
5　　that Rosaline,
　　Torments him so that he will sure run mad.

Benvolio. Tybalt, the kinsman to old Capulet,
　　Hath sent a letter to his father's house.

Mercutio. A challenge, on my life.

7–13 Tybalt . . . dared: The hot-headed Tybalt has sent a letter to Romeo, challenging him to a duel. He is obviously still angry about Romeo's crashing the Capulet party. Benvolio says that Romeo will do more than answer the letter; he will accept Tybalt's challenge and fight him.

10 **Benvolio.** Romeo will answer it.

Mercutio. Any man that can write may answer a letter.

Benvolio. Nay, he will answer the letter's master, how he
　　dares, being dared.

Mercutio. Alas, poor Romeo, he is already dead!
15　　stabbed with a white wench's black eye; shot through
　　the ear with a love song; the very pin of his heart
　　cleft with the blind bow-boy's butt-shaft; and is he a
　　man to encounter Tybalt?

17 blind bow-boy's butt-shaft: Cupid's dull practice arrows; Mercutio suggests that Romeo fell in love with very little work on Cupid's part.

Benvolio. Why, what is Tybalt?

20 **Mercutio.** More than Prince of Cats, I can tell you. O,
　　he's the courageous captain of compliments. He
　　fights as you sing pricksong—keeps time, distance,
　　and proportion; rests me his minim rest, one, two,
　　and the third in your bosom! the very butcher of a
25　　silk button, a duelist, a duelist! a gentleman of the
　　very first house, of the first and second cause. Ah,
　　the immortal passado! the punto reverso! the hay!

20–27 More than . . . hay: Mercutio mocks Tybalt's name. Prince of Cats refers to a cat in a fable named "Tybalt" that was known for its slyness. Then Mercutio makes fun of Tybalt's fancy new method of dueling, comparing it to precision singing (**pricksong**). **Passado, punto, reverso,** and **hay** were terms used in the new dueling style.

Benvolio. The what?

Mercutio. The pox of such antic, lisping, affecting
30　　fantasticoes—these new tuners of accent! "By Jesu, a
　　very good blade! a very tall man! a very good

29–37 The pox . . . their bones: As in his previous speech, Mercutio makes fun of people who, like Tybalt, try to impress everyone with their knowledge of the latest fashions in dueling.

whore!" Why, is not this a lamentable thing, grandsire, that we should be thus afflicted with these strange flies, these fashion-mongers, these
35 perdona-mi's, who stand so much on the new form that they cannot sit at ease on the old bench? O, their bones, their bones!

[*Enter* Romeo, *no longer moody.*]

Benvolio. Here comes Romeo! here comes Romeo!

Mercutio. Without his roe, like a dried herring. O,
40 flesh, flesh, how art thou fishified! Now is he for the numbers that Petrarch flowed in. Laura, to his lady, was but a kitchen wench (marry, she had a better love to berhyme her) Dido a dowdy, Cleopatra a gypsy, Helen and Hero hildings and harlots, Thisbe
45 a grey eye or so, but not to the purpose. Signior Romeo, bon jour! There's a French salutation to your French slop. You gave us the counterfeit fairly last night.

Romeo. Good morrow to you both. What counterfeit
50 did I give you?

Mercutio. The slip, sir, the slip. Can you not conceive?

Romeo. Pardon, good Mercutio. My business was great, and in such a case as mine a man may strain courtesy.

55 **Mercutio.** That's as much as to say, such a case as yours constrains a man to bow in the hams.

Romeo. Meaning, to curtsy.

Mercutio. Thou hast most kindly hit it.

Romeo. A most courteous exposition.

60 **Mercutio.** Nay, I am the very pink of courtesy.

Romeo. Pink for flower.

Mercutio. Right.

Romeo. Why, then is my pump well-flowered.

Mercutio. Well said! Follow me this jest now till thou
65 hast worn out thy pump, that, when the single sole of it is worn, the jest may remain, after the wearing, solely singular.

Romeo. Oh, single-soled jest, solely singular for the singleness!

39–45 without his roe: he is only part of himself. Mercutio makes fun of Romeo's name and his lovesickness. **numbers:** verses. Mercutio mentions Petrarch, who wrote sonnets to his love, Laura. He then makes insulting comments about famous lovers of the past.

46–51 bon jour: (French) good day. Here's a greeting to match your fancy French trousers **(slop).** You did a good job of getting away from us last night. (A piece of counterfeit money was called a **slip**.)

51–97 In these lines, Romeo and Mercutio have a battle of wits. They keep trying to top each other with funnier comments and cleverer puns.

63 pump: shoe; **well–flowered:** shoes were "pinked," or punched out in flowerlike designs.

70 **Mercutio.** Come between us, good Benvolio! My wits faint.

Romeo. Switch and spurs, switch and spurs! or I'll cry a match.

72–73 **Switch . . . match:** Keep going, or I'll claim victory.

Mercutio. Nay, if our wits run the wild-goose chase, I
75 am done; for thou hast more of the wild goose in one of thy wits than, I am sure, I have in my whole five. Was I with you there for the goose?

77 **Was . . . goose?:** Have I proved that you are a foolish person **(goose)?**

Romeo. Thou wast never with me for anything when thou wast not there for the goose.

80 **Mercutio.** I will bite thee by the ear for that jest.

Romeo. Nay, good goose, bite not!

Mercutio. Thy wit is a very bitter sweeting; it is a most sharp sauce.

Romeo. And is it not, then, well served in to a sweet
85 goose?

Mercutio. O, here's a wit of cheveril, that stretches from an inch narrow to an ell broad!

86 **cheveril:** kid skin, which is flexible. Mercutio means that a little wit stretches a long way.

Romeo. I stretch it out for that word "broad," which, added to the goose, proves thee far and wide a
90 broad goose.

Mercutio. Why, is not this better now than groaning for love? Now art thou sociable, now art thou Romeo; now art thou what thou art, by art as well as
95 by nature. For this driveling love is like a great natural that runs lolling up and down to hide his bauble in a hole.

95–97 **great natural:** an idiot like a jester or clown who carries a fool's stick **(bauble)**. Mercutio is happy that Romeo is his old playful self again.

Benvolio. Stop there, stop there!

Mercutio. Thou desirest me to stop in my tale against
100 the hair.

Benvolio. Thou wouldst else have made thy tale large.

Mercutio. O, thou art deceived! I would have made it short; for I was come to the whole depth of my tale, and meant indeed to occupy the argument no
105 longer.

[*Enter* Nurse *and* Peter, *her servant. He is carrying a large fan.*]

Romeo. Here's goodly gear!

Mercutio. A sail, a sail!

106–107 **Goodly gear:** something fine to joke about. A sail indicates that the Nurse in all her petticoats looks like a huge ship coming toward them.

Benvolio. Two, two! a shirt and a smock.

Nurse. Peter!

110 **Peter.** Anon.

Nurse. My fan, Peter.

Mercutio. Good Peter, to hide her face; for her fan's
the fairer of the two.

Nurse. God ye good morrow, gentlemen.

115 **Mercutio.** God ye good-den, fair gentlewoman.

Nurse. Is it good-den?

Mercutio. 'Tis no less, I tell ye, for the bawdy hand of
the dial is now upon the prick of noon.

Nurse. Out upon you! What a man are you!

120 **Romeo.** One, gentlewoman, that God hath made
himself to mar.

Nurse. By my troth, it is well said. "For himself to mar,"
quoth'a? Gentlemen, can any of you tell me where I
may find the young Romeo?

125 **Romeo.** I can tell you; but young Romeo will be older
when you have found him than he was when you
sought him. I am the youngest of that name, for fault
of a worse.

Nurse. You say well.

130 **Mercutio.** Yea, is the worst well? Very well took, i' faith!
wisely, wisely.

Nurse. If you be he, sir, I desire some confidence with
you.

Benvolio. She will endite him to some supper.

135 **Mercutio.** A bawd, a bawd, a bawd! So ho!

Romeo. What hast thou found?

Mercutio. No hare, sir; unless a hare, sir, in a lenten pie,
that is something stale and hoar ere it be spent.

[*Sings.*]

    "An old hare hoar,
140   And an old hare hoar,
    Is very good meat in Lent.
    But a hare that is hoar,
    Is too much for a score
    When it hoars ere it be spent."

145   Romeo, will you come to your father's? We'll to

110 Anon: Right away.

111 Fans were usually carried only by fine
ladies. The Nurse is trying to pretend that
she is more than a servant.

132–134 confidence: The Nurse means
conference; she uses big words without
understanding their meaning. Benvolio
makes fun of this by using endite instead
of invite.

135–145 Mercutio calls the Nurse a
bawd, or woman who runs a house of
prostitution. His song uses the insulting
puns **hare,** a rabbit or a prostitute, and
hoar, old.

dinner thither.

Romeo. I will follow you.

Mercutio. Farewell, ancient lady. Farewell, [*sings*] lady, lady, lady.

[*Exeunt* Mercutio *and* Benvolio.]

150 **Nurse.** Marry, farewell! I pray you, sir, what saucy merchant was this that was so full of his ropery?

Romeo. A gentleman, nurse, that loves to hear himself talk and will speak more in a minute than he will stand to in a month.

155 **Nurse.** An 'a speak anything against me, I'll take him down, an 'a were lustier than he is, and twenty such Jacks; and if I cannot, I'll find those that shall. Scurvy knave! I am none of his flirt-gills; I am none of his skainsmates. [*Turning to* Peter.] And thou must

160 stand by too, and suffer every knave to use me at his pleasure?

Peter. I saw no man use you at his pleasure. If I had, my weapon should quickly have been out, I warrant you. I dare draw as soon as another man, if I see

165 occasion in a good quarrel, and the law on my side.

Nurse. Now, afore God, I am so vexed that every part about me quivers. Scurvy knave! Pray you, sir, a word; and as I told you, my young lady bade me enquire you out. What she bid me say, I will keep

170 to myself; but first let me tell ye, if ye should lead her into a fool's paradise, as they say, it were a very gross kind of behavior, as they say; for the gentlewoman is young; and therefore, if you should deal double with her, truly it were an ill thing to be offered to

175 any gentlewoman, and very weak dealing.

Romeo. Nurse, commend me to thy lady and mistress. I protest unto thee—

Nurse. Good heart, and i' faith I will tell her as much. Lord, Lord! she will be a joyful woman.

180 **Romeo.** What wilt thou tell her, nurse? Thou dost not mark me.

Nurse. I will tell her, sir, that you do protest, which, as I take it, is a gentlemanlike offer.

Romeo. Bid her devise

151 ropery: roguery, or jokes.

158–161 The Nurse is angry that Mercutio treated her like one of his loose women (**flirt-gills**) or his gangsterlike friends (**skainsmates**). She then complains that Peter did not come to her defense.

169–175 The Nurse warns Romeo that he'd better mean what he said about marrying Juliet. She holds back her own news to make sure that Romeo's love is genuine.

176 commend me: give my respectful greetings.

185 Some means to come to shrift this afternoon;
And there she shall at Friar Laurence' cell
Be shrived and married. Here is for thy pains.

Nurse. No, truly, sir; not a penny.

Romeo. Go to! I say you shall.

190 **Nurse.** This afternoon, sir? Well, she shall be there.

Romeo. And stay, good nurse, behind the abbey wall.
Within this hour my man shall be with thee
And bring thee cords made like a tackled stair,
Which to the high topgallant of my joy
195 Must be my convoy in the secret night.
Farewell. Be trusty, and I'll quit thy pains.
Farewell. Commend me to thy mistress.

Nurse. Now God in heaven bless thee! Hark you, sir.

Romeo. What sayst thou, my dear nurse?

200 **Nurse.** Is your man secret? Did you ne'er hear say,
Two may keep counsel, putting one away?

Romeo. I warrant thee my man's as true as steel.

Nurse. Well, sir, my mistress is the sweetest lady. Lord,
Lord! when 'twas a little prating thing—O, there is a
205 nobleman in town, one Paris, that would fain lay
knife aboard; but she, good soul, had as lief see a
toad, a very toad, as see him. I anger her sometimes,
and tell her that Paris is the properer man; but
I'll warrant you, when I say so, she looks as pale as
210 any clout in the versal world. Doth not rosemary and
Romeo begin both with a letter?

Romeo. Ay, nurse, what of that? Both with an R.

Nurse. Ah, mocker! that's the dog's name. R is for the—
No; I know it begins with some other letter;
215 and she hath the prettiest sententious of it, of you
and rosemary, that it would do you good to hear it.

Romeo. Commend me to thy lady.

Nurse. Ay, a thousand times. [*Exit* Romeo.] Peter!

Peter. Anon.

220 **Nurse.** Peter, take my fan, and go before, and apace.

[*Exeunt.*]

184–187 Romeo tells the Nurse to have Juliet come to Friar Laurence's cell this afternoon using the excuse that she is going to confession (**shrift**). There she will receive forgiveness for her sins (**be shrived**) and be married.

193–194 tackled stair: a rope ladder. **topgallant:** highest point.

196–201 quit thy pains: reward you. The Nurse asks Romeo if his servant can be trusted and quotes the saying that two can keep a secret, but not three.

203–207 The Nurse, as is her way, begins to babble on and on. She mentions Paris' proposal but says Juliet would rather look at a toad than at Paris.

210–216 clout . . . world: old cloth in the entire world. **Doth not . . . hear it:** The Nurse tries to recall a clever saying that Juliet made up about Romeo and rosemary, the herb for remembrance, but she cannot remember it. She is sure that the two words couldn't begin with R because this letter sounds like a snarling dog. The Nurse mistakenly says **sententious** when she means sentences.

220 apace: quickly.

SCENE 5 *Capulet's orchard.*

Juliet is a nervous wreck, having waited for more than three hours for the Nurse to return. When the Nurse does arrive, she simply can't come to the point. Juliet gets more and more upset, until the Nurse finally reveals the wedding arrangements.

[*Enter* Juliet.]

Juliet. The clock struck nine when I did send the nurse;
    In half an hour she promised to return.
    Perchance she cannot meet him. That's not so.
    O, she is lame! Love's heralds should be thoughts,
5   Which ten times faster glide than the sun's beams
    Driving back shadows over lowering hills.
    Therefore do nimble-pinioned doves draw Love,
    And therefore hath the wind-swift Cupid wings.
    Now is the sun upon the highmost hill
10   Of this day's journey, and from nine till twelve
    Is three long hours; yet she is not come.
    Had she affections and warm youthful blood,
    She would be as swift in motion as a ball;
    My words would bandy her to my sweet love,
15   And his to me.
    But old folks, many feign as they were dead—
    Unwieldy, slow, heavy, and pale as lead.

[*Enter* Nurse *and* Peter.]

    O God, she comes! O honey nurse, what news?
    Hast thou met with him? Send thy man away.

20 **Nurse.** Peter, stay at the gate.

[*Exit* Peter.]

Juliet. Now, good sweet nurse—O Lord, why lookst
    thou sad?
    Though news be sad, yet tell them merrily;
    If good, thou shamest the music of sweet news
25   By playing it to me with so sour a face.

Nurse. I am aweary, give me leave awhile.
    Fie, how my bones ache! What a jaunce have I had!

Juliet. I would thou hadst my bones, and I thy news.
    Nay, come, I pray thee speak. Good, good nurse,
30   speak.

4–6 Love's . . . hills: Love's messengers should be thoughts, which travel ten times faster than sunbeams.

14 bandy: toss.

16 feign as: act as if.

21–22 The Nurse teases Juliet by putting on a sad face as if the news were bad.

26–27 give me . . . I had: Leave me alone for a while. I ache all over because of the running back and forth I've been doing.

Nurse. Jesu, what haste! Can you not stay awhile?
　Do you not see that I am out of breath?

Juliet. How art thou out of breath when thou hast
　　breath
35　To say to me that thou art out of breath?
　The excuse that thou dost make in this delay
　Is longer than the tale thou dost excuse.
　Is thy news good or bad? Answer to that.
　Say either, and I'll stay the circumstance.
40　Let me be satisfied, is't good or bad?

Nurse. Well, you have made a simple choice; you know
　not how to choose a man. Romeo? No, not he.
　Though his face be better than any man's, yet his leg
　excels all men's; and for a hand and a foot, and a
45　body, though they be not to be talked on, yet they are
　past compare. He is not the flower of courtesy, but, I'll
　warrant him, as gentle as a lamb. Go thy ways, wench;
　serve God. What, have you dined at home?

Juliet. No, no. But all this did I know before.
50　What say he of our marriage? What of that?

Nurse. Lord, how my head aches! What a head have I!
　It beats as it would fall in twenty pieces.
　My back o' t' other side—ah, my back, my back!
　Beshrew your heart for sending me about
55　To catch my death with jauncing up and down!

Juliet. I' faith, I am sorry that thou art not well.
　Sweet, sweet, sweet nurse, tell me, what says my
　　love?

Nurse. Your love says, like an honest gentleman, and a
60　courteous, and a kind, and a handsome, and, I
　warrant, a virtuous—Where is your mother?

Juliet. Where is my mother? Why, she is within.
　Where should she be? How oddly thou repliest!
　"Your love says, like an honest gentleman,
65　'Where is your mother?'"

Nurse. 　　　　　　　　O God's Lady dear!
　Are you so hot? Marry come up, I trow.
　Is this the poultice for my aching bones?
　Hence forward do your messages yourself.

70　**Juliet.** Here's such a coil! Come, what says Romeo?

Nurse. Have you got leave to go to shrift today?

39–40 Say . . . bad: Tell me if the news is good or bad, and I'll wait for the details.

41 simple: foolish.

54–55 Beshrew . . . down: Curse you for making me endanger my health by running around. Considering the Nurse's feelings for Juliet, is this really an angry curse?

66–69 O God's . . . yourself: Are you so eager? Control yourself (come up). Is this the treatment I get for my pain? From now on, run your own errands.

70 coil: fuss.

Juliet. I have.

Nurse. Then hie you hence to Friar Laurence' cell;
There stays a husband to make you a wife.

75   Now comes the wanton blood up in your cheeks:
They'll be in scarlet straight at any news.
Hie you to church; I must another way,
To fetch a ladder, by the which your love
Must climb a bird's nest soon when it is dark.

80   I am the drudge, and toil in your delight;
But you shall bear the burden soon at night.
Go; I'll to dinner; hie you to the cell.

Juliet. Hie to high fortune! Honest nurse, farewell.

[*Exeunt.*]

73–74 Then hie . . . a wife: Then go quickly to Friar Laurence's cell, where Romeo wants to marry you.

77–79 The Nurse will get the ladder that Romeo will use to climb to Juliet's room after they are married.

SCENE 6 *Friar Laurence's cell.*

Friar Laurence cautions Romeo to be more sensible in his love for Juliet. When she arrives, the two confess their love to each other and prepare to be married by Friar Laurence.

[*Enter* Friar Laurence *and* Romeo.]

Friar Laurence. So smile the heavens upon this holy act
That after-hours with sorrow chide us not!

Romeo. Amen, amen! But come what sorrow can,
It cannot countervail the exchange of joy

5   That one short minute gives me in her sight.
Do thou but close our hands with holy words,
Then love-devouring death do what he dare—
It is enough I may but call her mine.

Friar Laurence. These violent delights have violent

10   ends
And in their triumph die, like fire and powder,
Which, as they kiss, consume. The sweetest honey
Is loathsome in his own deliciousness
And in the taste confounds the appetite.

15   Therefore love moderately: long love doth so;
Too swift arrives as tardy as too slow.

[*Enter* Juliet.]

1–2 So smile . . . us not: May heaven bless this act and not blame us for it in the future **(after-hours)**.
3–8 come what . . . mine: No future sorrow can outweigh **(countervail)** the joy Juliet brings me. Once we're married, I don't even care if I die.

9–16 These . . . slow: The Friar compares Romeo's passion to gunpowder and the fire that ignites it: both are destroyed; then to honey, whose sweetness can destroy the appetite. He reminds Romeo to practice moderation in love. *How likely is it that Romeo will follow this advice?*

VIEW AND COMPARE

(Zeffirelli, 1968)

What view of marriage is reflected in each of these images?

(Luhrmann, 1996)

Here comes the lady. O, so light a foot
Will ne'er wear out the everlasting flint.
A lover may bestride the gossamer

20 That idles in the wanton summer air,
And yet not fall; so light is vanity.

Juliet. Good even to my ghostly confessor.

Friar Laurence. Romeo shall thank thee, daughter, for
us both.

25 **Juliet.** As much to him, else is his thanks too much.

Romeo. Ah, Juliet, if the measure of thy joy
Be heaped like mine, and that thy skill be more
To blazon it, then sweeten with thy breath
This neighbor air, and let rich music's tongue

30 Unfold the imagined happiness that both
Receive in either by this dear encounter.

Juliet. Conceit, more rich in matter than in words,
Brags of his substance, not of ornament.
They are but beggars that can count their worth;

35 But my true love is grown to such excess
I cannot sum up sum of half my wealth.

Friar Laurence. Come, come with me, and we will
make short work;
For, by your leaves, you shall not stay alone

40 Till Holy Church incorporate two in one.

[*Exeunt.*]

19–21 A lover . . . vanity: A lover can walk across a spider's web (**gossamer**), almost like walking on air.

22 ghostly confessor: spiritual advisor.

25 As much to him: The same greeting to Romeo that he offers to me.

26–31 If you are as happy as I am and have more skill to proclaim it, then sweeten the air by singing of our happiness to the world.

32–33 Conceit . . . ornament: True understanding (**conceit**) needs no words.

39–40 you shall . . . one: Until I have performed the wedding ceremony, I will not allow you to be alone together.

Thinking *through the* LITERATURE

Connect to the Literature

1. What Do You Think? What were your reactions to the balcony scene, in which Romeo and Juliet profess their love?

> **Comprehension Check**
> - What does Friar Laurence hope will be the result when he agrees to marry Romeo and Juliet?
> - Who challenges Romeo to a duel?
> - What important message from Romeo does the Nurse bring to Juliet?

Think Critically

2. Compare and contrast the ways that Romeo and Juliet respond to each other and their situation.

3. Much of the language that Romeo and Juliet use to express their love in Act Two, Scene 2, contains **imagery.** What effects does the imagery produce? Do you think it conveys more than literal statements would? Explain your answers.

4. `ACTIVE READING` `READING SHAKESPEAREAN DRAMA` Try to **visualize** the balcony scene (Act Two, Scene 2) as it might appear on stage. How do you imagine Romeo and Juliet would speak and move? What would their facial expressions be like? Read some of the lines aloud to help get a sense of the emotions the actors might be expressing, and then jot down notes in your **READER'S NOTEBOOK** about how you visualize the scene.

5. Do you think Romeo and Juliet marry too soon? Explain.

> THINK ABOUT
> - how long they have known each other
> - how they describe their feelings for each other in the balcony scene
> - possible reasons why Juliet is the one to suggest marriage
> - what the families might do if they find out about the romance

Extend Interpretations

6. Comparing Texts In what ways is the relationship between Romeo and Juliet similar to the relationship between the narrator and Eugene in "American History"?

7. Connect to Life Think about Romeo and Juliet's behaviors and decisions. How much do you think their relationship resembles modern love and courtship?

Literary Analysis

`SOLILOQUY/ASIDE` To reveal characters' private thoughts and feelings to the audience, Shakespeare frequently makes use of two devices, the soliloquy and the aside. A **soliloquy** is a speech that a character makes while alone on stage or when no one on stage is supposed to be listening. An **aside** is a remark that a character says in an undertone to the audience or to another character but that everyone else on stage is not supposed to hear.

Paired Activity Working with a partner, identify soliloquies and asides in Act Two of *Romeo and Juliet,* and explain what each reveals about the character who speaks it. You might organize your ideas on a chart like this one.

Scene and Line Numbers	Character Who Speaks	Soliloquy or Aside?	What Is Revealed

`REVIEW` `FORESHADOWING`
Foreshadowing is the technique of giving clues that hint or warn of events to come later in a plot. Which details in Act Two seem like they may foreshadow future events? What do you think they foreshadow?

ACT *Three*

SCENE 1 *A public place.*

Act Two ended with the joyful Romeo and Juliet secretly married. Their happiness, however, is about to end abruptly. In this scene, Mercutio, Benvolio, and Romeo meet Tybalt on the street. Tybalt insults Romeo, but Romeo, who has just returned from his wedding, remains calm. Mercutio, on the other hand, is furious with Tybalt, and they begin to fight. As Romeo tries to separate them, Tybalt stabs Mercutio, who later dies. Romeo then challenges Tybalt, kills him, and flees. The Prince arrives and demands an explanation. He announces that Romeo will be killed if he does not leave Verona immediately.

[*Enter* Mercutio, Benvolio, Page *and* Servants.]

Benvolio. I pray thee, good Mercutio, let's retire.
The day is hot, the Capulets abroad,
And if we meet, we shall not scape a brawl,
For now, these hot days, is the mad blood stirring.

> **3–4 we shall . . . stirring:** We shall not avoid a fight since the heat makes people angry.

5 **Mercutio.** Thou art like one of those fellows that, when he enters the confines of a tavern, claps me his sword upon the table and says "God send me no need of thee!" and by the operation of the second cup draws him on the drawer, when indeed there is
10 no need.

> **8–9 by the . . . drawer:** feeling the effects of a second drink, is ready to fight (**draw on**) the waiter who's pouring drinks (**drawer**).

Benvolio. Am I like such a fellow?

Mercutio. Come, come, thou art as hot a Jack in thy mood as any in Italy; and as soon moved to be moody, and as soon moody to be moved.

> **13–14 as soon moved . . . to be moved:** as likely to get angry and start a fight.

15 **Benvolio.** And what to?

Mercutio. Nay an there were two such, we should have none shortly, for one would kill the other. Thou! why, thou wilt quarrel with a man that hath a hair more or a hair less in his beard than thou hast. Thou
20 wilt quarrel with a man for cracking nuts, having no other reason but because thou hast hazel eyes. What eye but such an eye would spy out such a quarrel? Thy head is as full of quarrels as an egg is full of meat; and yet thy head hath been beaten as addle as

> **16–31** Picture Mercutio and Benvolio playfully roughing each other up as this conversation proceeds. Mercutio teases his friend by insisting that Benvolio is quick to pick a fight. However, everyone knows that Benvolio is gentle and peace loving. Mercutio could have been describing himself.

25 an egg for quarreling. Thou hast quarreled with a
man for coughing in the street, because he hath
wakened thy dog that hath lain asleep in the sun.
Didst thou not fall out with a tailor for wearing his
new doublet before Easter? with another for tying
30 his new shoes with old riband? And yet thou wilt tutor
me from quarreling!

Benvolio. An I were so apt to quarrel as thou art, any
man should buy the fee simple of my life for an hour
and a quarter.

35 **Mercutio.** The fee simple? O simple!

[*Enter* Tybalt *and others.*]

Benvolio. By my head, here come the Capulets.

Mercutio. By my heel, I care not.

Tybalt. Follow me close, for I will speak to them.
Gentlemen, good den. A word with one of you.

40 **Mercutio.** And but one word with one of us?
Couple it with something; make it a word and a
blow.

Tybalt. You shall find me apt enough to that, sir, an you
will give me occasion.

45 **Mercutio.** Could you not take some occasion without
giving?

Tybalt. Mercutio, thou consortest with Romeo.

Mercutio. Consort? What, dost thou make us minstrels?
An thou make minstrels of us, look to hear nothing
50 but discords. Here's my fiddlestick; here's that shall
make you dance. Zounds, consort!

Benvolio. We talk here in the public haunt of men.
Either withdraw unto some private place
And reason coldly of your grievances,
55 Or else depart. Here all eyes gaze on us.

Mercutio. Men's eyes were made to look, and let them
gaze. I will not budge for no man's pleasure, I.

[*Enter* Romeo.]

Tybalt. Well, peace be with you, sir. Here comes my
man.

60 **Mercutio.** But I'll be hanged, sir, if he wear your livery.

29–30 doublet: jacket. **riband:** ribbon or laces.

32–34 An I . . . quarter: If I picked fights as quickly as you do, anybody could own me for the smallest amount of money.

36 What do you predict will happen now that Tybalt has appeared?

38–57 As you read this exchange, ask yourself, Who is responsible for starting this fight?

41–44 Mercutio dares Tybalt to add a punch (**blow**) to whatever he has to say. Tybalt says he'll do so if Mercutio gives him an excuse.

47–51 consortest: keep company with. Tybalt means "You are friendly with Romeo." Mercutio pretends to misunderstand him, assuming that Tybalt is insulting him by calling Romeo and himself a **consort,** a group of traveling musicians. He then refers to his sword as his **fiddlestick,** the bow for a fiddle.

52–55 Benvolio steps between Tybalt and Mercutio, trying to keep peace between them. What does he suggest they do?

58–61 When Romeo enters, Mercutio again pretends to misunderstand Tybalt. By **my man,** Tybalt means "the man I'm looking for." Mercutio takes it to mean "my servant." (**Livery** is a servant's uniform.) He assures Tybalt that the only place Romeo would follow him as a servant is to the dueling field.

Marry, go before to field, he'll be your follower!
Your worship in that sense may call him man.

Tybalt. Romeo, the love I bear thee can afford
No better term than this: thou art a villain.

65 **Romeo.** Tybalt, the reason that I have to love thee
Doth much excuse the appertaining rage
To such a greeting. Villain am I none.
Therefore farewell. I see thou knowst me not.

Tybalt. Boy, this shall not excuse the injuries
70 That thou hast done me; therefore turn and draw.

Romeo. I do protest I never injured thee,
But love thee better than thou canst devise
Till thou shalt know the reason of my love;
And so, good Capulet, which name I tender
75 As dearly as mine own, be satisfied.

Mercutio. O calm, dishonorable, vile submission!
Alla stoccata carries it away.

[*Draws.*]

Tybalt, you ratcatcher, will you walk?

Tybalt. What wouldst thou have with me?

80 **Mercutio.** Good King of Cats, nothing but one of your
nine lives. That I mean to make bold withal, and, as
you shall use me hereafter, dry-beat the rest of the
eight. Will you pluck your sword out of his pilcher
by the ears? Make haste, lest mine be about your ears
85 ere it be out.

Tybalt. I am for you.

[*Draws.*]

Romeo. Gentle Mercutio, put thy rapier up.

Mercutio. Come, sir, your passado!

[*They fight.*]

Romeo. Draw, Benvolio; beat down their weapons.
90 Gentlemen, for shame! forbear this outrage!
Tybalt, Mercutio, the Prince expressly hath
Forbid this bandying in Verona streets.
Hold, Tybalt! Good Mercutio!

[Tybalt, *under* Romeo's *arm, thrusts* Mercutio *in, and
flies with his Men.*]

65–68 I forgive your anger because I have reason to love you. What reason is Romeo referring to? Who else knows about this reason?

69 Boy: an insulting term of address to Romeo.

74 tender: cherish.

76–78 Mercutio is disgusted by Romeo's calm response to Tybalt and assumes that Romeo is afraid to fight. **Alla stoccata** is a move used in sword fighting. Mercutio calls Tybalt a **ratcatcher,** an insult based on Tybalt's name. Then he dares him to step aside and fight **(walk).**

81–83 I mean . . . eight: I intend to take one of your nine lives (as a cat has) and give a beating to the other eight.

88 Be on your guard; I'm about to attack. (A **passado** is a move used in sword fighting.)
89–93 Imagine a sword fight between Tybalt and Mercutio. Romeo, off to the side with Benvolio, is frantic at what is happening. He wants desperately to stop this fighting **(bandying)** between his friend and his new in-law. He steps between the duellers and manages to hold Mercutio, but Tybalt stabs Mercutio under Romeo's arm.

Act Three, Scene 1. Mercutio, injured by Tybalt, curses the houses of Capulet and Montague. (Zeffirelli, 1968)

Mercutio. I am hurt.

95   A plague o' both your houses! I am sped.
    Is he gone and hath nothing?

Benvolio.   What, art thou hurt?

Mercutio. Ay, ay, a scratch, a scratch. Marry, 'tis
    enough.

100   Where is my page? Go, villain, fetch a surgeon.

[*Exit* Page.]

Romeo. Courage, man. The hurt cannot be much.

Mercutio. No, 'tis not so deep as a well, nor so wide as a
    church door; but 'tis enough, 'twill serve. Ask for me
    tomorrow, and you shall find me a grave man. I
105   am peppered, I warrant, for this world. A plague o'
    both your houses! Zounds, a dog, a rat, a mouse, a
    cat, to scratch a man to death! A braggart, a rogue, a
    villain, that fights by the book of arithmetic! Why the
    devil came you between us? I was hurt under your
110   arm.

95 A plague . . . sped: I curse both the Montagues and the Capulets. I am destroyed.

102–110 Picture Mercutio lying on the ground, bleeding, surrounded by horrified friends. Even as he is dying, he continues to joke and to make nasty remarks about Tybalt. He makes a pun on the word **grave.**

Romeo. I thought all for the best.

Mercutio. Help me into some house, Benvolio,
    Or I shall faint. A plague o' both your houses!
    They have made worms' meat of me. I have it,
115   And soundly too. Your houses!

[*Exit, supported by* Benvolio.]

Romeo. This gentleman, the Prince's near ally,
    My very friend, hath got this mortal hurt
    In my behalf—my reputation stained
    With Tybalt's slander—Tybalt, that an hour
120   Hath been my kinsman, O sweet Juliet,
    Thy beauty hath made me effeminate
    And in my temper softened valor's steel!

[*Re-enter* Benvolio.]

Benvolio. O Romeo, Romeo, brave Mercutio's dead!
    That gallant spirit hath aspired the clouds,
125   Which too untimely here did scorn the earth.

Romeo. This day's black fate on mo days doth depend;
    This but begins the woe others must end.

[*Re-enter* Tybalt.]

Benvolio. Here comes the furious Tybalt back again.

Romeo. Alive in triumph, and Mercutio slain?
130   Away to heaven respective lenity,
    And fire-eyed fury be my conduct now!
    Now, Tybalt, take the "villain" back again
    That late thou gavest me, for Mercutio's soul
    Is but a little way above our heads,
135   Staying for thine to keep him company.
    Either thou or I, or both, must go with him.

Tybalt. Thou, wretched boy, that didst consort him
      here,
    Shalt with him hence.

140 **Romeo.**   This shall determine that.

[*They fight.* Tybalt *falls.*]

Benvolio. Romeo, away, be gone!
    The citizens are up, and Tybalt slain.
    Stand not amazed. The Prince will doom thee death

116–122 My true friend is dying because of me. My reputation has been damaged by a man who has been my relative for only an hour. My love for Juliet has made me less manly and brave.

124 aspired: soared to.

126–127 This awful day will be followed by more of the same.

129–136 Romeo sees Tybalt still living, while Mercutio lies dead. What challenge does Romeo make to Tybalt?

140 Imagine the sword fight between the two men, which probably goes on for several minutes. The fight ends with Romeo running his sword through Tybalt.

141–144 Don't just stand there! The Prince will sentence you to death if he catches you.

Act Three, Scene 1. Romeo, avenging Mercutio's death, duels with Tybalt. (Zeffirelli, 1968)

If thou art taken. Hence, be gone, away!

145   **Romeo.** O, I am fortune's fool!

Benvolio.   Why dost thou stay?

[*Exit* Romeo.]

[*Enter* Citizens.]

Citizen. Which way ran he that killed Mercutio?
  Tybalt, that murderer, which way ran he?

Benvolio. There lies that Tybalt.

150   **Citizen.**   Up, sir, go with me.
  I charge thee in the Prince's name obey.

[*Enter* Prince *with his* Attendants, Montague, Capulet,
their Wives, *and* others.]

Prince. Where are the vile beginners of this fray?

Benvolio. O noble Prince, I can discover all
  The unlucky manage of this fatal brawl.

145 I am fortune's fool: Fate has made a fool of me.

153–154 Benvolio says he can tell (**discover**) what happened.

155　　There lies the man, slain by young Romeo,
　　　That slew thy kinsman, brave Mercutio.

Lady Capulet. Tybalt, my cousin! O my brother's child!
　　　O Prince! O cousin! O husband! O, the blood is spilled
　　　Of my dear kinsman! Prince, as thou art true,
160　　For blood of ours shed blood of Montague.
　　　O cousin, cousin!

Prince. Benvolio, who began this bloody fray?

Benvolio. Tybalt, here slain, whom Romeo's hand did
　　　　slay.
165　　Romeo, that spoke him fair, bid him bethink
　　　How nice the quarrel was, and urged withal
　　　Your high displeasure. All this—uttered
　　　With gentle breath, calm look, knees humbly
　　　　bowed—
170　　Could not take truce with the unruly spleen
　　　Of Tybalt deaf to peace, but that he tilts
　　　With piercing steel at bold Mercutio's breast;
　　　Who, all as hot, turns deadly point to point,
　　　And, with a martial scorn, with one hand beats
175　　Cold death aside and with the other sends
　　　It back to Tybalt, whose dexterity
　　　Retorts it. Romeo he cries aloud,
　　　"Hold, friends! friends, part!" and swifter than his
　　　　tongue,
180　　His agile arm beats down their fatal points,
　　　And 'twixt them rushes; underneath whose arm
　　　An envious thrust from Tybalt hit the life
　　　Of stout Mercutio, and then Tybalt fled,
　　　But by-and-by comes back to Romeo,
185　　Who had but newly entertained revenge,
　　　And to't they go like lightning; for, ere I
　　　Could draw to part them, was stout Tybalt slain;
　　　And, as he fell, did Romeo turn and fly.
　　　This is the truth, or let Benvolio die.

190　**Lady Capulet.** He is a kinsman to the Montague;
　　　Affection makes him false, he speaks not true.
　　　Some twenty of them fought in this black strife,
　　　And all those twenty could but kill one life.
　　　I beg for justice, which thou, Prince, must give.
195　　Romeo slew Tybalt; Romeo must not live.

159–160 as thou . . . Montague: If your word is good, you will sentence Romeo to death for killing a Capulet.

163–189 Benvolio explains what has just happened. How accurate is his retelling?

165–166 Romeo, that . . . was: Romeo talked calmly (**fair**) and told Tybalt to think how trivial (**nice**) the argument was.

170–171 Could . . . peace: All this could not quiet Tybalt's anger; he would not listen to pleas for peace.

180–181 His agile . . . rushes: He rushed between them and pushed down their swords.

185 entertained: thought of.

190–191 Why does Lady Capulet think Benvolio is lying? What wild accusation does she go on to make?

Prince. Romeo slew him; he slew Mercutio.
Who now the price of his dear blood doth owe?

Montague. Not Romeo, Prince; he was Mercutio's
friend;

200 His fault concludes but what the law should end,
The life of Tybalt.

Prince.   And for that offense
Immediately we do exile him hence.
I have an interest in your hate's proceeding,
205 My blood for your rude brawls doth lie a-bleeding;
But I'll amerce you with so strong a fine
That you shall all repent the loss of mine.
I will be deaf to pleading and excuses;
Nor tears nor prayers shall purchase out abuses.
210 Therefore use none. Let Romeo hence in haste,
Else, when he is found, that hour is his last.
Bear hence this body, and attend our will.
Mercy but murders, pardoning those that kill.

[*Exeunt.*]

200–201 Romeo is guilty only of avenging Mercutio's death, which the law would have done anyway.

203–213 The Prince banishes Romeo from Verona. He angrily points out that one of his own relatives, Mercutio, is now dead because of the feud. The Prince promises that if Romeo does not leave Verona immediately, he will be put to death.

SCENE 2 *Capulet's orchard.*

The scene begins with Juliet impatiently waiting for night to come so that Romeo can climb to her bedroom on the rope ladder. Suddenly the Nurse enters with the terrible news of Tybalt's death and Romeo's banishment. Juliet mourns for the loss of her cousin and her husband and threatens to kill herself. To calm her, the Nurse promises to find Romeo and bring him to Juliet before he leaves Verona.

[*Enter* Juliet *alone.*]

Juliet. Gallop apace, you fiery-footed steeds,
Toward Phoebus' lodging! Such a wagoner
As Phaëton would whip you to the West,
And bring in cloudy night immediately.
5 Spread thy close curtain, love-performing night,
That runaways' eyes may wink, and Romeo
Leap to these arms, untalked of and unseen.
Lovers can see to do their amorous rites
By their own beauties; or, if love be blind,
10 It best agrees with night. Come, civil night,
Thou sober-suited matron, all in black,

1–4 Juliet is wishing for nightfall, when Romeo is to come to her room. **Phoebus** is the god whose chariot pulls the sun across the sky; **Phaeton** was his son, who lost control of the chariot when he drove it too fast.

And learn me how to lose a winning match,
Played for a pair of stainless maidenhoods.
Hood my unmanned blood bating in my cheeks.

¹⁵ With thy black mantle; till strange love, grown bold,
Think true love acted simple modesty.
Come, night; come, Romeo, come; thou day in night;
For thou wilt lie upon the wings of night
Whiter than new snow on a raven's back.

²⁰ Come, gentle night; come, loving, black-browed
    night;
Give me my Romeo; and, when he shall die,
Take him and cut him out in little stars,
And he will make the face of heaven so fine

²⁵ That all the world will be in love with night
And pay no worship to the garish sun.
O, I have bought the mansion of a love,
But not possessed it; and though I am sold,
Not yet enjoyed. So tedious is this day

³⁰ As is the night before some festival
To an impatient child that hath new robes
And may not wear them. Oh, here comes my nurse,

[*Enter* Nurse, *wringing her hands, with the ladder of cords in her lap.*]

And she brings news; and every tongue that speaks
But Romeo's name speaks heavenly eloquence.

³⁵ Now, nurse, what news? What hast thou there?
    the cords
That Romeo bid thee fetch?

Nurse.   Ay, ay, the cords.

Juliet. Ay me! what news? Why dost thou wring thy
⁴⁰   hands?

Nurse. Ah, well-a-day! he's dead, he's dead, he's dead!
We are undone, lady, we are undone!
Alack the day! he's gone, he's killed, he's dead!

Juliet. Can heaven be so envious?

⁴⁵ **Nurse.**   Romeo can,
Though heaven cannot. O Romeo, Romeo!
Who ever would have thought it? Romeo!

Juliet. What devil art thou that dost torment me thus?
This torture should be roared in dismal hell.

⁵⁰ Hath Romeo slain himself? Say thou but "I,"

14–16 Hood . . . modesty: Juliet asks that the darkness hide her blushing cheeks on her wedding night.

22–26 What does Juliet think should happen to Romeo after he dies?

27–32 I have . . . wear them: Juliet protests that she has gone through the wedding ceremony (**bought the mansion**) but is still waiting to enjoy the rewards of marriage. She then compares herself to an excited, impatient child on the night before a holiday or festival.

36–37 cords . . . fetch: the rope ladder Romeo told you to get.

41–47 well-a-day: an expression used when someone has bad news. The Nurse wails and moans without clearly explaining what has happened. Juliet misunderstands and assumes that Romeo is dead.

And that bare vowel "I" shall poison more
Than the death-darting eye of a cockatrice.
I am not I, if there be such an "I,"
Or those eyes shut, that make thee answer "I."
55   If he be slain, say "I," or if not, "no."
Brief sounds determine of my weal or woe.

Nurse. I saw the wound, I saw it with mine eyes,
(God save the mark!) here on his manly breast.
A piteous corse, a bloody piteous corse;
60   Pale, pale as ashes, all bedaubed in blood,
All in gore blood. I swounded at the sight.

Juliet. O, break, my heart! poor bankrout, break
at once!
To prison, eyes; ne'er look on liberty!
65   Vile earth, to earth resign; end motion here,
And thou and Romeo press one heavy bier!

Nurse. O Tybalt, Tybalt, the best friend I had!
O courteous Tybalt! honest gentleman!
That ever I should live to see thee dead!

70   **Juliet.** What storm is this that blows so contrary?
Is Romeo slaughtered, and is Tybalt dead?
My dear-loved cousin, and my dearer lord?
Then, dreadful trumpet, sound the general doom!
For who is living, if those two are gone?

75   **Nurse.** Tybalt is gone, and Romeo banished;
Romeo that killed him, he is banished.

Juliet. O God! Did Romeo's hand shed Tybalt's blood?

Nurse. It did! it did! alas the day, it did!

Juliet. O serpent heart, hid with a flow'ring face!
80   Did ever dragon keep so fair a cave?
Beautiful tyrant! fiend angelical!
Dove-feathered raven! wolvish-ravening lamb!
Despised substance of divinest show!
Just opposite to what thou justly seemst,
85   A damned saint, an honorable villain!
O nature, what hadst thou to do in hell
When thou didst bower the spirit of a fiend
In mortal paradise of such sweet flesh?
Was ever book containing such vile matter
90   So fairly bound? O, that deceit should dwell
In such a gorgeous palace!

50–55 Juliet's *I* means "aye," or yes. She is in agony, thinking Romeo dead, and begs the Nurse to answer clearly. A **cockatrice** is a mythological beast whose glance killed its victims.

58–61 God . . . mark: an expression meant to scare off evil powers, similar to "Knock on wood." The Nurse says she saw the corpse (**corse**), covered (**bedaubed**) in blood and gore. She fainted (**swounded**) at the sight of it.

62–66 Juliet says her heart is broken and bankrupt (**bankrout**). She wants to be buried with Romeo, or share his casket (**bier**).

70–74 Juliet is trying to make sense of what the Nurse has said.

79–91 In her grief Juliet cries out a series of contradictory phrases, which show her conflicting feelings. A **fiend** is a demon. How are **fiend angelical** *and* **dove-feathered** *raven* contradictory? What is Juliet's first reaction to the news that Romeo killed Tybalt?

Nurse. There's no trust,
No faith, no honesty in men; all perjured,
All forsworn, all naught, all dissemblers.
95 Ah, where's my man? Give me some aqua vitae.
These griefs, these woes, these sorrows make me old.
Shame come to Romeo!

Juliet. Blistered be thy tongue
For such a wish! He was not born to shame.
100 Upon his brow shame is ashamed to sit;
For 'tis a throne where honor may be crowned
Sole monarch of the universal earth.
O, what a beast was I to chide at him!

Nurse. Will you speak well of him that killed your
105 cousin?

Juliet. Shall I speak ill of him that is my husband?
Ah, poor my lord, what tongue shall smooth thy
name
When I, thy three-hours' wife, have mangled it?
110 But wherefore, villain, didst thou kill my cousin?
That villain cousin would have killed my husband.
Back, foolish tears, back to your native spring!
Your tributary drops belong to woe,
Which you, mistaking, offer up to joy.
115 My husband lives, that Tybalt would have slain;
And Tybalt's dead, that would have slain my
husband.
All this is comfort; wherefore weep I then?
Some word there was, worser than Tybalt's death,
120 That murdered me. I would forget it fain;
But O, it presses to my memory
Like damned guilty deeds to sinners' minds!
"Tybalt is dead, and Romeo—banished."
That "banished," that one word "banished,"
125 Hath slain ten thousand Tybalts. Tybalt's death
Was woe enough, if it had ended there;
Or, if sour woe delights in fellowship
And needly will be ranked with other griefs,
Why followed not, when she said "Tybalt's dead,"
130 Thy father, or thy mother, nay, or both,
Which modern lamentation might have moved?
But with a rearward following Tybalt's death,
"Romeo is banished"—to speak that word
Is father, mother, Tybalt, Romeo, Juliet,

92–94 There's . . . dissemblers: All men are liars and pretenders.

95 where's . . . vitae: Where's my servant? Give me some brandy.

98–103 Blistered . . . him: Juliet has now recovered a bit from the shock of the news. How does she respond to the Nurse's wish that shame come to Romeo?

106–117 Shall . . . husband: Juliet is in turmoil. She is ashamed that she criticized her husband. She realizes that if he hadn't killed Tybalt, Tybalt would have killed him.

119–125 What is Juliet wishing she hadn't heard?

125–137 Juliet says that if the news of Tybalt's death had been followed by the news of her parents' deaths, she would have felt normal **(modern)**, or expected, grief. To follow the story of Tybalt's death with the terrible news of Romeo's banishment creates a sorrow so deep it cannot be expressed in words.

135 All slain, all dead. "Romeo is banished"—
There is no end, no limit, measure, bound,
In that word's death; no words can that woe sound.
Where is my father and my mother, nurse?

Nurse. Weeping and wailing over Tybalt's corse.
140 Will you go to them? I will bring you thither.

Juliet. Wash they his wounds with tears? Mine shall be
spent,
When theirs are dry, for Romeo's banishment.
Take up those cords. Poor ropes, you are beguiled,   **144 beguiled:** cheated.
145 Both you and I, for Romeo is exiled.
He made you for a highway to my bed;
But I, a maid, die maiden-widowed.   **147–149 But I . . . maidenhead:** I will
Come, cords; come, nurse. I'll to my wedding bed;   die a widow without ever really having
And death, not Romeo, take my maidenhead!   been a wife. Death, not Romeo, will be
                            my husband.
150 **Nurse.** Hie to your chamber. I'll find Romeo
To comfort you. I wot well where he is.   **151 wot:** know.
Hark ye, your Romeo will be here at night.
I'll to him; he is hid at Laurence' cell.

Juliet. O, find him! give this ring to my true knight
155 And bid him come to take his last farewell.

[*Exeunt.*]

SCENE 3 *Friar Laurence's cell.*

*Friar Laurence tells Romeo of his banishment, and Romeo collapses in
grief. When he learns from the Nurse that Juliet, too, is in despair, he
threatens to stab himself. The friar reacts by suggesting a plan. Romeo
is to spend a few hours with Juliet and then escape to Mantua. While
he is away, the friar will announce the wedding and try to get a pardon
from the Prince.*

[*Enter* Friar Laurence.]

Friar Laurence. Romeo, come forth; come forth, thou
fearful man.
Affliction is enamored of thy parts,   **3–4 Affliction . . . calamity:** Trouble
And thou art wedded to calamity.   follows you everywhere.

[*Enter* Romeo.]

5 **Romeo.** Father, what news? What is the Prince's doom?   **5 doom:** sentence.
What sorrow craves acquaintance at my hand
That I yet know not?

Friar Laurence.   Too familiar
Is my dear son with such sour company.
10   I bring thee tidings of the Prince's doom.

Romeo. What less than doomsday is the Prince's doom?

Friar Laurence. A gentler judgment vanished from his
        lips—
Not body's death, but body's banishment.

15   **Romeo.** Ha, banishment? Be merciful, say "death";
For exile hath more terror in his look,
Much more than death. Do not say "banishment."

Friar Laurence. Hence from Verona art thou banished.
Be patient, for the world is broad and wide.

20   **Romeo.** There is no world without Verona walls,
But purgatory, torture, hell itself.
Hence banished is banisht from the world,
And world's exile is death. Then "banishment,"
Is death mistermed. Calling death "banishment,"
25   Thou cuttst my head off with a golden axe
And smilest upon the stroke that murders me.

Friar Laurence. O deadly sin! O rude unthankfulness!
Thy fault our law calls death; but the kind Prince,
Taking thy part, hath rushed aside the law,
30   And turned that black word death to banishment.
This is dear mercy, and thou seest it not.

Romeo. 'Tis torture, and not mercy. Heaven is here,
Where Juliet lives; and every cat and dog
And little mouse, every unworthy thing,
35   Live here in heaven and may look on her;
But Romeo may not. More validity,
More honorable state, more courtship lives
In carrion flies than Romeo. They may seize
On the white wonder of dear Juliet's hand
40   And steal immortal blessing from her lips,
Who, even in pure and vestal modesty,
Still blush, as thinking their own kisses sin;
But Romeo may not—he is banished.
This may flies do, when I from this must fly;
45   They are free men, but I am banished.
And sayst thou yet that exile is not death?
Hadst thou no poison mixed, no sharp-ground knife,
No sudden mean of death, though ne'er so mean,
But "banished" to kill me—"banished"?

11 doomsday: death.

12 vanished: came.

15 Why does Romeo think death would be a more merciful punishment than banishment?

20–26 without: outside. Being exiled to the rest of the world (that is, the world away from Juliet) is as bad as being dead. And yet you smile at my misfortune!

27–31 The Friar is very angry at Romeo's reaction to the news. He reminds Romeo that the crime he committed deserves the death penalty, according to law. The Prince has shown Romeo mercy, and Romeo doesn't appreciate it.

32–46 Romeo refuses to listen to reason. He is obsessed with the word *banished*, just as Juliet was. He compares himself to the animals—and even the flies that live off the dead (**carrion**)—that will be able to see Juliet while he will not.

47–49 Hadst . . . to kill me: Couldn't you have killed me with poison or a knife instead of with that awful word?

50   O friar, the damned use that word in hell;
     Howling attends it! How hast thou the heart,
     Being a divine, a ghostly confessor,
     A sin-absolver, and my friend professed,
     To mangle me with that word "banished"?

55   **Friar Laurence.** Thou fond mad man, hear me a little
           speak.

     Romeo. O, thou wilt speak again of banishment.

     Friar Laurence. I'll give thee armor to keep off that
           word;
60   Adversity's sweet milk, philosophy,
     To comfort thee, though thou art banished.

     Romeo. Yet "banished"? Hang up philosophy!
     Unless philosophy can make a Juliet,
     Displant a town, reverse a prince's doom,
65   It helps not, it prevails not. Talk no more.

     Friar Laurence. O, then I see that madmen have no
           ears.

     Romeo. How should they, when that wise men have
           no eyes?

70   **Friar Laurence.** Let me dispute with thee of thy estate.

     Romeo. Thou canst not speak of that thou dost not
           feel.
     Wert thou as young as I, Juliet thy love,
     An hour but married, Tybalt murdered,
75   Doting like me, and like me banished,
     Then mightst thou speak, then mightst thou tear
           thy hair,
     And fall upon the ground, as I do now,
     Taking the measure of an unmade grave.

     [Nurse *knocks within.*]

80   **Friar Laurence.** Arise; one knocks. Good Romeo, hide
           thyself.

     Romeo. Not I; unless the breath of heartsick groans
     Mist-like infold me from the search of eyes.

     [*Knock.*]

     Friar Laurence. Hark, how they knock! Who's there?
85   Romeo, arise;
     Thou wilt be taken.—Stay awhile!—Stand up;

55 fond: foolish.

60–62 The Friar offers philosophical comfort and counseling (**adversity's sweet milk**) as a way to overcome hardship.

70 dispute: discuss; **estate:** situation.

71–79 You can't understand how I feel because you haven't been through what I have.

80–91 When a knock sounds, the Friar frantically tries to get Romeo to hide.

[*Knock.*]

    Run to my study.—By-and-by!—God's will,
    What simpleness is this.—I come, I come!

[*Knock.*]

    Who knocks so hard? Whence come you? What's
90   your will?

Nurse. [*Within.*] Let me come in, and you shall know
    my errand.
    I come from Lady Juliet.

Friar Laurence.   Welcome then.

[*Enter* Nurse.]

95 **Nurse.** O holy friar, O, tell me, holy friar,
    Where is my lady's lord, where's Romeo?

Friar Laurence. There on the ground, with his own tears
    made drunk.

Nurse. O, he is even in my mistress' case,
100   Just in her case! O woeful sympathy!
    Piteous predicament! Even so lies she,
    Blubb'ring and weeping, weeping and blubbering.
    Stand up, stand up! Stand, an you be a man.
    For Juliet's sake, for her sake, rise and stand!
105   Why should you fall into so deep an O?

Romeo. [*Rises*] Nurse—

Nurse. Ah sir! ah sir! Well, death's the end of all.

Romeo. Spakest thou of Juliet? How is it with her?
    Doth not she think me an old murderer,
110   Now I have stained the childhood of our joy
    With blood removed but little from her own?
    Where is she? and how doth she? and what says
    My concealed lady to our canceled love?

Nurse. O, she says nothing, sir, but weeps and weeps;
115   And now falls on her bed, and then starts up,
    And Tybalt calls; and then on Romeo cries,
    And then down falls again.

Romeo.   As if that name,
    Shot from the deadly level of a gun,
120   Did murder her; as that name's cursed hand
    Murdered her kinsman. O tell me, friar, tell me,
    In what vile part of this anatomy

99–105 O, he . . . an O: The Nurse says that Romeo is in exactly the same condition as Juliet. She tells Romeo to stand up and be a man and asks why he's in such deep grief (**so deep an O**).

113 concealed lady: secret bride.

118–124 that name: the name *Romeo*. Romeo says his name is a bullet that kills Juliet just as his hand killed her kinsman Tybalt. Romeo asks where in his body (**hateful mansion**) his name can be found so that he can cut the name out. What is Romeo about to do?

Doth my name lodge? Tell me, that I may sack
The hateful mansion.

[*Draws his dagger.*]

125   **Friar Laurence.**   Hold thy desperate hand.
        Art thou a man? Thy form cries out thou art;
        Thy tears are womanish, thy wild acts denote
        The unreasonable fury of a beast.
        Unseemly woman in a seeming man!
130   Or ill-beseeming beast in seeming both!
        Thou hast amazed me. By my holy order,
        I thought thy disposition better tempered.
        Hast thou slain Tybalt? Wilt thou slay thyself?
        And slay thy lady too that lives in thee,
135   By doing damned hate upon thyself?
        Why railst thou on thy birth, the heaven, and earth?
        Since birth and heaven and earth, all three do meet
        In thee at once; which thou at once wouldst lose.
        Fie, fie, thou shamest thy shape, thy love, thy wit,
140   Which, like a usurer, aboundst in all,
        And usest none in that true use indeed
        Which should bedeck thy shape, thy love, thy wit.
        Thy noble shape is but a form of wax,
        Digressing from the valor of a man;
145   Thy dear love sworn but hollow perjury,
        Killing that love which thou hast vowed to cherish;
        Thy wit, that ornament to shape and love,
        Misshapen in the conduct of them both,
        Like powder in a skilless soldier's flask,
150   Is set afire by thine own ignorance,
        And thou dismembered with thine own defense.
        What, rouse thee, man! Thy Juliet is alive,
        For whose dear sake thou wast but lately dead.
        There art thou happy. Tybalt would kill thee,
155   But thou slewest Tybalt. There art thou happy.
        The law, that threatened death, becomes thy friend
        And turns it to exile. There art thou happy.
        A pack of blessings light upon thy back;
        Happiness courts thee in her best array;
160   But, like a misbehaved and sullen wench,
        Thou poutst upon thy fortune and thy love.
        Take heed, take heed, for such die miserable.

125–142 Hold: stop. You're not acting like a man. Would you send your soul to hell by committing suicide (**doing damned hate**)? Why do you curse your birth, heaven, and earth? You are refusing to make good use of your advantages just as a miser refuses to spend his money.

152–158 The Friar tells Romeo to count his blessings instead of feeling sorry for himself. He lists the things Romeo has to be thankful for. What three blessings does the Friar mention?

Go get thee to thy love, as was decreed,
Ascend her chamber, hence and comfort her.
165   But look thou stay not till the watch be set,
For then thou canst not pass to Mantua,
Where thou shalt live till we can find a time
To blaze your marriage, reconcile your friends,
Beg pardon of the Prince, and call thee back
170   With twenty hundred thousand times more joy
Than thou wentst forth in lamentation.
Go before, nurse. Commend me to thy lady,
And bid her hasten all the house to bed,
Which heavy sorrow makes them apt unto.
175   Romeo is coming.

Nurse. O Lord, I could have stayed here all the night
To hear good counsel. O, what learning is!
My lord, I'll tell my lady you will come.

Romeo. Do so, and bid my sweet prepare to chide.

[Nurse *offers to go and turns again.*]

180   **Nurse.** Here is a ring she bid me give you, sir.
Hie you, make haste, for it grows very late.

[*Exit.*]

Romeo. How well my comfort is revived by this!

Friar Laurence. Go hence; good night; and here stands
all your state:
185   Either be gone before the watch be set,
Or by the break of day disguised from hence.
Sojourn in Mantua. I'll find out your man,
And he shall signify from time to time
Every good hap to you that chances here.
190   Give me thy hand. 'Tis late. Farewell; good night.

Romeo. But that a joy past joy calls out on me,
It were a grief so brief to part with thee.
Farewell.

[*Exeunt.*]

163–166 Go and spend the night with Juliet. But leave before the guards take their places at the city gates, so you can escape to Mantua.

167–171 till we . . . lamentation: The Friar intends to announce (**blaze**) the marriage at the right time, get the families (**friends**) to stop their feud, ask the Prince to pardon Romeo, and have Romeo return to a happier situation.

176–177 How does the Nurse react to the advice the Friar has just given Romeo?

179 bid . . . chide: Tell Juliet to get ready to scold me for the way I've behaved.

182 How has Romeo's mood changed since he threatened to kill himself?

183–189 and here . . . here: This is what your fate depends on: either leave before the night watchmen go on duty, or get out at dawn in a disguise. Stay awhile in Mantua. I'll find your servant and send messages to you about what good things are happening here.

SCENE 4 *Capulet's house.*

In this scene, Paris visits the Capulets, who are mourning the death of Tybalt. He says he realizes that this is no time to talk of marriage. Capulet, however, disagrees; he decides that Juliet should marry Paris on Thursday, three days away. He tells Lady Capulet to inform Juliet immediately.

[*Enter* Capulet, Lady Capulet, *and* Paris.]

Capulet. Things have fall'n out, sir, so unluckily
That we have had no time to move our daughter.
Look you, she loved her kinsman Tybalt dearly,
And so did I. Well, we were born to die.
⁵ 'Tis very late; she'll not come down tonight.
I promise you, but for your company,
I would have been abed an hour ago.

Paris. These times of woe afford no time to woo.
Madam, good night. Commend me to your
¹⁰   daughter.

Lady Capulet. I will, and know her mind early
      tomorrow;
Tonight she's mewed up to her heaviness.

[Paris *offers to go and* Capulet *calls him again.*]

Capulet. Sir Paris, I will make a desperate tender
¹⁵ Of my child's love. I think she will be ruled
In all respects by me; nay more, I doubt it not.
Wife, go you to her ere you go to bed;
Acquaint her here of my son Paris' love
And bid her (mark you me?) on Wednesday next—
²⁰ But, soft! what day is this?

Paris.   Monday, my lord.

Capulet. Monday! ha, ha! Well, Wednesday is too soon.
A Thursday let it be—a Thursday, tell her,
She shall be married to this noble earl.
²⁵ Will you be ready? Do you like this haste?
We'll keep no great ado—a friend or two;
For hark you, Tybalt being slain so late,
It may be thought we held him carelessly,
Being our kinsman, if we revel much.
³⁰ Therefore we'll have some half a dozen friends,
And there an end. But what say you to Thursday?

1–2 Such terrible things have happened that we haven't had time to persuade **(move)** Juliet to think about your marriage proposal.

8 Sad times are not good times for talking of marriage.

11–13 and know . . . heaviness: I'll know early tomorrow what she intends to do; tonight she's locked up with her sorrow. What reason do Lord and Lady Capulet think causes Juliet to be sad?

14–31 Capulet thinks Juliet will obey him and pledges her in marriage to Paris (makes a **desperate tender,** or bold offer). He decides the wedding will be on Thursday and only a small ceremony, since the family is mourning Tybalt's death. He is so sure that Juliet will accept Paris that he calls Paris "son" already.

Paris. My lord, I would that Thursday were tomorrow.

Capulet. Well, get you gone. A Thursday be it then.
Go you to Juliet ere you go to bed;
35   Prepare her, wife, against this wedding day.
Farewell, my lord.—Light to my chamber, ho!
Afore me, it is so very very late
That we may call it early by-and-by.
Good night.

[*Exeunt.*]

34–36 Capulet tells his wife to go to Juliet right away and inform her of his decision .

37–38 it is . . . by-and-by: It's so late at night that soon we'll be calling it early in the morning.

SCENE 5 *Capulet's orchard.*

Romeo and Juliet have spent the night together, but before daylight, Romeo leaves for Mantua. As soon as he leaves, Lady Capulet comes in to tell Juliet of her father's decision—that she will marry Count Paris on Thursday. Juliet is very upset and refuses to go along with the plan. Juliet's father goes into a rage at her disobedience and tells her that she will marry Paris or he will disown her.

The Nurse advises Juliet to wed Paris, since her marriage to Romeo is over and Paris is a better man anyway. Juliet, now angry with the Nurse, decides to go to Friar Laurence for help.

[*Enter* Romeo *and* Juliet *above, at the window.*]

Juliet. Wilt thou be gone? It is not yet near day.
It was the nightingale, and not the lark,
That pierced the fearful hollow of thine ear.
Nightly she sings on yond pomegranate tree.
5   Believe me, love, it was the nightingale.

Romeo. It was the lark, the herald of the morn;
No nightingale. Look, love, what envious streaks
Do lace the severing clouds in yonder East.
Night's candles are burnt out, and jocund day
10   Stands tiptoe on the misty mountain tops.
I must be gone and live, or stay and die.

Juliet. Yond light is not daylight; I know it, I.
It is some meteor that the sun exhales
To be to thee this night a torchbearer
15   And light thee on thy way to Mantua.
Therefore stay yet; thou needst not to be gone.

Romeo. Let me be ta'en, let me be put to death.
I am content, so thou wilt have it so.

2–5 It was . . . nightingale: The nightingale sings at night; the lark sings in the morning. What is Juliet trying to get Romeo to believe?

6 herald: messenger.

9–10 night's candles: stars. How is day personified here?

12–25 Juliet continues to pretend it is night to keep Romeo from leaving, even though she knows that it is morning. Romeo gives in and says he'll stay if Juliet wishes it, even if staying means death.

VIEW AND COMPARE

(Zeffirelli, 1968)

(Luhrmann, 1996)

*E*ach of these images depicts Romeo and Juliet after their night together and before Romeo leaves for Mantua. What mood is evoked in each one?

I'll say yon grey is not the morning's eye,
'Tis but the pale reflex of Cynthia's brow;
Nor that is not the lark whose notes do beat
The vaulty heaven so high above our heads.
I have more care to stay than will to go.
Come, death, and welcome! Juliet wills it so.
How is't, my soul? Let's talk; it is not day.

Juliet. It is, it is! Hie hence, be gone, away!
It is the lark that sings so out of tune,
Straining harsh discords and unpleasing sharps.
Some say the lark makes sweet division;
This doth not so, for she divideth us.
Some say the lark and loathed toad changed eyes;
O, now I would they had changed voices too,
Since arm from arm that voice doth us affray,
Hunting thee hence with hunt's-up to the day!
O, now be gone! More light and light it grows.

Romeo. More light and light—more dark and dark our
woes!

[*Enter* Nurse, *hastily.*]

Nurse. Madam!

Juliet. Nurse?

Nurse. Your lady mother is coming to your chamber. The
day is broke; be wary, look about.

[*Exit.*]

Juliet. Then, window, let day in, and let life out.

Romeo. Farewell, farewell! One kiss, and I'll descend.

[*He starts down the ladder.*]

Juliet. Art thou gone so, my lord, my love, my friend?
I must hear from thee every day in the hour,
For in a minute there are many days.
O, by this count I shall be much in years
Ere I again behold my Romeo!

Romeo. Farewell!
I will omit no opportunity
That may convey my greetings, love, to thee.

Juliet. O, thinkst thou we shall ever meet again?

Romeo. I doubt it not; and all these woes shall serve

20

25

30

35

40

45

50

26–28 Romeo's mention of death
frightens Juliet. She becomes serious and
urges Romeo to go quickly.

29 division: melody.

31–34 The toad's large, brilliant eyes
would be more suitable for the lark.
affray: frighten. **hunt's-up:** a morning
song for hunters.

47 much in years: very old.

For sweet discourses in our time to come.

55 **Juliet.** O God, I have an ill-divining soul!
Methinks I see thee, now thou art below,
As one dead in the bottom of a tomb.
Either my eyesight fails, or thou lookst pale.

Romeo. And trust me, love, in my eye so do you.
60 Dry sorrow drinks our blood. Adieu! adieu!

[*Exit.*]

Juliet. O Fortune, Fortune! all men call thee fickle.
If thou art fickle, what dost thou with him
That is renowned for faith? Be fickle, Fortune,
For then I hope thou wilt not keep him long
65 But send him back.

Lady Capulet. [*Within.*] Ho, daughter! are you up?

Juliet. Who is't that calls? It is my lady mother.
Is she not down so late, or up so early?
What unaccustomed cause procures her hither?

[*Enter* Lady Capulet.]

70 **Lady Capulet.** Why, how now, Juliet?

Juliet.   Madam, I am not well.

Lady Capulet. Evermore weeping for your cousin's
death?
What, wilt thou wash him from his grave with tears?
75 An if thou couldst, thou couldst not make him live.
Therefore have done. Some grief shows much of
love;
But much of grief shows still some want of wit.

Juliet. Yet let me weep for such a feeling loss.

80 **Lady Capulet.** So shall you feel the loss, but not the
friend
Which you weep for.

Juliet.   Feeling so the loss,
I cannot choose but ever weep the friend.

85 **Lady Capulet.** Well, girl, thou weepst not so much for
his death
As that the villain lives which slaughtered him.

Juliet. What villain, madam?

Lady Capulet.   That same villain Romeo.

55–57 I have . . . tomb: Juliet sees an evil vision of the future. What is her vision?

60 Dry . . . blood: People believed that sorrow drained the blood from the heart, causing a sad person to look pale. Romeo leaves Juliet by climbing down from her balcony.

61–63 fickle: changeable in loyalty or affection. Juliet asks fickle Fortune why it has anything to do with Romeo, who is the opposite of fickle.

69 What . . . hither: What unusual reason brings her here?

72–74 What does Lady Capulet think Juliet is crying about?

76–78 have . . . wit: stop crying (**have done**). A little grief is evidence of love, while too much grief shows a lack of good sense (**want of wit**).

90   **Juliet.** [*Aside.*] Villain and he be many miles
        asunder.—
      God pardon him! I do, with all my heart;
      And yet no man like he doth grieve my heart.

    Lady Capulet. That is because the traitor murderer
95   lives.

    Juliet. Ay, madam, from the reach of these my hands.
      Would none but I might venge my cousin's death!

    Lady Capulet. We will have vengeance for it, fear
      thou not.
100   Then weep no more. I'll send to one in Mantua,
      Where that same banished runagate doth live,
      Shall give him such an unaccustomed dram
      That he shall soon keep Tybalt company;
      And then I hope thou wilt be satisfied.

105   **Juliet.** Indeed I never shall be satisfied
      With Romeo till I behold him—dead—
      Is my poor heart so for a kinsman vexed.
      Madam, if you could find out but a man
      To bear a poison, I would temper it;
110   That Romeo should, upon receipt thereof,
      Soon sleep in quiet. O, how my heart abhors
      To hear him named and cannot come to him,
      To wreak the love I bore my cousin Tybalt
      Upon his body that hath slaughtered him!

115   **Lady Capulet.** Find thou the means, and I'll find such
      a man.
      But now I'll tell thee joyful tidings, girl.

    Juliet. And joy comes well in such a needy time.
      What are they, I beseech your ladyship?

120   **Lady Capulet.** Well, well, thou hast a careful father,
      child;
      One who, to put thee from thy heaviness,
      Hath sorted out a sudden day of joy
      That thou expects not nor I looked not for.

125   **Juliet.** Madam, in happy time! What day is that?

    Lady Capulet. Marry, my child, early next Thursday
      morn
      The gallant, young, and noble gentleman,
      The County Paris, at Saint Peter's Church,

90–114 In these lines Juliet's words have double meanings. In order to avoid lying to her mother, she chooses her words carefully. They can mean what her mother wants to hear, but they can also mean what we know Juliet really has in mind.

101 runagate: runaway.
102 unaccustomed dram: poison. What does Lady Capulet plan to do about Romeo?

105–114 Dead could refer either to Romeo or to Juliet's heart. Juliet says that if her mother could find someone to carry a poison to Romeo, she would mix **(temper)** it herself. What hidden meaning lies In lines 108–112?

130 Shall happily make thee there a joyful bride.

Juliet. Now by Saint Peter's Church, and Peter too,
He shall not make me there a joyful bride!
I wonder at this haste, that I must wed
Ere he that should be husband comes to woo.
135 I pray you tell my lord and father, madam,
I will not marry yet; and when I do, I swear
It shall be Romeo, whom you know I hate,
Rather than Paris. These are news indeed!

Lady Capulet. Here comes your father. Tell him so
140 yourself,
And see how he will take it at your hands.

[*Enter* Capulet *and* Nurse.]

Capulet. When the sun sets the air doth drizzle dew,
But for the sunset of my brother's son
It rains downright.
145 How now? a conduit, girl? What, still in tears?
Evermore show'ring? In one little body
Thou counterfeitst a bark, a sea, a wind:
For still thy eyes, which I may call the sea,
Do ebb and flow with tears; the bark thy body is,
150 Sailing in this salt flood; the winds, thy sighs,
Who, raging with thy tears and they with them,
Without a sudden calm will overset
Thy tempest-tossed body. How now, wife?
Have you delivered to her our decree?

155 **Lady Capulet.** Ay, sir; but she will none, she gives you
thanks.
I would the fool were married to her grave!

Capulet. Soft! take me with you, take me with you,
wife.
160 How? Will she none? Doth she not give us thanks?
Is she not proud? Doth she not count her blest,
Unworthy as she is, that we have wrought
So worthy a gentleman to be her bridegroom?

Juliet. Not proud you have, but thankful that you have.
165 Proud can I never be of what I hate,
But thankful even for hate that is meant love.

136–138 and when . . . Paris: Once again, Juliet uses a double meaning. She mentions Romeo to show her mother how strongly opposed she is to marrying Paris, yet what she really means is that she loves Romeo.

143 my brother's son: Tybalt.

145–153 conduit: fountain. Capulet compares Juliet to a boat, an ocean, and the wind because of her excessive crying.

158 take me with you: Let me understand you. Capulet, like his wife, simply can't believe that Juliet won't go along with his plan for marriage.

164–166 I'm not pleased, but I am grateful for your intentions.

Capulet. How, how, how, how, choplogic? What is this?
"Proud"—and "I thank you"—and "I thank you
not"—
170 And yet "not proud"? Mistress minion you,
Thank me no thankings, nor proud me no prouds,
But fettle your fine joints 'gainst Thursday next
To go with Paris to Saint Peter's Church,
Or I will drag thee on a hurdle thither.
175 Out, you green-sickness carrion! out, you baggage!
You tallow-face!

Lady Capulet.   Fie, fie; what, are you mad?

Juliet. Good father, I beseech you on my knees,

[*She kneels down.*]

Hear me with patience but to speak a word.

180 **Capulet.** Hang thee, young baggage! disobedient
wretch!
I tell thee what—get thee to church a Thursday
Or never after look me in the face.
Speak not, reply not, do not answer me!
185 My fingers itch. Wife, we scarce thought us blest
That God had lent us but this only child;
But now I see this one is one too much,
And that we have a curse in having her.
Out on her, hilding!

190 **Nurse.**   God in heaven bless her!
You are to blame, my lord, to rate her so.

Capulet. And why, my Lady Wisdom? Hold your
tongue,
Good Prudence. Smatter with your gossips, go!

195 **Nurse.** I speak no treason.

Capulet.   O, God-i-god-en!

Nurse. May not one speak?

Capulet.   Peace, you mumbling fool!
Utter your gravity o'er a gossip's bowl,
200 For here we need it not.

Lady Capulet.   You are too hot.

167–176 How . . . tallow-face: Capulet is furious with Juliet. He rages, calls her names, and threatens her. He calls her a person who argues over fine points (**choplogic**), and says she is a spoiled child (**minion**). He tells her to prepare herself (**fettle your fine joints**) for the wedding or he'll haul her there in a cart for criminals (**hurdle**). He calls her an anemic piece of dead flesh (**green-sickness carrion**) and a coward (**tallow-face**).

177 Fie . . . mad: Lady Capulet is worried by her husband's violent anger and tries to calm him.

185 My fingers itch: I feel like hitting you.

189 hilding: good-for-nothing person.

190 The Nurse dares to stand up for Juliet but is rudely dismissed by Capulet, who considers her nothing more than a lowly servant.

194 Smatter: chatter.

199 Utter . . . bowl: Save your words of wisdom for a gathering of gossips.

Capulet. God's bread! it makes me mad. Day, night, late, early,
　　At home, abroad, alone, in company,
205　　Waking or sleeping, still my care hath been
　　To have her matched; and having now provided
　　A gentleman of princely parentage,
　　Of fair demesnes, youthful, and nobly trained,
　　Stuffed, as they say, with honorable parts,
210　　Proportioned as one's thought would wish a man—
　　And then to have a wretched puling fool,
　　A whining mammet, in her fortunes tender,
　　To answer "I'll not wed, I cannot love;
　　I am too young, I pray you pardon me"!
215　　But, an you will not wed, I'll pardon you.
　　Graze where you will, you shall not house with me.
　　Look to't, think on't; I do not use to jest.
　　Thursday is near; lay hand on heart, advise:
　　An you be mine, I'll give you to my friend;
220　　An you be not, hang, beg, starve, die in the streets,
　　For, by my soul, I'll ne'er acknowledge thee,
　　Nor what is mine shall never do thee good.
　　Trust to't. Bethink you. I'll not be forsworn.

[*Exit.*]

Juliet. Is there no pity sitting in the clouds
225　　That sees into the bottom of my grief?
　　O sweet my mother, cast me not away!
　　Delay this marriage for a month, a week;
　　Or if you do not, make the bridal bed
　　In that dim monument where Tybalt lies.

230　**Lady Capulet.** Talk not to me, for I'll not speak a word.
　　Do as thou wilt, for I have done with thee.

[*Exit.*]

Juliet. O God!—O nurse, how shall this be prevented?
　　My husband is on earth, my faith in heaven.
235　　How shall that faith return again to earth
　　Unless that husband send it me from heaven
　　By leaving earth? Comfort me, counsel me.
　　Alack, alack, that heaven should practice stratagems
　　Upon so soft a subject as myself!

202–223 Capulet complains that day and night he's tried to get Juliet a good husband, and now that he has, she acts like a crying **(puling)** fool, a whining doll **(mammet).** He will not put up with this. She will marry or he'll put her out of his house. He will not break his promise to Paris **(be forsworn).**

233–237 how shall . . . earth: Juliet is worried about the sin of being married to two men. She goes on to ask how heaven can play such tricks **(practice stratagems)** on her.

240   What sayst thou? Hast thou not a word of joy?
        Some comfort, nurse.

Nurse.   Faith, here it is.
        Romeo is banisht; and all the world to nothing
        That he dares ne'er come back to challenge you;
245   Or if he do, it needs must be by stealth.
        Then, since the case so stands as now it doth,
        I think it best you married with the County.
        O, he's a lovely gentleman!
        Romeo's a dishclout to him. An eagle, madam,
250   Hath not so green, so quick, so fair an eye
        As Paris hath. Beshrew my very heart,
        I think you are happy in this second match,
        For it excels your first; or if it did not,
        Your first is dead—or 'twere as good he were
255   As living here and you no use of him.

Juliet. Speakst thou this from thy heart?

Nurse. And from my soul too; else beshrew them both.

Juliet. Amen!

Nurse. What?

260 **Juliet.** Well, thou hast comforted me marvelous much.
        Go in; and tell my lady I am gone,
        Having displeased my father, to Laurence' cell,
        To make confession and to be absolved.

Nurse. Marry, I will; and this is wisely done.

    [*Exit.*]

265 **Juliet.** Ancient damnation! O most wicked fiend!
        Is it more sin to wish me thus forsworn,
        Or to dispraise my lord with that same tongue
        Which she hath praised him with above compare
        So many thousand times? Go, counselor!
270   Thou and my bosom henceforth shall be twain.
        I'll to the friar to know his remedy.
        If all else fail, myself have power to die.

    [*Exit.*]

242–251 The Nurse gives Juliet advice. She says that since Romeo is banished, he's no good to her; Juliet should marry Paris. Romeo is a dishcloth (**dishclout**) compared to Paris.

251 beshrew: curse.

252–254 This new marriage will be better than the first, which is as good as over.

258 Amen: I agree. Curse your heart and soul!

260–263 What message does Juliet give to the Nurse for her parents?

265–270 Now that Juliet is alone, she says what she really thinks. She calls the Nurse an old devil (**ancient damnation**). She doesn't know whether to be angrier at the Nurse for telling her to break her wedding vows or for criticizing Romeo after having praised him.
Go . . . twain: Leave me. You and my secrets will be separated (**twain**) from now on. How has Juliet's relationship with the Nurse changed?

Thinking through the **LITERATURE**

Connect to the Literature

1. What Do You Think? What were your thoughts about Lord Capulet's behavior toward Juliet?

> **Comprehension Check**
> - In what way is Romeo accidentally responsible for Mercutio's death?
> - What is Romeo's punishment for killing Tybalt?
> - Why is Lord Capulet so angry with Juliet?

Think Critically

2. Which event in this act do you think causes the most problems for Romeo and Juliet, and why?

3. How well do you think Romeo handles difficult circumstances?

THINK ABOUT
- his behavior to Tybalt before and after Mercutio's death
- his behavior in Friar Laurence's cell
- his state of mind when he parts from Juliet

4. Describe Juliet's situation at the end of this act.

THINK ABOUT
- her mixed feelings of hate and love when she learns of Tybalt's death
- the future of her marriage with Romeo
- changes in her relationship with her parents
- the Nurse's advice

5. Compare and contrast the behavior of the Nurse and Friar Laurence in Act Three. Which of the two would you trust more if you were Romeo or Juliet? Why?

6. **ACTIVE READING** **READING SHAKESPEAREAN DRAMA** Review carefully the graphic you have been filling out in your **READER'S NOTEBOOK.** Look at the events that occur in Act Three. Which one of those events do you consider to be the **climax,** or turning point, of the play? Explain your answer.

Extend Interpretations

7. What If? If you were the Prince, would you have banished Romeo? If so, why? If not, what would you have done to punish him?

8. Connect to Life What messages might the outcome of events in Act Three, Scene 1, convey to those who resort to violence to resolve conflicts?

Literary Analysis

ALLUSION An **allusion** is a brief reference, within a work, to something outside the work that the audience or reader is expected to know. Shakespeare's plays, for example, often contain allusions to historical and current events, ancient Greek and Roman mythology, and the Bible. Line 20 from Act Three, Scene 5, alludes to Cynthia, another name for Diana, Roman goddess of the moon. Cynthia was often depicted with a crescent moon on her forehead (*reflex* here means "reflection"):

> *'Tis but the pale reflex of Cynthia's brow*

This allusion has a somewhat chilling, distancing effect, which anticipates the separation that Romeo and Juliet are facing at this point in the play.

Activity Find another allusion in Act Three, and explain what it means. Why do you think Shakespeare includes the allusion?

Shakespeare's plays have themselves become a source of allusions. For example, what do you think people today mean when they call someone "a regular Romeo"?

REVIEW **IRONY** **Irony** exists when there is a contrast between what is expected and what actually occurs. **Situational irony** occurs when a character or the reader expects one thing to happen but something else actually happens. **Dramatic irony** occurs when the reader or viewer knows something that a character does not know. Identify at least three examples of irony in Act Three.

ACT *Four*

Act Four, Scene 1. Verona

SCENE 1 *Friar Laurence's cell.*

When Juliet arrives at Friar Laurence's cell she is upset to find Paris there making arrangements for their wedding. When Paris leaves, the panicked Juliet tells the Friar that if he has no solution to her problem, she will kill herself. The Friar explains his plan. Juliet will drink a potion he has made from his herbs that will put her in a deathlike coma. When she wakes up two days later in the family tomb, Romeo will be waiting for her, and they will escape to Mantua together.

[*Enter* Friar Laurence *and* Paris.]

Friar Laurence. On Thursday, sir? The time is very
    short.

Paris. My father Capulet will have it so,
    And I am nothing slow to slack his haste.

5 **Friar Laurence.** You say you do not know the lady's
    mind.
    Uneven is the course; I like it not.

Paris. Immoderately she weeps for Tybalt's death,
    And therefore have I little talked of love;
10   For Venus smiles not in a house of tears.
    Now, sir, her father counts it dangerous
    That she do give her sorrow so much sway,
    And in his wisdom hastes our marriage
    To stop the inundation of her tears,
15   Which, too much minded by herself alone,
    May be put from her by society.
    Now do you know the reason of this haste.

Friar Laurence. [*Aside.*] I would I knew not why it
    should be slowed.—
20 Look, sir, here comes the lady toward my cell.

3–4 My . . . haste: Capulet is eager to have the wedding on Thursday and so am I.

5–7 You say . . . not: You don't know how Juliet feels about this. It's a difficult (**uneven**) plan, and I don't like it. What is the Friar's real reason for wanting to slow down the wedding preparations?

8–17 According to Paris, what is Capulet's reason for wanting Juliet to marry so quickly?

[*Enter* Juliet.]

Paris. Happily met, my lady and my wife!

Juliet. That may be, sir, when I may be a wife.

Paris. That may be must be, love, on Thursday next.

Juliet. What must be shall be.

25 **Friar Laurence.**   That's a certain text.

Paris. Come you to make confession to this father?

Juliet. To answer that, I should confess to you.

Paris. Do not deny to him that you love me.

Juliet. I will confess to you that I love him.

30 **Paris.** So will ye, I am sure, that you love me.

Juliet. If I do so, it will be of more price,
　　Being spoke behind your back, than to your face.

Paris. Poor soul, thy face is much abused with tears.

Juliet. The tears have got small victory by that,
35 　　For it was bad enough before their spite.

Paris. Thou wrongst it more than tears with that
　　report.

Juliet. That is no slander, sir, which is a truth;
　　And what I spake, I spake it to my face.

40 **Paris.** Thy face is mine, and thou hast slandered it.

Juliet. It may be so, for it is not mine own.
　　Are you at leisure, holy father, now,
　　Or shall I come to you at evening mass?

Friar Laurence. My leisure serves me, pensive
45 　　daughter, now.
　　My lord, we must entreat the time alone.

Paris. God shield I should disturb devotion!
　　Juliet, on Thursday early will I rouse ye.
　　Till then, adieu, and keep this holy kiss.

[*Exit.*]

50 **Juliet.** O, shut the door! and when thou hast done so,
　　Come weep with me—past hope, past cure, past
　　help!

Friar Laurence. Ah, Juliet, I already know thy grief;
　　It strains me past the compass of my wits.
55 　　I hear thou must, and nothing may prorogue it,
　　On Thursday next be married to this County.

22–32 As in the last scene of Act Three, Juliet chooses her words carefully to avoid lying and to avoid telling her secret. Whom does *him* refer to in line 29?

34–35 The tears . . . spite: The tears haven't ruined my face: it wasn't all that beautiful before they did their damage.

40 Paris says he owns Juliet's face (since she will soon marry him). Insulting her face, he says, insults him, its owner.

46 We must ask you to leave.

54–55 compass: limit. **prorogue:** postpone.

Juliet. Tell me not, friar, that thou hearst of this,
Unless thou tell me how I may prevent it.
If in thy wisdom thou canst give no help,
60   Do thou but call my resolution wise
And with this knife I'll help it presently.
God joined my heart and Romeo's, thou our hands;
And ere this hand, by thee to Romeo's sealed,
Shall be the label to another deed,
65   Or my true heart with treacherous revolt
Turn to another, this shall slay them both.
Therefore, out of thy long-experienced time,
Give me some present counsel; or, behold,
'Twixt my extremes and me this bloody knife
70   Shall play the umpire, arbitrating that
Which the commission of thy years and art
Could to no issue of true honor bring.
Be not so long to speak. I long to die
If what thou speakst not of remedy.

75 **Friar Laurence.** Hold, daughter, I do spy a kind
         of hope,
Which craves as desperate an execution
As that is desperate which we would prevent.
If, rather than to marry County Paris,
80   Thou hast the strength of will to slay thyself,
Then is it likely thou wilt undertake
A thing like death to chide away this shame,
That copest with death himself to scape from it;
And, if thou darest, I'll give thee remedy.

85 **Juliet.** O, bid me leap, rather than marry Paris,
From off the battlements of yonder tower,
Or walk in thievish ways, or bid me lurk
Where serpents are; chain me with roaring bears,
Or shut me nightly in a charnel house,
90   O'ercovered quite with dead men's rattling bones,
With reeky shanks and yellow chapless skulls;
Or bid me go into a new-made grave
And hide me with a dead man in his shroud—
Things that, to hear them told, have made me
95   tremble—
And I will do it without fear or doubt,
To live an unstained wife to my sweet love.

Friar Laurence. Hold, then. Go home, be merry, give
     consent

59–62 If . . . hands: If you can't help me, at least tell me that my plan (**resolution**) is right.

64–74 Before I sign another wedding agreement (**deed**), I will use this knife to kill myself. If you, with your years of experience (**long-experienced time**), can't help me, I'll end my sufferings (**extremes**) and solve the problem myself.

79–84 If you are desperate enough to kill yourself, then you'll try the desperate solution I have in mind.

85–97 Juliet replies that she will do anything. What does Juliet say she would rather face than marry Paris? **charnel house:** a storehouse for bones from old graves; **reeky shanks:** stinking bones; **chapless:** without jaws. The description in lines 89–93 comes closer to Juliet's future than she knows.

98–130 The Friar explains his desperate plan to Juliet.

Act Four, Scene 1. Juliet reaches for the potion that will make her appear to be dead. (Zeffirelli, 1968)

100　To marry Paris. Wednesday is tomorrow.
　　Tomorrow night look that thou lie alone:
　　Let not the nurse lie with thee in thy chamber.
　　Take thou this vial, being then in bed,
　　And this distilled liquor drink thou off;
105　When presently through all thy veins shall run
　　A cold and drowsy humor; for no pulse
　　Shall keep his native progress, but surcease;
　　No warmth, no breath, shall testify thou livest;
　　The roses in thy lips and cheeks shall fade
110　To paly ashes, thy eyes' windows fall
　　Like death when he shuts up the day of life;
　　Each part, deprived of supple government,
　　Shall, stiff and stark and cold, appear like death;
　　And in this borrowed likeness of shrunk death
115　Thou shalt continue two-and-forty hours,
　　And then awake as from a pleasant sleep.
　　Now, when the bridegroom in the morning comes
　　To rouse thee from thy bed, there art thou dead.
　　Then, as the manner of our country is,
120　In thy best robes uncovered on the bier
　　Thou shalt be borne to that same ancient vault

103 vial: small bottle.

106 humor: liquid.

107–116 Your pulse will stop (**surcease**), and you will turn cold, pale, and stiff, as if you were dead. This condition will last for forty-two hours.

117–122 What will happen when Paris comes to wake Juliet?

Where all the kindred of the Capulets lie.
In the meantime, against thou shalt awake,
Shall Romeo by my letters know our drift;

124 **drift:** plan.

125 And hither shall he come; and he and I
Will watch thy waking, and that very night
Shall Romeo bear thee hence to Mantua.
And this shall free thee from this present shame,
If no inconstant toy nor womanish fear

129–130 **inconstant toy:** foolish whim.
Abate thy valor: weaken your courage.

130 Abate thy valor in the acting it.

Juliet. Give me, give me! O, tell me not of fear!

Friar Laurence. Hold! Get you gone, be strong and
prosperous
In this resolve. I'll send a friar with speed

135 To Mantua, with my letters to thy lord.

Juliet. Love give me strength! and strength shall help
afford.
Farewell, dear father.

[*Exeunt.*]

SCENE 2 *Capulet's house.*

Capulet is making plans for the wedding on Thursday. Juliet arrives and apologizes to him, saying that she will marry Paris. Capulet is so relieved that he reschedules the wedding for the next day, Wednesday.

[*Enter Capulet, Lady Capulet, Nurse, and Servingmen.*]

Capulet. So many guests invite as here are writ.

[*Exit a* Servingman.]

Sirrah, go hire me twenty cunning cooks.

Servingman. You shall have none ill, sir; for I'll try if
they can lick their fingers.

1–8 Capulet is having a cheerful conversation with his servants about the wedding preparations. One servant assures him that he will test (**try**) each cook he hires by making the cook taste his own food (**lick his own fingers**).

5 **Capulet.** How canst thou try them so?

Servingman. Marry, sir, 'tis an ill cook that cannot lick
his own fingers. Therefore he that cannot lick his
fingers goes not with me.

Capulet. Go, begone.

[*Exit Servingman.*]

10   We shall be much unfurnished for this time.
        What, is my daughter gone to Friar Laurence?

Nurse. Ay, forsooth.

Capulet. Well, he may chance to do some good on her.
        A peevish self-willed harlotry it is.

[*Enter* Juliet.]

15   **Nurse.** See where she comes from shrift with merry
        look.

Capulet. How now, my headstrong? Where have you
        been gadding?

Juliet. Where I have learnt me to repent the sin
20   Of disobedient opposition
        To you and your behests, and am enjoined
        By holy Laurence to fall prostrate here
        To beg your pardon. Pardon, I beseech you!
        Henceforward I am ever ruled by you.

25   **Capulet.** Send for the County. Go tell him of this.
        I'll have this knot knit up tomorrow morning.

Juliet. I met the youthful lord at Laurence' cell
        And gave him what becomed love I might,
        Not stepping o'er the bounds of modesty.

30   **Capulet.** Why, I am glad on't. This is well. Stand up.
        This is as't should be. Let me see the County.
        Ay, marry, go, I say, and fetch him hither.
        Now, afore God, this reverend holy friar,
        All our whole city is much bound to him.

35   **Juliet.** Nurse, will you go with me into my closet
        To help me sort such needful ornaments
        As you think fit to furnish me tomorrow?

Lady Capulet. No, not till Thursday. There is time
        enough.

40   **Capulet.** Go, nurse, go with her. We'll to church
        tomorrow.

[*Exeunt* Juliet *and* Nurse.]

Lady Capulet. We shall be short in our provision.
        'Tis now near night.

Capulet. Tush, I will stir about,
45   And all things shall be well, I warrant thee, wife.
        Go thou to Juliet, help to deck up her.

---

10 unfurnished: unprepared.

14 A silly, stubborn girl she is. What does calling Juliet "it" suggest about Capulet's attitude toward her?
15 shrift: confession.

17–18 How are you, my stubborn (**headstrong**) daughter? Where have you been wandering around (**gadding**)?

19–23 Where I . . . pardon: where I have learned to regret disobeying your orders (**behests**). Friar Laurence has ordered (**enjoined**) me to bow before you and ask you to forgive me.

25–26 knot knit up: wedding, from the expression "tying the knot." Capulet declares that the wedding will be the next day, Wednesday, instead of Thursday. What does moving the wedding up by one day do to Friar Laurence's plan?

33–34 What is ironic about Capulet's praise of Friar Laurence?

35 closet: bedroom.

38–44 Lady Capulet urges her husband to wait until Thursday as originally planned. She needs time to get food (**provision**) ready for the wedding party.

45–51 Capulet is so set on Wednesday that he promises to make the arrangements himself.

I'll not to bed tonight; let me alone.
I'll play the housewife for this once. What, ho!
They are all forth; well, I will walk myself
50   To County Paris, to prepare him up
Against tomorrow. My heart is wondrous light,
Since this same wayward girl is so reclaimed.

[*Exeunt.*]

SCENE 3 *Juliet's bedroom.*

Juliet sends her mother away and prepares to take the drug the Friar has given her. She is confused and frightened but finally puts the vial to her lips and drinks.

[*Enter* Juliet *and* Nurse.]

Juliet. Ay, those attires are best; but, gentle nurse,
I pray thee leave me to myself tonight;
For I have need of many orisons
To move the heavens to smile upon my state,
5   Which, well thou knowest, is cross and full of sin.

[*Enter* Lady Capulet.]

Lady Capulet. What, are you busy, ho? Need you my
help?

Juliet. No madam; we have culled such necessaries
As are behooveful for our state tomorrow.
10   So please you, let me now be left alone,
And let the nurse this night sit up with you;
For I am sure you have your hands full all
In this so sudden business.

Lady Capulet.   Good night.
15   Get thee to bed and rest, for thou hast need.

[*Exeunt* Lady Capulet *and* Nurse.]

Juliet. Farewell! God knows when we shall meet again.
I have a faint cold fear thrills through my veins
That almost freezes up the heat of life.
I'll call them back again to comfort me.
20   Nurse!—What should she do here?
My dismal scene I needs must act alone.
Come, vial.

3–5 orisons: prayers. Why is Juliet's upcoming marriage "cross and full of sin"?

8–9 we have . . . tomorrow: We have picked out (**culled**) everything appropriate for tomorrow.

16–25 farewell . . . there: Juliet wonders when she'll see her mother and nurse again. She starts to call back the Nurse but realizes she must be alone to drink the potion. She keeps her knife near her in case the potion doesn't work.

What if this mixture do not work at all?
Shall I be married then tomorrow morning?

25   No, no! This shall forbid it. Lie thou there.

[Lays down a dagger.]

What if it be a poison which the friar
Subtly hath ministered to have me dead,
Lest in this marriage he should be dishonored
Because he married me before to Romeo?

30   I fear it is; and yet methinks it should not,
For he hath still been tried a holy man.
How if, when I am laid into the tomb,
I wake before the time that Romeo
Come to redeem me? There's a fearful point!

35   Shall I not then be stifled in the vault,
To whose foul mouth no healthsome air breathes in,
And there die strangled ere my Romeo comes?
Or, if I live, is it not very like
The horrible conceit of death and night,

40   Together with the terror of the place—
As in a vault, an ancient receptacle
Where for this many hundred years the bones
Of all my buried ancestors are packed;
Where bloody Tybalt, yet but green in earth,

45   Lies fest'ring in his shroud; where, as they say,
At some hours in the night spirits resort—
Alack, alack, is it not like that I,
So early waking—what with loathsome smells,
And shrieks like mandrakes torn out of the earth,

50   That living mortals, hearing them, run mad—
O, if I wake, shall I not be distraught,
Environed with all these hideous fears,
And madly play with my forefather's joints,
And pluck the mangled Tybalt from his shroud,

55   And, in this rage, with some great kinsman's bone
As with a club dash out my desp'rate brains?
O, look! methinks I see my cousin's ghost
Seeking out Romeo, that did spit his body
Upon a rapier's point. Stay, Tybalt, stay!

60   Romeo, I come! this do I drink to thee.

[She drinks and falls upon her bed within the curtains.]

26–31 Why does Juliet think the Friar might have given her poison?

32–37 In these lines what fear does Juliet express?

38–45 Next Juliet fears the vision (**conceit**) she might have on waking in the family tomb and seeing the rotting body of Tybalt.

46–56 She fears that the smells together with sounds of ghosts screaming might make her lose her mind. **Mandrake** root was thought to look like the human form and, when pulled from the ground, to scream and drive people mad.

57–60 Juliet thinks she sees Tybalt's ghost searching for Romeo. She cries to the ghost to stop (**stay**) and, with Romeo's name on her lips, quickly drinks the potion.

SCENE 4 *Capulet's house.*

It is now the next morning, nearly time for the wedding. The household is happy and excited as everyone makes final preparations.

[*Enter* Lady Capulet *and* Nurse.]

Lady Capulet. Hold, take these keys and fetch more
    spices, nurse.

Nurse. They call for dates and quinces in the pastry.

[*Enter* Capulet.]

Capulet. Come, stir, stir, stir! The second cock hath
    ₅ crowed,
    The curfew bell hath rung, 'tis three o'clock.
    Look to the baked meat, good Angelica;
    Spare not for cost.

Nurse.   Go, you cot-quean, go,
    ₁₀ Get you to bed! Faith, you'll be sick tomorrow
    For this night's watching.

Capulet. No, not a whit. What, I have watched ere now
    All night for lesser cause, and ne'er been sick.

Lady Capulet. Ay, you have been a mouse-hunt in your
    ₁₅ time;
    But I will watch you from such watching now.

[*Exeunt* Lady Capulet *and* Nurse.]

Capulet. A jealous hood, a jealous hood!

[*Enter three or four* Servants, *with spits and logs and baskets.*]

                     Now, fellow,
    What is there?

₂₀ **First Servant.** Things for the cook, sir; but I know not
    what.

Capulet. Make haste, make haste. [*Exit* Servant.] Sirrah,
    fetch drier logs.
    Call Peter; he will show thee where they are.

₂₅ **Second Servant.** I have a head, sir, that will find out
    logs
    And never trouble Peter for the matter.

3 pastry: the room where baking is done.

4–6 Capulet tells everyone to wake up
(**stir**).

7–8 In his happy mood he even calls the
Nurse by her name, Angelica. He tells her
to attend to the meat and to spend any
amount of money necessary.

9 cot-quean: The Nurse playfully calls
Capulet a "cottage queen," or a
housewife. This is a joke about his doing
women's work (arranging the party).

12–13 I've stayed up all night for less
important things and never gotten sick.

14–17 Lady and Lord Capulet joke about
his being a woman chaser (**mouse-hunt**)
as a young man. He jokes about her
jealousy (**jealous hood**).

Capulet. Mass, and well said, merry whoreson, ha!
Thou shalt be loggerhead. [*Exit* Servant.] Good faith,
'tis day.
30   The County will be here with music straight,
For so he said he would. [*Music within.*] I hear him
   near.
Nurse! Wife! What, ho! What, nurse, I say!

[*Reenter* Nurse.]

35   Go waken Juliet; go and trim her up.
I'll go and chat with Paris. Hie, make haste,
Make haste! The bridegroom he is come already:
Make haste, I say.

[*Exeunt.*]

28–31 The joking between Capulet and his servants includes the mild oath **Mass,** short for "by the Mass," and **loggerhead,** a word for a stupid person and a pun, since the servant is searching for drier logs. **straight:** right away.

SCENE 5 *Juliet's bedroom.*

The joyous preparations suddenly change into plans for a funeral when the Nurse discovers Juliet on her bed, apparently dead. Lord and Lady Capulet, Paris, and the Nurse are overcome with grief. Friar Laurence tries to comfort them and instructs them to bring Juliet's body to the Capulet family tomb. The scene abruptly switches to humor, in a foolish conversation between the servant Peter and the musicians hired to play at the wedding.

[*Enter* Nurse.]

Nurse. Mistress! what, mistress! Juliet! Fast, I warrant
   her, she.
Why, lamb! why, lady! Fie, you slugabed!
Why, love, I say! madam! sweetheart! Why, bride!
5   What, not a word? You take your pennyworths now,
Sleep for a week; for the next night, I warrant,
The County Paris hath set up his rest
That you shall rest but little. God forgive me,
Marry and amen, how sound is she asleep!
10   I needs must wake her. Madam, madam, madam!
Aye, let the County take you in your bed,
He'll fright you up, i' faith. Will it not be?

[*Opens the curtains.*]

What, dressed and in your clothes and down again?
I must needs wake you. Lady! lady! lady!

1–12 The Nurse chatters as she bustles around the room arranging things. She calls Juliet a **slugabed,** or sleepyhead, who is trying to get her rest now, since after the wedding, Paris won't let her get much sleep. When Juliet doesn't answer, the Nurse opens the curtains that enclose the bed.

15   Alas, alas! Help, help! my lady's dead!
     O well-a-day that ever I was born!
     Some aqua vitae, ho! My lord! my lady!

[*Enter* Lady Capulet.]

Lady Capulet. What noise is here?

Nurse.   O lamentable day!

20   **Lady Capulet.** What is the matter?

Nurse.   Look, look! O heavy day!

Lady Capulet. O me, O me! My child, my only life!
     Revive, look up, or I will die with thee!
     Help! help! Call help.

[*Enter* Capulet.]

25   **Capulet.** For shame, bring Juliet forth; her lord is
         come.

Nurse. She's dead, deceased; she's dead! Alack the day!

Lady Capulet. Alack the day, she's dead, she's dead,
     she's dead!

30   **Capulet.** Ha! let me see her. Out alas! she's cold,
     Her blood is settled, and her joints are stiff;
     Life and these lips have long been separated.
     Death lies on her like an untimely frost
     Upon the sweetest flower of all the field.

35   **Nurse.** O lamentable day!

Lady Capulet.   O woeful time!

Capulet. Death, that hath ta'en her hence to make me
     wail,
     Ties up my tongue and will not let me speak.

[*Enter* Friar Laurence *and* Paris, *with* Musicians.]

40   **Friar Laurence.** Come, is the bride ready to go to
         church?

Capulet. Ready to go, but never to return.
     O son, the night before thy wedding day
     Hath death lain with thy wife. See, there she lies,
45   Flower as she was, deflowered by him.
     Death is my son-in-law, Death is my heir;
     My daughter he hath wedded. I will die
     And leave him all. Life, living, all is Death's.

Paris. Have I thought long to see this morning's face,
50   And doth it give me such a sight as this?

17 **aqua vitae:** an alcoholic drink.

19 **lamentable:** filled with grief;
mournful.

33–34 **Death . . . field:** What simile does
Capulet use to describe what has
happened to Juliet?

48 **Life . . . Death's:** Life, the living, and
everything else belongs to Death.

Lady Capulet. Accursed, unhappy, wretched, hateful
   day!
Most miserable hour that e'er time saw
In lasting labor of his pilgrimage!
55 But one, poor one, one poor and loving child,
But one thing to rejoice and solace in,
And cruel Death hath catched it from my sight!

Nurse. O woe! O woeful, woeful, woeful day!
Most lamentable day, most woeful day
60 That ever, ever I did yet behold!
O day! O day! O day! O hateful day!
Never was seen so black a day as this.
O woeful day! O woeful day!

Paris. Beguiled, divorced, wronged, spited, slain!
65 Most detestable Death, by thee beguiled,
By cruel, cruel thee quite overthrown!
O love! O life! not life, but love in death!

Capulet. Despised, distressed, hated, martyred, killed!
Uncomfortable time, why camest thou now
70 To murder, murder our solemnity?
O child! O child! my soul, and not my child!
Dead art thou, dead! alack, my child is dead,
And with my child my joys are buried!

Friar Laurence. Peace, ho, for shame! Confusion's cure
75   lives not
In these confusions. Heaven and yourself
Had part in this fair maid! now heaven hath all,
And all the better is it for the maid.
Your part in her you could not keep from death,
80 But heaven keeps his part in eternal life.
The most you sought was her promotion,
For 'twas your heaven she should be advanced;
And weep ye now, seeing she is advanced
Above the clouds, as high as heaven itself?
85 O, in this love, you love your child so ill
That you run mad, seeing that she is well.
She's not well married that lives married long,
But she's best married that dies married young.
Dry up your tears and stick your rosemary
90 On this fair corse, and, as the custom is,
In all her best array bear her to church;

53–57 This is the most miserable hour that time ever saw in its long journey. I had only one child to make me happy, and Death has taken (**catched**) her from me.

64 Beguiled: tricked.

69–70 why . . . solemnity: Why did Death have to come to murder our celebration?

74–88 The Friar comforts the family. He says that the cure for disaster (**confusion**) cannot be found in cries of grief. Juliet's family and heaven once shared her; now heaven has all of her. All the family ever wanted was the best for her; now she's in heaven—what could be better than that? It is best to die young, when the soul is still pure, without sin.

89–93 Do what is customary. Put rosemary, an herb, on her corpse (**corse**), and take her, in her finest clothes (**best array**), to church. Though it's natural to cry, common sense tells us we should rejoice for the dead.

For though fond nature bids us all lament,
Yet nature's tears are reason's merriment.

Capulet. All things that we ordained festival
95 Turn from their office to black funeral—
Our instruments to melancholy bells,
Our wedding cheer to a sad burial feast;
Our solemn hymns to sullen dirges change;
Our bridal flowers serve for a buried corse;
100 And all things change them to the contrary.

Friar Laurence. Sir, go you in; and, madam, go with
him;
And go, Sir Paris. Every one prepare
To follow this fair corse unto her grave.
105 The heavens do lower upon you for some ill;
Move them no more by crossing their high will.

[*Exeunt* Capulet, Lady Capulet, Paris, *and* Friar.]

First Musician. Faith, we may put up our pipes, and be
gone.

Nurse. Honest good fellows, ah, put up, put up,
110 For well you know this is a pitiful case.

[*Exit.*]

Second Musician. Aye, by my troth, the case may be
amended.

[*Enter* Peter.]

Peter. Musicians, oh, musicians, "Heart's ease, heart's
ease." Oh, an you will have me live, play "Heart's
115 ease."

First Musician. Why "Heart's ease"?

Peter. Oh, musicians, because my heart itself plays "My
heart is full of woe." Oh, play me some merry dump,
to comfort me.

120 **First Musician.** Not a dump we, 'tis no time to play
now.

Peter. You will not, then?

First Musician. No.

Peter. I will then give it you soundly.

125 **First Musician.** What will you give us?

94 ordained festival: intended for the wedding.

98 sullen dirges: sad, mournful tunes.

105–106 The heavens . . . will: The fates (**heavens**) frown on you for some wrong you have done. Don't tempt them by refusing to accept their will (Juliet's death).

113–158 After the tragedy of Juliet's "death," Shakespeare injects a light and witty conversation between Peter and the musicians. Peter asks them to play "Heart's Ease," a popular song of the time and a **dump,** a sad song. They refuse, and insults and puns are traded. Peter says that instead of money he'll give them a jeering speech (**gleek**), and he insults them by calling them minstrels. In return they call him a servant. Then both make puns using notes of the singing scale, re and fa.

Peter. No money, on my faith, but the gleek. I will
    give you the minstrel.

First Musician. Then will I give you the serving
    creature.

130 **Peter.** Then will I lay the serving creature's dagger on
    your pate. I will carry no crotchets. I'll re you, I'll fa
    you, do you note me?

First Musician. An you re us and fa us, you note us.

Second Musician. Pray you put up your dagger, and
135   put out your wit.

Peter. Then have at you with my wit! I will drybeat you
    with an iron wit, and put up my iron dagger. Answer
    me like men:
        "When griping grief the heart doth wound
140   And doleful dumps the mind oppress,
        Then music with her silver sound—"
    Why "silver sound"? Why "music with her silver
    sound"?—What say you, Simon Catling?

First Musician. Marry, sir, because silver hath a sweet
145   sound.

Peter. Pretty! What say you, Hugh Rebeck?

Second Musician. I say "silver sound" because
    musicians sound for silver.

Peter. Pretty too! What say you, James Soundpost?

150 **Third Musician.** Faith, I know not what to say.

Peter. Oh, I cry you mercy, you are the singer. I will
    say for you. It is "music with her silver sound"
    because musicians have no gold for sounding.
        "Then music with her silver sound
155   With speedy help doth lend redress."

[*Exit.*]

First Musician. What a pestilent knave is this same!

Second Musician. Hang him, Jack! Come, we'll in here.
    Tarry for the mourners, and stay dinner.

[*Exeunt.*]

Thinking through the LITERATURE

Connect to the Literature

1. What Do You Think? How would you **summarize** the way circumstances have worked out so far for Juliet?

> **Comprehension Check**
> - What reason does Paris give for Capulet's decision to move up the marriage plans?
> - At first, what does Juliet believe is the only solution to her problem?
> - What does Friar Laurence suggest that Juliet do to avoid the wedding?

Think Critically

2. What aspects of Juliet's character do you think are most apparent in this act?

3. Explain whether you think Juliet was right to follow Friar Laurence's plan.

THINK ABOUT
- her hatred of the idea of marrying Paris and her love for Romeo
- her fears about the plan
- whether she could have turned to someone else for help

4. Dramatic irony exists when the reader or viewer knows something that one or more characters does not know. Find examples of dramatic irony in Act Four. What effect do these instances of irony create at this point in the play?

5. Do you feel sympathy for the Capulets, the Nurse, or Paris when they express grief over Juliet's death? Why or why not?

6. **ACTIVE READING** **READING SHAKESPEAREAN DRAMA** Reread Juliet's soliloquy at the end of Act Four, Scene 3. In your **READER'S NOTEBOOK**, write down vocabulary and sentence structures in the passage that are unfamiliar. Use the sidenotes and, if necessary, a dictionary, to help you figure out the meaning of the difficult language, and jot down your ideas. Then, with a partner, review your notes. Compare your interpretations, and work together to clarify any remaining obscure passages.

Extend Interpretations

7. What If? If the Nurse had accompanied Juliet to Friar Laurence's cell, do you think Juliet would have made a different decision? Explain your answer.

8. Connect to Life If you were Juliet, would you try Friar Laurence's solution? If so, why? If not, what would you do?

Literary Analysis

COMIC RELIEF In his tragedies, Shakespeare often includes **comic relief,** or humorous incidents that relieve the overall emotional intensity. An example is the conversation between Peter and the musicians at the end of Act Four, Scene 5. This humorous interchange follows the grief-filled scene in which Juliet's body is discovered. The audience does not yet know whether Friar Laurence's plan for Romeo and Juliet will work, and the comical exchanges between Peter and the musicians are intended to provide a change of pace and a lightening of the atmosphere.

Paired Activity With a classmate, discuss your response to these questions:
- If you were producing a stage or film version of *Romeo and Juliet,* would you leave this incident out, or do you think it contributes to the effectiveness of the play? Explain your responses.
- What additional examples of comic relief do you find in Act Four?

REVIEW **MOTIVATION**

Character Motivation refers to the reasons characters act or think in a certain way. Why do you think Juliet's father moves up the wedding? Why do you think Friar Laurence fails to tell Juliet's parents the truth?

ACT *Five*

SCENE 1 *A street in Mantua.*

Balthasar, Romeo's servant, comes from Verona to tell him that Juliet is dead and lies in the Capulet's tomb. Since Romeo has not yet received any word from the Friar, he believes Balthasar. He immediately decides to return to Verona in order to die next to Juliet. He sends Balthasar away and sets out to find a pharmacist who will sell him poison.

[*Enter* Romeo.]

Romeo. If I may trust the flattering truth of sleep,
    My dreams presage some joyful news at hand.
    My bosom's lord sits lightly in his throne,
    And all this day an unaccustomed spirit
5   Lifts me above the ground with cheerful thoughts.
    I dreamt my lady came and found me dead
    (Strange dream that gives a dead man leave to
       think!)
    And breathed such life with kisses in my lips
10   That I revived and was an emperor.
    Ah me! how sweet is love itself possessed,
    When but love's shadows are so rich in joy!

[*Enter* Romeo's *servant*, Balthasar, *booted.*]

    News from Verona! How now, Balthasar?
    Dost thou not bring me letters from the friar?
15   How doth my lady? Is my father well?
    How fares my Juliet? That I ask again,
    For nothing can be ill if she be well.

Balthasar. Then she is well, and nothing can be ill.
    Her body sleeps in Capels' monument,
20   And her immortal part with angels lives.
    I saw her laid low in her kindred's vault
    And presently took post to tell it you.
    O, pardon me for bringing these ill news,
    Since you did leave it for my office, sir.

1–5 If I can trust my dreams, something joyful is about to happen. My heart (**bosom's lord**) is happy and I am content.

6–10 What was Romeo's dream?

17 If Juliet is well, no news can be bad.

18–24 Balthasar replies that Juliet is well, since although her body is dead, her soul (**her immortal part**) is with the angels. As soon as he saw her in the tomb, he immediately rode to Mantua (**presently took post**) to tell Romeo. He asks forgiveness for bringing bad news but reminds Romeo that he had given Balthasar the duty (**office**) of bringing important news.

25 **Romeo.** Is it e'en so? Then I defy you, stars!
Thou knowst my lodging. Get me ink and paper
And hire posthorses. I will hence tonight.

Balthasar. I do beseech you, sir, have patience
Your looks are pale and wild and do import
30 Some misadventure.

Romeo. Tush, thou art deceived.
Leave me and do the thing I bid thee do.
Hast thou no letters to me from the friar?

Balthasar. No, my good lord.

35 **Romeo.** No matter. Get thee gone
And hire those horses. I'll be with thee straight.

[*Exit* Balthasar.]

Well, Juliet, I will lie with thee tonight.
Let's see for means. O mischief, thou art swift
To enter in the thoughts of desperate men!
40 I do remember an apothecary,
And hereabouts he dwells, which late I noted
In tattered weeds, with overwhelming brows,
Culling of simples. Meager were his looks,
Sharp misery had worn him to the bones;
45 And in his needy shop a tortoise hung,
An alligator stuffed, and other skins
Of ill-shaped fishes; and about his shelves
A beggarly account of empty boxes,
Green earthen pots, bladders, and musty seeds,
50 Remnants of packthread, and old cakes of roses
Were thinly scattered, to make up a show.
Noting this penury, to myself I said,
"An if a man did need a poison now
Whose sale is present death in Mantua,
55 Here lives a caitiff wretch would sell it him."
O, this same thought did but forerun my need,
And this same needy man must sell it me.
As I remember, this should be the house.
Being holiday, the beggar's shop is shut.
60 What, ho! apothecary!

[*Enter* Apothecary.]

Apothecary. Who calls so loud?

25 I defy you, stars: Romeo angrily challenges fate, which has caused him so much grief.

29–30 import some misadventure: suggest that something bad will happen.

37 What does Romeo mean?
38–43 Let's see for means: Let me find a way (**means**) to join Juliet in death. **apothecary:** pharmacist. **tattered weeds:** ragged clothes. **Culling of simples:** sorting herbs.

45–51 Romeo describes the items in the apothecary's shop.

52 penury: poverty.
53–55 Although it is a crime to sell poison, the apothecary is such a miserable person (**caitiff wretch**) that he would probably do it for the money.

Romeo. Come hither, man. I see that thou art poor.
    Hold, there is forty ducats. Let me have
    A dram of poison, such soon-speeding gear
65   As will disperse itself through all the veins
    That the life-weary taker may fall dead,
    And that the trunk may be discharged of breath
    As violently as hasty powder fired
    Doth hurry from the fatal cannon's womb.

70 **Apothecary.** Such mortal drugs I have; but
      Mantua's law
    Is death to any he that utters them.

Romeo. Art thou so bare and full of wretchedness
    And fearest to die? Famine is in thy cheeks,
75   Need and oppression starveth in thine eyes,
    Contempt and beggary hangs upon thy back:
    The world is not thy friend, nor the world's law;
    The world affords no law to make thee rich;
    Then be not poor, but break it and take this.

80 **Apothecary.** My poverty but not my will consents.

Romeo. I pay thy poverty and not thy will.

Apothecary. Put this in any liquid thing you will
    And drink it off, and if you had the strength
    Of twenty men, it would dispatch you straight.

85 **Romeo.** There is thy gold—worse poison to men's
      souls,
    Doing more murder in this loathsome world,
    Than these poor compounds that thou mayst
      not sell.
90   I sell thee poison; thou hast sold me none.
    Farewell. Buy food and get thyself in flesh.
    Come, cordial and not poison, go with me
    To Juliet's grave; for there must I use thee.

[*Exeunt.*]

63–69 ducats: gold coins. Forty ducats was a large sum of money. Romeo asks for fast-acting (**soon-speeding**) poison.

70–72 Such . . . them: I have such deadly drugs, but selling them is a crime punishable by death.

73–79 Romeo argues that the man lives in such misery he has no reason to fear death or the law. He urges the apothecary to improve his situation by selling the poison.

80 I'm doing this for the money, not because I think it's right.

81 I'm not paying your conscience.

84 dispatch you straight: kill you instantly.

92 Romeo refers to the poison as a **cordial,** a drink believed to be good for the heart.

SCENE 2 *Friar Laurence's cell in Verona.*

Friar Laurence's messenger arrives saying that he was unable to deliver the letter to Romeo. Friar Laurence, his plans ruined, rushes to the Capulet vault before Juliet awakes. He intends to hide her in his room until Romeo can come to take her away.

[*Verona.* Friar Laurence's *cell.*]

[*Enter* Friar John.]

Friar John. Holy Franciscan friar, brother, ho!

[*Enter* Friar Laurence.]

Friar Laurence. This same should be the voice of
    Friar John.
    Welcome from Mantua. What says Romeo?
5   Or, if his mind be writ, give me his letter.

Friar John. Going to find a barefoot brother out,
    One of our order to associate me,
    Here in this city visiting the sick,
    And finding him, the searchers of the town,
10   Suspecting that we both were in a house
    Where the infectious pestilence did reign,
    Sealed up the doors, and would not let us forth,
    So that my speed to Mantua there was stayed.

Friar Laurence. Who bare my letter, then, to Romeo?

15 **Friar John.** I could not send it—here it is again—
    Nor get a messenger to bring it thee,
    So fearful were they of infection.

Friar Laurence. Unhappy fortune! By my brotherhood,
    The letter was not nice, but full of charge,
20   Of dear import, and the neglecting it
    May do much danger. Friar John, go hence,
    Get me an iron crow and bring it straight
    Unto my cell.

    Friar John.   Brother, I'll go and bring it thee.

[*Exit.*]

6–13 Friar John explains why he didn't go to Mantua. He had asked another friar (**One of our order**), who had been caring for the sick, to go with him. The health officials of the town, believing that the friars had come into contact with the deadly disease the plague (**infectious pestilence**), locked them up to keep them from infecting others.

14 bare: carried (bore).

19–21 The letter wasn't trivial (**nice**) but rather contained instructions (**charge**) of great importance (**dear import**). The fact that it wasn't sent (**neglecting it**) may cause great harm. What would the letter have told Romeo that he does not know?

22 iron crow: crowbar. Why might Friar Laurence need a crowbar?

25 **Friar Laurence.** Now must I to the monument alone.
　　Within this three hours will fair Juliet wake.
　　She will beshrew me much that Romeo
　　Hath had no notice of these accidents;
　　But I will write again to Mantua,
30 　And keep her at my cell till Romeo come—
　　Poor living corse, closed in a dead man's tomb!

[*Exeunt.*]

25–28 Now I must hurry to Juliet's side, since she'll awaken in three hours. Juliet will be furious with me (**beshrew me**) when she discovers that Romeo doesn't know what has happened.

Scene 3 *The cemetery that contains the Capulets' tomb.*

In the dark of night Paris comes to the cemetery to put flowers on Juliet's grave. At the same time Romeo arrives, and Paris hides. Romeo opens the tomb and Paris assumes that he is going to harm the bodies. He challenges Romeo, who warns him to leave. They fight and Romeo kills Paris. When Romeo recognizes the dead Paris, he lays his body inside the tomb as Paris requested. Romeo declares his love for Juliet, drinks the poison, and dies. Shortly after, Friar Laurence arrives and discovers both bodies. When Juliet wakes up, the Friar urges her to leave with him before the guard comes. Juliet refuses and when the Friar leaves, she kills herself with Romeo's dagger. The guards and the Prince arrive, followed by the Capulets and Lord Montague, whose wife has just died because of Romeo's exile. Friar Laurence and both servants explain what has happened. Capulet and Montague finally end their feud and promise to erect statues honoring Romeo and Juliet.

[*Enter* Paris *and his* Page *with flowers and a torch.*]

Paris. Give me thy torch, boy. Hence, and stand aloof.
　　Yet put it out, for I would not be seen.
　　Under yond yew tree lay thee all along,
　　Holding thine ear close to the hollow ground.
5 　So shall no foot upon the churchyard tread
　　(Being loose, unfirm, with digging up of graves)
　　But thou shalt hear it. Whistle then to me,
　　As signal that thou hearst something approach.
　　Give me those flowers. Do as I bid thee, go.

10 **Page.** [*Aside*] I am almost afraid to stand alone
　　Here in the churchyard; yet I will adventure.

[*Withdraws.*]

1–9 Paris wants nobody to know that he is visiting Juliet's tomb. He tells his servant to keep his ear to the ground and whistle if anyone comes near.

Paris. Sweet flower, with flowers thy bridal bed I strew

[*He strews the tomb with flowers.*]

(O woe! thy canopy is dust and stones)
Which with sweet water nightly I will dew;

15   Or, wanting that, with tears distilled by moans.
The obsequies that I for thee will keep
Nightly shall be to strew thy grave and weep.

[*The* Page *whistles.*]

The boy gives warning something doth approach.
What cursed foot wanders this way tonight

20   To cross my obsequies and true love's rite?
What, with a torch? Muffle me, night, awhile.

[*Withdraws.*]

[*Enter* Romeo *and* Balthasar *with a torch, a mattock, and a crow of iron.*]

Romeo. Give me that mattock and the wrenching iron.
Hold, take this letter. Early in the morning
See thou deliver it to my lord and father.

25   Give me the light. Upon thy life I charge thee,
Whate'er thou hearest or seest, stand all aloof
And do not interrupt me in my course.
Why I descend into this bed of death
Is partly to behold my lady's face,

30   But chiefly to take thence from her dead finger
A precious ring—a ring that I must use
In dear employment. Therefore hence, be gone.
But if thou, jealous, dost return to pry
In what I farther shall intend to do,

35   By heaven, I will tear thee joint by joint
And strew this hungry churchyard with thy limbs.
The time and my intents are savage-wild,
More fierce and more inexorable far
Than empty tigers or the roaring sea.

40   **Balthasar.** I will be gone, sir, and not trouble you.

Romeo. So shalt thou show me friendship. Take thou
that.
Live, and be prosperous; and farewell, good fellow.

12–17 Paris promises to decorate Juliet's grave with flowers, as he does now, and with either perfume (**sweet water**) or his tears. He will perform these honoring rites (**obsequies**) every night.

19–22 What cursed . . . awhile: who dares to interrupt my ritual? Is he even carrying a torch? Let the darkness hide me. **mattock . . . iron:** ax and crowbar.

23–24 What might Romeo have written to his father?

28–32 What two reasons does Romeo give for going into Juliet's tomb?

32 In dear employment: for an important purpose.

33–39 Romeo threatens that if Balthasar returns because he is curious (**jealous**), Romeo will rip him apart and throw his bones around the churchyard. His intention is more unstoppable (**inexorable**) than a hungry (**empty**) tiger or the waves of an ocean.

Balthasar. [*Aside*] For all this same, I'll hide me
    hereabout.
His looks I fear, and his intents I doubt.

[*Withdraws.*]

Romeo. Thou detestable maw, thou womb of death,
    Gorged with the dearest morsel of the earth,
    Thus I enforce thy rotten jaws to open,
    And in despite I'll cram thee with more food.

[Romeo *opens the tomb.*]

Paris. This is that banisht haughty Montague
    That murdered my love's cousin—with which grief
    It is supposed the fair creature died—
    And here is come to do some villainous shame
    To the dead bodies. I will apprehend him.
    Stop thy unhallowed toil, vile Montague!
    Can vengeance be pursued further than death?
    Condemned villain, I do apprehend thee.
    Obey, and go with me; for thou must die.

Romeo. I must indeed; and therefore came I hither.
    Good gentle youth, tempt not a desp'rate man.
    Fly hence and leave me. Think upon these gone;
    Let them affright thee. I beseech thee, youth,
    Put not another sin upon my head
    By urging me to fury. O, be gone!
    By heaven, I love thee better than myself.
    For I come hither armed against myself.
    Stay not, be gone. Live, and hereafter say
    A madman's mercy bid thee run away.

Paris. I do defy thy conjuration
    And apprehend thee for a felon here.

Romeo. Wilt thou provoke me? Then have at
    thee, boy!

[*They fight.*]

Page. O Lord, they fight! I will go call the watch.

[*Exit.*]

Paris. O, I am slain! [Falls.] If thou be merciful,
    Open the tomb, lay me with Juliet.

[*Dies.*]

44–45 Balthasar decides to hide in the cemetery in spite of what he has just promised Romeo. Who else is hiding in the cemetery at this point?

47–50 Romeo addresses the tomb as though it were devouring people. He calls it a hateful stomach (**detestable maw**) that is filled (**gorged**) with the dearest morsel of earth, Juliet. He uses his crowbar to open its **rotten jaws** and feeds himself to it.

51–55 Paris speaks these lines to himself. He is angry with Romeo, believing that Romeo's having killed Tybalt caused Juliet to die of grief for her cousin. What does he think Romeo intends to do at the tomb?

60–69 Romeo rejects Paris' challenge. He tells Paris to think of those already killed and leave before Romeo is forced to kill him too. Romeo swears that he has come to harm himself, not Paris.

70–71 I reject your appeal (**defy thy conjuration**) and arrest you as a criminal.

Romeo. In faith, I will. Let me peruse this face.
Mercutio's kinsman, noble County Paris!
What said my man when my betossed soul
80 Did not attend him as we rode? I think
He told me Paris should have married Juliet.
Said he not so? or did I dream it so?
Or am I mad, hearing him talk of Juliet,
To think it was so? O, give me thy hand,
85 One writ with me in sour misfortune's book!
I'll bury thee in a triumphant grave.
A grave? O, no, a lantern, slaughtered youth,
For here lies Juliet, and her beauty makes
This vault a feasting presence full of light.
90 Death, lie thou there, by a dead man interred.

[*Lays* Paris *in the tomb.*]

How oft when men are at the point of death
Have they been merry! which their keepers call
A lightning before death. O, how may I
Call this a lightning? O my love! my wife!
95 Death, that hath sucked the honey of thy breath,
Hath had no power yet upon thy beauty.
Thou art not conquered. Beauty's ensign yet
Is crimson in thy lips and in thy cheeks,
And death's pale flag is not advanced there.
100 Tybalt, liest thou there in thy bloody sheet?
O, what more favor can I do to thee
Than with that hand that cut thy youth in twain
To sunder his that was thine enemy?
Forgive me, cousin! Ah, dear Juliet,
105 Why art thou yet so fair? Shall I believe
That unsubstantial Death is amorous,
And that the lean abhorred monster keeps
Thee here in dark to be his paramour?
For fear of that I still will stay with thee
110 And never from this palace of dim night
Depart again. Here, here will I remain
With worms that are thy chambermaids. O, here
Will I set up my everlasting rest
And shake the yoke of inauspicious stars
115 From this world-wearied flesh. Eyes, look your last!
Arms, take your last embrace! and, lips, O you
The doors of breath, seal with a righteous kiss

77–90 Romeo discovers that the man he has just killed is Paris, whom he vaguely remembers was supposed to marry Juliet. He says that like himself, Paris has been a victim of bad luck. He will bury him with Juliet, whose beauty fills the tomb with light. Paris' corpse (**Death**) is being buried (**interred**) by a dead man in that Romeo expects to be dead soon.

95–99 Romeo notices that death has had no effect on Juliet's beauty. The sign (**ensign**) of beauty is still in Juliet's red lips and rosy cheeks.

101–103 O, what . . . enemy: I can best repay you (Tybalt) by killing your enemy (myself) with the same hand that cut your youth in two (**twain**).

105–108 Romeo can't get over how beautiful Juliet still looks. He asks whether Death is loving (**amorous**) and whether it has taken Juliet as its lover (**paramour**).

112–115 O, here . . . flesh: Here I will cause my death (**everlasting rest**) and rid myself of the burden (**shake the yoke**) of an unhappy fate (**inauspicious stars**).

View and Compare

(Zeffirelli, 1968)

*E*ach of these images shows Romeo's discovery of Juliet. Which has the more powerful impact on the viewer?

(Luhrmann, 1996)

A dateless bargain to engrossing death!
Come, bitter conduct; come, unsavory guide!
120 Thou desperate pilot, now at once run on
The dashing rocks thy seasick weary bark!
Here's to my love! [*Drinks.*] O true apothecary!
Thy drugs are quick. Thus with a kiss I die.

[*Falls.*]

[*Enter* Friar Laurence, *with lantern, crow, and spade.*]

Friar Laurence. Saint Francis be my speed! how
125   oft tonight
Have my old feet stumbled at graves! Who's there?

Balthasar. Here's one, a friend, and one that knows
       you well.

Friar Laurence. Bliss be upon you! Tell me, good
130   my friend,
What torch is yond that vainly lends his light
To grubs and eyeless skulls? As I discern,
It burneth in the Capels' monument.

Balthasar. It doth so, holy sir; and there's my master,
135   One that you love.

Friar Laurence. Who is it?

Balthasar.   Romeo.

Friar Laurence. How long hath he been there?

Balthasar. Full half an hour.

140 **Friar Laurence.** Go with me to the vault.

Balthasar.   I dare not, sir.
My master knows not but I am gone hence,
And fearfully did menace me with death
If I did stay to look on his intents.

145 **Friar Laurence.** Stay then; I'll go alone. Fear comes
       upon me.
O, much I fear some ill unthrifty thing.

Balthasar. As I did sleep under this yew tree here,
I dreamt my master and another fought,
150   And that my master slew him.

Friar Laurence.   Romeo!

[*Stoops and looks on the blood and weapons.*]

118 dateless: eternal; neverending.
Romeo means that what he is about to
do can never be undone.

120–121 thy seasick weary bark:
Romeo compares himself to the pilot of a
ship (**bark**) who is going to crash on the
rocks because he is so weary and sick.

141–144 I can't go with you to the
tomb. My master threatened me with
death if I stayed here.

145–147 The Friar fears that something
unlucky (**unthrifty**) has happened.

Alack, alack, what blood is this which stains
The stony entrance of this sepulcher?
What mean these masterless and gory swords

155 To lie discolored by this place of peace?

[*Enters the tomb.*]

Romeo! O, pale! Who else? What, Paris too?
And steeped in blood? Ah, what an unkind hour
Is guilty of this lamentable chance!
The lady stirs.

[*Juliet rises.*]

160 **Juliet.** O comfortable friar! where is my lord?
I do remember well where I should be,
And there I am. Where is my Romeo?

Friar Laurence. I hear some noise. Lady, come from
   that nest

165 Of death, contagion, and unnatural sleep.
A greater power than we can contradict
Hath thwarted our intents. Come, come away.
Thy husband in thy bosom there lies dead;
And Paris too. Come, I'll dispose of thee

170 Among a sisterhood of holy nuns.
Stay not to question, for the watch is coming.
Come, go, good Juliet. I dare no longer stay.

Juliet. Go, get thee hence, for I will not away.

[*Exit Friar Laurence.*]

What's here? A cup, closed in my true love's hand?

175 Poison, I see, hath been his timeless end.
O churl! drunk all, and left no friendly drop
To help me after? I will kiss thy lips.
Haply some poison yet doth hang on them
To make me die with a restorative.

[*Kisses him.*]

180 Thy lips are warm!

Chief Watchman. [*Within*] Lead, boy. Which way?

Juliet. Yea, noise? Then I'll be brief. O happy dagger!

[*Snatches Romeo's dagger.*]

152–155 Why are these bloody swords lying here at the tomb (**sepulcher**), a place that should be peaceful? (The swords are also **masterless,** or without their owners.)

160 comfortable: comforting.

163–173 The Friar hears noise and wants Juliet to get out of the awful tomb. He says that a greater force than they can fight (**contradict**), meaning God or fate, has ruined their plans (**thwarted our intents**). He informs her of Romeo's and Paris' deaths and says he'll find a place for her in a convent of nuns. Why is the Friar so anxious to leave?

175 timeless: happening before its proper time.

176–180 Juliet calls Romeo a miser (**churl**) for not leaving some poison for her. She kisses him, hoping that perhaps (**haply**) some of the poison is still on his lips.

This is thy sheath; there rust, and let me die.

[*She stabs herself and falls.*]

[*Enter* Watchmen *with the* Page of Paris.]

Page. This is the place. There, where the torch doth
185   burn.

Chief Watchman. The ground is bloody. Search about
    the churchyard.
    Go, some of you; whoe'er you find attach.

[*Exeunt some of the* Watch.]

    Pitiful sight! here lies the County slain;
190   And Juliet bleeding, warm, and newly dead,
    Who here hath lain this two days buried.
    Go, tell the Prince; run to the Capulets;
    Raise up the Montagues; some others search.

[*Exeunt others of the* Watch.]

    We see the ground whereon these woes do lie,
195   But the true ground of all these piteous woes
    We cannot without circumstance descry.

[*Reenter some of the* Watch, *with* Balthasar.]

Second Watchman. Here's Romeo's man. We found
    him in the churchyard.

Chief Watchman. Hold him in safety till the Prince
200   come hither.

[*Reenter* Friar Laurence *and another* Watchman.]

Third Watchman. Here is a friar that trembles, sighs,
    and weeps.
    We took this mattock and this spade from him
    As he was coming from this churchyard side.

205 **Chief Watchman.** A great suspicion! Stay the friar too.

[*Enter the* Prince *and* Attendants.]

Prince. What misadventure is so early up,
    That calls our person from our morning rest?

[*Enter* Capulet, Lady Capulet, *and others.*]

183 From this point on, the churchyard will be filled with people and lights.

188 attach: arrest.

193 Raise up: awaken.

194–196 We see the earth (**ground**) these bodies lie on. But the real cause (**true ground**) of these deaths is yet for us to discover (**descry**).

199–205 The guards arrest Balthasar and Friar Laurence as suspicious characters.

Capulet. What should it be, that they so shriek abroad?

Lady Capulet. The people in the street cry "Romeo,"
210 Some "Juliet," and some "Paris"; and all run,
    With open outcry, toward our monument.

Prince. What fear is this which startles in our ears?

Chief Watchman. Sovereign, here lies the County
        Paris slain;
215 And Romeo dead, and Juliet, dead before,
    Warm and new killed.

Prince. Search, seek, and know how this foul
    murder comes.

Chief Watchman. Here is a friar, and slaughtered
220   Romeo's man,
    With instruments upon them fit to open
    These dead men's tombs.

Capulet. O heavens! O wife, look how our daughter
        bleeds!
225 This dagger hath mista'en, for, lo, his house
    Is empty on the back of Montague,
    And it missheathed in my daughter's bosom!

Lady Capulet. O me! this sight of death is as a bell
    That warns my old age to a sepulcher.

[*Enter* Montague *and others*.]

230 **Prince.** Come, Montague; for thou art early up
    To see thy son and heir now early down.

Montague. Alas, my liege, my wife is dead tonight!
    Grief of my son's exile hath stopped her breath.
    What further woe conspires against mine age?

235 **Prince.** Look, and thou shalt see.

Montague. O thou untaught! what manners is in this,
    To press before thy father to a grave?

Prince. Seal up the mouth of outrage for a while,
    Till we can clear these ambiguities
240 And know their spring, their head, their true
        descent;
    And then will I be general of your woes
    And lead you even to death. Meantime forbear,

212 startles: causes alarm.

225–227 This dagger has missed its target. It should rest in the sheath (**house**) that Romeo wears. Instead it is in Juliet's bosom.

232–234 My son's exile has caused my wife to die. What other sadness plots against me in my old age?

236–237 what manners . . . grave: What kind of behavior is this, for a son to die before his father?

238–245 Seal . . . descent: Stop your emotional outbursts until we can find out the source (**spring**) of these confusing events (**ambiguities**). Wait (**forbear**) and let's find out what happened.

And let mischance be slave to patience.
245 Bring forth the parties of suspicion.

Friar Laurence. I am the greatest, able to do least,
Yet most suspected, as the time and place
Doth make against me, of this direful murder;
And here I stand, both to impeach and purge
250 Myself condemned and myself excused.

Prince. Then say at once what thou dost know in this.

Friar Laurence. I will be brief, for my short date
    of breath
Is not so long as is a tedious tale.
255 Romeo, there dead, was husband to that Juliet;
And she, there dead, that Romeo's faithful wife.
I married them; and their stol'n marriage day
Was Tybalt's doomsday, whose untimely death
Banisht the new-made bridegroom from this city;
260 For whom, and not for Tybalt, Juliet pined.
You, to remove that siege of grief from her,
Betrothed and would have married her perforce
To County Paris. Then comes she to me
And with wild looks bid me devise some mean
265 To rid her from this second marriage,
Or in my cell there would she kill herself.
Then gave I her (so tutored by my art)
A sleeping potion; which so took effect
As I intended, for it wrought on her
270 The form of death. Meantime I writ to Romeo
That he should hither come as this dire night
To help to take her from her borrowed grave,
Being the time the potion's force should cease.
But he which bore my letter, Friar John,
275 Was stayed by accident, and yesternight
Returned my letter back. Then all alone
At the prefixed hour of her waking
Came I to take her from her kindred's vault;
Meaning to keep her closely at my cell
280 Till I conveniently could send to Romeo.
But when I came, some minute ere the time
Of her awaking, here untimely lay
The noble Paris and true Romeo dead.

246–250 Friar Laurence confesses that he is most responsible for these events. He will both accuse (**impeach**) himself and clear (**purge**) himself of guilt.

260 It was Romeo's banishment, not Tybalt's death, that made Juliet sad.

272 borrowed: temporary.

She wakes; and I entreated her come forth
285   And bear this work of heaven with patience;
But then a noise did scare me from the tomb,
And she, too desperate, would not go with me,
But, as it seems, did violence on herself.
All this I know, and to the marriage
290   Her nurse is privy; and if aught in this
Miscarried by my fault, let my old life
Be sacrificed, some hour before his time,
Unto the rigor of severest law.

    Prince. We still have known thee for a holy man.
295   Where's Romeo's man? What can he say in this?

    Balthasar. I brought my master news of Juliet's death;
And then in post he came from Mantua
To this same place, to this same monument.
This letter he early bid me give his father,
300   And threatened me with death, going in the vault,
If I departed not and left him there.

    Prince. Give me the letter. I will look on it.
Where is the County's page that raised the watch?
Sirrah, what made your master in this place?

305   **Page.** He came with flowers to strew his lady's grave;
And bid me stand aloof, and so I did.
Anon comes one with light to ope the tomb;
And by-and-by my master drew on him;
And then I ran away to call the watch.

310   **Prince.** This letter doth make good the friar's words,
Their course of love, the tidings of her death;
And here he writes that he did buy a poison
Of a poor 'pothecary, and therewithal
Came to this vault to die and lie with Juliet.
315   Where be these enemies? Capulet, Montague,
See what a scourge is laid upon your hate,
That heaven finds means to kill your joys with love!
And I, for winking at your discords too,
Have lost a brace of kinsmen. All are punished.

320   **Capulet.** O brother Montague, give me thy hand.
This is my daughter's jointure, for no more
Can I demand.

289–293 and to . . . law: Her nurse can bear witness to the secret marriage. If I am responsible for any of this, let the law punish me with death.

297 in post: at full speed.

303–304 Where . . . this place: The Prince asks for Paris' servant, who notified the guards (**raised the watch**). Then he asks the servant why Paris was at the cemetery.

307–309 Soon (**Anon**), someone with a light came and opened the tomb. Paris drew his sword, and I ran to call the guards.

310 Romeo's letter shows that Friar Laurence has told the truth.

315–319 Where are the enemies whose feud started all this trouble? Capulet and Montague, look at the punishment your hatred has brought on you. Heaven has killed your children (**joys**) with love. For shutting my eyes to your arguments (**discords**), I have lost two relatives (Mercutio and Paris). We all have been punished.

321 jointure: dowry, the payment a bride's father makes to the groom. Capulet means that no one could demand more of a bride's father than he has already paid.

Montague.   But I can give thee more;
        For I will raise her statue in pure gold,
325   That whiles Verona by that name is known,
        There shall no figure at such rate be set
        As that of true and faithful Juliet.

Capulet. As rich shall Romeo's by his lady's lie—
        Poor sacrifices of our enmity!

330   **Prince.** A glooming peace this morning with it brings.
        The sun for sorrow will not show his head.
        Go hence, to have more talk of these sad things;
        Some shall be pardoned, and some punished;
        For never was a story of more woe
335   Than this of Juliet and her Romeo.

        [*Exeunt.*]

324–327 at such rate be set: be valued so highly. What does Montague promise to do for the memory of Juliet?

328–329 Capulet promises to do the same for Romeo as Montague will do for Juliet. Their children have become sacrifices to their hatred (**enmity**).

Act Five, Scene 3. Citizens of Verona gather to mourn Romeo and Juliet. (Zeffirelli, 1968)

Thinking *through the* LITERATURE

Connect to the Literature

1. **What Do You Think?** What effect did the multiple deaths in Act Five have on you?

> **Comprehension Check**
> - What prevents Friar John from delivering the letter to Romeo?
> - Why does Paris attack Romeo at the Capulets' tomb?
> - What mistaken belief about Juliet causes Romeo to take his life?

Think Critically

2. The Prologue of Act One speaks of Romeo and Juliet as "a pair of star-crossed lovers." Do you think that fate or individual characters are more responsible for the deaths of Romeo and Juliet?

THINK ABOUT

- how likely it is that their love could have overcome their families' hate
- the actions of Juliet's parents, Tybalt, the Prince, the Nurse, Friar Laurence, the apothecary, and Romeo and Juliet themselves
- the extent to which accidents and coincidences contribute to the outcome
- what other choices Romeo and Juliet might have made

3. Does your opinion of Paris change in the final scene? Explain your answer.

4. **ACTIVE READING** **READING SHAKESPEAREAN DRAMA** The final stage of the plot of a drama is the **resolution.** In Shakespearean drama, the resolution occurs in the last act. Look back at the graphic you have been keeping in your **READER'S NOTEBOOK.** What events contribute to the resolution? Do you think this sequence of events brings the play to a satisfying conclusion? Why or why not?

Extend Interpretations

5. **What If?** If Capulet and Montague had not reconciled, how would the meaning of the play be affected?

6. **Connect to Life** In the lives of individuals as well as of communities and nations, important and necessary changes are often not made until a catastrophe occurs. List some current examples of situations that often are ignored until a crisis looms. What alternatives do you think there are to this way of dealing with problems?

Literary Analysis

TRAGEDY In drama, a **tragedy** is a particular kind of play in which events turn out disastrously for the main character or characters. Usually the tragedy traces the downfall of someone who is otherwise noble except for a character flaw that leads to disaster. Most often, the hero or heroine dies at the end of the play, after facing death with courage and nobility. Fate often plays a role as well in bringing on the final catastrophe.

Cooperative Learning Activity
Discuss the following questions as a class:
- What is the character flaw that leads to catastrophe in the play?
- Who is the play's hero?

REVIEW **THEME** A **theme** is a central idea or message about life conveyed by a work of literature. Think about how each of the human values and experiences listed in the chart below is conveyed in *Romeo and Juliet.* Then choose four of the topics, and for each one write a statement of how it is expressed as a theme in the play.

Values and Experiences	Statement of Theme
Fate	There are forces in life over which people have no control.
Communication and Its Importance	
Family Ties	
Friendship	
Loyalty	
Impulsive Behavior	
Love	

Choices & CHALLENGES

Writing Options

1. Production Notes Assume that you are going to stage a performance of one scene from *Romeo and Juliet*. After choosing the scene, think about the characters, setting, and action involved. Make notes detailing how you envision each character, what kinds of sets and props you want to use, and how the action sequences should be carried out. Consider the purpose, audience, and occasion. Place your notes in your **Working Portfolio.**

Sets & Props

2. Essay on Imagery Write an essay exploring the imagery in *Romeo and Juliet,* especially the light and dark imagery used in the main characters' speeches.

Writing Handbook
See pages 1157–1158: Analysis.

Activities & Explorations

1. Set Design Choose another time and place as the setting for a production of *Romeo and Juliet.* Design sketches for the sets of three or four major scenes. The sketches may be simple drawings or more elaborate finished works, and they may include suggestions for costumes and lighting. ~ **ART**

2. Falling in Love on Screen Look at the two film versions of Romeo and Juliet's first meeting provided on the video that accompanies this program. What does seeing and hearing the scene add to your understanding of the language and imagery in these lines? Do the characters seem believable? natural? With a partner, compare the two versions. ~ **VIEWING AND REPRESENTING**

VIDEO Literature in Performance

Inquiry & Research

1. West Side Story With classmates, read *West Side Story*, the stage musical based on *Romeo and Juliet*, or view a videocassette of the Oscar-winning 1961 film adaptation. Then, in a group discussion, compare and contrast the musical with Shakespeare's play. Consider similarities in characters, settings, events, social concerns and other themes, and language. Also consider differences, including the endings.

2. Modern Stagings of a Classic Play One reason for Shakespeare's long-standing popularity is the universal nature of his themes. Research modern stagings of *Romeo and Juliet.* Where have these been performed? Have modern stagings tinkered with the setting, characters, or plot events?

Real World Link Read the news article on page 1106 for information on one special production.

Grammar in Context: Parallelism

In the following passages, Shakespeare uses parallelism to emphasize ideas and to create rhythms.

> **Friar Laurence.** . . . Each part, deprived of
>   supple government,
> Shall, stiff and stark and cold, appear like death;
>   —Act Four, Scene 1

Parallelism is the repetition of a grammatical feature within a sentence or paragraph. In the example above, parallel elements are shown in colored type.

When you group ideas as in the example above, make sure that the sentence elements are parallel grammatically as well as logically. For example, Friar Laurence's statement would be less effective if Shakespeare had written "stiff and stark and without warmth," mixing a prepositional phrase *(without warmth)* with the two adjectives.

WRITING EXERCISE Rewrite each sentence, making the related elements grammatically parallel.

Usage Tip: Clauses also can serve as parallel elements.

Example: *Original* Loyalty, trust, and to have respect characterize Romeo and Mercutio's friendship.

Rewritten Loyalty, trust, and <u>respect</u> characterize Romeo and Mercutio's friendship.

1. The play begins with an insult, a fight, and with a warning.
2. Romeo arrives at a party, he sees Juliet, and falls in love with her.
3. Friar Laurence is compassionate, kindhearted, and he shows loyalty.
4. Romeo reacts to the news of Juliet's death with shock, distress, and becoming angry.

William Shakespeare
1564–1616

Other Works

Hamlet
Julius Caesar
King Lear
Macbeth

A Midsummer Night's Dream
Much Ado About Nothing
Othello
Richard II
Twelfth Night

Bard of Avon Although William Shakespeare is probably the most famous writer who ever lived, it is largely through his plays and poetry that we know him. The known facts about his personal life are surprisingly few. We know that he came from Stratford-on-Avon, a small town on the River Avon about ninety miles northwest of London. His father was a glove maker who later became the town's mayor; his mother was a distant connection of a wealthy family who lived just outside town. Church records indicate that Shakespeare was baptized on April 26, 1564, which suggests that he was born a few days earlier. He probably went to the local grammar school, although school records no longer exist. There he would have studied Latin and read works by ancient Roman writers, including Virgil and Seneca.

Making His Way At eighteen, Shakespeare married Anne Hathaway, a local farmer's daughter apparently seven or eight years his senior. The couple had a daughter named Susanna in 1583 and boy and girl twins named Hamnet and Judith two years later. There are no records of what Shakespeare did in the next seven years, which some scholars call the "lost years" of his life. During that time he apparently left his family back in Stratford, where they could live comfortably, and made his way to London, center of the theater world. He probably joined a theater company and traveled with them as an actor, most likely making London his home base. When next we hear of Shakespeare, he is a successful playwright and sometime actor in London. His earliest plays include *Richard III, The Comedy of Errors,* and *The Taming of the Shrew;* he also was writing lyric and narrative poetry. For example, in 1593 he published his long poem *Venus and Adonis,* apparently written during the 1592–1593 season, when London's theaters were shut because of an outbreak of the plague.

A Highly Successful Author By 1596, the year in which *Romeo and Juliet* was probably first performed, ten of Shakespeare's plays had already been produced in London, and Shakespeare was a shareholder in the Lord Chamberlain's Men. The theater company had as its patron at that time the high-ranking royal official, known as the Lord Chamberlain. Shakespeare's plays helped make the theater company the most successful of its day. In 1599, he and the other shareholders became part owners of London's popular new Globe Theatre. In 1603, when James I succeeded Elizabeth I to the throne of England, the new king himself became the patron of Shakespeare's theater company, which became known as the King's Men. Shakespeare's business interests and revenues from plays brought him a good deal of money, enough to purchase a beautiful home for his family in Stratford. He was also able to purchase a coat of arms for his father, an important symbol that allowed his father to move officially into the ranks of gentlemen.

Later Years In 1609, Shakespeare took advantage of his fame by publishing his sonnets, a series of poems about love and friendship that most scholars feel he wrote in the 1590s. Shakespeare also began spending more time in Stratford, retiring there permanently in 1613. He wrote no plays after that year; his last complete plays are believed to be *Cymbeline, The Winter's Tale, The Tempest,* and *Henry VIII.* While there are no documentary records of the date of his death, the monument that marks his grave indicates that he died on April 23, 1616.

Author Activity

Quarto and Folio Nicknamed the Bard of Avon (*bard* is a synonym for *poet*), Shakespeare wrote a total of 37 verse dramas. The earliest editions of his plays appear in small quartos and in folios of larger size. Find out more about these two different formats and about the famous First Folio of 1623.

Romeo and Juliet Are
Palestinian and Jewish

by Carol Rosenberg

William Shakespeare's Romeo and Juliet, *a tale of love, hate, and revenge, has proven to be lasting and compelling. Versions of the play have been set in different eras and produced in theaters all over the world. This article describes a 1994 production in Jerusalem that was based on the Palestinian-Israeli conflict.*

Most actors would be delighted to have their mothers in the audience as they played Romeo, scaling a moonlit balcony, matching wits with the Capulets.

Not so for Khalifa Natur, who makes his national debut later this week as the misguided young Montague in a politically charged production of Shakespeare's romantic tragedy being staged jointly by two Jerusalem theater troupes.

"It'll be a little bit embarrassing, that's for sure," said Natur, referring in particular to the part when he plants a not-so-chaste kiss on Juliet.

That's because Juliet is a Jew, Tel Aviv actress Orna Katz—and Natur is a Palestinian who grew up in a tiny Israeli-Arab village, Kalanswa.

❶ Katz and Natur, both 29, were scripted as the star-crossed lovers more than a year ago specifically because of their separate identities.

And both have rehearsed in on-again, off-again fashion for more than a year in the landmark production, which portrays the Montagues as Palestinians and the Capulets as Jews by shifting between Hebrew and Arabic dialogue.

Co-directors Eran Daniel (a Jew) and Fouad Awad (a Muslim) say they are largely faithful to the original text, whose translations were written by leading Israeli and Palestinian songwriters.

Three years in the making, it is an ambitious and contentious project of the Israeli Khan Theater in Jewish West Jerusalem and the Palestinian Al-Kasaba Theater in the Holy City's once predominantly Arab east side.

❷ Art has never been above the Arab-Israeli conflict. Some Palestinian artists refused to participate, arguing that Arabs should not collaborate with the occupier, Israel. Some Israeli

Reading for Information

Do you think cultural events have the power to help resolve deep-seated conflicts? This production is one example of using art to further understanding.

TAKING NOTES

Note taking is a useful skill when collecting and organizing the information that you read. There are three basic note-taking techniques:

- **outlining:** a visual display of the main ideas and supporting details in a text (in formal outlines, Roman numerals are used for main ideas, capital letters for subtopics, and numbers for details)
- **paraphrasing:** restating the main ideas in your own words
- **summarizing:** condensing an article's main ideas into shorter paragraphs, sentences, or phrases

YOUR TURN Use the questions and activities below to help you take notes on this article.

❶ Outlining Important Ideas Use the outline format shown here as you take notes on the article. Write down only key points; don't try to copy every word.

> I. Palestinian and Israeli production of Romeo and Juliet
>
> A. Jews and Palestinians shared both acting and production tasks.
>
>   1. Palestinians play Montagues and Jews play Capulets
>
>   2. Co-directed by a Jew and a Muslim

patrons were uncomfortable with the themes—particularly its violence, including a knife-fight in place of more traditional sword-play, and its gloomy message on coexistence.

"We had lots of difficulties—political difficulties, technical difficulties," said George Ibrahim, a celebrated Palestinian actor and general-manager of the Kasaba Theater, who plays the elder Montague. . . .

Artists on both sides feared for a time that—between army curfews and closures on Palestinian communities and anger and distrust between sides—the project would be abandoned. Simultaneously, the nascent Palestinian-Israeli peace process was thrown into turmoil.

But in the end, they agreed to resume their work for the same reason that they all agreed to participate in the first place.

3 "As performers, we believe that through culture we can make peace—not only through peace treaties," Ibrahim said. "Our destiny is to be with each other and live with each other." . . .

4 Comparisons between the story and the Palestinian-Israeli crisis are inevitable and accentuated by the staging.

At one point, the young Arab Montague men come on stage with handfuls of rocks—to play a sidewalk game—but looking much like the teenage stone-throwers in the Palestinian uprising, the intifada.

In another, the Montagues gather up a dead Mercutio and the Capulets carry off a slain Tybalt to separate funerals that are inescapably and eerily reminiscent of the ritual of burying dead street fighters and soldiers in Israeli and Palestinian communities. . . .

Between themselves, the Montagues speak Arabic while the Capulets speak Hebrew. In a reflection of real life in Israel and the occupied territories, the Montagues switch to Arabic-accented Hebrew when addressing the Capulets.

Yet Juliet, like many Israelis, fumbles through an Arabic greeting when meeting Romeo's priest, Friar Lawrence. "This is the reality. The Israelis can't speak Arabic. But the Arabs speak Hebrew," said Ibrahim.

Another reality for Palestinians is the part in which Romeo is banished from Verona after Tybalt is killed in a knife fight. It strikes a chord in a community where the theme of exile runs deep.

Natur agreed that some might interpret the play to mean that coexistence of the kind envisioned by Palestinians and Israelis in their peace accord is doomed. But he said he and his Jewish counterparts hoped that they would see Shakespeare's message: Blood feuds like those between the Montagues and Capulets are folly.

"Absolutely. He shows they are all stupid," said Natur. "The struggle between the families—each for their own place. It's foolish."

2 Paraphrasing In this section the author explains many of the difficulties that have plagued the production. In your own words, describe those problems.

3 Would you consider the information in this quote a main idea or a subtopic? Explain.

4 What aspects of the Palestinian-Israeli crisis are reflected in this production of *Romeo and Juliet*? Be sure your notes include this information.

Summarizing Reread the explanation of summarizing given on the opposite page. Using your notes, write a short summary of this article.

Inquiry & Research

Activity Link: *Romeo and Juliet*, p. 1104 Now that you have read about an unusual production of *Romeo and Juliet*, what features of the play do you think make it so adaptable to other cultures? In what ways might the play be relevant to your own culture? What insight does this give you into Shakespeare's knowledge of human nature? Discuss these questions with a partner.

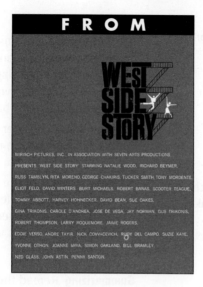

FROM

WEST SIDE STORY

MIRISCH PICTURES, INC. IN ASSOCIATION WITH SEVEN ARTS PRODUCTIONS
PRESENTS 'WEST SIDE STORY' STARRING NATALIE WOOD, RICHARD BEYMER.
RUSS TAMBLYN, RITA MORENO, GEORGE CHAKIRIS, TUCKER SMITH, TONY MORDENTE,
ELIOT FELD, DAVID WINTERS, BURT MICHAELS, ROBERT BANAS, SCOOTER TEAGUE,
TOMMY ABBOTT, HARVEY HOHNECKER, DAVID BEAN, SUE OAKES.
GINA TRIKONIS, CAROLE D'ANDREA, JOSE DE VEGA, JAY NORMAN, GUS TRIKONIS,
ROBERT THOMPSON, LARRY ROQUEMORE, JAIME ROGERS.
EDDIE VERSO, ANDRE TAYIR, NICK COVVACEVICH, RUDY DEL CAMPO, SUZIE KAYE,
YVONNE OTHON, JOANNE MIYA, SIMON OAKLAND, BILL BRAMLEY,
NED GLASS, JOHN ASTIN, PENNY SANTON.

Song Lyrics by
Stephen Sondheim

There's a place for us,
Somewhere a place for us.
Peace and quiet and open air
Wait for us
Somewhere.

There's a time for us,
Someday a time for us,
Time together with time to spare,
Time to learn, time to care
Someday!
Somewhere.

We'll find a new way of living,
We'll find a way of forgiving
Somewhere.

There's a place for us,
A time and a place for us.
Hold my hand and we're halfway there.
Hold my hand and I'll take you there
Somehow,
Someday,
Somewhere!

Stephen Sondheim
1930–

Other Works
*A Funny Thing Happened on the
Way to the Forum*
A Little Night Music
Into the Woods
Sunday in the Park with George

Early Aptitude Stephen Sondheim displayed an
early aptitude for music, learning to play the piano
and the organ when he was just a boy. Oscar

Hammerstein II, a family friend, took part in
Sondheim's musical education, and by the time he
was 15, he had had a musical performed at his
high school.

Breaking New Ground Sondheim's complex
melodies and unusual lyrics have been well
received in the world of music criticism. His
Broadway musicals have won many Tony awards.
Sunday in the Park with George, based on the
Seurat painting, won the Pulitzer Prize.

Choosing Among Word Meanings

Over time, many English words have developed multiple meanings. Other words, called **homonyms,** are spelled and pronounced alike but have different meanings and origins. In the passage on the right, for example, Shakespeare plays on the multiple meanings of *heavy* and the meanings of the homonyms *light* (a source of illumination) and *light* (not heavy or serious). The word *heavy* in Romeo's speech means "sad," but the phrase "I have a soul of lead" shows that his emotional state is also being likened to a physical weight. *Light,* on the other hand, refers primarily to a torch; but by contrasting the word with *heavy,* Romeo shows that he also has in mind its

> **Romeo.** Give me a torch. I am not for this ambling;
>   Being but heavy, I will bear the light.
> **Mercutio.** Nay, gentle Romeo, we must have you
>   dance.
> **Romeo.** Not I, believe me. You have dancing shoes
>   With nimble soles; I have a soul of lead
>   So stakes me to the ground I cannot move.
>   —*The Tragedy of Romeo and Juliet,* Act One, Scene 4

homonym. His pun emphasizes the difference between his mood and the light and playful mood of his companions.

Strategies for Building Vocabulary

The strategies that follow can help you in your encounters with homonyms and with words having more than one denotation.

❶ Examine the Context When you come across a familiar word used in an unfamiliar way, consider the context in which it appears. In Act Two, Scene 3, of *Romeo and Juliet,* Romeo approaches Friar Laurence with a request. As you read the friar's response, note the highlighted words.

> **Friar Laurence.** Be plain, good son, and
>   homely in thy drift.
> **Riddling confession finds but riddling
>   shrift.**

Although the word *homely* is often used to mean "not good looking," it can also mean "simple." Because Friar Laurence is urging Romeo to speak plainly, you can assume that in this case "simple" is the intended sense. Context clues can also help you infer that *drift* is used to mean "the thought running through something spoken or written," not "a movement produced by a current" or "a heap of snow or sand."

❷ Look Up the Word in a Dictionary If a familiar meaning of a word does not make sense in the context of a sentence and there are no clues to help you figure out the meaning, it's time to consult a dictionary. Read through the dictionary definitions, looking for the one that gives the meaning most suited to the context.

❸ Match the Meaning to the Context Writers often give their works richness and depth by using words to convey more than one meaning. For example, in Act Three, Scene 1, of *Romeo and Juliet,* Mercutio receives a deadly sword thrust. When told that the wound cannot be serious, he responds, "Ask for me tomorrow, and you shall find me a grave man." *Grave* means "serious," but the meaning of the homonymous *grave,* "a burial place," is also intended. Through a pun, Mercutio is revealing that he knows he is about to die. In this case the use of a word in more than one sense conveys an ironic humor. In other cases it may provide an important clue to a work's theme.

EXERCISE Locate these words in the indicated passages of *Romeo and Juliet.* Explain the meanings with which they are used there, then write sentences of your own in which you use them with those meanings.

1. *bound* (Act One, Scene 4, lines 20 and 21)
2. *sentence* (Act Two, Scene 3, line 85)
3. *execution* (Act Four, Scene 1, line 77)
4. *state* (Act Four, Scene 3, line 4)
5. *soundly* (Act Four, Scene 5, line 124)

Communication Workshop

Staging a Scene

Acting out a dramatic work . . .

From Reading to Staging Most people would agree that William Shakespeare was one of the greatest dramatists of all time. His plays examine universal themes with great insight, humor, and eloquence. His tragedy of the star-crossed lovers Romeo and Juliet, for example, has moved audiences for over 400 years. During that time, actors, directors, composers, dancers, and musicians have interpreted *Romeo and Juliet* in many different formats, ranging from very traditional presentations to ballets to a stage musical. Now you can try your own hand at **staging a scene** from this great play.

For Your Portfolio

WRITING PROMPT Create a staged presentation of a scene from *Romeo and Juliet*.

Purpose: To interpret and perform a scene

Audience: Your classmates and other interested students and adults

Basics in a Box

GUIDELINES & STANDARDS Staging a Scene

A successful script should

- include an overall description of the setting, props, lighting, and costumes
- include specific stage directions, indicating the gestures, movements, and tones of voice the performers should use
- note details of pacing, stage location, and other aspects of the interpretation

A successful performance should

- demonstrate an awareness of the audience
- present a clear and consistent interpretation of the script
- maintain the audience's interest through strong acting, good pacing, and effective staging

Analyzing a Model Script

Excerpts from Director's Script
Romeo and Juliet, Act One, Scene 5

Characters

Capulet	Mercutio	Five "maskers"/Montagues
Tybalt	Benvolio	Five Capulet men and women
Lady Capulet	Nurse	Three servingmen
Romeo	Juliet	Musicians

Props

Chairs; glittery masks for main characters; cloth masks for other actors; cassette player with recorded music cued on cassette tape

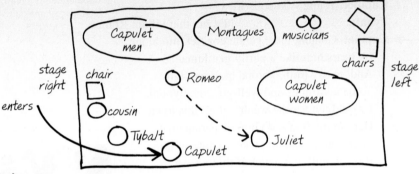

Capulet enters stage right and speaks loudly to all

Capulet. Welcome, gentlemen! Ladies that have their toes
Unplagued with corns will have a bout with you.
Ah ha, my mistresses! which of you all
Will now deny to dance? She that makes dainty,

Capulet walks around stage, addressing first men, then women; shows great humor.

She I'll swear hath corns. Am I come near ye now?
Welcome, gentlemen! I have seen the day
That I have worn a visor and could tell
A whispering tale in a fair lady's ear,
Such as would please. 'Tis gone, 'tis gone, 'tis gone!

Stagehand plays tape while musicians onstage pretend to play instruments.

You are welcome, gentlemen! Come, musicians, play.
A hall, a hall! give room! and foot it, girls.

[*Music plays and they dance.*]

More light, you knaves! and turn the tables up,
And quench the fire, the room is grown too hot.
Ah, sirrah, this unlooked-for sport comes well.

Capulet walks over to his cousin who is sitting; cousin begins to stand.

Nay, sit, nay, sit, good cousin Capulet,

Capulet greets his guests.

Capulet calms Tybalt.

For you and I are past our dancing days.
How long is't now since last yourself and I
Were in a mask?
Second Capulet. By'r Lady, thirty years.

- -

Tybalt acts angry, clenches fist.

Tybalt. Uncle, this is a Montague, our foe;
A villain, that is hither come in spite
To scorn at our solemnity this night.
Capulet. Young Romeo is it?
Tybalt.   'Tis he, that villain Romeo.

Capulet places a hand on Tybalt's shoulder.

Capulet. Content thee, gentle coz, let him alone.
'A bears him like a portly gentleman,
And, to say truth, Verona brags of him
To be a virtuous and well-governed youth.
I would not for the wealth of all this town
Here in my house do him disparagement.
Therefore be patient, take no note of him.
It is my will; the which if thou respect,
Show a fair presence and put off these frowns,
An ill-beseeming semblance for a feast.

Pause for Capulet to walk stage right, then Tybalt whispers angrily.

Tybalt. It fits when such a villain is a guest.
I'll not endure him.

- -

Romeo walks to Juliet, takes her hand, and bows before speaking.

Romeo. If I profane with my unworthiest hand
This holy shrine, the gentle fine is this:
My lips, two blushing pilgrims, ready stand
To smooth that rough touch with a tender kiss.

Romeo and Juliet meet.

Juliet. Good pilgrim, you do wrong your hand too much,
Which mannerly devotion shows in this;
For saints have hands that pilgrims' hands do touch,

Touch hands, palm to palm

And palm to palm is holy palmers' kiss.

Staging Your Scene

❶ Planning Your Scene

With your classmates, choose a scene from *Romeo and Juliet* to stage. One way to begin is to **brainstorm** a list of favorite scenes from the play and then pick one of these scenes. See the **Idea Bank** in the margin for other suggestions. After selecting a scene, follow the steps below.

Steps for Planning Your Scene

▶ **1. Assign acting roles.** Does the group want to have tryouts, draw lots, or have interested students choose their own roles? If the scene has fewer parts than the number of students, perhaps the main roles can be double cast.

▶ **2. List and assign responsibilities.** What other tasks need to be assigned? How will the group assign those tasks? Here are some possible positions:

- director
- prompter
- choreographer
- lighting manager
- prop manager
- set designer
- costumer
- acting coach
- sound crew

▶ **3. Decide on an interpretation.** What type of interpretation does the group want to present? A traditional theater performance? A restaging in modern setting and clothes? A choral reading? A musical?

▶ **4. Create a "director's script."** Mark a copy of the script with notes on the staging, sets, action, and delivery that will serve to convey the interpretation the group has chosen.

▶ **5. Gather the props, costumes, and lighting materials you will need.** What materials will indicate the time and place of the scene and help establish the characters' personalities? Remember that the simpler your materials, the more smoothly your staging will go.

❷ Developing Your Stage Presentation

Discuss the scene with your classmates to make sure everyone has read and understood it thoroughly. Resolve any disagreements in interpretations of the characters' motivations, actions, or emotions. Students should look up any unfamiliar words in their parts and make sure they can pronounce them.

Get interpretations on paper. As the actors rehearse, they should mark up their scripts with the actions and emotions their roles require. Consider the following elements:

- pacing
- facial expressions
- entrances, exits, and other movements
- inflections
- gestures
- use of props, lighting, or music

IDEABank

1. Your Working Portfolio
Look for ideas in the **Writing Option** you completed earlier in this unit:
- **Production Notes,** p. 1104

2. Get Up-to-Date
Look for a scene that will lend itself to a modern interpretation.

3. Get Real
Choose your scene based on the number of students and the space you have to work with.

PRACTICING
TIP

Make audiotapes of the rehearsals so that you can listen for parts that need to be delivered more loudly, more slowly, or with more emotion.

Get everyone involved. Students who don't have roles can serve as acting coaches or script markers. While the student playing a role acts it out, another student could provide coaching, and a third could mark the appropriate actions and emotions on the script.

❸ Practicing and Presenting

The entire cast should practice the scene several times before presenting it.

- **Read through the parts.** The actors should understand what their lines mean so that they can deliver them with the appropriate expression.
- **Walk through the action.** Actors should act out their parts while delivering their lines. Don't worry about costumes, props, or lighting at this point. Concentrate on making sure the actions support and help clarify the words.
- **Do a complete staging.** Finally, set up the stage and incorporate the costumes, props, and lighting that the group has decided on.

After several rehearsals with just the cast, ask one or two other people to watch a rehearsal and offer feedback.

Ask Your Peer Reviewers

- What did you like best about the performance?
- What parts were hard to follow? Why?
- What did you learn about this scene that you didn't know before?
- Which actions and emotions seemed most real to you? Which were least believable?

❹ Refining Your Performance

TARGET SKILL ▶ EVALUATING YOUR INTERPRETIVE CHOICES Think about the decisions you and your classmates made in interpreting your scene. Use the following standards to evaluate how effective those decisions were.

- **Naturalness and clarity.** Do the actors deliver their lines and interact in a realistic way? Do the movements on stage add liveliness and interest without becoming distracting? Do the lines and actions clearly present what is going on in the scene?
- **Conveying mood and character.** Do all parts of the performance work together to show the emotions and values of the characters?
- **Consistency.** Does each actor's approach to his or her part fit the overall interpretation? Do the props, lighting, and costumes all work together to support the interpretation?

❺ Reflecting

FOR YOUR WORKING PORTFOLIO What did you learn about staging a scene? How did performing your task help you learn more about *Romeo and Juliet?* Attach your reflections to your marked-up script. Save your script in your **Working Portfolio.** 🗀

Publishing
IDEAS

- Have someone make a videotape of your performance to be kept in the school library.
- Present your scene for other classes.

**More Online:
Publishing Options**
www.mcdougallittell.com

Read this paragraph from the first draft of a student essay. The underlined sections may include the following kinds of errors:

- **run-on sentences**
- **spelling errors**
- **double negatives**
- **verb tense errors**

For each underlined section, choose the revision that most improves the writing.

> The drama club presented three short scenes from different plays. <u>The first scene was from *Romeo and Juliet,* even though the actors wore regular clothes, the scene was quite convincing</u>. All the actors wore eye masks in different (1)
>
> colors. The masks made the actors seem <u>mysterius</u> and interesting. Lord (2)
>
> Capulet <u>speaks</u> in a very soft voice. <u>I couldn't hardly hear</u> what he was saying (3)   (4)
>
> at first. Soon he began to speak up and was very good. Romeo and Juliet stole
>
> the show. <u>When Juliet said her lines, she seemed completely unaware of anyone but Romeo, the audience was absolutely silent</u>. After the scene was over, the (5)
>
> actors <u>received</u> a well-deserved standing ovation. (6)

1. A. The first scene was from *Romeo and Juliet,* even though the actors wore regular clothes. The scene was quite convincing.

  B. The first scene was from *Romeo and Juliet*. Even though the actors wore regular clothes, the scene was quite convincing.

  C. The first scene was from *Romeo and Juliet*. Even though the actors wore regular clothes. The scene was quite convincing.

  D. Correct as is

2. A. mysterious
  B. mystereous
  C. mysteryous
  D. Correct as is

3. A. spoke
  B. had spoken
  C. have spoken
  D. Correct as is

4. A. couldn't barely hear
  B. could hear
  C. could hardly hear
  D. Correct as is

5. A. When Juliet said her lines, she seemed completely unaware of anyone but Romeo the audience was absolutely silent.

  B. When Juliet said her lines, she seemed completely unaware of anyone but Romeo. The audience was absolutely silent.

  C. When Juliet said her lines. She seemed completely unaware of anyone but Romeo, the audience was absolutely silent.

  D. Correct as is

6. A. receved
  B. recieved
  C. reiceved
  D. Correct as is

Need extra help?

See the **Grammar Handbook**

Correcting Run-on Sentences, p. 1197

Double Negatives, p. 1188

Verb Tense, p. 1184

The Classic Tradition

The *Odyssey* and *Romeo and Juliet* represent very different historical periods, cultures, genres, themes, and styles. Yet each is recognized as a literary classic that contains meaning and beauty for people of every time and place. How has reading the selections in this unit added to your understanding and appreciation of the classic tradition? Complete one or more of the following options to help you explore this question.

Winged Victory, Victor Higgins. Oil on canvas, 40″ × 43¼″. Collection of the Museum of Fine Arts, Museum of New Mexico, Gift of Joan Higgins Reed. Photo by Blair Clark.

Reflecting on Theme

OPTION 1

Analyzing Heroism With a small group of classmates make a word web to illustrate Odysseus' character traits. Make your web similar to the one you made for the activity on page 886. On the left side, write down as many qualities as you can think of that help make Odysseus an effective hero. On the right side, note qualities that you think hinder him from being an effective hero. Then compare this web to the one you made before reading the *Odyssey* and discuss the following questions: In what ways does Odysseus fit the picture you had of a hero? In what ways does he surprise you?

OPTION 2

Appreciating Shakespeare Imagine that your class has been assigned the task of introducing *Romeo and Juliet* to a group of students with no experience of Shakespeare or Shakespearean theater. With a partner, outline the points you would want to make in your introduction, along with your ideas for how to illustrate these points in ways that the inexperienced students could easily understand. Think back to the discussion of Shakespeare you had for the activity on page 982 in order to get ideas for your introduction.

OPTION 3

Understanding What a Classic Is Think about the quotation at the beginning of the unit: "When you reread a classic you do not see more in the book than you did before; you see more in *you* than there was before." With a small group of classmates, discuss how this statement could apply to one of the selections in this unit.

Self ASSESSMENT

READER'S NOTEBOOK

Which classic work—the *Odyssey* or *Romeo and Juliet*—do you think you understand and appreciate more thoroughly? In a paragraph, write your answer to this question and explain why you feel as you do.

Reviewing Literary Concepts

OPTION 1

Analyzing Imagery Both the *Odyssey* and *Romeo and Juliet* are rich in imagery—language that appeals to one or more of the five senses. Homer's imagery is most evident in his epithets and epic similes. Shakespeare often has his characters use images to communicate their thoughts, as when Romeo compares the sight of Juliet to a sunrise:

> But soft! What light through yonder window breaks?
> It is the East, and Juliet is the sun!

In a chart like the one shown, identify your favorite images from these selections, noting the sense or senses that each image appeals to and explaining why you think those particular images are effective. Compare your findings with those of your classmates.

Image	Sense(s)	Why Effective
"Juliet is the sun!"	sight	shows clearly how Romeo feels about her

OPTION 2

Assessing the Influence of Setting Often a story's setting—the time and place in which the action occurs—plays an important role in the development of the plot and makes a strong contribution to the impact of the story as a whole. Write a brief description of the settings of the *Odyssey* and *Romeo and Juliet*. Then choose one of these works and write a paragraph explaining the influence its setting has in making it an effective story.

Self ASSESSMENT

READER'S NOTEBOOK

Copy the following list of literary terms introduced or reviewed in this unit. Next to each term that you do not fully understand, put a question mark. Then consult the **Glossary of Literary Terms** (page 1126) to clarify the meanings of the terms you've marked.

epic	soliloquy
epic hero	aside
epithet	foreshadowing
epic simile	allusion
theme	irony
blank verse	comic relief
iambic	motivation
pentameter	tragedy
imagery	

Building Your Portfolio

- **Writing Options** Most of the Writing Options in this unit asked you to build on aspects of plot, character, or style found in the two works of the classic tradition included here. From these assignments, choose the one that you think best shows your strengths as a writer. Explain how it does so on a cover sheet, attach the sheet to the assignment, and place both in your **Presentation Portfolio.**

- **Writing Workshops** In this unit you wrote a Research Report on a literary topic that interests you. Reread the report and decide what you think are its strengths and weaknesses as a piece of writing. Write a paragraph explaining your thinking, attach it to the report, and place both in your **Presentation Portfolio.**

- **Additional Activities** Think about the assignments that you completed under **Activities & Explorations** and **Inquiry & Research**. Which kind of activity do you think you especially excelled in? Drawing? Dramatization? Oral presentation? Write an assessment of your ability in a cover note, attach it to your record of the assignment, and add both to your portfolio.

Self ASSESSMENT

Presentation Portfolio
Look through your portfolio for examples of writing or activities that you think are particularly well done. Then take time to reflect on all you've accomplished during this year.

Setting GOALS

Think about important learning experiences you've had during this year. What key strategies and processes have helped you improve as a reader and as a writer? Jot them down so that you can remember to use them again.

LITERATURE CONNECTIONS

LITERATURE CONNECTIONS
A Tale of Two Cities

CHARLES DICKENS

In this Victorian novel, set against the violent upheaval of the French Revolution, love and self-sacrifice prove to be the virtues of a true hero. The action of the story alternates between England and France. As in his other novels, Dickens includes vivid characters from every rung of the social ladder.

These thematically related readings are provided along with *A Tale of Two Cities*:

A Short "History" of the French Revolution
BY OLYMPE DE GOUGES AND MAXIMILIEN ROBESPIERRE

***from* Hind Swarj or Indian Rule**
BY MOHANDAS K. GANDHI

***from* Guillotine: Its Legend and Lore**
BY DANIEL GEROULD

Five Men
BY ZBIGNIEW HERBERT

The Pit and the Pendulum
BY EDGAR ALLAN POE

***from* Darkness at Noon**
BY SIDNEY KINGSLEY

The Strike
BY TILLIE OLSEN

And Even *More* . . .

West Side Story

IRVING SHULMAN

Based on the stage and screen musical, this novel sets Shakespeare's *Romeo and Juliet* in the slums of 1950s New York City. Like Shakespeare's tragic lovers, Tony and Maria find love and brief happiness in the midst of hatred and prejudice.

Books

Mythology
EDITH HAMILTON
Hamilton retells the stories of the gods and heroes of Greek and Roman mythology.

The Iliad
HOMER
TRANSLATED BY ROBERT FAGLES

In one of the greatest war stories of all times, gods and heroes clash on the battlefields of ancient Troy.

Antigone
SOPHOCLES
In this classic Greek tragedy, the heroine Antigone defies the state and buries her brother.

A Midsummer Night's Dream

WILLIAM SHAKESPEARE

Love and magic rule the world of this fanciful comedy. The fair maiden Hermia loves Lysander, but her father insists that Demetrius be her mate. To escape a forced marriage, Hermia runs away with Lysander to the woods, followed by Demetrius (who is madly in love with Hermia) and Helena (who is hopelessly in love with Demetrius). Unknowingly, the lovers enter the kingdom of fairies, where love potions and magical transformations are the order of the night.

These thematically related readings are provided along with *A Midsummer Night's Dream*:

A Midsummer Night's Dream
By NORRIE EPSTEIN

The Song of Wandering Aengus
By WILLIAM BUTLER YEATS

The Sweet Miracle/El Dulce Milagro
By JUANA DE IBARBOUROU
TRANSLATED BY ALICE STONE BLACKWELL

April Witch
By RAY BRADBURY

Come. And Be My Baby
By MAYA ANGELOU

Love's Initiations *from* Care of the Soul
By THOMAS MOORE

The Sensible Thing
By F. SCOTT FITZGERALD

***from* Love and Marriage**
By BILL COSBY

Idylls of the King
ALFRED, LORD TENNYSON
These narrative poems are based on the legends of King Arthur and the knights and ladies of his court.

Emma
JANE AUSTEN
One of Austen's best-loved heroines, Emma Woodhouse is a self-appointed matchmaker who finds true love after turning the lives of her friends upside down.

Other Media

The Odyssey
The adventures of Ulysses are brought to life in this 1997 adaptation of Homer's epic.
(VIDEOCASSETTE)

Romeo and Juliet
Directed by Franco Zeffirelli, this critically acclaimed version of Shakespeare's tragedy features Leonard Whiting and Olivia Hussey as the star-crossed lovers.
(VIDEOCASSETTE)

The Voyages of Ulysses and Aeneas
This CD recounts the voyages of Homer's Ulysses and Virgil's Aeneas. The two heroes' adventures are illustrated with fine art and photographs showing how the sites they visited appear today.
(CD-ROM)

2001: A Space Odyssey
This classic and highly influential space epic pits two astronauts against a talking computer named HAL.
(VIDEOCASSETTE)

EMILY DICKINSON

AMY TAN

HOMER

STEPHEN KING

BARBARA KINGSOLVER

MAYA ANGELOU

NELSON MANDELA

STEPHEN VINCENT BENET

AGATHA CHRISTIE

O. HENRY

W. H. AUDEN

JACK LONDON

FRANK McCOURT

RICHARD WRIGHT

LANGSTON HUGHES

SANDRA CISNEROS

JUDITH ORTIZ COFER

RITA DOVE

BERYL MARKHAM

ROBERT FROST

JULIA ALVAREZ

GUY DE MAUPASSANT

TIM O'BRIEN

TRUMAN CAPOTE

EDGAR ALLAN POE

GABRIEL GARCÍA MÁRQUEZ

SAKI

WILLIAM SHAKESPEARE

MARTIN LUTHER KING, JR.

DORIS LESSING

Student *Resource Bank*

Words to Know: Access Guide

A

abominably, 930
absurd, 762
abusive, 295
accost, 209
adamant, 461
adulation, 30
adversary, 910
affable, 45
affirmation, 717
affront, 793
aghast, 32
agile, 153
agitated, 623
alien, 657
aloof, 961
amalgam, 121
amenity, 45
amnesty, 447
anesthetic, 534
anguish, 936
animosity, 622
anthology, 695
antibiotic, 665
apathetically, 530
appalled, 903
appeasingly, 534
appendage, 521
appropriation, 176
aristocrat, 481
articulate, 659
ascetic, 164
askew, 33
assertion, 156
aura, 487
authenticity, 792
avenge, 902

B

banish, 181
beguiling, 918
beleaguered, 164
bereaved, 332
beseech, 379
betrayal, 98
bias, 431
bland, 268
blatant, 461
bleakly, 831
bolster, 858
bravado, 79
brevity, 753

C

careen, 596
cascade, 154
cascading, 487
casually, 69
cavort, 284
chaos, 932
chasm, 837
chide, 921
chronicle, 157
clamoring, 254
cognizant, 539
commandeer, 944
compassion, 84
compel, 240
competent, 458
compulsively, 544
concretely, 267
concur, 456
condone, 49
conformity, 791
conical, 66
conjecture, 865
conniving, 188
consequently, 179
consolation, 69

conspiracy, 277
contaminated, 265
contemplation, 857
contemptible, 954
contemptuously, 427
contender, 921
contrition, 375
conventional, 240
convey, 262
coveted, 157
critical, 545

D

default, 440
defiant, 379
degradation, 83
degraded, 178
demeanor, 623
denunciation, 461
deplorable, 52
depreciate, 792
deprivation, 634
desolation, 964
despondent, 121
despondently, 749
destined, 214
devastate, 96
devastated, 267
devoid, 623
diffuse, 66
dilapidated, 300
dire, 936
disarming, 43
disconsolate, 921
discord, 444
discordant, 94, 417
disdain, 912
disjunction, 621
dispel, 745
disperse, 867
dissenting, 792

distraught, 299
dithering, 952
doggedness, 601
droll, 49
dwindle, 933

E

egotistical, 751
elation, 299
elegantly, 69
elude, 50
embroider, 696
enigmatic, 750
ensue, 529
enticing, 921
entreat, 902
enveloped, 164
escalate, 544
essence, 487
evoke, 560
evolve, 713
exception, 246
execute, 69
exhilarate, 275
exorbitant, 33
exotic, 602
expertise, 744
extremity, 525

F

facetiously, 783
familiarity, 481
fanatic, 164
fanaticism, 421
fathom, 763
feigned, 418
fetter, 212
fiasco, 96, 792
flail, 118
foreboding, 765

formidable, 896
fortitude, 458
frenzy, 952
fulfill, 697
futile, 76

G

gall, 950
gamut, 32
garish, 278
goad, 281
grievously, 860
grotesque, 620
guile, 896

H

harass, 747
hedge, 658
heedless, 659
heresy, 604
hierarchy, 295
hindsight, 541
hoist, 118
homage, 417
hospitable, 761
hull, 117
hypothermic, 118

I

identity, 166
idiom, 666
illiteracy, 486
imminent, 598
impeccable, 790
imperative, 53
impersonally, 766
implacable, 958
implore, 212
impotent, 81

impoverished, 76
improbable, 365
impunity, 209
inadvertently, 456
inaugurate, 275
inception, 717
incessantly, 483
inconsequential, 156
incredulous, 381
incredulously, 118
indifferent, 898
indignity, 90, 566
indolent, 859
indomitable, 566
induced, 249
indulge, 238
indulgently, 175
inertia, 67
inexplicable, 753
inextricably, 442
infallibility, 599
infatuated, 297
infernal, 329
influx, 793
infuse, 485
ingest, 715
inhospitable, 668
initiative, 545
innumerable, 665
inscrutable, 238
insinuatingly, 417
instigate, 153
insubordinate, 672
intangible, 519
interim, 835
interminable, 365
intermittently, 114
intimately, 445
intimidation, 431
intrigue, 621
intuition, 837

intuitively, 656
invalid, 595
iridescent, 599
irreparable, 237
irreproachable, 186
irreverence, 795

J

justification, 944

K

kin, 337

L

lament, 95
languorous, 761
legitimate, 442
lethargy, 560
lodge, 165
lull, 765
lurk, 930

M

maelstrom, 119
magnanimous, 865
malice, 363
mandate, 562
maneuvering, 296
martyrs, 295
meander, 544
mobility, 443
mode, 659
mortified, 670
mystic, 560

N

naive, 659
noncommittal, 281
nostalgia, 696

O

obscuring, 540
obstinacy, 541
omen, 954
oppressor, 434
oratory, 455
oversight, 860

P

pagan, 251
pauper, 30
peremptorily, 531
perfidy, 252
peril, 934
pernicious, 445
perverse, 79
placidly, 425
plagiarized, 672
plunder, 946
poignantly, 76
ponderous, 903
potent, 249
potential, 181
precariously, 601
preclude, 209
predominating, 153
presumption, 715
primitive, 64
privation, 33
privilege, 254
procrastinating, 266
prodigy, 90
proliferate, 868
prone, 828
prosaic, 278

Pronunciation Key

Symbol	Examples	Symbol	Examples	Symbol	Examples
ă	at, gas	m	man, seem	v	van, save
ā	ape, day	n	night, mitten	w	web, twice
ä	father, barn	ng	sing, anger	y	yard, lawyer
âr	fair, dare	ŏ	odd, not	z	zoo, reason
b	bell, table	ō	open, road, grow	zh	treasure, garage
ch	chin, lunch	ô	awful, bought, horse	ə	awake, even, pencil, pilot, focus
d	dig, bored	oi	coin, boy		
ĕ	egg, ten	ŏŏ	look, full	ər	perform, letter
ē	evil, see, meal	ōō	root, glue, through		
f	fall, laugh, phrase	ou	out, cow		**Sounds in Foreign Words**
g	gold, big	p	pig, cap	KH	*German* ich, auch; *Scottish* loch
h	hit, inhale	r	rose, star		
hw	white, everywhere	s	sit, face	N	*French* entre, bon, fin
ĭ	inch, fit	sh	she, mash	œ	*French* feu, cœur; *German* schön
ī	idle, my, tried	t	tap, hopped		
îr	dear, here	th	thing, with	ü	*French* utile, rue; *German* grün
j	jar, gem, badge	*th*	then, other		
k	keep, cat, luck	ŭ	up, nut		
l	load, rattle	ûr	fur, earn, bird, worm		

Stress Marks

′ This mark indicates that the preceding syllable receives the primary stress. For example, in the word *language,* the first syllable is stressed: lăng′gwĭj.

′ This mark is used only in words in which more than one syllable is stressed. It indicates that the preceding syllable is stressed, but somewhat more weakly than the syllable receiving the primary stress. In the word *literature,* for example, the first syllable receives the primary stress, and the last syllable receives a weaker stress: lĭt′ər-ə-chŏŏr′.

Adapted from *The American Heritage Dictionary of the English Language, Third Edition;* Copyright © 1992 by Houghton Mifflin Company. Used with the permission of Houghton Mifflin Company.

Glossary of Literary Terms

Act An act is a major unit of action in a play, similar to a chapter in a book. Depending on their lengths, plays, such as William Shakespeare's *Romeo and Juliet,* can have as many as five acts. Susan Glaspell's *Trifles* is a one-act play.

See also **Scene.**

Alliteration Alliteration is the repetition of consonant sounds at the beginnings of words. Note this example of repetition of the *h* sound in these lines:

> The angels, not half so happy in Heaven,
>   Went envying her and me;
>   —Edgar Allan Poe, from "Annabel Lee"

See pages 139, 204, 611.
See also **Sound Devices.**

Allusion An allusion is an indirect reference to another literary work or to a famous person, place, or event. Maya Angelou's title *I Know Why the Caged Bird Sings* is an allusion to the poem "Sympathy" by Paul Laurence Dunbar.

See pages 490, 986, 1071.

Analogy An analogy is a point-by-point comparison between two things that are alike in some respect. Often, analogies are used in nonfiction, when an unfamiliar subject or idea is explained in terms of a familiar one.

See also **Extended Metaphor; Metaphor; Simile.**

Antagonist An antagonist is usually the principal character in opposition to the **protagonist,** or main character, of a narrative or drama. Sometimes the antagonist is not a character, but something else, like a force of nature, some aspect of society, or an internal force within the protagonist.

Examples: In "Brothers Are the Same" by Beryl Markham, Medoto is the antagonist. In *The Devil and Daniel Webster,* by Stephen Vincent

Benét, Mr. Scratch is the antagonist.

See pages 321, 371.
See also **Conflict; Protagonist.**

Aside An aside is a dramatic device in which a character speaks his or her thoughts aloud, in words meant to be heard by the audience but not by the other characters. In Act Four, Scene 1, of *Romeo and Juliet,* Paris is urging that his marriage to Juliet take place soon. Friar Laurence expresses his uneasiness in an aside.

> Friar Laurence. *[Aside.]* I would I knew not
>   why it should be slowed.—
> Look, sir, here comes the lady toward my cell.
>   —William Shakespeare, from *Romeo and Juliet*

See pages 987, 1043.
See also **Soliloquy.**

Assonance Assonance is the repetition of vowel sounds within nonrhyming words. An example of assonance is the repetition of the short *e* sound in the following lines.

> My grandmothers are full of memories
> Smelling of soap and onions and wet clay
>   —Margaret Walker, from "Lineage"

See pages 139, 204, 611.
See also **Sound Devices.**

Author's Perspective Author's perspective refers to an author's beliefs and attitudes as expressed in his or her writing. These beliefs may be influenced by the author's political views, ethnic background, economic position, education, or religion, for example. Julia Alvarez in "Daughter of Invention" and Sandra Cisneros in "Only Daughter" both write from the perspective of a daughter in an immigrant family.

See pages 651, 676, 684.
See also **Author's Purpose.**

Author's Purpose A writer usually writes for one or more of these purposes: to express himself or herself, to inform or explain, to persuade, and to entertain.

Examples: Pat Mora's purposes for writing "A Voice" are to express herself and to explain. Luisa Valenzuela's purposes for writing "The Censors" are to persuade and to entertain.

See also **Author's Perspective.**

Autobiography An autobiography is an account of a person's life written by that person and usually told from the first-person point of view. *I Know Why the Caged Bird Sings* by Maya Angelou is an autobiography, as is *Black Boy* by Richard Wright. An autobiography is usually book length because it covers a long span of time. Other forms of autobiographical writing include personal narratives, journals, memoirs, diaries, and letters.

See pages 233, 285, 490.
See also **Memoir; Personal Narrative.**

Ballad A ballad is a poem that tells a story and is meant to be sung or recited. **Folk ballads,** written by unknown authors and handed down orally, usually depict ordinary people in the midst of tragic events or adventures of love and bravery. A **literary ballad** is written by a known author. "O What Is That Sound" by W. H. Auden is an example of a **literary ballad.**

See page 144.
See also **Poetry.**

Biography Biography is a true account of a person's life told by someone else. The skilled biographer strives for a balance between fact and interpretation of fact. "The United States vs. Susan B. Anthony" by Margaret Truman is an example of a biography. Some biographical writings select a specific time or event in a subject's life to highlight a certain personality trait. These shorter pieces may be in the form of **character sketches.** Maya Angelou's "Encounter with Martin Luther King, Jr." is an example of a character sketch.

See pages 233, 463, 490, 504.

Blank Verse Blank verse is unrhymed poetry written in iambic pentameter. That is, each line of blank verse has five pairs of syllables. In most pairs, an unstressed syllable is followed by a stressed syllable. The most versatile of poetic forms, blank verse imitates the natural rhythms of English speech. Shakespeare's plays are written in blank verse.

> But soft! What light through yonder window breaks? / It is the East, and Juliet is the sun!

See pages 987, 1019.
See also **Iambic Pentameter.**

Character Characters are the people who take part in the action of a story, a novel, or drama. Sometimes characters can be animals or imaginary creatures, such as beings from another planet. The most important characters are the **main characters.** The other characters in a story, called **minor characters,** interact with the main characters and help move the story along. In "Where Have You Gone, Charming Billy?" by Tim O'Brien, Paul Berlin is the main character and Toby (Buffalo) is a minor character. Often main characters undergo changes as the plot unfolds. Such characters are called **dynamic characters,** as opposed to **static characters,** who remain the same. In "The Beginning of Something" by Sue Ellen Bridgers, Roseanne, the narrator, is a dynamic character in that she changes her reaction to her mother and her opinion about Melissa. Travis, in the same story, is a static character. Characters such as Roseanne, whose many personality traits are revealed by the author, are sometimes referred to as **round characters.** Characters who are described more simply, such as Cousin Roy or Travis, are referred to as **flat characters.**

See pages 24, 71, 100, 321, 340, 410.
See also **Characterization.**

Characterization Characterization refers to the methods that a writer uses to develop characters. There are four basic methods of characterization.

1. A writer may describe a character's physical appearance. In Beryl Markham's "Brothers Are the Same," the narrator describes Medoto: "He was lean and proud, and upon his level stare he weighed each movement Temas made, though these were hesitant and few."

2. A character's nature may be revealed through his or her own speech, thoughts, feelings, or actions. In "The Beginning of Something" by Sue Ellen Bridgers, the narrator describes her own feelings: "Ever since late this morning, I've had this fever. There's a cool dampness inside my clothes but my cheeks are burning. I feel like I've been on fire inside my face all this time but nobody seems to notice. I have a date!"

3. The speech, thoughts, feelings, or actions of other characters can be used to develop a character. The daughter's feelings about her father in "Daughter of Invention" help the reader to understand him better. "Probably, if I had thought a moment about it, I would not have done what I did next. I would have realized my father had lost brothers and comrades to the dictator Trujillo. For the rest of his life, he would be haunted by blood in the streets and late night disappearances. Even after he had been in the states for years, he jumped if a black Volkswagen passed him on the street."

4. The narrator can make direct comments about a character. The narrator in "Brothers Are the Same" comments about Temas: "He did not fear the beast. He was sure that in his bones and in his blood and in his heart he was not afraid."

See pages 182, 504, 676.
See also **Character.**

Chorus In early Greek tragedy, the chorus commented on the actions of the characters in the drama. In Elizabethan plays, such as Shakespeare's *Romeo and Juliet,* the role of the chorus is spoken by a single actor who serves as a narrator and speaks the lines in the prologue (and sometimes in an epilogue). The chorus serves to foreshadow or to summarize events.

Climax Often called the **turning point,** the climax is the moment when the reader's interest and emotional intensity reach the highest point. The climax usually occurs toward the end of a story, after the reader has understood the conflict and become emotionally involved with the characters. The climax sometimes, but not always, points to the resolution of the conflict. In "American History" by Judith Ortiz Cofer, the climax comes when Elena encounters Eugene's mother at the door of Eugene's house.

See pages 23, 302, 754.
See also **Plot.**

Comedy A comedy is a dramatic work that is light and often humorous in tone, usually ending happily with a peaceful resolution of the main conflict. A comedy differs from farce by having a more believable plot, more realistic characters, and less boisterous behavior.

Comic Relief Comic relief is a humorous scene, incident, or speech that is included in a serious drama to provide a change from emotional intensity. Because it breaks the tension, comic relief allows an audience to prepare emotionally for events to come. The sharp contrasts afforded by comic relief may intensify the themes of a literary work.

Example: In many of Shakespeare's plays, a scene involving a fool or bawdy interplay among common folks or between a servant and his or her master provides comic relief. Comic relief in *Romeo and Juliet* is provided by the Nurse in Act Two, Scene 5, when she returns to Juliet after learning the wedding plans from Romeo. Although Juliet is anxious to hear of the plans, which the audience already knows, the Nurse deliberately withholds the information until the end of the scene.

See pages 986, 1086.

Conflict The plot of a story always involves some sort of conflict, or struggle, between opposing forces. An **external conflict** involves a character pitted against an outside force, such as nature, a physical obstacle, or another character. An **internal conflict** is one that occurs within a character.

Examples: In "The Most Dangerous Game" by Richard Connell, Rainsford is in conflict with General Zaroff and with the traps Zaroff sets for him. In "The Bass, the River, and Sheila Mant" by W. D. Wetherell, the narrator is torn between his longing for Sheila and his desire to reel in the big fish that is on the line.

See pages 23, 35, 58, 71, 302, 371, 754.
See also **Plot.**

Connotation Connotation refers to the attitudes and feelings associated with a word, in contrast to **denotation,** which is the literal or dictionary meaning of a word. The connotation of a word may be positive or negative. For example, *enthusiastic* has positive associations, but *rowdy* has negative ones. Connotations of words can have an important influence on style and meaning and are particularly important in poetry. In Gary Soto's poem "Oranges," the connotations of the words *December, frost,* and *cracking* help to create an image of cold. The connotations of the words *orange, bright,* and *fire* help to create an image of warmth.

See page 555.

Couplet A couplet is a rhymed pair of lines.

> I was angry with my foe:
> I told it not, my wrath did grow.
> —William Blake, from "A Poison Tree"

Critical Essay *See* **Essay.**

Denotation *See* **Connotation.**

Description Description is writing that helps a reader to picture scenes, events, and characters. To create description, writers often use **imagery**—words and phrases that appeal to the reader's senses—and **figurative language.** Effective description also relies on precise nouns, verbs, adjectives, and adverbs, as well as carefully selected details. The following passage contains clear details and images.

> There was a low place in the meadow by that corner. The fall rains made a pond there, and in the evenings sometimes ducks would be coming in—a long line with set wings down the winds, and then a turn, and a skimming glide to the water. The wind would be blowing and the grass bent down.
>
> —William Stafford,
> from "The Osage Orange Tree"

See also **Figurative Language; Imagery.**

Dialect Dialect is a form of language as it is spoken in a particular geographic area or by a particular social or ethnic group. A group's dialect is reflected in its pronunciations, vocabulary, expressions, and grammatical constructions. Writers use dialect to establish setting, provide local color, and develop character. In "Two Kinds" by Amy Tan, the narrator's mother uses grammatical constructions that are not common in English and thus speaks a kind of dialect.

> "Who ask you be genius?" she shouted. "Only ask you be your best. For you sake. You think I want you be genius? . . ."

Dialogue Written conversation between two or more characters in either fiction or nonfiction is called dialogue. Writers use dialogue to bring characters to life and to give readers insights into the characters' qualities, personality traits, and reactions to other characters. Realistic, well-paced dialogue also advances the plot of a narrative. The words each character speaks are commonly set off with quotation marks. The following dialogue between a newspaper editor and Richard, the narrator of the autobiography *Black Boy,* helps to characterize Richard.

> "Where's my story?" I asked.
> "It's in galleys," he said.
> "What's that?" I asked; I did not know what galleys were.
> "It's set up in type," he said. "We're publishing it."
> "How much money will I get?" I asked, excited.
> "We can't pay for manuscript," he said.
> "But you sell your papers for money," I said with logic.
>
> —Richard Wright, from *Black Boy*

In a play, the story is told primarily through dialogue. Dramatists use **stage directions** to indicate how they intend the dialogue to be interpreted by the actors. Here is an example of dialogue from *The Devil and Daniel Webster.*

> **Jabez.** *(uncomfortably)* A man can't always be proud of everything, Mary. There's some things a man does, or might do—when he has to make his way.
> **Mary.** *(laughing)* I know—terrible things—like being the best farmer in the county and the best State Senator—

See pages 350, 410, 660, 676.
See also **Characterization; Drama; Stage Directions.**

Diction A writer's or speaker's choice of words and way of arranging the words in sentences is called diction. In her poem "A Voice," Pat Mora uses ordinary language (*meat, potatoes, gravy*) and arranges her words in an informal, conversational style, as in "This is America, Mom." In line 3 of "The Road Not Taken," Robert Frost arranges some of his words in unusual order. He writes "long I stood" instead of "I stood there a long time." The words *diverged* and *trodden* in his poem are more formal than the words in Mora's poem.

See pages 514, 547, 555, 684.
See also **Inversion; Style.**

Drama Drama is literature in which plot and characters are developed through dialogue and action; in other words, drama is literature in play form. Stage plays, radio plays, movies, and television programs are all types of drama. Most plays are divided into acts, with each act having

an emotional peak, or climax, of its own. Some modern plays, such as *The Devil and Daniel Webster,* have only one act. Most plays have stage directions, which describe setting, lighting, sound effects, the movement of actors, and the way in which dialogue is spoken. *The Devil and Daniel Webster* begins with long stage directions, which are a guide to directors, set and lighting designers, performers, and readers. A part of the directions follows:

> The scene is the main room of a New Hampshire farmhouse in 1841, a big comfortable room that hasn't yet developed the stuffiness of a front parlor. A door, right, leads to the kitchen—a door, left, to the outside. There is a fireplace, right. Windows, in center, show a glimpse of summer landscape.
>
> —Stephen Vincent Benét, from *The Devil and Daniel Webster*

See pages 409, 436.
See also **Act; Scene; Stage Directions.**

Dramatic Irony *See* **Irony.**

Dramatic Monologue A dramatic monologue is a lyric poem in which a speaker addresses a silent or absent listener in a moment of high intensity or deep emotion, as if engaged in private conversation. The speaker proceeds without interruption or argument, and the effect on the reader is that of hearing just one side of a conversation. This technique allows the poet to focus on the feelings, personality, and motivations of the speaker. The poem known as "The Seven Ages of Man," spoken by Jaques, a character in Shakespeare's play *As You Like It,* is a dramatic monologue.

See page 350.
See also **Lyric Poem.**

Epic An epic is a long narrative poem about the adventures of a hero whose actions reflect the ideals and values of a nation or race. Epics address universal concerns, such as good and evil, life and death, sin and redemption, or other serious subjects. The *Odyssey* is an epic.

See pages 890, 965.

Epic Hero An epic hero is a larger-than-life figure who embodies the ideals of a nation or race. Epic heroes take part in dangerous adventures and accomplish great deeds. Many undertake long, difficult journeys, displaying great courage and superhuman strength. Odysseus is an epic hero.

See pages 890, 914, 965.

Epic Simile An epic simile (also called a Homeric simile) is a long, elaborate comparison that often continues for a number of lines. Here is an example of an epic simile:

> Just as a farmer's hunger grows, behind
> the bolted plow and share, all day afield,
> drawn by his team of winedark oxen: sundown
> is benison for him, sending him homeward
> stiff in the knees from weariness, to dine;
> just so the light on the sea rim gladdened
>   Odysseus.
>
>   **—Homer, from the *Odyssey***

See pages 891, 926.
See also **Simile.**

Epilogue An epilogue is a short addition at the end of a literary work, often dealing with the future of characters. The concluding speech by Prince Escalus in *Romeo and Juliet* serves as an epilogue.

Epithet An epithet is a brief descriptive phrase that points out traits associated with a particular person or thing. An epithet is often an aid to characterization. In the *Odyssey*, Odysseus is often called the ". . . master strategist."

See pages 891, 926.

Essay An essay is a brief composition on a single subject that usually presents the personal views of the author. Essays are often found in newspapers and magazines. Generally, an **expository essay** seeks to explain something and therefore fosters readers' understanding, as does David Raymond's essay "On Being Seventeen, Bright—and Unable to Read." A **narrative essay** tells a story, as in Tony Hillerman's "The Great Taos Bank Robbery." A **persuasive essay** attempts to convince readers

to adopt a certain point of view or to take a particular action. A **critical essay,** such as Sandra Cisneros's "On Writing *The House on Mango Street,"* evaluates a situation, a course of action, or a work of art. In a **personal essay,** such as "Life Without Go-Go Boots" by Barbara Kingsolver, writers express their viewpoints on subjects by reflecting on events or incidents in their own lives in an informal, highly personalized style.

See pages 233, 241, 717.

Exposition In fiction, the structure of the plot normally begins with exposition. In the early part of the story, the exposition sets the tone, establishes the setting, introduces the characters, and gives the reader important background information. In Richard Connell's "The Most Dangerous Game," the exposition leads up to the time when Rainsford falls overboard.

See pages 23, 754.
See also **Plot.**

Expository Essay *See* **Essay.**

Extended Metaphor An extended metaphor is a figure of speech that compares two essentially unlike things at some length and in several ways. It does not contain the word *like* or *as.* For example, in the poem "Metaphor" by Eve Merriam, an extended metaphor compares each day in one's life to a new sheet of paper.

See pages 471, 660.
See also **Metaphor.**

External Conflict *See* **Conflict.**

Fable A fable is a brief tale told to illustrate a moral or teach a lesson. Often the moral of a fable appears in a distinct and memorable statement near the tale's beginning or end. "The Princess and the Tin Box" by James Thurber is a humorous fable.

See also **Moral.**

Falling Action In a plot structure, the falling action, sometimes called the **resolution,** occurs after the climax of a story. The conflict is usually resolved at this time, and any loose ends of the story are tied up. In "American History" by Judith Ortiz Cofer, the falling action begins when the narrator turns away from the door of Eugene's house.

See pages 23, 35, 302, 754.
See also **Climax; Plot.**

Fantasy Fantasy is a type of fiction that is highly imaginative and portrays events, settings, or characters that are unrealistic. The setting might be a nonexistent world, the plot might involve magic or the supernatural, or characters might employ extrahuman powers. *The Devil and Daniel Webster* by Stephen Vincent Benét is an example of a fantasy since it involves supernatural events.

See also **Magical Realism.**

Fiction Fiction refers to works of prose that have imaginary elements, such as the novel and the short story. Although fiction is sometimes based on actual events and real people, it primarily comes from the imagination of the writer. The basic elements of fiction are plot, character, setting, and theme.

See also **Character; Novel; Plot; Setting; Short Story; Theme.**
See pages 23, 285.

Figurative Language Figurative language is language that communicates ideas beyond the ordinary, literal meanings of words. Special types of figurative language called **figures of speech** include personification, hyperbole, simile, and metaphor.

See pages 139, 149.

See also **Hyperbole; Metaphor; Onomatopoeia; Personification; Simile; Style.**

Figures of Speech *See* **Figurative Language.**

First-Person Point of View A story told from the first-person point of view has a narrator who is a character in the story and uses the pronouns *I, me,* and *my.* The short story "Powder" by Tobias Wolff and the eyewitness account "Into Thin Air" by John Krakauer are told from the first-person point of view. In these examples of a first-person account, the reader knows what the narrator is feeling and thinking but must infer from the narrator's descriptions what other characters are feeling or thinking.

See pages 813, 861.
See also **Point of View.**

Flashback A flashback is a conversation, an episode, or an event that happened before the beginning of a story. Often a flashback interrupts the chronological flow of a story to give the reader information to help in understanding a character's present situation. In "Marine Corps Issue" by David McLean, the narrator interrupts the flow of the story to look back at his first memory of his father.

See page 636.

Foil A foil is a character who provides a striking contrast to another character. By using a foil, a writer can call attention to certain traits possessed by a main character or simply enhance a character by contrast. In Shakespeare's *Romeo and Juliet,* Mercutio serves as a foil to Romeo.

See page 987.

Foreshadowing Foreshadowing is a writer's use of hints or clues to indicate events and situations that will occur later in a plot. The use of this technique creates suspense while preparing the reader for what is to come. In the Stephen King play "Sorry, Right Number," the opening camera close-up and the first line of dialogue seem to indicate that the telephone and Bill's health will be important to the drama.

See pages 840, 1043.

Form Form refers to the way a poem is laid out on the page—the length and placement of the lines and the grouping of lines into stanzas. In Ishmael Reed's "Beware: Do Not Read This Poem," for example, some stanzas consist of one sentence, and other stanzas are made up of several short sentences.

See pages 138, 847.
See also **Stanza.**

Free Verse Free verse is poetry that does not contain a regular pattern of rhyme and meter. The lines in free verse often flow more naturally than do rhymed, metrical lines. "Song of the Open Road" by Walt Whitman is an example of free verse.

See page 291.
See also **Meter; Rhyme.**

Historical Fiction Historical fiction is contemporary fiction that is set in the past. It may contain references to actual people and events of the past. "Plainswoman" by Williams Forrest and "The Sniper" by Liam O'Flaherty are examples of historical fiction.

Horror Fiction Horror fiction contains strange, mysterious, violent, and often supernatural events that create suspense and terror in the reader. Edgar Allan Poe and Stephen King are famous authors of horror fiction.

Humor In literature there are three basic kinds of humor, all of which may involve exaggeration or irony. **Humor of situation** arises out of the plot of a work. It usually involves exaggerated events or situational irony, which occurs when something happens that is different from what was expected. **Humor of character** is often based on exaggerated personalities or on characters who fail to recognize their own flaws, a form of dramatic irony. **Humor of language** may include sarcasm, exaggeration, puns, or verbal irony, which occurs when what is said is not what is meant. In "The Great Taos Bank Robbery," Tony Hillerman uses these three kinds of humor.

See page 796.
See also **Irony.**

Hyperbole Hyperbole is a figure of speech in which the truth is exaggerated for emphasis or for humorous effect.

Example: In "Life Without Go-Go Boots," Barbara Kingsolver uses hyperbole when she visits a small, exclusive clothing shop and comments, "You could liquidate the stock here and feed an African nation for a year."

Iambic Pentameter Iambic pentameter is a metrical line of five feet, or units, each of which is made up of two syllables, the first unstressed and the second stressed. Iambic pentameter is the most common form of meter used in English poetry; it is the meter used in blank verse and the sonnet. The following lines, from *Romeo and Juliet*, are examples of iambic pentameter:

> Lĕt twó mŏre súmmĕrs wíthĕr ín thĕir príde
> Ĕre wé măy thínk hĕr rípe tŏ bé ă bríde.

See pages 987, 1019.
See also **Blank Verse; Sonnet.**

Idiom An idiom is an expression that has meaning different from the meaning of its individual words. For example, "go to the dogs" is an idiom meaning "go to ruin."

Imagery Imagery consists of descriptive words and phrases that re-create sensory experiences for the reader. Imagery usually appeals to one or more of the five senses—sight, hearing, smell, taste, and touch—to help the reader imagine exactly what is being described. The imagery in the poem "Incident in a Rose Garden" by Donald Justice helps the reader to see Death, wearing a black coat, black gloves, and a black hat. In the story "To Build a Fire" by Jack London, the description of a fire snapping, crackling, and dancing appeals to the senses of sight and hearing.

See pages 139, 515, 535, 616.

Informative Article An informative article gives facts about a specific subject. This type of writing is found primarily in newspapers, magazines, pamphlets, textbooks, anthologies, encyclopedias, and reference books. "'Who Killed My Daughter?': Lois Duncan Searches for an Answer" is an example of an informative article.

See page 234.

Internal Conflict *See* **Conflict.**

Interview An interview is a conversation, such as that conducted by a writer or reporter, in which facts or statements are elicited from another, recorded, and then broadcast or published. "Unfinished Business" is based on an interview with Elisabeth Kübler-Ross, who in turn describes some of her interviews with terminally ill children. "An Interview with Maya Angelou" is a record of George Plimpton's conversation with the famous author.

See pages 234, 269.

Irony Irony is a special kind of contrast between appearance and reality—usually one in which reality is the opposite from what it seems. One type of irony is **situational irony,** the contrast between what a reader or character expects and what actually exists or happens. The unexpected twist at the end of "The Censors" by Luisa Valenzuela is an example of situational irony. Another type of irony is **dramatic irony,** where the reader or viewer knows something that a character does not know. For example, in Susan Glaspell's play *Trifles,* the audience knows that Mrs. Peters and Mrs. Hale have discovered evidence leading to a motive for the crime, and therefore the guilty person, while the men in the play are still clueless. **Verbal irony** occurs when someone knowingly exaggerates or says one thing and means another. In "The Great Taos Bank Robbery," when Tony Hillerman refers to a "litany of notable events" in Taos, the reader knows that he does not really mean that the events are notable, since at least one, a Great Flood, was managed without a river.

See pages 159, 167, 189, 739, 784, 796, 1071.

Lyric Poem A lyric poem is a short poem in which a single speaker expresses personal thoughts and feelings. Most poems other than dramatic monologues or narrative poems are lyrics. Lyrics can be in a variety of forms and cover many subjects, from love and death to everyday experiences. "Theme for English B" by Langston Hughes and "The Writer" by Richard Wilbur are examples of lyric poems.

Magical Realism Magical realism is a literary genre, or type of literature, that combines fantastic or magical events with realistic happenings in a matter-of-fact way to delight or surprise the reader. "In the Family" by María Elena Llano and "A Very Old Man with Enormous Wings" by Gabriel García Márquez are examples of magical realism.

See pages 861, 871.

Memoir A memoir is a form of autobiographical writing in which a person recalls significant events in his or her life. Although basically personal, memoirs may deal with newsworthy events having a significance beyond the confines of the writers' lives. Memoirs often include the writers' feelings and opinions about historical events, giving the reader insight into the impact of history on people's lives. *Angela's Ashes* by Frank McCourt is a memoir.

See page 255.
See also **Autobiography.**

Metaphor A metaphor is a figure of speech that makes a comparison between two things that are basically unlike but that have something in common. Unlike similes, metaphors do not use the word *like* or *as.* In these lines from the poem known as "The Seven Ages of Man," the world and the people in it are compared to a stage and actors.

> All the world's a stage,
> And all the men and women merely players:
> —William Shakespeare, from *As You Like It*

A **dead metaphor** is one that has been overused, such as "Life is a bowl of cherries," and thus does not delight or surprise. A **mixed metaphor** results in a combination of images that seems absurd, such as "Her dreams have wings and are the foundation for her beliefs."

See pages 139, 149, 471.
See also **Extended Metaphor; Figurative Language; Simile.**

Meter Meter is the regular pattern of accented and unaccented syllables in a line of poetry. The accented, or stressed, syllables are marked with ´, while unaccented, or unstressed, syllables are marked with ˘. Although all poems have rhythm, not all of them have regular meter. Each unit of meter is known as a foot, which consists of one accented syllable and one or two unaccented syllables. The feet and the meter are marked on these lines from Emily Dickinson's poem "Surgeons must be very careful."

> Súrgeŏns | múst bĕ | véry | cáreful
> Whĕn thĕy | tákĕ thĕ | knífe!
> Úndĕr | néath thĕir | fíne ĭn | císiŏns
> Stírs thĕ | Cúlprĭt– | Lífe!

See page 139.
See also **Rhythm.**

Mood In a literary work, the feeling or atmosphere that the writer creates for the reader is called mood. Descriptive words, the setting, and figurative language contribute to the mood of a work, as do the sound and rhythm of the language used. In "The Cask of Amontillado," Edgar Allan Poe creates a mood of dread and horror.

See pages 216, 535, 555.
See also **Tone.**

Moral The moral of a piece of literature is the lesson taught in a work such as a fable. For example, the moral "Do not count your chickens before they are hatched" directs that one should not number one's fortunes or blessings until they appear. In James Thurber's "The Princess and the Tin Box," the moral, like the fable itself, is satirical.

See also **Fable; Satire.**

Myth A myth is a traditional story, usually concerning some superhuman being or unlikely event, that was once widely believed to be true. Frequently, myths attempt to explain natural phenomena, such as solar and lunar eclipses and the cycle of the seasons. For some peoples, myths were both a kind of science and a religion. In addition, myths served as literature and entertainment, just as they do for modern-day audiences.

Greek mythology forms much of the background for Homer's *Odyssey.* For example, the myth of the judgment of Paris describes events that led to the Trojan War. Athena, Hera, and Aphrodite asked a mortal—Paris—to decide which of them was the most beautiful. Paris chose Aphrodite and was rewarded by her with Helen, wife of the Greek king Menelaus.

Narrative Essay *See* **Essay.**

Narrative Nonfiction Narrative nonfiction tells a true story that includes a real setting, all the elements of plot, actual people, and a point of view. It may also have a theme. It is often, but not always, told in chronological order. *The Perfect Storm* by Sebastian Junger and *Into Thin Air* by Jon Krakauer are examples of narrative nonfiction.

See page 122.
See also **Nonfiction.**

Narrative Poem A narrative poem tells a story. Like a short story or a novel, a narrative poem has the following elements: characters, setting, plot, and point of view, all of which combine to develop a theme. "The Wreck of the Hesperus" by Henry Wadsworth Longfellow is a narrative poem, as is the *Odyssey.*

See page 128.

Narrator The narrator is the character or voice from whose point of view events are told. In "The Scarlet Ibis" by James Hurst, the narrator is a character in the story, Doodle's brother. In "The Great Taos Bank Robbery," the narrator is the author, Tony Hillerman.

See also **Persona; Point of View; Speaker.**

Nonfiction Nonfiction is prose writing that deals with real people, events, and places. The major types of nonfiction are autobiography, biography, and the essay. Other examples of nonfiction include newspapers, informative articles, true-life adventures, personal diaries, and letters. *The Perfect Storm,* a true account by Sebastian Junger, is nonfiction.

See page 233.
See also **Autobiography; Biography; Essay; Memoir.**

Novel A novel is a long work that takes the average reader several days, or even weeks, to finish. Typically, a novel tells a complex story that unfolds through the actions, speech, and thoughts of the characters.

Onomatopoeia Onomatopoeia is the use of words such as *pow, buzz,* and *crunch* whose sounds suggest their meanings.

Example: In Homer's *Odyssey,* the speaker says "Eyelid and lash were seared; the pierced ball / *hissed* broiling, . . ."

See page 139.
See also **Sound Devices.**

Paradox A paradox is a statement that seems to contradict itself but is, nevertheless, true, as in the beginning of this poem:

> Much Madness is divinest Sense
> To a discerning Eye;
> Much Sense the starkest Madness.
>
> —Emily Dickinson,
> from "Much Madness is divinest Sense"

Parallelism Parallelism is the use of similar grammatical constructions to express ideas that are related or equal in importance. The parallel elements may be words, phrases, sentences, or paragraphs. Parallelism occurs in the last line of the following speech. (*Sans* means "without.")

> . . . Last scene of all,
> That ends this strange eventful history,
> Is second childishness and mere oblivion,
> Sans teeth, sans eyes, sans taste, sans
> everything.
>
> —William Shakespeare,
> from "The Seven Ages of Man"

See page 515.

Persona A persona is the voice or mask that a writer assumes in a particular work. For example, W. D. Wetherell is the author of "The Bass, the River, and Sheila Mant," but the persona is someone remembering his 14th summer. The persona in "The Beginning of Something" is a character named Roseanne, the voice that author Sue Ellen Bridgers assumes. Both authors assume other voices in their other writings.

See also **Speaker.**

Personal Essay See **Essay.**

Personal Narrative A personal narrative is a short form of autobiographical writing in which the writer focuses on a significant experience in his or her life. William Nolen's "The First Appendectomy" is a personal narrative.

See also **Autobiography; Memoir.**

Personification Personification is a figure of speech in which human qualities are attributed to an object, animal, or idea. In "Incident in a Rose Garden" by Donald Justice, death is personified as someone who wears black and grins. In this line, morning is personified:

> The grey-eyed morn smiles on the frowning
> night, . . .
> —William Shakespeare, from *Romeo and Juliet*

See pages 139, 149.
See also **Figurative Language; Metaphor; Simile.**

Persuasive Essay See **Essay.**

Plot The sequence of events in a story is called the plot. Generally built around a conflict, the plot tells what happens, when, and to whom. A story's plot usually includes four stages: exposition, rising action, climax, and falling action.

Example: In "Full Circle" by Sue Grafton, the exposition establishes the freeway setting and the identity of the narrator. The rising action includes details of an accident and the narrator's search for a murderer. The climax comes when the narrator discovers the murderer, and the falling action tells what happens after the murderer is identified.

See pages 23, 35, 302, 409, 754.
See also **Climax; Conflict; Exposition; Falling Action; Rising Action.**

Poetry Poetry is a type of literature in which words are chosen and arranged to create a certain effect. Poets use a variety of sound devices, imagery, and figurative language to express emotions and ideas.

See pages 138–139.
See also **Alliteration; Assonance; Ballad; Free Verse; Imagery; Meter; Rhyme; Rhythm; Stanza.**

Point of View Point of view refers to the method of narrating a short story, novel, narrative poem, or work of nonfiction. Point of view is usually either first person or third person. In **first-person** point of view, the narrator is a character in the story, as in "The Cask of Amontillado" by Edgar Allan Poe. In **third-person** point of view, the story is told by a narrative voice outside the action, not by one of the characters. If a story is told from a **third-person omniscient,** or all-knowing, point of view, as in "The Gift of the Magi" by O. Henry, the narrator sees into the minds of more than one character. If events are related from a **third-person limited** point of view, as in Doris Lessing's "Through the Tunnel," the narrator tells only what one character thinks, feels, and observes.

See pages 216, 813, 821, 861.
See also **Author's Perspective; Narrator; Style.**

Prop The word *prop,* an abbreviation of *property,* refers to any physical object that is used in a stage production. In Stephen Vincent Benét's *The Devil and Daniel Webster,* the props include a cider barrel and a fiddle.

See also **Stage Directions.**

Protagonist The protagonist is the central character or hero in a narrative or drama, usually the one with whom the audience tends to identify.

Examples: In "Brothers Are the Same" by Beryl Markham," Temas is the protagonist. In Judith Ortiz Cofer's "American History" Elena is the protagonist as well as the narrator.

See pages 321, 371.
See also **Antagonist.**

Pun A pun is a joke that comes from a play on words. Puns can make use of a word's multiple meanings or of a word's rhyme. In *Romeo and Juliet* when Mercutio is fatally wounded, he says, "Ask for me tomorrow, and you shall find me a grave man," with a pun on the word *grave,* meaning both "solemn" and "a tomb."

Realistic Fiction Realistic fiction is a type of fiction that creates a truthful imitation of ordinary life. "Through the Tunnel" by Doris Lessing and "A Christmas Memory" by Truman Capote are examples of realistic fiction.

Refrain A refrain is the repetition of one or more lines in each stanza of a poem. Edgar Allan Poe's "The Bells" contains repeated lines in each of four stanzas.

See also **Stanza.**

Repetition Repetition is a technique in which a sound, word, phrase, or line is repeated for effect or emphasis. The word *they* is repeated for emphasis in the poem "Lineage."

See pages 291, 515, 611.
See also **Sound Devices.**

Resolution *See* **Falling Action.**

Rhyme Rhyme is the occurrence of a similar or identical sound at the ends of two or more words, such as *suite, heat,* and *complete.* **Internal rhyme** occurs within a line; **end rhyme** occurs at the ends of lines. **Slant rhyme** (also known as **approximate** or **near rhyme**), occurs when the sounds are not quite identical, as in the words *care* and *dear* in W. H. Auden's "O What Is That Sound." Edgar Allan Poe's "Annabel Lee" has end rhyme. "The Bells" has both end rhyme and internal rhyme.

> How it swells!
> How it dwells
> On the Future! how it tells
> Of the rapture that impels
> To the swinging and the ringing
> Of the bells, bells, bells!—
>
> —Edgar Allan Poe, from "The Bells"

See pages 138, 204, 611.

Rhyme Scheme The pattern of end rhyme in a poem is called a rhyme scheme. The pattern is charted by assigning a letter of the alphabet, beginning with the letter *a,* to each line. Lines that rhyme are given the same letter. Notice the rhyme scheme for the first stanza of Robert Frost's "The Road Not Taken."

Two roads diverged in a yellow wood,	*a*
And sorry I could not travel both	*b*
And be one traveler, long I stood	*a*
And looked down one as far as I could	*a*
To where it bent in the undergrowth;	*b*

See pages 138, 144, 291.

Rhythm Rhythm refers to the pattern or flow of sound created by the arrangement of stressed and unstressed syllables in a line of poetry. The accented, or stressed, syllables are marked with ´, while unaccented, or unstressed, syllables are marked with ˘. A regular pattern of rhythm is called meter.

> Ŏ whát ĭs thắt sóund whĭch sŏ thrĭ́lls thĕ eár
> Dŏw´n ĭn thĕ vállĕy drŭ́mmĭng, drŭ́mmĭng?
>
> —W. H. Auden, from "O What Is That Sound"

See pages 139, 144.
See also **Meter.**

Rising Action Rising action refers to the events in a story that move the plot along by adding complications or expanding the conflict. Rising action usually builds suspense to a climax, or turning point. In "American History" by Judith Ortiz Cofer, the rising action begins when Elena first speaks to Eugene.

See pages 23, 35, 302, 754.
See also **Plot.**

Satire Satire is a literary technique in which ideas or customs are ridiculed for the purpose of improving society. Satire may be gently witty, mildly abrasive, or bitterly critical. "The Censors" by Luisa Valenzuela bitterly satirizes the policies of a repressive government. "The Princess and the Tin Box" is a satire on a type of moralistic literature.

Scene In drama, the action is often divided into acts and scenes. Each new scene in a play indicates a different time and place. For example, Stephen Vincent Benét's *The Devil and Daniel Webster* is a one-act play, with two scene changes. In long plays, each act may have several scenes.

See also **Act.**

Science Fiction Science fiction is prose writing in which a writer explores unexpected possibilities of the past or the future, using known scientific data and theories as well as his or her creative imagination. Most science fiction writers create a believable world, although some create a fantasy world that has familiar elements. Ray Bradbury and Ursula Le Guin are just two of many writers of science fiction.

See also **Fantasy.**

Sentence Structure *See* **Diction; Style.**

Setting Setting is the time and place of action of a story. Some stories, such as "The Utterly Perfect Murder," have only a minimal description of setting. In other literary works, such as Doris Lessing's "Through the Tunnel," Eugenia Collier's "Marigolds," and Edgar Allan Poe's "The Cask of Amontillado," setting is described in detail and becomes a major contributor to the story's total effect.

See pages 24, 85, 322, 340, 385.
See also **Fiction.**

Short Story A short story is much shorter than a novel and can usually be read in one sitting. Generally, a short story has one main conflict that involves the characters, keeps the story moving, and makes it interesting.

See also **Fiction.**

Simile A simile is a figure of speech that makes a comparison between two things using the word *like* or *as.* In "Incident in a Rose Garden" by Donald Justice, the line "Dressed like a Spanish waiter" contains a simile.

See pages 139, 149.
See also **Epic Simile; Figurative Language; Metaphor.**

Soliloquy In drama a soliloquy is a speech in which a character speaks thoughts aloud. Generally, the character is on the stage alone, not speaking to other characters and perhaps not even consciously addressing the audience. At the beginning of Act Two, Scene 3, of *Romeo and Juliet,* Friar Laurence has a long soliloquy. There are several other soliloquies in *Romeo and Juliet.*

See pages 350, 987, 1043.
See also **Dramatic Monologue.**

Sonnet A sonnet is a lyric poem of 14 lines, commonly written in iambic pentameter. The sonnet may be classified as Petrarchan or Shakespearean. The Shakespearean (or Elizabethan) sonnet consists of three quatrains, or four-line units, and a final couplet. The typical rhyme scheme is *abab cdcd efef gg.*

See also **Iambic Pentameter; Rhyme Scheme.**

Sound Devices Sound devices, or the use of words for their auditory effect, can convey meaning and mood or unify a work. Some common sound devices are alliteration, assonance, consonance, onomatopoeia, repetition, and rhyme. The following lines contain much alliteration and consonance, which help to convey both meaning and mood.

> But whenever I see you, I burst apart
> And scatter the sky with my blazing heart.
> It spits and sparkles in stars and balls,
> Buds into roses—and flares, and falls.
>
> —Amy Lowell, from "Fireworks"

See pages 138, 144, 204.
See also **Alliteration; Assonance; Onomatopoeia; Repetition; Rhyme.**

Speaker In poetry the speaker in the poem is the voice that talks to the reader, similar to the narrator in fiction. The speaker is not necessarily the poet. In "A Voice" by Pat Mora, the experiences related may or may not have happened to the poet. In "Young" by Anne Sexton, since the poet uses the pronoun *I,* the poem may well be autobiographical.

See pages 139, 346.
See also **Persona.**

Speech A speech is a talk or public address. The purpose of a speech may be to entertain, explain, persuade, or inspire, or it may be any combination of these aims. "I Have a Dream" by Martin Luther King, Jr., and "Glory and Hope" by Nelson Mandela are speeches to inspire.

See page 448.

Stage Directions A play normally includes a set of instructions called stage directions, which are often printed in italic type at the beginning of a play and at the beginning of acts and scenes. They are a guide to directors, set and lighting designers, performers, and readers. When used to explain how actors should move and speak, they are separated from the dialogue by parentheses.

> Mrs. Peters *(Starts to speak, glances up, where footsteps are heard in the room above. In a low voice).* Mr. Peters says it looks bad for her. Mr. Henderson is awful sarcastic in a speech and he'll make fun of her sayin' she didn't wake up.
>
> —Susan Glaspell, from *Trifles*

See pages 409, 436.

Stanza A stanza is a grouping of two or more lines in a pattern that is repeated throughout a poem. A stanza is comparable to a paragraph in prose. Each stanza may have the same number of lines, or the number of lines may vary. "The Road Not Taken" by Robert Frost is divided into four stanzas.

See also **Form; Poetry.**

Stereotype In literature, simplified or stock characters who conform to a fixed pattern or are defined by a single trait are called stereotypes. Such characters do not usually demonstrate the complexities of real people.

Examples: Familiar stereotypes in popular literature include the absent-minded professor, the hard-boiled private eye, and the mustache-twirling villain. The figure of the rejected lover in many ballads is another example of a stereotype.

Structure Structure is the way in which the parts of a work of literature are put together. In poetry, structure refers to the arrangement of words and lines to produce a desired effect. A common structural unit in poetry is the stanza, of which there are numerous types. In prose, structure is the arrangement of larger units or parts of a selection. Paragraphs, for example, are a basic unit in prose, as are chapters in novels and acts in plays. The structure of a poem, short story, novel, play, or nonfiction selection usually emphasizes certain important aspects of content.

See also **Act; Stanza.**

Style Style is the particular way in which a piece of literature is written. Style is not *what* is said but *how* it is said. It is the writer's uniquely individual way of communicating ideas. Many elements contribute to style, including word choice, sentence length, tone, figurative language, and point of view. A literary style may be described in a variety of ways, such as *formal, conversational, journalistic, wordy, ornate, poetic,* or *dynamic.*

Examples: Short sentences, sentence fragments, short paragraphs and the first-person point of view mark the style of "My Wonder Horse" by Sabine R. Ulibarrí. The style of "A Very Old Man with Enormous Wings" by Gabriel García Márquez is marked by long sentences and paragraphs, third-person point of view, and detailed imagery.

See pages 217, 505, 514, 569, 871.
See also **Diction.**

Surprise Ending A surprise ending is an unexpected twist in the plot at the end of a story. The surprise may be a sudden turn in the action or a revelation that gives a different perspective to the entire story.

Examples: The final paragraph of "The Sniper" by Liam O'Flaherty is a tragic surprise. The ending of "The Wasp's Nest" by Agatha Christie upsets the reader's expectations about the nature of a crime.

See pages 167, 768.

Suspense Suspense is the excitement or tension that readers feel as they become involved in a story and eager to know the outcome of the plot.

Example: In "The Sniper," Liam O'Flaherty uses suspense-building techniques as he describes the struggle between the sniper and his enemy across the street.

See pages 167, 636, 739, 754.

Symbol A symbol is a person, a place, an activity, or an object that stands for something beyond itself.

Examples: In "Through the Tunnel" by Doris Lessing, the rocky bay represents challenge, danger, and adulthood; the beach represents both safety for Jerry and his childhood.

See pages 385, 605, 784.

Tall Tale A tall tale is a humorously exaggerated story about impossible events, often relating the supernatural abilities of the main character. The tales about folk heroes such as Paul Bunyan and Davy Crockett are typical tall tales.

Theme Theme is the main idea in a work of literature. It is a perception about life or human nature that the writer shares with the reader. In most cases, the theme is not stated directly but must be inferred. A statement of theme may, but does not usually, tell one how to live and should not be confused with a **moral.**

Examples: The theme of the story "The Scarlet Ibis" by James Hurst might be expressed as "Pride, love, and cruelty are often intermingled in human relationships." The theme of the poem "Theme for English B" by Langston Hughes might be expressed as "Despite the fact that the instructor is white and the theme writer is black, they are a part of each other." The theme of "New Directions" by Maya Angelou is stated directly in the final paragraph.

See pages 24, 100, 471, 498, 589, 605, 699, 939, 1103.
See also **Moral.**

Third-Person Point of View In the third-person point of view, the narrator is someone outside of the action, not a character writing the story. The characters are referred to by name or by the pronouns *he, she,* and *they.* "Through the Tunnel" by Doris Lessing is told from the third-person point of view.

See pages 814, 821.
See also **Point of View.**

Tone Tone is the attitude a writer takes toward a subject. Unlike mood, which is intended to shape the reader's emotional response, tone reflects the feelings of the writer. To identify tone, you might find it helpful to read the work aloud. Try to decide what emotions you feel as you read. For example, *The Devil and Daniel Webster* has a light, humorous tone. The tone of "Grape Sherbet" by Rita Dove is tender and loving.

See pages 514, 547, 616, 708.
See also **Mood.**

Tragedy A tragedy is a dramatic work that presents the downfall of a dignified character or characters who are involved in historically or socially significant events. The events in a tragic plot are set in motion by a decision that is often an error in judgment. Succeeding events are linked in a cause-and-effect relationship and lead inevitably to a disastrous conclusion, usually death. Shakespeare's *Romeo and Juliet* is a tragedy.

See pages 986, 1103.

True-Life Adventure A true-life adventure is a type of nonfiction found in popular magazines and books. *The Perfect Storm* by Sebastian Junger is a true-life adventure.

See page 234.

Turning Point *See* **Climax.**

Understatement Understatement is a technique of creating emphasis by saying less than is actually or literally true. It is the opposite of hyperbole, or exaggeration. One of the primary devices of irony, understatement can be used to develop a humorous effect, to create satire, or to achieve a restrained tone.

Example: Tony Hillerman makes use of understatement in "The Great Taos Bank Robbery" when he writes, "The reader might well pause here and recollect that it is traditional among robbers to steal escape vehicles, not to borrow them from friends."

See also **Humor; Hyperbole; Irony; Tone.**

Verbal Irony *See* **Irony.**

Voice The term *voice* refers to a writer's unique use of language that allows a reader to "hear" a human personality in his or her writing. The elements of style that determine a writer's voice include sentence structure, diction, and tone. For example, some writers are noted for their reliance on short, simple sentences, while others make use of long, complicated ones. Certain writers use concrete words, such as *lake* or *cold,* which name things that you can see, hear, feel, taste, or smell. Others prefer abstract terms like *memory,* which name things that cannot be perceived with the senses. A writer's tone also leaves its imprint on his or her personal voice.

Examples: In "On Writing *The House on Mango Street,*" Sandra Cisneros uses a personal, informal, and conversational voice.

See page 717.

Word Choice *See* **Diction.**

The Writing Process

Different writers use different processes. Try out different strategies and figure out what works best for you. For some assignments, it is best to start by figuring out what you need to end up with, make a plan or outline, and stick to it. Other writing assignments may be more successful if you start by writing everything you know about the topic, allow things to get messy, and then reshape and revise the writing so it fits the assignment. Try both approaches and get to know yourself as a writer.

Also consider whether the assignment is high-stakes or low-stakes writing. When the success of the piece is very important, such as in a test, you might choose to focus on meeting the requirements or criteria of the assignment. When the purpose of the writing is to develop your ideas, there is more opportunity to experiment and take risks. Take into account the time factor as well. In a timed writing test, you may not have time to explore and revise.

Correct grammar and spelling are very important in your final product. You don't need to focus on these as you shape your ideas and draft your piece, but be sure you allow time for a careful edit before turning in your final piece.

1.1 Prewriting

In the prewriting stage, you explore your ideas and discover what you want to write about.

Finding Ideas for Writing
Try one or more of the following techniques to help you find a writing topic.

Personal Techniques

- Practice imaging, or trying to remember mainly sensory details about a subject—its look, sound, feel, taste, and smell.

- Complete a knowledge inventory to discover what you already know about a subject.

- Browse through magazines, newspapers, and on-line bulletin boards for ideas.

- Start a clip file of articles that you want to save for future reference. Be sure to label each clip with source information.

Sharing Techniques

- With a group, brainstorm a topic by trying to come up with as many ideas as you can without stopping to critique or examine them.

- Interview someone who knows a great deal about your topic.

Writing Techniques

- After freewriting on a topic, try looping, or choosing your best idea for more freewriting. Repeat the loop at least once.

- Make a list to help you organize ideas, examine them, or identify areas for further research.

Graphic Techniques

- Create a pro-and-con chart to compare the positive and negative aspects of an idea or a course of action.

- Use a cluster map or tree diagram to explore subordinate ideas that relate to your general topic or central idea.

Determining Your Purpose
Your purpose for writing may be to express yourself, to entertain, to describe, to explain, to analyze, or to persuade. To clarify it, ask questions like these:

- Why did I choose to write about my topic?

- What aspects of the topic mean the most to me?

- What do I want others to think or feel after they read my writing?

LINK TO LITERATURE One purpose for writing is to clarify a subject. For example, Sandra Cisneros wrote "On Writing *The House on Mango Street*," page 711, to clarify how she came to write the book.

Identifying Your Audience

Knowing who will read your writing can help you focus your topic and choose relevant details. As you think about your readers, ask yourself questions like these:

- What does my audience already know about my topic?

- What will they be most interested in?

- What language is most appropriate for this audience?

1.2 Drafting

In the drafting stage, you put your ideas on paper and allow them to develop and change as you write.

Two broad approaches in this stage are discovery drafting and planned drafting.

Discovery drafting is a good approach when you are not quite sure what you think about your subject. You just plunge into your draft and let your feelings and ideas lead you where they will. After finishing a discovery draft, you may decide to start another draft, do more prewriting, or revise your first draft.

Planned drafting may work better for research reports, critical reviews, and other kinds of formal writing. Try making a writing plan or a scratch outline before you begin drafting. Then, as you write, you can fill in the details.

LINK TO LITERATURE Some writers plan and outline. Others write in a great flurry, without much previous planning, as ideas occur to them; of course, the ideas have been generating within them before they begin to write. Agatha Christie, who wrote "Wasps' Nest," on page 759, had to prepare with many notes about murder methods, effects of poison, and other details about death before she could write a crime story.

1.3 Revising, Editing, and Proofreading

The changes you make in your writing during this stage usually fall into three categories: revising for content, revising for structure, and proofreading to correct mistakes in mechanics.

Use the questions that follow to assess problems and determine what changes would improve your work.

Revising for Content

- Does my writing have a main idea or central focus? Is my thesis clear?

- Have I incorporated adequate detail? Where might I include a telling detail, revealing statistic, or vivid example?

- Is any material unnecessary, irrelevant, or confusing?

WRITING TIP Be sure to consider the needs of your audience as you answer the questions under Revising for Content and Revising for Structure. For example, before you can determine whether any of your material is unnecessary or irrelevant, you need to identify what your audience already knows.

Revising for Structure

- Is my writing unified? Do all ideas and supporting details pertain to my main idea or advance my thesis?

- Is my writing clear and coherent? Is the flow of sentences and paragraphs smooth and logical?

- Do I need to add transitional words, phrases, or sentences to make the relationships among ideas clearer?

- Are my sentences well constructed? What sentences might I combine to improve the grace and rhythm of my writing?

Proofreading to Correct Mistakes in Grammar, Usage, and Mechanics

When you are satisfied with your revision, proofread your paper, looking for mistakes in grammar, usage, and mechanics. You may want

Writing Handbook

to do this several times, looking for different types of mistakes each time. The following checklist may help.

Sentence Structure and Agreement

- Are there any run-on sentences or sentence fragments?
- Do all verbs agree with their subjects?
- Do all pronouns agree with their antecedents?
- Are verb tenses correct and consistent?

Forms of Words

- Do adverbs and adjectives modify the appropriate words?
- Are all forms of *be* and other irregular verbs used correctly?
- Are pronouns used correctly?
- Are comparative and superlative forms of adjectives correct?

Capitalization, Punctuation, and Spelling

- Is any punctuation mark missing or not needed?
- Are all words spelled correctly?
- Are all proper nouns and all proper adjectives capitalized?

WRITING TIP For help identifying and correcting problems that are listed in the Proofreading Checklist, see the Grammar Handbook, pages 1179–1213.

You might wish to mark changes on your paper by using the proofreading symbols shown in the chart below.

Proofreading Symbols

∧	Add letters or words.	/	Make a capital letter lowercase.
⊙	Add a period.	¶	Begin a new paragraph.
≡	Capitalize a letter.	⸜	Delete letters or words.
⊃	Close up space.	∾	Switch the positions of letters or words.
∧	Add a comma.		

 1.4 Publishing and Reflecting

Always consider sharing your finished writing with a wider audience. Reflecting on your writing is another good way to bring closure to a project.

Creative Publishing Ideas

Following are some ideas for publishing and sharing your writing.

- Post your writing on an electronic bulletin board or send it to others via e-mail.
- Create a multimedia presentation and share it with classmates.
- Publish your writing in a school newspaper or literary magazine.
- Present your work orally in a report, a speech, a reading, or a dramatic performance.
- Submit your writing to a local newspaper or a magazine that publishes student writing.
- Form a writing exchange group with other students.

WRITING TIP You might work with other students to publish an anthology of class writing. Then exchange your anthology with another class or another school. Reading the work of other student writers will help you get ideas for new writing projects and find ways to improve your work.

Reflecting on Your Writing

Think about your writing process and whether you would like to add what you have written to your portfolio. You might attach a note in which you answer questions like these:

- What did I learn about myself and my subject through this writing project?
- Which parts of the writing process did I most and least enjoy?
- As I wrote, what was my biggest problem? How did I solve it?
- What did I learn that I can use the next time I write?

1.5 Using Peer Response

Peer response consists of the suggestions and comments your peers or classmates make about your writing.

You can ask a peer reader for help at any point in the writing process. For example, your peers can help you develop a topic, narrow your focus, discover confusing passages, or organize your writing.

Questions for Your Peer Readers

You can help your peer readers provide you with the most useful kinds of feedback by following these guidelines:

- Tell readers where you are in the writing process. Are you still trying out ideas, or have you completed a draft?

- Ask questions that will help you get specific information about your writing. Open-ended questions that require more than yes-or-no answers are more likely to give you information you can use as you revise.

- Give your readers plenty of time to respond thoughtfully to your writing.

- Encourage your readers to be honest when they respond to your work. It's OK if you don't agree with them—you always get to decide which changes to make.

Tips for Being a Peer Reader

Follow these guidelines when you respond to someone else's work:

- Respect the writer's feelings.

- Make sure you understand what kind of feedback the writer is looking for, and then respond accordingly.

- Use "I" statements, such as "I like . . . ," "I think . . . ," or "It would help me if . . . ." Remember that your impressions and opinions may not be the same as someone else's.

WRITING TIP Writers are better able to absorb criticism of their work if they first receive positive feedback. When you act as a peer reader, try to start your review by telling something you like about the piece.

The chart below explains different peer-response techniques to use when you are ready to share your work.

Peer-Response Techniques

Sharing Use this when you are just exploring ideas or when you want to celebrate the completion of a piece of writing.

- *Will you please read or listen to my writing without criticizing or making suggestions afterward?*

Summarizing Use this when you want to know if your main idea or goals are clear.

- *What do you think I'm saying? What's my main idea or message?*

Replying Use this strategy when you want to make your writing richer by adding new ideas.

- *What are your ideas about my topic? What do you think about what I have said in my piece?*

Responding to Specific Features Use this when you want a quick overview of the strengths and weaknesses of your writing.

- *Are the ideas supported with enough examples? Did I persuade you? Is the organization clear enough for you to follow the ideas?*

Telling Use this to find out which parts of your writing are affecting readers the way you want and which parts are confusing.

- *What did you think or feel as you read my words? Would you show me which passage you were reading when you had that response?*

---

2 Building Blocks of Good Writing

Whatever your purpose in writing, you need to capture your readers' interest, organize your ideas well, and present your thoughts clearly. Giving special attention to some particular parts of a story or an essay can make your writing more enjoyable and more effective.

2.1 Introductions

When you flip through a magazine trying to decide which articles to read, the opening paragraph is often critical. If it does not grab your attention, you are likely to turn the page.

Kinds of Introductions

Here are some introduction techniques that can capture a reader's interest.

- Make a surprising statement
- Provide a description
- Pose a question
- Relate an anecdote
- Address the reader directly
- Begin with a thesis statement

Make a Surprising Statement Beginning with a startling statement or an interesting fact can capture your reader's curiosity about the subject, as in the model below.

> MODEL
>
> W.H. Auden is one of the major poets of the twentieth century. Until he was 16 years old, however, Auden's greatest interests were machinery and mining. He had intended to become a mining engineer.

Provide a Description A vivid description sets a mood and brings a scene to life for your reader. Here, details about heating the air for a hot air balloon set the tone for a narrative about a balloon ride.

> MODEL
>
> Whoosh! The red and yellow flame shot up into the great nylon cone. The warm air filled the balloon so that the cooler air below held the apparatus aloft. A soft breeze helped to push the balloon and basket along. The four passengers hardly noticed the noise or the heat as they stared in awe at the hilly farmland and meandering streams below.

Pose a Question Beginning with a question can make your reader want to read on to find out the answer. The following introduction asks a question about the breadth of a popular author's imagination.

> MODEL
>
> Between 1915 and 1973, Agatha Christie wrote 184 works of crime fiction. How was it possible for her to create so many clever plots that depend on intricate puzzles, clues, and solutions?

Relate an Anecdote Beginning with a brief anecdote, or story, can hook readers and help you make a point in a dramatic way. The anecdote below introduces a first-hand account of a rescue from a burning apartment building.

> MODEL
>
> A red light began blinking. A siren started up slowly but built to a screeching pitch. Twenty-five sleepy faces appeared a few at a time in the hallway. As I recall, each of us looked to left and right almost in unison as if watching an imaginary tennis match that would give some clue to the source of this midnight disturbance.

Address the Reader Directly Speaking directly to readers establishes a friendly, informal tone and involves them in your topic.

> MODEL
>
> **Find out how to maintain your cardiovascular system while enjoying yourself. Come to a free demonstration of Fit for Life at the Community Center Friday night at 7:00 P.M.**

Begin with a Thesis Statement A thesis statement expressing a paper's main idea may be woven into both the beginning and the end of nonfiction writing. The following is a thesis statement that introduces a literary analysis.

> MODEL
>
> **In "The Great Taos Bank Robbery," Tony Hillerman presents eccentric characters with loving detail. It is clear that he has affection for the hapless criminals as well as for the fascinated, easygoing townspeople.**

WRITING TIP In order to write the best introduction for your paper, you may want to try more than one of the methods and then decide which is the most effective for your purpose and audience.

2.2 Paragraphs

A paragraph is made up of sentences that work together to develop an idea or accomplish a purpose. Whether or not it contains a topic sentence stating the main idea, a good paragraph must have unity and coherence.

Unity

A paragraph has unity when all the sentences support and develop one stated or implied idea. Use the following techniques to create unity in your paragraphs.

Write a Topic Sentence A topic sentence states the main ideas of the paragraph; all other sentences in the paragraph provide supporting details. A topic sentence is often the first sentence in a paragraph. However, it may also appear later in the paragraph or at the end, to summarize or reinforce the main idea, as shown in the model that follows.

> MODEL
>
> **Tomás lifted the skimmer baskets and emptied the small collection of bugs and leaves. Then he filled the small vials with water and carefully measured four different solutions to test the pH, chlorine, total alkalinity, and acid demand. Next he got out all the equipment for vacuuming. Tomás had not realized that taking care of a swimming pool would require so many tasks.**

Relate All Sentences to an Implied Main Idea A paragraph can be unified without a topic sentence as long as every sentence supports the implied, or unstated, main idea. In the example below, all the sentences work together to create a unified impression of baking an apple pie.

> MODEL
>
> **The chef carefully poured in the mixture of freshly sliced apples, sugar, flour, salt, cinnamon, and nutmeg. Then she floured her hands again before adding strips of pastry in crisscrosses across the top. She dotted some butter all along the top and sprinkled a little more sugar and cinnamon. Finally she placed the masterpiece in the oven.**

Coherence

A paragraph is coherent when all its sentences are related to one another and flow logically from one to the next. The following techniques will help you achieve coherence in paragraphs.

- Present your ideas in the most logical order.
- Use pronouns, synonyms, and repeated words to connect ideas.
- Use transitional devices to show the relationships among ideas.

In the model below, the writer used some of these techniques to create a unified paragraph.

> MODEL
>
> **Just the name "alligator snapping turtle" brings to mind a ferocious, frightening creature. But this fascinating creature is protected by law. The alligator snapping turtle can grow to more than 200 pounds. In fact, whereas common snapping turtles rarely weigh 30 pounds, alligator snappers have been recorded with weights up to 300 pounds.**

2.3 Transitions

Transitions are words and phrases that show the connections between details. Clear transitions help show how your ideas relate to each other.

Kinds of Transitions

Transitions can help readers understand several kinds of relationships:
- Time or sequence
- Spatial relationships
- Degree of importance
- Compare and contrast
- Cause and effect

Time or Sequence Some transitions help to clarify the sequence of events over time. When you are telling a story or describing a process, you can connect ideas with such transitional words as *first, second, always, then, next, later, soon, before, finally, after, earlier, afterward,* and *tomorrow.*

> MODEL
> The orchestra members were seated. At first, the sounds conflicted with one another as the players tuned and tested their instruments. Then the concertmaster stood and played one note on her violin. Next all the instruments tuned to that tone so that one great sound on the same pitch filled the auditorium.

Spatial Relationships Transitional words and phrases such as *in front, behind, next to, along, nearest, lowest, above, below, underneath, on the left,* and *in the middle* can help readers visualize a scene.

> MODEL
> Gardeners have kept the tall grass maze in perfect order. They have mowed the paths that weave in and out within the 15-foot diameter of the maze. At the left, a clearly marked entrance invites walkers to try the maze. At the center, a small clump of clover signals to the careful observer that the path winds toward the exit on the right.

Degree of Importance Transitional words such as *mainly, strongest, weakest, first, second, most important, least important, worst,* and *best* may be used to rank ideas or to show degree of importance.

> MODEL
> Nathan has several qualifications that make him a good candidate for class representative; his greatest strength is his tolerance of more than one point of view.

Compare and Contrast Words and phrases such as *similarly, likewise, also, like, as, neither . . . nor,* and *either . . . or* show similarity between details. *However, by contrast, yet, but, unlike, instead, whereas,* and *while* show difference. Note the use of both types of transitions in the model below.

> MODEL
> Like dogs, cats are wonderful pets. Dogs give unconditional affection and have a great desire to please. You will find out, however, that there is no substitute for the comfort of a cat's purr.

WRITING TIP Both *but* and *however* may be used to join two independent clauses. When *but* is used as a coordinating conjunction, it is preceded by a comma. When *however* is used as a conjunctive adverb, it is preceded by a semicolon and followed by a comma.

Cause and Effect When you are writing about a cause-and-effect relationship, use transitional words and phrases such as *since, because, thus, therefore, so, due to, for this reason,* and *as a result* to help clarify that relationship and to make your writing coherent.

> MODEL
> Because a tree fell across the electric wires Monday night, we lost our electricity for four hours.

2.4 Conclusions

A conclusion should leave readers with a strong final impression. Try any of these approaches.

Kinds of Conclusions

Here are some effective methods for bringing your writing to a conclusion:

- Restate your thesis
- Ask a question
- Make a recommendation
- Make a prediction
- Summarize your information

Restate Your Thesis A good way to conclude an essay is by restating your thesis, or main idea, in different words. The conclusion below restates the thesis introduced on page 1147.

> MODEL
> **The kind humor with which Hillerman portrays the would-be bank robbers as well as the curious townspeople in "The Great Taos Bank Robbery" shows his affection for all his characters.**

Ask a Question Try asking a question that sums up what you have said and gives readers something new to think about. The question below concludes a request to consider a visit to a place of educational entertainment.

> MODEL
> **If you enjoy science experiments and you like puzzles, shouldn't you plan soon to visit the Magic House?**

Make a Recommendation When you are persuading your audience to take a position on an issue, you can conclude by recommending a specific course of action.

> MODEL
> **You can make your research work much easier by taking advantage of the Internet. Develop a list of key words that will help you narrow your search of the Internet.**

Make a Prediction Readers are concerned about matters that may affect them and therefore are moved by a conclusion that predicts the future.

> MODEL
> **If this state continues to permit landowners to drain wetlands, we will see a tremendous decline in the number and variety of wildlife.**

Summarize Your Information Summarizing reinforces the writer's main ideas, leaving a strong, lasting impression. The model below concludes with a statement that summarizes a literary analysis of the works of Agatha Christie.

> MODEL
> **Although there are a few examples of unrealistic situations in Agatha Christie's novels, for the most part each story is well-crafted, providing an excellent plot and entertaining reading.**

2.5 Elaboration

Elaboration is the process of developing a writing idea by providing specific supporting details that are relevant and appropriate to the purpose and form of your writing.

- **Facts and Statistics** A fact is a statement that can be verified, while a statistic is a fact stated in numbers. Make sure the facts and statistics you supply are from a reliable, up-to-date source. As in the model below, the facts and statistics you use should strongly support the statements you make.

> MODEL
> **Female cicadas cut little slits in the bark of twigs on trees and lay their eggs inside the slits. The eggs hatch after 6 to 10 weeks. When the eggs hatch, the twigs drop from the trees. Although this might seem threatening to the host trees, in fact there is little danger.**

- **Sensory Details** Details that show how something looks, sounds, tastes, smells, or feels can enliven a description, making readers feel they are actually experiencing what you are describing. Which senses does the writer appeal to in this paragraph?

MODEL

About 4:00 in the afternoon, the racket would begin in earnest. The cicadas must have dozed all day, but they seemed to awake in the heat of the afternoon to begin their persistent mating screeches. In lush suburban areas with large trees, the din was almost deafening. Even talking on the telephone was a challenge if the windows were open. The next morning there would be only little carcasses of spent insects that had apparently died happy after 17 years under-ground and a few days of discordant squawking.

- **Incidents** From our earliest years, we are interested in hearing "stories." One way to illustrate a point powerfully is to relate an incident or tell a story, as shown in the example below.

MODEL

Some of our most valuable sources of historical knowledge come from events that were disastrous for the people who were involved. The eruption of the volcano Vesuvius in A.D. 79 was a nightmare for the people of Pompeii. Many fled the city, but about 2,000 died, and their homes were buried under tons of volcanic ash. But the long-buried city has provided the modern world detailed knowledge of everyday life in ancient Pompeii.

- **Examples** An example can help make an abstract or a complex idea concrete or can provide evidence to clarify a point for readers.

MODEL

Many fiction writers use real locations for their settings. For example, Tony Hillerman uses cities and towns in New Mexico and Arizona for his mystery novels. Other writers make up locations that they continue to use. For example, Agatha Christie created St. Mary Mead as the setting for her novels in which Miss Jane Marple was the main character.

- **Quotations** Choose quotations that clearly support your points and be sure that you copy each quotation word for word. Remember always to credit the source.

MODEL

The sky is blue because air is not completely transparent. In *The Cosmological Milkshake*, Robert Ehrlich explains that "a fraction of sunlight is scattered by the molecules of the atmosphere, with blue light scattered the most." Even without smog and other forms of pollution, the sky would still look blue.

2.6 Using Language Effectively

Effective use of language can help readers to recognize the significance of an issue, to visualize a scene, or to understand a character. The specific words and phrases that you use have everything to do with how effectively you communicate meaning. This is true of all kinds of writing, from novels to office memos. Keep these particular points in mind.

- **Specific Nouns** Nouns are specific when they refer to individual or particular things. If you refer to a *city*, you are being general. If you refer to *London*, you are being specific. Specific nouns help readers identify the *who, what,* and *where* of your message.

- **Specific Verbs** Verbs are the most powerful words in sentences. They convey the action, the movement, and sometimes the drama of thoughts and observations. Verbs such as *trudged, skipped,* and *sauntered* provide a more vivid picture of the action than the verb *walked.*

- **Specific Modifiers** Use modifiers sparingly, but when you use them, make them count. Is the building *big* or *towering*? Are your poodle's paws *small* or *petite*? Once again, it is the more specific word that carries the greater impact.

3 Descriptive Writing

Descriptive writing allows you to paint word pictures about anything and everything in the world, from events of global importance to the most personal feelings. It is an essential part of almost every piece of writing, including essays, poems, letters, field notes, newspaper reports, and videos.

RUBRIC   Standards for Writing

A successful description should

- have a clear focus and sense of purpose.
- use sensory details and precise words to create a vivid image, establish a mood, or express emotion.
- present details in a logical order.

3.1 Key Techniques

Consider Your Goals What do you want to accomplish in writing your description? Do you want to show why something is important to you? Do you want to make a person or scene more memorable? Do you want to explain an event?

Identify Your Audience Who will read your description? How familiar are they with your subject? What background information will they need? Which details will they find most interesting?

Think Figuratively What figures of speech might help make your description vivid and interesting? What simile or metaphor comes to mind? What imaginative comparisons can you make? What living thing does an inanimate object remind you of?

MODEL

He typed away on the old dinosaur, his fingers chomping at the keys as the long metal claws imprinted the black ribbon onto the paper rolled into the top. This was just fine, thank you—none of those new-fangled computers for this writer.

Gather Sensory Details Which sights, smells, tastes, sounds, and textures make your subject come alive? Which details stick in your mind when you observe or recall your subject? Which senses does it most strongly affect?

MODEL

She had to admit that though her own skin was clammy, the skin she touched was soft, dry, and almost velvety. She began to consider that her damp and shaking hands might frighten the totally calm reptile the zoo keeper held. She wasn't sure she wanted those coils around her shoulders, but she was rapidly changing her mind about this warm cold-blooded creature.

You might want to use a chart like the one shown here to collect sensory details about your subject.

Sights	Sounds	Textures	Smells	Tastes

Create a Mood What feelings do you want to evoke in your readers? Do you want to soothe them with comforting images? Do you want to build tension with ominous details? Do you want to evoke sadness or joy?

MODEL

The Condors were one run ahead. Just one more strike by the Cranes' batter would end the game. The crowd stood. Orange and white streamers waved desperately on one side of the stadium while blue and gold ones mimicked on the other side. One more strike—just one. The pitcher wound up. The batter poised. Here came the ball.

3.2 Options for Organization

Spatial Order Choose one of these options to show the spatial order of a scene.

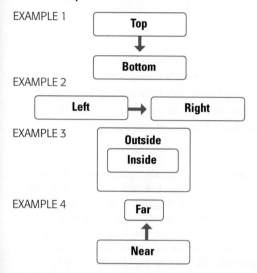

EXAMPLE 1

Top → Bottom

EXAMPLE 2

Left → Right

EXAMPLE 3

Outside / Inside

EXAMPLE 4

Near → Far

MODEL

The tour group squeezed through the door and into the long, narrow entryway. The leader began describing what they would see when it was their turn to enter the great center room. Some in the group tried to steal a glimpse of the enormous spectacle just ahead of them. At the end of the hall, a light illuminated a magnificent marble sculpture.

WRITING TIP Use transitions that help the reader picture the relationship among the objects you describe. Some useful transitions for showing spatial relationships are *behind, below, here, in the distance, on the left, over,* and *on top.*

Order of Impression Order of impression is how you notice details.

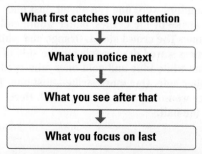

What first catches your attention

↓

What you notice next

↓

What you see after that

↓

What you focus on last

MODEL

When I first looked at the painting, I saw a brightly illuminated, sophisticated face looking toward me and well-manicured hands turning pages of a book. The longer I looked at the painting, the more I saw. I noticed that a letter seems just to have been opened, read, and set down. Before long my eyes fastened on bits of paper or maybe flower petals that might have come with the letter. At this point, I studied the expression on the young man's face. He seems very serious, maybe sad or worried. Suddenly, I really wanted to know more about this subject. I stared at the painting a long time.

WRITING TIP Use transitions that help readers understand the order of the impressions you are describing. Some useful transitions are *after, next, during, first, before, finally,* and *then.*

Order of Importance You might want to use order of importance as the organizing structure for your description.

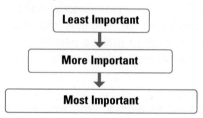

Least Important

↓

More Important

↓

Most Important

MODEL

Crowds of tourists mill amid the bookstalls and souvenir stands of the Left Bank, seeking a piece of Paris to take home. On the riverside promenade, couples stroll hand in hand, taking no notice of the bustle of the city. A sightseeing boat chugs along the Seine River as its passengers try to take in all the sights at once. Beyond on the island rises the magnificent Cathedral of Notre Dame, with its massive towers and delicate stonework that have graced the city since the Middle Ages.

WRITING TIP Use transitions that help the reader understand the order of importance that you attach to the elements of your description. Some useful transitions are *first, second, mainly, more important, less important,* and *least important.*

4 Narrative Writing

Narrative writing tells a story. If you write a story from your imagination, it is a fictional narrative. A true story about actual events is a nonfictional narrative. Narrative writing can be found in short stories, novels, news articles, and biographies.

Standards for Writing

A successful narrative should

- include descriptive details and dialogue to develop the characters, setting, and plot.
- have a clear beginning, middle, and end.
- have a logical organization with clues and transitions to help the reader understand the order of events.
- maintain a consistent tone and point of view.
- use language that is appropriate for the audience.
- demonstrate the significance of events or ideas.

4.1 Key Techniques

Identify the Main Events What are the most important events in your narrative? Is each event part of the chain of events needed to tell the story? In a fictional narrative, this series of events is the story's plot.

MODEL

Event 1	An electrical storm approaches while two ranchers search for Kid Turner, a missing ranch hand.
Event 2	They find his horse and follow its hoof prints up a dry riverbed.
Event 3	The storm breaks as they find Kid lying helpless with his leg broken.
Event 4	They carry him to safety just before a flash flood rolls down the riverbed where he was lying.

Describe the Setting When do the events occur? Where do they take place? How can you use setting to create mood and to set the stage for the characters and their actions?

MODEL

The gray sky was turning increasingly dark across the plains. A few streaks of lightning could be seen in the far distance. Two riders on horseback called Kid's name and listened intently for a reply. The sounds they heard were the brisk wind and distant thunder.

Depict Characters Vividly What do your characters look like? What do they think and say? How do they act? What vivid details can show readers what the characters are like?

MODEL

Jake had the hard, lined face of a veteran cowhand. His dark, piercing eyes scanned the countryside from beneath the shadow of his hat brim. He studied the clouds rolling in from the western horizon, gauging how severe the coming storm would be.

WRITING TIP Dialogue is an effective way of developing characters in a narrative. As you write dialogue, choose words that express your characters' personalities and show how the characters feel about one another and about the events in the plot.

MODEL

"Better find 'im soon," was Jake's simple declaration.

Edna Mae could barely make out the words that were muffled by the wind.

"We'll find him, Jake," was her reply, given with somewhat more confidence than she felt.

"I'll know the hoof prints of the Kid's horse if we ever pick up the trail," Jake answered.

4.2 Options for Organization

Option 1: Chronological Order One way to organize a piece of narrative writing is to arrange the events in chronological order, as shown below.

MODEL

Introduction *characters and setting*	Kid Turner hasn't come back to the ranch in three days. Fearing that he is hurt, Jake and Edna Mae set out to search for him.
Event 1	As a thunderstorm approaches, they find his horse and backtrack up a dry wash.
Event 2	They find Turner just as the storm breaks. He has a broken leg, so he can't drag himself out of the dry wash.
End *perhaps show the significance of the events*	They carry him out of the riverbed and find shelter under a rock ledge. As they watch, a flash flood surges through the riverbed where Kid had been lying.

Option 2: Flashback It is also possible in narrative writing to arrange the order of events by starting with an event that happened before the beginning of the story.

Flashback
Begin with a key event that happened before the time in which the story takes place.

↓

Introduce characters and setting.

↓

Describe the events leading up to the conflict.

Option 3: Focus on Conflict When the telling of a fictional narrative focuses on a central conflict, the story's plot may follow the model shown below.

MODEL

Describe the main characters and setting	The brothers arrive at the school gym long before the rest of the basketball team. Although the twins are physically identical, their personalities couldn't be more different. Mark is outgoing and impulsive, while Matt is thoughtful and shy.
Present the conflict	Matt realizes his brother is missing shots on purpose and believes they will lose the championship.
Relate the events that make the conflict complex and cause the characters to change	• Matt has a chance at a basketball scholarship if they win the championship. • Mark needs money to buy a car. • Matt and Mark have stood by each other no matter what.
Present the resolution or outcome of the conflict	Matt retells a family story in which their grandfather chose honor and integrity over easy money. Mark plays to win.

5 Explanatory Writing

Explanatory writing informs and explains. For example, you can use it to evaluate the effects of a new law, to compare two movies, to analyze a piece of literature, or to examine the problem of greenhouse gases in the atmosphere.

5.1 Types of Explanatory Writing

There are many types of explanatory writing. Think about your topic and select the type that presents the information most clearly.

Compare and Contrast How are two or more subjects alike? How are they different?

> MODEL
> Guy de Maupassant's story "The Necklace" and O. Henry's story "The Gift of the Magi" are similar in that they both involve objects that the characters can't afford and both use the device of irony. They are different, however, in that the former story has a sad ending whereas the latter has an upbeat ending.

Cause and Effect How does one event cause something else to happen? Why do certain conditions exist? What are the results of an action or a condition?

> MODEL
> Because Madame Loisel in "The Necklace" did not let the owner of the necklace know immediately that it was lost, she spent ten years paying for its replacement only to find it had been worth very little.

Analysis How does something work? How can it be defined? What are its parts?

> MODEL
> To repair a broken window you must remove the old glass, clean the window frame, fit the new glass in place, secure it with glazier's points, and seal its edges with glazing compound.

Problem-Solution How can you identify and state a problem? How would you analyze the problem and its causes? How can it be solved?

> MODEL
> In "The Possibility of Evil," the townspeople apparently thought of the best way to take revenge on Miss Strangeworth. They ruined her beloved rose garden.

5.2 Compare and Contrast

Compare-and-contrast writing examines the similarities and differences between two or more subjects. You might, for example, compare and contrast two short stories, the main characters in a novel, or two movies.

RUBRIC Standards for Writing

Successful compare-and-contrast writing should

- clearly identify the subjects that are being compared and contrasted.
- include specific, relevant details.
- follow a clear plan of organization dealing with the same features of both subjects under discussion.
- use language and details appropriate to the audience.
- use transitional words and phrases to clarify similarities and differences.

Options for Organization

Compare-and-contrast writing can be organized in different ways. The examples that follow demonstrate feature-by-feature organization and subject-by-subject organization.

Option 1: Feature-by-Feature Organization

MODEL

Feature 1 **I. Both women want something that they cannot afford.**

> **Subject A. Mathilde of "The Necklace":** new dress and fancy jewelry to go to a ball

> **Subject B. Della of "The Gift of the Magi":** special Christmas present for her husband

Feature 2 **II. Both make sacrifices that turn out to be ironic.**

> **Subject A. Mathilde:** works for years to replace a necklace that turns out to be a cheap imitation

> **Subject B. Della:** sells her hair to buy a watch chain, but her husband has sold the watch

Option 2: Subject-by-Subject Organization

MODEL

Subject A **I. Mathilde of "The Necklace"**

> **Feature 1. Wish:** new dress and fancy jewelry to go to a ball

> **Feature 2. Ironic sacrifice:** works for years to replace a necklace that turns out to be a cheap imitation

Subject B **II. Della of "The Gift of the Magi"**

> **Feature 1. Wish:** special Christmas present for her husband

> **Feature 2. Ironic sacrifice:** sells her hair to buy a watch chain, but her husband has sold the watch

WRITING TIP Remember your purpose for comparing and contrasting your subjects, and support your purpose with expressive language and specific details.

Cause and Effect

Cause-and-effect writing explains why something happened, why certain conditions exist, or what resulted from an action or a condition. You might use cause-and-effect writing to explain a character's actions, the progress of a disease, or the outcome of a war.

RUBRIC   Standards for Writing

Successful cause-and-effect writing should

- clearly state the cause-and-effect relationship.
- show clear connections between causes and effects.
- present causes and effects in a logical order and use transitions effectively.
- use facts, examples, and other details to illustrate each cause and effect.
- use language and details appropriate to the audience.

Options for Organization

Your organization will depend on your topic and purpose for writing.

- If you want to explain the causes of an event such as the closing of a factory, you might first state the effect and then examine its causes.

Option 1: Effect to Cause Organization

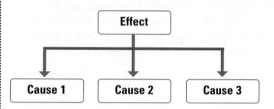

- If your focus is on explaining the effects of an event, such as the passage of a law, you might first state the cause and then explain the effects.

Option 2: Cause to Effect Organization

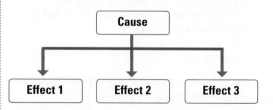

- Sometimes you'll want to describe a chain of cause-and-effect relationships to explore a topic such as the disappearance of tropical rain forests or the development of home computers.

Option 3: Cause-and-Effect Chain Organization

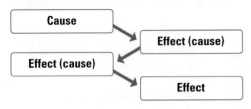

WRITING TIP Don't assume that a cause-and-effect relationship exists just because one event follows another. Look for evidence that the later event could not have happened if the first event had not caused it.

Problem-Solution

Problem-solution writing clearly states a problem, analyzes the problem, and proposes a solution to the problem. It can be used to identify and solve a conflict between characters, analyze a chemistry experiment, or explain why the home team keeps losing.

RUBRIC **Standards for Writing**

Successful problem-solution writing should

- identify the problem and help the reader understand the issues involved.
- analyze the causes and effects of the problem.
- integrate quotations, facts, and statistics into the text.
- explore possible solutions to the problem and recommend the best one(s).
- use language, tone, and details appropriate to the audience.

Options for Organization
Your organization will depend on the goal of your problem-solution piece, your intended audience, and the specific problem you choose to address. The organizational methods that follow are effective for different kinds of problem-solution writing.

Option 1: Simple Problem-Solution

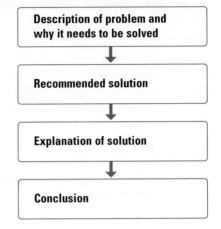

Option 2: Deciding Between Solutions

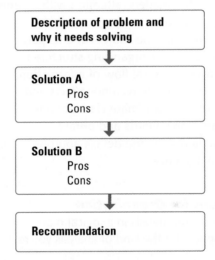

WRITING TIP Have a classmate read and respond to your problem-solution writing. Ask your peer reader: Is the problem clearly stated? Is the organization easy to follow? Do the proposed solutions seem logical?

Analysis

In writing an analysis, you explain how something works, how it is defined, or what its parts are. The details you include will depend upon the kind of analysis you write.

Process Analysis What are the major steps or stages in a process? What background information does the reader need to know—such as definitions of terms or a list of needed equipment—to understand the analysis? You might use process analysis to explain how to program a VCR or prepare for a test, or to explain how to replace a window pane.

Definition Analysis What are the most important characteristics of a subject? You might use definition analysis to explain a quality such as proficiency, the characteristics of a sonnet, or the features of a lever.

Parts Analysis What are the parts, groups, or types that make up a subject? Parts analysis could be used to explain the makeup of an organization or the anatomy of the intestinal tract.

RUBRIC   Standards for Writing

A successful analysis should

- hook the readers' attention with a strong introduction.
- clearly state the subject and its parts.
- use a specific organizing structure to provide a logical flow of information.
- show connections among facts and ideas through subordinate clauses and transitional words and phrases.
- use language and details appropriate for the audience.

Options for Organization

Organize your details in a logical order appropriate for the kind of analysis you're writing.

Option 1: Process Analysis A process analysis is usually organized chronologically, with steps or stages in the order they occur.

MODEL

Introduction	Repairing a window is easy.
Background	When I broke a window, my dad taught me how to fix it.
Explain Steps	Step 1: Remove broken glass and clean frame.
	Step 2: Put glazing compound in the frame, set new glass.
	Step 3: Push in glazier's points to secure glass.
	Step 4: Apply glazing compound to space where glass meets frame.

Option 2: Definition Analysis You can organize the details in a definition or parts analysis in order of importance or impression.

MODEL

Introduce Term	A lever allows a person to move heavy loads with less effort.
General Definition	A lever is a simple machine that consists of a rigid bar pivoted on a fixed point.
Explain Features	Feature 1: Force
	Feature 2: Fulcrum (pivot point)
	Feature 3: Load

Option 3: Parts Analysis The following parts analysis explains the parts of the intestinal tract.

MODEL

Introduce Subject	The intestinal tract breaks food into particles the body can use.
Explain Parts	Part 1: Mouth, esophagus, stomach
	Part 2: Small intestine
	Part 3: Large intestine, rectum, appendix

WRITING TIP Try to capture your readers' interest in your introduction. You might begin with a vivid description or an interesting fact, detail, or quotation. For example, an exciting excerpt from the narrative could open the process analysis.

An effective way to conclude an analysis is to return to your thesis and restate it in different words.

6 Persuasive Writing

Persuasive writing allows you to use the power of language to inform and influence others. It can take many forms, including speeches, newspaper editorials, billboards, advertisements, and critical reviews.

RUBRIC **Standards for Writing**

Successful persuasion should
- state the issue and the writer's position.
- give opinions and support them with facts or reasons.
- have a reasonable and respectful tone.
- answer opposing views.
- use sound logic and effective language.
- conclude by summing up reasons or calling for action.

6.1 Key Techniques

Clarify Your Position What do you believe about the issue? How can you express your opinion most clearly?

MODEL
The city needs to air-condition the Community Center.

Know Your Audience Who will read your writing? What do they already know and believe about the issue? What objections to your position might they have? What additional information might they need? What tone and approach would be most effective?

MODEL
Open windows and fans are no longer sufficient to keep our citizens comfortable at the many functions held during the summer in the Community Center.

Support Your Opinion Why do you feel the way you do about the issue? What facts, statistics, examples, quotations, anecdotes, or opinions of authorities support your view? What reasons will convince your readers? What evidence can answer their objections?

MODEL
According to the National Weather Service, this summer has been the hottest on record. Perhaps because of that fact and perhaps because air conditioning is way overdue anyway, attendance at the Little Theater and the Summer Arts and Crafts Show was down 10 percent from last year.

Ways to Support Your Argument	
Statistics	Facts that are stated in numbers
Examples	Specific instances that explain your point
Observations	Events or situations you yourself have seen
Anecdotes	Brief stories that illustrate your point
Quotations	Direct statements from authorities

Begin and End with a Bang How can you hook your readers and make a lasting impression? What memorable quotation, anecdote, or statistic will catch their attention at the beginning or stick in their minds at the end? What strong summary or call to action can you conclude with?

BEGINNING
If you want to spend an enjoyable evening with your neighbors seeing a live performance or shopping for homemade crafts or food, will you come down to the Community Center? Probably not. It's too hot!

CONCLUSION
Many people put hours and weeks and even months into providing our town with entertainment. Many more people have participated in events that others planned. But those numbers have decreased because the Community Center is not comfortable on hot summer evenings. Let's purchase an air-conditioning system for the center so people can enjoy the special events of this great town.

6.2 Options for Organization

In a two-sided persuasive essay, you want to show the weaknesses of other opinions as you explain the strengths of your own.

The example below demonstrates one method of organizing your persuasive essay to convince your audience.

Option 1: Reasons for Your Opinion

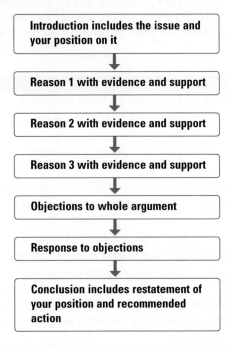

Introduction includes the issue and your position on it

↓

Reason 1 with evidence and support

↓

Reason 2 with evidence and support

↓

Reason 3 with evidence and support

↓

Objections to whole argument

↓

Response to objections

↓

Conclusion includes restatement of your position and recommended action

Option 2: Point-by-Point Basis

In the organization that follows, each reason and its objections are examined on a point-by-point basis.

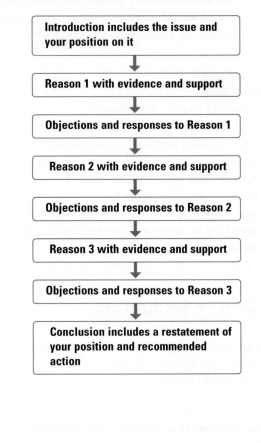

Introduction includes the issue and your position on it

↓

Reason 1 with evidence and support

↓

Objections and responses to Reason 1

↓

Reason 2 with evidence and support

↓

Objections and responses to Reason 2

↓

Reason 3 with evidence and support

↓

Objections and responses to Reason 3

↓

Conclusion includes a restatement of your position and recommended action

---

Beware of Illogical Arguments Be careful about using illogical arguments. Opponents can easily attack your argument if you present illogical material.

Circular reasoning—trying to prove a statement by just repeating it in different words

> The Community Center is too hot because it is not cool enough for people to be comfortable.

Overgeneralization—making a statement that is too broad to prove

> Nobody wants to attend events in a hot building.

Either-or fallacy—stating that there are only two alternatives when there are many

> Either we get first-class air conditioning or everybody will stop attending community events.

Cause-and-effect fallacy—falsely assuming that because one event follows another, the first event caused the second

> Because Monday's high was over 90 degrees, only 15 people came to the crafts fair.

⑦ Research Report Writing

A research report explores a topic in depth, incorporating information from a variety of sources.

RUBRIC **Standards for Writing**

An effective research report should

- clearly state the purpose of the report in a thesis statement.
- use evidence and details from a variety of sources to support the thesis.
- contain only accurate and relevant information.
- document sources correctly.
- develop the topic logically and include appropriate transitions.
- include a properly formatted Works Cited list.

---

⑦.① Key Techniques

Develop Relevant, Interesting, and Researchable Questions Asking thoughtful questions is an ongoing part of the research process. You might begin with a list of basic questions that are relevant to your topic. These would focus on getting basic facts that answer the questions *who, what, where, when, how,* and *why* about your topic. If you were researching the history of detective stories, you might develop a set of questions similar to these.

> MODEL
>
> **When did detective stories become popular?**
>
> **What are the different kinds of detective stories?**

As you become more familiar with your topic, think of questions that might provide an interesting perspective that makes readers think.

> MODEL
>
> **What makes modern detective stories so different from early ones?**

Check that your questions are researchable. Ask questions that will uncover facts, statistics, case studies, and other documentable evidence.

Clarify Your Thesis A thesis statement is one or two sentences clearly stating the main idea that you will develop in your report. A thesis may also indicate the organizational pattern you will follow and reflect your tone and point of view.

> MODEL
>
> **The detective story reflects the times, customs, and special interests of the culture in which it is written.**

Document Your Sources You need to document, or credit, the sources where you find your evidence. In the example below, the writer uses and documents a quotation from the introduction to a collection of critical essays.

> MODEL
>
> **In her introduction to *And Then There Were Nine: More Women of Mystery*, Bakerman comments on the relationship of the mystery story to the culture of the times by saying that the works under study show that "serious social commentary can spring fruitfully from entertaining escapist fiction, and that the most absorbing of all human questions—the presence of evil and the human propensity to engage in evil—are ever new, ever fresh, ever present" (5).**

Support Your Ideas You should support your ideas with relevant evidence—facts, anecdotes, and statistics—from reliable sources. In the example below, the writer includes a fact about the popularity of mystery fiction.

> MODEL
>
> **In the last two decades over 20 percent of all books sold have been mystery novels (Klein 1).**

7.2 Gathering Information: Sources

You will use a range of sources to collect the information you need to develop your research paper. These will include both print and electronic resources.

General Reference Works To clarify your thesis and begin your research, consult reference works that give quick, general overviews on a subject. General reference works include encyclopedias, almanacs and yearbooks, atlases, and dictionaries.

Specialized Reference Works Once you have a good idea of your specific topic, you are ready to look for detailed information in specialized reference works. In the library's reference section, specialized dictionaries and encyclopedias can be found for almost any field. For example, in the field of literature, you will find specialized reference sources such as *Contemporary Authors* and *Twentieth-Century Literary Criticism.*

Periodicals Journals and periodicals are a good source for detailed, up-to-date information. Periodical indexes, found in print and on-line catalogs in the library, will help you find articles on a topic. The *Readers' Guide to Periodical Literature* indexes many popular magazines. More specialized indexes include the *Humanities Index* and the *Social Sciences Index.*

Electronic Resources **Commercial information services** offer access to reference works such as dictionaries and encyclopedias, databases, and periodicals.

The **Internet** is a vast network of computer networks. News services, libraries, universities, researchers, organizations, and government agencies use the Internet to communicate and to distribute information. The Internet gives you access to the World Wide Web, which provides information on particular topics and links you to related topics and resources.

A **CD-ROM** is a research aid that stores information on a compact disk. Reference works on CD-ROMs may include text, sound, images, and video.

Databases are large collections of related information stored electronically. You can scan the information or search for specific facts.

RESEARCH TIP To find books on a specific topic, check the library's on-line catalog. Be sure to copy the correct call numbers of books that sound promising. Also look at books shelved nearby. They may relate to your topic.

7.3 Gathering Information: Validity of Sources

When you find source material, you must determine whether it is useful and accurate.

Credibility of Authorship Check whether an author has written several books or articles on the subject and has published in a well-respected newspaper or journal.

Objectivity Decide whether the information is fact, opinion, or propaganda. Reputable sources credit other sources of information.

Currency Check the publication date of the source to see whether the information is current.

Credibility of Publisher Seek information from a respected newspaper or journal, not from a tabloid newspaper or popular-interest magazine.

WEB TIP Be especially skeptical of information you locate on the Internet since virtually anyone can post anything there. Read the URL, or Internet address. Sites sponsored by a government agency (*.gov*) or an educational institution (*.edu*) are generally more reliable.

7.4 Taking Notes

As you find useful information, record the bibliographic information of each source on a separate index card. Then you are ready to take notes on your sources. You will probably use these three methods of note-taking.

Paraphrase, or restate in your own words, the main ideas and supporting details of the passage.

Summarize, or rephrase in fewer words, the original materials, trying to capture the key ideas.

Quote, or copy word for word, the original text, if you think the author's own words best clarify a particular point. Use quotation marks to signal the beginning and the end of the quotation.

For more details on making source cards and taking notes, see the Research Report Workshop on pages 974–980.

7.5 Options for Organization

Begin by reading over your note cards and sorting them into groups. The main-idea headings may help you find connections among the notes. Then arrange the groups of related note cards so that the ideas flow logically from one group to the next.

Option 1: Topic Outline

The Mystery Story As a Sign of the Times
Introduction Began in 1841 and continues today
I. Forms
    A. Classic puzzles
    B. Private eyes and police detectives
    C. Espionage and thrillers
II. Content and Culture
    A. Settings and characters
    B. Specialized information

Like other forms of writing, research reports can be organized in several different ways. Some subjects may fit in chronological order. For other subjects, you may want to compare and contrast two topics. Other possibilities are a cause-and-effect organization or least-important to most-important evidence. If your material does not lend itself to any of the above organizations, try a general-to-specific approach.

Whatever your organizational pattern, making an outline can help guide the drafting process. The subtopics that you located in sorting your note cards will be the major topics of your outline, preceded by Roman numerals. Make sure that items of the same importance are parallel in form. For example, in the Option 1: Topic Outline below, topics I and II are both phrases. So are subtopics A and B.

A second kind of outline, shown below in Option 2, uses complete sentences instead of phrases for topics and subtopics.

Option 2: Sentence Outline

The Mystery Story As a Sign of the Times
Introduction The mystery story began with Edgar Allan Poe in 1841 and continues in many popular forms today.
I. There are several distinct forms of the mystery story.
    A. The classic puzzles are stories that are often humorous, in which all the suspects are kept together and the detective is an amateur.
    B. The private-eye stories usually have professional detectives, and the locations are likely to be rough neighborhoods.
    C. Espionage stories often involve government agents; they rely on fast pace and surprise.
II. Mystery stories reflect the times and the culture in which they are written, often with a secondary purpose of explaining specialized information.
    A. Settings and characters are important and include such diverse examples as Arthur Upfield's Australian aborigines and Tony Hillerman's Navajo police officers.
    B. Specialized information is detailed and factual and covers such areas as effects of poisons (Agatha Christie), Jewish law (Harry Kemelman), and Navajo and Hopi legends and customs (Tony Hillerman).

7.6 Documenting Sources

When you quote, paraphrase, or summarize information from a source, you need to credit that source. Parenthetical documentation is the accepted method for crediting sources. You may choose to name the author in parentheses following the information, along with the page number on which the information is found.

> MODEL
> **The classic detective novel (also called traditional, cozy, village mystery, domestic malice, and Golden Age mystery) "is primarily a puzzle or intellectual game" (Klein 4).**

In parenthetical documentation, you may also use the author's name in the sentence, along with the information. If so, enclose, in parentheses after the sentence, only the page number on which the information is found.

> MODEL
> **Tony Hillerman writes about Navajo and Hopi traditions because he feels a kinship with the people. He says his biggest honor was being voted "most popular author" by students of St. Catherine Indian School. (128, 147).**

In either case, your reader can find out more about the source by turning to your Works Cited page, which lists complete bibliographical information for each source.

PUNCTUATION TIP When only the author and page number appear in parentheses, there is no punctuation between the two items. Also notice that the parenthetical citation comes after the closing quotation marks of a quotation, if there is one, and before the end punctuation of the sentence.

The examples above show citations for books with one author. The list that follows shows the correct way to write parenthetical citations for several kinds of sources.

Guidelines for Parenthetical Documentation

Work by One Author
Put the author's last name and the page reference in parentheses: (**Klein 149**).

If you mention the author's name in the sentence, put only the page reference in parentheses: (**149**).

Work by Two or Three Authors
Put author's last names and the page reference in parentheses: (**Nichols and Thompson 165**).

Work by More Than Three Authors
Give the first author's last name followed by *et al.* and the page reference: (**Gorman et al. 97**).

Work with No Author Given
Give the title or a shortened version and (if appropriate) the page reference: (**"Poe" 1194**).

One of Two or More Works by Same Author
Give the author's last name, the title or a shortened version, and the page reference: (**Klein, Woman Detective 78**).

Selection from a Book of Collected Essays
Give the name of the author of the essay and the page reference: (**Hillerman 128**).

Dictionary Definition
Give the entry title in quotation marks: (**"Detective"**).

Unsigned Article in an Encyclopedia
Give the article title in quotation marks, followed by a shortened source title: (**"Upfield, Arthur W[illiam]," Encyclopedia of Mystery & Detection**).

WRITING TIP Presenting someone else's writing or ideas as your own is plagiarism. To avoid plagiarism, you need to credit sources. However, if a piece of information is common knowledge—information available in several sources—you do not need to credit a source.

7.7 Following MLA Manuscript Guidelines

The final copy of your report should follow the Modern Language Association (MLA) guidelines for manuscript preparation.

- The heading in the upper left-hand corner of the first page should include your name, your teacher's name, the course name, and the date, each on a separate line.
- Below the heading, center the title on the page.
- Number all the pages consecutively in the upper right-hand corner, one-half inch from the top. Also, include your last name before the page number.

- Double-space the entire paper.
- Except for the margins above the page numbers, leave one-inch margins on all sides of every page.

The Works Cited page at the end of your report is an alphabetized list of the sources you have used and documented. In each entry all lines after the first are indented an additional one-half inch.

WRITING TIP When your report includes a quotation that is longer than four lines, set it off from the rest of the text by indenting the entire quotation one inch from the left margin. In this case, you should not use quotation marks.

Works Cited

Models for Works Cited entries

Works Cited

Berkeley, Anthony, et al. The Floating Admiral. London: Hodder, 1931.

❶ Book with more than three authors; note that publishers' names are shortened

Cawelti, John G. Adventure, Mystery, and Romance. Chicago: U of Chicago P, 1976.

❷ Book with one author

Gray, W. Russel. "The 'Eyes' Have It: Reflections on the Private Detective as Hero." Clues: A Journal of Detection. 6:2 (1985): 41–52.

❸ Article in scholarly journal

Hillerman, Tony. Hillerman Country: A Journey Through the Southwest with Tony Hillerman. New York: Harper, 1991.

___. "Mystery, Country Boys, and the Big Reservation." Colloquium on Crime. Ed. Robin W. Winks. New York: Scribner's, 1986. 127–147.

❹ Selection from a book of collected essays; second work by same author

Mitchell, B. R., and Phyllis Deane. Abstract of British Historical Statistics. Cambridge: Cambridge UP, 1962.

❺ Work with two authors

Reilly, John M., ed. Twentieth Century Crime and Mystery Writers. 2nd ed. New York: St. Martin's, 1985.

❻ Book with editor but no single author

7.8 MLA Documentation: Electronic Sources

As with print sources, information from electronic sources such as CD-ROMs or the Internet must be documented on your Works Cited page. You may find a reference to a source on the Internet and then use the print version of the article. If so, document it as you do other printed works. However, if you read or print out an article directly off the Internet, document it as shown below for an electronic source. Although electronic sources are shown separately below, they should be included on the Works Cited page with print sources.

Internet Sources Works Cited entries for Internet sources include the same kind of information as those for print sources. They also include the date you accessed the information and the electronic address of the source. Some of the information about the source may be unavailable. Include as much as you can. For more information on how to write Works Cited entries for Internet sources, see the MLA guidelines posted on the Internet or access this document through the McDougal Littell website.

More Online: Style Guidelines
www.mcdougallittell.com

CD-ROMs Entries for CD-ROMs include the publication medium (CD-ROM), the distributor, and the date of publication. Some of the information shown may not be always available. Include as much as you can.

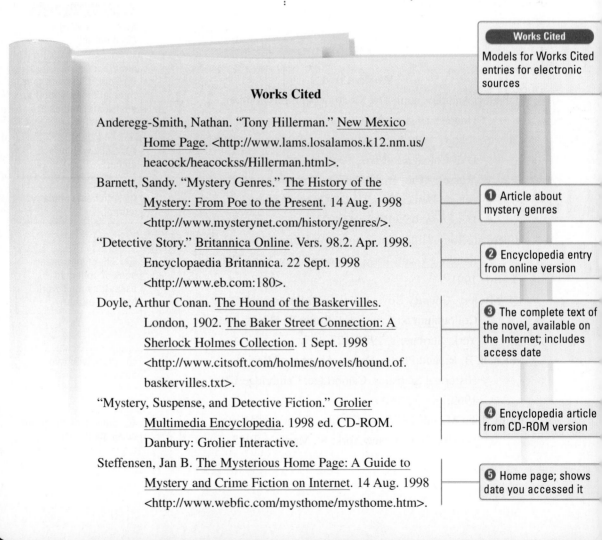

Works Cited

Models for Works Cited entries for electronic sources

Works Cited

Anderegg-Smith, Nathan. "Tony Hillerman." New Mexico
Home Page. <http://www.lams.losalamos.k12.nm.us/
heacock/heacockss/Hillerman.html>.

Barnett, Sandy. "Mystery Genres." The History of the
Mystery: From Poe to the Present. 14 Aug. 1998
<http://www.mysterynet.com/history/genres/>.

"Detective Story." Britannica Online. Vers. 98.2. Apr. 1998.
Encyclopaedia Britannica. 22 Sept. 1998
<http://www.eb.com:180>.

Doyle, Arthur Conan. The Hound of the Baskervilles.
London, 1902. The Baker Street Connection: A
Sherlock Holmes Collection. 1 Sept. 1998
<http://www.citsoft.com/holmes/novels/hound.of.
baskervilles.txt>.

"Mystery, Suspense, and Detective Fiction." Grolier
Multimedia Encyclopedia. 1998 ed. CD-ROM.
Danbury: Grolier Interactive.

Steffensen, Jan B. The Mysterious Home Page: A Guide to
Mystery and Crime Fiction on Internet. 14 Aug. 1998
<http://www.webfic.com/mysthome/mysthome.htm>.

❶ Article about mystery genres

❷ Encyclopedia entry from online version

❸ The complete text of the novel, available on the Internet; includes access date

❹ Encyclopedia article from CD-ROM version

❺ Home page; shows date you accessed it

Business Writing

The ability to write clearly and succinctly is an essential skill in the business world. As you prepare to enter the job market, you will need to know how to create letters, memos, and résumés.

Standards for Writing

Successful business writing should

- have a tone and language geared to the appropriate audience.
- state the purpose clearly in the opening sentences or paragraph.
- use precise words and avoid jargon.
- present only essential information.
- present details in a logical order.
- conclude with a summary of important points.

8.1 Key Techniques

Think About Your Purpose Why are you doing this writing? Do you want to "sell" yourself to a college admissions committee or a job interviewer? Do you want to order or complain about a product? Do you want to set up a meeting or respond to someone's ideas?

Identify Your Audience Who will read your writing? What background information will they need? What questions might they have? What tone or language is appropriate?

Support Your Points What specific details clarify your ideas? What reasons do you have for your statements? What points most strongly support them?

Finish Strongly How can you best sum up your statements? What is your main point? What action do you want others to take?

8.2 Options

Model 1: Letter

> 92 Hillside Acres
> Longacre, NY 10331
> April 16, _____

Heading *Where the letter comes from and when*

Inside Address *To whom the letter is being sent*

> Professor Leslie Lord, Dean
> Arts and Humanities College
> Brokow University
> 30880 Timberlake Drive
> Silver Lake, PA 19088

Salutation *Greeting*

> Dear Professor Lord:

Body *Text of the message*

> I am a junior at Albert Einstein High School and am beginning to consider where I would like to go to college.
>
> My art classes have been exciting for me. I would like to take college courses in art, especially commercial art.
>
> I will appreciate it if you will send me information about the art program as well as general information about applying to Brokow University.
>
> Thank you.

> Sincerely,
> *Tom Michael*

Closing

Model 2: Memo

Heading *Whom the memo is to and from, what it's about, and when it's being sent*

To: Tracy Alan
From: Leslie Lord
Re: Prospective Student
Date: 4/20/__

Body

Please send our Arts and Education brochure and a general catalog to this high school student.

Also, notify the Pennsylvania Alumni group to keep in touch with Tom. Thanks.

Model 3: Résumé A well-written résumé is invaluable when you apply for a part-time or full-time job or to college. It should highlight your skills, accomplishments, and experience. Proofread your résumé carefully to make sure it is clear and accurate and free of errors in grammar and spelling. It is a good idea to save a copy of your résumé on your computer or on a disk so that you can easily update it.

State your purpose. *This résumé is for a job application. A modified style can be used for a college application.*

List your previous employment experience *in reverse chronological order.*

Extracurricular activities and hobbies *can give a fuller picture of you and point out special job-related skills.*

TARA LEWIS
4656 McKinley Boulevard
Sanford, NC 27331

Objective Position as evening receptionist in an apartment building or other residential institution

Qualifications Facility with switchboard and computer
Friendly attitude
Pleasant voice

Work Experience 1998–present—Part-time secretarial assistant at Hughes & Lewis Real Estate, Sanford
1997—Temporary hostess at North Carolina State Fair

Education Currently senior at Granville High School
Extra summer courses in drama at Center Community College, 1998

Extracurricular Activities Drama Club, Glee Club, Granville Cubs cheerleader

Hobbies Reading, gymnastics, swimming

References Available upon request

1 Inquiry and Research

In this age of seemingly unlimited information, the ability to locate and evaluate resources efficiently can spell the difference between success and failure—in both the academic and the business worlds. Make use of print and nonprint information sources.

1.1 Finding Sources

Good research involves using the wealth of resources available to answer your questions and raise new questions. Knowing where to go and how to access information can lead you to interesting and valuable sources.

Reference Works

Reference works are print and nonprint sources of information that provide quick access to both general overviews and specific facts about a subject. These include

Dictionaries—word definitions, pronunciations, and origins

Thesauruses—lists of synonyms and antonyms for each entry

Glossaries—collections of specialized terms, such as those pertaining to literature, with definitions

Encyclopedias—detailed information on nearly every subject, arranged alphabetically (*Encyclopaedia Britannica*). Specialized encyclopedias deal with specific subjects, such as music, economics, and science (*Encyclopedia of Economics*).

Almanacs and Yearbooks—current facts and statistics (*World Almanac, Statistical Abstract of the United States*)

Atlases—maps and information about weather, agricultural and industrial production, and other geographical topics (*National Geographic Atlas of the World*)

Specialized Reference Works—biographical data (*Who's Who, Current Biography*), literary information (*Contemporary Authors, Book Review Digest, Cyclopedia of Literary Characters, The Oxford Companion to English Literature*), and quotations (*Bartlett's Familiar Quotations*)

Electronic Sources—Many of these reference works and databases are available on CD-ROMs, which may include text, sound, photographs, and video. CD-ROMs can be used on a home or library computer. You can subscribe to services that offer access to these sources on-line.

Periodicals and Indexes

One kind of specialized reference is a periodical.

- Some periodicals, such as *Atlantic Monthly* and *Psychology Today,* are intended for a general audience. They are indexed in the *Readers' Guide to Periodical Literature.*

- Many other periodicals, or journals, are intended for specialized or academic audiences. These include titles and subject matter as diverse as *American Psychologist* and *Studies in Short Fiction.* These are indexed in the *Humanities Index* and the *Social Sciences Index.* In addition, most fields have their own indexes. For example, articles on literature are indexed in the *MLA International Bibliography.*

- Many indexes are available in print, CD-ROM, and on-line forms.

Internet

The Internet is a vast network of computers. News services, libraries, universities, researchers, organizations, and government agencies use the Internet to distribute information and to communicate. The Internet can provide links to library catalogs, newspapers, government sources, and many of the reference sources described above. The Internet includes two key features:

World Wide Web—source of information on specific subjects and links to related topics

Electronic mail (e-mail)—communications link to other e-mail users worldwide

Other Resources

In addition to reference works found in the library and over the Internet, you can get information from the following sources: corporate publications, lectures, correspondence, and media such as films, television programs, and recordings. You can also observe directly, conduct your own interviews, and collect data from polls or questionnaires that you create yourself.

 Evaluating Sources

Not all information is equal. You need to be a discriminating consumer of information and evaluate the credibility of the source, the reliability of the specific information included, and its value in answering your research needs.

Credibility of Sources

You must determine the credibility and appropriateness of each source in order to write an effective report or speech. Ask yourself the following questions:

Is the writer an authority? A writer who has written several books on a subject or whose name is included in many bibliographies may be considered an authoritative source.

Is the source reliable and unbiased? What is the author's motivation? For example, a defense of an industry in which the author has a financial interest may be biased. A profile of a writer or scientist written by a close relative may also be biased.

WEB TIP Be especially skeptical of information you locate on the Internet, since virtually anyone can post anything there. Read the URL, or Internet address. Sites sponsored by a government agency (*.gov*) or an educational institution (*.edu*) are generally more reliable.

Is the source up-to-date? It is important to consult the most recent material, especially in fields, such as medicine and technology that undergo constant research and development. Some authoritative sources have withstood the test of time, however, and should not be overlooked.

Is the source appropriate? What audience is the material written for? In general, look for information directed at the educated reader. Material geared to experts or to popular audiences may be too technical or too simplified and therefore not appropriate for most research projects.

Distinguishing Fact from Opinion

As you gather information, it is important to recognize facts and opinions. A **fact** can be proven to be true or false. You could verify the statement "Congress rejected the bill" by checking newspapers, magazines, or the *Congressional Record.* An **opinion** is a judgment based on facts. The statement "Congress should not have rejected the bill" is an opinion. To evaluate an opinion, check for evidence presented logically and validly to support it.

Recognizing Bias

A writer may have a particular bias. This does not automatically make his or her point of view unreliable. However, recognizing an author's bias can help you evaluate a source. Recognizing that the author of an article about immigration is a Chinese immigrant will help you understand that author's bias. In addition, an author may have a hidden agenda that makes him or her less than objective about a topic. To avoid relying on information that may be biased, check an author's background and gather a variety of viewpoints.

 Collecting Information

People use a variety of techniques to collect information during the research process. Try out several of those suggested below and decide which ones work best for you.

Paraphrasing and Summarizing

You can adapt material from other sources by quoting it directly or by paraphrasing or summarizing it. A paraphrase involves restating the information in your own words. It is often a simpler version but not necessarily a shorter version. A summary involves extracting the main ideas and supporting details and writing a shorter version of the information.

Remember to credit the source when you paraphrase or summarize. See the Writing Handbook—Research Report, pp. 1161–1166.

Strategies for Paraphrasing
1. Select the portion of the article you want to record.
2. Read it carefully and think about those ideas you find most interesting and useful to your research. Often these will be the main ideas.
3. Retell the information in your own words.

Strategies for Summarizing
1. Read the article carefully. Determine the main ideas.
2. In your own words, write a shortened version of these main ideas.

Avoiding Plagiarism

Plagiarism is copying someone else's ideas or words and using them as if they were your own. This can happen inadvertently if you are sloppy about collecting information and documenting your sources. Plagiarism is intellectual stealing and can have serious consequences.

How to Avoid Plagiarism

1. When you paraphrase or summarize, be sure to change entirely the wording of the original by using your own words.

2. Both in notes and on your final report, enclose in quotation marks any material copied directly from other sources.

3. Indicate in your final report the sources of any ideas that are not general knowledge—including those in the visuals—that you have paraphrased or summarized.

4. Include a list of Works Cited with your finished report. See the Writing Handbook—Research Report, pp. 1161–1166.

② Study Skills and Strategies

As you read an assignment for the first time, review material for a test, or search for information for a research report, you use different methods of reading and studying.

2.1 Skimming

When you run your eyes quickly over a text, paying attention to overviews, headings, topic sentences, highlighted words, and graphic features, you are skimming.

Skimming is a good technique for previewing material in a textbook or other source that you must read for an assignment. It is also useful when you are researching a self-selected topic. Skimming a source helps you determine whether it has pertinent information. For example, suppose you are writing a research report on the detective story. Skimming an essay or a book on Edgar Allan Poe can help you quickly determine whether any part of it deals with your topic.

2.2 Scanning

To find a specific piece of information in a text, use scanning. To scan, place a card under the first line of a page and move it down slowly. Look for key words and phrases that signal the information you are looking for.

Scanning is useful in reviewing for a test or in finding a specific piece of information for a paper. Suppose you are looking for a discussion of hard-boiled private eyes for your research report. You can scan a book chapter or an essay, looking for the key names *Raymond Chandler* and *Dashiell Hammett*.

2.3 In-Depth Reading

When you must thoroughly understand the material in a text, you use in-depth reading.

In-depth reading involves asking questions, taking notes, looking for main ideas, and drawing conclusions as you read slowly and carefully. For example, in researching your report on detective fiction, you may find an article on police procedural stories. Since this is closely related to your topic, you will read it in depth and take notes. You also should use in-depth reading for reading textbooks and literary works.

2.4 Outlining

Outlining is an efficient way of organizing ideas and is useful in taking notes.

Outlining helps you retain information as you read in depth. For example, you might outline a chapter in a history textbook, listing the main subtopics and the ideas or details that support them. An outline can also be useful for taking notes for a research report or in reading a piece of literature. The following is an example of a topic outline that summarizes, in short phrases, part of a chapter.

> MAIN IDEA: **Agatha Christie is extraordinarily popular for good reasons.**
> **I. The Stories**
>   **A. Many variations on the mystery formula**
>   **B. Told well**
>   **C. Plays fair with readers**
> **II. The Detectives**
>   **A. Hercule Poirot, eccentric Belgian**
>   **B. Jane Marple, observant spinster**

2.5 Identifying Main Ideas

To understand and remember any material you read, identify its main idea.

In informative material, the main idea is often stated. The thesis statement of an essay or article and the topic sentence of each paragraph often state the main idea. In other material, especially literary works, the main idea is implied. After reading the piece carefully, analyze the important parts, such as characters and plot. Then try to sum up in one sentence the general point that the story makes.

 ## 2.6 Taking Notes

As you listen or read in depth, take notes to help you understand the material. Look and listen for key words that point to main ideas.

One way to help you summarize the main idea and supporting details is to take notes in modified outline form. In using a modified outline form, you do not need to use numerals and letters. Unlike a formal outline, a modified outline does not require two or more points under each heading, and headings do not need to be grammatically parallel. Yet, like a formal outline, a modified outline organizes a text's main ideas and related details. The following modified outline gives historic reasons why some words are not spelled like they sound.

> **Lost Sounds**
> • **Anglo-Saxon *gh***
> • **hard to pronounce *t* as in castle**
> • ***k* with *n* as in knight**
> • ***b* with *m* as in lamb**
> • ***w* with *r* as in write**
> **Added Letters**
> • **Dutch printers: unneeded *g* before *h***
> • **French scribes: unneeded *u***
> • **Latin scholars: unneeded *b***

Use abbreviations and symbols to make note taking more efficient. Following are some commonly used abbreviations for note taking.

w/	with	re	regarding
w/o	without	=	is, equals
#	number	*	important
&, +	and	def	definition
>	more than	Amer	America
<	less than	tho	although

③ Critical Thinking

Critical thinking includes the ability to analyze, evaluate, and synthesize ideas and information. Critical thinking goes beyond simply understanding something. It involves making informed judgments based on sound reasoning skills.

3.1 Avoiding Faulty Reasoning

When you write or speak for a persuasive purpose, you must make sure your logic is valid. Avoid these mistakes in reasoning, called **logical fallacies**.

Overgeneralization

Conclusions reached on the basis of too little evidence result in the fallacy called overgeneralization. A person who saw three cyclists riding bicycles without helmets might conclude, "Nobody wears bicycle helmets." That conclusion would be an overgeneralization.

Circular Reasoning

When you support an opinion by simply repeating it in different terms, you are using circular reasoning. For example, "Sport utility vehicles are popular because more people buy them than any other category of new cars." This is an illogical statement because the second part of the sentence simply uses different words to restate the first part of the sentence.

Either-Or Fallacy

Assuming that a complex question has only two possible answers is called the either-or fallacy. "Either we raise the legal driving age or accidents caused by teenage drivers will continue to increase" is an example of the either-or fallacy. The statement ignores other ways of decreasing the automobile accident rate of teenagers.

Cause-and-Effect Fallacy

The cause-and-effect fallacy occurs when you say that event B was caused by event A just because event B occurred after event A. A person might conclude that because a city's air quality worsened two months after a new factory began operation, that new factory caused the air pollution. However, this cause-and-effect relationship would have to be supported by more specific evidence.

3.2 Identifying Modes of Persuasion

Understanding persuasive techniques can help you evaluate information, make informed decisions, and reject persuasive techniques intended to deceive you. Some modes of persuasion appeal to your various emotions.

Loaded Language

Loaded language is words or phrases chosen to appeal to the emotions. It is often used in place of facts to shape opinion or to evoke a positive or negative reaction. For example, you might feel positive about a politician who has a *plan.* You might, however, feel negative about a politician who has a *scheme.*

Bandwagon

Bandwagon taps into the human desire to belong. This technique suggests that "everybody" is doing it, or buying it, or believing it. Phrases such as "Don't be the only one . . ." and "Everybody is . . ." signal the bandwagon appeal.

Testimonials

Testimonials present well-known people or satisfied customers who promote and endorse a product or idea. This technique taps into the appeal of celebrities or into people's need to identify with others just like themselves.

3.3 Logical Thinking

Persuasive writing and speaking require good reasoning skills. Two ways of creating logical arguments are deductive reasoning and inductive reasoning.

Deductive Arguments

A deductive argument begins with a generalization, or premise, and then advances with facts and evidence that lead to a conclusion. The conclusion is the logical outcome of the premise. A false premise leads to a false conclusion; a valid premise leads to a valid conclusion provided that the specific facts are correct and the reasoning is correct.

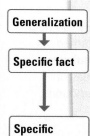

Generalization	We still have much to learn about the healing role of plants.
Specific fact	In some developing countries, many plants are being destroyed as people burn off forests so they can make a living.
Specific Conclusion	It is in our best interests to help these developing nations so that they can preserve their plants.

You may use deductive reasoning when writing a persuasive paper or speech. Your conclusion is the thesis of your paper. Facts in your paper supporting your premise should lead logically to that conclusion.

Inductive Arguments

An inductive argument begins with specific evidence that leads to a general conclusion.

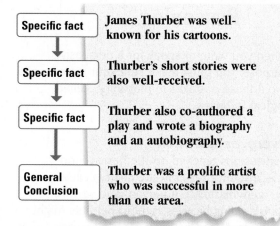

Specific fact	James Thurber was well-known for his cartoons.
Specific fact	Thurber's short stories were also well-received.
Specific fact	Thurber also co-authored a play and wrote a biography and an autobiography.
General Conclusion	Thurber was a prolific artist who was successful in more than one area.

The conclusion of an inductive argument often includes a qualifying term such as *some, often,* or *most.* This usage helps to avoid the fallacy of overgeneralization.

4 Speaking and Listening

Good speakers and listeners do more than just talk and hear. They use specific techniques to present their ideas effectively, and they are attentive and critical listeners.

4.1 Giving a Speech

In school, in business, and in community life, giving a speech is one of the most effective ways of communicating. Whether to persuade, to inform, or to entertain, you may often speak before an audience.

Analyzing Audience and Purpose

In order to speak effectively, you need to know to whom you are speaking and why you are speaking. When preparing a speech, think about how much knowledge and interest your audience has in your subject. A speech has one of two main purposes: to inform or to persuade. A third purpose, to entertain, is often considered closely related to these two purposes.

A speech **to inform** gives the audience new information, provides a better understanding of information, or enables people to use information in a new way. An informative speech is presented in an objective way.

In a speech **to persuade,** a speaker tries to change the actions or beliefs of an audience.

Preparing and Delivering a Speech

There are four main methods of preparing and delivering a speech:

Manuscript When you speak from **manuscript,** you prepare a complete script of your speech in advance and use it to deliver your speech.

Memory When you speak from **memory,** you prepare a written text in advance and then memorize it so you can deliver it word for word.

Impromptu When you speak **impromptu,** you speak on the spur of the moment without any special preparation.

Extemporaneous When you give an **extemporaneous** speech, you research and prepare your speech and then deliver it with the help of notes.

Points for Effective Speech Delivery

- Avoid speaking either too fast or too slow. Vary your **speaking rate** depending on your material. Slow down for difficult concepts. Speed up to convince your audience that you are knowledgeable about your subject.

- Speak loud enough to be heard clearly, but not so loud that your voice is overwhelming.

- Use a **conversational tone.**

- Use a change of **pitch,** or inflection, to help make your tone and meaning clear.

- Let your **facial expression** reflect your message.

- Make **eye contact** with as many audience members as possible.

- Use **gestures** to emphasize your words. Don't make your gestures too small to be seen. On the other hand, don't gesture too frequently or wildly.

- Use **good posture**—not too relaxed and not too rigid. Avoid nervous mannerisms.

 4.2 Analyzing, Evaluating and Critiquing a Speech

Evaluating speeches helps you make informed judgments about the ideas presented in a speech. It also helps you learn what makes an effective speech and delivery. Use these criteria to help you analyze, evaluate, and critique speeches.

CRITERIA — How to Evaluate a Persuasive Speech

- Did the speaker have a clear goal or argument?
- Did the speaker take the audience's biases into account?
- Did the speaker support the argument with convincing facts?
- Did the speaker use sound logic in developing the argument?
- Did the speaker use voice, facial expression, gestures, and posture effectively?
- Did the speaker hold the audience's interest?

CRITERIA — How to Evaluate an Informative Speech

- Did the speaker have a specific, clearly focused topic?
- Did the speaker take the audience's previous knowledge into consideration?
- Did the speaker cite sources for the information?
- Did the speaker communicate the information objectively?
- Did the speaker present the information in an organized manner?
- Did the speaker use visual aids effectively?
- Did the speaker use voice, facial expression, gestures, and posture effectively?

Using Active Listening Strategies

Listeners play an active part in the communication process. A listener has a responsibility just as a speaker does. Listening, unlike hearing, is a learned skill.

As you listen to a public speaker, use the following active listening strategies:

- Determine the **speaker's purpose.**
- Listen for the **main idea** of the message and not simply the individual details.
- **Anticipate the points** that will be made based on the speaker's purpose and main idea.
- Listen with an open mind, but **identify faulty logic, unsupported facts,** and **emotional appeals.**

4.4 Conducting Interviews

Conducting a personal interview can be an effective way to get information.

Preparing for the Interview
- Read any articles by or about the person you will interview. This background information will help you get to the point during the interview.
- Prepare a list of questions. Think of more questions than you will need. Include some yes/no questions and some open-ended questions. Order your questions from most important to least important.

Participating in the Interview
- Listen interactively. Be prepared to follow up on a response you find interesting.
- Avoid arguments. Be tactful and polite.

Following Up on the Interview
- Summarize your notes while they are still fresh in your mind.
- Send a thank-you note to the interviewee.

5 Viewing and Representing

In our media-saturated world, we are immersed in visual messages that convey ideas, information, and attitudes. To understand and use visual representations effectively, you need to be aware of the techniques and the range of visuals that are commonly used.

 Understanding Visual Messages

Information is communicated not only with words but with graphic devices. A **graphic device** is a visual representation of data and ideas and the relations among them.

Reading Charts and Graphs
A chart organizes information by arranging it in rows and columns. It is helpful in showing complex information clearly. When interpreting a chart, first read the title. Then analyze how the

information is presented. Charts can take many different forms. The following chart shows some techniques for using sounds in poetry.

Sounds in Poetry	
Technique	**Example**
Onomatopoeia	the slow **clip clop** of the ox
Alliteration	**r**ough **r**eaches of **r**anch and sky
Assonance	the c**o**stly t**o**ssing of l**o**st dreams
Consonance	his mea**g**er nu**gg**ets of be**g**rudging praise
Rhyme	A truth that's told with bad **intent** Beats all the lies you can **invent.**

There are several different types of **graphs,** visual aids that are often used to display numerical information.

- A **circle graph** shows proportions of the whole. The following circle graph shows the countries that governed Africa in 1913.

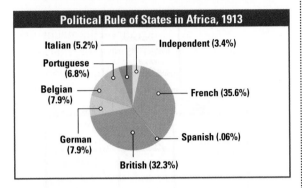

Political Rule of States in Africa, 1913

Italian (5.2%)
Independent (3.4%)
Portuguese (6.8%)
Belgian (7.9%)
French (35.6%)
German (7.9%)
Spanish (.06%)
British (32.3%)

- A **line graph** shows the change in data over a period of time. The following line graph shows attendance at the Linwood High School Drama Fair over five years.

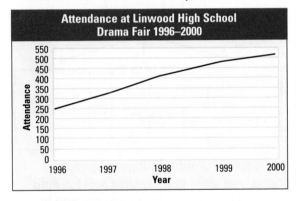

Attendance at Linwood High School Drama Fair 1996–2000

Attendance
550 500 450 400 350 300 250 200 150 100 50 0
1996 1997 1998 1999 2000
Year

- A **bar graph** compares amounts.

Interpreting Images

Speakers and writers often use visual aids to inform or persuade their audiences. These aids can be invaluable in helping you understand the information being communicated. However, you must interpret visual aids critically, as you do written material.

- **Examine photographs critically.** Does the camera angle or the background in the photo intentionally evoke a positive or negative response? Has the image been altered or manipulated?
- **Evaluate carefully the data presented in charts and graphs.** Some charts and graphs may exaggerate the facts. For example, a circle graph representing a sample of only ten people may be misleading if the speaker suggests that this data represents a trend.

 Evaluating Visual Messages

When you view images, whether they are cartoons, advertising art, photographs, or paintings, there are certain elements to look for.

CRITERIA **How to Analyze Images**

- Is color used realistically? Is it used to emphasize certain objects? to evoke a specific response?
- What tone is created by color and by light and dark in the picture?
- Do the background images intentionally evoke a positive or negative response?
- What is noticeable about the picture's composition, that is, the arrangement of lines, colors, and forms? Does the composition emphasize certain objects or elements in the picture?
- For graphs and charts, does the visual accurately represent the data?

 Using Visual Representations

Tables, graphs, diagrams, pictures, and animations often communicate information more effectively than words alone do.

Use visuals with written reports to illustrate complex concepts and processes or to make a page look more interesting. Computer programs, CD-ROMs, and on-line services can help you generate

- **graphs** that present numerical information;
- **charts** and **tables** that allow easy comparison of information;
- **logos** and **graphic devices** that highlight important information;
- **borders** and **tints** that signal different kinds of information;
- **clip art** that adds useful pictures;

- **interactive animations** that illustrate difficult concepts.

You might want to explore ways of displaying data in more than one visual format before deciding which will work best for you.

Making Multimedia Presentations

A multimedia presentation is an electronically prepared combination of text, sound, and visuals such as photographs, videos, and animation. Your audience reads, hears, and sees your presentation at a computer, following different "paths" you create to lead the user through the information you have gathered.

Planning Presentations

To create a multimedia presentation, first choose your topic and decide what you want to include. Then plan how you want your user to move through your presentation. For a multimedia presentation on the suspense story through the ages, you might include the following items:

- text defining the suspense story and discussing key elements
- taped reading from Appalachian ghost stories
- taped reading from an Edgar Allan Poe story
- chart comparing the novel *Frankenstein* with one of the movies
- video interview with a scholar on the elements of suspense in fairy tales and folk tales
- video from a modern suspense film
- photos of settings from suspense movies

You can choose one of the following ways to organize your presentation:

step by step, with only one path, or order, in which the user can see and hear the information

a branching path that allows users to make some choices about what they will see and hear, and in what order

A flow chart can help you figure out the paths a user can take through your presentation. Each box in the flow chart that follows represents something about suspense stories for the user to read, see, or hear. The arrows on the flow chart show the possible paths the user can follow.

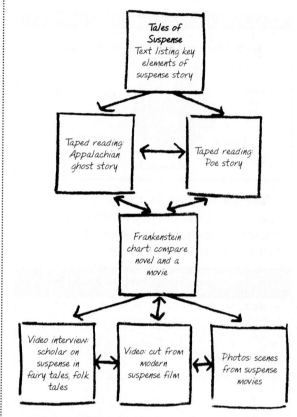

TECHNOLOGY TIP You can download photos, sound, and video from Internet sources onto your computer. This process lets you add to your presentation various elements that would usually require complex editing equipment.

Guiding Your User

Your user will need directions to follow the path you have planned for your multimedia presentation.

Most multimedia authoring programs allow you to create screens that include text or audio directions that guide the user from one part of your presentation to the next.

If you need help creating your multimedia presentation, ask your school's technology adviser. You may also be able to get help from your classmates or your software manual.

Grammar Handbook

1 Quick Reference: Parts of Speech

Part of Speech	Definition	Examples
Noun	Names a person, place, thing, idea, quality, or action.	Odysseus, Greece, boat, freedom, joy, sailing
Pronoun	Takes the place of a noun or another pronoun.	
Personal	Refers to the one speaking, spoken to, or spoken about.	I, me, my, mine, we, us, our, ours, you, your, yours, she, he, it, her, him, hers, his, its, they, them, their, theirs
Reflexive	Follows a verb or preposition and refers to a preceding noun or pronoun.	myself, yourself, herself, himself, itself, ourselves, yourselves, themselves
Intensive	Emphasizes a noun or another pronoun.	(Same as reflexives)
Demonstrative	Points to specific persons or things.	this, that, these, those
Interrogative	Signals questions.	who, whom, whose, which, what
Indefinite	Refers to person(s) or thing(s) not specifically mentioned.	both, all, most, many, anyone, everybody, several, none, some
Relative	Introduces subordinate clauses and relates them to words in the main clause.	who, whom, whose, which, that
Verb	Expresses action, condition, or state of being.	
Action	Tells what the subject does or did, physically or mentally.	run, reaches, listened, consider, decides, dreamt
Linking	Connects subjects to that which identifies or describes them.	am, is, are, was, were, sound, taste, appear, feel, become, remain, seem
Auxiliary	Precedes and introduces main verbs.	be, have, do, can, could, will, would, may, might
Adjective	Modifies nouns or pronouns.	**strong** women, **two** epics, **enough** time
Adverb	Modifies verbs, adjectives, or other adverbs.	walked **out, really** funny, **far** away
Preposition	Relates one word to another (following) word.	at, by, for, from, in, of, on, to, with
Conjunction	Joins words or word groups.	
Coordinating	Joins words or word groups used the same way.	and, but, or, for, so, yet, nor
Correlative	Join words or word groups used the same way and are used in pairs.	both . . . and, either . . . or, neither . . . nor
Subordinating	Joins word groups not used the same way.	although, after, as, before, because, when, if, unless
Interjection	Expresses emotion.	wow, ouch, hurrah

2 Nouns

A noun is a word used to name a person, place, thing, idea, quality, or action. Nouns can be classified in several ways. All nouns can be placed in at least two classifications. They are either common or proper. All are also either abstract or concrete. Some nouns can be classified as compound, collective, and possessive as well.

2.1 Common Nouns are general names, common to an entire group.
  EXAMPLES: *poet, novel, love, journey*

2.2 Proper Nouns name specific, one-of-a-kind things. (See Capitalization, page 1203.)
  EXAMPLES: *Jackson, Pleasant Street, Lewis*

2.3 Concrete Nouns name things that can be perceived by the senses.
  EXAMPLES: *roof, flash, Dublin, battle*

2.4 Abstract Nouns name things that cannot be observed by the senses.
  EXAMPLES: *intelligence, fear, joy, loneliness*

	Common	Proper
Abstract	peace	Christianity
Concrete	sniper	O'Connell Street

2.5 Compound Nouns are formed from two or more words but express a single idea. They are written as single words, as separate words, or with hyphens. Use a dictionary to check the correct spelling of a compound noun.
  EXAMPLES: *haircut, father-in-law, Christmas Eve*

2.6 Collective Nouns are singular nouns that refer to groups of people or things. (See Collective Nouns as Subjects, page 1200.)
  EXAMPLES: *army, flock, class, species*

2.7 Possessive Nouns show who or what owns something. Consult the chart above for the proper use of the possessive apostrophe.

Possessive Nouns

Category	Rule	Examples
All singular nouns	Add apostrophe plus -s	Stafford's, tree's, Bess's, town's, great-grandfather's
Plural nouns not ending in -s	Add apostrophe plus -s	children's women's people's
Plural nouns ending in -s	Add apostrophe only	witnesses' churches' males' Johnsons'

GRAMMAR PRACTICE

A. For each underlined noun, first tell whether it is common or proper. Then tell whether it is concrete or abstract.

1. Miss Adela Strangeworth lived alone in the <u>house</u> her <u>grandfather</u> had built.

2. <u>Adela</u> had lived on <u>Pleasant Street</u> all her life, tending the roses her grandmother had planted.

3. She knew everyone in <u>town</u>, though she kept a formal distance from people of lower <u>status</u>.

4. Although she and <u>Tommy Lewis</u> had been in the same high school <u>class</u>, she called him only "Mr. Lewis" after he opened his grocery store.

5. Mr. Lewis seemed worried; he even forgot to remind Miss Strangeworth to buy her <u>tea</u> on Tuesday.

6. Helen Crane looked at her baby with <u>wonder</u>, but she worried that the child might be slow.

7. Miss Strangeworth wanted <u>society</u> to be alert for the possibility of <u>evil</u>.

8. She wrote anonymous <u>letters</u>—the one to Don Crane, Helen's husband, suggested that their <u>child</u> was an idiot.

9. At the <u>post office</u>, Miss Strangeworth opened her <u>pocketbook</u> and dropped one of her letters.

10. A boy delivered the letter to Don Crane, and he took <u>revenge</u> by destroying Miss Strangeworth's <u>roses</u>.

B. 11–15. From the sentences above, write three compound nouns and two collective nouns.

C. Write the possessive form of the following nouns.

16. Shirley Jackson
17. Mr. Lewis
18. children
19. minister
20. bus
21. tourists
22. box
23. roses
24. Miss Strangeworth
25. princess

③ Pronouns

A pronoun is a word that is used in place of a noun or another pronoun. The word or word group to which the pronoun refers is called its antecedent.

3.1 *Personal Pronouns* are pronouns that change their form to express person, number, gender, and case. The forms of these pronouns are shown in the chart that follows.

	Nominative	Objective	Possessive
Singular			
First Person	I	me	my, mine
Second Person	you	you	your, yours
Third Person	she, he, it	her, him, it	her, hers, his, its
Plural			
First Person	we	us	our, ours
Second Person	you	you	your, yours
Third Person	they	them	their, theirs

3.2 *Pronoun Agreement* Pronouns should agree with their antecedents in number and person. Singular pronouns are used to replace singular nouns. Plural pronouns are used to replace plural nouns. Pronouns must also match the gender (masculine, feminine, or neuter) of the nouns they replace.

3.3 *Pronoun Case* Personal pronouns change form to show how they function in a sentence. This change of form is called *case.* The three cases are **nominative, objective,** and **possessive.**

A nominative pronoun is used as the subject or the predicate nominative of a sentence.

An objective pronoun is used as the direct or indirect object of a sentence or as the object of a preposition.

SUBJECT OBJECT

He will lead them to us.

OBJECT OF PREPOSITION

A possessive pronoun shows ownership. The pronouns *mine, yours, hers, his, its, ours,* and *theirs* can be used in place of nouns.

EXAMPLE: *This horse is mine.*

The pronouns *my, your, her, his, its, our,* and *their* are used before nouns.

EXAMPLE: *This is my horse.*

USAGE TIP To decide which pronoun to use in a comparison, such as *He tells better tales than (I or me),* fill in the missing words: *He tells better tales than I tell.*

WATCH OUT! Many spelling errors can be avoided if you watch out for *its* and *their.* Don't confuse the possessive pronoun *its* with the contraction *it's,* meaning *it is* or *it has.* The homonyms *they're* (contraction for *they are*) and *there* (a place or an expletive) are often mistakenly used for *their.*

3.4 *Reflexive and Intensive Pronouns* These pronouns are formed by adding *-self* or *-selves* to certain personal pronouns. Their forms are the same, and they differ only in how they are used.

Reflexive pronouns follow verbs or prepositions and reflect back on an earlier noun or pronoun.

EXAMPLES: *He likes himself too much. She is now herself again.*

Intensive pronouns intensify or emphasize the nouns or pronouns to which they refer.

EXAMPLES: *They themselves will educate their children. You did it yourselves.*

Singular	
First Person	myself
Second Person	yourself
Third Person	herself, himself, itself

Plural	
First Person	ourselves
Second Person	yourselves
Third Person	themselves

WATCH OUT! Avoid using *hisself* or *theirselves.* Standard English does not include these forms.

> **NONSTANDARD:** *The sniper kept hisself hidden behind a chimney.*
> **STANDARD:** *The sniper kept himself hidden behind a chimney.*

USAGE TIP Reflexive and intensive pronouns should never be used without antecedents.

> **INCORRECT:** *Read a tale to my brother and myself.*
> **CORRECT:** *Read a tale to my brother and me.*

3.5 Demonstrative Pronouns point out things and persons near and far.

	Singular	Plural
Near	this	these
Far	that	those

WATCH OUT! Avoid using the objective pronoun *them* in place of the demonstrative *those.*

> **INCORRECT:** *Let's dramatize one of them tales.*
> **CORRECT:** *Let's dramatize one of those tales.*

3.6 Indefinite Pronouns do not refer to specific persons or things and usually have no antecedents. The chart shows some commonly used indefinite pronouns:

Singular	Plural	Singular or Plural	
each	both	all	half
either	few	any	plenty
neither	many	more	none
another	several	most	some

Here is another set of indefinite pronouns, all of which are singular. Notice that, with one exception, they are spelled as one word:

anyone	everyone	no one	someone
anybody	everybody	nobody	somebody
anything	everything	nothing	something

USAGE TIP Since all these are singular, pronouns referring to them should be singular.

> **INCORRECT:** *Did everybody play their part well?*
> **CORRECT:** *Did everybody play his or her part well?*

If the antecedent of the pronoun is both male and female, *his or her* may be used as an alternative, or the sentence may be recast:

> **EXAMPLES:** *Did everybody play his or her part well?*
> *Did all the students play their parts well?*

GRAMMAR PRACTICE

Write the correct form of all incorrect pronouns in the sentences below.

1. Jim needed money for a present for Della, so he took his watch to the pawn shop hisself.

2. Would anybody else sell their watch to buy a Christmas present?

3. He chose a beautiful pair of them jeweled combs that Della could wear in her hair.

4. He was surprised to learn that she had sold her long hair to buy a watch chain for himself.

5. They gave theirselves better Christmas presents than they knew.

3.7 Interrogative Pronouns tell a reader or listener that a question is coming. The interrogative pronouns are *who, whom, whose, which,* and *what.*

> **EXAMPLES:** *Who is going to rehearse with you? From whom did you receive the script?*

USAGE TIP *Who* is used for subjects, *whom* for objects. To find out which pronoun you need to use in a question, change the question to a statement:

> **QUESTION:** *(Who/Whom?) did you meet there?*
> **STATEMENT:** *You met (?) there.*

Since the verb has a subject *(you),* the needed word must be the object form, *whom.*

> **EXAMPLE:** *Whom did you meet there?*

WATCH OUT! A special problem arises when you use an interrupter such as *do you think* within a sentence:

> **EXAMPLE:** *(Who/Whom) do you think will win?*

If you eliminate the interrupter, it is clear that the word you need is *who*.

3.8 *Relative Pronouns* relate, or connect, clauses to the words they modify in sentences. The noun or pronoun that the clause modifies is the antecedent of the relative pronoun. Here are the relative pronouns and their uses:

Replacing:	Subject	Object	Possessive
Persons	who	whom	whose
Things	which	which	whose
Things/Persons*	that	that	whose

* That generally will not replace specific names, such as Edgar Allan Poe.

Often short sentences with related ideas can be combined using relative pronouns to create a more effective sentence.

> **SHORT SENTENCE:** *Poe wrote "The Raven."*
> **RELATED SENTENCE:** *"The Raven" is one of the most famous poems in American literature.*
> **COMBINED SENTENCE:** *Poe wrote "The Raven," which is one of the most famous poems in American literature.*

GRAMMAR PRACTICE

Choose the appropriate interrogative or relative pronoun from the words in parentheses.

1. Poe, (who/that) wrote "The Bells," made each verse sound like a different kind of bell.

2. I hear silver sleigh bells. (Who/Whom) has the sledge been sent for?

3. The couple (who/whom) are coming from their wedding hear the golden bells.

4. When the brass alarm bells ring, the people (who/whom) live nearby run to help put out the fire.

5. The iron bells ring for a funeral. Do you know for (who/whom) the bells toll?

Verbs

A verb is a word that expresses an action, a condition, or a state of being. There are two main kinds of verbs: action and linking. Other verbs, called auxiliary verbs, are sometimes used with action verbs and linking verbs.

4.1 *Action Verbs* tell what action someone or something is performing, physically or mentally.

> **PHYSICAL ACTION:** *You <u>hit</u> the target.*
> **MENTAL ACTION:** *She <u>dreamed</u> of me.*

4.2 *Linking Verbs* do not express action. Linking verbs link subjects to complements that identify or describe them. Linking verbs may be divided into two groups:

> **FORMS OF *TO BE*:** *She <u>is</u> our queen.*
> **VERBS THAT EXPRESS CONDITION:** *The writer <u>looked</u> thoughtful.*

4.3 *Auxiliary Verbs,* sometimes called helping verbs, precede action or linking verbs and modify their meanings in special ways. The most commonly used auxiliary verbs are parts of the verbs *be, have,* and *do.*

> **Be:** *am, is, are, was, were, be, being, been*
> **Have:** *have, has, had*
> **Do:** *do, does, did*

Other common auxiliary verbs are *can, could, will, would, shall, should, may, might,* and *must.*

> **EXAMPLES:** *I always <u>have</u> admired her.*
> *You <u>must</u> listen to me.*

4.4 *Transitive and Intransitive Verbs*
Action verbs can be either transitive or intransitive. A transitive verb directs the action towards someone or something. The transitive verb has an object. An intransitive verb does not direct the action towards someone or something. It does not have an object. Since linking verbs convey no action, they are always intransitive.

> **Transitive:** *The storm <u>sank</u> the ship.*
> **Intransitive:** *The ship <u>sank</u>.*

4.5 **Principal Parts** Action and linking verbs typically have four principal parts, which are used to form verb tenses. The principal parts are the *present*, the *present participle*, the *past*, and the *past participle*.

If the verb is a regular verb, the past and past participle are formed by adding the ending -*d* or -*ed* to the present part. Here is a chart showing four regular verbs:

Present	Present Participle	Past	Past Participle
risk	(is) risking	risked	(have) risked
solve	(is) solving	solved	(have) solved
drop	(is) dropping	dropped	(have) dropped
carry	(is) carrying	carried	(have) carried

Note that the present participle and past participle forms are preceded by a form of *be* or *have*. These forms cannot be used alone as main verbs and always need an auxiliary verb.

> **EXAMPLES:** *The man is risking his life.*
> *The man has stopped running.*

The past and past participle of irregular verbs are not formed by adding -*d* or -*ed* to the present; they are formed in irregular ways.

Present	Present Participle	Past	Past Participle
begin	(is) beginning	began	(have) begun
break	(is) breaking	broke	(have) broken
bring	(is) bringing	brought	(have) brought
choose	(is) choosing	chose	(have) chosen
go	(is) going	went	(have) gone
lose	(is) losing	lost	(have) lost
see	(is) seeing	saw	(have) seen
swim	(is) swimming	swam	(have) swum
write	(is) writing	wrote	(have) written

4.6 **Verb Tense** The tense of a verb tells the time of the action or the state of being. An action or state of being can occur in the present, the past, or the future. There are six tenses, each expressing a different range of time.

Present tense expresses an action that is happening at the present time, occurs regularly, or is constant or generally true. Use the present part.

> **EXAMPLES**
> **NOW:** *That snow looks deep.*
> **REGULAR:** *It snows every day.*
> **GENERAL:** *Snow falls.*

Past tense expresses an action that began and ended in the past. Use the past part.

> **EXAMPLE:** *The storyteller finished his tale.*

Future tense expresses an action (or state of being) that will occur. Use *shall* or *will* with the present part.

> **EXAMPLE:** *They will attend the next festival.*

Present perfect tense expresses action (1) that was completed at an indefinite time in the past or (2) that began in the past and continues into the present. Use *have* or *has* with the past participle.

> **EXAMPLE:** *Poetry has inspired readers throughout the ages.*

Past perfect tense shows an action in the past that came before another action in the past. Use *had* before the past participle.

> **EXAMPLE:** *He had built a fire before the dog ran away.*

Future perfect tense shows an action in the future that will be completed before another action in the future. Use *shall have* or *will have* before the past participle.

> **EXAMPLE:** *They will have finished the novel before seeing the movie version of the tale.*

4.7 **Progressive Forms** The progressive forms of the six tenses show ongoing action. Use a form of *be* with the present participle of a verb.

> **PRESENT PROGRESSIVE:** *She is rehearsing her lines.*
> **PAST PROGRESSIVE:** *She was rehearsing her lines.*
> **FUTURE PROGRESSIVE:** *She will be rehearsing her lines.*

PRESENT PERFECT PROGRESSIVE: *She has been rehearsing her lines.*
PAST PERFECT PROGRESSIVE: *She had been rehearsing her lines.*
FUTURE PERFECT PROGRESSIVE: *She will have been rehearsing her lines.*

WATCH OUT! Do not shift tense needlessly. Watch out for these special cases.

- In most compound sentences and in sentences with compound predicates, keep the tenses the same.

  INCORRECT: *His boots freeze, and he shook with cold.*

  CORRECT: *His boots freeze, and he shakes with cold.*

- If one past action happens before another, do shift tenses—from the past to the past perfect:

  INCORRECT: *They wished they started earlier.*
  CORRECT: *They wished they had started earlier.*

GRAMMAR PRACTICE

Write the verb(s) in each sentence and identify their tenses.

1. Many people have benefited from the civil rights movement.

2. Martin Luther King, Jr., remains a towering figure in the history of nonviolent protest.

3. King became the leader of the Montgomery bus boycott.

4. When he spoke to the crowds in Washington, D.C., more than 200,000 people heard his words.

5. You will be reading his speech "I Have a Dream."

4.8 *Active and Passive Voice* The voice of a verb tells whether the subject of a sentence performs or receives the action expressed by the verb. When the subject performs the action, the verb is in the active voice. When the subject is the receiver of the action, the verb is in the passive voice.

Compare these two sentences:

ACTIVE: *Richard Wilbur wrote "The Writer."*
PASSIVE: *"The Writer" was written by Richard Wilbur.*

To form the passive voice use a form of *be* with the past participle of the main verb.

WATCH OUT! Use the passive voice sparingly. It tends to make writing less forceful and less direct. It can also make the writing awkward.

AWKWARD: *"The Writer" is a poem that was written by Richard Wilbur.*
CORRECT: *Richard Wilbur wrote the poem "The Writer."*

There are occasions when you will choose to use the passive voice because

- you want to emphasize the receiver: *The king was shot.*

- the doer is unknown: *My books were stolen.*

- the doer is unimportant: *French is spoken here.*

4.9 *Mood* The mood identifies the manner in which the verb expresses an idea. There are three moods.

The indicative mood states a fact or asks a question. You use this mood most often.

EXAMPLE: *His trust was shattered by the betrayal.*

The imperative mood is used to give a command or make a request.

EXAMPLE: *Be there by eight o'clock sharp.*

The subjunctive mood is used to express a wish or a condition that is contrary to fact.

EXAMPLE: *If I were you, I wouldn't get my hopes up.*

GRAMMAR PRACTICE

Identify the verbs as active or passive.

1. The wild bird flies on the back of the wind.

2. Behind its bars, the caged bird sings beautifully.

3. The song is filled with sorrow and longing.

4. The bird longs for the freedom of the wild bird.

5. The book was written by Maya Angelou.

For the following items, identify the boldfaced verb as indicative or subjunctive in mood.

6. Do you **understand** the bird's frustration and fear?

7. If I **were** a bird, I wouldn't want to be caged.

8. Angelou **was inspired** by Paul Laurence Dunbar's poem "Sympathy."

9. His poems **were** inspirational for many.

10. If he **were** alive today, he would probably continue to write about freedom.

⑤ Modifiers

Modifiers are words or groups of words that change or limit the meanings of other words. The two kinds of modifiers are adjectives and adverbs.

5.1 *Adjectives* An adjective is a word that modifies a noun or pronoun by telling *which one, what kind, how many,* or *how much.*

WHICH ONE: *this, that, these, those*
EXAMPLE: *That bird is a scarlet ibis.*

WHAT KIND: *small, sick, courageous, black*
EXAMPLE: *The sick bird sways on the branch.*

HOW MANY: *some, few, thirty, none, both, each*
EXAMPLE: *Both brothers stared at the bird.*

HOW MUCH: *more, less, enough, scarce*
EXAMPLE: *The bird did not have enough strength to remain perched.*

The **articles** *a, an,* and *the* are usually classified as adjectives. These are the most common adjectives that you will use.

EXAMPLES: *The bridge was burned before the attack.*
A group of peasants led the procession in the town.

5.2 *Predicate Adjectives* Most adjectives come before the nouns they modify, as in the examples above. Predicate adjectives, however, follow linking verbs and describe the subject.

EXAMPLE: *My friends are very intelligent.*

Be especially careful to use adjectives (not adverbs) after such linking verbs as *look, feel, grow, taste,* and *smell.*

EXAMPLE: *The weather grows cold.*

5.3 *Adverbs* modify verbs, adjectives, or other adverbs by telling *where, when, how,* or *to what extent.*

WHERE: *The children played outside.*
WHEN: *The author spoke yesterday.*
HOW: *We walked slowly behind the leader.*
TO WHAT EXTENT: *He worked very hard.*

Unlike adjectives, adverbs tend to be mobile words; they may occur in many places in sentences.

EXAMPLES: *Suddenly the wind shifted. The wind suddenly shifted. The wind shifted suddenly.*

Changing the position of adverbs within sentences can vary the rhythm in your writing.

5.4 *Adjective or Adverb* Many adverbs are formed by adding *-ly* to adjectives.

EXAMPLES: *sweet, sweetly; gentle, gently*

However, *-ly* added to a noun will usually yield an adjective.

EXAMPLES: *friend, friendly; woman, womanly*

5.5 *Comparison of Modifiers* The form of an adjective or adverb indicates the degree of comparison that the modifier expresses. Both adjectives and adverbs have three forms, or degrees: the positive, comparative, and superlative.

The positive form is used to describe individual things, groups, or actions.

EXAMPLES: *His father's hands were strong. His father was courageous.*

The comparative form is used to compare two things, groups, or actions.

EXAMPLES: *His father's hands were stronger than his own. His father was more courageous than the others.*

The superlative form is used to compare more than two things, groups, or actions.

> **EXAMPLES:** *His father's hands were the strongest in the family. His father was the most courageous of them all.*

5.6 **Regular Comparisons** One-syllable and some two-syllable adjectives and adverbs form their comparative and superlative forms by adding *-er* or *-est.* All three-syllable and most two-syllable modifiers form their comparative and superlative by using *more* or *most.*

Positive	Comparative	Superlative
small	smaller	smallest
thin	thinner	thinnest
sleepy	sleepier	sleepiest
useless	more useless	most useless
precisely	more precisely	most precisely

WATCH OUT! Note that spelling changes must sometimes be made to form the comparative and superlative of modifiers.

> **EXAMPLES:** *friendly, friendlier* (change *y* to *i* and add the ending)
> *sad, sadder* (double the final consonant and add the ending)

5.7 **Irregular Comparisons** Some commonly used modifiers have irregular comparative and superlative forms. You may wish to memorize them.

Positive	Comparative	Superlative
good	better	best
bad	worse	worst
far	farther or further	farthest or furthest
little	less or lesser	least
many	more	most
well	better	best
much	more	most

5.8 **Using Modifiers Correctly** Study the tips that follow to avoid common mistakes.

Farther and Further *Farther* is used for distances; use *further* for everything else.

Avoiding double comparisons You make a comparison by using *-er/-est* or by using *more/most.* Using *-er* with *more* or using *-est* with *most* is incorrect.

> **INCORRECT:** *I like her more better than she likes me.*
> **CORRECT:** *I like her better than she likes me.*

Avoiding illogical comparisons An illogical or confusing comparison results if two unrelated things are compared or if something is compared with itself. The word *other* or the word *else* should be used in a comparison of an individual member with the rest of the group.

> **ILLOGICAL:** *The narrator was more curious about the war than any student in his class.* (Was the narrator a student in his class?)
> **LOGICAL:** *The narrator was more curious about the war than any other student in his class.*

Bad vs. Badly *Bad,* always an adjective, is used before nouns or after linking verbs to describe the subject. *Badly,* always an adverb, never modifies a noun. Be sure to use the right form after a linking verb.

> **INCORRECT:** *Ed felt badly after his team lost.*
> **CORRECT:** *Ed felt bad after his team lost.*

Good vs. Well *Good* is always an adjective. It is used before nouns or after a linking verb to modify the subject. *Well* is often an adverb meaning "expertly" or "properly." *Well* can also be used as an adjective after a linking verb, when it means "in good health."

> **INCORRECT:** *Helen writes very good.*
> **CORRECT:** *Helen writes very well.*
> **CORRECT:** *Yesterday I felt bad; today I feel well.*

Double negatives If you add a negative word to a sentence that is already negative, the result will be an error known as a double negative. When using *not* or *-n't* with a verb, use *"any-"* words, such as *anybody* or *anything,* rather than *"no-"* words, such as *nobody* or *nothing,* later in the sentence.

> **INCORRECT**: *I don't have no money.*
> **CORRECT**: *I don't have any money.*
>
> **INCORRECT**: *We haven't seen nobody.*
> **CORRECT**: *We haven't seen anybody.*

Using *hardly, barely,* or *scarcely* after a negative word is also incorrect.

> **INCORRECT**: *They couldn't barely see two feet ahead.*
> **CORRECT**: *They could barely see two feet ahead.*

Misplaced modifiers A misplaced modifier is one placed so far away from the word it modifies that the intended meaning of the sentence is unclear. Place modifiers as close as possible to the words they modify.

> **MISPLACED**: *We found the child in the park who was missing.* (The child was missing, not the park.)
>
> **CLEARER**: *We found the child who was missing in the park.*

GRAMMAR PRACTICE

Choose the correct word from each pair in parentheses.

1. *The House on Mango Street* gives (better/more better) insights into Mexican-American culture than any other book I've read.
2. Sandra Cisneros's family moved so often that she hardly had (any/no) friends.
3. She felt (bad, badly) that she didn't live in a perfect house like the ones she saw on TV.
4. When she went to graduate school, there wasn't (anybody, nobody) like her there.
5. Living in such a different culture made her feel so (bad, badly) that she could hardly talk about it.
6. Cisneros realized that she hadn't (ever/never) read a book about a house like her own.
7. She decided to write about things that (no one/no one else) in her class knew about.

8. She searched for the (ugliest/most ugliest) subjects she could find.
9. Now Cisneros feels (good, well) about her "otherness"—her difference from other people.
10. She is glad when people tell her that her book describes their own lives (clear/clearly).

6.1 ***Prepositions*** A preposition is a word used to show the relationship between a noun or a pronoun and another word in the sentence.

Commonly Used Prepositions			
above	down	near	through
at	for	of	to
before	from	on	up
below	in	out	with
by	into	over	without

The preposition is always followed by a word or group of words that serve as its object. The preposition, its object, and modifiers of the object are called the **prepositional phrase.** In each example below, the prepositional phrase is underlined and the object of the preposition is in boldface type.

> **EXAMPLES**
> *The future of the entire **kingdom** is uncertain.*
> *We searched through the deepest **woods.***

Prepositional phrases may be used as adjectives or as adverbs. The phrase in the first example is used as an adjective modifying the noun *future.* In the second example, the phrase is used as an adverb modifying the verb *searched.*

WATCH OUT! Prepositional phrases must be as close as possible to the word they modify.

> **MISPLACED**: *We have clothes for leisure wear of many colors.*
> **CLEARER**: *We have clothes of many colors for leisure wear.*

6.2 Conjunctions A conjunction is a word used to connect words, phrases, or sentences. There are three kinds of conjunctions: **coordinating conjunctions, correlative conjunctions,** and **subordinating conjunctions.**

Coordinating conjunctions connect words or word groups that have the same function in a sentence. These include *and, but, or, for, so, yet,* and *nor.*

Coordinating conjunctions can join nouns, pronouns, verbs, adjectives, adverbs, prepositional phrases, and clauses in a sentence.

These examples show coordinating conjunctions joining words of the same function:

EXAMPLES

I have many friends but few enemies. (two noun objects)

We ran out the door and into the street. (two prepositional phrases)

They are pleasant yet seem aloof. (two predicates)

We have to go now, or we will be late. (two clauses)

Correlative conjunctions are similar to coordinating conjunctions. However, correlative conjunctions are always used in pairs.

Correlative Conjunctions

both . . . and	neither . . . nor	whether . . . or
either . . . or	not only . . . but also	

Subordinating conjunctions introduce subordinate clauses—clauses that cannot stand by themselves as complete sentences. The subordinating conjunction shows how the subordinate clause relates to the rest of the sentence. The relationships include time, manner, place, cause, comparison, condition, and purpose.

SUBORDINATING CONJUNCTIONS

TIME	*after, as, as long as, as soon as, before, since, until, when, whenever, while*
MANNER	*as, as if*
PLACE	*where, wherever*
CAUSE	*because, since*
COMPARISON	*as, as much as, than*
CONDITION	*although, as long as, even if, even though, if, provided that, though, unless, while*
PURPOSE	*in order that, so that, that*

In the example below, the boldface word is the conjunction, and the underlined words are called a subordinate clause:

EXAMPLE: *I recall his advice **whenever** I must make a hard decision.*

I recall his advice is an independent clause because it can stand alone as a complete sentence. *Whenever I must make a hard decision* cannot stand alone as a complete sentence; it is a subordinate clause.

Conjunctive adverbs are used to connect clauses that can stand by themselves as sentences. Conjunctive adverbs include *also, besides, finally, however, moreover, nevertheless, otherwise,* and *then.*

EXAMPLE: *She loved the fall; however, she also enjoyed winter.*

6.3 Interjections are words used to show strong emotion, such as *wow* and *cool.* Often followed by an exclamation point, they have no grammatical relationship to the rest of a sentence.

EXAMPLE: *You've written ten poems? Wow!*

GRAMMAR PRACTICE

Label each of the boldfaced words as a preposition, conjunction, or interjection.

1. Elena lived **in** Patterson, New Jersey, **near** streets named Straight and Narrow.
2. She didn't like school, **although** she liked to read.
3. **While** she read by her window, she could watch the people in the house **below** the fire escape.
4. Then after the old man died, the house **where** the older couple had lived was vacant for weeks.
5. **When** Eugene's family moved **into** the house, Elena liked him because he read books, too.
6. She **and** Eugene wanted to study American history.
7. **As soon as** she got home **from** school, she prepared to visit Eugene.
8. **Stop!** Don't go out **because** Kennedy has died.
9. She knew something dreadful had happened, **yet** she wanted to see her new friend.

7 Quick Reference: The Sentence and Its Parts

The diagrams that follow will give you a brief review of the essentials of the sentence—subjects and predicates—and of some of its parts.

The speaker's **pockets** **bulged** with oranges.

The **complete subject** includes all the words that identify the person, place, thing, or idea that the sentence is about.

The **complete predicate** includes all the words that tell or ask something about the subject.

pockets

bulged

The **simple subject** tells exactly whom or what the sentence is about. It may be one word or a group of words, but it does not include modifiers.

The **simple predicate**, or **verb**, tells what the subject does or is. It may be one word or several, but it does not include modifiers.

At the drug store, an understanding clerk **had given** the speaker **a chocolate bar.**

A **prepositional phrase** consists of a preposition, its object, and any modifiers of the object. In this phrase, *at* is the preposition and *drug store* is its object.

subject

A **direct object** is a word or group of words that tells who or what receives the action of the verb in the sentence.

Verbs often have more than one part. They may be made up of a **main verb,** like *given,* and one or more **auxiliary,** or **helping, verbs,** like *had.*

An **indirect object** is a word or a group of words that tells *to whom* or *for whom* or *to what* or *for what* about the verb. A sentence can have an indirect object only if it has a direct object. The indirect object always comes before the direct object in a sentence.

8 The Sentence and Its Parts

A sentence is a group of words used to express a complete thought. A complete sentence has a subject and predicate.

8.1 Kinds of Sentences

Sentences make statements, ask questions, give commands, and show feelings. There are four basic types of sentences.

Type	Definition	Example
Declarative	states a fact, wish, intent, or feeling	Audre Lorde understands youths.
Interrogative	asks a question	Did you read "Hanging Fire"?
Imperative	gives a command, direction	Read the poem.
Exclamatory	expresses strong feeling or excitement	The poem is amazing!

WRITING TIP One way to vary your writing is to employ a variety of different types of sentences. In the first example below, each sentence is declarative. Notice how much more interesting the revised paragraph is.

SAMPLE PARAGRAPH: *You have to see Niagara Falls in person. You can truly appreciate their awesome power in no other way. You should visit them on your next vacation. They are a spectacular sight.*

REVISED PARAGRAPH: *Have you ever seen Niagara Falls in person? You can truly appreciate their awesome power in no other way. Visit them on your next vacation. What a spectacular sight they are!*

WATCH OUT! Conversation frequently includes parts of sentences, or **fragments.** In formal writing, however, you need to be sure that every sentence is a complete thought and includes a subject and predicate. (See Correcting Fragments, page 1197.)

8.2 Complete Subjects and Predicates

A sentence has two parts: a subject and a predicate. The complete subject includes all the words that identify the person, place, thing, or idea that the sentence is about. The complete predicate includes all the words that tell what the subject did or what happened to the subject.

Complete Subject	Complete Predicate
The poets of the time	wrote about nature.
This new approach	was extraordinary.

8.3 Simple Subjects and Predicates

The simple subject is the key word in the complete subject. The simple predicate is the key word in the complete predicate. In the examples that follow, they are underlined.

Simple Subject	Simple Predicate
The poets of the time	wrote about nature.
This new approach	was extraordinary.

8.4 Compound Subjects and Predicates

A compound subject consists of two or more subjects that share the same verb. They are typically joined by the coordinating conjunction *and* or *or*.

EXAMPLE: *A short story or novel will keep you engaged.*

A compound predicate consists of two or more predicates that share the same subject. They, too, are usually joined by the coordinating conjunction *and, but,* or *or*.

EXAMPLE: *The class finished all the poetry but did not read the short stories.*

8.5 Subjects and Predicates in Questions

In many interrogative sentences, the subject may appear after the verb or between parts of a verb phrase.

INTERROGATIVE: *Was Shakespeare a poet as well as a playwright?*
INTERROGATIVE: *Why has this poem been quoted many times?*

8.6 **Subjects and Predicates in Imperative Sentences** Imperative sentences give commands, requests, or directions. The subject of an imperative sentence is the person spoken to, or *you*. While it is not stated, it is understood to be *you*.

> EXAMPLE: *(You) Please tell me what you're thinking.*

8.7 **Subjects in Sentences That Begin with There and Here** When a sentence begins with *there* or *here*, the subject usually follows the verb. Remember that *there* and *here* are never the subjects of a sentence. The simple subjects in the example sentences are underlined.

> EXAMPLES
> *Here is the solution to the mystery.*
> *There is no time to waste now.*
> *There were too many passengers on the boat.*

GRAMMAR PRACTICE

Copy each of the following sentences. Then draw one line under the complete subject and two under the complete predicate.

1. Melissa's mother had been sick a long time.
2. There were many arrangements to make before driving to the funeral.
3. Melissa nibbles at her sandwich and leaves the milk glass half full.
4. Carnations and chrysanthemums and gladioli decorate Cousin Jessie's casket.
5. The four teenagers will go to get burgers and then sit by the river after the visitation.
6. Why does Melissa's father let her go out?
7. Don't stay out past 11 o'clock.
8. On the way to the funeral, Mama, Daddy, Cousin Roy, and Buddy rode in the back seat of the limousine.
9. What should the narrator say to the grieving people?
10. Melissa and the narrator will be close friends.

8.8 **Complements** A complement is a word or group of words that completes the meaning of the sentence. Some sentences contain only a subject and a verb. Most sentences, however, require additional words placed after the verb to complete the meaning of the sentence. There are three kinds of complements: **direct objects, indirect objects,** and **subject complements.**

Direct objects are words or word groups that receive the action of action verbs. A direct object answers the question *what?* or *whom?* In the examples that follow, the direct objects are underlined.

> EXAMPLES
> *The students asked many questions.*
> (asked what?)
>
> *The teacher quickly answered them.*
> (answered what?)
>
> *The school accepted girls and boys.*
> (accepted whom?)

Indirect objects tell *to* or *for whom* or *what* the action of the verb is performed. Indirect objects come before direct objects. In the examples that follow, the indirect objects are underlined.

> EXAMPLES
> *My sister usually gave her friends good advice.* (gave to whom?)
>
> *Her brother sent the post office a heavy package.* (sent to what?)
>
> *His kind grandfather mailed him a new tie.*
> (mailed to whom?)

Subject complements come after linking verbs and identify or describe the subject. Subject complements that name or identify the subject of the sentence are called **predicate nominatives.** These include **predicate nouns** and **predicate pronouns.** In the examples that follow, the subject complements are underlined.

> EXAMPLES
> *My friends are very hard workers.*
> *The best writer in the class is she.*

Other subject complements describe the subject of the sentence. These are called **predicate adjectives.**

EXAMPLE: *The pianist appeared very _energetic_.*

Write all of the complements in the following sentences, and label them as direct objects, indirect objects, predicate nouns, predicate pronouns, or predicate adjectives.

1. Jack London was a writer and an adventurer.
2. As a young man, London worked and got an education.
3. He traveled the world.
4. When the Klondike Gold Rush began in 1897, London was eager to go.
5. Old timers told London stories of the North.
6. The experiences gave him ideas for many novels and stories.
7. One of Jack London's most famous stories is "To Build a Fire."
8. This story is characteristic of London's stories of the North.
9. London wrote 50 books before dying at age 40.
10. He was one of the most popular writers of his time.

⑨ Phrases

A phrase is a group of related words that does not have a subject and predicate and functions in a sentence as a single part of speech.

9.1 **Prepositional Phrases** A prepositional phrase is a phrase that consists of a preposition, its object, and any modifiers of the object. Prepositional phrases that modify nouns or pronouns are called **adjective phrases.** Prepositional phrases that modify a verb, an adjective, or another adverb are **adverb phrases.**

> **ADJECTIVE PHRASE:** *The central character _of the story_ is a wicked villain.*
> **ADVERB PHRASE:** *He reveals his nature _in the first scene_.*

9.2 **Appositives and Appositive Phrases** An appositive is a noun or pronoun that usually comes directly after another noun or pronoun and identifies or provides further information about that word. An appositive phrase includes the appositive and all its modifiers. In the following examples, the appositive phrases are underlined.

> **EXAMPLES**
> *The book is about Richard Wright, _a famous writer_. The book, _an autobiography_, tells how he began writing.*

Occasionally, an appositive phrase may precede the noun it tells about.

> **EXAMPLE:** *_A famous writer_, Richard Wright grew up in poverty.*

⑩ Verbals and Verbal Phrases

A verbal is a verb form that is used as a noun, an adjective, or an adverb. A verbal phrase consists of a verbal, all its modifiers, and all its complements. There are three kinds of verbals: infinitives, participles, and gerunds.

10.1 **Infinitives and Infinitive Phrases** An infinitive is a verb form that usually begins with *to* and functions as a noun, adjective, or adverb. The infinitive and its modifiers constitute an infinitive phrase. The examples that follow show several uses of infinitives and infinitive phrases. Each infinitive phrase is underlined.

> **NOUN:** *_To know her_ is my only desire.* (subject)
> *I'm planning _to walk with you_.* (direct object)
> *Her goal was _to promote women's rights_.* (predicate nominative)
> **ADJECTIVE:** *We saw his need _to be loved_.* (adjective modifying *need*)
> **ADVERB:** *She wrote _to voice her opinions_.* (adverb modifying *wrote*)

Like verbs themselves, infinitives can take objects (*her* in the first noun example), be made passive (*to be loved* in the adjective example), and take modifiers (*with you* in the adverb example).

Because *to*, the sign of the infinitive, precedes infinitives, it is usually easy to recognize them. However, sometimes *to* may be omitted.

> EXAMPLE: *Let no one dare [to] <u>enter this shrine</u>.*

10.2 *Participles and Participial Phrases*

A participle is a verb form that functions as an adjective. Like adjectives, participles modify nouns and pronouns. Most participles use the present participle form, ending in *-ing*, or the past participle form, ending in *-ed* or *-en*. In the examples below, the participles are underlined.

> MODIFYING A NOUN: *The <u>dying</u> man had a smile on his face.*
> MODIFYING A PRONOUN: *<u>Frustrated</u>, everyone abandoned the cause.*

Participial phrases are participles with all their modifiers and complements.

> MODIFYING A NOUN: *The dogs <u>searching for survivors</u> are well trained.*
> MODIFYING A PRONOUN: *<u>Having approved your proposal</u>, we are ready to act.*

10.3 *Dangling and Misplaced Participles*

A participle or participial phrase should be placed as close as possible to the word that it modifies. Otherwise the meaning of the sentence may not be clear.

> MISPLACED: *The boys were looking for squirrels <u>searching the trees</u>.*
> CLEARER: *The boys <u>searching the trees</u> were looking for squirrels.*

A participle or participial phrase that does not clearly modify anything in a sentence is called a **dangling participle.** A dangling participle causes confusion because it appears to modify a word that it cannot sensibly modify.

Correct a dangling participle by providing a word for the participle to modify.

> CONFUSING: *<u>Running like the wind</u>, my hat fell off.* (The hat wasn't running.)
> CLEARER: *<u>Running like the wind</u>, I lost my hat.*

10.4 *Gerunds and Gerund Phrases*

A gerund is a verb form ending in *-ing* that functions as a noun. Gerunds may perform any function nouns perform.

> SUBJECT: *<u>Running</u> is my favorite pastime.*
> DIRECT OBJECT: *I truly love <u>running</u>.*
> SUBJECT COMPLEMENT: *My deepest passion is <u>running</u>.*
> OBJECT OF PREPOSITION: *Her love of <u>running</u> keeps her strong.*

Gerund phrases are gerunds with all their modifiers and complements. The gerund phrases are underlined in the following examples.

> SUBJECT: *<u>Wishing on a star</u> never got me far.*
> OBJECT OF PREPOSITION: *I will finish before <u>leaving the office.</u>*
> APPOSITIVE: *Her avocation, <u>flying airplanes,</u> finally led to full-time employment.*

GRAMMAR PRACTICE

Identify the underlined phrases as appositive phrases, infinitive phrases, participial phrases, or gerund phrases.

1. "Daughter of Invention," <u>a short story</u>, was written by Julia Alvarez.
2. The narrator loves <u>to write about her experiences</u>.
3. She has been asked <u>to give a speech</u>.
4. <u>Working feverishly for hours</u>, she finally finishes her speech.
5. <u>Standing before the bed</u>, she reads the speech to her parents.
6. Her father rages at her for <u>insulting her teachers</u>.
7. <u>Seeing her speech in torn-up pieces</u> makes her weep.

11 Clauses

A clause is a group of words that contains a subject and a verb. There are two kinds of clauses: independent clauses and subordinate clauses.

11.1 *Independent and Subordinate Clauses*

An independent clause can stand alone as a sentence, as the word *independent* suggests.

INDEPENDENT CLAUSE: *Taos is famous for its Great Bank Robbery.*

A sentence may contain more than one independent clause.

EXAMPLE: *Many people remember the robbery, and they will tell you all about it.*

In the example above, the coordinating conjunction *and* joins the two independent clauses.

A subordinate clause cannot stand alone as a sentence. It is subordinate to, or dependent on, the main clause.

EXAMPLE: *Although the two men needed cash, they didn't get it from the bank.*

Although the two men needed cash cannot stand by itself.

11.2 *Adjective Clauses*

An adjective clause is a subordinate clause used as an adjective. It usually follows the noun or pronoun it modifies.

EXAMPLE: *Tony Hillerman is someone whom millions know as a mystery writer.*

Adjective clauses are typically introduced by the relative pronouns *who, whom, whose, which,* and *that* (see Relative Pronouns, page 1183). In the examples that follow, the adjective clauses are underlined.

EXAMPLES

A person who needs money should get a job.

The robbers, whose names were Gomez and Smith, had guns.

The robber needed a disguise that would fool Taos's residents.

WATCH OUT! The relative pronouns *whom, which,* and *that* may sometimes be omitted when they are objects of their own clauses.

EXAMPLE: *Hillerman is a writer [whom] millions enjoy.*

11.3 *Adverb Clauses*

An adverb clause is a subordinate clause that is used as an adverb to modify a verb, an adjective, or another adverb. It is introduced by a subordinating conjunction (see Subordinating Conjunctions, page 1189).

Adverb clauses typically occur at the beginning or end of sentences. The clauses are underlined in these examples.

MODIFYING A VERB: *When we need you, we will call.*

MODIFYING AN ADVERB: *I'll stay here where there is shelter from the rain.*

MODIFYING AN ADJECTIVE: *Roman felt good when he finished his essay.*

11.4 *Noun Clauses*

A noun clause is a subordinate clause that is used in a sentence as a noun. A noun clause may be used as a subject, a direct object, an indirect object, a predicate nominative, or an object of a preposition. Noun clauses are often introduced by pronouns such as *that, what, who, whoever, which,* and *whose,* and by subordinating conjunctions, such as *how, when, where, why,* and *whether.* (See Subordinating Conjunctions, page 1189.)

USAGE TIP Because the same words may introduce adjective and noun clauses, you need to consider how the clause functions within its sentence.

To determine if a clause is a noun clause, try substituting *something* or *someone* for the clause. If you can do it, it is probably a noun clause.

EXAMPLES: *I know whose woods these are.* ("I know something." The clause is a noun clause, direct object of the verb *know.*)

Give a copy to whoever wants one. ("Give a copy to someone." The clause is a noun clause, object of the preposition *to.*)

Identify each underlined clause as an adjective clause, an adverb clause, or a noun clause.

1. The sheriff investigated whether the killer was Mrs. Wright or an intruder.
2. Did Mrs. Hale, who was Mrs. Wright's neighbor, feel guilty for not visiting her?
3. When Mrs. Hale saw the empty bird cage, she wondered what had become of the bird.
4. The two women decided to hide the dead canary, which was in a box, from the sheriff.
5. The sheriff and county attorney think that Mrs. Wright killed her husband.

12 The Structure of Sentences

When classified by their structure, there are four kinds of sentences: simple, compound, complex, and compound-complex.

12.1 Simple Sentences A simple sentence is a sentence that has one independent clause and no subordinate clauses. The fact that such sentences are called "simple" does not mean that they are uncomplicated. Various parts of simple sentences may be compound, and they may contain grammatical structures such as appositives and verbals.

EXAMPLES

Ray Bradbury, a science fiction writer, has written short stories and novels. (appositive and compound direct object)

The narrator, recalling the years of his childhood, told his story. (participial phrase)

12.2 Compound Sentences A compound sentence has two or more independent clauses. The clauses are joined together with a comma and a coordinating conjunction (*and, but, or, nor, yet, for, so*), a semicolon, or a conjunctive adverb with a semicolon. Like simple sentences, compound sentences do not contain any dependent clauses.

EXAMPLES

I enjoyed Bradbury's story "The Utterly Perfect Murder," and I want to read more of his stories.

The narrator had lived a normal, complete life; however, he decided to kill his childhood playmate.

WATCH OUT! Do not confuse compound sentences with simple sentences that have compound parts.

EXAMPLE: *A subcommittee drafted a document and immediately presented it to the entire group.* (here *and* signals a compound predicate, not a compound sentence)

12.3 Complex Sentences A complex sentence has one independent clause and one or more subordinate clauses. Each subordinate clause can be used as a noun or as a modifier. If it is used as a modifier, a subordinate clause usually modifies a word in the main clause, and the main clause can stand alone. However, when a subordinate clause is a noun clause, it is a part of the independent clause; the two cannot be separated.

MODIFIER: *One should not complain, unless she or he has a better solution.*

NOUN CLAUSE: *We sketched pictures of whomever we wished.* (noun clause is the object of the preposition *of* and cannot be separated from the rest of the sentence)

12.4 Compound-Complex Sentences A compound-complex sentence has two or more independent clauses and one or more subordinate clauses. Compound-complex sentences are, simply, both compound and complex. If you start with a compound sentence, all you need to do to form a compound-complex sentence is add a subordinate clause.

COMPOUND: *All the students knew the answer, yet they were too shy to volunteer.*

COMPOUND-COMPLEX: *All the students knew the answer that their teacher expected, yet they were too shy to volunteer.*

GRAMMAR PRACTICE

Label each of the following sentences simple, compound, complex, or compound-complex.

1. Recovering from a nervous condition, Framton Nuttel moved to the country and visited his neighbors.

2. A young woman meets him when he first arrives at the house.

3. Framton knows few people in the neighborhood, and the young woman tells him about the death of her uncles.

4. Framton visits with Mrs. Sappleton and her niece until he sees three men crossing the lawn; then he flees from the house.

5. Nuttel believed that the hunters had died three years ago.

⓭ Writing Complete Sentences

A sentence is a group of words that expresses a complete thought. In writing that you wish to share with a reader, try to avoid both sentence fragments and run-on sentences.

⓭.1 **Correcting Fragments** A sentence fragment is a group of words that is only part of a sentence. It does not express a complete thought and may be confusing to the reader or the listener. A sentence fragment may be lacking a subject, a predicate, or both.

FRAGMENT: *waited for the boat to arrive* (no subject)

CORRECTED: *We waited for the boat to arrive.*

FRAGMENT: *people of various races, ages, and creeds* (no predicate)

CORRECTED: *People of various races, ages, and creeds gathered together.*

FRAGMENT: *near the old cottage* (neither subject nor predicate)

CORRECTED: *The burial ground is near the old cottage.*

In your own writing, fragments are usually the result of haste or incorrect punctuation. Sometimes fixing a fragment will be a matter of attaching it to a preceding or following sentence.

FRAGMENT: *We saw the two girls. Waiting for the bus to arrive.*

CORRECTED: *We saw the two girls waiting for the bus to arrive.*

FRAGMENT: *Newspapers appeal to a wide audience. Including people of various races, ages, and creeds.*

CORRECTED: *Newspapers appeal to a wide audience, including people of various races, ages, and creeds.*

⓭.2 **Correcting Run-on Sentences**

A run-on sentence is made up of two or more sentences written as though they were one. Some run-ons have no punctuation within them. Others may use only a comma where a conjunction or stronger punctuation is necessary. Use your judgment in correcting run-on sentences, as you have choices. You can make two sentences if the thoughts are not closely connected. If the thoughts are closely related, you can keep the run-on as one sentence by adding a semicolon or a conjunction.

RUN-ON: *We found a place by a small pond for the picnic it is three miles from the village.*

MAKE TWO SENTENCES: *We found a place by a small pond for the picnic. It is three miles from the village.*

RUN-ON: *We found a place by a small pond for the picnic it was perfect.*

USE A SEMICOLON: *We found a place by a small pond for the picnic; it was perfect.*

ADD A CONJUNCTION: *We found a place by a small pond for the picnic, and it was perfect.*

WATCH OUT! When you add a conjunction, make sure you use appropriate punctuation before it: a comma for a coordinating conjunction, a semicolon for a conjunctive adverb. (See Conjunctions, page 1189.) A very common mistake is to use a comma instead of a conjunction or an end mark. This error is called a **comma splice**.

INCORRECT: *He finished the apprenticeship, then he left the village.*

CORRECT: *He finished the apprenticeship, and then he left the village.*

GRAMMAR PRACTICE

Rewrite the following paragraph, correcting all fragments and run-ons.

In "A Christmas Memory," Truman Capote. He tells the story of two best friends. Although one is seven years old and the other is more than sixty. Both are children. Spend all their time together. They make fruitcakes they cut a Christmas tree and decorate it they fly kites. Soon, however, time pulls them apart. He goes off to military school she stays home alone, although she lives with relatives.

⑭ Subject-Verb Agreement

The subject and verb of a sentence must agree in number. Agreement means that when the subject is singular, the verb must be singular; when the subject is plural, the verb must be plural.

14.1 **Basic Agreement** Fortunately, agreement between subject and verb in English is simple. Most verbs show the difference between singular and plural only in the third person present tense. The present tense of the third person singular ends in *-s*.

Present Tense Verb Forms	
Singular	**Plural**
I sleep	we sleep
you sleep	you sleep
she, he, it sleeps	they sleep

14.2 **Agreement with Be** The verb *be* presents special problems in agreement because this verb does not follow the usual verb patterns.

Forms of *Be*			
Present Tense		**Past Tense**	
Singular	**Plural**	**Singular**	**Plural**
I am	we are	I was	we were
you are	you are	you were	you were
she, he, it is	they are	she, he, it was	they were

14.3 **Words Between Subject and Verb** A verb agrees only with its subject. When words come between a subject and its verb, ignore them when considering proper agreement. Identify the subject and make sure the verb agrees with it.

EXAMPLES

A story in the newspapers tells about the 1890s.

Dad as well as Mom reads the paper daily.

14.4 **Agreement with Compound Subjects** Use a plural verb with most compound subjects joined by the word *and*.

EXAMPLE: *My father and his friends read the paper daily.*

You could substitute the plural pronoun *they* for *my father and his friends*. This shows that you need a plural verb.

If the compound subject is thought of as a unit, you use the singular verb. Test this by substituting the singular pronoun *it*.

EXAMPLE: *Peanut butter and jelly [it] is my brother's favorite sandwich.*

Use a singular verb with a compound subject that is preceded by *each, every,* or *many a*.

EXAMPLE: *Each novel and short story seems grounded in personal experience.*

With *or, nor,* and the correlative conjunctions *either . . . or* and *neither . . . nor,* make the verb agree with the noun or pronoun nearest the verb.

EXAMPLES

Cookies or ice cream is my favorite dessert.

Either Cheryl or her friends are being invited.

Neither ice storms nor snow is predicted today.

14.5 **Personal Pronouns as Subjects** When using a personal pronoun as a subject, make sure to match it with the correct form of the verb *be*. (See the chart in 14.2.) Note especially that the pronoun *you* takes the verbs *are* and *were*, regardless of whether it is referring to the singular *you* or to the plural *you*.

WATCH OUT! *You is* and *you was* are nonstandard forms and should be avoided in writing and speaking. *We was* and *they was* are also forms to be avoided.

> **INCORRECT:** *You was a good student.*
> *They was starting a new school.*
> **CORRECT:** *You were a good student.*
> *They were starting a new school.*

14.6 *Indefinite Pronouns as Subjects*

Some indefinite pronouns are always singular; some are always plural. Others may be either singular or plural.

Singular Indefinite Pronouns			
another	either	neither	other
anybody	everybody	nobody	somebody
anyone	everyone	no one	someone
anything	everything	nothing	something
each	much	one	

> **EXAMPLES**
> *Each of the writers was given an award.*
> *Somebody in the room upstairs is sleeping.*

The indefinite pronouns that are always plural include *both, few, many*, and *several*. These take plural verbs.

> **EXAMPLES**
> *Many of the books in our library are not in circulation.*
>
> *Few have been returned recently.*

Still other indefinite pronouns may be either singular or plural.

Singular or Plural Indefinite Pronouns			
all	enough	most	plenty
any	more	none	some

The number of the indefinite pronouns *any* and *none* depends on the intended meaning.

> **EXAMPLES**
> *Any of these topics has potential for a good article.* (any one topic)
>
> *Any of these topics have potential for a good article.* (all of the many topics)

The indefinite pronouns *all, some, more, most,* and *none* are singular when they refer to a quantity or part of something. They are plural when they refer to a number of individual things. Context will usually give a clue.

> **EXAMPLES**
> *All of the flour is gone.* (referring to a quantity)
>
> *All of the flowers are gone.* (referring to individual items)

14.7 *Inverted Sentences* Problems in agreement often occur in inverted sentences beginning with *here* or *there*; in questions beginning with *why, where*, and *what*; and in inverted sentences beginning with a phrase. Identify the subject—wherever it is—before deciding on the verb.

> **EXAMPLES**
> *There clearly are far too many cooks in this kitchen.*
>
> *What is the correct ingredient for this stew?*
>
> *Far from the embroiled cooks stands the master chef.*

GRAMMAR PRACTICE

Locate the subject of each clause in the sentences below. Then choose the correct verb.

1. Many Greeks sail home from Troy, but few (struggles/struggle) as hard as Odysseus to get there.

2. Neither Odysseus nor his men (know/knows) what dangers lie ahead.

3. There (is/are) more dangers awaiting him than there (is/are) gods to save him.

4. Everybody who has read about Odysseus' trials (knows/know) what he endured.

5. There (is/are) few friends who can help him during his ten-year odyssey.

6. The herds of the Cyclops Polyphemus (gives/give) Odysseus an idea for escape.

7. Does anyone (escapes/escape) the spell of Circe?

8. Standing before the hogs that are his friends (is/are) Odysseus.

9. Some of the winds (blows/blow) favorably, but many (blows/blow) ill.

10. Penelope, Telemachus, and the suitors (awaits/await) Odysseus upon his return.

14.8 Sentences with Predicate Nominatives

When a predicate nominative serves as a complement in a sentence, use a verb that agrees with the subject, not the complement.

EXAMPLES

The speeches of Martin Luther King, Jr., are a landmark in American civil rights history. (*Speeches* is the subject—not *landmark*—and it takes the plural verb *are.*)

A landmark in American civil rights is the speeches of Martin Luther King, Jr. (The subject is the singular noun, *landmark.*)

14.9 Don't *and* Doesn't *as Auxiliary Verbs*

The auxiliary verb *doesn't* is used with singular subjects and with the personal pronouns *she, he,* and *it.* The auxiliary verb *don't* is used with plural subjects and with the personal pronouns *I, we, you,* and *they.*

SINGULAR

She doesn't know Martin Luther King's famous "I Have a Dream" speech.
Doesn't the young woman read very much?

PLURAL

We don't have the speech memorized.
Don't speakers usually memorize their speeches?

14.10 Collective Nouns as Subjects

Collective nouns are singular nouns that name a group of persons or things. *Team,* for example, is the collective name of a group of individuals. A collective noun takes a singular verb when the group acts as a single unit. It takes a plural verb when the members of the group act separately.

EXAMPLES

Our team usually wins. (the team as a whole wins)

Our team vote differently on most issues. (the individual members vote)

14.11 Relative Pronouns as Subjects

When a relative pronoun is used as a subject of its clause—*who, which,* and *that* can serve as subjects—the verb of the clause must agree in number with the antecedent of the pronoun.

SINGULAR: *I didn't read the poem about fireworks that was assigned.*

The antecedent of the relative pronoun *that* is the singular *poem;* therefore, *that* is singular and must take the singular verb *was.*

PLURAL: *William Blake and Amy Lowell, who are very different from each other, are both outstanding poets.*

The antecedent of the relative pronoun *who* is the plural compound subject *William Blake and Amy Lowell.* Therefore *who* is plural, and it takes the plural verb *are.*

GRAMMAR PRACTICE

Choose the correct verb for each of the following sentences.

1. (Don't/Doesn't) the play "The Devil and Daniel Webster" end happily?
2. The crowd of merrymakers (congratulate/congratulates) the newlyweds.
3. The fiddler who (confront/confronts) Scratch is chased away.
4. One problem with the trial (is, are) the prejudiced members of the jury.
5. A jury of the dead (hear/hears) the case of Jabez.
6. Scratch (don't/doesn't) know how clever Daniel Webster can be.
7. The objections of Webster (is/are) only a nuisance to Scratch.
8. Daniel Webster asks the jury why they (don't/doesn't) take pity on Jabez.
9. Jabez and Mary, who love each other dearly, (survive/survives) the ordeal.
10. Jabez is probably only one of many people who (is/are) tricked by Scratch.

Quick Reference: Punctuation

Punctuation	Function	Examples
End Marks period, question mark, exclamation point	to end sentences	We can start now. When would you like to leave? What a fantastic hit!
	initials and other abbreviations	Mrs. Dorothy Parker, C. P. Cavafy, McDougal Littell Inc., P.M., A.D., lbs., oz., Blvd., Dr.

	items in outlines	I. Volcanoes
		   A. Central-vent
		      1. Shield

	exception: P.O. states	NE (Nebraska), NV (Nevada)
Commas	before conjunction in compound sentence	I have never disliked poetry, but now I really love it.
	items in a series	She is brave, loyal, and kind. The slow, easy route is best.
	words of address	Maria, how can I help you? You must do something, soldier.
	parenthetical expressions	Well, just suppose that we can't? Hard workers, as you know, don't quit. I'm not a quitter, believe me.
	introductory phrases and clauses	In the beginning of the day, I feel fresh. While she was out, I was here. Having finished my chores, I went out.
	nonessential phrases and clauses	Ed Pawn, captain of the chess team, won. Ed Pawn, who is the captain, won. The two leading runners, sprinting toward the finish line, ended in a tie.
	in dates and addresses	September 21, 2001. Mail it by May 14, 2000, to Hauptman Company, 321 Market Street, Memphis, Tennessee.
	in letter parts	Dear Jim, Sincerely yours,
	for clarity, or to avoid confusion	By noon, time had run out. What the minister does, does matter. While cooking, Jim burned his hand.
Semicolons	in compound sentences that are not joined by coordinators *and,* etc.	The last shall be first; the first shall be last. I read the Bible; however, I have not memorized it.
	with items in series that contain commas	We invited my sister, Jan; her friend, Don; my uncle Jack; and Mary Dodd.
	in compound sentences that contain commas	After I ran out of money, I called my parents; but only my sister was home, unfortunately.

Punctuation	Function	Examples
Colons	to introduce lists	**Correct:** Those we wrote were the following: Dana, John, and Will. **Incorrect:** Those we wrote were: Dana, John, and Will.
	before a long quotation	Abraham Lincoln wrote: "Four score and seven years ago, our fathers brought forth on this continent a new nation. . . ."
	after the salutation of a business letter	To Whom It May Concern: Dear Leonard Atole:
	with certain numbers	1:28 P.M., Genesis 2:5
Dashes	to indicate an abrupt break in thought	I was thinking of my mother—who is arriving tomorrow—just as you walked in.
Parentheses	to enclose less important material	It was so unlike him (John is always on time) that I began to worry. The last World Series game (Did you see it?) was fun.
Hyphens	with a compound adjective before nouns	The not-so-rich taxpayer won't stand for this!
	in compounds with *all-, ex-, self-, -elect*	The ex-firefighter helped rescue him. Our president-elect is self-conscious.
	in compound numbers (to *ninety-nine*)	Today, I turn twenty-one.
	in fractions used as adjectives	My cup is one-third full.
	between prefixes and words beginning with capital letters	Which pre-Raphaelite painter do you like best? It snowed in mid-October.
	when dividing words at the end of a line	How could you have any reasonable expec-tations of getting a new computer?
Apostrophes	to form possessives of nouns and indefinite pronouns	my friend's book, my friends' book, anyone's guess, somebody else's problem
	for omitted letters in contractions or numbers in dates	don't (omitted **o**); he'd (omitted **woul**) the class of '99 (omitted **19**)
	to form plurals of letters and numbers	I had two A's and no 2's on my report card.
Quotation Marks	to set off a speaker's exact words	Sara said, "I'm finally ready." "I'm ready," Sara said, "finally." Did Sara say, "I'm ready"? Sara said, "I'm ready!"
	for titles of stories, short poems, essays, songs, book chapters	I liked McLean's "Marine Corps Issue" and Roethke's "My Papa's Waltz." I like Joplin's "Me and Bobby McGee."
Ellipses	for material omitted from a quotation	"When in the course of human events . . . and to assume among the powers of the earth. . . ."
Italics	for titles of books, plays, magazines, long poems, operas, films, TV series, names of ships	*The House on Mango Street, Hamlet, Newsweek,* the *Odyssey, Madama Butterfly, Gone with the Wind, Seinfeld,* HMS *Pinafore*

Quick Reference: Capitalization

Category/Rule	Examples
People and Titles	
Names and initials of people	**A**my **T**an, **W. H. A**uden
Titles used with or in place of names	**P**rofessor **H**olmes, **S**enator **L**ong, The **P**resident has arrived.
Deities and members of religious groups	**J**esus, **A**llah, the **B**uddha, **Z**eus, **B**aptists, **R**oman **C**atholics
Names of ethnic and national groups	**H**ispanics, **J**ews, **A**frican **A**mericans
Geographical Names	
Cities, states, countries, continents	**P**hiladelphia, **K**ansas, **J**apan, **E**urope
Regions, bodies of water, mountains	the **S**outh, **L**ake **B**aikal, **M**ount **M**cKinley
Geographic features, parks	**G**reat **B**asin, **Y**ellowstone **N**ational **P**ark
Streets and roads, planets	318 **E**ast **S**utton **D**rive, **C**harles **C**ourt, **J**upiter, **P**luto
Organizations and Events	
Companies, organizations, teams	**F**ord **M**otor **C**ompany, **B**oy **S**couts of **A**merica, **S**t. Louis **C**ardinals
Buildings, bridges, monuments	**E**mpire **S**tate **B**uilding, **E**ads **B**ridge, **W**ashington **M**onument
Documents, awards	the **D**eclaration of **I**ndependence, **S**tanley **C**up
Special named events	**M**ardi **G**ras, **W**orld **S**eries
Governmental bodies, historical periods and events	**U.S. S**enate, **H**ouse of **R**epresentatives, **M**iddle **A**ges, **V**ietnam **W**ar
Days and months, holidays	**T**hursday, **M**arch, **T**hanksgiving, **L**abor **D**ay
Specific cars, boats, trains, planes	**P**orsche, *Mississippi Queen*, *Orient Express*, **C**oncorde
Proper Adjectives	
Adjectives formed from proper nouns	**F**rench cooking, **F**reudian psychology, **E**dwardian age, **A**tlantic coast
First Words and the Pronoun *I*	
The first word in a sentence or quote	**T**his is it. **H**e said, "**L**et's go."
Complete sentence in parentheses	(**C**onsult the previous chapter.)
Salutation and closing of letters	**D**ear **M**adam, **V**ery truly yours,
First lines of most poetry The personal pronoun *I*	**T**hen am **I** **A** happy fly **I**f **I** live **O**r if **I** die.
First, last, and all important words in titles	*A **T**ale of **T**wo **C**ities*, "The **W**orld **I**s **T**oo **M**uch with **U**s"

Little Rules That Make A Big Difference

Sentences

Avoid sentence fragments. Make sure all your sentences express complete thoughts.

A sentence fragment is a group of words that does not express a grammatically complete thought. It may lack a subject, a predicate, or both. Fragments may be corrected by adding the missing element(s) or by changing the punctuation to make the fragment part of another sentence.

> **FRAGMENT:** *I read the poems of Walt Whitman. A poet who wrote about America.*
>
> **COMPLETE:** *I read the poems of Walt Whitman. He was a poet who wrote about America.* (adding a subject and a predicate)
>
> **COMPLETE:** *I read the poems of Walt Whitman, a poet who wrote about America.* (changing the punctuation)

Avoid run-on sentences. Make sure all clauses in a sentence have the proper punctuation and/or conjunctions between them.

A run-on sentence consists of two or more sentences written as though they were one or separated only by a comma. Correct run-ons by making two separate sentences, using a semicolon, adding a conjunction, or rewriting the sentence.

> **RUN-ON:** *James Galway is a great musician, he plays the flute.*
>
> **CORRECT:** *James Galway is a great musician. He plays the flute.*
>
> **CORRECT:** *James Galway is a great musician; he plays the flute.*
>
> **CORRECT:** *James Galway, who plays the flute, is a great musician.*

Use end marks correctly. Use a period, not a question mark, at the end of an indirect question.

An indirect question is a question that does not use the exact words of the original speaker. Note the difference between the following sentences, and observe that the second sentence ends in a period, not a question mark.

> **DIRECT:** *Lou asked, "What is that?"*
>
> **INDIRECT:** *Lou asked what it was.*

Do not use quotation marks with indirect quotations within a sentence.

A direct quotation uses the speaker's exact words. An indirect quotation puts the speaker's words in other words. Compare these sentences:

> **DIRECT:** *Jean said, "I'm going to be up all night writing my essay."* (quotation marks appropriate)
>
> **INDIRECT:** *Jean said that she was going to be up all night writing her essay.* (no quotation marks)

Phrases

Place participial and prepositional phrases as close as possible to the words they modify. Participial and prepositional phrases are modifiers; that is, they tell about some other word in a sentence. To avoid confusion, they should be placed as close as possible to the word that they modify.

> **INCORRECT:** *Tiny microphones are planted by agents called bugs.*
>
> **CORRECT:** *Tiny microphones called bugs are planted by agents.*

Avoid dangling participles. Make sure a participial phrase does modify a word in the sentence.

> **INCORRECT:** *Disappointed in love, a hermit's life seemed attractive.* (Who was disappointed?)
>
> **CORRECT:** *Disappointed in love, the man became a hermit.*

Clauses

Use commas to set off nonessential adjective clauses.

Do you need the clause in order to indicate precisely who or what is meant? If not, it is nonessential and should be set off by commas.

USE COMMAS: *Gary Soto, who is also a very good poet, visited the class to talk about his novels.*

NO COMMAS: *An award-winning novelist who is also a very good poet visited the class to talk about his novels.*

Verbs

Don't use past tense forms with an auxiliary verb or past participle forms without an auxiliary verb. (See Auxiliary Verbs, page 1183.)

INCORRECT: *I have saw her somewhere before.* (*saw* is past tense and shouldn't be used with *have*)

CORRECT: *I have seen her somewhere before.*

INCORRECT: *I seen her somewhere before.* (*seen* is a past participle and shouldn't be used without an auxiliary)

Shift tense only when necessary.

Usually, when you are writing in present tense, you should stay in present tense; when you are writing in past tense, you should stay in past tense.

INCORRECT: *When she watches television, she fell asleep.*

CORRECT: *When she watches television, she falls asleep.*

Sometimes a shift in tense is necessary to show a logical sequence of actions or the relationship of one action to another.

CORRECT: *After he had told his story, everybody went to sleep.*

Subject-Verb Agreement

Make sure subjects and verbs agree in number.

INCORRECT: *The other boys at the beach was older.*

CORRECT: *The other boys at the beach were older.*

INCORRECT: *Jerry, along with the older boys, were a strong swimmer.*

CORRECT: *Jerry, along with the older boys, was a strong swimmer.*

INCORRECT: *The boys and Jerry swims through the tunnel.*

CORRECT: *The boys and Jerry [they] swim through the tunnel.*

Use a singular verb with nouns that look plural but have singular meaning.

Some nouns that end in *-s* are singular, even though they look plural. Examples are *measles, news, Wales,* and words ending in *-ics* that refer to a school subject, science, or general practice.

EXAMPLES: *The news is good, for once.*
Genetics is an important branch of science.

Use a singular verb with titles.

EXAMPLE: *"The Seven Ages of Man" was written by Shakespeare.*
"The Sharks" tells about the day the sharks appeared.

Use a singular verb with words of weight, time, and measure.

EXAMPLES: *Five weeks is how long we have to complete this unit.*
Fifty pounds is a lot of weight to carry in your backpack.

Pronouns

Use personal pronouns correctly in compounds.

Don't be confused about case when *and* joins a noun and a personal pronoun; the case of the pronoun still depends upon its function.

INCORRECT: *Her and her mother took the train into the city.*

CORRECT: *She and her mother took the train into the city.*

INCORRECT: *John gave a copy of* The House on Mango Street *to Megan and I.*

CORRECT: *John gave a copy of* The House on Mango Street *to Megan and me.*

INCORRECT: *Take Sandy and they to the airport.*

CORRECT: *Take Sandy and them to the airport.*

Usually, if you remove the noun and *and,* the correct pronoun will be obvious.

Use *we* and *us* correctly with nouns.

When a noun directly follows *we* or *us,* the case of the pronoun depends upon its function.

INCORRECT: *Us students will read Maya Angelou's poems.*

CORRECT: *We students will read Maya Angelou's poems.* (*we* is the subject)

INCORRECT: *Jon gave a dramatic reading of "A Voice" to we students.*

CORRECT: *Jon gave a dramatic reading of "A Voice" to us students.* (*us* is the object of *to*)

Avoid unclear pronoun reference.

The reference of a pronoun is ambiguous when the reader cannot tell which of two preceding nouns is its antecedent. The reference is indefinite when the idea to which the pronoun refers is only weakly or vaguely expressed.

AMBIGUOUS: *Odysseus, not Agamemnon, visited Circe, and he* [who?] *saw Calypso, too.*

CLEARER: *Odysseus, not Agamemnon, visited Circe, and the former saw Calypso, too.*

INDEFINITE: Romeo and Juliet *was performed by the Royal Shakespeare Company, which is one of my favorite plays.*

CLEARER: Romeo and Juliet, *which is one of my favorite plays, was performed by the Royal Shakespeare Company.*

Avoid change of person.

If you are writing in third person—using pronouns such as *she, he, it, they, them, his, her, its*—do not shift to second person—*you.*

INCORRECT: *The feudal laborer had to obey his lord, and you needed to obey the king as well.*

CORRECT: *The feudal laborer had to obey his lord, and he needed to obey the king as well.*

Use correct pronouns in elliptical comparisons.

An elliptical comparison is a comparison from which words have been omitted. In order to choose the proper pronoun, fill in the missing words. Note the difference below:

EXAMPLES: *Margo respected Jack more than (she respected) him. Margo respected Jack more than he (respected Jack).*

Don't confuse pronouns and contractions.

Personal pronouns are made possessive without the use of an apostrophe, as is the relative pronoun *whose.* Whenever you are unsure whether to write *it's* or *its, who's* or *whose,* ask if you mean *it is/has* or *who is/has.* If you do, write the contraction. Do the same for *you're* and *your* and *they're* and *their,* except that the contraction in this case is for the verb *are.*

Modifiers

Avoid double comparisons.

A double comparison is a comparison made twice. In general, if you use *-er* or *-est* on the end of a modifier, you would not also use *more* or *most* in front of it.

INCORRECT: *We got to the theater more faster by taking the bus.*

CORRECT: *We got to the theater faster by taking the bus.*

INCORRECT: *That theater is the most largest I've seen.*

CORRECT: *That theater is the largest I've seen.*

Avoid illogical comparisons.

Can you tell what is wrong with the following sentence?

Plays are more entertaining than any kind of performance art.

This sentence is difficult to understand. To avoid such illogical comparisons, use *other* when comparing an individual member with the rest of the group.

Plays are more entertaining than any other kind of performance art.

To avoid another kind of illogical comparison, use *than* or *as* after the first member in a compound comparison.

ILLOGICAL: *Bradbury wrote as many good novels if not more than Capote.* (Did he write as many novels or as many good novels?)

CLEARER: *Bradbury wrote as many good novels as Capote, if not more.*

Avoid misplacing modifiers.

Modifiers of all kinds must be placed as close as possible to the words they modify. If you place them elsewhere, you risk being misunderstood.

MISPLACED: *The children always noticed the marigolds walking by Miss Lottie's house.*

CLEARER: *Walking by Miss Lottie's house, the children always noticed the marigolds.*

It is the children, not the marigolds, who are walking.

Words Not to Capitalize

Do not capitalize *north, south, east,* and *west* when they are used to tell direction.

EXAMPLES: *Chicago is north and east of St. Louis.*
Denver is located in the West. (The West is the name of a section of the United States.)

Do not capitalize *sun* and *moon,* and capitalize *earth* only when it is used with the names of other planets.

EXAMPLES: *The sun and moon are heavenly bodies in a solar system that includes Mars, Jupiter, and the Earth.*

We live on the Earth, not in heaven.

Do not capitalize the names of seasons.

EXAMPLES: *The summer will soon be over, and we'll return to school in the fall.*

Do not capitalize the names of most school subjects.

School subjects are capitalized only when they name a specific course, such as World History I. Otherwise, they are not capitalized.

EXAMPLE: *I'm taking physics, social studies, and a foreign language this year.*

Note: English and the names of other languages are always capitalized.

EXAMPLE: *Everybody takes English and either Spanish or French.*

GRAMMAR PRACTICE

Rewrite each sentence correctly.

1. Mrs. Flowers was a respected person in the town she took an interest in Marguerite.
2. A true gentlewoman, the tidy bungalow was perfect for Mrs. Flowers.
3. Many of the people in Stamps, Arkansas, was poor.
4. When Marguerite went to Mrs. Flowers's house, she puts on a school dress.
5. Momma takes care of Marguerite's brother and she.
6. Marguerite was so embarrassed she wanted to sink into the Earth.
7. Trying to encourage Marguerite, cookies were served by Mrs. Flowers.
8. Being liked by Mrs. Flowers made Marguerite feel more better about herself.
9. I think younger children look up to we teenagers.
10. Covered with a tea towel, Mrs. Flowers carried a tray of cookies.

Commonly Confused Words

accept/except	The verb *accept* means "to receive or believe"; *except* is usually a preposition meaning "excluding."	Except for some of the more extraordinary events, I can accept that the *Odyssey* recounts a real journey.
advice/advise	*Advise* is a verb; *advice* is a noun naming that which an *adviser* gives.	I advise you to take that job. Whom should I ask for advice?
affect/effect	As a verb, *affect* means "to influence." *Effect* as a verb means "to cause." If you want a noun, you will almost always want *effect*.	Did Circe's wine affect Odysseus' mind? It did effect a change in Odysseus' men. In fact, it had an effect on everyone else who drank it.
all ready/already	*All ready* is an adjective meaning "fully ready." *Already* is an adverb meaning "before or by this time."	We'll be all ready to go by noon. I have already seen that movie.
allusion/illusion	An *allusion* is an indirect reference to something. An *illusion* is a false picture or idea.	There are many allusions to the works of Homer in English literature. The world's apparent flatness is an illusion.
among/between	*Between* is used when you are speaking of only two things. *Among* is used for three or more.	Between *Hamlet* and *King Lear,* I prefer the latter. Emily Dickinson is among my favorite poets.
bring/take	*Bring* is used to denote motion toward a speaker or place. *Take* is used to denote motion away from such a person or place.	Bring the books over here, and I will take them to the library.
fewer/less	*Fewer* refers to the number of separate, countable units. *Less* refers to bulk quantity.	We have less literature and fewer selections in this year's curriculum.
leave/let	*Leave* means "to allow something to remain behind." *Let* means "to permit."	The librarian will leave some books on display but will not let us borrow any.
lie/lay	To *lie* is "to rest or recline." It does not take an object. *Lay* always takes an object.	Rover loves to lie in the sun. We always lay some bones next to him.
loose/lose	*Loose* (lo͞os) means "free, not restrained"; *lose* (lo͞oz) means "to misplace or fail to find."	Who turned the horses loose? I hope we won't lose any of them.
precede/proceed	*Precede* means "to go or come before." Use *proceed* for other meanings.	Emily Dickinson's poetry precedes that of Alice Walker. You may proceed to the next section of the test.
than/then	Use *than* in making comparisons; use *then* on all other occasions.	Who can say whether Amy Lowell is a better poet than Denise Levertov? I will read Lowell first, and then I will read Levertov.
two/too/to	*Two* is the number. *Too* is an adverb meaning "also" or "very." Use *to* before a verb or as a preposition.	Meg had to go to town, too. We had too much reading to do. Two chapters is too much.

Grammar Glossary

This glossary contains various terms you need to understand when you use the Grammar Handbook. Used as a reference source, this glossary will help you explore grammar concepts and the ways they relate to one another.

Abbreviation An abbreviation is a shortened form of a word or word group; it is often made up of initials. (B.C., A.M., *Maj.*)

Active voice. *See* **Voice.**

Adjective An adjective modifies, or describes, a noun or pronoun. (*happy* camper, she is *small*)

A **predicate adjective** follows a linking verb and describes the subject. (The day seemed *long.*)

A **proper adjective** is formed from a proper noun. (*Jewish* temple, *Alaskan* husky)

The **comparative** form of an adjective compares two things. (*more alert, thicker*)

The **superlative** form of an adjective compares more than two things. (*most abundant, weakest*)

What Adjectives Tell	Examples
How many	*some* writers *much* joy
What kind	*grand* plans *wider* streets
Which one(s)	*these* flowers *that* star

Adjective phrase. *See* **Phrase.**

Adverb An adverb modifies a verb, an adjective, or another adverb. (Clare sang *loudly.*)

The **comparative** form of an adverb compares two actions. (*more generously, faster*)

The **superlative** form of an adverb compares more than two actions. (*most sharply, closest*)

What Adverbs Tell	Examples
How	climb *carefully* chuckle *merrily*
When	arrived *late* left *early*
Where	climbed *up* moved *away*
To what extent	*extremely* upset *hardly* visible

Adverb, conjunctive. *See* **Conjunctive adverb.**

Adverb phrase. *See* **Phrase.**

Agreement Sentence parts that correspond with one another are said to be in agreement.

In **pronoun-antecedent agreement,** a pronoun and the word it refers to are the same in number, gender, and person. (*Bill* mailed *his* application. The *students* ate *their* lunches.)

In **subject-verb agreement,** the subject and verb in a sentence are the same in number. (A *child cries* for help. *They cry* aloud.)

Ambiguous reference An ambiguous reference occurs when a pronoun may refer to more than one word. (Bud asked his brother if *he* had any mail.)

Antecedent An antecedent is the noun or pronoun to which a pronoun refers. (If *Adam* forgets *his* raincoat, *he* will be late for school. *She* learned *her* lesson.)

Appositive An appositive is a noun or phrase that explains one or more words in a sentence. (Cary Grant, *an Englishman,* spent most of his adult life in America.)

An **essential appositive** is needed to make the sense of a sentence complete. (A comic strip inspired the musical *Annie.*)

A **nonessential appositive** is one that adds information to a sentence but is not necessary to its sense. (O. Henry, *a short story writer,* spent time in prison.)

Article Articles are the special adjectives *a, an,* and *the.* (*the* day, *a* fly)

The **definite article** (the word *the*) refers to a particular thing. (*the* cabin)

An **indefinite article** is used with a noun that is not unique but refers to one of many of its kind. (*a* dish, *an* otter)

Auxiliary verb. *See* **Verb.**

Clause A clause is a group of words that contains a verb and its subject. (*they slept*)

An **adjective clause** is a subordinate clause that modifies a noun or pronoun. (Hugh bought the sweater *that he had admired.*)

An **adverb clause** is a subordinate clause used to modify a verb, an adjective, or an adverb. (Ring the bell *when it is time for class to begin.*)

A **noun clause** is a subordinate clause that is used as a noun. (*Whatever you say* interests me.)

An **elliptical clause** is a clause from which a word or words have been omitted. (We are not as lucky as *they*.)

A **main (independent) clause** can stand by itself as a sentence. (*the flashlight flickered*)

A **subordinate (dependent) clause** does not express a complete thought and cannot stand by itself. (*while the nation watched*)

Clause	Example
Main (independent)	The hurricane struck
Subordinate (dependent)	while we were preparing to leave.

Collective noun. *See* **Noun.**

Comma splice A comma splice is an error caused when two sentences are separated with a comma instead of a correct end mark. (*The band played a medley of show tunes, everyone enjoyed the show.*)

Common noun. *See* **Noun.**

Comparative. *See* **Adjective; Adverb.**

Complement A complement is a word or group of words that completes the meaning of a verb. (The kitten finished *the milk.*) *See also* **Direct object; Indirect object.**

An **objective complement** is a word or a group of words that follows a direct object and renames or describes that object. (The parents of the rescued child declared Gus *a hero.*)

A **subject complement** follows a linking verb and renames or describes the subject. (The coach seemed *anxious.*) *See also* **Noun (predicate noun); Adjective, (predicate adjective).**

Complete predicate The complete predicate of a sentence consists of the main verb plus any words that modify or complete the verb's meaning. (The student *produces work of high caliber.*)

Complete subject The complete subject of a sentence consists of the simple subject plus any words that modify or describe the simple subject. (*Students of history* believe that wars can be avoided.)

Sentence Part	Example
Complete subject	The man in the ten-gallon hat
Complete predicate	wore a pair of silver spurs.

Compound sentence part A sentence element that consists of two or more subjects, verbs, objects, or other parts is compound. (*Lou* and *Jay* helped. Laura *makes* and *models* scarves. Jill sings *opera* and *popular music.*)

Conjunction A conjunction is a word that links other words or groups of words.

A **coordinating conjunction** connects related words, groups of words, or sentences. (*and, but, or*)

A **correlative conjunction** is one of a pair of conjunctions that work together to connect sentence parts. (*either . . . or, neither . . . nor, not only . . . but also, whether . . . or, both . . . and*)

A **subordinating conjunction** introduces a subordinate clause. (*after, although, as, as if, as long as, as though, because, before, if, in order that, since, so that, than, though, till, unless, until, whatever, when, where, while*)

Conjunctive adverb A conjunctive adverb joins the clauses of a compound sentence. (*however, therefore, yet*)

Contraction A contraction is formed by joining two words and substituting an apostrophe for a letter or letters left out of one of the words. (*didn't, we've*)

Coordinating conjunction. *See* **Conjunction.**

Correlative conjunction. *See* **Conjunction.**

Dangling modifier A dangling modifier is one that does not clearly modify any word in the sentence. (*Dashing for the train, the barriers got in the way.*)

Demonstrative pronoun. *See* **Pronoun.**

Dependent clause. *See* **Clause.**

Direct object A direct object receives the action of a verb. Direct objects follow transitive verbs. (Jude planned the *party.*)

Direct quotation. *See* **Quotation.**

Divided quotation. *See* **Quotation.**

Double negative A double negative is the incorrect use of two negative words when only one is needed. (*Nobody didn't care.*)

End mark An end mark is one of several punctuation marks that can end a sentence. See the punctuation chart on page 1201.

F

Fragment. *See* **Sentence fragment.**

Future tense. *See* **Verb tense.**

 G

Gender The gender of a personal pronoun indicates whether the person or thing referred to is male, female, or neuter. (My cousin plays the tuba; *he* often performs in school concerts.)

Gerund A gerund is a verbal that ends in *-ing* and functions as a noun. (*Making* pottery takes patience.)

 H

Helping verb. *See* **Verb (auxiliary verb).**

 I

Illogical comparison An illogical comparison is a comparison that does not make sense because words are missing or illogical. (My computer is *newer than Kay.*)

Indefinite pronoun. *See* **Pronoun.**

Indefinite reference Indefinite reference occurs when a pronoun is used without a clear antecedent. (My aunt hugged me in front of my friends, and *it* was embarrassing.)

Independent clause. *See* **Clause.**

Indirect object An indirect object tells to whom or for whom (sometimes to what or for what) something is done. (Arthur wrote *Kerry* a letter.)

Indirect question An indirect question tells what someone asked without using the person's exact words. (*My friend asked me if I could go with her to the dentist.*)

Indirect quotation. *See* **Quotation.**

Infinitive An infinitive is a verbal beginning with *to* that functions as a noun, an adjective, or an adverb. (He wanted *to go* to the play.)

Intensive pronoun. *See* **Pronoun.**

Interjection An interjection is a word or phrase used to express strong feeling. (*Wow! Good grief!*)

Interrogative pronoun. *See* **Pronoun.**

Intransitive verb. *See* **Verb.**

Inverted sentence An inverted sentence is one in which the subject comes after the verb. (*How was the movie? Here come the clowns.*)

Irregular verb. *See* **Verb.**

 L

Linking verb. *See* **Verb.**

 M

Main clause. *See* **Clause.**

Main verb. *See* **Verb.**

Modifier A modifier makes another word more precise. Modifiers most often are adjectives or adverbs; they may also be phrases, verbals, or clauses that function as adjectives or adverbs. (*small* box, smiled *broadly,* house *by the sea,* dog *barking loudly*)

An **essential modifier** is one that is necessary to the meaning of a sentence. (Everybody *who has a free pass* should enter now. None *of the passengers* got on the train.)

A **nonessential modifier** is one that merely adds more information to a sentence that is clear without the addition. (We will use the new dishes, *which are stored in the closet.*)

 N

Noun A noun names a person, a place, a thing, or an idea. (*auditor, shelf, book, goodness*)

An **abstract noun** names an idea, a quality, or a feeling. (*joy*)

A **collective noun** names a group of things. (*bevy*)

A **common noun** is a general name of a person, a place, a thing, or an idea. (*valet, hill, bread, amazement*)

A **compound noun** contains two or more words. (*hometown, pay-as-you-go, screen test*)

A **noun of direct address** is the name of a person being directly spoken to. (*Lee,* do you have the package? No, *Suki,* your letter did not arrive.)

A **possessive noun** shows who or what owns or is associated with something. (*Lil's* ring, a *day's* pay)

A **predicate noun** follows a linking verb and renames the subject. (Karen is a *writer.*)

A **proper noun** names a particular person, place, or thing. (*John Smith, Ohio, Sears Tower, Congress*)

Number A word is **singular** in number if it refers to just one person, place, thing, idea, or action, and **plural** in number if it refers to more than one person, place, thing, idea, or action. (The words *he, waiter,* and *is* are singular. The words *they, waiters,* and *are* are plural.)

 O

Object of a preposition The object of a preposition is the noun or pronoun that follows a preposition. (The athletes cycled along the *route.* Jane baked a cake for *her.*)

Object of a verb The object of a verb receives the action of the verb. (Sid told *stories.*) *See also* **Direct object; Indirect object.**

Participle A participle is often used as part of a verb phrase. (had *written*) It can also be used as a verbal that functions as an adjective. (the *leaping* deer, the medicine *taken* for a fever)

> The **present participle** is formed by adding *-ing* to the present form of a verb. (*Walking* rapidly, we reached the general store.)

> The **past participle** of a regular verb is formed by adding *-d* or *-ed* to the present form. The past participles of irregular verbs do not follow this pattern. (*Startled,* they ran from the house. *Spun* glass is delicate. A *broken* cup lay there.)

Passive voice. *See* **Voice.**

Past tense. *See* **Verb tense.**

Perfect tenses. *See* **Verb tense.**

Person Person is a means of classifying pronouns.

> A **first-person** pronoun refers to the person speaking. (*We* came.)

> A **second-person** pronoun refers to the person spoken to. (*You* ask.)

> A **third-person** pronoun refers to some other person(s) or thing(s) being spoken of. (*They* played.)

Personal pronoun. *See* **Pronoun.**

Phrase A phrase is a group of related words that does not contain a verb and its subject. (*noticing everything, under a chair*)

> An **adjective phrase** modifies a noun or a pronoun. (The label *on the bottle* has faded.)

An **adverb phrase** modifies a verb, an adjective, or an adverb. (Come *to the fair.*)

An **appositive phrase** explains one or more words in a sentence. (Mary, *a champion gymnast,* won gold medals at the Olympics.)

A **gerund phrase** consists of a gerund and its modifiers and complements. (*Fixing the leak* will take only a few minutes.)

An **infinitive phrase** consists of an infinitive, its modifiers, and its complements. (*To prepare for a test,* study in a quiet place.)

A **participial phrase** consists of a participle and its modifiers and complements. (*Straggling to the finish line,* the last runners arrived.)

A **prepositional phrase** consists of a preposition, its object, and the object's modifiers. (The Saint Bernard does rescue work *in the Swiss Alps.*)

A **verb phrase** consists of a main verb and one or more helping verbs. (*might have ordered*)

Possessive A noun or pronoun that is possessive shows ownership or relationship. (*Dan's* story, *my* doctor)

Possessive noun. *See* **Noun.**

Possessive pronoun. *See* **Pronoun.**

Predicate The predicate of a sentence tells what the subject is or does. (The van *runs well even in winter.* The job *seems too complicated.*) *See also* **Complete predicate; Simple predicate.**

Predicate adjective. *See* **Adjective.**

Predicate nominative A predicate nominative is a noun or pronoun that follows a linking verb and renames or explains the subject. (Joan is a computer

operator. The winner of the prize was *he.*)

Predicate pronoun. *See* **Pronoun.**

Preposition A preposition is a word that relates its object to another part of the sentence or to the sentence as a whole. (Alfredo leaped *onto* the stage.)

Prepositional phrase. *See* **Phrase.**

Present tense. *See* **Verb tense.**

Pronoun A pronoun replaces a noun or another pronoun. Some pronouns allow a writer or speaker to avoid repeating a proper noun. Other pronouns let a writer refer to an unknown or unidentified person or thing.

> A **demonstrative pronoun** singles out one or more persons or things. (*This* is the letter.)

> An **indefinite pronoun** refers to an unidentified person or thing. (*Everyone* stayed home. Will you hire *anybody?*)

> An **intensive pronoun** emphasizes a noun or pronoun. (The teacher *himself* sold tickets.)

> An **interrogative pronoun** asks a question. (*What* happened to you?)

> A **personal pronoun** shows a distinction of person. (*I* came. *You* see. *He* knows.)

> A **possessive pronoun** shows ownership. (*My* spaghetti is always good. Are *your* parents coming to the play?)

> A **predicate pronoun** follows a linking verb and renames the subject. (The owners of the store were *they.*)

> A **reflexive pronoun** reflects an action back on the subject of the sentence. (Joe helped *himself.*)

A *relative pronoun* relates a subordinate clause to the word it modifies. (The draperies, *which* had been made by hand, were ruined in the fire.)

Pronoun-antecedent agreement. *See* **Agreement.**

Pronoun forms

The *subject form* of a pronoun is used when the pronoun is the subject of a sentence or follows a linking verb as a predicate pronoun. (*She* fell. The star was *she.*)

The *object form* of a pronoun is used when the pronoun is the direct or indirect object of a verb or verbal or the object of a preposition. (We sent *him* the bill. We ordered food for *them.*)

Proper adjective. *See* **Adjective.**

Proper noun. *See* **Noun.**

Punctuation Punctuation clarifies the structure of sentences. See the punctuation chart below.

Quotation A quotation consists of words from another speaker or writer.

A *direct quotation* is the exact words of a speaker or writer. (Martin said, *"The homecoming game has been postponed."*)

A *divided quotation* is a quotation separated by words that identify the speaker. (*"The homecoming game,"* said Martin, *"has been postponed."*)

An *indirect quotation* reports what a person said without giving the exact words. (*Martin said that the homecoming game had been postponed.*)

Reflexive pronoun. *See* **Pronoun.**

Regular verb. *See* **Verb.**

Relative pronoun. *See* **Pronoun.**

Run-on sentence A run-on sentence consists of two or more sentences written incorrectly as one. (*The sunset was beautiful its brilliant colors lasted only a short time.*)

Sentence A sentence expresses a complete thought. The chart at the top of the next page shows the four kinds of sentences.

A *complex sentence* contains one main clause and one or more subordinate clauses. (*Open the windows before you go to bed. If she falls, I'll help her up.*)

A *compound sentence* is made up of two or more independent clauses joined by a conjunction, a colon, or a semicolon. (*The ship finally docked, and the passengers quickly left.*)

A *simple sentence* consists of only one main clause. (*My friend volunteers at a nursing home.*)

Punctuation	Uses	Examples
Apostrophe (')	Shows possession	Lou's garage Alva's script
	Indicates a contraction	I'll help you. The baby's tired.
Colon (:)	Introduces a list or quotation	three colors: red, green, and yellow
	Divides some compound sentences	This was the problem: we had to find our own way home.
Comma (,)	Separates ideas	The glass broke, and the juice spilled all over.
	Separates modifiers	The lively, talented cheerleaders energized the team.
	Separates items in series	We visited London, Rome, and Paris.
Exclamation point (!)	Ends an exclamatory sentence	Have a wonderful time!
Hyphen (-)	Joins parts of some compound words	daughter-in-law, great-grandson
Period (.)	Ends a declarative sentence	Swallows return to Capistrano in spring.
	Indicates most abbreviations	min. qt. Blvd. Gen. Jan.
Question mark (?)	Ends an interrogative sentence	Where are you going?
Semicolon (;)	Divides some compound sentences	Marie is an expert dancer; she teaches a class in tap.
	Separates items in series that contain commas	Jerry visited Syracuse, New York; Athens, Georgia; and Tampa, Florida.

Kind of Sentence	Example
Declarative (statement)	Our team won.
Exclamatory (strong feeling)	I had a great time!
Imperative (request, command)	Take the next exit.
Interrogative (question)	Who owns the car?

Sentence fragment A sentence fragment is a group of words that is only part of a sentence. (*When he arrived. Merrily yodeling.*)

Simple predicate A simple predicate is the verb in the predicate. (John *collects* foreign stamps.)

Simple subject A simple subject is the key noun or pronoun in the subject. (The new *house* is empty.)

Split infinitive A split infinitive occurs when a modifier is placed between the word *to* and the verb in an infinitive. (*to quickly speak*)

Subject The subject is the part of a sentence that tells whom or what the sentence is about. (*Lou* swam.) *See also* **Complete subject; Simple subject.**

Subject-verb agreement. *See* **Agreement.**

Subordinate clause. *See* **Clause.**

Subordinating conjunction. *See* **Conjunction.**

Superlative. *See* **Adjective; Adverb.**

Transitive verb. *See* **Verb.**

Unidentified reference An unidentified reference usually occurs when the word *it, they, this, which,* or *that* is used. (In California *they* have good weather most of the time.)

Verb A verb expresses an action, a condition, or a state of being.

An *action verb* tells what the subject does, has done, or will do. The action may be physical or mental. (Susan *trains* guide dogs.)

An *auxiliary verb* is added to a main verb to express tense, add emphasis, or otherwise affect the meaning of the verb. Together the auxiliary and main verb make up a verb phrase. (*will* intend, *could have* gone)

A *linking verb* expresses a state of being or connects the subject with a word or words that describe the subject. (The ice *feels* cold.) Linking verbs include *appear, be (am, are, is, was, were, been, being), become, feel, grow, look, remain, seem, smell, sound,* and *taste.*

A *main verb* expresses action or state of being; it appears with one or more auxiliary verbs. (will be *staying*)

The *progressive form* of a verb shows continuing action. (She *is knitting.*)

The past tense and past participle of a *regular verb* are formed by adding *-d* or *-ed.* (*open, opened*) An *irregular verb* does not follow this pattern. (*throw, threw, thrown; shrink, shrank, shrunk*)

The action of a *transitive verb* is directed toward someone or something, called the object of the verb. (Leo *washed* the windows.) An *intransitive verb* has no object. (The leaves *scattered.*)

Verb phrase. *See* **Phrase.**

Verb tense Verb tense shows the time of an action or the time of a state of being.

The *present tense* places an action or condition in the present. (Jan *takes* piano lessons.)

The *past tense* places an action or condition in the past. (We *came* to the party.)

The *future tense* places an action or condition in the future. (You *will understand.*)

The *present perfect tense* describes an action in an indefinite past time or an action that began in the past and continues in the present. (*has called, have known*)

The *past perfect tense* describes one action that happened before another action in the past. (*had scattered, had mentioned*)

The *future perfect tense* describes an event that will be finished before another future action begins. (*will have taught, shall have appeared*)

Verbal A verbal is formed from a verb and acts as another part of speech, such as a noun, an adjective, or an adverb.

Verbal	Example
Gerund (used as a noun)	Lamont enjoys *swimming.*
Infinitive (used as an adjective, an adverb, or a noun)	Everyone wants *to help.*
Participle (used as an adjective)	The leaves *covering the drive* made it slippery.

Voice The voice of a verb depends on whether the subject performs or receives the action of the verb.

In the *active voice* the subject of the sentence performs the verb's action. (We *knew* the answer.)

In the *passive voice* the subject of the sentence receives the action of the verb. (The team *has been eliminated.*)

Index of Fine Art

Index of Skills

Literary Concepts

Act (in a play), 1126

Action, 112, 787
> falling, 23, 35, 285, 293, 302, 409, 742, 754, 1131–1132
> rising, 23, 35, 285, 293, 302, 409, 742, 754, 1138

Alliteration, 139, 198, 204, 608, 611, 1126

Allusion, 151, 490, 986, 1071, 1126

Analogy, 1126

Antagonist, 321, 371, 410, 590, 1126

Approximate rhyme, 1137

Aside, 986, 1043, 1126

Assonance, 139, 198, 204, 608, 611, 1126

Audience, 493, 510, 511, 1174

Author's perspective, 651, 978, 1126. *See also* Author's perspective *under* Reading and Critical Thinking Skills.
> and characterization, 676
> and diction, 680, 684
> in fiction, 652

Author's purpose, 144, 448, 653, 757, 845, 1126–1127
> identifying, 185, 189
> reviewing, 861

Author's style, 217, 505, 583, 718

Autobiographical fiction, 272

Autobiography, 233, 235, 241, 285, 480, 490, 660, 1127

Ballad, 128, 141, 144, 1127

Biographical essay, 269

Biography, 233, 235, 453, 463, 490, 1127

Blank verse, 987, 989, 1019, 1127

Book review, 710, 968

Character
> analyzing, 23, 24, 38, 62, 71, 88, 100, 112, 122, 124, 128, 146, 159, 189, 323, 324, 340, 343, 346, 350, 409, 410, 412, 436, 463, 590, 605, 742, 768, 784, 787, 856, 914, 926, 965, 1127
> and conflict, 22, 58, 71, 88, 359, 1129
> development, 321, 411, 557, 569
> exploring, 411
> making inferences about, 591
> motivation, 768, 1086
> opinions of, 605
> and setting, 322, 605
> sketches, 1127
> study, 500
> traits, 35, 58
> visualizing, 25, 516

Characterization, 172, 182, 583, 654, 821, 926, 1128
> and author's perspective, 663, 676

Character types, 397
> antagonist, 321, 371, 410, 590, 1126
> dynamic, 24, 322, 340, 1127
> flat, 322
> hero, 890, 914, 965, 983, 1131
> main, 24, 62, 71, 85, 100, 285, 321, 323, 340, 346, 371, 1127

minor, 62, 71, 100, 285, 321, 323, 340, 1127
> protagonist, 321, 371, 410, 1137
> round, 322, 340, 1127
> static, 24, 322, 340, 1127
> tragic, 986

Chorus (in play or poem), 992, 1020, 1128

Climax of plot, 85, 285, 293, 302, 409, 590, 742, 754, 881, 1071, 1128. *See also* Falling action; Rising action.

Comedy, 1128. *See also* Tragedy.

Comic relief, 986, 1086, 1128. *See also* Humor.

Comparing literature texts, 75, 130, 144, 159, 182, 204, 205, 216, 269, 285, 291, 346, 350, 358, 389, 448, 463, 471, 490, 498, 551, 555, 569, 605, 616, 636, 676, 684, 699, 708, 784, 796, 821, 840, 855, 1043

Comparison, 128, 385

Complications of plot, 26, 35, 293, 302

Conflict
> analyzing, 22, 26, 35, 58, 71, 100, 113, 122, 124, 226, 293, 302, 359, 371, 726, 742, 745, 1019, 1128–1129
> external, 58, 71, 1129
> internal, 58, 71, 1129

Connecting to literature, 58, 71, 85, 100, 122, 144, 149, 167, 241, 255, 269, 285, 302, 344, 350, 371, 385, 436, 569, 660, 676

Connotation, 1129

Consonance, 139

Couplet, 1129

Crisis, 22. *See also* Climax of plot.

Critical essay, 1131

Critical thinking, 35, 58, 71, 85, 100, 122, 128, 144, 149, 159, 167, 182, 189, 200, 204, 206, 216, 241, 255, 269, 285, 289, 291, 302, 340, 344, 346, 350, 371, 385, 436, 444, 448, 463, 468, 471, 490, 493, 498, 504, 535, 547, 553, 555, 569, 605, 609, 611, 614, 616, 636, 660, 676, 682, 684, 699, 708, 717, 754, 768, 784, 796, 821, 840, 847, 855, 861, 871, 914, 926, 939, 965, 1019, 1043, 1071, 1086, 1103

Dead metaphors, 1134

Denotation, 1129. *See also* Connotation.

Descriptive writing, 122, 149, 547, 569, 965, 1129

Detective story, 740

Dialect, 410, 505, 1129

Dialogue, 122, 128, 144, 189, 350, 409, 410, 411, 412, 436, 505, 660, 676, 1129–1130. *See also* Interview; Monologue.

Diary, 233

Diction, 514, 680, 684, 1130. *See also* Word choice.

Drama, 409, 660, 784, 1130
> historical, 412, 436
> Shakespearean, 986, 989

Dramatic convention, 987

Dramatic irony, 189, 570, 739, 770, 784, 1071, 1134

Dramatic monologue, 348, 350, 1130. *See also* Soliloquy.

Dynamic character, 24, 322, 340, 1127. *See also* Static character.

End rhyme, 138, 1137. *See also* Rhyme.

Reading and Critical Thinking Skills

main ideas in, 350
narrative, 124, 128, 149, 890, 1135
theme in, 466, 467, 939, 965
understanding, 198, 204
Point of view, 813, 861, 970, 1121, 1137
first-person, 216, 255, 480, 490, 500, 608, 813, 861, 1132, 1137
and narrators, 813
third-person, 813, 814, 821, 1137, 1141
understanding, 490, 881
Points of comparison, 358, 371. *See also* Comparison and contrast.
Premise, 1174
Prior knowledge, activating, 38, 62, 74, 88, 124, 141, 146, 151, 162, 172, 185, 198, 207, 236, 243, 272, 288, 293, 324, 343, 348, 359, 373, 439, 453, 466, 480, 494, 500, 517, 538, 552, 557, 592, 608, 613, 618, 654, 663, 680, 694, 701, 711, 742, 759, 770, 823, 845, 856, 863, 893, 941, 989
Purpose, understanding, 387, 652. *See also* Author's purpose.
Reader's notes, 26, 35, 38, 58, 62, 70, 74, 85, 100, 111, 122, 128, 140, 141, 144, 146, 151, 172, 185, 198, 204, 207, 216, 226, 227, 236, 241, 243, 260, 272, 288, 291, 302, 346, 358, 359, 371, 373, 397, 412, 436, 439, 453, 463, 466, 471, 480, 494, 500, 547, 557, 572, 582, 591, 608, 613, 654, 663, 676, 680, 693, 694, 699, 701, 708, 711, 726, 727, 742, 754, 759, 768, 770, 784, 787, 796, 821, 823, 840, 845, 855, 856, 861, 871, 880, 881, 890, 914, 939, 940, 965, 989, 1019, 1043, 1071
strategies for using, 25, 140
Reading, 100, 149, 151, 272, 288, 291, 314, 340, 343, 348, 395, 439, 453, 498, 636, 989
actively, 38, 62, 71, 74, 88, 100, 122, 131, 141, 144, 146, 159, 172, 185, 198, 216, 269, 285, 344, 480, 490, 494, 572, 605, 940, 1103
aloud, 505
in depth, 1173
for details, 863
drama, 411, 988
evaluating, 582
extending, 228–229, 584–585, 728–729, 881
focusing, 38, 88, 112, 124, 141, 146, 151, 172, 185, 207, 236, 243, 260, 272, 323, 373, 466, 493, 494, 517, 538, 552, 613, 618, 654, 663, 680, 693, 701, 711, 742, 759, 770, 787, 823, 840, 845, 855, 893
guidelines, 387
for information, 61, 170, 235, 258, 387, 451, 550, 679, 757, 843, 968–969, 1106
news sources, 170
nonfiction, 235
Shakespearean tragedy, strategies for, 988, 1019
skills and strategies, 516, 653, 890
Realistic detail, 856
Recalling past events, 134, 317
Recognizing cause and effect, 618
Recognizing cultural influences, 385
Reflecting, 135, 224, 226, 318, 394, 582, 648, 726, 810, 878
Resolution, 226. *See also* Conflict.

Restatement clue, 103
Review. *See* Book reviews.
Scanning, 1172
Screenplays, visualizing, 823, 840
Sensory detail, 272, 285, 316, 613, 616
Sequence of events, 26, 302. *See also* Chronological order.
Setting, 871
assessing, 1117
drawing conclusions about, 591
visualizing, 787
Shakespearean drama, reading, 1071, 1086, 1103
Similarities, 390
Similes, 10
Skimming, 550, 1172
Sound, analyzing, 140
Sources, evaluating, 61
Speakers, understanding, 140, 144, 611
Statistics, 223
Storytelling, 124, 226, 806
Strategies for reading. *See also* Connections, making; Monitoring; Visualizing *under* Viewing and Representing.
clarifying, 7, 25, 140, 235, 411, 892
connecting to literature, 58, 71, 85, 100, 122, 144, 149, 167, 241, 255, 269, 285, 302, 344, 350, 371, 385, 436, 569, 660, 676
evaluating, 7, 25, 61, 88, 140, 170, 235, 323, 411, 653, 741, 892, 988
predicting, 7, 25, 58, 140, 151, 159, 323, 892, 893, 914, 926, 939, 988
questioning, 7, 25, 235, 323, 411, 516, 741, 768, 892
visualizing, 7, 25, 140, 235, 323, 411, 516, 787, 796, 892, 988
Strategies for reading types of literature
detective story, 739–741
drama, 409–411
epic, 890–892
fiction, 22–25
nonfiction, 233–235
poetry, 138–140
Shakespearean drama, 986–988
Structure of articles, identifying, 843
Study strategies, 1171–1172
Style, analyzing, 217, 505, 583, 718
Summarizing and main idea, 235, 711, 717
Summary, 679, 711
Supporting element, 439
Testimonial, 1173
Texts, comparing, 75, 85, 144, 159, 182, 204, 205, 216, 269, 285, 291, 346, 350, 448, 463, 471, 490, 498, 551, 555, 569, 605, 616, 636, 676, 684, 699, 708, 784, 796, 821, 840, 855, 1043
Text structure, analyzing, 439, 448
Theme, 694, 699
discovering, 591, 727
reflecting on, 226, 396, 582, 726
Thinking critically, 35, 58, 71, 85, 100, 122, 149, 159, 167,

189, 204, 205, 216, 241, 255, 269, 285, 289, 291, 302, 340, 344, 350, 371, 385, 436, 444, 448, 463, 471, 490, 493, 498, 535, 547, 552, 555, 569, 609, 611, 616, 660, 676, 684, 699, 708, 717, 754, 768, 821, 840, 845, 855, 861, 926, 939, 965, 1019, 1071, 1103

Thinking logically, 1174

Time lines, 134. *See also* Chronological order; Sequence of events.

Transitions, 439. *See also* Transition *under* Writing Skills, Modes, and Formats.

Viewpoint. *See* Bias; Point of view.

Vignettes, 708

Word choice, understanding, 686, 844. *See also* Diction; Word choice *under* Vocabulary Skills.

Word web, 172, 680, 708, 886

Vocabulary Skills

Analogies, 491, 641, 915, 1126

Antonyms, 59, 372, 606, 641, 755, 797, 849, 915

Assessing vocabulary, 168, 606, 636, 755, 796, 915

Assessment practice, 168, 606, 636, 755

Base words, 191

Building, 86, 103, 219, 242, 243, 255, 270, 286, 303, 341, 372, 386, 437, 449, 464, 473, 480, 491, 536, 538, 557, 570, 572, 641, 661, 663, 677, 769, 785, 798, 841, 862, 915, 927, 940, 966
  diagram of strategies for, 571
  strategies for, 103, 191, 305, 571, 572, 641, 686, 798, 849, 1109

Comparison clues, 798

Compound words, 973

Connotation, 684, 686. *See also* Connotation *under* Literary Concepts.

Context clues, 103, 183, 219, 256, 303, 305, 351, 437, 548, 570, 572, 661, 677, 719, 769, 785, 798, 872, 1109

Denotation, 686

Description clues, 351

Descriptive words, 85

Diction, 135, 514. *See also* Word choice.

Dictionaries, using, 572, 973, 1109

Eponyms, 973

Etymology, 219, 973

Formal diction, 514

Homonyms, 849, 1109

Idioms, 305, 536

Inference clues, 351

Informal diction, 514

Informal English, 305

Jargon, 351

Literal meanings, 686

Meaning clues, 72, 168, 270, 341, 449, 464, 570, 700, 841, 862, 1109

Meaning, roots of, 973

Metaphors, 798

Multiple-meaning words, 1109

Negative associations, 686

Positive associations, 686

Previewing vocabulary, 26, 38, 62, 74, 88, 112, 185, 207, 236, 260, 272, 293, 323, 412, 517, 591, 618, 653, 742, 759, 770, 823, 856, 863, 893, 940

Recording new words, 572

Reference tools, 305, 351

Related words, 536, 571

Relationship types, 641

Root words, 191, 973

Shakespearean, 985, 988

Similes, 798

Slang, 305

Specialized vocabulary, 351, 453, 463, 988

Synonyms, 59, 123, 242, 386, 637, 755, 849, 915, 966

Vocabulary in action, 36, 59, 72, 101, 123, 160, 168, 183, 190, 219, 242, 256, 270, 286, 303, 341, 386, 437, 449, 464, 491, 536, 548, 570, 606, 637, 661, 677, 700, 719, 755, 769, 785, 797, 841, 862, 872, 915, 927, 940, 966

Word choice, 135, 514, 538

Word families, 191, 973. *See also* Root words.

Word meanings, 123, 160, 190, 286, 386, 437, 927, 940. *See also* Dictionaries, using; Encyclopedias *under* Inquiry and Research.

Word origins, 973

Word parts, 571

Word relationships, 641. *See also* Etymology; Word families.

Words with multiple meanings, 1109

Grammar, Usage, and Mechanics

Abbreviations, 1209

Abstract nouns, 36, 1180, 1211

Action verbs, 465, 1179, 1183, 1214

Active voice of verbs, 648, 1185, 1214

Adjective, 1179, 1187, 1209
  clauses, 756, 1195, 1205, 1209
  and commas, 87
  compound, 87
  phrases, 1193, 1212

Adverb clauses, 786, 841, 1195, 1209

Adverb phrases, 1193, 1212

Adverbs, 73, 169, 811, 1179, 1186, 1209

Affixes, 473

Ambiguous reference, correcting, 1209

Antecedent-pronoun agreement, 135, 1181–1182, 1209

Antonyms, 59. *See also* Antonyms *under* Vocabulary Skills.

Apostrophes, 1202, 1213

Appositive phrases, 638, 1193, 1212

Appositives, 1193, 1209

Articles, 1186, 1209

Auxiliary verbs, 102, 1179, 1183, 1205, 1214

Be, forms of, 1198

Capitalization errors, 319, 1207

Capitalization, quick reference chart for, 1203

Case of nouns and pronouns, 1181

Clause punctuation, 1204

Clauses, 1195–1196, 1209
  as fragments, 878
  punctuating, 1205

Collective nouns, 1180, 1200, 1211. *See also* Subject-verb agreement.

Colons, 1202, 1213

Combining sentences, 319, 512. *See also* Conjunctions.

Comma errors, 225, 512, 649, 811

Commas, 1201, 1213

Writing Skills, Modes, and Formats

Inquiry and Research

Speaking and Listening

Viewing and Representing

Index of Titles and Authors

Page numbers that appear in italics refer to biographical information.

City News Publishing Company: "Glory and Hope" by Nelson Mandela, from *Vital Speeches of the Day*, Vol. LX, No. 16 (1 June 1994), page 486. Reprinted by permission of City News Publishing Company, Inc.

Georges Borchardt: "The End of Separateness" by André Brink, originally published in *Newsweek*, 9 May 1994. Copyright © 1994 by André Brink. Reprinted by permission of Georges Borchardt, Inc., on behalf of the author.

William Morrow & Company: Excerpt from "The United States vs. Susan B. Anthony," from *Women of Courage* by Margaret Truman. Copyright © 1976 by Margaret Truman Daniel. By permission of William Morrow & Company, Inc.

Alfred A. Knopf: "Theme for English B," from *Collected Poems* by Langston Hughes. Copyright © 1994 by the Estate of Langston Hughes. Reprinted by permission of Alfred A. Knopf, Inc.

Harcourt Brace & Company: "The Writer," from *The Mind-Reader* by Richard Wilbur. Copyright © 1971 by Richard Wilbur. Reprinted by permission of Harcourt Brace & Company.

Random House: "The Artist," from *Tales from Old China* by Isabelle C. Chang. Copyright © 1969 by Isabelle C. Chang. Used by permission of Random House, Inc.

Excerpt from *I Know Why the Caged Bird Sings* by Maya Angelou. Copyright © 1969 and renewed 1997 by Maya Angelou. Used by permission of Random House, Inc.

"Caged Bird," from *Shaker, Why Don't You Sing?* by Maya Angelou. Copyright © 1983 by Maya Angelou. Reprinted by permission of Random House, Inc.

"New Directions," from *Wouldn't Take Nothing for My Journey Now* by Maya Angelou. Copyright © 1993 by Maya Angelou. Reprinted by permission of Random House, Inc.

Excerpt from *The Heart of a Woman* by Maya Angelou. Copyright © 1981 by Maya Angelou. Reprinted by permission of Random House, Inc.

Paris Review: Excerpt from "The Art of Fiction," interview with Maya Angelou by George Plimpton in *The Paris Review*, Vol. 32, No. 116 (Fall 1990). Reprinted with permission of The Paris Review, Inc.

Villard Books: Excerpt from *Into Thin Air* by Jon Krakauer. Copyright © 1997 by Jon Krakauer. Reprinted by permission of Villard Books, a division of Random House, Inc.

USA Today: "The Summit: Next Stop for Those on Everest" by Tim Friend, from *USA Today*, 19 May 1998. Copyright © 1998 USA Today. Reprinted with permission.

New Directions Publishing Corporation: "The Sharks," from *Collected Earlier Poems, 1940–1960* by Denise Levertov. Copyright © 1949, 1979 by Denise Levertov. Reprinted by permission of New Directions Publishing Corporation.

Sabine R. Ulibarrí: "My Wonder Horse/Mi caballo mago," from *Tierra Amarilla: Stories of New Mexico* by Sabine R. Ulibarrí, translated from the Spanish by Thelma Campbell Nason. Reprinted by permission of the author.

Houghton Mifflin Company: "Fable for When There's No Way Out," from *Nature* by May Swenson. Copyright © 1994 by the Literary Estate of May Swenson. Reprinted by permission of Houghton Mifflin Company. All rights reserved.

New York Times: "On Being 17, Bright—and Unable to Read," by David Raymond, from *The New York Times*, 25 April 1976. Copyright © 1976 by the New York Times Company. Reprinted by permission.

Unit Four

James Hurst: "The Scarlet Ibis" by James Hurst. Copyright © 1960 by *The Atlantic Monthly* and renewed 1988 by James Hurst. Reprinted by permission of James Hurst.

Naomi Long Madgett: "Woman with Flower," from *Star by Star* by Naomi Long Madgett. Copyright © 1965, 1970 by Naomi Long Madgett. Reprinted by permission of the author.

The Estate of Margaret Walker Alexander: "Lineage," from *For My People* by Margaret Walker (Yale University Press, 1942). Reprinted by permission of the Estate of Margaret Walker Alexander.

Elizabeth Barnett, Literary Executor: "The Courage That My Mother Had" by Edna St. Vincent Millay. From *Collected Poems* (HarperCollins). Copyright © 1954, 1982 by Norma Millay Ellis. All rights reserved. Reprinted by permission of Elizabeth Barnett, Literary Executor.

Doubleday: "My Papa's Waltz," from *The Collected Poems of Theodore Roethke* by Theodore Roethke. Copyright 1942 by Hearst Magazines, Inc. Used by permission of Doubleday, a division of Bantam Doubleday Dell Publishing Group, Inc.

Rita Dove: "Grape Sherbet," from *Selected Poems* by Rita Dove. Copyright © 1983, 1993 by Rita Dove. Used by permission of the author.

David McLean: "Marine Corps Issue" by David McLean, originally published in *The Atlantic Monthly,* May 1993. Copyright © 1993 by David McLean. Reprinted by permission of the author.

"On Writing 'Marine Corps Issue'" by David McLean. Copyright © David McLean. Reprinted by permission of the author.

Tribune Media Services: "Vietnam Warfare Breeding Ground for Post-Traumatic Stress Disorder" by Dennis McEaneney, *Knight-Ridder Newspapers,* 2 October 1997. Copyright © 1997 Tribune Media Services, Inc. All rights reserved. Reprinted with permission.

Simon J. Ortiz: "My Father's Song" by Simon J. Ortiz. Originally published in *Woven Stone* (University of Arizona Press, 1992). Reprinted by permission of Simon J. Ortiz.

HarperCollins Publishers: Excerpt from *Black Boy* by Richard Wright. Copyright 1937, 1942, 1944, 1945 by Richard Wright. Copyright renewed 1973 by Ellen Wright. Reprinted by permission of HarperCollins Publishers, Inc.

Susan Bergholz Literary Services: "Daughter of Invention" by Julia Alvarez. This selection appears in a slightly different form in *How the García Girls Lost Their Accents* by Julia Alvarez. Copyright © 1991 by Julia Alvarez. Published by Plume, a division of Penguin USA Inc. Originally published in hardcover by Algonquin Books of Chapel Hill. Reprinted by permission of Susan Bergholz Literary Services, New York. All rights reserved.

"Only Daughter" by Sandra Cisneros, first published in *Glamour,* November 1990. Copyright © 1990 by Sandra Cisneros. Reprinted by permission of Susan Bergholz Literary Services, New York. All rights reserved.

"The House on Mango Street," from *The House on Mango Street* by Sandra Cisneros. Copyright © 1984 by Sandra Cisneros. Published by Alfred A. Knopf, a division of Random House, Inc., New York, in 1994. Reprinted by permission of Susan Bergholz Literary Services, New York. All rights reserved.

"My Name," from *The House on Mango Street* by Sandra Cisneros. Copyright © 1984 by Sandra Cisneros. Published by Alfred A. Knopf, a division of Random House, Inc., New York, in 1994. Reprinted by permission of Susan Bergholz Literary Services, New York. All rights reserved.

"Papa Who Wakes Up Tired in the Dark," from *The House on Mango Street* by Sandra Cisneros. Copyright © 1984 by Sandra Cisneros. Published by Alfred A. Knopf, a division of Random House, Inc., New York, in 1994. Reprinted by permission of Susan Bergholz Literary Services, New York. All rights reserved.

"A Smart Cookie," from *The House on Mango Street* by Sandra Cisneros. Copyright © 1984 by Sandra Cisneros. Published by Alfred A. Knopf, a division of Random House, Inc., New York, in 1994. Reprinted by permission of Susan Bergholz Literary Services, New York. All rights reserved.

"Mango Says Goodbye Sometimes," from *The House on Mango Street* by Sandra Cisneros. Copyright © 1984 by Sandra Cisneros. Published by Alfred A. Knopf, a division of Random House, Inc., New York, in 1994. Reprinted by permission of Susan Bergholz Literary Services, New York. All rights reserved.

Excerpt from the Introduction to *The House on Mango Street* by Sandra Cisneros. Copyright © 1984 by Sandra Cisneros. Published by Alfred A. Knopf, a division of Random House, Inc., New York, in 1994. Reprinted by permission of Susan Bergholz Literary Services, New York. All rights reserved.

"Cloud," from *Loose Woman* by Sandra Cisneros. Copyright © 1994 by Sandra Cisneros. Published by Vintage Books, a division of Random House, Inc., and originally in hardcover by Alfred A. Knopf, Inc. Reprinted by permission of Susan Bergholz Literary Services, New York. All rights reserved.

Marian Reiner, Literary Agent: "Metaphor," from *A Sky Full of Poems* by Eve Merriam. Copyright © 1964, 1970, 1973 by Eve Merriam. Copyright renewed by Dee Michel and Guy Michel. Used by permission of Marian Reiner, Literary Agent.

Entrepreneur Magazine: "If You Build It . . ." by Debra Phillips and Cynthia E. Griffin, from *Entrepreneur,* December 1997. Reprinted with permission from Entrepreneur Magazine.

Arte Público Press: "A Voice," from *Communion* by Pat Mora (Houston: Arte Público Press—University of Houston, 1991). Copyright © 1991 by Pat Mora. Reprinted with permission from the publisher, Arte Público Press.

Grove/Atlantic: "The Journey," from *Dream Work* by Mary Oliver. Copyright © 1986 by Mary Oliver. Used by permission of Grove/Atlantic, Inc.

Alfred A. Knopf: "Powder," from *The Night in Question* by Tobias Wolff. Copyright © 1996 by Tobias Wolff. Reprinted by permission of Alfred A. Knopf, Inc.

Rogers, Coleridge & White Ltd.: Excerpt from "A Local Universe" by Jenny Uglow. First published in *The Times Literary Supplement* (5.15.92). Copyright © Jenny Uglow, 1992. Reproduced by permission of the author c/o Rogers, Coleridge & White Ltd., 20 Powls Mews, London, W11 1JN.

National Geographic Society: Excerpt from "The Magic of Paper" by Jon R. Luoma, *National Geographic,* March 1997. Reprinted by permission of National Geographic Image Collection.

Unit Five

Aaron Priest Agency: "Full Circle" by Sue Grafton. Copyright © 1991 by Sue Grafton. Reprinted by permission of the Aaron Priest Agency.

Publishers Weekly: "Who Killed My Daughter?: Lois Duncan Searches for an Answer" by Maria Simson. Reprinted from the April 20, 1992, issue of *Publishers Weekly.* Copyright © 1992 by Publishers Weekly.

Putnam Publishing Group and Harold Ober Associates: "Wasps' Nest," from *Double Sin and Other Stories* by Agatha Christie. Copyright © 1929, 1957 by Agatha Christie Ltd. Reprinted by permission of the Putnam Publishing Group and Harold Ober Associates, Inc.

University of New Mexico Press: Excerpt from "The Great Taos Bank Robbery," from *The Great Taos Bank Robbery and Other Indian Country Affairs* by Tony Hillerman. Copyright © 1973 by Anthony G. Hillerman. Reprinted by permission of the University of New Mexico Press.

Don Congdon Associates: "The Utterly Perfect Murder" by Ray Bradbury. Copyright © 1971 by Ray Bradbury. Reprinted by permission of Don Congdon Associates, Inc.

Susan Frank: Adapted from "The Intruder" by Susan Frank, from *Statement,* Vol. 33, No. 2 (Spring 1997). Copyright © 1995 by Susan Frank. Reprinted by permission of the author.

Stephen King: *Sorry, Right Number* by Stephen King. Copyright © 1993 by Stephen King. All rights reserved. Reprinted with permission.

Thacher Proffitt & Wood: "Beware: Do Not Read This Poem," from *New and Selected Poems* by Ishmael Reed. Copyright © 1972 by Ishmael Reed. Reprinted by permission of Thacher Proffitt & Wood on behalf of the author.

Sue Doro: "The Cultural Worker," from *Blue Collar Goodbyes* by Sue Doro. Published by Papier-Mache Press, 1992. Copyright © 1985 by Sue Doro. Reprinted by permission of the author.

Farrar, Straus & Giroux: "Poetry," from *Isla Negra: A Notebook* by Pablo Neruda, translated by Alastair Reid. Translation copyright © 1981 by Alastair Reid. Reprinted by permission of Farrar, Straus & Giroux, Inc.

Agencia Literaria Carmen Balcells: "La poesía," from *Memorial de Isla Negra* by Pablo Neruda. Copyright © 1964 by Pablo Neruda. Reprinted by permission of Agencia Literaria Carmen Balcells S.A. on behalf of Fundacíon Pablo Neruda.

Arte Público Press: "In the Family" by María Elena Llano, from *Short Stories by Latin American Women: The Magic and the Real,* edited by Celia Correas de Zapata (Houston: Arte Público Press—University of Houston, 1990). Copyright © 1990 by Arte Público Press. Reprinted with permission from the publisher, Arte Público Press.

HarperCollins Publishers: "A Very Old Man with Enormous Wings," from *Leaf Storm and Other Stories* by Gabriel García Márquez, translated by Gregory Rabassa. Copyright © 1971 by Gabriel García Márquez. Reprinted by permission of HarperCollins Publishers, Inc.

Philadelphia Inquirer: Excerpt from "An Invasion from the Planet Mars" by George M. Mahawinney, from *Philadelphia Inquirer,* 1 November 1938. Reprinted by permission.

Unit Six

Vintage Books: Excerpts from *The Odyssey* by Homer, translated by Robert Fitzgerald. Copyright © 1961, 1963 by Robert Fitzgerald and renewed 1989 by Benedict R. C. Fitzgerald. Reprinted by permission of Vintage Books, a division of Random House, Inc.

Houghton Mifflin Company and Oxford University Press Canada: "Siren Song," from *You Are Happy: Selected Poems, 1965–1975* by Margaret Atwood. Copyright © 1976 by Margaret Atwood. All rights reserved. Reprinted by permission of Houghton Mifflin Company and Oxford University Press Canada.

Insight on the News: Excerpt from "Book, Tape, TV—It's All Greek" by Stephen Goode, from *Insight on the News,* 26 May 1997. Copyright © 1997 News World Communications, Inc. All rights reserved. Reprinted with permission from *Insight.*

Viking Penguin: "Penelope," from *The Portable Dorothy Parker* by Dorothy Parker. Copyright 1928, renewed © 1956 by Dorothy Parker. Used by permission of Viking Penguin, a division of Penguin Putnam Inc.

Princeton University Press: "Ithaka" by C. P. Cavafy, from *C. P. Cavafy: Collected Poems,* translated by Edmund Keeley and Philip Sherrard. Translation copyright © 1975, 1992 by Edmund Keeley and Philip Sherrard. Reprinted by permission of Princeton University Press.

Tribune Media Services: "Romeo and Juliet are Palestinian and Jewish in Politically Charged Jerusalem Production" by Carol Rosenberg, *Knight-Ridder Newspapers,* 15 June 1994. Copyright © 1994 Tribune Media Services. All rights reserved. Reprinted with permission.

Boosey & Hawkes, Inc.: "Somewhere" from *West Side Story.* Copyright © 1957 by the Estate of Leonard Bernstein and Stephen Sondheim. Copyright renewed. Leonard Bernstein Music Publishing Company LLC, Publisher Boosey & Hawkes, Inc., Sole agent. Reprinted by permission.

The editors have made every effort to trace the ownership of all copyrighted material found in this book and to make full acknowledgment for its use. Omissions brought to our attention will be corrected in a subsequent edition.

Art Credits

Cover, Frontispiece
llustration copyright © 1998 Michael Steirnagle.

Front Matter

xi *bottom* The Granger Collection, New York; **xiii** *The Ages of Man* (17th century), English school. Oil on canvas. Norfolk Museums Service (Norwich Castle Museum), U.K./Bridgeman Art Library, New York; **xiv** *top right, People Flying,* Peter Sickles. SuperStock; *center right* National Museum of American History, Smithsonian Institution, Washington, D.C.; *bottom left* Copyright © 1998 Jim Stratford/Black Star; **xv** Copyright © David Fritts/Tony Stone Images; **xvii** AP/Wide World Photos; **xviii** *top right* Detail of *The Pantry,* Art Gore; **xix** Copyright © Kamil Vojnar/Photonica; **xx** *top right* The Granger Collection, New York; **xxi** *center left* Copyright © 1996 Twentieth Century Fox. All rights reserved. Photo by Merrick Morton; **xxi** *bottom center,* **2** *top* Photofest; **2** *bottom* Copyright © Chris Noble/Tony Stone Images; **3** *top* Copyright © Twentieth Century Fox/Shooting Star; *bottom* Photofest; **6–7** Copyright © Seny Norasingh/Light Sensitive; **8** *Fresh Eggs* (1874), Winslow Homer. Collection of Mr. and Mrs. Paul Mellon, copyright © 2000, Board of Trustees, National Gallery of Art, Washington, D.C.

Unit One

27 *top, background, Suzanne Poirson* (1884), John Singer Sargent. Oil on canvas, 24¹³⁄₁₆″ × 18⅞″. Private collection, photo courtesy of Adelson Galleries, Inc., New York; **27** *bottom,* **29, 32** Copyright © Buenos Dias Bildagenturt/Liaison International; **37** Copyright © Culver Pictures; **38** Detail of *Casanova* (1987), Julio Larraz. Oil on canvas, 60″ × 69½″. Private collection, courtesy of Nohra Haime Gallery, New York; **39, 45, 49, 54** Illustrations by Tinan Valk; **60** Schlesinger Library, Radcliffe College; **61** AP/Wide World Photos; **62** Detail of *Infantry* (1997), James E. Faulkner. Oil on canvas. Collection of Nature's Nest Gallery, Golden, Colorado. Courtesy of the artist; **64, 66, 68, 70** *ferns* Copyright © Greg Vaughn/Pacific Stock; **73** Copyright © Jerry Bauer; **74, 78, 81, 82–83, 84** Photos by Sharon Hoogstraten; **101** Brown Brothers; **102** AP/Wide World Photos; **104** Grant Heilman Photography; **105, 109, 110** *top* Runk/Schoenberger from Grant Heilman; **110** *bottom* Photo by Larry W. Smith; **111** Photofest; **113** *background* Copyright © Ernst Haas/Tony Stone Images; *foreground* Copyright © 1995 PhotoDisc; **115** Copyright © Arnulf Husmo/Tony Stone Worldwide; **116** Copyright © Ernst Haas/Tony Stone Images; **120** Copyright © 1986 J. B. Diederich/Contact Press Images/PNI; **123** Photo by Dan Deitch; **124** *top* Detail of *Holding the Lines,* James E. Buttersworth. Christie's Images; *bottom* Copyright © 1995 Culver Pictures/PNI; **129** *left* Stock Montage; *right* Copyright © 1986 Woods Hole Oceanographic Institution; **131–135** Photos by Sharon Hoogstraten; **142, 143** *backgrounds* Copyright © P. Degginger/H. Armstrong Roberts; **145** *left* The Granger Collection, New York; *right* Copyright © 1994 Archive Photos/Frank Driggs Collection/PNI; **147, 148** *backgrounds* Copyright © SuperStock; **150** Photo by Nathaniel Justice; **151, 152** *top right* Copyright © Susumu Yasui/Photonica; **152** *background* Copyright © Kei Muto/Photonica; **154** Copyright © Susumu Yasui/Photonica; **157** Copyright © Kei Muto/Photonica; **160** *Golden Fall* (1940), Joseph Stella. Oil on canvas, 26″ × 20″. Courtesy of Spanierman Gallery, New York; **161** Stock Montage; **163, 165** Corbis; **169** AP/Wide World Photos; **171** Copyright © 1988 Kenneth Jarecke/PNI; **173** *top, bottom,* **177** Copyright © 1997 FoodPix; **184** AP/Wide World Photos; **186** *left,* **187** *top* Photos by Sharon Hoogstraten; **190** Copyright © Layle Silbert; **193** *bottom* The Granger Collection, New York; **194–198** *border* Photo by Sharon Hoogstraten; **194** *top right* The Granger Collection, New York; *frame* Photo by Sharon Hoogstraten; *bottom center* Edgar Allan Poe Museum, Richmond, Virginia; **195** *bottom* Holsinger Studio Collection, Special Collections Department, Manuscripts Division, University of Virginia Library; **196** The Granger Collection, New York; **197** *top, clockwise from right* Photofest; Photofest; Photofest; Copyright © S.S.

Archives/Shooting Star International. All rights reserved; *center right* Edgar Allan Poe Museum, Richmond, Virginia; *bottom right* Copyright © 1986 Simon Marsden, The Marsden Archive; **200** Study of a head for *The Mill,* Sir Edward Coley Burne-Jones. Graphite and wash, 7¼″ × 6½″. Bankside Gallery, London; **201** Copyright © 1991 Klaus Reisinger/Black Star/PNI; **202, 203** Copyright © 1989 Richard During/AllStock/PNI; **204** *border,* **205–206, 207** *border* Photos by Sharon Hoogstraten; **207** *top left* Copyright © 1993 Jean-Claude Carton/Bruce Coleman/PNI; **209** Copyright © The Image Bank; **213** Copyright © 1995 Jay Maisel; **216–219** *border* Photo by Sharon Hoogstraten; **217, 218** Edgar Allan Poe Museum, Richmond, Virginia; **220–224** Photos by Sharon Hoogstraten.

Unit Two
236 Photo by Irving Solero, courtesy of the Museum at the Fashion Institute of Technology, New York; **238** Copyright © SuperStock; **239** Copyright © 1994 Ron Chapple/FPG International; **240** Photo by Sharon Hoogstraten; **242** Copyright © Susan Pearce; **243** Reprinted with the permission of Scribner, a division of Simon & Schuster, from *Angela's Ashes: A Memoir* by Frank McCourt. Copyright © 1996 by Frank McCourt; **247** Copyright © 1996 Al Hamdan/Image Bank; **257** Copyright © 1997 Andrea Renault/Globe Photos; **259** UPI/Corbis-Bettmann; **261** Photo by Sharon Hoogstraten; **271** AP/Wide World Photos; **273** Copyright © 1992–94 Aridi Computer Graphics, Inc. All rights reserved; **276, 281** Illustrations by Rebecca McClellan; **286** Copyright © Bob Daemmrich/PNI; **287** Copyright © Henri Cartier-Bresson/Magnum Photos; **288** Copyright © Ron Watts/Westlight; **289** Copyright © W. Warren/Westlight; **290** *road in desert* Copyright © Cliff Riedinger/Natural Selection; *road in forest* Copyright © Ron Watts/Westlight; **292** *left* Museum of the City of New York; *right* The Granger Collection, New York; **293** *Little Girl Reading #3* (1973), Simon Samsonian. Oil on canvas, 42″ × 32″. Private collection, New York; **303** Copyright © 1994 Archive Photos/PNI; **304** Courtesy, Arte Público Press; **306–307, 308, 312** Cy DeCosse, Inc.; **313** Photo by Greg Tousignant; **314–318** Photos by Sharon Hoogstraten; **324** *Boy and Car* (1955), David Park. Oil on canvas, 18″ × 24″. Collection of Mrs. Wellington S. Henderson; **325, 326** Photo by Sharon Hoogstraten; **341** *Katie on Sofa* (1959), Fairfield Porter. Oil on canvas, 24¼″ × 25¼″. Collection of Mr. and Mrs. Edward W. Andrews, Jr.; **343** Detail of *By the Gate* (1953), Ernest Crichlow. Oil on board, 10½″ × 14½″. The Harmon and Harriet Kelley Collection; **347** *left* Copyright © Layle Silbert; *right* AP/Wide World Photos; **348** Detail of *The Ages of Man* (17th century), English school. Oil on canvas. Norfolk Museums Service (Norwich Castle Museum), U.K./Bridgeman Art Library, New York; **353** Photo by Sharon Hoogstraten; **354** M. Howell/Camerique/ H. Armstrong Roberts; **358** Copyright © 1990 K. Muller/PNI; **359** Copyright © Don Carl Steffen/Photo Researchers, Inc.; **360** *trees at sunset* Copyright © Richard J. Green/Photo Researchers, Inc.; **360** *border,* **361, 364, 365, 366, 368, 369, 370** Copyright © 1995 PhotoDisc; **362** Copyright © Nigel J. Dennis/Photo Researchers, Inc.; **372** AP/Wide World Photos; **373** Detail of *Reflections* (1970), Ken Danby. Original egg tempera, 38″ × 52″. By permission of the artist and Gallery Moos, Toronto; **386** Globe Photos; **387** Amos Nachoum/Corbis; **388** Copyright © Kevin Cullimore/Tony Stone Worldwide; **390–394, 400–403** Photos by Sharon Hoogstraten.

Unit Three
410 Photofest; **419** Photo by Sharon Hoogstraten; **438** National Archives; **439** National Museum of American History, Smithsonian Institution, Washington, D.C.; **441, 442** UPI/Corbis-Bettmann; **443** *left* Copyright © 1963 FPG International; **446** AP/Wide World Photos; **450** *left* National Museum of American History, Smithsonian Institution, Washington, D.C.; *right* AP/Wide World Photos; **451** Reuters/Corbis-Bettmann; **453** Photo by Sharon Hoogstraten; **454** From the collections of the Library of Congress; **460–461** Photo by Sharon Hoogstraten; **465** AP/Wide World Photos; **472**

left National Portrait Gallery/Art Resource, New York; *right* Smith College, Northampton, Massachusetts; **474** *top* Copyright © Ron Watts/Westlight; *bottom* Culver Pictures; **475** *top* R. Krubner/H. Armstrong Roberts; *bottom* By permission of the Houghton Library, Harvard University; **476–480** *border* Photo by Sharon Hoogstraten; **476** *top right* Copyright © 1998 Jim Stratford/Black Star; *frame* Copyright © 1997 Sense Interactive; *bottom right* Copyright © Archive Photos/PNI; **477** Philip James Corwin/Corbis; **478** *bottom left* FPG International; *center right* AP/Wide World Photos; **479** *bottom left* Photofest; *center right, bottom right* Reuters/Corbis-Bettmann; **480** *Portrait of Dorothy Porter, Librarian* (1952), James Porter. Oil on canvas. National Portrait Gallery, Smithsonian Institution/Art Resource, New York; **490–491** *border* Photo by Sharon Hoogstraten; **491** Photofest; **493** AP/Wide World Photos; **494** *border* Photo by Sharon Hoogstraten; *top right* Detail of "In many places, because of the war, food had doubled in price," panel 11 from *The Migration Series* (1940–1941), Jacob Lawrence. Tempera on masonite, 18″ × 12″. The Phillips Collection, Washington, D.C., acquired 1942;**496, 497** *background* Artbeats; **498–500** *border* Photo by Sharon Hoogstraten; **499** UPI/Corbis-Bettmann; **500** *top right* Copyright © 1979 U.S. Postal Service/Hamilton Projects/King Visual Technology/Estate of Martin Luther King, Jr. License granted by Intellectual Properties Management, Atlanta, Georgia, as manager for the King Estate; **501** UPI/Corbis-Bettmann; **502** *left* License granted by Intellectual Properties Management, Atlanta, Georgia, as manager for the King Estate; right Corbis-Bettmann; **504–506** *border* Photo by Sharon Hoogstraten; **505, 506** UPI/Corbis-Bettmann; **507–509** Photos by Sharon Hoogstraten; **517** Copyright © Skye Chalmers/The Stock Market; **518, 519** Copyright © Charles Michael Murray/Westlight; **520** Copyright © Nawrocki Stock Photo, Inc./Mauritius; **522–523** Copyright © 1987 Steve Satushek/Image Bank; **527** Copyright © John Beatty/Tony Stone Worldwide; **528** Copyright © Peter Pearson/Tony Stone Images; **530** Copyright © Monica Dalmasso/Tony Stone Images; **534** Copyright © Skye Chalmers/The Stock Market; **537** Jack London Museum and Bookstore, Glen Ellen, California; **538** Copyright © Nicholas DeVore/Tony Stone Images; **539** Copyright © Neal Beidleman/Woodfin Camp & Associates; **540** Copyright © Jess Stock/Tony Stone Images; **542** *left* Copyright © John McCombe; *right* Copyright © Scott Fischer/Woodfin Camp & Associates; **546, 548** Copyright © Chris Noble/Tony Stone Images; **549** AP/Wide World Photos; **550** From a map by Heinrich Berann; **553** *top right* Copyright © David Fritts/Tony Stone Images; **554** Copyright © Bill Ivy/Tony Stone Images; **556** *top center* Copyright © Richard Shiell/Animals Animals; *bottom left* The Luce Studio; *bottom right* The Granger Collection, New York; **557, 558–559** Photo by Robert Vavra, reprinted by permission of the author and the Watkins/Loomis Agency; **561** Copyright © Jose Carrillo; **563** Photo by Robert Vavra, reprinted by permission of the author and the Watkins/Loomis Agency; **566–567** Photos by Sharon Hoogstraten; **570** Copyright © Eastcott/Momatiuk/Animals Animals; **571** Courtesy, Arte Público Press; **576–580** Photos by Sharon Hoogstraten.

Unit Four
589 Copyright © 1995 Skye Chalmers/The Stock Market; **593, 594** *foregrounds* Copyright © L. L. T. Rhodes/Animals Animals; **593, 594** *backgrounds,* **596, 600** H. Armstrong Roberts; **606** *Richard at Age Five* (1944), Alice Neel. Oil on canvas, 26″ × 14″. Courtesy of Robert Miller Gallery, New York. Copyright © Estate of Alice Neel; **610** John Heseltine/Science Photo Library/Photo Researchers, Inc.; **612** *left* Handy Photo Studios; *right* The Bettmann Archive; **613** Copyright © PhotoDisc; **614** Copyright © 1993 FPG International; **615** Copyright © PhotoDisc; **617** *left* UPI/Bettmann Newsphotos; *right* Photo by Fred Viebahn; **619, 629** Photos by Sharon Hoogstraten; **637** *Solitary Confinement: Insects Witness My Agony* (1982), Theodore Gostas. Collection of the U.S. Air Force, Washington, D.C.; **643** *bottom*

Multicultural Advisory Board *(continued)*

Teacher Review Panels *(continued)*

Bunny Schmaltz, Assistant Principal, Ozen High School, Beaumont Independent School District

Michael Urick, A. N. McCallum High School, Austin Independent School District

Ohio

Glyndon Butler, English Department Chairperson, Glenville High School, Cleveland City School District

Ellen Geisler, English/Language Arts Department Chairperson, Mentor Senior High School, Mentor School District

Dr. Paulette Goll, English Department Chairperson, Lincoln West High School, Cleveland City School District

Lorraine Hammack, Executive Teacher of the English Department, Beachwood High School, Beachwood City School District

Marguerite Joyce, English Department Chairperson, Woodridge High School, Woodridge Local School District

Sue Nelson, Shaw High School, East Cleveland School District

Dee Phillips, Hudson High School, Hudson Local School District

Carol Steiner, English Department Chairperson, Buchtel High School, Akron City School District

Nancy Strauch, English Department Chairperson, Nordonia High School, Nordonia Hills City School District

Ruth Vukovich, Hubbard High School, Hubbard Exempted Village School District

Florida

Judith H. Briant, English Department Chairperson, Armwood High School, Hillsborough County School District

Beth Johnson, Polk County English Supervisor, Polk County School District

Sharon Johnston, Learning Resource Specialist, Evans High School, Orange County School District

Eileen Jones, English Department Chairperson, Spanish River High School, Palm Beach County School District

Jan McClure, Winter Park High School, Orange County School District

Wanza Murray, English Department Chairperson (retired), Vero Beach Senior High School, Indian River City School District

Shirley Nichols, Language Arts Curriculum Specialist Supervisor, Marion County School District

Debbie Nostro, Ocoee Middle School, Orange County School District

Barbara Quinaz, Assistant Principal, Horace Mann Middle School, Dade County School District

California

Steve Bass, 8th Grade Team Leader, Meadowbrook Middle School, Ponway Unified School District

Cynthia Brickey, 8th Grade Academic Block Teacher, Kastner Intermediate School, Clovis Unified School District

Karen Buxton, English Department Chairperson, Winston Churchill Middle School, San Juan School District

Bonnie Garrett, Davis Middle School, Compton School District

Sally Jackson, Madrona Middle School, Torrance Unified School District

Sharon Kerson, Los Angeles Center for Enriched Studies, Los Angeles Unified School District

Gail Kidd, Center Middle School, Azusa School District

Corey Lay, ESL Department Chairperson, Chester Nimitz Middle School, Los Angeles Unified School District

Myra LeBendig, Forshay Learning Center, Los Angeles Unified School District

Dan Manske, Elmhurst Middle School, Oakland Unified School District

Joe Olague, Language Arts Department Chairperson, Alder Middle School, Fontana School District

Pat Salo, 6th Grade Village Leader, Hidden Valley Middle School, Escondido Elementary School District

Manuscript Reviewers (continued)

Kathleen M. Anderson-Knight, United Township High School, East Moline, Illinois

Susan Arabie, Marshall High School, Marshall, Texas

Anita Arnold, Thomas Jefferson High School, San Antonio, Texas

Cassandra L. Asberry, Dean of Instruction, Carter High School, Dallas, Texas

Jolene Auderer, Pine Tree High School, Longview, Texas

Don Baker, English Department Chairperson, Peoria High School, Peoria, Illinois

Beverly Ann Barge, Wasilla High School, Wasilla, Alaska

Louann Bohman, Wilbur Cross High School, New Haven, Connecticut

Rose Mary Bolden, Justin F. Kimball High School, Dallas, Texas

Lydia C. Bowden, Boca Ciega High School, St. Petersburg, Florida

Angela Boyd, Andrews High School, Andrews, Texas

Hugh Delle Broadway, McCullough High School, The Woodlands, Texas

Glyndon B. Butler, English Department Chairperson, Glenville High School, Cleveland, Ohio

Stephan P. Clarke, Spencerport High School, Spencerport, New York

Kathleen D. Crapo, South Fremont High School, St. Anthony, Idaho

Dr. Shawn Eric DeNight, Miami Edison Senior High School, Miami, Florida

JoAnna R. Exacoustas, La Serna High School, Whittier, California

Linda Ferguson, English Department Head, Tyee High School, Seattle, Washington

Ellen Geisler, English Department Chairperson, Mentor Senior High School, Mentor, Ohio

Ricardo Godoy, English Department Chairman, Moody High School, Corpus Christi, Texas

Meredith Gunn, Secondary Language Arts Instructional Specialist, Katy, Texas

Judy Hammack, English Department Chairperson, Milton High School, Alpharetta, Georgia

Robert Henderson, West Muskingum High School, Zanesville, Ohio

Martha Watt Hosenfeld, English Department Chairperson, Churchville-Chili High School, Churchville, New York

Janice M. Johnson, Assistant Principal, Union High School, Grand Rapids, Michigan

Eileen S. Jones, English Department Chair, Spanish River Community High School, Boca Raton, Florida

Paula S. L'Homme, West Orange High School, Winter Garden, Florida

Bonnie J. Mansell, Downey Adult School, Downey, California

Linda Maxwell, MacArthur High School, Houston, Texas

Ruth McClain, Paint Valley High School, Bainbridge, Ohio

Rebecca Miller, Taft High School, San Antonio, Texas

Deborah Lynn Moeller, Western High School, Fort Lauderdale, Florida

Bobbi Darrell Montgomery, Batavia High School, Batavia, Ohio

Bettie Moody, Leesburg High School, Leesburg, Florida

Margaret L. Mortenson, English Department Chairperson, Timpanogos High School, Orem, Utah

Marjorie M. Nolan, Language Arts Department Head, William M. Raines Sr. High School, Jacksonville, Florida

Julia Pferdehirt, Free-lance writer, former Special Education teacher, Middleton, Wisconsin

Cindy Rodgers, MacArthur High School, Houston, Texas

Pauline Sahakian, English Department Chairperson, San Marcos High School, San Marcos, Texas

Jacqueline Y. Schmidt, Department Chairperson and Coordinator of English, San Marcos High School, San Marcos, Texas

David Schultz, East Aurora High School, East Aurora, New York

Milinda Schwab, Judson High School, Converse, Texas

John Sferro, Butler High School, Vandalia, Ohio

Brad R. Smedley, English Department Chairperson, Hudtloff Middle School, Lakewood, Washington

Faye S. Spangler, Versailles High School, Versailles, Ohio

Rita Stecich, Evergreen Park Community High School, Evergreen Park, Illinois

GayleAnn Turnage, Abiline High School, Abiline, Texas

Ruth Vukovich, Hubbard High School, Hubbard, Ohio

Kevin Walsh, Dondero High School, Royal Oak, Michigan

Charlotte Washington, Westwood Middle School, Grand Rapids, Michigan

Tom Watson, Westbridge Academy, Grand Rapids, Michigan

Linda Weatherby, Deerfield High School, Deerfield, Illinois